The Right Honourable Lord Lane
Legum Scriptor Illustris
With Kind Wishes
[illegible]
16th February 2004

ESTABLISHED 1834.

THOS. FRASER & SONS,

Blenders of Scotch Whiskies, Wine Merchants and Family Grocers,

DUNBAR.

We have much pleasure in directing attention to the undernoted Wines, &c., which we have every confidence in recommending.

CLARET—

Good Dinner Wine	*12/- per doz.*
Chateau Fronsac	*18/- „*
„ Mille Secousses	*24/- „*
, Pomerol, 1888	*30/- „*

PORT—

30/- to 48/- per dozen. Special Value.
Old Tawny Wine . . . 36/- per doz.
Royal Dry . . . . . 42/- „

SHERRY—

20/- to 48/- per dozen
Special Value at 36/- per dozen

FRENCH BURGUNDY—

24/- to 42/- per dozen

CHAMPAGNE, Best Brands, at Lowest Prices
HOCK. MOSELLE. CALIFORNIAN and AUSTRALIAN WINES. Prices on application

WHISKY—

From 14/- to 20/- per gall. Special Value, Celebrated Blend, 18/- per gall. No. 1 Special, 20/- per gall.
Put up for England in Jars, 5, 6, and 7 gallons, and in Casks, 10, 12, and 15 gallons and upwards packed in Cases. Also sent abroad under Bond.

BRANDY—

Old Cognac, 48/- to 72/- per doz. All kinds of Malt Liquors, Aerated Waters, &c.

ESTABLISHED 1830.

ALEXANDER BAILLIE,

Grocer, Tea, Wine, and Provision Merchant,

46 & 48 HIGH STREET, DUNBAR.

PROVISIONS A SPECIALITY.—Hams, Bacon, Butter and Cheese.
TEAS AND COFFEES.—Blended and Pure.
WINES.—Port, Sherry, and Claret. Burgundy in Quarts, Pints, and Flagons.
WHISKY.—Blend of Old Scotch, Antiquary, and Extra Special. As supplied to Royal Navy.
Brandies, Gin, Rum, and Champagnes. Best Brands Stocked.
MALT LIQUORS.—Beers, Stouts, and Lager. All kinds from Leading Brewers. Always in Prime Condition. Hotels Supplied at Wholesale Prices.

FULL LIST ON APPLICATION.

WINES . . .

"Special" Port	*at 18/-, 24/- and 36/- per doz.*
„ Sherry	*18/-, 20/-, 24/- and 30/- „*
„ Claret	*12/-, 18/-, 20/- to 36/- „*

WHISKY . . .

Fine Old Scotch	*30/- per doz.*	*2/6 per bottle.*
Glenara Blend, "Special"	*36/- „*	*3/- „*
Extra Special Liqueur	*42/- „*	*3/6 „*

TEAS . . .

Exceptional Value in Blends - at 1/6, 1/8, 2/- and 2/6 per lb.

Robert Cunningham,

Wine Merchant, Family Grocer, and Italian Warehouseman,

ESTABLISHED 1837. **DUNBAR.**

ORDERS FOR MILK AND CREAM

Punctually attended to.

VAN DELIVERIES:—
Three Times Daily to all Parts of Town and Distric

ESTIMATES
GIVEN FOR LARGE SUPPLIES.

WALTER COWAN & SONS

Dairymen and Grocers,

157 High Street, DUNBAR.

ANDREW MELVILLE & SONS,

(ESTABLISHED 1810)

Plumbers, Gasfitters, Ironmongers & Cycle Agents,

Glass, China, and Fancy Goods Merchants,

AND AT EAST LINTON. 114 & 115 HIGH STREET, DUNBAR.

Choice Selection of Newest Photographic Views of Dunbar and Vicinity.
FORGAN'S GOLF CLUBS. CLUB CARRIERS. BALLS, &c.
CAMP STOOLS, SPADES, PAILS, AND ALL SEASIDE REQUISITES.
ELEY'S SPORTING AMMUNITION.
FISHING RODS AND TACKLE FOR RIVER, SEA, AND LOCH.
LADIES' AND GENTLEMEN'S SAFETY BICYCLES
Lamps and Accessories of every kind. Repairs carefully and promptly executed.
We would direct special attention to our Extensive Stock of
HOUSE FURNISHING IRONMONGERY, KITCHEN AND COOKING UTENSILS.
Choice and Varied Selection of Fancy Goods. Visitors are invited to inspect our Showrooms Replete with all the Latest Novelties in Glass, China, and Earthenware.

Experienced & Registered Plumbers & Gasfitters sent to Town or Country,
AND ALL ORDERS ARE PUNCTUALLY ATTENDED TO.

We devote Special Attention to SANITARY PLUMBING and DRAINAGE WORK which is carried out under our practical personal supervision. Buildings examined and reported upon, and our long experience is always at the command of our Clients as to the latest and most approved methods of Sanitary Science.

Agent for—"NEW HOWE," "THE SWIFT," "THE STAR," SAFETY BICYCL
LADIES' BICYCLES ON HIRE.

GEORGE GRAHAME,

IRONMONGER,

Glass and China Merchant, Plumber and Gasfitter

A Large Assortment of all the Latest Novelties in
FANCY GOODS of Home and Foreign Manufacture
Suitable for Gifts and Presentations.

GOLD AND SILVER JEWELLERY. ELECTRO-PLATE AND CUTLE
CAMP CHAIRS AND SEASIDE REQUISITES.
SPECIALITIES IN DOMESTIC UTENSILS.
PERAMBULATORS AND MAIL CARTS.

AGENTS FOR WILSON'S PHOTOGRAPH
INSPECTION CORDIALLY INVITED.

Note—Plumbing, Gas, and General Repairs receive Prompt Attention.

99 HIGH STREET, DUNBAR.

GEO. MURRAY,

Pharmaceutical Chemist,

THE LABORATORY,

39 HIGH STREET, DUNBAR

Strict personal attention given to the dispensing of Prescriptions and Family Recipes.

All kinds of Patent and Proprietary Articles.
Photographic Materials.
Mackay's Kola and Aerated Waters.

LORNE HOTEL,

132 HIGH STREET,

DUNBAR.

H. HUNTLY, Proprietor.

JOHN G. GRAHAME,

Family Baker & Confectioner,

84 HIGH STREET,

DUNBAR.

Large Variety of Fancy Breads & Cakes.
Specialities—Lunch Loaves & Ginger Cakes.

W. MAYNE,

Confectioner, Fruiterer, Florist, and Refreshment Rooms,

146 HIGH STREET,

All kinds of . . . Fruit and Vegetables. DUNBAR.

Wreaths, Crosses, Cut Flowers, Hand and Table Bouquets, Sprays, &c.

R. C. & J. SHIELL,

FAMILY

Butchers & Poulterers,

103 HIGH STREET,

DUNBAR.

PRIME BEEF & WEDDER MUTTON

Selected from the Best Farms in East Lothian.

AT LOWEST PRICES.

Vans Deliver in Town and Country.

WM. BEATTIE PURVES

HOUSE AGENT,

Cabinetmaker and Upholstere

8 HIGH STREET,

DUNBAR.

Furniture of all kinds. Beds & Beddin

PIANOS ON HIRE FOR SUMMER MONT

TERMS MODERATE.

Enquiries for
FURNISHED HOUSES & APARTMEN
Promptly attended to.

SWORDS, LOAVES
&
FISHES

A History of Dunbar
from earliest times to the present
(Birthplace of John Muir, the father of conservation)

By

R J M Pugh

HARLAW HERITAGE

First published in 2003 By
Harlaw Heritage
21 Marchbank Gardens
Balerno, Midlothian
EH14 7ET
Scotland

Websites: www.harlawheritage.com
www.dunbar.org.uk

ISBN 0 9540465 1 X

Origination by Harlaw Heritage and Transcolour (Scotland) Ltd

Printed and bound by
Belfast University Press

RCAHMS

Frontispiece: *Aerial view of Dunbar from the NE. A number of landmarks shown on this late 1970s photograph have either disappeared or have been greatly modified, notably the outdoor swimming pool in the middle distance, the barracks to the left of the castle ruins and the granary at the Broadhaven, now flats. The vacant lot this side of the granary, the site of the Old Custom House, is now occupied by more modern housing. The layout of the Battery on Lamer Island can also be seen clearly.*

In fond memory of my mother Jean
and two redoubtable Dunbar historians, J I W (Jack) Milne and John (Jack) Steele,
also for the people of Dunbar past, present and future.

CONTENTS

List of Illustrations

CONTENTS

List of Illustrations

Figures

PREFACE

Convention

It is the practice of some historians to express dates in double years in the first three months of years prior to 1600 because until then, in accordance with the Old or Julian calendar, years legally began on 26 March. Thus dates occurring between 1st January and 25th March are often expressed in both old and new years eg 28th February 1345-46. Where possible, this accurate but clumsy procedure has been avoided and the relevant date is given according to the New or Gregorian calendar which was adopted in Scotland in 1600; England did not convert until 1752. In the above example therefore, in Scotland the date would be 28th February 1346. In 1752, when Britain fully adopted the Gregorian calendar, 11 days were removed from the calendar - from 3 to 14 September - because the former Julian calendar was incorrect by one day every 160 years. With all dates therefore, the year is deemed to begin on 1st January for the purposes of this book.
Names have been modernised except when quoted from original manuscripts and primary sources. The Notes to each chapter which appear at the end of the book provide additional information which would interrupt the flow of the text; they also give brief details of sources consulted which are given in abbreviated form as full titles, author/editor names, place and date of publication appear in the *Bibliography*.

Abbreviations

The following abbreviations are used in the text and in the notes to each chapter; most follow the guidelines laid down in the *List of Abbreviated Titles of the Printed Sources of Scottish History to 1560* as shown in the *Scottish Historical Review, xlii* (1963)

ADCP	*Acts of the Lords of Council in Public Affairs 1501-54*
Annals, Tig.	*Annals of Tigernach*
APS	*Acts of the Parliaments of Scotland 1174-1707*
AR	*Anglo-Scottish Relations 1174-1328*
ASC	*Anglo-Saxon Chronicle*
Asloan MSS	*Asloan Manuscripts*
Beaugue, Hist.	*Histoire de la Guerre d'Ecosse pendant les Campagnes 1548 et 1549,* Jean de Beaugue
Bede, Historia Venerable	*Historia Ecclesiastica Gentis Anglorum* (A Church History of the English Nation), The Bede
Blind Harry, Wallace	*Schir William Walleis, The Actis and Deidis of the Illustere and Valzeand Campioun Schir William Walleis, Knicht of Elderslie,* Harry the Minstrel, known as Blind Harry
Boece, Hist.	*Scotorum Historiae* (History of Scotland), Hector Boece
Bruce	*Bruce, The,* J Barbour
Buchanan, Hist.	*History of Scotland,* George Buchanan
CWAAS	*Cumberland and Westmoreland Antiquarian and Archaeological Society*
CBP	*Border Papers, The: Calendar of Letters and Papers relating to the Affairs of the Borders of England and Scotland*
CCR	*Calendar of the Close Rolls*
CDS	*Calendar of Documents relating to Scotland 1104-1516*
C. Hat	*Calendar of Manuscripts at Hatfield House*
CEPR	*Calendar of Entries in the Papal Registers for Great Britain and Ireland*

CFR	*Calendar of the Fine Rolls, Edward 1 1272-1307*
Chron. Auchinleck	*Auchinleck Chronicle: Ane Schort Memoriale of Scottis Cornikilis for Addicioun*
Chron. England	*Chronicle of England,* J Capgrave
Chron. Fordun	*Chronica Gentis Scotorum* (Chronicle of the Scottish Nation) Johannis de Fordun
Chron. Froissart	*Chronicle of England, France, Spain (Chroniques, 1329-1400), Jean Froissart*
Chron. Holyrood	*Chronicle of Holyrood*
Chron. Roger Hoveden	*Chronica Magistri,* Roger Hoveden
Chron. Henry of Huntingdon	*Historia Anglorum* (Chronicle of Huntingdon)
Chron. Lanercost	*Chronicon de Lanercost* (Chronicle of Lanercost Priory 1201-1346)
Chron. Melrose	*Chronicon Mailros* (Chronicle of Melrose)
Chron. Matthew Paris	*Chronica Majora Historia Anglorum* (Chronicle of the History of England 1242), Matthew Paris
Chron. Picts and Scots	*Chronicles of the Picts: Chronicles of the Scots and other Memorials of Scottish History*
Chron. Pluscarden	*Liber Pluscardenis* (Chronicle of Pluscarden)
Chron. Rishanger	*Chronica,* William Rishanger
Chron. Walsingham	*Historia Anglicana* (Chronicle of Walsingham)
Chron. Florence of Worcester	*Florenti Wigorniensis Monachi, Chronicon ex Chronicis* (Chronicle of *Florence of Worcester 1171-1265)*
Chron. Wyntoun	*Orygynale Cronikyl of Scotland* (Chronicle of Andrew of Wyntoun 1420)
Cotton, Hist.	*Historia Anglicana* (History of England) Bartholomew Cotton
CP	*Complete Peerage, The,* G E Cockayne
CPL	*Calendar of Papal Letters to Scotland of Benedict XIII of Avignon 1394-1418 Benedict XIII*
CPL Clement VII	*Calendar of Papal Letters to Scotland of Clement VII of Avignon 1378-1394*
CPR	*Calendar of Patent Rolls*
CSP Dom.	*Calendar of State Papers, Domestic Series* (England)
CSP Scot.	*Calendar of State Papers relating to Scotland and Mary Queen of Scots 1547-1603*
CSP Thorpe	*Calendar of State Papers relating to Scotland 1509-1603,* M J Thorpe
CSSR ii	*Calendar of Scottish Supplications to Rome 1423-28, vol. ii*
CSSR vii	*Calendar of Scottish Supplications to Rome 1428-32, vol. vii*
Cumberland Hist.	*History of the County of Cumberland*
Diurnal Occurrents	*Diurnal of Occurrents That Have Passed Within the Country of Scotland 1513-75*
Dowden, Bishops	*Bishops of Scotland, The,* J Dowden
Dryburgh Liber	*Liber Sancti Marie de Dryburgh* (Dryburgh Cartulary)
Dunbar, Scot. Kings	*Scottish Kings: A Revised Chronology of Scottish History 1005-1625,* A Dunbar
Easson, Religious Houses	*Medieval Religious Houses Scotland,* I B Cowan and D Easson
EHD	*English Historical Documents 1042-1189*
EHR	*English Historical Review*
EHS	*English History Society*
ER	*Exchequer Rolls of Scotland 1264-1600* (see also *Rotuli Scaccarii Regum Scotorum*)
ESC	*Earliest Scottish Charters*
ES Scot. Hist.	*Earliest Sources of Scottish History 500 to 1286* (comprising extracts from various chronicles)
Fraser, Douglas	*Douglas Book, The,* W Fraser
Fraser, Wemyss	*Memoirs of the Family of Wemyss,* W Fraser
Hamilton Papers	*Hamilton Papers, The, vols. i and ii*
Hume, Douglas & Angus	*History of the House and Race of Douglas and Angus, A,* D Hume of Godscrot
Keith, Bishops	*Historical Catalogue of the Scottish Bishops, An.* R Keith
Kelso Liber	*Liber Sancti Marie de Calchou* (Kelso Chartulary)
Laing Chrs.	*Calendar of the Laing Charters 854-1837*
Lawrie, Annals	*Annals of the Reigns of Malcolm and William 1153-1214,* Sir A Lawrie
Lawrie, ESC	*Early Scottish Charters Prior to AD 1153,* Sir A Lawrie
Lesley, Hist.	*History of Scotland,* Bishop A Lesley
Lockhart	*History of the Lockharts of Lee and Carnwath: Seven Centuries,* S Lockhart

Major, Hist.	*History of Greater Britain, A,* John Major
Mary of Lorraine Corresp.	*Scottish Correspondence of Mary of Lorraine 1543-60*
Melrose Liber	*Liber Sancti Marie de Melros* (Melrose Chartulary)
Miller, Dunbar	*The History of Dunbar,* J Miller
Nat. MSS Scot.	*Facsimiles of the National Manuscripts of Scotland*
Northumberland County Hist.	*History of Northumberland, The,* The Northumberland County History Committee
Palgrave, Docs. Hist.Scot.	*Documents and Records Illustrating the History of Scotland,* A Palgrave
Pat. Rolls	*Patent Rolls*
Pickering, Dunbar, Hume and Dundas	*Histories of Noble British Families, The,* H Drummond and W Pickering
Pitcairn, Trials	*Criminal Trials in Scotland 1488-1624,* R Pitcairn
Pitscottie, Hist.	*Historie and Cronicles of Scotland, The 1437-1575,* Robert Lindsay of Pitscottie
PRO	*Public Record Office (England)*
PRS	*Pipe Roll Society*
PRS Henry II	*Pipe Rolls of Henry II of England*
PSAS	*Proceedings of the Society of Antiquaries of Scotland*
Raine, North Durham	*Appendix to* J Raine's *The History and Antiquities of North Durham*
RCAHMS	*Royal Commission on Ancient and Historical Monuments of Scotland: East Lothian*
RCRB	*Records of the Convention of the Royal Burghs of Scotland*
RMS	*Registrum Magni Sigilli Regum Scotorum* (Register of the Great Seal of Scotland 1306-1688)
RPC	*Registers of the Privy Council of Scotland 1545-1691*
RRS	*Regesta Regum Scottorum* (Acts and Charters by Scottish Kings)
Rot. Scot.	*Rotuli Scotiae in Turri Londinensi et in Domo Capitulari Westmonasteriensi Asservati* (being a collection of transactions between Scotland and England from 1290 to 1516)
RSRS	*Rotuli Scaccarii Regum Scotorum* (Exchequer Rolls of Scotland 1264-1600)
RSS	*Registrum Secreti Sigilli Regum Scotorum* (Register of the Privy Seal of Scotland 1488-1584)
SAEC	*Scottish Annals from English Chroniclers 500-1286*
St Andrews Liber	*Liber Cartarum Prioratus Sancti Andree in Scotia* (St Andrews Cartulary)
SBRS	*Miscellany of the Scottish Burgh Records Society*
Scalacronica	*Scalacronica,* Sir Thomas Gray of Heton, Knight (1356) (a history of Scotland)
Scotichronicon	*Scotichronicon* (The Chronicle of Inchcolme): a continuation of *Chron. Fordun* by Water Bower, Abbot of Inchcolme, 1440-45
Scott, Fasti.	*Fasti Ecclesiae Scoticanae* (The succession of the ministers of the Church of Scotland from the Reformation (Synod of Lothian and Tweeddale) H Scott
Seton	*History of the Family of Seton, A,* G Seton
SP	*Scots Peerage,* J Balfour Paul
SHR	*Scottish Historical Review*
SHS	*Scottish History Society*
Spottiswoode Misc	*Spottiswoode Miscellany (Civil and Ecclesiastical)*
SRO	*Scottish Record Office*
Stevenson, Documents	*Historical Documents of Scotland 1286-1306,* J Stevenson
Symeon of Durham	*Historia Regum in Symeonis monachi opera omnia* (Chronicle of Simeon of Durham)
TA	*Accounts of the Lord High Treasurer of Scotland (Compota Thesaurorium Regum Scotorum) 1473-1574*
TELAS	*Transactions of the East Lothian Antiquarian and Field Naturalists' Society*
Warrender Letters	*Warrender Letters; The Correspondence of Sir George Warrender of Lochend 1715*
Warrender Papers	*Warrender Papers, The: King James' Secret;* also *Warrender Papers 1301-1603*
Watt, Fasti	*Fasti Ecclesiae Scoticanae Medii Aevi ad Annum 1638* (The succession of priests etc up to and beyond the Reformation) D E R Watt
Watt, Fasti Ecclesiae	*Fasti Ecclesiae Scoticanae* (The succession of ministers of the Church of Scotland from the Reformation ed. Hew Scott *et al*)

ACKNOWLEDGEMENTS

A book which has taken thirteen years to prepare cannot possibly register exhaustive thanks to named individuals employed by the many organisations which offered assistance and provided advice. My debt to these individuals is immeasurable. Particular thanks go to the staff of the National Library of Scotland who located the more obscure titles used in my research. Similarly, I wish to record my gratitude to the staff of the National Archives of Scotland in the various branches, the Public Record Office, London, the Scottish and Edinburgh Rooms, George IV Bridge Library, Edinburgh.

I am also indebted to Veronica Wallace, Local History and Promotions Librarian, Chris Roberts, Local Studies Officer, East Lothian Local History Centre, Haddington, Peter Gray, Museums Officer, East Lothian Council Museums Service, Mark Beattie, Gordon Easingwood and Pauline Smeed of the Dunbar and District History Society.

Thanks are due to Jim Thompson and Duncan Smeed of Dunbar's John Muir Association, who kindly read Chapter 11, correcting factual errors and supplying information about the Association and its aims.

Thanks are also due to David Watson, my colleague in the Scottish Office, Edinburgh for his assistance with Appendix I; to J Ritchie, Mortonhall Crematorium, Edinburgh who located the burial register for New Calton Cemetery, Edinburgh, which provided conclusive proof of the burial places of Richard Gall in 1801 and James Miller in 1865; to Helen Nicoll, Picture Library and Heather Brunton, Scottish Life Archive, both of the National Museum of Scotland; Colonel I Shepherd and the Scottish National War Memorial for information about the casualties of the two World Wars.

My greatest debt goes back further than the years spent researching and writing this book. Perhaps the most significant and lasting influence on me has been that generated by my former history teacher at Dunbar Grammar School, Miss Lena Mackay (now Mrs Lena Glass). From her, I learnt to be impartial about history, particularly that of Scotland; she instilled in me a continuing interest in a fascinating subject, even when I was unaware of her efforts. That is the mark of a good teacher. In the same vein, a debt is also owed to the late J I W Milne, a good friend and mentor who taught me Latin and Roman history at Dunbar Grammar School. He also taught me much about life during many Saturday pub lunch sessions in the George Hotel

To the Rev. Eric Foggitt and Douglas Laird of Dunbar Parish Church, thanks for permission to investigate the lead coffin in the Roxburghe vault. To James and Pam Mason for access and kind permission to photograph the stained glass window in their home at the East Links, Dunbar.

Finally I wish to end my acknowledgements by thanking Robin Murdoch for his enthusiasm in the preparation of this book. Without his advice, encouragement and personal commitment, the book would have taken considerably longer to produce. I am also grateful to Robin for his painstaking care in stripping out my typing and spelling errors and for challenging me with occasional withering honesty on my flights of fancy and moralising - these, I think have been excised (well nearly - editor's comment!!).

I hope that Lena Glass and other friends in Dunbar and far beyond will enjoy the end result.

Roy Pugh
Balerno, Midlothian, Autumn 1990 - Dunbar, East Lothian, Spring 2003

Illustration acknowledgements

Each illustration is accompanied by a code of initials. The author is indebted to the following individuals and organisations who have allowed their own images or images within their collections to be used.

Individuals

KA	Kenny Ainslie
MB	Mark Beattie
MD	Margaret Dann
RF	Richard Fawcett

HM	Hope Mason
J&PM	James and Pam Mason
KM	Keith Milligan
KLM	Keith Mitchell
RM	Richard Morgan
KRM	Robin Murdoch
PS	Pauline Smeed
RCM	Redcar and Cleveland Museum, per D Anderson
WF	Warrender family
RJP	The author's collection

Organisations

DDHS	Dunbar and District History Society
ELCMS	East Lothian Council Museum Services
HLHC	Haddington Local History Centre
HH	Hillside Hotel
LRM	Lauren Rogers Museum
NAS	National Archives of Scotland
NMS	National Museum of Scotland - Picture Library
RCAHMS	Royal Commission on the Ancient and Historical Monuments of Scotland
RCM	Redcar and Cleveland Museum
RA	Regimental Asoociation
SLA	National Museum of Scotland - Scottish Life Archive
SP	Scotsman Publications

INTRODUCTION

The soft gentle topography of Dunbar's modern landscape belies its sometimes dark past. Being a small Lowland community, culturally it has little to do with tartan, bagpipes or haggis; although these things are of Scotland, they are not all of it. There are different regions and districts with their distinct identities which contribute to Scotland's richly diverse culture. In another existence, I once had to write a speech for the Secretary of State for Scotland who was hosting a conference on *Television in a Small Country* to which the smaller European countries like Luxembourg and Belgium were invited. During my research into suitable subjects for the speech, I was taken aback by the variety and shades of colour in the Scottish kaleidoscope. If in nineteenth century society, monarchs like George IV, Victoria and men like Sir Walter Scott indulged themselves in embracing all things Highland, the interested observer could be forgiven for thinking that the rest of Scotland warranted little attention. To a certain extent, this was true; Victoria and Scott were basically seeking to promote Scotland's cultural identity. This book is not concerned with tartan, bagpipes or haggis but it is no less Scottish for that.

From earliest times, Scotland was inhabited by an amalgam of races and tribes - Picts, Celts, Britons, Scots from Ireland, Anglo-Saxons, Norsemen and finally, Norman-Flemish-French. Despite the differences in Lowland and Highland culture, both regions contain people who descend from this rich Scotch Broth. In Dunbar's case, descent was from ancient Celtic-British and Anglo-Saxon races until 1018; although among the last communities to become Scottish, no Scot would dare impugn its Scottishness. In the past two centuries, Dunbar became a garrison town for militia, then regular units of the British Army; thus yet again, the community experienced an invasion of new people from all over the UK, some of whom married and settled in the community, introducing new and alien surnames. I know that only too well. Despite the biological fact that I had a Welsh-English father, I consider myself Scottish first and foremost. After all, nationality is mostly a matter of how we feel about ourselves.

Dunbar's history was well researched by one of its famous sons, James Miller (1791-1865). Miller published *The History of Dunbar* in 1830; it was reprinted in 1859 with additional material which proved its popularity. So why another history of Dunbar? Some justification is needed for adding yet another book to the shelves. Inevitably, given Miller's excellent account, there are bound to be those who will consider this book superfluous; perhaps the chapters which follow will convince such critics that a revised version is long overdue.

There are also practical reasons for writing this book. The most obvious is that Miller's account appeared over a century and a half ago; this book contains source material either not available to Miller or used by him.

Some of his errors of fact have also been rectified. Miller occasionally paid scant attention to whole centuries without any apparent reason; this too has been rectified although the volumes of municipal and kirk records has obliged me, like Miller to be selective. I am also fortunate in having the benefit of recent archaeological discoveries which have thrown more light on obscure aspects of our history. However, I have attempted to avoid simply quoting from archival material in order to give the skeleton clothes as well as flesh. Having said that, I hasten to add that my approach has been to use primary sources rather than received knowledge from legend, individual memory and folk memory, these being notoriously untrustworthy. In the process, I hope I have not over-indulged my imagination to the detriment of this account.

In the first half of the twentieth century, very little Scottish - and no local - history was taught in Scottish schools. Thankfully, this has changed. Much of Dunbar's past was learnt at the fireside; many of its tales- colourful though they were - paid scant attention to fact. While it is true that in history as in life, legend and myth are always more popular than fact, it is also true that they contain grains of truth. Fact and legend are irretrievably interwoven and legend usually prevails. Most people who were born in Dunbar have heard of Black Agnes and her famous defence of Dunbar Castle against the English in 1338, the longest siege in the castle's history. Less is known about her husband, the 9th Earl of Dunbar and his ancestors and descendants. For example, it came as a complete surprise to me that the Dunbar dynasty was founded by a former earl of Northumberland whose daughter became queen of Scotland in 1094, albeit only for six months.

Some educationalists used to believe that history has little relevance in modern society. I disagree. History is not a record of kings and queens and battles. It is about the doings and sayings of men and women and is therefore important because of that. Thomas Carlyle wrote that history is simply the biographies of individuals, how they lived their lives and how they affected those of the people around them. This makes history a subject worthy of study. One could go as far as to accuse the historian of being a failed novelist; the opposite is true in the case of Sir Walter Scott, who gives us a convincing impression of having been a failed historian. But, like literature, history is about people; one lesson it teaches is that we ignore it at our peril. I like the line from the song about the Spartans of ancient Greece which for me effectively sums up history:

> 'We are what you were; we shall be what you are.'

Dunbar has existed as a living community since at least the first century AD which makes it one of the oldest settlements in Scotland. It formed part of the kingdom of the Votadini, an Iron Age British-Celtic tribe which once occupied the area from Lindisfarne, Northumberland to Stirling across the Firth of Forth. Dunbar was in the forefront of the conflict between the Picts and the Votadini, then the Angles of Bernicia, or old Northumbria. Situated in an unstable area, it is likely that Dunbar experienced Pictish sea-raiding since it was some distance away from the Votadini stronghold and capital, Traprain Law. A recent suggestion that the Votadini invited the Romans to settle in their territory or acquiesced in the process seems highly unlikely even if the motive was to contain the expansion of the Pictish kingdom southwards across the Firth of Forth. The northward thrust of the Angles from Hadrian's Wall was gradual and took almost a century to complete; by the seventh century, the Votadini were isolated in their new stronghold of Din Eidyn (Edinburgh) with only pockets of their former kingdom surviving in places like Traprain Law, Dunbar.and perhaps some of the Merse (Berwickshire). Finally, the warrior tribe was overwhelmed around the early part of the seventh century by the Angles. By 638AD, Dunbar had become an important Anglian shire centre. This alone does not suggest a peaceful colonisation; more to the point, the Angles wasted no time in erasing surviving traces of the Votadini, replacing their stronghold on Doon Hill with their own.

Dunbar's history may be summarised by the following key events:

- c 638 establishment of Anglian shire centre
- 1018 annexation of Lothian by Scotland
- 1296 battle of Dunbar which began the Wars of Independence
- 1338 defence of Dunbar Castle and the disruption of English strategy for continued occupation of south-east Scotland
- 1370 elevation of Dunbar to a free burgh
- 1445 elevation of Dunbar to a royal burgh
- 1650 second battle of Dunbar which was the prelude to the loss of Scotland's independence
- 1803 Dunbar becomes a garrison town to meet the threat of Napoleon's expected invasion
- 1914 Dunbar forms part of the shore defence system guarding the Firth of Forth
- 1976 establishment of the John Muir Country Park and the start of an international movement to promote environmental protection

Of these ten events, the majority had national, even international significance - a crude but effective benchmark of Dunbar's role in Scotland's development. The list is by no means exhaustive; other events which had their effect on the wider community of Scotland are given due attention.

With the annexing of Lothian by the Scots in 1018, the next major influence on the community of Dunbar was its earls, founded by a former earl of Northumberland in 1072. The Dunbar dynasty began with Gospatric, a noble whose family had connections with the royal houses of both Scotland and England. The Dunbars held considerable power in south-east Scotland until the mid fifteenth century. They have been incorrectly - and irritatingly - accused of continuous defection to England, described as the'mighty but wavering' earls. There is of course more than a grain of truth in that but the fact is that the majority of the eleven blood-line earls were loyal to Scottish kings.

The most controversial of the earls, Patrick, 9th Earl of Dunbar and 3rd of March continued his father's pro-English stance. Although absent from the field of Bannockburn, he was never deprived of his earldom or lands as were others in Scotland; they became known as the *Disinherited.* The least attractive of all the earls was the 9th Earl's father; his is a classic example of how a single sentence can sum up a whole life, as ably evinced by Plutarch:

> 'A slight thing like a phrase or jest often makes a greater revelation of character than battles where thousands fall.'

Writing of the 8th Earl of Dunbar, Edward I of England put it another way, as we shall see in Chapter Two.

This book is about the history and the economic development of Dunbar over the past thirteen centuries. The modern historian may perceive evidence of a community which once thrived, its wealth based on agriculture and fishing, local, national and international trade. In its heyday between 1700 and 1960, it was a prosperous royal burgh, with its impressive tolbooth and its broad, well-appointed High Street and its impressive Parish Church. Other modern eyes may see only decay, but there is still evidence of its former greatness in some of its surviving buildings and houses.

In the course of this account, it will be seen that East Lothian in general and Dunbar in particular made a considerable contribution to the welfare of the country as a whole, particularly in the agriculture and fishing industries. Its importance as a fishing port and trading centre extended well into the nineteenth century. During the Middle Ages, Scottish exports were limited to wool, hides and skins; the Border abbeys grew mighty from the wool clip, a fact which David II acknowledged by raising Dunbar to the status of a free burgh in 1370, thereby creating an outlet for these commodities when Berwick and Roxburgh were in English hands with the consequential loss of a significant element of royal revenue. Because of agrarian reforms heralded by statutes in 1661, 1669, 1685 and 1686 which improved the crop yield through enclosure, the bumper grain crop of 1685 allowed Scotland to export grain to the Baltic. Dunbar undoubtedly contributed to this surplus, having a rich hinterland of productive land. Before the Union of 1707 - which Dunbar initially opposed-the pattern of Scottish trade and the economy itself were affected by the state of Anglo-Scottish relationships. Even during peace, English continental wars disrupted Scottish trade and made it difficult for her ships to travel without interference. While Dunbar never became a major export centre like Leith, its proximity to England should have guaranteed a healthier trade in grain and other exports. Much of the problem stemmed from the English *Navigation Acts* which prevented any goods being taken to England except in English vessels. Despite this however, Dunbar's *East Lothian and Merse Fishing Company* and *Fall, Melville and Company* which dealt in extensive overseas trade thrived for almost a century; these companies had a considerable share of the fish-processing and import-export trades; at one time, the Fall initiative put Dunbar second only to Leith in the whaling industry.

In 1633, the privileges enjoyed by Scottish Royal Burghs were upheld by statute which recognised that in bearing their share of the national tax burden, they would enjoy lucrative monopolies. The local burgesses and merchants were the *nouveaux riches* of their time; they engaged freely in foreign as well as domestic trade, importing luxuries such as fine Continental wines. James II's charter of 1445 which bestowed royal burgh status on Dunbar compelled all foreign and domestic merchants from lesser burghs to buy and sell only within the royal burgh precincts, thus generating wealth for Scottish kings through customs and excise revenue as well as enriching the local traders. All fish, wool and other commodities had to be bought and sold within the burghs and all cloth was required to be finished by burgh craftsmen. Like other royal burghs, Dunbar strove to protect its privileges, jealously guarding them until finally, legislation was enacted to break their monopolies and allow other burghs - burghs of barony and regality - to export locally-produced goods and import articles which until then could only be obtained in royal burgh markets. Nonetheless, Dunbar prospered until the turn of the twentieth century, even if by then, its days as a major fishing port were numbered.

While Dunbar played an important role in the political, military and economic life of the country, the community was not always well served by those in administrative control. Much of its rich heritage has been lost through thoughtless, narrow-sighted and short-term planning decisions. 'Historic' Dunbar has a rather hollow ring to it today. Much of the failure to preserve the town's antiquities is a direct result of poor or expedient planning aimed at short-term gain. This continues. Officialdom will always put forward outwardly logical arguments and reasons to justify its decisions. Apart from the abject failure to preserve more of Dunbar Castle in the nineteenth century - a century more than any other which saw societies dedicated to preserving national monuments - greater effort could have been made to enlist the support of some national agency like the Royal Commission on the Ancient and Historic Monuments of Scotland to assume responsibility for the castle. The errors of local administration go back much further however. A classic example occurred in the eighteenth century when the local bailies decided to dismantle the town's mercat cross because it stood in the way of such traffic as existed at the time. Dunbar's symbol of wealth and history was, in these mens' minds, a nuisance; they ordered it to be taken apart and used to line a street drain! Such behaviour by men who personally benefited from the town's burgh status with its trade and commerce is nothing short of a scandal.

The contribution of generations of the working population is, with one or two individual exceptions, poorly documented. A book dealing with a long period and many diverse themes is inevitably the product of several years of research, yet in many respects, I am conscious that I have barely scratched the surface in some of those themes. Some readers may be interested only in the last one or at most two centuries, having had their appetite for history dulled by the history lessons they endured at school - and usually English or European history at that. Perhaps a fresh approach will rekindle their interest and perhaps local and recently arrived people will want to know more about Dunbar's niche in the history of Scotland. For me, this has been a fearsome responsibility in attempting to predict what people will expect from this book. If it runs to a further print, I would welcome the views of local people on any of my more glaring sins of omission.

That I am not a professional or academic historian is perhaps evident in the style in which this book is written However, I believe that modern historians recognise that they have to combine the talents of the actor with those of a disciplined spectator cum psychologist. The spectator observes and records, the actor attempts to get beneath the skin of his subject. My impressions of Dunbar in general and its earls and castle in particular do not reinforce any political attitude; I am simply interested in the attractions of history rather than political theory although it is difficult to separate the two. Hopefully, I have managed to avoid the amateur historian's greatest pitfalls - reaching conclusions and filling gaps in knowledge with glib personal views. In attempting to interpret bald statements and brief facts in official documents, I have also tried to avoid passing judgement on individuals, viewing them in the light of the standards of their time. There is a growing demand for history written in this way today; at last it is being seen as literature worthy of study, not simply a dry subject written by academics for academics.

The true historian is not the implacable enemy of myth and legend. While he or she must pay due attention to folklore, the prime objective is to record fact. I believe that fact is more interesting than fiction. And Dunbar is steeped in fact, which is confirmed by what has survived the depredations of progress. Its tolbooth or town house is its most direct statement, indicating what once was.

If I were asked to explain my reason for writing this book, I wouldn't hesitate in my reply. It is a tribute to a town where I was born and grew up, a town that shaped me. It is also in recognition of the efforts of two local men, George and James Miller, the forgotten men of Dunbar who between them did much to put this small community on the Scottish map.

1

The Castle

Today, Dunbar exudes an atmosphere of long-settled peace. Looking down on it from the Lammermuir Hills, the community drowses at the edge of well-cultivated, almost lovingly arranged fields. In summer, great cloudscapes sweep across land and sea, casting moving shadows over Belhaven Bay and its long beach which stretches beyond West Barns Links, culminating at the floodwater plain of the river Tyne. The overall effect is that of a sleepy postcard scene which contains little to suggest a past which was often violently disturbed.

It is appropriate that a book about Dunbar should begin with its castle. Not only was the castle the reason for much of the town's history; it also gave the burgh its heraldic seal. In return, the community provided the local ruling family with its surname; in their time, the Dunbars gave the town status, first as a free burgh in 1370 which ultimately led to its elevation to a royal burgh in 1445.

Throughout the Middle Ages, Dunbar Castle was a key fortress in south-east Scotland, guarding the east coast route to Edinburgh. It withstood several sieges and became a bargaining counter in the incessant wars with England. Today's pathetic ruin conveys little impression of its considerable strength and importance, unlike the better preserved East Lothian strongholds at Hailes, Dirleton and Tantallon. By Scottish standards, it was large, at one time accommodating a garrison of nearly two hundred foot soldiers and archers. James Miller, *The History of Dunbar* (1830) (*Miller, Dunbar*) rightly acknowledges the contribution the castle made to Scotland's history - not always, it has to be said, in Scotland's interest. Why then has it received scant attention in contemporary and modern histories? Why was it never preserved by such organisations as the National Trust for Scotland or the Royal Commission on the Ancient and Historical Monuments of Scotland? Was national indifference compounded by lassitude on the part of the local authorities? Perhaps after more than a century and a half, *Miller, Dunbar* needs to be re-assessed and Dunbar Castle's story re-told before what little of it is left tumbles into the sea.

We do not know for certain when a fort first appeared on the rock adjacent to the Victoria Harbour, nor do we know who built the original version. In all probability, the first fortified dwelling was constructed by the Votadini, one of the many disparate British-Celtic tribes which settled in Scotland at the end of the Bronze Age. Archaeological excavations in the Castle Park between 1987 and 1993 confirmed the presence of an Iron Age fort or settlement on which was superimposed a later Anglian settlement. However, it wasn't until Dunbar was fortified in stone in the mid-thirteenth century that references to it - scant though they are - begin to appear in state documents like the *Exchequer Rolls* (*ERs*) and the *Register of the Great Seal of Scotland* (*RMS*)

Through the efforts of archaeologists, we now know that fortifications existed in and near Dunbar from early times (see *Castle Park Dunbar:* Two Thousand years of a Fortified Promontory). Probably the first to establish defensive camps in the vicinity were the late Bronze and early Iron Age colonists whose hill forts are scattered throughout the Lammermuir Hills. These forts were constructed on high ground for security; whether the sites were chosen to form a cohesive defence system or as part of a larger military strategy is not obvious, although this is possible. Did the earliest settlers establish the community of Dunbar on its present-day site? Possibly not. Archaeological finds corroborate the existence of small isolated sites which were occupied for long periods, particularly where conditions permitted crop cultivation and animal husbandry. We know that the Votadini predominated in the vicinity from the Iron Age until the late sixth century. The warrior tribe was one of several Brythonic-Celtic peoples who settled various regions in Scotland long before the Roman and Anglian invasions occurred. At one time, the Votadini kingdom extended from Lindisfarne (Northumberland) to Stirling. In the first century, when the Roman legions marched into Scotland, the Votadini appear to have made a mutually beneficial treaty with the invaders and possibly assisted the Romans in subduing a revolt in Wales. There is evidence that Roman auxiliaries lived close by Traprain Law, site of the Votadini capital at that time; in recent years, the remains of a Roman farm have been detected north of Traprain Law by aerial photography near the modern A1 road. This suggests a peaceful co-existence either by arrangement or by conquest, although the latter is unlikely; the Votadini were allies of the Romans who trusted them sufficiently to bear arms and quell a Welsh revolt.

When the Romans withdrew from Scotland in the fourth century AD, the Votadini appear to have been strong enough to withstand attacks from their northern neighbours, the Picts who, while scorning them as former clients and allies of Rome, were unable to dislodge them from the Lothians. The Votadini warrior-class ensured that their civilian population could follow a relatively peaceful existence, engaging in agriculture and living in their stone, wood and earth settlements in the hills until late in the sixth century. That the Votadini were predominantly a warrior race is confirmed in one the earliest Scottish poems to survive; *The Goddodin*, written in c.600 by the contemporary poet Aneirin, describes how the Votadini knights attempted to halt the advance of the Angles of Bernicia (old Northumbria) into Scotland but were decisively defeated at Catterick. The poem is written in epic style and describes the exploits of several hundred knights, some of whom are named. Out of an army of several thousand which left Edinburgh, only Aneirin and the warrior-knight Cynon the Stubborn returned to their king Mynyddog to tell of the defeat. After that defeat followed the battle of Degsastan - thought to be modern day Dawston in Liddesdale, in 603AD which ensured that the days of Votadini dominance in the Lothians were numbered. Much speculation surrounds the fate of the Votadini, who fade from history about this time. Did they retreat north only to be enslaved by the Picts, their temporary allies against the Angles or were they forced to join the Strathclyde Britons in the west? We will never know. An obscure race, the Votadini have left little of their history other than a few hill fort sites and, of course, the famous Traprain Law treasure discovered in 1919. Archaeologists believe that Traprain Law was settled as early as 700BC which comes as no surprise; the great whale-backed hill is a natural fortress commanding a clear view of most of East Lothian and the sea coast. Occupied continuously until the late fifth century, it offered security against Pictish sea-raiders. In its final days, Traprain probably served as an outpost monitoring Anglian probing expeditions.

Looking at Dunbar from its dominant feature, Doon Hill, logic and perhaps some speculative imagination suggest the hamlet of Dunbar probably evolved as a result of the expanding population among the hill-top dwellers. To be able to leave Doon Hill suggests two possibilities - either the threat of external attack had diminished or else a powerful authority had been established which encouraged the tribe to settle and cultivate the lower ground. It was probably the Votadini warrior-class who provided the necessary security to allow the Doon Hill dwellers to farm the lower slopes, then the flat plateau which stretches from Stenton in the west, through Spott, Easter and Wester Broomhouse, Pinkerton and the farms at Eweford, Hallhill, Lochend and Oxwellmains-Broxburn. Dunbar or *Dynbaer* (Old British-Celtic) translates as 'the fort on the point' or 'the strength on the height' but was it situated on the promontory above Victoria Harbour known as Castle Park which isn't particularly high, nor indeed is the Castle Rock! It is not beyond the realms of possibility that *Dynbaer* originated on and was named for the Iron Age fort on the summit of Doon Hill, which we know the Votadini occupied till the late fifth or early sixth century AD. Further support for this theory is that while it is traditionally accepted that Dunbar is named after its fortress, it is mentioned in Eddius Stephanus, *Vita S. Wilfridi* a century and a half before a castle is first mentioned in 856AD

Considerable excitement in archaeological circles occurred some thirty or so years ago when excavations on Doon (*Dyn* or *Dun*?) Hill revealed the traces of an Anglian timbered hall; even more exciting was the uncovering of an earlier structure beneath it, believed to have been British (Votadini). Either the Votadini built the structure or supplanted those who had, modifying it to suit their own needs. Perhaps the earlier settlers were Bronze Age farmers and hunters who recognised the relative safety and the proximity of water and good pastureland. Were these early settlers forced to farm the lower ground, dominated by the warlike Votadini? Were they the real founders of the hamlet of Dunbar? This is a broad assumption but it is entirely feasible.

We know that the pre-Iron Age inhabitants of Scotland were agriculturalists from the few standing stones which have survived at Easter Broomhouse, near Doon Hill, at Kirklandhill and Pencraig Hill, both near East Linton, some five miles from Dunbar. It is thought that the stones were primitive calendars used to deduce the seasons by plotting the sun's position in the sky; they may also have had some religious purpose. Evidence of the Iron Age farmers' existence near Doon Hill was discovered in 1962, when a long cist cemetery was uncovered near Lochend Woods and in full view of the hill. Were the several skeletons those of farmers who cleared the woods and cultivated new fields while remaining within safe distance of their fortified camp? The discovery suggests the beginning of a movement to lower ground, probably out of necessity, thus giving further weight to my theory that Dunbar derived its name from the Doon Hill settlement.

After the Romans evacuated Britain in c.410AD, England was colonised by Angles, Jutes and Saxons; by the sixth century, the Angles had occupied middle and northern England; from Northumberland, they began to infiltrate south-east Scotland. In the course of a century, Anglian aggression forced the Votadini into flight or submission; the Pictish elements in Lothian were also pushed back across the Firth of Forth. At one point, the Anglian empire stretched from the Humber to beyond the Forth. As peace is the first requirement of human development, it is certain that by 638AD, the former Votadini hamlet of Dunbar was fortified to ensure that peace was maintained. Dunbar, with its natural harbour at Belhaven undoubtedly expanded within less than three decades after Degsastan. It was occupied by Anglian soldiers and became an important shire centre in East Lothian. The Anglian chieftains were not slow to appreciate the strategic value of Doon Hill; they built a new stronghold on its summit to forewarn them of invasion by sea and the hinterland of the Lammermuirs. As for the Votadini in *Din Eidyn* (Edinburgh), they may have joined with their Strathclyde allies or even emigrated to Wales to join those whom the Votadini chief Cunedda had led and settled there after helping the Romans to put down the Welsh revolt mentioned above.

Anglian influence was pre-dominant in south-east Scotland for the next three centuries. Consequently, East Lothian and Berwickshire became the most Anglicised shires in Scotland. A military presence in Dunbar began in the Dark Ages and continued until the twentieth century. *Miller, Dunbar* and others suggest that fortifications existed in or prior to the fifth century AD; Miller considered these were Pictish but this is unlikely as the Votadini preceded the Picts in the Lothians, ruling there until relatively late in the sixth century. Excavations which took place in 1989 on the site of the former Castle Park confirmed the presence of human habitation from at least 75AD.[1] There is little doubt that the Angles occupied a settlement which had been established in the Roman-Iron Age period; whether they inherited a land-based fort or one on the Castle Rock cannot be established with certainty.

By 638AD, Edinburgh had fallen to the Bernician Angles who controlled the whole of the Merse (modern Berwickshire), East Lothian and Midlothian.[2] At that time, Dunbar was administered and occupied by officials and soldiers of king Ecgfrith, or Egfrid, one of the most ambitious Bernician-Anglian rulers. The Angles certainly brought stability to the Lothians; Belhaven was a natural haven for Anglian shipping and fishing boats, providing a landing stage for Bernician vessels engaged in trade. We know that Dunbar was sufficiently important to warrant the presence of a fairly senior royal official from two accounts - one almost contemporary and another written in the eleventh century.[3] Both accounts confirm that in 680, Dunbar was under the jurisdiction of Tydlin, a reeve or prefect in Egfrid's service.

Anglian expansion continued until it was challenged in southern Pictland. Initially, Egfrid defeated the Picts in 672 and was able to occupy territory north of the Forth; by 685 however, Pictish hopes were regenerated by a new king called Bridei mac Bili who encouraged his people to throw off the Anglian yoke. Egfrid was not a man to allow any affront to his authority to go unchallenged, particularly by a people he considered were no better than savages. In order to restore Anglian hegemony and salve his injured pride, he crossed the Forth in 685. Bridei lured Egfrid ever northwards, then attacked him in strength at Nechtansmere, or Dunnichen Moss, in Forfarshire, where the Anglian king was decisively defeated and killed. The battle marked the high-water mark of Anglian ambitions in Scotland. Defeat was thought to be a divine judgement on Egfrid, who in 680 had incarcerated Wilfrid, the opinionated and overbearing Bishop of York, at Dunbar,[4] ostensibly because of the cleric's haughty manner in pursuing ecclesiastical politics, his vulgar show of wealth but most importantly, his influence over Egfrid's beautiful first wife. Wilfrid's biographer, the monk Eddius Stephanus recounts that one of Egfrid's jailers had refused to punish Wilfrid, so the king '....angrily ordered the holy bishop to be sent to his town of Dunbar, to the reeve named Tydlin, whom he considered a more cruel man.' Tydlin kept Wilfrid in solitary confinement and tried to chain him. Eddius records that a minor miracle occurred; the smiths found that the chains they'd forged for the bishop's arms and legs were either too large or too small. Unfettered, the holy man was left alone, no doubt defiantly singing hymns and saying prayers to while away the eight or nine months of his captivity in a dark cell overlooking the North Sea. This occurred while Egfrid and his second wife Erminburga were lodging at Coldingham '.... making their progress with worldly pomp and daily rejoicings and feasts, through cities, fortresses and villages ....' presumably a royal tour intended to impress the local population.

There is a suggestion, possibly based on the fact that, having become a frontier town, Dunbar was the seat of an English *eorl* or earl in c.680; it is more likely that the town formed part of an area under the jurisdiction of an *ealdorman* who had similar status to an earl and governed his district with the assistance of *thengs* or thanes. After Egfrid's death, Anglian influence in Lothian was undoubtedly shaken but it was slow to wane. The Angles were gradually pushed southwards during the reign of Kenneth mac Alpin, king of the Dalriadic Scots and Picts (843-58). Kenneth invaded Lothian no fewer than six times, burning Dunbar on at least one occasion. For some years, suzerainty over Lothian would be bitterly contested although the Scots do not appear to have been strong enough to keep it. Scottish raids were probably intended for plunder rather than territorial gain at this time.

Then in about 973, Kenneth II of Scotland (971-95) received Lothian as a gift from Edgar, king of a by now united England on condition that he did homage for it.[5] Lothian remained under Scottish jurisdiction until 1005, when it was taken by Uchtred or Uhtred, Earl of Northumbria in retaliation for Malcolm II's attack on

Durham that year. Lothian became permanently Scottish in 1018, when at Carham-on-Tweed, Malcolm II (1005-34) defeated Eadulf Cudel, the late Uhtred's half-brother and weak successor. During the prolonged Anglian retreat from south-east Scotland, Dunbar must have again experienced upheaval and was forced to adjust to yet another cultural change; even if the common people were left to continue their largely agricultural existence, their lives would have changed to some extent.

It is perhaps appropriate here to briefly summarise the story of the castle at Dunbar during the Middle Ages. At the beginning of the eleventh century, Dunbar was controlled by Patrick de Dunbar, a soldier in Malcolm II's army; in 961, there had been a Thane Patrick of Lothian in the army of the Scottish king Indulfus, or Indulf (954-62) but it is unlikely he was the same Patrick who fought for Malcolm. *Miller, Dunbar* states that Patrick de Dunbar was killed in 1005 fighting the Danes at the battle of Mortlake '....a town of Mar.'[6] Being without male heirs, Patrick's thanedom was possibly given to a Nothumbrian noble when Uhtred re-took Lothian the same year. When Lothian was annexed permanently by Scotland in 1018, the thanedom was held by the crown until 1072, when Malcolm III (1034-93) gave Dunbar and its surrounding lands to his cousin Gospatric, the deposed Earl of Northumberland.

It is not possible to establish whether an Anglian fort still existed when Gospatric settled in Dunbar; however, we know there was a fort of sorts there in 856, built either on the Castle Rock or on the nearby site known as the Castle Park. One source implies that a wooden fort existed and was 'burnt in 856'[7]- probably by Kenneth mac Alpin - then it was made impregnable; it is likely that a stockade was erected on the Castle Rock at some point and that its creator may have come from Bamburgh, Northumberland, possibly Eadwulf, ruler of Old Bernicia (c.890-913) who could not have failed to compare the site at Dunbar with Bamburgh Castle. The Eadwulfings - so-called after the dynasty's founder, Eadulph or Eadwulf (see **Fig 1**) - were Gospatric's ancestors.

Fig 1: The Eadwulfing Dynasty of Bernicia-Northumberland c.890-1072

Northumberland County Hist. vol ii indicates that Gospatric of Northumberland (Gospatric I of Dunbar)may have been descended from the Anglian Eadwulfings, so-called after the dynasty's founder, Eadulf I, as follows:

Eadwulf I	c.890-913	
Ealdred	c.913-927	Son of Eadwulf and *ealdorman* of Bernicia; he was responsible for the defence of the church lands of Lindisfarne in the Wear Valley
Danish rule	927-754	
Oswulf	954-	A native Anglian earl
Eadred	945-955	King of Englan who ruled Bernicia-Northumberland direct
Eadwulf II (Eadulf Yvelcild)	955-973?	Named Yvecild in *de Regibus Saxones* or *Primo Saxonium Adventa;* during his reign King Edgar gave Lothian to Kenneth I of Scotland
Waltheof	975-1006	Son of Eadwulf II?
Uchtred or Uhtred	1006-1016	Gospatric I's maternal grandfather
Eadwulf III (Eadulf Cudel)	1016-1018	Uhtred's half brother who lost Lothian after the battle of Carham-on-Tweed in 1018
Ealdred II	c1019-1038	
Eadwulf IV	1038-1041	

From 1041 until 1067, the earldom was ruled by men appointed by English and Danish kings although the line of the Eadwulfings continued through Gospatric of Northumberland (Gospatric I of Dunbar), then Waltheof from 1072-1075.

The Eadwulfings ruled Northumbria from the ninth to the eleventh centuries. The same account referred to above suggests that Gospatric made improvements to and extended an existing fort when he arrived in Dunbar in 1072. It may well have been Gospatric who re-fortified the Castle Rock because, like Eadwulf, he was familiar with Bamburgh and would have readily appreciated the strategic value of a stronghold built on a sea-girt promontory.

It is probable that Gospatric or his son, Gospatric II replaced the crude stockade at Dunbar with a structure on the Castle Rock. Gospatric's fort probably consisted of a wooden tower within a defensive timberwork. When stone castles appeared two centuries later,[8] skilful use of the natural rock made Dunbar's castle virtually impregnable, able to withstand the missile-throwing artillery used in siege warfare until the advent of gunpowder and roundshot.

Because it was dismantled several times, it is impossible to determine when the first stone castle appeared in Dunbar but it may have been one of the earliest to be built in East Lothian, probably in the mid-thirteenth century. We cannot tell what the original structure looked like since much of the ruins visible today are those of James IV's castle built between 1497 and 1501. However, James' version probably differed little in design and size from earlier structures. One thing is certain; it was impressive. James employed the foremost master masons of his day, men who had worked on other royal buildings such as Holyroodhouse in Edinburgh. The meagre ruins which survive today give little impression of the castle's strength or size - large by Scottish standards of the time. With the help of several eighteenth and nineteenth century engravings and using imagination, we can envisage the austere beauty of the castle walls and sea-towers dominating the immediate coastline in what is still a romantic setting today.

At the end of 1567, parliament decided the fate of Dunbar Castle; it was to be dismantled. The gates were locked, the keys handed over to burgh officials, then it was gifted by James VI to a local burgess, William Boncle or Buncle, along with its policies. Parts of the castle were demolished in 1568, the spoil probably used by local builders for cottages, walls and dykes; we also know that a century later, Cromwell plundered the ruin to repair the east pier at the Old Harbour. Only the shell survives today; sections of the curtain walls and their sea-towers have tumbled into the sea over time. About a third was blasted out of existence in 1842 to form the entrance to the New or Victoria Harbour. Only the forework, part of the gatehouse and main ward and one wall

NMS

Illus 1: *Dunbar Castle in a storm*

of a tower survive; the last is arguably Dunbar's most familiar landmark from the sea. The engraving of painting of Dunbar Castle in a storm by J M W Turner (**ill 1**), a moment of high - if romanticised - drama is particularly interesting as it gives us a fair idea of what the castle looked like prior to 1842.

As far as can be established, it is probable that Dunbar's first stone castle was built by Patrick, 6th Earl of Dunbar (1232-48) since in his time, Scotland experienced a boom in castle-building. Dunbar ranked alongside Dirleton, Yester and Hailes and probably pre-dates them.[9] Strategically, it was more important than these castles since it dominated the east coast land and sea routes into Scotland. Whoever built Dunbar Castle had considerable resources at his disposal. A large workforce of masons, stonecutters and labourers was required; stone, timber, tiles and other materials had to be moved from distant sites. It is thought that the red sandstone quarry at Bowerhouse or Bourhouse provided the stone; the same quarry supplied the stone for the Parish Church which was re-built in 1819-21. The expense of building a castle was met from its owners's coffers so he had to be rich; at that time, wealth derived from rented landholdings so the local vassals and tenants met some of the cost. However, a castle offered protection - in theory at least - to the local population. That the 6th Earl possessed considerable resources is beyond doubt; by the early thirteenth century, the earldom was prosperous and Scotland had enjoyed peace and stability for many years. The 6th Earl also owned several manors and vills in Northumberland from which he received rents from his vassals and tenants. The Dunbars made full use of the administrative system of the day, maximising their income and influence in their earldom, which was virtually a petty kingdom in a fertile and productive region of Scotland.

The assumption that the 6th Earl built the first stone castle is supported to some extent by an event which took place in 1244. For some reason, Patrick failed to pay annual homage to Henry III of England for his Northumbrian possessions, a serious breach of feudal law which did not pass unnoticed. Perhaps Earl Patrick, now secure in his new stronghold, deliberately ignored his legal obligations to the English king. This is not improbable, though the consequences would have been loss of rights to feudal service and revenues due to Dunbar from his manors and vills in Northumberland. Another explanation for the Earl's contumacy may have stemmed from a continuing and long-standing dispute his family had with the monks of Tynemouth concerning the ownership of two manors in the parish of Tynemouth. Perhaps the 6th Earl had grown tired of the squabbling and asked himself whether the diminishing rents being paid by his English tenants in 1244 were worth the trouble of collecting.

Dunbar ranked next to Roxburgh as the most important castle in the south-east; perhaps this is difficult to appreciate today, as the scant remains of the castle do little justice to what was once an impregnable stronghold with several stout sea towers. Tytler, *History of Scotland,* describes Dunbar as 'a castle of great strength and extent, one of the keys of the kingdom, by which the Earls of [Dunbar and] March commanded so much influence in an age of war and invasion.' Chapters 2 and 4 examine in greater depth the part Dunbar Castle played during the Dunbars' occupation of it from 1244 to 1435. This chapter concentrates on the castle's various roles in Scottish history after the forfeiture of the Dunbars in 1435.

Stone castles were a major development in Scottish architecture; traditionally, they have been associated with war and military strategy. Their appearance certainly marked the end of the relatively peaceful early Middle Ages and with it, predominantly wooden defensive structures. It was the arrival of post-Conquest Norman, Flemish and French knights in Scotland which led to the introduction of stone castles north of the Border. Those who built them were men of instinct and action rather than rationalisation and contemplation. Their aim was purely and simply to dominate. Castles were symbols of power rather than military outposts; they were physical evidence of an authoritative presence. Owners of castles upheld the king's peace and enforced the king's laws. The castle was a symbol of the rigid, hierarchical society in which power, wealth and influence were concentrated in the hands of a few families such as the Dunbars with their hereditary titles and estates. Castles are usually associated with the cult of chivalry and knightly conduct, highlighted by historically naive novelists like Sir Walter Scott. In point of fact, they were the visible sign of the presence of a powerful lord in the neighbourhood. A castle was the focal point of jurisdictional, governmental and fiscal control of the area in which a baron lived. Just as a castle dominated the landscape, its owner regulated the lives of the inhabitants; very little was done without his knowledge and permission. Thus the castle was the appropriate setting in which a noble fulfilled his feudal and social obligations to medieval feudal kings and their courts which travelled about the country. It stood for power and power was integral to the apparatus of government of the realm which aimed to keep the population at large under control. Its owner was automatically entitled to a seat in parliament and membership of the king's councils. And of course, in time of war, it was the rallying point for the local noble's feudal knights and their retainers. Thus the castle was a statement in stone, indicative of status and authority. The nobles of the Middle Ages were practical men; they knew how to influence those around them with an outward show of wealth. They were accustomed to snapping their fingers at their inferiors and they expected - demanded - instant obedience.

The emphasis on defence was however uppermost; it allowed few concessions to luxury. Castles were cold, draughty and ill-lit, especially in winter. Even so, they were home to the noble, his family and personal retainers; very few castles maintained a standing garrison and only in time of war was the castle's domestic population swollen with soldiers and archers. Today, they are significant reminders of the fabric of rural social life and the administrative machinery of the time, although the modern view that they were primarily military establishments undoubtedly predominates.

As noted earlier, while more than one castle was built on the Castle Rock between the thirteenth and sixteenth centuries, it is unlikely that the several versions differed significantly until the arrival of gunpowder and roundshot influenced architectural styles. A castle's strength depended not only on its method of construction but also on the topography of its site, owing much to nature as well as art; this explains why most castles rarely conform to any set style, although many share similar features. The castle at Dunbar was literally grafted on to living rock. The strongest point was the barbican, or forework, since the main entrance was its only vulnerable feature. The barbican and its associated gatehouse were particularly well constructed which is the main reason why a substantial part of the forework has survived at Dunbar to the present day. The stonework still looks solid, even if the facing has long since disappeared. The gate was probably made of wood rather than iron; at the time of the famous siege of 1338, we know from contemporary accounts that the gate was of wood and shod with iron. What survives of the forework today was built in 1497-50; while the gatehouse itself no longer exists, there is a surviving inverted 'keyhole' type of gunloop - used for discharging hand-held firearms - today blocked by fallen masonry.

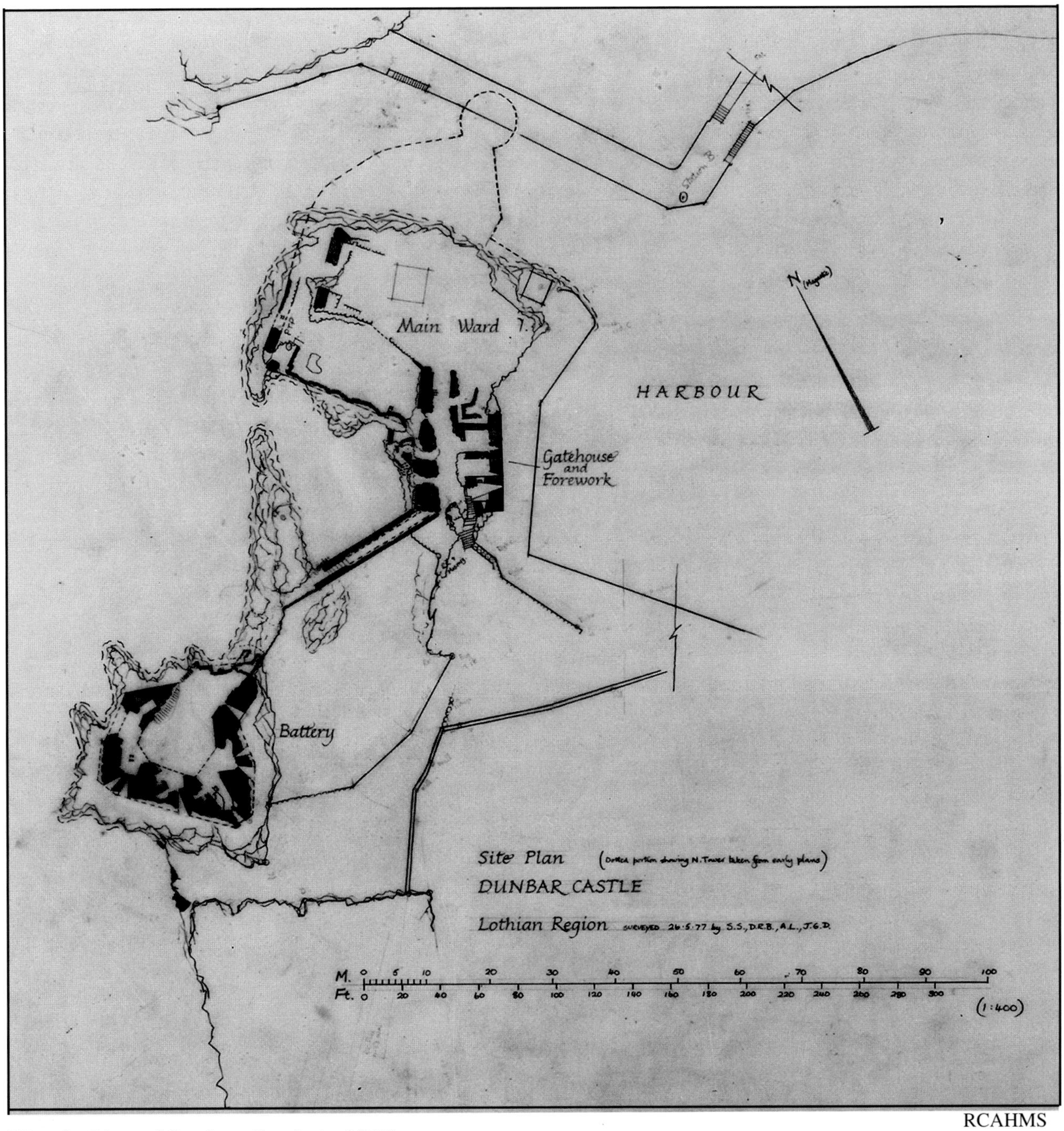

RCAHMS

Illus 2: *Plan of Dunbar Castle in 1977*

The approach through the barbican is steep and steps were added later for the benefit of sightseers; during the Middle Ages, access to the main ward may have been more gradual. The gateway led to an inner courtyard from which the living quarters diverged. Some of the cellars and rooms can be seen in the western aspect; they appear as irregular holes which have been exposed by the collapse of the curtain walls. One of the largest holes is locally known as Mary, Queen of Scots' bedchamber which she reputedly occupied in 1567 but this is highly unlikely; the queen's bedroom was probably on the upper floor, looking seaward. (**ill 2**)

Dunbar's original size and outline can be seen from the plan of its two floors, which also shows the portion

Illus 3: *Castle from the east, c.1830* KLM

lost when the Castle Rock was blasted in 1842 to create the new harbour entrance. Scottish strongholds of the time were usually built to suit the site on which they were constructed and were usually several sided enclosures with a courtyard, curtain walls of between seven and nine feet thick and between 20 and 30 feet high. Angles in the curtain walls were protected by square or round towers, the latter being the case at Dunbar. These towers were placed strategically to defend adjoining walls and support other towers. The principal tower was known as the *donjon*, invariably situated in the innermost court where the lord, his family and their retainers could make a last stand during sieges. The lower part of the *donjon* was commonly used as a prison - hence the word dungeon. In Dunbar's case, according to a plan of 1860 by John Mason, a Belhaven surveyor, the dungeon was situated on the site now occupied by the harbourmaster's office.

While it is impossible to confirm whether the curtain walls had rampart walks, this is likely, as we are informed by one of the contemporary chronicles that during the famous siege of 1338, Black Agnes led her maids on to the walls to dust them whenever a stone projectile struck home. The garrison usually lived in the corner towers, evidenced by the existence of *garderobes* (primitive privvies) in towers that survive elsewhere.

The main hall - centre of castle life - with its adjacent kitchen was probably situated in the north-west aspect; most of the living quarters were on the safer northern aspect, both areas presenting difficult targets for land-based siege artillery and cannon. There may have been a small family chapel in the castle during the Dunbars' occupancy; we know for certain that one dedicated to St John of the Cross existed in James IV's castle as money was paid to a painter to decorate it in 1501.

Illus 4: *Castle from the east, 1789* NMS

Miller, Dunbar tells us that one or two of the castle's towers rose from sea-level; we also know from the above plan that there was access by a stairway rising from sea-level at the northern aspect, as well as a waterstair in the eastern aspect which allowed access to the gatehouse. The frontispiece from Miller's history (**ill 3**) shows what the structure looked like in his day; the earlier drawings by Francis Grose (**ill 4**) give an impression - if somewhat out of scale - of the exterior facing west. Miller considers that a remnant of the cross wall (**ill 5**) which survived after the harbour was built, succumbing a few years later to a violent storm; since it incorporated a panel bearing the Dunbar heraldic insignia, it pre-dates the castle built by James IV. The wall probably shielded the principal apartments occupied by the earls and their families (see also description in 1760 by Richard Pococke in Chapter 3). The insignia consisted of a large triangular shield with a lion rampant with a

NMS

Illus 5: *Castle from the north, 1789*

bordure of eight roses - the Dunbar coat-of-arms - the shield being adorned with a helmet and crest of a horse's head bridled. On the left was a shield bearing the three-legged symbol of the Isle of Man and on the right, a saltire and the insignia of Annandale. The Man and Annandale honorifics were added after 1346, when the 9th Earl acquired these lands through his Countess Agnes, daughter of Thomas Randolph, 1st Earl of Moray.

A well was situated to the left of the castle forework (**ill 6**); it is not known whether there was a fresh water

NMS

Illus 6: *Castle gatehouse with well in foreground, 1820s*

supply within the castle, although this is likely. The engraving also shows the entrance to the natural undercroft within the rock, used in its day for access, part of which is now utilised as storage by local fishermen with access through an iron grilled gate, added after the Victoria Harbour was built. An engraving of the exterior from the east (**ill 7**) gives an idea of the approach to the castle from the east and a view from the west is reproduced from an engraving dated 1814 (**ill 8**). The portion of the castle lost at the time of the construction of the new harbour is indicated by the plan shown earlier. The Blockhouse (**ill 9**) constructed between 1515 and 1521 was a half-moon battery which was unroofed; it was connected to the main building by a covered walkway built from sea level, the last vestiges of which collapsed in 1993 (**ill 10**). A modern panorama (**ill 11**) gives an impressive view

Illus 7: *Castle from the NW, c.1900* RJP

of both Blockhouse and castle. The beach which allowed access by sea on the northern side survives at the Grippes or Grips and is known locally as Johnstone's Hole; a portion of the outer limit of the castle rock incorporated into the north facing harbour wall marks the limit of the castle rock, with the free-standing rock stack which can be clearly seen in the illustration taken from the *frontispiece* of *Miller, Hist.* Although much of the castle was destroyed on parliament's orders in 1567, a substantial portion remained until 1842, when the new harbour was built. Much of the structure has fallen prey to the elements, tumbling inwards and on more than one occasion, into the harbour mouth and the sea. We may share the frustration of a

Illus 8: *Castle from the SW, 1820s* NMS

Illus 9: *The Blockhouse from the N* DDHS

disgruntled correspondent who wrote to the *Haddingtonshire Courier* at the beginning of the twentieth century, complaining about the failure to preserve more of the castle in her time.[10] It is somewhat ironic that a significant portion was destroyed in 1842 to create the harbour entrance - now widely accepted as being in the wrong place as it is accessible only with care and the benefit of experience at certain stages of the tide; in the opinion of many modern seafarers, the entrance to the Old Harbour - now blocked - is a safer point of entry whatever the state of the tide.

RJP

Illus 10: *The walkway from castle to blockhouse before it collapsed in 1993*

Thus Dunbar's strategic value lay in its geographical position, guarding both land and sea approaches to Edinburgh. Whether for Scotland's good or ill, Dunbar could never be ignored or discounted by invading English armies. When Berwick was in English hands, the castle formed part of the vital chain of fortifications in the south-eastern defence system, both as a base from which raids could be mounted and where troops and supplies could be concentrated. It also served as a signal station to warn the east coast population of invasion. The castle's offensive and defensive value altered when Berwick changed hands, one of the main reasons why the Scots could never make up their minds whether to maintain or dismantle it. Being relatively close to the Border, its owners were often lured by the promise of gold or other rewards by offering it as a bargaining counter. The fortunes, political attitudes and allegiances of the Dunbars and those who came after them were governed to a great extent by the geographical location of their castle. (The various owners and governors of the castle appear in Appendix A).

Dunbar was the principal seat of the old earldom of Dunbar and March, the strongest of the Dunbars' several residences in East Lothian and the Merse, or Berwickshire. In addition to Dunbar, the earls built defensive towers and fortalices in Berwickshire. These included Cockburnspath Tower (**ill 12**), Stoneypath Tower, Innerwick Castle (**ill 13**), Thornton and Billie Castles - neither has survived - and a fortalice at Dunglass; with Dunbar, these formed what the 8th Earl termed his 'Seven War Steeds'. Most of these small strongholds were primarily used as summer residences when the earls and their families went hunting, visited their vassals and tenants in the Merse to collect rents or attended the fairs at Roxburgh, Kelso and Berwick.

RM

Illus 11: *Panorama of the remains of the castle in 2000*

When James I deprived George, 11th Earl of Dunbar and March of his title and lands in 1435, Dunbar Castle again reverted to the crown. Initially, it was held for James I and James II by the Hepburns of Hailes Castle (**ill 14**),[11] former vassals of the Dunbars; James II subsequently gave the earldom and its principle castle to his infant son Alexander, 3rd Duke of Albany which encouraged the latter to engage in a power struggle with his brother, James III. From 1435 to 1567, Dunbar Castle played paradoxical roles in the history of Scotland, occupied by those who were either hostile to the crown or at odds with the prevailing political scene. During the first half of the sixteenth century, Dunbar served as a signal station, a base for both English and French troops, a prison for unruly Highlanders and briefly, Scotland's main arsenal. It continued to be the official residence of the wardens of the East March, men whose loyalties were sometimes suspect because they often entertained English ambassadors and were tempted by English gold. Several Stewart monarchs resided within the castle's walls; it sheltered a desperate Mary, Queen of Scots after Riccio's murder in 1566; it was the scene of Mary's alleged rape by the Earl of Bothwell and the signing of the subsequent contracts that gave her consent to their short and tragic marriage in May 1567.

NMS

Illus 12: *Colbrands' Path (Cockburnspath) Tower, 1789*

When James I was murdered by some of his disaffected nobles in 1437, rival factions - the Douglases, Livingstons and Crichtons - vied with each other for power. The Queen Dowager, Joan Beaufort and her young son, James II, were constantly threatened by the shifts and swings in court politics. Finally, the Douglases and the Livingstons formed an alliance to counter the queen's party which included the Crichton and Kennedy faction led by Bishop Kennedy and James Stewart of Lorne, the queen's second husband. Queen Joan died at Dunbar Castle on 15th July 1445, an event which obliged its keeper, Adam Hepburn of Hailes, to surrender it to James II. However, Hepburn's son Patrick re-occupied it in 1446; on 28th April,[12] James, still in his minority, accused Patrick Hepburn of '.... the maist treasonable takyn [taking]of our castell of Dunbar, bernying [burning]her schippis [ships], slaughtyr, prissonying, oppression of our peple, and destruction of our land, and mony other detestabill enormyties and offence.' The accusation of imprisonment relates to Hepburn's capture of John Oll, Prior of Coldingham, in retaliation for raids made on Hepburn possessions by Sir Alexander Home of Dunglass. The Hepburns and the Homes had both benefited from the Dunbars' forfeiture in 1435 and Alexander Home began to cast acquisitive eyes on Hepburn's considerable Merse possessions.[13] Coldingham, a rich Benedictine priory and dependency of Durham, once under the protection of the Dunbars and their vassals the Hepburns, had favoured the Douglases as their protectors earlier in the fifteenth century, a fact which not only alienated the Dunbars but rattled the Homes as well. As for the Hepburns, they had little respect for the Dunbars, particularly after 1433, when the 11th Earl of Dunbar and William Drax, a former Prior of Coldingham supported their rivals the Homes. Robert Lindsay of Pitscottie's *Historie and Cronicles of Scotland (Pitscottie Hist.)* informs us that the Earl of Northumberland ravaged Dunbar in 1448, probably in retaliation for the kidnap of John Oll; then on 30th November 1466, the deposed 11th Earl of Dunbar's son Archibald burnt Dunbar but unable to take its castle,[14] he proceeded to capture the Hepburn stronghold at Hailes, near East Linton. Archibald's motives are somewhat obscure; he may have intended to secure Dunbar and use it to bargain with James II in an unrealistic attempt to force the king to reinstate his father in his earldom. Whatever his reasons, Archibald had little choice but to surrender Hailes to the Douglas faction, then disappear from the political scene. James II besieged Dunbar unsuccessfully and was forced into a compromise with Hepburn which restored the castle to the crown and resolved the Home-Hepburn feud.

NMS

Illus 13: *Innerwick Castle, 1820s*

After James II was accidentally killed by an exploding cannon during an attempt to recapture Roxburgh Castle from the English in 1460, his widow, Mary of Gueldres, took up residence in Dunbar Castle, probably with her nine year-old son, James III. Mary distrusted several of the nobles whom she rightly suspected would attempt to seize the boy king to achieve their political ambitions.. As a precaution, she replaced the governors of Stirling, Edinburgh and Dunbar Castles with her own supporters. Mary remained at Dunbar until 1462;[15] from 1460 until her death in 1463, the Queen Mother acted as Guardian of Scotland, attempting to control her

Illus 14: *Hailes Castle, 1820s* NMS

nobles through the usual Stewart stratagem of divide and rule, playing factions against each other. At this time, the York-Lancaster Wars of the Roses were in progress and as a consequence, England posed less of a threat; Roxburgh fell to the Scots, Berwick was handed back to Scotland by Lancastrians sheltering there and for the first time in many years, the Borders were free from English occupation.

The Stewart dynasty was bedevilled by monarchs who ascended the throne in their minorities. From the outset, James III faced the same problem as his father. This time, the country was split between the Kennedy and Boyd factions who attempted to gain control over the young king.[16] Throughout his reign, James III resorted to ill-chosen favourites for counsel; he further complicated matters by alienating his brother Alexander in 1476. The reasons for their quarrel is obscure but Alexander, aided by their youngest brother John, Earl of Mar, had designs on the throne. Unwisely, James gave Alexander the governorship of Berwick, the guardianship of the East March and the earldom and castle of Dunbar. Created 3rd Duke of Albany, an honorific revived by James II for his second son, the title had unfortunate associations; it had been last used by two ambitious guardians of Scotland in whose interests it was to keep James I a prisoner in England from 1406 to 1424. The 1st Duke of Albany, Robert Stewart, son of Robert II, was renowned for his deviousness; his son Murdoch, 2nd Duke was equally venal and the 3rd Duke would prove even more troublesome than his predecessors. Alexander was determined to have the Scottish throne and when his brother and co-conspirator the Earl of Mar died, he turned to England for help

Aware at last of the fact that a hostile presence in Dunbar could put national security at risk, James III updated the arrangements for warning of invasion, possibly to subtly remind Albany that Dunbar was a key fortress in the early warning system. In October 1465, parliament met at Stirling and enacted regulations which provided for watchmen at the traditional fording places of the Tweed; on the approach of an English army, beacons were to be lit at Hume and Edgerton Castles, then Soutra, Dunbar, Haddington and Dalkeith. Beacons ignited on Traprain and North Berwick Laws would also be the signal for all able-bodied men in East Lothian to muster at Haddington.

Albany was ideally placed to begin clandestine negotiations with England. Although there is no reliable documentary evidence to explain James' sudden attack on his brother in the Spring of 1479, he accused him of 'treasonably stuffing' Dunbar Castle with hostile troops, breaking a truce with England and causing the death of one John of Scougall. Some historians consider James' actions unjustified and Albany's indictment suspect; Scougall's murder seems to have occurred somewhat inconveniently *after* James made his allegations which may suggest that Scougall was a spy in James' pay who was discovered and suitably dealt with by Albany's men; equally credible is that Scougall was murdered by the king's supporters in a bid to bring about a confrontation between the king and his rebel brother. Whatever the truth, James acted on evidence which suggested his brother's complicity in some intrigue or other and he had Albany arrested and put in Edinburgh Castle. Albany escaped soon afterwards by dirking his drunken guards and using knotted bedsheets - were there enough to negotiate Edinburgh's high walls? - lowered himself to freedom. One is tempted by the view that James - or more accurately, his advisers - allowed Albany to escape to involve himself in further hostile attempts against the king, thereby discrediting himself further. At any rate, Albany rode to Dunbar, munitioned and garrisoned the castle with pro-English forces, then set off for France where he hoped to enlist Louis XI's support for his claim to the Scottish throne. Albany was politely received by the French king who took pity on his destitute state; Louis even tried to effect a reconciliation between the brothers. Albany persisted with his requests for French military aid to depose James. Louis was the wrong choice however; the French king's reign was one of a progressive strengthening of the French crown at the expense of the nobility. A shrewd and autocratic monarch, Louis laid the foundations for absolute monarchy in his own country and was hardly likely to encourage a usurper in another, particularly a country whose king he regarded not only as legitimate but friendly towards

France. Unable to secure Louis' help, Albany turned yet again to England in April 1482, finding a more sympathetic ear in Edward IV.

After Albany's escape from Edinburgh in 1479, James III ordered his Chancellor, Andrew, Lord Avandale, to recover Dunbar Castle. Although it cannot be proven, Avandale's ensuing siege was probably the first occasion cannon were used by and against the castle.[17] The garrison put up a spirited defence and never formally surrendered. As the adjacent Blockhouse wasn't built until the following century, the castle's artillery were mounted on its ramparts; operated by expert gunners, a well-placed shot killed three of the besieging nobles - Colquhoun of Luss, James III's chamberlain, Wallace of Craigie and Shaw of Sauchie. When Avandale finally got inside Dunbar Castle in December, he found it empty; not only had the entire garrison slipped away by sea during the night, they had removed most of the castle's valuable furnishings!

Albany was declared a traitor before the gates of Dunbar and at the mercat [market] cross in Edinburgh in July 1479. His confederates at Dunbar - the Merseman John Ellem of Butterdean,[18] constable of the castle, Gavin Home of Manderston and Jacobus de Edington - were charged with high treason, unlawfully occupying a royal castle and causing the deaths of several score of individuals, including of course the three unfortunate nobles mentioned above.

By 1482, despite rejection by France and the loss of his estates, titles and royal appointments, Albany persevered with his claim to the throne; he contrived successfully to convince Edward IV of his right to be king of Scotland on the entirely spurious grounds of James' illegitimacy. Edward heard what he wanted to hear and on 10th and 11th June,[19] Edward and Albany signed two documents, one of which was a treaty regarding Scotland's future government. Now styling himself Alexander IV of Scotland, Albany swore allegiance to the English king, promising that within six weeks of conquering Scotland, he would pay homage to Edward for his crown. He also undertook to end the *Auld Alliance* with France and give Berwick to England within fourteen days of entering Edinburgh. In return, Edward promised English military aid and even offered his daughter Cecille in marriage to Albany.

Everything was in place by the summer. At the end of June, Albany and the Duke of Gloucester - the future Richard III - began their march north. Meanwhile, the Scottish nobles, irked by the resumption of hostilities on the Border in 1481 and the rapidly deteriorating political scene persuaded James to act timeously and prevent the fall of Berwick, Albany's obvious choice to begin hostilities. The Scottish army got no further than Lauder. Angered by James' persistent courting of favourites and lesser men, several disgruntled nobles gathered in Lauder Kirk to decide how best to resolve the situation. The nobles opted for the most effective and direct way of showing their disaffection. Their ringleader, Archibald Douglas, 5th Earl of Angus ordered several of James' sycophants to be hanged from Lauder Bridge, an incident which earned him history's epithet *Bell-the-Cat* for getting rid of the hated minions, reputedly in the king's presence. James survived the conspiracy which even his queen had supported. In their minds, the nobles' demonstration of lack of confidence in the king was more important than resisting the imminent invasion. James was led back to Edinburgh where he was warded in Edinburgh Castle

Meanwhile, Berwick held its own against Albany and Gloucester who consoled themselves by laying waste to Jedburgh before resuming their march on Edinburgh. Thereafter, the 'invasion' began to assume the elements of farce; faced with Albany's *coup d'etat* and squabbling at the Scottish court, the nobles agreed to negotiate with Albany without the king. On 2nd August, Chancellor Avandale came up with a pathetically naive compromise; if Albany swore allegiance to James III, his former rank, titles and estates would be restored. However, Albany had to agree to return any money he had received from Edward IV as dowry for his proposed marriage to the English princess. Albany accepted these terms willingly on the understanding that James III would be freed and the invasion force would go home peacefully. Gloucester, encamped outside Edinburgh, was totally unaware of these proceedings; he was showered with gifts and 8,000 merks from the local merchants, fearful that the city would be burnt. On learning of Albany's deal with Avandale, a disgusted Gloucester turned south; ignoring the treaty to which he wasn't party to in any case, he took Berwick on 24th August 1482, when it became permanently English. Gloucester had little else to offer Edward IV by way of recompense for the expense of the invasion.

The treaty signed at Edinburgh came apart almost as soon as the ink was dry. Albany bided his time. Although his attempted coup on the throne had been premature, Albany could see that James had lost the support of the majority of his nobles; to ingratiate himself with these nobles, boasted that he would recapture Berwick for Scotland. He had no intention of doing so but made a half-hearted attempt through the Lammermuir Hills, turning back at the eleventh hour. It was no more than empty posturing, a ruse to wrong-foot James' remaining supporters. In the months that followed, he publicly announced that he and his brother were reconciled while privately continuing to plot against him, manipulating the disaffected nobles. At first, Albany favoured the nobles who declared for him, then he upbraided them for their treatment of the king. To confuse them even further, Albany had James set free to convince those still loyal to James that he had no further designs on the throne. His double-dealing backfired however; several nobles began to doubt his sincerity and decided that James was the lesser of two evils. By December 1482, James commanded more support than he had all summer.

James III, a stubborn, self-willed and delinquent king reverted to type on regaining his freedom. He surrounded himself with favourites again and incurred parliament's displeasure by adopting a placatory policy towards England. Even if he hadn't learnt the lessons of Lauder, he at least set about undermining any residual support among the nobles for Albany, forcing him to turn again to England. Albany issued letters on 12th January 1483 from Dunbar Castle;[20] these authorised the Earl of Angus to negotiate with the English king on his behalf. Then on 11th February, Edward IV came up with a proposal similar to that of the previous year; Albany accepted it and urged Edward to invade Scotland via the East March, promising him Dunbar as a base. By the end of February, James had knowledge of his brother's continuing duplicity; Albany had played his last desperate card and support in Scotland for him dwindled rapidly. Isolated in Dunbar Castle with only a few soldiers, the frustrated Duke was forced to sign a humiliating and curious indenture on 19th March;[21] its terms required him to end his intrigues against James and not to come within six miles of the king's person. Albany honoured the second of these terms but shortly afterwards, he went to England to conduct fresh negotiations with Edward. Before leaving Dunbar, he reinforced his garrison with English troops to convince the English king of his resolve. Added to the farce that was never far from Albany's dealings, fate finally went against him. Edward IV died on 9th April 1483 and English support for him was forgotten in the ensuing constitutional crisis which gave England three kings in one year - the others being Edward V and Richard III. Albany was forced to go into exile in France where in 1485, jousting in a tournament, he was accidentally killed by a splinter from a shattered lance.

A truce was arranged between the Scots and the English on 21st September 1483 which would last for three years.[22] The treaty made specific provision for Dunbar Castle; it was to be neutral for the first six months of the truce; thereafter, the Scottish king was obliged to inform England that he desired removal of English troops by the end of the six-month period. The treaty also made provision for meetings between Scottish and English commissioners on the Border and at Dunbar to settle any affairs relating to the Scottish and English Marches. James III ratified the treaty on 21st October.[23] Dunbar was occupied by English troops purely as a precautionary measure to dissuade the Scots from resuming Border warfare at a time of political uncertainty in England and possibly because of the threat Albany might pose should he return to Scotland. The Scots left the castle to its own devices until February 1485, when parliament ordered it to be retaken. An army was raised with provisions for a 28-day siege; in the event, the castle held out from May till December 1485, probably because of Dunbar's impregnability, the tenacity of the besieged and the poor morale of the besiegers. The Scottish forces were given no cannon to reduce the castle; presumably James was reluctant to antagonise the English king or he intended to starve the garrison into submission. The latter view is perhaps reinforced by parliament's order that all grain stored at West Barns, Newtonlees and Oswald Dean - hamlets within a radius of two miles of the castle - was to be removed for safekeeping. This is perhaps a comment on the freedom of movement the castle garrison enjoyed during the siege. When James' troops finally entered the castle in December 1485, Henry VII made no protest at the violation of the treaty. The phoney war which had begun in 1481 finally flickered out.

With Berwick permanently English, the Scots regarded Dunbar with understandable ambivalence; the question was whether to maintain it for defensive purposes or dismantle it, thus denying its use to the English or perhaps a home-grown troublemaker like Albany. Even before the trouble with Albany, Dunbar was considered a mixed blessing; the chronicler of *Liber* Pluscarden was moved to write '...of the many evils wrought by this castle.'

After James recovered the castle, he gave it to Lord Bothwell, then changed his mind because of growing tension between himself and the nobles. One dispute may have been over the revenues of Coldingham Priory which involved the Homes and the Hepburns. By 1488, James III saw southern Scotland slipping out of his control; a faction of nobles including the Earls of Angus and Argyll, Lords Gray, Home, Hailes and Drummond seized Dunbar Castle and its gold, arms and ammunition, then proceeded to Leith where they captured the king's personal baggage train and treasure, awaiting removal to Stirling. The rebels declared James' son king. An infuriated James confronted the rebels at Sauchieburn, near Stirling; he reputedly bore Bruce's sword but the Bruce luck was not with him that day of 11th June 1488. During the fighting, the king's horse bolted from the field, then threw him. A concussed James was taken to a nearby cottage where an unknown assailant murdered him. Thus the crown passed to his son, James IV who never forgave himself for conspiring against his father. For the rest of his life until his death at Flodden, he wore a heavy iron chain about his waist, adding another link every year.

Never an effective or popular king, James III may have ordered Dunbar Castle to be demolished as, shortly after his death, parliament did so, justifying its decision on the grounds that the East Lothian coast could no longer be defended and because the castle '.... hes done gret scaith in tyme begane ....' . Perhaps in referring to previous trouble, parliament had in mind not only the 3rd Duke of Albany but one or two earls of Dunbar. During James IV's minority, the Great Chamberlain, Alexander Home [24] was appointed steward of Dunbar and probably supervised the dismantling of its castle; it would remain in ruins until 1496, when James IV, rejecting parliament's advice,[25] decided to rebuild it. He was right to do so as by then relations between himself and Henry VII were rapidly deteriorating and full-scale war was imminent. In 1496, administrative responsibility for Dunbar passed to Andrew Wood of Largo,[26] one of Scotland's most renowned sailors. Perhaps it was Wood who persuaded James to rebuild the castle as a supply base for his navy as he was appointed its governor.

Because of James' support for the pretender to the English throne, Flemish-born Perkin Warbeck, relations with England swiftly deteriorated; James was prepared to assist anyone who challenged the Lancastrian king and he made no secret of the fact that he supported the Yorkist alternative in the person of Warbeck. For his part, Warbeck agreed to restore Berwick to Scotland in exchange for military assistance against Henry VII. Warbeck was pronounced rightful king of England by Margaret of York, Dowager-Duchess of Burgundy. Warbeck declared he was her nephew Richard, Duke of York, one of the little princes allegedly murdered by Richard III in the Tower of London. Warbeck married a daughter of the Earl of Huntly, thus reinforcing his acceptance in the Scottish court. James IV, best remembered as a builder of ships, palaces and castles, was resolved to pursue an aggressive policy towards England and appointed a diplomatic mission to promote recognition of the Stewart dynasty in Europe. His support for Warbeck was a foretaste of the full-scale war that would culminate at Flodden in 1513.

One of James' initial preparations for the expected war with England was the rebuilding of Dunbar Castle. Records indicate that the work began in March 1496, when Andrew Wood of Largo received £5 Scots (under £1 sterling) to buy lime.[27] Early in April, James was on site, personally supervising the quarriers cutting stone, the labourers clearing the rubble for the masons and 'wynning' the nearby freshwater well; for the latter, John the quarrier received a payment of £21:17:3 (about £3-4 sterling). The master mason was Walter Merlioune,[28] one of a family of stonemasons in the king's employment; his initial work - for which he was paid £20 (just over £3 sterling) - was completed by Whitsun. In April, the forework was strengthened and roofing beams were ordered for ' Hannis' Toure'; Hans was one of James' master gunners from the Low Countries.[29] On 1st April, John Mawar received a part payment of £3 (ten shillings sterling or 50p) for wheels he was making for the 'bombardis and mons'- obviously cannon - and in May, nails for the gate and bolts and rivets were delivered. A blacksmith called Thom Barker arrived thereafter to measure and weld the great cross-barred iron 'yett' or outer gate. James must have been well pleased with progress at that time as he authorised payments of 35 shillings (9 shillings sterling or 45p) as 'drinksilver' for the masons and six shillings (one shilling sterling or 5p) for a fiddler to entertain them.

James next ordered a bedchamber identical in size to the royal bedchamber at Edinburgh Castle; Pate Falconer was paid two shillings (4p) and sent to Edinburgh to 'mak Dunbar sic lik'.[30] In June, Master Merlioune returned to 'pend' the hall, erect Hans' Tower - possibly the upright which survives on the Castle Rock today - and complete various other works. Rafters were delivered by sea in August; the roof of Hans' Tower was almost complete by September, when more rafters were delivered. The armoury was augmented by three breech-loading guns as we know from a payment made to John Lam [Lamb], a smith. The castle wasn't finally completed until 1501 with the installation of iron grills for the windows; shortly afterwards, a chapel dedicated to St John was added at a cost of £10 (just under £2 sterling). On 30th August 1505, a painter received five French crowns (about £3 sterling) for decorating it. Dunbar remained a royal castle until its demolition in 1568. However, in 1497, no doubt an embattled Henry VII was aware of its rebirth through his spies in the East March. Faced with domestc crisis and a rebellion in support of Warbeck in Cornwall, Henry was obliged to sue for peace. In 1503, James IV married Margaret Tudor as part of the 'Treaty of Perpetual Peace', subsequent events would prove this treaty somewhat hollow. The marriage was celebrated in William Dunbar's famous poem *The Thistle and the Rose*.[31] When Margaret passed Dunbar on her way to meet James at Dalkeith, the castle guns gave her a royal salute. As marriage gifts, Margaret received the Earldom of March and the Lordship of Dunbar and Cockburnspath; James kept Dunbar Castle for himself however. At Dunbar's mercat t] cross on 29th May 1503, James Logan, sheriff of Edinburgh, publicly announced that he was granting *saisin* [ownership] and corporeal possession 'of the earldom of Dunbar and lordship of Cowburnspecht' [Cockburnspath] to the queen's attorney; this was witnessed by two local bailies, John Lermonth and William Liddell and others present such as Robert Ross, canon at Dunbar Collegiate Church.[32]

From 1503 until Henry VII's death in 1509, Scotland and England enjoyed peaceful relations. Little of historical moment occurred at Dunbar Castle until Flodden although on 5th November 1512, a few quixotic Highlanders made an unsuccessful attempt to rescue their kinsman Farquhar MacIntosh from imprisonment;[33] MacIntosh had no doubt been warded in the castle as guarantor of his clan's good behaviour. His kinsmen were caught and hanged; he was released the following year.

After the tragic defeat and death of James IV at Flodden (**ill 15**) on 9th September 1513, castles near the Border were hurriedly reinforced to meet the expected English invasion which never materialised. On 10th January 1514, the Lords of the council appointed to govern Scotland during James V's minority prepared a memorandum '....to consider how the strenthis and castellis of Fasscassell [Fast Castle, Berwickshire] and Dunbar salbe providit in men, artazelry [artillery], and vittale [victuals]........in all possible hast [haste].'[34] James' cousin John, 4th Duke of Albany, a Frenchman by birth and education, was appointed regent, a task he performed with limited success. Albany understandably was more interested in maintaining the *Auld Alliance* between Scotland and France, an alliance which often as not was detrimental to Scotland's well-being. In the incessant hostility and open warfare between England and France, Scotland was often a French pawn. However, Albany was astute enough to make Dunbar Castle his principal base and he installed a French garrison and French gunners to guard the east coast route into Scotland. The castle, then under the governorship of Robert Forman, Dean of Glasgow Cathedral, was passed to Anthony d'Arcy, Sieur de la Beaute at some point after 20th November 1514. While it cannot be established beyond doubt, it is thought that sometime between 1514 and 1517, Albany drew up plans for an artillery blockhouse adjacent to the south-west of the castle. Public records are strangely silent about the Blockhouse - even the building costs are not recorded - but we know it existed in 1521. *The Accounts of the Lord High Treasurer of Scotland* (*TA*) record a payment made to 'Robert of Borthwick' in July 1515 to hire workmen for Dunbar Castle. For what reason? And to what use was put deliveries of timber, deal boards, lead and iron between September and December that year?[35] Known locally in more recent times as the *Gunholes* or the *Magazine*, the Blockhouse reflected the evolving pattern of warfare in the sixteenth century. The Blockhouse was without doubt the work of d'Arcy, Sieur de la Beaute, more commonly known to history as Sieur de la Bastie.

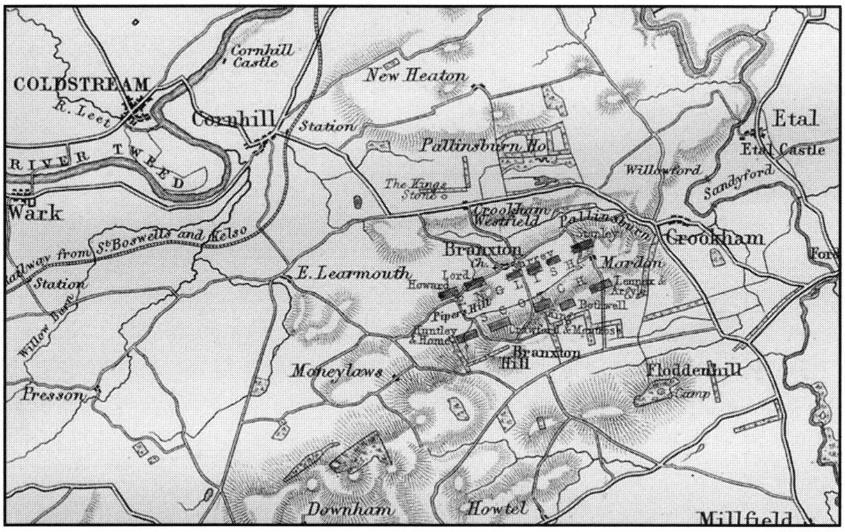

KRM

Illus 15: *Flodden battlefield*

The French master masons who built the Blockhouse used the rock formation to good effect, protecting the castle's flank with a clear field of fire. The Blockhouse was built on what today appears to be a freestanding rock; however, modern archaeological investigation has proved that the Blockhouse was built on a promontory connected to the mainland by a natural ditch which was artificially widened and deepened between 1515 and 1521. Stonework beneath the edge of this enlarged ditch facing the sea to the west suggests that the 'ditch' was protected from attack by sea; there is also stonework above the remains of part of the fish hatchery on the foreshore which to the imaginative appears to be a stone throne. The Blockhouse could be reached only from the castle by means of a 69-foot long screen or traverse wall with a roofed-in walkway leading from the forework. *Miller, Dunbar* informs us that the building was octagonal, measuring 54 by 60 feet and was 72 feet high. Five gunports are visible today; these measure four feet at the loading platform and sixteen inches at the mouth. The Blockhouse was only partially roofed to allow maximum light. The guns could fire at two levels i.e. from a parapet above and a casement below; they could also be manoeuvred out of their landward-facing positions to face any threat from the sea. The wide-mouthed gunports allowed use of heavy artillery pieces; the oval embrasures were deeply splayed with large mural niches for storing ammunition and incorporated air shafts to draw off the smoke from the guns. Squat bastions like that at Dunbar were built to absorb cannon shot and prevent the stone shattering on impact. The design and style of the Blockhouse are undisputedly French; the gunports are identical to those in French castles of the period. Much of the seaward aspect of the Blockhouse fell into the sea many years ago; the remains of two vaulted chambers with evidence of a fireplace suggest that these were used as accommodation for the gunners. In its time, the Blockhouse was a state of the art artillery battery, making Dunbar even more formidable.[36] Although the Blockhouse lost its upper storey and facework many years ago, it is an important example of one of the earliest artillery fortifications in Scotland.[37]

De la Bastie was appointed governor of Dunbar Castle some time after 20th November 1514.[38] As Albany's knight, he was made warden of the East March, an hereditary office of the Homes; this was a grave error on Albany's part and one which would have tragic consequences. In December 1515, the French ambassador met Albany at Dunbar Castle to discuss matters of state, as payments were made to Adam Dundas and John Balfour to take official papers from Dunbar 'to the Queen.' (Margaret Tudor, James IV's widow and Henry VIII's sister had married Archibald Douglas, 6th Earl of Angus in August 1514). A new pro-English alliance was formed; an uneasy truce with England in 1516 was formed as a result of French diplomacy which gave those Scottish nobles hostile to Albany and his man at Dunbar an opportunity to intrigue against them. Albany's insult to the Homes did not go unnoticed; Alexander, 3rd Earl of Home, former Chamberlain of Scotland and warden of the East March put Dunbar to the torch. It was said that Home's mother had been roughly ejected from her family residence in the Borders and imprisoned at Dunbar for six weeks because she had visited queen Margaret at Coldstream. As Home was one of Margaret's chief opponents in Scotland, Margaret no doubt embellished the tale to cause mischief; she had never liked Scotland and took every opportunity to encourage squabbling between the Stewarts and their supporters as well as acting as a spy for her brother, Henry VIII. The queen complained that Home's mother had been forced to live on a diet of bread and water during her warding at Dunbar. Alexander Home, already insulted when Albany deprived him of his hereditary office, decided this latest affront to the honour of his house could not go unanswered.

After raiding Dunbar, Home was decoyed to Edinburgh, supposedly as part of the queen's plan to rid herself of the troublesome Lord Home; to justify Home's family's subsequent actions, it was reputedly de la Bastie who lured the 3rd Earl to the capital on what seems a suspiciously weak charge. According to *Diurnal Occurrents*, Home's crime was to allow 'work' to proceed at Norham [Castle?] On 8th October, 1516, Home and his brother were executed at Edinburgh. From that day on, de la Bastie's name was odious to those Merse families who were vassals of the Homes. It is thought that Thomas Fiennes, Lord Dacre, warden of the English East March had been engaged in clandestine negotiations - probably at the behest of queen Margaret - with certain disaffected Scottish nobles wishing to discredit de la Bastie.

Matters got worse as the summer of 1517 progressed. On 7th June, Albany left Scotland for France, appointing de la Bastie as his deputy and specifically charging him with the command of his base at Dunbar. By September, the Frenchman had increased the complement of gunners at Dunbar to six (see note 35). Determined to avenge the death of his kinsman the previous year, David Home of Wedderburn lured the Frenchman out of Dunbar by feigning an attack on Langholm. Home ambushed de la Bastie near Duns on 17th September;[39] attempting to escape, the French knight rode his horse into a bog, forcing him to continue on foot. Home easily overtook the Frenchman and decapitated him at Broomhouse, near Duns;[40] the spot is known locally as Battie's Bog. (A cairn reputedly marking the Frenchman's burial place stood there until the nineteenth century, when the stones were used to resurface one of the district roads).

The south of Scotland remained on a permanent war footing after Flodden; in June 1523, Kelso was burnt and raids occurred almost daily as Henry VIII threatened to invade Scotland. Then in September the same year, the Earl of Surrey crossed the Border and with Lord Dacre, torched Jedburgh; Scottish resistance and constant harrying forced Surrey and Dacre back to England. An armed camp was established at Douglasdale, as is shown in *TA;* the fisher folk of Musselburgh, Gullane, North Berwick and Dunbar were ordered to supply the camp with fish. Now back in Scotland, Albany mounted an attack on Wark Castle with his French troops but bad weather forced him to abandon the siege and leave 300 of his countrymen dead on the field. Queen Margaret continued to provide intelligence for Surrey and Dacre, informing them that Isabella Hoppringion, Prioress of Coldingham was another friendly spy.

At the age of twelve, James V inherited a lawless kingdom; when he ascended the throne in 1524, he was bedevilled by a pro-English faction of nobles led by his mother and his stepfather, Archibald, 6th Earl of Angus. This faction had grown confident during Albany's government; with his reputation tarnished over the Home affair and faced with the rise of the powerful pro-English faction, Albany left for France in May 1524. Although he promised the young king he would come back to Scotland, Albany never returned, preferring to serve Scotland as a diplomat at the French court.

From the outset, James V was determined to stamp his authority on Scotland. At age sixteen, he confronted his stepfather Archibald, 6th Earl of Angus, who took refuge in Tantallon Castle (**ill 16**). With only 500 troops, James advanced on Tantallon but Angus had fled to Coldingham, where he was no doubt well received by the co-operative Prioress Isabella Hoppringion. When James arrived at the Priory, Angus had gone to Billie Cas-

Illus 16: *Tantallon Castle, 1850s* KRM

tle, near Boncle. Resting at Coldingham, James awaited further intelligence of his stepfather's whereabouts when the elusive Earl suddenly attacked him with several hundred men. Angus chased the king and his allies the Homes to Dunbar Castle. James later besieged Angus in Tantallon but failing to reduce the castle with his artillery, he negotiated Angus out; Angus went to England, seizing every chance to stir up trouble for Scotland at Henry VIII's court.

Meanwhile, Henry VIII, preoccupied with his disputes with the pope in Rome, wanted no problems on his northern frontier. Despite a concerted effort to delay any major confrontation with the Scottish king, Border hostilities commenced in 1523. On 25th July the following year, the sheriffs of Edinburgh, Peebles, Selkirk and the bailies and magistrates in towns such as Dunbar were ordered to muster their local levies at 24 hours' notice and with 20 days' rations. The coastal dwellers in and near Dunbar were also ordered to keep a constant watch for enemy vessels in the North Sea.[41] This was one of the regular drills for protecting the south-east of Scotland, of which several examples are recorded in fifteenth and sixteenth century State documents.

Despite efforts by James V and Henry VIII to maintain peace, Border raiding continued, carried along on its own momentum. In October 1533, English troops burnt Coldingham; in retaliation, 3,000 Scots invaded Northumberland, destroying several villages. A further raid by Lord Dacre in the south-west provoked James V although nothing came of his threatened invasion of northern England. James also resented the presence of French troops at Dunbar who remained there until 1538, when as part of his marriage contract with Marie of Guise-Lorraine, they were evacuated as a placatory gesture in the interests of the *Auld Alliance.* Perhaps the French presence reminded James of the 4th Duke of Albany's less than satisfactory rule during his minority.

We know that after 1521, Dunbar Castle contained both garrison and field artillery. From 1538 onwards, *TA* records several payments to the gunners at Dunbar Castle, of which there were never less than five. It is also clear from the 1537 accounts that Dunbar possessed a foundry or arsenal as it is recorded that a payment was made to the castle's master mason for making 'sindry [sundry] munitionis to the Kingis schippis.'

By 1535, Henry VIII had rejected the authority of Rome and sought James V's support in furthering the cause of Protestantism; in 1541, he proposed that James meet him at York, then London but James refused to go further than York on the advice of his councillors who believed that because the death of James' two young sons had left the country without an heir, Henry intended to take him hostage and force Scotland to submit to him. Negotiations finally broke down and both countries began to prepare for war in 1542. Deterioration in the relations between France and England meant that Scotland was dragged into yet another war because of the *Auld Alliance.* Hostilities began with Scottish raids across the Border, then a retaliatory English raid intent on destroying Kelso. The English were ambushed and defeated by the Earl of Huntly at Hadden Rigg in the Borders. A humiliated Henry VIII then ordered a full-scale invasion of Scotland, the main purpose of which was to take Edinburgh. Preliminary preparations were made by the Duke of Norfolk who soon realised the logistical problems he faced in provisioning an army of 40,000. Henry's invasion ran out of steam and Norfolk limited his campaign to the burning of Eccles, Kelso and a score or so of small villages in the Borders. James V, eager to mount a retaliatory attack, was frustrated by his nobles' lack of interest although he nonetheless managed to gather a force of about 18,000 men. It was now James' turn to be shamed by his army's feeble resistance at Solway Moss on 24th November 1542, where casualties amounted to seven English and twenty Scots, with 1,200 Scots taken prisoner, including a score or so of prominent nobles. News of the defeat was carried to the king lying in his sick bed at Caerlaverock Castle. James died three weeks later; some said his heart was broken. He is remembered for his weary words on learning that his newly-born heir was a girl: 'It cam wi' a lass and it will gang wi' a lass.'[42] (This is a reference to the founding of the Stewart Dynasty through the marriage of Marjorie Bruce to Walter, the High Steward of Scotland in the fourteenth century; James' daughter was of course the future Mary, Queen of Scots).[43] Yet again, Scotland would be ruled by a French regent, this time for almost eighteen years.

Henry VIII gained considerable political advantage after Solway Moss since he netted a rich haul of Scots nobles - men like the Earls of Glencairn and Cassillis, Lords Maxwell, Fleming, Sommerville, Oliphant and Grey being among the *prominentes.* Henry would put these hostages to good use in his attempts to bring Scotland to her knees by a combination of political and diplomatic pressure. He also saw a way of destroying the *Auld Alliance* and tying Scotland to England's interests by marrying his son Edward to the infant Mary. But he reckoned without the strength of character of James' widow, Marie of Guise, among the most formidable women in Scotland's embattled history.

At first, Henry attempted to effect peace through negotiation and gentle persuasion. He argued that the disruption between the two countries had been caused by David Beaton, Cardinal of St Andrews. Beaton, he said, was totally opposed to the English Reformation and looked to France and Rome for support at the expense of Scotland's stability. To show good faith, Henry released the prominent peers of the realm taken at Solway Moss, although before doing so, he made them agree to help him gain custody of the infant Mary, intending she should marry his son Edward. To reinforce this, he separately and secretly coaxed signed statements from ten of the twenty nobles who swore they would recognise and support his claim as lawful king of Scotland if Mary did not survive.

The baby became the subject of intense diplomatic posturing; the English envoy, Sir Ralph Sadler, one of Henry's Secretaries of State, arrived in Dunbar with orders to secure the royal marriage of Mary and Edward, Henry's sole heir. These overtures achieved nothing and Mary was sent to France to marry the Dauphin in 1558.

As noted above, Dunbar Castle had been strengthened by the French around 1515x1521, a fact which greatly troubled Cardinal Wolsey who was virtually governing England. At that time, Wolsey requested Lord Dacre, warden of the English East March to report on the developments at Dunbar. Dacre's reply of 26th June 1521[44] does not mince words: '......it is a thing in manner unprenable [impregnable]; it standeth upon a crag and there is no way to go to it but one which is strongly and substantially made with ai new bulwar [a new bulwark] and sett with ordnance.....' This is unmistakeably a description of the Blockhouse - which *Pitscottie Hist.* describes as 'the utward [outward] blokehouse'. One of James V's final acts before Solway Moss had been to increase Dunbar's artillery firepower in October 1542. After Solway Moss, several Merse nobles sheltered in Dunbar Castle; its keeper, William Wemyss of Raith refused to deliver it to the hastily-formed Council of Scotland and the country's new governor and regent, James Hamilton, 2nd Earl of Arran. Perhaps Wemyss suspected that Arran superficially supported Scottish resistance to Henry VIII by his public show of murdering Henry's herald at Dunbar, a man who was travelling south presumably under diplomatic immunity several days after Solway Moss. Arran also had Cardinal Beaton arrested and imprisoned and paradoxically pardoned the pro-English Earl of Angus and Sir George Douglas who had fought at Hadden Rigg for England and managed to escape capture by the Earl of Huntly. It is clear that Arran was playing a double game, courting Henry VIII when it suited him, no doubt justifying actions which he believed were in Scotland's interests.

State documents reveal that in February 1543, two men in the services of the Earls of Arran and Moray were installed at Dunbar Castle to monitor travellers passing through the town - but to what purpose? Arran, ambitious and chameleon-like, changed the colour of his loyalty to Scotland, camouflaging his intentions to further his political aims. One day he would promise to introduce the Reformed religion to Scotland, the next he would champion Rome. In March that year, Arran took custody of Dunbar; in April, Henry VIII wrote to Sadler in Scotland, urging him to persuade Arran to send both Mary and his arch enemy in Scotland, Cardinal Beaton, to England. Sadler was also directed to ensure that Arran and Sir George Douglas got inside Dunbar Castle 'now or never'; this phrase perhaps underlines Henry's accurate appraisal of Arran's duplicity at this time. At first, Arran refused Sadler's requests on the grounds that both he and Douglas were detested by the majority of Scots for their placatory attitude to England and that the Scottish people would never allow themselves to be ruled by Henry. Then in July, Arran offered Henry several castles including Dunbar and Tantallon, while the nobles hastily re-aligned themselves between the two main contenders seeking a power-base; on the 'Nationalist' side were the Earls of Huntly, Argyll and Moray and on the pro-English side were Arran, Angus and Douglas. Arran, surprisingly appointed governor was as slippery as the proverbial eel. He was publicly opposed to the pro-French, pro-Catholic Beaton and declared his support for the Reformation which tacitly meant he was pro-England. However, Sir George Douglas, his ally, warned Sir Ralph Sadler that if Henry VIII exerted too much pressure on Arran to remove the young Mary, Queen of Scots to England, Arran would be forced to go over to the Beaton faction and the Catholic party in Scotland. Governor Arran the survivor was double-faced like the god Janus, presenting one face to Henry and Sadler and another to Beaton and the Catholic Marie of Guise, Mary's mother. With the Beaton faction in the ascendancy, Henry offered Arran 5,000 troops to subdue Scotland; Arran declined, remarking that 5,000 Englishmen in Scotland would raise an army of 20,000 Scotsmen to expel them. Yet still Arran kept ahead of the political dimension which grew ever more sensitive. A solution seemed to present itself in 1543, when Arran ratified the Treaty of Greenwich which promised peace if a contract of marriage between Mary and Edward were effected as soon as Mary reached the age of ten years. The stumbling block was English insistence on the end of the *Auld Alliance*; a more preposterous condition was that Mary should be educated in England. To complicate matters, France began to exert pressure on those in power in Scotland with tempting offers, including the payment of generous cash subsidies. Would a friendly but Catholic France or a hostile but Protestant England succeed? Arran finally threw in his lot with Beaton; money, France and Catholicism had won the struggle for dominance in Scotland. Or so it seemed.

In September that fateful year, Henry instructed Sadler to buy Dunbar Castle for a 'staple of money'; Henry needed Dunbar or Tantallon as a secure place for storing his 'treasour'- money to be used as bribes to weaken the resolve of those in Scotland who were proving unreceptive to his demands. Sadler had no hope of purchasing Dunbar; in October, he wrote to Henry informing him that the castle was held by a 'stout man who beareth none affection for Englonde'; that man was Robert Hamilton of the Briggs.[45] Tantallon, a Douglas stronghold, was a better choice since its owner, the Red Douglas Earl of Angus was pro-England. Although the Scots had trodden the road to union with England in 1503 with the marriage of James IV and Margaret Tudor, that road was no smoother in 1543; in December that year, the Scottish parliament revoked the Treaty of Greenwich and with Arran now reconciled with Beaton, war between the two countries was inevitable.

In the mid-sixteenth century, Scotland experienced English aggression to a degree unknown for many years, with East Lothian and the Merse bearing the brunt of the subsequent hostilities. With the Treaty of Greenwich in ruins, Arran was obliged to seek French military assistance, hoping unrealistically to marry his son to Mary, Queen of Scots. The *Auld Alliance* was restored. Arran received the honorific title Duke of Chatelherault and Scotland braced herself for invasion in 1544. Proclamations were issued for beacons to be ready along the east coast at Fast Castle, St Abbs Head, Domilaw, perhaps modern day Dowlaw - under the charge of Hamilton of the Briggs at Dunbar - and Traprain and North Berwick Laws; Lord Borthwick, keeper of Hailes Castle at East Linton was instructed to apply for assistance to Hamilton of the Briggs which made Dunbar Castle a key link in the Border defensive system.

After some preliminary raiding in the autumn and winter of 1543-44, the Earl of Hertford launched an impressive amphibious attack on Leith and Edinburgh in which a number of townspeople were killed and Holyroodhouse was looted, although the English somewhat exaggerated their claim that the city had been devastated. Arran lost his nerve completely, making a feeble attempt to halt Hertford at Leith. After burning parts of Edinburgh save for its castle which Hertford was unable to take and which continued to bombard his position, the countryside around Edinburgh was destroyed for a radius of seven miles. Hertford felt he had punished the Scots sufficiently to bring them back to the negotiating table. Virtually no resistance was offered against Hertford on his return overland to England; marching through East Lothian, his troops burnt Tranent, Haddington, Markle, Traprain, Kirklandhill, Belton, Hedderwick, Dunbar and East Barns. The worst atrocity took place at Dunbar, where the townspeople expected their wooden houses to be fired. Their fears were realised; on the morning of 26th May, when the frightened folk finally went to their beds, the English torched the town. Many men, women and children were either burnt to death or suffocated by the smoke.[46] Informing Henry VIII of his success, Hertford wrote that 'We have brent [burnt] the townes of Haddington and Donbarre, which we dare assure your majeste be well brent, with asmany [sic] other piles, gentlemens and others houses and villagies.'[47]

In November, Hertford destroyed Jedburgh and Kelso and took Coldingham Priory which he converted into an armed camp for his Irish levies. On 29th November, Arran gathered an army of 8,000 and borrowing a large cannon and several small pieces from Dunbar's armoury, marched to Coldingham to batter away fruitlessly at the Priory for a whole day and night,[48] then he rode back to Dunbar, leaving Angus with the artillery train to make his way back to Dunbar as best as he could.[49] The wily Earl of Angus had learnt his lesson from Arran; he was again engaged in secret negotiations with England while serving in the Scottish army.

Lothian and the Merse would not forget Hertford easily, nor he they. Now well appraised of the terrain and with little prospect of serious opposition from Arran, Hertford mustered his forces at Norham and returned in the winter of 1544 to destroy several small hamlets, burn Melrose Abbey and desecrate the tombs of the Earls of Douglas, the ancestors of the Earls of Angus. Despite his pro-English sympathies, Angus could not allow this insult to his house to go unpunished. With Arran's help, he attacked and defeated the destroyer of Melrose, Sir

Ralph Evers, at Ancrum Moor in February 1545. In retaliation, Hertford revisited the Borders later in the year, burning the harvest and the Abbeys of Kelso, Jedburgh and Dryburgh which like Melrose, were never restored.

The years 1544-45 are known to Scottish history as the *Rough Wooing* [50] because Scotland had repudiated that part of the Treaty of Greenwich providing for the marriage of Edward VI and Mary, Queen of Scots. During this period, the country was in turmoil, fuelled by the religious upheavals which would ultimately bring about the Reformation. Marie of Guise, James V's spirited widow, was Catholic and determined that her infant daughter would marry the Dauphin of France to ensure the continuation of the *Auld Alliance.* After Henry VIII's death in 1547, Edward VI's uncle Edward Seymour - Hertford - became king of England in all but name; he was to wage an even more destructive war against Scotland that year to further Henry's aims. Hertford maintained that his intention was to unite the two countries, not prostrate Scotland; he set his mind on a marriage of the royal children to unite the two kingdoms in an empire to be called Great Britain. It is perhaps worth pausing here to examine Hertford's political aspirations; before 1547, he vigorously denied his aim was the domination of Scotland, insisting that he only intended to free Scotland from the authority of Rome. Hertford's manifesto highlighted the material advantages which a royal marriage would guarantee. The united nation would be ruled by an emperor in the person of Edward VI and any heirs born of Mary Stewart. Hertford was anticipating the union of the crowns in 1603; however, he believed both countries should retain their separate legal systems and enjoy freedom of trade, thus pre-empting the union of the parliaments in 1707. To many in Scotland, it was an *auld sang* which sounded suspiciously like the dirge of English domination but with different words.

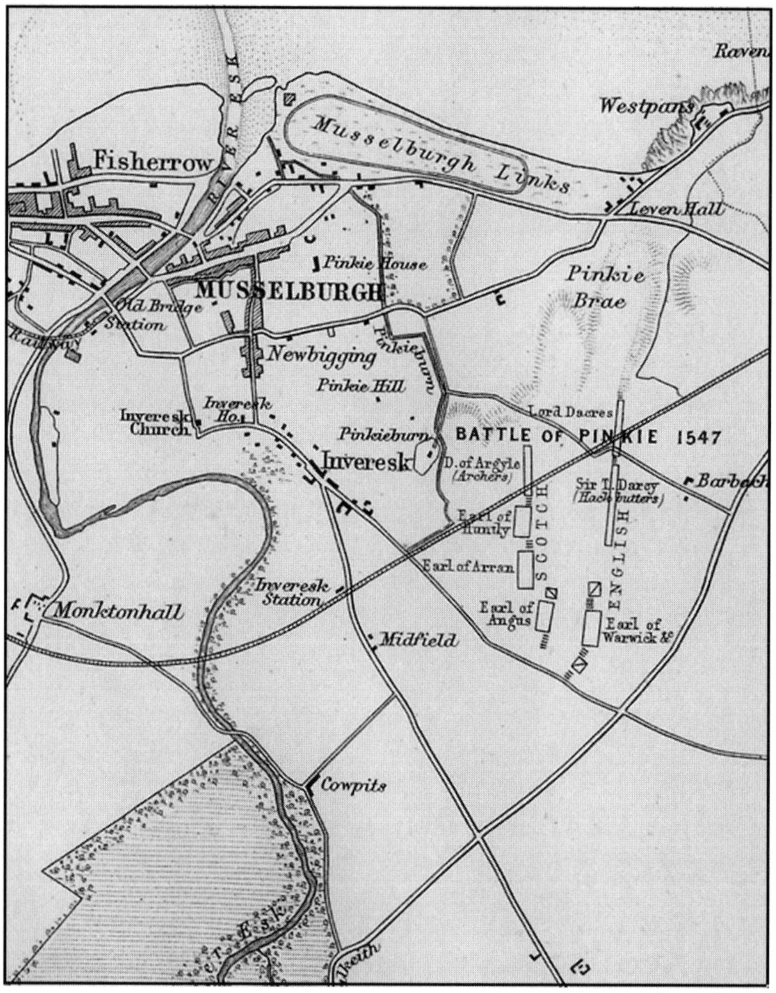

KRM

Illus 17: *Pinkie battlefield*

Hertford's expeditions of 1544 and 1545 had been aimed at bringing a recalcitrant Scotland to heel by a short, sharp shock. With the increasing threat of a full-scale invasion, many Scottish nobles began to have second thoughts about their anti-English stance; some even foresaw benefits from a closer relationship with England although whether the majority were prepared to go as far as constitutional union remained to be seen. A number of lairds expressed interest in the English proposals, particularly where religion was concerned; those in East Lothian for whom Rome was anathema - Heriot of Trabroun, Broun of Coalston, Cockburn of Ormiston, Crichton of Brunstane and Douglas of Longniddry - saw an opportunity to topple the Catholic Church. These men were among many who had supported the martyred Protestant George Wishart and harboured the arch-architect of Reformation, John Knox. The strength of feeling against Catholicism was steadily gathering momentum and the East Lothian lairds were in the forefront of the movement which brought the Reformation into being. This was particularly the case after the battle of Pinkie, when several of these lairds actually assisted the English victors, even accommodating the officers in their houses. For once, Scotland and England were joined against what they saw as their common enemy - Rome.

In 1547, Hertford, now styled Duke of Somerset and Lord Protector of England was a virtually unopposed dictator.[51] He was quick to exploit the religious unrest in Scotland and invaded for the third time. On this occasion, he was determined to achieve his aims with cannon rather than casuistry; his political reputation was at stake and he knew that the voices of opposition in England would not remain silent should he fail to bring the Scots to heel. He crossed the Border with the largest army ever to invade Scotland; his idea of reasonable force was demonstrated by a dreary succession of burnt monasteries, market towns, villages and fortalices throughout the Merse; reaching East Lothian, he burnt Dunbar and Haddington yet again. Somerset's final invasion was a wantonly destructive campaign which equalled the excesses of Edward I; he was equipped for war on a grand scale and was determined to give no quarter and thereby force the Scots to the negotiating table. The positive consequence of his bloody advance into Scotland was the temporary unification of Scots of all shades of religious belief and political opinion. Internal differences were laid aside; Arran's request for an army was direct as it was unique. He sent the fiery cross through the whole realm of Scotland, a war symbol of rebellion hitherto used only to raise the clans in the North. The summons was obeyed.

James Hamilton, 2nd Earl of Arran and Duke of Chatelherault was indeed a mixed blessing for Scotland; he had been deprived of the governorship of Scotland for his indecision after opposing Marie of Guise's attempt to become regent. He filled Holyroodhouse with his supporters and supplied them with powder and ammunition from Dunbar and grain from Leith. Civil war was averted when Arran climbed down and accepted parliament's censure of his behaviour. While the 1547 emergency restored him as governor of Scotland, Arran was a poor match for the experienced Somerset and was distrusted by a number of the nobles. Forced to accept his re-appointment, Marie of Guise nevertheless urged parliament to watch him closely; she became a member of a special war council formed ostensibly to advise Arran but in reality to monitor his activities.[52] In that troubled year, Marie was too weak to oppose Arran; she would have to wait seven years to obtain the regency she so desperately sought.

In the course of his destructive march through the Borders to Musselburgh, Somerset's route was marked by the smoke of burning communities. In that late summer of 1547, he created a base at Eyemouth to supply his troops remaining in the Merse as a rearguard screen; he destroyed the fortalice of Dunglass and the castles at Thornton and Innerwick.[53] Somerset was surprised that Arran had made no serious attempt to bar his way at the Paths of Pease - Pease Glen, outside Cockburnspath, an ideal place for blocking tactics. Even today, with the modern AI and its rail bridge, the ravine is a sickeningly deep and dangerous natural obstacle whose defensive potential is obvious. Although a few trenches had been dug in the vicinity, Arran's preparations were inadequate - perhaps deliberately so to follow the age-old Scottish tactic of luring the enemy from supplies while pursuing a scorched earth policy. Somerset's invasion occurred before the harvest, so there was no time to set fire to or gather the crops. The local lairds and nobles made no attempts to impede the English advance, which is curious. Once again, the poor Merse tenant farmers were forced to watch their homes, possessions and the labour of a year confiscated or go up in smoke. The ferocity of the invasion had at least instilled courage in the East Lothian fighting men as they answered Arran's summons to arms in droves at Musselburgh's market cross.

Somerset passed within cannon-shot of Dunbar Castle; its garrison did little more than discharge 'diverse shottes' into the English army, as an eye-witness informs us.[54] No attack was pressed home and Somerset brushed aside Arran's cavalry near the town. Apart from a few desultory shots fired from Hailes Castle, the English proceeded virtually unopposed through East Lothian. Another ideal opportunity for ambush at East Linton was lost; contact between the two armies was limited to some cavalry skirmishing on the narrow Linton Bridge across the river Tyne. By early September, Somerset had reached Pinkie on the outskirts of Musselburgh, having sustained negligible casualties on the march. His provisioning fleet commanded by Admiral Clinton was already anchored off the town, having sailed parallel with the army from Berwick, a tactic Cromwell would imitate in 1650.

At first, the Scots were strongly entrenched with the North Sea on their right flank and the Shire Moss, a marsh, on their left - an ideal position as it denied Somerset the use of his cavalry. Then for some reason - possibly overconfidence or perhaps because Somerset's redeployment movements led Arran to believe he was retreating - the Scots crossed the river Esk and reformed on the vulnerable plain of Pinkie Cleugh (**ill 17**). Even so, they were drawn up in good order and held a strong position, forcing Somerset to occupy Fa'side Ridge which limited the effectiveness of his cavalry. The Scots were drawn up in traditional *schiltroms* - densely-packed squares of infantry equipped with twelve or eighteen-foot long spears to repulse cavalry attacks. The Scottish army reputedly contained 30,000 infantry, outnumbering the English by more than two to one. Morale was high in the Scottish army. The battle opened with a cannonade from the English fleet anchored off Fisherrow; the shots fell amongst the advancing infantry squares which kept good order, beating off a cavalry charge and even breaking the English vanguard until they were halted by English archers. As the Scottish army fell back to regroup, the Highland elements mistook the movement for a general retreat and they broke ranks to loot the English baggage train. Panic spread through the army; the lines shivered, then shook and dissolved into a heaving mass of men intent on flight. Somerset ordered in his cavalry and the rout was complete. Casualties were 6,000 dead and 2,000 taken prisoner;[55] among the latter were the Earl of Huntly, Lord Hay of Yester, Colquhoun, Laird of Luss and Robert Hamilton of the Briggs, captain of Dunbar Castle.[56] English losses were estimated at between 500 and 600. Pinkie was almost as serious a defeat for Scotland as Flodden had been. The sole success story in the dismal campaign was that Dunbar Castle was never taken; writing to Somerset on 16th November,[57] Lord Grey of Wilton informed him that 'the king has few enemies in the Merse except in the castle of Dunbar.'

After Pinkie, the Scots had no option but to renew the *Auld Alliance* which Arran negotiated in December; in the process, he was required to hand over to the French certain key castles including Dunbar. By 1548, Somerset's war was concentrated in East Lothian and Dundee. In the same year, the infant Mary was taken to France and under Arran's treaty, she would marry the Dauphin in return for French support against the occupying English forces. The French set about creating a chain of defensive forts along the east coast, incorporating existing strongholds such as Dunbar, Eyemouth and Inchkeith into their system. In that year, Dunbar was burnt yet again, this time by Somerset's German mercenaries returning from an attempt to relieve the English forces occupying Haddington during its long siege of 1548-49. It is curious that Lord Grey of Wilton believed '....the keeping of Haddington to be the winning of Scotland.' Haddington had fallen easily to Wilton in April and he spent the next three months fortifying it; by the end of June,[58] he was surrounded by 14,000 French and Scots troops commanded by Andre Montalembert, Sieur d'Esse. Grey delegated the command of Haddington to Sir James Wilford so that he could direct operations from Berwick; on 7th July, he sent a small relief force of 2,000 troops with powder and shot, 400 of whom were able to get inside the town walls.[59] Throughout the siege, both armies engaged mercenaries; d'Esse's army contained Germans, Spaniards and Swiss *landsknechts*, while the English forces included troops from Italy, Spain and Germany, among them engineers with specialist knowledge of offensive and defensive siege warfare. During the siege, of which there are graphic accounts in Miller's *Lamp of Lothian* and Forbes-Gray's *A Short History of Haddington*, Dunbar remained in French hands, serving as a vital depot for fresh troops and stores from the Continent; its cannon were also hauled up to Haddington for use in the siege.

By August, the war had reached stalemate although operations would continue for a further year. Another relief column of 15,000 led by the Earl of Shrewsbury came by ship from Berwick to Longniddry; on learning that Haddington was in no danger and being short of supplies, Shrewsbury returned to Berwick, torching Dunbar yet again. Before crossing the Border, he rebuilt and strengthened Dunglass and installed 3,000 German troops in the area, a forward-thinking move to cover the inevitable withdrawal from Haddington.

The siege dragged on until September 1549.[60] There were long spells of inactivity caused by a serious defeat sustained by the French and traditional desertions among the Scots at seedtime and harvest. An outbreak of plague within the walls of Haddington in October 1548 limited English operations to occasional skirmishing. In one sortie, the English commander Wilford managed to raid as far as Dunbar; arriving before the castle with only 50 mounted *arquebusiers*, he was easily surrounded by the garrison and in the ensuing firefight, Wilford was wounded and taken prisoner to Stirling with his entire troop. He was succeeded at Haddington by Sir James Croft.[61]

Faced with the prospect of dwindling supplies and the onset of winter which would have made Haddington difficult to provision from Berwick, Croft evacuated the town in September 1549.[62] A relief column of 6,000 men under the Earl of Rutland was despatched from Berwick to screen Croft's withdrawal. Retreating via Dunbar, Croft's men were ambushed by the French garrison, a sight no doubt enjoyed by the townspeople. Jean de Beague, a French historian accompanying d'Esse's army, wrote that the French captains 'Achault, Corroman and Desme were in garrison at Dunbar'; he describes how these officers posted their musketeers in houses near the Parish Church from which positions they fired their muskets at the English from loopholes.[63] (This is an invaluable comment for the historian; either the main street in Dunbar then was Castle Street - Church Street, or the High Street was already in existence). The French harried Croft through the Merse, cutting to pieces the German garrison at Coldingham; only the isolated strongpoints at Lauder, Home[64] and Dunglass held out for a further few months. A court coup toppled Somerset in October, bringing the war to an end. Somerset was executed and the war he waged so ruthlessly seemed to have achieved nothing.

Dunbar played a vital role in the events of 1548-49; it is surprising therefore that only ten years later, it is recorded that the castle was rapidly crumbling and could be taken easily;[65] this has to be accepted at face value as the description is contemporary but it is difficult to believe that the stronghold had deteriorated to such an extent in a relatively short time. It was never neglected and was even repaired and strengthened in 1550; the French [69] were reluctant to leave it and they had to be negotiated out in 1561. However, as recorded in the *Acts of the Lords of Council in Public Affairs* 1501-54 (*ADCP*) on 8th November 1550, 'The Governors and lords of secret council having considered it expedient to build a fort [sic] "about the toun and castell of Dunbar for strenthing [sic] and fortificatioun of the same and resisting of sik [such] danger and inconvenientis [inconvenience] as may herefter follow" the following lairds shall be responsible for a specified number of roods "and send men to that effect with pik, mattock, spaid and schule [shovel], and remane....unto the tyme that every man for his owne part have biggit his rudis [built his roods] conform to the taxt roll said thereupon." ' A total of 197 roods were to be fortified, with one man provided for every rood from various towns and villages in East Lothian and the Merse. The workforce was ordered to gather at Dunbar on 10th December 1550 and to complete the work 'on pain of horning'- loss of the protection of the law. As 197 roods would enclose roughly 50 acres, it is certain that the 'fort' was in fact a town wall which we know was built some time after the siege of Haddington as de Beague comments on its lack in 1548-49. The 1550 wall was earthen; a stone version did not appear until the next century (see account by J Brome in Chapter 3). By that time, stone walls were not intended solely for defence but to control human and animal traffic entering and leaving the burgh.

In addition to these preparations, large sums of money were made available for improvements to the castle in 1550. *TA* show that payments were made for building, strengthening and repairing 'divers warkes [various works] within the Castell'. Three payments were made; £1,254 for materials and £1,321 and £221 for labour and further materials, making a total of £2,800, a not inconsiderable sum for the time even in pounds Scots (more than £900 sterling.) A separate bill for food and wages for the gunners came to £547. Clearly, the French regarded Dunbar as crucial to the defence of southern Scotland. Even so, the garrison was greatly reduced at the end of the *Rough Wooing* by the Treaty of Boulogne in 1550. Three years later, the castle was commanded by Captain Corronant (de Beaugue's Corroman?) and ninety pikemen and hagbutters, five officers, two sergeants, a fifer and a drummer.[66]

The French were not an unqualified success in Dunbar. When French troops were in Scotland, they were unpopular in the communities they occupied as they commandeered livestock and grain to feed themselves. At Dunbar, *TA* for this time records that an impoverished woman, Isobel Lauder, received £10 compensation (about £1:13:0 sterling or £1.65) for four cows taken by the garrison. Even if such acts of plunder did not endear them to the local populace, now turning to the new Protestant religion, the French held the castle and the town. *TA* for 1558 shows that French justice was decisive; the burgh authorities received a payment for expenses incurred in the execution at the castle of two local men who had led 'certane companeis of Inglismen in Teviotdale and the Mers.'

By 1559, the Reformation was gathering momentum. As regent from 1554, Marie of Guise followed the traditional Stewart policy of attempting to reconcile the various interests in the country; but as added precaution, she concentrated her forces in key areas such as Leith, Inchkeith and Dunbar to allow the movement of French vessels carrying fresh troops and supplies. The Protestant Lords of the Congregation, aware that the marriage contract between Mary, Queen of Scots and the Dauphin contained a clause which stipulated that the Dauphin would succeed to the Scottish throne in the event of Mary's death, saw this as a threat to the new religion. In October 1559, they deposed Marie of Guise but were unable to eject her supporters from the three fortresses. The disturbances which John Knox had manufactured earlier in the year had not spread as quickly and widely as had been anticipated and the Lords' rebellion crumbled, forcing them to leave Edinburgh. Marie's support was thinner than in 1554 but she was a survivor; her political position was by no means untenable and until her death in 1560, she remained a queen in more than name alone and held in awe by friend and foe alike. Marie played for time, keeping Scotland a French satellite until the royal couple could return from France and take up their thrones. Meanwhile, political developments in France itself had upset the English who discovered that Mary, Queen of Scots had been proclaimed queen of the four kingdoms, a fact which led to English intervention in the Scottish civil war of 1560.

In the growing unrest in the capital, 'the queen and her faction........with all due diligence, departed from Edinburgh to Dunbar....' [67] where she hoped to receive fresh troops and consolidate French control. Marie remained optimistic and self-assured, which is more than can be said about her distraught ambassador, Sieur d'Oysel; faced with an increasingly hostile local population and mutinous, half-starved troops within the castle, he was at his wits' end.[68]

Then news arrived from Edinburgh of mass desertions from the Lords' army; Marie held a council of war at Dunbar on 22nd July and with her morale high, she decided to take the initiative. She ordered part of her small force of 3,000 to Edinburgh on 23rd July, where a truce was agreed in order to allow the Lords to consider her terms.[69] Before leaving Dunbar, Marie prudently doubled the garrison which required the creation of a separate fort or redoubt in the Castle Park.[70] This necessary precaution would have consequences in the peace negotiations a year later.

Never was there truer saying that war makes strange bedfellows. The English administration, now under pressure to mobilise against the French in Scotland, began making overtures to the Scottish Lords, promising to support them in the interests of Protestantism. Faced with the constant threat of war from Catholic Spain and France and with the young Elizabeth on the throne for less than a year, a cautious England put out feelers to the

Scots in the name of the reformed religion; at the same time, the English saw there was now an opportunity to end the age-old alliance between France and Scotland. Sir James Croft, governor of Berwick, was authorised to receive John Knox and offer funds to finance the Protestant army's occupation of Stirling, gateway to the Catholic North. Knox successfully completed his mission and rode back to Edinburgh with the good news although his small band was attacked by a French patrol from Dunbar, an incident to which he obliquely refers in a letter dated 6th August to Croft.

The *Auld Alliance* was now in jeopardy. By the end of 1559, Marie of Guise could count on few supporters apart from the Earl of Bothwell and Lord Seton. As Elizabeth of England (**T120**) nervously contemplated military intervention in the Scottish civil war which she well knew might precipitate French and Spanish aggression against her kingdom, she decided to give only token assistance to the Scottish Lords. When the English threat receded, Marie's attitude to the Lords abruptly changed; she staged yet another recovery and openly reinforced Leith. Plagued by a shortage of money to pay their army, the Lords decided to attack Leith immediately, no doubt promising the spoils of war to their troops on its capture. Despite such acute financial difficulties - there was no gold or silver to make coinage - Knox informs us that the Lords denied Marie the use of 'the printing irons'; the tools for minting coinage were 'stayed, for fear that she should privily cause transport them to Dunbar' and use them to buy further support.

A disgruntled Scottish army made a lacklustre attempt on Leith, then deserted in droves which forced the Lords to fall back on Stirling yet again. The initiative was with Marie until an English fleet arrived in the Firth of Forth to cut communications between the French bases in Edinburgh and Fife and prevent any reinforcements reaching Leith and Dunbar. Elizabeth, now growing in confidence, sent the fleet and an army of 7,000 under Lord Grey of Wilton to assist the Lords investing Leith. Wilton made good progress after he crossed the Border but as he passed Dunbar, the French gunners inflicted some casualties on his troops. Despite the English blockade and the superior number of Anglo-Scottish troops, the French clung tenaciously to Leith.

Added to this new threat, Marie of Guise was now terminally ill; true to character, she attempted to negotiate her way out of difficulty. She proposed that if the Protestant Lords would end their alliance with England, she would send her French troops home except for the garrisons at Inchkeith and Dunbar - a force of about 1,000 men. Her proposal was unacceptable. Her health deteriorated rapidly and on 11th June, she died of dropsy. When they heard of her death, the dispirited French surrendered. The subsequent Treaty of Leith was concluded by French and English diplomats on 6th July 1560; its terms sealed the fate of the *Auld Alliance*. The French were ordered out of Scotland save for token forces at Dunbar and Inchkeith, strongholds they were permitted to occupy with 60 men in each case until arrangements could be made for Scottish troops to replace them.[71] The English negotiators imposed a further condition - that the military works 'lately erected by the French at Dunbar' were to be dismantled.[72] These works were described in detail in the treaty; rampart, counterscarp - the exterior of a ditch supporting a covered way, presumably giving access to the castle proper - platform, flanker and the in-fill of a ditch leading from the castle cross to the captain's garden.[73] *Miller, Dunbar* states that the fort extended 136 feet in front of the castle. Its demolition was subsequently supervised by local lairds.[74]

KRM

Illus 18: *Mary, Queen of Scots*

The dismantling of Marie of Guise's redoubt did not proceed quite as smoothly as expected. Randolph, the English ambassador, wrote to Elizabeth's chief minister Lord Cecil of Burleigh on 1st August 1560 informing him that six ships had arrived at Dunbar and were inspected by a Captain Forbes who found they contained nothing more sinister than biscuit, lard and cider for the garrison.[75] Then he refers to 'Sarlabos', the French captain at Dunbar: 'Sarlabos showed himself very gentle in receiving the lords' message [to dismantle the fort] and in words, willing enough to observe all points of the contract and has sent to them for a copy. [Captain] Forbes thinks the fortifications not sufficiently demolished and that 10 days' labour would restore it [sic].......' Sarlabos is an English corruption of Sieur Labois, the French officer in charge of Dunbar from 1560 to 1561.[76] It would appear that Labois had only *said* he would level the fort which troubled the English and was the cause of a further letter from Randolph to Cecil on 23rd September;[77] 'It is said the [French] men in Dunbar exceed 60, the number agreed. The munition house yet stands: Sarlabos would not suffer the pioneers to overthrow it. He stands always on guard, and goes not far abroad.' The reference to the pioneers relates to the arrival of 100 men under an officer on 15th August with orders for Labois to allow demolition work to proceed. Clearly, the Frenchman was determined to make life awkward for the Scots by delaying the demolition and the French evacuation as long as he possibly could. Did he entertain hopes of a French army accompanying Mary, Queen of Scots when she returned to Scotland in August?

Although to all intents and purposes the French were forced out of Scotland in 1561, there was a small French presence and influence in the early months of Mary, Queen of Scots' reign. Mary Stewart (**ill 18**) stepped ashore at Leith on 19th August 1561, ten months after her mother's remains had been taken to France for burial at Rheims.[78] Mary hated leaving France; it had been her home from the age of six and it was natural that she should bring French companions to the Scottish court. However, her Protestant nobles were suspicious of French aims and demanded that they return to France as they believed a French presence at court threatened the Protestant religion.

The French left their mark in a an enduring way - in the Scottish tongue. Miller, *Lamp of Lothian* suggests that a few words in use in his time and still used today were introduced into the language during the French occupation of Haddington. Some examples of French derivation are *ruckle*, from *recueil*, a collection; *ashet,* from *assiette*, a plate; *gigot*, from *jigot*, a cut of lamb. Miller also believes that the Haddington place-name *Poldrate* is a corruption of *L'Epaule Droit*, literally *the right shoulder* which may have been part of a fortification.

After the French evacuated Dunbar Castle in 1561, Simon Preston of Craigmillar became its governor; he was serving in that capacity when he received into custody the eldest son of the Earl of Huntly. George Gordon, 4th Earl of Huntly, the head of the clans in the north-east, rebelled against Mary - or to be precise, her Protestant advisors. A devout Roman Catholic, Huntly urged the queen to reinstate Catholicism as the national religion. Already at odds with some of her nobles over her policy of religious tolerance, Mary was embarrassed by Huntly's ultimatum; the more bigoted nobles dismissed the Earl of Huntly's view that his opinion should carry more weight than any other noble because he claimed to be first in rank among the Scottish nobility. The Protestant nobles called his bluff and an army was sent north to help him change his mind. After some indecision, Huntly was persuaded by his wife to take the field. He was 'defeated' by Mary's half-brother James Stewart, Earl of Moray on 28th October at the farcical 'battle' of Corrichie, where Huntly died of an apoplectic stroke before a shot was fired.

Huntly's eldest son and heir George, not even present at the battle, was charged with treason and sent to prison in Dunbar Castle. George Gordon narrowly escaped execution and subsequently became 5th Earl of Huntly and one of Mary's staunchest supporters. Unwittingly, Mary had signed his unauthorised death warrant which it is thought had been slipped in among a sheaf of state documents requiring the queen's signature by some Protestant official possibly in the pay of the Earl of Moray or another Protestant noble who considered Huntly a nuisance because he was Catholic. Fortunately, Huntly's jailer at Dunbar, Preston of Craigmillar, refused to carry out the order without the queen's personal confirmation and Mary subsequently cancelled the warrant. Huntly remained a 'guest' at Dunbar for the next three years. On 12th May 1565, the English statesman Throckmorton was entertained to dinner at Dunbar by Secretary Maitland of Lethington; writing to queen Elizabeth, Throckmorton described Huntly as a 'condemned man for highe treason'[79] which was not of course the case. Huntly was restored to Mary's favour in 1565.

At about this time, the last male in the blood-line of Dunbar earls died leaving no male issue; coincidentally, Dunbar Castle was to play its final role in Scottish history during the brief and tragic reign of Mary, Queen of Scots. She visited Dunbar on at least three occasions, all arising from violent events. At the outset of her reign, Mary was a popular queen although inevitably, she fell foul of John Knox (**ill 19**) by continuing to practise Roman Catholicism; in more than one stormy lecture, the bullying Knox reduced the young queen to tears, upbraiding her for allowing mass to be said in her private chapel at Holyroodhouse. Although Knox could not persuade her to convert to Protestantism, infinitely more subtle and powerful forces would destroy her. Mary's misfortunes were compounded by two imprudent marriages after the death of her first husband, the Dauphin of France. She remained a widow for five years, although she briefly contemplated marrying one of Elizabeth's favourites, Robert Dudley, created Earl of Leicester to make him more acceptable to the Scottish queen. Mary's

Illus 19: *John Knox* KRM

marriage to Dudley would have strengthened her claim to the English throne, a course her nobles favoured. Between 1561 and 1565, Mary was successful in reorganising the Crown's finances and status, ably assisted by the capable and loyal Secretary Maitland of Lethington until their relationship deteriorated. Her detractors tend to the view that her political disasters arose from unwise marriages to Darnley, then Bothwell, which is largely true. Marriage to her Catholic cousin Henry, Lord Darnley, son of the Stewart Earl of Lennox certainly avoided a foreign marriage which might have proved unpopular; Darnley also had a claim on the English throne through his mother which strengthened Mary's claim. However, Darnley was a catastrophe both as a man and a husband. Weak, dissolute and of little intellect or charm, he had a violent temper and an overbearing attitude. In addition, the marriage isolated Mary's half-brother, the Earl of Moray and the Hamiltons, a powerful family in Scotland. The royal wedding had scarcely been solemnised when Moray and the Hamiltons, displaced in the pecking order by the Lennox Stewarts, rebelled against Mary. The insurrection went by the name of the *Chaseabout Raid*, which accurately sums up its farcical nature; no battle was fought and the incident ended with Moray in exile in England and James Hamilton pardoned on condition that he go into voluntary exile in France. Moray sought Elizabeth's assistance in his intrigues, believing she would be sympathetic to his support for Protestantism in Scotland. However, he received a cool reception at the English court, although shortly afterwards he received a full pardon from his half-sister which allowed his return to Scotland.

Relations between Mary and Darnley were strained from the outset; she refused to grant him the crown matrimonial which would have made him king. Darnley blamed Mary's Italian secretary, David Riccio, of whom he said had exercised undue influence over her, even declaring the little Italian had cuckolded him. The real reasons for Riccio's murder on the night of 9th March 1566 are obscure; some historians consider he was a threat to the Protestant religion while others have suggested that he persuaded the queen to allow the exiled James Hamilton to return from exile in France which alone would have guaranteed Riccio's murder by the Lennox Stewarts. At any rate, the conspirators led by Lord Ruthven dragged Riccio from Mary's presence in Holyrood, took him to an adjacent room and repeatedly stabbed him (**ill 20**). The shock so unnerved Mary that believing herself the next victim, she urged Darnley to escape with her to Port Seton, then Dunbar. By joining her, Darnley alienated his fellow conspiratotors who had used his dagger on Riccio, deliberately leaving it beside the Italian's body to leave no room for doubt concerning the political if not physical part he played in Riccio's murder.

One of Mary's staunchest supporters, Sir James Melville states in his memoirs [80] that Moray was involved in the plot as Mary begged Melville to persuade Moray to distance himself from the conspirators; this may have been a fabrication to discredit Moray. However, on the morning of 12th March, a surprised Simon Preston of Craigmillar found the queen, Darnley and seven companions at the gate of Dunbar Castle 'hungry and clamouring for fresh eggs to breakfast.'[81]

Despite her virtual isolation, Mary possessed some of her mother's spirit and she retaliated quickly. She issued a proclamation from Dunbar on 16th March inviting all men loyal to the crown to gather at the mercat crosses at Haddington and Musselburgh and advance on Edinburgh. The inhabitants of the sheriffdom of Edinburgh, Haddington and several Border towns were requested to ' meit thair Hienesses at Hadingtoun and Musilburgh respective[ly], the xvi., xvii and xviii of Marche instant, with viii dayis provisioun and victualis eftir thair cuming....and that thair Majesteis, God willing, being of porpois to be at Hadingtoun this nixt Sonday, the xvii of Marche instant, ordainis thairfor lettres to be direct to officiaris of armes, to pas to the mercat croces of the said burgh of Hadingtoun and utheris places neidful....and to attend and pas furthwart with thair Majesteis towart thair Heinesses burgh of Edinburgh or uther place as thai salbe commandit.....'[82]

Illus 20: *Murder of David Riccio* KRM

An understandably troubled Melville met Mary and Darnley en route from Dunbar to Haddington. Darnley, no doubt fearful for his own position, immediately asked him what had happened to Ruthven, Morton and the other conspirators; the answer was that they had probably fled the city. Darnley, affecting injured innocence, reputedly replied: 'As they have brewed, so let them drink.' Melville later wrote probably for posterity and with an eye on political correctness: 'it appeared to me that he was troubled he had deserted them finding the Queen's favour cold.' The next day, the Marian forces were outside the gates of Edinburgh Castle where some of those responsible for guarding the entrance to Holyroodhouse on the night of Riccio's murder were summarily executed.

James Hepburn, Earl of Bothwell and the Earl of Huntly had led Bothwell's fighting men into Dunbar, picking up more at Haddington and Musselburgh. On 18th March, Mary entered the capital in euphoric mood at the head of 8,000 men, an apprehensive Darnley at her side. The rebels had indeed fled and it seemed that Mary would be firmly restored to her throne. For the moment, she was safe.

By now, Mary was carrying Darnley's child, the future James VI. During their escape on horseback to Dunbar, Mary had feared for the baby's survival but Darnley had urged her on, shouting that they could have another child. From his point of view, he had much to gain from the deaths of both mother and child and he began to form wildly misguided plans for accession to the thrones of both Scotland and England. He even went as far as to seek the support of Philip II of Spain, suggesting that Philip invade England and declare him king of both countries. This unrealistic idea never got beyond the discussion stage.

Meanwhile, Riccio's assassins, anxious to restore themselves to Mary's favour, made it known that Darnley had been involved in Riccio's murder. Mary maintained a pretense of matrimonial harmony but by now she detested her husband; Darnley persisted with his excuse that he had sanctioned the murder to avenge his and her honour as the Italian had seduced her. Now sorely in need of friends, Mary turned to the Earl of Bothwell whose influence and confidence were growing daily. In January 1567, Bothwell met Morton, Maitland and one of the Morton Douglases at Whittingehame, East Lothian to discuss what was ostensibly an alliance but is believed by some historians to have been a plan to get rid of Darnley.[83] Tradition has it that they met under an ancient yew in the grounds of Whittingehame House - safe from prying ears if the topic was indeed murder - to discuss matters of government. Whatever the subject of their conversation, Darnley had only a few weeks to live. It is almost certain that Mary had no part in or knowledge of this meeting but subsequent events were distorted to incriminate her. She placed her trust in Bothwell, another disastrous if understandable choice as he was one of the few men who went with her to Dunbar the previous year. Grateful for his help, she had unwisely rewarded Bothwell with 'the whole inheritance of Dunbar' on 7th June 1566, making him governor of the castle. Bothwell was also given the crown lands of East Barns, Newtonlees and West Barns with the latter's mills, a £10 annual rent (about £1.65) from the Lochend estate at Dunbar and several lesser benefits.[84] With his other lands and castles in the south-east, Bothwell became extremely powerful in a very short space of time.

It was inevitable that Bothwell would be accused of Darnley's murder at Kirk o'Field on the night of 9th February 1567. One of history's most celebrated murders, the real casualty was truth; we will never know for certain the full facts of the plot - or plots - nor the identities of those directly involved. Official records are unhelpful as they contain contradictions, improbabilities and falsehoods; many of those who were involved became enemies after the event which led to accusation and counter-accusation. Attempts to unravel the mystery have been the subject of several speculative and well-constructed theories. The main body of evidence suggests that Darnley planned to murder Mary by means of an explosion, obtain the crown and discredit the Protestant nobles. It is believed that his plan went wrong and that he encountered a group of hostile nobles hurrying to Kirk o' Field, men who already suspected he was plotting the queen's death and who dispatched him that fateful night as he was attempting to escape from the house. Darnley certainly had a strong motive and he was the kind of man who would resort to desperate measures to achieve his aims. Mary's death would have automatically secured for him the crown matrimonial or the regency of Scotland; perhaps he might also have succeeded in restoring the Catholic religion in Scotland which would have attracted support for him from Spain, if not France. The plan had considerable political and emotional appeal; it might well have swayed public opinion; given his devious mind, it is likely that Darnley would have blamed his wife's death on the Protestant nobles, thus discrediting them and their religion.

It was a reasonable gamble but it went awry. One possible reason was that Darnley's plans were leaked to his enemies, including the Earls of Bothwell and Moray. If there is any credibility to the Darnley theory, it was fortunate indeed that Mary was delayed on her way to join him at Kirk o' Field that night. Mary was at Holyroodhouse attending the wedding of Bastien Pagez, one of her closest allies and not as has been said, an obscure servant in her retinue; she had every reason to be there that night, given the importance of the occasion. We must therefore rule out any involvement on her part in the murder, although she had every reason to welcome it.

Darnley is thought to have deposited gunpowder in the cellar below Mary's bedchamber over several days in small amounts; on the day of the murder, Mary visited the house and remarked on how grimy one of the servants was - not in itself proof of her innocence but modern historians accept that most of the evidence against her was circumstantial. At any rate, Darnley lit the fuse to the gunpowder prematurely, expecting the queen to return to the house at any moment. After setting the fuse, he didn't even bother to warn the other servants in residence; he and one servant escaped over the garden wall in their nightgowns where they ran into a group of nobles coming through the garden to investigate the explosion. They must have been very close to the house to have been able to intercept Darnley; this suggests they were in fact lying in wait for him. Whatever words passed between them, the nobles acted swiftly; the bodies of Darnley and his servant were found in the garden with only marks of strangulation on them. Beside the bodies were a chair and a rope. Was Darnley hanged from a nearby tree?

There are other aspects of the murder which warrant further investigation. At the time, Dunbar Castle was the country's arsenal; several historians have suggested that the gunpowder used at Kirk o' Field came from Dunbar, which conveniently implicates Bothwell - no friend of Darnley - and possibly Mary herself.[85]

Theories abound as to the murderers' identities but it is now widely accepted that Mary played no part in the deed. Darnley was certainly the intended victim that night; it is likely that he would have met with a violent end even if Kirk o'Field had not occurred. He had many enemies and betrayed many friends; it is almost certain that he, his father the Earl of Lennox and Balfour - Catholics with a vested interest in Mary's demise - had planned her murder. These plans were undoubtedly leaked to the nobles whom he had insulted or discredited, thus giving them a motive for getting rid of him. It was a tragic coincidence that two separate plots conjoined that night of 9th/10th February. We will never know the true facts. The identities of the murderers have remained a mystery because of the crude attempts of the State archives to point the finger at the chief suspect, Bothwell. What is beyond doubt is the consequences Darnley's murder had on the remainder of Bothwell's tragic life. The Scottish crown lay tantalisingly within Bothwell's reach; he was close to the queen, her husband was out of the way. Lesser men could not have resisted the temptation.

News of Darnley's murder reached England via Dunbar - or more precisely, Sir William Drury, the governor at Berwick learned of it from an English official visiting Dunbar Castle. Drury sent a courier to Lord Cecil in London with a letter dated 11th February - less than two days after the event - informing the minister that '....there be advertisement come unto me and sent from Dunbar that the lord Darnley was upon Sunday night slain.' This set in motion a flurry of gossip in the English court, encouraged by nobles on both sides of the Border who were eager to discredit Mary and the religion she so stubbornly refused to abandon.

There were too many unanswered questions, too many Scottish voices raised against Mary and her hopes for a stable throne and as always, personal happiness eluded her. She was driven to rely more on Bothwell, a man who was as volatile and calculating as most of his contemporaries, even Darnley, inept though he was. James Hepburn, 4th Earl of Bothwell, Lord High Admiral of Scotland and Sheriff of Haddington had become extremely powerful in a very short time. An excellent administrator possessed of independent political thought, Bothwell was becoming increasingly dangerous mainly because of the influence he now had over the queen. With his power-base firmly established in the south-east - castles at Borthwick, Hailes and Dunbar - and with many friends in the Merse, Bothwell posed a threat to the stability of the realm after Darnley's death.

Although a Protestant in February 1566, Bothwell had married the Catholic Lady Jean Gordon, the 5th Earl of Huntly's sister. Almost immediately, he was openly unfaithful to her. In April 1567, Lady Gordon brought a civil action against her husband which was judged in her favour. (Bothwell had apparently seduced a young serving lass in Haddington's church). Bothwell's response was to raise an action to annul their marriage which, as was the practice, was remitted to a commission of six churchmen to investigate on 27th April. The commissioners appear to have been either unable to agree or were reluctant to give a decision. Finally, judgement rested on the jurisdiction of one man, commissioner John Manderston, a canon of Dunbar Collegiate Church. Bothwell's servants threatened Manderston with physical violence and a decision in Bothwell's favour was reached almost immediately.[86] The reason for the pressure on Manderston is made clear by events which occurred only two weeks later.

Bothwell's mercurial personality drove him to further boldness. Having survived a rigged trial in Edinburgh on 12th April for his alleged part in the murder of Darnley - he got his way by appearing in the streets of Edinburgh at the head of a large band of followers - he suddenly found he had friends in places he least expected. Despite growing unrest in the streets of Edinburgh - Bothwell was accused of Darnley's murder in pamphlets in which he was depicted as a hare and Mary as a mermaid, the latter a symbol of the prostitute - he managed to maintain his position. By now, the common people had decided that even if he had not personally despatched Darnley, his hands weren't clean. Before his 'trial' the city streets were thronged with 4,000 of his men - the figure was more likely 400. His judges had no option but to acquit him. Bothwell then met some thirty nobles and senior churchmen at an Edinburgh tavern where a bond was signed by friends who pledged support for him. Did this encourage him to abduct the queen a week later? Was he lulled into a sense of false security to commit greater acts of folly? Perhaps his 'friends' handed him the rope with which he would hang himself.

On 24th April, Bothwell with 700 - 800 men intercepted Mary at Kirkliston on her way back to Edinburgh from a visit to her infant son James in Stirling. Contemporary sources hostile to Bothwell claimed he abducted the queen, Secretary Maitland, the Earl of Huntly and Sir James Melville, making them his prisoners at Dunbar.[87] Some historians have interpreted Bothwell's move as a pre-emptive strike to prevent others taking Mary into custody, while others maintain she was a willing partner in her 'abduction.' Sir James Melville states in his memoirs that at Dunbar, Bothwell boasted he would marry the queen 'whether she would herself or not'; this may be hostile propaganda written in retrospect, given Melville's loyalty to Mary. In any event, at some point between 24th April and 6th May, Bothwell not only reputedly - and repeatedly - raped Mary, he persuaded her to sign two marriage contracts, one written in Scots and the other in French. To give the proceedings an air of respectability, Bothwell enlisted the support of his kinsman, Thomas Hepburn, parson of nearby Oldhamstocks who was present to witness the signing of the documents. On 7th May, Bothwell's divorce was conveniently settled so he was free to marry the queen, a wedding which took place with almost indecent haste on 15th May. May was then considered an unlucky month for marriages. Subsequent events vindicated the superstition.

The consequences of the marriage were immediate. It was one thing to offer Bothwell support but quite another to suffer his audacity. Several nobles - many of whom had undoubtedly signed the bond promising support only a month ago - formed a coalition; styling themselves the Confederate Lords, they attempted to capture Bothwell at Borthwick Castle. He escaped to Haddington, then to Dunbar, where Mary joined him a day later, leaving Borthwick dressed in male clothing.[88]

The citizens of Edinburgh were by now convinced that Bothwell and Mary were instrumental in Darnley's murder and eagerly responded to the Confederate Lords' call to arms against the queen. Many of the rebel lords had private scores to settle, while others affected a sympathy for Bothwell they'd never shown before, opportunists who were hedging their bets in the power struggle. Bothwell gathered a force of about 2,000 from East Lothian and the Merse, recruited mainly by the few remaining loyal nobles such as Lords Seton and Hay of Yester, the most resolute among the Catholic minority. The armies met at Carberry Hill near Musselburgh on 15th June; both sides were about equal in numbers, although the Marian force had the advantage of seven or eight artillery pieces from Dunbar. Perhaps for good luck, Bothwell and Mary occupied the old earthworks which Lord Protector Somerset had prepared before the battle of Pinkie twenty years earlier.

Most of that sultry afternoon, the two small armies glowered at each other, neither willing to make the first move. Bothwell's artillery fired an occasional shot into the rebel pickets but inflicted no damage. The Confederate Lords who confronted Mary were by no means united, nor were they all Protestants; at least two - the Earls of Borthwick and Sempill - were Catholics and the Earl of Cassillis had changed his religion no fewer than three times since 1560. The publicly proclaimed aim of the Confederates was to free Mary and her infant son from Bothwell's influence but as will be seen, their real purpose was to force Mary to abdicate in James' favour.

Neither side wanted bloodshed; the Confederate Lords believed that delay would bring them success. With growing impatience, Mary waited for reinforcements which never materialised; as the day wore on, her force dwindled as men deserted, ignoring her taunts of cowardice. No sword was drawn, no horses put to spur except those carrying away the remnants of her army. Finally, Mary and Bothwell stood with only sixty men; she knew she would have to capitulate. The nobles on the other side urged her to come over to them and at last a compromise was reached. Bothwell was given safe conduct to Dunbar - probably by those among the rebels whom he might have identified as party to Darnley's murder. He rode to Dunbar, garrisoned the castle with kinsmen and friends, leaving it in the charge of Patrick Whitelaw,[89] then he took ship for Orkney. On one of the saddest days of her life, exactly one month after her marriage to Bothwell, Mary was led to Edinburgh dressed in a short red petticoat, the only female clothing she was able to find at Dunbar before leaving for Carberry. The colour of the garment said it all; not only was it the detested scarlet of Rome, it was also the garb of the common whore. As Mary entered the capital, she was jeered in the streets by a hostile citizenry.

On 26th June,[90] a proclamation was issued to the defenders at Dunbar:

'Patrick Quhytlaw of that Ilk, Capitane, the Constabill, Keparis [keeper] and all utheris personis [other persons] being in the said Castell of Dunbar, to render and deliver the samyn [same] with all artaillieris [artillery] and munitioun being thairin, to the Officiar executor of the saidis [said] letters and personis being with him.'

Further pronouncements were made on 26th August and 10th September,[91] the latter identifying some of the defenders - Hepburn of Wauchton, Patrick Hepburn and his son, Patrick Whitelaw, William Newton and his son John, Thomas Hepburn of Oldhamstocks, Adam Hepburn of Smeaton and William Hepburn of Gilmerton. These desperate men prepared for the final siege in the castle's long history. On 11th September, the regent Moray's herald Adam McCulloch stood before the castle gate, demanding that Whitelaw surrender the castle within twenty-four hours.[92] The defenders ignored him. In Edinburgh, Moray raised a force to march on Dunbar; four companies under Captains Cunningham, Haliburton, Melville and Murray [93] were joined by bakers, butchers and brewers from Haddington who were instructed by the Privy Council to supply the besieging forces with food 'at competent prices.'[94] Two days later, the Council forbade merchants to sell food to the castle's occupants.[95] On 28th September, four cannon and six smaller pieces were brought from Edinburgh to reduce the castle. Moray himself directed the operations. Having been stripped of most of its guns for the confrontation at Carberry, the castle contained few artillery pieces to withstand a siege.[96] The small garrison surrendered on 1st October. The castle was handed over the local magistrates until parliament decided its future.

Bothwell's accomplices received only token prison sentences; less than six months later, Thomas Hepburn, the Oldhamstocks parson, was set free and even attempted to recapture Dunbar with 20 men in March 1568, a fiasco easily rebuffed by the Earl of Home, now in charge of the castle. Hepburn of Oldhamstocks was something of a character;[97] shortly after officiating at the signing of the marriage contracts between Bothwell and Mary, he was appointed Master of Requests to the Privy Council, a fairly important position and clearly a reward for his services to Bothwell. He was thus able to move about Edinburgh freely. After Carberry, Bothwell asked Hepburn to get into Edinburgh Castle to retrieve some of his personal papers. Hepburn and two companions located the documents; whether or not he knew their contents, Hepburn certainly knew they were of importance to the Confederate Lords. He managed to slip out of Edinburgh but his two companions were caught; under torture, they revealed that the letters had been hidden in a house in Potter Row. These became known as the *Casket Letters,* copies of which were used in evidence against Mary to force her to abdicate the throne in favour of her son, James VI. The originals of these letters mysteriously disappeared although eight letters were copied as well as some poetry; modern investigators have concluded that the originals were probably altered deliberately to incriminate Mary. One historian has convincingly argued that several were written by Anna Throndsen, a Norwegian lover whom Bothwell had jilted years before.[98] These were tampered with and copied to suggest Mary was the author; the copied correspondence also includes genuine letters from the queen but it is believed that these were also doctored to prove her personal complicity and involvement in Darnley's murder. The Confederate Lords ruthlessly used this highly suspect evidence to secure a guilty verdict and force her to abdicate in favour of her son James.

Mary's fate is well documented. After her abdication, she was put in custody in Loch Leven Castle from where she escaped in 1568; her army was decisively defeated by the Earl of Moray at Langside on 13th May that year. Forced to cross the Border, Mary had little choice but to place herself under the protection of Elizabeth of England. At first, Elizabeth was sympathetic but refused to grant her an interview until she cleared herself of the charge of murder. (Most modern historians agree that Mary played no part in Darnley's murder, although she probably had foreknowledge of it, which technically makes her an accessory to the crime). The two queens never met. Mary spent the next 19 years engaging in unrealistic schemes to recover her throne. Finally, accused of complicity in the Babington Plot on Elizabeth's life, she was executed at Fotheringhay Castle on 8th February 1587. History is silent on whether she expressed any concern about Bothwell's fate. The martyrology of Mary causes controversy even today. Was she the victim of two of her ambitious husbands?

Probably. But she was ambitious herself, seeking the throne of England. There was hardly a noble in Scotland who didn't want Darnley, then Bothwell dead - or at least out of the way. Sympathy for Mary's disastrous marriages is appropriate but she wasn't by any standards the victim of doomed love. Her tragedy is that she was less politically astute than her cousin Elizabeth of England who outwitted her at every turn.

As for James Hepburn, 4th Earl of Bothwell, his subsequent life is classic Greek tragedy. After leaving Dunbar, he went to Orkney, then took ship for Norway. Arriving at Bergen on 2nd September, his past caught up with him. As mentioned earlier, he had had an affair with Anna Throndsen in 1556; Anna was a well-connected lady who loaned him money and who followed him to Scotland to renew the love affair - or retrieve her gold. At Bergen in 1568, Bothwell had the misfortune to meet Anna's cousin, Eric Rosenkrantz, the Norwegian Viceroy. Anna learnt of his arrival and filed a lawsuit for the return of her money, which Bothwell was unable to pay, so he was imprisoned for the rest of his life. At first, he was well-treated in accordance with his rank and status. However, international politics moved on and Bothwell outlived his usefulness as a hostage. He spent his remaining years at Dragsholm Castle on the Danish island of Zealand. Chained-up in solitary confinement, he went insane and died on 14th April 1578. For four centuries, his mummified body lay in the church in Faarvejle, about nine miles from Dragsholm. The mummy was on show at a cost of a few pence until in the latter half of the twentieth century, when Scottish tourists complained to the Danish authorities, obliging them to give the dehydrated remains a decent burial.[99]

Illus 21: *Queen Elizabeth I of England* KRM

As for the royal castle at Dunbar, parliament decided in December 1567 that it should be dismantled. An order of parliament decreed that

> '...the castell of Dunbar........[shall] be demolischit [demolished], and cassin [cast]downe utterlie to the ground, and distroyit in sic wise that no foundment thairof be occasioun to big [build] thairupon in tyme cumming.....'[100]

On 13th October 1568, *TA* records that thirty-five shillings and sixpence (6 shillings sterling or 30p) was spent on locks to make the castle secure; at some point in that year, William Boncle, burgess of Dunbar, was paid £319 (about £54 sterling) to meet the expenses of ten guards and three watchmen to keep out intruders. The guards appear to have been unnecessary, as subsequent payments of 12 shillings a day (2 shillings sterling or 10p) were made only to three watchmen.

Dismantling work proceeded in 1568 but parts were still standing in the nineteenth century; perhaps those charged with its demolition were reluctant to do so 'utterlie'. In 1573, James VI granted to the above-mentioned William Boncle [101] 'burgess of Dumbar [sic] of the forthe [fort] of Dumbar'.[102] Boncle presumably also received the castle policies which included grazing land.

And yet Dunbar almost rose phoenix-like from its ruins. In 1597, Lord Scrope, warden of the English West March, had spies in the Scottish court. Despatching intelligence to the English statesman Cecil, Lord Burleigh that year, he wrote thus of Dunbar:

> 'Her[e] is a new matter put into the King's [James VI] head, to wit that the Earldom of Marche did sometime apperteyne [belong] to the Croune [crown] and therfor should now be called back. The ground [arguement] whereof proceeds, that they would have the castle of Dunbar buylden [built] agayne, and his Majestie to dowell [dwell] there as in an ordinar [ordinary] palace.'[103]

The proposal was no more than court gossip or perhaps a ruse to alarm the English.

During the seventeenth century, the castle site was owned by Sir George Home, Baron Berwick and Earl of

Dunbar until his death in 1611. It was inherited by his daughter, Lady Anne Home in 1613, then it passed to James Baillie of Lochend in 1617.[104] The site was then sold to the Maitland family, the future Earls of Lauderdale. On 27th December 1653, the ruined castle and its policies were in the possession of John Maitland who assigned them to Stephen Thornley 'citizen and goldsmith of London' apparently as collateral to cover Maitland's debts of £2,000 (about £330 sterling) while he was a prisoner in England after the battle of Worcester in 1651. After the Restoration, the property was returned to Maitland on 25 May 1661.[105] John Maitland was then elevated to the peerage, becoming 1st Duke of Lauderdale and Marquis of March in 1672. The property remained in the Lauderdale family until they left Dunbar in the mid-nineteenth century. When Lauderdale House was purchased by the War Office in 1855, the castle site appears to have been excluded from the transaction, as it was then owned by the Earls of Home, descendants of the Earls of Dunbar. The ruin was incorporated in the chain of coastal batteries to counter any Russian reprisals in response to the British Navy's operations in the Baltic during the Crimean War (1854-56)

Visiting Dunbar in 1857 while researching his book *Feudal and Military Antiquities of Northumberland and the Scottish Borders*, C H Hartshone described the castle in somewhat purplish prose to convey the extent to which he was impressed by what were depleted remains after the Victoria Harbour was built:

> 'How red and shattered does it look, rising in its jagged and fantastic form from its ocean bed! Nature has done everything to clothe it with a harsh and frowning aspect: the sea roaring around and dashing through its darkened caverns, or washing its sides precipitously rising above the water, makes it a rock of horror for sailor or landsman to gaze upon.'

On the contrary, after a hard day at sea in winter, many a fisherman returning to harbour has no doubt been glad to see the solitary stack of Hans' Tower, sometimes called 'the camel' because of its profile.

As mentioned above, much of the ruin was destroyed in 1842, when the New or Victoria Harbour was constructed. The surviving stonework was further reduced in October 1869, when a violent storm blew down the cross-wall with the heraldic insignia. Since then, stones have crumbled and fallen into the sea, the worst occurring in 1980. On 24th January 1980, the *Edinburgh Evening News* reported that the lifeboat and the fishing fleet were trapped in the harbour by a fall of rock which took with it some of the castle's foundations; about 100 tons of rock collapsed into the harbour mouth and even at high tide, some skippers felt uneasy when entering or leaving the harbour. After the 1980 fall, the Castle Rock was declared unsafe for the Coastguard Signal Station which overlooked the harbour entrance. The last vestige to disappear was perhaps one of the castle's remaining attractive features; the arch , which was all that remained of the enclosed walkway from the castle to the Blockhouse, collapsed the week before Christmas 1993. (The arch in better shape is shown in a postcard in *Old Dunbar* by David Anderson, a local historian; however, the manuscript note - not the author's - which appears on the reproduction incorrectly describes it as 'the watergate where Mary Queen of Scots escaped'- it was neither watergate, nor did Mary escape by way of it).

As one of East Lothian's oldest and strongest castles, Dunbar deserved a better end. About a century ago, a less important castle at Hailes was better preserved because it didn't stand in the way of commercial development. However, street names in Dunbar commemorate the castle - Castlegate, Castle Street, Castle Place - and of course, the eponymous pub. Generations of fishermen who have lived and worked in its shadow are shyly sentimental about the old ruin, now almost indistinguishable from the Castle Rock itself. To many of the fishing community of the past and perhaps even today, it was Black Agnes' castle rather than the family seat of the Dunbars.

Writing in 1929 for *Transactions of the East Lothian Antiquarian and Field Naturalists' Society ((TELAS)*[106] T Wilson Fish of Dunbar ruefully lamented the lack of memorials to Dunbar's past, drawing attention to Grose's sketches of the castle. Wilson Fish rightly says that 'the castle was of imposing proportions and national importance'. Why therefore was no serious attempt made to conserve what survived? Local and national authorities alike must bear the blame. In its time, the castle was first the seat of the Dunbars from whom sprang several extant Scottish families,[107] then it became part of the defensive system guarding the east coast of Scotland. In so many respects, the castle ***was*** Dunbar.

Ancient buildings are preserved because they shed light on the world in which our ancestors lived. The local burgh council - defunct under local government reorganisation since 1975 - cannot be said to have been over-anxious about preserving the ruins. It wanted to be absolved of the responsibility, theirs from 1936. On 11th March 1936, the town council minutes recorded that the castle had been adopted by HM Office of Works as a monument whose preservation was of national importance. An extract from the minutes shows that 'The Council has long desired the recognition of the Castle as an ancient monument and the view was expressed that, in the hands of the Commissioners [of HM Office of Works] the conditioning and preserving of the Castle ruins will be adequately carried out. In the immediate future, the ruins of Dunbar's historic Castle should have a leading place among the old Burgh's attractions for visitors.' At the same meeting, it was suggested that a museum should be established in the Town House but the Council decided there was no space available for it. (This decision has been reversed in recent years; Dunbar Town House is one of the county museums promoted by East Lothian Council Museum Services in association with the Dunbar and District History Society).

The castle's future remained uncertain. On 13th October 1937, the council minutes record that both the Ancient Monuments Board [The Royal Commission on the Ancient and Historical Monuments of Scotland] and HM Office of Works had declined to make repairs to the castle as their limited resources were needed for more prestigious sites. In the minutes for 1st July 1938, the burgh applied for a grant of £350 from HM Office of Works for restorative work; a grant of £170 was provided for repairs, the burgh meeting the shortfall. At that time, the council decided to replace the wooden door at the entrance to the undercroft with an iron gate so that visitors could view the interior. The council had to meet the entire cost of this alteration as it wasn't classed as restorative work.

The decay continued. In 1955, the burgh surveyor of the time reported a fall of masonry from the gunport in the eastern side of the forework which had to be shored-up in the interests of safety. The castle was surveyed and recorded by the Royal Commission on the Ancient and Historical Monuments of Scotland in 1977. After a serious rock fall in 1980, the next major incident occurred in December 1993, when the remains of the covered walkway collapsed and the site was closed to the public.

Soon there will be precious little of Dunbar Castle to stir the imagination of future generations. That is a great pity, as the castle provided the town with an appropriate motif for its burgh seal; in turn, the town is the source of a great clan or family which played a part in the history of Scotland for more than three centuries.

2

The Earls (1072-1289)

The history of the Earls of Dunbar began and could be said to have ended in England. Unlike many of the other great Scottish families whose ancestry originated south of the Border, the founder of the Dunbar dynasty was neither Norman adventurer, nor a stranger to the Celtic culture of his adopted country. The earls who descended from Cospatrick or Gospatric of Northumberland in the eleventh century survived for twelve generations; the blood-line continued into the reign of Mary, Queen of Scots in the sixteenth century. The Dunbars and their cadets flourished on both sides of the Border; some of the oldest and noblest families in Scotland and the north of England have their roots in the House of Dunbar. It is curious therefore that the family has received meagre attention from modern historians. Intermittent and brief references are made to the Dunbars in contemporary historical accounts but usually only when their political affinities had an adverse effect on Scotland; this is particularly the case after 1291, when the relative peace between Scotland and England of more than a century came to an end. On occasion the Dunbars favoured England for entirely understandable reasons for which they were censured by biased chronicles which lack the objective approach of modern accounts. Perhaps that is inevitable; it is difficult to understand however why the family has been neglected by modern historians who usually have smaller axes to grind and are not swayed by the crude propaganda of a more hysterical time. History is about people and how and why they acted in certain ways; we must therefore judge individuals according to the conditions prevailing in their own time. The Dunbars undoubtedly played a major part in Scotland's history and they deserve appropriate recognition for that. As no full account of the family has been written since 1859,[1] further appraisal of it is long overdue.

Who were the Dunbars and what was their contribution to the state of medieval Scotland? The first question is easily answered; the second less so. This chapter will address the second aspect by examining the family's activities between the years 1072 and 1289. Appraisal of the family continues in Chapter 4 after 1289, when the subsequent earls figure more prominently in Scottish history - usually in accounts by their critics. In the process of this examination, bias and error are highlighted, as are fair and just criticism.

The amateur historian may be forgiven for accepting the Dunbars at face value, given the fact that several historians have argued that at best, they were ineffective and at worst, unpatriotic. As always in history, the truth lies somewhere in between. With exceptions, the Dunbars were loyal to the Scottish crown. It may be said with some justification however that their political stance during crucial periods of Scottish history brought their loyalty and credibility into question. Sometimes, their role may best be described as whimsical if not irresponsible; they were often misguided in their attitude to Scottish politics, as will be seen. At least two earls were friendly towards England and isolationist during the Wars of Independence but we should not judge the entire family in this light. Lack of patriotic fervour was not always the underlying reason for their contumacy as has been claimed by their several critics; often, affront to the honour of their house was the real issue which drew them towards England, seeking restitution for wrongs, real or imagined.

Patriotism did not have the same significance or universal appeal during the early Middle Ages as it would acquire in later centuries. The surge of patriotic zeal came about in 1296 only after the defeat of John Balliol's army at Dunbar, when patriotism or nationalism was the only logical response to an aggressive Edward I of England. England's attitude to her smaller neighbour was invariably arrogant, resulting from poor foreign policy and lack of diplomacy; faced with continuous war with France and the need to keep Wales and Ireland under control, the obsession of several English kings who aspired to control Scotland demanded nothing less than Scotland's submission as a subservient or vassal state. Such a policy was understandably resisted by the nationalist families situated chiefly in the less vulnerable north of Scotland; families in the south were more at risk from the depredations of war which inevitably coloured their political thought.

The Dunbar line descended from Gospatric of Northumberland, who had Celtic blood in his veins. Subsequent Dunbars were drawn by culture and preference to the feudal aristocracy rather than the old Celtic nobility. Neither of these factions were exclusively nationalistic however. Some ancient Celtic families aligned themselves with those of Norman-Flemish descent who came to Scotland after the Norman Conquest, the reverse also being the case. Nationalism did not emerge as a political force until late in the thirteenth century, when Alexander III's reign was brought to an abrupt and untimely end by his fatal accident. Alexander was probably the first king to achieve a harmony among his elite; while the nobles were not a homogenous group, the squabbling among them did not show itself markedly until Alexander's tragic death at Kinghorn in 1286. He had ruled Scotland through his nobles whether they were indigenous Celtic or *parvenu* aristocrats, achieving a stability which subsequent events would bring to an end, inducing many to look on Alexander's reign as Scotland's golden age.

The Dunbars' role in Scottish history was to a large extent governed by the geographical location of their earldom. Undoubtedly, it exerted considerable influence over the way they thought and acted. In theory at least, under the feudal system, every Scottish noble was subservient to the king, in whose power it was to distribute land and titles in return for feudal service. Certain Scottish nobles were charged additionally with specific functions in government, which in turn meant there was a closer relationship with the crown. The Dunbars were no exception, becoming in time hereditary wardens of the East March of Scotland, which sometimes brought their political ambitions into conflict with those of several Scottish kings, notably the Stewarts. For several centuries, they performed their duties in the Merse (modern Berwickshire) with greater or lesser success but they were also under a formal obligation to English kings in what was a unique arrangement regarding the governorship of part of Northumberland, an obligation which began in the reign of Henry I and is described below. Historians have tended to ignore or underplay this arrangement but in some ways, it explains the dual nature of some of the Dunbars in their dealings with the two countries.

It was sometimes because of this dual role that the Dunbars were guilty of an ambivalent attitude towards Scotland; also, their earldom was vulnerable to attack from the south. East Lothian and the Merse were difficult to defend, falling easy prey to professional English armies and Scottish guerrillas alike. Some Dunbars came into conflict with Scottish kings simply as a result of jealousies deliberately engineered to create divisions among the major noble families whose loyalty could rarely be taken for granted. Having said that, one of history's many ironies is that the last blood-line earl was deprived of his lands and titles, not because his personal loyalty to James I was in any doubt but simply because he was rich.

In studying the Dunbars, we musn't lose sight of the first rule of history - that individuals are judged by the standards prevailing in their time. A common and erroneous impression of the Dunbars is that they constantly wavered between Scotland and England. While this is of course true to some extent, it is equally true of their contemporaries. For example, the Douglases, rightly celebrated for their patriotism during the troubled reign of Robert the Bruce, later grew overmighty and thought nothing of allying themselves with England when it suited their ambitions. We may censure at least two Dunbar earls for their political affinities with England but it is patently irresponsible to tar the whole family with the same brush. It is unfair to describe them as 'the great and wavering earls' as one account puts it.[2] Like most generalisations, this unqualified statement is suspect. It is also a superficial view that the Dunbar countesses were heroic and the earls ineffective; two countesses - Marjorie Comyn in 1296 and Agnes Randolph in 1338, wives of the 8th and 9th Earls respectively - deserve our admiration for their heroic defence of Dunbar Castle. The legend of 'Black' Agnes Randolph is well-known; arguably, she gave the family its finest hour, but hers is only part of the story.

It has been suggested that the Dunbars' failure to secure major royal appointments was to a great extent due to the fact that they were 'unstable' and therefore untrustworthy. Again, that is not the case, nor is it accurate; one Dunbar held the post of Justiciar for Lothian in the twelfth century (see note 61). *Scots' Peerage (SP)* informs us that 'the Earls of Dunbar held great territories both in Scotland and in England and they had the guardianship of the East March, a charge which either seems to have been sufficient to occupy them, or they were not ambitious, as although they were perhaps the most powerful of the Scottish nobility they do not appear to have held any of the high offices of the king.' Tytler's *History of Scotland* makes it quite clear that William I 'the Lion' redefined the duties of the Scottish law officers, establishing two major judges he termed Justiciars. One was responsible for applying the law in Lothian, which covered the whole of the Lowlands from the Firths of Forth and Clyde; the other controlled the rest of Scotland. Tytler leaves us in no doubt that the judicial authority of these officers was 'pre-eminent and that it embraced a civil and criminal jurisdiction which was next to that of the sovereign.'

Undoubtedly, the Dunbars preferred to live the life of country gentlemen rather than statesmen, fulfilling their feudal obligations to king and community while indulging in the universal and popular sport of hunting. Having said that, they were shrewd politicians when the occasion arose, keeping an eye on the state of the country when it affected their personal ambitions. They were in effect medieval businessmen. They were most emphatically not 'an obscure east coast family' as one recent account describes them.

Almost from the outset of his arrival in Scotland in 1072, Gospatric of Northumberland - from here on known as Gospatric I - proceeded to extend his land-holdings in East Lothian and the Merse. In the thirteenth century, Dunbar lands covered the area from East Linton to the Tweed, spreading inland beyond Melrose

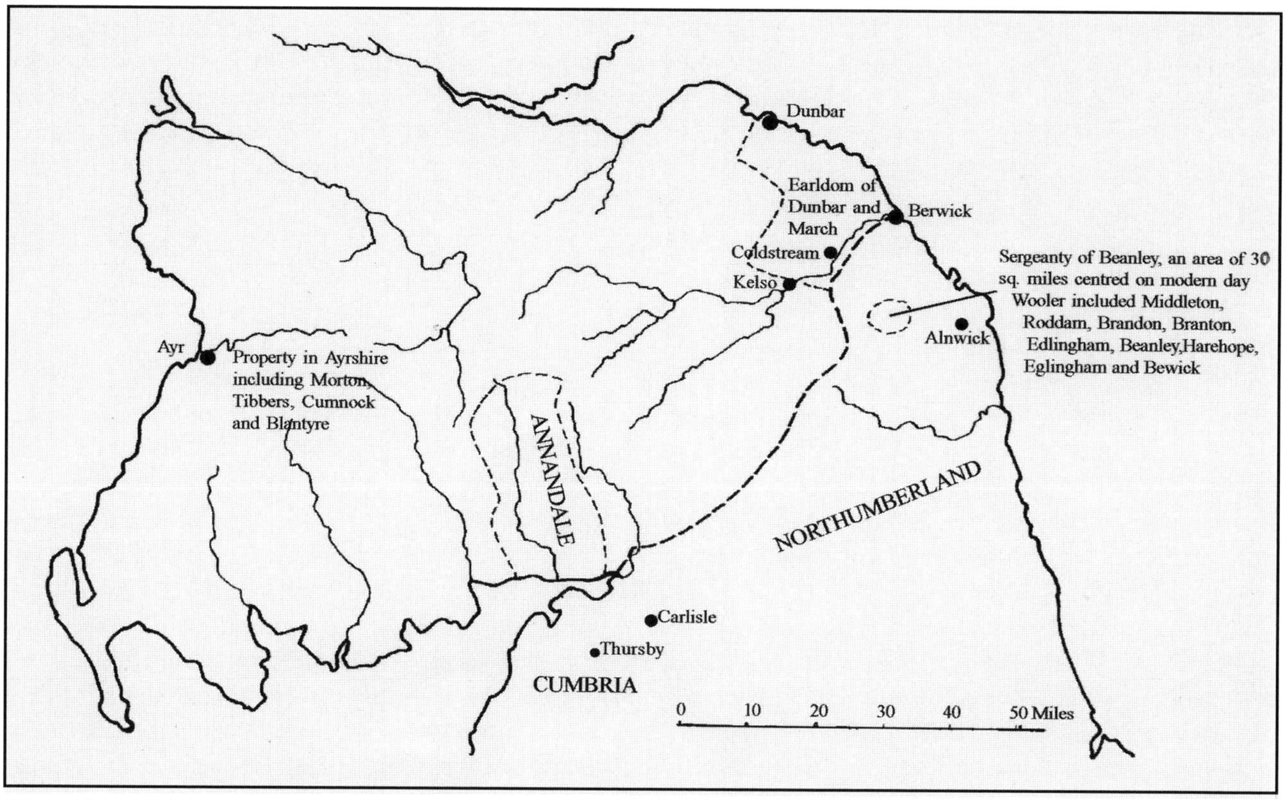

Illus 22: *Lands held by the Earls of Dunbar and March in southern Scotland and northern England 1072-1435* KRM

(**ill 22**). By the fourteenth century, the Dunbars had acquired territory in the south-west, in Ayrshire and Dumfriesshire and from 1346 to 1429, they enjoyed the rents from the earldom of Moray, some styling themselves as its earls until the title was given to the Douglases through marriage. The last three earls were among the richest and most powerful nobles in Scotland. In the south east, their prestigious stone castle at Dunbar was second only to Roxburgh and no English army invading by the east coast route could afford to ignore it.

Any study of the Dunbar earls must necessarily begin with a brief account of their earldom, which is no easy matter, given the dearth of documented source material in the period known as the Dark Ages and prior to the reign of David I. As noted in Chapter I, Dunbar became an important Anglian shire centre in c.638. In the interval between the evangelistic era of the early Christian Church and the Norman Conquest, the history of Britain is one of periodic invasion and mass migration of tribes from northern Europe. We know something of the Anglian newcomers however. In northern England, Ida, an Anglian war chief established himself in his castle at Bamburgh in c.547; he founded the dynasty of petty kings who ruled Bernicia or old Northumbria, men whose influence allowed them to annex a considerable part of south-east Scotland and found the town of *Beorwic* (Berwick). At the height of its power, Bernicia embraced most of modern Northumberland, Roxburgh, Selkirk, Peebles and the Lothians. In Ida's time, Dunbar was a minor community occupied by the Celtic-British Votadini, who had supplanted earlier Bronze Age settlers. When the Angles of Bernicia-Northumbria invaded southern Scotland in c.603, Lothian was among the first shires to be occupied from then until 1018, by which time it became permanently Scottish. By the end of the eleventh century however, a Northumbrian would again occupy Dunbar.

In pre-feudal Scotland, Dunbar was part of the thanage of Lothian. The term *thane* derives from the Anglo-Saxon *theng*, or high-born vassal of the king. The powers and duties of a Scottish thane corresponded roughly to those of an earl; both exercised jurisdiction over civil and criminal matters on the king's behalf. Thanes were put in charge of the local population to ensure public order and prompt payment of taxes, including the *teinds* or *tithes* - the tenth part of everything produced by a community - due to the Church. The term *earl* also existed in pre-feudal Norman Scotland; an earl was responsible for mustering and leading the men of his earldom in times of war. An earldom could include more than a single shire but the shire was the unit recognised for calculating the number of men required for military service.

Buchanan's fifteenth century *History of Scotland (Buchanan, Hist.)* refers to Patrick de Dunbar, Thane of Lothian, who was present at the battle of Cullen Fields in 961. Buchanan credits Dunbar with a significant role in the defeat of the Danes in Morayshire that year. It is possible that Thane Patrick was a Scot but it is equally likely that he was a Northumbrian as Lothian was then part of the kingdom of Bernicia. He may have been recruited for the army of Indulfus or Indulf of Scotland, who like the English, suffered from periodic invasions by Danish war-bands intent on plunder and permanent settlement. At Cullen, the Danes were thrown into confusion by the arrival on the field of a noble known only as Graeme who, with Thane Patrick, led the troops from Lothian to victory. Cramond, *Annals of Cullen* refers to 'Dunbar, Thane of Lothian....a commander.'[3]

The next we hear of Thane Patrick is in 1010; he is probably not the same man who served in Indulf's army in 961. We know very little about him other than the year of his death. In about 971x975, Kenneth II (971-95) was formally granted Lothian by king Edgar of a united England on condition that he paid homage to English kings for the privilege. At some point between 975 and 1018, Lothian was recovered by England; the precise year is in doubt but it is it is more than likely that the loss occurred in 1005 when Uchtred or Uhtred, Earl of Northumberland, reclaimed Lothian after defeating Malcolm II (1005-34) in that year. Malcolm made repeated raids in Northumberland and besieged Durham in 1005, where he was defeated by Uhtred. A Thane Patrick de Dunbar served in Malcolm's army between 1008 and 1010 but he is almost certainly not the same Patrick who fought at Cullen. In 1010, the second Patrick was slain along with two other thanes at the battle of Mortlake, near Banff, when Malcolm finally expelled the Danes from Morayshire.[4]

After Patrick's death, the thanage of Dunbar possibly remained vacant until 1018 when Malcolm II annexed Lothian after defeating Eadulf Cudel, the late Uhtred's half-brother. Had Uhtred been alive then, it is questionable whether the Scots could have taken Lothian. The thanage of Dunbar was probably administered by some other means after 1018 until 1072, in which year it was a vacant earldom.

The earls were the premier group in the Scottish nobility; numbering about a dozen, nearly all were descended from Celtic stock. The only exception was Gospatric I, who was of mixed Celtic-Anglian birth. The earls were successors to the *mormaers* - men like Macbeth - literally 'great officers'. They served Scottish kings as provincial governors and military commanders. The position created for Gospatric I in 1072 was unique; it was a post-Conquest honour bestowed upon a native of England in an area which had been Scottish for less than a century. At that time, the language and culture of Lothian were more akin to those of northern England than Gaelic Scotland; the men who laboured in the fields and felled trees near Dunbar had spoken English for four centuries. Gaelic influence, never strong in Lothian, was ultimately restricted to the north.

Gospatric I

About a year after Hastings, Gospatric I emerges from obscurity. Of Celtic-Anglo-Saxon stock, Gospatric, the son of Maldred of Scotland and Aldgytha or Algatha of Northumberland was born in either 1040 or 1045; the *Cumberland and Westmoreland Antiquarian and Archaeological Society (CWAAS) (vols. xiv, xii and xvii)* place his birth about 1026 but most sources accept 1040x1045. Gospatric's paternal grandfather was Crinan the Thane,[5] head of the House of Atholl from which the Alpin line of Scottish kings descended. Through his mother Algatha, the blood of the royal house of Wessex ran in Gospatric's veins and his maternal grandfather Uhtred was one of the last of a dynasty which had ruled the Northumbrian kingdom from the late ninth century (**Fig. 1**) Thus Gospatric's immediate ancestors linked him directly with the Scottish and English thrones. In 1005, Crinan the Thane married Bethoc, Malcolm II's daughter; their eldest son became Duncan I. Of their younger son Maldred, little is known other than that he appears to have ruled an area in Cumbria which formed part of the old British kingdom of Strathclyde. When Maldred married Algatha, daughter of Earl Uhtred of Northumberland by Elfgiva,[6] Uhtred's third wife, he may have entertained some hopes of the Northumbrian earldom, although his wife had male relatives with a stronger claim on the title. *Symeon of Durham* informs us that Maldred was a rich man. Gospatric couldn't have known his father or his paternal grandfather, being either a small child or recently born when Maldred and Crinan were slain in 1045 fighting Macbeth who after killing Duncan I, took the Scottish throne. (Despite Shakespeare, Macbeth was the more effective king). Before his death, Maldred had repulsed an attack on Cumbria in 1038 by Algatha's half-brother Eadolph or Eadwulf, Earl of Northumberland who may have been attempting to recover both Cumbria and Lothian from the Scots. Whatever his reasons, relationships within the family were far from congenial.

Thus Gospatric was born into a family at war with itself. Virtually no documentary records of him have survived but his immediate English ancestors were the Eadwulfings of Northumbria.. The first Eadwulf was a personal friend of Alfred the Great who fought the Danes; the Eadwulfing dynasty ruled Bernicia or Old Northumbria for over a century. A genealogical chart (**Fig. 2**) illustrates the complex route through which Gospatric I succeeded to the Northumbrian earldom. In his youth, Gospatric had much in his favour; he inherited his father's Cumbrian estates and through his marriage - his wife's name is unknown[7] - he gained lands in Northumbria.

When Earl Siward of Northumbria died in 1055, the Wessex warlord Tostig - brother of Harold Godwinson whom Duke William of Normandy defeated at Hastings - was appointed by Edward the Confessor as Siward's successor. It is thought that Gospatric I was the 'noble youth' who accompanied Tostig and Aldred, Archbishop of York, on a pilgrimage to Rome in 1061,[8] the year Malcolm III, Gospatric's cousin, made the first of several raids into Northumbria. Before his uncle Maldred was killed in 1045, Malcolm had been appointed prince of Cumbria and effectively ruled Lothian; *Scotichronicon* indicates that Duncan I had given him the province and Malcolm desired to annex Northumbria to extend the Scottish border to conform with Scottish Cumbria. When Malcolm became king in 1058, he would have confirmed his cousin Gospatric's hereditary rights in Cumbria. From 1055, Malcolm became obsessed with Northumbria; as a boy, he had fled there from Macbeth and received military aid from his uncle Siward against Macbeth who had, in his eyes, usurped the Scottish throne. On the eve of the Norman Conquest, Gospatric was styled Lord of Allerdale and Dalston, confirmed by a document known as *Gospatric's Writ* (see Appendix B).[9]

The unpopular Tostig was expelled from the Northumbrian earldom by the people - aided according to *CWAAS (vol iv)* by Gospatric - possibly because Tostig's sister Edith, Edward the Confessor's queen, had arranged the murder of Gospatric's half-uncle, also called Gospatric, in 1064. Disappointed by the lack of support from his brother Harold, Tostig went to Flanders where he was persuaded by Duke William of Normandy to join him against Harold. Tostig obtained support from Harold Hardrada of Norway and also visited Malcolm III's court seeking military aid. Harold, now king of England and faced with war on two fronts, dealt with the lesser threat first; in 1066, he marched north to defeat and kill Tostig and Hardrada at Stamford Bridge, Yorkshire, then turned south in a spectacularly swift and gruelling forced march to engage William at Hastings.

It is almost certain that any help Malcolm III had offered Tostig was conditional on the annexation of Northumbria to Scotland, a cornerstone of Malcolm's foreign policy; he probably saw first Tostig, then Gospatric I as a means to this end. After Tostig's death, the earldom changed hands four times between 1065 and 1067. With virtually no direct male heirs old enough to challenge him, Gosaptric I made his bid for the title, basing his claim on descent from Earl Uhtred, his maternal grandfather. William the Conqueror supported his claim and he became Earl of Northumberland at Christmas, 1067. William believed the locally popular Gospatric would bring stability to a lawless area and save him the trouble and expense of subduing it by force. For the privilege however, Gospatric was obliged to pay William a large sum of money; in this respect, William treated him no differently from other native English nobles since those he did not replace with his own knights were required to pay him a fee before their confiscated lands were returned to them. William must have been bitterly disappointed when his young protege joined a rebellion against him in 1068.

Malcolm III probably resented his cousin's elevated status, now backed by Norman might. To some extent, Cumbria was a factor in the political equation; the province see-sawed between Scotland and England from 945 until 1136, when it finally became English territory.

Thus Cumbria appears to have been a royal fiefdom possessed by heirs to the Scottish throne in much the same way as the princedom of Wales, created in 1284 by Edward I for heirs to the English throne. This arrangement continued well after the Conquest, even if England annexed 'Scottish' Cumbria in 1092; in name at least, Cumbria was considered Scottish in 1107 and along with unspecified parts of Lothian, continued to be an appanage of Scottish crown princes. Thus someone such as Gospatric I who had close connections with Cumbria would have been expected to promote Scottish rather than English interests.

In 1031-1034, Malcolm II and Cnut or Canute of England quarrelled over Cumbria because Malcolm's son Duncan, then prince of Cumbria, refused to swear his obligatory oath on the grounds that it was due to English kings and Cnut was a Dane. Semantics were swept aside in the ensuing invasion of Scotland and war was narrowly averted by the intervention of nobles and churchmen on both sides. The two kings agreed that provided the necessary fealty was sworn, Duncan and his heirs would hold Cumbria as freely as had Malcolm and his predecessors. Some accounts, including *CWAAS*, consider that Cumbria was restored in exchange for Lothian but this is not the case; the ownership of Lothian was never in dispute at any time after 1018.[10] The foregoing is supported by *The Anglo-Saxon Chronicle (ASC)* - for once reliable; the real purpose behind Cnut's invasion was probably to discourage further Scottish ambitions in northern England. For his part, Malcolm II needed to maintain a Scottish presence in Cumbria as it secured his continued occupation of Lothian and offered him a route into northern England. Although subject to the overlordship of England, Cumbria was considered Scottish after Maldred's death in 1045;[11] while Malcolm III paid homage for it from 1058, the area was part of the earldom of Northumberland in Earl Siward's time (1041-55). Cumbria was eventually integrated with Norman England after 1092, when Gospatric I's eldest son Dolphin was ejected from the governorship of Carlisle by William the Conqueror's successor, William Rufus.[12]

By 1068, Gospatric I, Earl of Northumberland and Lord of Allerdale and Dalston had become the most powerful noble in northern England; perhaps because of this, he grew over-ambitious. The impetuousity of youth - he was probably not yet thirty years old - induced him to join Edgar Atheling's ill-conceived insurrection against William the Conqueror that year. The inexperienced pair exploited the Northumbrians' desire for independence from Norman England and the population rose in rebellion; after initial success, it failed through lack of resources and military naivety. Joined by Morcar of Mercia and with the support of Malcolm III and Swein of Denmark, the rebels seized the town of Monkchester; the authority for this is unreliable but William came north to defeat the small army on Gateshead Fell.[13] Edgar, Gospatric and several nobles scuttled back across the Border,[14] reputedly accompanied by Edgar's mother and sisters Margaret and Christiana.[15] Margaret subsequently married Malcolm III and after her death became St Margaret of Scotland. One historian has suggested that Edgar Atheling publicly renounced his claim to the English throne and his exodus from England was to convince William the Conqueror of his intentions,[16] which is more than likely. The royal ship berthed at Bamburgh where Edgar supposedly met Gospatric I and planned the rebellion; when it failed, the invention of a storm, which had allegedly blown Edgar off course conveniently explained his presence in Scotland. Malcolm encouraged Edgar's wildly impractical schemes to depose William as he expected to receive Northumberland as reward for his support.

William's reaction was to deprive Gospatric of his Northumbrian earldom and give it to Robert Comines (Cumin or Comyn), a Norman knight, to hold for him.[17] Comines' tenure was brief; at Durham on 28th January 1069, he and 700 Norman soldiers were slain by Northumbrian peasants. [18] Encouraged by this, Edgar and Gospatric collected a second force and joined the Danish army, then investing York; on 20th September, York fell, allowing the Danes to over-run Lincolnshire. William marched north for a second time to eject the Danes from York, where he spent Christmas, then devastated large areas of the northern countryside. In 1070, William summoned the rebel Gospatric and Waltheof, Earl of Huntingdon and Northampton to submit to him; an apprehensive Gospatric couldn't face the king and made his peace by proxy.[19] Perhaps by now he realised that the only man strong enough to oppose William had died at Hastings.

Gospatric's earldom was restored, possibly because William dismissed his rebellion as youthful waywardness; he needed an ally against a potentially hostile Scotland and perhaps this time, Gospatric had learnt his lesson. The contrite Earl of Northumberland made a barefoot pilgrimage to the shrine of St Cuthbert on Holy Island (Lindisfarne); his penance was to atone for having removed the greater part of the church of Durham's rich ornaments in his flight from William at the end of 1069. [20] Now eager to prove his loyalty to the Norman king, Gospatric proceeded to raid Scottish Cumbria over which he had some jurisdiction; if it seems curious that he attacked his own as well as Scottish possessions, it is even more curious that Malcolm III raided Teeside and Cleveland in the same year yet spared Gospatric's lands there.

The Scottish king was enraged by his cousin's treachery; he crossed the Border to 'kill any of the English nation' he could find. He sacked Bamburgh, from whose castle Gospatric made sporadic but half-hearted attacks. *The History of Northumberland (Northumberland County Hist.) (vol vii)* states that Malcolm spared Gospatric's possessions because of his foreign policy and blood-ties but this is speculation. What *was* Malcolm's policy? The only logical answer is that the Scottish king did not wish to alienate Gospatric entirely, thereby endangering his hopes of annexing Northumberland. Malcolm's raid was severe and bloody. Contemporary chroniclers all testify to this fact; the usually unbiased *Symeon of Durham* states that many men, women and children were either slaughtered or taken in chains to become slaves in Scotland. Even allowing for the usual exaggerations, every chronicle confirms the harshness of Malcolm's raid.

William didn't respond to the Scots' aggressive invasion initially as he was engaged in formulating a national defence plan and a major castle-building programme. However, in 1072, he crossed the Border, pursuing Malcolm to the Tay, where he received Malcolm's submission at Abernethy. Under the peace treaty, Malcolm agreed not to shelter Edgar Atheling and handed over his son Duncan as hostage for his good behaviour.[21]

Despite the Treaty of Abernethy, William rightly surmised that Malcolm would continue to pursue his ambition to annex Northumberland so to dissuade him, he deprived Gospatric of his earldom again, this time for good. Knowing that Malcolm and Gospatric were related and shared a common interest in Northumberland, William could not rule out the possibility they would join forces in the future. William decided to leave nothing to chance. However, his reasons for expelling Gospatric do not stand up to examination; the first reason was Gospatric's alleged complicity in Robert de Comines' murder at Durham and his alliance with the Danes in York,[22] offences for which he had pardoned Gospatric. In 1072, William appointed Waltheof, son of the late Earl Siward as Gospatric's successor; Earl Waltheof of Huntingdon and Northampton was married to the Conqueror's niece Judith, so he seemed to be a sounder choice. Waltheof was as troublesome as his predecessor. In 1075, he unsuccessfully rebelled against William and was executed in 1076.

Now himself stateless, a chastened Gospatric visited Malcolm's court hoping to effect a reconciliation. On Malcolm's advice, he went to live in Flanders for a time, possibly to avoid antagonising William. He returned to Scotland later in 1072 and this time he would be no bird of passage. Forgiven for his Cumbrian adventure, Malcolm received Gospatric warmly; whatever the reason for his change of heart, Malcolm gave Gospatric Dunbar 'until happier times returned'. We may take this to imply that Malcolm hoped that Gospatric would regain his Northumbrian earldom at some point. Malcolm's motive is clear; he still had hopes of annexing Northumberland and extending the Border to the Tyne. For his part, William decided that as Northumberland was difficult to control, he ordered a 'new castle' to be built on the Tyne by his son Robert, creating debatable land for fifty miles to the Tweed. Thus the town of Newcastle got its name and became a frontier fortress.

Malcolm never gave up his hope of Northumberland. He invaded it in 1079, 1091 and 1093;[23] his final raid was in retaliation for the annexation of Cumbria as far as Carlisle by William's successor, William Rufus. On 13th November 1093, Malcolm was ambushed and killed by a party of Normans at Alnwick, an act which William Rufus publicly deplored but no doubt privately welcomed.

Gospatric was among the first post-Conquest nobles to arrive in Scotland and whose families possessed lands on both sides of the Border. Gospatric retained lands in Northumberland and Cumbria even after William Rufus took the latter from Scotland; Gospatric's son would later extend his land-holding in Northumberland when he became Earl of Dunbar. Thus from the beginning of the twelfth century, the Dunbars were vassals of both Scotland and England, one of the first families to pay homage to the kings of both countries for their lands.

When William Rufus took Cumbria, he gave it to Ranulph de Meschin,[24] one of his Norman knights who was created Lord of Carlisle; he also expelled Gospatric I's eldest son Dolphin from his governorship of the town. For some reason - undoubtedly political - de Meschin's brother William favoured Waltheof or Waldeve, Gospatric I's third son who lived in Cumbria; Waldeve received lands between the Cocker and Derwent rivers, an area containing the five 'towns' of Birgham, Eglesfield, Dean, Crakesotten and Clifton. Thereafter, Waldeve was known as Lord of Allerdale, a title subsequently confirmed by Henry I. For some years afterwards, Waldeve and his descendants had their country seat at Cockermouth.

Perhaps because he felt Dunbar was inadequate compensation for his Northumbrian earldom, Gospatric I never styled himself its earl. In Scottish charters, he signs himself simply 'Gospatric the Earl' or 'Earl Gospatric'. From 1072 onwards, he began to expand his Scottish possessions; shortly after settling in Dunbar, he reputedly pursued and butchered a band of outlaws in the Merse,[25] presenting the leader's head to Malcolm III. For this, he received the vill of Cockburnspath and other lands in the Merse. With territory stretching to the Border, Gospatric's descendants were described as having the keys of the kingdom hanging from their girdles. Dunbar lands were situated to the east of the old Roman road known as Dere Street. From Eccles and Birgham in Berwickshire and from the Stow of Wedale in Lauderdale to the Lammermuir Hills in the north-east, the whole probably amounted to only about 500 square miles but the land was fertile, productive and strategically important. After only thirty years in Scotland, the Dunbars became an extremely wealthy family.

The Dunbar genealogy (**Fig. 3**) is taken mainly from *SP* and is supplemented by notes on individual members of the family, not all of whom are direct descendants. Some sources contain conflicting material, particularly during the period 1139-1166; genealogies beginning as early as the Dunbars' inevitably suffer from a dearth of reliable source material.

Several noble families sprang from the House of Dunbar; these included the Homes, the Dundases, the Edgars and the Maitlands in Scotland and English families with the surnames Curwen, Lucy and Dacre. As late as 1673 - over two centuries after the death of the last blood-line earl - John Renton of Lamberton was granted an heraldic device for his family crest; it was based on the Dunbar coat-of-arms which consisted of a lion rampant surrounded by a bordure of roses. The family motto was *Forward.* The Rentons were Dunbar vassals in c.1344 and one member of the family attempted to claim the dormant earldom after 1435. The desire of a seventeenth century Renton to link his family with a defunct Scottish peerage is somewhat modern in its pretension. Put into perspective, whether their forbears agreed or not, they were obliged under the feudal system to ride to battle with

'.................................hundreds more
From the rich Merse and Lammermore
And Tweed's fair borders to the war
Beneath the crest of old Dunbar.'[26]

When Gospatric I made Dunbar his family seat, he would have occupied an existing stronghold; as noted in Chapter 1, there had been a wooden fortification as early as 856 and it is likely that Gospatric I inherited a timber stockade situated near the Castle Rock. No trace of any stronghold dating from the eleventh century has yet been discovered at Dunbar[27] and it seems reasonable to assume that Gospatric occupied one which already existed on the promontory now occupied by the leisure swimming pool or the Castle Rock which he or his son later improved.

In c.1090, Gospatric I's daughter Ethelreda married Malcolm's son Duncan who became Duncan II on 12th May 1094; Duncan had remained a hostage in England since 1072 and was Normanised in the intervening years. With William Rufus' help, he took the Scottish throne from Donald Ban, only to be murdered six months later by Malpeder Macloen, *mormaer* of the Mearns in Donald's service. Practically nothing is recorded of Duncan and Ethelreda's brief reign, although it was unique in two respects. Duncan II was the first contender for the Scottish throne to reject the Celtic *tanist* or election method of appointing Scottish kings; he styled himself 'Duncan, son of King Malcomb, by *hereditary right* (my italics) King of Scotland.' Also, one of Duncan's charters - perhaps his only one - is the oldest surviving in Scotland. [28] Had Duncan remained king longer, it is likely that his son William Fitzduncan would have succeeded him. Ethelreda's was the only successful occupancy of the throne by the Dunbars; it will be seen in Chapter 4 that the family made further bids in 1291, 1370 and 1395.

Where and when Gospatric died have given rise to speculation. *Chronica Magistri, Roger Hoveden (Chron. Roger Hoveden)* indicates that 'he did not survive long in Scotland' which could infer that he either died shortly after settling in Dunbar or that he left or was expelled from it. It is recorded that after Malcolm III's death in 1093, his nobles ordered all his English friends out of Scotland; [29] Gospatric I, being a blood-relative might have been able to remain however as there is no mention of his earldom falling vacant, given to a native-born Scottish noble or held in ward for his son, Gospatric II.

As to the date of Gospatric I's death, there is considerable difference of opinion; some accounts give 1073, 1074 and 1075, while others place it in 1115 and 1118; one source puts it as late as 1120x1130, [30] which means he would have been aged 80 or 90, untypical but not unlikely, even for that time. *Northumberland County Hist.* states that Gospatric died in 1075, which would have made his age about 30 or 35, when none of his sons would have been old enough to succeed him. Whatever the truth of it, Gospatric II inherited the earldom in c.1120 but didn't style himself earl until several years afterwards; could that have been because his father was still alive? Perhaps it is safe to assume that Gospatric I died between 1115 and 1120.

The uncertainty about Gospatric's year of death is further complicated by his burial place and the fact that he was confused with his grandson, Gospatric III. In 1161, *Chron. Roger Hoveden* indicates that Gospatric I died in 1074 and was buried at Ubbanford (Norham-on-Tweed);[31] other sources maintain that he spent his last years as a monk in Durham Cathedral and that he was interred there in the monks' burial ground. To add to the confusion, the Durham *Obituary* contains an entry dated 15th December 1166 in memory of 'Gospatricus comes et monachus'-Gospatric earl and monk - which one source believes to be Earl Gospatric III, who also died a monk at Durham in 1166.[32] Further controversy arose in 1821, when a grave cover was found in the crypt of the dormitory at Durham bearing the inscription 'Gospatricus Comes'- Earl Gospatric [33] - but which one? Dunbar, *Scottish Kings* suggests this was Gospatric I's grave; other sources contend that the Durham *Obituary* entry of 1166 was inscribed half a century after Gospatric I's death ie in 1116 - a suspiciously glib attempt to reconcile 'facts'. It cannot be a concidence that Gospatric III also died in 1166. I believe that Gospatric I died at some point in the early twelfth century, serving as a monk at Durham where he was interred and that the grave cover discovered in 1821 is his. The *Obituary* record of 1166 almost certainly refers to his grandson, Gospatric III who was given his 'immortality' in the *Obituary* because of his generosity to the Church.

Details of Gospatric I's family survive; Dolphin or Dolfin, the eldest son, expelled from Carlisle in 1092, may have pre-deceased his father which would explain why Gospatric the younger son succeeded to the earldom. According to Pickering, *The Histories of Noble British Families*, Dolphin was still alive in 1120, the year Gospatric II began to witness royal charters and identify himself as 'Gospatric frater Dolfini' - Gospatric, brother of Dolphin; he may not have styled himself earl as a mark of respect to a recently-deceased elder brother who should have inherited the title and the lands appertaining to Dunbar. Waldeve or Waltheof, the third son became Lord of Allerdale and may have been the lay Abbot of Croyland Abbey, although there are conflicting views about this. Gospatric I's daughters Octreda, Gunnilda and Matilda married into wealthy Cumbrian families and as noted earlier, his fourth daughter Ethelreda married Duncan II.

Gospatric II, 1st Earl of Dunbar

Gospatric II probably assumed responsibility for the earldom in his early thirties. Wood, *The Peerage of Scotland* states that he succeeded his father in his Scottish possessions but wasn't styled Earl of Dunbar until 1130. He often attended Alexander I's court and witnessed David I's charters before and after he ascended the throne. Lawrie, *Earliest Scottish Charters (ESC)* questions why Gospatric II, a Border noble, appears among the witnesses to Alexander I's possibly spurious charter of 1120 which founded the Priory of Scone. Why not? If the influential young man was popular at court, there is no reason to question his involvement in any royal charters. The same question might be asked about David I's *Inquisition* in c.1124 and c.1134 concerning the lands belonging to the church of Glasgow, the latter charter bestowing Govan on Glasgow;[34] both documents were witnessed by Gospatric II. It is perhaps less surprising that his name appears among those who witnessed David's important charter founding Holyrood, supposedly engrossed between 1128 and 1138.[35]

Although *SP* states that Gospatric never styled himself earl during his lifetime, this is incorrect as it was as

Illus 23: *Coldingham Priory* NMS

Earl Gospatric that he granted lands to Coldingham Priory (**ill 23**) in 1128x1138, a title also used in David I's charter confirming Gospatric's gift. Although he was the second to possess the earldom, he is regarded by most historians as the 1st Earl of Dunbar since his father never styled himself as such

We know that Gospatric's wife was Derdere or Deirdre, the proprietress of The Hirsel, in the Borders; this is substantiated by the fact that her son Patrick inherited the property from her. Thereafter, The Hirsel became the family seat of the Homes.

During Gospatric II's tenure of the earldom, the family's Northumbrian possessions were considerably extended at some point after Henry I's accession to the English throne in 1100. Henry granted either Gospatric I or II the grand-serjeanty of the barony of Beanley, situated between Morpeth and Wooler. This was given to the Dunbars for acting as constables to ensure the safe passage of English officials crossing the Border on state business. A serjeanty was land tenure granted for special duties; it could be a grand or a petty serjeanty according to the type of duties performed and it was the usual way of compensating members of the royal household of England for their services. The appointment was undoubtedly a political move on Henry I's part, a somewhat assiduous one to secure a foothold in south-east Scotland. Even so, with his other lands in Northumberland, Gospatric remained loyal to David I throughout his reign; he supported David's policies in Scotland and England. Thus from 1115 until the rise of the House of Douglas under Bruce in the early-fourteenth century, the Dunbars were among the foremost Scottish nobles. That their influence lessened after Bruce's reign through their wavering is a narrow view which is not confirmed by events, as will be seen in Chapter 4.

Gospatric II lived in the early years of Norman-Flemish influence in Scotland; Lothian and Fife were the first areas to be colonised by French knights who gradually spread throughout the Lowlands, then the north. The irony was that Scotland was never conquered by Norman arms; after 1066, there was a 'gentle' conquest of the country largely due to the fact that David I was impressed by the Norman institutions and administrators he had encountered in England. However, the impact of Norman-Flemish culture cannot be lightly dismissed; while the Normans were not the first to establish a system of knight-service in return for land, nor combine the use of cavalry and archers in warfare or create castles of stone as centres of administration and control, they were unique - and successful - in combining all three. With their energy and ability to adapt existing government machinery, their genius for organisation and control was an impressive achievement, which benefited Scotland.

Born in 1058, David I was the youngest of Malcolm III's sons and consequently had little expectation of the Scottish crown. It is thought that after his father's death in 1093, he was educated in England; he married Matilda, or Maud, daughter of Earl Waltheof of Northumberland whom William the Conqueror had executed in 1076. Through Maud's previous marriage to the Flemish baron Simon de Senlis, David obtained the vast estates of the Honour of Huntingdon and Northampton in 1114. Scottish by birth but Norman by persuasion, David was keen to re-invigorate his kingdom when he ascended the throne in 1124. Not surprisingly, he associated improvement with what he saw and experienced in Norman England. He admired Norman institutions and developed a passion for Norman forms of administration, particularly through the Church; his frequent and considerable generosity to religious communities in Scotland earned him the censure of James I who would later refer to him as a 'sair sanct [sore saint] to the Croun [Crown] because he gave away so much royal land to monasteries and abbeys. More significant was David's introduction of the fabric of Norman feudalism to consolidate and enforce his royal - political - authority. He believed that by imitating it, he would civilise his semi-barbaric kingdom within his own lifetime. As a consequence, he invited many Norman knights from the Honour of Huntingdon to settle in Scotland; these were mainly younger sons of Norman families - men with little prospect of inheriting their fathers' estates. The incomers didn't displace the native Celtic aristocracy. As with Gospatric I in 1072, grants to them came from Crown lands, those lacking an heir or which had been forfeited to the Crown. The Normans - a convenient title used to describe the Flemings, Picards, Angevins and those who had come to England with William the Conqueror from Normandy - soon made their presence felt in Scotland. At first, these knights acted as clerical and lay advisors to David, then administrators and finally as colonists, intermarrying with native Scottish families and thus ensuring land-holding. Continental culture was never imposed on Scotland at sword-point; it simply took root in soil which had been prepared for it. If the ultimate aim of military conquest is to shape and transform the society of the vanquished country, the 'gentle' conquest of Scotland encouraged by David I was a resounding success. That conquest not only brought about the creation of stone castles, it introduced a more efficient form of administration and organisation and in doing so, helped to forge the country's national identity.

David's Normans had an unquenchable thirst for land which brought wealth and influence. How far they individually influenced the imposition of the new feudal system on Scotland is difficult to determine. The new system certainly caught on; it brought benefits to both superior and vassal since to some extent a king could keep his nobles in control by reward. Thus the old feudal system was subsumed by the Norman version, which centred on the king as ultimate superior who delegated his power and authority through his nobles in exchange for land tenure and service. The main difference between the old and new systems was that there was a closer relationship between monarch and vassal; land given by the king became the hereditary property of every noble, not returned to the crown on the death of the holder.

The three Gospatrics of Dunbar lived through a period of intense change in Scotland; that their earldom not only survived intact, but expanded is a tribute to their perspicacity. By the time David I ascended the throne, the Dunbar earldom was considered one of the 'native' earldoms of Scotland;[36] it was never usurped by any incoming Norman.

Prior to his death, Gospatric II gave the church of Edlingham in Northumberland in alms to the Abbey of St Albans,[37] possibly in return for the 'gift' of lands in Bewick and Eglingham he had received from the Abbot of St Albans for the protection David I gave in a charter which Gospatric undertook to uphold - to the St Albans cell at Tynemouth during the brief war with England in 1138. More is heard of this particular exchange of gifts in the thirteenth century, as will be seen. Gospatric II also endowed the church of St Nicholas of Home in the Merse with a carucate of land,[38] the gift receiving the specific consent of his family. A significant endowment of Nesbit and Edrom made to the monks of Coldingham-Durham is of particular interest to the historian not only because it is an informative archive but also gives us insight into the character and identity of the Gospatric who witnessed it (see under Gospatric III).[39]

The death of Gospatric II in 1138 or 1139 came about as a result of David's foreign policy towards England. In 1127, as Earl of Huntingdon and Northampton, David supported the English barons who acknowledged Matilda, David's niece, as Henry I's rightful heir to the throne of England. After Henry's death, he was succeeded by Stephen, his nephew, third son of the Count of Blois and Adela, daughter of William the Conqueror. Matilda's claim was in fact stronger and in 1138, David I invaded England twice in her support. David's actions were not altogether altruistic; he sought Northumberland on the grounds of his marriage to Matilda of Senlis, the daughter of Earl Waltheof of Northumberland.

David and Stephen signed a peace treaty in 1136 but it didn't last long. In the following year, during Stephen's absence in France, David demanded the earldom of Northumberland for his son, prince Henry; after a flurry of diplomatic activity, another truce followed, then in 1138, Stephen invaded Roxburghshire, retreating almost immediately and giving the Scots the initiative. David and Henry ravaged Northumberland, although the St Albans cell at Tynemouth escaped destruction by paying the Scottish king 27 silver merks in return for the protection charter mentioned earlier. A Scottish force led by William Fitzduncan, Gospatric II and the Earl of Angus defeated the English at a skirmish near Clitheroe.[40] David raised a second army in August; he reached Yorkshire, where he was confronted by a hastily-gathered force of northern nobles, uncertain whether to fight the Scots. The aged Archbishop Thurstan of York, a staunch supporter of Stephen, rallied the wavering army until Bernard de Balliol arrived with king Stephen's commission to lead the army. The two armies met at Cowton Moor, near Northallerton and prepared to do battle.

The night before the battle, two Anglo-French knights arrived from the English camp at Thirsk to negotiate with David, hoping to persuade him to return to Scotland. The knights were Bruce and Balliol who owned extensive lands in Scotland; Bruce urged David not to fight with 'friends' who had helped him subdue an unruly Scotland. William Fitzduncan - son of the late Duncan II - launched into a tirade against Bruce - the great-grandfather of the future king - and David refused the terms offered by Bruce and Balliol, whereupon they renounced their fealty to him for their Scottish estates.

The armies drew up in battle formation. The Scottish van consisted of kilted Galwegians; mistaken for dancing girls by the English, they were lightly armed warriors rather than soldiers. In the second line, the Scotto-Norman cavalry was brigaded with the infantry from Cumbria and Teviotdale and were commanded by David's son Henry. The third line contained the men of Lothian and the Isles under Gospatric II. David led the reserve, which consisted of his royal bodyguard and the men of Morayshire.

Norman tactics,[41] already proven at Hastings proved a decisive factor in the outcome of the battle of Cowton Moor - better known as the battle of the Standard - on 22nd August 1138. The English standard was set on a ship's mast in a cart; attached to the mast were a silver pyx containing the consecrated host and the banners of St Cuthbert of Durham, St Wilfrid of York and St John of Beverley. The Anglo-Norman army was formed up in three divisions or 'battles' grouped tightly round the standard. The front line consisted of archers screening a second rank of spearmen; behind the standard stood a division of older horsed knights with a number of younger dismounted knights, a departure from the usual Norman plan of battle using mainly archers and cavalry. As at Hastings, the archers won the day. Galwegian leather bucklers offered no protection against arrows and steel-tipped lances; the semi-barbaric men in the Scottish vanguard were soon obliterated. English chroniclers would later write with unconcealed glee about the frenzied Galwegians struck by so many arrows they resembled porcupines. The English army then engaged the main force and routed it. In the ensuing Scottish flight, Balliol's army made no attempt to consolidate its victory, possibly because the main aim was to halt the Scottish advance. A spectacular English victory, it is said that almost 10,000 - the figure is suspect - of David's troops were buried on the site of the battle, an area known today as Scotspit Lane.

Gospatric II was mortally wounded in the fight. *Historia Anglorum (Chron, Henry of Huntingdon)*[42] indicates that 'the chief leader of the men of Lothian was struck by an arrow; he fell, and his whole nation turned to flight.' *Miller, Dunbar* asserts that Gospatric died on 16th August 1139,[43, 44] almost exactly a year after the battle; *SP* confines its comments to a cautious statement that Gospatric II was no longer alive after August 1139. It is entirely possible that he survived the battle but he was certainly dead by August 1139. *Miller, Dunbar* accepts that he was buried at Norham-on-Tweed which is possible; if he was fatally wounded, he may have died during the retreat from Yorkshire, his followers burying him in the conveniently-situated Border church. However, Dunbar's *Scottish Kings; A Revised Chronology of Scottish History (Dunbar, Scot. Kings)* makes an interesting comment on the final resting-place of Gospatric II's son, Gospatric III; Dunbar refers to a tradition which has it that Gospatric III's warhorse was buried with him at Norham-on-Tweed, although he maintains that the chroniclers have confused Gospatric I and III. The confusion is likely to have been between Gospatric II and III.

The aftermath of defeat brought unexpectedly favourable terms for Scotland. The battle of the Standard led to the Peace of Durham in 1139; under its terms, Stephen offered David Northumberland, probably because he no longer wanted it. In addition, Stephen recognised David's annexation of Carlisle in 1135 and allowed him to retain the Honour of Huntingdon. The sole conditions of the Peace of Durham were that the castles at Bamburgh and Newcastle remained in English hands. These were generous terms - some would say they were bribes - to allow Stephen a free hand to deal with rebellious nobles in the south who continued to fight for Matilda. Stephen was clearly protecting his back and David was only too pleased to aquiesce; he had got what he wanted and Matilda was forgotten.

As for Gospatric II, it is almost certain that he died in 1138. Lawrie's *Early Scottish Charters Prior to 1153AD (Lawrie, ESC)* states that from Gospatric II descended not only the ensuing Earls of Dunbar but other families; he considers that any who possess the surname Dunbar and who can trace their pedigree to Gospatric II may regard themselves 'of the best blood in Scotland.' If it is indeed the case that the eleventh and twelfth centuries produced men who weren't particularly intelligent and were brutal, Gospatric II wasn't among them.

Gospatric III

Gospatric II had four sons; the eldest named after him was by seniority among his siblings his heir. Did Gospatric III immediately inherit his father's earldom after the battle of the Standard? The treaty between David I and Stephen required the Scottish king to surrender Henry, his son and heir as hostage along with the sons of four prominent Scottish nobles; these included 'the son of Gospatric'. We do not know if the son was Gospatric III or Gospatric III's son Waltheof; it is certain that Gospatric II was dead by 1139 and that either Gospatric III or Waltheof was sent to England.[45] The hostages were surrendered to ensure the Peace of Durham agreed on 9 April 1139; the hostages were confined in England for several years, possibly even until Stephen's death in 1154. If Gospatric II did not die until August 1139 as *Miller, Dunbar* contends, then the hostage from Dunbar could only have been Gospatric III. So who ruled Dunbar after Gospatric II's death? *Miller, Dunbar, et al,* believe that Gospatric III inherited his father's title only for nine years and that there was a fourth Gospatric after 1147. Whether there is any basis of truth in this is in doubt. No modern historian accepts the existence of a Gospatric IV after 1147 until 1166, the latter being generally accepted as the year when Gospatric III died. While intrigued by the theory of a fourth Gospatric in *Miller, Dunbar,*[46] I have rejected it on the grounds of faulty research.

Be that as it may, *Miller, Dunbar* refers specifically to the curious absence of references to any Gospatric in *Chronicon Mailros (Chron. Melrose)*, a deliberate omission on the chronicler's part since Earl Gospatric III failed to endow Melrose with customary gifts of land between 1139 and 1165. The Dunbars were closely connected with Melrose Abbey; Gospatric II witnessed its foundation charter in 1136. Although the original has not survived, a subsequent version by David I dated prior to 1144 is thought to embody it; if the second version was endorsed by Gospatric III, his subsequent ungenerous treatment of Melrose certainly would have irked the monks to the extent of withdrawing the 'immortality' their chronicle conferred on those whose names are recorded therein for good deeds. It is certainly significant that there is no mention of any Dunbar Gospatric until 1166, the year of Gospatric III's death.

What is significant is that after 1147, Gospatric's attitude to the Church changes dramatically, as he made gifts to several religious communities. Before that, he contested his father's gift to Coldingham-Durham on several occasions in the full knowledge that he would suffer his father's curse contained in the endowment charter and thus consign himself to eternal damnation. And then, as if he was suddenly converted on some Scottish road to Damascus, we find Gospatric III positively brimming over with goodness and mercy. It is recorded that he allowed one of his Dunbar tenants to live rent-free for life as the man was of good faith but poor in wordly goods and suffering from a painful, incurable disease, possibly leprosy.[47] Gospatric III's generosity to church and poor alike alters dramatically in about 1147. His 'conversion' could have been simply caused by feelings of guilt, or because he survived some serious illness and wished to thank his god for saving his life. Either is possible. So too is the fact that Gospatric III may have been a hostage in England between 1139 and 1147 and that the Dunbar earldom was administered by a natural son of a relative eg William Fitzduncan's bastard son Gospatric, a man who had no obligation to underwrite a gift of land to Coldingham because he wasn't party to the agreement.

David I gave land liberally to whomever he pleased, expecting the usual knight-service based on acreage and crop-yield. The sliding scale of service might require a major landowner to provide 40 knights in the king's service whereas a modest estate would attract the service of a single knight or even a fraction of one.[48] The royal custom of endowing religious houses was imitated by the nobility and would continue in Scotland until the fourteenth century unlike in England, where the nobility recognised that they could not afford to give away land on which their power and wealth was founded. The Dunbars were among the first in Scotland to recognise this and found a less costly way of guaranteeing their salvation. Rather than give away precious acres, the 9th Earl of Dunbar established a self-financing Collegiate Church in Dunbar in 1342. Gospatric II's generous treatment of his sons Edgar and Edward left Gospatric III with little of the fees he might have expected from his Northumbrian possessions which could explain why he made no gifts to the church between 1139 and 1147 and tried unsuccessfully to recover lands from Coldingham-Durham. (He appears to have acquired additional land at Drem, East Lothian during the reign of Malcolm IV who succeeded David[49]). As mentioned earlier, his wife Deirdre was probably the proprietress of The Hirsel near Coldstream, herself a generous patron of the Church. Her marriage to Gospatric III produced two sons, Waltheof or Waldeve - some historians argue he was the 4th Earl of Dunbar although Gospatric I was never styled as such - and Patrick, who inherited the Manor of Greenlaw and his mother's property at The Hirsel.

Little more is known of Gospatric III. One of his last official duties was to act as witness to a charter by Malcolm IV in favour of Kelso Abbey. Before his death in 1165, Malcolm IV, a weak king known as *The Maiden* gave in to Henry II's demands for the return of Northumberland and Cumbria given to Scotland under the Peace of Durham. Henry argued that as an unconstitutional king, Stephen had no right to make grants of English territory to Scotland. As a consequence, Gospatric III and his brothers again became English vassals for their Northumbrian possessions. During Malcolm's reign, the Earls of Fife and Dunbar were the king's loyal supporters; although Anglo-Norman nobles predominated as witnesses of royal charters, Gospatric III's name is prominent among them.

Like his grandfather, Gospatric III probably became a monk of Durham near the end of his life. As indicated earlier, he is almost certainly the Gospatric whose name is entered in the Durham *Obituary* for 15th December 1166, when he died. Some historians believe he was interred at Durham while others maintain he was buried alongside his wife Deirdre at Eccles in the Borders [50] *Chron. Roger Hoveden* states that he was 'in Albania' [he meant Alba, the ancient name for Scotland]; Lawrie, *Annals of the Reigns of Malcolm and William (Lawrie, Annals)* believes that Hoveden implied he lived in Scotland, not that he died there. *Dunbar, Scot. Kings* considers it unlikely that he died in Scotland and that he was residing in Durham when he died. It is entirely possible that he ended his days as a monk of Durham and that his name was recorded by the brothers there in recognition of his generosity to the Church. It is also likely that he was buried in Eccles.

Waltheof, 4th Earl of Dunbar

Waltheof is known to us as Earl Waltheof or Waldeve the Earl. He administered the earldom from at least 1165.[51] He is regarded as the 4th Earl of Dunbar by modern historians even though his great-grandfather was never styled the first earl of Dunbar. If Gospatric II is considered the first earl, this implies that there were two subsequent holders of the title before Waldeve inherited the family's considerable Scottish and Northumbrian estates.[52] Be that as it may, his first charter confirmed his grandfather's gift of Edrom and Nesbit to Coldingham-Durham, possibly as a gesture to the mother house at Durham for honouring his father's memory in its *Obituary.* Waldeve also granted eight ploughgates (104 acres) of land to the Prior of Coldingham in an undated charter.[53] A further charter was made in favour of the nuns of Coldingham.[54] He also granted lands to Kelso and Melrose Abbeys and witnessed William I's decision on the settlement of a dispute between the churches [Abbeys?] of Durham and Croyland in 1167.[55]

Waldeve seems to have taken little interest in military matters; he was more of a courtier with some political acumen and clearly a very religious man. Although he never enjoyed a royal appointment, he regularly frequented William I's court, acting as the king's advisor and witnessing several royal charters between 1165 and 1182. Waldeve made a wise and well-balanced speech in the Scottish parliament in 1173 in an attempt to dissuade William I, known as the Lion, from invading England that year; advice which the king ignored. William I became obsessed with recovering the earldom of Northumberland, lost to Scotland before the death of Malcolm IV.

While the Norman-French influence encouraged by David I continued during William's reign, native Scottish nobles figure prominently as witnesses to his charters; for example, Waldeve's name appears in at least 30 charters and his son Patrick, the future 5th Earl of Dunbar witnessed about 27, an indication of the growing influence of the Dunbars. Waldeve also accompanied William on his travels throughout the kingdom; during William's reign, the royal court was constantly on the move, covering punishing distances for the time.

Having rejected Waldeve's sound advice in 1173, William - now openly supporting Henry II's sons Richard 'the Lionheart' and Geoffrey in their attempts to usurp their father's throne crossed the Border in 1173 in his attempt to recover Northumberland.[56] He reached Prudhoe on the outskirts of Newcastle, then immediately retreated to avoid a pitched battle with Henry's supporters. The price of William I's support for Richard the Lionheart was of course Northumberland.

The following year, William beseiged Carlisle, and took castles in Westmorland and Northumberland; investing Alnwick Castle, he was jousting with only 60 knight-companions on 13th July when English cavalry surprised him. William was taken prisoner by Ranulph de Glanville, and led in chains to Chinon in France where under the Treaty of Falaise, he was forced to submit to Henry II as his feudal superior. The Earls of Fife, Dunbar and Angus were required to provide hostages as well as the surrender of the castles at Roxburgh, Jedburgh, Berwick, Edinburgh and Stirling.[57] William's personal humiliation was visited on the Scottish bishops, earls and prominent barons who were also forced to swear an oath of fealty to Henry II on 10th August

1175. Henry II who ranks among the greatest statesmen-soldier kings of Europe had effectively removed any threat from Scotland which might interfere with his political aims in France. Scotland was in English vassalage until 1189, when Richard I, needing money to finance his participation in the Third Crusade, allowed William to purchase the quitclaim of his fealty for 10,000 silver merks.

As for Waldeve, he appears to have retired quietly to Dunbar, witnessing his last royal charter in 1182, one in which William granted lands in Lanark to Hugh Fitzwilliam for the fifth part of a knight's fee. Waldeve's wife Alina died in 1179;[58] he survived her by only three years.[59] By all accounts he seems to have been a loyal and peace-loving man who strove to achieve the best interests of church and state in Scotland.

Patrick, 5th Earl of Dunbar

Waldeve's eldest son Patrick succeeded him and became the first to style himself with the territorial title 'of Dunbar' and adopt it as his surname.[60] *Chronica Gentis Scotorum Johannis de Fordun (Chron. Fordun)* refers to Patrick as the Earl of Lothian, a title Patrick himself used when he became Justiciar for Lothian. At the energetic age of 30, Patrick soon made his presence felt in the community. Contemporary chronicles describe him as a man fascinated by the law; fond of a 'guid gaun plea'; his litigious nature made him the perfect choice as Justiciar of Lothian,[61] a royal appointment he held from 1195 to 1199.[62] His success brought his appointment as Chief Justiciar for the whole of Scotland in 1199 until at least 1205.[63] Patrick is thus unique in being the only Dunbar to have held an appointment of the crown. Power may have affected his judgement however as in 1208, he made himself extremely unpopular with the king concerning a dispute with the Church, a matter discussed later.

The 5th Earl was clearly a natural for the legal profession. In 1195, he was foremost among the Scottish nobles who protested against William's proposal to marry his daughter Margaret to Otto of Saxony which would have made Otto his heir-apparent in the absence of any male heirs to the throne.[64] In mitigation, William was severely ill at the time and his purpose was to ensure his successor; recovering from his illness, and with discretion in the face of overwhelming opposition, William withdrew his proposal.

As well as holding the offices of the justiciary, Patrick acted as warden of Berwick - another appointment which suited his temperament as it gave him endless opportunities to practise his legal skills in Border disputes. One example occurred in 1199, when William ordered him to rebuild the wooden bridge across the Tweed at Berwick after a storm washed away an earlier structure.[65] Patrick rebuilt most of the bridge but on reaching the English side of the river, Philip, Bishop of Durham withheld his permission for the supports to be placed on his land. Dunbar and Durham were locked in an acrimonious dispute in which neither would give way until an English knight, William de Estuteville, persuaded the tiresome bishop to let Dunbar complete the bridge.

Patrick was involved in a litigation which occurred between 1207 and 1208, a case almost as robust as that by Gospatric III who challenged the gift of Edrom and Nesbit to the monks of Coldingham-Durham in 1140. In 1207, Patrick granted lands in Wedale [66] to the monks of Melrose Abbey, then later 'vexed' them with a lawsuit on points of trespass and rights to pasturage. The monks argued that the terms of Patrick's charter were unequivocal but he persisted, forcing them to seek Papal intervention. Dunbar's Scottish estates were placed in interdict while Pope Innocent III referred the matter to Bricius [Brice] Douglas, Bishop of Moray, in a letter dated 17th October 1207. Both parties to the dispute appointed representatives to judge the case along with Bishop Douglas. After due deliberation, the committee settled in Melrose's favour. A subsequent charter confirmed the judgement,[67] one which Patrick accepted with bad grace, probably because he was under pressure from William the Lion who was sympathetic to the monks and anxious to please the Pope.

We can but speculate on the standard of justice the disputatious Earl delivered at his own baron courts in nearby Whittingehame. Baron courts were established to judge disputes about agricultural matters, labour and service, trespass, allegations of immorality and slander, theft, murder and assault. Men were usually fined for poaching, brawling or using false weights; women were physically punished for losing their virginity before marriage as this reduced their value. Cases were judged under arrangements very loosely based on the jury system; guilt or blame was decided by *compurgation* in which a number of compurgators gathered to publicly swear the innocence of one of the two parties to an offence. If an insufficient number supported one or other, this was an indication of guilt. Clearly, the system was open to abuse; a modestly well-off lawbreaker could buy his innocence. No doubt Patrick Dunbar followed the cases heard at his baron court with interest, personally participating in the more serious disputes.

In 1184, Patrick married Ada, one of William's several illegitimate children. Ada was pious and before she died in 1199, she reputedly founded a convent for Cistercian nuns at St Bothans (Abbey St Bathans).[68] Patrick possibly owed his royal appointments to his wife and as the king's son-in-law, he may have entertained some hopes of the crown; it comes as no surprise that he was among the most vociferous of the nobles who vetoed the marriage of Margaret to Otto of Saxony since by law, a woman could not inherit the throne of Scotland if there were extant males in the royal family. The constitutional problem was resolved in 1198, when William's queen produced a male heir, the future Alexander II.

In 1200, Patrick accompanied William to Lincoln to pay homage to king John;[69,70] Patrick witnessed the official document recording William's oath, styling himself Earl of Lothian. He endorsed many of William's charters, the last in 1212 which contains details of Alexander's future marriage.[71] After this, Patrick appears to have retired from public life; *SP* suggests he occupied himself with his Northumbrian estates which may be accurate as Scottish archives are silent about his activities south of the Tweed. One of the last references to him in state documents - an oblique one at that - relates to his son William who was made a hostage in England for the Scottish king's good behaviour; William Dunbar was placed in the custody of Roberto de Veteri Ponte.[72]

When Alexander II became king in 1214, Dunbar was one of the seven nobles of the realm who, along with Bishop Malvoisin of St Andrews, took the sixteen year-old boy to be crowned at Scone. The legacy Alexander inherited from his father was a unified Scotland; it was a kingdom he held in his own right, with no subordination to England other than what he was due for the lands he possessed south of the Border.

Young Alexander proved to be an energetic monarch; even during his minority, he conducted himself with dignity and authority. From the outset, his foreign policy towards England was confrontational; for example, he supported the English barons in their revolt against king John, even to the extent of assisting John Fitzwilliam in the capture of London which forced John to negotiate with his nobles at Runnymede and put his seal to the *Magna Carta.* Despite this setback, John resumed war with his nobles, who turned to France and Scotland for help. For his support, Alexander was promised the northern shires of England.

Alexander besieged Norham Castle while John, correctly assuming Scotland was the weakest of his adversaries, marched north before French troops could land in the south-east of England. Alexander retreated across the Border followed closely by John's army; by January 1216, John had reached Dunbar and while he was unable to take the castle, he burnt the town.[73] John reputedly swore he would 'hunt the red fox-cub in his lair' - Alexander had red hair - and he burnt Haddington, Roxburgh, Coldingham and Berwick during his campaign. A cruel and petulant king, John died in October that year and in the ensuing squabbles between England and France over the spoils of war, Scotland was ignored and the promise of Northumberland and Cumbria was conveniently forgotten.

In 1218, perhaps suffering pangs of conscience over his treatment of the Melrose monks ten years earlier, Patrick Dunbar made amends by granting land in Dunbar to the friars of the Holy Trinity.[74] The Trinitarian, or Red Friars' settlement became known as Friarscroft (**ill 24**), a name which survives today. His second wife Christian Bruce, the widow of William Bruce of Annandale may have influenced his decision as she later

Illus 24: *Friarscroft* KRM

founded a second Trinitarian establishment, a *maison de dieu* in Dunbar- confirmed by *Yester Writ No 14* - at some point between 1240 and 1248; it is likely that Patrick granted the land to the Red Friars because he had kinsmen fighting in the Crusades and the brothers raised ransom money to free captives of the Saracens. It is thought that Patrick also endowed Dunbar's Parish Church with either land or money; in the next century, his descendant Patrick, 9th Earl of Dunbar would elevate the church to Collegiate status.[75]

Patrick Dunbar appears to have enjoyed a close relationship with Alexander II. He was with the king at York on 18th June 1221[76] to witness the arrangements made for the dowry of Alexander's wife Joan, sister of Henry III. After that, little is known of him until 1230, when he confirmed a grant of land made to Kelso Abbey[77] by his son-in-law William who married his daughter Ada.[78] There is a reference to a Dunbar earl subduing a revolt in Galloway in c.1232 but this occurred several years later and involved the 6th Earl of Dunbar. In 1232, Patrick was aged 79; it is recorded that he spent a happy Christmas with his family at Dunbar and died six days later,[79] perhaps from a combination of old age, excitement and seasonal overindulgence. Falling ill on 29th December, he called for his friend and kinsman Adam de Harkares or Harkes,[80] Abbot of Melrose who administered the last rites. *Chron. Melrose* tells the story; after spending 'the festival of Our Lord's Nativity....he [Dunbar] was seized with a severe illness, wherefore he summoned the Abbot of Melrose....and received extreme unction and the dress of a monk at his hands.' Patrick, 5th Earl of Dunbar, died on 31st December 1232, in the fiftieth year of his succession to the earldom; he was buried in the church of St Mary's at Eccles where it is thought his grandfather and grandmother are buried.[81] The hoary old earl is believed to have sired several illegitimate offspring as well as three legitimate sons and a daughter. Only the latter are identified in *SP.*

Patrick, 6th Earl of Dunbar

It is more than likely that Patrick, 6th Earl of Dunbar had been managing his father's estates for some time before his death. Wood, *The Peerage of Scotland* describes the 6th Earl as a brave soldier who treated his vassals well; *Chron. Melrose* refers to him as a 'strenuous knight and nephew of the king'- his mother being Alexander II's half-sister. According to Kilconzie, *Dunbar's 1000 Years,* Patrick was first in rank among the 24 nobles of the realm. Succeeding formally to the earldom at the age of 46, Patrick paid the customary homage to Henry III for the family's Northumberland possessions (see Appendix C) on 22nd February 1233.[81] In 1235, he was in command of the army sent to Galloway to supress a revolt. The shire had been plunged into anarchy after its feudal lord, Alan Fitzroland died in 1234 without male heirs, leaving his three daughters' husbands to divide Galloway for themselves. The Galwegians, ill-disposed to the fragmentation of the shire, sought the king's help; Alexander refused to maintain it intact which he could have done by declaring it a crown fiefdom. Thomas, a natural son of Fitzroland was encouraged to claim the whole of Galloway for himself which led to a rebellion quickly subdued by the Earl of Ross. *Chron. Melrose* records that Thomas escaped to Ireland with his chief supporter Gilrod or Gilroy, returning later to stage a second uprising. This time, Patrick Dunbar defused the situation completely through a show of strength; he took Gilroy prisoner. For his decisive action, Alexander gave him lands in Dundaff and Strathcarron.[82] In 1237, Dunbar was first among the nobles who offered surety for the treaty with Henry III under which Alexander resigned any residual claims to the three northern counties of England which had by then been under English jurisdiction for nearly a century. In 1242x1243, Dunbar defeated Somerled, a rebel in Argyle who refused to recognise Alexander's authority in Scotland.[83] It is clear from these incidents that Dunbar made a considerable contribution towards keeping the king's peace in Scotland.

In 1244, Alexander offered his son and heir in marriage to Henry's daughter in the interests of peace, enshrined in a formal document witnessed by Patrick Dunbar and other prominent nobles; known as the Treaty of York,[84] the signatories were obliged to affirm they would personally guarantee the peace. Despite the earlier treaty of 1237, Alexander had again to formally surrender any claims to the northern counties of England; for good measure, he swore not to take up arms against England.

In 1244, Dunbar failed to renew his oath of obligation to Henry III for his Northumbrian estates as had William Comyn for his lands in England; Dunbar and Comyn appeared before the English court to clear themselves by oath for their default.[85] The incident suggests that Patrick had inherited his father's temperament. Perhaps the underlying reason for his contumacy was that by 1244, Patrick had built himself a stone castle at Dunbar at a time when relations with England were deteriorating. That he was a fractious individual is confirmed by two incidents which occurred in 1245 and 1247.

In 1245,[86] Dunbar accompanied David de Lindesay, the Justiciar of Lothian and several knights to meet Hugh de Bolbec, Sheriff of Northumberland and a party of English knights at Reddenburn on the Border. The meeting possibly stemmed from the Treaty of York in 1244 as it was convened to delineate the line of the Border across Wark Common. Six knights were chosen from either side to mark out the boundary line; the

English knights gave their ruling, the Scottish knights led by Dunbar disagreed with them. Two fresh teams were chosen with the same result. Finally, a third group of 24 English knights declared on their honour that the true and ancient March was as their friends had described it on the two previous attempts. Despite having sworn an oath to accept the verdict, de Lindesay and his companions did not consider themselves bound by a decision taken by force of numbers. Backed by his Scottish lances, de Lindesay began making threats but superior English numbers settled the matter. The disgruntled Scots could do little other than turn their destriers - warhorses - northwards.

Informing Henry III of the incident, de Bolbec's letter is not without a hint of injured moral rectitude:

> '....on the quinzaine [15th] of Michaelmas....with knights of Northumberland, [I] met in person at 'Revedenburne' [Reddenburn] David de Lindesay, Justiciar of Laoudie [Lothian], Patric earl of Dunbar, and many other knights sent by the King of Scotland. The business on which they had met being opened, they elected six knights for England, and six for Scotland, as jurors, to make a true perambulation between the kingdoms, viz., between Karham and Hawedene. Wheron the six English knights with one assent proceeded by the right and ancient marches between the kingdoms, the Scottish knights totally dissenting and contradicting them. Wherefore it was agreed between the Justiciar and Earl, [Dunbar] and the writer, to elect twelve other knights, six on either side, and to associate them in the perambulation with the first twelve, for greater security. These being selected and sworn, the English knights agreed on the said boundaries, and the Scottish knights to different ones, as before. And inasmuch as the Scottish knights thus stood in the way of business, the writer, in virtue of the King's command., elected and caused to be sworn, twenty-four discreet and loyal knights of his county, that they might settle the ancient marches between the kingdoms........as follows, viz., from Tweed by the rivulet of Revedenburne, ascending towards the south as far as 'Tres Karras' [Three Marshes], and from thence in a straight line ascending as far as Hoperichelawe [Hopringlaw], and from thence in a straight line to Witelawe [Whitelaw].'

The letter concludes with de Bolbec inviting Henry to indicate his pleasure on the matter. This was of course one of countless disputes on the Anglo-Scottish border, some of which led to full-scale war.

The Scots were back again in 1246.[87] This time, the dispute was between the canons of Carham-on-Tweed and Bernard de Hawden or Hadden. The English knights walked their horses in the reverse direction from that taken in 1245; they began at Whitelaw, arriving at Reddenburn via Hopringlaw. On this occasion, there were no dissenting Scots, probably because Dunbar was absent.

The second incident was more serious. On 11th April 1247, Henry III ordered an inquisition [88] into the lands included in Dunbar's serjeanty of Beanley; the inquiry sought to establish Patrick Dunbar's rights to estates granted to Gospatric I or II by Henry I in c.1100 (see Appendix C). Almost all of the Dunbar holdings[89] in Northumberland were let to tenants and were thus subject to rent payments so that by 1247, Patrick Dunbar had only the vills or manors of Beanley and Shipley for his own use. As noted earlier, the serjeanty of Beanley did not attract the usual knight-service since it was granted as a reward to the Dunbars for enforcing cross-border pledges and arranging the safe conduct of English officials visiting the Scottish court.

The reasons for Henry III's inquisition appear on the surface to have been a rebuke because as in 1244, Dunbar had failed to observe his feudal obligations to the English king; a year later, he had been involved in the Border dispute at Reddenburn. For good measure, Dunbar was now accused of causing a disturbance in Tynemouth Priory, a cell of St Albans. The English king probably decided that enough was enough and thought to punish him for his contumacy by threatening his English possessions. We may accept on face value the first and second of these accusations; that in 1247 was a separate affair, Dunbar being accused of what was technically blasphemy.[90] The real point of issue was in fact something entirely different. In Matthew Paris' *Chronica Majora Historia Anglorum* (*Chron, Matthew Paris),* Dunbar is accused of showing insulting behaviour to the Tynemouth brothers. Paris was the monk and chronicler of St Albans at that time, a personal friend of Henry III. Paris accused Dunbar of being sceptical about the authenticity of the Tynemouth relics of St Oswin, an early Christian king of Northumberland. Paris used his influence with Henry, enlisting his support to rid the Tynemouth brothers of a problem. But was the problem actually blasphemy, as Paris claimed?

In point of fact, the claim of Paris was a stalking horse which concealed the true purpose - that of financial gain. Dunbar mocked the relics simply because he was frustrated by the length of time it was taking the Tynemouth monks and Dunbar's tenants, the Lords of Beanley to agree that Dunbar owned the manors of Bewick and Eglingham. The manors had been given to Gospatric II by the Abbot of St Albans in c.1138 - in effect protection money - so that the Tynemouth cell of St Albans would not be molested during David I's short-lived campaign against Stephen of England. In the intervening years, St Albans had undoubtedly decided that the abbot in 1138 should not have given away the properties in perpetuity and that they should be returned by virtue of the Peace of Durham, which had removed the threat of further war. There are no Scottish records to support this, but we know that the dispute between the monks and the Dunbars had begun in 1201. Some 46 years on, Patrick Dunbar's patience was strained and he lost his temper that day in Tynemouth Priory, mocking the bones of a saint. That the property dispute was the real reason for his anger is accepted by *Northumberland County Hist. vol ii*; it is also a more plausible explanation for Henry's inquisition. Agitated by the dispute, the monks at Tynemouth complained to the mother-house at St Albans about Dunbar's insult, where a politically astute Matthew Paris saw an opportunity to turn the dispute into the more serious charge of blasphemy and restore the two manors to St Albans. In due course, a suitably chastened Dunbar was obliged to apologise to Tynemouth; in an act of contrition, he announced his intention of joining the Seventh Crusade then being organised by the 'Blessed' Louis XI of France. Louis had spent several years preparing for his Crusade and by 1247, he was ready to embark for the Holy Land.

Almost certainly, Dunbar had to return the manors of Bewick and Eglingham to St Albans as they do not appear in the list of Dunbar possessions after 1247 (see Appendix C). In that year, he began to make preparations for his journey to the Holy Land. To meet his expenses, he sold his stud of horses at Lauder to the Abbot of Melrose in August, a transaction witnessed by brothers William and Robert, the latter then acting as his *seneschal* or steward. Dunbar and his son and heir Patrick received 100 and 20 marks each respectively for the horses. The Earl's last official duty in Scotland took place on 14th April 1248, when with Alexander II, he confirmed a grant made by William of Greenlaw to Melrose Abbey. It has been suggested that Dunbar's pilgrimage was not simply personal and that he was appointed by the king to lead 3000 Scottish knights on the crusade.[91] However, the Seventh Crusade was predominantly French and only a small contingent of Scottish, English and Italian knights took part.

By 1248, the crusading ideal begun about 150 years earlier was politicised and degraded. Many knights 'took the Cross' with a degree of cynicism - undoubtedly so in Earl Patrick's case, one of eating humble pie. He probably had little thought of demonstrating his military skills which were limited to chivalric jousts and never put to the test of hostile battle

Louis XI's crusade was probably the best equipped expedition to the Holy Land. He sailed for Cyprus with 15,000 troops and 2,000 knights from Aigues-Mortes, a small fishing village near Marseilles, a port often used by embarking crusader armies. Forty ships from Genoa and Marseilles were contracted to transport the army and stores; Louis left Aigues-Mortes in August 1248 and landed at Limassol, Cyprus in May 1249. At first, all went well; the crusaders invaded Egypt, taking the key port of Damietta. Louis lost it the following year however as he was captured by the Saracens in April and was freed on payment of a large ransom and on condition that he evacuted Damietta. *Chron. Melrose* lamented Damietta's loss as it effectively ended the Seventh Crusade although Louis remained in the Middle East for another five years.[92]

Patrick Dunbar never reached the Holy Land. He never even left Europe. *Miller, Dunbar* and others state that he died at the seige of Damietta but this is incorrect; Damietta fell to the crusaders on 21st June 1249 which is confirmed by *Chron. Melrose* and *Chronicon de Lanercost (Chron. Lanercost).* We know that Earl Patrick died at some time between May and December 1248 at Marseilles although the precise date of his death his unknown.[93] On 13th December 1248, his son and heir Patrick did homage to Henry III for the Dunbars' Northumbrian estates [94] which means that by then he had inherited the Dunbar earldom. As noted earlier, the 6th Earl's last transaction in Scotland was to confirm a grant of land to Melrose Abbey[95] which *SP* considers took place at Easter, 1248. *Chron. Melrose* and *Chron. Matthew Paris* record the Earl's death but the latter account is slightly misleading;[96] *Northumberland County Hist. vol vii* states that Dunbar died at Marseilles and that 'his body was brought back to Tynemouth and buried there in the lands he had harassed.' No doubt the chronicler Matthew Paris was grimly satisfied with the outcome. It is ironic that the 6th Earl, embarking on the noblest knightly cause for the time, died ignominiously of some unspecified disease - probably syphilis - in a French backstreet lodging-house. It was a degrading end to a man who craved the immortality promised by his quest.

The Crusades were a constant drain on men and money, with little to show for the expense. While the Crusading fervour had largely run its course by the end of the thirteenth century, pilgrims continued to the Holy Land. The 5th Earl's cousins had died in the Fifth Crusade; the 6th Earl met an untimely end attempting to join the Seventh Crusade and his great-great-grandson Sir Patrick Dunbar would die at Candia, Crete on pilgrimage in 1357. At least the Crusades introduced certain luxury goods and new plant species to Western Europe; knights returning home brought carpets that were initially hung on walls as decorations, gauze, silks, plants, seeds, bulbs - the humble snowdrop is thought to have come to Europe this way - all hitherto unknown in the West.

Unfortunately for the historian, many Scottish records in the late twelfth and most of the thirteenth centuries were destroyed and save for a few fragments of *ER* (1254-66 and 1288-90), the only sources available are the monastic chronicles which are notoriously biased and unreliable. However, *Chron. Melrose* and *Chron. Lanercost* are considered accurate; the latter is very readable and is widely accepted as a true account of events because of its plausible and often humorous observations and anecdotes, two of which are about the 6th Earl of Dunbar. These stories are written in the typical style of medieval simplicity and quaintness which bridge the centuries, bringing the Earl alive for us.

The first incident is almost modern in its pretension. Once, Patrick Dunbar invited several important people to a feast at Dunbar Castle; he was subsequently informed by his steward that as more guests than expected had arrived, there wasn't enough food to go round. The resourceful Earl saved his family honour by ordering the kitchen set on fire, presumably announcing that dinner was most definitely off. (Shades of the popular TV series *Fawlty Towers* which featured the hapless and pretentious Basil!)

The second tale illustrates the nature of Scottish justice at the time. It concerns a robber whom Dunbar saved from the gallows then employed in his castle's household. The fellow showed his gratitude by attempting to wound his new employer by putting a dagger underneath his bedclothes so that it pierced his foot. The miscreant escaped but was captured three days later and brought before Patrick, who treated the whole matter as a joke and offered him his job again. The man declined, pretending he was going on pilgrimage; Patrick gave him a purse of money to help him on his way! The baron court at Whittingehame undoubtedly delivered many such arbitrary rulings; in the hands of the nobles, justice often came a poor second to whimsy

One of the consequences of the 6th Earl's pilgrimage was the creation of a medieval hospital at Dunbar. Some modern historians have attributed the founding of the Trinitarian or Red Friars community in Dunbar to the 6th Earl; a closer examination of the facts suggests this was more likely the work of his father in 1218. According to some sources, the 6th Earl founded a Carmelite hospital or *maison de dieu* in Dunbar between 1240 and 1248 or that his son was responsible for its creation in 1263. We know that the only establishment created in Dunbar after Friarscroft in 1218 was Trinitarian and that it was founded by the 6th Earl's stepmother, Christian Bruce in 1240x1248 as an annex to the main house at Friarscroft.[97] The evidence which survives[98] does not date the founding of the *maison de dieu* precisely but the identity of its founder is quite clear.

The 6th Earl's wife Euphemia, daughter of Walter, 3rd High Steward of Scotland, brought her husband lands in Birkenside, Lauderdale, where some cadets of the Dunbars subsequently settled. She survived her husband for 19 years but according to *Chron Lanercost,* she did not enjoy cordial relations with her son Patrick, 7th earl of Dunbar.[99] She lived out the years of her widowhood at Whittingehame, well away from the family seat; it is said that mother and son were reconciled at her deathbed in 1267 however. Her second son Waldeve became rector of Dunbar's church and is referred to as such in a letter from Pope Innocent IV.

Patrick, 7th Earl of Dunbar

Aged 35, Patrick inherited the earldom at a time when the great stone castles were beginning to make their appearance in Scotland. Along with Yester (Humbie), Dirleton (North Berwick) and Hailes (East Linton), Dunbar was among the first to be built in East Lothian and probably preceded them. In 1249, the year Alexander III became king, Patrick Dunbar reputedly declared loyalty to England but the sources which attempt to discredit him are biased, possibly deliberately; Patrick was simply paying the customary homage to the English king for his lands in Northumberland From about 1242 until 1250, the Dunbars appear to have kept a low profile in Scottish politics although they periodically fished in troubled waters during Alexander III's minority, as will be seen. It could be said that the 7th Earl wavered between Scotland and England between 1250 and 1260 but this is not strictly accurate; his activities were to a greater extent aimed at appeasing Henry III while he remained loyal to Alexander. His contemporary critics either misrepresented his actions or set out to discredit him during the political upheaval which Scotland experienced at the time.

During Alexander III's minority, the Dunbars and other families had short-term aims; their objectives were directed towards preserving their wealth and position. It was during this period that a distinct division among the ruling families arose. There were two factions, one led by the foremost family of the time, the Comyns in the north; the other faction was largely comprised of Lowland nobles, including the Dunbars. The aim of the first group was to maintain Scotland's sovereignty, one which commends them to its history. The second faction appears to have been simply to wield influence over the young king in order to suit personal interests. In reality, both groups had the similar aims; they differed only in the way by which they would achieve them. The 7th Earl of Dunbar was no different from his allies, nor was he the villain the Comyn faction painted him. Dunbar certainly looked to England for support but he was nonetheless loyal to the boy-king Alexander.

To understand the 7th Earl's motives from 1250 to 1260 requires a brief examination of the power struggle between the two factions uppermost during Alexander III's minority. The faction-fighting which began then continued for the next three centuries, ultimately transforming itself into a conflict between the crown and the nobility. In 1250, matters were complicated in Scotland by the constant interfering by Henry III which effectively split the nobles into national and pro-English factions. Although the pre-eminent position of the Comyns dominated mid-thirteen century Scottish politics, they were not the cause of the strife. That was caused by the lesser faction led by the Durwards who seeking prestige and a higher place in the pecking order, turned to Henry III for support to compensate for their lack of following in Scotland.

Alan Doorward or Durward, an Angus landowner, had married an illegitimate daughter of Alexander II; he possibly entertained some hopes of the crown and set out to discredit the Comyns, then regarded as 'the best men in Scotland.'[100] Several Scottish nobles manipulated by Henry III appointed Walter Comyn as Alexander III's chief advisor; Comyn soon proved himself no English puppet which discomfited the English king. In 1255, Henry came north to 'rescue' his son-in-law through marriage to his daughter;[101] Henry claimed that the Scottish nobles were treating the young king dishonourably and were discourteous to his equally young queen. Most contemporary English chronicles and records are almost hysterical in their depiction of Scotland as a country on the brink of civil war. Using the diplomatic and convenient ruse of parental concern, Henry made it known he would visit Scotland simply to restore order; his real purpose was to interfere in Scotland's domestic affairs and raise the ancient claim as Scotland's overlord.

In Edinburgh, Durward was supported by Patrick Dunbar and other nobles hostile to the Comyns; reinforced by English troops, Durward moved swiftly. He seized Edinburgh Castle, filled it with his supporters and removed the royal couple to Wark Castle on the Border. A 'grateful' Henry declared his support for the earls of Fife, Dunbar, Carrick, Strathearn, Alexander the Steward, Bruce of Annandale[102] and of course, Durward; in his eyes, these were the legitimate government. Most were Lowland nobles whom Henry felt would contain Comyn power in the north. Henry next wrote to the Durward-Dunbar faction on the strength of a letter he had received allegedly written by Alexander III and naming those in the Comyn faction who should be removed from the governing council of Scotland. Clearly, the pro-English faction had manipulated Alexander, exerting pressure on him to put his seal to the letter. As a consequence, the Comyn faction was excluded from government; the 7th Earl of Dunbar, foremost in the new council was 'caused.....to swear on our soul that we shall faithfully and inviolably observe all these provisions.'[103] Dunbar's name appears fourth in the council; the displaced Comyns, Buchans and Atholls would not easily forgive or forget Durward and Dunbar. In some respects, Dunbar's support for Durward was misguided; it is clear their association stemmed from their mutual opposition to the Comyns. Dunbar's decision to support the pro-English faction was hardly a serious attempt to establish a coup or to bend to Henry III's will. No matter, the chronicles of the time describe Scotland as a country divided into 'native' and 'pro-English' parties.

In 1257, Patrick Dunbar sent a letter dated 4th February, again allegedly written by Alexander III informing his father-in-law that both he and the queen were 'happy and prosperous' in Scotland. In September that year, Alexander was required to formally resign all claims to the northern English counties; this was now almost an automatic ritual when a Scottish king took the throne, aimed at maintaining the peace between Scotland and England. In that document, Dunbar's name appears first among the witnesses who swore to uphold the young king's quitclaim. In the same year, the Comyns took matters into their own hands; they 'kidnapped' the young king. This is regarded less as a retaliatory strike at the Durward faction than a somewhat clumsy attempt to restore the balance of power and knit together the squabbling nobles constantly re-aligning themselves with various factions. Perhaps for this reason, Henry withdrew his support for Durward-Dunbar in 1258; the Lowland coalition had little choice other than to accept Henry's decision. Durward conceded defeat, thus avoiding further conflict - for the time being.

Even during his adulthood, Alexander III relied more on his nobles than any other Scottish king before him; his reign was one of modest, steady development in the relatively peaceful period from 1260 until his death in 1286. As for Dunbar, he too accepted the inevitable and to show his good faith, agreed to the marriage of his son Patrick, the future 8th Earl of Dunbar to Marjorie Comyn, clearly a political move.

The pendulum of power swung back in 1260. Dunbar was once again one of those favoured by England and he became one of the nobles entrusted with the safe-keeping of Alexander's first-born that year.[104] Dunbar was indisputably loyal to Alexander and supported his policies which led to the virtual unification of Scotland by 1286. He also joined the army which defeated Haco of Norway in the west in 1263. Haco's purpose was to deter the Scots from harrassing the Norwegian Hebrides after Alexander took Bute, Cumbrae and Arran from Norway in 1248. Alexander was anxious to annex the Hebrides and thus consolidate his kingdom. Haco's fleet set sail in late summer when an eclipse of the sun occurred; it was considered a bad omen by those in the longships which set sail from Orkney. The fleet of 600 warships sailed into Arran Bay, closely watched by the Scots from the Ayr hills. Alexander played for time to allow his forces to consolidate; he sent envoys to negotiate with Haco but the Norwegian king refused to accept his peace initiatives which did not include the return of the Western Isles to Norway.

We can but speculate whether Dunbar, commanding a division in the left wing of Alexander's army, informed the king that the patron saint of Dunbar, Beya, was buried on nearby Little Cumbrae and that prayers to her would ensure success. Dunbar certainly played a part in the several small running fights subsequently known as the battle of Largs in 1263. Not unexpectedly, Scottish and Norwegian chroniclers differ in their treatment of the battle. The Norwegian saga predictably highlights the bravery of the Norsemen while admitting that Largs was a rout. The battle was important strategically and psychologically since it ended further Norwegian aspirations in Scotland for good. The Norwegian chronicler contents himself with praise for those of his countrymen who fought a rearguard action to allow Haco to recover most of his ships which had been driven ashore by a summer storm. *Chron. Melrose* attributes the victory to 'divine power' adding more prosaically that the Norsemen were 'defeated and overthrown by the foot and the horse of the land.' Haco was able to collect his dead and burn his unserviceable vessels which was hardly possible after a decisive defeat. A treaty signed at Perth in July 1266 ceded the Hebrides and the Isle of Man to Scotland; Dunbar was among those who witnessed it and it is perhaps ironic that his grandson would add Man to the family honours in 1346.

Miller, Dunbar states that the 7th Earl of Dunbar was severely wounded at Largs, implying that he celebrated his survival by founding a monastery for the Carmelites, or White Friars, at Dunbar in 1263. There may be a germ of truth in this but this account argues against the likelihood of a significant Carmelite presence in or near Dunbar.[105] It is more likely that the 7th Earl showed his gratitude to the existing Trinitarian communities founded in 1218 and 1240x1248.[106] The Earl may have expressed his gratitude by extending a grant made by his ancestor Gospatric III to the Cluniac monks at Belhaven, as he gave them five additional acres of land there; in 1553, the area was feued as 'Belhevyne Croft,' now the site of Belhaven Brewery.

Little more is known about Patrick, 7th Earl of Dunbar. It is thought that after 1263, he was mainly preoccupied with his Northumbrian estates and his inactivity is perhaps consistent with his having sustained a severe wound at Largs. However, he helped the Earls of Atholl and Carrick to subdue the Western Isles and annex them to Scotland. Also, in 1266, he witnessed the treaty signed by Magnus of Norway which ceded the Hebrides and the Isle of Man. Dunbar and his son and heir were second only to the Earl of Buchan in the number of royal charters they witnessed between 1262 and 1272, an indication of the extent of their influence at court. Perhaps other documents which might have shed light on his activities at this time were destroyed by Edward I in 1296.[107]

In his late sixties, Dunbar witnessed the marriage of Alexander III's daughter Margaret to Eric of Norway at Roxburgh on 25th July 1281. He was also present at the Scone parliament which accepted Alexander's decision that his daughter's child Margaret - known as the fair Maid of Norway - would inherit the Scottish throne if he died without a male heir. Along with twelve other nobles, Dunbar swore to uphold the accession proposal, a decision they took reluctantly but realistically.

After Alexander's accidental and tragic death at Kinghorn in March 1286, a strong party was formed with aims which remain obscure even today. On 26th September 1286, Robert the Bruce's grandfather, Patrick Dunbar, his sons and other nobles met at Turnberry to offer mutual support. Some historians believe the Turnberry Band as it was known was formed to oppose the Fair Maid of Norway's accession while others regard it as an early bid by the Bruces for the throne. The Band seems more likely to have been a compact in which the signatories pledged themselves to co-operate with each other against the powerful Comyns who were to remain the predominant family in Scotland until the next century. Even so, both Bruce and Dunbar's son Patrick, the 8th Earl of Dunbar would number among the Thirteen Competitors for the Scottish crown some five years later.

Alexander's death plunged Scotland into chaos. A strong-willed man, he was determined to visit his new queen Yolande in Fife on the night of 19th March 1286. After attending a council of state in Edinburgh, the king rode to South Queensferry that day of equinoctial gales and driving snow.[108] Even the ferryman at Queensferry advised against crossing the stormy Forth but Alexander insisted, reaching North Queensferry without mishap. By then, darkness had fallen and galloping ahead of his retinue, his horse stumbled and threw him over the cliffs at Kinghorn.

Alexander was the last of the kings descended from the Celtic House of Dunkeld founded by Crinan, Gospatric I of Dunbar's grandfather. The king's premature death was a tragedy for Scotland. During his reign, the country had begun to prosper; it has also been forged into a united kingdom enjoying peace and economic stability the like of which would not be known again for many years in the future. Alexander's reign has been described a golden age and in many ways this was true; peaceful relations with England had allowed him to concentrate on domestic policies without much foreign interference and apart from Largs, there had been no costly military campaigns to drain the nation's scant resources. The Scottish king had conducted himself with dignity when dealing with England, particularly in 1272, when he attended Edward I's coronation. After observing the customary homage he was due Edward for his English possessions, Alexander never hesitated in his reponse to the suggestion from one wily churchman that he should also pay Edward homage for his crown:

'To homage for my kingdom of Scotland, no one has a right except God alone.'

Nonetheless, modern historians do not consider Alexander's reign to be the golden age *Scotichronicon* would have us believe; his achievement lay in the unification of Scotland.

There is an interesting postscript - if it is true - which the 7th Earl of Dunbar witnessed the day after Alexander died. According to one account,[109] Thomas Learmonth of Earlston[110] also known as Thomas the Rhymer was a frequent visitor to Dunbar Castle and was there on the night Alexander was killed. Being something of a prophet, Thomas predicted that a dire event would take place. A minstrel whose talents were widely praised, Thomas was guilty of the egotism often present among poets; he became irascible when the Earl of Dunbar ridiculed his prediction that night. Dunbar challenged him to forecast a memorable event on that violent evening of wind and snow at Dunbar. Thomas responded with dramatic presence, choosing his words carefully; this is the version of his prediction which has come down to us:

'Alas for tomorrow, a day of calamity and misery! because before the stroke of twelve a strong wind will be heard in Scotland, the like of which has not been known since times long ago. Indeed its blast will dumfound the nations and render senseless those who hear it; it will humble what is lofty and raze what is unbending to the ground.' (quoted from *Scotichronicon*)[111]

If Thomas did in fact speak these words, they are intentionally obscure; his prediction is skilfully ambiguous, hinting of both natural and national disaster. How could he go wrong on that dreadful night of storm?

The following day, the old Earl assembled his family and gentlemen and summoned Thomas at nine o'clock. He teased him for being a false prophet. Then, as recorded in *Scotichronicon,* a rider on a foam-flecked horse arrived at noon before the castle gate demanding to speak to Dunbar. News of the tragedy at Kinghorn elicited the following from Thomas:

'This is the scathful wind and dreadful tempest which shall blow such a calamity to the whole of Scotland.'

The second part of the prophecy was soon to be fulfilled. After Alexander's death, the country descended into anarchy which allowed Edward I to extract an oath of homage from the Scottish nobles under pressure, then the appointment of John Balliol as king and finally, the long, dour Wars of Independence. In all probability, the Rhymer's story was recorded long after the event and was possibly embellished by him to emphasise what was indeed a black day for Scotland.

The tale of Thomas the Rhymer sheds some light on the 7th Earl's character; he was sceptical and had inherited the family inclination to argue. We have another glimpse into the man from an incident recorded in 1254.[112] In midsummer, a sheriff issued a writ ordering him to settle debts amounting to 130 merks which he and his father owed to Ada de Balliol. The debt was still unpaid a year on and a second writ demanded full payment within a year; by 1261, Ada was dead and some 29 merks were still outstanding. The records do not indicate whether the debt was ever cleared. For his own part, the 7th Earl brooked no dereliction of duty in his vassals responsibilities to him; in June 1263, he issued a writ against Roger de Merlay to do him 'the customary and right service demanded of him' for the freehold of de Merlay's tenancy of Dunbar land in Northumberland.[113]

Patrick, seventh of the Earls of Dunbar in 227 years did not live to witness the upheaval caused by the constitutional crisis after 1286. He died in his seventy-sixth year on 24 August 1289 at Whittingehame and was buried under in the north aisle of Dunbar Parish Church.[114] It is from this year onwards that we find both contemporary and modern historians alike referring to the Dunbars as wavering earls. Chapter 4 will examine the extent to which this description was justified during the period 1289 to 1435.

Fig 2 Relationship between the MacAlpin Dynasty of Scottish Kings through Crinan the Thane and the Earls of Northumberland between 967 and 1072

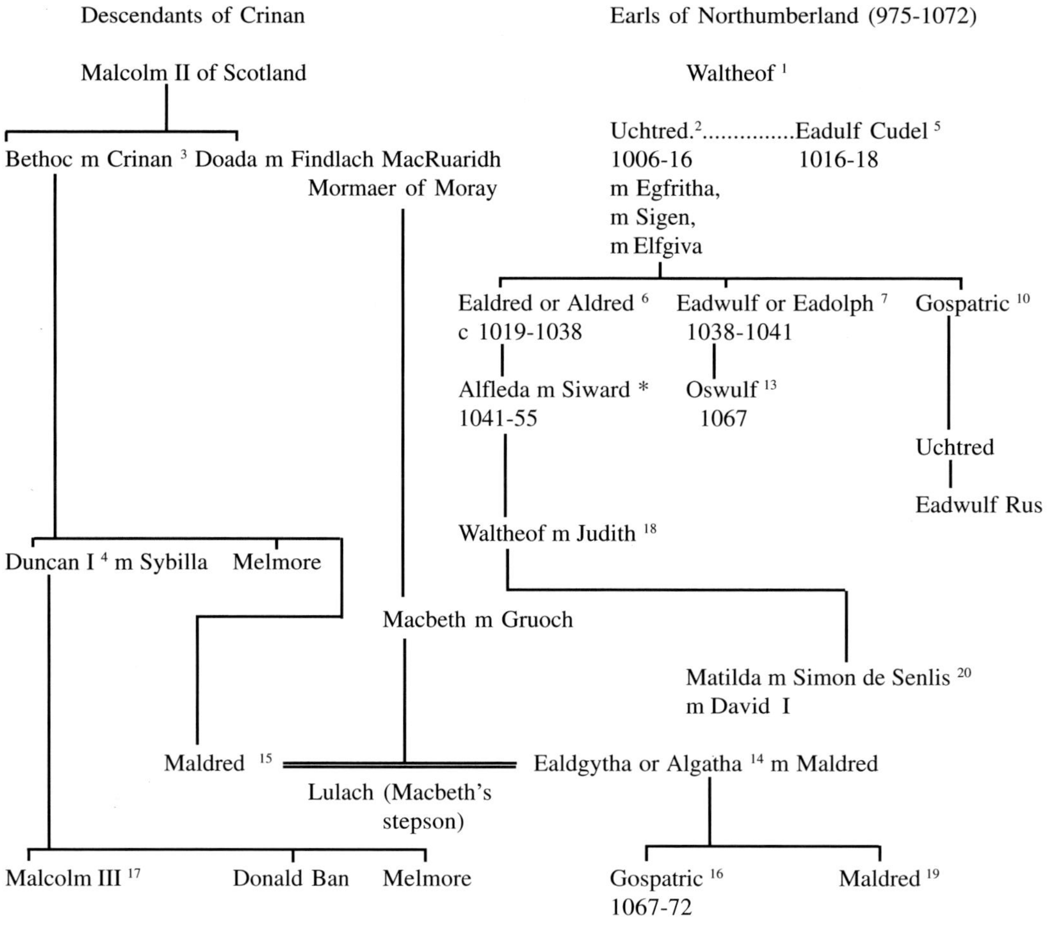

* Non-hereditary appointment; others were Tostig [9] (1055-63 and 1065), Morcar [11] and Copsig [12] (1066-67)

Notes to Fig 2

Introduction

Figs. I (Chap 1)and 2 clearly illustrate that from c.890 to 1075, Northumberland was governed by both hereditary and non-hereditary earls; the non-hereditary earls were officiary appointments made by Saxon and Danish kings, then William the Conqueror in 1067. These officiary earls acted as the king's deputies. There is evidence of a blood-feud between the families of Waltheof of Northumberland and Thurbrand, as will be seen from the notes below; the feud lasted for nearly 60 years.

The main concern here is with Gospatric of Northumberland, later Gospatric I of Dunbar; his tenure as Earl of Northumberland in 1067 was neither the longest or the shortest of these appointments, nor did it lack controversy. Gospatric was both a hereditary and officiary appointment since despite being descended from Uchtred, an Eadwulfing, William the Conqueror 'appointed' him in 1067. The chart in fig. 2 derives from several primary and secondary sources too numerous to list here; some are incompatible, which is only to be expected, given that the period 1034-1067 was one of repeated disruption in the government of Northumberland. The main primary sources consulted are the *Anglo-Saxon Chronicle* and the *Chronicle of Melrose;* secondary sources are Stenton, *Anglo-Saxon England;* Round, *Feudal England*; Barlow, *Edward the Confessor* and Clark, *Genealogical Collections*

Notes

1 Earl Waltheof (975-1006) is a convenient starting point for the chart; he was among the last of the Eadwulfings

2 Uchtred or Uhtred, Waltheof's son, was appointed by Aethelread or Ethelred 'the Unready'. He married that king's daughter Elfgiva; and thus was Edward the Confessor's brother-in-law. His previous wives were Egfritha, daughter of Bishop Aldune of Durham and Sigen, daughter of Styr, a Scandinavian noble. In 1005-1006, Uhtred defeated Malcolm II at Durham and re claimed parts of Lothian the Scots had annexed over the previous century. When Ethelred died during his struggle against Cnut or Canute of Denmark in 1016, Uhtred was murdered in obscure circumstances on his way to negotiate a peace with Cnut that year. (It is thought that his assassin was Thurbrand *the Hold* - the title is Scandinavian, denoting a military rank between thane and earl - who was reputedly acting on Cnut's orders. Cnut appointed Eric of Norway as Earl of Northumberland in 1017; Eric and Eadulf Cudel, Uhtred's half-brother jointly ruled Northumberland for a few months, Cudel taking charge of the north ern parts which by then included Lothian. It was perhaps the division of territory that induced Malcolm II to attack anddefeat the weaker Cudel at Carham-on-Tweed in1018, whereupon Cudel ceded Lothian to Scotland

3 Bethoc was Malcolm II's heir; Crinan, her husband and their son Maldred were slain by Macbeth in 1045 while attempting to avenge the murder of Duncan I; Melmore, the third son fled to Northumberland to escape Macbeth. Duncan's son Donald Ban

reputedly escaped to the Hebrides or Ireland

4 Duncan I was the head of the House of Alpin; Macbeth was head of the House of Moray; both were bitter rivals for the throne

5 As indicated in note 2, Eadulf Cudel was Uhtred's half-brother. After Carham, Cudel was ousted by Ealdred or Aldred, Uhtred's son. Cudel didn't live long after 1018; he obtained a manor in Peebles-shire which became known as Eadulfston [Eddleston]. *Symeon of Durham* describes him as ' a man very cowardly and timorous' who gave Lothian to the Scots to keep the peace

6 Ealdred or Aldred, son of Uhtred, murdered Thurbrand *the Hold* in revenge for his father's murder in 1016. He became Earl of Northumberland in 1019 and was murdered in 1038 by Thurbrand's son Carl

7 Eadwulf or Eadolph, Uhtred's second son succeeded to the earldom in 1038; he was slain by Siward of Denmark in 1041

8 Siward was appointed Earl of Northumberland in 1041 by Cnut's son Harthacnut. He married Aldred's daughter Alfleda, possibly against her will. He was a just and strong man who brought stability to the unruly northern earldom; he also as sisted the future Malcolm III in his struggle against Macbeth. Siward died in 1055, two years before Malcolm finally deposed Macbeth at the battle of Lumphanan

9 Tostig, Harold II's brother was next appointed earl by Edward the Confessor in 1055. Greedy, unstable and treacherous, Tostig was unpopular with the Northumbrians who expelled him in 1063 because he imposed heavy taxes on them. The Northumbrians invited Morkere or Morcar, brother of Edward of Mercia to act as their overlord. Tostig was briefly reinstated in 1065 after Gospatric, Uhtred's third son was murdered (see note 10). Gospatric, Uhtred's son, was Gospatric of Dunbar's half-uncle; he may have been Earl of Northumberland very briefly at some point between 1063 and 1064. Barlow, *Edward the Confessor* conjectures that he was never Earl of Northumberland and he also doubts that he was murdered by Tostig and his sister Edith, Edward the Confessor's queen. *Northumberland Hist. vol vii* accepts that Gospatric's murder was arranged by Edith

11 Morcar was reputedly appointed by Harold II in 1065 and remained earl until 1066. Neither Morcar or his brother assisted Harold at Hastings; it is thought that they hoped he would be defeated by William of Normandy and that they might benefit accordingly

12 Copsig, Tostig's brother was appointed earl by William the Conqueror; he was murdered by Oswulf, son of Eadolph

13 It is said that Morcar and his brother Edwin of Mercia gave the earldom to Oswulf, which is unlikely; Oswulf was murdered by a robber five weeks after his appointment

14 Ealdgyth or Algatha married Maldred, son of Crinan and Bethoc; she was the daughter of Uhtred and Elfgiva and she had two sons, Gospatric and Maldred. As she was half-sister to Uhtred's three sons by his first wife, her issue had a lesser claim on the earldom

15 Maldred, Gospatric's father was prince of Cumbria; he was killed by Macbeth in 1045

16 Gospatric, son of Maldred and grandson of Uhtred had a lesser claim on the earldom than others such as Waltheof, Uhtred's great-grandson who was Earl of Huntingdon and Northampton. Gospatric probably had years in his favour over any other male heirs and William the Conqueror supported him because he believed Gospatric's popularity in the north would bring stability

17 Malcolm was governor of Cumbria when he succeeded to the Scottish throne in 1057; he and Gospatric were cousins

18 Waltheof, son of Earl Siward joined Edgar Atheling and Gospatric in the rebellion against the Conqueror in 1069; he was married to the Conqueror's daughter Judith. Waltheof obtained the earldom after Gospatric was expelled in 1072; he also slew several of Carl Thurbrand's sons in revenge for the murder of his grandfather Aldred (see note 6 above). Waltheof took part in an ill-fated rebellion against William the Conqueror in 1075 and was executed in 1076

19 From Gospatric's brother Maldred descended the Nevilles, a titled Northumbrian family. Maldred had issue; one son, Robert Fitzmaldred may have had a son called Ulkyl, named in a charter by Gospatric II in 1138 (Raine, *North Durham*)

20 Matilda, daughter of Waltheof and Judith married Simon de Senlis, a wealthy Flemish baron. After his death, she married David I of Scotland, bringing him the Honour of Huntingdon and Northampton. David invited many Norman and Flemish knights to Scotland, probably under Matilda's influence

Fig 3 The Earls of Dunbar and March between 1072 and 1289
Dates indicate tenure of the Dunbar earldom

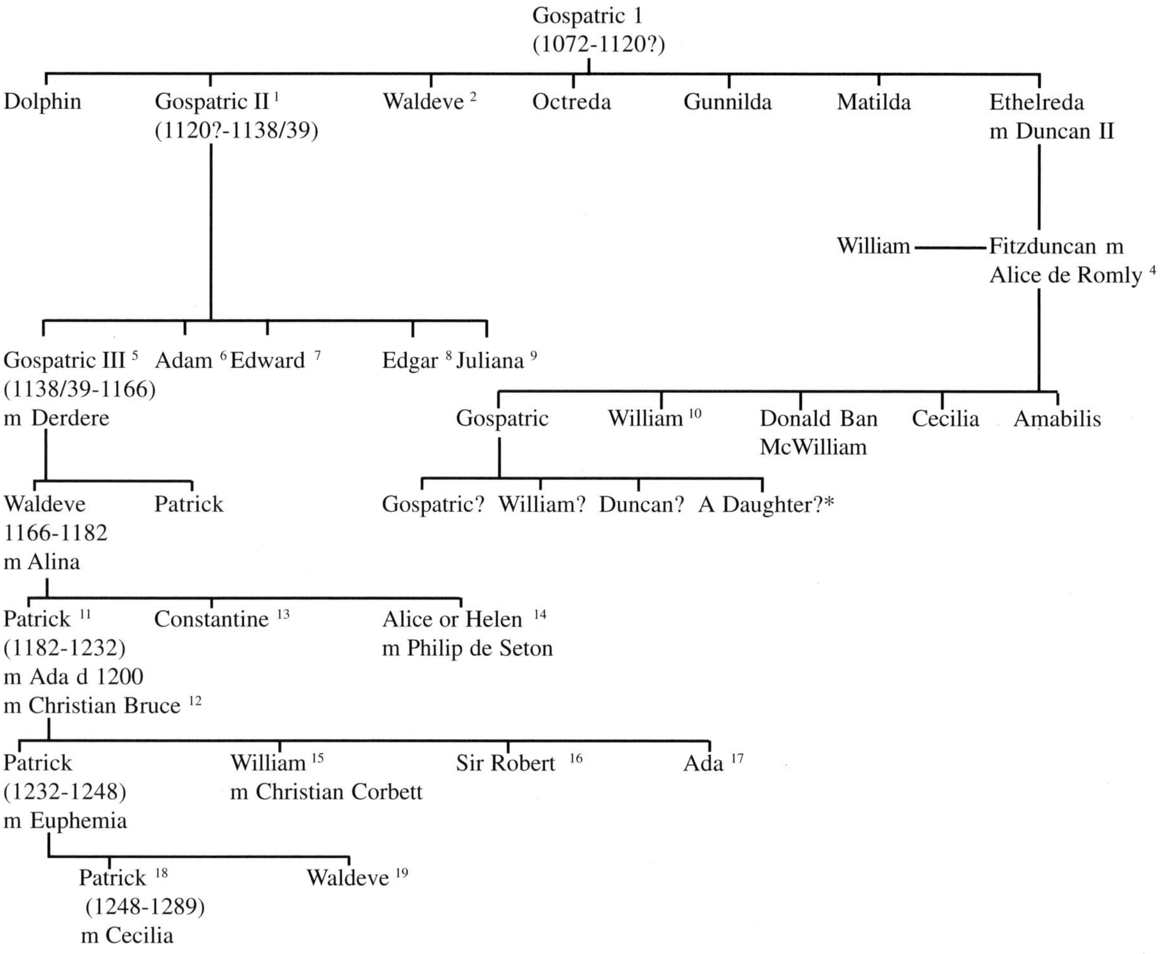

* Issue extracted from *The Dunbar Line* but not claimed by it to be this Gospatric's issue

Notes to Fig 3

1 Gospatric II's wife's name is unknown; *CWAAS vol ix* conjectures she was called Sibilla; but *SP* indicates she was his son Edward's wife

2 Waltheof or Waldeve married into a Cumbrian family; his wife's name was Sigareth or Sigrida. *GEC* states she was alive in 1126. Their issue were Alan, Waldeve, Gunnild and Octreda; another son, Gospatric was illegitimate. Octreda married Ranulf de Lindesay, a Flemish knight; Gunnild married Uhtred, son of Fergus, Lord of Galloway. Waldeve's issue owned lands in Bolton, Bassenthwaite and elsewhere in Derwentwater, together with Dundas on the south bank of the Firth of Forth. Inter esting is the fact that the natural son Gospatric was still alive in 1150 as he is supposedly the Gospatric who witnessed one of David I's charters (Lawrie, *ESC,* Charter No ccxxxii). It is conjectured that Waldeve, his father was Abbot of Croyland Abbey in 1124; Ordericus Vitalis, *Ecclesiastical History* states that an unnamed Abbot of Croyland died on 5 June [1119] 'and was succeeded by Waltheof, the brother of Gospatric, of noble English stock.'

3 Octreda, Gunnilda and Matilda married Cumbrian men; Octreda m. Waldeve, son of Gillimin; Gunnilda m. Orm, son of Ketel and Matilda m. Dolphin, son of Aylaward (*Northumberland County Hist. vol vii*). All three sisters are named in the Wetherall Register at about this time

4 William Fitzduncan, son of Duncan II and Ethelreda of Dunbar obtained the lands in Cumbria which belonged to Waldeve's son Alan (see note 2). William m. Alice de Romly, daughter of Robert de Romly, Lord of Skipton (*CDS vol ii* No 64). Through Alice, he inherited other lands in Cumbria and became Earl of Moray. William was still alive in 1151 as David I restored the Honour of Skipton to him that year. *SP* indicates that his male line ended with William 'the Boy of Egremont' (see note 10). There was another Gospatric of whom *SP* says nothing is known; *CWAAS vol ix* states that he died in infancy. (*Miller, Dunbar* contends there was a Gospatric IV who ruled the earldom of Dunbar between 1139 and 1147 while Gospatric III was an English hostage) It is curious that *The Dunbar Line* gives different issue for Gospatric II from those appearing in *SP*; the names look suspiciously similar to those we might expect to have found in the Duncan II-Ethelreda-Fitzduncan branch of the family de scended from Gospatric I. William's three daughters inherited his Derwent estates; Cecilia m. William the Gross, Earl of Albemarle to whom she brought the Honour of Skipton; Amabillis m. Reginald de Lucy, to whom she brought the Honour of Egremont; and Alicia m. Gilbert de Pypard, a member of the English royal household to whom she brought the Honour of Cockermouth (*CDS vol ii* No 64)

5 *Miller, Dunbar* considers there were two Gospatrics between 1139 and 1166

6 Adam may have changed his name for religious reasons; *Miller, Dunbar* refers to him as Uhtred. Adam was party and witness

to a charter by Gospatric II to the church of St Albans; along with yet another Gospatric, he witnessed Gospatric II's charter granting Edrom and Nesbit to Durham-Coldingham

7 Edward owned Edlingham, Hedgeley, Harehope and other lands in Northumberland which the monks of Durham held of him in *feu-ferme.* He m. Sibilla, probably a Northumbrian woman. To save the souls of himself and his family, he granted the Cluniac monks on the May Island a chalder of meal on the Feast of St Cuthbert from his mill at Belton, near Dunbar. Edward was estranged from his brother Edgar - probably on account of a dispute about land - the claim being settled in Edgar's favour. His descendants inherited some Northumbrian possessions for several generations.

8 Edgar - known as 'Unithing' or the Dauntless - is first named in records in 1138, when Richard of Hexham called him Bastard - more through anger than comment on his birth. He seems to have been the black sheep in the family and was deprived of Bewick and Eglingham in Northumberland, probably because of his bad behaviour in 1174. He m. Aliz of Northumberland who brought him 10 manors - five in Coquetdale and the others in Yorkshire, Cumberland and Westmoreland. Patrick, one of his sons inherited the estate of Caistron and took the surname Kestern as a consequence; his descendants gave lands to Newminster Abbey, founded by Juliana ofDunbar (see note 9)

9 Juliana m. Ranulph or Ralph de Merlay, Lord of Morpeth who owned Morpeth Castle. Her dowry consisted of the lands of Witton, Windygates, Horsley, Stanton, Ritton and Leverchild. She and her husband founded Newminster Abbey in 1138 and both were buried in the chapter-house. At the end of the nineteenth century, a single Gothic arch marked the site of the former Abbey

10 Although the issue of William Fitzduncan are not for the purposes of this genealogy direct in the Dunbar line, perhaps the ex istence of another Gospatric accommodates the theory of Gospatric IV in *Miller, Dunbar* (see note 5). *SP* recognises Fitzduncan's issue as the Boy of Egremont who was drowned in the river Strid near Bolton Abbey; the child is the subject of Wordsworth's poem *The Force of Prayer.* Donald Ban McWilliam was killed in 1187; nothing is known of Gospatric

11 Patrick was the first to style himself 'of Dunbar'.

12 Christian Bruce probably married the 5th Earl between 1215 and 1218; some accounts confuse her with the 7th Earl's wife (see note 18)

13 Constantine died young

14 Alice or Helen reputedly m. Philip de Seton; the Dunbars married into the Seton family on at least one other occasion (Seton, *A History of the Family of Seton* and note 9, Fig. 4)

15 William m. Christian Corbet or Corbett, daughter of William Corbet, Lord of Makerston, Roxburghshire; they had three sons - Nicholas, Patrick and Walter. The family owned Makerston and Langton, Northumber land. William died in 1253, twelve years after his wife. *Chron. Melrose* mentions him in 1240; when the monks were re-interring the remains of a former abbot of Melrose, William extracted a tooth from the corpse which he claimed was beneficial to the sick

16 Sir Robert, *seneschal* or steward to the 6th Earl is scarcely mentioned in any records; he seems to have given up his stewardship of Dunbar to Alan of Harcase [Herkess?] in 1249. Robert witnessed charters by the 6th and 7th Earls and is briefly mentioned in *CDS vol I* p539

17 Ada married three times; William de Courtenay (d. 1217); Theobald Lascelles (d. 1225); her third husband was her father's cousin, William of Greenlaw and their issue were ancestors of the Homes of the Hirsel. Sir George Home who received the honorific title of Earl of Dunbar in 1605 renewed the family relationship with Greenlaw in 1596, according to a charter at Falkland Palace dated 2nd July 1596

18 Patrick is said to have m. Christian Bruce but she married his grandfather. His wife was Cecilia *filia Johannis*, so-named in a charter by his son and heir; *GEC* considers Celia was of the House of Fraser as the 7th Earl added added a bordure of roses to the family armorial bearings, roses featuring as a device in the Fraser coat-of-arms. (Other sources maintain that the rose bordure in the Dunbar coat-of-arms comes from the proximity of the earldom to the English Border, which is not without foundation; however, this could be a propagandist attempt to prove that the Dunbars favoured England rather than Scotland)

19 Waldeve became rector of Dunbar Church; he was allowed to hold an additional benefice, authorised by Pope Innocent III at Lyons on 3rd February 1245. He is mentioned in a charter by Sir Alexander Seton of Seton in c. 1271

3

Indwellers and Visitors

The word *tourist* evokes ambivalent responses the world over. Dunbar did not have tourists - it had *visitors,* the term used today by the tourist industry to describe its clients. Perhaps Dunbar was ahead of its time.

Visitors came to Dunbar from Edinburgh, Glasgow and the north of England; the Scots took 'trades' fortnight holidays' in July while families from Newcastle and Yorkshire arrived in August. They spent their money, shivered in the chill North Sea breezes, consoled by the fact that year after year, Dunbar held the east coast record for sunshine - hence its epithet *Sunny Dunny*. When it rained during the holiday months - July often being wet - the local population expressed genuine sympathy for the Visitors. Little has changed since then except that there are fewer visitors today; most families expect the sunshine and warmth of Spain. However, Dunbar encountered a variety of incomers and visitors - not all of them welcome - over the centuries, as will be seen.

Scotland experienced a trickle, then a flood of European incomers centuries before records existed. Some were visitors while others took up permanent residence; some lingered briefly and others overstayed their welcome. The early incomers were shadowy people who left few clues to their identity. They were nomadic tribes of hunter-gatherers during the Mesolithic period. Since the earliest radio-carbon date, so far, of human habitation in Scotland is 8,500BC at Cramond, 30 miles east of Dunbar; it is reasonable to assume that Dunbar was known to peoples of that era or soon after. Permanent settlement would have taken place around 3,000 BC, when nomadic patterns of life in the Mesolithic period were supplanted by the settled farmers of the Neolithic period.

The first arrivals migrated from Europe soon after the end of the last Ice Age, when land bridges still connected Britain to mainland Europe. The melting of the ice caps raised the sea level and made them permanent residents. Although land access to mainland Europe was cut off by rising sea-levels, 'immigrants' would still make their way to East Lothian.

Bronze and Iron Ages

Changes in man's understanding and utilisation of his environment resulted in what we euphemistically describe as the Bronze and Iron Ages because of the widespread usage of these metals during these periods. The Bronze Age in Scotland dates from about 2,000BC to 700BC, the Iron Age from 700BC to 400AD. It is likely that the area around Dunbar was settled permanently quite early in the Neolithic period, given the fertile nature of the local soils.

Between 1,000 and 400BC, Scotland was colonised by Celts from Central and Western Europe; philologists have categorised the Celtic peoples by their language group, the 'P' group represented by the Welsh, Cornish and Breton dialects, the 'Q' group being Gaelic. The ancient Britons of Scotland and England were P-Celts; the Q-Celts came to Scotland from Ireland. That they conquered many of the non-Celtic indigenous tribes is beyond dispute; prior to the arrival of the Romans, they were the military aristocracy of their age. By 400BC, the east coast of Scotland was occupied by the Brythonic 'P' Celts or Britons who cleared woodland for farming land. As well as their agricultural pursuits, these early visitors were sea-faring men who used small fragile boats or coracles to fish and possibly travel short distances to trade with neighbouring tribes. Through them, we can detect the microcosm of Dunbar as it developed up to about 700AD.

We know very little about these early peoples apart from the traces of their hill-forts and random grave goods, reliable indicators of the cultural and social development of these obscure tribes which help us to date their existence. Even so, it is difficult to draw hard and fast conclusions from the occasional and scarce finds scattered around Dunbar. Those which have been hitherto discovered consist mainly of artefacts dating from the Bronze and Iron Ages. One of the oldest skeletons discovered in the county dates from about 2,000BC.[1] The earliest recorded find of human remains occurred in 1801 at Lauderdale House, when two intact skeletons and disarticulated human bones were uncovered during landscape gardening. A grave excavated at Bowerhouse (Bourhouse) in 1829 contained Bronze Age razors and a socketed axe;[2] a flint arrowhead was found at Hedderwick Hill near West Barns in the 1860s. Nine graves were uncovered at Belhaven in 1891 when a storm washed away part of the bank on the western boundary of what became Winterfield Golf Course, but the stone cists contained only a few bone fragments.[3] Between 1939 and 1972, no fewer than five short and long cists were uncovered at Skateraw. In May 1914, the *Haddingtonshire Courier* reported the find of a stone coffin containing a skull and bones at Ashfield, near the modern railway station. The remains were unearthed by workmen extending the north-bound platform but were re-interred without professional examination. In 1938, a Bronze Age (c.1,600BC) beaker was discovered at Thorntonloch, near Innerwick, then fragments of a beaker of the same period and similar in design was found at Kirkhill Braes, near Roxburghe Terrace in December 1951. This find was made a week after the discovery of several early Christian graves on the site which was being developed for private housing.

The most exciting find in the vicinity occurred in 1962, an excavation extensively recorded by the Society of Antiquaries of Scotland.[4] In the course of deep ploughing at Lochend, a local farmer uncovered a cemetery dating from the Iron Age; it contained the skeletons of at least 20 adults and one child. (This site may have had some connection with the remains discovered at nearby Ashfield; both may indicate the presence of a settlement within sight of the protecting Iron Age fort which existed to the west of the summit of Doon Hill, a site which is almost obliterated today). One of the cists at Lochend contained three iron ornaments, two penannular brooches of the Early Iron Age and an iron stud or dress fastener. At the time, the Dunbar discovery was the most significant find of Scottish Iron Age skeletal remains. In 1977, an Iron Age settlement containing two skeletons was excavated at Broxmouth; it has been suggested that this site was a dependency of the major *oppidum* at Traprain Law.

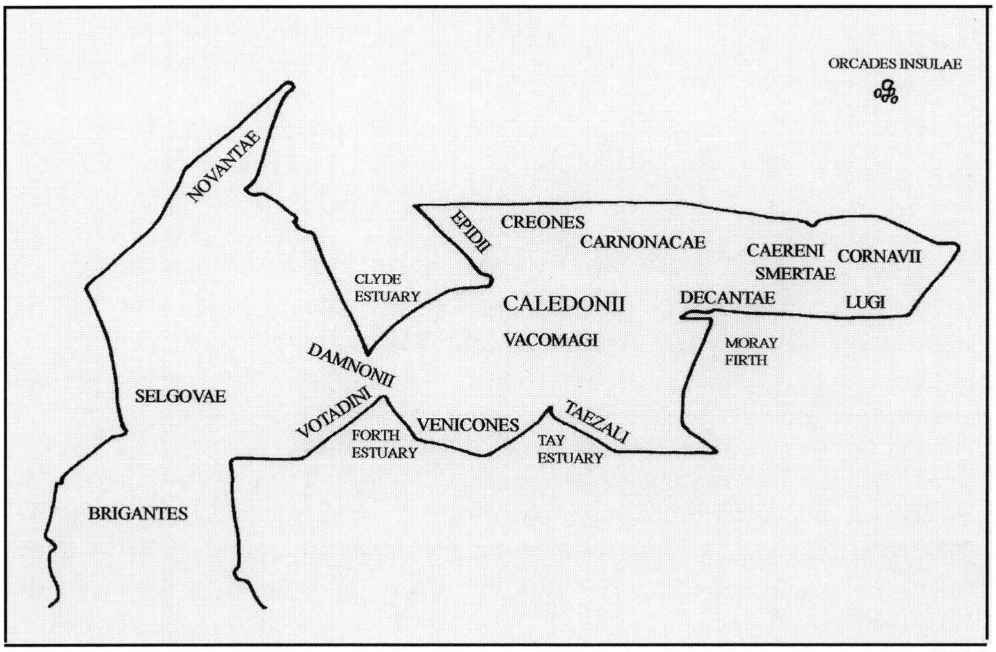

Illus 25: *Ptolemy's map of the tribes of Scotland and northern England in Roman times, some modern details added to assist orientation*

The most significant find of human remains occurred at the Castle Park, formerly Lauderdale House gardens, between 1993 and 1998; in 1993, 33 adult and 13 children's skeletons were uncovered, then in 1998, a further 127 skeletons were brought to light, probably part of the same burial ground. They may be Anglian or Scottish; although part of the Northumbrian kingdom until 1018, Dunbar was subject to Scottish jurisdiction between 973 and 1005 (see Chapter 1). Recent excavations in advance of the A1 improvements between Haddington and Dunbar have revealed traces of a number of sites including a substantial burial/ritual cairn of Late Neolithic to Early Bronze Age date near Eweford Cottages, not far from Lochend Estate. Several cremations, some in urns, were recovered from this site. On the hillside overlooking East Linton from the south, another substantial site was excavated, on this occasion of apparent Iron Age date and probably contemporary with the major occupation of nearby Traprain Law. Final reports from the excavations at Eweford and East Linton along with several other sites along the line of the new A1 have yet to be published.

The most reliable evidence of long-term settlement is evidenced by the remains of a series of forts in the Lammermuir Hills. The earliest of these systems appeared in Britain around the Late Bronze and Early Iron Ages, the end of the latter continuing throughout the Roman occupation. The earliest hill-forts pre-date the accepted Iron Age period and consist of a single rampart with a stone wall or turf bank with a ditch forework.

Palisaded settlements have also been discovered near Dunbar dating from 700BC until the early Christian period. The most well-known of these occurred at Dunpelder or Traprain Law which was occupied from at least 700BC until the fifth century AD. Traprain may well have been part of a series of defence works on a east-west alignment above Dunbar. Iron Age hill forts were discovered in the west at Chesters, near Little Spott, at Doon Hill and in the east at Blackcastle, near Innerwick. The major find in 1989 of a promontory fort consisting of five ditches and turf and stone walls in the Castle Park may have been connected with the major site at Traprain as it was in full view of the fort there.

Among the early visitors were the Votadini, Brythonic Celts who occupied the area from the Firth of Forth to the northern parts of Northumberland; other tribes in the south of Scotland were the Selgovae, the Novantae, the Damnonii, the Carvetti and in Northumberland, the Brigantae (**ill 25**). The history of these tribes is obscure. However it was probably the Votadini who gave Dunbar its name, as Dun or Din is a 'P' Celtic word for stronghold. The community of Dunbar is referred to in Eddius Stephanus' *Vita S. Wilfridi* (c.710) as 'urbem Dynbaer'. How long these disparate tribes were able to maintain their independence is uncertain since most were subsumed by the 'Q' Celtic Scots from Ireland - the Picts - or the Angles arriving in c.603 from Northumberland. In 731, in his *Historia Ecclesiastica Gentis Anglorum,* the Venerable Bede indentifies the inhabitants of Scotland as Scots, Picts, Angles and Britons.

Illus 26: *Doon Hill - Site of British and Anglian timber halls* KRM

Who were the Votadini? They probably descended from the Belgic Gauls; as shown on Ptolemy's second century AD map of Britain, they controlled modern East Lothian and Berwickshire from at least 175BC until about 600AD. The Votadini were certainly established in Dunbar by 75AD. It has been suggested that the tribe may have been the descendants of an earlier group of Celts from Hallstaatt who arrived in Britain around 700BC. As noted in Chapter 1, the Votadini Doon Hill site may have been the nucleus from which the community of Dunbar derived its name and modern location. We know that a British/Votadini timber hall was built on Doon hill around 540AD, a site which was burnt and on which an Anglian royal timber hall was later erected after the defeat of the Votadini in the early seventh century (**ill 26**). Between 1989 and 1993, archaeologists uncovered evidence at Castle Park Dunbar to support the existence of a Votadini settlement in the Late Iron Age and at the time of the Roman invasion in 79AD. Traprain Law, the Votadini capital, can be seen clearly from Dunbar; in times of danger, it would have served as a rallying point for satellite communities like Dunbar.

At Cairndinnie Farm, near Traprain Law, stands the Loth Stone, traditionally accepted as the burial marker of Loth, the eponymous king of Lothian. In 1861 the stone was moved 160 feet from its original position and a stone cist was found nearby. There is another stone at Pencraig Hill which may have been aligned with the Loth Stone for some purpose. Traprain is of course famous for its treasure, discovered in 1919; until then, finds had been limited to a few Roman coins dated between 395 and 408 AD, along with a few stone, bronze and iron relics and pottery shards. However, after the First World War, digging resumed and further excavation revealed the foundations of an early settlement; workmen then broke into what appears to have been a pit which contained 160 silver objects amounting to 770 ounces Troy weight. Some of the items had been hammered flat after folding, bowls had been crushed, flagons beaten and broken - all indicative of hurried concealment or possible use as scrap silver for re-working. The treasure is now on display in the National Museum of Scotland in Edinburgh. Speculation about the origins of the treasure has led to the theory that it had been plundered from churches and hidden during an attack on Traprain. Some of the pieces feature early Christian motifs and date from about the late 5th century. The Votadini were the likely owners. Modern opinion is that the hoard was probably a subsidy rather than plunder.

Apart from Traprain, the Votadini did not live in 'towns' but in scattered settlements, some of which may only have comprised of a single family group - perhaps confirmed by the major find at Lochend in 1962 and a long cist containing two skeletons at North Belton in 1989, both thought to date from between the first and third centuries AD. These groups would have been self reliant, growing or catching their food. Other dispersed sites have probably disappeared due to modern intensive farming but it is more than likely that each group would have been within reasonable distance of a protective hill-top fort such as that on Doon Hill.

The Roman legions which marched from Hadrian's Wall appear to have bypassed Dunbar; their main camps in the south-east of Scotland were situated near Dere Street, the Roman road which went past Newstead, Melrose - itself a major camp - Inveresk, near Musselburgh - another sizeable camp - and Cramond, where extensive excavations have been carried out. At the time of going to print, there is evidence of a Roman settlement in Prestonpans. We know there were two small camps in the Merse; one to the west of St Abbs' Head and at Chesterknowe, on the south bank of the river Whiteadder, a site long-since levelled but mentioned in the *Old Statistical Account* for Berwickshire. Absence of any other traces of Roman road systems in southern Scotland, particularly in the coastal strip from Berwick to Musselburgh - Votadini territory - suggests that perhaps after some initial resistance, the Votadini accepted the *pax Romana* and co-existed peacefully with the incomers.

The treasure found at Traprain included coins dating from the time of Mark Antony (first century AD) up to Accadius and Honarius (5th century AD). These may not in themselves support the theory that the Votadini were a client people of the Romans but the apparent absence of military marching camps suggests peaceful co-existence. To some extent, this is borne out by the discovery of a Roman farm at Overhailes, near Traprain Law. The presence of the site was revealed by aerial photographs taken in 1980; it is about 120 by 60 metres, surrounded by three ditches and containing a timber house. It is similar in style to settlements in Northumberland.

In the time of the great Roman general Theodosius, military operations extended to the Scottish Lowlands, which Theodosius named Valentia, although the precise location and extent of this province remains in doubt. The province couldn't have existed for long. When Roman power was threatened by an Irish invasion of Wales, Votadini warriors were recruited to help the hard-pressed auxiliaries. There is a tradition that Cunedda of the Manau, a sub-kingdom extending from Fife to Dunbar - Manau is thought to survive in the name Pressmennan in the Lammermuirs - was invited to assist the Romans in Wales, repulsing a major Irish invasion in the fourth century AD. Cunedda never returned to Scotland. The only other notable event in the history of the Votadini is the brave but futile attempt by their king Mynyddog in Edinburgh who tried to stem the tide of invading Angles by attacking them at or near Catterick in Yorkshire in c.600AD, an event celebrated - or more accurately, lamented - by one of the two survivors of the defeat, the poet Aneirin, in his contemporary work, *The Goddodin*, the earliest Scottish poem to have survived.

When the Romans were obliged to leave Scotland in c.210AD because of threats elsewhere in the empire, the Votadini appear to have remained in their citadel at Traprain. They were soon threatened by sea-raiding Picts from the other side of the Forth. At first, the Romanised tribe held its own against the Picts until the late sixth century, when they were attacked on a second front by the Angles, intent on expanding their kingdom of Bernicia in Northumberland. The eclipse of the Votadini occurred in the first four decades of the seventh century; however, we know they still possessed Dunbar in the early years of that century.[5] The expansion of the Dalriadic Scots from Ireland into the west of Scotland and the establishing of their stronghold at Dunadd challenged the kingdom of the Picts and in time, the two nations were united by Kenneth I to resist the Angles who by then had ousted the Votadini or enslaved them.

When political and military difficulties in the their Empire forced the Romans to abandon Hadrian's Wall by 409AD - as Bede informs us - the ensuing power vacuum brought to light the comparative weakness and petty factionalism of the British kingdoms on both sides of the Border. Power-seeking and land-hungry incomers - Angles, Jutes and Saxons - colonised large areas of England between the Thames and the Trent; their kingdoms included Mercia (the Midlands), Deira (modern Yorkshire) and Bernicia (Northumberland). As noted in Chapter 2, the Bernician kingdom was founded in the mid-sixth century AD, towards the end of the early Christian period in Scotland; however, few accounts of the Christian missionaries up to 950AD have survived. Bernicia controlled Lothian for nearly four centuries from about 638 until 1018. During that period, the Angles settled in Dunbar and made it one of their main shire centres.

The Dark Ages

In the mid-seventh century, Dunbar was probably little more than a small, smoky hamlet comprised of a group of timber buildings within the Anglian promontory fort mentioned above. The site was excavated in 1989-93 and provided conclusive evidence of an Iron Age, then an Anglian presence; brought to light were the remains of a number of Anglian timber-built dwelling houses, a stone mortar and an Anglian *grubenhaus* - a crude dwelling literally scraped in the ground, the first example found in Britain. These were within a stone-faced turf-and-earth rampart and palisade on an approximately north-east/south-west alignment. In the seventh century, Dunbar became an Anglian royal residence, as it was then described as an *urbs regis*, or royal town.

Other significant finds included a fragment of a gold and garnet pectoral cross dating from the seventh century of similar design to that found in the tomb of St Cuthbert (635-687) when it was opened at Durham Cathedral in 1827 and two Northumbrian *stycas* (coins) dated c.837-841 and c.844. In addition were two finger rings thought to be sixteenth century as they were found in the foundations of Mary of Guise's fort of 1559 (see Chapter 1). Comment in the first report of the dig[6] suggested that there was an Anglian presence in Dunbar before any full-scale conquest of Lothian had occurred. Anglian power in Scotland reached its peak in 685, when the Picts decisively defeated and killed Egfrid of Northumberland at the battle of Nechtansmere. Thereafter, Lothian was subjected to Scottish-Pictish raids with occasional incursions by the Danes in the ninth century. What little evidence there is to shed light on these dark times lies in the museum display case or under the earth; the nameless kingships in and beside the Lammermuir Hills are largely lost to us. Thus Dunbar saw its earliest visitors come and go; arrival of new visitors in the seventh century would continue until 1018, when Lothian became Scottish.

The ease with which the Angles were able to settle in Lothian was due in part to the internecine squabbling among the neighbouring British tribes. In 547AD, Angles led by Ida their 'king' - more pirate than monarch but regarded as the founder of the dynastic rulers of Bernicia - landed at Bamburgh and built a fort there. At first, British chieftains including those of the Votadini whose kingdom included Lindisfarne and the Tees, resisted the invaders, then they quarrelled amongst themselves, thus weakening their ability to contain the Anglian forces. In Scotland, the Strathclyde Britons known as the Damnonii were more successful against the Angles until the powerful Anglian king Aethelfrith (c592-617) - the founder of a combined Bernicia-Deira royal house -defeated a mixed Irish-Scottish-British force at Degsastan, thought to be Dawston, Liddesdale in about 603. By 638, Edinburgh had fallen to the Angles and the area from the Tweed to the Forth came wholly under the control of Oswald and Oswiu, Bernician-Deiran kings who ruled between 634 and 671.

In all probability, Oswald occupied Dunbar around 634 as he is almost certainly the architect of the Anglian palisaded hall excavated at the summit of Doon Hill in 1989, which also revealed an early cemetery of cremated burials. The Anglian structure was superimposed on an earlier structure of 23 metres in length and probably built for a Votadini chieftain in the sixth century. Oswald Dean at the base of Doon Hill may have been named for Oswald of Northumbria. The Doon Hill residence was probably that of an Anglian *ealdorman*; it is strikingly similar in construction to the palace on the hill of Yeavering Bell, near Kirknewton in Northumberland. Yeavering was a *villa regalia* or princely home defended by a wooden palisade, watchtowers and a ditch. Thus by 638, the Angles were firmly established in south-east Scotland, Dunbar being an important military and administrative centre. The annexation of Lothian coincided with the introduction of a strong Gaelic influence spread by the Columban clergy established at Iona.

Some of the Anglian settlers were content to leave unchanged the original place-names of British communities e.g. Peebles and Melrose. *Dynbaer* is thought to have been an old British name. It is highly improbable that the name Dunbar derives from a general called Bar or Barre in the service of king Kenneth MacAlpin in 839 who it is said rewarded Bar with lands in East Lothian. The name *Dynbaer* appears at least a century before, in c.710, when it is referred to by Eddius Stephanus in his *Vita S. Wilfridi* (Life of St Wilfrid). There are however a number of Anglian or English place-names surviving from the seventh century; those villages which have names ending in *-ham* or *-ingeham* (*ham* = a village) thus Tyninghame is Tyn's village and Whittingehame is Huita's village); other places ending in *-ton* or *-tun* (*ton, tun* = a settlement) thus Haddington is Hadin's settlement; *-wic* is rarer (*wic* = a farm) but at least two places survive near Dunbar at Innerwick and Hedderwick; Hedderwick was probably Hedda's farm.) The nucleated villages of East Lothian and the Merse are of undoubted Anglian origin and have more in common with Northumbrian hamlets with their attractive village greens.

Before his death in 670, Oswiu of Northumbria encouraged the spread of Christianity throughout his kingdom as well as enlarging it - policies which his son and successor Egfrid (670-85) followed. Egfrid's reign was the high-water mark of Anglian ambition in Scotland. While keen to allow conversion to Christianity, he wavered between the version founded at Iona (Celtic) and that espoused by Canterbury (Roman). Missionaries from Iona had evangelised the Scottish mainland as far north as Morayshire and by the seventh century, Scots, Picts, Britons and Angles had embraced the Ionian form of worship. St Cuthbert of Lindisfarne, the 'apostle of Lothian' did more than any other missionary to convert the population of south-east Scotland from paganism; born in the Lammermuir Hills near Lauder in c.635, Cuthbert was first based at Melrose, then Lindisfarne but he had no episcopal seat; his mission kept him constantly on the move, baptising converts and preaching throughout the Merse and Lothian. It is more than likely that he visited Dunbar before his death in 687 but there are no records to confirm this.

Egfrid, a strong individual who during his relatively short reign succeeded in annexing the whole of eastern

Scotland to the Forth and beyond it. He accepted and implemented the decisions of the Synod of Whitby in 664 which adopted the Canterbury version of Christianity. However, he quarrelled with Wilfrid (634-709), Bishop of York, ostensibly about ecclesiastical politics but in reality over a personal issue. Wilfrid ridiculed the Ionian or Celtic Church and became the chief mouthpiece for the pro-Rome faction at Lindisfarne, insensitively sweeping aside the opinions and feelings of his opponents. Implacably opposed to those who clung to the Celtic Church whose practices he declared sinful, he denounced Egfrid as a schismatic reprobate for favouring Iona. Egfrid resented the arrogant and overbearing bishop with his large episcopal *imperium.* Wilfrid's wealth, retinue and personality finally brought him into open conflict with the Anglian king, particularly after he encouraged Egfrid's wife to enter Coldingham Priory as a nun. Egfrid had married Etheldreda, the daughter of an Anglian noble; she is referred to as a 'virgin' wife in one ecclesiastical account of the time. Under Wilfrid's influence, she entered Coldingham 'clothed in chastity' in 672 - after twelve years of marriage!

Coldingham was then in the charge of Egfrid's aunt, Abbess Ebba[7] but this allowed him no special considerations as he had to resort to force in an unsuccessful attempt to release Etheldreda in 673. Accepting the situation, Egfrid took a second wife, Ermenburga, who was also hostile towards Wilfrid. Matters came to a head in 680 when on some pretext or other, Egfrid put Wilfrid in prison. Bede informs us that Wilfrid was '.....living...as a banished man out of his country in the coasts of the Marchmen.'[8] According to the monk Eddius Stephanus,[9] Egfrid and his queen cast Wilfrid into a prison whose location is unidentified, then transferred him to Dunbar where he was placed in the custody of the reeve Tydlin. Wilfrid remained at Dunbar for nine months until 681, when Abbess Ebba persuaded Egfrid to set the bishop free.

After Egfrid was defeated and killed at Nechtansmere in 685, the Angles were contained in the area south of the Forth, suffering a further defeat in 698. Peace was restored by king Aldfrith who preserved the integrity of Northumberland but with 'narrower boundaries.' East Lothian remained Anglian throughout the eighth century although it became a cockpit in the power-struggle between the Picts, then the Picts and Scots combined against the Angles after Kenneth mac Alpin united the two races. It is about this time that Bernicia-Northumberland was ruled by Eadwulf I (c.890-913), the founder of a native Anglian dynasty [10] which would continue almost unbroken until Gospatric I became Earl of Northumberland, then Dunbar. The Eadwulfings ruled Bernicia north of the river Tyne to Edinburgh; Eadwulf, to some extent isolated by the Danes, was a personal friend of Alfred the Great, united by their common interest in preventing Danish colonisation of England. It cannot be stated with certainty whether the Eadwulfing kings visited Dunbar but it is highly probable.

Although the Angles and the Picts were separated by the Firth of Forth, anarchy within Northumberland led to political collapse in the ninth century, leaving Lothian prey to the expansionist policy of Picts and Scots under Kenneth. The Angles were also challenged from the sea by Danish pirates who plundered Northumberland after they took York in c.867. We know that in the following century, Lothian suffered depredation at the hands of Norsemen as the priory at Tyninghame founded by St Baldred was attacked in 927 and 945, probably because the Angles were unable to protect the long eastern coastline with its flat, vulnerable beaches. Baldred's diocese included Dunbar and as an important cleric in the area, he undoubtedly enjoyed close relationship with the governing power, visiting the community regularly until his death in 757. Other churchmen followed him and while it is not known whether Dunbar had a church in the eighth and ninth centuries, this is more than likely. Norse forays increased between 939 and 945 but such raids were directed at places where there were rich pickings i.e. undefended churches with their silver and gold plate and religious vessels.

Kenneth I resolved to annex Lothian to Scotland and he made six attempts,[11] burning Dunbar at least once. Even after York fell to the Danes in 867, isolating Northumberland from its allies in Scotland, the Scots were unable to occupy the area from Dunbar to the Tweed. For the next century and a half, Kenneth and his successors attempted to wrest Lothian from the Angles; king Gregory (875-92) was able to prevent the Danes from colonising parts of Scotland but the Angles clung tenaciously to the Merse and Lothian. At some point between 859 and 934, the southern half of Lothian must have drawn closer to Scotland, evidenced by an apocryphal but in some respects possibly unlikely story recorded in the *Anglo-Saxon Chronicle* (*ASC*) in 934. Prior to this, *ASC* records that Constantine of Scotland (903-43), Owen of Strathclyde and Eadwulf of Bamburgh had acknowledged the supremacy of king Athelstan of England in 927. In 934, Athelstan invaded Scotland on some unspecified provocation - possibly the alliance between Constantine and Eadwulf, which suggests some basis for the *ASC* entry for 934. In that year, Athelstan came north to subdue Constantine and his Northumbrian ally; according to *Florenti Wigorniensis Monachi, Chronicon ex Chronicis (Chron. Florence of Worcester),* Athelstan invaded Scotland because Constantine had broken the treaty of 927. *ASC* indicates that all Scotland was subdued and that the English king remained in the north for three years, which is extremely unlikely.

The apocryphal tale referred to above relates to Athelstan's return to England by sea; the king swore that if god granted him a sign that Scotland would forever be a subject-state of England, he would offer everlasting thanks. *ASC* states that as he sailed past Dunbar, he delivered his promise to the heavens and passing some offshore rocks, he struck one with his sword. *ASC* tells us that the rock was 'as penetrable to his sword as if the stone had been butter or soft gravel'; so deep was the cleft made by his sword that Athelstan judged this to be divine acknowledgement of his wish. The story is mocked by Bower in *Scotichronicon*; by way of confirmation, there is no Athelstan's Rock in the sea off Dunbar. What is important about the story however is that it suggests that Dunbar and Lothian were either Scottish or territory under Scottish jurisdiction.

What happened to Dunbar during the centuries of Anglian occupation? The community had never been Pictish although it had formed part of the Brythonic-Celtic kingdom of the Votadini. The Celtic farmer/fishermen families no doubt intermarried with the Angles between 638 and 1018. When the area became part of Scotland, it would have made little difference to the majority of its inhabitants; the population of Dunbar was small, living in a poor economy, illiterate and working the fields for subsistence at a very basic level. If there were a church, it would have offered little more than spiritual comfort, crude and ineffective advice on health and perhaps some colour and entertainment on holy festival days. Other than these, the peasant labourer lived in much the same way as his forefathers had done, in small smoky hovels, sharing the house with domestic animals and falling sick a great deal during their brief lives. At least the humble folk were protected by their Anglian military overlords. The main threat came from the Danes who plundered the coastal area where there were churches and priories. It is not known whether these unwelcome visitors ravaged Dunbar but it is entirely possible.

The Middle Ages, 1018 to 1499

The next major influx of visitors came from post-Conquest Norman England. Malcolm III invited knights and soldiers of fortune to cross the Border, initiating a process of Normanisation which his descendent David I would complete in the twelfth century. The Middle Ages brought a succession of famous men and women to Dunbar, beginning with Gospatric, Earl of Northumberland who arrived in Dunbar at the time Malcolm III was favouring Anglo-Norman settlers. Under Gospatric, the community would experience change although the lives of the common people wouldn't have altered much. The Dunbars ruled the community and much of the Merse for almost four centuries, attracting royal and high-born visitors during their time.

It is more than likely that William the Conqueror passed through Dunbar in 1072 in pursuit of Malcolm III who 'became his man' at Abernethy that year. Malcolm probably resided at Dunbar as Gospatric I's guest in 1093, the year he launched his final, fatal attack on Northumberland. David I, Malcolm IV and William I (the Lion) almost certainly visited Dunbar, especially the last-named whose court was permanently on the move.

When stone castles began to proliferate in Scotland in the mid-thirteenth century, Dunbar grew in stature; its castle was visited by court officials and diplomats from England and the Continent. The English administrators were guaranteed a safe conduct through the Borders as a result of the arrangement whereby the Dunbars acted as special constables for England. The castle brought new blood to the community during its construction, which must have taken several years. The invasion of artisans and labourers must have given the local economy a boost and no doubt many a man employed by the 6th Earl of Dunbar settled in the district after the work was finished. The Earl probably hired a number of his tradesmen in the north of England as it is unlikely that there was an adequate workforce in the community; an army of masons, quarrymen, carpenters. smiths, labourers and carters descended on the small town, living in lodgings or camping in the Castle Park. The stone for the castle is thought to have come from the red sandstone quarry at Bowerhouse (Bourhouse) which would later provide the stone for the parish church built in 1821. Such tracks as existed between Bowerhouse and Dunbar would probably have skirted the Great Loch of Dunbar at Lochend and were unsuitable for heavy loads, so the stone would have been carted to Belhaven and taken by sea to the site of the castle.

We know that two English kings visited Dunbar between 1296 and 1314 - one to celebrate a victory, the other to escape a defeat. The visits of Edward I and Edward II are dealt with in greater detail in Chapter 4. The great William Wallace also came to Dunbar in 1297 to teach the haughty and overbearing 8th Earl of Dunbar some manners at the point of his claymore, reputedly at Corsekill Park, near Innerwick. Robert the Bruce almost certainly came to Dunbar as he raided Lothian and the Merse for supplies for his troops during the first War of Independence. His son David II was acquainted with Dunbar for two reasons; one was to swell his coffers by bestowing free burgh status on the community in 1370, an arrangement which brought him income from the Great Customs. The other reason swelled the chambers of his heart, as he paid court to Lady Agnes, the 10th Earl's daughter whom he hoped to marry and obtain an heir; unfortunately, he died before the marriage took place. By the 1380s, the main street of Dunbar was lively on market days, the local population increased by merchants from other towns and possibly traders from the Baltic, particularly after the 10th Earl wrote to the

Danzig authorities to reassure them that trade could resume as the second War of Independence had ended.

While senior churchmen tended to visit towns with Abbeys and large monasteries, one or two came to Dunbar and its satellite villages. Between 1240 and 1250, we know that David de Bernham, Bishop of St Andrews was a constant visitor; during that period, he re-dedicated many local churches which are listed in *Chron. Melrose*. Another religious dignitary who visited Dunbar was Aneas Sylvanus, the future Pope Pius II. Aeneas came to Scotland in the fifteenth century during James I's reign, a visit which would have lasting effect on the churchman's health. Sent on a papal diplomatic mission to encourage James to renew the *Auld Alliance* with France, Aeneas' ship nearly foundered in a severe storm. He vowed that if he reached dry land alive, he would make a pilgrimage to the shrine nearest the spot where his ship touched land. He arrived at Dunbar - or more correctly, Belhaven - and kept his promise by walking barefoot through snow to Whitekirk and the shrine founded there in 1297 by Marjorie Comyn, Countess of Dunbar. It is said that for the rest of his life, Aeneas suffered from rheumatism in his feet, the irony of which appears to have been lost on the Vatican authorities who recorded the miraculous cures effected at Whitekirk. Aeneas spent enough time in Dunbar to notice that its women were 'fair....comely and pleasing, but not distinguished for their chastity'! The men were bold, forward and enjoyed abusing the English. One wonders, if true to form, history is repeating itself today....

Another senior churchman who may have been in Scotland on ecclesiastical business in 1388 was Alexander Neville, the newly-appointed Archbishop of York; he was possibly combining business with pleasure as the Nevilles of Northumberland were related to the Earls of Dunbar. Possibly over-indulging in the 10th Earl of Dunbar's hospitality at the castle, the unfortunate man died during his stay. We also know that James I visited Dunbar Castle in 1429, en route to meet Cardinal Beaufort, his queen Joan's uncle, at Coldingham. Beaufort came north to persuade James not to send Scottish troops to France as reinforcements for Joan of Arc who had recently raised the English siege of Orleans. The agreement between James and Beaufort denied Joan Scottish recruits which some historians claim were directly responsible for her subsequent defeat and death. Taken prisoner by the Burgundians, Joan was handed over to the English in 1430 when she was found guilty of witchcraft and burnt at the stake in 1431. We know that James IV spent some considerable time at Dunbar between 1497 and 1500, when he was rebuilding its castle.

1500 to the Present

By the late Middle Ages, Dunbar was visited more often by commoners rather than kings and princes; some of these were famous on both sides of the Border. Among them was Hector Boece, his visit confirmed by his *History of Scotland* in 1527. Boece's account contains much romantic fiction, although his brief account of Dunbar is accurate:

> 'Nocht [not] far fra [from] the mouth of the Forth is the Castel of Dunbar; quhilk [which] be nature and crafty industrie of man, is the strenthiest house, this day, of Albion [Scotland]. Dunbar wes sum [some] time the chief chernis [residence] of the Erlis of Marche. Nocht far fra it is ane town under the same name, with ane magnificient and riche College of Chanons [the Collegiate Church] foundit and honoyrably dotat [endowed] by the said Erlis.'

Others who came to Scotland left brief but written accounts of their visits - Frenchmen like Jean de Beaugue who accompanied the French expeditionary force under Andre de Montalembert, Sieur d'Esse, sent to assist the Scots to free the Lowlands from English occupation in 1548-49, particularly the siege of Haddington discussed in Chapter I, an account of which is given in de Beaugue's history;[12] during the siege which lasted from June 1548 to September 1549, de Beaugue took time to visit Dunbar Castle, garrisoned by his countrymen. His description of the town contrasts with hostile accounts by later visitors from England:

> 'Donbarre [sic] is situated on the seashore ten leagues distant from Edinburgh on the side of Lothian, and in such an excellent tract of country, and accommodated with so many of the good things which profit the life of man, that if the town were enclosed with walls (since a harbour could easily be made, and at little cost) we might reckon it among the most beautiful towns in the isles of the ocean. And as for its castle, it is a very handsome and strong place built on a lofty rock on the edge of the sea, very difficult of approach, and on which so much art has been displayed, that few places are to be found anywhere at the present time, which are by nature more commodious, less exposed to battery, and all other methods of storming, than this castle......'

His account reads like a visitors' guidebook. His comments are of interest to the historian in two respects; de Beaugue confirms that Dunbar possessed neither man-made harbour or town wall in 1548. *Miller, Dunbar* has stated that there is no evidence to confirm whether Dunbar was completely enclosed although he knew that a wall of sorts had been constructed as fragments survived until the eighteenth century (see below). However, we know from *Acts of the Lords of Council in Public Affairs* (*ADCP)* that in December 1550, work began on an earthen wall (see Chapter I). We also know that a harbour existed in 1650 as Cromwell donated money for the repair of its pier; work on the original structure may have started as early as 1549 as Etienne Perlin, a French clergyman visiting Scotland in 1551-52 wrote an account of his trip which included a visit to Dunbar.[13] Perlin refers to the 'seaport of Dumbars [sic]' which suggests there was a harbour in his time; it is known that the Old or Cromwell Harbour was built by 1557 but it may have existed six years earlier.

At the end of the sixteenth century, a wholly different view of Dunbar than de Beaugue's colourful and pleasant report appears in the account of Fynes Morison, a lawyer and Fellow of Peterhouse College, Cambridge. In 1598, he wrote that it was '....said to have been of old, a Towne of some importance, but then it lay ruined, and seemed of little moment, as well for the povertie as the small number of inhabitants.' A common thread which runs through accounts by English travellers is their jaundiced view of Lowland Scotland in general. It is unlikely that Dunbar had deteriorated to the extent described by Morison only 50 years after de Beaugue's visit - academics are sparing with praise.

John Taylor, the Water Poet and Thames waterman, friend of John Donne, Beaumont and Fletcher and an acquaintance of Ben Johnson - the brilliant *literati* of the age - decided he would walk from London to Scotland in 1618, following in the footsteps of Ben Johnson who had set out two weeks before. No account of Johnson's visit has come down to us; if it ever existed, it was probably lost in the fire which burnt his lodgings in 1623. Taylor left an account of his travels however; returning south, he passed through Dunbar, describing how he rode down the coast from Edinburgh, staying at the now-vanished village of Auldhame, near North Berwick. From there, he proceeded with two companions to 'the towne of Dunbarre [sic]....where ten Scottish pints [sic- this is eqivalent to 33 imperial pints!] were consumed, and brought to nothing for a farewell; there at Master James Baylies house I tooke leave.' (This proves that the Baillie family seat at Lochend existed at least 66 years before the Romanesque arch bearing the date 1684 and the family motto was erected; in point of fact, a Jacobi [James] Baillie of Lochend is mentioned in *RMS* in 1614. The residual waters of the Great Loch of Dunbar - drained in the sixteenth century - mustn't have impressed the Water Poet or else the effects of drinking several pints of wine had dulled his muse since he wasn't moved to immortalise it.

Another traveller in 1639, Sir William Brereton, knight of Cheshire, was equally unimpressed by Dunbar. Brereton, a Puritan who subsequently distinguished himself as a general in Cromwell's Model Army during the English Civil Wars, was visiting Scotland because of his interest in ecclesiastical matters. At this time, Charles I was attempting to force Episcopacy on the Scots and Brererton, who had a 'human aversion to the government of the Church' possibly wanted to see for himself the extent of Presbyterian opposition to the king's religious policy. Although Charles 1 ascended the thrones of Scotland and England in 1625, he didn't return to Scotland until 1633 to celebrate his coronation; en route to Edinburgh, he stayed a night in Dunglass House as the guest of the Earl of Home, his retinue and baggage train being housed at Dunbar and Haddington. In Edinburgh, at Holyroodhouse, he upset the Kirk by insisting on an Anglican service to celebrate his coronation. Perhaps the good citizens of Edinburgh did not shed too many tears when his treasure ship was sunk between Burntisland and Leith, said to be the work of Lancashire witches. (His next visit in 1637 alienated him even further from the people; he attempted to force the English Book of Common Prayer on the Scots, provoking the ire of one Jenny Geddes, who threw her *creepie* stool at the Dean of St Giles, accusing him of Papistry).

However, as Brereton rode through the Merse in June 1636, his poor opinion of the country increased the further north he went. To be fair, he accurately described what is undoubtedly the bleak and desolate Coldingham Moor as

> 'the largest vastest moors [sic] that I have ever seen, which are now dry, andwhereupon (in most parts) is neither sheep, beast nor horse.'

It wasn't completely devoid of life however; Brereton met at least one man of whom he enquired

> '....how far to Dunbar....it was answered it was thrie [three] miles. I demanded whether so far; he said "Yes, it was thrie bonnie mile." About a mile from Dunbar, we observed this husbandry; the grass, weeds and wreck [seaweed or oarweed, known locally as tangle] brought by the sea and with the tide left upon the sands, was carried and laid thick on the ground. This used for corn.'

Thus we know that for several hundred years, local farmers fertilised their fields with seaweed, a common practice in Scotland. Brereton next encountered Broxburn:

> 'Here is my Lord Rocksburne's [Roxburghe] house or castle, seated with[in] six score [yards?] of the main sea, where groweth and prospereth many kinds of wood; the highest thorns that I ever saw; this I admired, because I have observed all the sea-coasts whereby we passed, almost one hundred miles, and could not find any manner of wood prospering near the sea-coast.'

Brereton's future commander-in-chief would become familiar with Broxmouth House fourteen years later. The Broxburn women came in for some adverse criticism; they were

'....sluttish....washing their clothes in a great tub with their feet, their coats, smocks and all, tucked-up to their breech.'

His Puritan moral sense outraged, he continued in similar vein when he reached Dunbar at noon. He was scathing about the Old Harbour:

'....it is not improperly called Dunbarr, because it is so environed with shelfs, bars and sands, as there is no manner of haven, though the main sea beat upon the town, which indeed is not seated upon any river, which might furnish it with an haven or navigable channel; only here is an haven made of great stones piled up, whereinto at a spring-tide a ship of one hundred ton may enter but not without much hazard.'

At some point in the seventeenth century, Sir John Hamilton of Broomhill visited Dunbar and decided to settle there. Created Lord Belhaven on 15th December 1647 for his loyalty to Charles I, he farmed at Bielside until his death in 1679, before which year he resigned his title to Charles II, having no male heirs. There is a strange tale told of Lord Belhaven; he feigned death from 1654 to 1661, remaining in hiding for seven years. When he re-appeared, he said the reason for his disappearance was simply because he believed creditors would confiscate his estate but believing him dead would allow his wife to inherit the property. It is more likely that he feared Cromwell's depredations during the Commonwealth, when Scotland was ruled from London; was it pure coincidence that Belhaven appeared, Lazarus-like in 1661, about the time of Charles II's Restoration? After Belhaven's death, Charles bestowed the title on John Hamilton, the husband of Hamilton of Broomhill's grand-daughter in 1675. Her husband, John Hamilton, 2nd Lord Belhaven is best remembered for his robust opposition to union with England in 1707.

Cromwell's visit to Dunbar in 1650 is described in detail in Chapter 6 so it needs no comment here. However, a letter from one of his troopers is worth mentioning here as it makes scathing comments on the hygiene in some of the houses in which he was billeted between Berwick and Edinburgh:

'.....we found not sheets in any house, and those beds that were left were most nasty and greazie, ful of lops [fleas] and covenanters [Cromwellian soldier-slang for lice] or both;' he continues: '....their drink hath such a filthy tange and so laxative that it brought the flux among our souldiers.....whoredome and fornication is the common darling sin of the nation.'[14]

The old sweat goes on to admit that at least the country side was well stocked with oats, barley, peas and beans but lacking entirely in trees save at a laird's house. Allowing for the universal grumbling of men in arms in a strange country, it should have come as no surprise that the beds were without sheets, lousy and brutish; Cromwell's men were invaders and no Scottish housewife would have given her linen to troopers, being uninvited guests. The comment about Scottish beer is however interesting - and grossly unfair.

The Civil Wars, then the Wars of the Covenant virtually ruined the already shaky Scottish economy; this is borne out by the perennial complaints from the royal burghs - not Dunbar however, possibly because of the events of 1650 - and on the authority of a report of 1656 entitled *Upon the Settlement of the Revenue of Excise and Customs in Scotland.* Its author, Thomas Tucker, visited Scotland in his official capacity as Registrar to the Commissioners for the Excise in England; he was ordered to go to Scotland on 17th August 1655 to set up the customs and excise service. On 18th March 1652, the English parliament had agreed that Scotland and England should become a Commonwealth; three years later, commissioners appointed to examine Scotland's economy found that the country was more of a burden than a benefit. Tucker's report assesses every community, including Dunbar, which he describes as a village rather than a town but

'a fisher towne, famous for the herring fishing, who [sic] are caught thereabout, brought thither and afterward made, cured and barrelled up either for merchandize, or sold and vended to the country people, who come thither farre and neere at that season, which is from about the middle of August to the latter end of September, and buy great quantityes of fish, which they carry away, and either spend them presently or els salt and lay up for winter provision of theyr familyes. The trade here is little else except salt, which is brought hither and layd up, and after sold to the fishing; the people of these parts which [sic] are not fishermen, employing themselves in tillage and in affaires of husbandry. But yett the conveniency of an indifferent good harbour and landing-place hath occasioned the placing of a wayter [exciseman] here, not only for preventing any goods from being brought privately on shoare, but alsoe to looke backward as farre as Eyemouth, and forward to Prestonpans and Newhaven.....'

As this was an impossible stretch of coastline for one man to police effectively, the potential for smuggling was considerable.

About 1661 - the exact date is uncertain - the Frenchman Jorevin de Rocheford visited 'Dunbart,' famous for its

'great fishery of herrings and salmon, which are carried into France and other parts of Europe.

The port would be good for nothing, if the road, which is before it, was not covered by high rocks, which border these coasts. At the foot of these is a part of the village, the habitation of fishermen and another above it, where there is a fine large street.'

De Rocheford lodged in the house of a local man who spoke French and had served Louis XIII in the *Garde d'Ecosse* - the Scots' bodyguard of French kings raised after the battle of Verneuil in 1424 - a man who had taken part in the siege of Protestant-held La Rochelle in 1628. De Rocheford does not identify his host though he tells us he gave him fish for dinner along with ale which he said was cheaper than English beer and 'the best in Europe'; few in Dunbar would disagree with the Frenchman's opinion of the local ale. Perhaps he pays its potency appropriate compliment as he describes his leave-taking of *Dunbarton* to visit 'Cobrspech.'

In 1662, the English naturalist John Ray, an unfriendly, supercilious observer, was scathing about his sojourn in Scotland in general and Dunbar in particular. Ray arrived in the town on 17th August; he described it as the place

'noted for the fight between the English and the Scots. The Scots generally (that is, the poorer sort) wear, the men blue bonnets on their heads, and some russet; the women only white linnen, which hangs down their backs as if a napkin were pinned about them. When they go abroad [outside] none of them wear hats, but a party [sic] coloured blanket which they call a plad [plaid], over their heads and shoulders,. The women generally to us seemed none of the handsomest. They are not very cleanly in their houses, and but sluttish in dressing their meat.'

Ray considered the Scots over-sensitive, unable to bear their country or their countrymen spoken against - is this not true of most countries, including England? He criticised the local domestic produce and habits as follows:

'They have neither good bread, cheese or drink. They cannot make them, nor will they learn. Their butter is very indifferent, and one would wonder how they could contrive to make it so bad.'

Bread, butter and cheese he may have disliked but the famous local ale? His diatribe gathers momentum:

'The ordinary country houses are pitiful cots, built of stone, and covered with turves, having in them but one room, many of them [have] no chimneys, the windows very small holes, and not glazed.'

Like Brereton in 1636, Ray describes the way the women laundered their clothes and he notes the custom of fertilising the fields with seaweed. The castle was 'quite ruined and falling down.' Dunbar at that time appears to have had two ministers whom Ray criticises for singing 'their Gloria Patria at the end of the psalm after sermon, as had been ordered by the Parliament' - Episcopacy having been restored in 1660. Ray notes that the herring fishing season was in full progress and that the locals told him about 20,000 joined the sea-harvest, a figure of which he was rightly sceptical.

Ray also describes burial services he witnessed in Dunbar as well as elsewhere in Scotland; he notes that when someone died, a bellman would walk through the streets ringing a small handbell,[15] announcing the deceased's name and inviting the local people to attend the funeral at the appointed time. Thereafter, the corpse was accompanied by the minister, bellman and chief mourners to the graveyard where the coffin was interred with no words spoken over it - possibly a comment on the Catholic burial service. Instead, a church service followed at which psalms were sung and a sermon preached; a collection was usually taken from the mourners when they entered the kirk and given to the family of the deceased; no doubt some of the money was used to pay the minister's and bellman's fees.

A more objective and less prejudiced observer of Dunbar life was James Brome who visited Scotland in 1669. Brome, a Church of England clergyman, describes the siege of Dunbar Castle in 1338 and Black Agnes' heroic defence of 'two and twenty weeks'- full marks to Brome for getting that right. He also confirms that the local people still lived in terror of Oliver Cromwell

'when e'er they call [recall] that bloody day [of Dunbar in 1650] to remembrance.'

Brome's account is of particular value as he states that

'the town hath been fenced in with a stone wall of great strength, though by the frequent batteries it hath of late years received, 'tis much impaired and gone to decay,'[16]

We know that an earthen wall was built around 1550, so the stone version must have been erected at some time between then and 1669. As indicated in *Miller,Dunbar,*fragments of the town wall survived until the eighteenth century although it is difficult to prove the year it was built. However, Brome's account narrows the date for us.

In the seventeenth and eighteenth centuries, visitors from England came north in trepidation for they thought the country was wild and savage. The English visitors who came to Scotland via Berwick experienced little that unnerved them which may to some extent explain their scathing descriptions of the first 60 miles of countryside. A traveller from England who entered the country via the Dumfries and Galloway mosses had their worst fears confirmed. Confronted by heather, bracken, wild and lonely hills, bogs, patchy cultivation and people who spoke a strange dialect, one Englishman leaving by that route was moved to write the following:

'I passed to English ground and hope I may never go to such a country again.'

It wasn't until Thomas Pennant wrote a comprehensive and reassuring account of his travels in the north that Scotland began to hold fewer terrors for over-sensitive Englishmen. Before that however, Daniel Defoe, the author of *Robinson Crusoe*, visited Scotland in 1724-25; the following is an extract from his account *A Tour through the Whole Island of Great Britain:*

> 'The first town of note....is Dunbar, a royal burgh, as they are call'd in Scotland, which is (much what) we call a corporation in England and which sent members to parliament ....only that in Scotland...they had some particular privileges to themselves; as that, for example, of holding parliament, or convention of burghs by themselves, a method taken from the Nans-Towns in the north, and not much unlike it, in which they meet and concert measures for the publick good of the town, and of their trade, and made by-laws, or Acts and declarations which bind the whole body........This town of Dunbar is a handsome well-built town, upon the sea-shore; where they have a kind of natural harbour, tho' in the middle of dangerous rocks. They are [sic] a great herring-fishery, and particularly, they hang herings here, as they do at Yarmouth in Norfolk, for the smoking [of] them; or, to speak the ordinary dialect, they make red herrings here; I cannot say they are cur'd so well as at Yarmouth.....However, they do it very well.......Between the town and the great road stands a little, but pleasant and agreeable seat of the Duke of Roxburgh, with a park well planted......On the south-west side of this town, under the mountain [Doon Hill], near a place call'd the battel of Dunbar, was fought, between Oliver Cromwell and General Lesly, who then commanded the royal army; when the desperate fear, for Cromwell's army was not above 8,000 men, defeated and totally overthrew the great army of the other side, kill'd 6,000 and took 10,000 prisoners, to the surprise of the world.'

Defoe's account, published in 1727, was reprinted no fewer than nine times until 1778, with alterations by other hands. The version quoted above appeared 20 years after the Treaty of Union; it is an account of Scotland's economic state at the time of his visit.

In 1713, Colonel John Blackadder of the Cameronian Regiment passed Dunbar on his way home, hoping to spend his remaining years as a kirk elder. His biographer Crichton *(Life of Lt-Colonel Blackadder)* recounts how he stepped out one evening to look at the Bass Rock, where his father, Rev. John Blackadder, the celebrated Covenanter minister and one of the Martyrs - as they are described in the monument in Greyfriars Churchyard, Edinburgh - had died and was buried in the graveyard of St Andrew's Church at North Berwick. Crichton informs us that Colonel Blackadder bore the Bass Rock no ill.

Dunbar was virtually unaffected by the two Jacobite rebellions of 1715 and 1745, although both events brought visitors to the town. The first of the rebellions led to a visit by a secret agent called John Macky who was employed by the Hanoverian government to spy on Jacobites on both sides of the Border; Macky was also ordered to investigate possible plots and treasonable correspondents. The date of his visit to Dunbar is not known but his account of it is quite colourful:

> '[Dunbar is] a famous Sea-port at the Mouth of the Firth of Forth. It hath formerly held out many a Siege from the English, and its Castle reckoned of that Consequence, that the French demanded it as a Pledge for the Troops they sent to Scotland in Queen Mary's time [Marie of Guise]; but it's now entirely demolish'd. The upper part of the Town and the Church stand very pleasantly; and by the sea-side are several good houses and a Pear [pier]; but their Trade consists chiefly in the herring-fishing. I must say that Dunbar stands in as delicious a Spot of Country as you can imagine.'

Fair praise indeed. For some reason, Macky fell under the suspicion of the very government he was serving some time after 1708 and until 1714, when the Elector of Hanover became George I of Britain. Macky died in Rotterdam in 1723; his *Memories of Secret Services* was published ten years later with notes by Dean Swift, the creator of *Gulliver's Travels.*

The second Jacobite rebellion in 1745 brought General Sir John Cope from Aberdeen to Dunbar by sea; having failed to intercept the army led by Charles Edward Stuart - Bonnie Prince Charlie - in the north, he decided the best way to contain the Jacobites in Scotland was to meet them on a Lowland field. Cope left no personal reminiscences of his one night stay in Dunbar. On 17th September 1745, the day the Jacobite army entered Edinburgh, Cope arrived at Dunbar with a mixed force of Hanoverian and English troops - the latter described as the sweepings of an English army whose best elements were serving in Flanders. Cope's strategy was simple; he wanted to prevent the Jacobites leaving Scottish soil which meant an engagement between Dunbar and Edinburgh. The English soldiers spent at least one night at Dunbar where they were joined by two regiments of dragoons under Colonels Gardiner and Hamilton;[17] Gardiner who was mortally wounded at the subsequent battle of Prestonpans was that night the guest of Alexander Pyott, the local minister. The parish kirk session minutes are uncommonly silent about Cope's arrival and the subsequent visit of the Duke of Cumberland the following year. There is however an oblique reference to the rebellion in the session minutes for December 1745, when it was recorded that the 4th Lord Belhaven had requested a list of all the able-bodied men in the parish to be sent to the Sheriff-depute in Haddington, presumably to serve as militia.

The Anglo-Hanoverian army left Dunbar and marched along the coast road via Dirleton and North Berwick and thence to Prestonpans, where Cope was spectacularly defeated on the 21st of September. Cope's alleged haste in vacating the field was mercilessly satirised by a ballad attributed to Alan Skirving, an East Lothian farmer and rhymer. There are few songs more popular in Scotland than *Johnnie Cope:*

> 'Cope sent a letter frae Dunbar,
> Charlie meet me an ye daur,
> And I'll learn you the art of war
> If you'll meet me in the morning
>
> Hey Johnnie Cope, are ye waukin' yet?
> Or are your drums a-beating yet?
> If ye are waukin, I would want
> To gang to the coals in the morning.
>
> When Johnnie Cope to Dunbar came,
> They spier'd at him, where's a' your men?
> The deil confound me gin I ken
> For I left them a' I' the morning.'

an=if; waukin'=waking; spier'd=asked

The ballad is in fact unfair to poor Cope; he was neither asleep nor was he a coward, but in the popular tradition, Cope's retreat was seen by Jacobite and non-Jacobite alike as a precipitous flight.

We do not know if Bonnie Prince Charlie visited Dunbar but we know it was spared by the rebel army because the son of Robert Lauder of the Bass was among the few Lowlanders who joined the rebels. Lauder senior was then living at Bielmouth; after the '45, Lauder's son was taken to Carlisle and executed. The Dunbar authorities had declared against Prince Charlie and brought bad luck first to Cope, then General Hawley a year later; Hawley and his staff were feted by the local population before continuing his pursuit of the Highland army. The exhausted clansmen summoned enough reserves of energy to turn on their pursuers and rout them at Falkirk in April 1746. Then Duke William of Cumberland came north with the rest of the Hanoverian army. He was enthusiastically received by the Dunbar burgesses who entertained him lavishly. Even those not sympathetic to the Jacobite cause censured Dunbar's hospitality to a man who after Culloden was known as Butcher Cumberland.

Richard Pococke, Bishop of Meath, visited Scotland on three separate occasions; his *Tours of Scotland* is a rich narrative even if it is flawed by errors.[18] Pococke, born in Southampton in 1704, lived for 62 years and came to Scotland in 1747, 1750 and 1760. His first trip barely touched Dunbar, when he relates that on 10th October, he 'rid [rode] through Dunbar, dined at Beltonford, saw the spot of Prestonpans [the 1745 battle-ground]; come to Edinburgh.' His visit in September 1760 was long enough to give a full account of Dunbar to his sister. On that occasion, he describes Dunbar as follows:

> '[it is] pleasantly situated....it chiefly consists of one broad street and another at right angles with it which leads to the harbour.'

He describes the former Collegiate Church as having small, narrow Gothic windows, with a large chapel built to the south:

> 'The east end is now separated from it, under which there is a vault for the family of Home,[19] Earls [sic] of Dunbar, the first [sic] being George Hume, who was made by King James VI Baron Hume of Berwick and afterwards in 1515 [sic] Earl of Dunbar, as some say for clearing the country of Robbers.'[20]

Pococke mentions the monastery of the Red Friars founded in 1218 as well as a convent of White Friars or Carmelites, supposedly founded in 1263 by Patrick, Earl of Dunbar, which we now know to be erroneous.

> 'There is a place they call the grey Friars which I suppose means the Carmelites,

a plain tower is standing but no other part, and some sheds seem to have been built against it.'[21]

He goes on to describe the Old Harbour as 'cut out of the rock', noting that the entrance was difficult to navigate and impracticable

'when the wind blows a little hard from the north-east. The Castle was built on a rock, which is peninsular; on the south side is a gateway leading to a ruined building, which seems to have consisted of two grand apartments in the Castle Way; over it in the middle are the Arms of Scotland [sic] and on each side of it a Coat of Arms.[22] From this apartment a high wall extended to an island near the shoar but it is every way a perpendicular Cliff. There is a covered way to it through the wall.'[23]

Pococke is clearly describing respectively the crosswall which bore the Dunbar coat-of-arms and the Blockhouse or Magazine. He goes on to describe nearby Lamer Island whose rock formation he compares with the Giant's Causeway in Ireland. He usefully summarises the condition of Dunbar's economy at the time:

'They have some linnen [sic] Manufacture, and Export of Corn and an import of boards, timber, hemp, flax,iron, etc. They have very little fishing trade, the Fish they say has failed, particularly the herring.'

He visited the Tolbooth, or Town House where he saw

'Militia pikes which are very large and a sort of bill on a handle with a hook on the back of it to draw a man from his horse. When Cromwell went against the Scotch, who took up arms in favour of Charles the 2nd, he was encamped where the Duke of Roxburgh's Park is within a small mile of Dunbar.'

His brief description of the ensuing battle is dismissive:

'....it being windy and beginning to rain their [the Scots'] flint locks would not fire so they turned their backs and were defeated.'

He visited Broxmouth and Skateraw the following day, writing to his sister of the old ruined chapel of 'Skitraw' built of 'soft blew [blue] slate.' The ruins of the chapel dedicated to St Denis have yielded to time, the elements and the local farmers who used its stone for dykes.[24]

A particularly interesting account of Scotland which unfortunately only briefly mentions Dunbar was written in 1750 by Dr John Clephane to his sister Elizabeth who was married to the Laird of Kilravock. Their father, Colonel William Clephane was a soldier of fortune in the pay of the Dutch government, serving in the Scots Brigade in Holland. From 1747 to 1749, Dr Clephane was one of the physicians at the hospital for British soldiers fighting the French in Flanders. Clephane returned to Britain in 1749 to superintend the military hospital at Ipswich. He visited his sister several times, the first occasion occurring in 1750, when his account of the journey comments on the turnpike road system in Scotland. Clephane started his journey at Scarborough; for his journey from Newcastle to Edinburgh, he '....hired a chaise and pair for 4 guineas £4.20) but I am to pay for the turnpikes' i.e. the tolls levied in the various shires through which he travelled, the money being used to pay for the upkeep of the roads. He continues with an account of his journey to Edinburgh:

'From Berwick to Old Camus [Aldcambus] is the Merse; but past Dunglass, or the glass mills, which belong to Sir John Hall, is East Lothian. A very fine open corn country, full of country seats. The next to Dunglass is....Broxton [Broxmouth], the Duke of Roxburghe's, on the right; then Sir John Warrender by Dunbar [Lochend] etc etc. Over the Tyne from Beltonford is Lord Haddington's seat, Tiningham [Tyninghame] etc. East Lothian fine corn country. From Beltonford to Edinburgh, there are two roads; the higher by Haddington, but the longest and worst road [the present A1]; the other, by Bangley Brae-foot, is said to be the best and shortest. From Beltonford to Bangley Brae-foot is 8 computed miles;[25] and from thence to Edinburgh is 10 computed miles. The 18 computed miles measure 26. From Beltonford, you pass by Seaton [Port Seton], Prestonpans and Preston and so to Musselburgh and Edinburgh, the road all along at a little distance from the sea.'

One eminent individual who visited Dunbar on at least one occasion between 1751 and his death in 1791 was John Wesley, the apostle of Methodism. He travelled all over Scotland in his mission to introduce his version of Christian worship. At Dunbar, he found lodgings near the harbour in the appropriately named Rock House which stood at right angles to the Cat's Row in what is now Victoria Street, sited just beyond the present day Methodist Church. Wesley does not appear to have left any account of his visit.

The most descriptive and unbiased account of all up to this time was made by Thomas Pennant. Pennant, a Welshman from Flintshire, undertook a grand tour of Scotland in 1769, the first of two visits. In 1769, he travelled up the east coast, beginning his journey on horseback at Chester; an overwhelming passion for natural history induced him to keep a journal in which he meticulously recorded the landscapes through which he rode. In mid-July, he entered Scotland via the Merse, referring en route to Halidon Hill where Edward III defeated the Scots in 1333. Pennant considered this route into Scotland as having an 'unpromising look' due to the ravages of Border warfare; like others before him, he found Coldingham Moor a '....bleak, joyless, heathy moor' which of course sums it up perfectly. Nearing Dunbar, he mentions Sir John Hall's estate at Dunglass, then the great woods and the home of the Duke of Roxburghe.

Pennant, a friendly observer, spent some time at Dunbar; his impressions of it differ vastly from other contemporary travellers in that he praises the town's affluence, represented by its High Street which he found

> '....broad and handsome...the houses built of stone.' (Perhaps his comments reflect relief at finding a decent town after the small, dismal villages he had encountered in the Merse, with their thatched roofs, unglazed windows and ruinous walls). He refers to the narrow mouth at the Old Harbour from where he watched boats sailing to Greenland - probably the whalers belonging to the Fall's *East Lothian and Merse Fishing Company.* Lamer Island is again compared with the Giant's Causeway because of its '....great red columns of a red grit stone.'

Pennant's description of Dunbar Castle deserves to be quoted almost verbatim:

> '....the ruins....seated on a rock above the sea; underneath one part is a vast cavern, composed of a black and red stone, which give it a most infernal appearance' only wanting '....to be peopled with witches to make the scene complete; it appears to have been the dungeon, there being a formed passage from above, where the poor prisoners might have been let down....There are in some parts, where the rock did not close, the remains of walls; but the founders of the castle, taking advantage of this cavity, adding a little art to it, rendered it a most complete and secure prison.[26] On the other side are two natural [sic] arches, through which the tide flowed; under one was a fragment of wall, where this seems to have been a portal for the admission of men or provisions from [the] sea; through which it is possible that Alexander Ramsey [of Dalhousie], in a stormy night, reinforced the garrison, in spite of the fleet which lay before the place, when closely besieged by the English, in 1337 [sic] and gallantly defended for nineteen weeks [sic] by that heroine black [sic] Agnes, Countess of March.'

There is a footnote referring to Agnes at this part of the account which gives Pennant's source as Buchanan's *History of Scotland*; the following additional note also explains that

> 'The English were obliged to desist from their enterprise. Agnes was the eldest daughter of Sir Thomas Randal [sic] of Stradown [sic], Earl of Murray and nephew to Robert Bruce. She was called black Annes, says Robert Lindesay [of Pitscottie], because she was black-skinned.'

Much of the remainder of the castle which he describes has since disappeared and was gone even by the time *Miller, Dunbar* was published in 1830. However, Pennant noted the Dunbar coat-of-arms, which *Miller, Dunbar* says appeared 'over the ruins of a window....three legs or arms of the Isle of Man, a lion rampant and a St Andrew's cross.'

Pennant visited the Parish Kirk - then still a Collegiate establishment; he draws attention to Sir George Home's statue which survives today. Pennant is remarkably well-informed about the man, whom he describes as

> '...the worthiest and best Scotch Minister of James VI....moderate, prudent and successful in the management of Scotch affairs; and as Spotswood [Spottiswoode] remarks "a man of deep wit, few words and in his Majesty's service no less faithful than fortunate; the most difficile [difficult] affairs he compassed without any noise; and never returned when he was employed without the work performed that he was sent to do.... ....and by his assistance gave peace to the Church of Scotland....." Dunbar's [ie Home's] merit is evident; for the weakness and the infamy of His Master's reign did not commence during the period of his [Home's] power.'

Even if this is a somewhat polarised view of Sir George Home, James VI's able but unpopular Privy Councillor in Edinburgh, Pennant is clearly an admirer, impressed with the man's undoubted dedication to public service during the early years of James VI's reign.

Oddly, Pennant writes little of the battles of 1296 and 1650; he states that the Scottish nobles captured in Dunbar Castle in 1296 were delivered to Edward I 'who with his usual cruelty, devoted them all to death' which is of course untrue. Mention is made of the tragedy of Mary, Queen of Scots and Bothwell, the latter having 'committed the simulated outrage on the person of the fair Mary Stuart'; Pennant ill-conceals his satisfaction as to Bothwell's fate after Carberry. As for Oliver Cromwell, he restricts his comments to the obvious; Cromwell had a 'well-founded confidence' on seeing the Scots descend from Doon Hill the day before the battle.

Pennant is among those who believe there was a Carmelite Priory founded at Dunbar in 1263; he correctly describes the Red or Trinitarian house as a 'convent of Matburines [Mathurines, as the Trinitarians in Paris dedicated their house to St Mathurine[27]] whose founding he attributes to the Earl of Dunbar in 1218.

Leaving Dunbar, Pennant rode within sight of Tantallon Castle on 18th July, describing the Bass Rock and its castle from a village he calls Castleton; he attempted to land on the Bass but heavy seas prevented him. The natural historian in him delighted in the gannets and kittiwakes; he tells us that the young gannets were bred for the table and sold in Edinburgh at 'twentypence Scots apiece' (about 3p) and served up roasted 'a little before dinner'. He also confirms that the price of this dubious *hors d'oevre* hadn't increased since 1662 as 'we learn from Mr Ray that it was equally dear about a century ago.' Anyone interested in the state of Scotland in 1769 should read Pennant's highly entertaining account. It is a delightfully candid book, filled with impressions of a country shunned by the English for being uncivilised and bleak. It was of course neither and Pennant clearly relishes his role as that of a pioneering spirit. His book, which runs to over 300 pages was so popular that the first two editions were quickly followed by a third and fourth, in larger format with impressive engravings and additional material. A traveller with a refreshingly open mind and literary turn of phrase, Pennant will always have admirers, not only in Scotland; a contemporary was moved to extol Pennant's descriptive account which he said was

> '.....beatified with his diction, historical illustrations or the charm he gave to things unknown before.'

This could be the description of a poet.

Pennant died aged 72 after a short illness in 1798 at Dowing, Flintshire. He was almost a modern tour guide; he wryly commented that he had proved that 'North Britain' could be visited safely, adding that since his trip, the country had experienced an invasion of Englishmen. His book undoubtedly helped. Perhaps he had proven one famous Englishman wrong. Dr Samuel Johnson had once said of Scotland that the only good thing that came out of it was the road south. Johnson, renowned for his critical views on every subject, stopped at Dunbar during his visit to Scotland in 1773 and sampled the local ale;[28] in the absence of any perceived Johnsonian wisdom, we assume he found it palatable. His biographer James Boswell certainly did; stopping on one London trip to refresh himself at Dunbar he declared the local brew 'the best small beer I have ever had.'

The next visitor to make an impression on Dunbar rather than the other way round never set foot in the town. John Paul, born in July 1747 on St Mary's Isle off the Kircudbrightshire coast, was the son of a gardener employed on the estate of the eccentric Earl of Selkirk. John, the fourth of seven Paul children went to sea when he was thirteen, serving on merchant shipping in the Caribbean and plying the seas to Virginia in North America. What he saw of the slave trade in the Americas disgusted him. As he was involved in a brawl in which he ran his cutlass through a seaman in 1773, he added Jones to his name for obvious reasons. Fearing a prejudiced trial by the Lords of the Admiralty, he jumped ship and ended up in America to settle in Virginia. He was subsequently commissioned in the fledgling Continental - later the USA - navy in April 1775

A mercurial character, John Paul Jones established his legend early on in the American War of Independence, operating against the British from American and French seaports. Of slight build - he was five feet five inches - and a pugnacious fighter, he eagerly accepted the Continental Congress commission to carry the war at sea to Britain. Congress recommended that cruisers be sent to wage a sea war on the enemy's shores to disrupt trade in the Baltic and Scandinavia. Strategically, this was a doubtful venture; the embryonic American navy was no match for or likely to pose the remotest threat to the mightiest sea power in the world. However, despite robust warnings from the British government about the consequences of raids carried out by vessels flying the American flag, a formal treaty was signed by an optimistic Congress and a somewhat nervous France on 6th April 1778; the treaty pledged both countries to disrupting in any way the shipping of their common enemy, England.

John Paul Jones had a fiery temper. He fell foul of the American High Command and both were relieved when he set his sails for his home shore in 1778. Captain Jones embarked on a career that was little short of piracy, much in the same way as had Drake and Frobisher in Elizabethan England. He attacked Whitehaven Harbour, in Cumberland, spiked some guns in a shore battery, then sailed to St Mary's Isle intending to take the Earl of Selkirk hostage. Fortunately the gentleman happened to be away from home at the time and in his frustration, Jones stole the family silver, then returned it afterwards with his apologies. These farcical attempts at naval warfare did however establish his reputation and no doubt the stocky, cocky little Scot believed in his own legend.

In 1779, the first year of her official war with England, France provided Jones with a slow, leaky 40-gun warship, the *Bon Homme Richard* and three smaller vessels. Jones had orders to raid the British coast in preparation for an invasion by 50,000 French troops; the weak and lumbering flotilla set sail, cruising aimlessly and posing more of a nuisance than a threat to the British navy. Curiously - he seems to have been one of those Scots who would die for his country but not live in it - he chose Scotland for his second raid. Posturing up and down the east coast in September 1779, he finally decided to attack Leith, probably because he knew the British men-o'-war were safely in the south. His captains were lukewarm about the idea; perhaps fortuitously, a sudden squall drove the little ships out of Leith Roads and into the open sea. When the storm abated, Jones anchored off Dunbar, where he lay from 20th to 25th September, possibly contemplating whether the town was worth raiding. The alarmed bailies of Dunbar sent to Edinburgh for a regiment of dragoons - an armed vessel would have been more appropriate - but we are told that the cavalry were intended to protect a battery of 4 guns loaned to the town by the *East Lothian and Merse Fishing Company* and hurriedly installed on the Kirkhill, near the modern Hillside Hotel. Finally, Jones was galvanised into action; he trained his cannon on the shore, firing a salvo which inflicted superficial damage on some chimney pots in the High Street.[29] Honour and ego thus satisfied, Jones sailed off to immortality at Flamborough Head, the scene of his only major sea-fight with the British navy.

Encountering a convoy of 41merchantmen being escorted to the Baltic by *HMS Serapis* (44 guns) and *HMS Countess of Scarborough* (20 guns), Jones engaged *Serapis* in late evening. In a desperate but one-sided fight, the *Bon Homme Richard* and the *Serapis* were locked together; unable to use her cannon, the *Richard* was raked from bow to stern by *Serapis'* guns. When Captain Pearson of the *Serapis* demanded Jones' surrender, he uttered his immortal challenge: "I have not yet begun to fight." By 10pm, Jones' ship was a wreck on fire with most of the crew dead or wounded; at 10.30pm, incredibly, Pearson surrendered the *Serapis* after her main mast was destroyed. Jones transferred the remnants of his command to the British ship, limped away to Holland and arrived in Paris, feted as a hero. On the strength of this single exploit, he sought promotion to the rank of rear-admiral in the Continental navy. When Congress refused to promote him, he resigned his commission and offered his services to Catherine the Great of Russia. He was given the rank he sought in the Russian navy but falling foul of Catherine's lover, Potemkin, he was banished to the Baltic, his reputation tarnished by an unlikely charge of rape. John Paul Jones died of jaundice and nephritis in Holland on 18th July 1792. In the twentieth century, the US ambassador to Holland located his grave, the remains later re-interred at the USA Naval Base, Annapolis. Jones is considered the founder of the American navy.

If the element of farce was never far away throughout John Paul Jones' naval career, it was equalled by yet another attack on Dunbar on 22nd May 1781. On this occasion, the aggressor was a Captain G Fall, a freebooter in the pay of the king of France. Although there appears to be no proof to substantiate it, Captain G Fall and Provost Robert Fall of Dunbar may have been related. Be that as it may, Provost Fall wasn't a man to be trifled with; he was determined to defend Dunbar to the hilt. Captain Fall attempted to capture a small vessel lying off the Old Harbour but by the time he went into action, a small battery of guns were positioned on Lamer Island. The guns were loaned by Robert Fall's *East Lothian and Merse Fishing Company*; two others salvaged from the wreck of the man-o-war *The Fox* on Tyne Sands in 1745 were hauled up to Dunbar Castle, more for effect than defence. Shots were exchanged but no damage was inflicted on either party. Robert Fall was as imaginative in war as he was resourceful in business. On 22nd June 1781, the bailies approved his suggested contract for the building of a permanent battery on Lamer Island at the town's expense. The Battery was constructed later in the year; eventually, it incorporated 16 embrasures for 9, 12 and 18-pounder guns; of questionable value, it is unlikely that it ever fired a hostile shot.

Robert Fall cultivated the great as well as the entrepreneur. On 23rd May 1787, Robert Burns was invited to Dunbar as Fall's guest during his Border tour. True to character, the poet was accompanied part of the way by a young woman about whom he was laconic and almost modern in his assessment of her character:

> 'Miss—— will accompany me to Dunbar, making a facile of me as a sweetheart of hers,
> among her relatives.'

Surely his lady companion was attractive, as he was in a good mood when he wrote:

> 'Past [sic] by the most glorious corn country that I ever saw till I reached Dunbar,
> a neat little town. Dine with Provost Fall, an eminent merchant and most respectable character.'

He later called on a Miss Clark, whom he desribes as 'a maiden guid enough, but no brent new.' Although she was curious about and impressed by Burns, the spirited Miss Clark took a certain delight in candidly pointing out to the poet that 'though Dunbar was but a little town, yet it was not destitute of people of parts.'[30] There is more than a hint of *Him? Kent his faither* in Miss Clark's reply. However, Burns was courteous to his host's wife Magdalen, whom he complimented on the quality of her watercolours.

Two visitors who came to Dunbar between 1786 and 1788 for a brief sojourn left no record of their visits. They couldn't afford to. One was the notorious William Brodie (**ill 27**), Deacon of the Wrights in Edinburgh, town councillor and professional burglar. The other was George Smith, one of Brodie's gang. Smith, a grocer in Edinburgh's Cowgate, carried out a successful burglary single-handed at Messrs Bruce of Bridge Street, Edinburgh in the early hours of Christmas Day, 1786. He divided the spoils with Brodie later that afternoon. The haul was worth £350 sterling (about £10,000 in modern currency). On the advice of Brodie, Smith left Edinburgh on foot on 28th December, intending to dispose of his share of the loot with a man called Tasker, a banished Scot and fence in Chesterfield. Smith stopped at Dunbar and caught the mail coach there.

By 1788, Deacon Brodie's crimewave was at its height and the net began to close on him and his gang. A reward was offered in Edinburgh for information on the gang, money eagerly claimed by John Brown, an Irishman and fugitive from English justice. Brown knew about Brodie's activities and led the Sheriff-Depute of Edinburgh's men to the Nor' Loch (now Waverley Station) where he showed them the hole in the wall where Brodie stashed his duplicate keys, jemmies and crowbars. Brown also turned King's evidence, naming the Englishman George Smith and Andrew Ainslie, an Edinburgh shoemaker, as Brodie's accomplices. Brown kept Brodie's name to the last for perhaps obvious reasons. Smith was taken into custody the following day attempting to board the Berwick coach; soon afterwards, Ainslie joined him in the Tolbooth. Smith sang like the proverbial canary, revealing all. Brodie, sensing that the net was closing, fled Edinburgh the following Sunday, 9th March 1788. He stopped at Dunbar, no doubt to refresh himself at Cossar's Inn (the future St George Hotel). Sheriff officers were sent after him. Yes, they remembered Brodie in Dunbar. The innkeeper couldn't help noticing his afternoon guest for Brodie was something of a dandy with his black cocked hat, frock coat and silver shoe buckles. Perhaps the innkeeper also noticed the man's sallow complexion and his dark brown eyes, one of which had a slight cast which made him look sinister. The livid scar under the other eye - the result of a tavern brawl - would have been enough to identify Brodie. He almost got away. Going to London, he took ship for Ostend, intending to emigrate to America, then at war with Britain. Informed of Brodie's whereabouts through three letters he foolishly wrote home, the Lord Admiral of Scotland contacted the Secretary of State in London who ordered the British consul in Ostend to arrest Brodie. The master cracksman was brought back to Edinburgh to stand trial. He had panache. During his imprisonment he constantly made light of his undoubted fate, unlike George Smith who wept and whined throughout. Brodie and Smith swung together in Edinburgh's Grassmarket on 1st October 1788.

Illus 27: *Deacon Brodie* KRM

In 1789, the antiquarian Francis Grose came to Scotland to illustrate the country's architectural antiquities. Grose, a dissolute army officer had squandered his inheritance and turned to engraving for a living. He never completed his pictorial record of Scottish castles and famous houses as he died in Ireland of apoplexy, probably brought on by drink. He left excellent engravings of the castles at Dunbar, Hailes, Innerwick and Cockburnspath Tower. Grose was reputedly immortalised by a line in Burns' *Tam o' Shanter*; he was 'the chiel amang ye, takin' notes.'

In the same year, Alexander Wilson the Paisley packman poet who later became a famous ornithologist in America passed through Dunbar on 2nd September. He writes of the High Street and Provost Robert Fall's house (now Lauderdale House) which then was fronted by a row of trees in the north-west aspect 'making a neat appearance.' Wilson notes that a new pier was being constructed for the battery on Lamer Island and he describes the castle as 'hollowed with gloomy caves, through which, in a storm, the waves roar horribly; which, joined to the ruins above, forms a most dismal appearance.

The anonymous author of *A Journey to the Northern Parts of Great Britain* recounts how in 1796, he arrived at the New Inn - first a hotel supposedly established in opposition to Lorimer's (the St. George Hotel), then a barracks for army officers and finally a nursing home - with three companions who 'were ushered into a spacious room, where we were informed a ball is held every week, under the patronage of Sir James Stewart, who commands a regiment in the neighbourhood.'

Before leaving the following morning, the four men went for a walk in the High Street, noting the house

> '.....being builded [extended in fact] by Lord Lauderdale and passed on to some bold rocks, upon which stand the trifling remains of an ancient castle. A cavern below, composed of black and red stone, appears, as Mr Pennant observes, like the pit of Acheron, and should seem to have been formerly the dungeon, there having been evidently a passage from above, formed with regular brickwork.
> On the other side are two natural arches, through which the tide flows; under one of which is the fragment where there seems to have been a portal, for the admission of assistance from the sea.'

The final sentence quoted above is almost *verbatim* from Pennant's account.

The author complains that the smell of whale blubber was 'extremely offensive'; at that time, Dunbar was among the main whaling ports on the east coast, at one time second only to Leith. He also states - probably basing his view on Pennant's erroneous belief - that Edward I executed the nobles in Dunbar Castle after the Scots' defeat at Spott Muir in 1296.

Passing what are not identified but to a native of Dunbar are clearly Belhaven Sands and West Barns Links, the anonymous traveller describes a cavalry camp to the right of the Edinburgh road - at that time the sea was closer to it than it is today - where he was able to identify three of the four regiments stationed there; these were the Cambridge Fencibles, the Windsor Foresters and the East Lothian Yeomanry which were 'exercising on the shore, as we passed, and made an interesting appearance.'

One frequent visitor to - or more accurately, traveller through Dunbar - was a friend of James Boswell, Johnson's biographer. James Burnet, Lord Monboddo, a respected member of the Bench in 1767 lived in St John's Street in Edinburgh's Canongate. Monboddo's title was an honorific granted for his services to the law; it is also in keeping with his eccentric character. Monboddo always travelled on official business to London on horseback rather than by coach, which says something about his stamina. His many trips south brought him through Dunbar and he may have spent the occasional night at Lorimer's Hotel in the High Street. Monboddo looked like a stuffed monkey and reputedly drank a bottle of port wine at a sitting, thought nothing of walking 50 miles in a day and despised sedan chairs, preferring his horse to any 'modern' city transport. Two of many stories told of him perhaps sum up his character. His simian features may have given him an interest in monkeys - or rather, human beings with monkey-like tails. He believed that babies lost the tails they were born with because the midwife cut them off with a knife before the newborn was presented to its mother. This belief led him to skulk around the chamber doors of expectant mothers, hoping to catch a glimpse of the dismembered appendage. The other story concerns his habit of strewing his dining table with fresh roses in emulation of the Roman poet Horace. (Judges then and now appear to have much in common). On what turned out to be his last visit to Dunbar en route to London in 1799, he fell ill and got no further than the small town. On being asked by his nephew why he had stopped at Dunbar, he replied 'Oh George, I find I am noo [now] aughty-four [eighty-four].' Monboddo's most celebrated work as an anthropologist was not, as we might suspect, about unwanted monkey tails - there is an obvious pun which I have resisted making - but a three-volume treatise *On the Origins and Progress of Language* which argued the case for an evolutionary view of human origin. Monboddo died on 26th May 1799 and was buried in Greyfriars Churchyard, Edinburgh.

Some who travelled by sea made unscheduled stops at Dunbar, particularly in stormy weather. In 1810, two naval frigates, *HMS Pallas* (32 guns) and *HMS Nymph* (36 guns) were driven on to the rocks near Broxburn and at Skateraw on 18th December. Apparently, the captains of both vessels were confused by the lights of the limekilns at Skateraw, mistaking them for the May Island lighthouse. A full account of the shipwreck appears in Chapter 10.

In 1822, George IV made his famous visit to Scotland, travelling by sea in the sensible summer month of August. Although he never set foot in Dunbar, the twelve bay horses which pulled his coach were disembarked at the Old Harbour and completed their journey to Edinburgh by road. The town provided a salute from the half-moon battery and small boats put out from the harbour to welcome the royal barge. A further gun salute was fired from Doon Hill, where a bonfire was lit. Returning south on 29th August, the king was treated to a repeat performance of salvoes from hill and shore, with a bonfire lit on the pier-head at the harbour. The loyal subjects of Dunbar saw nothing of the squadron that wet, dark night. History was repeated when queen Victoria came to Scotland in 1842; on that occasion, she resided at Broxmouth House as guest of the Duke and Duchess of Roxburghe for a day, planted a tree, then sailed into Leith Roads on 31st August after being treated to a 21-gun salute from the Dunbar battery and bonfires lit at Broxmouth, Dunbar Castle and on the summit of Doon Hill.

Approaching Dunbar from the south in 1832, the Surrey-born son of a publican, William Cobbett, who started life as a farmworker, then became a soldier, journalist and MP for Oldham, was moved to comment on the productive fields and the wooded valleys he saw. For him, all that was lacking was the people. He detested the new agricultural methods which had put people off the land and the rich landowners who produced food not for the local population but exclusively for the cities. Cobbett, quintessential Englishman had this to say about East Lothian:

> 'We found the road (which is very fine and broad) actually covered with carts....all loaded with sacks of corn. For several miles, it appeared to be a regular cavalcade of carts, each carrying about twelve English sacks of corn, and all going to DUNBAR [sic], which is a little sea-port (though a large town) apparently made for the express purpose of robbing Scotland of all its produce, and of conveying it away to be squandered in scenes of dissipation, of gambling, and of every vice tending to vitiate man and enfeeble a nation.'

Not entirely accurate but we must admire his sentiment for its honesty. After all, although Cobbett was something of a sensational journalist, he didn't exaggerate the living conditions of the poor farm labourers and abhorred the fact that English 'gentlemen' farmers employed the sons of Scottish farmers to act as bailiffs: 'Scotch bailiffs...are recommended to the grinding ruffians of England by the grinding ruffians of Scotland.' Clearly, Cobbett had arrived on a market day when corn was sold and shipped south. He is economic with his words about Dunbar itself, limiting his comments to the High Street, which he said was 'so wide as to be worthy of being called an oblong square.'

Apart from the excitement of queen Victoria's visit in 1842, Dunbar witnessed a ceremony the same year which the local population believed would solve the burgh's economic difficulties. On Tuesday, 27th September 1842, the Earl of Dalhousie - who else, given his family's long association with Dunbar - laid the foundation stone of the New or Victoria Harbour. Miller, *Lamp of Lothian* records that 'a bottle, hermetically sealed, containing newspapers, almanacs and coins' was laid beneath the stone. The guns of the Lamer Island battery added to the importance of the occasion and a dinner was held in the evening for 300 guests including Dalhousie, Sir George Warrender of Lochend, James Maitland Balfour, (father of A J Balfour, the future MP for East Lothian, Secretary of State for Scotland, then Prime Minister), Provost Christopher Middlemas and last but not least, the Duke of Roxburghe who provided blocks of stone from his Broxmouth estate for the harbour's construction.

There were other notables who made their brief appearances in Dunbar including James Hogg, the *Ettrick Shepherd* and poet who was made a freeman of the burgh. Like Hogg, few who visited Dunbar in later years have left any personal impressions of the town; General William Booth, leader of the Salvation Army held a meeting in the Parish Church on 29th June 1908 although the session minute-book omits further details of the visit. The arrival of Sir Reginald Wingate the year before perhaps went unnoticed save by the local gentry. Wingate brought several famous visitors to Dunbar - men like Rudolf Slatin, an eccentric Austrian who joined the British Army, the protege of the equally nonconforming Charles Gordon of Khartoum. Another famous visitor was Wingate's cousin Orde, an unconventional soldier in the mould of Gordon of Khartoum and Lawrence of Arabia, the latter being a distant relative. He stayed briefly at Knockenhair, organised the Jewish *Gideon Force* against the Arabs in Palestine and achieved fame by creating the *Chindits*, a commando group operating behind the Japanese lines in Burma during the Second World War.

One of the most eminent Victorians of the day who came to Dunbar was Herbert Horatio, Lord Kitchener with whom Wingate served in the Sudan and fought alongside at the battle of Omdurman. On 26th September 1902, the *Haddingtonshire Courier* reported that Lord Kitchener had been visiting Arthur J Balfour, recently appointed Prime Minister, at his country seat at Whittingehame. Kitchener may have been called there to be informed that he'd been appointed Commander-in-Chief of the British forces in India, as he left Britain a few weeks later to take up his appointment. (Conversely, he may have discussed security arrangements for King George V's visit to Whittingehame three weeks later). Kitchener, a shy man who hated being in the limelight, was besieged by curious Dunbar folk at the railway station at Dunbar that day; one man even attempted to shake his hand. A horrified Kitchener declined, although he recovered sufficiently to manage a goodbye wave as the train pulled out of the station.

At the turn of the century, Dunbar shared in a small but prosperous way the nationwide development of the *bourgeois* summer lifestyle which had become popular. As early as 1866, Dunbar was considered an 'agreeable summer resort'. In that year, the *Haddingtonshire Courier* lamented that 'no list of visitors was kept for the town to show the estimation it is held as a watering hole.' (Mr Downie the local bookseller remedied this failure by compiling a list). By 1870, at the time of the Franco-Prussian War, prominent Edinburgh businessmen bemoaned the fact that they were unable to find summer houses for let in Dunbar and that they would have to look elsewhere for summer accommodation. By 1893, Dunbar had moved from being merely 'agreeable' to 'fashionable', its chief attraction being golf at the East Links course.

The era immediately preceding the First World War is known nostalgically as *La Belle Epoque* – a period of two decades which saw the creation of garden suburbs for comfortable if not excessively well-off middle-class households. It became fashionable to take annual holidays by the sea. Bayswell in the west end of Dunbar was created to accommodate visitors in the summer months 'in handsome villas and cosy cottages'; some of these birds of passage remained and made their living in the town. Leisure holidays involving golf became an annual 'must'; it was golf that brought Sir Reginald Wingate to the town, where he rented the prestigious Stafford House overlooking what was then the Ladies Only Bathing Pool until he built his impressive manor at Knockenhair. In some respects, Dunbar became a Scottish version of the London 'season.'

Wingate wasn't the first to build a stylish house overlooking the sea at Dunbar. The town's popularity as a summer watering-hole led to the building of several impressive hotels such as the Bellevue - sadly now a ruin

- the Roxburghe, now demolished and the Royal Hotel - now known as The Barns Ness. The East and West promenades (the latter gifted to the town by Mrs James Baird of the Hays of Beltonford in 1893), the segregated bathing pools which gave way to the more enlightened 'safety' mixed swimming pool at the foot of the Glebe, the golf courses and the clean, broad beaches all contributed to Dunbar's success as a holiday resort, a success which lasted for about half a century. At the end of the nineteenth century, the town council sponsored the publication of *Picturesque Dunbar*, an annual illustrated guide and local history 'for the purpose of promoting the popularity of the Town of Dunbar and District as a Summer Resort and Golfing Centre.' The object of the guide was to 'assist those in search of a delightful place for a healthy summer holiday to decide for Dunbar. I have a much-worn copy dated about 1899 containing several interesting photographs, some of which are reproduced in this book.

For decades into the twentieth century, Dunbar was visited by *pierrot troupes* - stage performers whose unsophisticated song-and-dance routines in clown costumes were eagerly attended by visitors and locals alike. For many years The Zenith performers entertained the public in Winterfield Pavilion. A frequent visitor to the Old Harbour and Cromwell House was the French sea-captain Janion (**ill 28**) whose fine vessel the *Shoal Fisher* **(ill 29)** was often seen berthed near Cromwell House. There were also visits from celebrities on radio and in films; actors such as Douglas Fairbanks Jnr and Trevor Howard were guests at the Craig-en-gelt and Hillside Hotels, the latter brought to Dunbar by the war. The radio comedian Jack Anthony - John Herbertson, born in Glasgow in 1900 - became a pantomime star in 1931 until he retired and became proprietor of the Roxburghe Marine Hotel until his death in 1962. Anthony was famous for an unmemorable catchphrase 'Nae better at a' the meaning of which is obscure and cannot come near to competing with the sophisticated - and humorous - slogans of today. One casual visitor who arrived and tried to depart discreetly but was seen by my mother and myself was the actor James Mason. Mason's brother taught at Belhaven Hill School in the 1950s; during the making of the film *A Touch of Larceny*, Mason was in Scotland filming on location in the Western Islands and took the opportunity to visit his relative en route to London.

In the 1930s, new housing estates were built and the town began to expand from the cramped and unsanitary areas off the High Street and at the harbours; the houses near the sea were positively Dickensian - slums like the Cat's Row were infamous nests of vermin and disease. In the 1960s, perhaps acknowledging the fact that many of the town's summer visitors came from Glasgow, the county council decided that Dunbar should accommodate some of them permanently. The Glaswegians were welcomed; the hideous estate at Floors and Rig where they were housed was not.

Illus 28: *Captain Janion* HM

The final word on Dunbar's attractions must be left to the quaint but sincere sentiments of the anonymous author(s) of *Picturesque Dunbar*:

' ....it will be seen that the Town is of hoary antiquity, and possesses numerous points of interest forthe student of Scottish History. For the Geologists who will be attracted by the peculiar rock formation of the coast, which presents a series of low rocky ledges, generally of red sandstone in the east, and bold basaltic rocks under peculiar trap veins near the Castle. For the student of Natural History, who will find numerous specimens in the rock pools which abound the shore. The Botanist, the Angler, the Golfer, the Landscape Photographer, the Pedestrian and the Cyclist will each find in the district plenty of scope for the exercise of their particular pastime.' Reading these words today must evoke a sense of loss among those who enjoyed the town's quiet, natural beauty - particularly the area south of the railway which is fast disappearing through private housing development. As I write this, three estates are being built and there are plans for more houses which will almost double the population. It has always been my personal wish that road signs would one day advertise 'Historic Dunbar' but that seems unlikely now.

Dunbar is the first east coast holiday town encountered by those coming across the Border via the A1. More personable than its long-time rival, North Berwick, it still has the potential to attract visitors. At the time of writing, the long-promised Expressway from Haddington to Dunbar is under construction, so Dunbar will undoubtedly change. Its broad High Street is still picturesque, although recent modernisation has destroyed much of its character. Today, Dunbar is a community poised on the brink of what may be dramatic change; it is to be hoped that the change will be positive. Of the countless thousands who have visited Dunbar over the centuries - royal, noble, statesman and 'low-born' - it is the latter who have the power to ensure that the changes do not destroy what is essentially still a fine little town. I believe that 'Historic Dunbar' should be one of their foremost aims; the right moves have already been spearheaded by the creation of the Town House Museum by East Lothian Council's Museum and Library Service. The initiative of the Dunbar and District History Society, which in just over a decade since its inception has collected an impressive photographic archive and memorabilia which have added to our knowledge of the town's past. Hopefully, future generations will build on what a few dedicated individuals who care about the history of Dunbar have achieved.

Illus 29: *The Shoal Fisher* HM

4

The Earls 1289-1611

Scotland is probably foremost among the small nations which throughout history have experienced violent changes in culture and development out of proportion to their size. The instincts and customs of a nation may change little but Scotland was rarely free from the braying of foreign trumpets and the tramp of alien feet until 1746. It is a country which, like others, has a past which is inextricably linked with that of a larger, aggressive neighbour. The first large-scale invasion from England took place in 1296, the year of the struggle for independence. As a result, Scottish character remained conservative with a small c; successive kings and the ruling class clung tenaciously to the past because to them, therein lay the nation's strength and individuality. From 1291 to 1296, the security of the country was threatened by a ruthless English king and a weak, ineffective Scottish one; it was natural therefore that some Scottish nobles turned to the stronger of the two to protect their own interests. This explains the behaviour of at least two of the Earls of Dunbar during the Wars of Independence. In this Chapter, we shall examine the extent of the Dunbars' fluid loyalty and whether they deserve their reputation as the 'wavering earls' of popular Scottish history.

Perhaps the most notable achievement of thirteenth century Scottish kings was the political harmony they achieved, assisted by their nobles and senior churchmen. When the nobles were offered an opportunity to acquire insight into government and its problems, they were better placed to assist the monarch in overcoming them. After all, they were the government of the day. Thus when a king accepted the opinions of the majority of his nobles, he formed national policy in the knowledge that his decisions would be upheld as law. King and nobles were inextricably bound together under the feudal system; when the relationship between them was well-balanced, the nation moved forward. When the equilibrium was disturbed, the country was weakened and split by factions, intent on preserving their interests at the nation's expense.

The cohesion which had largely obtained during the reign of Alexander III was destroyed by his untimely death in 1286. The kingdom was left without a male heir to the throne which upset the balance of government. As a consequence, the country descended into anarchy which weakened its ability to resist England's intervention. The absence of a figurehead meant that the process of law and order crumbled; the ruling class knew this would happen and frantically cast about for a solution. Edward I of England, aware of the confusion in Scotland, was given a unique opportunity to bring the country under English overlordship in 1291.

The lawless period which occurred immediately after Alexander III's death lasted from 1286 to 1292. However, most of the nobles and senior churchmen were united by a common commitment to retaining the country's sovereignty. The problem was that they couldn't agree on the means to preserve that sovereignty. As a consequence, the behaviour of certain nobles was dictated by their own interests and how in the face of conflicting attitudes they could sustain them. The minds of many modern historians have been coloured by the belief that the nobles were wholly to blame for the disaster which beset Scotland after 1286. While this is of course largely the case, part of the problem was that from 1286 to 1293, Scotland lacked a king. On one aspect, historians agree that the nobility and churchmen desired independence and strong rule from within, even if they disagreed on how these could be achieved. Several nobles like the 8th and 9th Earls of Dunbar believed that England alone could ensure the stability which the country needed. Some nobles favoured the Bruces who seemed to offer the best hope even if Robert Bruce the Elder and his father had close connections with England; others put their faith in the nationalist faction in the north led by the Comyns who supported their preferred candidate John Balliol for king. That Balliol was chosen came as a disappointment to many, not simply because the Bruce faction had lost; he was a weaker man and for most of his brief rule, he was Edward I's puppet. The nobles were irreversibly split into rival factions which atrophied the will of the country to meet the challenge from England; it would take a man of different stamp than Balliol to unite the country again.

At the end of Chapter 2, we saw that in 1286, the Dunbars joined the Bruce-Stewart faction in what was known as the Turnberry Band. The three families had one thing in common - all possessed English estates and therefore owed allegiance to England. Modern historians tend to play down this aspect but it must have had an effect on the thinking of these and other families with English possessions. The factions which sprang up between 1286 and 1289 were aimed at self-preservation rather than resistance to England. The faction-forming occurred on a greater scale than ever before; many looked to England for stability because they had no time for John Balliol, little respect for the Bruces and no confidence in William Wallace. The political situation which came after Balliol's coronation forced Scotland into an alliance with France which did not always serve the country's best interests.

Thus in 1286, many nobles followed unpredictable courses of action in what was a mixture of confused political thought and quirks of personality. What were their motives? One thing is certain; few were driven by patriotism or the 'national' cause. The motives were complex and varied. However, we cannot assume that the Celtic north was the undisputed champion of independence or that the Lowland south was drawn to England; there were many in the north who belonged to the Comyn-Balliol faction simply because they opposed the Bruce-Stewart faction. In the Lowlands, it was hardly the case that the nobles there were lukewarm about independence but many were convinced that only England could offer a solution, provided they bided their time. The Dunbars supported Bruce because they refused to support Balliol; but this did not mean they were anti-England, a country which offered the best chance of stability for their vulnerable earldom, if not the whole of Scotland.

Of the three Dunbar earls who ruled the earldom from 1286 to 1368, the 7th Earl was pro-England until his death in 1289; the 8th Earl continued his father's policy and died in English service, despite being married to Marjorie Comyn; the 9th Earl was a waverer, first serving England until Bannockburn, then Scotland until 1333, when he again turned to England for two years, finally declaring for Scotland in 1335 until his death in 1368. It is these three individuals who have coloured the view of those who consider the Dunbars waverers. The 10th Earl defected to England in 1400 for purely chivalric reasons while his son, the last to hold the title was a loyal supporter of James I until his lands and titles were taken for that king's gain. This chapter will examine the motives of the last four earls of Dunbar (See Fig. 4 at end of chapter) to determine the extent to which they acted against Scotland's interests.

At the outset of the constitutional crisis in 1286, the 7th Earl of Dunbar was loyal to Scotland and outwardly supported the Fair Maid of Norway, the only individual with a legal claim to the Scottish throne. At the same time, Dunbar was party to the Turnberry Band.[1] We must examine the nature, aims and objectives behind the Band as it tells us much about the state of mind of its signatories.

The Band was probably instigated by Bruce the Competitor who in 1291 would make his bid for the throne.[2] What is curious about the Band is that the signatories declared their fealty to kings on both sides of the Border, so the prime objective was one of self-interest as all three owned lands in England. To a certain extent, the fact that the ancestry of Bruce and James the Steward was Anglo-Norman moved their strong desire to rule others while not wishing to be ruled themselves. The Band was skilfully drafted; while it preserved the signatories' fealty to who ruled Scotland 'by reason of the blood of the late King Alexander' it preserved an existing relationship with England which could be put to advantage in the event of constitutional problems. Dunbar was party to the document mainly because he wished to preserve his earldom in an area vulnerable to invasion and because he couldn't risk standing alone. It was logical that he should join Bruce and Stewart whose estates were also in the Lowlands.

The death of the Maid of Norway threw the country into further confusion. It forced those nobles still sitting on the constitutional fence into one or other faction so that the period 1289 to 1296 was one of tangled skeins of alliances and counter-alliances. After 1292, no Scottish king would sit easily on his throne - even Bruce had problems - and the period of kingship of the Stewart dynasty was one of coaxing, cajoling, negotiating with, bribing, conciliating or punishing the nobles. It became fundamental Stewart policy to create divisions among the strongest factions in order to control the whole.

The 7th Earl of Dunbar was among those who accepted the Maid of Norway as rightful heir to the throne; few among those who shared his view believed she would ascend the throne. He was never put to the test however as he died before the Maid's premature death plunged the country into a new constitutional crisis.

Patrick, 8th Earl of Dunbar and 1st of March

Patrick Dunbar had witnessed the Turnberry Band and followed in his father's footsteps, supporting the Bruce-Stewart faction. In May 1290, Dunbar lands in Northumberland taken by the English *escheator* [officer responsible for property confiscated by the Crown] were restored to him after he had 'done due homage' to Edward I.[3] Two months earlier, a parliament [4] held at Brigham-on-Tweed[5] engrossed a charter witnessed by twelve Scottish earls who gave their consent to the marriage of the Maid of Norway to Edward of Caernarvon, Edward I's son It seems self evident that Dunbar's signature was the price he paid to retain his Northumbrian possessions. A 'Solemn Treaty' was signed at Brigham on 18th July 1290 which not only ratified the proposed marriage but preserved Scotland's sovereignty; the treaty also stipulated that no vassal of the Scottish crown would pay homage to an English king for his Scottish lands. Finally, the agreement provided that Scotland's laws, rights and liberties would continue entire and inviolate. Clearly the nobles were uneasy; Edward I was a devious monarch who appeared to abide by the law but would stop at nothing to achieve his ends even if that meant breaking it. Edward ratified the treaty on 28th August 1290, only to dismiss it two years later; he argued that its terms had only held good while Scotland was without a king. However, that was in the future; the carefully laid plans went awry when the Maid of Norway died, invalidating Edward's 'respectable' solution to Scotland's problem.

Although no likenesses of any of the Dunbars have survived, we know that the 8th Earl was bearded; he was referred to as Patrick-with-the-Black-Beard at the Brigham parliament. He was also first to style himself Earl of Dunbar and March, although in official documents, he described himself as 3rd Earl of March, his full title reflecting his appointment as warden of the East March.

The Six Guardians who governed Scotland at this time until 1291 were equally divided in their support for Balliol-Comyn and Bruce-Stewart.[6] The two groups distrusted each other privately, although publicly they acted in tandem. From September 1290 until March 1291, the country was in turmoil. Many nobles supported Bruce the Competitor who had a strong claim to the throne by birth and because a childless Alexander II had in 1238 recognised him publicly as his heir, a promise made irrelevant by the birth of Alexander III. Even so, old Bruce never let his contemporaries forget it.

A majority of nobles might have redressed the fatuity of muddled political thinking. However, the country was on the brink of a civil war. The first signs occurred in the earldoms of Atholl and Mar, then in the south-west. Unrest spread like a bush fire; what happened next is almost inconceivable to modern Scottish minds. The nobles turned to Edward I for a solution. There was no one else. The dearth of state papers for 1290-91 makes it difficult to confirm[7] whether the Guardians formally approached Edward with a request to resolve their difficulties or whether he acted opportunely. The nobles had little choice in the matter; had they sought assistance from another head of state - France for example - Edward would have regarded that as a hostile act. The weight of opinion is that in their weak position, the Scots were unwilling to provoke England. Perhaps even more remarkable was Edward I's patience and restraint in the face of such an opportunity; he could have crossed the Border and taken the country by force. For the moment, he was careful to observe the law, for which he had a qualified respect.

John Balliol moved swiftly. On 16th November 1290 at Gateshead, he issued a charter which declared him heir to the Scottish throne and illegally handed over the crown estates in Northumberland to the Bishop of Durham. Bruce the Competitor was more ingenuous; he protested about Balliol's precipitous action in the names of seven of the thirteen earls of Scotland - including the 8th Earl of Dunbar - insisting that the thirteen earls alone had the right to appoint the king's successor, not one or two of the Guardians such as Bishop William Fraser of St Andrews and John Comyn of Badenoch, both Balliol supporters. It can be surmised that Balliol's actions in Northumberland weren't lost on the 8th Earl of Dunbar, concerned about the albeit temporary loss of his lands there. From then on, the *Great Cause* - as the succession question became known - marked the beginning of Edward I's ruthless ambition to subjugate Scotland. From the outset, he demanded nothing less than full recognition of his claim as Lord Superior of Scotland before he would lift a finger to resolve the constitutional question.[8]

From what little we know of the 8th Earl of Dunbar in the confused period from 1289 to 1291, outwardly he appears to have detached himself from the political upheaval but this cannot be true. Apart from busying himself in consultation with scribes and lawyers about his ancestry in order to formulate his claim to the throne, he seems to have continued his father's alliance with the Bruces and the Stewarts while maintaning a foot in the Balliol-Comyn camp through his marriage to Marjorie Comyn. He, Bruce the Competitor and Stewart were among the seven earls [9] who voluntarily placed themselves under Edward I's protection in 1290 - tantamount to recognising the English king as their feudal superior. There is nothing particularly sinister or, given the absence of a Scottish king, unusual in this; however, in Dunbar's case, there is a definite sign he was hedging his bets at an early stage in the constitutional question. Sooner or later he would have to choose one faction or the other - if indeed he had any real choice in the matter.

Events reached a watershed in the spring of 1291. The Scottish Guardians agreed to meet the English king at Norham-on-Tweed on 10th May; Edward's response was to demand acknowledgement of his feudal superiority over Scotland within three weeks. The Guardians' written response at the end of the month was courteous, diplomatic but unequivocal; they informed Edward they had no knowledge of his right to claim superiority over Scotland 'nor did they [the Guardians] ever see it claimed and used by you and your ancestors; therefore they answer you, as far as in them lies, that they have no power to reply to your statement in default of a lord to whom that demand ought to be addressed, and who will have power to answer about it.'[10] The reply ignores the facts of Malcolm III's submission to William the Conqueror in 1072 and William the Lion's to Henry II in 1173. Not that it mattered. Edward would sweep aside their defensive argument as mere semantics; he was growing tired of the shadow-play, determined to enforce his claim as self-styled lord of Scotland who alone had the power and authority to appoint a Scottish king.

By now, there were thirteen Competitors for the crown (see Appendix D); at Norham on 2nd and 5th June,[11] nine acknowledging Edward's supremacy. They could do little else. On 4th and 6th June,[12] the same nine agreed that Edward should receive the royal castles so that he could formally hand them over to whomever was successful in his bid for the throne. Their submission effectively ended any further opposition by the six Guardians. On 5th June, nine Competitors agreed to accept Edward's judgement on the succession question and be bound by his decision as overlord of Scotland.[13] No doubt in the Dunbar alehouses, men took wagers on their own lord's chance of success.

On 5th June, 140 commissioners or auditors were appointed - 40 each for Bruce and Balliol and 60 for the remaining eleven Competitors. On 6th and 11th June, nine of these solemnly swore that *saisin* of Scotland and its royal castles be surrendered to Edward I who had by then promised to give his decision on the throne by 2nd August.[14] Shabby though the proceedings of June 1291 appear to us, they were inevitable and necessary. A system of government had collapsed; underlying this was the serious division among the nobility as to who should rule the country. Edward, a self-professed champion of the code of chivalry and feudal law - when it suited him - was a devious man, devoid of any real compassion for a country he knew was on its knees; all he had to do was call for his scribes and dictate terms in the full knowledge that the Scots couldn't refuse him even if they wanted to.

The way was now clear for Edward's decision. Before this, on 12th June,[15] Edward demanded that every Competitor swear to accept him publicly as lord superior of Scotland, thus rubbing salt into already smarting wounds. After some initial hesitation, each Competitor gave his oath. On 13th June at Upsettlington,[16] the Guardians and other Scottish magnates present swore fealty individually to Edward. Among the 27 barons and knights who took this oath were the Bruces of Annandale and Carrick - Bruce the Competitor's son and grandson - Balliol, Atholl, Mar, Dunbar, Randolph, Comyn of Buchan - Dunbar's father-in-law - two Umfravilles and Stewart of Menteith. Also included was John de Soules who would take up the Guardianship of Scotland after Wallace's defeat at Falkirk in 1298.

On 3rd August,[17] twelve of the Thirteen Competitors submitted their petitions to Edward at Berwick; the claims were laid before the auditors appointed to advise the king. Five of the claims, including that of Dunbar, were based on blood-line kinship with four natural daughters and one natural son of William the Lion; these claims were immediately dismissed on the grounds of illegitimacy. Gradually, the remaining names were reduced to three - John Hastings, John Balliol and Bruce. Bruce's claim was the strongest under modern law as he was closer to the throne through his mother Isabella, daughter of William the Lion's brother, David of Huntingdon. However, under feudal law, Balliol had the stronger claim; although he was the great-grandson of Isabella's sister Margaret, the latter was older which gave him precedence over Bruce. Bruce tried to argue that Balliol's claim was weaker than his own since it rested on his mother Dervorgilla's relationship to the royal line whereas his was direct through his father's marriage to Isabella. He also reminded those present that he had been named as Alexander II's heir in 1238 and that he was supported by the Seven Earls of Scotland. It was to no avail. Edward chose Balliol for legal as well as political reasons; furthermore, in Bruce he saw a man who would be less compliant than Balliol. Bruce accepted the king's decision and on 7th November, quietly transferred his claim to the throne to his son, Bruce the Elder and his heirs; two days later, the Elder Bruce gave the earldom of Carrick to his son Robert, then aged eighteen. These acts were intended to ensure the continuity of the Bruce claim; moreover, Robert's grandfather Bruce the Competitor had foreseen that there would be a more favourable opportunity to press the claim when his grandson reached maturity. In any event, parliament ratified the choice of Balliol as king in August 1293.

Balliol, the vassal king of Scotland, was promised the throne at Berwick on 17th November 1293; that unhappy man's coronation took place on 30th November at Scone. He was the last king to be crowned on the Stone of Destiny. At Newcastle on 26th December, Balliol did homage to Edward for his kingdom, addressing him as 'Lord Superior of the realm of Scotland.'[18] The historian Fordun makes the point that Bruce the Competitor withdrew from the ceremony; he died in 1295 without swearing fealty to Balliol.

As for the unsuccessful Competitors, none went away empty-handed. Sums of money or land were given to every candidate, the value determined by status. At the top of the scale, Comyn of Badenoch - the Red Comyn's father - received £1,600; at the other end, the 8th Earl of Dunbar was given lands to the value of £100. Dunbar remained in the Bruce camp; Edward would find Bruce the Elder and Dunbar his main supporters in the future, chiefly because of their opposition to Balliol and his champion, William Wallace. Both men's failure to offer their allegiance to Balliol was in no way treasonable; it was about the need to preserve law, order and a life-style - all guaranteed by Edward I, their powerful superior. Whether Dunbar genuinely supported the Bruce cause is doubtful; more than likely, he acted out of self-interest, courting Edward as the best means of preserving his position.

While Scottish history has traditionally held John Balliol in contempt, it must be said in mitigation that he was the victim of a strong and aggressive English king. He was also the lamb among wolves in his own court. Even so, he managed to summon enough courage to defy Edward but he was neither powerful nor effective enough to match the English king.

From 1292, the Dunbars abandoned any lingering interest in an independent Scotland and became wholly occupied with increasing their land-holdings through service to the English crown. The 8th Earl was ultra-conservative even for the time and he abided by the oath which bound him to Edward. The earldom of Dunbar had become a petty kingship in the Merse and eventually included estates in the south-west of Scotland, then the earldom of Moray and the Isle of Man, although the last was little more than an honorific. Dunbar was a realist who ingratiated himself with England purely to preserve his power and with an eye on possible financial gain. Also, we must not lose sight of the unique arrangement which had existed since c.1100 regarding the Dunbars' possession of the grand serjeanty of Beanley in Northumberland. Every earl from Gospatric II onwards had a duty to England as special constables enforcing cross-border pledges and the safe conduct of English officials travelling to Scotland. When this unusual arrangement ceased is not clear but it may have continued until Bannockburn. Scottish kings were aware of the arrangement and allowed it to continue so that the Dunbars were in some respects subject to a degree of dual allegiance not required of other nobles in Scotland. Apart from the Beanley arrangement, most of the Dunbars' other Northumbrian possessions had been sub-infued to their vassals there, although nominal rents were still forthcoming from their tenants. The residual feudal association with northern England was insignificant and the Dunbars' association with the district was cultural rather than economic. However, the Beanley arrangement lessened the likelihood of any invading English army destroying Dunbar's possessions in Scotland; Earl Patrick felt confident that this would be sufficient insurance.

While the 8th Earl of Dunbar never wavered in his loyalty to England, it is odd that he allowed himself to be declared in default for his 'contumacy' in 1292 when he delayed answering a summons to prove his rights to Beanley. Perhaps he believed he no longer needed to bend his knee to England but he later paid due homage to Edward; his estates with all liberties and rents were restored on 20 July 1293. He defaulted a second time in 1295, when his Northumbrian lands were withheld until 30th December 1296.[19] It is hard to put these lapses down to poor memory; Patrick Dunbar had a healthy respect for and fear of Edward and he wouldn't have wanted to antagonise him. Perhaps the real reason was that he over-estimated his worth in the English king's eyes.

In 1294, the Bruces, the de Umfravilles of Angus and Dunbar renewed their oath of allegiance to Edward. In the same year, Edward ordered Balliol to muster troops to assist him against Philip IV of France who was menacing English interests in Gascony, a fiefdom constantly in revolt and encouraged by French kings. On 29th June, Edward expected Balliol to accompany him on his French campaign along with 10 Scottish earls and 14 barons who had lands in England. Dunbar was among those summoned; he alone went to London on 1st September that year. The French campaign never materialised; it was abandoned because of rebellion in Wales. On 5th July 1295, the Scottish parliament effectively removed the reins of government from the lack-lustre Balliol. Twelve magnates - four earls, four barons and four bishops - formed a council to govern Scotland. Earlier that year, Philip of France had appealed to the Scots to enter - or renew - an alliance which was accepted by the council of twelve and which most historians consider the original *Auld Alliance,* although an arrangement between the two countries had existed since 1173.[20]

Balliol was carried along by subsequent events. Following parliament's ratification of the treaty with France in October 1295, a *wapinshaw* was ordered in February 1296.[21] Not unexpectedly, Bruce the Elder, de Umfraville of Angus and Dunbar ignored the summons for war; Bruce and Dunbar even warned Edward of these events, Balliol's reaction was to declare their Scottish estates forfeit;[22] Bruce and Dunbar weren't troubled, knowing Edward would restore them.

When Edward learnt of the forfeiture of Bruce and Dunbar, he issued writs for the seizure of all English estates held by Scottish nobles who refused to join him against Balliol. Perhaps because Scottish morale was low, more than 80 nobles met Edward at Wark Castle to offer homage; among them were Bruce, de Umfraville and Dunbar who swore they would serve him

'well and loyally against all mortal men, on every occasion that we are so required or instructed by our lord the king of England or his heirs.'[23]

In acknowledging their oath, Edward referred to Balliol as the former king of Scotland; thus even before he crossed the Border on 25th March 1296, Edward effectively removed the allegiance due to Balliol from his nobles. This was important since when Dunbar joined Edward at Berwick - a town which, as warden of the East March, he was under obligation to defend on behalf of the Scottish crown - his oath of allegiance to the Scottish king was invalid. Edward took Berwick on 30th March, ruthlessly slaughtering 8,000 men, women and children. Only the Flemish merchants in the Red Hall put up a fight and were killed to a man. The brutal and needless sack of Berwick is a stain on Edward's character.

Meanwhile, young John Comyn of Badenoch led the Scottish host to Cumberland to plunder Tynedale and Redesdale and make an unsuccessful attempt to take Carlisle, then under the command of Bruce the Elder. It was rumoured at the time that Edward had promised Bruce the Elder the Scottish throne after the rebellion was crushed.[24] Comyn re-crossed the Border on 1st April and led an inconclusive raid on Northumberland later in the month.[25] Edward, encamped in a smoking, ruined Berwick contemplated his next move. Balliol's response to the dreadful news of Berwick was to remove his *diffidato* or homage to Edward, delivered to the English king at Berwick on 5th April by the Abbott of Arbroath.[26]

In April 1296, war broke suddenly and brutally. The populations of Lothian and the Merse were panic-stricken; in the Dunbar earldom, the knight-tenants were aware that their feudal lord had declared for England and were thus obliged to follow his banner. In Dunbar itself, the merchants and common folk probably went about their normal business, confident that the English would spare the community.

News reached Berwick on 23rd April that the Scottish army was besieging Dunbar Castle and Edward acted quickly (see Appendix E). The English army contained 30,000 infantry and 5,000 cavalry; perhaps on Patrick Dunbar's advice, he ordered the Earl of Warenne to advance on Dunbar with 10,000 troops and 1,000 cavalry to re-take the castle and force the Scots to fall back on Edinburgh. When Warenne arrived in Dunbar on 24th April, the castle gate was shut. In defiance of her husband, Marjorie Comyn, Countess of Dunbar had handed over the castle to her kinsman. An undoubtedly embarrassed Dunbar, upstaged by a disobedient wife, may have accompanied Warenne in his anxiety to restore his credibility.

Marjorie Comyn, the daughter of the late Alexander Comyn, Earl of Buchan, did not share her husband's enthusiasm for England; whether she acted on the spur of the moment or simply accepted the reality of the situation isn't clear. According to one source,[27] the Earl of Mar had publicly denounced Dunbar a traitor and apparently persuaded Marjorie to surrender his castle as a matter of honour. With a pitifully small garrison, Dunbar's brother Alexander knew that he couldn't resist the besiegers. The Scots were admitted to the castle on 25th April.

The castle was placed under the command of Sir Richard Siward, a 'man renowned in war and respected in arms.' Warenne immediately laid siege to it by land and sea on 26th-27th April. An account written sixty years later deviates from what is generally accepted as the true version of events:[28]

> '....the Earl of March, Patrick-with-the-Black-Beard who alone [sic] of all lords of Scotland had remained obedient to the king of England and was with the king at the taking of Berwick, came to announce to the king that his wife had received into his castle of Dunbar her kinsmen, enemies of Scotland, who had imprisoned his officers and taken the castle against him. He therefore asked assistance from the king and wished to set out that very night. The king gave him the Earls of Warenne and Warwick, with great supplies by sea and land so that before sunrise the next day he had laid siege to the castle of Dunbar. On learning of the siege, the assembled [Scottish] nobles marched by night upon the place and came in the morning to Spott, between which place and Dunbar, they gave battle to the besiegers, when the Scots were defeated [in] the first battle of the war.'

We know of course that Dunbar wasn't the only noble to support Edward and it is not absolutely certain he was with Warenne and Warwick at the siege; he was certainly not present on the field of Spott Glen on 27th April.

On that day, Warenne learnt of the Scottish host's advance; leaving the siege of the castle in charge of a few junior officers and a token force of soldiers - the defenders were going nowhere - he marched to Spott. The valley known as Spott Glen, or Oswald Dean (**ill 30**), is a long winding scar at the foot of Doon Hill, its unimpressive burn enters the North Sea at Broxburn, the site of Oliver Cromwell's victory in 1650. An obscure glen of dull grass, straggling gorse and stunted, windswept hawthorn then as now, it is a cold place in early spring which a profusion of primroses fails to soften. Here it was that steel decided Balliol's fate. The battle which followed has been described as the forgotten field of Dunbar. It is well-named; few places in Scotland have witnessed such an effusion of blood.[29] Today, a quiet and eerie silence, a sweet sadness pervades Oswald Dean; to those who know its history, it cannot be walked through with a quiet mind. In winter and spring, the burn in spate turns a bloody colour from the red earth. There is no monument to identify the site on which the

KRM

Illus 30: *Oswald Dean, reputed site of the 1296 battle of Dunbar*

first battle for independence was fought and lost. In 1296, Dunbar did not merely add another date to history; it altered it in a way that would continue until 1707.

John Comyn led the amateur feudal host of men and boys that passed as an army; most of them had never seen action before. While presenting a formidable barrier to the smaller but professional English army, the Scots were no match for it. The two armies wasted no time on chivalrous niceties. Warenne made the first move. In addition to outnumbering him four to one, the Scots occupied a strong defensive position on the upper slopes of Spott Glen with their backs to Doon Hill. Warenne knew that with his small force he would have no chance of success with a frontal attack. The tactics he used suggest that it was his intention to engage one of the Scottish flanks, defeat it and roll up the entire line. He began to deploy his troops accordingly, possibly intending to attack the thickly massed Scottish right wing; to do so he had to descend his side of the Glen. The scene is easily imagined; steel glinting in the weak April sunshine, the ranks of armour broken by the terrain and hidden from view here and there by the dense gorse so that only pennants and banners whipping in the cold wind betrayed his position. Among Warenne's knights was the redoubtable Henry Percy, 5th Earl of Northumberland who particularly distinguished himself that day, his family thus beginning a long association with Dunbar.[30]

The Scots seem to have had no other battle plan other than to engage the enemy. Weak in cavalry and archers, few troops were kept in reserve. It is certain that the front line was a crowded, undisciplined mass. The Scottish van apparently mistook Warenne's deployment for retreat which precipitated a premature charge. Blowing their horns, the front line elements rushed down into the valley, drawing the main body after them. They met the English in small unco-ordinated groups which were systematically destroyed in a way reminiscent of the battle of the Somme in 1916. In the brief but bloody encounter, the Scots staggered, then broke whatever ranks they had managed to maintain. They scattered, suffering heavy loss from the pursuing cavalry while the archers decimated those that stood their ground. It is said that a number of the survivors stopped flight only when they reached the Forest of Selkirk, some 40 miles south. Contemporary English chroniclers quote 10,005 casualties[31] - a suspiciously precise and probably exaggerated figure. (Medieval chroniclers are prone to exaggerate the size of armies and casualties; for them, a thousand men was a host). The population of thirteenth century Scotland is estimated at 400,000, that of England about two million. It is unlikely that the Scottish army at Dunbar numbered 40,000 - ten per cent of the entire population. A more realistic figure is 4,000, with 1,000 casualties.

Whatever the precise figure, Spott was a bloody and decisive defeat; among the dead lay Sir Patrick Graham of Montrose who gave and received no quarter, alone praised by the English for standing his ground. Another noble, Walter, Earl of Menteith aged 76, was taken prisoner and executed on Edward's orders. The only force capable of resisting Edward melted away into the Lammermuir Hills and the Border forests. The battle demonstrated the inadequacy of Scottish troops in the face of a battle-hardened and disciplined professional army. The knights who had led the free men of Scotland knew little of warfare other than what they had learnt at tournaments. The Scots hadn't fought in any major engagement since the battle of the Standard in 1138 - we may disregard the series of minor skirmishes against Haakon of Norway at Largs in 1263. A grossly inadequate military establishment was destroyed because the nation was wholly unprepared for war. The message that came from the defeat at Dunbar was clear. Patriotism wasn't enough. However, England had forged a dangerous weapon in 1296 - nationalism became a cohesive political and military force as a result of Edward's invasion.

As for the Earl of Dunbar, he was preoccupied with regaining his castle. He played a minor but significant role in the campaign of 1296. Whoever it was that prompted Marjorie Comyn to hand over the castle to the Scots, she wasn't prepared to defend it for more than three days, after which time she had promised to surrender it if she wasn't relieved by the Scottish army. She had put the three days to good use, taunting Warenne's young knights from the battlements.[32] The castle surrendered on 27th April, the day of the battle. Siward, its commander, was later accused of giving in too readily but he swore to abide by Marjorie Comyn's promise. Sheltering within the walls was a rich haul of ransomable hostages; while accounts differ as to numbers, several important men were among those taken prisoner. They included John de Strathbogie, Earl of Atholl, Alexander Menteith and the Earl of Ross - members of three of the oldest Celtic families. The knights included John Comyn of Buchan - the Red Comyn whom Bruce would slay in 1306.[33] Most of the knights were from Lothian and the Merse.[34] The prisoners were removed in chains and taken to 25 castles in England and Wales, the most valuable taken to the Tower of London.[35]

There is no evidence to confirm whether Marjorie Comyn was punished for her rebellion by her husband or Edward I. The latter may have questioned the extent of the Dunbars' reliability in an age when loyalty was personal as well as political. On the other hand, the soldier-king may have been impressed by Marjorie's courage; we know it failed her after the battle as there is a document - albeit slightly inaccurate - in the Vatican which gives an account of Marjorie's flight from Dunbar after the siege.[36] She was injured getting into the boat which was taking her to safety in Fife, a slightly erroneous account of which is quoted in Chapter 5.[37] In all probability, Marjorie suffered a rebuke from her husband; as far as is known, none came from Edward. Despite his reputation as *Hammer of the Scots,* Edward showed compassion to the wives and daughters of the high-ranking prisoners taken at Dunbar. Some accounts state that he executed many of the prisoners from Dunbar, which is untrue. Edward was chivalrous when it suited him; he awarded pensions to the wives and daughters of the men taken prisoner at Dunbar and few of those who had fought under Balliol's banner had their estates forfeited permanently.

Scotland was prostrate. Bruce the Elder gave way to lethargy, becoming as impotent as Balliol had been; Robert the Bruce wavered indecisively. The 8th Earl of Dunbar remained a staunch ally of England but pro-English Scots and English alike held him in low esteem. Edward himself was irritated by him; he tolerated Dunbar for purely political reasons as he was ineffective in military matters. Dunbar was so afraid of Edward that he galloped about the countryside in desperate, inconclusive sorties that he hoped would impress him. He constantly travelled between Dunbar and Ayr and was incompetent in both places,[38] a fact Edward summed up by saying this of his Scottish ally:

'When the war was finished, Audegier drew his sword.'

Dunbar was at the mercy of events; he wanted to maintain his lifestyle at all costs, enjoying fine food and hoping for English gold. Despite his loyalty to Edward, he lost his Northumberland estates for a third time,[39] possibly on account of his wife's behaviour.

Until his death in 1304, Bruce the Elder remained a passive English supporter after the battle of Dunbar in 1296, possibly because when he asked Edward for the Scottish crown afterwards, Edward answered him thus:

'Have we nothing to do but win a kingdom for thee?'[40]

Even so, his son Robert the Bruce again renewed his oath of fealty to Edward and entered a phase in his life which perhaps reflected the mood of the nation. The young Earl of Carrick would have several changes of heart before he finally declared for Scotland; while he undoubtedly shared his family's aversion to Balliol, he remained with Edward during most of the heady days of Wallace, fighting in Balliol's name.

After April 1296, Edward no longer referred to Scotland as a kingdom; he regarded it in the same way as Wales and Ireland, conquered territory. Determined to stamp out any lingering resistance in Scotland, he marched from Dunbar to receive word of Balliol's surrender at Montrose on 5th July, given in person by the hapless former king at Brechin two days later. On 10th July, Edward learnt of the alliance with France which turned his disgust for Balliol into anger. *Toom Tabard* [41] as Balliol is known to history, was ignominiously stripped of his regalia, insignia and titles in the king's presence. Edward then sent his army to Elgin to discourage any risings in the wild and less accessible north; he returned to Lothian on 20th August and spent the night on the Earl of Dunbar's estate at Pinkerton, moving on to Coldingham the following day. But he wasn't finished with Scotland yet.

On 28th August, at a parliament in Berwick, Edward ordered over 1,500 Scottish nobles, churchmen and freemen to pledge oaths to him; the names are recorded in the 35 great parchment rolls which were so festooned with seals that they are known as the *Ragman Roll.* Among the names are those of the 8th Earl of Dunbar and his falconer, Elias de Spott, Bruce the Elder, Robert the Bruce and Gilbert de Umfraville - men who would remain loyal to Edward longer than most of the others who signed the document that day. The Stone of Destiny

- returned to Scotland in 1996 on the 700th anniversary of its removal to England - the Holy Rood of St Margaret and much of the Scottish crown archives were taken to London. Edward showed his contempt for Scotland in a petulant display; the Great Seal of Scotland was broken up, reputedly in Edward's presence, as he is alleged to have made the caustic comment that 'A man does good business when he rids himself of a turd.' Balliol was imprisoned in the Tower of London until 1297, when the Pope intervened on his behalf and he was allowed to retire quietly to the family estates in Ballieul, France. He died in obscurity in the year of Bannockburn.

Scotland was now merely *terre* or 'land' in the same way as the lordship of Wales and Ireland. The country was governed by Hugh Cressingham, Earl of Surrey and English Treasurer and William Ormsby, the English Justiciar. Patrick Dunbar was made governor of Berwick on 28th May 1297; in November the same year, he was appointed commander-in-chief of all English forces south of the Forth, his jurisdiction extending westwards to Ayr. Despite Dunbar's marriage to Marjorie Comyn, his power was greatly curtailed by 1297 and he was increasingly isolated, forced to serve England because he had few friends in Scotland, even among those who were lukewarm towards England. The 8th Earl of Dunbar served Edward I largely because of self-interest, his lands on both sides of the Border secured by that service. Like Bruce at the time, he placed a higher value on protection that came from the south. The fact that he refused to serve under Balliol's banner might be construed as tacit support for Robert the Bruce, although this is unlikely.

In 1297, William Wallace began his rebellion. Bruce joined him for a time which is odd since Wallace fought for Balliol and he would have been aware of Bruce ambitions. At this time, the deep divisions among the Scottish nobility were such that one disgusted knight remarked it was folly to fight for men who fought each other, so he joined the English. The Bruces did the same.

Dunbar appears to have curried favour with Edward at every opportunity; in March 1297, he sent the English king a gift of a goshawk,[42] although this may have been a *blanche-ferme* [43]- an 'empty' or token feu for his Northumberland estates. In September, as premier noble in Lothian and the Merse, Dunbar met and welcomed the English army under Warenne at the Tweed; Edward, then in Flanders had ordered a full-scale campaign aimed at destroying Wallace. The invasion ended with the spectacular Scottish victory at Stirling Bridge on 11th September. Dunbar's sole contribution to the campaign was to guide Warenne's shattered remnants through Lothian and the Merse to safety over the Border, pursued by Wallace's jubilant cavalry. It is interesting to note that on this occasion, Wallace's army contained the young Earl of Carrick, Robert the Bruce; perhaps less important but significant was the fact that many of Dunbar's Coldingham tenants fought for Wallace, ignoring their feudal - and legal - oath to Dunbar because of his pro-English policy.[44]

In a matter of months, the revolt which had sparked in the north under Andrew Murray, son and heir of a local baron soon spread south. Wallace,an obscure knight from Elderslie in Ayrshire, joined Murray and shared the guardianship of Scotland with him briefly until Murray was mortally wounded at Stirling. Wallace became a legend almost overnight; despite the inaccuracies in the film *Braveheart,* Wallace neither painted his face blue, nor did he wear a kilt - he was a knight who wore armour - though he was venerated by the common people.

Shortly after Stirling Bridge, Wallace formed a governing council at Perth to which high and low alike were invited. At the same time, the 8th Earl of Dunbar and other pro-English nobles received letters from England dated 25th September commending them for their continued support for Edward. If we are to believe Blind Harry, the minstrel whose adulatory life of Wallace often strays from the truth, Dunbar summarily dismissed Wallace's invitation. In his long celebratory poem, Harry has Dunbar mocking Wallace thus:

'That king of Kyll I can nocht undirstand
Off him I held nevir a fur[long?] of land.'

If Dunbar did refer to Wallace as the king of Kyll, he may have meant Kyle, his birthplace; however, it is thought that the description derives from the Celtic word *coille* - a wood or forest - so that Dunbar was implying that Wallace was no more than an outlaw in the same manner as Robin Hood, king only of the woods.

Many of Wallace's supporters wanted to attack Dunbar but Wallace was prepared to attempt diplomacy for a second time; he sent Dunbar a conciliatory note, promising he would be forgiven if he were to join the governing council, admit the error of his ways and declare for Scotland. Dunbar's response was that he was free to reign as lord in his own right as any prince or king and that he did not need Wallace's council to uphold his rights. Dunbar is but one example of Wallace's failure to convince the nobles of the rightness of his cause. They refused to give him what they had given to Edward; even after Stirling Bridge, their lack of resolve may be attributed to their refusal to follow a man from an obscure background.

In the face of Dunbar's second rebuff, Wallace took the advice of his supporters. He gathered a small force, crossed the Forth and was joined at Musselburgh by minor nobles such as Crystal Seton and Lauder who increased his band to 400 men. Believing Dunbar to be in the vicinity of Cockburnspath, Wallace by-passed the community of Dunbar and according to Andrew of Wyntoun's *Orygynale Cronikyl of Scotland (Chron. Wyntoun),* confronted the haughty Earl and 900 of his men at a place called Corsikill Park, near Innerwick. After a brief skirmish, Dunbar retreated to his fortalice at Cockburnspath, then to Boncle Wood and finally to Norham-on-Tweed from where he sought English help. Wallace gave up the chase, took Dunbar Castle and left it in the care of Crystal Seton while he raised a fresh force to pursue Dunbar.

Meanwhile, Dunbar conveyed news of Wallace's foray into Lothian to the military commander at Norham.[45] Blind Harry tells us that he enlisted the support of Antony Bek or Beck, the warrior cleric who ruled the Bishopric of Durham in the fashion of his Norman ancestors. Harry adds that Dunbar was joined by Bruce the Elder, no doubt suspicious that Wallace was attempting to claim the Scottish throne for himself. According to Harry, a large force was raised and the wing of the army commanded by Dunbar was detached to recover his castle. Then Bruce the Elder learnt that Wallace had gathered a considerable army and was at Yester Castle, intent on re-taking Dunbar Castle. Bruce marched through the Lammermuirs and according to Blind Harry, reached Spott Muir where he received word that the 8th Earl would join him to ambush Wallace.[46] Heavily outnumbered, Wallace nonetheless attacked Dunbar's element of the army; at first, Dunbar held his ground but gradually gave way until Bruce arrived with reinforcements. After a bloody encounter,[47] both sides were relieved to draw apart in the evening. A running fight was resumed the following day when Dunbar and Bruce retreated through the Lammermuirs to Norham.[48] They were shadowed by a few of Wallace's men, the bulk of which were engaged in slighting Dunbar's fortalices in the Merse.

So much for Blind Harry. Most modern historians do not accept his account insofar as a major battle at Spott Muir is concerned. There may have been a skirmish near Innerwick and Dunbar Castle was certainly occupied briefly by Wallace's men. Harry had no need to lionise his hero in the way he did; Wallace's legend persisted in his own day and continues today. However, the tale may have some basis in truth.

In October 1297, Dunbar, smarting from his encounters with Wallace, wrote to Edward I, urging him to invade Scotland and end the revolt. However, his ire may have been occasioned by another incident. Wallace carried the war to northern England and for a month, he devastated parts of Northumberland and looted Cumberland as far as Cockermouth; in the list of properties destroyed in Northumberland was Shipley Manor, a Dunbar possession.[49] At this time, Edward was in Flanders but his miltary intelligence-gathering machine was working well; he received an anonymous letter from Scotland appraising him of the situation.[50] The writer informs the king of

'....news of the borders. Earl Patrick has come to Scotland from France and, among his news, a great quarrel is beginning between 'them' [the Scottish nobles]. Also, the Scottish nobles are now at Scone for their council but no one knows yet what they are doing. As to the king's faithful men of the same [parts?], men [say?] divers things, as the writer will inform the king in person more fully than he can by letter. He will do his best to get news, and, as soon as he has any, will come to the king as quickly as he can.'

A curious letter, it has been attributed to the 8th Earl's son and heir, Patrick. Apparently, the Earl had made a flying visit to France, possibly to report to Edward in person the news of Wallace's invasion of northern England.

Edward returned from Flanders, no doubt in bad fettle; he quickly raised an army at York and summoned those Scottish nobles who had attached their seals to the *Ragman Roll* in 1296. Most ignored his call to arms, more it must be said out of fear of reprisals by Wallace than love of Scotland. Edward's second invasion began in midsummer 1298, when he pursued an elusive Wallace, busy raising an army, conducting a scorched-earth policy and drawing the English away from their supply ships. After much marching and counter-marching, a near-starving and mutinous English army pitched their tents at Kirkliston, where Edward ordered a general withdrawal to Edinburgh and his supply ships at Leith.

And then unexpectedly, Patrick Dunbar obtained intelligence of Wallace's position; he and the Earl of Angus learnt that the Scottish army was camped in the forest of Falkirk. They were so afraid of Edward that they informed Bishop Beck as they'd hitherto failed to pinpoint Wallace's position.[51,52]

On 22nd July, the battle Wallace hoped to avoid broke his extraordinary run of successes; Falkirk was a decisive defeat which ended Wallace's governorship of Scotland. It is thought that Robert the Bruce was among the sparse Scottish cavalry who took no part in the battle. Edward went to Ayr two weeks later to deal with Bruce but he had fled; in an undated letter to the king, Bruce apologised for his defection to the Scots through 'evil advice'; even so, Edward took possession of his castle at Lochmaben. From 1299 to 1300, Bruce and Comyn of Badenoch were appointed joint Guardians of Scotland but both conspired against each other with English connivance, if not open encouragement; during this time, Bruce held a position of trust in Edward's court.[53] Neither Bruce nor Comyn played any part in Edward's campaigns however.

From 1298 to 1305, Scotland was forced to endure the rule of Edward's officials, agents and soldiers; for all that, the English king was obliged to come over the Border no fewer than five times to subdue various risings. To increase his mobility, Edward transferred his administration from London to York, which Dunbar visited on several occasions to discuss military strategy.[54] As mentioned earlier, Dunbar had been appointed governor of Berwick on 28th May 1298,[55] then on 19th November, he took command of the English forces in the East March.[56] His was an independent command, although he was ordered to mount forays against any nationalist forces active in his area. For the next five years, south-east Scotland was virtually English territory; elsewhere the Scots under Sir John de Soules who had replaced Wallace as Guardian of Scotland began to consolidate their position.

Not surprisingly, Dunbar's military appointments also included responsibility for judicial matters; one of his cases in 1299 concerned the abduction of a noblewoman by a minor noble in East Lothian. The case was known to Edward who ordered Dunbar and the Constable of Edinburgh Castle to appoint a jury to enquire into charges made by Joanne de Clare, Countess of Fife, against Robert de Morham, who lived near Haddington. Apparently, de Morham had waylaid the Countess - travelling to England under Edward I's personal safe conduct-somewhere between Stirling and Edinburgh, taking her against her will to his brother's castle at Morham where he put the lady in prison as she refused to marry him. Joanna was in fact under oath to Edward not to marry without his consent. De Morham also appropriated her possessions - valued at £2,000 - and defied initial demands to release her. Eventually, he was taken and placed under arrest in Edinburgh Castle; he and his father were still incarcerated in 1304, the only prisoners not released under an exchange arranged by Comyn of Badenoch. There appears to be no record of any trial.[57]

Despite his victory at Falkirk, Edward had insufficient troops to occupy the whole of Scotland and until 1303, only Lothian was under English control; more castles there than anywhere else were held by English or pro-English garrisons. As for Dunbar, his poor military skill irritated Edward; even when he planned strategic moves other than those ordered by the king, they were never blessed with success. Dunbar functioned incompetently as militarist and politician but English resources ensured that his earldom and his vassals were protected from molesting nationalists.

During the period 1299 to 1306, Dunbar appears to have spent a considerable amount of time at Ayr. Why he was put in charge of Ayr is unclear but the records confirm that several payments were made to him between 1301 and 1307 to buy food and pay the garrison at Ayr Castle. On 11th April 1300, Edward ordered Dunbar and his bailiffs in Scottish castles not to allow any silver money or silverware, or any other coin from the royal mint to leave the country without his permission. This proclamation was made at several seaports 'under pain of forfeiture of life and goods.'[58] The threat didn't work; in February 1301, Edward had to reissue the *diktat* as 'certain persons scheming together' had carried off sums of money and silverware hidden in sacks of wool, hides and bales of straw. The wardens at all ports like Dunbar - or to be precise, Belhaven - had orders to search all persons and ships' cargoes before they left port.

On 1st July 1300, Edward led yet another army against Caerlaverock Castle, near the Solway Firth; Dunbar's standard flew among others at the action.[59] The siege lasted only three days; the garrison of 60 men sought honourable terms of surrender which an insulted Edward disregarded. The castle was battered into submission and every soldier taken alive was hanged in a nearby wood. After this event, the Comyns of Badenoch and Buchan sought a truce with Edward; they asked for the reinstatement of John Balliol and the restoration of the rights of Scottish nobles dispossessed of their lands in England by buying them back. Edward not unexpectedly rejected these requests out of hand. In October, he was at Dunipace and ordered Dunbar to send him a *ballista* or siege machine from Dunbar to reduce a castle in the neighbourhood. Whether Edward was successful is not recorded but he achieved very little in that campaign.

The nobles who remained loyal to Edward didn't impress his officers or even those Scots in his army, yet the king persisted in placing his trust - and scarce resources - in men like the 8th Earl of Dunbar. A letter dated October 1301 indicates that Edward's troops were deserting and that he was in financial straits:

> 'But for lack of money, he [Edward] would have completed the bridge across the Firth of Forth; he [the writer of the letter] is sure that if he [Edward] had crossed this season he would have done such exploit against his enemies that his business would have quickly reached a satisfactory and honourable conclusion.'[60]

The letter ends by urging the English Treasurer to send money to the king himself and specifically only to the garrisons at Dumfries and Lochmaben, those guarding the West March and Earl Patrick 'at Noef Chastel sur Are' [the New Castle at Ayr]. The year before, Dunbar had been stationed at Roxburgh Castle, acting as warden and assisted by his son and heir Patrick, who received 10 merks for his personal subsistence.[61]

As a senior nobleman of the realm, Dunbar was expected not only to be well versed in military tactics but to lead as well. He was a disappointment to Edward in both aspects. In 1301, he was criticised in a petition to

Edward from the pro-English Scots garrison at Ayr. The soldiers at Ayr complained about Dunbar's lack of military skills and that they were being threatened by the nationalist Scots in Turnberry Castle; as a consequence, they asked for help from their English allies. The petition does not mince words, ending as follows:

'....[The men at Ayr] have heard nothing from Earl Patrick, to whom they understand the king has given the keeping of the country, at which they wonder much.'[62]

Eventually, Dunbar appeared with a relief force and lifted the siege of Ayr; at least he rescued his reputation on that occasion. He seems to have paid more attention to Ayr after that as several payments were made to him during 1302 for the Ayr garrison.[63] In September 1301, Turnberry Castle fell to the English but in October, both it and Ayr were threatened by the Scots of Carrick - vassals of Bruce the Elder who no longer adhered to England. In February 1302, Dunbar received the forfeited lands of several Annandale and Galloway vassals fighting against England.

A truce was signed at the end of 1301; it would last from January to November 1302. At some point during this period, Edward removed Dunbar from Ayr and placed it under the command of Robert the Bruce who by this time had returned to the English camp. Between 1302 and 1304, Bruce actively opposed the nationalists at every opportunity. At the end of this period, Dunbar and Sir Archibald Livingstone were the only other nobles who supported Edward. Dunbar must have begun to feel insecure as on 6th May 1302, he sent all his jewels and valuable plate to Newcastle for safe-keeping.[64]

The period from 1302 to 1304 were years of gloom for Scotland, both at home and abroad. Their French allies were defeated by the Flemish at Courtrai at the 'battle of the spurs' which also lost Scotland the support of Pope Boniface VIII. On the plus side, John the Red Comyn severely mauled an English force at Rosslyn in 1304. However, before that, Edward ordered Dunbar to bring 'as many men-at-arms'[65] as he could to Roxburgh, probably to subdue a rebellion there. Then on 20th May, the Scots suffered yet another set-back; Philip IV of France and Edward signed the Peace of Paris, a treaty which effectively ended the prospect of any French support. By 1304, the nationalist cause was almost extinguished.

The 8th Earl of Dunbar was an unimaginative leader; the arrival of any orders from Edward seemed to reduce him to impotence, such was his fear of him. Although not personally cowardly, he was prepared to fight only when he enjoyed superiority in numbers. On 2nd May 1304, he was treated to yet another royal rebuke for failing to capture several nationalists;[66] Edward had specifically ordered him to keep watch on the garrison at Stirling Castle and to cut them off if they attempted to leave the castle, which they did. In that year, Wallace was declared an outlaw and Dunbar took part in the intensifying hunt for the fugitive knight.

If he didn't rate Dunbar much, Edward had developed a fondness for his son and heir, Sir Patrick; it is recorded [67] that Ralph de Wotton, Sir Patrick's valet, acknowledged receipt at Berwick of a cask of new wine from Edward to Lady Ermigarda, the young man's pregnant wife; [68] further gifts of wine, malt and wheat arrived at Dunbar in August and more wheat and malt in September.

By 1305, Edward was convinced that resistance had ended in Scotland even if Wallace was still at large; he knew however that no Englishman could sleep soundly until he was taken. Then the unthinkable happened; Wallace was captured, supposedly through the treachery of the Earl of Menteith. He was taken to London and declared a traitor, suffering an agonising death. Wallace's slaughter - it could hardly be termed judicial execution - on 23rd August 1305 is probably as significant to many Scots as the Crucifixion; Edward I's vindictive cruelty is vividly described in Blind Harry's martyrology which has ensured that the great patriot's name will never be forgotten.

In 1304, Robert Bruce inherited the Bruce earldom on the death of his father. In yet another change of heart, he and the Red Comyn briefly became pro-English joint Guardians of Scotland. It is difficult to gauge Bruce's attitude to Wallace immediately prior to his capture since Wallace fought for John Balliol to the end. Meanwhile, the Earl of Dunbar was suffering Edward's displeasure yet again; this time, the king demanded that Dunbar pay £54:8:0 (£54.40) to Walter de Bedwynd, cofferer to the royal wardrobe, to balance a discrepancy in the royal funds. Dunbar was ordered to make good the deficit. The deficiency was apparently the fault of Ralph de Menton, late cofferer to the king; we can detect more than a hint of mismanagement or misappropriation of royal funds. Perhaps Dunbar and de Menton had been entertaining themselves at Edward's expense. Whether de Menton was alone responsible for the shortfall is not clear but his lands were sequestered. Edward wasn't known as *le roi coveyteux* for nothing; in 1305 several nobles sought financial help from him, Dunbar requesting money for the sustenance of his family and castle as his lands had been ravaged. Under feudal law, Dunbar was entitled to protection from his superior, Edward, who agreed to consider his request 'and do remedy at a fitting time.' We do not know if Dunbar received compensation but we do know that Edward refused to grant lands in Polwarth to Dunbar's son, Sir Patrick from a letter written on the king's behalf:

'The king is not advised to give his lands to any one.'[69]

By 1305, Scotland was at Edward's feet; her leadership lost heart and nobles submitted to Edward in droves in order to keep their lands. On 15th September, the king put forward his policy for governing Scotland.[70] The country was to be put under the supervision of a Lieutenant, a Chancellor, a Chamberlain and a Controller, with pairs of Justiciars - one Scottish, one English - in each of the judiciary regions. Lothian's Scottish Justiciar was Sir Adam de Gordon, a friend of Dunbar's. The Lieutenant was to work with a council of English officers, officials and 22 Scots - four bishops, four abbots, five earls including Dunbar and nine barons. Dunbar was one of ten commissioners who attended the English parliament in September to agree these arrangements; he had been appointed a commissioner in February but had inexplicably absented himself from a meeting,[71] sending John Stewart of Menteith in his place. The new arrangements were about to come into effect the following year when an incident at Dumfries on 10th February changed everything.

With Wallace the great patriot dead, what hope was there for Scotland? Once more, Bruce reconsidered his position. History presents us with several Robert Bruces; there is only one William Wallace. In that crucial year of 1306, Bruce became fully committed to Scotland. Widely recognised as one of the greatest Scottish and European kings, Robert the Bruce inspired his countrymen with a concept of nationhood by sheer force of personality and dedication. For all Wallace's stubborn and heroic resistance, everything he achieved was done in John Balliol's name, vested in his traditional and conservative view of the Scottish monarchy. Wallace's greatest gift was to lay the foundations of Bruce's ultimate victory as military king and statesman. If Bruce is regarded today as a great king, Wallace endures as an untarnished patriot.

Bruce might not have made his bid for the throne in 1306 if he hadn't learnt that an unnamed rival had accused him of treachery at Edward's court. Bruce left England in haste. If as is highly likely his accuser was John Comyn of Badenoch, the Red Comyn, there are no surviving records to confirm it. Abbot Bower of Inchcolm, pro-Bruce and a Scottish patriot tells us in his *Scotichronicon* that the subsequent murder of the Red Comyn at Dumfries was justified because he had 'slanderously given away Robert's secrets.' The statement is probably not without foundation. Some modern historians have conjectured that Comyn had given Edward I details of Bruce's movements in Galloway and that he had persuaded the Galwegians to rise against the English. Whatever the truth of it, the two rivals met at Greyfriars Church, Dumfries to discuss plans for renewing the struggle against Edward. It is believed they accused each other of treachery. Bruce lost his temper and wounded Comyn with his dagger at the altar - why were knights carrying weapons within a church? - one of Bruce's retinue finished him off or made 'siccar' [certain] Comyn was dead. This was the first of a series of setbacks for Bruce; he needed the Comyns' support, he was excommunicated from the Church for sacrilege and murder and he took the throne because - to quote a popular maxim of the time - 'necessity needs no law.'

It all went wrong from the outset. Alienating a powerful Scottish family was bad enough but no medieval king could afford to be excommunicated. Bruce lacked significant support among the nobility, many of whom regarded him as a mere Pretender who had turned his coat so many times he couldn't be trusted. The common people must have been appalled by his act in Greyfriars Church. And yet on 25th March 1306 - almost the tenth anniversary of the battle of Dunbar - Bruce had himself crowned at Scone. Even his coronation did not observe the traditional ceremonials; there was of course no Stone of Destiny and the Earl of Fife whose hereditary right it was to place the crown on the king's head was absent, supporting Edward.[72] Nobles such as the Earls of Ross, Angus and Sutherland who had hitherto promised to support Bruce deserted him. He could count on the support of less than a third of the nobility; even Bruce's great captain and nephew, Thomas Randolph, later 1st Earl of Moray, left his side after his defeat at Methven in 1306. His other great commander, James Douglas 'the Good Sir James' joined him only because Edward I refused to restore lands taken from his father; however, Douglas rightly considered the Bruce offered a reasonable prospect of regaining them.

In that heady year of 1306, the Dunbars were among the minority who refused to break with England, no matter what Bruce might have to offer. In an undated letter probably written in 1306[73] - the identities of the author and his correspondent are also unknown - Dunbar is described as having been 'assigned as warden of the counties of Roxburgh and Selkirk' and their castles. Perhaps because of prolonged absences from his base, the 8th Earl took the sensible precaution of storing his grain in the church at Dunbar for safekeeping so that he was able to feed his garrison.[74]

Bruce had reigned for less than six months when he suffered his first defeat at Methven, near Perth, on 20th June; many of his immediate family were made prisoners[75] while he became a fugitive in the heather, reputedly spending some time on Rathlin Island off the coast of Antrim,[76] one of several places where he is said to have studied arachnology in a cave. The following year brought some consolation; on 7th July, Edward I died at Burgh-on-Sands, leading yet another invasion of Scotland.

Dunbar and his eldest son were among the first to swear fealty to Edward II. Leaving for France in December, Edward invited several Scottish clergymen and nobles including the Dunbars to keep the peace in Scotland

and to obey its governor, the Earl of Richmond. The 8th Earl did not serve his new master long; he died on 10th October 1308 aged 66; he was survived by his redoubtable Countess, Marjorie Comyn. Perhaps his life can be summed up as one lived in the shadow of other, greater men, in timidity and self-preservation through association with England.

Patrick, 9th Earl of Dunbar and 2nd of March

Edward I's, then Edward II's policy towards Scotland was supported by the Dunbars until 1314, then some wavering occurred between 1333 and 1335. Patrick, 9th Earl of Dunbar remained firmly in the English camp possibly because of his father's influence and under his guidance. On 11th November 1308, an army raised in the northern counties of England and Scots under Dunbar, Robert de Keith and Alexander Abernethy descended on Galloway and 'freed' it from the ravages of Bruce, who was forced to retreat into the Highlands.

The 8th Earl of Dunbar had refused to join Wallace, considering him no better than an outlaw; it was patently obvious that his son would not join Bruce for the same reason. The 9th Earl had seen his father benefit from his adherence to England and he benefited also, receiving a cash payment for expenses defrayed in upholding a truce in 1308-09 between Edward II and Bruce,[77] although he would pay dearly for his loyalty to England. The East March was constantly raided for food, the resident English and their Scottish sympathisers' lands were terrorised which in turn meant loss of income for the Dunbars. To the nationalists, Dunbar was a traitor like his father; in his own eyes, he was honouring an oath of allegiance he had sworn first to Edward I, then his son. He considered Bruce a usurper and a murderer but one must ask why he refused to join the Comyns especially after Bruce murdered his mother's kinsman? The answer may have been in the territorial positions of their earldoms; the Comyns were relatively safe in the north, while Dunbar was insecure at England's front gate, vulnerable to attack at any time from both sides of the Border. In 1308, Comyn of Buchan did attempt to avenge the murder of the Red Comyn, attacking Bruce unsuccessfully at Inverurie. Whether the Earl of Dunbar expressed any sympathy for his murdered relative is not recorded.

What were East Lothian's politics between 1296 and 1314? Several historians have commented unfavourably on the county's apparent lack of interest or involvement in the independence movement. At first all of Lothian had declared for Balliol; the army defeated at Dunbar in 1296 contained many Lothian knights, although afterwards, many had little choice but to attach their seals to the *Ragman Roll*. Also, it must be remembered that Lothian and the Merse was the most anglicised area in Scotland. However, by 1308, many Lothian/Merse barons and knights began to loosen their ties with England, declaring for Bruce; among them were William de Vieuxpoint of Langton in the Merse - virtually the only fatal casualty among the nobles present at Bannockburn - Thomas Hay of Yester, Robert Keith de Marischal and Broun of Coalston, all from East Lothian. For the most part, Dunbar's tenants and vassals abided by their oaths of fealty to him as they were obliged under law. We have seen that there were exceptions however; for example, Dunbar's tenants in Coldingham defied him.

In 1311-12, *Chron. Lanercost* records that the men of the earldom of Dunbar 'in the king's [ie Edward II's] peace' paid heavily for 'immunity' from Bruce's foragers; that peace became progressively worthless, driving more and more local men to Bruce until by 1313, only the Earl of Dunbar and Sir Adam de Gordon supported Edward II - and even Gordon had begun to waver by then, as Bruce controlled the whole country save for Lothian and the Merse. *Chron. Lanercost* describes the pitiful state of Lothian in 1312. Soon a small civil war was in progress, with fathers fighting for Edward against sons fighting for Bruce and vice-versa. *Chron. Lanercost* adds that those Scots who remained with the English did so 'insincerely' or to preserve their English estates. The Border was open, with predators from both sides simply appropriating what they needed, irrespective of nationality or political persuasion.

Despite their continued occupation of Stirling and Edinburgh Castles and the defensive line of Dirleton, Yester, Dunbar, Berwick, Roxburgh, Jedburgh and Selkirk, the English were powerless to contain Bruce's roving bands. By 1313, sickened by the devastation inflicted by both sides, the lesser barons and knights in the south-east threw their lot in with Bruce which was of course his intention. In the rapidly deteriorating political climate, the 9th Earl of Dunbar should have seen the writing on the wall; for reasons best known to himself, he clung tenaciously to England, hoping for a dramatic reversal. Lothian was close to exhaustion; its rural population had been burnt out of their farms, crops were devastated or stolen and much of the livestock and horses were taken.[78] Dunbar's lands were at the mercy of forays from the Berwick garrison - supposedly his allies - which demanded ransom money and food at every turn; when Dunbar entertained Edward II to dinner at Dunbar Castle on the night of 31 October 1311,[79] he may have been confident about his position; by 1313, he was a desperate man.

On 26th January 1312, Dunbar, the Earl of Atholl, Alexander de Abernethy and Adam de Gordon attended an English parliament and were appointed as commissioners to negotiate a treaty with Bruce. This was the best Edward II could do to forestall the raids on his remaining Scottish possessions. The negotiations proved fruitless. By 1313, Lothian was fast approaching the end of its usefulness to either side. Dunbar clung stubbornly and unrealistically to the forlorn hope that England would save him; his lack of political acumen is clear; only his oath to Edward justified his continued support for England. At the beginning of 1313, Edward held 13 castles; by midsummer, only Stirling, Yester, Dirleton, Dunbar, Selkirk, Jedburgh and Berwick remained in English hands.

In the autumn of 1313, Dunbar had reached the end of his tether; he wrote a despairing letter to Edward II, complaining bitterly about the blackmail and plundering in his earldom,[80] amounting to a staggering £20,000 in the past three years. His letter is quoted in part below:

> 'Petition to the king from the people of Scotland [sic] by their envoys, Sir Patrick Dunbar, earl of March and Sir Adam de Gordon.....Matters are daily getting worse, and for the 'suffraunce' [freedom from molestation] they have till this Martinmas, they had to give 1000 qurs [quarters] of corn.
> Yet their livestock is plundered, partly by the enemy and partly by the garrisons of Berwick and Roxburgh, especially by Gilbert de Medilton [Middleton] and Thomas de Pencaitlande and their company at Berwick.....When 'upplaunde' [people from the hills] got to buy their 'vivers' [provisions] in Berwick, the garrison spy out and seize them, confining some in houses and carrying off others to Northumberland, holding them in concealment and 'duresce'[restraint] there till they get a ransom - and the Scots are fined in Northumberland for resetting them.......Some of them, at the end of the 'suffraunce' at midsummer purchased from Sir Robert de Bruys [Dunbar refuses to acknowledge Bruce as king] at his late coming, a truce of fifteen days, and on his retreat, after they had returned to their houses, the next morning the warden and the whole garrison of Berwick came and took the people in their beds, carrying them off dead and alive to Berwick, and held them to ransom, viz on this foray within the bounds of the earldom of Dunbar, both gentlemen and others, to the number of 30. Also 300 fat beasts, 4,000 sheep besides horses and dead stock....some of the Berwick garrison, with Thomas de Pencaitlande as 'Guyde'[guide] carried of [sic] some of the poor people to Berwick. Those who had wherewithal were ransomed; those who had nothing were killed and thrown into the Water of the Tweed.'[81]

A sorry tale indeed. But was it enough to bring Edward to Scotland? Dunbar's letter to Edward II may be yet another example of history's capricious accidents, as the immediate consequences for the earl following Bannockburn would prove.

Edward responded on 29th November,[82] promising an English army the following midsummer. According to most contemporary and modern histories, the invasion was about chivalry and honour; modern historians appear to have ignored the letter which Dunbar wrote to Edward, which must have had some effect. The official version is that in 1313, Bruce's brother Edward laid siege to Stirling Castle and its commander, Sir Philip de Mowbray negotiated an end to the siege; de Mowbray promised that if an English army did not appear within three leagues [nine miles] of the castle by Midsummer's Day 1314, he would hand it over to the Scots. Under the terms of chivalry, Edward II could not refuse the challenge but was Stirling vital to his continued occupation of the south-east of Scotland? It seems incredible that Edward - not noted for his enthusiasm for warfare - even contemplated invading Scotland, particularly Stirlingshire where only Stirling Castle was still in English hands. I am not convinced that chivalry was indeed the main reason behind Edward's invasion; many English knights and even pro-English Scots were growing tired of living in a country where guerrilla warfare brought sudden and bloody attacks.[83] Political credibility rather than chivalry demanded a response. The 9th Earl of Dunbar's impassioned letter was bound to have an effect on Edward's thinking, a fact which modern historians have either discounted or failed to appreciate.

For his part, Robert Bruce was alarmed by his brother's actions. He had no wish to fight a full-scale battle in defence of a castle he would have slighted. Bruce excelled in guerrilla warfare, recognising that he was unlikely to command a force large enough to engage Edward II in a pitched battle. Edward Bruce had forced him into this position and he was apprehensive that he would have to meet the English on their own terms. A defeat could easily topple him from his still far from secure throne.

In midsummer, only seven castles in Scotland remained in English hands and six were of little account, being in East Lothian and the Borders; even so, Edward could be reinforced or supplied by them. On 10th June, Edward assembled his army at Berwick. Estimates vary as to its size but most accounts accept that it consisted of 20,000 foot and archers and 2,000 cavalry. Bruce was about to face the greatest challenge of his reign with only 8,000 foot and 500 horse; his lack of cavalry was a significant weakness, so he knew he would have to pick ground which would reduce the effectiveness of the mounted English knights. Bannockburn was ideal, the area being marshy and criss-crossed by streams.

It is unnecessary here to go over the already well-trampled ground of the days of 23rd and 24th June 1314. Bannockburn was a signal victory of which any nation could be proud, even if the battle didn't immediately realise Bruce's dream of independence. On the eve of the battle, Bruce may have hoped that a Scottish victory would bring Edward II to the negotiating table at last. Bannockburn's political significance was that afterwards, Bruce was accepted as rightful king of Scotland and he commanded the respect of most of the nobles.

The destruction of the English army complete, Edward and the Earl of Pembroke attempted to seek refuge in Stirling Castle; they were politely refused entry by the honourable Sir Philip de Mowbray. The frustrated and terrified king forced his way through the mass of fleeing men with 500 horse, galloping from Stirling to Dunbar and hotly pursued by the Good Sir James Douglas and only 80 light horse - his knights shed their armour to travel faster. Edward could have easily withstood such a small force but he believed Sir James was the vanguard of a large body of Scottish horse. Douglas pressed the English so hard that they 'had not even time to make water.' [84]

With a greatly reduced escort, Edward managed to reach Dunbar Castle and vanished inside. Dunbar received the king 'full gently' but shocked by and apprehensive about Edward's defeat,[85] he could only offer the king a boat to take him to safety to Bamburgh Castle in Northumberland. It is fruitless to speculate on the exchange between Edward and Dunbar during their brief encounter. An account of Bannockburn written 42 years later states that those who managed to escape with Edward to Dunbar '....were saved; all the rest came to grief.[86] Patrick Dunbar received the king honourably and even put his castle at his disposal, removing all his people so that there would be no doubt nor suspicion that he would do nothing short of his devoir [duty] to his lord for at that time he was his liegeman. Thence the king went by sea to Berwick [sic] and afterwards to the south.' Even after England's defeat, Patrick remained loyal. He would soon discover how Edward rated his loyalty.

A contemporary English account of Bannockburn states that

> 'our costly belongings were ravished to the value of £200,000; So many fine noblemen and valiant youth.......all lost in one unfortunate day, one fleeing hour.......Assuredly the proud arrogance of our men made the Scots rejoice in their victory.'[87]

The colossal sum of money was lost in the capture of the baggage train.

Safe in England, Edward II's response to Dunbar's courtesy was swift and uncompromising, possibly persuaded by his court favourites that in writing to him the previous autumn, Dunbar's letter had been part of Bruce's strategy to entice him north. Edward was not noted for his political acumen and relied on favourites for advice. He denounced Dunbar as a traitor on 25th June - the very day after his flight from Dunbar Castle - and his English possessions were forfeit.[88] One has a measure of sympathy for a man who had worked himself into a heads-you-win-tails-I-lose situation. Dunbar was now regarded as hostile to Scotland and England. Had he been less chivalrous about his oath to Edward and made him his prisoner, his reward would have been great. Ingratiating himself with Bruce, he would have been undoubtedly enriched by lands forfeited by those Scottish nobles who were absent from the field of Bannockburn. As it was, Dunbar had little choice but to submit to Bruce, who extended his policy of leniency and moderation to late adherents - somewhat surprisingly in the circumstances - and welcomed him to his court.

Bruce's probation period was now at an end. Even the English chronicler at Lanercost referred to him as king of Scotland, although Edward refused to do so. At Cambuskenneth Abbey in November 1314, Bruce declared those earls, barons and knights who were not present at the field of Bannockburn and whose fealty to England remained would forfeit their Scottish estates. These men became known as the *Disinherited.* Bruce's words were uncompromising; all those who

> 'had not come into his faith and peace....are to be disinherited forever of lands and tenements and all other status in the realm of Scotland. And they are to be held in future as foes of the king and the kingdom, debarred forever from all claims of hereditable right....on behalf of themselves and their heirs.'[89]

Bruce also extended this decree to include the English lands held by Scottish nobles from Edward II so that no Scottish male or female could thereafter be subject to dual allegiance. This is an important point which to some extent undermines certain modern historians view that the ownership of English estates wasn't a major factor in the occasional lapses of loyalty in some Scottish nobles. It must be said that Bruce had scarcely a knight in his army at Bannockburn who at one time or another hadn't sworn allegiance to England for possessions they held there

Why in the light of this draconian but necessary *diktat* was Dunbar pardoned? It is likely that Bruce wanted Dunbar on his side, given the location of his earldom; he could have easily disinherited Dunbar and rewarded one of his more loyal supporters with the strategically important earldom. It is unlikely that he felt pity for

Dunbar but perhaps he was moved by his plight; more realistic was his need to have a stable East March from which he could mount expeditions into northern England. Even so, he could have achieved that by installing another earl who had proven more trustworthy - Thomas Randolph for example. Although he readily accepted Dunbar's submission, Bruce kept him at arms' length during the rest of his reign; in all of 200 royal charters, Dunbar witnessed less than 20, which is a telling comment. Even so, Dunbar attended the important parliament at Ayr on 27th April 1315 which formally settled the crown on Bruce and his heirs. Afterwards, the 9th Earl set about rebuilding Dunbar Castle which was partially dismantled shortly after Bannockburn to deny it to the English.

In 1318, Dunbar was with Douglas and Randolph at the siege of Berwick and according to one source 'James de Douglas with the assistance of Patrick, Earl of March, captured Berwick from the English by means of treason of one of the town, Piers de Spalding.'[90] Berwick fell on 28th March, although its castle held out until 20th July.

And then on 6th April 1320, almost six years after the justifiably exaggerated and resounding victory which should have ensured England's recognition of Scotland's sovereignty, the *Declaration of Arbroath* was sent to Pope John XXII. Dunbar's seal is among those of the first three signatories, one of eight earls and 31 barons. The *Declaration* ranks among the most significant documents in the history of Scotland and the Western world. It is unique not only because it asserts a nation's right to independence, it proclaims that right to the international community. It is also remarkable for its economy of words and therefore its clarity. The *Declaration of Arbroath* has been favourably compared with that other famous statement of personal freedom, the American *Declaration of Independence* in that it expresses the protest of a small nation against the illegal aggression of another larger one; *Arbroath* presents a direct and challenging promise that

'for as long as a hundred of us are left alive, we will never be subject to the domination of England. It is not for glory, riches or honour that we fight, but for that liberty which no good man will consent to lose but with his life.'

No mention of God, nor of the Divine Right of His will. Propaganda and a surrogate Scottish constitution it may be; rhetorical it most certainly is but the text is free from judicial, legalistic and bureaucratic language which would have detracted from the directness of its message. If the *Marseillaise* comes closest to expressing the comradeship of common citizens in arms, the *Declaration of Arbroath* evokes a similar response from the soldier-nobles of Scotland who were sworn to defend the common man.

The document was taken to the Pope John in Avignon appropriately by Sir Adam de Gordon who received as reward the lordship of Strathbogie, thus transplanting a Border family to the north.[91] However, the *Declaration of Arbroath* did not discourage England's ambitions regarding Scotland; nor did it achieve its primary purpose - that of persuading the Pope to remove the sentence of excommunication from Bruce. Even so, a thirteen-year truce was agreed at York in May 1323 - ostensibly giving Bruce a breathing space to consolidate his kingdom - until Edward II was dethroned in 1326 then murdered in 1327 by his queen Isabella and her lover Roger Mortimer who governed England during Edward III's minority.

The truce had almost expired when Edward III was crowned on 1st February 1327, although Bruce, in failing health, technically broke it by unsuccessfully besieging Norham Castle and making minor raids in the north of England which were not serious enough to bring England to the conference table. Perhaps it was Douglas and Randolph who persuaded Bruce to abandon his ineffective raids in favour of annexing English territory in the north. The Scots invaded Westmoreland and the fifteen year-old Edward III took to the field in what became known as the Weardale Campaign. For England, the invasion was pure impudence and ignominy; the boy-king was led up hill and down dale by Douglas who mocked him at one point by positioning himself so close to the English that only a rain-swollen river separated the two armies. Then Douglas attacked the English camp at Stanhope Park and Edward III was nearly taken prisoner. The young king was learning bitter lessons in warfare; on 6th April 1327, the entire Scottish army simply melted away during the night, leaving large bonfires and two trumpeters in their abandoned camp. By the time the English discovered they had been tricked, Douglas was safely away with his booty, met by a relief force led by the Earls of Dunbar and Angus, sent south by an anxious Bruce. The impetuous Edward was said to have burst into tears as he returned to York empty-handed. Loss of face induced Edward to concede to Bruce's demands and on 17th March 1328, the Scottish king set his seal to what became known as the Treaty of Northampton. Its terms insisted on the recognition of Bruce as rightful king of an independent Scotland, restored the Border to that during Alexander III's reign and provided for the marriage of Bruce's son David to Edward's sister Joan. Ratified by Isabella and Mortimer on Edward's behalf, the treaty was in effect the quitclaim of English overlordship of Scotland. The English considered it a humiliating failure of arms.

At the eleventh hour, Bruce finally achieved his objective. For all his flawed character and changes of heart during Wallace's time, Bruce was one of the greatest medieval kings of Scotland. He had surmounted incredible obstacles; he is almost a romantic figure in the mould of king Arthur of Camelot; patient, wise, diplomatic, daring and courageous, he inspired his countrymen as no other king before him. His greatest fault lay in his policy of dissipating his royal authority amongst the nobles, a policy which would become the curse of the Stewart dynasty of kings who followed him. At the end of his reign, there was harmony among the leading Scottish families. A giant of a man, Bruce is proof of the truism that he whom propaganda makes mighty no man can readily cast aside. He needed no empty propaganda however; his heroic resistance, unflinching will and a conviction in the rightness of his cause finally restored Scotland's sovereignty - at least for a few years. At least he lived to realise his dream of a free Scotland; it is thought he died of leprosy in 1329. He was succeeded by his son David, by his second wife, Elizabeth de Burgh.

Absolute peace was not achieved however. Border bickering - usually the benchmark for the imminence of resumed warfare between the two countries - continued for the next four years. On 3rd February 1331,[92] Edward wrote to David II requesting that the Earl of Dunbar evacuate his armed occupation of Uppsettlington opposite Norham Castle. The Border was restless which gave Edward an excuse to resume hostilities, intent on subjugating Scotland once more. He wrote to David again, intimating that he would meet him at Berwick on 18th March; similar letters were sent to the leading Scottish nobles including the Earls of Fife, Dunbar and Moray. Edward knew he could not press his ambitions too robustly however as the compensation the Scots had agreed to pay the English Treasury under the Treaty of Northampton would not be paid in full until midsummer 1331, after which Edward could afford to be more aggressive. Besides, Edward had a key card to play; he was creating what today would be termed a fifth column in Scotland, men who were only too eager to assist him. The *Disinherited* of Bannockburn.

After their alienation by Bruce, the *Disinherited* had lived as exiles in England under their leader, Edward Balliol, son of the deposed king. The *Disinherited* were predominantly Scottish but also included some English knights excluded like the *Disinherited* Scots from the Treaty of Northampton; these men were intent on recovering their Scottish estates and to make Edward Balliol king of Scotland. They easily convinced Edward III of the justness of their demands. Edward, an impetuous but politically astute king disguised his political aspirations under the cloak of chivalry. Although not strong enough in his own kingdom to launch an all-out invasion of Scotland, his support for the *Disinherited* was a cheaper option in perpetuating the war.

Edward Balliol and his force of between 1,500 and 2,000 sailed into the Firth of Forth in August 1332; landing at Kinghorn in Fife, he marched unopposed to Perth.[93] Thomas Randolph, Earl of Moray, [94] regent during David II's minority had died at Musselburgh on 20th July - not without suspicion of poisoning according to some accounts - and was succeeded by the less popular Earl of Mar. There are indications that Balliol expected covert assistance from Mar who sympathised with several nobles among the *Disinherited.* The Earl of Dunbar was given command of the south-east forces; aware of Mar's sympathies, he must have felt less than confident of success against Balliol.

Mar took up position near the river Earn, on the heights of Dupplin Moor. On the night of 10th/11th August, the Scots were so sure of victory that they began drinking heavily. At midnight, one of Balliol's captains, Sir Alexander Mowbray, led a picked force over the Earn at a ford shown to him by Murray of Tulliebardine, a traitor from the Scottish camp. In the ensuing battle, Mar's superiority in numbers proved fatal. Dupplin Moor was a wild and desperate fight in which numbers were a hindrance; more Scots were killed by their own men as the front line collapsed, crushed underfoot by those who followed them. Among the dead was a bastard son of Robert Bruce who had openly accused Mar of treachery; galloping towards Balliol's men, he was killed instantly. Estimates of casualties ranged from between 2,000 to 13,000 to Balliol's 35. It was the worst defeat for Scotland since Wallace's disaster at Falkirk.

Dunbar's army was about as strong as Mar's and intact; he could have easily defeated Balliol's meagre force but there was uncertainty in Dunbar's camp; honesty and national pride were the real casualties at Dupplin Moor. The sight of the Scots dead - piled it is said higher than a spear's height - may have unnerved Dunbar. He decided not to face the English archers and blockaded of Perth. Balliol's position was precarious; he knew escape or reinforcement lay in the Firth of Tay, his ships guarded by Henry de Beaumont. The fleet was attacked by John Crabb, a Flemish sailor and engineer in the pay of the Scots who captured Beaumont's flagship. Then the English recovered and destroyed Crabb's force, securing Balliol's escape route by sea.

Dunbar has been censured for not attacking Balliol at Dupplin Moor but it is doubtful whether further numbers would have affected the outcome. He had thrown his force across the Firth of Forth in haste, marched through Stirlingshire and camped at Auchterarder, some eight miles from Balliol's position at Forteviot. Perhaps his intention was to outflank Balliol who recognised that he had to prevent Dunbar and Mar from joining forces.

Dunbar and Sir Archibald Douglas made painfully slow progress after Balliol, marching to Perth too leisurely for some of his critics. Dunbar undoubtedly felt less secure with the regents Moray and Mar dead and David II in his minority. He may have been hedging his bets, hoping to regain his English possessions by not menacing Balliol over robustly.

At Perth, Dunbar unaccountably halted his army some distance away from the town; he placed faggots in the defensive ditches beneath the town wall, giving the impression that he planned to storm the town, then did nothing. *Chron. Wyntoun* records that the English 'saw friends in Dunbar's army.' In fairness, Dunbar had no idea of the size of Balliol's force; it had destroyed Mar's army and John Crabb's ten ships had failed to capture Balliol's fleet at the mouth of the Tay on 24th August. Dunbar and Douglas abandoned Perth after a few days, giving as reason a revolt in support of Balliol in Galloway; they were joined by the recently appointed regent Andrew Murray and marched off to loot and take cattle. The 'seige' lifted, Balliol left a small garrison in the town and proceeded to Scone, where he had himself crowned king. Perth was relieved by the nationalist Scots in October, when Murray of Tulliebardine was executed for treason.

Balliol left Scone for Roxburgh, establishing lines of communication with Edward III. Over the next two months, he issued charters which declared Scotland a vassal state of England. However, his arrogance did not go unchallenged; in December 1332, Sir Archibald Douglas and John Randolph, 3rd Earl of Moray attacked Balliol at Moffat. The 'king' narrowly avoided capture, escaping across the Border partially clothed on an unbridled horse.

But matters got worse in 1333, when Berwick surrendered to the English. Tytler's *History of Scotland* blames Dunbar for its loss, stating that 'Berwick was imprudently committed' to Dunbar's keeping. If that were so, why did the 9th Earl of Dunbar repair and strengthen the town wall and the castle defences, even requisitioning a load of timber bound for the Franciscan Friars at Roxburgh?[95]

Balliol, still smarting from his ignominious flight from Moffat besieged Berwick in March and was joined by Edward III in May. The engineer John Crabb who had failed to destroy Balliol's small fleet the year before had by now switched sides; he knew the Berwick defences well, having assisted Bruce in the siege of 1318. Archibald Douglas, now Guardian of Scotland, was faced with a dilemma all too familiar for the time - the terms under which Berwick would surrender if it wasn't relieved by a Scottish army. In the game of war, these terms were typical of the period. A Scottish army was required to relieve Berwick from the Scottish side of the Tweed; alternatively, if a single division of 200 Scottish men-at-arms entered Berwick between sunrise and sunset with the loss of no more than thirty men, the siege would be lifted. If neither of these conditions was met by 20th July, Dunbar was pledged to surrender the town and its castle. Edward was executing two hostages each day, one of whom was the third and only surviving son of the town's commander, Alexander Seton, who watched his son being hanged; that would stop when Dunbar gave up the town.

The loss of Berwick in 1318 had become a matter of honour for Edward III. The Guardian Archibald Douglas - known as the Tyneman [Loser] - had little choice but to fight the English king on difficult ground. Edward's men occupied the crest of Halidon Hill, the 500-foot high moor dominating the approach to Berwick. His army was arranged in three divisions or battles; the left flank was commanded by Edward Balliol, Edward held the centre and Sir Henry de Bohun commanded the right and seaward flank; the three flanks were protected by archers.

Douglas confronted Edward on 19th July, the day before the surrender terms would take effect. The battle began badly from the start; the three Scottish divisions had to march downhill, cross a marsh, then climb Halidon Hill. The troops were exhausted even before they struck a blow; as they struggled up the hill, the English archers took their toll. Finally, when the Scots engaged Balliol's wing, the second division had to stand by, ineffective because of their inability to deploy. Douglas commanded the third division with 200 hand-picked men-at-arms ready to storm into Berwick and lift the siege. During the battle, Dunbar sent Douglas 50 men-at-arms, a useless gesture which had no effect on the outcome.

Halidon Hill was a battle lost before it began. Douglas suffered a defeat not repeated until Flodden nearly 200 years later. He and many prominent nobles were killed; the lowest estimate of casualties was 14,000.[96] The survivors were pursued through Berwickshire, some running into the sea to avoid capture. Berwick's fate was sealed; both castle and town surrendered when news of the defeat was formally announced in the market place.

Even before Halidon Hill was fought, the Earl of Dunbar had reconsidered his position. Before the battle, he and 80 landed gentry had extracted letters of protection from Edward. In the subsequent negotiations, Edward granted Dunbar, his Countess Agnes and their male heirs £100 of English land on 28th July;[97] any of Dunbar's tenants who refused to swear allegiance to England would forfeit their lands to those who did. Dunbar was a broken reed, following the prevailing wind. In addition to receiving English land, he was permitted to repair his slighted castle of Dunbar at England's expense. Ironically, this would have consequences for the English forces occupying the south-east in 1338, as will be seen. Despite the censure of several historians for his actions at Berwick, Dunbar had no intention of remaining in the English camp for longer than necessary. In 1333, it was said that he had no preference for either side.[98]

Holinshed's *Chronicles of Englande, Scotlande and Irelande* tells us that in 1333, the Earl of Dunbar was ordered to rebuild his castle at Dunbar

> 'upon his own costs and charges, for that he had thrown it down, when he saw that he was not able to defend it against the English power cumming toward him'

Holinshed wrote this in the sixteenth century, possibly in an attempt to save Edward III's face for allowing a mere Scottish earl to outwit him; the records are precise and show that Dunbar received a sum of 600 marks from the English Treasury in 1333-34.[99]

In 1333, Robert the Bruce would have found much to disappoint him. While Edward III concentrated his energies on bestowing honours on his victorious knights and holding feasts and tournaments, Edward Balliol was given authority to subdue Scotland. Balliol had never forgotten or forgiven those who had chased him out of Scotland or those who supported Bruce who disinherited him and subsequently favoured some of his English confederates.[100] However, for some reason, Dunbar benefited from Balliol's policies; he was allowed to extract rents from the tenants of those lands forfeited by Scottish tenants who refused to accept Edward III's peace.[101,102] It is to Dunbar's discredit that he was one of the seven Scottish nobles[103] present at the obsequious parliament of February 1334 - Alexander Seton who had lost all three sons fighting the English was also present - to witness Balliol's proclamation of 12th June 1334 which ceded 2,000 librates of Scottish land to England 'for ever'; the area he handed over stretched from the Solway Moss to the Firth of Forth and included the important castles of Edinburgh, Roxburgh, Berwick and Dunbar.

The Bruce faction under Sir Andrew Murray who had ransomed himself out of an English prison staged a minor uprising and the nationalist cause flickered into life again. Balliol was beset by other problems caused by quarrelling supporters, one or two of whom defected to Murray. Once more, the Earl of Dunbar found himself the sole Scottish noble in the English camp; whatever his private thoughts on the future, he was busily milking the English Treasury of money, payments which continued until November 1334.[104]

Then suddenly, Dunbar returned to the nationalist camp in February 1335. Not unexpectedly, his Northumbrian knights' fees from his lands there were forfeited and given to Henry Percy, Earl of Northumberland;[105] then he lost his manors in Duns and Chirnside in August 1335,[106] followed by several possessions between Cockburnspath, seven miles south of Dunbar and Markle, five miles north of it, since technically, he held his earldom by virtue of his fealty to the English crown. From 1335, the 9th Earl of Dunbar would fight the English at every opportunity

Edward's response was to come north to Carlisle, from where he mounted a robust campaign in July, moving into the south-west and plundering Roxburgh and other nearby towns. At the same time, Edward Balliol advanced from Berwick up the east coast, followed by Guy de Namur[107] and 2,000 Flemish mercenaries. Namur had arrived too late to join the main body and he was harried on his way to Edinburgh by the Earl of Dunbar, Douglas of Liddesdale and Randolph of Moray.[108] On 30th July, Namur was attacked in strength by Dunbar, Douglas, Randolph and Ramsay of Dalhousie. A brief running fight developed [109] until Namur disengaged and led his command up what is now Edinburgh Castle's Esplanade to seek refuge in the ruins of the castle.[109] The beleaguered Flemings slaughtered their horses to form a barricade but disheartened by their losses, lack of food and water, they surrendered the following day. Young Randolph, who had inherited the earldom of Moray on the death of his brother at Dupplin Moor, chivalrously offered to escort Namur to the Border. Acompanied by James and William Douglas - and Dunbar for part of the way - Moray and the Douglases were ambushed by a raiding party of English soldiers out of Roxburgh. James Douglas was killed, William escaped and Moray was taken prisoner, first to Bamburgh, then to Windsor Castle;[110] he would remain in captivity until 1341 and was used as a bargaining counter in the siege of Dunbar in 1338.

The 9th Earl of Dunbar 'lightly esteemed by all parties' in 1333 prosecuted the war for the nationalists with all the bitter righteousness of the convert. In addition to losing his English possessions, his Scottish lands were also declared forfeit - on parchment at least.[111] Towards the end of 1335, the nationalist cause was beginning to founder; there was disaffection among the nobles and a small civil war flared up between Balliol's supporters led by David de Strathbogie who was gradually gaining ground; Strathbogie had been forced to transfer his allegiance from Balliol to David II [112] but he had returned to the Balliol cause after the Peace of Perth in August 1335, when he swore allegiance to him and thereby regaining the earldom of Atholl; he was also appointed Constable of Scotland. In the autumn of 1335, Strathbogie raised a small army and with some siege engines, set off to conquer the north-east in Balliol's name. His plan was simple; he intended to oust the Bruce following, replacing them with the heirs of the *Disinherited.* Being autumn, every knight and cottar alike was at the harvest; Strathbogie's campaign was marked by burning ricks and slaughtered cattle. Then he halted at Kildrummy Castle and laid siege to it; sheltering inside was David II's aunt, Christian Bruce, the wife of Sir Andrew Murray, the son of the patriot who had fought alongside Wallace in 1297 and now appointed Guardian of Scotland as a consequence of the capture of the young Earl of Moray. Strathbogie took Kildrummy's captain prisoner and forced him to agree that that the castle would be surrendered on 30th November - St Andrew's Day - if not relieved by then.

Sir Andrew Murray was at Bathgate, negotiating with Balliol's commissioners when the news reached him; he broke off the talks and marched north with 800 men, among them the Earl of Dunbar, Douglas of Liddesdale and Sir Alexander Seton. Learning of the relief column, Strathbogie withdrew from Kildrummy to bivouac in the Forest of Culblean, where he positioned his forces on the main approach road at the top of a hill. Sir John of Craig, Kildrummy's commander and 300 of the garrison shadowed Strathbogie, linking up with Murray on 30th November.

Early on St Andrew's Day, Murray split his force; he commanded one half and Douglas the other. A half-asleep sentry in Strathbogie's camp heard the sound of approaching armour and in the growing light, the camp was made ready for an attack in the rear. On that grey autumn morning, a force of 1,000 men from the Lothians, the Merse and elsewhere stood in the Forest of Culblean, awaiting their orders.[113] Strathbogie attacked Douglas in a headlong charge reminiscent of the fight at Dunbar in 1296. As the two groups clashed, Murray pressed forward with his battalion and in the ensuing fight, his men chased Strathbogie into the wood. It was soon over; attended by five of his knights, Strathbogie placed his back against an oak tree and fought bravely until he fell mortally wounded, pierced by several swords.

Culblean was no Bannockburn but it brought back shades of its glory; it gave Murray the courage to continue the struggle. It was the turning-point in the third War of Independence. The struggle was no longer one of loyalty to Edward Balliol or David Bruce but to Scotland. Culblean was a victory in the north achieved by men from the Lowlands, the Earl of Dunbar playing a major part. The fight was a matter of honour for the men of Lothian and the Merse, so long accused of being in the pocket of the English. Even the chroniclers of later years would look back on Culblean as a decisive factor in the struggle for Scotland's independence.

Dunbar's role at Culblean would cost him dearly; his earldom was again occupied by English troops although it is unlikely that they took the town of Dunbar, defended by its strong castle. Dunbar Castle was about to know its greatest hour in Scotland's history.

After the death of his wife Ermigarda who bore him two sons, only one of whom grew to manhood, Dunbar married Agnes Randolph, the elder of the late Earl of Moray's two daughters. Black Agnes was the great-neice of Robert Bruce and daughter-in-law of Marjorie Comyn who had resisted the English in 1296. According to *Pitscottie, Hist.*and others, she was swarthy like the Black Douglas; however, the patrynomic of Agnes and Douglas may derive from heraldry, as the heraldic colour black - sable - signifies constancy. The date of Agnes' marriage to the 9th Earl of Dunbar is uncertain but a papal dispensation dated 16th January 1324 from Pope John XXII allowed them to marry despite being cousins and within the forbidden degrees of consanguinity. Agnes inherited her father's fierce nationalism; she hated the English with impunity, having lost two of her three brothers fighting them. While a woman's political opinions didn't carry much weight openly in medieval Scotland, it is certain that she encouraged her husband to fight against England at every opportunity. Although Agnes' star burnt briefly, the light it cast over a war-weary Scotland was an inspiration to her countrymen. She is remembered not only in Dunbar or Scotland for her heroic defence of Dunbar Castle in 1338.

Mainstream Scottish history touches the siege of Dunbar briefly; most accounts are sparing in assessing its significance. Why was Dunbar the focal point and not some other castle like Roxburgh or even Stirling? The reality is that after Edward III rebuilt Edinburgh Castle, he lost interest in the subordinate strongholds in the south-east - Dunbar, Roxburgh and Berwick - as he regarded Edinburgh as the key to controlling the area and allowing continued English occupation of East Lothian. The events leading to the siege of Dunbar are straightforward; by 1337, Edward was more interested in his ambitions in France than in Scotland, probably because France offered more likelihood of financial gain since Scotland was financially and physically exhausted. Edward also unrealistically entertained hopes of the French crown. With Edinburgh in English hands, Dunbar assumed a new importance for the Scots as it kept open the lines of communication with France. However, to allow him to prosecute his French aims in 1338 - the start of the Hundred Years' War - Edward appointed Thomas de Beauchamp, Earl of Warwick as his lieutenant representing 'the person of the lord King' in Scotland.[114]

Throughout 1337, the Earl of Dunbar campaigned alongside Sir Andrew Murray in Fife and Lanarkshire, reducing every castle which held out for Edward Balliol or Edward III. *Chron. Fordun* tells us that in the summer of that year, Lothian suffered wholesale destruction at the hands of Scots and English alike; the ineffective Beauchamp was replaced by Richard Fitzalan, Earl of Arundel and William Montague, Earl of Salisbury; Arundel and Salisbury were appointed joint commanders of the English forces in south-east Scotland.[115] Probably aware that the Earl of Dunbar was campaigning in central Scotland, the two commanders planned to attack and capture Dunbar which they considered a threat to the stability of the south-east. Their strategy was also aimed at relieving pressure on other English garrisons. A morale-boosting course of action, it appeared to offer a good chance of success and would have the effect of subduing the entire area at little cost and dissuading the Scots from challenging English authority in the district.

The plan might well have succeeded but for the young, spirited Countess of Dunbar, Black Agnes Randolph.[116] Agnes had been left in charge of Dunbar while her husband was campaigning with Murray - one hostile account accuses Dunbar of having 'cautiously absented himself' from Dunbar which is patently untrue. We know that Dunbar and Douglas of Liddesdale defeated an English force at Panmure, then slighted the castles at St Andrews and Leuchars and Falkland Tower. When the siege of Dunbar was well under way, Murray received siege engines from France which enabled him to reduce the formidable Bothwell Castle in Lanarkshire.[117]

The siege of Dunbar was a medieval set-piece affair. It began in January 1338 and lasted for 155 days until 16th June.[118] William Montague, Earl of Salisbury and Richard Fitzalan, Earl of Arundel, with a corps of military engineers and 4,000 men began the siege on 13th January. Agnes with her small garrison of 40 men knew it was unlikely that any help would be forthcoming from outside; time was on her side however as the castle appears to have been well-provisioned in anticipation and there was a ready supply of fish from the sea. The siege would last longer than that of Stirling in 1304. Salisbury knew Agnes was in sole command but he badly misjudged her tenacity, even if he knew of her temperament. In 1337, Agnes' brother John - the only remaining male heir to the earldom of Moray - was imprisoned in the Tower of London after his capture in 1335. Agnes wrote to him there on 3rd June; her letter attracted the personal interest of Edward III. The king commanded Nicholas de la Beche in the Tower to allow Adam de Cailly, an English captive released from Dunbar to deliver her letter to John Randolph; however, de la Beche was ordered to examine the contents and to send it to the king or his counsel 'if it contains anything sinister or notable.'[119] Clearly, Agnes' reputation was well known to the English.

The main reason Agnes held out for so long is obvious; it was a combination of grit, determination and stubborn refusal to give in. Although Dunbar Castle was reckoned the strongest in the area, it was Agnes and the men she commanded who frustrated the English aggressors; to misquote Oscar Wilde slightly, stone walls do not a castle make. Agnes inspired her small force by her personality and courage; Dunbar would prove an unforgiving experience for England in general and Salisbury and Arundel in particular.

At the time of the siege, the Blockhouse to the west of the castle did not exist so the rock could have been used as a natural platform for archers and perhaps even a small siege engine. The Castle Park also provided an excellent field of fire for the heavy siege equipment to batter away at the entrance since only a frontal attack was likely to meet with success. The sketches by Miller, Grose and others (see Chapter 1) give an impression of the castle of 1497-50 but the version in 1338 would not have differed greatly from it. Probably having its own water supply, well-stocked larders and an endless supply of fresh fish, the castle was protected on three sides by the sea. Even if breaches had been made in its curtain walls by the crude siege engines of the time, the attackers faced a 30-40 foot climb with no shelter from the garrison's arrows, spears, rocks and boiling oil. Salisbury - or Montague, as Agnes addressed him during the siege - knew that he must destroy the barbican or starve the occupants into submission. To ensure the latter, he anchored two Genoese galleys and some smaller craft in a semi-circle off the north aspect of the castle; these were manned round the clock by crossbowmen.

Thus Dunbar was sealed off by land and sea. Salisbury maintained a constant barrage with his siege machines; *mangonels* - the crude artillery of the day styled on the Roman *ballista* - catapulted large rocks against the walls to little effect. Salisbury's crossbowmen were probably stationed on the Blockhouse rock, protected by *pavises* - large moveable wooden shields normally used to protect those whose task it was to in-fill defensive ditches with *fascines*, or bundles of faggots. We also know from a crude couplet attributed to Agnes that Salisbury used a *sow* or battering ram with a stout wooden roof to protect the sappers attempting to undermine the walls at their base.

Salisbury had the services of the Flemish engineer John Crabb, former Scottish mercenary but in English pay since the fall of Berwick in 1333.[120] He had brought with him William Hurley from London; Hurley was a carpenter whose specialty was the construction of siege machines. One account states that Hurley dismantled 'a great siege engine in the Tower of London' and brought it to Dunbar with four expert carpenters and three smiths for its reassembly.[121] With the heavy machines pounding away daily and escape by sea impossible, Salisbury believed it was only a matter of time before Agnes surrendered.

A lesser spirit might have succumbed. Agnes thrived on adversity and challenge, becoming ever more defiant as the days wore on. Perhaps like Louis XIV who, when queen Anne of Britain declared war on France in 1702 at the outbreak of the War of the Spanish Succession, Salisbury was moved to comment that he must be getting old 'when ladies declare war on me.' If he did, it was appropriate. At age 25, Agnes was in her prime and nothing Salisbury quite literally threw at her daunted her. Described by one chronicler as a 'manly heroine,' she was a born leader, combining spirit with flamboyance while keeping her head. Daily, she walked along the battlements, encouraging her small force of men-at-arms and archers and taunting the English below. On at least one occasion, she is said to have ordered her housemaids to dust the walls when they were struck by stone missiles. Salisbury soon realised that his *mangonels* were having little effect so he changed tactics.

The vulnerable point of most castles was the barbican or front gate. Salisbury used the *sow* - virtually a reinforced shed on rollers - to protect the sappers who with their mining equipment began to chip away at the foundations at the gate. Advancing with massed archers and crossbowmen to keep the defenders from the walls, the *sow* lumbered forward; the work had barely begun when Agnes, with complete disregard for her safety, leant over the battlements and reputedly delivered two lines of what was hopefully her only attempt at poetry:

'Beware Montagow
For farrow sall [shall] thy sow.' [122]

She then ordered a massive boulder to be dropped over the wall, crushing the machine, reputedly shouting 'behold, the litter of English pigs!' [123] but this is probably embellishment added later by the Scottish chroniclers.

Salisbury tried everything, even blackmail. He sent to London for Agnes' brother John; on 12th April, young Moray was brought in chains before the castle and shown to his sister. Salisbury threatened to execute him on the spot unless Agnes surrendered. Her response was brief and dramatic; she said the castle belonged to her lord and that while it was in her custody, she would never give it up unless he ordered it. Then she called Salisbury's bluff; she said she had everything to gain from her brother's death as he was the last male heir to the earldom of Moray which she would inherit.[124] Salisbury sent John Randolph back to England probably with mixed feelings about his sister.

Salisbury then attempted a more subtle approach; he bribed the castle gatekeeper to allow a small party of men under his personal command to enter the castle gate. The gatekeeper took the English gold, then informed his mistress of the plan. Agnes let a few soldiers inside the gate, then dropped the portcullis, trapping them. Salisbury escaped capture because one of his young esquires, John de Copeland begged the honour of going in first.[125] Copeland was taken prisoner and Agnes called out to the frustrated commander

'Adieu Monsieur Montagow; I intended that you should have supped with us, and
assisted in defending this fortress against the robbers of England.' [126]

One further incident illustrates Salisbury's frame of mind at the end of the siege. One summer morning he was before the castle, accompanied by a knight in full armour when a Scottish defender, William Spens, shot an arrow at them, killing the knight immediately. Salisbury reputedly withdrew the arrow, remarking

'There comes one of my lady's tire-pins; Agnes' love-shafts go straight to the heart.' [127]

But sieges could not last indefinitely; for all her resilience, Agnes was running out of food. The nationalist forces knew of the siege but were unable to break the English blockade. Elements of a relief force were forced to sit in the hills, watching the events from afar. The same force did however manage to frustrate two attempts to reinforce Salisbury. The first English column was routed by Laurence Preston, the second by William Keith of Gaston. After these failures, Salisbury assaulted the castle 'more sharply, with more serious attacks' [128] possibly urged on by Henry Percy of Northumberland who at some point had joined him, certainly by 28th April. [129]

Then literally at the eleventh hour, one resilient Scottish baron found a way to relieve Agnes. Sir Alexander Ramsay of Dalhousie set off from the Bass Rock one moonless night with 40 men and a boatload of provisions; probably with muffled oars, Dalhousie managed to slip past the cordon of Genoese galleys and other vessels. *Miller, Dunbar* maintains that Dalhousie entered the castle by means of a postern near the sea; this may have been the stairway to the gatehouse at the east side of the forework.

When Dalhousie arrived, the siege had entered its twenty-second week. An exasperated Salisbury was making no progress, his own stores were dwindling and by now, the empty town of Dunbar was stripped of any food. Starvation, Salisbury's original weapon to reduce the castle was now staring his own men in the face. On the morning of Dalhousie's arrival, Agnes ordered newly-baked white bread to be catapulted into Salisbury's camp, a direct way of letting him know that she had been relieved. The English commander finally conceded defeat.

Edward III had of course learnt of the time it was taking to reduce Dunbar; he was impatient and required

Salisbury's men for a forthcoming expedition to France. He came north and reputedly held a war conference at Whitekirk, urging Salisbury and Arundel to renew their attack on Dunbar. However, when he learnt that Dalhousie had brought fresh supplies into the castle, Edward accepted the reality of the situation. Contemporary English chronicles maintain that Salisbury was ordered to England on 16th June;[130] there is more than a hint of face-saving in this. Before the retreat began, Dalhousie had remained only one night at Dunbar; some contemporary accounts have him leading an 'army' out of Dunbar Castle and inflicting a serious defeat on Salisbury but this is highly improbable. The garrison numbered only 40 men and Dalhousie had brought only another 40 with him.[131,132] Dalhousie's legend was secure for posterity without such embellishments.

The siege of Londonderry in 1689 lasted 105 days and the population was reduced to eating cats, dogs and even rats; Dunbar had held out for an incredible 155 days, bettered only by another famous siege - Baden-Powell's 187 days at Mafeking during the Boer War in 1899-1900. The defenders at Dunbar appear to have been well-fed throughout most of their siege however. Agnes is commemorated in *Chron. Wyntoun*; Andrew Wyntoun's long pastoral poem is certainly rooted in fact; the verse he dedicated to Agnes was modernised by Sir Walter Scott as follows:

'She kept a stir in tower and trench
That brawling, boisterous Scottish wench.
Came I early, came I late,
I found Agnes at the gate.'[133]

It would be wrong to say of medieval women of status that they were mere supervisors of their husbands' households; they may appear to have played a subsidiary role but in truth, many were strong-willed and had firm opinions of their own. Agnes may not be unique in medieval social history but she is certainly amongst the bravest of her sex - then and since. We do not know what Edward III said of her; his words are not important for he expressed himself directly when he ordered Salisbury and Arundel back to England.[134] Dunbar remained intact. The siege cost the English Treasury £6,000,[135] a considerable sum for the time; it ended in a truce which would last until Martinmas 1339.[136] An English chronicler wrote ruefully that the siege and its outcome had been

'wasteful and neither honourable nor secure, but useful and advantageous to the Scots,'[137]

Edward III, now completely preoccupied with matters in France, was able to release some of his forces from guard duty in Scotland because of the truce which of course also benefited the Scots who were thus able to continue reducing castles and towers still holding out for Edward Balliol. Perth was captured for David II by the Robert the Steward and Earls of Dunbar and Ross on 17th August 1338. Agnes Dunbar's triumph was yet another boost to the morale of the nationalists; looked at in the broad context of Scottish history, Dunbar was a sideshow although if it had fallen, the setback to the nationalist cause would have been damaging. England would have won a victory of immeasurable propaganda value and allowed their continued occupation of the south-east. Even so, Edward still held six castles including Edinburgh, Stirling, Roxburgh and Berwick but from 1338, the trickle of Scots who deserted Balliol became a flood.

As for the principal characters in the siege of Dunbar, William Montague, Earl of Salisbury was dead by 1344. Alexander Ramsay of Dalhousie continued to fight the English from Hawthornden, his base in Midlothian. The Dalhousie family maintained a Dunbar connection; in 1364, his nephew Sir Patrick held lands in Easter Spott, first granted by the 9th Earl of Dunbar to his constable, Alexander de Ryklington. As for Alexander Dalhousie himself, he met a tragic end in 1341; he was appointed warden of the East March by a well-meaning David II as reward for taking Roxburgh Castle from the English that year. David also gave him the sheriffdom of Teviotdale,[138] an hereditary office held by William Douglas of Liddesdale. Outwardly, Douglas affected friendship, then while Dalhousie was holding his court in Hawick Church, Douglas wounded him and carried him across his saddle to Hermitage Castle, where he put the ailing knight into a dungeon and starved him to death.[139]

As for the heroine 'Black' Agnes,[140] little is known of her after the siege. She died in 1369-70, possibly surviving her husband whom it appears died between 1368 and 1369. Two centuries later, Mary, Queen of Scots owned a small black palfrey which was called Black Agnes, a gift from her half-brother James Stewart, Earl of Moray who may have consciously wished to commemorate Agnes Randolph of Moray. She was unconventional, of strong and uncompromising character and independence of mind. The siege of Dunbar was probably the most exciting thing that ever happened to her. It is certain that Countess Road and Countess Park were named for her.

David II's exile in France came to an end in 1341; from the outset of his return to Scotland relations between himself and the regent Stewart were anything but congenial. This caused many of the Stewart supporters to change their allegiance to the Stewart family, the effects of which follow later. David came back to Scotland in the knowledge that the English were still present in the south-east and west and cross-border raiding was common. An anonymous letter thought to have been written at some time between 1340 and 1348 - the earlier date is accurate - complains to Edward III about raids made on Bamburgh in June by the earls of Dunbar and Sutherland; the raiders took '2,000 fat beasts and many prisoners'[141] and burnt the land as they left. However, it appears that they were intercepted by the English from Roxburgh who occupied the castle until it fell to Ramsay of Dalhousie in 1341; in the ensuing fight, over half the Scots were killed or captured and all the English hostages were freed, 'the two earls escaping with difficulty'. Despite the audacity of the raid, the English parliament was reluctant to provide funds to support English garrisons in the south-east. Many English knights found their feudal duties in Scotland a nuisance and by 1341, most of them simply wanted to go home. Edward Balliol and the *Disinherited* were forgotten, never again posing a threat to Scotland's security. David II held his first parliament at Scone in September 1341 and effectively took over the reins of government; his return to Scotland could be said to have been due in part to the successful defence of Dunbar three years earlier.

Perhaps to express his gratitude for his wife's heroic stand in 1338, the 9th Earl of Dunbar founded the Collegiate Church of Dunbar in 1342, the second or third of its kind in Scotland.[142] Collegiate churches were little more than song schools which offered some teaching to the young; they enjoyed privileges not available to other churches. They were smaller versions of the monasteries, abbeys and minor cathedrals, endowed at a fairly modest expense to their patron and largely self-financing. In return, the canons said daily masses for the souls of their benefactor and his family. It was cheaper than giving away valuable land. In modern terms, Collegiate churches were extremely good value for money. In elevating Dunbar to Collegiate status, Dunbar started a fashion which spread throughout Scotland during the fourteenth and fifteenth centuries. Dunbar Collegiate Church was founded by charter on 21st September 1342; dedicated to St Bega or Beya, it was built along the same lines as Ladykirk, near Norham. Dunbar's church thus became a minor cathedral, more important than the usual Scottish chantry.[143]

The 9th Earl of Dunbar acted as David II's envoy or ambassador to England. On 29th April 1342, Dunbar and the bishops of St Andrews and Brechin wrote to Edward III about the truce between the English king and the king of France, enquiring whether the truce held good for Scotland.[144] It did, although four years later, the *Auld Alliance* dragged Scotland into war again after Edward III's spectacular victory over Philip IV at Crecy on 26th August 1346. The French king wrote desparately to David II, begging him to invade England to divert English troops from France. On 17th October, David led an army of 15,000 to Durham, where he was confronted by an English force at Neville's Cross. Personally brave, David II was a poor strategist and chose unfavourable ground - a field networked with enclosures which disrupted the cohesion of his advance. The battalion commanded by John Randolph, Earl of Moray (sole surviving brother of Black Agnes) on the right flank broke apart on a series of dykes so that his men were crushed against the battalion commanded by the king. Both battalions had little room for manoeuvre and were forced to fall back on the reserve battalion commanded by Robert the Steward and the Earl of Dunbar who occupied better ground. These commanders appeared hesitant; *Chron.Fordun* accuses the Steward and Dunbar of leaving the field prematurely and English chroniclers pour scorn on them. A more logical explanation is that the reserve battalion panicked and the Steward and Dunbar had little option but to follow their men, leaving David and Randolph to face the main English army.

The bulk of the Scottish army scattered before the English horse; no longer an effective fighting force; the knights at David's side began to fall in great numbers. The king was wounded in the head and attacked a second time by an esquire, John Coupland (possibly the Copeland who was captured by Black Agnes in 1338) who lost two teeth to the king's dagger-hilt before he made David his prisoner.[145] During the battle, John Randolph was killed - a bitter irony since it fulfilled his sister Agnes' prediction eight years earlier as he stood before Dunbar Castle in chains.

After Neville's Cross, the English overran Lothian and the Merse once again. All the gains of the recent past were lost almost overnight. Although Dunbar's castle remained secure, he lost his fortalice at Cockburnspath. Neville and Percy boasted that the English East March now began at 'Colbrandspath to Soutra and from thence to Carlops and Crosscryne.'[147] The Scots were able to keep the English out of the castles at Dunbar, Edinburgh and Stirling which restricted their movements until a more powerful enemy weakened the forces against the Scots - the Black Death; the plague would reach Scotland in 1349 with devastating effect. There are no statistics to measure the effects on manpower but Bower's *Scotichronicon* gives some indication of the plague's severity in 1349;[148] he tells us that of 24 canons of St Andrews, only one third survived. It is now believed that the Black Death was less virulent in Scotland than elsewhere but it took its toll.

The consequences of Neville's Cross were disastrous for Scotland. Along with the king, 50 barons were taken prisoner and a weak Robert the Steward was left to rule the country. Negotiations for David II's release in 1348 by the Earl of Dunbar and the Bishop of St Andrews came to nothing. Edward III asked for ransoms, first of £40,000 then £60,000 - enormous sums for the time.[149]

In August 1355, Dunbar captured Sir Thomas Gray, the constable of Norham Castle, no doubt hoping to enrich himself with his ransom. (Gray was taken to Edinburgh Castle where he whiled away the months of captivity writing the Scotichronicon, a history of Britain). Later in the same year, the French sent a pitiful force of 50 men-at-arms and 40,000 gold francs to encourage further raids in England. They joined the Earl of Dunbar and in November, took the town of Berwick, only to lose it to Edward again on 20th January 1356.[150]

By now, the Dunbars were considerably wealthy. The 9th Earl's wife Agnes and her sister Isabella [151] - the latter had married the Earl's cousin Sir Patrick of Biel - inherited the feudal superiority of Moray (**Fig. 5**); with the earldom came the Isle of Man,[152,153] the Lordship of Annandale, Longformacus, Duns and lands in Mochrum Cumnock and Blantyre. With these acquisitions, the Dunbars now controlled areas of the East and West Marches (**ill 31**) as well as in the north-east, giving the 9th Earl of Dunbar unprecedented power. Along with Annandale came the castles of Annan and Lochmaben wich guarded the western approaches to Scotland, a fact which sparked off animosity between the Douglases and the Dunbars. During Robert the Steward's weak administration, families like the Dunbars and the Douglases grew overmighty. The extent of the jealousy between the two families is underlined by the fact that neither attempted to draw closer to the other through the usual course of marriage. The two families would remain at loggerheads until both were forfeited in the next century.

After taking Berwick, Edward invaded Scotland, laying waste to villages and towns in the Merse and Lothian. It was during this campaign - known as the *Burnt Candlemas* - that Haddington's famous church of the Grey Friars - the *Lamp of Lothian* - was destroyed.[154] However, January and February were months of severe

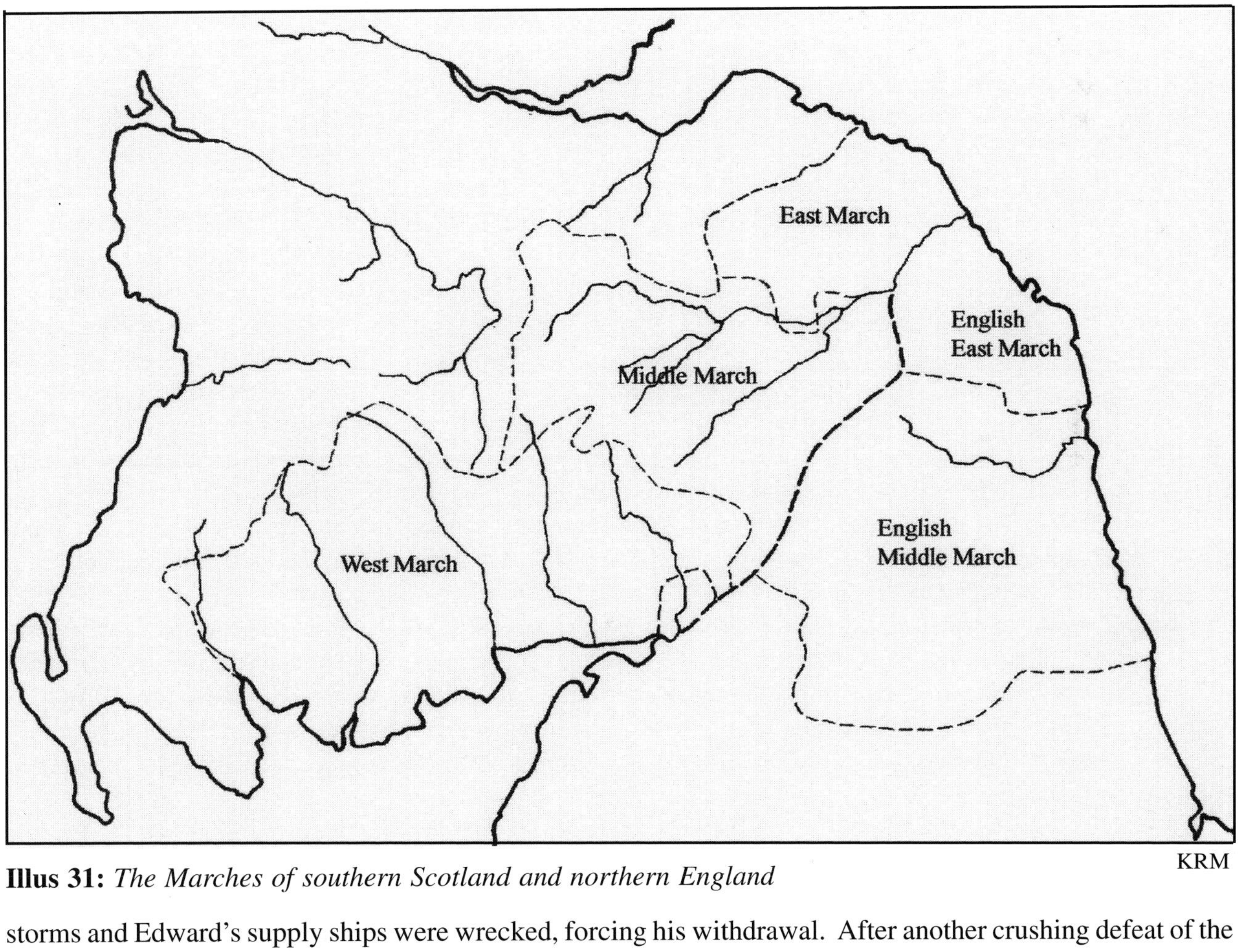

KRM

Illus 31: *The Marches of southern Scotland and northern England*

storms and Edward's supply ships were wrecked, forcing his withdrawal. After another crushing defeat of the French at Poitiers, Edward agreed to a Scottish request for a truce.[155]

On 17th January 1357, Robert the Steward appointed Dunbar[156] as one of the commissioners to negotiate David II's release; Robert knew he could expect no help from France, so he would have to bargain for the king's freedom. The Scots asked for a ten-year truce and agreed to pay a heavy ransom for David's return. On 8th May,[157] Dunbar and several nobles were named as those required to send three hostages to England to ensure there was no default in the ransom payments. This was agreed; the Earl of Dunbar signed the treaty on 30th September at Berwick.[158,159] Under the treaty, the Scots were required to pay a staggering 100,000 merks (£66,667) over ten years.

David II came home to a nation racked by feuds and disease. Almost immediately, he alienated three of his most powerful nobles. He quarrelled with Robert the Steward and the Earl of Angus over some administrative matter and the Earl of Dunbar lost the earldom of Moray; David argued that Dunbar had no right to the earldom as it was a male fief and because there were no surviving male heirs, it belonged to the Crown.[160] In 1358, David added insult to injury by giving the earldom to the Duke of Lancaster with the further insulting proviso - to Dunbar - that if Lancaster had no male heirs, any surviving *female* heirs might inherit. Clearly, David had never forgiven the Steward and Dunbar for their flight from Neville's Cross in 1346. Even so, Dunbar continued to style himself Earl of March and Moray; in 1363, he is so named in a charter granting the sheriffdom and constabulary of Elgin to a William de Vaus. David II was determined to curb the power of overmighty nobles by various means; it is probable that he elevated William, Lord of Douglas as 1st Earl of the 'Black' Douglases, to act as a counterbalance to Dunbar's power. The Black Douglases would play a major role in Scotland's history for almost a century; they posed a threat to the stability of several Stewart kings even if they restricted the ambitions of overmighty men like the Dunbars.

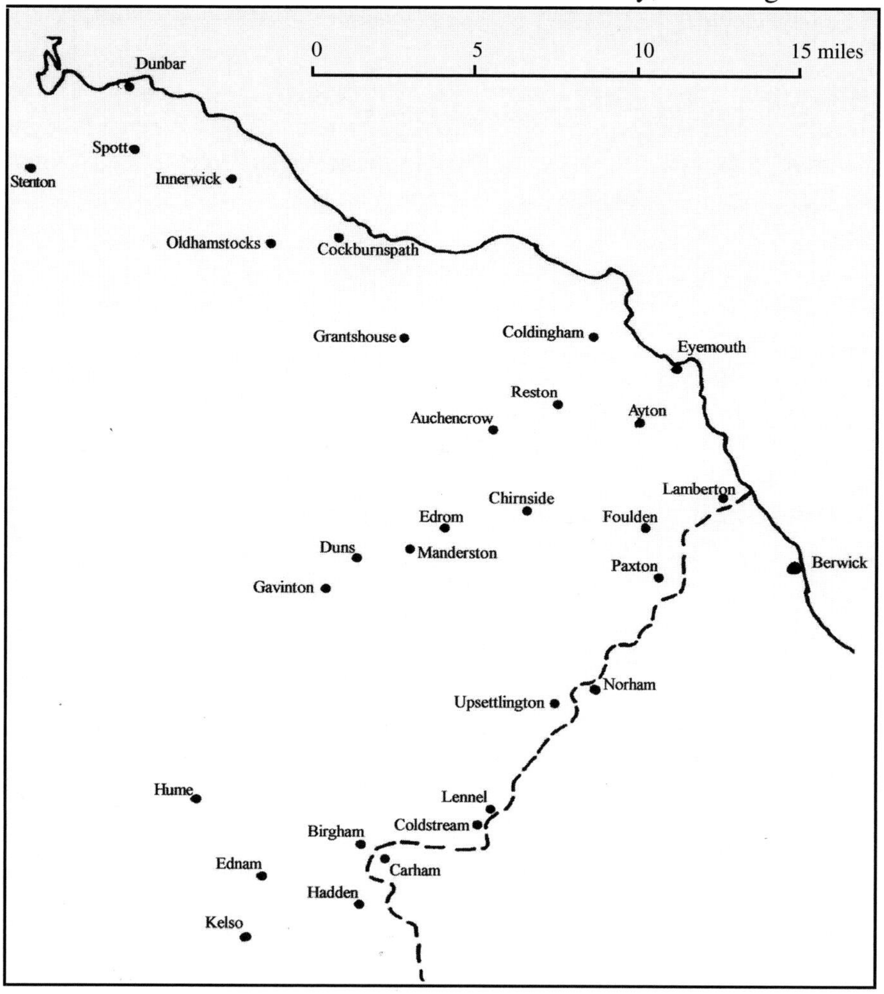

Illus 32: *Some of the more important settlements in the Scottish East March* KRM

In 1363, David II came up with a preposterous suggestion as to the succession question as he had no male heirs at that time. His proposal was that Edward III's son would become heir to the throne and any residual amount of his ransom due to England would be cancelled. It is interesting to note that at this time, several Dunbar and several provincial barons and churchmen went to England, ostensibly on pilgrimages to the shrine of Thomas a Beckett - usually a cover for political dealings. For example, when Dunbar quarrelled with David about the Moray earldom in 1358, he made a pilgrimage south with a retinue of knights and esquires.[161] Was he courting English support for his claim to Moray? And if so, what did he promise in return? As late as 1367, Dunbar was still styling himself Earl of March and Moray when he addressed a precept or writ to his chancellor in Moray that year.[162]

In 1363, in what was ostensibly a protest by the landowning taxpayers, Robert the Steward, the Earl of Dunbar and the Earl of Douglas rebelled against David. The latter two were aggrieved by personal matters - in Dunbar's case, the question of the earldom of Moray. On the surface, the rebellion was attributed to the fact that the king was wilfully squandering money 'by evil counsel' which should have been paid as ransom to England. After all, it was the taxpayers who were footing the bill. Another reason was that after the death of David's queen Joan, he proposed marriage to Dame Margaret Logie, a Drummond and a commoner who might bear the king a son. Robert the Steward was in direct line of succession if David were to die childless; his protest was therefore understandable. Dunbar supported him for factional reasons but only Douglas took action; he embarked on a series of running raids, throwing the king's supporters into prison and seizing their lands until David captured him and received his submission. The revolt quickly collapsed, the rebels being ordered to attend the wedding of David and Margaret Logie in April 1363.

By June the same year, Dunbar appears to have been restored to the king's favour, styling himself Earl of Moray as is confirmed by a charter dated 9th June 1363;[163] he was also allowed to collect revenues from his Moray tenants. However by then, some of his possessions in the south-west were in English hands - Annandale and Lochmaben Castle, the latter occupied by the Earl of Hertford.[164, 165] Even so, benefiting from the considerable income from the Moray and Dunbar earldoms, the 9th Earl could afford to be generous with his vassals and servants. For example, he rewarded Alexander Ryklington, constable of Dunbar Castle with land in Duns, the Merse and Easter Spott, confirmed by two charters in 1363 and 1365.[166]

In January 1364, the Scottish parliament met to discuss a further treaty with England and decide the amount of ransom to be paid annually; to meet the payments, it was agreed to levy a wool tax - an unpopular measure in general but particularly so in the Merse and the Lothians, major wool-producing areas. David's clandestine negotiations with England continued which perhaps explains the absence of Dunbar and Douglas from the January parliament; they had been 'detained' on a pilgrimage to Beckett's shrine. In March 1364, David announced his Westminster Proposal to a shocked parliament which reacted in the only way they could:

'We never will allow an Englishman to rule over us.'[167]

The marriage to Dame Margaret Logie and the Westminster Proposal whereby one of Edward III's sons would inherit the Scottish throne plunged the country into further petty feuding and faction-forming. Nobles put their own interests before those of the realm and several took to visiting England regularly, attending tournaments and going on pilgrimages. In 1367, the Earls of Dunbar, Douglas and Ross again absented themselves from parliament by going on pilgrimage; it may be that Dunbar went to England to plead for the return of the last of his Northumbrian possessions in Shipley, lands given to Earl Percy of Northumberland.[168]

The 9th Earl of Dunbar, March and Moray was now nearing the end of his long life. Although he had vacillated between Scotland and England for nearly thirty years before 1335, his advice to David II on the succession question and the ransom payments to England was based on realistic judgement. It could be said that having lost the last of his English possessions, he had more to gain from supporting David and Scotland, even if he lost his lands in Moray. Dunbar never missed an opportunity to fatten his purse as illustrated by an incident in 1367. On 28th August, he inspected the charter which his ancestor Gospatric II had made in favour of the monks of Coldingham-Durham and granting them Nesbit and Edrom in c.1138 (see Chapter 2). He wanted to make sure that while he had no claim to income from Edrom, Gospatric's charter had provided for a payment of thirty shillings a year to the Dunbars; the money was by way of compensation for giving land to the priory from which Gospatric II had not been freed - the feudal burdens of providing the king with food whenever he passed through Coldingham and for supplying part of a knight's service for the king's army. The priory had agreed to meet part of the royal food bill and supply men for the army, so Gospatric was paid thirty shillings annually to cover his share of the food.[169] The fact that the 9th Earl felt it necessary to check on this payment after two centuries tells us much about him!

Patrick, 9th Earl of Dunbar and March probably died in 1368; *SP* simply states that he was dead by June 1369. He and the king were on good terms at the end of his life, largely because of the arrangements made for the disposal of his Dunbar earldom since he had no surviving male heir.[170] The 9th Earl's last public duties took place in 1367-68 when he assisted David in formulating a treaty with England at Roxburgh and attended a parliament at Stirling. Some accounts suggest that Dunbar died before 25th July 1368, the date of David II's charter conferring his earldom on George Dunbar. George was the son of the 9th Earl's cousin, Sir Patrick, who married Isabella Randolph, sister to Agnes, Dunbar's wife. George is first mentioned in a charter of 1364 which confirmed the 9th Earl's gift to him of half of the baronies of Morton and Tibbers in Dumfriesshire.[171] On 24th May 1367, George was described as Earl of Dunbar and the 9th Earl's cousin - he was his great-nephew - when David II confirmed further gifts of lands from his great-uncle. *Miller, Dunbar* mistakenly identifies George's parents as the 9th Earl and Agnes Randolph who had no children; George's parents were Sir Patrick Dunbar of Biel and Isabella Randolph. Two further charters in 1369 granted George the free barony of Cumnock, Glenken, Mochrum and – significantly - the earldom of Dunbar.[172]

That David II disposed of a rich earldom willingly - it could have become crown property - may not have been unconnected with the fact that he had fallen in love with Agnes, George Dunbar's sister.[173] Margaret Logie, David's wife for six years had produced no children, so desperate for an heir, he began to pay court to Agnes Dunbar. Agnes was already married to Robert Maitland and had borne his children; in one contemporary account, she is described as young and nubile but her child-bearing years were probably over in 1369. She and Maitland received Tibbers from her brother George as confirmed by George's inspection charter of 1369;[174] when she became the king's mistress, Agnes' marriage was annulled, although Maitland retained Tibbers.[175] probably as a sweetener. When David divorced Margaret Logie, the small but powerful political faction led by Sir Robert Erskine which included the Dunbars was in the ascendancy over Robert the Steward and his faction.

A marriage between Agnes Dunbar and the king would consolidate Erskine's position, particularly if Agnes produced an heir. The Dunbars were set to become greater than they had ever been throughout their long history. David heaped honours on the family. The town of Dunbar was elevated to a free burgh on 8th February 1370, which speaks volumes about the power of love. Agnes herself received money payments from the king's customs at Aberdeen and Haddington; these included 1,000 merks as a pension for life, granted in January 1371.[176]

Then at the eleventh hour, the unexpected happened. David II aged only 46 and about to marry Agnes Dunbar and hopefully end the isolation of the House of Bruce, died suddenly on 22nd February 1371. There would be no queen Agnes, no added power and influence for the Dunbars. For the third time in their history, the throne was denied to the House of Dunbar.

Robert the Steward, heir-in-waiting since the battle of Halidon Hill in 1333, finally came into his own. The late king's men - Erskine, Dunbar and others - were relegated to a minority faction. Although David II had given George Dunbar's brother John the earldom of Fife, the honour was withdrawn by Robert the Steward in the first two years of his reign as Robert II. However, by way of compensation, John Dunbar was given the earldom of Moray. As for Agnes Dunbar, she married into the Douglas family, clearly a political move perhaps intended to soften the reversal of the Dunbars' fortunes. Agnes' second husband was James Douglas of Dalkeith;[177] her dowry brought him Morton, then Mordington in 1372.[178] The Dalkeith branch of the Douglas family would later take the name of Morton, probably after the Douglases were disinherited and declared outlaws in the fifteenth century.

George, 10th Earl of Dunbar and 3rd of March

George Dunbar was in the prime of life when he inherited the Dunbar earldom.[179] He owned considerable tracts of land, was wealthy and counter-balanced the rival House of Douglas in Galloway, posing a threat to their ascendancy. George was initially styled Earl of March and Moravia [Moray], Lord of Man and Annandale until 1372, when his brother was created 5th Earl of Moray. George's name is refreshing after the confusing succession of Patricks from the twelfth century.

When Robert the Steward was proclaimed king, William, 1st Earl of Douglas apparently refused to recognise him; this is now seen as more of a demonstration against royal patronage rather than a serious attempt to seize the throne. After meeting with Sir Robert Erskine and George Dunbar, Douglas prudently withdrew his objections. Perhaps to keep Douglas in check, Robert II appointed Dunbar and Douglas joint wardens of the East March and Douglas became Justiciar for the area south of the Forth. Dunbar, anxious to find favour with the new king, appears to have done so with remarkable speed as he soon began to receive cash payments for his services to Robert.[180] In 1370, John Dunbar married the future king's daughter Marjorie and perhaps because of this, he was created Earl of Moray by parliament at Scone on 9th March 1372. Thus began the short but royally-sanctioned Dunbar occupation of the Moray earldom.

From the outset of George Dunbar's tenure of the Dunbar earldom, the community prospered. Becoming a free burgh in 1370 with a free port at Belhaven and other privileges, the town fathers quickly grasped the commercial possibilities this presented; they became rich and cosmopolitan over the next three centuries. On the international scene, during the ill-observed truce of 1370 between Scotland and England, Dunbar lands were relatively untouched by raids although constant bickering between the 10th Earl and the Percys of Northumberland threatened the fragile peace. Dunbar's possessions in Annandale were still occupied by the English, so he made a wasteland of the area in 1376, sacking vills and hamlets whose occupants refused to pay taxes to him.[181] Although all-out war was averted, Border incidents were becoming more frequent, often under the guise of chivalry. There is a classic example of this in 1377, when one of Dunbar's equerries was in Roxburgh possibly buying goods for his master was murdered at the fair by the English. *Chron. Wyntoun* informs us that Dunbar unsuccessfully sought redress from Percy of Northumberland; he waited until the next fair, when he descended on the town and murdered every Englishmen he could find.[182] This provoked a retaliatory raid into Dunbar's territory by Henry Percy, warden of the English East March; Percy complained about the outrage to Robert II on 14th October 1377 and receiving no satisfaction, embarked upon what was known as the Warden's Raid. It was a fiasco. Percy and his knights were asleep in camp when they were surrounded by the common folk who brought heavy wooden rattles to scare away their horses. The largely mounted force had to walk back to England in armour, carrying their heavy lances on their shoulders.

Yet another incident occurred in 1378, when the English warden of Lochmaben Castle was forced to abandon it to Dunbar and Douglas. By April, the two earls were harassing the English side of the Border and ransoming hostages for large sums of money.[183] The extent to which Dunbar benefited from such raids is illustrated graphically: Sir Thomas de Musgrave, one of Dunbar's prisoners, was released on parole and on condition that he would return to Scotland within a stipulated period or else his bail money of 1,000 merks would be forfeit. Musgrave was a week overdue; Dunbar demanded his money, promising that if it wasn't forthcoming, he would

'take a distraint on the inhabitants of the [English] March, which will ruin the country as the people are not able for that amount.'

As a consequence Richard II of England issued a writ dated 5th March 1382 ordering that the money be raised from Musgrave lands. The reigns of both Robert II and Robert III saw a sharp rise in the activities of Border barons like Dunbar who not only ransacked the English Border counties but repeatedly asked for payments for their services to both kings. The money was usually met from the Great or King's Customs, raised by the royal burghs.

While Robert II publicly spoke out against these incidents, he privately condoned them although he knew there was always the danger of war breaking out. An eight-year truce to last until 31st May 1387 was signed at Billymire on 27th June 1379 by Lord Neville, newly appointed warden of the English East March and his opposite numbers, Dunbar and Douglas.[184] The truce was never observed; fighting continued until June 1380, when a second truce was negotiated at Ayton Church by John of Gaunt, Duke of Lancaster and Archibald Douglas, Lord of Galloway, George Dunbar and the Bishops of Dunkeld and Glasgow which brought an uneasy peace until 1384. The second truce fared no better than the first; in 1382, hostilities resumed largely as a result of Scottish negotiations with Charles V of France who was planning to invade England.

As noted above, Dunbar received money payments from Robert II for his services; he was also given resources to arm and equip a vessel to ward off attacks on the east coast by English pirates. [185] Dunbar was so wealthy he was able to lend money to the king for his personal use.[186] Border bickering continued; in 1382, Archibald 'the Grim' Douglas took Lochmaben Castle from the English who had re-occupied it. This brought John of Gaunt back across the Border with a large army which encountered the rigours of a Scottish winter and its attendant sickness. For a time, he camped outside Edinburgh while the citizens carried off anything of use to the English saving - even the straw from their roofs - so that when Gaunt entered the city he found it stripped bare and was forced to retreat. During this invasion, the English were anxious about the security of Roxburgh Castle, one of their key fortresses; accordingly, Baron Greystoke of Cumberland was sent to provision the Roxburgh garrison. George Dunbar was in the vicinity at the time and he ambushed Greystoke, taking him prisoner to Dunbar along with the rich baggage train. With supreme irony, Dunbar entertained Greystoke with his own food eaten off his own silver plates! [187] Later in the year, Greystoke complained to John of Gaunt that his ransom was too much and that he could not possibly raise enough cash to satisfy Dunbar;[188] he also protested that he had done nothing to infringe the truce, nor had he harmed any Scot on either side of the Border.

In 1384, the French were determined to carry their war to England through Scotland and a forward party of 30 knights and esquires arrived in Edinburgh with promises of support for a major invasion. A treaty signed the following year brought John de Vienne, the French admiral, to Leith and Dunbar at the end of May. His force consisted of 2,000 auxiliaries and 50,000 *livres* or gold francs. The money was distributed among the foremost nobles, James Douglas and George Dunbar receiving 7,500 and 4,000 *livres* respectively. According to *Chron. Fordun*, the French army consisted of 50 nobles, 26 bannerets [knights with vassals serving under their banners, usually those knighted on the field for their bravery], 1,050 men-at-arms and 80 suits of armour. Vienne received a warm welcome at Leith and Dunbar; his men were billeted in Dunfermline, Queensferry, Dalkeith, Dunbar and Kelso. The common folk didn't share their lords' enthusiasm for their French guests; the rural communities regarded them with suspicion, knowing that war was imminent. And the visitors did not endear themselves to their hosts; they foraged for their food, taking whatever they pleased until at one point, the local populace slaughtered about a hundred Frenchmen who had exceeded their welcome.

The truth was that Robert II neither wanted nor could afford a war with England but he allowed himself to be persuaded into invading the northern counties by his nobles. An army supposedly 30,000 strong but mainly comprised of poorly armed foot soldiers attacked the Border strongholds. The Franco-Scots troops failed to capture Roxburgh Castle and went on to storm Wark Castle. Then word came that an English army of 67,000 under the command of Richard II was on its way and the Scots retreated, laying waste to the countryside as they went, much to the dismay of the French knights who had hoped to win battle honours. The sole material gain was a series of treaties which guaranteed peace until 1388 although Border hostilities continued. On 11th June 1385,[189] Richard II issued a warrant for the safe-conduct of Dunbar's son's servant and six others to buy food in northern England for the relief of the garrison at Cockburnspath Tower. (A similarly curious event occurred on 12th December 1387, when the 10th Earl and 100 Scottish horse were allowed to enter York, Northumberland and Durham to buy 100 chalders each of flour and malt for the Christmas festivities and take them to Dunbar Castle in an English vessel hired for the purpose.[190])

A year on, yet another truce was negotiated by the English and Scottish March wardens in which both sides swore not to mount major raids and allow local disputes to be settled at their level. The truce, drawn up in June 1386 was again signed at Billymire, Dunbar and Douglas being among the signatories. The style of this document is interesting:

> ' At Billymire the 27th day of June, the year of grace 1386, it is accordit [agreed]
> betwen the Lord Nevill, wardyn of the este [east] marche of Ingland agaynes [against]
> Scotland on the ta [one] part, and the erles of Douglas and the Marche [Dunbar]
> wardeynes of the este marche of Scotland agaynes Ingland on the tother [the other]
> part.'[191]

The truce required the signatories not to burn or slaughter men or take or ransom them. Billymire was a burn that marked the Border between Chirnside and Coldingham. Billie Castle in the old parish of Buncle and Preston belonged to the Earls of Dunbar and was situated in the Billymire which as the name suggests was a quagmire; it could only be crossed by large boulders placed in it as a causeway and passable at two places. When a truce expired, the causeway was removed so that the marsh became a natural barrier against enemies. There were several fortalices or towers in the area - Billie, which no longer exists, Fairney Castle, Old Castle and Stoneshiel Castle - all of which were under Dunbar's control.

At this time, the 10th Earl of Dunbar and the 2nd Earl of Douglas appear to have enjoyed a warmer relationship, co-operating with each other in the interests of acquiring booty and wealth. Then came the most renowned incident of the period, celebrated in ballads on both sides of the Border by minstrels eager to dramatise the deeds of the March Lords in the intersets of chivalry which disguised the real reason-plunder. On a summer night in August 1388, a relatively minor fight took place at Otterburn, the culmination of a successful Scottish raid on Northumberland. The 'battle' of Otterburn - known as Chevy Chase in English history - was fought in moonlight exactly two months after a recent truce had expired. For years it has been heralded as a classic chivalrous episode in which the banners of Douglas and Dunbar flew together against those of the Percys of Northumberland.

The events leading up to Otterburn are well-documented. A Scottish raiding party raised with Robert II's tacit consent entered Northumberland intent on collecting as much booty as could be carried. According to Froissart's *Chroniques (Chron. Froissart)* the Scottish force consisted of 1,200 lances and 40,000 foot including archers; a quarter of these figures is more likely. Mustering at Yetholm, the army was split into two groups or battles; the larger with the baggage train entered England via Carlisle, while the smaller under James, 2nd Earl of Douglas and the 10th Earl of Dunbar took the Newcastle road. Douglas reputedly commanded 6,000 men - again a suspiciously high figure; with Dunbar was his brother John and the Earl of Mar. This group marauded as far south as Durham and returning north, brushed with Ralph and Henry Percy outside the walls of Newcastle. Douglas allegedly captured Henry Percy's pennon - probably a romantic addition by the minstrels - and boasted that it would fly from his castle walls unless Percy reclaimed it. Young Henry Percy was not known as *Hotspur* for nothing; arguably one of England's bravest - if not brightest - knights, Percy couldn't let this insult go unchallenged.

The Scots made their way to the Tweed via Ponteland, wasting an unrewarding and unnecessary day besieging Ponteland Tower owned by Sir Edmund Alphel [Aymer de Atholl?]. Word reached Hotspur about Douglas' position and he set off immediately, meeting up with the Scots about 35 miles from Newcastle. By the time he located the Scottish camp it was night; Hotspur true to his epithet surprised the Scots at supper. Perhaps Douglas had intended to delay the retreat to allow Hotspur to catch up with him because by now, the Carlisle contingent had rejoined him and the Scots outnumbered the English. On the night of 19th August under a full moon, Percy attacked without hesitation;[192] in his haste to get into action, Dunbar forgot his *bascinet* or steel helmet as he ran to join the Lindsays and Sinclairs rallying on Douglas.

The battle was fought in bright moonlight. George Dunbar and his brother John fought well alongside Douglas who hewed a path through his opponents with a two-handed axe. Wounded three times, he finally fell, rallying his men with cries of 'a Douglas!' The balladeers had a field day, milking the fight for all it was worth. A dead man won the fight. English casualties were given as 1,840 dead, 1,000 wounded and 1,040 prisoners to the Scottish loss of 100 dead and 200 captured, largely pursuing the English. These figures are quoted in *Chron. Froissart*, sympathetic to the Scots, although the figures were given by those who took part in the engagement. Whatever the true figures, there were many empty saddles among the English force. George Dunbar took Hotspur prisoner to Dunbar for ransom. Perhaps it was Percy's capture which brought Alexander Neville, Archbishop of York to Dunbar in 1388 where he died (see Chapter 3) possibly to negotiate Percy's freedom.

Otterburn was irresponsible and unwarranted; it almost destroyed the shaky peace between the two countries and made the Border volatile once more. On 12th July 1389, a safe-conduct was granted to the 'Countess of March of Scotland' - Christian, George Dunbar's wife who was in Northumberland to negotiate the safety of '1,000 sheep and 2 shepherds to pasture at Colbrandspath and 5 leagues around at the Countess' pleasure for 3 years.'[193] This writ was issued at the request of Henry Percy by the English chancellor but there was a condition; if the English king entered Scotland in person with an army during the three years, the safe conduct was void. Clearly, the intention was to prevent English knights from marauding in the Cockburnspath vicinity, possibly a promise extracted from Hotspur while he was a prisoner in Dunbar Castle. Such measures were necessary after Otterburn as knights on both sides of the Border were continually taunting each other. At one point, the Scots took up the gauntlet and sent word to the custodians of the English East March who had replaced the disgraced Percys; the challenge was refused.[194]

In 1390, Robert II died; little is known of his reign except that it appears to have been undistinguished by anything other than the fact he established the Stewart dynasty of kings. Tytler credits him with 'admirable qualities' including an unbending love of justice although he admits the king was irresolute, timid and over-anxious to placate his nobles - hardly qualities to be admired. In an age where comparisons were made, the nobles were uneasy at the coronation of Robert III - he changed his name from John to remove any association - real or imagined - with the unlucky John Balliol. Robert III was also disabled permanently by a kick from his horse. He was lame in other respects; his reign was as unremarkable as that of his father, both fraught with lawlessness and disorder. The nobles did as they pleased; they sought glory in skirmishes and tournaments instead of helping to rule the country. However while the people loved the chivalry and the pageantry of knightly behaviour, chivalry would finally die out during Robert III's reign. And those who had no respect for the new king - men like Alexander Buchan, Wolf of Badenoch who burnt Forres and sacked Elgin Cathedral in contempt of the king even before he was crowned - showed how the country was split once more into a north-south divide, the Highlands becoming increasingly estranged from mainstream Scottish society.

As noted earlier, Robert III's reign marked the end of feudal service in the traditional sense; land formerly held of the king had become heritable. In England the practice of paying pensions for feudal service had existed since the reign of Henry II who rewarded his nobles with cash payments that were only introduced in Scotland in the late fourteenth century. The 10th Earl of Dunbar was the first of many to receive a royal pension - £100 a year from Robert II, then Robert III.[195,196] The nobles no longer accepted that monarchs had the right to deprive them of lands granted by earlier kings and the concept of cash payments introduced a new and dangerous element of independence. Thus the practice known as 'bastard' feudalism became more prevalent; the king was obliged to hire vassals for service, meeting the cost from the royal purse which meant generating more revenue from taxation, largely provided by the royal burghs. The prospect of young knights who openly swaggered about with a have-sword-will-travel attitude would have shocked earlier generations. Even so, trade with England increased and safe conducts for Scottish knights travelling to England became commonplace.[197]

Stability in Scotland was weakened by Robert III and the behaviour of his dissolute son and heir, the Duke of Rothesay and the aggressive ambitions of the 3rd Earl of Douglas. David, Duke of Rothesay, was awarded an annuity of £640 for several years from the customs of nine royal burghs including Dunbar.[198] As a result, Rothesay may have been a frequent visitor to Dunbar from 1392 onwards; on one of his visits he met George Dunbar's daughter Elizabeth. Earlier in 1395, Dunbar sanctioned - he may have even proposed - marriage between Elizabeth and Rothesay in the hope of reversing the earlier disappointment of his other daughter Agnes. At any rate, Dunbar offered Robert III a large dowry for his daughter's betrothal and the young couple went through a form of marriage which was the subject of two papal dispensations.[199]

Despite Rome's blessing, an angry Robert III declared the marriage 'irregular' in 1395. He even contemplated besieging Dunbar Castle in 1396 and sent a sizeable army to Haddington [200] by way of threat; the king justified his actions by accusing the Dunbar of what today would be called sharp practice, as the marriage hadn't been discussed by the Three Estates of parliament.[201] George Dunbar wondered what would happen next; yet again, his family had the prospect of the crown in view only to have that prospect removed at the last minute. Then Rothesay himself changed his mind, probably at the prompting of his father or the 3rd Earl of Douglas, who was probably alarmed by the prospect of Dunbar extending his power in south-east Scotland. Douglas went further; not only did he persuade parliament to declare the marriage null and void, he offered Robert III an even larger dowry than Dunbar for a marriage between his daughter Marjorie and Rothesay. An infuriated Dunbar demanded an audience with Robert III; he upbraided the king for going back on his word, for the insult to his daughter - the marriage had been consummated - and he demanded the return of his money. Robert was completely unmoved; his reaction was crude, unsympathetic and insensitive. He simply turned his back on Dunbar when he appeared at court, making a frustrated man angry, then desperate. The slight to the great name of Dunbar demanded apology at least, let alone financial recompense; neither was forthcoming. Then Dunbar threatened Robert; either his daughter's good name would be restored or he would take such revenge as would have 'dire consequences for Scotland.'[202] Robert again ignored him, sanctioning the marriage of his son to Marjorie Douglas, daughter of Dunbar's bitterest rival. Tytler describes Dunbar's 'designs' as having been 'defeated by the intrigues of a family more powerful than his own'; he does admit however that Dunbar had little choice but to retaliate in some way. Rothesay's marriage to Marjorie Douglas in February 1400 precipitated Dunbar's defection to England. Both *Scotichronicon* and *Chron. Wyntoun* suggest that Dunbar was forced into this course of action by Archibald Douglas, who at some point after February 1400 bullied Sir Robert Maitland, governor of Dunbar Castle, into handing it over to him while Dunbar was in England.[203]

As for poor Elizabeth Dunbar, she accepted the consequences of her ill-advised 'marriage' and retired from public life to become Prioress of St Leonard's Hospital in Perth.[204] She took the veil as was the custom of the time. Dunbar was genuinely distraught about his daughter's rejection as any father would be; her withdrawal from secular life also denied him her company. The rivalry between the Dunbars and the Douglases had reached a dangerous stage and having made his threat to the king, Dunbar was committed to action which *Scotichronicon* accepts. It is unlikely that Dunbar would have received much support from other noble families against the all-powerful Douglases so he turned for help to his distant relative, the recently enthroned Henry IV of England. Dunbar had suffered yet another insult to his House; obliged to attend Rothesay's wedding [205] as one of the premier nobles of Scotland; on what should have been his daughter's wedding day, he was ostracised by Robert III and other guests at the ceremony. He rode home to write an impassioned letter to Henry IV on 18th February. The letter is direct and wastes no time on courtly etiquette or style; the bitterness is self-evident :

> 'I am gritly [greatly] wrangit [wronged] by ye Duc de Rothesay, the quhilk [who]spousit my doughter and now agaynes his oblysing [against his word] to me made by hys letter and hys seal and agaynes the laws of halykirk [against the laws of the holy church] spoused ane other wif [wife].'

Dunbar reminds Henry that he and the king's mother were within the fourth degree of consanguinity (fourth cousins in effect) 'the quhilk in alde tymes wes callit neire [near]' and seeks Henry's support in redressing 'ye wrong and ye defowls [default] that ys done to me.' Dunbar's relationship with Henry was based on his 'graunde-dame' or great-grandmother, Marjorie Comyn, who had married the 8th Earl of Dunbar and Henry's great-grandmother Alice Comyn (Beaumont) whom Dunbar erroneously claimed were sisters; Alice was in fact Marjorie's niece. Be that as it may, there was a family connection.

Dunbar apologised to Henry for writing in English rather than French: perhaps here he was making a subtle point, seeking to convince Henry that he disapproved of the Franco-Scottish alliance or the fact that Scotland was refusing to abide by the Anglo-French truce of 1396:

> 'Mervaile [marvel] yhe nocht that I write my lettres in Englis for that ys mare [more] clere [clear] to myne understandying than latyn or fraunche [Latin or French]............writyn at my castel of Dunbar the 18th Februar 1399.'[206]

The letter is signed 'le Comte de la Marche d'Ecosses.'[207] In it, Dunbar asks that Neville of Furnival or the Earl of Westmoreland [208] be sent to confer with him on the Border Marches and he requests a safe-conduct through England for himself and 100 companions.[209]

Medieval history abounds with instances of men who put family honour before political ambition although often both were inextricably combined. The 10th Earl of Dunbar was no traitor in 1400; Robert III and his advisors had insulted his family name and he turned to England for redress. Of all the Dunbars, the 10th Earl was renowned for his personal bravery and his military skill; his defection to England was a severe loss to Scotland at a time of political unrest. Dunbar was an unexpected ally whom Henry could usefully employ in his planned invasion of Scotland; the sight of the 10th Earl's banner in his army might induce other Scottish nobles to join him.

Before setting off for north England in March 1400, the 10th Earl entrusted his castle at Dunbar to Robert Maitland of Thirlestane, his sister Agnes' son by her first marriage. At first, Maitland refused to surrender the castle to Robert III's herald and for this, his Thirlestane estates were declared forfeit. Then Archibald, heir to the Douglas earldom arrived at the castle, threatening him with his life if he refused to hand over the keys. Maitland had little choice in the matter. Then the king ordered the deputy warden of the East March to seize Dunbar's strongholds at Billie and Cockburnspath, to remove whatever provisions were within them and distribute them to the monks at Coldingham Priory 'on account of the rebellion of George, Earl of March.'[210] Robert was being somewhat presumptuous unless he had spies in the area; so far as is known, Dunbar had not given any hint of his defection to the king or any of his advisors. At any rate, he was declared a traitor and

Archibald Douglas received all Dunbar's lands and Maitland became his vassal, although he received compensation for the loss of Thirlestane in October 1400,[211] when Douglas gave him certain Dunbar possessions. On the death of Archibald 'the Grim' 3rd Earl of Douglas on 24th December 1400, his son Archibald became 4th Earl of Douglas, Lord of Galloway, Annandale and Dunbar.

At some point between 8th March and 21st June, Dunbar attempted to contact Dunbar Castle but his intermediaries found the gate firmly closed against them. In vain, Dunbar wrote an angry letter to Robert III protesting at the unjust seizure of his castle and lands. He said he was on business in England and that he had not withdrawn his allegiance to Robert, nor had he transferred it to Henry. His appeal was rejected, effectively removing any lingering prospect of Dunbar's return to Scotland. He was granted a further safe-conduct to England on 21st June and met Henry IV at York where invasion plans were underway.[212] Henry issued a safe conduct dated 2nd August granting permission for Dunbar, his Countess Christian, his sons and daughters including Elizabeth at Perth and a retinue of 80 persons to come to England, valid for a year until Martinmas [November] 1401. Now that his family was safe, Dunbar may have mounted a raid in East Lothian even before he crossed the Border. There are no details of this raid, the first of two between 1400 and 1401.

On 7th August 1400, Henry IV issued a proclamation from Newcastle to every Scottish noble 'to induce their king to do him [Henry] homage and fealty in person at Edinburgh on Monday, 23rd of the same month or failing this, to do it themselves.'[213] This was much more than mere diplomatic manoeuvring about the Anglo-French treaty; it was a repeat of the *auld sang* of English kings from Edward I onwards. The reason appears to have been because an unidentified Scottish noble had written to the French court calling Henry a traitor and that letter had come into his possession somehow. Henry was testing the nobles' loyalty to Robert III, hoping they would submit to him. Henry had no sense of history.

What followed contained an element of farce. Henry crossed the Border on 17th August and marched to Leith via Haddington. It is unlikely that Dunbar was with him since it is recorded that during May and September, Henry paid Dunbar's esquire £20 who 'came on his lord's message to the king then in the war in those parts [ie Lothian].[214] Unable to capture Edinburgh, Henry sustained some losses from guerrilla attacks and concerned about his ability to feed the army, he extracted little more than a promise from a diplomatic official in Edinburgh to consider the matter of his overlordship of Scotland.

Henry had in fact 'invaded' Scotland to appease some of his more impetuous nobles demanding action; now he needed a spectacular victory to justify the expense of his Scottish tour. George Dunbar would shortly give him that victory. Meanwhile, on 4th December 1400, Dunbar was paid the second of many cash gifts and lands he would receive from Henry over the next seven years.[215,216]

George Dunbar's defection made sure that the royal or Great Customs due from Dunbar were denied to Robert III, as no taxable goods were able to enter or leave Belhaven between 1401 and 1405 because of the conflict with England.[217] Perhaps the money was diverted to Dunbar in England.

Dunbar learnt of the death of his rival Archibald, 3rd Earl of Douglas at Threave Castle on Christmas Eve, 1400. His successor, the 4th Earl had been granted Dunbar's titles, yet another insult to the family. Perhaps Douglas' death encouraged him to mount another raid on East Lothian. With Henry Percy of Northumberland, Dunbar set off to attack Patrick Hepburn of Hailes, near East Linton in February 1401. The small force marched through the Lammermuir Hills to avoid detection, attacking Hailes Castle, burning the villages of Hailes, Papple, Traprain and Markle - lands he had formerly held, now in the hands of the 4th Earl of Douglas. In Edinburgh, Douglas learnt of the raid; gathering a sizeable force, he surprised the raiders at supper near Pencraig Hill, East Linton. According to Bower's *Scotichronicon,* the invaders left their booty and roast meat on the cooking spits as Douglas chased them to Cockburnspath, taking several prisoners; he did not break off pursuit until Dunbar and Percy reached Berwick.[218]

Thus Dunbar became an English mercenary, receiving English gold for his services. Dunbar himself, his Countess, his sons Gawain and Columba all received gifts of money. Columba the cleric was appointed Dean of the church of St Mary Magdalen at Bridgenorth, a living he neglected abominably in order to line his own pockets. On 22nd June 1402, Dunbar and two of his sons justified their expensive existence with a victory over Patrick Hepburn the younger of Hailes. Hepburn and 400 men had raided Northumberland for booty and Dunbar and Henry Percy chased him over the Border, overtaking him at Nesbit Moor, near Duns.[219] In the sharp and bloody fight, the day was saved by Dunbar's son who arrived with 200 reinforcements from the Berwick garrison. Hepburn and several barons were killed along with - according to Bower's *Scotichronicon* - 'the flower of the fighting men of a great part of Lothian' who were taken prisoner. Percy is credited with the victory, although Dunbar played a major part. Hepburn's raid had been a decoy for the movements of a larger force led by Murdoch, the son of Robert III's illegitimate half-brother, the Duke of Albany. Murdoch and the Earls of Douglas, Moray and Angus menaced Carlisle, then switched to the east after plundering in the west for several weeks. The Scots were caught on the wrong side of the Tweed at Homildon Hill, near Wooler, on 14th September 1402.[220]

A precise account of the ensuing battle is given in *Historia Anglicana (Chron. Walsingham).* Percy and Dunbar jointly commanded the English forces, Dunbar proving the more able commander. He urged the impatient Hotspur to allow the Scots attack so that the English archers could do their work;[221] *Chron.Walsingham* states that the English knights were simply spectators, leaving the bowmen to settle the outcome. Here we see an example of Dunbar's military skill; patience, knowledge of Scottish tactics and the use of the bow brought him a decisive victory. He knew what to do, how to do it - and did it. Bower's *Scotichronicon* records that the Scots, maddened by the showers of arrows, clamoured to go on the offensive. Sir John Swinton and Adam de Gordon led a charge of 100 knights and were hacked to pieces; killed with them was Alexander Ramsay of Dalhousie whose father had raised the siege of Dunbar in 1338. Among the prisoners were the Earl of Douglas, Murdoch and Dunbar's brother Sir Patrick of Biel, his nephew Thomas, Earl of Moray and his brother-in-law, Sir James Douglas of Dalkeith. In all, seven prominent barons were taken along with 80 knights - 30 of them French - and 1,000 Scots and French foot. About 500 Scots were drowned attempting to swim the Tweed. Contemporary English chronicles report a loss of five English soldiers, which must be suspect. Homildon Hill was the last major battle the Scots would fight until Flodden in 1513; it was a defeat which sapped Scottish confidence and the will to wage war.

Tytler is petulant about Dunbar's victory at Homildon Hill; he writes that 'if he could be so base as to enjoy the triumph [he] would have been amply satiated with revenge; for his rival, Douglas, was defeated, cruelly wounded and a captive.'[222] Of course Dunbar enjoyed his triumph; he had vindicated Henry's faith in him and he may have felt 'amply satiated' because he had avenged his family for Robert III's insensitivity, Douglas' intrigues and Rothesay's waywardness. After all, Dunbar was now a stateless person; he had lost titles, lands and castles. He had every right to indulge in self-congratulation. At least Tytler admits that Dunbar was motivated more by his hatred of Douglas than his love of England.

The sight of Douglas, wounded in five places and Henry Hotspur's prisoner was the real victory for Dunbar. Hotspur was also jubilant; a Douglas had defeated and humiliated him at Otterburn. On learning of Homildon, Henry IV wrote to the victors on 22nd September instructing them not to release any prisoners on parole or ransom them; the reason was clearly political, since the prisoners were high-ranking men and valuable bargaining counters. Percy was enraged; he felt it was his right under the code of war to be free to ransom his prisoners; possibly as an excuse for his subsequent behaviour, Hotspur argued that his uncle, Edmund Mortimer, Earl of March had a claim on the English throne so he had every right to ignore Henry's wishes. From this point onwards, Percy began to plot against Henry, using Douglas when it suited him. It is unlikely that Dunbar was aware of this development at the outset but he would learn of it eventually. Percy took most of the captives to Whitehall on 20th September where they knelt before Henry - a chivalrous and merciful man - to pay homage. Percy kept Douglas in his own custody which angered the king and soured their relationship. As for Dunbar, all he sought as reward was the restoration of his lands and titles, which of course Henry could only promise to do when the Dunbar earldom came under English control.

The political situation on the Scottish side of the Border changed rapidly, perhaps too quickly for the Percys' liking; Henry Percy had hoped to enlist the support of Robert III in his rebellion against Henry IV but that came to nothing. His scheme to depose Henry would result in the battle of Shrewsbury which consolidated Henry IV's monarchy. Before proceeding to describe the battle, it is appropriate here to mention a curious anecdote about a visit George Dunbar made to the Scottish court on 10th June 1403. Despite his defection to England, Dunbar appears to have obtained a safe-conduct allowing him into Scotland to seek not the return of his lands but to obtain a pardon for his oath of allegiance given to Richard II in 1385 ,[223] the king whom Henry IV had deposed! That year, Richard invaded Scotland and Dunbar had done nothing to impede his advance. Perhaps Robert III wanted to appease Dunbar for having insulted his House or else he desired to know the extent of Dunbar's loyalty to England. Whatever the reason, Dunbar's Scottish journey achieved nothing except that it allowed him to stop at Cockburnspath and stock his tower which could be used to English advantage.

Although of little strategic value, it is perhaps appropriate to describe Cockburnspath Tower as it was in Dunbar's time. A small, square building of rough stone, it housed about twenty men. It had a circular staircase at its south-west aspect and adjoining the southernmost side was a gate with an arch; on entering it, there were a number of vaulted buildings, possibly living quarters and storehouses. In Dunbar's day, it dominated the road to Dunbar and Edinburgh; the ruin faces the now disused Pease Bridge.

Driven by his all-consuming hatred of Douglas, Dunbar made his suspicions known to Henry; by now, the murmurings of revolt were growing louder when the king learnt that Owen Glendower in Wales had joined the

Percy-Douglas coalition. Glendower promised Percy an army of 10,000; Percy, his brother Thomas, Earl of Worcester and Douglas had raised another army on the pretext of subduing Glendower's revolt. Dunbar prudently advised Henry to await further developments. Henry believed the real threat to his kingship would come from Wales, supported as he thought by a few Scots and French troops. Then on 13th July, he learnt of the Percys' rebellion. The younger Percy had made a proclamation stating that Richard II was alive and therefore Henry had no right to call himself king. Dunbar advised Henry to attack the Percys before they had time to link up with Glendower. At last, Henry was galvanised into action; he finally realised that his survival depended on eliminating the Percys. He marched from Burton-on-Trent to Shrewsbury in three days, surprising the Percys who were about to occupy Shrewsbury to provision their army and hopefully capture the Prince of Wales - the future Henry V - who was in the vicinity with a small force. At first, Henry IV attempted to negotiate with Thomas Percy, Earl of Worcester and his nephew, the younger Percy of Northumberland; they refused his offer, hoping that Owen Glendower would arrive to reinforce them. Dunbar urged Henry to attack the Percys; it was due to his promptings that the battle of Shrewsbury was fought on 21st July, two days earlier than had been planned.

Both armies were of roughly equal strength at 14,000;[224] as in most civil wars, Shrewsbury was a desperate affair, since the Percys and Henry each knew that defeat would mean the headsman's axe. The royal army made the first move, fighting uphill against companies of Cheshire archers who took a heavy toll. The battle was fought at close-quarters so that friend or foe couldn't be identified by their coats-of-arms; at one point, Dunbar advised Henry not to expose himself to danger and the king reluctantly withdrew from his battle station. It was just as well, as Douglas almost reached him with his sword. The fight was going in the rebels' favour when the younger Percy raised his visor for air and was pierced through the skull by an arrow. The Scottish auxiliaries lost heart when Percy fell; they gave ground along with large groups of English and the three-hour fight ended in Henry's favour. One of many decisive battles in medieval history, Shrewsbury determined the dynasty of English kings for the next 60 years. Henry was secure on his throne. He had Dunbar to thank for his life as it may have been he who ordered two knights to dress in royal surcoats to deceive the enemy. According to *Scotichronicon*, the wounded Douglas - the man's body must have only begun to heal after Homildon Hill - maintained later he had killed three men disguised as the king that day. A prisoner once more, at least his life was spared. Thomas Percy, Earl of Worcester and others were beheaded two days later. The younger Percy's dead body was dismembered and hung in chains; his father in Northumberland was placed under house arrest until 1405 when he escaped with his grandson to Scotland, where he died in exile in 1408. The dead numbered about 1,600 on both sides and a further 3,000 were wounded. *Historia Anglicana (Chron. Walsingham)* states that men 'fell as leaves fall to the ground after a frosty night, at the approach of winter.' Most of the wounded subsequently died or were despatched by pillagers seeking booty after the battle.

Henry IV had fought the only major engagement of his reign; it is ironic that a Scottish noble gave him the victory. Henry later founded the Collegiate Church of Battlefield in memory of all those who fell at Shrewsbury. The Dunbars were honoured guests at the English court; the Percys were toasted in Scotland. Dunbar and his son Gawain were well rewarded after the battle; Dunbar received lands in Lincolnshire, a house or inn in London and Gawain received a vill and lordship. In April 1404, John Herying or Herring, Dunbar's herald, was styled 'Shrewsbury Herald' as a special honour in recognition of Dunbar's contribution to the battle.

Early in 1404, Dunbar petitioned Henry to licence four ships at Newcastle to provision his tower at Cockburnspath, still holding out against the Scots under his son George.[225] Despite the many English cash payments and gifts of land, the Dunbars were in financial difficulties by 1404. George Dunbar informed Henry of his parlous state; also Henry Percy's followers were preventing his return to Cockburnspath. In February that year, Percy was pardoned and ordered by parliament to allow Dunbar to visit Cockburnspath - hence the provisioning of 4 vessels. Even so, as late as 1407, Countess Christian of Dunbar complained to Henry that she and her husband were unable to visit Cockburnspath because of pestilence and continuing Percy hostility.

After Shrewsbury, Henry increasingly desired peace with Scotland as he was chronically short of money due to the drain on his resources in suppressing Glendower's rebellion and because of commitments in France. Dunbar was a stumbling block in the subsequent negotiations; earlier peace initiatives had excluded him and Henry felt it was duty to protect one of his chief advisors. The Dunbars were now unpopular in England. They were in dispute with the English Church - probably over land - and Henry was obliged to issue a pardon in favour of

> 'Dunbar and his people....who have componed their quarrel with the Dean and Chapter of Lincoln at Navenby, and with the widow of John Blessewell of Navenby, for his murder.' [226]

Five years after Shrewsbury, the Dunbars had become an acute embarrassment to Henry. For example, after the incident at Navenby, Dunbar's cleric son Columba was censured for allowing his living at the Collegiate

Church of St Mary Magdalene, Bridgenorth to fall into disrepair, pocketing the money intended for its upkeep. When Columba returned to Scotland in 1409 with his family, he was declared a traitor in England, guilty of 'leaving dilapidations to granges, stables, roofs, and gutters' which would cost 900 merks (£600) to make good.

In 1409, Henry negotiated a treaty with the Duke of Albany, regent of Scotland after Robert III's death in 1406 and the capture of James I off Flamborough Head by English seamen. The treaty conveniently accommodated the return of George Dunbar to Scotland; that suited Henry and Albany as the former no longer needed him and the latter did, as Dunbar would counterbalance the might of the Douglases. Archibald Douglas was back in Scotland and broke his parole to Henry to return to captivity; he gave up the Dunbar earldom but Albany allowed him to keep Annandale. George Dunbar and his son George appeared before a Haddington parliament on 2nd October 1409 to formally resign his Annandale possessions to Douglas so that he could regain his other titles and lands.[227] Even so, Dunbar didn't completely sever his ties with Henry IV; on 2nd April 1410, the English king granted his protection to Elizabeth Dunbar, Rothesay's slighted mistress, when she gave up the veil and took up residence in the vill of Mordington, near Berwick. Elizabeth and the population of Mordington enjoyed Henry's favour for the next two years.[228]

Despite the overtures of the peace negotiations, war flared up with England the following year which gave the Dunbars an opportunity to restore their standing in Scotland. By 1410, only Berwick and Roxburgh Castles and the small but impregnable Fast Castle, near St Abbs remained in English hands. Fast was held by Thomas Holden, more of a freebooter than a king's man. With 100 men, Patrick Dunbar of Biel re-took Fast Castle 'with as much cunning as bravery'[229] as we are told in *Scotichronicon*, hinting of bribery, although Holinshed writes that Patrick with a hundred

> 'hardie persons, came earlie one morning somewhat before the breake of day to Fast castell, and wan [won] the same, takeing the Capteine prisoner, whose name was Thomas Holden,'

Holden, pirate at sea and marauder on land, had terrorised the countryside from St Abbs to Coldingham for some time.[230] With Dunbar, Fast, Cockburnspath and Billie Castles again held by the Dunbars for Scotland, the East March was secure. Then on 28th June 1411, Gawain or Gavin Dunbar and Douglas of Drumlanrig attacked the English in Roxburgh, torching the town and destroying the bridge across the Tweed.[231]

These Dunbar successes were small compared with the major attacks made by Richard de Umfraville, Admiral of the English fleet; with a squadron of 10 ships, de Umfraville ravaged the coast on both sides of the Firth of Forth, capturing 14 Scottish merchantmen and considerable booty, including a large quantity of grain which was then in short supply in England. This exploit earned him the epither *Robin Mendmarket.*

On 23rd May 1411,[232] Dunbar and Douglas were among the commissioners Albany appointed to treat for peace with England; in December, Dunbar was one of the ambassadors sent to Henry IV to negotiate the return of Albany's son Murdoch, in English custody since Homildon Hill. The point is significant. Albany made no moves to secure the release of James I; the future king would not forget the slight when he returned to Scotland in 1424. In January 1412, James sent his chaplain to the Scottish court with several letters requesting that fresh negotiations for his release; one of the letters was addressed to the Earls of Douglas and Dunbar and James Douglas of Dalkeith and refers to James' special trust in those in whose hands his best chances of freedom lay.

During the negotiations, Henry IV died suddenly on 20th March 1413. His son, Henry V refused to free either James or Murdoch as he wanted to ensure Scotland's good behaviour while he pursued his ambitions in France. On 7th August, Albany gave a commission to Sir Patrick Dunbar of Biel and two other knights to treat for a trade agreement with England but Henry V was preoccupied with his claim to the French throne.[233] Albany continued to petition for the release of his son but not James I. Murdoch was finally freed in 1417 and James was allowed to visit Scotland on parole.

By 1417, on the surface at least, the feud between Dunbar and Douglas seems to have lessened although Dunbar made it clear that while he had resumed his place in the East March, he was no longer prepared to undertake one of his traditional obligations. In October, he wrote to the Countess of Westmorland from his 'castell of Dunbar' in response to the Countess' plea that he should protect Coldingham Priory, a cell of Durham. In the past, Coldingham had looked to the Dunbars and their vassals the Homes for protection. However, Dunbar reminded the Countess that while he and his ancestors had willingly supported the Priory in the past, this was now the responsibility of the Douglases as the Earl of Douglas had been appointed 'sovereign baillie' of Coldingham by the Dean and Chapter of Durham in 1414 against Dunbar's wishes. Furthermore, Douglas had been granted the lordship or superiority of Coldingham in 1406 and Dunbar wanted to wash his hands of it all.

Despite Henry V's continued absence in France, hostility towards England was limited to a half-hearted, two-pronged attack on Berwick by the ageing Albany and on Roxburgh by the Earl of Douglas; this adventure went by the appropriately named *Foul Raid* - foul meaning foolish -which brought retaliation from Richard de

Umfraville, now governor of Berwick. De Umfraville and Henry IV's brother, the Duke of Bedford burnt Dunbar, Hawick, Selkirk, Jedburgh and Lauder. Albany died on 3rd September 1420, his regency marked by a certain success in the extent to which he controlled his nobles; however, not unnaturally, he had tended to please the stronger families like the Douglases. In 1424, James I returned to a Scotland wracked with anarchy, his nobles acting like petty kings. George Dunbar and Archibald Douglas were two such men; the former did not live to see the return of James, as he died of pestilence some time between 1422 and 1423;[234] one account places his death even earlier in 1416. A facsimile copy recording the 10th Earl of Dunbar's death survives;[235] an entry added in a sixteenth century hand states that the Earl's epitaph within Dunbar Collegiate Church bore the following inscription:

> 'Here lyis Erll George the Brytane to thir thre kingis that bair the crown ves of
> thair blud and of thair kyn and hes governit this land wit in xlviii [48] yeiris space
> and in the yer of Grace 1416 Scotland, Ingland and Denmark.'

George, 10th Earl of Dunbar and March had succeeded to the earldom in 1368 and so by 1416, he had held the title for 48 years. The inscription appears to have been lost after the Collegiate Church was demolished in 1819; it is difficult to understand its meaning - especially as to the three kings of whose blood the Earl was other than Henry IV and perhaps one of the Stewards who took the throne. The reference to Denmark is obscure. However, according to another source,[236] the 10th Earl was admitted to the monastic confraternity of Durham in January 1418, a tradition of earlier Dunbars. A more precise reference to his death occurs in a letter dated 3rd January 1424 to Pope Martin V seeking a successor to Dunbar as patron of the church of Cumnock - part of Dunbar lands which had fallen vacant 'lately....by the death....of George Dunbar.'[237] Bower's *Scotichronicon* is grudgingly complimentary about George Dunbar:

> 'He was accounted most fortunate in every encounter, for his side always prevailed, whether he was
> the commander or in the company of greater men, as was clear in the battle[s] of Otterburn, Nisbet,
> Humbleton [Homildon], Shrewsbury and other laudable fights.'

George, 10th Earl of Dunbar and 3rd of March left a quiverful of children who should have ensured the continuation of the Dunbar line.

George, 11th Earl of Dunbar and 4th of March

George, 11th Earl of Dunbar, aged 50 in 1423 is mentioned in English state documents that year for the first time, he being one of the commissioners appointed to negotiate James I's freedom. From 1423, his name figures prominently in several documents and accounts. One of the first of these was the seven-year truce agreed between Scotland and England, a condition of James' release; Dunbar's seal is among those of other nobles who agreed to guarantee the peace.[238] George's brothers Sir Patrick of Biel, Sir David of Cockburn and the illegitimate Nicholas were hostages in the Tower of London for James I when he visited Scotland on parole between 1421 and 1423;[239] David was set free briefly in 1421 at James I's personal request, a gesture David never forgot and repaid to some extent when James was assassinated in 1437, as will be seen.

In 1424, George Dunbar and his brother Patrick were among the nobles who escorted James I and his queen Joan of Beaufort across the Border. James was crowned on 21st May at Scone, installed by the regent Murdoch, Duke of Albany whose son Alexander was knighted along with 18 of the principal barons, including Dunbar. Five days later, James investigated the abuses of government under the Albany regime. He appointed 11 auditors to report on the state of the crown revenues, a Domesday Book survey in microcosm; one of the auditors was Sir Patrick Dunbar of Biel. A parliament convened in Edinburgh in July passed several new measures to enhance the king's income. These included a 5% tax on land and goods, new export duties on certain commodities such as salted herring and cloth; there was also legislation concerning crown lands and the government of town burghs. The new laws affected not only George Dunbar personally but the free burgh of Dunbar. From the outset of his reign, James was determined to break the power of his nobles; at a parliament in Perth on 12th March 1425, he declared that the country was in poor shape, exhausted by mismanagement, violence, anarchy and corruption. On 21st March, he had Murdoch arrested along with his son Alexander and 26 nobles including the Earls of Dunbar and Douglas, Hay of Errol, Hepburn of Hailes, Hay of Yester and Ramsay of Dalhousie. Most were imprisoned at Perth.

James sent a clear message to his nobles; there would be no half measures, no leniency towards wayward spirits. He set about cleaning the Augean stables in the most direct and public manner. After eleven months' rule, he now felt strong enough to take action, particularly after the death of John, Earl of Buchan and Archibald, 4th Earl of Douglas, both of whom fell at the battle of Verneuil in France, 1424. (Buchan and Douglas commanded the Scottish army in France). His successor, Archibald, the 5th Earl was favoured by James who enlisted his support to isolate Murdoch and his faction. On 24th May 1425, James' parliament at Stirling, with

Dunbar and the 5th Earl of Douglas among the jurors, found Murdoch's son Walter guilty of robbery. Murdoch and his sons Alexander and Walter were executed along with their associate, the 80 year-old Earl of Lennox. James confiscated their estates, thereby enriching the crown with an annual income of £1,000.

The 11th Earl of Dunbar lived quietly in Dunbar from 1425 onwards; there are practically no references to him or his family in state records for the next decade apart from a petition to England in 1426 by 'Sir Patrick of Dunbarre [the heir to the earldom] and Gilbert of Hay esquire' for safe-conduct for a year ' for their wives to come to them and make a pilgrimage to Canterbury if they wish.'[240] In 1432, Dunbar was accused of 'putting violent hands' on 'Laurence' the Dean of Dunbar Collegiate Church for some unspecified reason, possibly connected with the appointment of the Earl of Angus as warden of the East March in 1430. Perhaps he encouraged William Drax, Prior of Coldingham and David Home of Wedderburn to plot against Angus who was supported by Hepburn of Hailes, Dunbar's vassal. By 1434, Dunbar's standing in the king's esteem had evaporated; for some reason, James chose to ignore him.

In 1429, the burgh of Dunbar played a small and indirect part in the fate of Joan of Arc in France. The French, again at war with England, had been inspired by Joan who lifted the siege of Orleans. Under the continuing *Auld Alliance*, Scottish troops served in the French army, mainly the remnants of the Earl of Buchan's forces destroyed at Verneuil in 1424. These Scots fought under Joan's banner and entered Orleans with her on 14th April 1429. England protested to James about the part played by Scottish soldiers as the two countries were technically at peace. Cardinal Beaufort, James' uncle-in-law came north to meet James at Coldingham in May 1429. The king stayed at Dunbar to refresh himself then proceeded to Coldingham and the historic meeting with Beaufort.[241] On that 'day of truce' a treaty was proposed and drawn up on 12th July whereunder no more Scottish troops would be sent to France, nor would Scotland wage war on England. These measures contributed to Joan of Arc's increasing difficulties in fighting the English. While it would be overstating the case to attribute her capture to the lack of Scottish support, this certainly affected France's ability to prosecute the war. Despite the treaty, no Scottish soldier serving in France deserted Joan; there were Scots with her to the very end, when she was burnt at the stake for witchcraft on 30th May 1431.

James continued to lean heavily on his nobles, particularly the 11th Earl of Dunbar. He knew the earldom was rich and prosperous and that at any time, a renegade Dunbar earl might invite an English army into the East March. On the surface, relations between James and Dunbar were congenial. George Dunbar sponsored - some accounts say he was godfather to - James' baby son, the future James II.[242] As already noted, Dunbar had been replaced by the Earl of Douglas - a Red Douglas - as warden of the East March so that by 1430, the Red and Black Douglases controlled the three Border Marches. The death of James Dunbar, 8th Earl of Moray in 1430 left two daughters in an earldom which was a male fief; George Dunbar was James' second cousin and he made an unsuccessful bid for the earldom. By now, matters had turned decidedly sour for the Dunbars.

James was at his deadliest when he affected friendship. A shrewd businessman, he cast his eyes on the lucrative income to be derived from the earldom of Dunbar. To this end, he began to isolate George Dunbar in 1431. James then contended that the Duke of Albany had acted outwith his authority as regent in alienating any lands which on the death of an illegitimate heir would have reverted to the crown. The words are meaningless; what James was saying was that he would not underwrite anything Albany had done in his name. A test case arose about lands in Yetholm in which James challenged Albany's decision; he would use this as a precedent to justify further attacks on his nobles.

For George Dunbar, matters came to a head in 1434. James accused him of holding his titles and lands falsely on the grounds of his father's treason in 1400. He apparently based his claim to the earldom of Dunbar and March by right of inheritance from his late brother, the Duke of Albany. In the spring of 1434, Dunbar went to Edinburgh to plead the case of some of his vassals when he was suddenly and unexpectedly detained in Edinburgh Castle. Bower tells us that Dunbar was examined by a parliament at Perth in August and that his estates were declared forfeit to the crown. Again according to Bower, James I ordered the Earl of Angus, his chancellor William Crichton and Hepburn of Hailes to occupy Dunbar Castle; Hepburn was appointed its governor. Dunbar protested that he had been pardoned for his conduct in 1400 but the king wasn't moved; he declared that Albany had no right to pardon him or his father in 1409 and that as a consequence, his lands were forfeit. James I has been variously described as a family man, a poet and a king who cared about the common people; he was also mean and vindictive. Many nobles were shocked by his treatment of the Dunbars; they began to ask themselves on whom the axe would next fall.

James had deliberately alienated George Dunbar, acting coldly towards him to pave the way to confiscate his earldom. Dunbar was probably astute enough to recognise James' motives. In desperation, he wrote to Henry VI seeking a safe-conduct to England for himself, his son and heir Patrick and several servants; the warrant was granted and would last from January 1435 to January 1436. It was the worst decision Dunbar could have made, given the circumstances of his forfeiture.

In January 1435, a parliament at Perth appointed a committee of nine - three each of barons, clergymen and burgesses - to adjudicate on certain matters before it; it is not clear whether Dunbar's case was on the agenda but during the sitting, Dunbar was publicly informed that 'in consequence of the forfeiture of Lord George of Dunbar, Earl of March, all title of property to the lands and earldom of March and lordship of Dunbar, with whatever lands the same baron held of the Crown, [now]belonged of right to the king.'[243] Abbot Bower of Inchcolm was present when Dunbar's forfeiture was announced. The sins of the father had been visited on the son; there were no mitigating circumstances, no right of appeal, no voices raised in protest or support. Dunbar appears to have accepted the king's decision quietly, a decision parliament ratified immediately.[244]

The last blood-line Earl of Dunbar deserved better treatment than he received. Bower tells us that James had it in mind to mitigate his harshness by creating Dunbar Earl of Buchan in the north, where he would pose less of a threat; however, there is no documentary evidence to support this, nor is there any basis for Bower's belief that a pension of 400 merks (£133) was paid to Dunbar and his heir, Patrick. George Dunbar retired quietly to Kilconquhar, part of the barony of St Monans in the East Neuk of Fife, near modern Thornton Junction; the parish contained the hamlets of Earlsferry, Pitcorthie, Largo, Williamsburg and Liberty. In 1435, George Dunbar became plain Sir George Dunbar of Kilconquhar;[245] like his father, he sought English help but this time it was not forthcoming..[246]

James did not keep all Dunbar's possessions for himself; he gave Dunbar Castle to Sir Walter Haliburton of Dirleton and Hepburn of Hailes also benefited from Dunbar's forfeiture.[247] Meanwhile, although England was anxious to maintain the truce made in 1429, Border hostility erupted once more. Dunbar's son Patrick received a safe-conduct to visit Henry VI on 12th July 1435, no doubt to inform the English king of his plans. Patrick had formed an association with Sir Robert Ogle, governor of Berwick and Henry Percy of Northumberland. The three broke into the East March in early autumn with a strong body of men, plundering former Dunbar possessions. James complained to the English Privy Council on 26th September about Ogle's foray which he said was in support of the deposed Earl of Dunbar's son, Patric, described as 'Paton of Dunbar, the king's rebel'. By this time, Ogle had been captured by the Earl of Angus, Adam Hepburn of Hailes and Alexander Ramsay of Dalhousie at Piper Dene or Piperdean [248] on 10th September where a skirmish had gone against Ogle and Dunbar.[249] Patrick Dunbar managed to escape capture but from then on, the Dunbars fade into obscurity although the family did not die out until the reign of Mary, Queen of Scots. Visits to England in July, October and November failed to convince Henry VI of any Dunbar claims for restitution, nor did Henry see any political advantage in pressing the family's claims with James I. George Dunbar remained in Kilconquhar and his son Patrick was forced to live in England, declared a traitor. With English assistance, Patrick and Archibald his brother - probably the Archibald who seized Hepburn's castle at Hailes near East Linton in 1446 - raided Perth but this was no more than banditry. Archibald Dunbar burnt Dunbar in 1446; it was burnt again in 1448 by Henry Percy and Robert Ogle, more by way of insult to the House of Douglas than a determined attempt to start a war.

These incidents were no more than the dying throes of a once-proud family which had existed for almost four centuries. Little is known of George Dunbar's brothers and sisters after 1435. Sir Gawain or Gavin died in 1418. Columba de Dunbar was a controversial churchman who held the incumbency of Dunbar in 1411 after he returned to Scotland in 1409. (It will be remembered that he misappropriated funds for the repair of Bridgenorth chapel and stolen the lead from its roof; he was fined *in absentia* by Henry IV's commissioners but it is unlikely the fine was ever paid.) In Dunbar he was in contempt of the papal court in 1420 for refusing to surrender the benefice of Archdeacon of Lothian which he maintained was his along with other benefices. Of the Pope, he once said 'there was very little holiness about him.' When the papal executor arrived at Dunbar Castle to deliver the Pope's warrant forbidding him to hold any benefices, the executor 'in the presence of Columba was seized in the said castle by his mother and violently dragged away as if he were a robber and the letter of citation snatched from him with threats.' These misdeeds didn't prevent Columba's subsequent appointment as Bishop of Moray in 1422, when he completed the repairs to Elgin Cathedral (**ill 33**), sacked by the Wolf of Badenoch in 1390. It is believed that Columba installed the large circular window which survives in the ruined cathedral today. On his death, he was interred in the grounds of Elgin, in the Aisle of Thomas the Martyr, subsequently known as the Dunbar Aisle, burial place of the Morayshire Dunbars, hereditary sheriffs and constables of Moray. Today, Columba's much defaced effigy (**ill 34**) lies in the north transept; beside it is the effigy of Sir Alexander Dunbar of Westfield who died in 1498. On the west wall is a plaque commemorating the remains of John Dunbar of Bennetfield, the last Dunbar to be buried at Elgin in 1648.

As for the remaining members of the family, Sir Patrick of Biel survived until at least 1469; John, the youngest son appears to have died before 1438; Sir David of Cockburn who alone pursued James I's assassins

Illus 33: *Elgin Cathedral* KRM

in 1437 and was wounded - he lost fingers from his left hand - received as reward the barony of Auchtermonzie, Cairnie, in Fife,[250] lands which passed to his daughter who married Sir William Wallace of Craigie, 4th Earl of Crawford. Nicholas who was illegitimate was last heard of in 1421-24 while a hostage for James I in the Tower of London. Of Dunbar's sisters, the fortunes of Lady Elizabeth have already been discussed; little is known of Lady Jane who may have married a Crichton, as a Janet Dunbar is mentioned as the mother of William Crichton who supported the 3rd Duke of Albany against James III and escaped abroad in 1483.

George's own children appear to have adjusted to their new life. His heir Patrick, at first exiled in England after 1435 was pardoned as he returned to Scotland and married Elizabeth Dishington of Murthly. He was known as Patrick Dunbar of Kilconquhar, Master of March; he was still alive in 1503, when he is mentioned in a legal action concerning the lands of Balbully in Fife, within the lordship of Kilconquhar.[251]

Illus 34: *Tomb of Columba Dunbar, Elgin Cathedral* RJP

As for George Dunbar, 11th Earl of Dunbar and 4th of March, he died an old man in 1455. He lived long enough to learn of the murder of James I and the downfall of his great rivals the Earls of Douglas; he may have derived some grim satisfaction from the beheading of the 6th Earl of Douglas in 1440, the murder by James II of the 8th Earl of Douglas in 1452 and the death of Archibald Douglas, Earl of Moray at the battle of Arkinholm in 1455, a futile attempt to preserve the Black Douglas dynasty. George Dunbar died a proud if defeated man; he continued to use the family seal until his death on 4th August 1455,[252,253] just two months after an Edinburgh parliament issued a proclamation pronouncing the Black Douglases outlaws and announcing the forfeiture of the 9th Earl of Douglas after whose death in 1488, that line of the Douglas clan became extinct.[254] The manor at Kilconquhar where the Dunbars resided has long since disappeared; the chapel at which they worshipped had been granted to the nuns at North Berwick years earlier, in 1200, so in a sense, the last of the family retained a connection with East Lothian. A recently-discovered recumbent gravestone in Kilconquhar Parish Church graveyard bears an effigy of a knight (**ill 35**). It is quite possible that the grave is that of the 11th Earl of Dunbar, as the family continued to possess lands there until the reign of Mary, Queen of Scots. The effigy is badly weathered however and it is impossible to identify the heraldic markings which

Illus 35: *Possible effigy of 11th Earl of Dunbar in Kilconquhar Parish Church graveyard, Fife* RF

would confirm the identity of the incumbent.

The honour of Dunbar did not die out however. In the second half of the fifteenth century, James III's brother Alexander, 3rd Duke of Albany was styled Earl of March, Lord of Annandale and Man and he was given the lordship of Dunbar. In 1580, Robert Stewart, Earl of Lennox resigned his earldom to become Earl of March and Lord of Dunbar, honours confirmed by James IV's charter of 1582. Lennox held the title until 1586 when his honours became extinct. A few years later, Chancellor John Maitland of Thirlestane, Maitland of Lethington's brother, was rewarded by James VI for services to the crown; among many of the property rights he assumed was the lordship of Dunbar. However, because of hostility between James VI and Thirlestane in his final years, the king deprived him of all his titles and lands in 1593.

Geoge Home, Baron Berwick and Earl of Dunbar

The last incumbent of the earldom was George Home, the third child of Sir Alexander Home of Manderston and Jean or Janet Home of Spott; his parents married in 1552 and George was born in c.1556. George was presented at court by Alexander, 6th Lord Home in c.1582 and he became Gentleman of the Bedchamber to James VI in 1585. In 1591, he was given the lands of Horseley in the Merse, then Easter Spott in 1592. Shortly afterwards, he succeeded his uncle as Laird of Spott and from then on styled himself Sir George Home of Spott. His star continued to rise; in 1599, he was appointed sheriff of Berwick and in 1601, became provost of Dunbar and Lord High Treasurer of Scotland. George married Elizabeth, daughter of Sir Alexander Gordon of Gight by Agnes, the illegitimate daughter of Cardinal Beaton, Archbishop of St Andrews who was assassinated in 1546.[255] He received his knighthood in 1590, probably for accompanying James VI to Denmark to marry his queen, Anne; Home would have therefore known of the North Berwick Witches who reputedly raised the storms which first delayed the queen's voyage to Scotland, then almost sank the ship carrying the royal couple from Denmark (see Chapter 5).

With the union of the crowns in 1603, James VI and I took several Scottish officials with him to England; most were administrators and not surprisingly, Home was among them. He had already proven his worth as financial advisor to the king, contributing to the maintenance of law and order and implementing the king's religious policy. Home's meteoric rise seemed unstoppable; in England he became one of the few Privy Councillors from Scotland; he was appointed Keeper of the Wardrobe - the royal household finances - and in 1604, he was created Baron Home of Berwick. In the following year, he was elevated to the Dunbar earldom - technically the 12th Earl of Dunbar - on 5th July 1605. Despite his considerable contribution to the running of the country between 1600 and 1611, George Home has been largely ignored by English historians probably because his major contribution was to Scottish rather than English affairs of state - despite the fact that the two countries were united under one king.

George Home enjoyed the patronage of James VI and I, not only because of his close association with the king but because of his ability to get things done. He recognised the difficulties of governing Scotland from Whitehall, so he acted as the king's agent in the north from 1603, making punishing journeys to Scotland until his death in 1611.

In the first year of the union of the crowns, considerable progress was made in the administration of Scotland, even if it was ruled *in absentia*. The bureaucratic machinery there remained intact, as many Scottish officials who had gone south in 1603 returned home within the year. There was however a London group which consisted of the Duke of Lennox, the Earl of Mar, Lord Kinloss, Sir James Elphinstone and Sir George Home -

KRM

Illus 36: *Monument to Sir George Home, Earl of Dunbar 1605-1611, in Dunbar Parish Church*

a quintumverate of advisors to the king on Scottish matters. Some officials had stayed on in minor government posts and became naturalised Englishmen; members of the quintumverate, or inner circle, were admitted to the English Council of State but their influence on English affairs was negligible. Of the five barons, George Home alone was appointed to a prestigious government post - that of Chancellor of the Exchequer. His tenure was brief however.

An Anglo-Scottish commission was set up on 20th October 1604 to examine the possible union of the two parliaments; it contained 48 English and 31 Scottish members, broadly representative of the representatives in the indigenous parliaments - nobles, gentry, civil lawyers, clerics, merchants and burgesses. Several Scottish nobles such as the Catholic Earl of Huntly were excluded on religious grounds; George Home and his colleagues were also excluded on the grounds that the 31 Scottish commissioners would properly represent Scotland's interests.

In 1605, Home received an unexpected commission. The Border question - a thorn in the sides of both countries for centuries - would be settled once and for all. Henceforth, the Borders would be known as the Middle Shire, thus ending Border feuding. George Home was given the unenviable task of bringing law and order into the new shire; it was for this reason he was created Earl of Dunbar in 1605.[256] At this time, he was also appointed an English Privy Councillor and became a naturalised Englishman under an act of the English parliament In 1604, he had been appointed as Lieutenant of the East, Middle and West Marches of Scotland and a member of the Northumberland Commission of Peace. Things had gone full circle. The last Earl of Dunbar was determined to stamp his authority on these districts and he did just that. One account says of him:

> 'This quiet, ruthlessly efficient man had more influence in shaping policy in Northumberland and the Middle Shires than did any other single counsellor of state with the possible exception of Sir Robert Cecil.'[257]

A joint Border commission was established in February 1605 to pacify the area; its activities resulted in an unprecedented number of summons and convictions. George Home pursued a robust law enforcement policy. He was so successful that on 4th March 1604, the Council of Scotland wrote to the king and the Council of England, recommending that Home be made sole commissioner for both sides of the Border. In September that year he 'condemned and caused hang above 140 of the nimblest and most powerful thieves in all the Borders.' Home was given a free hand to administer justice; ruthless and draconian, his suppression of the criminal elements gave rise to the expression *Jeddart [Jedburgh] Justice* - hanging without trial - an instance of which occurred at Dumfries in 1609, when Home ordered a mass hanging there.

After pacifying the Borders, James turned his attention to the Scottish Kirk. He was determined to continue his pre-1603 policy of introducing Episcopacy, having created titular bishops in 1601. His aim was to secure a place for bishops in the Presbyterian Church, thus bringing it in line with England. Again he used Home who set about implementing the king's policy with his usual single-mindedness. His first task was to smooth the ruffled feathers of the more radical elements in the mixed Presbyterian and Episcopalian General Assembly; to this end, he summoned the Assembly to a conference in London to discuss church reform. Why London? Perhaps Home felt there was less likelihood of pressure from within Scotland; his 'guests' could enjoy the delights of London and contemplate the king's proposals in a relaxed atmosphere. More significant perhaps is the fact that Home chose London as the venue to justify payments of generous 'travelling expenses' - bribery in other words - as these payments were much criticised. However, Home was scrupulously honest where money was concerned; he accounted for every penny he spent, even if the way he spent it was suspect.

In 1605, there was a minor rebellion in which several Scottish Kirk ministers defied the crown in the matter of Episcopacy. Home supervised their trial and in 1606, a verdict was given in the king's favour. The so-called *Red Parliament* enacted two Articles; one gave the king absolute authority over all persons and causes; the other confirmed the restoration of bishops.

During the protracted negotiations with the Scottish Kirk, Home was involved in a matter of doubtful honesty relating to two significant trials. In August 1608, he extracted a dubious confession from George Sprott concerning his part in the Gowrie Conspiracy - a strange episode which occurred in 1600, when the Earl of Gowrie attempted to detain James VI at Gowrie House. Sprott was executed in Home's presence. The second trial concerned James Elphinstone, 1st Lord Balmerino who in 1605 had opposed Home in the Scottish Council of Session. Before that, in 1599, Balmerino had inserted a letter among others to be signed by James VI; the letter was addressed to Pope Clement VIII and sought a favourable position in the Catholic Church for one of Balmerino's kinsmen. Elizabeth I somehow received information about this and she complained to James; the business thus created a minor diplomatic incident. Even though James punished the offending Lord Balmerino, Home indicted him a second time, probably for personal reasons. While Balmerino escaped the headsman's axe, he was imprisoned in 1609 and ended his days quietly on his Fife estate in 1612. Home never missed an opportunity to get his revenge on any who opposed him.

Home was also involved in matters stemming from the infamous Powder Treason or Gunpowder Plot discovered on the 4th - not the 5th - of November 1605, the day before parliament was due to meet.[258] As is well-known, the Plot was organised by Catholics who planned revenge on the king and his government for the severe treatment of those of the old faith. They intended to blow up thc king and Parliament but one of the conspirators, Guido or Guy Fawkes was caught in the cellars handling barrels of gunpowder; he and his fellow conspirators were hanged. About seventeen months later, in March 1607, George Home apprehended George Jarvis, a seminary priest in Berwick and sent him to Dunbar under suspicion of involvement in the attempt on the king's life in 1605. On 30th August 1609, Home sent two priests to the Tower of London under suspicion of their collusion in the same plot.[259] In these and matters like the subjugation of the Borders, Home was assisted by the horse and garrison of Berwick Castle; he had his own private army so to speak.[260] In October 1609, Home, with the characteristic sentimentality of the ruthless, presented the king ' "with a little book, written in his mother's own hand " very wisely and [offering] good counsel to her son [George].'[261]

From 1605 to 1610, Home worked closely with Archbishop James Spottiswoode, implementing James' policy of restoring diocesan Episcopacy in Scotland. Spottiswoode (1565-1639) was the son of a Midcalder minister who had caught James' ear, being an avid supporter of Episcopacy. Spottiswoode became Archbishop of Glasgow, then St Andrews and in 1635 was appointed Chancellor of Scotland. He was excommunicated by the Covenanter Church in 1638 possibly for criticising the Kirk's persecution of so-called witches.

Home effectively carried through the legislation for the restoration of bishops at a parliament in Perth in 1606. There was some talk of Home forcing - and bribing - recalcitrant elements in the Kirk but by 1610, Episcopacy was firmly established in Scotland. On 19th August 1608, the Council of Scotland issued a warrant requesting letters patent from the king to appoint Home - by now a Knight of the Garter - Treasurer or Lord Chancellor of Scotland, an appointment James I readily confirmed.

James showered Home with gifts - the revenues from towns in Annandale, effective from 15th January 1610; under his charter of that year, Home became sheriff of Annandale and heritable keeper of the castle of Lochmaben. History was repeating itself. Within the year however, Home sold his rights and appointments in Annandale for 20,000 merks (£1,110 sterling) to John Murray of Rampatrick, groom to the Royal Bedchamber, later created Earl of Annandale. The sale was probably to meet the costs of the sumptuous marriage festivities Home arranged for his daughter Elizabeth and her husband, Lord Walden, later Earl of Suffolk, shortly after Home's death.[262] At this time, Home had begun to build himself an impressive 'palace' in Berwick which was almost completed in 1611 when he died unexpectedly at Whitehall 'not without suspicion of poison' on 29th January. There is a cryptic reference to him in English state papers dated 8th December 1610: 'Lord Dunbar ill.'

Whether or not George Home was the victim of an assassination plot is difficult to prove. Some tongues inevitably wagged. He had made many enemies in his lifetime and several English nobles were jealous of his influence over the king. According to Sir John Scot's *Scotstarvit's Staggering State*, Home was given tablets of sugar by Secretary Robert Cecil to alleviate a cold. The tablets were thought to have been poisoned as Sir James Baillie, Home's associate and servant saw Cecil hand over the tablets; he swallowed a piece of one and came out 'all blisters; but by strength of body, he escaped death.' Rumour? Fact?

Home's death caused a stir in Scotland; some said a great tree had fallen in the forest. His body was embalmed and brought from London to Dunbar in a lead coffin which was interred within the Collegiate Church. *Miller, Dunbar* states that the last Earl of Dunbar was placed in the vault beneath his marble monument (**ill 36**), a tomb which was subsequently vandalised by persons unknown, probably because of Home's unpopularity in Scotland.

Home's name lingered on sporadically in English state papers. Before his death, he had been concerned about the condition of the bridge over the Tweed at Berwick.[263] In March 1611, part of it fell down so that horses couldn't cross it as two of the wooden support arches had collapsed.[264] In 1620, the Bishop of Durham gave a full account of the recently erected wooden bridge 'irrespective of what was spent by the Earl of Dunbar between 1608 and 1611,'[265] Immediately after Home's death, the teinds and herring assize of Dunbar which were due to Home were collected by the Homes of Renton until his estate was settled.

Home's possessions were considerable and an inventory was required. Like his predecessors, he owned lands, manors and castles on both sides of the Border, although his Northumberland property reverted to the crown on 10th August 1611. By all accounts, Home had been the king's staunch and loyal supporter; scrupulous in anything he undertook, he was consequently unloved in his own country. Spottiswoode once described him as 'a man of deep wit, few words and in His Majesty's service, no less fulfilled than fortunate.' Home seems to have been adept at carrying out the king's orders at the precise psychological moment to achieve maximum effect. The English may have detested him for his close relationship with the king and because he was Scottish and powerful. His own countrymen certainly shared their view.

In 1987, when Dunbar Parish Church was gutted by fire, the Earl of Dunbar's impressive black, brown and white marble monument - the work of the Dutch sculptor Maximilian Colt who also sculpted Elizabeth I's monument in Westminster Abbey in 1603 - was badly damaged and had to be restored by skilled craftsmen. It is 26 feet high and Dunbar is represented bareheaded and kneeling at prayer on a cushion. He is wearing armour beneath his knight's robes; two knights in full armour stand on each side. Above the knights are female figures representing Justice and Wisdom; between them is Fame while opposite is Peace. The monument was moved from a central position against the E wall of the main part of the church when the eastern apse was added in 1895. That central position is now occupied by the pulpit added after the fire of 1987. The inscription on the monument reads:

> 'Here lyeth the body of the Reight Hoble [Honourable], George, Erle of Dvnbar, Baron Howme of Barwick, Lord Heigh Tressr. [Treasurer] of Scotland, Knight of the most Noble Order of the Garter, and one of His Matte. [Majesty's] most Hoble. Privie Covnsell, Whoe depted [departed] this life the XXIX day of Iannvary,MDCX,' [Under the Gregorian calendar adopted in Scotland in 1600, the date should be MDCXI]

The honorific Earl of Dunbar did not disappear on George Home's death. With no male heirs, George's honorific was dormant. Several *de jure* earls followed him however:

John Home (1611-28): son of George Home of Spott; succeeded in none of the Dunbar estates; the Lord Advocate's certificate of 6th August 1634 states that the earldom descended to him but that he 'conceiving his fortune too mean, forebore to assume the dignity'.

George Home (1630-51?): nephew and heir of Alexander Home of Manderston

Sir Alexander Home (165175): son and heir of Alexander Home's first wife; Charles II confirmed the earldom, setting out that he 'well deserved more than a bare confirmation of what in so much right belongs to him' on 6th May 1651

Alexander Home of Manderston: first son and heir of George Home of Manderston (1651?- 75): served heir to his father on 24th September 1663; captained a troop of horse in Dutch service; on 14th October 1689, William III [of Orange] confirmed the earldom and undersigned the earlier confirmation of Charles II; the family reputedly lived in Holland and became extinct in the male line before the end of the seventeenth century.

The title was never used again officially although it refused to disappear. James Stewart, the Old Pretender, created James Murray, second son of Lord Stormont and brother of Lord Mansfield proleptic Earl of Dunbar in 1727 by way of reward for acting as proxy at the wedding ceremony of James and Clementine Sobieski, parents of Charles Edward Stewart, known as Bonnie Prince Charlie. Murray became Charles' tutor in 1729.[266] The Old Pretender's will is preserved at Avignon with other Jacobite papers, presumably including the warrant conferring the Dunbar title on James Murray.[267] The 'last' Earl of Dunbar died at Avignon in 1770 aged 80. The title has been dormant for about four centuries, although the Earl of March honorific has never died out; Lord William Douglas, second son of the 1st Marquis of Queensberry became Earl of March in 1697; his grandson William, 3rd Earl of March succeeded as 4th Marquis of Queensberry but as he died without issue, the title went to the Earls of Wemyss who today are styled Wemyss and March.

The name Dunbar is a modern surname. It exists in profusion in the north-east and south-west of Scotland, the USA, Canada, Australia, South Africa and oddly, in Scandinavia. Many of the slaves in the cotton plantations in the Southern States of the USA took the surname Dunbar from their masters - hence its preponderance there. Most of the Scottish Dunbars descend from the last Dunbar Earl of Moray who was murdered at Frendraught in 1429. Many of the clan Dunbar owe their origins to the Dunbars of Westfield in Morayshire; others occur in the old Dunbar lands of Mochrum, Ayrshire. The family name lives on and baronetcies continue today - the Dunbars of Durn, Banffshire, the Westfield Dunbars, the Dunbars of Hemprigge in Caithness. One or two adopted the name Gospatric - notably Sir Alec Douglas Hume, the Prime Minister whose line descended from Ada, daughter of one of the blood-line earls.

The Dunbars are part of Scotland's history and their name lives on in countries all over the world.

Fig 4 The Earls of Dunbar and March between 1289 to 1435

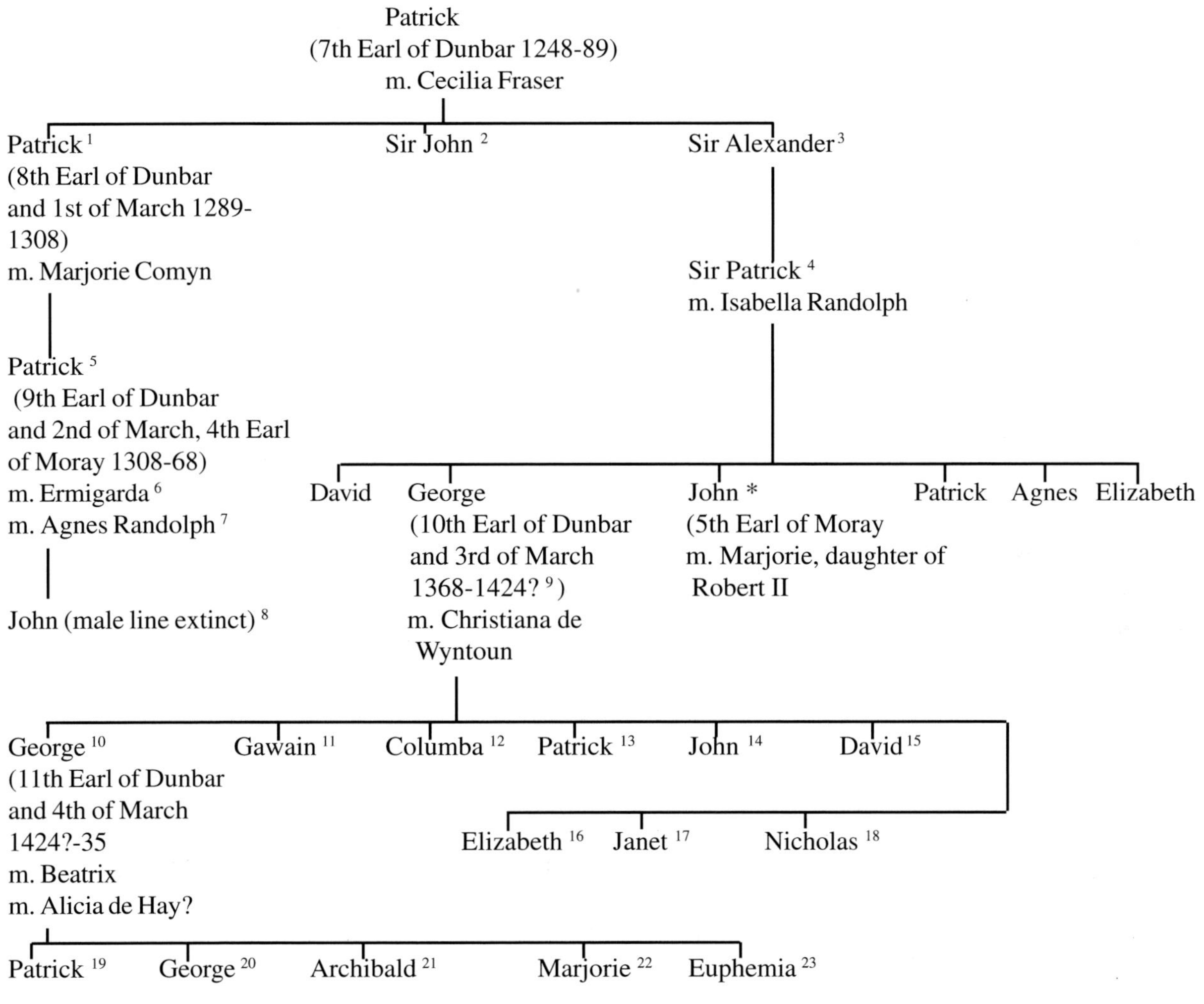

* See fig. 5 for the Dunbar Earls of Moray

Notes to Fig 4

1 Patrick (b. 1243) was the first to style himself 'of March' referring to himself as 3rd of March, known as Patrick-with-the-Black-Beard (*Scalacronica*), he married Marjorie Comyn of Buchan, daughter of Alexander Buchan

2 He may have been Sir John Dunbar of Birkenside, Lauderdale who witness *Yester Writ* No 17 (1250-1267). He is named in the Turnberry Bond of 1286

3 Sir Alexander is also mentioned in the Turnberry Bond along with brothers Patrick and John. Alive in 1231, the date of his death is uncertain. He received several payments of 18 and 20 merks from Alexander III (*Hist. Docs. Scotland vols I, ii* Nos XXXVI, LXVI, LXXIII and *CDS vol v* No 65 dated 7th June 1289, three years after the king's death.) Is it possible that he was the fruit of a liaison between the 7th Earl's wife Cecilia (see fig. 3) and the king who was notoriously fond of the ladies?

4 Alexander's son Patrick fought at Neville's Cross in 1346 and at Poitiers in 1356 against England. He died en route to the Holy Land in 1356-57 and was buried at Candia, Crete. His issue included the future 10th Earl of Dunbar:

George	as the 9th Earl died without male heirs, he was given the earldom by David II
John	the first officially recognised Dunbar Earl of Moray
Patrick	known as Sir Patrick of Biel, he was an English prisoner after Homildon Hill in 1402, when he fought against brother George. He was alive in 1438 and is reputedly the ancestor of William Dunbar, the renowned medieval poet
David	received lands in Cumnock, Blantyre and elsewhere in 1374; the Dunbars of Mochrum and Cumnock descend from him
Agnes	but for the untimely death of David II, she would have become queen of Scotland
Elizabeth	m. John Maitland of Lethington, ancestor of the Lauderdale family; their daughter m. Johannes de Haga, which may links the Dunbars to the Haigs of Bemersyde, ancestors of Earl Haig (World War I)

5 Patrick, 9th Earl of Dunbar was 24 when he succeeded his father. He was a wavering earl who more than any other has attracted the censure - and bias - of historians

6 Ermigarda, the 9th Earl's first wife is a mystery lady; nothing is known of her except that she was pregnant - probably with John who pre-deceased his father - when she received two casks of wine from Edward I in 1303-04

7 Ermigarda was dead by 1320. The 9th Earl married Agnes, daughter of Thomas Randolph, a Border lord who owned Broxburn, near Dunbar, among other lands which were forfeited for his support for Bruce. (By way of compensation, Bruce gave him lands in Moray and he assumed the title Earl of Moray). Agnes Randolph and Patrick Dunbar were granted a papal dispensation on 18th August 1320 to marry; they became man and wife some time afterwards as a second dispensation dated 16th January 1324 noted that they were within the 3rd and 4th degrees of consanguinity but were permitted to remain married, any issue being considered legitimate. 'Black' Agnes brought her husband no children but much wealth, as she and her sister Isabella inherited the Moray earldom after their sole surviving brother John was killed at Neville's Cross in 1346. Through this marriage, Dunbar became related to Robert Bruce, Thomas Randolph's cousin

8 John died before his father and appears to have been the sole issue of Lady Ermigarda. *Boece, Hist.* suggests there were other children, which is unlikely as the earldom passed to George, the son of the 9th Earl's cousin. John was heir to the Dunbar earldom; he became a hostage for David II after Neville's Cross and is thought to have died between 1354 and 1356

9 George was 28 when he unexpectedly inherited the Dunbar earldom and the Lordship of of Annandale and Man in 1368. He married Christiana who according to Cockayne, *Peerage (GEC)* was the daughter of Alan de Wintoun and Margaret, daughter and heir of Sir Alexander Seton of Seton. (*A History of the Family of Seton* claims Christiana was the daughter of Christopher Seton and Agnes Dunbar ' a daughter of the 7th Earl of Dunbar' which is incorrect. Their son Sir William became the first Lord of Seton). The date of the 10th Earl's death is reputedly 1416 but he appears to have been alive in 1422, as he named Christiana his spouse in a charter dated that year. He also enacted a charter in September 1422 giving his armour-bearer, George Inglis lands in Lochend; he is also referred to as the late lay patron of the church of Cumnock in a papal document of 3rd January 1423

10 George, 11th Earl of Dunbar and 4th of March is first mentioned in a charter of 1385, when he commanded the garrison at Cockburnspath Tower. On 27th March 1390, Robert II granted him all wards and reliefs due from the Earldom of Moray and the Lordship of Annandale; failing this, these rights were to be granted to his brothers in descending age order ie Gawain, Colin or Columba, Patrick and John. George was given a safe conduct to 'go beyond the sea' in March 1399 but this is thought to have been a reference to the fact that he joined his father in his rebellion against Robert III. George certainly inherited the earldom in 1423x1424. He married Beatrix [?] after 27th March 1390 and she died before 7th August 1421, when he received a papal dispensation to marry Alicia, daughter of Sir William Hay of Yester; it is doubtful whether this marriage was solemnised. George was the last blood-line Earl of Dunbar, dying in August 1455, known simply as Sir George Dunbar of Kilconquhar after 1435, the year his titles and lands were forfeited to James I.

11 Sir Gawain or Gavin is named in Robert II's charter of 1390 (see note 10) and also in a safe conduct from Henry IV dated 1402 which permitted him to enter England. He received money and land for his services to the English king and on his return to Scotland in 1409, received payments from the Scottish Exchequer and grants from cus toms in the East March until about 1417, when he is thought to have died

12 Colin or Columba was born in c.1390 and educated at Oxford in 1402-03. He was something of a lax churchan, possibly on account of his tender years. He was put in charge of the church in Bridgenorth, England between 1402 and 1409, robbing it of money and materials. In 1411, aged 21, he became Dean of Dunbar Collegiate Church which carried a stipend of £40 a year. He witnessed the charter founding St Andrews University on 28th February 1412 (*PSAS vol 22* 1988). According to *SP*, he received the hospital at Ruthven as an adddtional benefice valued at £30 in 1413; the hospital is not listed in *Medieval Houses, Scotland*. Columba became Bishop of Moray on 3rd April 1422 and was called to Rome in c.1429 - possibly to be rewarded for his restora tion of Elgin Cathedral. He died at Spynie Palace in 1435. He is named as Sir Columba, Bishop of Moray in a charter by his sister Elizabeth dated 24th April 1438

13 Patrick of Biel is mentioned in Robert II's charter of 1390 (see note 10) and in an English safe conduct of 1400. He m. Dame Annabelle Boyd (*Yester Writs* No 151); the date of his death is uncertain but he was alive in 1469

14 John is thought to have died young

15 Sir David of Cockburn is mentioned in an English safe conduct dated 1402. He received for life the lands of Cockburn and Birgham in Berwickshire some time before his father died. His daughter or grand-daughter brought the lands of Cockburn to her husband Alexander, 4th Earl of Crawford; she may be the Margaret who 'sprung from the Dunbar family and was seduced by James III' (*Buchanan, Hist*)

16 Elizabeth was the jilted lover of the Earl of Rothesay, heir to the throne. She took the veil and entered the hospital of St Leonards, Perth. On 23rd November 1411, Robert Clarkson, master of St Leonards renounced it and all gifts attaching thereto to 'Dame Elizabeth Dunbar that she may be governor of the hospital which had formerly been governed by women.' She resigned the post on 24th April 1438 to Henry Wardlaw, Bishop of St Andrews, in favour of the prior and brethren of the Charterhouse of the Vale, near Perth; in return, Elizabeth asked that prayers be said for herself, her father and mother and brothers George, Gavin, Patrick, John and 'Sir Davy'; also included were Henry Wardlaw, Henry Wardlaw of Spott, his brother William, sister Jonet and Margaret, daughter of the late Henry Wardlaw of Spott

17 Lady Jonet or Janet is obscure. *Miller, Dunbar* says she was married to John, 2nd Lord Seton, which is accurate, then Sir Adam Johnston of Johnston

18 Nicholas was illegitimate. In 1394, his family petitioned the pope for his ordination into the church but there is no surviving evidence to prove that he took holy orders

19 Sir Patrick was another hostage for James I from 1421 to 1427; he appears to have died in 1453 (*Ers vol v* No 664). He married Elizabeth Sinclair and their issue ended the blood-line of the Gospatrics. Their descendant Andrew died childless in 1564, having inherited the lands of the last of the family estates along with his sisters Margaret, Janet, Elizabeth and Alison. Margaret married William MacDowel of Freugh; their son John was named as their heir in 1582. (Margaret had other husbands - John Vaus or Vaux, John Wemyss whom she divorced to marry John Giffart of Gorme. She is described in Riddell's *Inquiry* as the 'frail adultress Margaret, the eldest of the co-heiresses of the remains of Dunbar's earldom [sic] of Kilconquhar.') In about1574, Margaret disposed of Kilconquhar to Sir John Bellenden of Achnoull; she died in 1582. The second sister Janet married William Mundale, then left him for William Adair of Altoun; they had a daughter Christian Adair. Elizabeth died a spinster in 1566. The fourth sister Alison married David McCulloch of Drouchtan and she was alive in 1576 when she and Sir John Dunbar of Mochrum agreed that she should sell her half of Mochrum Loch and Kilconquhar. There is an interesting anecdote about Alison in Riddell's *Inquiry*; he describes her as 'a direct desendant and co-heiress of the ancient and once-powerful and illustrious House of the Dunbars, Earls of March.' Riddell goes on to say that she pursued an action of bastardy in 1573 with her husband's consent against her sister Janet's child, Christian. Alison contended that as Christian, the issue of Janet's liaison with William Adair was illegitimate, she couldn't inherit property since Janet was legally mar ried to William Mundale, by whom she also had issue. In due course, Christian Adair was declared an adultress and bastard in 1568. Thus two of the sisters ended the Dunbar line in a blaze of notoriety

20 George, named in his father's charter of 1423, styled himself George, Earl of March in charters infefting his kinsman, Hugh de Spense, with lands in Chirnside on 8th April and 15th November 1431. Little else is known about him and he may have died in 1432

21 Archibald is mentioned in a charter of 1423. He had lands in Wester [Little ?] Spott, granted by his father's charter of 8th March 1426. He is also probably the Archibald Dunbar who held the lands of Little Spott from the crown in 1452 until 1467; he also owned land in Balbuthie, Fife. He was alive in 1472 in (*Yester Writs* No 169); his son Gawain or Gavin of Little Spott was also alive that year as he witnessed *Yester Writs* Nos 169 and 172 dated 14th and 15th February 1472

22 Marjorie married Sir John Swinton, the grandson of Robert, Duke of Albany, in 1423-24 and theyhad a son. Sir John was killed at the battle of Verneuil in 1424. Marjorie then married Lucas Stirling of Keir; she died before 1433

23 Euphemia received a pension from James II between 1453 and 1574, continued by James III, when it ceased on her death in the latter year. It is thought she was the mistress of James II

Figure 5: The Dunbar Earls of Moray

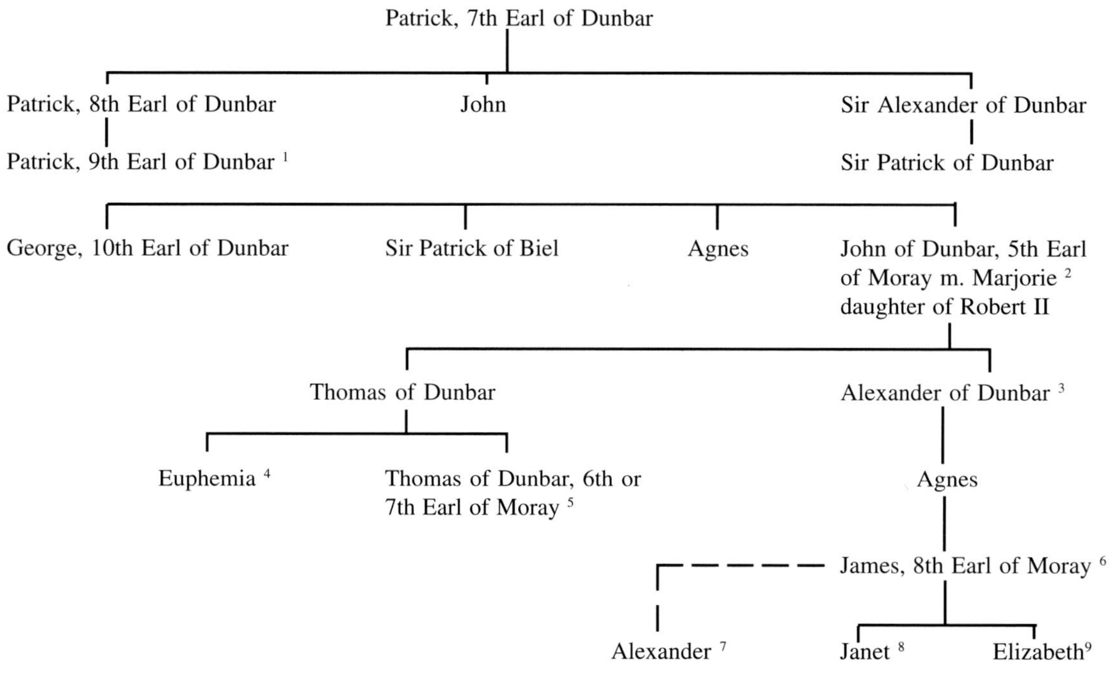

Sources; Dunbar's *Scottish Kings* and *SP*

Notes to Fig 5

1 Thomas Randolph, Earl of Moray was succeeded by his two sons. After the second son's death at Neville's Cross in 1346, his daughters Agnes and Isabella technically inherited the earldom. Agnes m. the 9th Earl of Dunbar who after 1346 styled him self 4th Earl of Moray, a title never formally ratified by David II. After George, 10th Earl of Dunbar inherited the Dunbar lands, his brother John m. Marjorie, daughter of Robert II who in 1372 created his son-in-law 5th Earl of Moray

2 When John died in 1391x1392, Marjorie and son Thomas jointly governed the earldom until 1402, when Thomas was taken prisoner at Homildon Hill, fighting against his uncle, George 10th Earl of Dunbar

3 Alexander may have taken over Thomas' role but neither were formally recognised as Earls of Moray. Alexander m. Matilda (Mauld), daughter and heiress of James Fraser of Frendraught (*Melrose Liber*); he was dead by 1421

4 Euphemia was probably the daughter of John, 5th Earl of Moray

5 There is no surviving evidence to confirm whether this Thomas was ever formally created 6th (or 7th) Earl of Moray, although historians tend to regard him as 7th Earl from 1415. He married Euphemia, Countess of Ross ((*CPL Benedict XIII*)

6 James took as mistress Isabella, daughter of Sir Walter Innes. *Pitscottie, Hist.* states that the pair were *handfast* (literally, the hand of one bound to that of the other) but she died before the marriage was solemnised. James later m. Margaret or Janet, daughter of Alexander of Seton, 1st Earl of Huntly. James was murdered - probably by an Innes as the two families continued a feud for many years - at Frendraught in 1429. Although James' wife is referred to as Janet in several writs, she appears in a letter of 26th July 1432 as Margaret de Seton, married to the late 'James de Dunbar' (*CSSR vii*). She subsequently m. Alex ander Stewart, Earl of Mar after receiving a papal dispensation, the pair being within the forbidden degrees of consanguinity

7 Alexander was the illegitimate issue of James, 8th Earl of Moray and Isabella Innes (see note 6). He became sheriff of Westfield and m. Isobel Sutherland from whom descended the Mochrum and Cumnock branch of the Dunbars

8 Janet m. Sir James Crichton, Great Chamberlain of Scotland and Master of the Great Seal on 15th October 1470; she died between 1494 and 1506

9 Elizabeth married Archibald Douglas who was created Earl of Moray at some point between 1442 and 1445. Douglas was forfeited in 1455 and killed at the battle of Arkinholm. Elizabeth then married George Gordon, heir to the earldom of Huntly. The Gordons hoped to add Moray to their honours but this never occurred as the earldom passed to James II's son David

5

Ecclesiastical

This chapter consists of four sub-headings which examine the main aspects of local church history. Part I deals with the churches in and around Dunbar; Part II investigates the witchcraft trials which took place in the area, cases initiated by the Presbytery of Dunbar; Part III contains examples of kirk discipline (people who were accused of being 'scandalous in their person') and poor relief, cases recorded in Dunbar Parish Church session minutes; and Part IV deals with burial grounds past and present.

Part I: The Churches

The site of Dunbar's first church is virtually impossible to locate, although we are on firmer ground in estimating its date. There may have been more than one church or chapel, certainly by the seventh century, during the Anglian (Christian) occupation from c.638 onwards. When the Roman legions marched out of south-east Scotland, disappearing into the misty Cheviot Hills, they left a people who still adhered to the native pagan beliefs and customs of tribal existence. A full century would elapse before the Word was spread by St Ninian, then missionaries such as Columba, Kentigern (St Mungo), Cuthbert and Baldred of the Bass, the last two being particularly active evangelists in the Anglian kingdom of Bernicia which from the seventh century included Dunbar. Cuthbert was born in an unidentified village on the river Leader; he became Bishop of Lindisfarne from where he spread the Gospel in remote villages in the Lammermuir Hills. Baldred built one of the earliest churches near Dunbar and others in the vicinity were dedicated to him. Baldred reputedly built his first chapel on the southern aspect of the Bass Rock; he was celebrated in James Miller's poem, *St Baldred of the Bass. Scotorum Historiae (Boece Hist.)* tells us that St Baldred died on the Bass Rock in 606; other sources say 608. If Cuthbert was the apostle of Lothian, Baldred deserves the title vicar of North Berwick and Tyninghame, the latter being the site of one of his churches.

Tradition has it that Dunbar's first church was founded by a woman which is not unusual; the cult of feminism featured prominently in pagan religions, women being closer to nature - hence the Virgin Mary's appeal to the Roman Catholic Church, which 'Christianised' [borrowed] many of the old religious rituals. The patron saint of Dunbar is Bey or Beya; she originated in County Down, Ireland and came to Scotland in the seventh century, befriending other holy women such as Ebba of St Abbs, Hilda of Whitby and Ethelreda of Ely - all associates of St Aidan of the monastery at Lindisfarne, Northumberland. Aidan came from Iona and was the first Bishop of Durham in the seventh century, tutoring Oswald, king of Northumberland in c.635. Bey reputedly challenged Ebba - daughter of the Anglian king Aethelfrith and aunt of king Egfrid - and Helen of Aldcambus, near Coldingham to a contest to determine which of the three could build a church closest to the North Sea. St Bey won; tradition has it that her church was built on the sands near Dunbar Castle, which is probable, as a cave south of the Blockhouse and facing west was known as St Bey's; the stretch of beach which contained the now-demolished open air swimming pool was once called St Bey's Shore and St Bey's Well was further west - hence the modern names Bayswell and Bayswell Park. Her church was built before 683, as Ebba, one of the contestants died in that year. The legend is commemorated in a Northumbrian folk-rhyme written several centuries later:

'St Abb, St Helen and St Bey,
They a' [all] built kirks, whilk to be nearest the sea;
St Abbs upon the Nabbs *
St Helen's upon the lea
St Ann[e]'s upon Dunbar sands
Stands closest to the sea.'

* The Nabbs is the name of a rocky peninsula near St Abb's Head in Berwickshire; the ruins of St Helen's on the Lea - not the original church - survive today at Aldcambus, south of Cockburnspath

Illus 37 : *St Helens Church, Aldcambus* KRM

Where was Bey's church of St Anne? An old tradition has it that a church dedicated to St Anne - supposedly the mother of the Virgin Mary and patron saint of married women - stood on the site of the modern Coastguard rocket station at the East or Coastguard Beach; it could be the church built by St Bey. The discovery in 1951 of a fairly large burial ground at Kirkhill Braes, near Roxburghe Terrace and east of the Coastguard Beach (see Chapter 3) may have been connected with a church, possibly Bey's. Whatever the facts, Bey didn't live long in Dunbar; some time after she built her church dedicated to St Anne, she went to the Island of Little Cumbrae in the Firth of Clyde. Preferring the life of a hermit, she died there, surrounded by her beloved birds and animals. At some point before the Reformation, a Dunbar rector proposed to remove her relics from Little Cumbrae and install them in the parish church but a 'miraculous storm' prevented him from doing so. We know that a parish church existed on the site of the modern church in the early twelfth century; whether it was also the site of Bey's church is impossible to verify. However, Dunbar Parish Church was dedicated to St Bey and remained so until the Reformation in 1560.

Cuthbert, Prior of Melrose, then Lindisfarne, did not possess an episcopal seat until he was appointed Bishop of Lindisfarne in 684, where he remained until his death in 687. He began life as a shepherd in the Lammermuir Hills, then became a monk in Melrose Abbey, from where he travelled extensively through the Northumbrian kingdom of Bernicia. Known as the Apostle of Lothian, Cuthbert was dedicated to the life of an itinerant missionary, preaching, baptising, confirming souls and dedicating rural churches; his journeys undoubtedly brought him to Dunbar which became an important Anglian shire centre during his lifetime. As noted in Chapter 3, Wilfrid, the controversial monk of Lindisfarne, then Bishop of York, was a reluctant guest of the Anglian king Egfrid at Dunbar for several months. A fervent spokesman for the pro-Rome faction at Lindisfarne, Wilfrid called into question the validity of the practices of the Celtic Church established at Iona. Egfrid supported the Ionian version which held that Easter should be celebrated on the same day every year, whereas Rome declared it a moveable feast. In the end, the word of Rome prevailed in this and other minor matters such as the size of monks' tonsures; by c.690, Northumbria had accepted Rome's jurisdiction. In challenging Roman jursidiction, Egfrid was in a sense the first 'Protestant'; Wilfrid of York once described the practices and traditions of the Celtic Church as sinful.

Although Cuthbert of Lindisfarne was a particular favourite of the Earls of Dunbar from the eleventh century onwards, Baldred of the Bass, a less well-known churchman founded the church or priory at Tyninghame near East Linton, one of the earliest religious houses to appear in the district. At one time, the lands between the Lammermuir Hills and the river Esk at Musselburgh belonged to Tyninghame which may or may not have included Dunbar, as it had its own church. Tyninghame Priory thrived until c.927, when Olaf, a Danish warlord raided and sacked parts of Lothian, including Tyninghame; according to *Symeon of Durham* and *Chron. Melrose*, the church suffered destruction a second time by the Vikings between 941 and 946. Tyninghame church was rebuilt in or before the twelfth century; all that survives of it today are two Norman-style arches near the private cemetery in the grounds of Tyninghame House, where the Earls of Haddington were buried between 1628 and 1761.

The parish church at Dunbar is first recorded in 1173 when its *teinds* or tithes were in dispute;[1] it is next mentioned in the *Taxatio* for St Andrews in 1176.[2] The *Taxatio* (assessment for tax) listed the religious houses in the Deanery of Haddingtonshire, as East Lothian was then known; the document was in effect an inventory of church lands and the income deriving from them. The *Ecclesia de Dunbar cum capella de Whytngeham* [church of Dunbar and chapel of Whittingehame] were assessed at 180 merks (£120) per annum which indicates that it was a larger establishment than Haddington church, valued at only 120 merks (£80).

The parish is the oldest administrative unit in Scotland, dating from the end of the twelfth century. Every acre of land had to be allocated to a territorial parish, thus every individual belonged to a parochial presbytery with access to a priest for the well-being of his or her soul. The parish was one of the most important developments in Scotland; parish authorities controlled the local population and gave the community an identity. The priest at Dunbar had responsibility for subordinate chapels at Belton, Pitcox, Spott, Pinkerton and Whittingehame; his authority approached that of an English Dean whose diocese might include up to ten parishes or ten churches within a parish.

The predominant religious orders - Franciscans (Grey Friars), Augustines and Dominicans (Black Friars), Carmelites (White Friars) and Benedictines - scarcely touched Dunbar, although these mendicant Orders travelled the length and breadth of the country and would certainly have visited Dunbar. The most common sight would have been the Cistercians of Melrose, a branch of the Benedictines. Orders which settled in Dunbar were the Cluniacs (Benedictines) and the Trinitarians (Red or Crutched Friars); we also know that there was a small Carmelite settlement consisting of a house and two to three acres of land in the vicinity of Newtonlees, near Broxburn. The Benedictine, Trinitarian and Carmelite Orders were certainly favoured by the patronage of the Dunbar family.

A Cluniac settlement was founded at Belhaven by Gospatric III in 1153; the 5th Earl of Dunbar granted the Order additional land at Mayshiel in the Lammermuir Hills - both sites serving the brothers at their monastery on the May Island. The chapel on the May was dedicated to St Adrian who, with all his companions, was murdered by Vikings in 970. David I endorsed the creation of the monastery in the mid-twelfth century; in granting it to the Benedictine Abbey at Reading, he made the condition that twelve monks would live there and say masses for himself and his family. In 1288, the rights of the Priory of the May were sold by the Abbot of Reading to William Fraser, Bishop of St Andrews, much against the wishes of the resident brothers. It changed hands again largely through Edward I's influence in 1296; Wallace reclaimed it from Reading for St Andrews in 1297-98, then it reverted to Reading once more in 1305 until 1318 when it became Scottish again and was abandoned. The monastery fell into ruin after the Cluniacs departed in 1318. It remained undisturbed until 1868, when the shell of the building was cleared of rubbish and the walls repointed; the site was recently investigated by a team of archaeologists.

The May Island was reputed to make barren women fertile if they drank from the pilgrims' well there. Mary of Gueldres landed on the island in June 1449 en route to marry James II, possibly taking the waters for this reason, as she was expected to produce a son and heir to the throne. In 1548, Jean de Beaugue described the island as the haunt of pirates; in 1549, it was used to isolate people 'infectit with the pest [plague].' The Jacobites briefly occupied the May in 1715 and the last of the resident villagers died in 1730. During both World Wars, there were garrisons on the island. It is now a bird sanctuary.

The Cluniac presence in Dunbar was unobtrusive, tucked away in the sleepy little hamlet of Belhaven, near the natural harbour there and on the site of the modern Belhaven Brewery. The brothers grew food on their toft and brewed ale for those on the May. A more obvious presence was that of the Trinitarians or Red Friars. The 5th Earl of Dunbar founded a major settlement at Friarscroft, near the West Port in 1218; the founding charter is considered spurious in one minor respect - it describes the granter as the 5th Earl of Dunbar and March, the latter half of the title reputedly used unofficially by the 6th Earl and formally used until 1289, when the 8th earl styled himself as the 3rd Earl of March. This could be stretched to include the 5th Earl as in his time, the East March was controlled by the Dunbars. (Perhaps a copy of the original charter of 1218 was made at a later date by a scribe at the time when the Dunbars were styled the Earls of March). It is certain that the Dunbars granted the Order land at Friarscroft. The 5th Earl's widow Christian Bruce endowed the Order with a gift of land at the east end of the High Street for a *hospicium* or *maison de dieu* at some point between 1240 and 1248, the later date is more likely, as her son the 6th Earl left Dunbar to go on crusade that year. It was logical that the Dowager Countess should make such a gift; the Order took their name from the Holy Trinity and divided its income from the sale of produce and public donations into thirds. One third was used to ransom Crusaders captured by the Saracens in the Holy Land; another was devoted to the care of the sick, the poor and to provide accommodation for pilgrims; the remaining third was for the support of the brothers themselves. The success of the Trinitarians in effecting the release of Crusaders in a three-year period was considerable, although the figure of 90,000 is suspiciously high. There is a traditional local belief that the Carmelites were in possession of the *maison de dieu* but the weight of evidence favours the Trinitarians. (For example, Walter Bower, Abbot of Inchcolm, who wrote his *Scotichronicon* in 1447, lists every religious house in Scotland; there is no Carmelite establishment mentioned at Dunbar, a parish he would have known intimately, being a native of Haddington). The minor Carmelite settlement at Newtonlees farm in the sixteenth century is verified by *Registrum Magni Sigilli Regum Scotorum (RMS),* the Register of the Great Seal of Scotland. The Register identifies its location and other reliable sources describe it as having consisted of little more than a dwelling house with a few acres for growing food, the surplus possibly being sent to the Carmelite settlement at Luffness, near North Berwick. The Trinitarian and Carmelite Orders have often been confused because they both wore white habits; the Trinitarians affected a red cross on their habits, probably to distinguish themselves from the Carmelites.

The relatively minor presence of religious orders in Dunbar means there are few records to inform us about the state of the community in the Middle Ages; we have to rely on *Chron. Melrose* for information and even that is patchy. Most Orders maintained *chartuleries* which listed the endowments and charters made in their favour and recorded the names of their benefactors, often providing additional - and to the historian - invaluable information. Some abbeys went to the trouble of recording historical events; those chiefly consulted for the purposes of this Chapter include *Chron. Melrose, Chron. Holyrood, Chron. Pluscarden* and the *chartuleries* maintained by Kelso Abbey (*Kelso Liber*) and Dryburgh Abbey (*Dryburgh Liber*). Despite the much-vaunted claim that the great abbeys and monasteries were thriving seats of learning prior to the creation of universities, less was recorded or preserved than might be imagined; nevertheless, the religious establishments deserve credit for their painstaking care in keeping records at all, for they provide us with interesting glimpses into the society of the time.

Undoubtedly, there were holy shrines in the Dunbar area but virtually all of these have disappeared. The most famous was at Whitekirk, founded by Marjorie Comyn, Countess of Dunbar in 1297. As mentioned in Chapter 4, when the Wars of Independence began in 1296, Marjorie's husband, the 8th Earl of Dunbar supported Edward I. Learning of the approach of the English army from Berwick in April 1296, Marjorie handed over Dunbar Castle to the Scots; after their defeat at Spott Glen a few days later, Marjorie had little option but to surrender the castle and make her escape by boat. Intending to make for Fife, she was blown off course and landed on the shore near North Berwick. The details are recorded in a document held in the Vatican, an account written after the Reformation which contains at least two errors of fact:

> 'In 1294 [sic] when Edward the First had defeated the Scots army at Dunbar, many of the enemy [sic] fled into the castle, then commanded by Black Agnes[3] [sic] Countess of Dunbar who seeing the number within so great that the place must soon be surrendered, rather than fall into the hands of her enemies, [she] made her escape by water in the night in order to have gone to Fife. But she, receiving a hurt when getting into the boat, and the winds against her, was obliged to be landed on that part of the shore nearest Fairknowe,[4] to which she was carried. The English however, ravaging the country, they were obliged to halt while a party of them passed, during which time, being in great agony, she prayed to the Holy Mother for relief, when an hermit came and told her, if she had faith, to drink of that holy well she would find relief: which she did, and had no sooner done drinking than she was perfectly recovered from all bruises and made whole. This miracle she made known to Andrew Forman, prior of Coldingham and in the year following, she built a chapell [sic] and a chantry in honour of Our Lady, and endowed it with two marks a year forever,'

The document does not tell us if Marjorie was punished for disobeying her husband and Edward I. However, it indicates that by 1309, the number of miracles occurring at Fairknowe induced Melrose Abbey to erect and dedicate a shrine to the Virgin Mary. During Edward III's invasion in 1356, a story is told of an English sailor who entered the church and stole a ring from the finger of the statue of the Virgin, only to be killed by a crucifix falling from the roof; for good measure, his ship was wrecked off Tynemouth. In 1386, the papal authorities announced that an indulgence - remission of temporal punishment of either one year and 40 days or three years if visits fell on certain feast days - would be granted to those who visited Fairknowe. As repenting sinners were expected to make an offering, the granting of indulgences - literally season tickets for freedom from damnation - was a convenient way of paying for the upkeep of holy places. In April 1397, the centenary of the shrine's creation, Robert II, then Fairknowe's patron, consented to its appropriation by the Abbot of Holyrood to compensate for revenues lost by the Abbey due to 'the incursions of the English.'[5] In 1413, no fewer than 15,653 pilgrims visited the shrine, donating 1,422 merks (about £1,000 Scots).

In 1430, James I placed the chapel of Fairknowe under his personal protection and made it a dependency of the Abbey of the Holy Cross (Holyrood, in Edinburgh). James also built houses for the itinerant pilgrims and frequently visited the shrine. Adam Hepburn of Hailes added a choir in 1439 and the chapel prospered until 1540, when one of James V's favourites, Oliver Sinclair, petitioned the king to allow him to build himself a house at Fairknowe. It is known that he demolished the pilgrims' houses for stone for his own. There is today what is described as a good example of a Scottish tithe barn but the structure has clearly been extended from a free standing tower or keep, possibly that occupied by Sinclair. At some point after the Reformation the shrine was destroyed, as noted by the Catholic Church of the time:

> 'That holy chapell also shared the fate of many more, and was made a parochial church for the preaching of heresy, and by then called "Whitekirk".'

It is now believed that Countess Marjorie landed at Seacliff, slightly south of Tantallon Castle where there was a hermitage associated with the chapel of St Mary Fairknowe. Churches were usually built at a distance from any existing chapel, shrine or hermitage dedicated to some saint or other; this explains the distance between Seacliff Hermitage and Whitekirk, to which Marjorie was carried. The hermitage was still occupied in 1427 as it is recorded then that 'John Vussale, layman, poor hermit, St Andrews diocese, has ruled the hermitage of the chapel of St Mary, called Whitekirk.'[6] Vussale had sought permission from the Vatican to remain there as he was lame and infirm. Part of Seacliff Hermitage survives today; its quiet ruin still offers shelter to those who have need of it in sudden rainy squalls. There is no trace of the holy well at Whitekirk - also known as Hamer at one time - however, it is thought to have disappeared in the course of drainage improvements around 1830. To date, no coins - the usual votive offerings cast into wells even in pre-Christian times - have been found in the immediate vicinity of the church.

Front View.

View from South-East.

KLM

Illus 38: *Dunbar Collegiate Church*

Dunbar Collegiate Church

A major ecclesiastical innovation at Dunbar occurred on St Matthew's Day, 21st September 1342, when the 9th Earl of Dunbar granted a charter conferring collegiate status on the parish church, Dunbar becoming one of the earliest in Scotland.[7] The word *collegiate* derives from the Latin *collegia,* which in the fourteenth century meant 'a community or corporation of secular clergy living together on a foundation for religious service.' In effect, Collegiate churches were literally praying corporations for the dead. They were institutions created by the nobility for purely economical reasons, being a less expensive way of patronising the Church without granting land which was a source of revenue and much-needed by their heirs. The Dean or Provost of a Collegiate church was able to enrich himself from the revenues of the parish church in which the collegiate establishment was incorporated; he could also legitimately acquire the tithes and revenues of other churches and chapels in the district. A Collegiate church was therefore self-financing, a benefice much sought-after for obvious reasons. Dunbar Collegiate Church was the responsibility of a Provost (known as a Dean in Dunbar)[8] an Archpriest and eight Canons, all of whom benefited from the revenues of smaller chapels, provided they did not absent themselves from the College establishment; a condition of their employment was that they had to be resident in the building to qualify for their stipends. If the Dean or Archpriest were absent from the church without the appropriate episcopal dispensation, they forfeited their rights to income; similarly, any canon absent without leave would not only receive nothing but also forfeit a third of his prebend [stipend] to those who were resident. Thus the Dean, Archpriest and canons obtained their stipends from the parish church revenues of Dunbar, Linton (Prestonkirk), Duns, Chirnside and the revenues of the annexed chapels at Whittingehame, Pinkerton, Spott, Pitcox (later transferred to Stenton), Penshiel and Belton - sometimes known as Heatherwick (Hedderwick).[9] The charter of Dunbar Collegiate Church makes provision for the Bishop of St Andrews to erect at the request of the patron, Patrick, Earl of March

> '....the parish churches of Dunbar, Linton, Duns and Chirnside with their chapels into a collegiate church, so that....in all time coming [there will be] a dean, an archpriest having the cure [charge of souls] of the parishioners and the parochial chapels....'

The Dean's prebend were the whole teinds and altar-dues of the parish of Whittingehame; the Archpriest's prebends were the whole teinds [tithes, or tenths of all taxes generated in a parish] and altar-dues of the parish of Dunbar 'except the teinds of the chapel of Whittingehame and excluding the teind of wool, sheep and lambs'. Each of the eight canons received prebends as follows:

canon prebendary of Dunbar	:	the whole township with all its pertinents
" " of Pinkerton	:	" " "

"	" of Spott :	"	"	"
"	" of Belton :	"	"	"
"	" of Pitcox :	"	"	" save those assigned to the Archpriest
"	" of Linton	"	"	" less ten merks he paid to a local vicar
"	" of Duns :	"	"	"
"	" of Chirnside	"	"	"

The design of the former Collegiate Church (**ill 38**) has given rise to speculation that it was based on a similar establishment at Ladykirk on the north bank of the Tweed opposite Norham Castle. This is logical, given that the Earls of Dunbar regularly visited the area which until 1844 formed part of the county of Durham. The church at Dunbar was cruciform and built on the usual east-west axis; it had aisles and a square tower in the west, conforming to the mixed Saxon-Gothic style prevalent in the fourteenth century. About half of Scotland's Collegiate churches were erected within existing parish churches which usually involved some rebuilding and extension. Usually additions were made - at Dunbar, an apsidal choir (the arched or dome-roofed recess in churches) with a sacristy or repository for vessels and vestments; the choir or eastern aspect reserved for the clergy or the choir after which it was named incorporated the altar, the *piscina* or arched recessed niche containing holy water, the *sedilia* or arched and recessed benches used by the celebrants of mass - the Dean and Archpriest - and most important, the location of the tomb of the patron. Appendix F identifies most of the incumbents of the collegiate church between 1342 and 1560.

The 9th Earl of Dunbar began a fashion which was quickly adopted by other Scottish nobles; Dunbar was founded after St Andrews and possibly Abernethy. Collegiate churches also ran song schools and taught grammar (Latin) to the choir and altar boys. Some incorporated existing or installed 'hospitals' known as *maisons de dieux*; these were little more than lodging houses for the poor, the sick and pilgrims. Dunbar's *maison de dieu* was founded by Countess Christian Bruce of Dunbar in 1240x1248 and granted to the Red or Trinitarian Friars who were responsible for the establishment until the Reformation.

Of all the Deans, Columba de Dunbar was probably the most well-known, being the privileged son of the 10th Earl of Dunbar and nephew of John Dunbar, Earl of Moray. Columba was appointed Dean of Dunbar on 7th October 1413; he enjoyed the fat slumber of rural clerical life until 1423, when he translated to the See of Moray. As noted in Chapter 4, he completed the rebuilding of Elgin Cathedral which had been sacked in 1390 by Alexander Stewart, Earl of Buchan, known as the Wolf of Badenoch. Columba is credited with the installation of the large circular window at the eastern end of the cathedral. We know that he visited Rome in 1433 since he received a safe-conduct for himself and 30 servants to travel through England to attend the Council of Basle founded by Pope Martin V two years earlier. The Council's aims were to stamp out heresy, unite all Christian nations under the Catholic Church and to introduce reforms. Columba died in 1435 and was buried in Elgin Cathedral; his remains lie in what is known as the Dunbar Aisle; his much-defaced and weathered effigy in mitre and robes with the Dunbar arms - a lion rampant charged with a bordure of eight roses - has barely survived. The Dunbar Aisle was created by the Dunbar Earls of Moray whose descendants became hereditary sheriffs and constables in Morayshire.

In January 1435, when the 11th Earl of Dunbar's titles and estates were forfeited to James I, the Collegiate Church at Dunbar became crown property. The *Accounts of the Lord High Treasurer of Scotland (TA)* for 1497 show that 20 shillings (£1) were paid to 'Maister William [Sandilands, probably the Dunbar canon prebendary] to ger say [have said] a trentale of massis [30 successive masses for the dead] of Sanct Bay [the parish church]'. In 1501, when James IV received the translation of his Chapel Royal at Stirling as a Collegiate church, Pope Alexander VI granted him the right to incorporate Dunbar's canonries; even as late as 1617 - more than half a century after the Reformation - the Dean of Dunbar was 'named' to the re-erected Chapel at Stirling.[10] James VI refers to Dunbar as the 'Ecclesia Collegiata Sancti Bae.' In addition to the Collegiate Church, there was a chapel dedicated to St John in Dunbar Castle; the chaplaincy of St John in the Collegiate Church had some acres of land associated with it as *TA* for 1571 show these were leased for £20 to Henry Smyth, a burgess in Edinburgh. It comes as no surprise to learn that the field in question in the vicinity of Lochend was known as St John's Croft.

Although it became an ordinary parish church in 1562, two years after the Reformation, Dunbar was still referred to as Collegiate as late as 1611; within living memory local inhabitants native to the town called it the 'high' church of Dunbar. *Miller, Dunbar* describes it as a building of the workmanship of several ages; in Miller's day, the church measured 100 feet in length and 20-25 feet in breadth, the transept or cross-aisle measuring 83 feet. In 1779, the building was badly in need of repair, particularly the west part beyond the transept, thought at that time to have been the original existing in 1342 or even 1176. Writing in the *Old Statistical Account* in 1793, the minister at Dunbar, the Reverend George Bruce described the building as follows:

'The fabric is very old....It is built exactly in the form of a cross....the floor was sunk below the ground, which made it always damp and cold....till lately one of the worst, and most inconvenient in Scotland. It was repaired by the heritors in 1779, floored with deal and ceiled [ceilinged] in the roof. A part of the long body was cut off, by a partition, as useless and it was regularly seated; so that now it looks clean and neat, the quire [choir] only remains unaltered.'

Illus 39: *Interior of Dunbar Parish Church before the fire of 1987* HM

The heritors simply adapted the interior of the old medieval version to save money. The last service in the Collegiate Church was held on 7th March 1819. The foundation stone of the new parish church was laid by the provost on 17th April the same year. Built by James Gillespie Graham, a well-known architect of the time, the new building was made of red sandstone from the quarry at the Bowerhouse (Bourhouse) not the best building material as it is soft and weathers badly; the corrosive salt air causes further problems. The building cost approximately £6,000 and although unfinished, its doors were opened on 20th April 1821 for the ordination of the Reverend John Jaffrey; normal worship began on 16th September that year. Among its heritors were the Duke of Roxburghe, the Hays of Spott, Belton and Linplum, Sir George Warrender of Lochend and Anderson of Winterfield Farm. The inauguration ceremony was performed by the Reverend John Jaffray, the new incumbent. The church was badly damaged twice in the last century; on the first occasion, its 107 foot tower was struck by lightning, after which lightning conductor rods were installed. The second and more tragic incident occurred on 3rd January 1987 when the church was gutted by a fire reputedly caused by an electrical fault. Structural damage required complete rebuilding; the new interior is functional and bright but it lacks the character of the original (**ill 39**)

In the Middle Ages, the parish church and the castle between them dominated the lives of the community. Being the only public building, the church met the spiritual, social and cultural needs of its parishioners. There would have been several outbuildings in the churchyard precincts, mainly the area now occupied by the local bowling club and the railway station. There was probably a tithe barn nearby, no doubt demolished when the railway was constructed.[11] Prior to the Reformation, churches provided entertainment - religious plays - held courts and were administrative centres. It is recorded that because the Town House or Tolbooth was in such a ruinous state prior to its rebuilding in the early seventeenth century that trials were held in the churchyard - a fact which in c.1597 brought protests from the criminal fraternity and their friends among the local population that open-air trials were illegal; the felons were set free. The bells of the church which summoned the parishioners to worship were also a means of telling the time - useful to workers in the outlying fields - when they were rung to announce the canonical hours of prayer e.g. matins in early morning and vespers in the evening. As churches were built on an east-west axis, they also acted as massive sundials.

Churches were frequented by nobility and commoner for secular pursuits. They were places of business, where deals were struck and families signed dynastical agreements; for example, on 18th March 1468, John Hay, son of Sir David Hay of Yester, granted Sir William Cunningham and his son George 1,000 merks on his marriage to George Cunningham's daughter Elizabeth. The dowry was paid in annual instalments at the altar of Belton Chapel on condition that Elizabeth became the Cunningham heiress. On 28th August 1515,[12] Elizabeth Hay of Yester, then in possession of the Belton estates, is named as patron of the altar of St Monan 'in the Parish Kirk of the town and College [Collegiate Church] of Dunbar'; Sir John Leis [Lees] was appointed chaplain of the altar for life and received £10 a year from the 'corn mill and the wauyk [cloth] mill' at Belton and a house and an acre of land there. In return, Lees was required to celebrate mass at the altar of Dunbar and every Sunday at the Chapel of Belton.[13] Business and religion were easily accommodated in pre-Reformation Scotland.

In addition to the 'curing' of souls - the main object of the clergy - the church provided rudimentary education; at Dunbar, there was a school of sorts run by the clerics, its standard of dubious quality although it was probably better than the teaching provided by the smaller, non-Collegiate establishments. The parish priest also instructed women about such matters as childbirth and how to prevent a child sharing its mother's bed from being smothered! Very little 'sin' is recorded prior to the Reformation, since by definition, a confession made to a priest was a conversation between sinner and God. When the church was reformed in 1560, sin became a matter of public concern, as is evinced by extracts from the Kirk session records.

The four main feast days in the medieval Christian calendar were Christmas (Yule), Easter (Pasche), the feast of the patron saint of the church and the anniversary of every church's dedication with perhaps at Dunbar, the anniversary of its elevation to Collegiate status. On these important days, every household was expected to make an offering known as the mass penny; the rich were expected to give much more however, the poor gave what they could afford, usually a halfpenny. If church records had existed in the fourteenth century, we might have learnt that on 21st September 1343 - the first anniversary of the founding of Dunbar Collegiate Church - the 9th Earl would have donated several shillings on the morning of 21st September, when he took the sacrament that day. Similar payments were expected at Christmas and Easter for the *howselle,* or act of communication. As the humble folk were not only required to pay for the cure of their souls but to contribute to these special days, festivals to celebrate a successful harvest literally took the bread out of their mouths. However, these special feast days brought some colour into the monotony of their lives, particularly during the gloomy medieval winters, when Christmas brightened an otherwise cheerless time.

The medieval church affected the lives of the rich and the poor in many ways. In the case of the rich, the Abbot or Bishop and in the poor, the rector or vicar were concerned with one aim - control.[14] They wielded a great deal of power; every clergyman in charge of a chapel, church, cathedral, monastery, abbey or diocese was entitled by law to the church tithes or tenth part of everything produced in the parish. Nobles, knights, tenant farmers and freemen alike were obliged to surrender a tenth part of their livestock and harvest to support the local clergy. Fishermen handed over a tenth of their catches, very important during the herring season when the fish were dried or salted for use during winter. The history of the medieval church abounds with anecdotes of rascally rectors and venal vicars demanding more than their lawful share; the local magnate's bailiffs were often called in to settle disputes between tenant farmers and priests. The peasants were dependent on the integrity of their local priest who laboured to instil in them a fear of God - often to extract more than that to which he was entitled.

In return for the tithes, the clergy cured souls and gave alms to the poor. The pre-Reformation church was as much preoccupied with sexual morality as was its post-Reformation successor, the only difference being that the Reformed Church made sin a matter of public concern. The most common secular crimes were wife-beating and adultery; fornication between unmarried couples or married men and single girls - usually servants - were cardinal sins. The humbler miscreants were dealt with personally by the parish priest; the middle and upper classes came under the censure of the local abbot or bishop - if at all - since confession had to be heard by a churchman of equal status to that of the sinner. In reality, because those in the upper hierarchy of the church were as guilty of fornication as those they were expected to admonish, few nobles were brought to book. Women were harshly treated; usually, their punishment was delivered publicly in the market place or at the mercat cross. There were minor offences such as talking or falling asleep in church, association with excommunicated persons of both sexes - usually women outwith the protection of the law - and giving shelter and help to adulterous couples. All of these carried monetary penalties. The medieval church rigidly enforced the marriage laws - on the surface at least - and meted out punishment according to the degree of severity of the irregularity.

Though they undoubtedly exercised considerable power, Catholic churchmen weren't held in the awe modern society believes existed at the time. The late fourteenth century statutes of St Andrews diocese show that many clergymen were obliged to carry weapons for self-defence, especially at events held within the church precincts. These included fairs, markets, archery contests, play-acting, bear-baiting, wrestling matches and dancing - the latter being considered a preliminary to sexual liaison. Gambling was rife and often ended with blood being shed. It would also be a mistake to assume that while religion played an important part in daily life and behaviour, medieval man did not particularly venerate sacred places or indeed hold the Sabbath special. For example, John Major's *A History of Greater Britain* indicates that the poor were often obliged to reap their crops on a Sunday as they spent the weekdays harvesting their masters' corn; also, pedlars were allowed to stand in church porches on Sundays to sell their wares to farmers who weren't able to come to towns from outlying districts through the week. So much for the modern sensitivity about Sunday trading. At Dunbar, pedlars and traders would have crowded the entrance to the church, selling their wares in the churchyard.

Priests did not set a good example. In many cases, even allowing for the hostile propaganda fomented after the Reformation, there is evidence of hypocrisy among the clergy. They ignored their vow of celibacy by openly taking 'hearth wives' into their manses; others celebrated mass more often than necessary for financial gain. The priest acted as parochial officer, giving alms to the poor and the sick. There was no authority to monitor the rascally clergy however; on the surface, the poor were given the last rites without charge, though many priests expected - and received - recompense from the deceased's family 'in the name of God'. With very few official duties, the clergy could devote much of their time to secular pursuits, undertaken under the guise of church business but invariably to satisfy their usually prodigious appetites. The Church of Rome was desperately in need of reform by the end of the fifteenth century; many questioned the sale of indulgences and absolution for personal gain, the practice of allowing plural benefices and the keeping of concubines. It was time for change. Even if the Church co-operated with the crown, parliament and the secular authorities, receiving protection from the king and his nobles as of right, there was much that was known to be wrong in it. While the Scottish Church played a leading role in the struggle for independence, it has to be said that it was primarily concerned with its own survival, identity and independence.

Excluding the canonry of Dunbar itself, five of the eight canons attached to the Collegiate Church enjoyed income derived from local chapels such as Belton. The barony of Belton with its chapel was first part of the Dunbar earldom, then the Yester-Hay estates. Belton is first mentioned in a writ of 1366 which granted an annual rent of 45 merks from Belton and 'Petkokis' [Pitcox] to Neil Cunningham.[15] Some time after that, the 10th Earl of Dunbar granted Belton to Cunningham 'for his homage and service'; the latter writ is a typical example of the way feudal documents were engrossed at the time.[16] The writ bestows on the beneficiary land

> '....in fee and heritage, in woods, and plains, meadows, fields, and pastures, moss, marshes, waters, stanks [pools or ditches], mills, multures [share of corn ground at the lord's mill] and their sequels with the tenandries [tenancies] of Edynton [Edington] which are held of Belton, and with smithies, brewhouses, hawkings, huntings and fishings, and with all other commodities, liberties and easements, beneath and above the earth, named or not, belonging to the said lands.....'

Nothing was left to chance or dispute. The writ ends with the 10th Earl's guarantee that he would forever defend the lands on Neil Cunningham's behalf and those of his heirs and assignees 'gainst all men and women'. Belton passed to the Yester Hays in 1472 but only six years later, the lands were appropriated by the 3rd Duke of Albany [17] with the proviso that if he died without male heirs, the lands would revert to Elizabeth de Cunningham (Hay) or her grandson John Hay, who in fact ultimately inherited them. Hays lived at Belton until the twentieth century; sadly, their fine mansion, Belton House, was demolished in the 1960s and there is no trace today of Belton Chapel.

South of Dunbar were the chapels of Pinkerton and Skateraw; neither exist today. Skateraw was dedicated to St Denis; the ruins were still visible in the nineteenth century. Pinkerton was a canon prebend of the Collegiate church. It was probably in existence in 1296 as Edward I resided there after his campaign in Scotland which removed John Balliol from the throne. Perhaps Edward gave thanks for his victories the day he stayed there.

To the west of Pinkerton is the first reasonably-sized church of Spott, the steep approach to which is still called the Canongate, named for the canons of the Collegiate church. There was a church at Spott in 1327; the modern church has a bell cast in 1639 which Cromwell would have heard on Sunday, 1st September 1650, two days before his momentous victory. The entrance to the churchyard is guarded by a watch-house where local men kept a lookout for the resurrectionists in the early nineteenth century. At the door hangs the *jougs*, near the pre-Reformation holy water stoup; the jougs were used to punish sinners, those who talked in church and the local witches.

Spott Kirk deserves particular attention as it has a somewhat colourful history; three of its incumbents met violent ends and it was a notorious place for trying witches, of which more later. The first minister to meet death out of bed was Robert Galbraith, Senator of the College of Justice founded in Edinburgh in 1532. Galbraith was attending a meeting in Edinburgh in c.1554 and became involved in a brawl with a city burgess who stabbed him to death. Next came John Hamilton, the natural son of the Earl of Arran; he became Archbishop of St Andrews after leaving Spott. He was hanged at Stirling in 1571, suspected of complicity in the murder of the Regent Moray in 1570.

But the most infamous of all was undoubtedly John Kello; Kello strangled his wife on the Sunday morning of 24th September 1570, then went to the church where he proceeded to deliver a more than usually eloquent sermon, no doubt fired by adrenalin rather than divine inspiration. Later, Andrew Simson, schoolmaster and minister at Dunbar reminded Kello of a dream he had related to him a few weeks after he committed his crime, one in which he claimed to have seen his wife's murderer. Simson, something of a psychologist replied "Ye are,

I fear, the author yourself of this cruel murder." Apparently, Kello wanted rid of his wife since he was ambitious and sought the favours of the daughter of a local rich landowner. No account of the trial has survived other than the details of the sentence passed on 4th October 1570. Kello was hanged

'to the deid, and theirefter his body [was] to be cassin [cast] in ane fyre [fire] and brint [burnt] in assis [ashes], and his guidis and gear [possessions] to be confiscat etc.'

The sentence was carried out the same day, in Edinburgh.

One or two of the Spott Kirk session minutes bring to life the otherwise sleepy little church:

> 'August 1685 :
> Thanksgiving day for victory over the rebels in the West headed by Argyle.'[18]
> 'December 1688:
> Mr Buchan the minister taken out of his bed by 3 fanatics with swords and guns; led down to the church half-naked; in his presence they took away the church bible and keys; discharged him to officiate any longer in that parish as minister at his peril.'

The reference to 'Argyle' related to the ninth earl of Argyll's association with the ill-fated Monmouth rebellion against the Catholic James VII and II who was deposed in 1688 by the Bloodless Revolution which gave the throne to William of Orange. The reason for the expulsion of the Reverend Archibald Buchan from Spott was clearly his refusal to swear an oath to William. In 1688, the residents of Spott were anxious to show their loyalty to the new king, which is why they ran their minister out of the village

In Spott graveyard lie the remains of Covenanters who were mortally wounded and hastily buried in the grounds of Spott House after the battle of Dunbar in 1650. In the nineteenth century, during the building of hothouses at Spott House, several skeletons, buttons, swords and shreds of uniforms were discovered. The remains were exhumed and given a decent burial, reputedly in the north-east corner near the kirk entrance; the grave is not marked. Spott Kirk is today the responsibility of the minister at Belhaven Church, Dunbar - almost a case of history repeating itself, as Spott was part of the Collegiate establishment at Dunbar.

Nearby Pitcox - once a bustling hamlet with its adjacent deer park at Biel faded when its chapel fell into disuse in 1561. All that remains of the community is a small grassed square with a farm cottage. Stenton or 'Stane-toun' subsumed Pitcox in its reformed church, the ruins of which are close to the modern Gothic-style building of 1829. The old churchyard contains the remains of John Hamilton of Biel, 2nd Lord Belhaven who died in 1708. Outside Stenton is a rather attractive feature, the Rood Well, known as the Cardinal's Hat on account of its shape. It is thought that the Rood Well was erected on the site of a natural spring by the monks of Melrose Abbey for the refreshment of pilgrims.

Prestonkirk, or Linton as it was once known, was another canon-prebend of Dunbar. A chancel there dates from the thirteenth century, by far the most impressive example of church architecture in the vicinity of East Linton and Dunbar. The original church was dedicated to St Baldred; the present version is late Georgian c.1770, renovated in 1891.

After the Reformation, the Presbytery of Dunbar included several churches formerly outwith the jurisdiction of the Collegiate Church. These were Whitekirk - already described, Innerwick, Oldhamstocks and Cockburnspath. Little of note occurred at Whitekirk after the Reformation which no doubt hastened the demise of the holy well there; such Romish places were anathema to the reforming fathers. However, Whitekirk was the scene of civil disobedience in 1914, when on the night or early morning of 26th February, the church was set on fire by suffragettes. Although the building escaped serious damage, some valuable furnishings were lost; these included chairs of the William and Mary period (1688-1702) and a 1611 version of the *Old Testament* which had come from the ruined church at Tyningehame. The miraculous well is mentioned in the *New Statistical Account*; in 1845 the minister wrote that

> 'the well and its virtues have been sacrificed to what the creed of those times would have considered a sordid and unhallowed agriculture. Drains and ditches have left the pilgrim not a drop to drink.'

A remarkably restrained comment on the old faith.

Oldhamstocks and Innerwick lie just inside the boundary of East Lothian, whereas Cockburnspath - once a dependancy of Oldhamstocks in religious matters - is in Berwickshire, having become a separate parish in 1609. Innerwick's plain kirk was built in 1784, although there must have been an earlier establishment under the patronage of the Hamiltons who owned the now derelict castle. Oldhamstocks dates from 1581 but there are traces of an earlier building which probably dates from the twelfth century; there is a reference to a rector called Adulf - perhaps a derivative of the Anglian Eadwulf - in a charter of c.1127. Oldhamstocks Church was consecrated in 1242 by David de Bernham, Bishop of St Andrews as is recorded in *Chron. Melrose*. In 1296, a rector called Thomas de Hunsingoure swore fealty to Edward I as his signature appears on the *Ragman Roll*. The church was patronised by four Hepburns of Blackcastle and a Hepburn Aisle was added in 1581. As noted in Chapter 1, one of Oldhamstocks priests was Thomas Hepburn, the eccentric kinsman of the Earl of Bothwell. The present church dates from 1701. Not far distant is Dunglass Collegiate Church, founded it is thought in c.1443 by Sir Alexander Home. Cockburnspath had a small chapel in 1255 which may have been erected in 1163. Not far from it is St Helen's Aldcambus, closed in 1609 and now a ruin; recent attempts have been made to retrieve fallen gravestones which over the years were covered by turf so that many of these have remarkably clear inscriptions, some dating from the late seventeenth century. The small graveyard has an irregular surface which suggests the presence of other grave covers. A bag of gold coins was unearthed in the graveyard in the nineteenth century.

KRM

Illus 40: *Dunbar Parish Church in 2003*

The modern churches in Dunbar date from 1764, the year the Wesleyan or Methodist Chapel was built. (The first Methodist Society was set up in Dunbar in 1755, four years after John Wesley visited the burgh). The parish church built in 1819-21 had an apse added in 1896; the interior gutted by fire in 1987 had to be reconstructed entirely (**ill 40**). In 1776, the Parish Church manse was situated in the High Street - probably at No 44, since it is shown on the 1830 Town Plan as being occupied by the Reverend John Jaffrey. A new manse was built in 1852 in Bayswell Road; the present manse adjacent to it was built only a few years ago.

The modern Parish Church is solid and assured, its crenellations a reminder of Dunbar's embattled past. It is a landmark more striking than Dunbar Castle. Built of Old Red Sandstone, it exudes a warm glow on sunny summer evenings.

In1835, the Parish Church session minutes record that local parishioners were seeking a second Church of Scotland establishment as the population of Dunbar had grown to almost 4,000. However, the session pointed out that as the parish church built in 1819 could accommodate 1,800 people - 40 more than the number required by law - there was no need for another church as most of the parishioners lived within three or four miles of the existing church. (The elders also drew attention to the fact that the local roads 'were the best in the kingdom' which strikes me as a somewhat irrelevant - and undoubtedly fallacious statement). However, the local people persisted and Belhaven Church was built in 1839-1840. Almost immediately, it was taken over by the Free Church of Scotland after the Disruption of 1843. The Church of Scotland took the case to the House of Lords which judged in its favour. Belhaven re-opened its doors to Church of Scotland worshippers on 22nd August 1858. (When Belhaven was disjoined from the Parish Church by the Council of Teinds in 1863, its congregation regarded this as a victory over what they termed the 'High' Kirk). The next church to be built was the Abbey or Free Kirk in 1850;

KLM

Illus 41: *Free or Abbey Church*

it merged with the Parish Church in the 1960s. Then came Our Lady of the Waves Roman Catholic chapel in 1877, followed in 1889 by St Anne's Episcopal Church. (A list of some of the incumbents of the local churches appears in Appendix F).

Despite the advent of the Reformation in 1560, the Collegiate church carried on until the next century; at the time of the Reformation, it was well-endowed, enjoying a minimum income of £690, a considerable sum for the time. While scathing attacks were made on the wordly pursuits of monks, friars and nuns, the Deans and canons of the Collegiate establishments were not seen in quite the same light by the reformers. Today, the excesses reputedly carried out at the time of Reformation must be treated with caution; while there is evidence of vandalism, much of the accusations against the reformers were made by those who supported a discredited Catholic Church which failed to reform itself in time to resist the challenge of Protestantism. The clergy were often the arbiters of their own fate; for example, it is recorded that the Trinitarian friars in Dunbar's *maison de dieu* were banished to the Trinitarian house at Peebles for unspecified immorality.[19] In the sixteenth century, the 'massin dew' or 'maidendew' was annexed by the Collegiate Church which proves that it wasn't incorporated into the Collegiate Church in 1342, as some maintain; a reference to the *maison de dieu* appears in an inventory dated 28th July 1558 listing the lands and properties leased to the minister and convent of the Trinitarian house at Peebles.[20] A charter of 1586 gave the former Trinitarian establishment at Friarscroft - about 3.5 acres - to a James Home or, according to Keith's *Historical Catalogue of the Scottish Bishops, (Keith, Bishops)* George Hume of Friarsland.

Allowing for the equally hysterical and censorious Protestant propaganda of the Reformation, the Church of Rome was corrupt and inefficient from top to bottom; parsons, vicars, rectors, priests, monks, friars and nuns as well as the senior hierarchy were ignorant, venal and immoral. The vicars and parsons appropriated as much of the fruits of their humble parishes as they could, engaging young curates to do their work while they enjoyed the good life at the expense of their poverty-stricken parishioners. Some parish priests hardly knew the alphabet and neglected the repair of their churches which more often than not simply collapsed in the course of time rather than fell prey to the depredations of the so-called 'fanatics' of the new religion. While Protestant mobs undoubtedly destroyed buildings and interior furnishings, smashed statues, stained glass windows and stole valuable silver plate, the truth is that a substantial percentage of Catholic chapels were in a semi-ruinous state when they were taken over by the reformers. The teachings of Martin Luther of Germany and John Calvin of France and Geneva along with the invention of the printing press sounded the death knell of the old autocratic Roman Church. Tyndale's translation and printing of the *Bible* allowed the literate to interpret the *Gospels* for themselves; they no longer needed to rely on the word of the often illiterate clergy who naturally clung to the version authorised by the Vatican. For the man - or to be more precise, the woman - at the parish pump, religion became a subject discussed more than ever before but in a spirit of freedom.

Part II: The Witch Hunt in Dunbar and District

Witches. Did such creatures exist? The *Old Testament* says they did. What was written in Holy Scripture was followed to the letter by the Protestant Reformers in Scotland.

The persecution of women for witchcraft wasn't of course confined to Scotland, nor was it the worst in terms of excessive zeal. It was however an aberration and remains a dark chapter in Scotland's church history, one which Christian apologists have attempted to minimise. That a reformed church, dedicated to 'freedom' from the autocracy of Rome should have hunted witches is perhaps surprising; what is even more remarkable is the extent of the hunt and the length of time it took for the epidemic to run its course. Much that is reprehensible has been said and done in the name of God; the witch-hunt in Scotland is a classic example. It is a story of mass hysteria, bigotry, superstition, fanaticism and egomania - all pursued in the name of orthodox religion. The persecutors - the clergy of the Church of Scotland - were driven by religious fervour, misogyny, superstition, narrow-mindedness and sheer ignorance, aided by the civil authorities. The majority of those accused were women, regarded as lesser creatures than men, subject to illogical mood swings, uncivilised and unreasonable creatures; it was argued that their unpredictable, illogical behaviour made it easy for the Devil to corrupt them. Women were more animal than human. They had brought about Original Sin and the expulsion of man from the Garden of Eden. They were dangerous, manipulative and thereby themselves prone to manipulation.

There was another reason for the outbreak of witch persecution between 1560 and 1727, especially in the early years of the Reformation. The Scottish Church, separated from Rome in 1560, already knew that the Vatican condemned witches for heresy, a crime or sin of which the Reformers held that Catholics themselves were guilty. Those who clung to the old religion were heretics and witches were no better. Rome's *Inquisition* under the Spanish Inquisitor Thomas de Torquemada (1420-1498) had discovered several witches among the 2,000 or so victims he tortured for heresy. The only difference between Torquemada and the Reformed Church of Scotland was that Torquemada rarely executed those he found guilty; torture was usually sufficient to induce heretics to recant and return to the holy fold like strayed sheep. The Church of Scotland would prosecute at least twice the number of Torquemada's victims - all for the crime of witchcraft which, after 1563, carried the death penalty in Scotland.

No historian interested in Scotland's past can ignore the curious phenomenon of the witch-hunt which affected about two-thirds of the country between 1560 and 1727. Would the hunt have occurred with or without the Reformation? One can but speculate but the weight of evidence and a more enlightened attitude of the Church of Rome towards the witch-heretic suggest that the Reformed Church followed a more aggressive policy, as did the Protestant German states and to a lesser extent, Protestant England. Was the witch-hunt in Scotland causal or was it a manifestation of a brutality inherent in the national character? To subscribe to the latter view is to admit the presence of some flaw in personality which drove men in Scotland - particularly in the Highlands - to slaughter each other simply because they belonged to different clans, practising different religions. Did Scotsmen burn women simply for being female? Perhaps the only response is to echo Nietzsche's cynical and pessimistic view of all mankind - it realises its true self at bullfights and crucifixions. Scotland, a country which had suffered from the tyranny and aggression of its larger neighbour south of the Border for almost four centuries should have learnt the lesson of humanity and the peace forgiveness brings. So why were witches hunted more ruthlessly in Scotland than in England and for many more years?

Witchcraft, sorcery and magic are as old as man himself. When the Christian religion was adopted as the official religion of the West, witchcraft was known to exist; it was a manifestation of evil and the existence of the Devil. To begin with, Holy Scripture warned man that as witches were real creatures, they should be exterminated. 'You shall not permit a sorceress to live' as *Exodus,* chapter 22, verse 18 in the King James or authorised version of the *Bible* rather lamely puts it; earlier versions do not mince words:

'Thou shalt not suffer a witch to live.'

To understand the witch hunt in Scotland, we have to examine the attitude to witches prior to the Reformation. Although the word witch derives from the Anglo-Saxon *wicca*, witches existed in earliest times; the Witch of Endor - more of a medium than a sorceress - is referred to in the First Book of *Samuel,* chapter 28, verse 7. At least she escaped execution. Witches existed in Scotland during the reign of Kenneth 1 in the ninth century, confirmed by an act he passed outlawing wizardry, juggling (!) and necromancy. In the following century, king Duffus was tormented by the Witches of Forres who were caught in the act of roasting his image over a fire, thus making the king ill. The Forres witches were probably the very first victims of the witch hunt in Scotland. During the superstition-ridden Middle Ages, witchcraft actually posed less of a threat since faith was strong and the Devil and his disciples could be banished by Holy Mother Church and the judicious use of holy water whose efficacy against witchcraft was well-known - or at least well-publicised. At the time of the Crusades, the Devil was relegated in the hierarchy of evil, taking second place to the infidel Muslims who allegedly defiled places in the Holy Land significant in Christian mythology. The crusading fervour began in 1096, when Pope Urban II launched the First Crusade to free Jerusalem from the Saracens; his appeal brought an immediate response from the pious, the chivalrous, the adventurous and the parsimonious. When these wasteful and largely irrelevant expeditions ended in the fourteenth century, Rome had to find new threats to the true religion and not unexpectedly turned her attention once again to heretics and witches. It is a paradox that witch persecution did not occur on a large scale until the later Middle Ages. Most medieval Christians gave little thought to witches and wizards which were seen in the same light as elves, fairies, goblins and other supernatural creatures. The Church was able to deal with such nuisances when they acted capriciously or spitefully; for the most part, medieval man accepted the existence of the little people and often regarded them as friendly creatures who only needed to be placated in order to reap the rewards they could offer.

After the last crusading pope died in 1464, Rome began to investigate heresy which of course included witchcraft, condemned in the papal bulls of Popes Innocent VIII (1484), Julius II (1504) and Adrian IV (1523). On the heels of the fifteenth century edicts came *Malleus Maleficarum* - Hammer of Witches - literally a textbook for identifying and prosecuting witches. *Malleus Maleficarum* was compiled in 1489 by two bigoted and fanatical Dominican priests Jacob Sprenger and Heinrich Kramer; it is a monumental work of superstition, prejudice, injustice, bigotry, hypocrisy and hysteria, the blueprint for judges in ecclesiastical and secular courts which led to the wholesale slaughter of European witches.

Once discovered, a witch was automatically excommunicated from Mother Church. Before the Scottish Reformation, a few witches had been executed but the victims attracted no more attention than would common felons. The Reformation swept away the old world of good and evil spirits; the worship of saints and images was blasphemous and it was sinful - heretical - to adhere to the old religious ways. If this were so, why was the Reformed Church in Scotland so preoccupied with evil spirits? Perhaps it was impressed by the zeal of the

German states where Protestantism had originated and where in excess of 100,000 women and men were executed. Was the epidemic simply an acceptable way of disposing of Roman Catholics who refused to recant and were therefore considered heretical and superstitious? This seems more than likely. On the other hand, was there some psychological flaw in the national character of Scotland? We have come full circle.

Incredibly, the reformed Church in England and Scotland believed witches existed; they argued logically that evil did not stop at the coast of France. There was clamour on both sides of the Border for civil laws to outlaw witchcraft. The first Acts against 'witchcraftis, sorsarie and necromancie' were passed in 1563 in both England and Scotland, by Elizabeth I and Mary, Queen of Scots. The Witchcraft Acts remained on the statute books for nearly two centuries until they were repealed in 1735-36 and even then, there was a saving provision which allowed the authorities to prosecute women who *pretended* [my italics] to be witches. (This provision was last invoked in 1944 at the trial of Helen Duncan, an Edinburgh medium practising in Portsmouth).

In the eyes of the Church of Scotland, witches existed because Holy Scripture said they did. The earlier quote from *Exodus* was eagerly grasped by an 'enlightened' clergy anxious to ensure that the fledging Protestant church would survive. They also did not wish to be outdone by the faith which had been proscribed; they took pains to make the people aware of the fact that witches would be punished under the new religion as they had been under the old.

In my earlier book, *The Deil's Ain,* a history of the witch hunt in Scotland between 1560 and 1727, I fully examined the ways by which a witch could be detected and the measures taken by the ecclesiastical and secular authorities in dealing with their victims. There is no need here to revisit these measures; suffice it to say that the Church of Scotland led the way, interrogating suspects and often torturing them by depriving them of sleep, food and water to obtain a confession. Thereafter, a suspected witch was handed over to the local civil authorities for trial.

What or who was a witch? According to Rogers, *Scotland Social and Domestic*, witches 'stopped mills, placed boulders in the path of the plough, raised storms, upset fishing boats, entered houses through the keyholes and hid or destroyed goods, rode on broomsticks shod with dead men's bones, stole the bodies of children from graves to concoct ointments from the corpses to make spells, promoted the sweating sickness, made waxen images and stuck pins in them, cast *glamour* or the evil eye on animals to make them die or, in the case of milking cows, dried up their milk.' All fairly representative of what people had been encouraged to believe at that time.

Witchcraft in Scotland, an article by F Legge which appeared in the *Scottish Review* (October 1891) is rightly critical of the Church in the sixteenth and seventeenth centuries. Legge wrote convincingly:

> 'It is with no feeling of pleasure that a writer of the present day can enter upon the task of sketching the sad history of Scottish witchcraft.....Here [in Scotland] the victims are, with hardly a[n] exception, such poor and wretched old women as are still to be found in every parish in town and country; while the persecutors are the pious, zealous, and, on the whole learned clergy, with whom we have accustomed to reverence as the very....exemplars of the milder virtues of Christianity.'

Written no doubt more in sorrow than in anger, we will return to Legge's pronouncements later.

The Scottish church was obsessed with witchcraft, backed by the authority of the civil power; both church and state were gripped by hysteria, convinced that in their midst was an ever-increasing menace which had to be eradicated. There is no single satisfactory explanation for such behaviour, although the most likely answer was that the authorities simply wanted to control a population which was largely uneducated. Certainly, an accusation of witchcraft soon put paid to women who were nuisances, beggars, unmarried mothers, viragoes and plain nasty-minded old crones who had outlived their usefulness and were a drain on the parish poor box. Many of these women were victims of sexual harassment; when they reacted to such treatment, they were censured for having cast a spell on the perpetrator. Others were outspoken and roundly cursed their employers, neighbours or those from whom they unsuccessfully begged alms. To curse anyone in that society was to risk an accusation of witchcraft and non-capital punishment of some sort and death in the 'extreme' cases - usually those where the witch had allegedly brought about death or sickness in both people and animals. It is interesting to note that after the Reformation, the Catholic Church turned the tables on its rival by denouncing the persecution of witches on the grounds that it considered the Reformed church heretical! One man's heretic is another man's martyr....

In Scotland, witchcraft was not only an ecclesiastical offence, it was a secular crime which along with murder and other crimes attracted the death penalty. And the Scottish Church went one better; it declared that refusing to believe in witches and witchcraft was also heretical, equally as bad as practising the Black Arts; this technicality effectively tied the hands of lawyers defending a suspect - when the accused could afford to hire one. The Church of course made it known that it was waging war on the evil ones to protect the godly; it also reminded the faithful that like plague and famine, the effects of witchcraft were visited on them because of their sins. If the Catholic Church was priest-ridden, the Reformed Scottish Church was people-ridden; Kirk elders exercised considerable power over their ministers well into the twentieth century and no clergyman - young or old - could afford to risk his livelihood by upsetting the local session or presbytery which had the power to remove him from his incumbency. There must have been many instances where to placate their elders, the weaker vessels were eloquent in denouncing witches from the pulpits, eagerly interrogating suspects when these were brought before the session. The Church was not ashamed of the contagion it spread; it positively revelled in it, welcoming it almost with a sense of relief, since if the good book and the General Assembly of the Church of Scotland said witches existed, no presbytery would dare disagree. When a suspect was identified, self-congratulatory presbyteries paraded their diligence; here was God's work being done and being seen to be done. Praise the Lord....

The process began with the apprehending of the suspect and placing her in custody- usually the kirk steeple to make escape virtually impossible. She would be 'watched' by volunteers - in effect kept awake for a period of days and nights until she was softened-up for interrogation. Presbyteries and kirk sessions conducted themselves as if in a court, acting as both judge and jury; these bigoted assemblies were often more feared than the secular trials which followed. Church spies were everywhere, usually the elders who walked the streets at night, reporting any odd behaviour. Every church also had a wooden box with a slot - like a ballot box - so that anyone might leave a note of a suspected witch's name and remain anonymous; the kirk authorities justified this method by telling their congregations it was their duty to 'delate' or inform on those they suspected of practising witchcraft and that their anonymity would be preserved in case the witch might take revenge before she was brought to justice. A certain Chancellor in Nazi Germany would have found this practice quite acceptable.

There are scarcely any records of witch trials in the pre-Reformation archives and executions were rare. In England, less than a dozen witches were put to death in the five centuries following the Norman Conquest. When James VI's minority ended in 1589 and he took the throne, he developed a morbid curiosity in witches and their craft, especially after a personal brush with an East Lothian coven in 1590-1591. The trials of the so-called North Berwick Witches in fact began the first of four epidemics which would send countless hundreds of women and a few men to their deaths. James VI believed that two of the suspects, Agnes Sampson of Nether Keith and Dr Fian of Prestonpans were the ringleaders, aided and abetted by Barbara Napier, Euphame McCalzean [McLean](an unrepentant Catholic) and the warlock Richard Graham, all resident in Edinburgh. The North Berwick Witches were said to number over a hundred although at first, only the above-named four were tried along with a young serving girl from Tranent, Geilie Duncan. Apparently, the coven was working under the instruction of the 5th Earl of Bothwell whose family had entertained hopes of the Scottish crown for three generations. Geilie Duncan was first to be tried; she broke down under torture and named the others. These five were taken into custody and examined by the king in person. At first, James treated the episode as treason until he learnt that the coven had attempted to sink the ship carrying him and his bride, Anne of Denmark to Scotland. He was astonished when Agnes Sampson virtually repeated *verbatim* a conversation he had with his bride on their wedding night; he changed the indictment to one of witchcraft. Of the so-called ringleaders, only Barbara Napier, who pleaded she was with child, escaped death; the others were executed on Edinburgh's Castlehill. In all, something in the region of 80 women and men - about two-thirds of the North Berwick Witches - were put to death. The first phase of the witch hunt had begun.

Over the next hundred years or so, it is thought that something in excess of 2,000 witches and warlocks were put to death in Scotland compared with about half that number in England. In *The Deil's Ain,* I have argued the case for a higher figure - about 4,000 - on the grounds that many cases went unrecorded or records were destroyed; where these exist, they are often deliberately vague about numbers. It is also interesting that a further one hundred cases were brought to light in 2001 by a researcher conducting a study into crime and punishment in the seventeenth century; these cases had not been incorporated in the Privy Council *Register* for the period, an omission which has since been rectified. How many more cases are yet to be discovered in some dusty archive? As this book goes to print, an in-depth study is being conducted by a team of researchers; the results of the Witch Survey will not be published until about 2004. However, an earlier study undertaken by the late Dr Christina Larner in 1977 examined 1,891 witchcraft trials involving over 2,000 people, most of whom were executed. It became apparent to Dr Larner that there was a predominance of cases in the east of Scotland, starting in the north-east, continuing down the coast, then crossing to Dumfries and Galloway and thence to Bute, in the manner of the shape of a fish-hook The highest number of trials occurred in the Central Belt - not only because it was the most densely populated area but also because certain counties like the Lothians and Fife were particularly active in the witch hunt and were within a day's ride of Edinburgh, where warrants to hold trials locally were granted by the Privy Council. Other areas such as West Scotland, Berwickshire, the Western Borders and Galloway were also hotspots as **Fig. 6** shows.

Fig 6: Witchcraft Trials in Scotland 1560-1727

Area	No of Trials (usually involving more than one person)
Lothian and Edinburgh *	331
East Lothian**	297
West Scotland	237
Berwickshire	231
Fife	169
Central Scotland	147
Western Borders and Galloway	106
Unlocated cases	100
Highlands and Islands	89
North-east Scotland	50
Orkney and Shetland	47
Total	1891 (possibly as many as 3,500 + persons)

**A single trial could include more than one accused, the figure for East Lothian may have been as high as 500 persons - or more. There are conflicting accounts and wild guesswork as to the number of trials, convictions and outcomes. Modern accounts give figures ranging between 1,500 and 20,000 executions; my estimate in *The Deil's Ain* is that a realistic figure is in the region of 3-4,000

* Includes Midlothian and West Lothian. East Lothian was the third highest of the Scottish counties for trials. For Dunbar and district covered by the Presbytery of Dunbar, there appears to have been about 70 documented cases with perhaps a further 30 where the figures are not stated eg in 1649, when 'several unnamed persons were tried at Tyninghame'. Taking as a conservative estimate 600 cases in East Lothian, Dunbar accounted for 20% (see fig 7). There appears to have been only about twenty commissions for local trials; these are recorded in the *Registers* of the Privy Council which issued warrants for trial by local magistrates and usually under members of the local landed gentry, often themselves Privy Councillors. Trials authorised for named individuals often led to further trials eg when a woman accused of witchcraft identified others; these persons were tried under the same warrant and were often unnamed or unrecorded. It is virtually certain that the majority tried locally under these conditions were executed.

The late Dr Larner made these findings but her figures must be approached with caution as they are only indicative; many trials were not recorded or were incompletely recorded. Some authorities held trials without obtaining the necessary commission from the Privy Council, Dunbar Burgh magistrates among them in 1649-50. It is difficult to decipher the entries in sixteenth and seventeenth century kirk session minute books - where those exist. Also, central records are patchy even where they have survived and no effort was made to record outcomes of the cases tried locally under Privy Council commissions. Even local magistrates' books are unhelpful, again where they exist. Also, surviving documentation often contains imprecise entries; for example, Spott Kirk session minute book simply records that 'many witches' were burnt there in 1705.

When a suspect was identified, she was apprehended almost immediately and brought before the kirk session. Skilful questioning and mild torture such as sleep deprivation usually resulted in a confession of guilt. Some ministers were over-zealous, not only pricking the suspect to find a witch-mark- a sure sign of guilt- but beating particularly stubborn individuals with a rod. Once a confession was extracted, the minister would inform the local magistrates and request a civil trial. Although cases were tried in the High Court of Justiciary and the circuit courts, the majority were tried in their own localities, under commissions granted by the Privy Council. Suspects were warded in the local kirk steeple or the tolbooth. In Dunbar, the dangerous cases were dragged through the streets for all to see, often being subjected to verbal and physical abuse before being put in one of the two cells on the first floor of the Tolbooth or Town House. Once there, anything could - and did - happen to a suspect. She might be tortured by the lockman - town executioner- or her jailers, although sleep deprivation or 'waking' was more common. The prisoner survived on a restricted diet and was often denied visitors while the burgh authorities awaited the necessary Privy Council commission appointing judges for the assize or trial. This was only the beginning of the ordeal.

Most authorities used the services of a witchfinder or witchpricker. East Lothian's high proportion of cases was due partly to the zeal of these brutish, greedy men. Notorious amongst witchprickers was David Seaton, the Earl of Winton's chamberlain in 1590. The Privy Council gave Seaton a roving commission to seek out witches throughout the county. The most famous of all however, was John Kincaid of Tranent. Kincaid's patch covered Berwickshire to Aberdeen. A deft wielder of the 'preen,' a six to eight inch long brass pin, he was paid six shillings for every witch he pricked, receiving £1 for every witch executed. Kincaid is mentioned in trials up and down the country but he was particularly active in the Lothians and Berwickshire. The witchpricker searched for the *stigmata sagurum* or Devil's Mark on the skin; he stuck the pin in various parts of the body and if the victim produced no blood or felt no pain, she was guilty. The pin might be stuck quite deep into the flesh, usually areas of dead skin and lumps, moles and warts; the presence of a fleabite indicated that the Devil or one of his familiars had been sucking the victim's blood. Women were subjected to the most demeaning examinations; their heads and other hair-covered parts of the body were shaved, searches were made under the armpits, the eyebrows, and often - with no doubt added relish - the private parts. Shut in a dark cell, denied food, water, sleep and suffering 'physical persuasion' or 'strict dealing' - euphemisms for torture - a suspected witch was reduced to such a poor physical and mental shape that she would confess to anything.

Instruments of torture devised for felons in general were often used on suspected witches who were stubborn and refused to confess their crimes. These included the *pilniewinks* (thumbscrews to crush the thumbs), the *boot* (a wooden contraption) into which the victim's leg was inserted and the ankles broken by wedges driven into it. The *cashieclaws* or *caspieclaws* was a particularly nasty instrument which is graphically described in the Privy Council *Register* (1599-1604); the instrument drew 'body, nek, armes and feit togider.........[the torturer] straik wedges betwix...the schailbanes [shoulder-blades] ....[until] the blude bursit oute......' Although the contraption is difficult to envisage, it was undoubtedly a cruel method to extract a confession. Victims might also be put in the stocks with the added refinement of having heavy iron bars placed on their legs while they were whipped. The scold's or witch's bridle was another cruel instrument; it was a kind of open helmet which was placed over the head and had a mouthpiece with a cruciform attachment so that when the mouth-piece was padlocked into place, the 4 points of the cross pierced the tongue, the palate and both cheeks when the victim attempted to speak. In his article for *Scottish Review*, F Legge describes other tortures such as burning the soles of the feet with lighted candles, putting lit candles in the victim's mouth or burning the head with them. Hair or hemp shirts were also used; the victim might be whipped and the shirt soaked in vinegar was put on their backs to lift off the flesh. Sometimes, the victim was put on a bread-and-water diet, made to lie on the cold stone floor of her cell with only a hair-shirt for covering. Less common in Scotland was the 'ducking' or 'floating' test where the victim's toes were tied to her thumbs, then she was lowered into a pond. If she floated she was guilty. This practice was common in Berwickshire and in certain areas like Dunfermline; it was more widely used in England.

After enduring these terrible ordeals, the suspect still had to face her or his accusers and attempt to deny their accusations. Few could afford the luxury of a defence lawyer, although a fair percentage of cases were held by the High Court of Justiciary in Edinburgh or the circuit and sheriff courts, where justice was applied more fairly, resulting in several acquittals. However, the majority of cases were held locally and almost always resulted in the death penalty. Local commissions were rarely noted for leniency; they were literally kangaroo courts conducted by ignorant or biased men with no legal skills. Usually chaired by a local landowner who was also a church heritor, it was in no one's interest to allow a suspect to go free. There were cases where tenants threatened to leave their rented land unless the landowner took action against those they considered witches. And the church was of course obsessed with sin and the need to control the population.

Confused by pain and lack of sleep, most women were at the end of their tether by the time they appeared before their judges; they confessed and named others in the hope that either the torture would cease or their lives would be spared. Some women even volunteered to confess without torture - deranged souls who mouthed a stream of nonsense which made them seem possessed by evil spirits; some of them wanted death because they were simply sick of their miserable existence.

We will never know for certain how many women and men were tried, how many were found guilty and how many were executed. Documented cases are usually brief and inconclusive; seldom is there a hint of pity expressed for the accused. As the majority of trials were by Privy Council commission, there was no incentive for reporting the outcome to the Council unless it expressed a wish to know. To obtain a commission, a man had to ride on horseback to Edinburgh and back which cost money; once the trial was over, the local authorities did not trouble themselves to incur more expense in reporting the verdict to Edinburgh. Also, to keep local taxes down, the Privy Council ruled in 1628 that a witch's heritable goods should be used to pay for the cost of maintaining her in prison, her trial and the materials used to burn her remains. Once found guilty, a witch was taken from prison to the place of public execution, 'werrit' [hanged] then burnt; her ashes were scattered since no witch could be interred in consecrated ground. Sometimes, especially where the victim's crimes were considered more evil than usual, she was tied to a stake and burnt alive, thereby adding a certain *frisson* to the mob's enjoyment.

As indicated earlier, there were peaks and troughs in the witch-hunt and four distinct epidemics. After James VI's experience with the so-called North Berwick Witches - only one of the hundred-plus actually lived in the parish - the period 1591-97 saw a crescendo of cases which peaked in 1597, the year James published his famous (infamous?) treatise *Daemonologie* which encouraged church and civil authorities alike to seek out witches and destroy them. The second epidemic erupted in the late 1620s and lasted until 1632. The third occurred shortly after the National Covenant of 1638, the document signed in Greyfriars Churchyard, Edinburgh which established the reign of the Covenanters in the Scottish Church. The Covenanters took an oath to adhere to the 'pure' principles of Presbyterianism; they refused to accept Charles I's English Book of Common Prayer which was considered Popish and they deprecated the installation of bishops and Episcopacy, also considered Popish. These grim and humourless men were also determined to stamp out witchcraft; they brought about the third and fourth epidemics in the witch hunt; these occurring between from 1647 to 1650, then again in 1660 until 1662. After 1640, the Covenanters dominated the General Assembly; several acts were passed urging congregations to be more vigilant in identifying witches so that by 1649, wholesale slaughter was in progress. In the summer of 1649, no fewer than 350 commissions were issued by the Privy Council, mainly in East Lothian, Fife and Berwickshire. A commission might involve the trial of more than one person, which gives some indication of the scale of the epidemics.

The trough which occurred between 1650 and 1658 was wholly due to Cromwell's Commonwealth - more relaxed at least where witches were concerned - established after the battle of Dunbar in 1650. By that time, the English had all but ceased to prosecute people accused of witchcraft south of the Border. The English commissioners appointed to administer justice in Scotland during the period of the Commonwealth were appalled to discover large numbers of women in Scottish prisons accused of witchcraft. They released most of these unfortunate women on the grounds that their so-called crimes were unproven. However, after Cromwell's death and the Restoration brought Charles II to the throne, the witch hunt resumed with added virulence; cases dismissed by the English commissioners were resuscitated, bringing about the final phase of the epidemic in 1660 until it lost momentum in 1662. One of the worst years was 1661 when 'innumerable witches were pricked, tried and executed in East Lothian. The list in that dreadful year seems to be endless.'[21] In the area controlled by the Presbytery of Dunbar, almost two-thirds of the recorded cases - and many went unrecorded - occur after 1658; Dunbar also conforms to the national pattern of peaks of activity in the witch hunt i.e. 1624-32 and 1648-50.

East Lothian was a county prominent in furthering the cause of Protestantism and made a considerable contribution to the establishment of the Reformation. John Knox, the arch-architect of reform was born in Haddington and much of his support came from local lairds and landowners. It is not surprising that East Lothian was prominent among those counties which prosecuted witches. According to Dr Larner,[22] East Lothian was second only to 'Lothian and Edinburgh' (which included Mid- and West Lothian) in the prosecution of witches; East Lothian was among the foremost counties which continued to execute witches up to the early part of the eighteenth century, although it wasn't the last.

The first recorded case in the Presbytery of Dunbar occurred in 1593, when Jonet or Janet Lindsay of Linton (Prestonkirk) was tried for witchcraft; she was acquitted however as no one came forward to verify the accusations made against her. Jonet was released on condition that if anyone in the future brought charges against her, she would be tried again by the Presbytery.[23] In all, about 72 women and men out of 297 recorded trials involving possibly twice that number of people were from the Dunbar district, a considerable percentage for such a small area, as shown in **Fig. 7**.

Fig 7: Approximate No. of Persons Tried for Witchcraft in and around Dunbar from 1593 to 1705

The statistics on an all-Scotland basis given in fig. 6 are drawn from the late Dr Christina Larner's *A Source-Book of Scottish Witchcraft.* Despite her painstaking research, she admitted that it is virtually impossible to quantify precise numbers of cases; also, her study contains errors of fact which would require extensive research to correct. At present, a team of statisticians are working on a comprehensive witch survey; its objective is to create a website on the Internet by the year 2004 identifying 'hot spots' for witchcraft trials in Scotland and hopefully correcting errors in Dr Larner's study - and no doubt my own in *The Deil's Ain*, my earlier book which deals specifically with witch persecution in Scotland.

The following are cases of witchcraft discovered and tried in the area under the jurisdiction of the Presbytery of Dunbar The total for the Presbytery is as follows:

Belton, Dunbar	1 female, verdict unknown but probably executed			
Bourhouse (Corhouse?), Dunbar	1 male, 1 female	"	"	"
Broxburn	1 female	"	"	"

Cockburnspath	1 female " " "
Dunbar	24 females and males (18 females, 1 male and 'five persons'; this figure is not precise as an unspecified number of'supected persons' were tried in 1644. Of these, 11 females and 'five persons' were recorded as having been executed; verdict unknown in the case of 7 females and 1 male but probably executed
East Barns	2 females, 1 male; 1 female executed; verdict unknown for others but probably executed
Innerwick	2 females, 1 male, verdict unknown but probably executed
Prestonkirk/Nether Hailes	2 females; 1 executed, 1 acquitted
Skateraw	2 females, verdict unknown but probably executed
Spott/Pinkerton	6 females, 2 males and 'many witches' burnt on Spott Loan in 1705; 2 females executed, verdict unknown for 4 females and 2 males but probably executed
Stenton	16 females, 1 male; 13 females executed, 2 females escaped from or died in prison, verdict unknown for 1 female and 1 male but probably executed
Tyninghame	1 female, 1 male and 'several unnamed persons including a farmer's wife' in 1649; 1 female and 1 male executed, verdict unknown for the unnamed persons but probably executed
Whittingehame	3 females and 1 male executed

Thus we arrive at 72 persons (57 females, 10 males, 5 'persons' to which must be added an unquantified number of persons at Dunbar, Tyninghame and Spott) accused of witchcraft within the Presbytery. Records confirm the execution of 38 females, 2 males, '5 persons' and an unquantified number of witches at Spott in 1705; 2 females escaped from or died in prison and only 2 females were acquitted. A further 21 females and 7 males have no verdict recorded but as the number of acquittals is less than 1% of the number tried, it is almost certain they were put to death.
Estimating the unquantified people at Dunbar, Tyninghame and Spott at 30 - not an unreasonable figure, given that covens usually operated in groups of 13 - we arrive at a total of 101 females and males. Estimating the total for East Lothian at about 500 suspects, the Presbytery of Dunbar accounted for 20% of the county total; on an all-Scotland total of say 3,500, Dunbar's share is about 3%

If we estimate that about 600 persons were tried in East Lothian - a not unreasonable figure - adjusting the total for Dunbar to take account of the unquantified number tried, the Dunbar figure may have been as high as 100 or about 17% of the county total. Other communities where witch trials were predominant include were Prestonpans (79), Tranent (51), Haddington (50) and the nearby farm-town of Samuelston (43) Penston and Peaston (30), Musselburgh (19), Stenton (14), Ormiston (15), Longniddry (10) and Spott/Pinkerton (8+). The Presbytery of Dunbar covered several parishes, where the number of suspected persons amounted to 72 which is on the low side; for example, in addition to these cases, the records include unquantified 'suspected persons' at Dunbar, 'unnamed persons' at Tyninghame and 'many witches' at Spott. We will never know how many. Dunbar, with Bourhouse, Broxburn, Belton and Pinkerton heads the list with more than 30 victims; next is Stenton (16), Spott (8+) and Whittingehame (4). Smaller communities near Dunbar such as East Barns, Skateraw, Innerwick, Cockburnspath, Tyninghame and Prestonkirk tried more than 14 between them. Although on these figures, the total is 72, I would be prepared to defend my estimate of a hundred.

The following is a chronological table of witches and warlocks tried in the Dunbar area:

1593	Jonet Lindsay, Prestonkirk	Acquitted (*Synod Records of Lothian and Tweeddale*)
1612	Christian Grintoun, Dunbar	Executed (*RPC vol ix)*
	Jonet Litstar or Lister, Innerwick	Probably executed (*RPC vol ix*)
	Jonnet Henrie, Skateraw	"
	Agnes Smyth, Skateraw	"
	Katherine Vertie or Virtue, Corhouse (Bourhouse?)	"
	Robert Allane, fisherman, Dunbar	"
	Katherine Hammiltoune, his wife	"
1613	Unnamed wife of Alexander Burghie, Dunbar	"
	Ewphame Young, Cockburnspath	"
	Alesoun Denis or Deans, Dunbar	"
1624	Marioun Boyd, Spott	"
1628	Margaret Baxter, Dunbar	"

1628	Marion Bathcat or Bathgate, East Barns	"
1629	Margaret Mewros/Melvis or Melrose, Pinkerton	Executed after previous acquittal in 1624 *(SRO ref JC2/6)*
	Jonnet Achesoun or Aitcheson, Pinkerton	"
	Isobel Young, East Barns	Executed (*RPC 2nd Series vol iii*)
1644	'Suspected persons' in Dunbar	Probably executed (*An Old Kirk Chronicle*)
	Jonet Kempe, Belton, Dunbar	Probably executed
1649	Janet Nicolsone, Prestonkirk/Nether Hailes	Executed (*An Old Kirk Chronicle* and Tyninghame Kirk session minutes)
	'Several unnamed persons including a farmer's wife' at Tyninghame	Probably executed (*Tyninghame Kirk session minutes*)
	John Bronne, Bourhouse, Dunbar	Probably executed (*RCE PA 11/8*)
	Elspet Scongall or Scougal, Whittingehame	Executed (*RCE PA 11/8*)
	Beatrix Doulson, Whittingehame	Executed "
	Marion Hongman, Whittingehame	Executed "
1650	Unnamed male, Whittingehame	Executed (*An Old Kirk Chronicle*)
	Six witches in Stenton	Executed "
1650	Ten witches in Dunbar	Executed (*Tyninghame Kirk session minutes*)
	David Stewart, Tyninghame	Executed (*An Old Kirk Chronicle*)
	Agnes Kirkland, Tyninghame	Executed "
1659	Marion Wilsoune, Stenton	Executed (*SRO JC26/26C*)
	Isobel Kemp, Stenton	Executes "
	Bessie Luost or Lacost, Stenton	Executed "
	Helen Heriot, Stenton	Executed "
	Alleson Fermor, Stenton	Executed "
	Marion Angus, Stenton	Executed "
	Jean Sydserf, Stenton	Executed "
	Five persons in Dunbar	Executed (*An Old Kirk Chronicle*)
	Jonet or Janet Wood, Stenton	Acquitted (*SRO JC 26/26C*)
	Helline Cumming, Stenton	Escaped from/died in prison (*SRO JC 26/26C*)
	Jonnet Man, Stenton	"
1661	Margaret Nisbitt, Spott	Probably executed
	Margaret Moffatt, Spott	"
	Margaret Elleot, Spott	"
	George Watson, Spott	"
	James Jonstoun, Spott	"
	Elspeth Yester, Spott	"
1662	John Task, East Barns	Probably executed (*SRO JC 2028)*
	Jeane Martin, Dunbar	"
	Unnamed woman in Broxburn	"
	George Binnie, Stenton	"
	William Cowan, Innerwick	"
1663	Jonet Harlaw, Innerwick	Probably executed (*RPC Third Series vol x*)
	Alesoun Angus, Dunbar	"
1688	Catherine McTarget or McTaggart, Dunbar	Probably executed (*RPC Third Series vol xiii*)
1698	Marion Lillie, Spott	Almost certainly executed (*Old Statistical Account, Spott Parish*)
1705	'Many witches' burnt on Spott Loan	Executed (*Spott Kirk session minutes*)

Code: SRO=Scottish Record Office with reference number for documents relating to specific cases
RPC =Register of the Privy Council
RCE= Register of the Committee of Estates of the Scottish parliament

A closer examination of these cases shows that they occurred in clusters at about the same time. For example, the cases given for 1612-13 all occur within a space of three months which clearly indicate that when one witch was discovered, she named others in the area. A similar cluster occurs in 1628-29 and again in 1649-50, then

KRM

Illus 42: *The author viewing the Witch's Stane near Spott.*

in 1659 when the last epidemic began. The numbers for Dunbar conform to the national pattern of epidemics, which proves that everywhere in Scotland, the pulpits were getting the message across.

There are few local 'memorials' to witches; Spott has its Witch's Stone (**ill 42**) - reputedly on or near the place of execution of Marion Lillie, known locally as the Rigwoody Witch in 1698. Stenton has its Witch's Knowe and the Witch's Cairn - the latter supposedly where witch sabbats were held every quarter. There is a Witch's Cairn at Crystal Rig, Innerwick, the place where the local witches cast spells to sink fishing boats they saw out at sea.

No account of the local witches would be complete without closer examination of at least two of the more infamous cases. Before doing so, it may be of interest to know that between 1612 and 1688, no fewer than twenty commissions were granted by the Privy Council for trials in Dunbar. The earliest recorded trials occurred in December 1612 when a commission was granted to 'Sir Alexander Hammyltoun of Innerweik, Sir James Douglas of Spott, knight, [blank] Home of Pinkartoun, Jasper Home of Lawfield [rector of Dunbar Parish Kirk] and the provost and bailies of Dunbar, or any two of them, to send for and apprehend Jonnet Litstar, spous to Johne Chancellar in Innerweik, Katherine Vertrie [sic], spous to George Wallace in Corhouse [possibly Bourhouse?], Agnes Smyth, relict of umquhile [the late] Hew Hammyltoun in Scaitraw and [name omitted], spous to Alexander Burghie in Dunbar.' Unusually, the Privy Council requested it be informed of the outcome of the trial (*RPC vol ix*).

Less than two weeks later, a further commission was granted - undoubtedly arising from information about women indicted in the earlier trial. On that occasion, the commission was for the apprehending of

> 'Robert Allane, fisher, induellar in Dumbar [sic], and Katherine Hammiltoun, his spous, being in ward in thetolbooth of Dunbar "as suspect guiltie of the divilische and detestable cryme of witchcraft, quhairof thair wes cleir evidenceis gevin aganis thame be some personis who lailtie sufferit death within the said burgh." '

It is unlikely that the pair - obviously named by the women in the first trial - were acquitted. (*RPC vol ix.*). Another commission was granted in February 1624 to Hammilton of Innerwick, Sir Archibald Douglas of Whittingehame, Sir James Baillie of Lochend [provost of Dunbar], Patrick Hepburn of Smeaton, George Home of Friarlands, William Sydserf of Ruchlaw, James Hopper of Bourhouse and the bailies of Dunbar or any two of them with the bailies to 'apprehend Margaret Mewros and Jonnet Achesoun, induellars in Pinkertoun, who have been long suspected of witchcraft &c., and to keep them in sure ward [the tolbooth] and examine them on the depositions already made by the said Margaret and others, and to report in writing to the Council.' A later entry appears in *RPC* on 28th April which suggests that the two women had named a third, one Marion Boyd 'wife of James Small in Spott "who is suspected of witchcraft &c.," as by the depositionis of certane personis of whom some wer brunt for witcheis." ' (*RPC vol xiii*). Mewros [Melrose] and Achesoun [Aitchison] were acquitted but tried again in 1628 as they were named in the trial of Isobel Young of East Barns, more of whom follows

A further commission in 1628 directed the provost and bailies of Dunbar, Douglas of Kilspindie, John Gilmour of Cockburnspath, John Hepburn of Gilmerton and George Home of Furde as justices 'to apprehend and imprison in the tolbooth of Dunbar, and therefter to any three of them to hold courts and try Margaret Baxter in Dumbar [sic], and Marioun Bathcat in Eistbarns, who have long been suspected of witchcraft.' (*RPC vol ii*) Although there are no records to confirm it, Marion Boyd of Spott, Margaret Baxter of Dunbar and Marion Bathgate of East Barns were executed on the depositions of other witches. An earlier case tried on 9th November 1612 - that of Christian Grintoun who was undoubtedly executed - is mentioned in the Melrose-Aitchison-Young trials in 1628-29.

The case of Isobel Young has been well-researched by Simon Lockhart in his family's geneaology *A History of the Lockharts of Lee and Carnwath: Seven Centuries.* Isobel Young of East Barns was accused of using witchcraft to cure sick animals using the *Lee Penny*, a semi-precious stone in the possession of the Lockharts of Lee and which came from Moorish-occupied Spain. The talisman came to the family after Robert the Bruce's death in 1329. It transpires that Sir Simon of Lee, later known as Locard (Lockheart) because he was entrusted with the key to the casket containing Bruce's heart, was campaigning in Spain with the Good Sir James Douglas, custodian of the casket. In a skirmish with the Moors, Douglas reputedly threw the casket before him shouting to his men that Bruce was again leading them to victory. Douglas was killed in the fight but the casket was retrieved and brought back to be interred in Melrose Abbey - recently authenticated by experts on its discovery in the grounds of Melrose. Locard had also captured a rich emir whom he put to ransom; when the young man's mother was handing over the ransom money, a jewel fell from her purse and Locard claimed it also. At first she was reluctant to part with it but Locard persisted; she told him it had magical powers, was a remedy against bleeding and fever, the bite of rabid dogs and that it could cure sick horses and cattle. It later became known as the *Lee Penny* after one of Locard's descendants mounted it on a silver groat [worth four old pennies] minted in the reign of Edward IV (1422-83). The jewel is in the family's possession today. Tales were told of its efficacy against hydrophobia and as a styptic. A member of the family, Sir James Lockhart used the jewel to cure some ailment after the Reformation; Sir James was accused of sorcery by the Synod of the Church of Glasgow but being a wealthy landowner, he was admonished with a rebuke.

No such consideration was given to poor Isobel Young of East Barns in 1628-29. According to the records, the 'Routting evil'- bellowing or roaring among cattle - broke out in the Haddingtonshire herds. Isobel Young, a mature woman married to a farmer decided to visit James Lockhart, Laird of Lee in Ayrshire to beg the loan of the *Lee Penny* to cure the animals near Dunbar. The legend was that if the *Penny* were dipped in water which was then given to sick animals, they were made well again. Isobel was given a flagon of the 'treated' water and returned to East Barns to cure the animals. Word got to the Presbytery of Dunbar who applied for a commission to try her for witchcraft.

The commissioners appointed by the Privy Council contained influential men - Adam, Bishop of Dunblane, Sir Thomas Hope of Craighall, the King's Advocate, Sir George Elphinstone of Blythswood, Justice Clerk, Sir John Scott of Scotstarvit, Director of the Chancellery and Alexander Colville, Justice Depute to Scott of Scotstarvit. Perhaps in view of the involvement of Lockhart of Lee, the authorities were nervous about making the charge or that they questioned the reliability of the evidence and therefore the legality of the trial.

Isobel Young was taken to Edinburgh for trial. She was accused of both causing and curing the sickness in the herd at East Barns. In the course of the trial, she named Margaret Melrose and Jonet Aitchison as her accomplices; that they had met the Devil to arrange the murder of George Clarkson in Dunbar and that Isobel was also guilty of causing the death of her own husband who apparently knew more than was good for him about the local witches. For good measure, Isobel was found guilty of associating with Christian Grintoun of Dunbar who was probably executed for witchcraft in 1612. Convicted on all counts including her witchcraft, Isobel Young was burnt at the stake on Edinburgh's Castlehill on 4th Febraury 1629. Her accomplices were also executed as were in all probablity Margaret Baxter and Marion Bathgate.

Sentence was passed on a person found guilty of witchcraft by the *dempster* or *doomster* who assisted the clerk of court. The usual form of words in the pronouncement were as follows:

> 'The judge acceptis the determination of the assyse and deferrs sentence to the morn.'

Then on the following day:

> 'The judges ordainis the panell [defendant] to be caryit be the locksman [public executioner] to the Gallowhill worryit [strangled] to death and brunt to asches [burnt to ashes].' (*RPC vol v*)

Thus in a relatively short period from 1593 to 1629, of more than 72 persons brought to trial, there were only two acquittals - Jonet Lindsay in 1593 and Janet Wood in Stenton in 1659. After 1629, near the end of the second epidemic of witch burning, Dunbar conforms to the national pattern of epidemics, the third of which began in the mid-1640s, then again in 1659-62. In 1661, a commission was granted by the Privy Council for the trial of 'Margret Moffat, Margret Elleot, George Watson, James Jonstoun, Elspeth Yester and Margert Nisbitt, all induellars and residenters within the parochin [parish] of Spott in entering into paction with the divell, renounceing ther baptismes and otherwayes'; they confessed to the "abominable sin of witchcraft". Tried locally, they were probably executed.

Visiting Scotland in 1662, the English naturalist John Ray (see Chapter 3) wrote in his account that 120 witches were executed in the month of August; unfortunately he does not expand on the event. We know however that the years 1660-62 saw the last of the major outbreaks of the witch hunt although women were still being executed in large numbers in localities which were infamous for the hunt - places like Inverkeithing, Torryburn, Culross and Pittenweem in Fife.

One of the most well-documented cases recorded in the Privy Council *Register* is that of Catherine McTarget or McTaggert of Dunbar in 1688. The wife or perhaps widow of a weaver at the time of her trial, Catherine had taken to begging for her living. She had been tried locally and at first, she was declared innocent of the charges; she was tried a second time and found guilty of practising witchcraft, but for some reason, the local bailies approached the Privy Council for a decision on the matter. On 14th May 1688, the Council issued summons for witnesses to attend yet another hearing. A detailed account of the twenty-seven charges brought against her and the conduct of the trial can be found in my book *The Deil's Ain.* Catherine McTaggart's case is typical of its kind as far as the charges against her are concerned; where it differs is in the amount of detail recorded in the Privy Council *Register.*

Catherine was married to William Brown, a local weaver; Brown is briefly mentioned in the course of the trial and as she had become a beggar, it is likely that he was dead or estranged from her when she was arrested. She was imprisoned in Dunbar's Tolbooth and accused of witchcraft contrary to Mary Queen of Scots' Witchcraft Act of 1563. The Procurator Fiscal charged with examining her was Patrick Brown, a qualified lawyer - such was the gravity and compexity of her case. The charges against her detailed incidents which took place between 1658 and 1688; no fewer than forty-six people from Dunbar and district were brought before Mr Patrick Brown to testify against her on 30th May 1688. The charges included allegedly causing the deaths of five men, two women, two children, a horse, eight cows and bullocks, bringing sickness to four women, three of whom she 'cured', inducing sickness in a cow and last but not least, interfering in the brewing of ale in two households. She was feared by all who knew her; when people saw her coming, they would try to avoid her or bless themselves - some making the sign of the cross, a Popish practice which the authorities seem to have thought justified. A jury was appointed to deliberate on the charges against her; the majority of the fifteen jurors were from outside Dunbar. Perhaps the Procurator Fiscal took particular care to make the trial as fair as possible - in spite of the preponderance of nonsense which passed for evidence. Catherine McTaggart was found guilty of the three counts of witchcraft, sorcery and superstitious libel. The verdict should have assured her execution but it is not confirmed in the Privy Council *Register.* According to Chambers, *Domestic Annals of Scotland*, Catherine McTaggart was sent to Dunbar to be burnt 'if her judges pleased.' It is certain that they were pleased to dispose of her on the Gallow's Green.

One of the later cases in the Dunbar district - but not the last, as we know that several witches were burnt at Spott in 1705 - was that of Marion Lillie, also from Spott. Marion was known locally as the *Rigwoody Witch - rigwoody* means thin or bony. She was tried in 1698 by the Spott Kirk session for imprecations and witchcraft practices. What on earth did they mean? In actual fact, Marion was little more than a poor beggar woman who roundly cursed those who refused her alms. She was also accused of having once frightened a pregnant woman 'to a rather unpleasant extremeity by handling her rudely.' In fact, Marion's career as a witch was quite unremarkable, given the more colourful tales told of so many others. Her nickname appears to be her only real claim to fame, surely an example of the saying to 'give a dog a bad name'. There is a certain sinister ring to *rigwoody.* Marion was brought before the Dunbar magistrates and while her fate may be recorded somewhere - the local records are difficult to decipher - it is almost certain that she was executed. The Kirk session minutes make it perfectly clear the elders meant business:

> 'The Session, after long examination of witnesses, refer the case of Marion Lillie for imprecations and supposed witchcraft to the presbytery who refer her for trial to the civil magistrates - said Marion known as the Rigwoody Witch.'

The site of her immolation is probably that marked by the Witch's Stone - west of Spott village - an unprepossessing rock enclosed by railings. At one time, the railings bore a small plaque identifying the stone; as the plaque has long-since disappeared, the boulder could be mistaken for the grave of some pet animal. As mentioned earlier, many witches were 'burnt on Spott Loan' in 1705; a 'Loan' is described as public ground, in the manner of a village green in England. How many were put to death? The Kirk session records are silent on the matter. As covens usually numbered thirteen, it is possible that about a dozen unfortunate women met a horrible death in that quiet and beautiful landscape near Dunbar. Another Witch Stone was once sited at Thistley Cross, at the side of the B-road from West Barns to Stenton where it intersects with the modern A1 Bypass; identified on the OS map, the stone disappeared many years ago.

On more than one occasion, the Privy Council in Edinburgh voiced its concern about the number of trials taking place up and down the country. This was particularly so during the 1620s and even more so in the period 1643-50, when the Covenanters dominated the General Assembly of the Church of Scotland and literally ran the country until Cromwell's invasion. The further outbreak in 1660 following the Restoration exceeded that of the 1640s. After 1663, the hysteria died down, although there were sporadic local outbreaks in 1676 and 1697 - despite a more enlightened attitude towards witchcraft by the legal and medical professions and the efforts by the Privy Council to restrict trials after 1688. Compared with England's four cases between 1660 and 1712, the Scottish authorities continued to try and execute women until 1727. By 1663, even the Privy Council was sickened by the excesses of the church and the local authorities. Even so, lawyers defending those individuals who were brought to court were frustrated in their attempts to defend their clients in the face of certain stubbornly conservative judges who obstructed their efforts to obtain justice. Legge quotes one instance where the victim of an alleged witch had been declared officially dead but the lawyer proved he was alive eleven years after a 'fatal' spell had been visited on him! (The man had sired several children in the intervening period but this evidence was dismissed as 'contrary to the indictment '). A more enlightened attitude was prevalent, even if certain judges remained obdurate; a few took the view that if an accused witch was found not guilty, the witnesses for the prosecution were told they would 'die for it' ie their refusal to co-operate with the authorities.

The last cases in the Dunbar area took place at Spott, where 'many witches' were burnt. After that, suspects were simply admonished for abusing the people. Elsewhere in Scotland, the witch hunt continued sporadically in isolated places until the last witch was burnt alive in the parish of Loth, Dornoch in 1727. Janet Horn and her daughter were indicted for witchcraft and meeting with the devil. Janet's daughter managed to escape from jail but poor Janet was led out on a cold June day to be burnt alive. The poor woman was so confused that she stood before the bonfire which would immolate her, warming her hands....

The Christian apologists who today dismiss the whole subject as folklore and the executions as an exaggeration - some have insisted that no more than 100 people were put to death for witchcraft. Clearly, they are somewhat uneasy about the role played by the Scottish Church. On the subject of statistics, Legge states that Mackay's appropriately titled book *Memoirs of Extraordinary Popular Delusions* gives the unlikely figure of 21,000 executions for the period 1562-1660; Rogers, *Scotland Social and Domestic* claims there were 7,500 persons tried between 1479 and 1735; Black, *A Calendar of Witchcraft Cases in Scotland* 1510-1727 considers the number was 4,500. Legge himself is more cautious and suggests 3,400 for the period 1590-1680 but he admits the figure could be higher because of the lack of records or ambiguity in those which have survived. Although the High Court of Justiciary kept accurate records, a low proportion of suspects were tried in the courts. In *The Deil's Ain,* I estimated the number at around 4,000 but again this figure must be approached with caution. A more precise figure may be established by the Witch Survey presently being conducted under the guidance of Dr Louise Yeoman, National Library of Scotland, but she admits that estimating the number of women and men executed for witchcraft will remain an inexact science. What is beyond doubt is that the intensity of the witch hunt may not be unfairly compared with the visitation of a medieval plague.

Modern psychologists would explain the witch phenomenon as a manifestation of the fear of women, with their biological make-up and their unpredictable mood swings. That is an oversimplification. Even if to seventeenth century man, women were a mixture of sensuality and malice, spite and bewitchment - in the sexual sense, these characteristics do not fully explain the phenomenon of the witch hunt - apart from the fact that only about 20% of the victims were men. However, when a woman instilled evil - sexual - thoughts in men because she was attractive, they believed they were possessed. Jealousy and acrimony between neighbours had a good deal to do with the discovery of witches; one woman might curse another in the heat of an argument - society was much more close-knit than today - and often the aggrieved person sought redress by informing the church that her neighbour was a witch. Many of the victims were simply old women and beggars who were a drain on the scarce resources of the parish poor box. A fair proportion were viragos. The majority came from the working and lower middle classes. The elderly were prime targets - the crone who lived alone on the fringe of society with only a cat - invariably black - for company. The eccentric, the wandered in mind, the lonely, the persistent beggars - uninvited guests at baptisms, weddings and funerals with their palms held out for alms - formed a fair proportion of the victims. Add to this the heady brew of hysteria preached from the pulpit and it is not difficult to understand how the witch-hunt came about.

As late as 1705, an East Lothian minister - John Bell of Gladsmuir, near Haddington - prepared a manual describing ways to detect a witch;[24] it appears to have been based on the practices used by the Earl of Haddington to identify many witches on his estate at Samuelston in 1661-1662. One hopes that Bell was merely recording an aspect of social history when he wrote

'....the witch's mark was like a blue or red spot or like fleabiting....'

to be found on parts of the body where detection was difficult eg the body hair including the eyebrows, the lips and under the armpits. Bell freely admits that he had personally pricked witches but he confesses that much mischief had been wrought on innocent women in the course of the witch-hunt.

Scotland was the last country in Europe to abandon the witch-hunt. The execution of witches did not end until 1727.[25] Today, if the conversation turns to witchcraft at all, many claim that theirs was the last community to burn a witch, often said with ill-disguised pleasure. The subject is now a matter of folklore. No one seriously believes that witches existed. But they did. And they do. I met one in Fife in 2001. She is an unreconstructed, candidly open white witch who assures me that witches never practised their art with intent to harm people. I believe that. I also believe that the majority were early herbalists whose potions were intended to heal the sick and control natural disorders by perhaps unnatural or unorthodox means which were treated with suspicion by the conservative-minded medical profession of the day. Little has changed. The medical confraternity oppose new treatments even in our own times. However, the witch of popular belief, the woman who dabbled in the Black Arts, cast spells for evil and mischief was but one aspect of the propaganda of a bygone age when the church was at pains to put the fear of God into people so that they maintained a rigid control over their behaviour. For that was the real reason for the witch hunt. Control.

Incredible though it may seem, the Witchcraft Acts of 1563 and 1604 weren't repealed until 1735-36. As mentioned earlier, the repealing measure made it lawful to prosecute anyone who pretended to be a witch; a one-year jail sentence was imposed and the individual was put on display in the stocks on market days every quarter to be seen by those whom she had supposedly abused. Such a case - that of Jean Maxwell - occurred in Kirkcudbright in 1805, then during the Second World War, when Helen Duncan, a medium, was prosecuted for 'abusing the people' with her fraud; she was also suspected of passing information to the Germans. The'witch' legislation wasn't finally repealed until 1951 when the Fraudulent Mediums Act was passed. Until at least 1831, supposed witches were subjected to 'scoring'- drawing blood from above the breath i.e. under the nose or on the forehead. Compared with other countries which prosecuted witches, Scotland has much to answer for - or at least the post-Reformation Church, which must take the credit for the witch-hunt. After the legislation was repealed, urban society considered it absurd for anyone to be accused of witchcraft. Not so in the remote parishes. The Scottish Church outlawed the practice of hunting for witches although the Associate Presbytery of the Established Church of Scotland (The Auld Lichts), a seceding branch of the Kirk, deprecated the repeal of the Witchcraft Acts. At their General Assembly of 1743, these grim and cheerless men pronounced that the government had acted 'contrary to the express law of God.'[26] In the eyes of that austere body of Christians, witchcraft remained one of several personal sins.

Even today, the ugly practice of witch persecution persists in the minds of those in America's Bible Belt, an area known to have more churches per 100,000 of the population than in the whole country. The congregations in Tulsa, Arizona were recently treated to a sermon delivered in old-style hell-and-damnation prose denouncing witches. As for Scotland, the General Assembly has allowed the subject to quietly fade into the mists of time; however, the ministers cannot avoid the reality that their forebears hellish fires consumed several thousand Scots women and men in the name of God.

Part III: Sinners and Paupers

After the initial upheaval subsequent to the Reformation, the General Assembly was instrumental in rationalising the thirteen former dioceses which between them had charge of ten ecclesiastical districts and set about establishing the new church's role. In matters of polity, the kirk session was a crucial element in the imposition of church discipline, a subject close to the reforming fathers' hearts. A kirk session's prime duty was to improve the moral climate in its parish; however, in the process, the Kirk grew ever more bureaucratic and interfered in the lives of the people to a much greater extent than had the medieval church. In this respect at least, progress was dramatic, although the reformed church was less successful in making adequate financial provision for matters such as the upkeep and rebuilding of churches, ministers' stipends, poor relief and the provision of parish schools.

At first, the old habits took a long time to die. Although Dunbar's church lost its Collegiate status as early as 1562, the local population continued to follow at least one pre-Reformation custom for several years. In May 1568, the Bishop of London wrote to Sir William Cecil, Lord Burleigh, the English Privy Councillor and Minister of State that he was 'credibly informed that in Dunbar on Good Friday....certain persons go barefoot and barelegged to the church, to creep to the Cross'. He censoriously added that if this was indeed the case, the Kirk of Scotland would 'not be pure enough for our men.' I have no idea how widespread Creeping to the Cross was in post-Reformation Scotland nor when it ceased in Dunbar; it is unlikely to have continued for long, given the anathema to the Roman Church and the enforced abdication of Catholic Mary, Queen of Scots in 1567.

Because of an acute shortage of qualified ministers, the quality of services in many churches varied considerably although this was gradually eased by increasing the student places in theology at the main universities. In the early stages of the Reformation communion was celebrated quarterly in the burghs but only twice a year in the rural parishes because of the manpower shortage. These and other deficiencies would be resolved in time. However, it is not my intention to catalogue the progress made by the Reformed Church in addressing its problems except in two respects - church discipline and poor relief.

We have seen how in the medieval church, sin went unrecorded because it was generally private and auricular, disclosed to the priest in the confidentiality of the confessional; an individual made his or her confession and paid the penalty by doing penance and the sin was absolved. The Reformed church changed all that by returning to the practice of the early Christian church where confession was made before the entire congregation until Pope Leo the Great changed this to secret confession in 450AD. After 1560, not only did sin again become a matter of public concern, detailed records were kept of every sin committed in the parish and every sinner was obliged to sit on the stool of repentance before the congregation for a stipulated number of Sundays depending on the severity of the sin. The session minute books for Dunbar contain many cases of what were considered sinful practices, a sample of which appear below as examples of the extent to which the kirk controlled the lives of the humble folk.

It would tax the skills of a professional calligrapher to decipher the hands which compiled Dunbar Kirk session minute books prior to the eighteenth century. Occasionally, the hand changes and entries are clear for a few pages. These provide tantalising glimpses of the problems which came before the session. On 5th October 1591, the Presbytery of Dunbar was taken to task for failing to excommunicate two men, James Hume, guilty of the murder of Patrick Craw and Thomas Home of Spott who had killed an unidentified person in 1594. Home had added fornication to his crimes and fornication was the *Magnus Criminis,* or great crime, as will be seen. By contrast, some incidents which were censured seem absurd and petty in our enlightened times. For example, in 1648, the Kirk session in Dunbar allowed the children of Irish widows to be baptised and admitted to communion as long as they possessed a testimonial from a minister in Ireland who knew them. Perhaps the intention was to identify possible closet Catholics.

But fornication and all That Sort of Thing - within and outwith the state of holy matrimony was the Kirk's obsession - next to hunting for witches that is, at least until the turn of the eighteenth century, when fornication headed the long list of sins. While most cases occurred in the eighteenth century, a few appear in earlier records, involving soldiers from the Covenanter and Cromwellian armies. Although meetings of the General Assembly were suspended from 1653 until 1690, the Kirk bided its time. As we have seen, the Restoration bought back the witch-hunt; other matters left to simmer away came to the surface. For example, in 1659, the year after the end of the Cromwellian Protectorate, Margaret Home, a local woman, was 'rebuked for her fall in fornication ' in 1651 with Trooper John Bahill in Cromwell's regiment. Untypically, she was fined £3 Scots (25p), a payment usually made by the man. Perhaps she was fined for sleeping with the enemy; it is more than likely she was obliged to meet the fine as her erstwhile lover had left the parish.

The sullen Covenanter General Assemblies of the 1640s censured men and women for wearing new fashions, the sin being pride or vanity. Frivolity of any kind was discouraged; for example *Penny Bridals,* where large numbers of well-wishers gathered to celebrate a young couple's marriage were seen as an excuse for drunken and licentious behaviour - which it has to be said was often the case. In the climate of unremitting gloom, who could blame the humble folk for indulging themselves in what for the most part was a day of innocent fun every now and then? The Kirk took steps to control these bridals; it ruled that no more than twenty persons should attend such gatherings and expenditure on the wedding feast was not to exceed ten shillings Scots (about 5p).[27] 'Promiscuous' dancing was banned by the General Assembly in 1650.

Commerce and trade did not escape the net either. Monday markets were banned as that meant travelling on a Sunday, when the faithful were expected to attend church morning and evening and sometimes in the afternoon as well. Trading with Catholic countries was of course expressly forbidden - whether the merchants paid any attention to this stricture is doubtful - money-lending was prohibited and merchants were obliged to close their booths to observe Kirk fasts. Even the harvest - the most important event in the agricultural calendar after spring sowing - took second place to church attendance. Oppressed and tormented by the constant meddling in their lives, it says much for the patient endurance of the Scottish people that they did not rise against these grim, humourless men. For centuries, Scotland was immersed in holy gloom, subjected to an unremitting regime which has thankfully lessened in the last fifty years. Those born after the middle of the twentieth century are fortunate indeed that church membership and attendance is a matter of personal choice and that unorthodox views on religion are tolerated much more so than they were in the recent past.

The session minutes are not without subconscious humour. In May 1649, certain profane and wicked people 'induellars in Petcokis [Pitcox]' baptised a bitch dog and called it Marion Tod; this harmless rustic prank elicited a stern rebuke from the Stenton Kirk session. The farm workers had to stand in the porch of the kirk for several Sundays, wearing 'saccloath'. Some misdeeds were punished by both kirk and the civil authorities or individuals authorised by law to do so. For example, a parishioner censured by the session for using profane language might be employed by one of the elders who as his employer was entitled to scourge him. The kirks imposed fines, often used the kirk steeple as a prison and had the power to banish individuals from the parish; those suspected as being of bad character who were unable to produce testimonials to the contrary were automatically expelled from the parish. Excommunication meant that the offender was denied civil liberties and classed as an outlaw, boycotted and spurned by everyone. An excommunicant could also be arrested and imprisoned at any time and on any pretext.

Kirk discipline was imposed using the same procedures as in a civil court. Hearings were undertaken in a solemn, orderly fashion and legal phrases were used in the session minutes. The intention was to deter other potential wrongdoers by subjecting those who misbehaved to admit their disgrace before the entire congregation. Some ministers were more empathetic than others, very occasionally betraying the merest hint of humanity; a minister wrestled with human failing while attempting to reconcile himself with an overbearing kirk session whose elders, though subordinate to him, could dismiss him from his living. Few ministers were prepared to risk their livelihood in the face of such men; many elders were vindictive, often stupid and certainly hypocritical. If the objective was to improve the moral climate in the parish, the community leaders did not always set a good example themselves. After 1560, sin became a matter of public confession, becoming a kind of weekly entertainment in the kirks. When fines were levied, the money was used for the relief of the poor.

The Kirk maintained and encouraged an army of snoopers, spies and informants who followed courting couples, noted down the names of Sunday whistlers and singers and those who indulged in smoking, inhaling snuff and - horror of horrors - taking strong drink on the Sabbath. A few West Barns men were rebuked for playing *pennystone* - a form of quoits - on the Lord's Day. The Dunbar Kirk did however allow the local fishermen to set their nets on Sunday afternoon and evening during the annual herring drave in August and September as long as they didn't haul them; an example of this is recorded for Sunday, 8th September 1639:

> '.....gude order [was] keepit by the seamen of the draife; no hering
> brocht in nor nets hauled but only set at efternoon.'[28]

Fishermen were fair game for the kirk spies who followed them along the shore to see if they were catching 'poos' - crabs - or forking 'flooks' - flounders - in the sea or trapping 'cunnies'- rabbits - on the links. The barbers in Dunbar came under censure on 13th June 1734 for 'the vile and scandalous practice of shaving and dressing on the Lord's Day.' One or two examples of similar occurrences which show the extent of the kirk's power follow:

> 'August 7, 1709
> : ....two elders, with ane officer, [to] go through the town after services in the afternoon, and reprove such as they find going or parading either in the streets, shore or castle, or any who sitt at their doors intertaining idle discourses, and reprove such; and to bring in a list of those who will not refrain.
> August 19, 1710
> : The elders, whose dutie it is to search the town, found severall persons in Janet Hunter's [alehouse] drinking a glass of twopeney [sic] beer and smoaking [during] the time of divine service. The persons were cited before the session, and confessed they were humbly sorrie for such heinaiss [heinous] breach of the Lord's Day; but they declared they wauld [would] drink no more twopenny beer or smoak tobacco again on Sundays, so they were absolved.'[29]

The elders kept particular watch on strangers lately arrived in the community as indicated in the session minutes for 30th April 1732 :

> '....to prevent disorderly persons to reside in this parish [the Session] do appoint that Elders both in Town and Country go thorough [sic] once every half year at least, their Bounds and demand, Testimonials from all strangers, that came from other parishes with certification.'

In other words, any interlopers causing trouble in the community were banished.

The records contain several references to instances of petty pilfering from the collection plate by the elders in charge of it. This ruefully reminds us of the Greek Cynic philosopher Diogenes who, when asked why he was walking about the streets in daylight with a lighted lamp replied that he was looking for an honest man.

Rural communities like Dunbar were undoubtedly the worst - or best, depending on your viewpoint - for surveillance. The elders had a field day - literally. They crept along the hedgerows bordering the fields, pouncing on amorous couples, tipsy revellers and those shearing sheep or threshing corn when they should have been in church.

It wasn't all gloom and doom however. The church struggled against overwhelming odds to care for the poor and the needy. There were few pensions in payment although there were quarterly payments made to the deserving poor in the eighteenth century; generally however, the humble folk had to make provision for their old age as best they could. When they fell on hard times as they inevitably did, they were often near starvation by the time the kirk came to the rescue. Widows were usually the most needy, although on occasion those of men who had served in an official capacity received a one-off payment. For example, in the sixteenth century, the Dunbar widow of a minor official who died in the service of James V was given £6 in 1542 (*TA*). A yearly payment of twenty merks was however made to a gunner who retired from Dunbar Castle.[30]

After the Reformation, the ministers' stipends and their manses were provided by the church heritors (major local landowners) who were also responsible for the provision of statute road labour, education and poor relief; the weekly collections were therefore largely used for relief of the poor. Before the advent of the rudimentary social security schemes provided by central government, the Kirk undertook the role, making payments to those in the parishes whose straitened circumstances were usually long-term. The recipients went through a form of means test; with a woefully inadequate budget, harsh decisions had to be made and the amounts awarded were meagre even by the economic standards of the time. Some of the needy received coal or food instead of cash and there are several examples recorded where the church officer personally bought shoes and breeches for impoverished schoolboys who also occasionally received cash payments - bursaries in effect - to enable them to attend school.

The unemployed did not qualify to any relief whatsoever. Those who left their native parish and returned later ill or disabled were refused help; they were advised to apply to the parish in which they last resided for relief. Some who lived temporarily in another parish were told to apply to their native parish for assistance. The church sanctioned *gaberlunzies* or 'official' beggars - including children - who wore badges or blue gowns signifying their right to beg. Relief was given to 'broken' men - those whose livelihoods were taken away by fire, accident or shipwreck; a sailor or fisherman described as 'ane poor, ship-broken man' would be entitled to some payment from the parochial poor box. Those sailors taken prisoner by pirates also benefited; at Dunbar in 1617, the session minutes record the local congregation's contribution of £3:18:4 (about 33p sterling) towards the ransom of John Muir of the town who had been taken at sea by Turkish freebooters. This happened again in 1620 when about the same amount was collected for the relief of 'the Scottishmen lying in Algiers, taken by the Turks.'[31] Some cases nearer to home are quoted below which illustrate the difficulties faced by those in need and the way the Kirk dealt with them.[32]

Fig 8 Dunbar Parish Church: Account of Income and Expenditure from 1730 to 1731

The treasurer's accounts were examined and show the following:

	£	s	d	£	s	d
Balance at date of last audit	228	2	8			
Amounts owing to the church (deficits) for mortcloths, gravestones, church seats, penalties and private baptisms	145	9	8			
Receipts:						
Mortcloths from January 1730 to September 1731	298	11	4			
Hearse money from March to August 1731	16	8	0			
Magazines from February 1730 to October 1731	21	12	0			
Headstones from January 1730 to October 1731	14	0	0			
Seats from Candlemas 1729 to Candlemas 1731	73	5	0			
Penalties in the years 1730 and 1731	45	16	0			
Private baptisms in 1730 and 1731	6	6	0			
Given to the poor by a private hand	8	4	0			
Collections from January 1730 to October 1731	972	8	3			
Received from the Town Treasurer for the fisher men that were cast in here twenty-four A[pril or August]	24	0	0			
Credit charge (total)	1,854	2	11			
	£	s	d			
Paid out to the poor from February 1730 to October 1731	651	0	0			
Paid to vagrants and the 'caring of the fisher men'	615	8	8			
Total	1,266	8	8			
Deficiencies in mortcloths and seats unpaid	192	7	8			
Total	1,458	16	4	1,854	2	11

Income less expenditure = £395:6:7 credit which was accepted and duly handed over to the new treasurer
Source: Dunbar (Old) Parish Church Session minutes 1730-1731: SRO ref. CH/2/647

The session kept a close eye on the balance sheet, making difficult decisions in a climate of abject poverty. We have a typical account of income and expenditure for January 1730 to October 1731 (**Fig. 8 opposite**).

Nearly a century later, the kirks faced even greater difficulties after the Napoleonic Wars, when the economy was depressed; after Waterloo in 1815, the minutes abound with applications for poor relief, more in the whole of the previous century. The entire country suffered from the soaring price of grain which meant that bread became prohibitively expensive and many businesses faced economic ruin. Inevitably, disagreements arose between parochial boards as to which was responsible for individuals who had resided in more than one parish. Dunbar kirk session refused point blank to accept liability for several people in this plight which meant that their cases had to go before Haddington Sheriff Court for a ruling. A single line entry in the session minute book can prise open the door of a humble country cottage, allowing us a brief glimpse inside. The following cases are typical examples of the time:

September 26, 1824:

Elizabeth Brown appeared before the session to declare she had been born and resident at Innerwick for a number of years with her parents; 'being lame and impotent [sic] she received from the parish of Innerwick a regular allowance of Five Shillings per quarter for many years - she does not remember how long.' The allowance was withdrawn as she had left the church at Innerwick and went to 'The Meeting'- probably one of the breakaway 'free' sects in Dunbar. She confessed that Mr Rogers, her former minister called on her 'at Godspeed, gave her a shilling and advised her not to tell us [ie the Dunbar session] the circumstances of her getting anything from Innerwick, or as she expressit "not to tell us unless she was sair put."

On 9th December 1824, the session unanimously agreed that Elizabeth Brown had no claim on Dunbar and she was advised to apply to Innerwick for relief. The case went to the Sheriff Court which ruled on 13th July 1827 that Innerwick was liable for her upkeep.

November 27, 1825:

John McHenrie and his son-in-law, married to McHenrie's recently deceased daughter Jean applied for relief for three surviving children. After questioning by the session, the men admitted that the children were 'begotten in fornication' with other men; one of the children was aged thirteen, one was the daughter of John Laurie and the third was the son of James Lumsden. The session ruled that the pair should apply to the fathers for maintenance for the children.

There are cases of women in their 60s - probably former farm servants who were too old to work in the fields - applying for parish relief. The majority were made redundant after Whitsuntide or May, the traditional time for hiring and firing farm workers. In a number of instances, the women had recently arrived in Dunbar from outlying parishes seeking less onerous work; when they could find none, obviously because of their age, they were forced to seek relief. In practically every case, the applicant was advised to apply to the parish from whence they'd come. It wasn't easy to get 'on the parish', as church relief was known. Some cases were complicated:

October 10, 1827

:George Brock informed the session that his daughter Beatrix had lost the power of one leg at age 12 and was then aged 23. She had lived in Prestonkirk for 9 years before coming to live with him in Dunbar. 'Immediately she was delivered of a Bastard child, he applied to the parish of Prestonkirk for aliment for the said child.' He was advised to apply to Dunbar 'being the parish in which the child was born.' An application to Dunbar two years earlier had been refused; Brock said his daughter was unable to work out of doors but she could earn two or three shillings sewing at home, or looking after neighbours' children in return for some meal or a few potatoes. As she was unable to support herself, Brock and the neighbours had had to do so. The session decided that because Beatrix Brock had never had 'an industrial residence in Dunbar and could not obtain a settlement in Prestonkirk, then she should take her father's settlement which was Athelstaneford, never having been able to acquire a settlement for herself.'

Thus the kirk session went to great lengths to avoid accepting liability.

From 1821, the beginning of the Reverend John Jaffray's incumbency at Dunbar Parish Church, the session minutes are briefer than formerly. There are longer intervals between entries and the tone is less sombre and harsh. Jaffray was one of the more enlightened ministers of his day; he comes across as human and caring. It is perhaps not a coincidence that in his time, there were more applications for parish relief than previously; there is also less hysteria about the evils of fornication and practically no cases were brought before the session in his time. In October 1833, the session examined the case of Isabella Dickson, a pauper whose state of mind had deteriorated to such an extent that she had to be put in jail prior to her removal to the House of Confinement in

Edinburgh, where most mentally ill people were sent. In 1839, four years after the death of George Miller, the local businessman, printer and publisher (see Chapter 7), his son George appeared before the session seeking parish relief. George had a history of instability and drunkenness; aged 45, he had no means of supporting himself. For a time he had worked for his uncle John, a printer in Dunfermline - he it was who published the original editions of the *Dunfermline Advertiser* - who had 'presumed too much [word deleted] him by allowing him only 6/6 (about 32p) per week and keeping the rest of his wages in his own hands.' John Miller clearly did so to ensure the money wasn't wasted on drink. Losing his job in Dunfermline, George had wandered through East Lothian seeking what work he could get, then depending on charity. He also claimed he was ill so the session ordered him to be examined by 'two Medical Gentlemen and sent to the Royal Infirmary [in Edinburgh] if the medical men think it necessary.' The doctors found George free from any illness which would require him to be admitted to hospital so the session refused his application for aid. The poor creature eventually became an in-patient in the local mental hospital at Haddington in 1849, where he died twenty years later.

Occasionally, the session came up with humanitarian solutions, as in the case of the tragic drowning of five men who attempted to save the life of a fisherman in 1845. On 20th August that year a small boat - presumably a herring-boat as the herring drave was in progress - got into difficulties just outside the Victoria Harbour mouth; one of the fisherman managed to get out of the boat and cling to a rock. Attempts to rescue him resulted in the deaths of five men and the kirk arranged a collection for the widows, children and the relatives of those who 'lost their lives in the generous effort'. The collection raised slightly less than £108. A commemorative tablet was erected in the cemetery by the community of Dunbar and vicinity in memory of the drowned - Lieutenant S Wyllie, RN, W Lucas, Coastguard P Darg, W Miller and W Clements, fishermen.[33] It survives today.

But of all sins, fornication - an ugly word in any century for an act which is the ultimate expression of love - was the greatest. The kirk regarded sexual congress sinful, even between married couples. In the eighteenth century, unmarried and pre-nuptial sex was a manifestation of 'unclean lives and scandalous behaviour.' The truth was, rather than offending against moral principles, those who indulged in sex brought unwanted mouths to the parish - children for whom the session would have to provide. The minutes are full of references to sexual misconduct between single women and single and married men as well as married couples found guilty of pre-nuptial sex - confirmed by premature birth - all commanded to appear before the session to answer for their behaviour. There were no exceptions. Even the nobility, the ministers and the elders did not escape the Kirk's censure. For example, on 5th May 1647, David Robertson, minister at Dunbar was required to repent for his unlawful fornication with a single woman whom he later married. Perhaps this left its mark on him as in the autumn and winter of 1649-50, he played a prominent part in the trial and execution of ten women accused of witchcraft. Did one or more of them report him to the session? Anything was possible where accusations of witchcraft were concerned. The session minutes exhorted that the Presbytery be vigilant in the detection of scandalous behaviour in its ministers - clearly a reference to Robertson who, like others of his calling, were expected to set a good example to their flocks.

The following are but a few examples of the cases which abound in the session minutes of the time. To illustrate the lengths to which the presbyteries would go in disciplining those who transgressed, one of the earliest cases involved John Hamilton, 3rd Lord Belhaven, a respected landowner and one of the 16 representative Scottish peers in the Westminster parliament after the Treaty of Union in 1707. In 1709, Lord Belhaven entered a *liaison adultere* with Lady Wigtown, whom he may have met through politics or business. Whatever the way of it, he and Lady Wigtown were married - unfortunately not to each other. Margaret Lindsay, second daughter of the 3rd Earl of Balcarres, was married to John, 6th Earl of Dunfermline, a Jacobite sympathiser and opponent of the Treaty of Union with England. Discovering his wife's affair with Belhaven, he divorced her on the grounds of her infidelity in December 1708. The Presbytery of Glasgow was informed of the affair and the Glasgow Brethren felt it incumbent upon them to report the matter to the Presbytery of Dunbar so that they might take appropriate steps to admonish Lord Belhaven for his licentious behaviour. The kirk session minutes of 1709 take up the story.

June 1st, 1709:

> 'This day, the Presbyterie resuming the affair of My Lord Belhaven, Mr [Robert] Stark [minister at Dunbar] acquainted them that he [Lord Belhaven] was now returned to the Kingdome .....because of the Notoritie of the Scandal of Adulterie betwixt the said Lord and My Lady Wigtoune flagrant in this Countrieside and the said Lord's residence here [near Dunbar] the Presbyterie judged themselves bound to do something in that affair and did therefore for that end appoint Mr Brown [a kirk elder?] to join with Mr Stark, Minister in this parish where the Lord Belhaven lived to conferre with him in order to bring him to comply with the discipline of the Church.'

Belhaven wriggled on the religious hook. At Dunbar on 25th September 1709, the Reverend Robert Stark reported to the Presbytery that

> 'Lord Belhaven is delayed and cannot attend the Presbyterie as he was.......obliged to go abroad this morning on business but that he promised to wait upon the Presbyterie at their next meeting. Mr Stark [was ordered] to acquaint him [Belhaven] not to delay his appearance any longer.'

On 10th October, we learn that

> 'This day compeared [appeared before the session on summons] My Lord Belhaven and was by the Moderator verrie seriously rebuked for the offence he had given by his scandalous conversatione [*Old Scots* for sexual intercourse] with the Ladie Wigtoun and taken against all future correspondence with her [ie he wasn't to contact her again]. He [Lord Belhaven] professed his heartie sorrow for the offence he had given to God and His people by his conversatione with My Lady Wigtoune and resolved through Grace never to give anie such offence againe.......He was absolved and dimissed. And for the Publick Removal of this Scandal, Mr Stark was appointed to intimat [make known] to the Congregatione of Stenton [the church Lord Belhaven attended] from the Pulpit on a Lords Day the Presbyterie's procedure in This matter.'

Hamilton, 3rd Lord Belhaven was married to Anne, daughter of Edward Bruce, an Edinburgh merchant. In 1721, he was appointed Governor of Barbados but was lost at sea on the voyage on 17th November.

Most of the cases which follow involve the lower and middle classes.

March 29, 1728:

> Thomas Skedsley and Mary Haggins or Huggins were found guilty of their sin but Skedsley would not agree that the guilt had occurred in the place named in Mary's deposition. When asked where it had occurred, Skedsley cheekily replied that he 'kept not a pocket book for such things.' Clearly, this was not the first time he had 'fallen'. (It is interesting that the session were keen to learn where the act had taken place; this was for the benefit of the kirk elders who patrolled the burgh looking for likely secluded places for physical trystings).

September 15, 1728:

> Margaret Ritchie 'fell' with not one but two men and was duly rebuked. 'This is a relapse into fornication the aggravations of her sin were fully represented to her and her danger shown. She was gravely rebuked and......led to repent, that iniquity might not be her ruin.' Perhaps one of her sins was doubly serious as it had occurred in the yard behind Bailie Fall's house!

November 3, 1728:

> John Denholm of Lochend's wife gave birth to a child six months after their wedding. Denholm was made to confess publicly their pre-nuptial fornication before the minister would baptise the child.

April 9, 1729:

> Mary Carlyle had an illegitimate child but 'parted with it.' She named the father as James Brown, the servant of her father John Carlyle, tenant of South Belton Farm. She confessed that the sin had been committed 'on Thursday before Hansel Monday [the first Monday of the New Year.] in the Barn.' Brown denied being the father and said he didn't even know Mary. She refused to alter her testimony, claiming to have said to Brown 'are you going to bring your self and me to shame and upon that he said he was going to do her no ill.' It is certain that they served their time on the stool of repentance.

August 16, 1730:

> Thomas Smith, a married maltster and Margaret Oseburn, single, were accused of 'Scandalous Behaviour and lewd Practices.' John Crumbie, an elder, reported that he had seen Smith enter Margaret's house at 10pm; he stayed there for two hours. At last, Crumbie and his companions knocked on the door and were admitted by Margaret who 'had nothing upon her but her shirt and the said Thomas was found buttoning up his waistcoat, which being looked upon as scandalous behaviour, and a presumption of guilt.' When the pair appeared before the session, Thomas explained that he had visited Margaret to pay for some shirts she had made for his son. Both denied any sinful acts had been committed and stuck to their story; the case was remitted to the Presbytery of Dunbar which presumably found them guilty.

Fines were frequently levied for sexual misconduct, ranging from a few shillings to several pounds or gold guineas which were paid into the poor box. As already noted, the session sometimes resorted to blackmail:

May 18, 1731:

> John Cochran, mason, was found guilty of anti-nuptial [sic] fornication whose penaltie was modified to forty shillings Scots, refused payment of the same. The Session ordained that in time coming his child should not be baptised until he paid the same.

There is more than a hint of pathos in the case of John Horie and Mary Hogg:
December 5, 1731:

John Horie was seen coming from Mary Hogg's bed early on the morning of 18th November in the house of her master, Alexander Nisbet. Mary insisted she was unaware of Horie's presence until one of the children with whom she was sleeping began to cry. When asked to explain his behaviour, Horie said he'd been worse for the drink and was looking for a bed for the night. He 'owned his Cloathes were off, but did not lye down within the Bed Cloathes.' A witness in the house said she'd risen at 5am, lit a candle and went to Mary's room where she found Horie 'with all his Cloathes off but his breeches and stockings and that he had come out of the bed.' The session was satisfied that no misconduct had occurred and Horie was let off with an admonition to be more sober in future.

There were sad stories which speak volumes about the human condition:
May 7, 1736 :

The session heard the case of Alison Dawson, Linlithgow, pregnant by Thomas Dundas, son of a Linlithgow surgeon. Lodging with her sister in Dunbar, she gave birth prematurely although her sister, Mrs Nicolson, had administered 'red corral and claret wine' to prevent her miscarrying after her long and uncomfortable journey. The baby was born dead, allegedly 'decayed, black and bruised on the Back Part of the Head.' The pathetic little bundle was buried at night in a 'Piece of Cloath' in the Nicolsons' back yard. The remains were exhumed and examined by a local surgeon who pronounced the baby older than the 5 months its mother claimed it to have been, that there were no blemishes other than the appearance of a contusion and putrefaction in the back of the head. Did Alison and her sister strike the baby on the back of the head to make sure it wouldn't live? It seems likely. Their failure to inform the authorities of the baby's death was taken as evidence of guilt and the pair were referred to the Dunbar magistrates to deal with as they judged. There are no surviving records to indicate the outcome of their trial.

Some cases dragged on for months, even a whole year:
July 1739-40:

Janet Penman, servant to Provost Fall named a local man, James Pringle, as the father of her child. Pringle had visited her at 11pm and stayed with her until 4 or 5am, although it transpired his intentions were honourable; he had asked Janet to marry him. She refused but he kissed her on the mouth. On 18th July 1739, Janet altered her statement to the session, naming Harry Knox as the father. Knox was a local brewer who would become a town councillor in 1744. Along with two friends - Melvin, master of the local linen factory and Nisbet, an employee - Knox had first exhorted Janet to blame a recently deceased carpenter, then a soldier and finally poor love-stricken James Pringle. Knox denied 'any carnall dealing' with the girl yet he he confessed he had offered to pay the girl's fare to Edinburgh to have the baby in secret. Knox then tried to divert attention from himself by accusing Melvin and Nisbet of having bedded Janet. Accusations and counter-accusations were made during 1739 and into 1740, when in July that year, Knox finally admitted he was the father of Janet's baby. Melvin was cited in another case the following year when on 20th December 1741, Janet Duncan named him the father of her child. The third member of this colourful threesome, Nisbet, said he had warned Melvin that Janet Duncan, 'that half-witted creature,' might name Melvin as the father. Melvin was a quick learner. Following Harry Knox's example, he first attempted to get Janet to go to Edinburgh to have the baby, then he offered her sister Isobel three guineas to coax her sister to get rid of it. Associated with this case was Nisbet's sexual misconduct with Janet Goodman whom the session confused with Janet Duncan. Whatever happened subsequently is not clear but we will encounter Melvin and Nisbet again.

Sometimes, there seem to have sexual epidemics in Dunbar:
November 1, 1739 :

The session recorded that three of Provost Fall's servants had fallen pregnant; Janet Kid[d] and Alison Cockburn by local sailors and Jean Jardin by George Lauder, a tenant farmer at Broxburn who had died 7 months previously. The three women were duly rebuked for their sins.

There was no escaping justice either. Girls who found themselves in the family way and who ran away from their parish had to live somewhere; sooner or later her native parish minister informed the new one of her misdeeds and directed that a public rebuke be arranged.
September 11, 1742:

Isobel Duncan, Janet Duncan's sister (see entry for July 1739-40 above) was brought before the session to confess she was with child by James Wauch, a soldier in Perth. Then she confessed she possessed no marriage certificate and that Thomas Meik or Meek, a Dunbar merchant was the father. She said

Meek had told her to name Wauch otherwise 'he would treat her the way Mr Melvin had treated her sister Janet.' Meek and co were nothing better than confidence tricksters at best and downright liars and blackguards at worst. Thomas Meek was the most devious of all. He told the session he had no case to answer as Isobel Duncan had already admitted she was married and so '....by law, her Charge cannot in the lest [least] affect me, and tho I can freely refuse it, yet it is not incumbent on me either to deny or affirm, or in the least to mind it. But Gentlemen, as I would be very loath to give you or my self any trouble, which is in my power to prevent. I am willing to receive a Sessional rebuke, and give your poor two Guineas. But you must not construct this offer as an acknowledgement of Guilt, it is only to save yourselves and me a great deal of trouble and noise at Superior Courts.'

Meek's statement is a mixture of arrogance, hypocrisy and threat. Clearly well-educated - he was a successful merchant in Dunbar - he clearly regarded the whole affair as a nuisance which he wished to end as quickly as he could. He spared no thought for the serving girl he had wronged because he was, to put it mildly, a snob. The session somewhat mealy-mouthed decided 'out of tenderness to the young man who appears penitent and seems to be sorry for the offence given, they will accept his said offer, upon his making a full confession....' Meek was 'severely' rebuked on 17th September 1742. By May 1744, Meek had been made a burgess, there is nothing about his persuasive manner which appeals to us today. His grave and that of his wife adorn the west boundary wall of the kirkyard; the inscription drips with pious unction.......

October 9, 1742:

Incredibly, Melvin's name crops up again, this time to confess to his sin of the previous year with Janet Duncan. Like Meek, he offered to buy himself out of trouble. The session suggested he pay five guineas; Melvin beat them down to four on 19th December on condition that the payment was not regarded as an admission of guilt. Even so he accepted his rebuke.

October 6, 1743:

The elders at least were treated no differently from others. We learn that Alexander Pringle tendered his resignation on 6th October 'for reasons known to himself ' The reason was soon made clear. Mary Heron 'servitrix to Messrs Pringles, Merchant' was with child and named Pringle as the father. Pringle admitted his guilt and was publicly rebuked.

Occasionally babies were abandoned. The same entry continues with the case of Elspeth Craig who left her illegitimate child in a cart at Belhaven. Elspeth was put in prison and appeared before the session in due course. She told the session she'd been walking to Abbey St Bathans one day when she was seized by a man with yellow hair who 'took hold of her and lay with her.' The poor girl was a beggar and already had a ten year-old child. She was put in Dunbar Tolbooth but was allowed to keep the baby with her until 6pm every evening. She asked to speak with an elder to whom she confessed her story about the yellow-haired man was untrue and that the father was John Hume, sevant to John Lorimer. She said she'd told Hume about the expected child and asked him for two shillings. He said he had no money and 'if she be with child, it was not to him.' Hume denied the same before the kirk session. On 16th January 1745, Elspeth Craig was banished from the parish.

January 10, 1744:

A case of violent rape was recorded although it was never referred to as such. The case of Janet Speirs is particularly poignant. She told the session that the father of her child was Captain James Hay, brother of John Hay of Belton and that ' it [the child] was begot of him at one o' clock in ye morning on ye fourth day of December last at ye foot of Crow's Wynde [Cossar's Wynd] when he threw her down and was guilty with her, being sent by her Master to light him up ye town to his quarters.' The poor girl said she hadn't informed Hay of her pregnancy. Hay was of course a member of a well-respected family who had lived at Belton since the Middle Ages. At any rate, the session interviewed him. He denied he was the father; he said he'd been in the company of Bailie John Pollock, Mr Castellau and Town Clerk Higgins who conveyed him to his lodgings at Mr Castellau's house [then on the outskirts of Dunbar, in a wooded area at the foot of the West Port. Castellau House now contains the town library]. The session asked Captain Hay if he'd had any prior carnal knowledge of the girl, which he denied. On re-examining Janet, the session learnt that the incident hadn't taken place in Crow's Wynd but in the vennel [close] leading from Clerk Higgins' house to that of Martin Sibbald and that long before that night, Captain Hay had had dealings with her in the stable at the back of the St George Hotel. Hay had no choice but to admit he'd had sex with Janet in the stable at the coaching inn but that had happened three months earlier. On 30th September 1744, the session minute book records that although an elder had written to Hay about removing his scandal by public rebuke, he reported he'd received no reply to his summons and that Hay had gone to Ireland. As for the unfortunate Janet, she had to accept public rebuke first for having willingly fallen, then taken against her will and bearing a childout of wedlock.

The session minutes are virtually silent about the '45 rebellion. However, the brief presence of the Hanoverian army in Dunbar had its consequences. On 5th October 1746, the minutes record that Margaret Hunter confessed to marrying a Denis Calachan in Hamilton's Regiment of Dragoons at Norham-on-Tweed but that she had mislaid her marriage 'lines' [certificate]. She was however able to produce a letter in which Calachan confesses he 'owns her as his wife.' She was ordered to inform the session when Trooper Calachan returned to Dunbar - presumably to confirm the marriage. Another case involving a soldier took place on 18th October 1747 when Catherine Sinclair was cited for her fourth incident of fornication with John Bell ' in the [cavalry] troop in this town'. Bell's regiment is not identified.

Entries in much the same vein continued into the early part of the nineteenth century although by the 1820s, there are more cases of applications for parish relief. Fornication crops up here and there but very rarely after 1821 and not at all in the second half of the century. The session minutes actually become mundane at the end of that century. Such highlights as are recorded concern national events such as the death of queen Victoria in 1901 and Edward VII in 1910. In 1906, the Reverend William Borland, minister at Dunbar from 1901 to 1912 addressed the General Assembly in Edinburgh, complaining that the Presbyteries acted as both prosecutor and judge in matters of Kirk discipline, a brave stance in which he was supported by at least one colleague who described the practice as that of a medieval system. The church was becoming more enlightened at last.

Part IV: Burial Grounds

In 1565, the General Assembly of the Church of Scotland ordered every parish in Scotland to maintain a record of burials in their graveyards. Some were lax in complying with this order as the Church backed by the Privy Council were obliged to reissue the order in 1616.

There are two graveyards in Dunbar today. The first at the Parish Church dates from the late sixteenth century; the second at Deer Park near Broxburn was opened in the second half of the twentieth century. However, two major ancient burial grounds have been found in recent years. As briefly mentioned in Chapter 3, the first of several small grave sites was uncovered at the Castle Park in 1821. The first major find occurred in December 1951 during the construction of a few private dwelling houses at Kirkhill Braes, Roxburghe Terrace, not far from the modern Deer Park cemetery on the outskirts of Dunbar. The graves were about a foot below the surface; the cists were mainly of red sandstone though unfortunately, many were destroyed by the bulldozers levelling the site. Experts from Edinburgh University concluded that the site was early Christian, dating between the sixth and tenth centuries. The remains had been laid to rest facing west, a characteristic of Christian interments. Because the heavy machinery had ploughed through the graves, it was impossible to quantify the number of burials but more than thirty intact skeletons were found. It is tempting to suggest that the graveyard was associated with St Bey's church 'upon Dunbar sands' but there is no proof of that.

Another important discovery was made in 1962, when in the course of deep ploughing at Lochend, several cists were uncovered. The cists contained at least 21 skeletons - 12 males, eight females and a child, possibly members of the same family. The remains were later confirmed as Iron Age - Votadini - the site was the largest Iron Age burial place discovered in Scotland at that time. In 1972, three long cists each containing a single skeleton were found at Dryburn, near Dunbar; then in 1979-80, Bronze and Iron Age burial sites containing 14 skeletons were discovered at Oxwellmains. Burials discovered between Broxmouth and Skateraw over the past century provide ample evidence of an area which has sustained human habitation for many years in the past. Neolithic and Bronze Age burials were excavated at Eweford in 2001-02.

The second major cemetery was discovered at Castle Park, on the site of and adjacent to the modern Leisure Centre and Indoor Swimming Pool. Cists were uncovered in 1993 and 1997; the first find consisted of the remains of 31 adults and 13 children, thought to be Anglian and dating from the seventh century. The discovery in 1997 was by far the greatest; 127 skeletons being uncovered; the remains are thought to have been buried between the ninth and eleventh centuries and are probably Anglian. Two skeletons were of particular interest; one was a male aged between eleven and fourteeen, the other a female aged betweeen sixteen and eighteen. Both showed signs of having been assaulted. According to one archaeologist, the male had been killed by a knife or other sharp instrument driven into his skull. The nature of the wound in the female skull indicated that she'd been killed by an axe wielded by someone who had stood facing her. Speculation is that the pair were executed for transcribing some code of behaviour- possibly sexual in nature. All the skeletons had been interred in east-west positions with their arms crossed, a feature of Anglo-Saxon burials.

The Parish Kirk cemetery was said to have contained two ancient graves, supposedly two captains of Dunbar Castle in 1350 and 1351; the headstones were reputedly inscribed with Saxon characters, but so far, no trace of

Illus 43: *Lead coffin in vault below the pulpit in Dunbar Parish Church, possibly Janet Home, (Cockburn) died c.1605, sister of Sir George* KA

Illus 44: *Coffin from the head end showing crushing/collapse* KA

them has been found. It is unlikely that the current survey of the graves in the churchyard by Dunbar and District History Society will prove successful in locating them It is thought that only one or at most two of the blood-line Earls of Dunbar and possibly their countesses are interred within the church vaults; there are no commemorative plaques to help us identify them. As will have been noted in Chapters 2 and 4, Dunbars found resting places at Durham Cathedral, Eccles, Norham and Tynemouth. Also mentioned in Chapter 4 is the lead coffin discovered in the vault in the east-facing part of the church after the fire of 1987; recent investigations suggest it is post-medieval. A preliminary investigation of the coffin in February 2003, followed by consultation with Dr Julian Litten (retired) of the Victoria and Albert Museum, London, has led to the following interpretation. It is the repository of a female and although high status, the moulding of the lid of the coffin is crude and may be local i.e. Scottish manufacture. These so-called anthropoid coffins were in general use for high status burials from around 1450 till the last decade of the 17th century. We know that Sir George Home died in 1611 in London, was transported to Dunbar in a lead coffin and interred in a vault below the then Collegiate Church. It is believed that Sir George may be buried at a lower level underneath the vault containing the illustrated lead coffin. The initials I[J?]C can be seen inscribed below the left breast on the coffin and they may refer to Janet Home, sister of Sir George, who married John Cockburn of Ormiston, Lord Justice-Clerk of Scotland. The coffin has sustained some damage, it has blown at the foot end and appears also to have been crushed and perhaps dropped. It was not unusual for these coffins to be moved around whilst tidying the vaults.

Bishop Richard Pococke of Meath, writing of his visit to Dunbar in 1760 (see Chapter 3), gives an account of his visit to the church, where he described - and probably viewed - a coffin in the vault in the east end of the church, placed there in 1611. (Although interior church burials were forbidden after the Reformation, if a family 'owned ground' within a church ie a family vault, relatives could - and did - insist on an indoor interment, especially if the family was powerful. For example, an even later interior burial occurred in 1629 at Tyninghame Church, which proves that the practice was still permitted nearly seventy years after the Reformation). The monument to Sir George Home, originally situated directly above the vault containing the lead coffin, was moved to its present position when the apse was added in 1897. This monument was one of two similarly impressive memorials in East Lothian, the other being that in the Lauderdale Aisle in St Mary's,

Haddington. The Home Monument was the work of a Dutch sculptor, Maximilian Colt who also created the effigy of Elizabeth I in Westminster Abbey. Another interesting interment is that in the Hay Vault which contains the remains of a factor to the Hay family and several members of his family. The wall inscription identifies the family:

'Within this wall is interred the bodys [sic] of Alexander Ramsay, Factor to David Hay of Belton and Eliz. Eagle his wife with 7 of their 20 children. She was daughter to Gilbey Eagle esq. Great Horse Equery [sic] to their macesties [majesties] K[ing] Cha[rles] the 2th K[ing] James the 7th and dyed [died] the 1st of August 1720, and he [Alexander Ramsay] died 2th Aprill 1731.'[34]

Illus 45: *William Ramsay's grave* KRM

The earliest external grave is dated 1604 but no inscription survives which might identify its occupant. A notable external wall monument (**ill 45**) is that set in the west boundary wall, the resting place of a relative of the Earl of Dalhousie. In the *Dunbar Register* for 1828, James Miller records the following:

'A monument built into the west side of the church-yard wall records the burial place of a youth conjectured to have been slain at Doon Hill [ie in 1650]. The words still readable are:- "What was mortal of WILLIAM RAMSAY lyeth heir [here], he was sonne of Jhone Ramsay, laird of Edington, brother the right honourable William earl of Dalhousie, a linage [sic] for all virtues in peace and warre, renouned and second to one, a youth ingenuous, comly [sic], of a sweet disposition, pleasant aspec[t], faire........." (All that we can trace is that it was erected by a fond mother in remembrance of her son').

The stone is decorated with the Angel of the Resurrection with trumpet and ornamented with two pillars on a plain pedestal surmounted by the crest and arms of Ramsay of Dalhousie. It bears carvings of weapons - swords, spears, muskets and banners - and contains the almost indecipherable inscription *Mors Ianva Vitae* (Death in the Cycle of Life). Another impressive wall monument nearby is that of the Purves family, many of whom were seventeenth century burgesses.

One touching memorial near the Ramsay monument commemorates the life of a John Jamieson:

'His most faithful wife, Margaret Parwes [Purves] had her very dear husband John Jamison [sic] commemo rated by this monument for love and honour.'

The inscription continues thus:

'Seven good things - man, citizen, husband, neigh bour, companion, merchant, bailie - but the same person.'

Who could ask for a more succinct and fine tribute?

Several gravestones bear symbolic carvings which identify their occupants' profession or trade - farmers are depicted sowing corn, butchers and craftsmen are represented by the tools of their trade. One grave marks the resting place of a butcher, William Mackie who was one of 46 witnesses who gave evidence at the trial of Catherine McTaggart, the Dunbar beggar accused of witchcraft in 1688.[35] Unfortunately the tombstone has been deliberately pushed over, but I managed to decipher the inscription a year before that occurred; the stone was inscribed thus:

'Heir lyes William Mackie flesher [butcher] andburgess of Dunbar who depairted this lyfe the 17 October 1704 and of his age 65.'

The gravestone bore an hourglass and skull with a shield in relief incised with an axe and a pair of callipers - the butcher's insignia. Another epitaph in quaint and touching verse appears on the tombstone of William Martin, an East Barns farmer; he died in 1729 aged 76, his wife predeceasing him in 1704. She was clearly a great loss:

'Here lyes interred ye crops [corpse] of Jennet Deans Loving to husband obleedging to her frend[s] Alace [alas] short while on earth she did remain Her godly life has freed hir from all pain Spouse childrend [sic] friends doe not her death deplore Her sad soul enjoys Hevens eternal glore.

She died the 19 April 1704 at 47.'

Near the entrance at the western boundary wall is the grave of William Hendrey, Poor Inspector at Dunbar who died on 6th August 1866; nearby is the grave of Ellis Dudgeon, owner of Belhaven Brewery who died in 1861, aged 68. Also in that part of the kirkyard is the grave of William Rennie of Oxwellmains, described as 'a man of very superior mind, great knowledge and sterling intelligence' ; Rennie died in 1830. Nearby is the grave of John Jaffrey, the enlightened minister of the Parish Church in 1821; he gave evidence to the Royal Commission set up to investigate the relief of the poor in 1843-1844 and contributed to the *New Statistical Account* of 1845.

There are graves of several former provosts - Christopher Middlemass of Underedge, successively Burgh Council treasurer in 1789, bailie (magistrate) in 1789, provost for several periods between 1794 and 1847 totalling twenty-six years in that office and burgh councillor in the intervening years. Middlemass began life as an employee of *Fall, Melville and Company*, became a successful merchant, was appointed major in the local militia and served as Deputy Lieutenant of Haddingtonshire - an impressive career indeed. Known as The Major, he lived in Cromwell House [now demolished] at the Old Harbour until his death in 1850. The nearby Sawers' monument commemorates members of the family, one of whom was a provost and two others who were respectively an officer in the Bengal Army (with a *bas relief* of his likeness) and an administrator in the Ceylon (Sri Lanka) Civil Service. In the same part of the graveyard is a wall monument to Elizabeth Delisle 'Spoufe [spouse] of Mr Thomas Meik, merchant' who died in 1790 aged 52. Meik whom we encountered earlier in a fornication trial managed the Falls' *East Lothian and Merse Fishing Company* until it ceased trading; he sued the Falls for money due to him as company manager. Thomas Meik followed his wife to the grave in 1802, aged 83. Not far away is the pathetically small headstone of Ann Merry, servant to the Duke and Duchess of Roxburghe until her death in 1869. Ann was probably too poor to afford a headstone; at least her employers had the decency to recognise her years of faithful - and undoubtedly poorly paid - service. Further over in the main section of the graveyard is the headstone of John Hogg, (**ill 46**) the local bellman who announced funerals. The bellman was an important - if part-time employee of the burgh. In addition to ringing his handbell through the town streets to advertise a funeral, he was charged with maintaining the hearse, looking after the mort cloths and collecting the fees for their use; he also dug the graves. The fees from the hire of mort cloths were used to supplement the poor box, so the bellman had to be scrupulously honest. Hogg died in 1840 having clearly met the requirements of his job, his headstone informs us that he was

'an honest man and lived an inoffensive life'

ELCMS

Illus 46: *John Hogg, bellman*

Another poignant memorial mentioned earlier is the plaque set in the west boundary wall commemorating Lieutenant Sydenham Wylde RN commanding Dunbar Coastguard who on 24th August 1845 led a doomed rescue attempt to save one of the 5-man crew of the fishing boat the *Red Rover,* skippered by William Thomson of Buckhaven. *Red Rover* had capsized outside Victoria Harbour. Three crewmen were drowned; skipper Thomson managed to reach land. His brother sought refuge on a rock which today is identified by its iron pole, not far from the entrance to the Victoria Harbour. Wylde and five volunteers set out in their cutter to rescue Thomson's brother from the rock which they knew would be submerged at high tide. Wylde almost reached him, even grasping his hand but didn't manage to bring him to safety as a large wave overturned the cutter. Wylde, his chief boatman William Lucas and local fishermen Peter and David Darg, William Miller and William Clements were drowned along with Thomson's brother. The plaque in the wall was raised by public subscription and a collection was taken for the widows and orphans of the drowned men. James Miller commemorated the tragedy in verse.

Another reminder of tragedy is the grave of Benjamin Wilson near the Church entrance(**ill 47**); Benjamin was the father of Robert Wilson who was among those who developed the screw propellor. Benjamin Wilson

KRM

Illus 47: *Benjamin Wilson's grave*

was one of the lifeboat crew who lost his life in 1810 attempting to rescue the crew of *HMS Pallas.*

There are several gravestones which prove that some Dunbar people lived well over 100 years. One example is the grave of Lieutenant-Colonel William Steil [Steel?] of Belhaven who served in the 3rd Regiment of Foot (the Scots Guards) for 60 years and died on 7th February 1810 aged 104. Another grave contains the remains of the Reid family whose headstone records ages of 104 and 105. According to the inscription, one of the family, Magnus Reid, lived to the incredible - if accurate - age of 114! Magnus was a travelling chapman at age 80 and followed the trade until his death in 1786; if his age is indeed correct, he was 16 years old when Catherine McTaggart was tried as a witch in Dunbar. Graves of notable businessmen include William Annandale of Bielside paper manufacturing factory on the outskirts of West Barns; the factory was destroyed by fire at the end of the nineteenth century. Other notable graves are those of Rear-Admiral James Hay of Belton who died on 3rd February 1857 aged 71. Hay served on *HMS Defiance* at Trafalgar, *HMS Aramantae* at Martinique and commanded *HMS Papillon* between 1810 and 1815. He was Deputy Lieutenant of Haddingtonshire. His son Lieutenant David Hay served in the 22nd Oude irregular cavalry regiment and was among the defenders of Lucknow during the Indian Mutiny who at age 25 died of fatigue on his way home. Hay's first son Lauderdale Hay was an ensign in the 39th Foot Regiment, dying in 1851 aged only 21. A third son, Commander Edward Hay RN served at the siege of Sebastopol in the Crimean War and took part in the Chinese war of 1860-61; at age 29, Edward Hay was fatally wounded in New Zealand, leading a storming party against a Maori position on 30th April 1864. The Hays certainly served their country to the full. Other military men interred at Dunbar include the Andersons of Winterfield Farm, one of whom served in the Indian Army; Major General William Cochran Anderson, Royal Artillery, was present on the field of Waterloo (see Chapter 11). Another soldier who saw action in India was Lieutenant-General George Handyman of the Bengal Lancers whose grave shows he died in September 1836 aged 87. The monument to Sergeant John Penn (**ill 48**) who survived the disastrous Charge of the Light Brigade at Balaclava during the Crimean War (1854-56) is difficult to read today but a rubbing I made in 2002 deciphered the following:

> 'John Penn late sergeant E.L. & B.Y. CAV.
> [EastLothian and Border Yeomanry Cavalry]
> a brave soldier served with 3rd Light Dragoons
> in India at Moodkee Sobraon Soodoolapore
> Llianwalla and Goojerat with 17th Lancers in
> the Crimea at Alma Balaklava [sic] Inkerman
> Born 31 Dec. 1820Died 31 January 1886.' (**ill 49**)

KRM

Illus 48: *Sgt. John Penn's grave*

At the base of the obelisk are two pairs of crossed lances with pennants on which is superimposed the Death's Head cap badge of the 17th Lancers. Further details of Sergeant Penn's military career appear in Chapter 12. There is a row of impressive monuments running across the breadth of the graveyard from east to west, dividing the old and new parts of the cemetery. Among these are the graves of Lieutenant-General Sir Robert John Hay KCE, second son of Rear-Admiral

Illus 49: *Sgt. John Penn, survivor of the Charge of the Light Brigade* PS

Hay of Belton. Sir Robert Hay was the Colonel Commandant of the Royal Artillery; he died on 5th November 1910. Nearby is the equally impressive grave of Sir James Grant Suttie of Balgonie (1830-1878), Colonel Commanding the Haddington, Berwick, Linlithgow and Peebles [Militia] Artillery.

Last but not least is the plain, unprepossessing Celtic cross which marks the grave of Sir Reginald Wingate, Sirdar (Commander-in-Chief) of the Egyptian Army and Governor of the Sudan. Wingate was among the small party who said goodbye to General Charles 'Chinese' Gordon on the platform of Cairo railway station, from where he proceeded to his destiny at Khartoum. Wingate was intelligence officer to Kitchener after the fall of Khartoum and he was present at the battle of Omdurman, where Gordon's needless death was finally avenged. During the Great War, Wingate supported Lawrence of Arabia in the Arab Revolt against the Turks.

East Lothian didn't escape incidents of grave-robbing, just as today it is beset by vandals intent on pushing over headstones in graveyards. In the latter half of the eighteenth and the first half of the nineteenth centuries, robbing graves was a lucrative occupation, highlighted by the celebrated case of William Burke - whose name was used to coin the word burking or death by suffocation - and his accomplice Hare who provided fresh corpses for the anatomy school in Edinburgh. It is not possible to prove that they visited the Dunbar area, although during their time, a robber was caught removing the corpse of a newly buried woman in Prestonkirk Cemetery. The incidence of grave-robbing led to the creation of watch-houses. An intact example survives at Spott; that at Dunbar was erected in 1822 and was used in living memory by cemetery employees until it was partially destroyed in what appears to have been an act of arson. Another method used to deter the resurrectionists was the formation of mort-safe societies. Mort-safes were iron-grills placed over recently-dug graves and removed a few months later when the corpse was no longer of any value to the surgeons or their accomplices. Mort-safes were often permanent fixtures, as can be seen in practically every nineteenth century Scottish graveyard.

In summing up this chapter, one aspect of Scottish life transformed by the post-Reformation Church was education; the country must acknowledge its debt to the reforming fathers for that at least. Knox's First Book of Discipline called for a school in every parish with an education system open to all children whatever their parents' wealth or social status. Although Knox's vision was never wholly achieved by the church, it is generally acknowledged that Scotland's standard of literacy was higher than that in England and most other European countries until the twentieth century. The parish dominie was often a *stickit* or failed minister or divinity student. Learning was seen as its own reward and at the outset of the Reformation, it ensured that the ordinary people were able to read the Bible as well as the Shorter Catechisms. The reformers believed that an educated, god-fearing populace would be more biddable. For too many centuries, it was. However, that isn't meant to imply that the church's excessive discipline and control were exclusively counter-productive. Today, we live in a more enlightened climate and in our society, religion no longer has the stranglehold it once possessed. There is more emphasis on tolerance, spirituality and love within the Kirk which was hard on women from the outset of the Reformation and until fairly modern times. Those who profess to be Christians must surely be grateful that times have changed.

6

The Protector

After the ignominious defeat of the Army of the Covenant at Dunbar on 3rd September, 1650, the mere mention of Oliver Cromwell's name (**ill 50**) brought fear and terror to the local population for many years after the battle; even today, he is still held in awe. Little did the inhabitants realise the part their small community would play in the events following Charles I's execution at Whitehall on 30th January 1649. That day, the London mob cheered. They cheered again when Cromwell rode out of the city at the head of an army to invade Scotland in June 1650. On the day he left London, Cromwell - ever the pragmatist - remarked to his aide John Lambert:

> 'Do not trust the cheering, for those very persons would shout
> as much if you and were going to be hanged.'

Had the Scots been victorious at Dunbar, his observation might well have come to pass.

KRM

Illus 50: *Oliver Cromwell*

Every battle is unique in its own way and Dunbar is no less so; it deserves the epithets given by history - *Dunbar Drove, Dunbar Race* and *Tyseday's* [Tueday's] *Chase.* Just as the defeat of the medieval Scottish army in 1296 began the Scottish Wars of Independence, the defeat of the Army of the Covenant of Scotland in 1650 began the political process which culminated in the Treaty of Union in 1707. Dunbar has the dubious distinction of being the site of both battles, with their momentous consequences, a fact which appears to have escaped the notice of most modern historians. In less than 60 years after Cromwell's spectacular victory, England would achieve its long-cherished vision of a united kingdom whose subsequent empire would last until the twentieth century. A crushing defeat, the battle of 1650 was fought over ground which had been unlucky for Scotland three and a half centuries before; the site is within about two miles of Edward I's victory in April 1296. It is indeed ironic that the struggle for independence began and ended on the same killing ground.

When news of Charles I's execution reached Edinburgh on Sunday, 4th February 1649, few among the city's population reacted against it. On 5th February, Lord Chancellor Loudon proclaimed the late monarch's eldest son Charles king, although constitutionally, he had no right to do so as the crowns had been united in 1603. By all accounts, the proclamation was a lifeless event; the heralds' trumpets brayed in the streets of a largely indifferent Edinburgh. Charles II was then in exile at The Hague in Holland, to where Scottish commissioners were despatched to negotiate with a man who would prove more politically astute than his devious, incompetent father. To understand the events which led to Dunbar, it is necessary to briefly examine the complicated political and religious scene which then existed on both sides of the Border.

The Scots had their problems with the later Stuart monarchs, largely in the context of religious worship and practices. James VI had successfully re-introduced bishops to the Scottish Church chiefly by skilfully exploiting the differences which existed within the established Church's hierarchy. James effected the restoration of Episcopacy by means of the Five Articles of Perth, which provided for private baptism, private communion, confirmation by a bishop, observance of holy days and kneeling during communion. At first the Articles were rejected by the staunchly Presbyterian church, then accepted reluctantly by the General Assembly when they were ratified by parliament in 1621. Charles I had followed his father's policy with one significant difference. He favoured the English Book of Common Prayer compiled by Archbishop Laud and wanted it to be univer-

sally adopted throughout the kingdom. Attempts to force it on the Scottish Church at the Kirk of St Giles, Edinburgh in 1637 elicited a wave of public protest which led directly to the signing of the National Covenant the following year. Scotland was in open revolt which brought about the Bishops' Wars - one of five weeks' duration and the other of ten days - which were civil wars, the fighting waged not between the forces of king and Covenant but royalist and anti-royalist premier families in Scotland. The Bishops' Wars were in effect the forerunners to the Wars of the Covenant.

KRM

Illus 51: *General David Leslie*

By 1639, relations between Charles I and the English parliament had deteriorated to such an extent that he was forced to promise the Scottish Church certain concessions in return for military aid. Early in 1640, the Scottish army commander, David Leslie (**ill 51**), marched his troops from Duns to Berwick where he expected to negotiate a treaty with Charles whereunder the General Assembly of the Church of Scotland would be formally recognised as having complete authority and jurisdiction in religious matters. The king kept none of his promises however; the disgusted Covenanters returned home, having achieved nothing. Then in July the same year, the army was mustered at Leslie's headquarters at Dunglass, Berwickshire; consisting of 2,500 horse and 20,000 foot it included a regiment of East Lothian troops raised by the Laird of Waughton and chaplained by the Tyninghame parish minister.[1] Waughton's regiment marched with the main army to Newcastle which Leslie easily took from the Royalists in occupation. An uneasy peace was agreed; more important was the fact that the almost bloodless success of the Covenanters had shaken the Stuart claim to absolute monarchy, one of the main causes of the subsequent English Civil Wars. Charles was obliged to placate the disgruntled Scots by paying their army £850 a day for the duration of their occupation of northern England which didn't end until the summer of 1641. The Tyninghame minister John Lauder, who would be ordered by the Presbytery of Dunbar in February 1650 to witness the execution of ten unnamed women in Dunbar for witchcraft, was chaplain to Waughton's regiment until its return to Dunbar, where it was disbanded in the Parish kirkyard in August 1641.

The following year brought the outbreak of the First English Civil War. In 1643, the Scots and English parliamentarians were bound together - superficially as it transpired - by the Solemn League and Covenant; under the Covenant, the English agreed to establish the Scottish version of Presbyterianism in England in return for the Scots' military assistance against Charles I. The English parliament had of course no intention of honouring the Covenant. However, Leslie crossed the Tweed on 19th January 1644, marching through snow to Newcastle, which he besieged until April. The Scots played a decisive part in the parliamentary victories at Marston Moor and Naseby, the bloodiest battles of the Civil Wars. East Lothian men were present at both battles, commanded by Lord Humbie of Yester.

Meanwhile in Scotland, the Royalists were encouraged by the brilliant strategies of the Marquis of Montrose who in a series of spectacular victories - not in themselves significant to the outcome of the Civil Wars - ran circles round every Covenanter army sent against his small Highland-Irish force. Montrose was finally defeated by Alexander Leslie at Philiphaugh in 1644; he was sentenced to death but managed to escape to the Continent.

Acceptance of the treaty with England was based on the clear understanding that the Elizabethan Protestant Church would be refashioned 'according to the Word of God and the example of the best reformed churches.' Naturally, the Scots took this to mean the Scottish Church whose leaders set about abolishing Episcopacy, completing this by 1646. Despite their commitment to the National Covenant of 1638 however, the Scots felt bound by the lawful authority of their sovereign; when Charles I was executed in 1649, there was a sense of outrage in Scotland. This was an affront to national pride and as a result, diplomatic relations with England were severed. Even so, when the Scots commissioners departed for Holland to negotiate with Charles II at Breda, they made it abundantly clear that Scotland would accept nothing less than Charles' promise to allow liberty of conscience in religious worship.

In many respects, the Covenanters displayed considerable naivety in their dealings with Charles II. The future king was as determined and disruptive as his grandfather, James VI and I had been. Outwardly supporting the Presbyterian faith and the Church of the Covenant, Charles privately detested both. At the same time as he was engaged in negotiations with the Presbyterian commissioners, he approached Catholic Ireland to assist him in his claim to the throne. At the talks in Breda, Charles promised he would agree to the Scots' demands for the adoption of Presbyterianism in the three kingdoms. However, with Irish support doubtful and at a crucial stage of the negotiations, Charles gave the Marquis of Montrose his royal commission to raise an army against the very men he was soliciting in constitutional talks.

This time, Montrose's luck deserted him; unsuccessful in his attempts to incite rebellion in the north of Scotland, he was defeated at Carbisdale, near Bonar Bridge, captured with Charles' commission on his person. He was taken to Edinburgh to be executed - he had already been sentenced to death in 1644 - suffering the indignity of death as a common felon by the hangman's rope rather than the headsman's axe. Perhaps those responsible were not over-anxious to draw attention to Charles' dealings with Montrose for obvious reasons; for his part, while Charles detested the National Covenant and all it stood for, he arrived in Scotland within a week of Montrose's death, acting in the role of Covenanter king-designate.

Thus a complex political and religious situation had existed in Scotland for most of the decade preceding the battle of Dunbar. Charles I had been forced to surrender to the Scots at Newark in 1644 but he refused to acknowledge the Covenant. By then, the English parliament was split into two factions - one supporting Presbyterianism and the other a radical Independent party; both were at odds with each other which of course benefited the Royalists. After nine months of frustrating talks during which the Scots at Newark suffered Charles I's subterfuges, they ran out of patience; about to break off negotiations with the king, the Scots were taken unawares when English troopers abducted the king from their camp. The Scots were infuriated; they had recently informed the dominant Independent Party in the English parliament that they would resist any attempts to remove the king from their custody. Several months of nervous and clandestine negotiations culminated with Scottish promises of military aid to Charles in return for even yet more absurdly unrealistic religious demands. This time, Charles agreed to introduce Presbyterianism in England for a three-year experimental period and to complete the political union of the three kingdoms in accordance with James I's proposals after 1603. To some Scottish minds, these were inseparable. However the heady principles of the National Covenant had been somewhat diluted and the Kirk Party in Scotland lost influence in what became a search for peace and security. The arrangement between Charles I and the Scots was supported by more than half the nobles and lairds and just under fifty percent of the burgh representatives in the Scottish parliament. Known as the Engagement, the deal with Charles was doomed to failure. The Kirk Party sat on one side, biding its time. It did not have long to wait to recover the high moral ground and the political domination of the country. The Engagers' army was defeated at Preston in 1648 which had the immediate effect of restoring the Kirk Party to power. In 1649, the Act of Classes was passed by the Scottish parliament; it banned Engagers and Royalists alike from holding state or local government appointments as well as officers and men in the Scottish army known to have Royalist sympathies. The army was purged from 1649 until the very eve of Dunbar in 1650. In its revolutionary regime which lasted from 1648 until the autumn of 1650, the Kirk Party spearheaded what was in effect a Second Reformation.

The differences between the Kirk Party and their several opponents contributed adversely to Scotland's ability to wage effective war against Cromwell when the time came. Apart from a scarcity of war *materiel* and trained men, the constant purging of competent officers and seasoned troops weakened the Army of the Covenant. In the eyes of men like Archibald Johnston of Wariston - one of the architects of the National Covenant - the army contained too many *Malignants* or Engagers and Royalists. The extremists in the Kirk Party took every opportunity to hamper the work of the locally-formed war committees in their attempts to recruit replacements. Several shires such as Haddington were under firm Kirk control and consequently provided few if any recruits for the army; this may explain to some extent why there were no exclusively East Lothian regiments present on the field of Dunbar in 1650, although the Earl of Leven's Horse was drawn largely from Haddington and Berwick.

When the Engagers were discredited after Preston, Cromwell invaded Scotland in 1648 and remained in the country for six months. He supported the Kirk Party at that time but sought to obtain knowledge of the lie of the land in the area. Expediency forced the Kirk Party's leaders to accept such support although the majority

in the Party had no desire to ally themselves with Cromwell or the Independents in the English parliament. In the midst of this confused situation, Charles I was executed and the Kirk Party turned to his son in Holland.

The future Charles II was a more able and ambitious politician than his father had been; outwardly, he seemed to be the kind of king the Scots had sought since 1638. After the Montrose incident, however, Charles was under surveillance day and night. Meanwhile, the Purging Committee continued to purify the army; its effect on the officer *cadre*, military morale and discipline would tell on the morning of Dunbar. David Leslie was denied the services of about 4,000 valuable men including the vital middle-ranking officers.

The population greeted Charles II's arrival in Edinburgh enthusiastically; bonfires were lit, bells were rung and there was dancing in the streets of the Old Town which must have sorely vexed the sterner Presbyterian leaders. The Scots' jubilant welcome of the king presumptive angered the English parliament; had it not recently demonstrated how it regarded the monarchy by the most violent means ? The English Council of State ordered an immediate invasion to pre-empt any Scottish invasion which might encourage the English Royalists. Neither the English or Scottish administrations appear to have assessed the political situation. The English parliament had until 1650 done precious little to exploit the confusion in Scotland immediately after the execution of Charles I. It was common knowledge that factions in Scotland were committed to church and king, church and no king and king and no church. In Scotland, the Kirk party failed to assess the reasons why England was reluctant to invade the country. Fairfax, commanding the New Model army was pressed to take the initiative but refused, insisting he would only fight the Scots on English soil. He resigned and Cromwell was offered the appointment which he reluctantly accepted.

Prelude to the Battle

Aware that he faced no threat from the small Scottish navy, Cromwell planned his campaign accordingly; in June 1650, he marched up the east coast, his supply ships keeping pace with his progress. He left London with 4,000 men and recruited the bulk of his army in the north of England. When he crossed the Border on 22nd July, he had between 16,000 and 25,000 in his force; the former figure seems more likely. He still hoped to avoid a pitched battle as by this time, he was weary of war and had considerable respect for his adversary, General David Leslie, his former ally. Leslie had been trained in the army of Gustavus Adolphus of Sweden and was a master of strategy. Leslie knew that Cromwell was accustomed to the cut and thrust of set-piece battles, so to compensate for his army's relative inexperience, he decided to play a waiting game, wearing down his opponent until a suitable opportunity arose to attack him. Had his strategy been carried through to its logical conclusion, Dunbar might have been a brilliant success for the Scots.

As the Ironsides advanced through the Merse, they found the Berwickshire villages empty of young men; the troopers didn't think much of the Scots and found their women 'pitiful sorry creatures' who wailed about their menfolk being forced by 'the maisters tae gang tae the Muster.'- no doubt a reference to the shire levies raised by the Homes of Wedderburn.

Cromwell quartered his men at Mordington, then advanced to Cockburnspath where he spent the night of 23rd July in the house of Sir James Nicholson;[2] some of his troops camped beside the walls of Cockburnspath Tower,[3] once the stronghold of the Earls of Dunbar. The low bridge which spanned the nearby Pease Burn was afterwards known as Cromwell's Bridge. That night, one of his soldiers wrote home dejectedly:

> 'Tomorrow we march, I believe, very near Dunbarn [sic] where we are like to
> lie in the fields, day after day, till the issue of the business be known, and if the
> ships with the biscuit and cheeses meet us not about Dunbarn, we shall be put to
> extraordinary straits, for this town [Cockburnspath] affords us little.'

The Ironsides reached Dunbar on 26th July, where some of the badly needed supplies were unloaded at Belhaven Bay and what became known as Cromwell Harbour, then the Old Harbour; during the campaign, Belhaven and Dunbar remained the main English supply bases, both being less exposed than Eskmouth and Musselburgh. Two days later, Cromwell was at Haddington, brushing with Leslie's *vedettes* at Gladsmuir. It may have been at this point that some officers in Leslie's army-notably Colonel Gilbert Ker and Lieutenant-Colonel Strachan of Ker's Light Horse - a regiment which fought well at Dunbar - had secret talks with Cromwell's officers; they reputedly urged the English to allow the godly of Scotland to rid the country of *Malignants.* Was that the real reason for the talks? We shall never know. Ker's and Strachan's loyalty remains in doubt to this day. It was perhaps no coincidence that at Leslie's Council of War on the summit of Doon Hill the day before Dunbar, both men urged him to leave the hill and attack Cromwell rather than let sickness and starvation take their course. This does not necessarily mean they were disloyal; more likely they were poor tacticians.

About 1,300 troopers in the English vanguard caught up with Leslie's retreating *vedettes* at Musselburgh and a short, sharp fight took place at Fisherrow, the first blood of the campaign. Cromwell camped in Musselburgh that night while Leslie fell back on his defensive line of trenches running from Arthur's Seat to Leith. The tactics Leslie employed throughout the campaign were dictated by the fact that Cromwell's smaller army was superior in discipline and experience; Leslie's aim was to contain and wear down the English so that shortages of food, sickness and the effects of the deteriorating weather would destroy their morale. The weather was particularly advantageous to the Scots; 1650 was the worst in a succession of bad summers, being colder and wetter than usual. In addition, the rich Merse and Lothian crops had been destroyed and the livestock driven into the Lammermuir Hills.

Cromwell fretted before Leslie's Edinburgh trench system. Monck's field guns shelled the city from the Salisbury Crags while the English supply ships, unable to land their stores, bombarded Leith. Attacks were mounted on the trenches; in one sortie, the English lost 500 officers and men including Colonel Lambert, Cromwell's capable cavalry commander who was wounded and briefly taken prisoner, only to be rescued almost immediately by his men. Lambert would later distinguish himself fighting on the right wing of the English army at Dunbar.

Despite these probing attacks, Leslie refused to leave his position and Cromwell was forced to fall back on Musselburgh on 29th July. He still hoped to lure the Scots into a battle. Denied the port of Leith, the English were compelled to withdraw to Dunbar on 6th August for much-needed supplies. They destroyed part of Hailes Castle at East Linton on their way. At Dunbar, Cromwell was allegedly generous to the townspeople, feeding the near-starving population from his own stores.[4]

Unable to take Edinburgh from the east, Cromwell attempted a flanking attack from the south. Scouts were sent through the Braid Hills on 10th August, reporting back to Musselburgh with encouraging news three days later. On 19th August, the English advanced through the Braids and took Colinton; Cromwell then made a feint towards South Queensferry only to find Leslie blocking his way at Corstorphine Hill. The campaign was assuming all the characteristics of a Scottish country dance. A brief skirmish occurred at Gogarburn in the last week in August; poor use was made of the artillery in boggy ground although according to English sources, 80 Scots were killed. The Scots reported one killed and eleven wounded. On 29th August Cromwell fell back to Jock's Lodge on the outskirts of Edinburgh while Leslie shadowed his retreat round the base of Arthur's Seat. The English burned their huts at Musselburgh and retreated to Haddington on 31st August, where Cromwell offered Leslie battle on ground of his choosing. Leslie declined. He knew that the army returning to Dunbar was hungry and discouraged. Men were falling sick daily from dysentery; despite the cold and the rain, the Ironsides were too exhausted to carry their tents and the Scots took heart when they saw them being thrown away. All Leslie had to do was to march parallel to the dispirited army, then bottle them up at Dunbar.

On 2nd September, Leslie held the crest of Doon Hill; he had also secured the pass at Cockburnspath thus effectively containing the entire English army in the narrow confines of the Belhaven-Dunbar-Broxburn shoreline. For the second time, Dunbar acted as host to a Covenanter army; in January 1644, the 21,000-strong Army of the Covenant had camped briefly outside the town before crossing the Border to capture and garrison the towns of Berwick, Morpeth, Alnwick and Newcastle. By and by, many in Leslie's army would visit these towns again but under less auspicious circumstances.

The Battle

Acutely aware that his army was disintegrating, Cromwell made plans to ship those too weak to travel by land to Newcastle. A council of war at Musselburgh had decided that Dunbar should be fortified, either to entice Leslie into the field or to allow evacuation of the entire army by sea. The stores were dwindling, dysentery was rife and the weather had worsened. Cromwell knew he had only one alternative to surrender so he prepared for withdrawal, intending to resume the campaign in the spring.

On 2nd September - a Monday - Leslie surveyed the enemy lines from his vantage point on Doon Hill. No doubt he was satisfied with the outcome of his cat-and-mouse tactics. The hill which 'lays its shoother [shoulder] to the shore' at Dunbar is impressive, even if not particularly high; its front is steep, its base is protected by the deep fault of Oswald Dean and Spott Glen and it dominates Broxmouth House where Cromwell made his headquarters. His shattered, hungry and discouraged soldiers were strung out for two miles from Broxmouth to Belhaven from where they could see the Scots massed on the hill. Some of the cavalry and artillery were quartered in Dunbar Parish Kirk. A regular occurrence during the Civil Wars, churches were ideal for accommodating men and the kirkyard provided grass for the horses. Apparently so much damage was done to the Dunbar kirk interior - the troopers probably used the pews for firewood - that it remained in disrepair for several years after the battle. The men billeted there would have had a clear view of Leslie's 22-25,000 troops,[5] (see Appendix G) an army outnumbering the English by more than two to one. The Scots held the high ground, the English had their backs to the sea; defeat stared them in the face even before a single shot was fired. And yet, when Leslie's forward outposts captured a veteran English trooper on 2nd September and asked him if Cromwell intended to fight, he replied without hesitation:

'What do you think we came here for?'

Impressed by his courageous reply, Leslie let the man go. Later, when reporting to Cromwell, the old sweat complained that the Scots had robbed him of twenty shillings; Cromwell gave him £2 from his own pocket.

And then incredibly, the Scots began to move down the hillside late that afternoon. Historians continue to debate the extent to which Leslie was responsible for bringing the army off Doon Hill; he certainly gave the order but was it his own, freely given? Apologists for Leslie insist he allowed himself to be manipulated by the Covenanter ministers accompanying the army. There is probably more than a grain of truth in that. It is said that Archibald Johnston of Wariston, the intelligent but fanatical Presbyterian persuaded the kirk men to order Leslie off the hill. Whether this has any basis in truth cannot be verified as there seems to have been no written orders. We know that all wasn't well in the Scots' army. Apart from the attempts of two of Leslie's senior officers to negotiate with Cromwell at Gladsmuir the previous month, many officers were inexperienced or downright incompetent. Leslie had made no secret of his opposition to the purging of the army all summer; a major purge of between three and four thousand officers and men had taken place at Leith Links before the army moved off to Dunbar. More men were dismissed the day before the battle. One disgruntled reject commented that the army was being left 'to be run by ministers' sons, clerks and other unlikely creatures who had never touched a sword in their lives.' Johnston of Wariston, the dour and implacable enemy of Engagers and Royalists noted in his diary that on 16th August that

'wee spent al day in going through al the regiments of Horse and Foote, and
purging out and placing in of officers, wherein I [im]pressed upon their consciences.....
the guilt and the blood and mischiefs that may follow on haiving Malignant, profan[e],
scandalous persons and Ingagers in our airmy.'[5]

This clearly illustrates the difficulties Leslie faced; despite his superior position, the committee of ministers set to 'guide' him insisted he follow the tactics revealed to them by the Lord of Hosts. We will never know the extent to which Leslie was manipulated or even threatened; he was a man of strong character but in truth, he probably had little say in the matter.

The ministers proclaimed to the army that the Lord had 'delivered ten thousand of the Moab into thine hand'. Theirs was a fairly accurate estimate of the English strength, even if they acted like men possessed - blinded might be more appropriate - by their Old Testament vision. Urging Leslie to attack, it is said they enlisted the support of the Scottish parliament's Committee of Estates whose members were there to see a battle so they ordered him off Doon Hill. Perhaps Leslie was compliant because he knew he had neither enough tents or supplies to sit out a siege in a very exposed position in the terrible weather. He also knew that traditionally, Scottish troops deserted in droves for the harvest and many were already slipping away under cover of darkness. Whatever his reasons, he came off the hill on the Monday afternoon to occupy the flat Oxwellmains and Pinkerton fields in front of Broxmouth House.[6]

Until that moment, Cromwell had ridden through the camp on a wiry Scottish pony, an eyewitness recalling later that he had bitten his lip 'till the blood ran down his chin without his perceiving it.' Cromwell probably studied the Scottish army from a slight rise in the grounds of Broxmouth Park, later known as Cromwell's Mount. Watching the Scots coming off the hill, some of his nearby staff heard him mutter

'God is delivering them into our hands, they are coming down to us.'

The terrain and numerical odds were still in the Scots' favour - almost an identical situation which faced Edward I's men in 1296. The only difference was the weather which was neutral or more accurately, it disadvantaged both sides to the same degree. September had come in cold and blustery, with driving rain. At Dunbar's small harbour, the English seamen were slowly unloading the last of the stores, piling them on the quay and filling the empty holds with scores of sick soldiers. Cromwell had prepared himself mentally and physically for a siege; now he hastily made a battle plan on ground which favoured his superior cavalry. He was confident; the troops who were fit were veterans whose calibre more than compensated for the Scots' superior numbers.

The two armies faced each other across the Brox Burn, normally a small stream but now swollen by rain. Leslie's right flank was anchored on the old A1 road to Berwick where he placed the bulk of his army; his left flank stood south of Easter Broomhouse Farm (**ill 52**). Cromwell's army faced roughly in the direction of Berwick; his left wing had its back to the sea where he husbanded a crack reserve to roll up the Scottish line as soon as an opportunity presented. Broxmouth House, seat of the Duke of Roxburghe[7] - about whom history appears to be silent on that momentous day - provided an excellent vantage point from which Cromwell could direct operations.

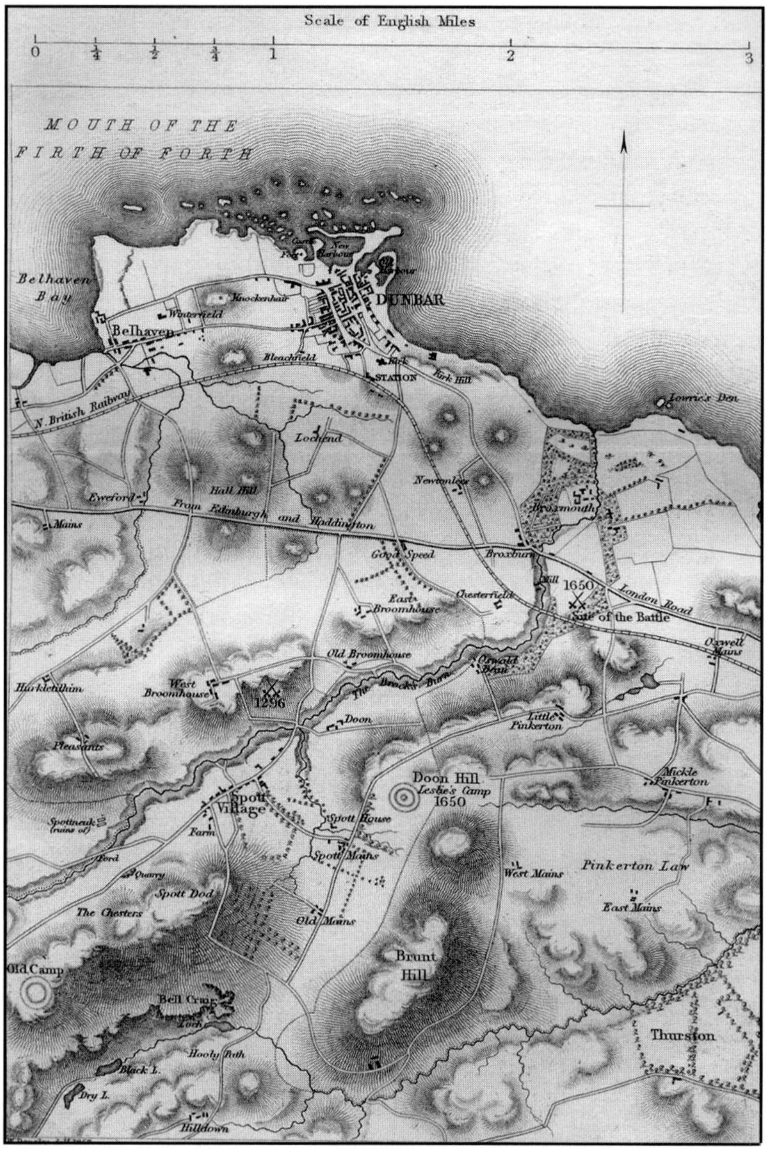

Illus 52: *Map of the 1650 Battle of Dunbar* KRM

On the eve of the battle, Cromwell visited his men drawn up on the left bank of the Brox Burn, offering words of encouragement. That day, he wrote to Sir Arthur Hesilrige, the governor of Newcastle: 'The Enemy hath blocked our way at the Pass of Copperspath [Cockburnspath], up on the hills, that we know not how to come that way without difficulty; and our lying here daily consumeth our men, who fall sick beyond imagination.'[8]

Cromwell knew he had only one option - to attack the Scots from his left flank, a tactic which didn't succeed initially; it was however on the cramped Scottish right where he achieved victory.

Both armies spent a miserable night in a thunderstorm and driving rain. The Scots lay down in the wet grass and flattened corn; a number of officers left their men to seek shelter in nearby small farms and villages such as Pinkerton and East Barns, the latter nearly a mile from the battlefield. Major General Sir James Holborn, a brigadier commanding troops from Stirlingshire and Clackmannanshire ordered his entire command to stand down and extinguish the saltpetre matches for their muskets an hour or two before dawn in case the light gave away their positions, understandable but a serious error. Without the slow-burning matches, the muskets were useless and this undoubtedly contributed to the panic which began when the English attacked. Holborn is a controversial figure, his loyalty to the Covenanters' cause suspect, confirmed by his dismissal from the key post of governor of Stirling Castle a year later.

The English attacked at 4am in bright moonlight. Leslie was taken completely by surprise although the main phase of the battle came two hours later. Lambert's regiment of dragoons attacked the Scottish left wing, the bulk of which was unable to manoeuvre at the base of Doon Hill. Even so, their long Spanish lances were able to repulse Lambert's troopers in the initial stages. Then two English foot regiments with cavalry support crossed the Brox Burn and were fiercely resisted by the opposing Scottish foot until the tired, soaked men began to give ground gradually. After a desperate push of pike, the Roundhead cavalry cut through the disintegrating infantry, scattering the Scottish horse and driving a wedge between the foot battalions. The Scots were forced back on to the lower slopes of Doon Hill, where their numerical superiority became a hindrance.

Cromwell husbanded his scarce reserves carefully; he held back his own regiment of horse and three infantry regiments, committing the whole brigade when the Scottish right wing began to crumble. The reserve pitched into the heaving mass of men, rolling up the flank in support of General Monck's thrusting attack in the centre. All the pent-up frustration of the previous month went into the charge. A so-called 'Highland' brigade - probably the Perthshire regiments of Sir George Preston of Valleyfield and Gleneagles' Foot - resisted and was slaughtered almost to a man. The Scots' on the right and in the centre groaned, shuddered then broke and scattered; unnerved by the shock of the English onslaught, the Scottish Horse were driven into the foot soldiers and panic developed quickly. The left flank of Leslie's army had been scarcely involved and soon succumbed to General Lambert's renewed assault.

It was all over in two hours. The sun rose over the North Sea to the echoes of the English cry 'the Lord of Hosts!' as they chased the Scots nearly eight miles from the field. Many casualties were sustained during the scramble to escape the Roundhead troopers who slashed at and cut into the running men, riding them down ruthlessly. Adrenalin changed Cromwell's euphoria into religious fervour; he was heard saluting the sun which dispersed the mist on that bloody September morning. Quoting from the 63rd Psalm, he shouted

'Now let God arise and His enemies be scattered!'

On seeing the Scots break, he remarked that they were 'made by the Lord of Hosts as stubble to our swords.' So legend has it. Miller, *The Lamp of Lothian* describes how the fleeing Scots were chased to Cockburnspath, Dunbar and Haddington; the majority who escaped were of course the cavalry who rode to Edinburgh and Stirling, shouting the news as they went. Many of the infantry were buried where they were cut down; fatally wounded Covenanters were hastily buried in the grounds of Spott House and at West Barns at Battleblent - so-named as tradition has it that both men and horses were buried in a communal pit there, discovered many years later.

Dunbar was arguably the greatest of Cromwell's military successes; he should have been defeated at Dunbar or forced to surrender. The social gossip John Aubrey wrote in his *Monumenta Britannica* that he once met a soldier who was present at Dunbar and who told him that Cromwell had been possessed of a divine impulse that day:

'....he did laugh so excessively as if he had been drunk; his Eyes sparkled with Spirit. He obtained a great Victory but the action was said to be contrary to Human Providence.'

The same fit of laughter had taken Cromwell at Naseby in 1645. After Dunbar, he is said to have remarked that the Scots' cause was doomed from the start; as he put it:

'...there may have been a covenant with death and hell.'[9]

As for Charles Stuart, king of Scotland but not of England, while he may not have exactly laughed on learning of Leslie's defeat, he is said to have gone on his knees and thanked the Almighty, such was his hatred of the Presbyterian Church and all it stood for. Charles would have even greater cause for regret as Cromwell repeated his success at Worcester exactly twelve months after Dunbar when on September 3rd 1651, he routed Leslie a second time. The date wasn't always lucky for Cromwell however; he died on 3rd September 1658, in his 60th year.

There are varying estimates of the Scottish casualties at Dunbar. However, most accounts accept these were between 3-4,000 dead and over 10,000 soldiers and 200 officers taken prisoner out of an estimated 23,000. The English claimed they lost only 30 men.[10] The English version of the battle was reported to parliament as follows:

'The night proved bluftery [blustery] and wet, fo [so] that our Army fell not upon the Enemy at the hour appointed, till it was fomewhat [somewhat] later in the morning.....opposition was made by the Enemy with very great Refolution [resolution]; a very hot difpite [dispute] at Swords' point being between our Horfe [horse] and theirs. Five Companies of our Foot that were firft [first] commanded out, after they had difcharged [discharged] their duties, being over-poured [overpowered] by the Enemy, received fome repulfe [some repulse], [from] which they foon [soon] recovered: the Genral's Regiment [ie Cromwell's] timeofly [timeously] coming in....at the pufh [push] of Pike, did break the ftouteft [stoutest] Regiment the Enemy had, and totally routing them, did full execution on them.... And now the beft [best] of the Enemies Horfe [horse] and Foot, who after the firft Repulfe [first repulse] were as stubble before them....it became a total Rout, our men having the chafe [chase] and execution of them near eight miles; in all.... our Army loft [lost] not thirty men....In this battle were killed upon the place and near about it, above four thoufand [thousand] men. Of private Soldiers taken prifoners [prisoners], above four thoufand [thousand]. Of their Horfe [horse] taken, killed and made unserviceable, about two thoufand [thousand]. Commission[ed] officers taken prifoners, as Colonels Lieutenant Colonels....about Two hundred and ninety [which included ' Lord Libberton' ?] and Sir James Lumsden of Innergelly, Fife along with some of the ministers]. The foot Arms taken, were about fifteen thoufand. About Two hundred Colours taken. Two and Thirty pieces of Ordnance with the reft of their Artillery, Bag and Baggage, and all their Ammunition taken,'[11]

The battle of Dunbar deserves the epithets history has given it - *Dunbar Drove, Dunbar Race* as well as *Tyseday's Chase* [Tuesday's Chase, which appears in McDonald's *Burgh Registers and Guide to Dunbar*]. The site of the main English attack was marked by a single rough stone (**ill 53**) at the junction of the old Oxwellmains road with the former A1 near the modern Lafarge cement factory. It is inscribed as follows:

'3 September 1650 Here took place the brunt or essential agony of the Battle of Dunbar Thomas Carlyle' to which is added 'The Covenant'.

Because of road improvements, the stone has been moved some way from its original position; for the purist, this makes a nonsense of the inscription; the only saving grace is that the memorial is now more accessible to

KRM

Illus 53: *Memorial of the Battle of Dunbar in 1650*

the general public, on the right hand side of the B-road into Dunbar, just before Broxmouth House.

After the battle, Cromwell was aware that any exit through the Lammermuirs might still be barred by the section of Leslie's army sent to guard the road to Berwick. As he was unsure whether this element of the army had fled on hearing the news of the defeat, he sent two soldiers to spy out the land. The troopers masqueraded as Royalist soldiers, intending to ride to Newcastle for reinforcements. The men hadn't gone more than a few miles when a gust of wind lifted their cloaks and revealed their Roundhead uniforms to the watching Covenanters. The troopers were overtaken and shot dead on the bank of the Whiteadder river, their bodies subsequently buried under a whin bush.[12]

That autumn, few regretted the Covenanters' defeat - even those who supported Charles Stuart. The English parliament, already alerted to the possibility of a Royalist conspiracy in England, formed an intelligence unit of *agent provocateurs* who enticed Royalists to join fake conspiracies then turned them over to the army. One such agent was Captain George Bishop who after Dunbar wrote smugly:

> 'Upon the route at Dunbarr, the royall partie were much comforted in seeinge us destroy their enemy, as well as ours.'[13]

Thus despite the Scots being Charles' sole hope of ever regaining the throne of England as well as Scotland, there were few tears shed over the defeat.

The way was now open for the complete subjugation and annexation of Scotland by the English Commonwealth. Monck had virtually achieved this by 1652 although before then, the defeat at Dunbar had forced the main political factions in Scotland to settle their differences in order to continue the struggle. Initially, the Kirk Party rode out the storm; they had a significant following in the west and south-west - an army which was called the Western Association. By the end of 1651, Engagers and Royalists were back in favour, much to the Kirk Party's disgust. Worcester ended any further attempts to resist the English and by 1652, Cromwell and Monck controlled the whole of Scotland apart from gangs of moss troopers, disaffected Highlanders and thieves who were more of a nuisance than a threat. The last royalist castles at Brodick, Dunottar and the Bass Rock had capitulated by the spring of 1652 and Highland resistance finally flickered out in July 1654. Archibald Campbell, 9th Earl of Argyll who had fought at Dunbar took part in the ill-fated Glencairn Rising and was defeated by Monck at Dalnaspidal.

By 1654, Scotland was a divided nation again. One faction remained loyal to Charles Stuart and against England; the other faction wanted neither. Moves to forge closer links between the two parliaments were inevitable after the Cromwellian occupation which lasted until 1658. It has to be said that the Protectorate in Scotland brought an unprecedented efficiency in the executive and the judiciary. Justice was administered impartially and effectively and witch hunts and executions were proscribed.

What then were the consequences of the Battle of Dunbar? It was certainly a stain on the nation's honour even if at local level, the town benefited from the improvements made to its harbour. Unlike other seaports on the east coast, Dunbar escaped destruction so that it was able to continue its fishing and coastal trade. Some historians regard the battle of Dunbar and not the Union of 1707 as the 'end of ane auld sang.' Dunbar has also the dubious honour of having the first military medal struck for the ordinary soldier, albeit the auld enemy. The battle was commemorated by the general issue of a campaign medal to British [English] soldiers who took part irrespective of rank or merit.[14] An original of the medal is owned by Dunbar Golf Club. The obverse bears the head of Oliver Cromwell and is inscribed 'The Lord of Hosts Word at Dunbar Septem y 3 1650'. The reverse shows the House of Commons in session. It is doubtful whether any Scot received or would have wanted to receive such a memento. Well might General David Leslie have agreed with George V's sentiments in 1915 when he was petitioned to strike a medal for those who took part in the Gallipoli campaign: 'We do not issue medals for retreats.'

In the aftermath of the battle, Cromwell did not impose free quartering of his soldiers on the small community of Dunbar as he had done elsewhere during the English Civil Wars. Compensation was paid to those who billeted his troops and provided stabling and feed for his horses. In addition, any corn crops destroyed in the course of the battle were paid for. The burgh records provide examples of costs; the account for 1651 comes to £134,638 (£22,460 sterling),[15] a considerable sum for the time. Some expenses appear in detail. The payment for Colonel Saxby's regiment of 1,200 men was 8 shillings Scots (40p) per man per day; Thomlinson's regiment of 1,200 stationed in the district from 31st January to 16th April 1651 cost a total of £5,000 Scots (about £800) each man and his horse requiring 30 shillings a day (£1.50). There were several regiments billeted in and around Dunbar throughout that year; Aldridge's Dragoons and the regiments of Twistleton, Cobbet, Finch, Cotterell, Lilburne, Overton, Morgan and Syllerese [Syllers or Sillars?]. The town of Haddington was benevolent to the local surgeon's widow; as late as 1663, the magistrates continued to pay her a fee for her husband's care of 'the hurt sojers at Dunbar fecht.'[16] But even though the good people of Dunbar were spared the upkeep of their conquerors, the mere mention of Cromwell's name terrified them for years afterwards.

On 3rd September 1843, Thomas Carlyle visited the battlefield to take part in the dedication ceremony at which the commemorative stone was laid at Oxwellmains road-end. Ever since the seventeenth century, local farmers ploughing the site of the battle have found rusted swords, pike-heads, helmets and cannon balls which were invariably cast onto spoil heaps of stones at the side of the fields. The *Sealed Knot Society,* an organisation which takes its name from the somewhat ineffective Royalist secret society in the English Civil Wars reenacts Cromwellian battles. The *Society* has staged several impressive displays at Dunbar. The first occurred in the 1960s - marred by the blinding in one eye of a local boy who took part in the mock fighting. The site of the battles of 1296 and 1650 does not readily betray the eerie quiet which pervades some Scottish battlefields yet on still days, there is a melancholy silence and an indescribable heaviness about the place.

The Useless Mouths

More tragic than a battle lost is a battle won. Wellington said something of the kind after Waterloo, where he lost many friends on the field. Dunbar was a defeat for Scotland but in many ways, its aftermath was even more tragic than the fighting. Thousands of men and boys were netted like shoals of herring that day, giving Dunbar its nickname *Dunbar Drave* or *Drove.* It is the fate of these prisoners which is perhaps more heartbreaking than the lives that were lost. As we have seen, most of those who escaped were the 4,000 cavalry; many of the foot soldiers got no further than Spott or West Barns, both within a mile or so radius of Dunbar.

It is impossible to state with accuracy how many were taken prisoner on the day of the battle; nor is it possible to quantify the number marched to the north of England afterwards. Under the rules of war, Cromwell had no right to remove prisoners of war from Scotland, then a separate country whose soldiers had fought in its defence. Not only were about 4,000 forced to march south, a few were exiled to the American colonies and the West Indies to be indentured to various owners and treated little better than slaves. More than half of the 3,900 died needlessly from malnutrition and neglect on the road to England in what today would be considered a war crime.

Most accounts agree that at least 10,000 men and boys were taken prisoner at Dunbar - they alone outnumbered Cromwell's effective strength. The logistics of feeding and supporting so many prisoners would have stretched the resources of a modern day commander and Cromwell was desperately short of supplies for his own men. He did what he could for the beaten army. In a letter dated 4th September, he admitted to the Lord President of the Council of State in England that he didn't have sufficient men to guard his prisoners, let alone feed them:

> 'We have been constrained....to dismiss betwen 4 and 5 thousand almost starved,
> sick and wounded; the remainder....I am fain to send to Berwick and so on to
> Newcastle.'[17]

Cromwell was not a vindictive man; he had treated prisoners of war well on other occasions and yet it is stretching credibility to argue that he sent several thousand men to Newcastle purely in the interests of their welfare and his own security. Knowing as he did the state of many of these wretched men, a man of his intelligence could not fail to appreciate the fate of many of them along the weary, dusty roads to the north of England. In mitigation, from a purely military point of view, Cromwell couldn't allow so many men to go free.

He culled out the weakest, the most severely wounded, the elderly and the young before sending the remainder south. Cromwell claims that about 4,500 were set free; we also know that he released a further 1,000 into the care of the Countess of Winton in East Lothian. How many began that long march? Something in the region of about 4,000 men set off from Dunbar on 5th September. The number who reached Durham was considerably less than that.

The escort for the prisoners was provided by Colonel Hacker who commanded four troops of cavalry. On 5th September, Cromwell wrote to Sir Arthur Heselrige at Newcastle:

'After much deliberation, we can prise [think of] no way how to dispose of those prisoners that will not be consistory with these two ends (to wit, the not losing them and the not starving them, neither which we would willingly incur) but by sending them to England. We have despatched away [in Scotland] near 5,000 poor wretches of men, very many of them will die of their wounds.'[18]

The letter ends by suggesting that the English Council of State

'....may exercise their wisdom and better judgement in so dispersing and disposing of them.'

A recent article in a quality Scottish Sunday newspaper accused Cromwell of selling 150 Scots into slavery in America which is quite without foundation. In the same article, the eminent professor of history, T C Smout stated that Cromwell simply wanted to be rid of the prisoners, which is of course true. Cromwell's letter makes it abundantly clear that he was neither willing nor able to decide what should be done with the prisoners and he at least expressed concern about their welfare. Why did he not simply release them after obtaining their *parole* that they would never again take up arms against England as had often occurred in similar situations during the English Civil Wars? The answer may be that he didn't trust the word of Scotsmen who had already defied England and appointed Charles Stuart king of Scotland. Be that as it may, he did what he could for the poor wrecks left lying in the fields around Broxburn and Oxwellmains, issuing the following proclamation in Dunbar on 4th September, the day after the battle:

'Forasmuch as I understand there are Soldiers of the Enemy's Army yet abiding in the Field, who by reason of their wounds could not march from thence; These are therefore to give notice to the inhabitants of this Nation that they may and 'hereby' have free liberty to repair to the field aforesaid and with their carts or 'in' any other peaceable way, to carry away the said Soldiers to such places as they shall think fit: provided that they meddle not 'with' or take away any the Armour there. And all [English] Officers and Soldiers are to take notice that the same is permitted.

Given under my hand, at Dunbar, 4th September 1650'

As mentioned earlier, in addition to the 5,000 he had set free, Cromwell made a 'gift' of 1,000 to the Countess of Winton who presumably fed and tended them. Were they included in the global figure? If they were, the number of men who marched south was even greater than the estimated 4,000. No less than 3,900 were ordered on the march but the true figure may have been nearer 5,000. Colonel Hacker seems to have delegated his responsibilities to a Major Dobson who had no means of feeding the men on their 8-day route march to Newcastle. Several accounts of the march - including Miller's *Lamp of Lothian* - tell us that some prisoners were shot attempting to escape while others literally fell by the wayside, unable to march because of their poor condition. The march soon deteriorated into a straggle of sick, exhausted spirits; starving men stole cabbages from the gardens in Morpeth and ate leaves, roots and twigs in their desperation - much to the amusement of their escort. Even so, it is not outward behaviour which decides whether the human frame can survive but what is within to sustain it. In desperate situations, survival depends on that inner strength; if it does not remain intact, men will break. When the weary column staggered into Newcastle on 13th September, deaths along the way had reduced the prisoners by half.[19]

On 9th September, Cromwell wrote again to Heselrige:

'I hope that your northern guests are come to you by this time. I pray you let humanity be exercised towards them....let the officers be left at Newcastle, some sent to Lynn [King's Lynn, Norfolk] some to Chester [the port for Cheshire].'[20]

Perhaps Cromwell, anxious about the welfare of men he had defeated under honourable arms, distrusted the wily Heselrige and whether he would attend to hungry and sick men for whom he had little regard. The Scots were a nuisance. Heselrige was not noted for his kindness. A closer examination of the facts is difficult, given the dearth of surviving records; however, we have a glimpse of the subsequent events - albeit a biased one - from correspondence between Heselrige and the English Council of State. His treatment of his prisoners was nothing short of scandalous, as we shall see.

An American account by A E Smith *Colonists in Bondage: White Servitude and Convict Labour in America* (1607-1776) quotes from government records for 1650 which indicate that a Committee of Examinations was delegated the task of disposing of the fit and able men from Dunbar. Hesilrige was instructed to send as many as possible to the Durham coalmines; 900 were to be delivered to Samuel Clark, a ship's master, by 19th September; thereafter, they were to be transported to Virginia to be sold to Joshua Foot and John Bese, New England - all to be fit, strong and free from wounds. A further 200 were to be allocated to Isaac le Gay, Virginia; 2,300 were to be sent to Ireland for miltary service - excluding Highlanders because of their cultural affinities with the Irish; and 300 were destined for France, presumably for military service. Thus the Committee believed that Heselrige had in captivity 3,700 men, excluding up to 200 officers left behind at Newcastle in accordance with Cromwell's instructions - a total of 3,900 men.

The reality was quite different. Heselrige did not have anywhere near that figure in Newcastle and Durham. In fact he couldn't account for less than half that number, as will be seen from his response to the Council of State dated 31st October 1650.[21] His letter, reproduced in full in Appendix H, is a laboured explanation of why he was unable to comply with the Council's instructions. The Council of State was treated to a detailed account of how much he had done for the survivors - in public administration, this is often the approach taken by culpable people who disguise the truth in the interests of self-preservation. It is a document remarkable for its insincerity. One thing is abundantly clear; apart from his undoubted mismanagement of the prisoners, he is unable to account for the deficit in the number he was supposed to have in custody. In mitigation, he had no idea of the true facts of the march from Dunbar to Newcastle. What is more important, he didn't care. His letter is carefully structured to keep the bad news to the very last; his compilation reminds one of the drunk man in the hotel room above who drops one shoe to the floor, keeping the person below awake waiting for the second shoe to fall. Extracts from his response to the Council of State dated October 1650 follow:

'Gentlemen,

> I received your Letter dated the Twenty-sixth of October, in that you desire me, that Two Thousand three hundred of the Scotch prisoners now at Durham or elsewhere, able and fit for Foot Service, be selected, and marched thence to Chester and Liverpool, to be shipp'd for the South and West of Ireland; and that I should take special Care not to send any Highlanders............'

Heselrige continues by giving 'a full accompt of the Prisoners' and intimates that Cromwell had informed him that of the 9,000 [sic] prisoners taken at Dunbar, 5,100 had been freed. He then explains that the remaining 3,900 were sent under Major Hobson's charge to Berwick and from there to Newcastle under escort of elements from the garrison at Berwick. Hesilrige is at pains to describe the Morpeth incident - men eating raw cabbages which resulted in several deaths on the road to Newcastle. He doesn't provide precise details, although further on, we are informed that 3,500 left Berwick for Newcastle. On arrival there, the men were put in the town's largest church [St Nicholas Cathedral] and on the following day, 140 were 'found to be sick and unable to march, while three had died in the night and some fell down on their march from Newcastle to Durham and dyed.'

On reaching Durham, Heselrige says there were 3,000 prisoners, although Colonel Fenwick - an officer from the Berwick garrison - had informed him there should have been 3,500. Heselrige explains that this discrepancy was due to the fact that a head count wasn't made at Berwick and that of 'most that were lost, it was in Scotland.' This is an out and out lie (see **Fig. 9** which gives details of the prisoners held at Newcastle, Shields and Durham). Heselrige was without doubt economical with the truth. At this juncture of his tortuous narrative, he infers that he has no idea of the fate of the missing prisoners - he leaves that to the last - although he states that the officers in charge '....were necessitated to about kill 30, fearing the Loss of them all, for they fell down in great Numbers and said they were not able to march, and they brought them far in the Night so that doubtless many ran away '

Fig 9: Prisoners from the Battle of Dunbar

Deported to America: Lynn contingent from the *Unity*

Adams, James
Archbell, [Archibald?] John
Banke, John
Braband, Alexander
Burgess, Alexander
Clarke, John
Danielson, James
Darling, George
Gourdon [Gordon?], James
Grant, Peter
Gualter, [Walter?]Thomas
Grimes, Alexander
Jempson, Andrew
Jourdan, [Jordan] William
Kelton, Thomas
Luddle [Liddle], James
MacCallum, Micam
Meeme, Richard
Mudie, Engram [Ingram]
Pardee, [Purdy?] John
Rupton, John
Steward [Stewart], John
Thomson, George
Taylor, James

Downing, Micam	Mason, John	Toish [MacKintosh?] John
Dugle[Dougal], Alexander	MacKall [McKail/ McColl?], James	Tower, Thomas
Dunsmore, James	MacMallen[McMillan], John	
Eaton, Alexander	MacShane, John	
Ennis [Innes?], Alexander	Mackwater[McWalter?] William	Total: 36

Deported to America: Kittery, Unity Parish (now Berwick) from the *Unity*

Agnew, Niven	Gray, George	Neal , John
Barry, James	Gowan [Cowan?], William	Ross, John
Cooper, Alexander	Hamilton, David	Taylor, John
Furbush, William	Holme [Hume?], Thomas	Thomson, William
Ferguson, Daniel	Key [Kay?], John	Warren, James
Grant, Peter	Maxwell, Alexander	Total: 17

Prisoners from Dunbar were included with the batch from the battle of Worcester in September 1651 which sailed in the *John and Sarah* from London on 8th December 1651, arriving at Boston in February 1652:

Danielson, James	Innes, Alexander	Tosh [MacKintosh?], William
Guthrie, Robert	Rose, Thermot [Dermot?]	Others
		Total: at least 5

In 1655, a further 8 prisoners from Dunbar were put to work in [New] York, possibly taken to America on the *John and Sarah*:

Carmichael, John	Junkins [Jenkins?], Robert	
Grant, James 'The Scot'	McIntire [McIntyre], Micum	
Grant , James 'The Drummer'	MacNair, Alexander	
Jackson, James	Rankin, Andrew	
		Total: 8

3,900 prisoners left Dunbar on 5th September 1650. Of these, less than 500 came back to Scotland. The figures which I have extrapolated from records do not prove the precise figure; I have attempted to determine what happened to those who never came home.

Shot escaping	30
Died of malnutrition between Dunbar and Newcastle	1600
Sick soldiers at Newcastle	140
Officers held in Newcastle 'At the Marshal's' (ordered by Cromwell)	60
Put to work in 'Sheels' [North or South Shields]	92
Missing between Berwick and Newcastle	500
Possible deaths between Berwick and Newcastle	78?
In prison at Durham	1400

This totals 3,900, the figure given in several sources (see below). Of that number, it is probable that 1,708 died, a further 500 were missing, leaving 1,742 in the 'care' of Governer Heselrige if we include 92 prisoners put to work in Shields. The fate of these is difficult to determine precisely, although records confirm that the majority were either deported to the Colonies or forced to join Cromwellian regiments in Ireland and France. An approximate breakdown of this figure follows:

Deported to Boston on the *Unity* (1650)	53
Deported to Boston on the *John and Sarah* (1651)	13+
Enforced military service in Ireland	500
" " " " France	300
Allocated to Major Clark for deportation to Virginia	350 (300 from Durham and 50 from Newcastle) *
Deported to Barbadoes (1655)	100

Total = 1316

* Of this contingent, 200 died between Newcastle and London or in the Blackwall plague-house and 150 were deported

The final figures are thus:

Dead	1,908 (approx.)
Missing	500
Deported	316 (approx.)
Military service	800
Released from captivity	376 (approx.)
Total	3,900

Accepting these figures as roughly accurate, 62% of the total died or were missing, presumed dead; 8% were deported; 21% were put into military service; only 9% were released from captivity. (It can be assumed however that those who served in the Cromwellian army would have been discharged after completing their term of enforced enlistment)

Sources: *Miller, Dunbar; Prisoners from the Battle of Dunbar*, Massachusetts History Society, 1927; Suffolk Court Files No 1228 Massachussetts Archives LXIX 49; *Colonists in Bondage*; Directory of Scots Banished to the American Plantations etc

The long and convoluted preamble to Heselrige's letter is a classic example of the civil servant who wishes to soften unwholesome facts and for which he must bear responsibility. His letter displays the unease of a man who is intent on placating his superiors - a case of *s'excuse, s'accuse.* The next part of the letter describes his sterling efforts in the matter; he spared no expense to ensure the well-being of his charges at Durham. He is growing ever more desperate. He states that he gave orders to the mayor of Durham to ensure that the Scots should want for

> 'not anything that was fit for Prisoners' - what on earth does he mean? - 'and what he [the mayor] should disburse for them, I would repay it. I also sent them a daily Supply of Bread from Newcastle and an Allowance equal to what had been given to former Prisoners;[22] but their Bodies being infected, the Flux [dysentery] increased among them. I sent many Officers to look to them and appointed that those that were sick should be removed out of the Cathedral Church [at Durham] and sent to the Bishop's Castle [Durham]....and provided Cooks and they had Pottage, made with Oatmeal, Beef and Cabbages a full Quart at a Meal for every Prisoner. They had also Coals daily brought to them as many as made a hundred Fires both Day and Night, and Straw to lie upon.'

As for the men, they were

> '....unruly, sluttish and nasty.....they acted rather like Beasts than Men so that the Marshal was allowed forty men to cleanse and sweep them every Day.'

How could men suffering from chronic dysentery keep themselves clean? All of this is a thinly disguised attempt to exonerate himself and to distract attention from the real issue - the unaccountably depleted number of survivors.

In Durham Castle, the sick allegedly received mutton and veal broth 'boiled together'; they had elderly women to look after them as well as physicians to bleed them, dress their wounds and administer 'physick'. Why was it necessary to dress wounds? We are informed by none other than Oliver Cromwell himself that only those who were sound in limb and fit to travel were selected to march south. Heselrige continues in the same placatory vein:

> 'I dare confidently say, There was never the like care taken for any such Numbers of prisoners that were ever in England.'

One is tempted to comment - Oh really? Heselrige admits that many of his charges died - victims of the flux - although some were killed by their own:

> '.........they were exceedingly cruel one towards the other. If a Man was perceived to have any Money, it was two to one but he was killed before Morning and robb'd; and if any had good Cloaths, he that wanted, if he was able, would strangle the other and put on his Cloaths.'

This last sentence does not ring true in the least. It would have been as untypical then as it is today of Scotsmen in adverse circumstances, particularly of men in the hands of the Auld Enemy. It is part of the character of a Scot to ridicule one's own countrymen - Highlander against Lowlander for example - but put a mixed group together - in England or anywhere else for that matter - and Scotsmen will forget their differences and unite against the common enemy. Heselrige paints a bleak picture of men who were most definitely united by hostility towards their captors. His comments are pure fabrication, as any psychologist who has studied the national character would have informed Heselrige.

There is no doubt that dysentery was rife in the camps; to contain it, Heselrige is again at pains to inform his masters in London that he sent men to obtain milk at market prices in nearby towns and villages. The milk was then mixed with water, bean flour was added and the concoction was boiled before it was given to the sick - a remedy Hesilrige states was prescribed by the doctors. His letter continues with niggling pettyfogging detail- how he went about obtaining milk, sending men 'to three score towns and farms as well as twenty towns near Durham.' All this is camouflage intended to impress; the opposite was probably close to the truth. Why waste good money on sick and dying men, enemies of the State?

Then at last, Heselrige lets the other shoe drop, the shoe he has held on to for so long.

'Gentlemen, You cannot but think strange of this long Preamble and to wonder what the matter will be, in short it is this.'

He blatantly informs the Council of State that of the 3,000 [sic] men delivered to Durham

'....300 from there and 50 of the 140 left behind [at Newcastle] were delivered to Major Clark by Order of the Council and there are also 500 Sick in the Castle and about 600 yet in Health in the Cathedral, the most of which are in probability Highlanders, they being hardier than the rest.....About 1,600 are dead and buried.'

A further 60 officers were held 'at the Marshal's in Newcastle' as Cromwell had specifically ordered the officer class to be detained separately from the other ranks for perhaps the obvious reason that they might encourage the men to escape. Heselrige also reminds the Council that they had previously empowered him to use some prisoners as he saw fit; he explains that he gave 40

'.....to well appointed persons that have salt works at Sheels [South Shields][23] and 12 weavers to begin a trade of linen cloth like the Scottish cloth and 40 labourers.'[24]

The truth is abundantly clear. Heselrige had nowhere near the 2,300 prisoners the Council of State had ordered to be sent to Chester and Liverpool and from there to Ireland. Heselrige accounts for the total number of prisoners as follows:

shot escaping	30	
died on the march	1,600	
missing between Berwick and Newcastle	500	
sick at Newcastle	90	(after 50 were given to Major Clark)
officers 'at the Marshal's' in Newcastle	60	
put to work in Shields etc	92	
given to Major Clark	350	
sick and fit at Durham	1,100	

His figures account for 3,822 prisoners, 78 less than the original 3,900 of which 1,630 were already dead. What happened to the other 578 who left Dunbar on 5th September? Did they escape? Were they shot? It will be remembered that a discrepancy of 500 was reported on the march between Berwick and Newcastle, a discrepancy which Heselrige attributed to the failure to make a headcount at Berwick on the day the men left there. Were Cromwellian officers and troopers so incompetent that they allowed nearly an entire regiment to escape them? History does not confirm this view. Cromwell's New Model Army was well-discplined, efficient, one of the best armies in the Europe of the time. Heselrige damns himself by offering the lame excuse that a subordinate had not done his duty and kept a proper tally of his charges.

What was the reason for the discrepancy in the number of survivors? It can be but conjectured that a good deal more than 1,600 men died of malnutrition on the route march from Dunbar to Durham. We may speculate that Heselrige didn't want to spend money on those he considered useless mouths. The blame reputedly rests with Colonel Fenwick at Berwick, a clumsy excuse. It is inconceivable that a man of Fenwick's rank and experience would fail to conduct a headcount. It is more likely that the Roundhead troopers were not unduly concerned about their prisoners; hadn't they laughed at the sight of starving men scratching for roots and cabbages in the Morpeth gardens? It is entirely possible that many more managed to make their escape than was admitted but that is a damning indictment on the calibre of the escort's officers. Hesilrige is careful to state that the 30 who did attempt to escape were shot. There have been no mass burials found along the A1 between Dunbar and Berwick but this may be explained by the fact that when men dropped from exhaustion or starvation they were simply left to die by the roadside. If as Heselrige says, every care was taken to ensure the men's welfare during their time with him, the escorting officers must have been aware of their Commander-in-Chief's orders that the prisoners were be treated humanely. Perhaps Heselrige had privately expressed the view that he was not overly anxious to entertain his 'Scottish guests', as Cromwell had described the prisoners.

The elaborate preparations Heselrige describes are a red herring to cover the fact that instead of having nearly 3,000 men for the purposes of the Council of State, he had only 1,692. The only conclusions we can arrive at is that for the most part, Heselrige's letter is a tissue of lies - at least as far as the elaborate and expensive arrangements he made for the prisoner' welfare. Or conversely, when he found he had fewer men than expected, he was able to make above average provision for their keeping. Even if he had provided a single hot meal every day on the march, he could have saved many more lives although undoubtedly a few would have died. Perhaps it is unfair to lay the entire blame on Heserige for what happened between Dunbar and Durham but he was given adequate advance warning of the imminent arrival of nearly 4,000 prisoners and that he was to treat them well. The fact remains that he and only he had overall charge of them; it was his duty to provide for them during and after their long march south. But in his eyes, the Scots were an administrative headache; they had been defeated, they were prisoners of war and they deserved what happened to them. Why waste good money on enemies?

It is perhaps worth mentioning here that Heselrige was a rigid Republican, one of the five MPs Charles I had attempted to arrest in the Long Parliament in 1641 - one of the 'birds' who had flown from the House of Commons, as Charles reputedly described them when he entered the House with his soldiers. Heselrige, a quarrelsome and greedy man remained a member of the predominant Independent Radical Party in parliament; he was resolutely opposed to the introduction of Scottish Presbyterianism in England so he had no reason to be unduly concerned about the welfare of a few thousand Scots whom he regarded as little more than animals. After the Restoration, Heselrige, a man who made free with the confiscated lands of English bishops and lined his own pockets from them, was imprisoned in the Tower of London and remained there until his death.

Further confusion arises when we attempt to unravel the fate of 1,342 prisoners remaining in Newcastle, South Shields and Durham after 350 had been handed over to Major Clark to march to London, destined for Virginia. Many of Clark's prisoners fell sick on the way to London, ending up in the infamous 'pest-house' at Blackwall.[25] Clark was brought before the Committee of Examinations in London to answer the charge of maltreatment of his prisoners, a clear indication that the central authorities were far from happy about the way things were being done in the north of England regarding the Scots prisoners. Of those who survived the journey by sea from Newcastle to London, then the plague house at Blackwall, only 150 were shipped to Virginia on 11th November 1650.[26]

Thus Heselrige was left with about 1,400 prisoners in Newcastle and Durham, almost half of them in poor health. The 53 or so who sailed with Captain Walker of the *Unity,* out of London on 11th November may have been the more fortunate. On arrival in Boston, they were indentured as servants of 6-7 years' duration at £20-30 a head.[27] The men were put to work in the ironworks at Lynn, Massachusets and the sawmills in Unity parish, Kittery (now Berwick) in Maine. The men in Maine were subsequently released and given land worth £25 and became prosperous farmers.

A further 13 from the battle of Dunbar may have joined those on the *John and Sarah* from the battle of Worcester in 1651, as there is a plaque on the wall of a modern building in New York - thought to be the site of the old jail - which commemorates the imprisonment of several survivors from the battle of Dunbar. Of those remaining at Durham, 500 were deported to Ireland to serve in foot regiments in the Cromwellian army. Another 500 were ordered to France in 1651[28] but because of transport problems, 300 were left to rot in a Tynemouth jail until 1655, when the fittest - perhaps about 100 - were deported to the Barbados and literally worked to death. The 100 or so who remained in Durham were joined by other Scottish soldiers captured at the battle of Worcester on 3rd September 1651 - the anniversary of Dunbar. It is known that some of the Dunbar prisoners were put to forced labour in October 1651, draining the fens at King's Lynn.[29] On 13th November 1651, the English parliament announced that any Scottish prisoner leaving England without permission would be executed; this suggests that some had already escaped.

Thus despite the traditional view that most of the prisoners taken at Dunbar were put to work in the Colonies, it is unlikely that more than 300 went into permanent exile; those who ended up in Ireland and France were probably allowed home after completing their enforced military service. Many of the captives from Worcester taken to Durham died there; when infectious disease broke out at the end of 1651, the Council of State wrote to a James Powell of Bristol on 2nd December ordering him to remove the prisoners to a place where they would pose less of a risk to the Durham population. The officers were to be given daily subsistence of five pennies (about 2p) with four pennies for every foot soldier.[30] Powell was informed that '....these prisoners were to have been carried to the plantations but are left behind....you shall be paid your expenses herein.' Of those who returned to Durham later, some must have been well enough to return home as they were released under an order dated 1st March 1652, providing they swore never to take up arms against England again. The defacing of Durham Cathedral was attributed to 'these unhappy sufferers.'[31] The 200 left at Tynemouth weren't released until 1655.[32] As noted above, the number of Scots prisoners at Durham increased after Worcester; of the 261 prisoners who embarked on the *John and Sarah* in December 1651 for Boston, perhaps more than 13 prisoners from the battle of Dunbar were among them.[33] As for those who ended up in America, a Scots

Charitable Society was founded in Boston in 1657 to ease their plight but unfortunately, records of the names of most of the men have been lost.[34]

The treatment of the useless mouths from Dunbar is a grim postscript to England's prosecution of the war of 1650-52. Today, three and a half centuries later, it is well nigh impossible to establish the true facts of what might be called a death march. It is not unreasonable to suggest that more than half of the 4,000 prisoners died in England - twice the proportion of British soldiers from Scotland taken prisoner by the Japanese and who perished building the infamous Burma Railway. The campaign of 1650 heralded the beginning of the process which would culminate in the Union of the Parliaments in 1707. For Scotland, Dunbar was the worst defeat since Pinkie Cleugh in 1547; what sets it apart is the treatment of the prisoners. While to some extent Heselrige's and Cromwell's actions are understandable there was no justification under any acknowledged rules of war - had they existed then - for deporting uniformed soldiers taken prisoner in the lawful defence of their country. Even if only a few hundred went abroad never to return home, there was no excuse for the deliberate starving to death of more than half of them.

Perhaps not surprisingly, Dunbar was one of the first royal burghs to join the Cromwellian Union or Commonwealth proposed in 1651; fear undoubtedly played its part in the decision. The local population had seen how Cromwell had snatched victory out of the jaws of defeat. On 13th February 1652, the burgh [35] was among the 44 of 58 royal burghs which consented to union with England which became known as the Commonwealth, represented by an English parliament. It was the shape of other things to come. Under the Commonwealth, the export of wool, hides and skins - traditional Scottish goods - was banned; trade decayed, poverty increased and manufacturing was slow to develop. When General Monck, the governor of Scotland left his headquarters in Dalkeith in 1660 to persuade parliament to accept Charles II as king, he took with him petitions from the burghs requesting that union with England continue. The union took another half century to arrive but by then, Dunbar was opposed to it. The ultimate political settlement was of little consequence to those soldiers who either died on the field of Dunbar or perished afterwards. They paid the ultimate price for defending their country. There is no commemorative plaque to the useless mouths of Dunbar. They are forgotten.

7

Forgotten Men

George Miller, James Miller, Richard Gall and Robert Mennon

The previous chapter ends with a lament about the forgotten men of the battle of Dunbar. Perhaps it is appropriate therefore to continue the theme in relation to the above individuals. Two of these forgotten men were instrumental in putting Dunbar on the map by peaceable means, proving Bulwer Lytton's contention that the pen is mightier than the sword.

George Miller (1771-1835)

East Lothian - almost exclusively agricultural - does not spring readily to mind as a pioneering district in the publishing world, nor does it figure largely in the annals of Scotland's history of publishing. Yet surprisingly, the *East Lothian Press* founded in 1795 in Dunbar produced two monthly magazines which were to be found in every parish in Scotland between 1813 and 1815. Who today remembers the publisher George Miller of Dunbar? Like others in the business, George Miller (**ill 54**) made and lost a fortune and was quickly forgotten.

Illus 54: *George Miller* ELCMS

It is inconceivable to us today that anyone would have wanted to establish a publishing business in a small country town like Dunbar - not the least because of its proximity to Edinburgh, a major publishing centre in the early nineteenth century as it is today. To embark on such a venture in the late eighteenth century, someone would have needed to be self-assured, reasonably well-off but most important of all, prepared to take a gamble. Dunbar can boast of such a man who although he wasn't rich, became very successful in a relatively short space of time. At worst, Dunbar has forgotten George Miller; at best, he is occasionally confused with his son James who is perhaps slightly better known as the town's historian.

Although a mere country bookseller, George Miller was far-sighted; he was also a rare breed in the publishing world in that he successfully combined printing, bookbinding, publishing and journalism - all in the same premises. First at Dunbar, then additionally in Haddington, George built up a trade in books and magazines which for a few years was the envy of some of the Edinburgh publishing houses. Even so, nowhere in the town of his birth is he commemorated in any way whatsoever. If he is remembered at all, it is by the few who recognise his contribution to adult education and the popular literature movement in Scotland. While George Miller wasn't the first to promote either, he was among the first to pioneer cheap, wholesome literature, a trade which would be developed by other publishers such as the Chambers brothers in Edinburgh. Where George Miller differed from his predecessors was that he wanted to produce reading-matter at a cost which the ordinary working man could afford, something no one else had ever contemplated before.

George Miller's family came from East Lothian, originating in the small village of Gifford where they had worked on the land for several generations. His grandfather married Isabel Wilson, a Dunbar woman (**Fig. 10**) and the family were living in Dirleton in 1725 when George's father James was born. Shortly afterwards, the Millers moved to Dunbar, where James Miller became a general merchant; he was to marry three times, producing three sons and two daughters. James, the eldest son followed his father into the grocery trade while George and brother John became printers in Dunbar and Dunfermline.

Fig 10 The Millers of Dunbar and Dunfermline

James Miller (1725-57?)
m. Isabel Wilson (1726-?)

James Miller (1725-89)
m. ?
m. Elizabeth Wilson (1733-76)[1]
m. Mary Deans (1779-80)[2]

Other issue, some of whom are named on Gravestone B (see fig 11)

James Miller (1768-1851)
m. Eliza ? (?-1858)
(see fig 11 for issue)

George Miller(1771-1835)
m. Janet Jamieson (?-1802)
m. Helen Grieve (1803- post 1835)

John Miller (1780-1853)[3]
m Helen Laing (?-1851)

James (1791-1865
m. Janet Crow
George[5] 3 daughters
issue not known

George (1794-1869)

William (1796-1838)
m. Catherine Aitken (?-1835)
issue not known

Elizabeth (1799-1838)

John (1800-?)

Robert (1802-28)

A daughter (?-?)[4]

Notes

1 George Miller's mother
2 John Miller's mother who died giving birth to him on 4th September
3 Of his issue, Mary Miller (1808-90) m. Alexander Lyle, son of Peter Lyle, a Dalkeith bookseller and close friend of George Miller. The firm P D Lyle owned and published the *Dalkeith Advertiser* in 1914. John Miller's son John Laing Miller (1811-83) founded the *Dunfermline Advertiser* [now the *Dunfermline Press and Advertiser*]; his son George founded the printing firm George Miller and Co., Liverpool before he emigrated to America
4 Died in infancy
5 Died in infancy in 1823

It is conjectured that George Miller's headstone was demolished in 1895-96, when the east-facing apse of the church was created. As some of George Miller's family are buried not far from there, it is fairly certain that his burial place was nearby, possibly on the site now occupied by the apse

George was born on 14th January 1771; in later life, he was to reflect ruefully on the belief - real or imagined - that he was a man marked from the day he was born. In what is in effect his autobiography,[1] George mourned the passing of the old Scottish festival known as *Hansel Monday* which fell on the first Monday of the New Year. For many years in Scotland, Hansel [free gift] Monday was the alternative to Christmas, a festival regarded with suspicion by the Church of Scotland, it being considered Popish. On Hansel Monday - celebrated on the Monday closest to the 12th January under the Old Style or Julian Calendar rather than 25th December, children received presents - provided their parents observed the day. By 1771, those who continued to observe the custom did so on a different date, as eleven days had been removed from the calendar in 1752, when England finally adopted the Gregorian Calendar which had been introduced in Scotland on 1st January 1600.[2] As George wrote - perhaps somewhat tongue-in-cheek - under the Old Style calendar, his birthday would have fallen on 3rd January which in 1771 was celebrated as Hansel Monday. However, his parents were not only New Style people, they didn't recognise the custom either. As he puts it,

'disappointment shook hands with me on my entrance into life.'

More appropriately, he might have added that Dr Samuel Johnson, the famous lexicographer, referred to 1771 as the year of the Black Spring because the season came late and food prices rose steeply.

Between 1776 and 1785, George attended the local schools, including Dunbar's prestigious grammar school which taught Latin, a subject for which he showed little aptitude. His schooldays appear to have been happy however and he developed a lifetime fondness for teachers, regarding them as friends as well as customers. His mind was open to new ideas and in adult life, he enjoyed discussions with his teacher friends on such diverse subjects as natural science, philosophy, astronomy and geology. In later life, he repaid his mentors in a small way by providing accommodation for them in his shop for their regular meetings; he may have also printed leaflets free of charge for their main preoccupation - the creation of a national fund for the relief of widows and children of burgh and parish schoolteachers, which was ultimately achieved and which became the Scottish Teachers' Superannuation Scheme, administered first by the Scottish Office, now by an agency of the Scottish Executive.

George's mother, Elizabeth Wilson, the daughter of a Dunbar wright and his father's second wife, died when he was only five years' old; her burial place is marked by a badly weathered and broken headstone in the local cemetery (**see fig 11**). Her death on 9th October 1776 was an early and therefore lasting traumatic memory for George; years later, he recalled standing guard over her coffin as it was being made

'forbidding the profane touch of any of my little comrades'.

Another childhood memory was of John Paul Jones, the Scots privateer in American service during the American War of Independence whose small fleet lay off Dunbar for a few days in 1779. He tells us how several women gathered on the cliffs wearing red coats to fool Jones into thinking they were soldiers. Two years on, George also remembered the farcical attempt of another privateer, Captain G Fall, to capture a small vessel outside the Old Harbour. (Accounts of these incidents appear in Chapter 3). George wrote that Fall's desultory cannon-fire did little damage other than to rattle a few chimneypots in the High Street, although he claimed that his brother John was nearly killed

Leaving school in 1785, George was uncertain of a career. His father first suggested teaching, then selling books and stationery; the boy nursed a secret ambition to go to sea, his sense of adventure fuelled by books he'd read - *Robinson Crusoe* and the *Voyages of Captain Cook.* Parental influence prevailed however and George settled for the steady trades of bookbinding and bookselling. On 20th September 1785, he was apprenticed to Alexander Smart, an Edinburgh bookseller and bookbinder who had opened a shop in Dunbar in 1780 The shop closed due to lack of business and Smart took George to Edinburgh to complete his indentured term, first in premises in the Lawnmarket, then in Frederick Street. In September 1788, George's four-year indenture was prematurely terminated by mutual agreement due to Smart's failing business and a lack of interest in his young apprentice's training. George returned to Dunbar and reluctantly went into partnership with his elder brother James in the family grocery shop.

The brothers were as oil and water. Solid James and mercurial George quarrelled over a minor matter within a few weeks. George angrily pulled down the shop sign bearing their names and in April 1789 he went to South Shields and Newcastle where he met Smart again, now employed as a journeyman printer. George gained a knowledge of typesetting within a few days at South Shields - valuable experience for the future, when he began his own business. He was called home on 14th May to an ailing father who died on 27th June 1789. As often happens after a family bereavement, George and brother James were reconciled and entered a second partnership in November 1789. This time, they agreed to combine bookselling and bookbinding with the sale of general merchandise, George arguing convincingly that the trades would be mutually beneficial. Not content with selling books however, bibliophile George was keen to spread the written word and he established what was probably one of the first circulating lending libraries outside Edinburgh.[3] After only two years, his library contained more than 1,000 volumes.

The precise location of the Miller brothers' shop is not known but it was close to the St George Hotel, then known as Lorimer's Hotel, Dunbar's oldest inn. It was the venue for informal meetings of the local traders, the provost and bailies and the magistrates; it was also the watering-hole where the London-Edinburgh stage-coaches changed horses, allowing the passengers a brief comfort stop. Possibly the travel-weary people occasionally bought merchandise from the Millers; perhaps they didn't buy many books but they were a source of news and gossip from the two cities.

In 1790, the book trade was going through one of its periodic depressions; the Edinburgh booksellers were reluctant to take risks but the Millers were optimistic - or foolish - enough to sell books which needed capital and took up valuable shelf-space in their small premises. Books offered little prospect of an adequate return on the outlay, given the small proportion of reading public in the community. Even so, the Millers provided a service with their small library which undoubtedly brought customers into the shop.

In 1791, George married his late father's housekeeper, Janet Jamieson from North Berwick; before his death, old Miller had expressed a wish that the pair should marry but the relationship had developed in any event. George and his fiance kept their plans secret even from brother James, travelling to Edinburgh to get married.in the Tron Kirk on 3rd June. There was a reason for their secrecy; the pair went to Edinburgh to be wed because Janet was carrying their first child James. In 1914, George's biographer innocently stated that they did so 'without any necessity for such a course' although James was born about six months later. Today, their situation would hardly have attracted a passing comment but two centuries ago, the church interfered in the lives of its parishioners to a degree which a more enlightened age would have found unacceptable. The young couple soon found themselves in trouble with the local kirk session; George was fined 3 shillings and sixpence (17p) by the session clerk - the minister - for failing to post his marriage banns in Dunbar; the minister was probably also disgruntled at the loss of a marriage fee.

And that wasn't the end of it. Like many others in his predicament, George was ordered to appear before the session to answer for his sin of pre-nuptial fornication. George belonged to one of the secessionist churches - the Burghers or the Anti-Burghers, both of which had meeting-places in Dunbar. His biographer wrote that he put up a spirited defence, unlike many a poor farm hind in the same circumstances. George wasn't in the least intimidated by these grim men; he seems to have challenged his accusers to such an extent that one exasperated elder shouted

'What? Have ye come here to bamboozle [confuse] us a'[all]?'

Perhaps because of the incident, George left the secessionist church although he never gave up his faith; he became a member of the Church of Scotland which was growing more relaxed in its discipline.

George's marriage didn't only upset the kirk; it precipitated an important phase in his life, one which would set him on the road to his long-cherished dream of being his own master. His brother James had become a burgess in October 1790; being a burgess not only brought respectability and increased trade but entitled the burgess ticket-holder to vote in parliamentary elections. James' new status probably made him more sensitive about family prestige; he complained to George that their partnership didn't include marriage - or at least he said he hadn't envisaged George taking that step, as he was only twenty in 1791. The brothers dissolved their partnership - amicably as it turned out - and each decided to make a fresh start in separate businesses. By now, George had added bookbinding to his side of the business and he had enough work to employ two apprentices. His stock of library books was valued at twice that of the grocery side of the business but true to his nature, he insisted that the assets should be split fifty-fifty. This meant selling half of the stock, so George and his pregnant wife Janet travelled around the neighbourhood on horseback, selling enough books to give James his share. In the process however, George gained valuable experience in auctioneering which he put to good use later.

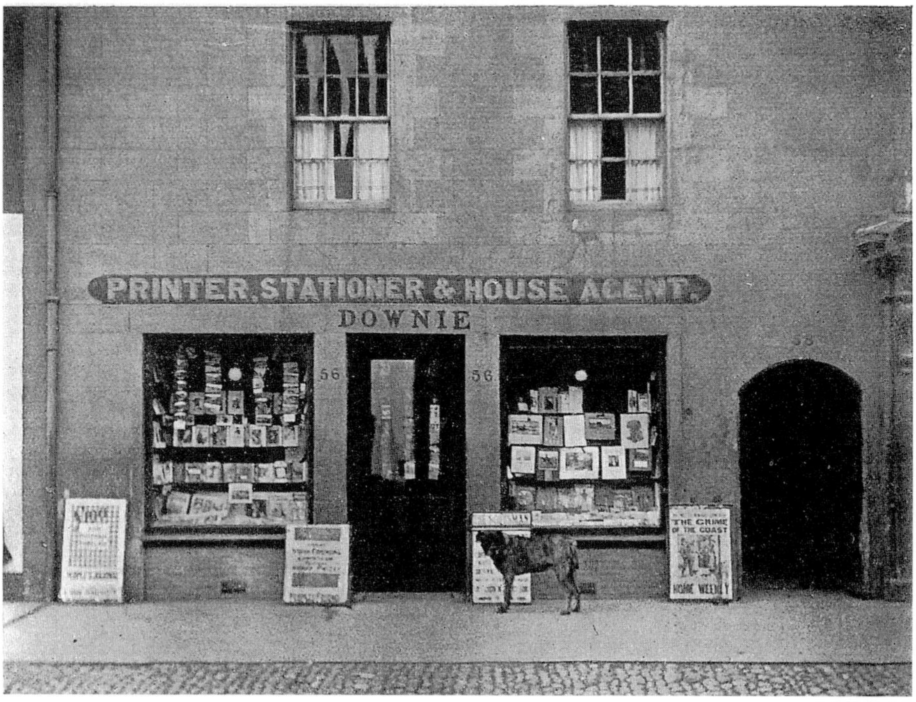

Illus 55: *George Miller's first shop at 56 High St, Dunbar* HLHC

The young couple set up their new business on 20th October 1791 at No 56 High Street Dunbar [3] (**ill 55**), living to the rear of the premises. As before, George sold groceries, stationery and books and continued bookbinding. He found the circulating library unprofitable and onerous but it brought in customers who might buy a few groceries. The library began life as *G Miller's Circulating Library, Dunbar*;[4] by 1809 it was known as *The Dunbar and Country Circulating Library* and contained 3,500 volumes - a considerable collection for the time. Although he was living a precarious existence and only just managing to keep his head above water, he advertised himself as a wholesale and retail bookseller, an exaggerated claim since he possessed neither sufficient stock or resources to supply wholesale. In 1792, the population of Dunbar was 3,700, with about 8,000 living within a ten-mile radius of the burgh. The majority were unlikely customers for books but somehow George managed to survive. Then in 1795, he embarked on his publishing career, purchasing second-hand printing equipment from a Berwick printer for an outlay of £23. In that year, he launched the *East Lothian Press*, the first publishing business in the county. A lesser man would have settled for jobbing work, printing advertisements, pamphlets and leaflets - the bread-and-butter trade of the small rural printer - but George had ambitions in other directions.

In 1795, there were print shops in Dumfries, Hawick, Kelso, Duns, Dundee, Perth, Inverness and Kilmarnock; Edinburgh, the main publishing centre was only 30 miles distant where men like William Creech (1745-1815) had cornered the bulk of the market for book sales. Creech occupied the premises formerly belonging to Allan Ramsay in the High Street, Edinburgh; a mean but very successful printer, Creech was reputedly worth £30,000 in 1799, a considerable sum for the time. He began his empire at a time when the publishing trade was beginning to expand in Scotland; the number of periodicals produced by presses north of the Border had begun to challenge London's claim as the nation's publishing capital.

Why did George Miller, living so close to Edinburgh, take the gamble that he did? Perhaps the driving force was the sudden upsurge of interest in the printed word but that is an oversimplification. While George appreciated the contribution books and magazines made to education, he also knew that the book-buying people in and around Dunbar were almost exclusively schoolmasters and those on the burgh council responsible for providing books for the parish schools. (At that time, a farm labourer earned £13 a year, the bulk of which was spent on feeding and clothing his family). Thus there were few in the area who could afford books even if they could read. *The Scots Magazine*, a more sophisticated publication then than now may have given George the germ of an idea for a similar publication but one which would have to suit the pockets of the readers he had in mind - working people. In 1801, *The Scots Magazine* was taken over by Alexander Constable in Edinburgh who it is claimed was the first publisher to identify a potential market for inexpensive literature. If that were so, Constable waited until 1827 before making a serious attempt to exploit that market - some fourteen years after George Miller in Dunbar.

When George went into business on his own account in 1791, the general state of the country was in good shape and the economic stagnation of the eighteenth century was coming to an end. Scotland had been slow to throw off the grinding poverty which had existed prior to the Union with England in 1707 but the general population was beginning to enjoy a standard of living unknown to the previous two generations. Even a small town like Dunbar was becoming solid and respectable, even if its days as a major fishing port were showing signs of decline. What was lost in the fishing industry was compensated to a certain extent by a developing grain trade which expanded as agricultural yields increased as a result of continuing improvements in production methods. Men like George Miller weren't slow to grasp the opportunities presented; many started small family businesses which would survive until the twentieth century. However, publishing - ever at the mercy of market forces and every twist and turn in the economy - was under threat from an unlikely quarter, the British parliament.

As the well-known saying has it - a little knowledge is a dangerous thing Recent moves to educate the masses were regarded with suspicion by the Whig and Tory parties; both were alarmed by the rise in debate and discussion among a working class which was reading newspapers as never before. Panic took hold in a government already concerned at the outbreak of revolution in France which they feared might spread across the Channel. Political discussions in the workplace were declared seditious; the upper and middle classes were gripped by hysteria because they feared they might lose control of the masses. Incredible though it may seem, at one point the Church suspended Sunday schools - established in Scotland in 1780 to prevent young child workers from running wild in the streets and fields on the Sabbath - lest they too become hotbeds for revolution! Added to this was the publication of Tom Paine's *Rights of Man* about the same time as the National Assembly in France arrested Louis XVI. Paine had supported the colonists during the American War of Independence; his pamphlet *Common Sense* had recommended the separation of the colonies from Britain. In 1787 he returned to Britain and wrote *Rights of Man* in response to Edmund Burke's *Reflections on the French Revolution.* Paine was about to be prosecuted for seditious libel when he escaped to France, there to take part in the trial of Louis XVI whom he recommended should not be executed but imprisoned and banished. Paine believed in universal suffrage and the redistribution of property; he made no secret of his view that the aristocracy were worthless drones who held power in a parliament which was unrepresentative of the people. He publicly expressed the hope that revolution in France would catch on in Britain. George Miller admired Paine and sold his book in Dunbar until it was proscribed by the government in May 1792 - a measure which increased its popularity. The following year, Britain was at war with France and any reaction by the British working class was, to Paine's disappointment, swept away on a tide of patriotism and war propaganda.

At the beginning of the eighteenth century, the book trade in Scotland was depressed because of the degree of risk and uncertainty involved; as a result, the London publishing houses were unchallenged and held the monopoly in output. A breakthrough of sorts occurred in 1774 however when the House of Lords overturned a case involving a London publisher's claim to perpetual copyright; the Lords introduced a limited term of copyright which largely survives in modern law. The outcome was that like other publishers, George Miller was able to print and market his own editions of popular books without fear of litigation.

In 1801, George obtained a second printing press which allowed him to produce the *Shorter Catechisms*, children's books, classics such as *Robinson Crusoe* and chapbooks. At that time, chapbooks were the staple reading matter of the rural workforce; of little or no educational value, they usually contained ghost stories, legends and occasionally, traditional ballads passed on orally by earlier generations before printing made them more accessible. Chapbooks were the tabloids of the day; despite his aversion to what he regarded as inferior reading material, George printed two chapbook stories - *The Cherry and the Slae* by Alexander Montgomery (c.1545-c.1611) and *A Strange Chapbook, or the Laird of Cool's Ghost* by W Ogilvie, an Innerwick minister who reputedly met the eponymous phantom in Dumfriesshire in 1722. These were innocuous enough tales but George later expressed regret for publishing for financial gain what he regarded as inferior reading matter.

George drove himself harder than ever before to produce publications which met his own increasingly high standards. He began in a small way, publishing inexpensive tracts on educational and social matters. Between 1802 and 1803, the series of tracts ran to twenty editions, each selling 3,000 copies and grossing £1,500 a year. Mostly cautionary tales about human failings, titles included *The Slave Trade* - George was an abolitionist - *The Magdalen, or the History of a Reformed Prostitute, The Generous Libertine, The Drunken Husband, or the Fatal Effects of Drunkenness, Moral Tales and Counsels to Young Men.* Others were written for children or extolled the beauties of nature. Whether his *Cheap Tracts* improved his customers' morals or their reading habits is impossible to judge; however, George's son James believed they

'superseded the common trash of the hawker's basket'

a comment on the chapbooks sold by the chapmen from door to door along with the clothes' pegs.[5]

Although Dunbar was in decline as a fishing port, new industries such as the cotton mill at Belhaven and cotton, flax and flour mills at West Barns provided employment for many local men and women. Also, after 1795, imports of foreign grain were subject to heavy duty so farmers were encouraged to improve crop yields; this made agriculture the main source of employment during the Napoleonic Wars and the period of the Industrial Revolution. Dunbar's corn markets thrived; the farmers met in the town once every week to sell their produce which was then taken by road or sea to the large towns and cities. Those who owned land or earned their living from it enjoyed a reasonable standard of living so that demand for popular entertainment increased. It was also a time when science and religion were becoming more empathetic and George Miller anticipated a demand for what today would be termed adult education. He met a hitherto unfulfilled need by publishing decent - if not particularly sophisticated - literature with a strong moral and educational message he believed would appeal to the poorer classes.

Inconceivable though it may seem today, those who published popular literature were regarded a threat by the Establishment. Reactionary elements in the government deprecated what they considered an unhealthy and irrelevant interest in education and knowledge among the working class.[6] In 1795, one of the foremost English critics of working class education in England made his views clear:

'Does it necessarily follow that the lower classes will become more industrious,
more virtuous, more happy, by learning how to read?'

This was endorsed by the appropriately-named David Giddy, an English MP who contended that

'Giving education to the labouring classes....would be prejudicial to their morals and happiness; it would teach them to despise their lot in life, instead of making them good servants in agriculture and other laborious employments. Instead of teaching them subordination, it would render them fractious and refractory.'

Unbelievably - or perhaps ominously so - the Bishop of London, another indefatigable critic of workers' education wrote:

'It is safer for both the Government and religion of the country to let the lower classes remain in that state of ignorance in which nature has placed them.'

Reactionary sentiments such as these were of course aimed at controlling the masses; the Bishop of London's views are refreshingly honest and we may applaud him for the absence of hypocrisy in his albeit narrow-minded attitude.

Such sentiments had little to do with the depression in the Scottish book trade in the early nineteenth century however; this was largely due to the timidity of the Edinburgh booksellers who left the risk-taking to the London publishing houses. That books sold at all in Dunbar is a tribute to George Miller's belief in the getting of knowledge through the printed word and his own determination and hard work to make it possible. In Edinburgh, Constable was impressed by George's prolific sales of Forsyth's *Beauties of Scotland*, a weighty travelogue and illustrated guide to Scotland. George also continued to add to the catalogue of volumes in his circulating library, a venture which at no time received any financial support from public funds. Industrious as ever, George printed booklets, ballads and other titles to such an extent which allowed him to sell wholesale. By 1802, he had established his reputation as a respectable small town publisher who produced good quality - if cheaply printed on inferior paper - reading matter. In that year, his shelves were crammed with stock, so he decided to advertise his intention to sell his surplus to the Edinburgh wholesale trade.

On 9th February 1802, George set out his catalogues and samples in Metcalf's Tavern in the Lawnmarket, Edinburgh, promising his clients a free dinner. In his autobiography *Latter Struggles*, George admitted that he took a gamble but cheerfully wrote that in the course of the two-day auction in the tavern - where the city magistrates were eating the *deid-chack* - the grim meal following a public execution - he grossed £300. His success was tempered with sadness however; his wife Janet died on 25th June, leaving him with six young children. In *Latter Struggles*, he wrote that a year after Janet's death, he himself almost died from what he called 'a severe disorder' probably brought on by stress and overwork. As one of his customers remarked that year:

'Dear man, I wonder if ye'll take time to dee [die]'

His wife's untimely death was a great loss to George, both in the care of his children and in his shop.

Visiting London on business, he met Helen Grieve, a Stenton woman who had turned down his earlier proposal of marriage. Perhaps the loneliness of the city drew them closer or made them less self-conscious; George described their chance encounter in *Latter Struggles*:

' "Well met!" said I! "The people will be saying we are away to be married. Suppose we go and get the business settled, and give them room to talk when we go home." '

While the encounter was romantic, the same cannot be said about George; however, publishers cannot afford to be sentimental - they leave that to their authors. Helen's response is reminiscent of Ruth's in the *Old Testament*:

"I'll go anywhere with you."

Their marriage of July 1805 proved a long and happy one; Helen was not only a much-loved step-mother but also a source of strength to George, supporting him in his business ventures to the end of hie life.

In 1802-03, George implemented his plan to produce cheap literature for the working people with the publication of his *Cheap Tracts* (1802-04); he would use much of the material in his subsequent monthly magazine. In 1804, his brother John helped him to establish a second printing-press in Haddington, commuting the 12 miles on horseback until October 1805, when a daily stagecoach service was introduced between Dunbar and Edinburgh. Ever the entrepreneur, George acted as agent for the coach owner; in return, his parcels were carried free of charge. The Haddington press was an instant success; the jobbing work for the second half of 1804 exceeded that for the whole of the previous year in Dunbar, bringing in nearly £300 a year. Haddington Town Council was a major customer and George printed many of the town's public notices; for example, on 2nd December 1805, he published a newsheet announcing Nelson's victory at Trafalgar on 21st October and he issued a subscription list for the fallen hero's memorial.[7]

The Haddington business expanded so rapidly that George had to lease two shops from the town council, one on either side of the Fleshmarket, an area levelled at the turn of the last century. For the first time, George kept the printing and grocery trades separate until he was forced to amalgamate the two shops when brother John opened his own printing business in Dunfermline in 1805. Obliged to move his family to Haddington, George left the Dunbar shop in the capable hands of his mother-in-law. The move to the county town wasn't a domestic success however. One by one, the family fell sick, servants were unreliable, then Mrs Grieve, his mother-in-law, fell ill and died in December 1806. Rumours were rife that George Miller was finished in Dunbar, that he was about to close his shop there and that a rival was ready to fill his place. Within the year, George moved back to Dunbar, maintaining the Haddington press for jobbing work only.

To discourage any likely opposition, George rented larger premises at No 71 High Street, Dunbar (**ill 56**), situated between the St George Hotel and the Eagle Inn. He was able to live above the shop, which he called *The India Tea Warehouse*; he also had the use of a small garden to the rear of the premises. In 1809, his circulating library contained over 3,500 books; the following year his son James was running the Haddington business and in 1811, George opened what he characteristically called *The Agricultural, Commercial, Military Intelligence, News and Reading Room* - he had a weakness for long titles and an inveterate tendency to over-use the comma - above his shop. It was a reading room patronised by local farmers, tradesmen and the soldiers in the cavalry, infantry and artillery units stationed in Dunbar.

HLHC

Illus 56: *George Miller's second shop and dwelling house at 71 High St.*

Now housed and working under one roof, George confidently took out a 17-year lease on his new premises. But small clouds were gathering on the economic horizon. The East Lothian Bank, founded in 1810 by businessmen and farmers in the county had its head office in Dunbar in premises at No 99 High Street. Not unnaturally, the local traders pressurised George into supporting the new enterprise. He reluctantly opened an account there, transferring some of his capital from the local branch of the British Linen Company Bank in what is now *Croft House,* a bank which had treated him well in the past. Not being a client of the East Lothian Bank might have meant loss of local business which he could ill-afford.

In 1812, the year Napoleon made his disastrous retreat from Moscow, George was preoccupied with other matters such as the growth of juvenile delinquency in Scotland, particularly in the streets of Edinburgh where three young men had been executed recently for their crimes. George felt something should be done for the young and he believed - somewhat naively - that the printed word was the most effective way to deter would-be lawbreakers. Also at this time, he was almost ready to launch his monthly magazine; he prepared the ground by issuing circulars - flyers - to ministers in the Presbytery of Dunbar and schoolteachers in the area, compiling the customary subscription list to give him some idea of likely demand. George was never the stereotype rural printer. He had already put his toe in the water and was now poised to enter the world of journalism on a larger scale than before. He would write and publish his own work in a monthly periodical pitched at a price within the pocket of the working people, a reading public largely ignored in the past.[8]

On 14th January 1813 - his forty-second birthday - George published the first issue of *The Cheap Magazine or the Poor Man's Fireside Companion* from his premises at No. 15 High Street, Haddington. Wisely, he dropped the sub-title from Issue No 2. Running to 48 pages, its editor and virtually sole contributor announced optimistically that the magazine was

> 'calculated to promote the interests of religion, virtue, and humanity, and to dispel the shades of ignorance, prejudice, and error among the lower classes of mankind.'

On the title page, he wrote that the magazine was directed at 'the prevention of crimes'; he expressed the hope that it would

> 'insure [sic] the peace, comfort, and security of society' in addition to giving young young minds 'a taste for reading subjects of real utility.'

To modern eyes, George's message is pompous, smug, patronising and narcissistic but his sentiments were expressed in a contemporary style and form of expression which reflected the values of the day. While *The Cheap Magazine* wasn't the first of its kind, it was the first to be written for a largely rural population which could afford its extremely modest price of fourpence (about 2p), something without precedent. It should be remembered that society then was rigidly class-oriented and few concessions were made to the humbler folk who, coming from grindingly poor and obscure backgrounds and scarcely educated, had little chance of bettering themselves. For example, it was an extremely rare occurrence for the son of a farm hind to become even a minor clerk. George's magazine was thus an integral part of the best social experiments of the time. Its objectives were two-fold - to improve minds in a style which would appeal to his readers and offer some diversion from the daily drudgery of work. George Miller was later to admit that his magazine was

> 'in the way of a duty as well as in the way of business.'

The Cheap Magazine was a resounding success. Published between 1813 and 1814, it was read in every parish in Scotland, even selling well in England. *The Cheapy* sold between 15,000 and 21,000 copies annually, an exceptional output for a small publisher at the time. George needed three printing presses in Haddington to keep pace with demand. Printed on inferior quality paper to keep production costs low, selling at fourpence an issue, *The Cheapy* grossed £4,200 a year (about £67,000 in today's terms). As was customary in the publishing trade, thirteen issues were produced each year, the final issue appearing as a supplement in December. While George wrote many articles himself, he commissioned other contributors including Mrs Beatrice Grant whose brother Sir Neil Campbell would accompany Napoleon to his first imprisonment on Elba. George's son James, now aged twenty-two, also contributed an occasional poem.

It is perhaps difficult today, in a superficially enlightened hot-house climate, to understand why the magazine was popular; its tone was severe, sermonising and written in a ponderous style. Then again, perhaps there might be a need for it - albeit qualified - in our own time. The titles of some of the articles speak for themselves: *Dreadful Consequences of Gambling; Fatal Effects of Anger; Piety the Foundation of Good Morals* and the cumbersome *The Progress of Genius from Obscure and Low Situations to Eminence and Celebrity.* The last was almost certainly written by George, a conservative moralist who favoured the long titles popular in his time.

Inexpensive, popular magazines weren't of course the brainchild of George Miller. *Ruddiman's Weekly,* a publication of the same genre, had been in existence since 1768. However, George's magazine was different in that it spoke directly to the farm labourer, the remote villager. *The Cheap Magazine* would have its imitators after it went out of production. In 1813, fulsome praise came from David Dale, Robert Owen and William Allen, co-founders of the model mills at New Lanark who ordered several copies of every issue for their workforce. Another enthusiastic supporter was William Wilberforce, the slave abolitionist. And J M Barrie, finding a copy in his father's house, referred to it as *The Cheapy* in *A Window in Thrums* (1899), his sentimental Kailyard-school tribute to humble Scottish life in his native Kirriemuir.

The Cheapy's popularity ensured a sequel in 1815. *The Monthly Monitor and Philanthropic Museum* - another example of George's predilection for long titles - matched the success of its predecessor. At the beginning of 1815, George Miller was financially buoyant but in that year, the battle of Waterloo ended the Napoleonic Wars which brought economic stagnation, then what today would be called a depression. Even before the year was over, money was harder to obtain and food prices and employment rose sharply. Publishers then as now were among the first to feel the effects of the recession. In the days before local authorities funded and ran public lending libraries, reading was a luxury and few could afford to buy new editions of good books. The majority of George Miller's customers were low wage earners; very soon they couldn't afford even the few pennies for his magazine. *The Monitor* issued for the last time in December 1815; its editor hinted that it might become a quarterly but it never re-appeared. George Miller was physically and mentally exhausted, his income and his inspiration were drying up and he believed that the novelty of his magazines was over. His financial troubles were about to begin.

Unhappy with the premises he had leased in Haddington, George secured another lease on the shop in the High Street there; *Messrs George Miller and Son* continued to trade until 1833, when his son James lost the shop through his habitual drinking. However, that was in the future; in June 1814, George had transferred his lending library to Haddington under James' care as most Dunbar people had read the books it contained. The library wasn't a success in Haddington, possibly because of competition from the *Itinerating Library* scheme started by Samuel Brown, a local man to whom George sold his entire library stock.

Before 1815 ended, George was considering an alternative to his magazine; his next venture was a form of pyramid bookselling - a bad choice as it turned out. In April that year, he entered into a disastrous partnership with William Gracie, a Berwickshire bookseller who persuaded him to join a subscription scheme selling quality books in instalments. This was by no means uncommon; other booksellers canvassed for customers under similar arrangements and like the chapmen, sold instalments at the doors. Gracie undertook to provide George with popular quality titles on easy terms for sale in areas not already covered by himself - which meant nearby Berwickshire. George, ever the optimist, overextended himself, buying a stock of books which cost him £2,600; initially, sales brought in about £140-150 a week, a theoretical £7,500 a year (about £120,000 in modern terms). It was too easy. The scheme had one major flaw; George had to canvass areas further afield than East Lothian, which meant that he had to hire agents up and down the country in places as far away as Newcastle, Aberdeen, Inverness, Caithness, Thurso and even Orkney in the days before railway transport. George had made his first mistake; he committed himself to long journeys up north, attending to his agents' problems in person. In addition to canvassing, he continued to make sales to the book trade, grossing £1,000 (about £18,000 today) at auctions in Edinburgh and Glasgow.

The slump worsened. Several booksellers who owed George money went bankrupt simultaneously. In 1816, his assets on paper amounted to £10,500 but with liabilities of about £9,500, George was forced to declare himself bankrupt, offering his creditors a respectable 16 shillings in the pound (80p), payable between 1816 and 1818. To reduce costs, he concentrated his business in Dunbar, moving son James and the printing of books from the Haddington press and leaving it in the hands of a jobbing printer - his second mistake. He was like a man caught in quicksand, sinking deeper at every turn.

By 1818, George's situation had worsened through the loss of a consignment of books in a shipwreck; he was unable to offer his creditors more than 14 shillings in the pound (70p). Disaster followed disaster; his wife Helen fell ill and his own health deteriorated, again probably through stress. A second cargo of books was lost at sea and a rival canvassing agent began to operate in East Lothian, joined by of all people William Gracie, whom George rightly accused of unprofessional conduct. He could do nothing about it however and this time, he was staring liquidation in the face. In April 1819, he invited his creditors to the Royal Exchange Coffee House in Edinburgh and declared that with debts of £6,100 and assets of £6,253 - largely stock which wouldn't fetch the price at which it was valued - he could pay only 8 shillings in the pound (40p) at periods of 6, 12 and 21 months. To some extent, his predicament was reflected throughout the country; writing his memoirs in 1822, Lord Cockburn expressed the fear that the continuing economic slump was driving the country ever closer to revolution. And then as if George didn't have enough problems, the East Lothian Bank crashed mainly because Borthwick, the chief cashier, had misappropriated funds into loss-making ventures aimed at enriching himself. He did what in Scotland is called a 'moonlight flit' to escape his employers. In his autobiography, George does not say whether he lost money in the crash but it is likely that he did.

George plunged himself into work; he turned to writing again and in 1821, he published *The Affecting History of Tom Bragwell*, a cautionary tale of a young man who turned to crime and was executed. Written out of his concern about wayward youth, George's style is occasionally sensational and sentimental although today, some might applaud his well-intentioned naivety. Later, he was to claim that 'since Tom Bragwell, we have had fewer delinquents of this description in our criminal records'

although he added ruefully but realistically that the drop in crime was probably coincidental.

The book was well-received and men whose opinions were valued praised George's effort. Encouraged by its modest success, he worked on a manuscript he'd begun writing in his youth which, together with some of the articles he'd written for volume 2 of *The Cheap Magazine* became *The Book of Nature Laid Open, or The Wisdom and Goodness of God or the Works of Creation Unfolded;* thankfully, in the course of its revision, he changed the title to the more attractive *Popular Philosophy* in 1826. An impressive piece of work whose theme is natural theology, it is by no means original but it ably demonstrated its author's ability to put across a moralistic message in an attractive and popular style. It elicited praise from Dr James Davidson, Professor of Civil and Natural History at Aberdeen University, to whom it was dedicated. Davidson described it a 'very excellent and instructive treatise.' It was also well-thought of by the famous church leader, Dr Thomas Chalmers, who bought a copy after visiting George so that he might study 'the Geographical Alphabet and the other curiosities along the coast of the Cove [at Cockburnspath] shore.' Although the book gave George intense personal satisfaction, its sales were affected by the failure of the Edinburgh publisher, Constable. The book had special significance for a local farm labourer, Alexander Somerville, who wrote in his *Autobiography of a Working Man* of how he scrimped and scraped to save 10 shillings and sixpence (52p) to buy it. Somerville lamented the lack of interest in the book locally:

'there were not 6 other copies of it sold in the 3 parishes of Cockburnspath,
Oldhamstocks and Innerwick, the geology of which it was chiefly devoted to.'

As George himself puts it, he was

'a poorer man in purse than when he began,'

And yet his Dunbar shop shelves were still well-stocked in 1825; Somerville tells us that he visited *The India Tea Warehouse* to increase his knowledge of measurement and accountancy so that he might train as a forester; he decided to buy a copy of Hutton's *Mensuration* at 4 shillings (20p); tramping the seven miles from his home in Branxton, near Innerwick, he begged George Miller to reserve a copy of the book for him until he could save up for it.

Like many in the publishing business who had lost money, despite his hard work, he never recovered sufficiently to resume publishing. In 1827, his liabilities exceeded his assets by nearly £1,800 (modern equivalent £28,800) and he was forced to sell off all his stock and equipment to meet some of his debts; added to these misfortunes, his son Robert died on 12th Augsut 1828 after a long illness. We know that George had ceased printing by 1830 as *The History of Dunbar,* written by his son James, was published by George's son William. Printing and publishing certainly ran in the Miller family; besides George, sons James and William and brother John in Dunfermline were printers. John's son established Dunfermline's first newspaper, the *Dunfermline Advertiser* between 1835 and 1863. Also, the proprietors of the famous publishing house of *T Fisher Unwin* were descendants of one of George's uncles and a great-nephew started the printing firm of *George Miller and Co* of Liverpool, which was still trading at the beginning of the twentieth century.

By 1832, George Miller was declared bankrupt and forced to sell his treasured private book collection as well as his furniture. About this time, he began to write his last book, *Latter Struggles*- a frank self-portrait and catalogue of his misfortunes. A curious book which might have enjoyed some commercial success with judicious editing, *Latter Struggles* is valuable as an account of the early printing and bookselling trades in East Lothian. Not quite autobiography, it is a dry and gloomy work, although its sombre tone is occasionally relieved by personal anecdotes which provide endearing glimpses of a man who came to terms with failure and yet never became bitter. George Miller was a creature of habit as we learn from his annual New Year's Day meditations; every Ne'er Day, he looked forward to his walk along the seashore at Dunbar, an area now occupied by the East Links Golf Course. He wrote that this customary walk was by way of a holiday ramble which gave him the opportunity to rid himself of his business worries for a time rather than indulge in the local New Year's Day custom of shooting sea-fowl for relaxation. On 1st January 1817, he lamented the fact that he could walk no further than the old Kirkhill Toll (near the site of the ruined Bellevue Hotel) owing to a leg injury caused by exposing a wound to frost. The following year found him in a similar predicament, unable to walk at all because he suffered from a painful ingrowing toenail which he treated successfully with 'an auld wife's cure' of herb poultices. He touchingly records the death in 1823 of his little grandson George - his son James' child - who died suddenly at Haddington on 30th July just as he was about to be taken on a visit to his grandfather. The little boy was buried in Dunbar churchyard. *Latter Struggles* contains a degree of invaluable information even if much of it is frustrating to biographers, as its author needlessly and deliberately omits place names and writes of himself in the third person.

George Miller undoubtedly possessed remarkable insight in many ways. He exploited a latent and hitherto untapped market for his publications; his prime objective was to encourage reading among the poor and the young and to that end, he provided them with cheap, good quality reading material. Dedicated to his task, he almost killed himself in the process.

No account of the businessman would be complete without mentioning his humanitarian concern for his fellow men. George Miller was a man who today would probably belong to Greenpeace or Friends of the Earth. He would have readily embraced the philosophy of John Muir, a Dunbar boy whom he probably never knew. In his day, George campaigned against the slave trade and collected subscriptions for the local abolitionist society; he wrote pamphlets against war [9] and in support of Tom Paine's *The Age of Reason* and *The Rights of Man.* He was also deeply concerned about loss of life at sea, so much so that in 1793, he formed a humane society to whose members he proposed that a lifeboat should operate from Dunbar. He also espoused an idea he had for life-saving equipment; his theory involved the use of a mortar which fired a rope line from shore to stricken ship instead of the other way round, a device which he contended would save more lives. He failed to convince his audience about the need for a lifeboat or to licence the prototype rocket apparatus with the Society for the Encouragement of the Arts, Manufactures and Commerce. His rocket or mortar proposal was taken up and developed by Captain George Manby RN (1765-1854) who patented the idea which was adopted by the Royal National Lifeboat Institution. True to his nature, George wrote 40 years later that he bore Manby no ill will; he simply lamented that he'd personally failed to encourage interest about the project among the members of the Dunbar Humane Society.

George was successful in obtaining a lifeboat for Dunbar, even if it took him 15 years to do so. Appalled by a particularly tragic shipwreck off Torness Point in October 1807, when even those who managed to struggle ashore died of exhaustion and hypothermia, George wrote to Henry Greathead of Newcastle. Greathead had designed and built a new type of lifeboat and George was determined that Dunbar should have the most up-to-date version.[10] Calling his lecture simply *Lifeboat*, George addressed a public meeting on 21st October 1807 - did he choose the second anniversary of Trafalgar on purpose? - and coaxed cash from his fellow businessmen and interested townspeople. The previous week, he had formed a small committee consisting of himself, William Brown, an accountant with the Dunbar branch of the British Linen Bank and David Laing, a local shipbuilder. George printed a subscription leaflet[11] at his own expense, wording it carefully so that it didn't offend anyone's sensibilities by implying there had been a lack of public spirit on his first attempt to have a lifeboat at Dunbar. He tactfully described that as a 'lack of opportunity'. Within a year, he raised £400. In 1808, Dunbar launched its first lifeboat; it cost £150, the equipment and boathouse accounting for a further £194; a formal committee was appointed under the chairmanship of the Earl of Haddington. In 1808, the boat was declared seaworthy. It gave good service over the next 8 years.

Dunbar's first lifeboat was apparently never named or else its name was never recorded. It was coxswained by David Laing; the very day it was declared ready for use, it was called to the assistance of the sloop *HMS Cygnet*. More than 22 vessels foundered off Dunbar in the next few years but there are few records of the part played by the lifeboat. There is however a detailed account of one successful mission in 1810, when two naval frigates, the *Pallas* (32 guns), once captained by the famous Admiral Thomas Cochrane, Lord Dundonald and then captained by Edward Clay, towing a prize commanded by Captain Paris Monk. Its sister ship, the *Nymph* (36 guns) strayed off course and ran aground between Skateraw and the Vaults, a rocky stretch of coastline near Barns Ness lighthouse. The frigates reputedly mistook the lights of the Skateraw limekiln for the May Island light. The *Nymph's* crew were lucky as the vessel ran aground and keeled over, allowing the sailors to crawl to the shore along the masts. The men on the *Pallas* were less fortunate; Captain Clay probably cut loose the prize he was towing but his action made little difference; the *Pallas* was pounded against the rocks at the Vaults, close to Broxmouth House. Daylight found the exhausted survivors clinging to the wreckage. Miller, *Lamp of Lothian* records that

> 'a party of the Royals [cavalry troop]....mounted guard over the wreck.......the lifeboat was launched under the direction of David Laing who succeeded in landing two cargoes of almost 50 men. On taking in her third cargo....she was overloaded;'

Laing was thrown into the sea but managed to climb on to the *Pallas*; however, one of his crewmen, Benjamin Wilson - father of Robert Wilson who developed a version of the screw propellor (see Chapter 10) - was drowned as his tombstone in Dunbar Churchyard tells us. In all, ten sailors were lost; the survivors were taken to Broxmouth House, where the Duchess of Roxburghe provided the men with blankets and hot drinks.

The lifeboat put to sea for the last time in 1816; by 1821, it was no longer seaworthy and it was sold by public *roup* or auction in 1829 by which time the Royal National Lifeboat Institution had been founded and funds for boats were collected nationally. Henry Greathead, the lifeboat designer, presented George Miller with an inscribed engraving of a lifeboat saving a crew near Tynemouth Castle; for many years it was displayed in the Burgh Council Chambers but it seems to have disappeared some time after 1914.

Despite his financial difficulties - especially those he could have laid at other doors - George Miller rarely spoke or wrote bitterly of anyone with whom he'd had business dealings. Although his was a minor publishing concern and while he never met the great writers of his day, his contribution to the popular literature movement remains his greatest achievement. Unorthodox in his religious beliefs, his journalism was didactic rather than literary; his sense of secular morality sometimes caused the orthodox Church of Scotland raised disapproving eyebrows but he remained a committed Christian until his death. Although made a burgess of Dunbar in 1800, George was never appointed to the Burgh Council, unlike his brother James.

In the history of printing, publishing and bookselling, there have been few who combined all three trades. George Miller was one of those who did and was successful for a time. Through his small magazines, he tried to open the minds of ordinary people. He clearly cared about the humble folk and attempted to alleviate the conditions of the imperfect and harsh world into which they'd been born. Living in an age when men and women knew more about their duties than their rights, George made his mark as a pioneer of adult education in his modest way. He set the format for those who came after him to further the development of the cheap literature movement - men like Robert and William Chambers whose *Edinburgh Journal* (1832) and *Chambers' Miscellany* (1859) carried on the tradition. Writing of George Miller in his *Gazetteer of Scotland* in 1832, Robert Chambers paid tribute to *The Cheap Magazine*, describing it as a periodical

> 'conducted on an unambitious plan......an undertaking in some respects in advance of the age......filled with matter calculated to instruct, as well as amuse, the two great classes who mostly require instruction, the young and the poor. Such a work, as it was rather a design of the present time than of that when it appeared, might surely be tried again with better hopes of success than at first.'

Fulsome enough praise and tribute to the foresight and determination of a small country printer.

An intensely happy man in both his marriages, George derived less joy from his children who were a source of grief as well as pride. James, his historian son became an alcoholic tramp, although George never lived to see his descent into darkness. His second son George was eccentric, went to sea, took to drink and ended up in the local asylum; Robert, a promising lad, died in his early twenties. His fourth son William became a successful printer; daughter Elizabeth never married but kept house for her parents and died two years after George. Helen, his second wife, survived him for many years. The family tree is shown in **Fig. 10.**

It is perhaps appropriate that George Miller's epitaph should be written by of his humble customers. In his *Autobiography of a Working Man*, Alexander Somerville of Branxton describes George Miller as 'the father of cheap literature' which is perhaps a somewhat exaggerated claim. However, paying tribute to a man he clearly respected, Somerville wrote:

> 'Nearly forty years ago, he brought out several works at a price so low as to secure the hostility of all booksellers and to make the learned and literary look on them as worthless.'

Somerville attributed George's failure to the problem of living in a small provincial town, together with his perhaps intentional policy of refusing to act as a mouthpiece for the orthodox Church of Scotland's propaganda in *The Cheap Magazine*; Somerville contended that the magazine's fate 'was sealed because of the latter' which is not entirely fair or true. His last words on the man who put aside books for him until he could save for them are brief and to the point:

'An unrequited and unappreciated George Miller died and was buried.'

George Miller's achievements and failures are well documented in a biography written nearly a century ago.[12] A balanced account of man and businessman, it emphasises his valuable contribution to social reform. Since then, George has been either confused with his historian son James or forgotten altogether, although in 1973, H V Morton's *In Scotland Again* makes a passing reference to him. Morton ventures that had George Miller lived today, he would have been a millionaire.

Two Miller graves in Dunbar Kirkyard

Fig 11 Two Miller Gravestones in Dunbar Parish Church Cemetery

Gravestone A

An east-facing headstone in very good condition; it may have been restored or replaced an earlier stone after 1851. Completely legible, it contains the remains of the following Millers:

'James Miller, [1]merchant, Dunbar, 20 November 1854
and
Isabella Forrest, his wife who died 22 September 1827
and the following members of their family

Isabella and John who died in youth [3]
and
James Miller, Ironmonger, who died 4 October 1851 [4]
Eliza Miller who died 27 November 1858 [5]
Isabella A Miller who died 16 December 1871
Robert Miller died 4 April 1881
Mary Miller died 17 November 1886
James Kemp Miller died 11 March 1895 [5] '

Gravestone B

This stone is not only badly weathered but has been vandalised; George Miller is not interred here. It is thought his grave may have been removed to make way for parking facilities

'.......the remains of Elizabeth
Wilson, spouse of James Miller [2]
born in Dunbar ......[died?] 29
October 1776 in the 44th year
of her age and also [obscured] 5
months James 3 December 1757
[obscured] days old 7 December
[1]1762
Also George 27 October 1764 aged
64 years old Robert [obscured]
Miller John died 1780 aged 19
years and 6 months..........'
There are no further names

Notes

1 This is probably James Miller's son (see note 4)
2 George Miller's mother and father resepctively
3 Issue of James and Isabella Forrest
4 George Miller's elder brother
5 Wife of James Miller (see note 4)
5 Minister, United Secession Church, Catrine, Ayrshire

George Miller died penniless on 26th July 1835. None of the local newspapers reported his passing, although *The Scotsman* published an obituary notice ten days later. The local register of burials which was available in 1914 recorded his death by prefixing his name with *Mr* which was unusual for the time; it also indicated that he was 'the author of several works.' Perhaps the clerk felt he warranted this distinction in absence of any official recognition. Although there are two Miller graves in the local churchyard (**Fig. 11**), my exhaustive search to locate his grave has proved fruitless; it is conjectured that it disappeared when the Parish Church apse was added in 1896-97, as the surviving family headstones are not far from it). A versatile, gifted amateur, George Miller put Dunbar and Haddington on the map. Visit either town today and ask about him in vain; it is unlikely that more than a handful of people will have heard of him, which is a great pity.

James Miller (1791-1865)

Born on 21st December 1791 - the day of least light, which is perhaps symbolic given his ultimate descent into vagrancy- James Miller (**ill 57**) shared his father's love of books from an early age. While his father was never more than a minor journalist, James became a historian of some considerable merit and standing. He began writing poetry, a medium in which he wasn't particularly good, although he was favourably compared with and received praise from Sir Walter Scott. Some of his early verses appeared in *The Cheap Magazine* and

Illus 57: *James Miller* ELCMS

the *Scots Magazine* published one in 1817. James was at his best writing of antiquity in prose; encouraged by his father from an early age, James produced two valuable books - *The History of Dunbar* (1830, rep. 1859) and *The Lamp of Lothian* (1844), a history of Haddington. While his book on Dunbar is short on the identification of his source material and suffers from a stilted style, James was thorough in his examination of family charter chests and scattered archives. In his time, there were no convenient repositories such as the National Library or the National Archives of Scotland, where many of the source documents he consulted are stored today.

One major criticism of his Dunbar book is that it ignores whole centuries or parts of them for no obvious reason; another is that he tended to concentrate on the lives of the great and he tells us little of ordinary Dunbar people. Even so, his book remains an important source of information and modern historians consult it as it has proved a reliable source for their own work. James Miller not only collected information about the development of Dunbar, he left impressions of buildings which have long since disappeared.

When his Dunbar history was published in 1830[13] it was favourably reviewed in the *Edinburgh Literary Journal* and James was feted by the Town Council at a dinner held in his honour. But who reads him today? Who has read his collection of poems *St Baldred of the Bass, The Siege of Berwick and Other Poems and Ballads* (1824)? None of James' poems or histories were made known to schoolchildren of subsequent generations in Dunbar. Perhaps James Miller was relegated to obscurity because of his chief character flaw - intemperance, or as his biographer euphemistically puts it, his 'unsteady habits'.

Was it an ill-omen that James was born on the shortest day of the year? He seems not to have been troubled by this fact unlike his father, who lamented that he'd been denied the delights of Hansel Monday on his birthday. Perhaps James' baptism on Christmas Day 1791 was consolation enough. Educated at the local school, in 1805, James began work in at the age of fourteen in the family business, training as a printer. Most of his apprenticeship was spent in his father's Haddington shop and despite his tender age and inexperience, he shared responsibility for the shop with his stepmother's brother who was dismissed, probably for theft. For a time, James ran the printing press at Haddington while a female relative took care of the grocery side of the business until one day, the wanderlust gripped him. In the winter of 1807, he simply walked out of the shop and went to Edinburgh to work in an office for several months until the novelty wore off and he came home in 1808, completing his apprenticeship in 1811.

In 1812, James entered a formal partnership with his father. In sole charge at Haddington, James hated the grocery side of the business, possibly because he was already developing a fondness for the spirits that were too readily at hand. He begged his father to close the grocery department, which George Miller did in 1815, perhaps when it was too late.

In 1819, James married Janet Craw or Crow of Garvald; their marriage produced three daughters and a son called George after his grandfather; the little boy died suddenly in 1823 which occasioned James to write his only personal poem, an ode to his dead child:

'Child of my love! why hast thou laid
 Thy gentle head beneath the willow?
Thy father's arms was warmer bed
 Thy mother's breast a softer pillow.'

As far as can be established there are no descendants from the marriage; at least one daughter appears to have been socially irresponsible - whatever that may mean - and the date of Janet Miller's death is unknown. James' other two daughters apparently didn't amount to anything.

Some of James' early poems showed promise, particularly *St Baldred of the Bass, Verses in Memory of Dunbar Collegiate Church* - the latter written in 1819, when the old medieval church endowed by the 9th Earl of Dunbar in 1342 was demolished - and *The Luckless Drave* or as it was known in 1824, *The Lost Drave,* a dramatic account of the herring fishing disaster in 1579 (see Chapter 9). By the time he married, James had collected all his poems in a slim volume which he called *St Baldred of the Bass, a Pictish Legend*; a second volume of poems entitled *The Wreck of the Czar and Other Poems* appeared in 1835. James' work is clearly influenced by Scott but possesses little of his lyricism. His verse suffers from quirky, irregular metrical construction, overworked metaphors and clumsy lines which clump along encased in leg-irons; even William McGonagall, the flawed poet, would have hesitated to use some of his rhyming couplets. An imperfect voice in Scottish poetry, James' verses are nevertheless valuable as local history, a subject he handled better in prose.

James took over the Haddington shop in his own name by 1817; at that time, he had probably started researching his history of Dunbar. A sympathetic and honest account of his character at that time appeared in Thomas Cowan's preface to a reprint of the *Lamp of Lothian.* Cowan, a Haddington bookseller knew James personally; he paid tribute to the young man's extensive reading and research undertaken after a long and hard working day; his research took him on journeys on horseback as far afield as Berwick. On one occasion, James was snowbound at Carfrae Mill in Berwickshire for three weeks! While there, he composed several verses of his narrative poem *The Gudewife of Tulloshill and the Lord Lauderdale.*

In 1825, James was appointed a merchant-councillor of Haddington; initially, he became a member of a committee which dealt with the *stent* - the contemporary equivalent of the council tax - and the town's accounts. However, his talents equipped him better for his second appointment - that of membership of a five-man committee established in 1826 to found a local library. James' interest in civic affairs ceased after he failed to become elected as a magistrate after three separate nominations, the last occurring in 1829; the reason may not have been unconnected with his by now regular sampling of *The Glenlivet.* Reasons for drinking are as diverse as people themselves; in James' case, one suggestion was that his membership of the St John Kilwinning Lodge of Freemasons in Haddington from 1815 might have encouraged him in his conviviality but he appears to have attended few of the Lodge's meeting or functions. Perhaps like many men, he was simply frustrated and bored with the mundanity of small town life and his humdrum existence as a printer which interfered with his urge to write. Whatever the reasons, by 1835 he had published his 300-page history of Dunbar (1830), left his wife, children, home and business; clearly, he missed the steadying influence of his late father whom he had loved and admired. At his own request, James' name was removed from the Haddington voters' list which suggests that he wanted to sever his ties with the town. James had become a drunkard, a friendless outcast who frequently moved lodgings, staying in Edinburgh and elsewhere, taking up work when and where he could until he was sacked for unreliability. Yet for all his rootless existence, he published a second history which he started to write in 1820. *Lamp of Lothian; A Short History of Haddington* was published in 1844. The title refers to St Mary's Parish Church, Haddington - not the famous Franciscan or Grey Friars Church known in the Middle Ages as the Lamp of Lothian and destroyed by Edward III's invasion of 1356, known as the *Burnt Candlemas.* Nonetheless, poetic licence gave James Miller an attractive title for his book. James nursed the proofs personally to the point of neurosis; he set up the type himself and no other printer was allowed to interfere. On one occasion, a typesetter in James Allan's Haddington print shop thought he would lend a hand while James was out of the shop; he soon learnt to his cost that this was a one-man labour of love. When James returned, he lost his temper, stripped down the man's work and restored it. Perhaps James knew the book would be his epitaph.

Lamp of Lothian is primarily about Scottish history but it is none the worse for that. Printed in a limited edition, after the subscribers' copies and secondary orders were sold, the unsold and unbound copies gathered dust on the shelves of James Allan's bookshop for several years. In his preface to the second edition, Thomas Cowan wrote that Allan sold the loose sheets to a local tobacconist for wrapping tobacco; fortunately, the man had the foresight to have two copies bound as the book had been out of print for many years. Originally published at 8 shillings (40p) - *The History of Dunbar* had cost 4/6 (about 22p) half a week's wage for a labourer - it later sold at 3 guineas (£3.15); the edition printed by the *Haddingtonshire Courier* in 1900 is in newspaper column style. The original is far superior and in addition, the second edition was adulterated by other hands which lost something of James' originality. Today, a decent second-hand copy of *The History of Dunbar* fetches in the region of £75.

It has often been said of the Scots that they never forgive success or forget failure. This is eminently so in James Miller's case. Once respected and respectable, a man of property, promise and talent, his best years were behind him in 1844, when he was aged 53. He was to live another 21 years, a vagrant walking the East Lothian and Berwickshire roads, hawking copies of his poems at a penny a time, begging food and whisky money and sleeping rough in all weathers. Although friendless and alone, even in adversity, James retained some vestiges of self-esteem, hating - and showing he hated - the charity on which he depended. For example, he once begged at a country mansion where the butler, who possibly knew of his reputation, felt obliged to ask his employer where he should seat the tramp. Not unexpectedly, the lady of the house told him to take James to the servants' quarters. With unintended irony, the butler replied that the man was 'dreadfully proud' and proceeded to feed the old poet in a quiet corner of the house. Often, James fell foul of the village boys who tormented him mercilessly until he retaliated by cursing them roundly in a torrent of Hebrew, Greek and dog Latin. A man of quick temper, James once laid out a pressman with a wooden stool; it cost a handful of bonny guineas to keep the man from taking him to court for assault.

Occasionally, James would scribble a few verses, usually dedicating them to some local dignitary who would subsequently find him on his doorstep, begging time and again. Such was his price for bestowing immortality on his 'betters'. The Earl of Haddington, to whom James dedicated *St Baldred of the Bass*, was always good for a handout; he fed and clothed the old historian on several occasions at Tyninghame House and even obtained £20 for him from the Literary Fund. The money was doled out in small amounts to prevent it all going on *Glenlivet.* Once when it was suggested he apply for parish relief, James retorted that he could make more money with a scrape of his pen in one hour than his do-gooder charity worker could earn in a whole month. James wrote his last poem in 1862; *Carmen Triumphalis*, a poem of 98 lines - why not 100? - is mostly doggerel; it was dedicated to the Earl of Haddington and describes the East Lothian and Berwickshire Yeomanry going into quarters at Dunbar in 1861.

It wasn't long before the country folk in East Lothian and Berwickshire referred to the old poet by an obvious nickname. Seen lying in a stream in Haddington one day, a passing lady enquired who it was in the miserable bundle of rags in the water. On being told, she ruefully replied 'Eh me! But the Lamp's burnin' low, low, the day.'

But even the strongest constitution must surrender to the inevitable; the rigours of James' rootless life began to take their toll in his final years. He fell ill and was forced to accept the help of the Poor Inspectorate, or the parish relief officers in Haddington, Tranent and Dunbar. This caused a dispute between the Dunbar and Haddington parishes which threatened each other with lawsuits in the county court as to which parish was responsible for James' welfare. Finally, commonsense prevailed over bureaucracy and the two parishes agreed to share the burden, finding lodgings for the old man in Queensberry House, Edinburgh's Home of Refuge. On 7th May 1864, at the age of 72, James took up residence in his first permanent address for many years, enjoying regular meals and warmth he'd not known for some time. On market days, he met up with old friends in the city but being true friends, they didn't tempt the bard into the Edinburgh alehouses, knowing this would lose him his place at Queensberry House. Thus for the last year of his life, James Miller knew relative comfort, security and tranquility in surroundings which for him must have been luxurious indeed.

Then on 23rd May, about six weeks after General Robert E Lee surrendered to General Ulysses S Grant at Appomattox Court House, ending the American Civil War, the old poet and historian died. Thomas Cowan of Haddington later wrote that he was in Edinburgh that day, attending the court for jury service. Having been discharged sooner than expected, Cowan decided to walk down the Canongate, hoping to meet the old bard 'on the prowl'. Cowan learnt of James Miller's death in the following day's newspaper. Two weeks later, the *Haddingtonshire Courier* published a fairly sympathetic obituary which lamented

> 'the shrivelled-up and wasted form of the old poet....feebly urging his steps along, uncertain where his next meal was to be had and where he was to lay his wearied limbs.'

Apart from the few pounds from the Literary Fund, James Miller received no official assistance until the very end of his life. Scotland has never been kind to her writers.

Thomas Cowan mourned his friend's passing in terms which were neither moralistic or patronising. He admits that Miller's was a tragic life and quotes Burns, who once asked 'Why is the bard so unfitted for the world?' Cowan ventures the view that the bard is different from the man in the street and condemns the self-righteous who shunned Miller, quoting classic Burns:

> 'O wad some Pow'r the giftie gie us
> To see oursel's as ithers see us.'

Cowan describes James Miller as a round man stuck in a square hole, someone labouring at a trade for which he had scant regard and which frustrated his attempts at writing. Perhaps James also rebelled subconsciously against his father's exuberant reforming spirit; whatever the reasons for his downfall, we shall never know the truth of it.

This book is in some way a tribute to - and hopefully an extension of - *The History of Dunbar.* Because of my admiration for James Miller, I couldn't accept his biographer's claim that 'No one seems to know where he is buried or where the vagrant rests from his wanderings.' So I made up my mind to try to locate his grave in Edinburgh. Since James died a pauper, I knew this would be difficult, since his burial place was unlikely to be marked by a headstone. However, my search didn't take too long; I was convinced that James must have been buried near Queensberry House to save on costs; this ruled out the prestigious Canongate Cemetery. On 22nd October 1992, my search took me to Edinburgh's Mortonhall Crematorium where many of the city grave records are stored. Fortunately I located the Record Book of Mortality for the New Calton Burial Ground which showed that James Miller had been interred there. The entry on page 262 is a blunt, official statement:

> 'James Miller from House of Refuge is buried in the New Ground 4 feet North
> the S.W. corner of Newground [sic].'

His age is given as 73 and the entry is dated 23rd May 1865. There is no reference to his books or poems. In the New Calton Cemetery, Regent Road, Edinburgh, the plot of ground referred to is grassed over; there is no memorial or headstone. I didn't expect there to be one.

The *Haddingtonshire Courier* celebrated the centenary of *The History of Dunbar* in 1930, praising its worth as an antiquarian account although lamenting that its appeal was limited for modern readers since it contained no information about the common people, their customs and social problems. However, the second edition published in 1859 contains additional material, albeit mainly about shipwrecks, floods and other disasters; again, the *Courier* regretted the lack of information about the development of burgh life. The article ends with a challenge:

> '.....no one has done anything better than James Miller. No one has appeared
> with a History that can displace his.'

Perhaps this book will go some way towards meeting this challenge.

George and James Miller aren't commemorated by any public memorial in Dunbar or Haddington. My attempts to locate George's grave in Dunbar have been unsuccessful although his mother's badly-weathered headstone stands beside that of George's brother James and his family, including James Kemp Miller who died in 1895. In 1896, the bailies of Dunbar record in the burgh minutes for 24th April that they had agreed to accept the bequest of a collection of books in the Reverend James Kemp Miller's will. The books were donated to the people of Dunbar and were to be used to form the nucleus of a public lending library. A love of books clearly ran in the family; I wonder if the library in Castellau House, Dunbar has any record of James Kemp Miller's generous gift. Dunbar didn't have a public library until 1947, 50 years after J K Miller's bequest and a century and a half after George Miller created the town's first library. In January 1946, David Balloch of Haddington donated £500 to Dunbar for a library; on 1st July 1947, Dunbar Public Library opened its doors to the public, offering 780 titles.[14]

George and James Miller did much for the towns of Dunbar and Haddington. They are forgotten men. Until 1945, Dunbar didn't even possess a copy of James Miller's history; the Town Council minutes of 4th May record that a copy was bought for five shillings (25p) from a private source in Brechin.[15] As mentioned earlier, today, the book would fetch £75 or more.

It isn't too late for Dunbar and Haddington to acknowledge the Millers in some small way. A plaque bearing their names would suffice. It could be located on George's last shop at 71 High Street, Dunbar. After all, while we rightly honour John Muir, we should not do so to the exclusion of other notable men born in the community.

Richard Gall (1776-1801)

Another of the forgotten men of Dunbar is Richard Gall. His name is almost all we know about him, a young poet who died prematurely at the threshold of a promising literary career. His brief life is commemorated in a small book published 18 years after his death - *Poems and Songs by the Late Richard Gall, with a Memorial of the Author* (Edinburgh, 1819)

Mary Burn and George Gall, the latter a notary, were married on 7th June 1771, the year of George Miller's birth. Their son Richard was born in December 1776 at Link House, near West Barns Links, not far from Hedderwickhill. The Galls weren't well-off which probably explains why they were not unduly concerned about the profession Richard chose for himself. For some unaccountable reason, young Gall didn't attend the burgh Grammar School at Dunbar; in 1781, at the age of five, he was sent to Haddington Burgh School, where he was taught the rudiments of reading, writing and arithmetic. At the age of eleven, he was apprenticed to his maternal uncle, James Burn, a Haddington house-carpenter and builder; at the time, Burn was employed in the building of Gosford House, home of the Earl of Wemyss, near North Berwick. Richard knew even then where his talents lay; when his parents moved to Edinburgh, he joined them there in 1789, taking up the trade of apprentice printer.

That Gall from Dunbar chose to enter the printing trade links him with the Millers, although it is unlikely that they ever met; when Gall died, George Miller was just beginning to establish his business and son James was only nine years old. Gall was apprenticed to David Ramsay, proprietor of the *Edinburgh Evening Courant*, a newspaper popular in the capital. About this time, his mother appears to have been widowed, as she took in a male lodger who assumed responsibility for her family's education. This unidentified gentleman spent considerable time and energy on young Gall; the thirteen year-old developed a passion for writing and literature and even at that early age, began planning a literary career.

His printing apprenticeship over, David Ramsay appointed the young man as his travelling clerk which not only increased his earning capacity but allowed him to travel the length and breadth of Scotland, seeing the beauty spots which would fire his imagination. Richard became a great admirer of Allan Ramsay, Robert Fergusson - who died the day before his twenty-fourth birthday in an Edinburgh asylum - Hector MacNeill, the author of *Will and Jean* and of course, last but not least, his mentor Robert Burns. In 1799, the Glasgow poet Thomas Campbell was preparing for publication *The Pleasures of Hope,* his book of poems which became an overnight success throughout Britain. Campbell was lodging in the same house as Richard Gall, who must have been enraptured by his work. To complete his introduction to the world of Scottish literature, Richard befriended the Reverend Dr Alexander Murray who wrote a biography of Robert the Bruce. Murray encouraged the young man, spending a good deal of his time with the poet until his untimely death.

By about 1800, Richard was becoming noticed. He wrote several songs including *Farewell to Ayrshire* which he submitted anonymously to Robert Burns' printer but with the poet's name prefixed to it to increase its chances of publication. For some time, the song was attributed to Burns until the real author became known. Another of Richard's poems, *Now Bank and Brae are Clad in Green* appeared in *Reliques of Burns* and is imitative. Richard's most accomplished works were *My Only Jo and Dearie* and *The Braes o' Drumlee*, both of which could have been written by Burns, such was the similarity in their style. Richard Gall wrote other poems with a local flavour - *Arthur's Seat* and *Address to Haddington*, the latter describing scenes of his childhood when he was 'a stranger yet to pain.'

Richard Gall never saw his collected works in print. He fell ill in 1801, suffering from what was diagnosed as an abscess of the breast - cancer - which proved malignant. During his lingering illness, Richard continued to write until he was too weak to sit upright, having been forced by then to lie in bed writing with a pencil instead of a pen. In his twenty-fifth year, he died on 10th May 1801.

For some years, Richard Gall had been a member of a Highland volunteer regiment, many of whose members admired the more patriotic of his poems. In fact, the officers clubbed together to meet the cost of printing one poem, every man in the regiment receiving a personal copy. The regiment buried Richard Gall with full military honours in the Old Calton Cemetery as a mark of their respect. The Record Book of Mortality for the Old Calton Cemetery simply records his name, as the headstone which marked his grave was removed with others when Regent Road was built during the nineteenth century.

After Richard Gall's death, Dr Murray edited his poems. In his brief biography of Gall, Murray describes him as gentle, sensible and well-mannered. Richard's favourite subjects were Scottish history and songs - another link with the Millers of Dunbar. When Richard spoke of poetry - especially Scots poetry - he was visibly moved and proud of his heritage.

Murray's labour of love was finally completed in 1819, when he published Richard Gall's collected works under the title *Poems and Songs.* Richard's output wasn't great - less than fifty poems - but the little book was well-received. His was a major talent in embryo, a talent which was sadly ended too soon.

Robert Mennon (1797-1884)

Although not a native of Dunbar, Robert Mennon of Ayton, the fourth of the forgotten men commemorated in this chapter lived in the town from 1850 to 1869. Mennon was the fourth of seven children born to James and Magdalene Mennon of Ayton, Berwickshire. Robert was born there on 29th April 1797. His father and grandfather were the village slaters, residing in one of six or seven cottages known as the Old Town, a narrow street that runs at right angles to the main road through Ayton. Robert was educated at the village school which provided a rudimentary education.

Robert was influenced by the quiet, reflective landscape that surrounds his sleepy little village then and now. After leaving school to take up work in his father's slating business, he began to write poetry. Unlike James Miller of Dunbar, Robert Mennon had no knowledge of Latin and Greek, consoling himself with his contention that an 'illiterate bard should follow nature's way.'

Robert's mother died in 1816, his father following her in 1824. Then aged 24, Robert decided to seek his fortune in London, leaving his siblings to carry on the family trade in Ayton. Thus he followed Dr Samuel Johnson's somewhat patronising advice that a move to England was the 'noblest prospect for any Scotsman.' It was sound advice nonetheless, followed earlier by the famous civil engineer, John Rennie of Phantassie, East Linton and Robert Wilson of Dunbar, reputedly the inventor of the screw propellor. Moving to London must have been a great culture shock to the young Mennon, a senstive, sentimental man whose love of nature and the countryside inspired his muse. He lived in London until 1850, though he never forgot his humble roots, his home-sickness showing through the poems he wrote while away from his native Ayton.

Mennon lived in the London of Nash the architect at the time of the transformation of Georgian to Victorian London. There was work in plenty for a skilled slaterer like Mennon, who in one of his London poems describes his feelings on a cold winter's day when he was repairing the roof of Westminster Hall. The poem *The Slater's Soliloquy on a Winter's Day* is, like much of his work, regrettably of little literary merit - his poetry at the time is little more than doggerel, although it is valuable in that in provides us with information on the kind of contracts the young man secured in London.

In 1850, Robert and his wife Sarah returned to Scotland, although not to live in Ayton, where his brothers had cornered the slating market. He moved to Dunbar, where he set up a commercial business as a slater and glazier. In 1861, he was living in a three-storey house on the corner of the High Street and Silver Street, sharing the building with two other families. Mennon worked on many of the roofs of the tall tenements in the High Street and he would have been a familiar figure at the time. He continued to write poetry, contributing to the *Haddingtonshire Courier* which at that time reserved a section of its back page for original poems.

Robert Mennon lived in Dunbar until 1869, when aged 72, he returned to his native Ayton. It was a momentous year in other respects, for he published his collected poems in a volume entitled *Poems Moral and Religious.*

His wife Sarah died in 1876, he continuing to live at No 10, Old Town, the cottage where he'd been born, until his death in January 1884 at the ripe old age of 87. His gravestone in Ayton Churchyard describes him as

> 'much beloved, pure in heart, of a meek and gentle nature, wide in sympathy and of poetic tone.'

Who could wish for more?

Mennon's poems about birds and animals are simple and gently humorous; poems like *The Big Armchair* are unashamedly sentimental and nostalgic, recalling days gone by. Perhaps one of his best poems is *Ayton Past and Present*, the style of which compares favourably with James Miller's *Bounce Dunbar.* Of all his works, perhaps the best is *Whoopers o'Ayton,* a rollicking celebration of the antics of local worthies, a poem whose style is reminiscent of Robert Burns.

Writing of Robert Mennon, the Ayton Bard, in his *Minstrelsy of the Merse* (1893), the Reverend W S Crockett describes him as

> 'a man of genuine piety, a keen observer of nature....good-humoured in conversation, a most agreeable companion, full of sage counsel and kindly warm-hearted encouragement. His poetical productions are not of the highest merit but they are generally pleasing and show the writer....[as] a man of refined feeling....an honest, god-fearing and patriotic Scot.'

There are no plaques to commemorate Dunbar's forgotten men. However, perhaps Dunbar and District History Society will publicise George and James Miller, Richard Gall and Robert Mennon, perhaps by memorial plaques. It is not too late to honour them.

8

Royal Burgh

The term *royal burgh* is Scottish, corresponding to the English *borough* and was applied to several different kinds of town corporations. A royal burgh was, as the title indicates, a corporate body created under Crown charter. The corporation consisted of magistrates and burgesses of the district erected in the burgh. The magistrates were appointed by the council, usually consisting of the provost and several bailies; other important appointments were the burgh clerk, dean of guild and the treasurer who assisted the full council. But when were royal burghs first formed and under what circumstances? The answer to the first question is simple - they were created during the reign of David I (1124-1153). The circumstances leading to their creation was that David saw them as cornerstones of his policy of introducing feudal institutions and ideas, based on similar institutions which he knew played a key role in the administration of Norman England.

In recent years, the Norman contribution to the development of Scotland has been re-appraised; some modern historians no longer support the view that the Normanisation of the country made a significant contribution to Scotland's development. However, the Norman-Flemish settlers who came north during David's reign undoubtedly exerted their influence in various ways, to varying degrees and with mixed results. Whatever the truth of it, it is fair to say that without the impact of this cultural change, David I wouldn't have civilised the semi-barbaric kingdom he inherited so rapidly and effectively as he did. Dynamic progress was made possible with the building of impressive stone castles in Scotland during the thirteenth century - they were administrative centres as well as strongholds - and with the proliferation of royal burghs, both imported from Norman England. The king's castles and royal burghs provided a firm base for the local sheriff or crown officer who worked in tandem with the local nobles to administer justice, regulate finance - particularly the Crown's income - and maintain law and order, all deriving from the post-Conquest legacy.

The importance of the castle has already been discussed in Chapter I. This chapter will examine the impact of the royal burghs, using Dunbar as example. The first royal burghs were established in the central belt and the Borders. As mentioned above, the word *burgh* derives from the English *borough* and is a legal term; in Scotland, the laws governing a burgh's constitution and powers are thought to have been drawn from the *Leges Burgorum*, the twelfth century code operating in Newcastle-upon-Tyne. While it is true that during the reign of Alfred the Great (872-901) there were Anglian *burhs* or fortified settlements and trade centres which grew haphazardly with sheriffs and nobles to administer them, these institutions came to an end in 1066. After that, Norman castles became the focal points for the administration of communities; in time, these became known as boroughs in England, places which were granted the right to hold fairs and markets and given trading rights defined by law.

David I's burghs were part of a calculated policy. Many shared similarities; they were dominated by a castle at one end of the main street and a church or religious house at the other and some were enclosed by a town wall. In a sense, David was the first Scottish town planner; the potential for control was obvious to a king who had witnessed the success of Norman administration south of the Border. His charters creating royal burghs granted rights and privileges to the community; in return, the inhabitants were directly answerable to him in person without interference from an intermediary feudal vassal such as a local earl or baron. Burghs flourished where geographical conditions were favourable i.e. in towns situated at the mouth of a river or within proximity of the sea, preferably with a good natural harbour. Thus royal burghs were also likely to be found in fertile areas prolific in agricultural yields; Haddingtonshire (**ill 58**) was such an area and Dunbar fulfilled the conditions for royal burgh status with its fertile soil, good fishings and natural harbour at Belhaven, a port or haven in use from at least the twelfth century. And yet although these preconditions were met long before the mid-thirteenth century, when Dunbar's first stone castle appeared, why did it take nearly three centuries after David's reign to achieve full royal burgh status? The answer is quite simple - the state of court politics.

An English borough enjoyed rights of self-government and internal and external trade which David I imitated in Scotland; Scottish royal burgh charters were modelled on the example of Newcastle - yet another instance of that northern English town's influence on medieval Scotland. About fifteen burghs can trace their foundation to David I's reign, among them Edinburgh, Stirling, Perth, Dunfermline, Berwick and Roxburgh.

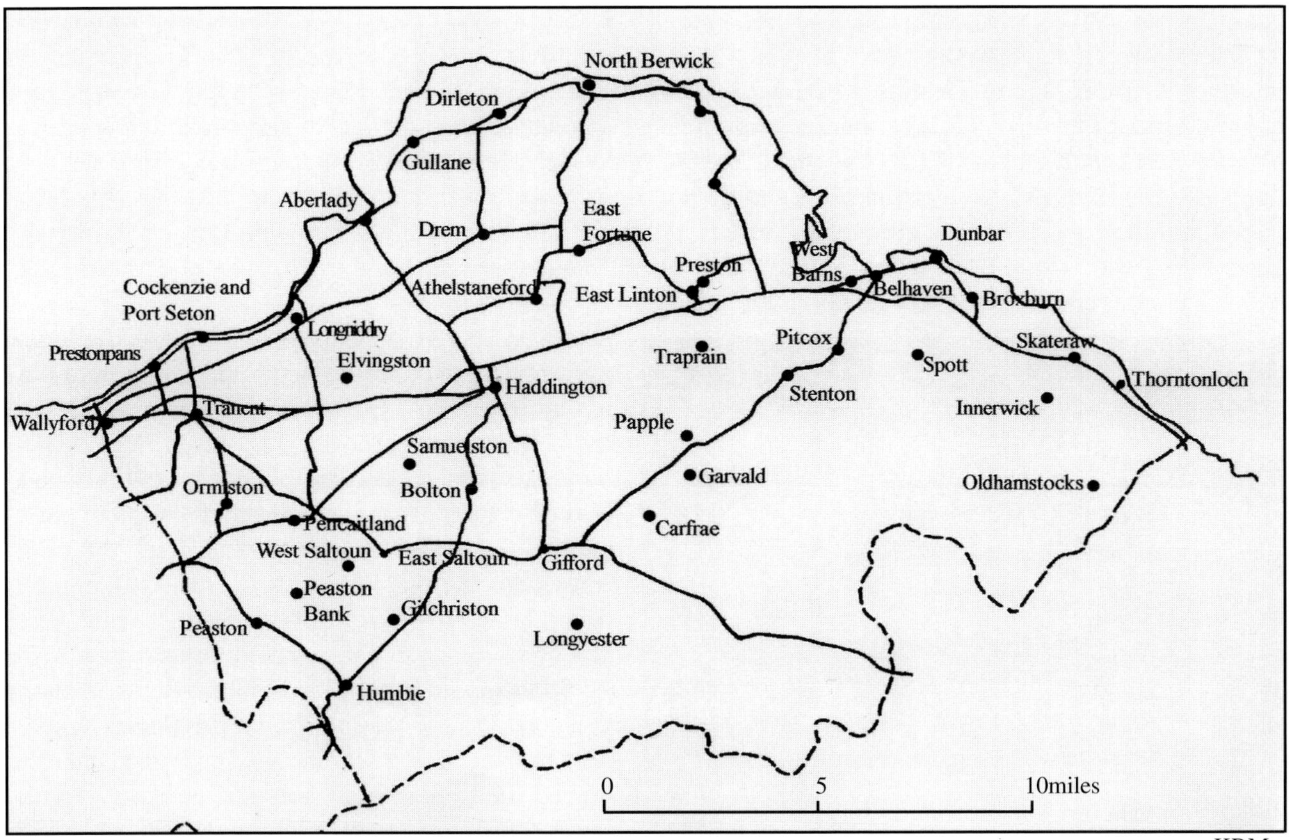

Illus 58: *Simplified map of East Lothian (Haddingtonshire)*

References to unnamed burghs appear in many of David's charters; it wasn't until the reign of William the Lion (1165-1214) that burghs began to be identified by name. Merchants were authorised to trade in wool, animal skins and hides both locally and on the Continent; they could also import wine and salt, selling these commodities in the local market, then to other burghs and parishes. Flemish cloth and fine wines were imported for re-sale on the domestic market for the simple reason that the king derived a large part of his income - known as the Great Customs - from import and export taxes. Royal burghs were concentrated in the central belt, binding together the southern half of Scotland; the tribal and largely Gaelic-speaking northern belt contributed little to the royal coffers because most of the income raised from trade and the sale of cattle went into the money chest of the clan chief.

Speculation as to the origins of Dunbar appears in Chapter I; this chapter will examine how the town achieved royal burgh status, the consequences for its inhabitants and how it enriched both king and community.

The 'planning' of Dunbar was well advanced by 1170, when it became one of about 1,200 Scottish parishes. At that time, few parishes or towns had been elevated to royal burghs, although many possessed the desired conditions for upgrading. What were these? A crude definition of a royal burgh is that of a community with a castle, a river or harbour, a mercat cross, a town seal and a tron or weigh-beam for weighing goods sold in the local market. Many Scottish towns met these criteria and Dunbar had a town seal in 1357, one of the oldest in Scotland. However, acquiring royal burgh status required more than symbolic insignia; a royal burgh could be created only by the monarch who gave it special privileges and who expected his due in return. Only the king had the power to establish a royal burgh; he could at any time alter the conditions under which it operated and the range of privileges it enjoyed.

There were three types of burgh - burghs of regality, burghs of barony - both of which might include ecclesiastical burghs - and royal burghs. The first two were creations of the feudal system - granted by the king to a subject inferior i.e. a noble, baron or senior churchman; burghs of regality and barony were similar in that they held their rights from a local lord and not directly from the crown. Burghs of barony were analogous to royal burghs, though the magistrates were elected by the superior of the barony or the inhabitants themselves; burghs of regality were a lesser form of barony burghs, with jurisdiction in the limited districts whose boundaries were defined by royal charter. Dunbar was a burgh of barony in c.1230, when it is first described thus in *Dryburgh Liber* charter No 121.

Royal burghs created under the royal prerogative enjoyed a direct relationship with the king. Although some historians consider that Dunbar became a royal burgh under David II's charter of 1369-70, the document doesn't refer to it as such; it is called a 'free' burgh, given to the 9th Earl of Dunbar, which means that technically, it remained a burgh of barony in 1370. A new town seal was struck in 1370 however; it was inscribed *David II D* [eo] *G* [racias] *Rex Scottor Burgi de Dunbar* or David II King of Scotland by the Grace of God Burgh of Dunbar. (A fine example of the seal is reproduced from a stained glass window in a private house at East Links, Dunbar (**ill 59 and back cover**). However, although the term *burgi* was common at that time, the terms *burgus regalis* or *burgus regius* do not occur in any Scottish document until Rothesay became a royal burgh in 1401; references to royal burghs are made infrequently in the fifteenth century so that the generic term was rare until late in that century. The sole difference between burghs of regality and royal burghs is that the latter could engage in overseas trade.

Illus 59: *Early 19th century stained glass window, East Links, Dunbar* KRM

The first four royal burghs - Stirling, Edinburgh, Berwick and Roxburgh - led to the creation of others until 1552, when they formed themselves into the Convention of Royal Burghs, an organisation which exercised considerable power and influence in the Scottish parliament. From the reign of Alexander I to the Treaty of Union (1107-1707), very few of the 71 royal burghs were created after 1600. Since James II's charter of 1445 rather than David II's of 1370 specifically named Dunbar as a royal burgh, it should be regarded as the 54th royal burgh in Scotland. Dunbar's original privileges - exclusive rights of trade within a defined area - also included the right to hold fairs and markets, a privilege not extended to other communities until 1517. The merchant oligarchies dominated the royal burghs from the outset, even keeping the craftsmen and tradesmen in a subordinate position despite the existence of powerful craft guilds like the hammermen, or metalworkers. The lesser burghs were also often at odds with their royally-favoured rivals in trade disputes.

Being created by kings, royal burgh freemen or burgesses were king's men, on king's land; the burgh rents belonged to him and burgh inhabitants were subject to the jurisdiction of the king's officers rather than local lords. Royal burghs were robust institutions, guarding their special position jealously; in many ways the spirit of exclusiveness and protectionism spelt out in their charters reflected the self-interest of the feudal barons. However, the king received the Great Customs, his share of the taxes and customs duties levied on goods imported and exported by sea; the taxes levied on goods bought and sold within the burgh, or entering or leaving by road were known as the Petty Customs and were for the exclusive benefit of the burgh council. To enforce the rights of royal burghs, legislation was enacted in 1457, 1466, 1488 and 1503 which upheld the special position of the burghs and their merchants. Dunbar exercised particular rights over the fishing industry from the sixteenth century onwards; in that century, it issued no fewer than 30 local acts to protect local interests. From the king's point of view, a royal burgh was a source of income; the Great Customs were collected by local officials and without cost to the Exchequer since these burghs were obliged to employ - and pay - *custumars* or customs officers for this purpose.

Thus it was not a one-sided arrangement; in return for privileges, a royal burgh contributed to the national taxation as well as bearing a share of specific national expenditure. For example, in 1590, the Privy Council *Register* records that along with other burghs, Dunbar and North Berwick were ordered to pay £20 and £19 respectively towards the cost of 'a bark [sic] hired by them [the Council] to convey the King [James VI] home' [with his bride and queen Anne from Denmark]. The two burghs were in fact charged almost double these amounts and took their case to the Privy Council which upheld the original charges. Perhaps there is a measure of irony in this for North Berwick; shortly after the royal couple came to Scotland, one of the earliest witchcraft trials - that of the so-called North Berwick Witches - took place. The witches were accused of causing the storm which blew the king's ship off course, sparking off the first of four epidemics of witch hunting in Scotland.

Royal burghs were a sound investment for Scottish kings. As well as providing the king with albeit fluctuating income, another source of regular income were the *firma* or rents paid to the king for their tofts (landholdings) and their tenements as evidenced from the frequent entries in *ERs.* As direct vassals of the Crown, bailies (the word *baillivi* used in the fourteenth century is probably the origin of the term) and burgesses paid specified rents for their possessions to the Royal Exchequer. In effect, the king was their landlord. Crown officers, known as comptrollers were appointed to receive these rents. Royal burghs were thus 'leased' by the Crown; rents were set at a fairly modest rate to allow each burgh, as a corporation, to retain sufficient income for its own upkeep and well-being. These arrangements continued for some time until burgesses obtained obtained individual Crown charters, known as *feu-charters*, converting their holdings into a perpetual right subject to the payment of an annual lump sum - invariably a few pounds - which were paid to the Exchequer. (To modern eyes, payments of £6 might seem negligible and hardly worth the trouble of collecting; the amounts were however significant at the time).

However, prior to the introduction of national income tax in 1798 from which the royal household was funded through the Privy Purse, the main source of royal income derived from the Great Customs paid on goods imported and exported through overseas trade. The income generated for use in the burgh itself were derived from taxes levied on goods bought and sold within its precincts and animals, goods and people simply passing through the town ports and toll gates. There was a general policy of allowing goods required by the burgesses and craftsmen for manufacture - wool for knitting yarn, flax for cloth and hides for leather goods - into the burgh free of tax or at a low rate, although the proper tax was levied when the finished goods were bought and sold. Animals brought to the burgh market for sale attracted a halfpenny tax for every ox, cow and sheep, a penny for every horse. Merchants who weren't burgesses of Dunbar or any other town and 'unfree' men from surrounding districts bore the brunt of the taxation. Most royal burghs charged other taxes - harbour and market dues, weigh-house charges, *thirlage* [a feudal tax formerly paid to the local lord and particularly despised as it was levied on corn ground into flour for bread] at the burgh mills at West Barns and of course, popular with Dunbar's burgh council, a penny or two on every pint of ale sold in the alehouses. The Petty Customs could bring in anything from a few hundred to several thousand pounds, depending on the size of the burgh and its trade activity. However, there were many more sources of income which were provided for in local byelaws and acts passed by individual councils, far too numerous and complex to mention here. Suffice it to say that in order to meet their liabilities - provision of schools, salaries for teachers, repair of buildings and roads and poor relief - burghs like Dunbar were obliged to raise income from every house-occupier, shop-owner and stall-holder. Ultimately, the Petty Customs were replaced by other taxes as the monopolies of royal burghs waned; a county rating system based on the former burghal rating - the stent - was introduced in the nineteenth century, the last vestiges of the complex system of Petty Customs disappearing around 1870. After the stent came local rates, apportioned between county councils and the burghs within the counties; the modern version is of course the council tax. Incredibly, possibly to simplify tax reckoning, Dunbar petitioned parliament in 1853 supporting the adoption of decimal currency - nearly 120 years before Britain converted.

Royal burgh provosts and bailies (both had first to obtain their burgess ticket before they were 'elected' by their colleagues) also served as magistrates, required to keep the king's peace; they were also liable for military service, attending *ex officio* at the periodic *wapinschaws*, or medieval musters of able-bodied men who had to show they possessed arms and accoutrements according to their station in life. In the Middle Ages, every provost and bailie swore an oath of personal loyalty to the king; contravening that oath was tantamount to treason. Later, it meant automatic expulsion from the town council, as occurred in at least one instant when one Dunbar bailie declared he was unable to swear the required oath to William and Mary in 1688 on grounds of conscience - he supported the deposed James VII and II

Provosts and bailies acting as magistrates were empowered to prosecute those who transgressed the burgh's laws or abused their rights; in turn, these men were subject to the scrutiny and regulation by the Convention of Royal Burghs and by the crown and its instrument, the Privy Council. While royal burghs were empowered to levy taxes they were not liberty to charge what they liked. The Council and the Convention could for example order a royal burgh not to fix the price of some locally-produced commodity such as bread without due regard to the prevailing price of wheat and flour; such directives usually resulted from petitions submitted to the Council by local tradesmen. Not unexpectedly, the burghs resented such interference and occasionally, some disputes never reached the ears of the Privy Councillors. For example, on 23rd March 1813, the bakers and others dealing in corn at Dunbar petitioned the local magistrates not to charge tolls on corn being transported from the town's mill in West Barns. The bakers argued that in 1758, when the town council instituted the arrangements for the *multure* - that part of every consignment of corn ground at the town mills and due to the town as *thirlage* - the multure fee also included carriage toll. The local magistrates side-stepped the issue by referring the bakers to the trustees of the turnpike road between Dunbar and West Barns!

Because their concerns were largely related to trade matters, burghal duties were not particularly onerous; however, the provost and bailies spent a good deal of their time judging respectfully worded petitions - for what would be regarded today as planning permission applications - to extend existing premises, build external stairs and gain access to various areas of the town, usually affecting the High Street. (One case in the nineteenth century concerned a long-standing bone of contention about the constant flooding caused by the dam at Beltonford used to power the flour mill at West Barns). Other burghal duties included punishing wrongdoers - witches included, although a Privy Council commission was required for local trials of persons accused of practising witchcraft, since it was a crime punishable by death; more common were the prosecution of unlicensed beggars, prostitutes, thieves, petty criminals and whoever else was considered a public nuisance. In the matter of witch prosecutions, the provost and bailies worked closely with the kirk session, as we have seen in Chapter 5. In matters of law however, the Crown reserved the right to prosecute any burgh indweller suspected of capital crimes which included treason and murder.

It is without doubt that Dunbar was already a thriving community before it was elevated from a burgh of barony to a royal burgh. Gradually, it conformed to the familiar pattern of the Scottish burgh - a broad main street dominated by a castle at one end and a church at the other. Every burgh possessed a mercat cross, a tron and a tolbooth. Little of what we would call public amenities were evident; the merchants were more concerned that their own self-interest didn't take second place to the needs of the community at large. Royal burghs were however able to invest more money in town improvements simply because whatever was produced in the community, they were able by law to exact the town's share of the profits.

Dunbar was regulated by six main royal charters. As noted earlier, the first was granted on 8th February 1370 by David II; it gave

'to the earl of March, of the erection of the town of Dumbarre in a free burgh' [1]

with the right to trade in wool, hides and other merchandise, with a free port at Belhaven and all the rights and privileges of a free burgh and port. The town was authorised to erect a mercat cross and hold a market every Monday; to possess a tron or weigh-beam; and most important, a *cochet*, or official seal used by the local customs officers to stamp documents certifying that a merchant had paid the appropriate customs on goods bought or sold. Taxes were imposed on all goods, no matter from whence they came - within or outwith the earldom of March and to or from overseas countries. The first charter also allowed reciprocity of trade with Haddington. David II's charter was of course intended to prevent the loss of royal revenue to England which occupied the important burghs of Berwick and Roxburgh in 1370, thus denying the Scottish Crown the vast revenues from wool produced by the great Border abbeys like Melrose. The revenues on the wool clip from Melrose, Dryburgh and Kelso were diverted south simply because there were no other royal burghs near at hand to buy and sell the wool. However, according to one source,[2] the customs collected at Dunbar in 1370 amounted to £2,097 but this cannot be accurate, given the amounts shown in the *ERs* for the period (**Fig. 13**). The revenue deriving from the Great Customs on a national scale rarely exceeded a few thousand pounds each year, although this was a colossal sum in its day.

The second charter in Dunbar's favour was granted by James II on 16th August 1445.[3] James' charter removes any doubt of Dunbar's royal burgh status; it confirms David II's charter and perpetuates the community's right to trade throughout the earldom of March, the lordship of Dunbar (including Stenton) and the baronies of Coldingham, Mordington, Bonkyl, Langtown and Innerwick within the sheriffdom of Berwick 'until the town of Berwick and the castle of Roxburgh shall have been recovered from the hands of the English.' Clearly, James was hoping to increase his income by awarding Dunbar added status and thus encourage increased trade in the south - east to thwart English ambitions. His charter granted Dunbar trading monopolies within its boundaries, its hinterland and most important of all, beyond the seas.

The third and fourth charters were granted in the reign of Mary, Queen of Scots on 18th June 1555 - five years before she came to live in Scotland - and 31st March 1567, the latter occuring at the time of the threat to her rule by those who had murdered David Riccio, when she was forced to seek refuge in Dunbar.

The fifth and sixth charters were granted by James I on 1st March 1603 and in 1618; the fifth charter confirmed all previous four charters.[4] The sixth measure - not in the nature of a charter proper - was granted by the king in 1618 which reinforced the burgh's rights and privileges.[5] In 1641,[6] the Scottish parliament ratified James' measures which spelt out the rights Dunbar enjoyed at

'.........the free portes and sea places of Bellheaven, Lamerheaven [the Old or later-known Cromwell

Harbour] and Lamercraige [Lamer Island, *craig* being Old Scots for a substantial projecting rock] and all bullwarkes made or to be made thereon Togidder with all other craiges ylandis Landis [rocks and landing] places and creekes betuixt [between] the forsaidis [aforementioned] portes of Bellheaven and Lamerheaven.'

In James VI's reign, trade was centred on the east coast of Scotland, Dunbar being one of the main burghs which generated a reasonable income from sea-trade, particularly with Holland which of course enriched the king.

It is not difficult to envisage Dunbar from the Dark to late Middle Ages. Its houses would have been huddled around the castle, single storey buildings of wood, clay and wattle, thatched with straw or turf, with a plot of ground to the rear for grazing animals. We know from the excavation report published in 2000, *Castle Park: Two Thousand Years of a Fortified Headland* that the earliest settlement was established in the Iron Age, concentrated on the promontory of Castle Park; after the demise of the Votadini, the site was occupied by the Angles who established a royal *burh*, or *urbis regis* in the seventh century until East Lothian became Scottish in 1018. After that, the lands were Crown property until the arrival of Gospatric from Northumberland who established the line of the Earls of Dunbar. This Gospatric either built a fort or strengthened an existing one, the nucleus of the community. The domestic buildings would have been haphazardly grouped near the fort, with paths rather than defined streets in the eleventh century. The work area probably began immediately outwith the castle policies; fields surrounded the Parish Church, an island of stone that brought comfort to the weary fieldworkers. When David II elevated Dunbar to a free burgh in 1370, attempts were undoubtedly made to improve its layout; the huddle of mean hovels and cottages slowly evolved in an orderly fashion, eventually forming the High Street which is recognisable in this remove of time. The first priority would have been the creation of a spacious market-place; once established and thriving, visitors from nearby towns and villages came first to buy and sell, then settled permanently and gradually increased the population. The incomers built houses, particularly those in the rapidly expanding merchant class after 1370.

At the close of the thirteenth century, the population of Scotland was about 400,000; there were 50 burghs of the three types described above, where about a tenth of the population resided. Even today, modern burghs maintain the standard blueprint - a straight main street with a castle at one end and a church at the other. We know from Jorevin de Rocheford's visit to 'Dunbart' in about 1661 that in that year, Dunbar consisted of a 'fine large street' above the lower part of the village which he describes as the 'habitation of fishermen'. At some point a tolbooth was erected to house the town jail and its administrative offices, serving also as an early form of bank where taxes were paid and kept in a strongbox. In Dunbar's case, the tolbooth or town house was deliberately situated near the West Port, probably the main entrance to the burgh in the fifteenth century.

The tolbooth was the focal point of the town; taxes and tolls were paid there, courts were held and wrongdoers were held in it, either to be tried locally or in the case of serious crimes, awaiting trial at the county sheriff court or the High Court in Edinburgh. At Dunbar, the ground floor eventually housed the local police station with its cells behind used until the mid-twentieth century; these were used to detain petty criminals and public nuisances overnight prior to appearance before the magistrates, justices of the peace or the sheriff at Haddington in the more serious cases. Many of the public 'nuisances' found their way there as a result of keeping too convivial company on a Saturday night.

The pecking order in the society of a royal burgh began with the heritors - those who owned land and property within the burgh boundary which were passed on to descendants. The heritors had considerable say in the running of the local church and often served on special assizes authorised by the Privy Council to try for example people suspected of witchcraft. They were given their due place, solicited for their wealth and influence - they were foremost among the few who were members of parliament - but the burgh council tried to keep them at arms' length, the provost and bailies taking their own decisions. Occasionally, the burgh came into conflict with their so-called betters, modifying or curbing the local inheritors' land improvement schemes, particularly where these encroached on burgh land or property. Because of the powers granted them by royal charter, the provost and bailies came next in the hierarchy, then the burgesses and merchants and finally, the craftsmen, all of whom could and did serve on the council. Burgesses played a diminishing part in burgh administration after the sixteenth century however.

Although few records survive to confirm it, municipal government in Dunbar was fairly rudimentary from 1370 until the mid-sixteenth century. By then, every royal burgh was subject to the overall direction and scrutiny of the Convention of Royal Burghs, a powerful organisation founded in 1552 (see Appendix J) which acted - in theory at least - for the good of the burgh inhabitants, taking to task overbearing or corrupt burgh councils. It is perhaps appropriate here to briefly examine the extent of central control exercised by the government in Scotland at that time. By European standards, Scottish government machinery - the executive - was ineffective and inefficient until the early eighteenth century. The main institution in Edinburgh was the Privy

Council whose members were appointed by the crown. The Council was responsible for day-to-day administration of the country, applying the laws passed by parliament. The Lords in Council controlled the unsophisticated and almost moribund Scottish parliament - the legislative in name at least - by means of a strange body known as the Committee of Articles whose members were drawn from the nobility. This committee was appointed when parliament met at the beginning of a new session; thereafter, parliament went into recess almost immediately, meeting on a few days during its session. After parliament recessed, the Committee of Articles proceeded to prepare a list of legislative measures which it later invited parliament to debate and ratify - virtually an automatic process. There was also a Convention or Committee of Estates - a kind of informal parliament which possessed similar powers ie the right to vote taxes and interpret and amend existing legislation. The Committee of Estates was however subordinate to the Privy Council, often undertaking its duties during the periodic recessions of parliament, particularly in summer.

Thus the legislative was concentrated not in parliament but in the hands of a small group of men which by the sixteenth century had virtually a monopoly over the measures of law passed - rubber-stamped is more appropriate - by parliament. There was endless scope for corruption. Scottish parliaments were notoriously derelict in their duty, largely because sittings were brief; for example in 1587, parliament sat for only seventeen days in the whole year, about average. The law was often flouted and there were problems with enforcement, the nobles invariably ignoring the laws they themselves had introduced whenever their personal interests were threatened. By 1552, those entitled to sit in parliament were drawn from four groups instead of the previous Three Estates of the Middle Ages. These initial three comprised of the nobility, the church and representatives of the royal burghs who were appointed as commissioners of the Convention of Royal Burghs. By 1650, most royal burghs had been established and their representatives were usually chosen by the burgh council, whereafter they rode in grand style to Edinburgh wearing fine livery.

The royal burghs' exclusive trading rights were re-affirmed by two acts of parliament in 1633 and 1690. The conduct of central government offered countless opportunities for graft and corruption, the statutory checks and balances of modern government being almost non-existent. The same applied at local level but provided the king's revenues were collected and paid promptly to the Exchequer, no one cared unduly. As in other burghs, Dunbar burgh council was dominated by a small group - usually three or four of the richest merchants - who ran the town almost like a personal fiefdom. In some burghs, municipal power was excessive, irresponsible and went virtually unchallenged. Like other burghs, Dunbar's provost and bailies repeatedly borrowed heavily especially during the eighteenth century and were eventually forced to sell the ancient patrimony of every royal burgh, the Common Land, to make good the difference between income and expenditure. Until the great reform legislation of the nineteenth century, burgh councils were not administered by elected representatives but by individuals who petitioned for office when vacancies occurred and were duly 'elected' by those already serving. These arrangements would never stand up to public scrutiny today even if the procedures - oath-taking for example - were dutifully observed. Burgesses were appointed by the provost and any two bailies which again offered an opportunity for favouritism and bribery. The 'elected' bailies appointed the provost from one of their own - usually a wealthy businessman like Robert Fall whose merchant family virtually dominated politics in Dunbar for practically the whole of the eighteenth century. Most burgh councils contained about twenty members - influential merchants and traders - outwardly displaying a sense of public duty but clandestinely serving their own ends and those of their families and friends when, for example, municipal contracts were awarded. In 1721, Dunbar burgh council consisted of a provost [post vacant], 3 bailies, one treasurer and 15 councillors; by 1831, the number hadn't changed.

By 1619, each royal burgh could send two representatives as commissioners to the Convention of Royal Burghs who also sat in parliament until the Act of Union in 1707. Dunbar seems to have sent only one. The town is first mentioned in the parliamentary roll of 1469 and the names of some commissioners are given in **Fig. 12**;[7] it will be seen that men bearing the same surname attended year after year - indisputable evidence of the nepotism which existed at the time. However, the Convention of Royal Burghs rigidly enforced its rules on the appointment of commissioners; failure to comply with them brought censure, as occurred on more than one occasion in the case of Dunbar. For example, in 1623, Dunbar was fined £100 Scots (about £8 sterling) for irregularities in the method of appointment of its provost, Sir James Baillie of Lochend. All bailies, councillors and burgesses were of course required to swear an oath to the king before being appointed; it is also interesting to note that in 1758, burgh councillors were also required to take an oath of abjuration against the Stuart dynasty as memories of the '15 and '45 Jacobite rebellions were still uppermost in the Establishment's mind. Dunbar was intensely loyal to the Crown as is evidenced by the heraldic panels (**ill 60 and 61**) in the former Burgh Chambers, the panels gifted by James VII and II in 1686 and George I in 1714. On the occasion of the government's victory at Culloden in 1746, the local councillors sent a letter of congratulation to George

KRM

Illus 60: *The James VII heraldic panel in the Council Chamber of the Town House, Dunbar*

II, extolling the benefits and virtues of his reign and the heroism of his son, William, Duke of Cumberland (see Chapter 12).

About twenty years before the Act of Union, Dunbar had an ambivalent attitude towards William of Orange who succeeded to the throne in 1688 after the Glorious Revolution. At the time, the town celebrated the birthday of James VII and II although two decades later, the 'Prince and Steward of Scotland [James VII, the Old Pretender] had been relegated to 'a mere Pretender' as is recorded in the council minutes of 29th March 1708. By 1745, Dunbar was staunchly pro-Hanoverian and denounced the rebellion, referring to the Young Pretender, Prince Charles Edward Stuart as a puppet of the king of France.

Despite the decidedly undernourished state of the Scottish economy in 1706, the Convention of Royal Burghs opposed union with England, Dunbar being among the dissenting burghs; only a third of the 66 burghs declared for the Act of Union despite the fact that the treaty upheld the existing rights of every royal burgh. The eccentric but implacable opponent of union, 2nd Lord Belhaven predicted that Scotsmen would soon be' walking the desolate Streets, hanging down their Heads with Disappointment.'

On 2nd November 1706, Dunbar burgh council instructed Robert Kellie, its commissioner to the Convention of Royal Burghs and member of the last Scottish parliament [8] to

'advysse with their Advocate to adress[sic] or not as they see fit'.

KRM

Illus 61: *The Hanoverian heraldic panel*

It seemed as if resolve was weakening yet only three weeks later, parliamentary records show that the burgh council, the burgesses and other inhabitants of Dunbar presented addresses against union with England in terms of the articles. Dunbar's chief concern about union with England were the consequential duties on salt and the effect on fishing. Perhaps by 1706, the local mood had changed however. After the union was ratified by a minority of the Scottish nobles, Lord Belhaven was victimised for his opposition; a resolute Whig and Presbyterian, Belhaven was ridiculed by his contemporaries not only for his 'eccentric' political views but also for his appearance; one hostile critic described him as 'rough, fat, black [in complexion], noisy, more like a butcher than a lord.' After the Treaty of Union was signed, he was arrested on suspicion of Jacobite sympathies and supporting the aborted French invasion in 1708 - a suspiciously convenient excuse. Committed to the Tower of London, he was examined by the Privy Council and allowed bail. A few days later, Belhaven died of what was termed inflammation of the brain.

It was perhaps successive poor harvests up to 1707 which convinced many gentlemen farmers union with England was necessary. The truth of the matter was simply this - Scotland was virtually bankrupt. The Scots pound was worth only 1/12th of English sterling (see Appendix I). The treaty signed in Edinburgh on 16th July 1707 was flawed in several respects, the main being that Scotland was inadequately represented in the British parliament for many years afterwards; the second rankled until the end of the twentieth century, when Scotland regained her parliament. In accepting union with England, Scotland gave up her hard-won sovereignty which consigned her to a minority position controlled by a legislative which being predominantly English put English interests to the fore.

However, in this second point, the constitutional lawyers differed from the politicians; in their opinion, both countries gave up their sovereignty in 1707, a reality not readily appreciated by modern English people. Be that as it may, legal niceties did nothing to remove the view which still remains today - that in English eyes, Scotland became a second-class country in 1707.

The imbalance in Scottish representation at Westminster was adjusted in later years but at the outset, only 16 out of 226 lords were Scottish-born - somewhat less than the 10% representation based on Scotland's proportion of the population of Great Britain. More significant at the time was the fact that the first united parliament was controlled by a small cabinet in which Scotland had no voice whatsoever; although there were Secretaries of State with responsibility for Scottish affairs from 1707. In 1720, the post of Secretary of State for Scotland was held by the Duke of Roxburghe; however, after the '45, it was abolished by Westminster for the simple reason that its continued existence played into the hands of those who still considered Scotland a separate and sovereign nation. The role of governing Scotland became the responsibility of the Home Secretary who had nominal control of a number of Scottish Boards set up to deal with matters such as the promotion of fisheries and industry; these boards were agencies rather than government departments, reporting their findings to the Home Office. The ministerial and cabinet post of Secretary of State for Scotland wasn't reinstated until 1885, which caused a certain degree of unease among the conservative factions at Westminster, men who argued that reviving the post would give encouragement to those who still hankered after an independent Scotland. The position was given to the Duke of Richmond and Gordon who was acceptable to those who expressed fears of the rise of neo-nationalism on the Celtic fringe. Gordon set up his headquarters in Dover House, Whitehall, where the Scottish boards were established to deal with matters such as education, agriculture and fisheries. The effectiveness of these boards was criticised for a variety of reasons at the turn of the nineteenth century; in 1919, it was decided to transfer their functions to proper government departments staffed by civil servants who ultimately became employees and officials of the Scottish Office based in St Andrew's House, Edinburgh. All this was of little import to the royal burghs which from 1707 onwards, struggled to retain their considerable power, privileges and independence. Gradually, their ability and need to raise local taxes were curtailed as central government increasingly assumed their former functions, particularly after the introduction of income tax at the end of the eighteenth century. Some of the unpopular tax-gathering measures were the poll tax, the hearth tax, the inhabited homes tax and the highly unpopular window tax.[9]

Nevertheless, burghs like Dunbar could maintain a sense of their special relationship with the Crown, petitioning the king and parliament on certain occasions. For example, on 28th June 1815, two months after Emperor Napoleon of France abdicated and a month after the First Treaty of Paris, the Dunbar magistrates received a resolution from

> 'the London Committee as to the Abolition of the Affrican [sic] Slave Trade. They think it very proper that petitions recommending the measure should be sent to both houses of parliament.'

This mild rebuke was in response to a petition from Dunbar whose magistrates were concerned that the terms of the peace treaty with France contained no provisions to proscribe possible attempts by France to resume this dreadful trade. Although slavery had been abolished by statute in Britain in 1807, the measure had led to increased trade with Africa; the fear was that France might choose to ignore the example set by Britain. The Dunbar magistrates sent their respectfully-worded petition to Westminster, expressing regret that the recent treaty made no provision for the prevention of slave trading by French overseas possessions; these humanitarian men wrote that slavery was

> 'a trade avowedly repugnant to every moral and religious principle.'

(One is tempted to speculate that George Miller (see Chapter 7) was perhaps one of the leading voices urging the burgh council to petition parliament). The magistrates were at pains to point out that if France resumed trade with Africa, this could lead to the clandestine importation of slaves from French to British colonies. While their sentiments were laudable, France did in fact abolish slavery in 1814, even if the practice wasn't completely outlawed until well into the first half of the century. Although the United States banned the traffic in slave in 1808, slavery would continue in the Southern States until the American Civil War, when President Lincoln issued his Emancipation Proclamation in 1863.

The burgh councils of the eighteenth century employed few officials although one important position - that of burgh treasurer - was never allowed to remain vacant for any length of time. His duty it was to guard and account for the money collected as tolls, taxes and customs duties and for ensuring that the correct amounts collected by the Custom House were remitted to the king's comptroller. He also administered the Common Good Fund whose income came chiefly from taxation, the lease of the burgh mills and the sub-let of common grazing land or fishing. The fund was used chiefly to repair public buildings e.g. slating the roof of the local church, meeting the expenses of the parish schools, improving the tolbooth and cleaning the streets. A burgh or common clerk recorded the business transacted at the weekly council meetings. Unfortunately, Dunbar's burgh records go back no further than 1688 as on the approach of Cromwell in 1650, the ship carrying the earlier records to the safety of the Bass Rock was wrecked. The kirk session minutes go back to 1658 however.

The most important officials were the provost and the bailies who doubled as magistrates and whose task it was to enforce the bylaws and regulations enacted by the burgh council as a whole. A dean of guild was appointed to ensure that trading standards met the legal requirements and to identify any craftsman or workman who produced shoddy goods or sub-standard work. An early form of quality control on which the reputation of the burgh rested, the dean of guild's duties were crucial to the administration. Items such as milk, bread, foodstuffs, ale, candles, and other household goods and commodities had to conform to standards and quality prescribed by regulations and sold at regulated prices. Not unexpectedly, this led to conflict between the merchant class and guild craftsmen, something which is unique to Scotland; Dunbar and 19 other burghs were involved in such a clash of interests arising from restrictive laws chiefly those concerning price-fixing to which the craftsmen and craft guilds objected.[10] The merchants invariably won as they had powerful friends on the burgh councils. Curious though it may seem, the craft guilds made no attempt to band together and thus increase their own power and influence in such matters.

Main burgh council meetings were known as Head Courts, held three times a year at Michaelmas (October), when new bailies and councillors were elected, Yule (Christmas) and Pasche (Easter). In more recent times, the appointment of new councillors was generally followed by the official recognition of the newly-formed council in a ceremony known as the Kirkin' of the Council, a tradition which is self-explanatory. (After the Great War, the Burgh council usually marched at the head of the Armistice Day parade to the War Memorial). Before that, weekly council meetings were held, the officials being summoned by tuck of drum to the council chambers in the tolbooth. These meetings were usually concerned with petitions from merchants and businessmen seeking to make alterations to their premises or the installation of water pipes to draw supplies from the public wells for such activities as brewing and distilling. Occasionally, individual traders took the burgh to task for failing in some duty or other. As mentioned earlier, a long-standing source of difficulty was that faced by landowners and tenants whose property bordered the water which provided the power for the town mills at West Barns whose dam at Beltonford caused frequent flooding.

Justice was dispensed from the town house by the magistrates who invoked the burgh's judicial powers. As mentioned earlier, cases of a more serious nature were tried at the sheriff court in Haddington, although cases of witchcraft were tried locally under special commissions appointed by the Privy Council in Edinburgh; whether the standard of justice administered locally compared favourably with that in Haddington is debatable but local nuisances were dealt with severely, those convicted of witchcraft being executed at the Gallows' Green (modern-day Gala Green). In James VI's and I's measures of 1603 and 1618, the Dunbar magistrates were given powers of sheriffship, the provost acting as sheriff-principal and the bailies as sheriff-deputes. They could initiate lawsuits, impose fines, bring actions against persons suspected of criminal behaviour and execute common criminals guilty of one of the four capital crimes which included murder and witchcraft. Trial was by compurgation where the innocence of an accused person was determined by the number of oaths sworn in his or her favour - a throwback to the old baron courts administered by the Earls of Dunbar. The burgh court also supported the rights of individuals eg the right to bequeath property and that of a married woman over property held in her own name. Up to the reorganisation of local government in 1975, burgh courts were held every Saturday morning at 10.00am in the Town Chambers. A court of three bailies presided over cases of petty crime, hearing evidence from the local police. These courts could impose monetary fines of a few pounds or sentences of up to five days' imprisonment in the local jail. More serious crimes were referred to the Sheriff Court at Haddington.

Minor officials found in every burgh were those concerned with the enforcement of local bylaws and regulations. In the early years, there were various types of inspectors - ale-tasters and flesh-prisers [pricers]. At Dunbar there were three *metsters* under the supervision of the dean of guild; these officers measured the weight of corn, coal and salt to ensure they complied with the regulations. Prior to 1839, when local police forces were authorised by parliament, the magistrates at Dunbar were attended by three officials, one of which was the Town Officer, a law enforcement officer or constable who also acted as the town jailer and commanded the town guard; his symbol of office was a halberd or long spear with an axe-head and a hook by which a man trying to escape by horse could be dragged to the ground. Until 1831, the duties of the Town Officer were combined with that of harbourmaster. In December 1831, the magistrates appointed a surveyor of works who superintended the work of the town's few employees. He was also required to be present at the weighing of grain in the weekly market 'when not required at the harbour' which implies he served as harbourmaster. In addition, he was responsible for the local fire engine. In 1776. the Sun Fire Office in Edinburgh wrote to the burgh council on 21st november about their claim for insurance after a gunpowder accident, offering for sale a 'no. 3 fire engine' to minimise the risk of future claims. In this connection, an important officer was the watchman. In the 17th century, an important burgh officer was the watchman. In 1617 the Convention of Royal Burghs decreed that every burgh should appoint a watchman to patrol the burgh precincts. In Dunbar, he did his rounds at the tolling of the curfew bell at 8pm and 10pm. His prime duty was to watch for fire - vital in the days when many houses were built of wood. [Curfew is of course French - *couvre-feu* - when household fires were put out or made safe]. As late as 1920, the 10pm bell was still being tolled although the burgh council decided that was no longer necessary and declared the practice would cease; no fewer than 628 inhabitants signed a petition to retain the custom. The burgh council went ahead nevertheless.

Among the town employees at the bottom of the small hierarchy were the town drummer, the town piper, the clock-keeper, the scavenger and the lockman (jailer/executioner); these last three occupations were undertaken by one man in 1638. In 1743, Charles Hastie was the Town Officer; his father Robert was the town piper. In 1761, David Lamb asked if he might be appointed town drummer as he was too old to undertake the strenuous duties of Town Officer. There was also a town herdsman who took the town's cattle to graze at the Bleachfield, situated in the Countess Park.

The natives of most burghs were distrustful of strangers who settled in their area; families who did so were required to possess some kind of written testimonial from a former landlord, parish, employer or minister of the church attesting to their good behaviour. Those who were unable to produce 'good conduct' certificates were regarded with suspicion; at the least sign of trouble, they were banished from the parish, some being branded on the cheek prior to the nineteenth century. *The Scottish Burgh Records Society* archives contain many examples of the treatment meted out to those whom the burgh council considered were undesirables. Religious intolerance was often the real cause. Fines were also imposed on burgh indwellers who entertained strangers in their homes for more than three days without informing the council; visitors were conspicuous as few other than merchants, pedlars, chapmen, drovers, the crews of ships or farm workers seeking new employment travelled any distance at all. Vagrants and beggars were discouraged from entering a burgh; if they were allowed in, they were kept under close observation.

Justice and law enforcement took up a good deal of the magistrates' time. In the seventeenth and eighteenth centuries, like most communities, Dunbar had its pillory, wooden stocks for the public humiliation of wrongdoers; the *branks* or scold's bridle used to silence women who spread malicious gossip, the *jougs* or iron collar which was fixed to the kirk wall near the entrance - an example survives at Spott Kirk - and of course the lockman or hangman who chained thieves in the stocks and scourged them with whips, broke their noses with an iron frame, nailed their ears to doors or cut them off and branded those guilty of fornication or banishment from the parish for one reason or other. Women who committed adultery were stripped half-naked, had their hair shorn and were publicly flogged; the death penalty was imposed only for the most serious crimes such as murder and witchcraft. Banishment from the parish was usually more common in the case of petty crime.

There are several executions recorded in the archives. In 1603, Joseph Boncle was executed for the murder of Joseph Loch [Lough?], the local blacksmith. In 1608, John Swan a burgess, killed George Clarkson 'by striking him with a fork on his head' and he was executed. In 1621, Sir James Baillie of Lochend, provost of Dunbar, was ordered to apprehend a local man, John Wilson, who was an habitual sheep stealer; on being caught, Wilson was to be sent to Edinburgh's Tolbooth, such was the gravity of his crime. In 1623-24, the Privy Council *Register* records that no fewer than six men were arrested for sheep and cattle stealing; among them was Robert Cowper, a housebreaker in Dunbar found guilty of burglary. Cowper stole £140 in gold and silver from the widow of William Lauder, burgess of Dunbar and robbed various other houses in the town. Some cases were minor breaches of the local bylaws such as that of Andrew Tod, a Dunbar burgess. Even so, he wrote to the Privy Council to complain that he'd been quietly walking along the High Street minding his own business when he was set upon by the bailies who 'hurled him into their tolbooth, committed him to close warde, suffering none to have access to him.' A few days earlier, the town drummer had been sent through the town proclaiming that no one should lease Tod or his servant any house or supply him with meat and drink. It transpired that Tod had been insolent, contemptuous and disorderly [drunk?]and that his name should be removed from the Burgess Roll. The Privy Council found in the bailies' favour. While there are several cases of summary justice, some individuals were fortunate to a certain extent as in the case of Katherine Graham in 1663. She was imprisoned in the tolbooth for some time for - in the words of the magistrate - the alleged 'accession to the death of James Brydie', later referred to as James Brydon, son of George Brydon of Skateraw although it was known that 'her innocence hereof is known to the whole country.' The Privy Council was petitioned for a decision; the Council ruled that the local magistrates should deliver a proclamation at the mercat cross on the next market day to the effect that 'any person desirous of pursuing the supplicant for the foresaid slaughter must insist before 2nd February next or she will be liberated.' The bad news was that if Katherine were released she was not to be seen in Scotland again under 'peine [pain] of death.' Although the magistrates were ordered to try her in 1664, there appears to be no record of Katherine's fate.

In 1668, the Privy Council considered an address from the justices of the peace in East Lothian to determine what should be done with Daniel Sanderson, a prisoner held in Dunbar and formerly servant to James Strang, minister at Tyninghame whose life Sanderson had threatened. Sanderson was found guilty and deported to the plantations.[11] In 1675, two gypsies called Faa and Shau were held in Dunbar, then sent to the Tolbooth in Edinburgh to be tried for law-breaking and causing wilful damage in Dunbar High Street 'armed with suords, durkes [swords and dirks]and pistols.' [12] As late as 1824, men were still being publicly flogged. In its glimpses into the past, the *Haddingtonshire Courier* reported that Robert Dunnett was found guilty of the crimes of 'assaulting, cutting and wounding with an intent to murder' on 27th July and was sentenced to receive 100 lashes. Dunnett received 20 lashes on leaving the tolbooth, 20 at the east end of the town, 20 at Thompson's Close where the crime had been committed, 20 at the seaport, whereafter he was marched along Castle Street to the foot of Silver Street where he received the final 20 - all laid on his naked back. He was then returned to jail to be examined by a doctor who certified that his punishment wouldn't endanger his life!

The town jail, housed for many centuries in the tolbooth was in considerable disrepair in 1818. During the course of a national survey of burgh jails conducted by the Convention of Royal Burghs, the Dunbar magistrates reported that the jail

> 'is by no means secure. It is a very old building at least 3 Hundred years old [ie it was built before 1518] Consisting of a Jailor's House on the first storry [sic and also meaning the ground floor], two apartments for Prisoners on the second, and a Court House on the third storry. From its insecurity it is often necessary to remove criminal prisoners for Capital offences to the neighbouring Burgh of Haddington....The usual average Prisoners is three or four but often it is necessary to imploy [sic] the Court House to house debtors frequently however no prisoners are confined.'

The magistrates' report admits that the number of prisoners was on the increase due to an expansion in the population; several prisoners had escaped 'but not being debtors, no loss was sustained.' The jailer's salary was given as £10 a year with a free house; his salary might be as much as £15 a year provided he obtained the customary fee paid by certain categories of prisoner. About fourpence (less than 2p) was paid by the burgh for each prisoner's daily upkeep. The report ends by intimating that the burgh's annual income was £600, most of which was spent on 'upholding the harbour'; the magistrates were making it abundantly clear there was no money available for much-needed improvements to security at the town jail.

In the days before the Poor Law Act of 1845 came into effect, the relief of the poor was the responsibility of each parish kirk; relief was provided on assessment, each parish making its own arrangements. Official beggars were licensed to beg within the burgh boundary; they were issued with a lead badge or ticket bearing the town seal or stamp. Beggars of this kind were known as *gaberlunzies*; often disabled, blind or elderly, many were children. The privilege could be withdrawn however; this barbaric and crude form of social security continued into the nineteenth century. As we noted in Chapter 5, parish kirk sessions never had enough money to meet the needs of their poor; money was raised from a variety of sources - chiefly the weekly collections, the hire of mortcloths - a government initiative in 1686, when parliament passed an act requiring all corpses to be wrapped in Scottish linen gravecloths which benefited the country's spinners during a depression in the linen trade - and of course the hiring fee for the parish hearse. Other sources of income were from the hire of church seats and the fines levied on those who breached kirk discipline, the majority being guilty of carnal behaviour.

The needy poor were numerous in Dunbar

> 'as is the case in all country towns such as are seaports'

where employment was precarious due to the elements and the capricious herring shoals. Fishermen often fell sick or were drowned, forcing their families to apply for parish relief. The poor were usually paid by the kirk session treasurer after he satisfied himself on the amount affordable and when he was instructed by the minister and the elders, these men being regarded

> 'as the fittest persons to judge and proportion the supplies according to the necessities of the poor.'

The statement is rich in subconscious irony. The burgh council contributed one sixth of the amount agreed by the session which was responsible for the Poor Relief Fund until the burden was transferred to the civil authorities after 1845. To give some idea of the amount disbursed to the local poor, the kirk session book for 1709 records in the flyleaf that £116:9:0 (£116.45) was paid out to the sick, the widows and the 'idiots' in the burgh compared with £435 over a century later - an increase of almost 400 per cent.

By 1843, the problem of the poor had at last achieved sufficient prominence in the national consciousness -

perhaps as a result of the publicity given to the Highland Clearances - to generate concern and alarm. Humanitarian voices were raised against the landlords in the North-West Highlands, to which were added those of like-minded men who demonstrated that there were wide variations in the way parish kirk sessions dealt with the problems of the poor. To silence these voices, the government appointed a Scottish Royal Commission on the Poor Law in 1843; the Poor Law Inquiry Commission obtained evidence from every parish in the country to assist parliamentary debates on a Poor Law Bill. The Commission visited Dunbar in 1844, where it heard submissions from the local minister and others on 9th January.[13] In submitting his evidence, the Reverend John Jaffray reported there were 114 paupers in the burgh in 1842 and £435 had been paid to them in that year. The population was given as 4,395 in 1841. Jaffray intimated that the heritors fixed the annual assessment for the parish, one sixth of the relief being borne by the town. The following is an extract from the Inquiry:

> 'Generally speaking, the paupers are of a better class [!], and do not beg....The chief cause of the number ....in Dunbar arises from the influx of persons from the landward parishes in the neighbourhood.'

Interrogated,

> "What do you consider to be the cause of this influx?"

Answered,

> "Because they are no longer efficient in the country. The hind has no other resources but to come into the town, where he hires a house, and after three years may come upon the poor funds....The age at which they come into the town may be above sixty. One inducement is....that houses are easily got ....and they come with the view to get work.......There is a want of employment for aged females in the town....The means for the education of the people are ample. There are two parish schools, and a charity school besides....Witness [John Jaffray] has seen a decided improvement in the habits of the people since his incumbency [1821]. They are more temperate, pay more attention to education and, on the whole, exhibit a greater spirit of Independence....The poor rates have been reduced more than one-half, and this he attributed in a great degree to the law being strictly and rigidly applied, so as to make every parish support its own poor. Witness thinks that the great secret in the management of the poor is, not to encourage them to come upon the poor roll, but rather to lead them to trust in their own exertions. There have been a great many cases of disputed settlements in Dunbar parish and witness thinks that extending the period to seven years [for disputes to be settled] would be a great improvement in the law.'

The next witness to be examined was Provost Simon Sawers who criticised what as he saw as the fishermen's imprudence:

> 'Their gains are at times large; yet if a storm happens, so as to throw them out of work for a fortnight or three weeks, they are reduced to great misery. Their houses are very wretched; the windows are often unglazed, and the bedding of the worst description....There was a soup kitchen during the period of the cholera [1831-32], but none of later years.'

The Session Clerk, George Combe reported that the allowances to the poor varied from five to 10 shillings a month (25-50p) and that some house rents were also paid, usually for those who were very old and had no relatives to support them. Widows with children were allowed two shillings (10p) per week for each child until the age of 13. Much of what is recorded more than a century and a half ago makes disturbing reading today.

The Royal Commission's findings were published in 1844. Its overall conclusion was that the existing Poor Law (of 1575) was 'not inadequate to deal with social distress.' The subsequent Poor Law Act of 1845, while maintaining the parish as the basic administrative unit, transferred responsibility for poor relief from Kirk to State; parochial boards were created with Poor Inspectors appointed to investigate individual cases. It was little more than a cosmetic exercise designed to combat the original complaint of variations in levels of relief meted out by individual kirk sessions. This is substantiated by the fact that the majority of the members of the parochial boards were drawn from kirk session elders and church heritors, with token representation from burgh councils. Thus the arbitrary - and often prejudiced - paternalism of the Kirk was replaced by a theoretically more democratic administrative body. The Poor Law Act of 1845 did not bring about a marked improvement in the lot of the poor, the level of relief being only marginally increased. The only positive aspect of the legislative change was that the new law provided a wider and more public forum for the investigation of individual cases. In Dunbar as elsewhere, the able-bodied (male) unemployed - the majority in Dunbar being fishermen - were still denied relief as before. Poverty continued.

From about the eighteenth century, Dunbar consisted of the main or High Street - so named because the town was built on two levels, the lower containing the castle, then the two harbours. The High Street was established by the mid-seventeenth century, although its present layout came much later; it was both a source of income and expenditure for the burgh, as will be seen. The tenements extending at right angles to the street were separated by closes, vennels and wynds; some of these gloomy and dilapidated thoroughfares survive to this day, although they are worth a visit. The tenements were built at the head of the burgage plots or tofts which were either cultivated for food or used to graze animals owned by local merchants, traders and burgesses - hence their name - creating a herring-bone pattern at right angles on both sides of the High Street (**ill 62**). In the early eighteenth

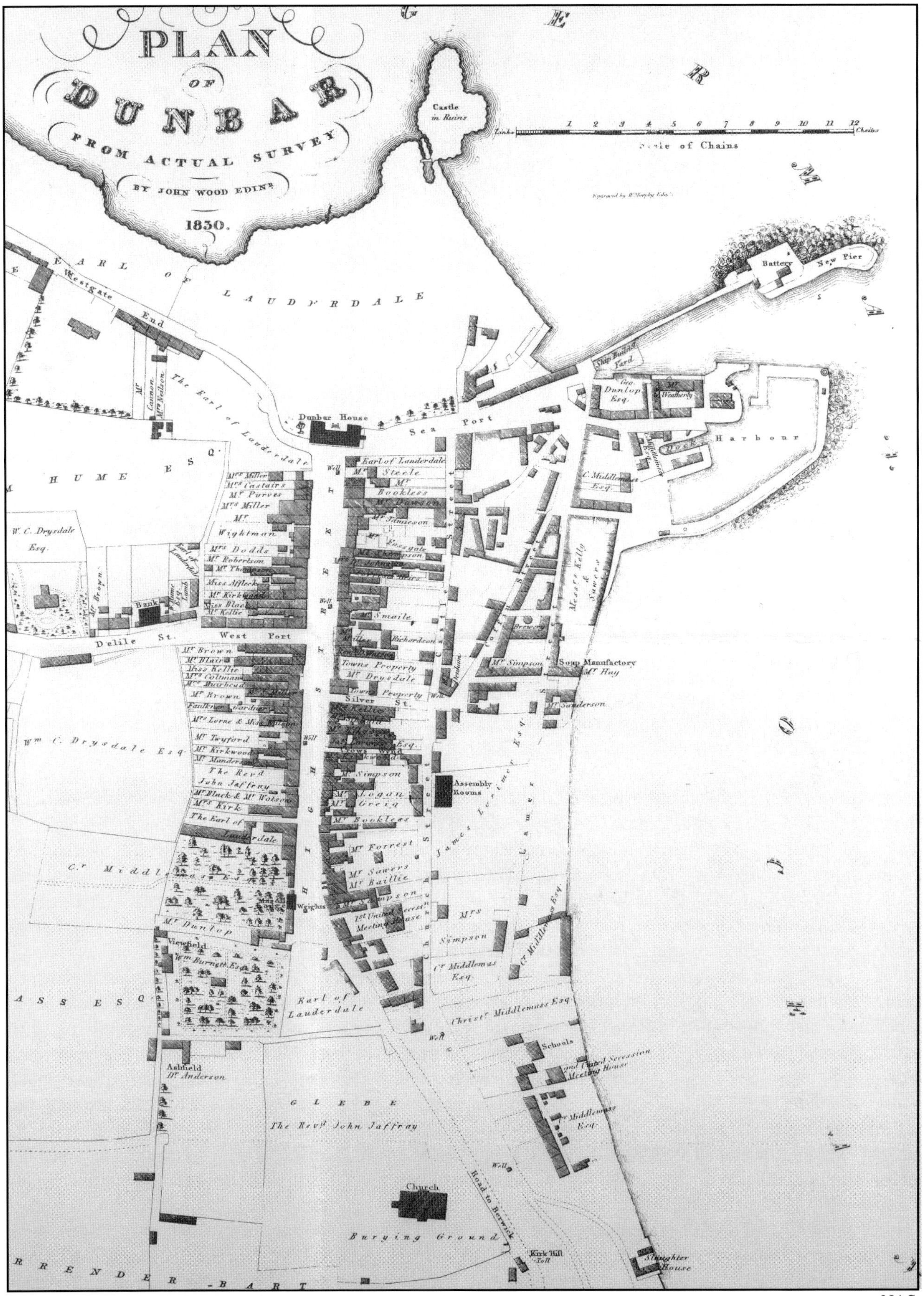

NAS

Illus 62: *John Wood's town plan of Dunbar, 1830*

century, merchants began to extend their houses into the street, incorporating their business premises which fronted them. Before then, business was largely conducted from temporary stalls with trestle tables to display goods at fairs and markets until finally, the merchants created permanent shops and incorporated them into their houses. Expansion was strictly controlled however and the burgh authorities took care to ensure that the High Street conformed to straight parallel lines.

Despite efforts by the burgh council to control the threat to public health from discarded refuse, sanitation was deplorable until the passing of several public health acts in the mid to late nineteenth century. The stews in the High Street, backstreets and closes were infamous; offal from the shops and abattoir, night soil from houses and general household and shop waste were dumped on the pavements - where they existed. It got so bad that large boulders were placed in the main thoroughfare - of beaten clay or earth until 1737 - to act as stepping stones to get from one side of the street to the other, a practice used in Pompeii up to its destruction by Vesuvius in 79AD. The High Street was often clogged with rubbish, excrement - human and animal - animals' heads, bones and entrails, rotten fish and fruit and vegetables, all of which not only gave off noxious smells but spread disease. To control the nuisance, the burgh council repeatedly issued bylaws and regulations but the very frequency of these is a telling comment on their effectiveness. Scavengers or muck-rakers were employed to collect the refuse and cart it away to the town refuse pit. Cesspits were regularly inspected and cleaned and gradually, public health improved. In the years up to the twentieth century, people washed less frequently and hardly any houses had running water or lavatories so there was a constant risk for passers-by in the street from the contents of slop pails emptied from the tenements to the shrill cry of *gardyloo*! often delivered too late. In the seventeenth century, most burghs were mean, dirty places containing broken-down hovels, ruinous and often empty tenements with middens at every corner or convenient nook and cranny. It is surprising that a large proportion of the population managed to escape the ravages of cholera and other fatal diseases.

At one time, animals were slaughtered in the streets, their carcasses and offal added to the filth which in summer stank to high heaven, was covered with flies that turned the public streets into a veritable breeding-ground for disease. Sickness was rife until sensible measures were taken - the creation of a slaughterhouse off the High Street and the regular removal of waste. Even so, it wasn't until the end of the nineteenth century that effective public health legislation was introduced, making it possible to impose realistic and collectable fines on those who transgressed the laws. Before that, it was left to the diligence of the local authorities themselves. An example of this occurred on 11th October 1773, when the Dunbar magistrates decreed that unless rubbish was removed from the streets within eight days of their public order to do so, a fine of sixpence (just over 2p) a day was payable. In August 1810, medical officers petitioned the burgh council to prevent the spread of disease by removing decaying animal and herring offal and vegetables every day to a distance of half a mile from the town; clearly, the earlier measures had been ineffective and a considerable amount of backsliding had occurred. The council immediately agreed to the doctors' request, intimating that it would prosecute offenders.

Not unexpectedly, cholera epidemics broke out; on 8th November 1831, the council was urged to take whatever steps were necessary to provide clean water and erect additional privvies. A soup kitchen was set up in 1832 by the local Cholera Committee to which the town contributed £10 for feeding over 100 paupers. At this time, no cases of cholera had been found in Dunbar but at West Barns 'the disease had been peculiarly fatal.' On 4th October 1832, the magistrates' minute-book recorded the death of Councillor George Turnbull, a local surgeon who died of 'asiatic cholera' in the course of his duties at East Barns. Smallpox was another killer, especially among the young; two schoolchildren died of the disease in 1874.

One of the earliest measures to rid the High Street of rubbish took place in the first half of the eighteenth century when the local medical officer recommended that the town's abattoir situated at the rear of the tolbooth on the left of Silver Street facing the sea should be moved some distance away. That there was such a place so close to human habitation is perhaps confirmed by an iron ring set in the wall at approximately the former site of the slaughterhouse. There has been much speculation about the purposes of this ring; some believe it was used to haul carts up the hill or to anchor them halfway to give the horses a rest. My view is that the ring was used to tether animals waiting to be slaughtered.

More effective measures to deal with public health came late in Scotland's development. First was the Public Health (Scotland) Act 1867 which gave parochial boards such functions as the keeping in good condition of waterworks, sewers, the prevention and mitigation of disease and the provision of local hospitals. Other legislation quickly followed but the main measure, the Public Health (Scotland) Act 1897, introduced a wide range of services which were to be provided by local authorities to reduce the incidence of diseases which had plagued earlier generations. At about this time, the burgh council used the old Battery at the Victoria Harbour as an isolation hospital; on the OS map of 1907, it is described as a 'casual sick house.'

A typical example of the regulations the magistrates drew up from time to time appears in the council minutes of 3rd December 1814; the wording has been modernised for easier reading:

'A magistrate and constable were to walk the streets on the Sabbath to ensure that no shops were selling excisable liquor and to apprehend any disorderly persons'

presumably those suffering from excessive drink taken the night before. The public wells in the street were to be shut during divine service and no one was permitted to carry water in cogs or pails. All articles were to be sold by English weight except for fresh butter which was allowed to contain 22 ounces to the pound - somewhat confusing for the shopkeeper and shopper alike. The following items were to be sold by Dutch weight:

'butcher meat of all kinds;
fresh or salt green fish;
oatmeal;
barley meal and mixed meal
undressed flour.

Coal was to be sold by weight of 11 hundredweight English to the boll.

Fishermen were ordered to sell their catches to the local people for one hour before selling them to retailers.

Potatoes delivered and sold in the burgh were to weigh 28 pounds English per peck, or 448 pounds English by the boll.

Bakers were to make twopenny, threepenny and sixpenny loaves to correspond to the weight of the Quartern loaf - weight to be inspected.

Publicans keeping disorderly houses would receive a reprimand for the first offence; a fine for the second and their licence removed after a third.

All strangers trading within the burgh were classified as *stallangers* [ie foreign or non-burgh dwellers who were permitted to set up stalls under licence bought from the council for a few shillings every year].

No carpets were to be shaken in the street after 7am in summer and 9am in winter otherwise a fine of five shillings [25p] would be imposed.

All dung was to be removed from where it was deposited to the land for which it was intended as manure otherwise a penalty of five shillings would be levied.

No person was allowed to throw filth or riddled ashes from domestic fires in the streets or pavements after 7am in summer and 9am in winter; the penalty was five shillings and the person's riddle would be confiscated.

All persons driving horses or cattle with wanton cruelty would be fined not less than five shillings.

No boys or other persons were to drive hoops or girds nor play at shinty nor make slides in time of frost, nor throw stones by hand or with a sling nor discharge firearms (!) under penalty of five shillings; crowds of boys who stood in pavements and obstructed people or insulted them would be cease doing so or be fined two shillings and sixpence

(Perhaps those who today are concerned about Human Rights might pause to ponder the wisdom of early nineteenth century legislators who didn't need to use physical violence to keep their young in check - effectively).

Dogs belonging to carters were to be kept under control.

No foul linen, fish or other dirty articles were to be washed in the public wells otherwisea fine of sixpence would be charged for each offence.

Loose horses were not to drink at public wells otherwise owners would be charged one shilling (5p) for each horse.'

The regulation about washing foul linen in public may be the derivation of the popular proverb!

Dunbar took care with and was proud of its fine main street. The houses of stone with their ordered facades gave the High Street a classical appearance. Prior to 1737, the street was of beaten earth or clay with stepping stones to allow pedestrians to cross without getting their feet or clothes soiled. We know it was causewayed or cobbled in 1737 and again in 1769-70. (Further improvements to the street were carried out in 1835, when on 20th April, the burgh council decided to re-pave both sides of the High Street and the West Port at an estimated cost of £700 to be raised by public subscription, chiefly from the proprietors of shops on the stretch of the pavements fronting their premises). In 1766, water was piped - first in wooden, then in lead pipes - from St John's Well at Spott to provide a clean public supply. Then in 1772, water was piped to the Bleachfield. In 1798, Dunbar obtained its first horse-drawn fire engine, the firemaster being George Combe, a local blacksmith. By then, Dunbar was a thriving market town and shopping centre, family shopkeepers having largely replaced the door-to-door travelling chapmen.

In 1785, street lighting was introduced, making Dunbar one of the first burghs to do so; many fairly large towns didn't light their streets until the third decade of the nineteenth century. In 1790, James Miller, ironmonger and elder brother of the printer and publisher George Miller was made a burgess and awarded the contract for tending the whale or paraffin oil street lamps in winter. On 18th September 1811, a cost conscious council decided in their wisdom that the town streets could be adequately lit by 38 lamps in all; this was reduced to seven lamps twenty years later. A few years after that, the council minutes record the council's thanks to those members of the council who had collected subscriptions from the inhabitants - probably the local traders who wanted lights in front of their shops - to meet the cost of lighting the streets in the winter months. In 1826, the Dunbar Gas and Light Company was formed to provide gaslight in the High Street. In 1886, the Burgh Council took over the company and formed the Dunbar Gas Company, its offices situated in the Edinburgh Road just beyond Doon Avenue road-end, two large gasometers being installed in what was then known as the Sailors' Park. The High Street was first to be lit by gas, then the tenements and harbour area, followed by the council housing estatates built between 1930 and 1935. For many years up to the mid-twentieth century, Dunbar's streets were lit by gas which required *leeries* (lamplighters) employed by the Gas Company to light and extinguish every lamp.

With a little imagination, it isn't difficult to picture the High Street in autumn and winter just over a century ago. In the months between October and March, particularly in winter, the afternoons grew dark early. By December, the gaslights would flicker into life, answered by the gas lamps in the shop windows that cast their pools of light on the cobbled stones. People went about their business, women dressed in long skirts that brushed the pavements as they hurried along with heavy shopping baskets on their arms. The few horse-drawn carts and fewer coaches and carriages occasioned the ladies to keep to the inside of the pavements to avoid being splashed by these passing vehicles. When the school came out, the relative quiet of the street would echo with the shouts of schoolchildren playing games or going home to do their homework. A few boys would dump their schoolbags and come out again to start work as delivery boys employed by the local shops, running with baskets on their heads and dressed in the white aprons supplied by their employers - the butchers, bakers and grocers. By 6pm, the street would be quiet again, the wet streets deserted save for a patrolling policeman and the shop owners locking their doors to hurry home for the evening meal by the fireside, their parlours also lit by gas.

Domestic gaslight and gas cooking were the norm in council and private homes until the early 1950s, when gas was replaced by electricity and the romantic appeal of the old lamps was lost forever. Electric lighting and power - for those who could afford it - were introduced to Dunbar by the Lothian Electrical Supply Company in 1925.

All these improvements may have led directly or indirectly to an increase in the town's population; while infant mortality was still unacceptably high until the early twentieth century, adults were beginning to live longer as can be seen from the following population census:

1755	3281	1831	4735*
1792	3700#	1881	5396
1801	3951	1911	4830
1811	4114	1931	5062
1821	5272	1951	5440

The writer of the Dunbar entry for the *Old Statistical Account for Scotland* complains that the figure might have been higher - and more accurate - as 'many neglect to get the names of their children entered in the public register.'
* The reduction may have been caused by the closure of the cotton mills at Belhaven which gave work to mainly Irish immigrants who moved to other burghs seeking work

Before examining some of the municipal and privately-owned buildings in and around Dunbar, it is appropriate here to discuss some of the features and amenities which were common to most royal burghs.

Mercat or Market Cross

What mercat cross? There isn't one. On the right hand side of the Town House stands what at first sight might appear to have been the mercat cross but it is too small (**ill 63**). Professional opinion is that the 'cross' is in fact a fake - or more accurately, it is made up of two sections - the base which is reputed to be that of the castle cross - no doubt the cross itself was snapped off by overzealous converts to the new Protestant faith after 1560, possibly in 1568, when the castle was dismantled on the orders of parliament the previous year; the upper part is a skewput thought to have come from the Collegiate Church which was demolished in 1819. The badly worn and grotesque faces are almost certainly medieval. It is believed that these genuine artefacts were found in the

Illus 63: *The fake mercat cross outside the Town House, Dunbar* KRM

garden to the rear of the former Commercial Bank in the High Street, now the Royal Bank, at the beginning of the twentieth century and someone in his wisdom decided to knit them together to either preserve them or to compensate for the missing mercat cross. When the modern police station was built at Castellau, the fake cross was probably placed on the vacated site to give added character to the town house without interfering with the growing modern traffic. The original mercat cross stood at or close to the West Port where most of the tolls and taxes were collected and deposited in the town house. The site of the cross had to be both convenient, practical and dominant in the High Street; all proclamations and local announcements were made from the mercat cross which also served as a rallying point for the medieval *wapinschaws.*

So what happened to the original mercat cross? We need look no further that the burgh council minutes for 26th August 1736 which recommended that

> 'the [Mercat] Cross and the Trone.....be removid [removed] as being *a sort of common nuisance* [my italics] by obstructing the passage on the [High] Street.'

It is regrettable that the town fathers who made their fortunes from the very symbol of the town's trade acted in this way, but progress then and now inevitably has its casualties. This is how the council dealt with the problem. The slaughterhouse to the rear of the tolbooth was converted first into a meat market, then used for the sale of butter, cheese, poultry and eggs

> 'commonly now sold at the Cross'

which meant that the cross had become redundant in 1736 and could be disposed of. What we might now regard as official vandalism did not end there however; it was later agreed to construct a new slaughterhouse at the foot of the yard above the dung pit - both sited to the rear of the tolbooth. In 1744, the council minutes of 24th December record that the existing well at the top of Silver Street would be *lined with the stones of the cross* [my italics]

> 'as far as the same will go.'

So the original mercat cross lies underneath the junction of Silver Street and the High Street! The minutes fail to inform us as to the fate of the 'Trone' or weighing beam although it still existed in 1830; a replica of a tron used at markets can be seen at the nearby village of Stenton.

Town Wall

Although the earliest royal burghs like Perth were enclosed with stout stone walls specifically for defence, the 'walls' in many of the smaller towns were little more than low earth and wooden ramparts with delineated gaps or portes for exit and entrance. Dunbar was first enclosed by an earth dyke in 1550-1551, then at some point between the sixteenth or seventeenth centuries, a stone wall was built; the date of its construction is difficult to establish. At Dunbar, the prime consideration would have been defence, given its proximity to the English border; even so, a secondary and later major function of the wall was to regulate the flow of human and animal traffic, the ports or gates being the focal points for tax-collections. In 1503, an act of parliament directed all Forth seaports to erect walls of stone and lime down to the sea. We know from the *Acts of the Lords in Council in Public Afffairs* (1501-54) (*ADCP*) that in December 1550 an earth wall was ordered to be built at Dunbar 'for strenthing [sic] and fortificatioun' possible because of the recent invasion by the English known in Scotland as the *Rough Wooing*. *ADCP* states that 197 roods (about 50 acres) were enclosed by the earth wall. We also know that a stone wall was in being by 1669, confirmed by James Brome (see Chapter 3); a medical officer accompanying Cumberland's army also commented on it in 1746 (see *Miller, Dunbar*). A fragment of the wall was discovered near No 25 High Street in 1949. The westward limit appears to have bounded the burgage plots to the rear of the west side of the High Street, running along Monks' Walk and Lawson Place, at right angles to the West Port. The wall was reputedly interrupted here and there by gaps which allowed the town's cattle to gain access to grazing in the Bleachfield. At the eastern end of the High Street, the wall probably followed what are now Church and Castle Streets near Bamburgh Close. It is unlikely that the stone wall extended further than the former Free or Abbey Church, the site of the *maison de dieu* which places the wall near No 25 High Street and located close to the site of the former East Port at Kirkhill, after which the prestigious house known as Port Lodge, near Logan's Close, was probably named.

Ports and Tollgates

Irrespective of whether Dunbar's municipal wall was of earth or stone, built originally for defensive purposes, its subsequent function was to prevent unsupervised or unauthorised entry to the burgh. People, goods and animals were admitted only by designated gates or ports where taxes were collected and goods entering or leaving the burgh could be inspected to ensure that the appropriate tax had been paid on them. There were three ports at Dunbar, the busiest being the West Port; the East Port is mentioned above and the North Port was probably situated at or near the top of Victoria Street, near Dunbar House, later known as Lauderdale House, where sea -borne imports and exports were also checked to make sure customs duty had been paid. Thus the ports not only controlled the flow of traffic, they were also customs posts. (It is perhaps appropriate here to mention the legendary passage which supposedly provided an underground escape route from the castle to No 25 High Street. My theory is that there may well have been such a passage but it wasn't an escape route from the castle; why escape into the midst of an enemy besieging you? It is more likely that a passage of sorts existed at some time to carry contraband goods from the harbour area to the High Street. Once these goods were beyond the North Port, they would have been distributed to their buyers - inns and individuals - thus avoiding customs duty. Times have not changed....).

Tollgates were set up outside the burgh, often as much as a mile away; this was to ensure that people and animals whose destination wasn't Dunbar didn't pass through the parish bounds without paying the turnpike tolls. One of the most lucrative sources of revenue for the burgh were the customs charged on animals, irrespective of whether they were bound for the Dunbar market for sale or slaughter or were simply being herded along its roads to another market. When a herd of cattle or a flock of sheep passed through a customs area such as Dunbar, the tollgate keeper collected the tax stipulated by the locally-determined scale of charges. For example, the tax due for every ten sheep, goats or swine might be a penny; a wagon and four oxen might attract fourpence; there were different charges made for persons on foot and on horseback, laden and unladen. The burghs claimed their right of levying duty on people, goods and animals passing through their bounds until the railways were built, when burghs waived their right to make charges on goods etc carried by the railway companies in return for lump sum compensatory payment.

Those with business within the burgh itself paid their toll tax and were given a metal token by the tollkeeper to prove to the keeper of the port that the appropriate toll charge had been paid; the token was returned at the tollgate of exit. Taxes and tolls charged by burghs were known as *tolsylvir*, the Petty Customs paid on goods traded locally or entering and leaving the burgh bounds. These taxes were collected by the tacksman or tollkeeper. Tacksmen resident in Dunbar stood at each port's Stent Stone - no example has survived at Dunbar, the tollkeepers living near the tollgates, of which there were three on the outskirts of Dunbar. One was at the Kirkhill, next to the Parish Church; the second was at Belhaven - known within living memory to bus drivers and their conductors as Belhaven Toll - and the third was Cleikimin Toll [cleik = to watch in Old Scots] at the crossroads where the Spott Road connects with the modern roundabout on the A1 bypass. (Cleikimin Road branched off the main A1 at Beltonford, following what is now the main bypass road).

The burgh benefited from the collection of what might be termed road tolls but the money wasn't necessarily used for the upkeep of the local roads which in the eighteenth century was the responsibility of turnpike managers empowered by statute to levy tolls for repairs and improvements. In the changing tax-raising climate of 1835, the imposition of tolls on road traffic ceased to be a burgh prerogative; on 27th May 1835, Dunbar petitioned parliament against a bill not only proposing to authorise Midlothian Roads Trust to charge two tolls instead of the single charge on the Great Post Road which ran through East Lothian to Edinburgh but to increase the charges due for the part of the road that ran through the county. The burgh council argued that the community had long enjoyed the privilege of a single toll and, in its opinion, the existing charge was adequate for keeping the road in good repair. The appeal was successful and the Haddingtonshire MP, Robert Stewart informed the council by letter that the offending clause had been removed from the Bill. The Roads and Bridges (Scotland) Act 1878 finally abolished both tolls and statute labour in relation to the main highways and set up county road trustees which consisted of commissioners, elected representatives from every parish ratepayer and others from burghs in the county which didn't manage the roads themselves.

Markets and Fairs

Royal burghs usually consisted of a wide main street to accommodate the weekly markets which in Dunbar probably took place at or near the Town House or Tolbooth, where taxes and tolls were deposited; to the rear of the Tolbooth was a slaughterhouse and dung-heap. The market place would have been centred on the mercat cross and the tron, the latter being used to weigh grain, coal and other heavy goods under the close supervision of the *metsters* mentioned earlier. There were also likely to have been temporary stalls and booths erected near these focal points on market days and at the periodic fairs held in the burgh. In the nineteenth century, temporary stallholders from outwith the burgh - known as *stallangers* - were able to trade at fairs and markets provided they purchased a licence to do so from the burgh council. During the Middle Ages, the weekly market must have been a colourful and lively event. Permeated by strong smells - perspiring bodies, the pungent, reeking smell of steaming cattle, animal droppings, rotten fruit, onions, leeks, herbs and the hot yeasty smell of freshly baked bread, meat pies and gingerbread. Then as now, the vendors vied with each other, haggling with their customers over prices shouted aloud. Would their cries have differed much from today's open markets and auctions?

'See what you lack! Will you buy?
Apples, lovely ripe apples, juicy pears! Ribbons! Fine cloth! Cakes! Ale!
Meat pies, all juicy and hot! Fat chickens!

And of course at Dunbar

'Poos! [crabs] ! Lobsters! Herrings, lovely fresh herrings! Come buy the silver darlings!'

All this to an accompaniment of bells ringing, cattle lowing, pigs grunting, hens [known as cloakers in these parts] clucking and scratching for spilt grain, dogs barking, children shouting, laughing and whistling. Shoppers jostled each other as they poked in sacks and baskets, picking up and smelling fish for freshness, knocking an escaping lobster or crab back into a barrel, inspecting cooking pots, buckets, candles, leather goods - all spread out on the stalls or the ground. Market days were a mass of heaving, pushing, squabbling, brawling, unwashed humanity; most of the men ended up in the local alehouses at the end of the day, comparing their purchases, counting their money, getting drunk and singing all the way home.

In 1641, the Scottish parliament altered Dunbar's market day from Fridays to Thursdays so that it didn't coincide with Haddington's market day.[14] The day was changed again in 1831, when the local authorities decided that the market for grain, dairy produce, poultry, pigeons and rabbits would be held on Tuesdays from 10am until noon. Fairs were held on Whitsunday in May, 8th September and 11th November (Martinmas) under royal charter. *Miller, Dunbar* tells us that the Whitsun Fair was marked by the boys of the burgh who decorated the town ports with flowers. When the Black Death came to Scotland in 1349-50, markets and fairs were cancelled by parliament for obvious reasons. In 1580 and 1584, the Privy Council ordered all fairs to be suspended because of outbreaks of the Pest or plague; the Council also ordered a Scottish vessel out of Norway and berthed at Dunbar in 1618 to return there as it had plague on board. In 1637, the Privy Council ordered Roxburgh and Selkirk people to stay away from the herring drave at Dunbar because plague was rife in both these towns.[15] In the nineteenth century, the great scourges were cholera and smallpox. The burgh council took such steps as they could to curtail the spread of these diseases but prevention was very difficult especially since epidemiology and cure were still in their infancy.

Granaries and Custom House

Illus 64: *The Old Custom House, Dunbar* HLHC

These once important buildings no longer exist, casualties of modern development. Spot's Granary at the harbour was the store for grain from the surrounding farms at Innerwick, Oldhamstocks and Stenton. It was probably financed to some extent by those who owned land in these parishes - men like Nisbet of Dirleton whose tenants farmed Innerwick and who insisted his tenants bring his share of the grain to Dunbar for transport by sea. The Granary site now accommodates modern flats but the name has been retained. A smaller granary in Shore Street once known as the *Dreadnought* opposite the Maltings (now Cromwell Anchorage) was built in 1817 by the enterprising

Christopher Middlemas, the prominent merchant who succeeded the Falls of Dunbar and served on the burgh council in various capacities, chiefly that of provost, between 1789 and 1848. The Custom House (**ill 64**) needs no explanation; built in 1710, it housed the local customs and excise officer until the last century. By the twentieth century, it had deteriorated so badly that it too had to be demolished.

Slaughterhouses and Public Wells

Every burgh was required to have a public slaughterhouse - an essential if unattractive building. Dunbar's main slaughterhouse was once situated at the top of Silver Street, then at the seashore near the East Links below Kirkhill Toll and finally on the Spott Road. There were five public wells, three of which were situated at various points in the High Street and two along the sea road towards the golf course. At the south end of the town was the weight beam or tron, situated in the exit road between the Barns Ness - formerly the Royal, then the Royal Mackintosh - Hotel and the Dolphin public house, which incorporated the former Railway Hotel in the 1960s.

Common or Town Land

As a royal burgh, Dunbar owned land which belonged to the community at large - in theory at any rate - so that any revenues deriving from it was paid into the Common Good Fund administered by the burgh council. Dunbar once possessed an Inner Common and an Outer Common, although the latter didn't amount to much and appears to have served little purpose other than to give the provost and the council an excuse to take a day's holiday every year to ride in the Lammermuir Hills to mark the town's boundary. In 1834, the burgh council decided to sell its holding in the Outer or Dunbar Common; the land was chiefly used for grazing sheep and had an annual value of £37:14:3 (£37.71) so it was proposed to sell it outright for £838 sterling.[16] The Inner Common was worth much more, being productive and used to graze the town cattle and those belonging to local burgesses.

The burgesses jealously guarded their common right to pasture; it was first mooted in 1835 that any railway line laid between Edinburgh and Glasgow should be extended to Dunbar and Berwick, which in Dunbar's case would impinge on common land. This proposal came to nothing at the time, so a possible conflict between the burgesses and the council never materialised. Two years later, the burgh council considered another proposal to sell common land to the railway company. This elicited a strongly-worded petition from the Dunbar burgesses on the future of the Inner Common

> 'which from time immemorial has been pastured by the Horses and Cows
> belonging to the Burgesses of the Town.'

The burgesses took legal advice which was to the effect that the town common could neither be sold or burdened with town debt; the right of pasture was thus upheld - for the time being. A few years later, virtually all of the town's land would be sold to meet the burgh's share of the cost of building the New or Victoria Harbour in 1844. Before that however, the burgesses complained again on 8th May 1839 because a council committee had been given the responsibility for deciding when cattle should enter and leave the grazing on the Inner Common. The burgesses weren't consulted on an issue which they rightly felt they were more entitled to judge. Perhaps the real cause for conflict was the continuing levy of ten shillings and sixpence per annum (52p) which was levied on every animal grazing the common, a charge originally introduced to meet the cost of enclosing the common with a stone wall, remnants of which survived well into the twentieth century. In the burgesses' considered opinion, the wall had been paid for long ago; they also complained that their servants were being ill-treated by the local fishermen who had a right to spread their nets on the common in order to repair them. The burgesses said they were perfectly willing to pay the wall tax provided the money went towards improving the area. By 1788, the greater part of the Common consisted of Gallows'Green (identified as such on the OS survey map of 1907) now Gala Green), what became known as the Bleachfield in Countess Park and the Kirkhill near the Parish Kirk. The town also owned small parcels of land elsewhere in the burgh, including the land occupied by the town mills at West Barns. (Perhaps it is appropriate here to mention the various industries at West Barns. In adddition to the Dunbar flour mill on the left side of the road to Edinburgh, almost opposite the modern West Barns Inn was a cotton mill; the flour mill was on the site of the modern Sheriff Agricultural Factory; on the other side of the road behind West Barns Inn were a brewery and distillery, a flax mill and the prestigious Distillery House which, with its Palladian stone columns, compares favourably with the plantation mansions of the Deep South depicted in the film *Gone With the Wind* set in the time of the American Civil War. There were also saltings on either side of the Biel Burn, near the modern electricity sub-station as well as brickworks and a cement factory which operated on a small scale behind the inn at West Barns).

In 1844, the Inner Common did not amount to more than 50 acres. A drying green, wash-houses and well were created at the Bleachfield in 1758; in 1802, the east area is described in the saisines as Jean Airth's croft, with three dwelling houses to the west of Lady Wynd, a site owned in 1805 by Jane Lamb of Tyninghame.

Before the Bleachfield was established, the land had been used for grazing. Other small, isolated plots such as the area then known as the Burrowdales [Boroughdales] near the Edinburgh Road was owned by Charles and Robert Fall who sold ten acres to the town for £369 in the second half of the eighteenth century. The Falls also owned land at Gunsgreen, near Gala Green, Underedge on the Dunbar Common; the seadykes at West Barns opposite Stenton Road was owned by Robert Fall's widow Magdalen. Some areas are mentioned in thirteenth century records e.g. Rig, Fleurus [Rigg and Floors] and Priestis Fauld [Knockenhair]. By the mid-nineteenth century, most of the town land and those parts owned privately had changed hands.

It is now appropriate to briefly describe some of the prominent buildings in and around Dunbar, some of which, like the tolbooth were made possible by tax generation or were built by prosperous businessmen and landowners who benefited from and contributed to the wealth of the burgh, many re-channelling a proportion of their wealth into the parish church as church heritors Most of the buildings described below which survive were built well before the beginning of the twentieth century and are of red sandstone, which was readily available locally. A belt of bright Old Red Sandstone runs through the Lammermuir Hills to Stenton and Bowerhouse, the latter for many years having a quarry which probably provided the stone for the castle built by James IV in 1497, both versions of the tolbooth between the fifteenth and sixteenth centuries and the new parish church in 1821. The stone has also given the local soil its distinctive red colour and richness in texture and fertility.

West Port and High Street

Entering Dunbar from the west, on the left is the impressive if somewhat gloomy Castellau House, named for the family who built it in the eighteenth century. Empty for many years, it was a First Aid Post and trained personnel in Air Raid Precautions and gas contamination attacks during the Second World War; it now houses the town library. On the right is **Friarscroft** of which all that remains of the former Trinitarian or Red Friar religious settlement is the tower of the thirteenth century church which stood between the nave and the choir, a building which had a fine tiled floor.[17] Nearby **Parson's Pool**, named from the deep depression which is now a children's play park - probably provided the monks with fish such as carp. Connected with Friarscroft but not shown on modern maps or plans was a path which once led from there to the High Street, then resumed its way to Church Street. The path or walk no longer exists because of commercial and housing developments; in 1958, I recollect clearing away undergrowth and rubbish to the rear of Lipton's Grocery Shop, now Ladbroke's (No 77 High Street) to reveal a stone plaque in the wall which identified the former vennel as St James' Walk - probably so-named by the Red Friars who used it.

The next prestigious building is No. 3 Delisle Street - named for Philip Delisle, an officer in the 13th Regiment of Dragoons who lived in Dunbar in the eighteenth century. (Was he a relative of the aristocratic family de L'Isle in England?) Now known as Croft House, it once housed the British Linen Bank; a late Georgian building, it has five bays and a flanking block with an archway leading to the former stables. Opposite Lawson Place is Friarbank Terrace which is adjacent to Monk's Walk, which aligns with the remnant of the Town Wall; on the corner of the building is a stone-carved plaque informing us that the tenement was built in AD 1879. At the junction of the West Port with the High Street is No. 94 High Street, another impressive building. Built of red sandstone in 1891, it accommodated a family butcher shop on the ground floor with flatted accommodation on several floors above; it has a turreted frontage with crow-step gables to the south

Illus 65: *High St. Dunbar looking east c.1900* RJP

There are a multitude of photographs of the High Street dating from the mid-nineteenth century, showing the cobbled street and gas lamps. One dating from about 1900 (**ill 65**) appears to have been taken during the funeral of some important person, judging by the large carriage in the centre and the mounted procession following it. Although it is impossible to substantiate when the High Street was created, we know from the visit of Jorevin de Rochefort (Chapter 3) that it existed in the mid-seventeenth century. (A street of sorts must have existed in the thirteenth century, as provisions for the castle would have been taken by that way. Also, if we accept that the Tolbooth was around in the mid-fifteenth century and associated with the main tax-gathering West Port, a High Street of sorts has been around for nearly six centuries.

Tolbooth or Town House

The tolbooth was the ultimate symbol of burgh status. It served as a council meeting place, court-house, toll house, town jail, police station, burgh record depository and finally, a library. The present building is thought to date from the early seventeenth century (c.1610) on account of its architectural style, the Dutch influence of crow-stepped gables becoming popular at that time. However, an earlier version existed, probably in the mid-fifteenth century, when Dunbar was elevated to full royal burgh status; to some extent, this is confirmed by its Tudor-style entrance. The Tudor period is generally accepted as occurring between 1400 and 1600, which accommodates the likely existence of a tolbooth in 1445. Extensively rebuilt and possibly enlarged in about 1610, it is Dunbar's - East Lothian's and possibly Scotland's - oldest civic building still in use. A glance at the frontage gives us an unmistakeable sense of age, antiquity and a charm not often found in Scottish municipal architecture. Built of red freestone in Renaissance style, it calls attention to itself as any important building should. The hexagonal tower is two storeys high with dormer windows; the ground floor was vaulted and there is a narrow winding stair near the entrance which leads to the upper storeys. Contemporary accounts state that the first (i.e. ground) floor housed the town jailer, the second (i.e. first) floor contained two jails and the third (i.e. second) floor accommodated the town chambers and court room. Access to the first floor jails was by a stout wooden door whose lock appears to have been deliberately attached upside down - possibly to confuse any would-be escapee who managed to acquire the key! At some point, a purpose-built jailer's house was created to the rear of the building. The two cells on the first floor are of different sizes; it is virtually certain that suspected witches were incarcerated in the smaller cell, as there are no windows to offer a means of escape - after all, it was believed that witches could fly! The municipal offices were situated in the first floor of the adjacent building, added in 1928 to extend the original burgh chambers which were accessed by the internal stairway from the jails. The council minutes of 12th February 1686 indicate an intention to paint the

'kings armes at the bak of the Counsell table'

these being the arms of James VII and II 1686; the royal Hanoverian arms of 1714 were a later addition and

Illus 66: *The Town House c.1900* NMS

Illus 67: *The Town House c.1900* RJP

both murals may be seen in what were the council chambers until burgh councils were abolished in 1975. On the side of the clock tower which overlooks Silver Street, windows look out from the town jailer's house and the cells; the spiral stone staircase continues to the council chambers where the burgh court sat until 1974. As can be seen from (**ill 66**) the local police station was added to the side of the tower nearest Silver Street; on the other side was a local watchmaker's shop. From 1947, the town library was housed in a separate and temporary wooden building on the ground floor to the rear until the early 1960s.

The exterior features crow-stepped gables, which as indicated above is an example of the Dutch architectural style which became popular in Scotland in the late sixteenth and early seventeenth centuries, particularly in communities like Dunbar and Culross, Fife, both of which enjoyed extensive trade with Holland. The semi-hexagonal clock tower has a conical roof which looks like an eighteenth century candle-snuffer and is topped by a cockerel weather vane; the spire is not the original and is pierced by oval *lucarnes.* There are two clock faces and sundials set beneath the steeple and here and there, small square windows. In 1913 the external rendering was removed in a misguided attempt to enhance the building's appeal. This has been done to many older Scottish buildings presumably to give them an air of antiquity, however in point of fact, most of these buildings were lime-rendered externally. Since the stonework was exposed, the fabric of the tolbooth at Dunbar is visibly deteriorating and will require attention before long. For many generations, the building has been known simply as the Town Clock (**ill 67**), where local people gather at Hogmanay to say goodbye to one year and welcome in the next.

The modern clock works extremely well. It wasn't always so. On 29th March 1720, the council minutes record that the Town Clock was causing problems which Baillie Charles Fall brought to the council's attention. He reported that after winding, the clock had to be rewound eight or nine hours later. Worse than that, it intefered withthe smooth running of council meetings as

> 'The noises come down the stair leading to the Council *Houfe* [house] which is both unconvenient [sic] and dangerous, and that going with [out?] a Ballance, her motion, *Efspecially* in high winds is very irregular, and the Belman [sic] has very much difficulty to obtain any just measure of time if the sun does not shine on the Dyall [dial]'

Presumably a reasonable estimate of time could be derived using the thing as a sundial; however, back to the minutes

> 'For remedying of these defaults the said Baillie Fall had concerted with one William Berrie Clockmaker in Edinburgh that the Town Clock might be made to go thirty or thirty four hours. After once winding up the noises [would] come no further than the underfloor of the Bellhouse and being fixed with a pendillum may measure time more Ju*f*tly and in order thereunto as also for the Equall Divi*f*ion of time betwixt hours that a minute hand may be fixed for performing of which work the Clockmaker demands that the soum[sum] of Six pounds Sterling and to furnish all materials iron and bra*fs*'

The council agreed with Fall's proposals and the clock was duly 'modernised '!

It is interesting to learn that the burgh council, in discussing a proposal to create new schools at Dunbar on 18th November 1813 decided to issue subscription lists for cash, then on 21st December agreed to demolish the town house and erect a new one on the same site. In the process, it was mooted that the new building should extend over Silver Street to join with the tenements opposite. The extension was to have held the council chambers and a new school. Thankfully, these proposals came to nothing. Even so, as late as 1818, George Miller, the local printer, was asked to prepare a subscription appeal but the project was finally dropped. The existing building was listed in 1951; it has character, style and charm. Today it is used for entirely appropriate purposes; it houses the Town Museum and Dunbar and District History Society; the latter rightly despairs of their inadequate accommodation which severely restricts the display of photographs and memorabilia they have collected in less than a decade since the society was formed.

Dunbar (Lauderdale) House

Illus 68: *Lauderdale House from the High St, Dunbar c.1900* DDHS

A friend recently asked me this question. Which came first, Dunbar (Lauderdale) House to align with an already established High Street or was the High Street laid out to conform to it? The answer is probably the former. We know that Dunbar had a 'fine large street' above the harbour from the account of Jorevin de Rocheford who visited Dunbar in c.1661 (see Chapter 3). Dunbar House - colloquially known in the eighteenth century as Dunbar Castle - built in either 1734 or 1740 by Captain James Fall, MP, one of the Fall merchant princes of Dunbar.[18] Over a period, Captain Fall acquired the five burgage plots which occupied the site (My guess is that James Fall built his house in 1734. A staunch Whig and Provost of Dunbar in 1706 as we know from the Court of Session records of that year, Fall and Sir James Suttie of Balgowan became bondsmen for the heirs of the estates of James, 6th Earl of Dunfermline who was forfeited in 1690 for supporting the Jacobite James VII and II. James Fall was appointed tacksman and factor of the Dunfermline estates at Urquhart and Fyvie and was given the family's river Spey fishing rights. He retained that position until 1733, when he and Suttie arranged the sale of the forfeited estates. No doubt he was well rewarded for his stewardship which enabled him to build Dunbar House in 1734. The central section of the house is of red sandstone and built in Anglo-Gothic style, the original entrance being from the High Street. The wings which give the building its distinctive modern H-shape were added after 1788, when the Falls sold the house to the Lauderdale family after whom it was re-named (**ill 68, ill 69**).

Illus 69: *Lauderdale House from the Castle Park c.1900* DDHS

Dunbar House and its policies occupied the most important historic site in the burgh; as indicated in Chapter 3, several recent excavations have confirmed the existence of human settlement from at least 75AD, spanning the late Iron Age, the early Christian period and the Anglian occupation from about 638 until 1018. When the Falls went bankrupt in 1788,[19] Dunbar House was bought by Captain James Maitland, the future 8th Earl of Lauderdale; Maitland hired the famous Adam brothers to make attractive interior and exterior alterations to the house, including their specialty - fireplaces and plasterwork. Maitland also added the winged sphinx motif. In 1792, probably at Maitland's request, Robert Adam changed the entrance from the High Street to the rear of the building, adding the Doric pillars which survive today. The modern north-facing portico was once screened by trees fronting a landscaped garden. Lauderdale House was probably Robert Adam's last commission as he died in 1792; brother James died two years later. In 1801, the 8th Earl of Lauderdale landscaped the area to the front of the new entrance; during the proceedings, workmen uncovered several skeletons and cannon balls.[20] Considerably more human remains were found between 1989 and 1997, as indicated in Chapter 3.

It was perhaps appropriate that the Lauderdales came to live in Dunbar. The family were cadets of the Earls of Dunbar; one of their ancestors, John Maitland of Lethington [Lennoxlove] married Elisabeth, the great-niece of the 8th Earl of Dunbar and March. Reinforcing the Dunbar connection, the 2nd Earl of Lauderdale married Anne, daughter of the 1st Earl of Home whose family also descended from the Dunbars. The 2nd Earl of Lauderdale was taken prisoner at Worcester in 1651; when he was rewarded for his loyalty to Charles II in 1672, he chose the appropriate honorific Marquess of March.

Before moving on to describe some of the other town buildings, it is perhaps appropriate to relate two interesting anecdotes about the 8th Earl of Lauderdale. He had a violent temper, was first a Whig, then a Tory and he became the personal friend of Jean Paul Marat, one of the most radical leaders of the French Revolution. Lauderdale, known then as plain Captain James Maitland was in Paris when the Revolution began; he witnessed the fall of the Bastille on 8th July 1789. His pro-revolutionary views earned him the epithet Citizen Maitland. He was something of a writer and produced several treatises on financial matters, employing a ghost writer, Thomas Ritchie who in 1807 wrote a little-known life of David Hume, the Scottish philosopher. Ritchie lived and worked in Dunbar and he met a sudden and somewhat farcical death. In 1810, he fell from a third floor window in the High Street, apparently trying to make himself sick! At the time, George Miller ventured that Ritchie had been over-convivial in celebrating George III's birthday on 4th June at Lorimer's Hotel [the St George]. He was buried in the parish kirkyard; his tombstone bears the following inscription:

'In Memory of Thomas Edward Ritchie historian and barrackmaster Belhaven Obit 1810'

The latter refers to his employment at the dragoon barracks in or near the grounds of what is now Summerfield House, Belhaven. (His grave was paid for by Dunbar Castle Lodge of Freemasons). In 1844, the Lauderdales left Dunbar to live in Thirlestane Castle, much to the town's regret. In 1855, the government bought Lauderdale House and its policies for conversion into barrack accommodation, building additional accommodation in 1911; along with officers' accommodation at the New Inn in the High Street which until recently housed the Church of Scotland St Andrews' Nursing Home, now closed. New Inn Barracks and Lauderdale served as a depot for the yeomanry and artillery militia, then the Royal Artillery until the middle of the twentieth century, when the house was vacated and left to rot until it was converted into flats in 1995.

In the early eighteenth century, by the time Dunbar House was built, the town undoubtedly experienced a revolution in High Street buildings due to the rising prosperity of the merchant-trading class. The burgh council took great pains to ensure that individual, selfish and competing interests were not allowed to interfere with their desire for a broad, orderly High Street. The tall tenements were required to conform to rigid, straight lines; not only did these house many families, they also freed the street from the smoke of the earlier, low-roofed and one-storey buildings. While a mixture of styles was acceptable - Georgian, Dutch etc - the frontages had to meet the strict criterion of parallel lines. Today, few buildings disturb this basic arrangement; exceptions are No. 97 High St, (the Bank of Scotland), No.99 High St (site of the ill-fated East Lothian Bank), and No.101 High St, (the Royal Bank of Scotland), although both these last-named have extended frontages which conform to a straight line. The only glaring exception to this rule is the Doric porch at the New Inn Barracks (see below) which projects onto the pavement.

Corn Exchange

Situated near the Town House is a surviving symbol of the town's former prosperity. The Corn Exchange opened its doors on 16th October 1855 - reported in the *Caledonian Mercury* the following day. Weekly grain markets were held there until the trade diminished; in 1916 it was used as a cinema and for many years served as dance hall, venue for pierrot summer shows, amateur dramatics and other social purposes; for example, the twice-annual payments from the Suddons' friendly society were paid out there (see Chapter 9). Today, it is used by senior citizens and for charity events. Diagonally opposite is No 126-128 High Street, the birthplace of John Muir (see Chapter 10).

St George Hotel

Among the oldest buildings in Dunbar is the George or St George Hotel, erected in 1625 and completely rebuilt in 1828. Originally named for its proprietors - eg Crow, Lorimer (1830s), Cossar (1850s) - for many centuries it was the town's principal coaching inn, the stables being situated at the rear, off Cossar's Wynd. Various photographs show it as the George and the St George. Its impressive Roman Doric porch has a mural of St George slaying the dragon on its ceiling; as the hotel wasn't known as the St George until the twentieth century, the painting is probably modern. Presently empty, the shell is likely to suffer the fate of many a fine historic building, that of conversion into modern flats.

Further up the south-end of the High Street and adjacent to **Templelands** is a group of impressive tenements adorned with unicorn statuary and ornamental stone balustrades. Templelands is named for the Knights Templar who owned the site until 1309, when the Order was suppressed by the Pope and its lands and property were given to the Order of the Hospitallers of St John of Jerusalem. The Knights of St John certainly owned property

Illus 70: *The New Inn Barracks, Dunbar* KRM

in Dunbar as is confirmed by rental records in 1533-47.[21]

Opposite Templelands and mentioned above is the **New Inn (ill 70)** with its Doric pillared porch. Dating from the late eighteenth century, it was reputedly built to compete with the St George because the property owner's daughter married against his wishes into the family which owned the St George. The New Inn subsequently became known as the New Inn Barracks, providing rooms for officers stationed at Castle Park Barracks. Most of the tenements in the High Street date from the mid to late eighteenth century, although No 56 High St, (Downie's Stationers and Booksellers) may well be much earlier, with its Dutch gable.

Closes and Wynds

Many of the closes are named for former tenement owners or the proprietors of shops beside them, although a few reveal their former use. Some of these decayed and neglected street entries offer a glimpse of the past; many have evidence of doors and windows blocked up and some have a distinctly eerie atmosphere which makes them places to avoid on dark winter nights. Many were re-named in the last century, I have come across earlier different references for the Old Post Office Close, Slaughterhouse Close, Thompson's Close and Ruchlaw Close, the last being the residence of Catherine McTaggart who was tried for witchcraft in 1688. At the south end of the High Street is **Logan's Close**, then **Old Kirk Close**, now the entrance to a developed area of modern flats on land once occupied by teh 1st United Meeting House, then Stark's Garage. Beyond that is **Bamburgh Close**, adjacent to No 25 High Street, a chemist's shop. The property was known as Bamburgh's Castle, probably because it was owned by someone of that name. There is absolutely no evidence to support a locally-held minority view that there was once a castle proper on the site. Why on earth would Dunbar require two castles? (It is more probable that it got the name Castle from the pretentiousness of a tenant or owner in the same way as A J Cronin's snobbish hat-seller named his tenement in the novel *Hatter's Castle*. Also, we know that Lauderdale House was colloquially referred to as Dunbar Castle simply because it was a large building). *Miller, Dunbar* tells the apocryphal tale of a piper who attempted to prove there was an underground passage from Bamburgh Close to Dunbar Castle; he reputedly played his bagpipes underground as far as Silver Street, when the playing stopped. He was never seen again.[22] Similar legends are recounted elsewhere in Scotland - at Currie, Midlothian for example - where a piper disappeared attempting to trace an underground passage from Lennox Tower to Curriehill Castle.

Illus 71: *Craig's fish van* DDHS

Beyond Bamburgh Close is **Gibson's Close**, then **Cossar's Wynd**, named for a former proprietor of the St George Hotel; Cossar's Wynd was formerly Crow's Wynd, by which name it was known in 1744, when the Kirk session minute-book recorded a case of rape which took place there (see Chapter 5). Next is **Kilgour's Close** beside the Eagle Inn; it was probably named for James Kilgour, one of the founding members of Dunbar Castle Lodge of Freemasons in 1758. Crossing Silver Street, we come to **Corn Exchange Close**, named for obvious reasons, then **Craig's Close** which wends beneath Craig's Buildings, now the Bank of Scotland; the ground floor once housed the shop of Thomas Craig, a well-patronised fishmonger whose van plied the streets for many years (**ill 71**). The shop interior was colourfully decorated with attractive ceramic tiles depicting fishing scenes, species of fish, crabs and lobsters. One of the closes which has disappeared is Johnstone's Close, now incorporated in No. 121 High St, (Umberto's Italian Restaurant). The remaining closes on that side of the street are **Legion Close** leading to the British Legion premises and finally, **Castle Wynd**, which once contained Castle Place, known locally as the Common Close, where my family once lived.

Crossing the street to retrace our steps eastwards, the first close is **Greco's**, named for its famous ice-cream selling owners. Next are **Melville's Close** (perhaps the abode of Robert Melville of the East Lothian and Merse Fishing Company or Andrew Melville, a local plumber), **Lawson's Court** (named after Peter Lawson, a local apothecary), **Innes Close** - named for a local family of hairdressers. Crossing the West Port, we encounter **Purves Close** - named for a former grocer - **Garden Close**, **Mason's Close** - the Masons being bootmakers and shoe sellers for many years and one of the few local family businesses still trading - **Flesher's Close**, which is self-explanatory; next is **Printing Close**, where George Miller began his business - **Empire Close** - named for the first of Dunbar's two cinemas - **Trinity Close**, which took its name from the Trinitarian establishment at Friar's Croft. Last of all is **New Inn Close**, adjacent to the New Inn Barracks.

Illus 72: *Former Buttercup Dairy* KRM

The High Street contains a few quaint reminders of the recent and not so recent past, mostly at street level. Prominent among these is No 138 High Street, currently a Chartered Surveyor's office. Within living memory it sold dairy goods, engagingly named *The Buttercup*; on the right-hand side of the entrance is a sentimental but attractive scene in tiles manufactured by J Duncan Ltd depicting a pretty little milkmaid offering a buttercup to a sleepy cow (**ill 72**). What else? Above it are the letters B[uttercup] D[airy] Co Ltd. (A similar scene occurs at No 15 West Port, where six tiles show a trio of cows ruminating by a stream; No 15 was once the premises of the *Renton Dairy*). On the frontage of No 64 High Street is what at first sight appears to be a gas bracket but in fact were flagholders installed in 1935 to commemorate George V's Silver Jubilee, as Tom Anderson, a former owner of the shop recently enlightened me. Another curiosity is found at the *Consignia* sorting office, formerly the General Post Office built in 1904; set in the wall are footholds shod with brass, with handrails on the window ledges above. These were used by night duty policemen to hoist themselves up and shine their torches on the night safe within. One yearns for the best of the old days....

A fine building which was destroyed by fire in the latter part of the twentieth century was Cromwell House, the home of Christopher Middlemass in the nineteenth century (**ill 73**). Middlemass married into the Belhaven Brewery family and probably sold them grain from his granary in Shore Street. In Church Street are the former **Assembly Rooms**, once the venue for prestigious balls, supper dances and musical evenings which were patronised by middle class merchants and businessmen. Built in 1822, it lay empty for many years; it has been scheduled for conversion into modern flats, although so far, only the basement has been developed. Nearly parallel to Church Street and Castle Street is Colvin Street, formerly Coffin Street, a distinctly sinister Dickensian name which derives from the undertaker trade once practised there.

Country Houses

It is now appropriate to describe some of the surviving and vanished country seats in the vicinity which with their prosperous farms once contributed to the wealth of Dunbar.

Lochend House

The remains of this once extensive property are situated to the south of Dunbar, bounded by the A1 bypass and extending almost to the town itself. Visible now is a gable end which is all that survives of the house built by Sir Gideon Baillie; once graced with a Renaissance gateway bearing the date 1684, it is probably the ruin (**ill 74**) marked on the OS map of 1852. There was probably a Baillie presence at Lochend before 1614; it certainly existed in 1618, as John Taylor the Water Poet visited 'Master James Baylies House' that year (see

Illus 73: *Cromwell House in the 1950s* HM

Chapter 3). For many years, a stone panel inscribed with the Baillie motto *Sedes Dent Fata Quietus* 'may the fates ensure a quiet seat' and the family coat of arms was incorporated in an adjacent archway. (The panel was illegally removed in 1990 and incorporated in a private house in Peebles; Dunbar and District History Society tried to retrieve the stonework, but was unsuccessful). The Baillie house was sold by Sir Gideon's grand-daughter on or before 1671 to Sir Robert Sinclair of Longformacus who sold it in 1708 to Sir George Warrender, a wealthy Edinburgh merchant who owned Bruntsfield House in Edinburgh in 1685. Sir George was a staunch Whig and supporter of the first Hanoverian king George I; he became Lord Provost of Edinburgh, then was elected as the city's Westminster MP in 1715. His letters of that year to the city fathers contain advice about the defence of the city during the Jacobite rebellion. Sir George's grandson, Lieutenant Colonel Patrick Warrender, 11th Dragoons, was present on the field of Minden in 1759, during the Seven Years' War. Patrick was elected MP for the Haddington burghs (1768-74) and served as King's Rembrancer to the Exchequer (1771-91). A Warrender presence continued at Lochend until 1859; the family owned the adjacent farms of Hallhill, Eweford, Newtonlees and Chesterhall - a total of 1,820 acres.The 4th baronet, Sir George, built a new house in 1826 (**ill 75**); it is described in the *New Statistical Account* (1845) as ' an elegiac mansion in the Anglo-Gothic style.' It was reduced to a shell by fire on 10th March 1859 [23] - reputedly because of a gypsy curse that predicted the Warrenders would lose three houses to fire. (There is a tradition that the estate boundary walls were built by Napoleonic prisoners of war, supposedly confirmed by marks cut in some of the stones. I have studied these marks but there is nothing to suggest they are French; it is likely they are spoil from the house dismantled in 1861. A similar tale is told of the boundary wall at Belhaven Brewery but like Lochend, this remains to be substantiated). After the fire of 1859, when the house was looted by locals who emptied the cellar of its fine wines, the Warrenders moved to Edinburgh shortly afterwards. The 7th baronet, another Sir George, served in the Royal Navy as rear-admiral and assisted in the relief of Peking where the European dipolomatic missions were besieged by the fanatical Boxer faction in 1900.[24] Sir George was naval commander-in-chief in 1917 when he died at Portsmouth aged 57 and was succeeded by his son Victor. Victor became an MP in 1923 and was Permanent Secretary to the Treasury in 1935. All that remains of the estate are the fine wood currently

Illus 74: *The ruins of Sir Gideon Baillie's House, Lochend* KRM

Illus 75: *The Warrenders' House at Lochend, built 1826, destroyed by fire 1859* WFC

being managed by Dunbar Community Woodland Group, the walled garden, the stables and the Retreat, a fine country house built in 1830. Also surviving is the attractive Lochend Cottages (**ill 76**), now a single dwelling house

Lochend got its name from the Great Loch referred to in Acts of parliament in the late Middle Ages. Dunbar's post-glacial freshwater loch had been drained by the seventeenth century under a land reclamation scheme but within living memory, the area has been subject to periodic flooding. (As a boy, I remember being warned not to venture into the woods to pick naturalised daffodils but doing so anyway. The flowers grew on little tussocky islands of grass separated by green-scummed ponds which on reflection, were probably dangerous). Even today, in the course of housing development, the water table is so high that areas have had to be pumped out to allow building.

Belton House

Sadly, this fine mansion was reduced to a heap of bricks and tiles in 1967, a ruin which is now almost indistinguishable from the landscape it once graced. There are traces of the terraced gardens and some exotic trees beside the walled garden. Situated near Pitcox, it is described in the *New Statistical Account* as standing 'in a beautiful winding glen....with its stream [the Biel Burn] gliding by.' For centuries, Belton was owned by the Hays who originated in Yester; the place is mentioned frequently in the *Yester Writs* which contains charters dating from 1369, the year when the 10th Earl of Dunbar and March granted Belton to a Nigel Cunningham. A further charter transferred the lands of West Barns and elsewhere to Cunningham in 1376, then all the property and lands passed to the Hays of Yester through marriage in 1482. There were Hays at Belton until the twentieth century. Belton - sometimes called Heatherwick (Hedderwick - see below) once possessed a small chapel, a canon-prebendary of the Collegiate Church of Dunbar (see Chapter 5). There was also an inn but no trace of either survives today.

Illus 76: *Lochend Cottages pre-1917* DDHS

Illus 77: *Biel House* DDHS

Biel House

The lands of Bele or Biel were held by the Earls of Dunbar until the fifteenth century; Sir Patrick Dunbar of Biel gave the property to his grandson, Sir Hugh who sold it in 1489 to Sir Robert Lauder of the Bass. There was a fortalice in the grounds at one time but it is thought to have been dismantled during the building of Biel House (**ill 77**) in the sixteenth century. The house was bought by the Earls of Melrose in 1625, then in about 1647, by James Hamilton of Broomhill, 1st Lord Belhaven. It is said that he built several of the surviving terrace walls prior to 1650. The 2nd Lord Belhaven was a keen agricultural improver, introducing many changes to the Biel estate during his lifetime. The 2nd Lord Belhaven is however better remembered for his unflinching opposition to Union with England in 1707; in that fateful year, he inscribed a stone at Biel House with the words *Traditionis Scotiae anno primo 1707,* or '1707, the first year of the betrayal of Scotland'. The house was partly demolished in 1953 although it is still occupied.

Bowerhouse or Bourhouse

This fine house is about a mile to the south of Dunbar. It was built by Major Carfrae of the East India Company and was occupied by a Reverend Robert Cunningham in 1799, then Dr Carfrae, the last minister of the old Collegiate Church of Dunbar in 1819. The grounds contain extensive gardens and an eighteenth century dovecote which, with its walled garden suggests the existence of an earlier residence. The gardens are said to contain the tracery or stone ornamental open-work of the Gothic windows from the church dismantled in 1819. Bowerhouse had a quarry which probably provided the red sandstone for the castle and the Parish Church. The 'fake' mercat cross in front of the Town House is of red sandstone; the three faces adorning it are of medieval design, thought to have come from the demolished Collegiate Church, again the stone probably came from the Bowerhouse Quarry. The stone for the second Parish Church built between 1819 and 1821 also came from Bowerhouse, a gift of Dr Carfrae who lived there after retiring from the incumbency in 1819.

Hedderwick House

Not far from Biel and Belton stood Hedderwick House [Heatherwick in pre-Reformation times] which was demolished in 1961. It dominated a rise on the left of the A1 approaching West Barns, where its walled garden and associated cottage still survive. Built in the seventeenth century, the *New Statistical Account* records that it stood 'on an eminence which is well wooded and commands views of the surrounding plains, the town of Dunbar, Belhaven and the extensive grounds of Tyninghame.' North-east of Hedderwick was Link House - now gone - where the poet Richard Gall was born (see Chapter 7).

DDHS

Illus 78: *Broxmouth House pre-1906*

Broxmouth House

Broxmouth House or Park (**ill 78**), originally owned by Sir Thomas Randolph, Robert Bruce's able lieutenant, has been occupied continuously since the fourteenth century. When Randolph was forfeited for supporting Bruce, his lands became part of the earldom of Dunbar, then, when the Dunbars were forfeit in 1435, the property was owned by several nobles, including the Homes of Broxmouth, until it was granted by royal charter to the Duke of Roxburghe in 1642. It is thought that the old mouldering ruin which was Cromwell's headquarters in September 1650 was demolished in 1774, when the present house was built. All that remains of the original is the walled garden; the fine house is obscured by trees which grow almost to the seashore. There is a folly or mock-tower nearby, dating from 1850. In 1830, the Duke of Roxburghe owned the highly productive farms at Oxwellmains, Broxmouth, Little and Meikle Pinkerton and the Brunt, near Spott village. The family also owned Oswald Dean at one time. Queen Victoria visited Broxmouth House in August 1878, her jubilee year; she planted an oak tree in the grounds. The Roxburghe family still own the estate, although the house was partially demolished in 1955. Not far away, the remains of an Iron Age settlement were excavated in 1977.

Conclusion

The monopolies and privileges of the royal burghs couldn't last forever. Before the Union of the Crowns in 1603, Scotland was rent by anarchy and quarrelling factions among the nobles; it was a wretched, economically depressed and ill-governed nation. The Borders harboured reivers, common thieves and broken men - those who were destitute for one reason or another and outlaws who hired themselves to those who paid the most - whether English or Scottish. Around 1610, their teeth were pulled by George Home, the last Earl of Dunbar at a time when royal burghs like Dunbar experienced a renaissance as a result of the royal union with England; the new prosperity allowed Dunbar to find the resources to rebuild its prestigious Town House and Tolbooth at this time. The population expanded, trade was on the increase and ships that went to London with raw and finished goods brought back luxury items for personal use but more often for resale.

For the next 60 years, royal burghs enjoyed their exclusive position until an act of parliament attacked their privileged position in 1672. It was the beginning of the end. In the previous century, parliament had for the first time licensed fairs outwith the royal burghs; the act of 1672 went much further by allowing ordinary burghs to hold their own markets and engage in overseas trade. The extension of market privileges to other burghs had a considerable impact on the royal burghs' revenues and they understandably complained about this infringement of their rights and privileges to parliament. While the Act of Union upheld their special status, they went into decline simply because their structure and organisation had become irrelevant to the economic needs of the time.

Thus in its heyday, the Scottish royal burgh was a self-contained, self-financing unit; its business was built on self-interest, restrictive practices and it must be said, nepotism and corruption. The most frequent complaint about the unreformed royal burghs prior to 1833, when the long-overdue reform legislation finally broke their stranglehold, was that many administrations were blatantly guilty of misuse of burgh patrimony, common land and the revenues deriving from these. Nearly 50 years before the great reform legislation, questions were being raised about the accountability of the royal burghs. In 1787, in response to a proposed reform of the royal burghs, a delegation from the Convention of Royal Burghs complained to the reformers that they had signally failed to cite a single case of corruption before 1783. The reformers countered this argument by quoting the case of burgh councillors in Glasgow who had wasted the town's patrimony in 1691 'for their own sinistrous ends and uses.' so that common land had to be sold to meet subsequent debts. A second case was that of thw small burgh of Dumbarton where the council had spent nearly £2,000 of burgh funds on food and drink![25] Such examples were typical and without number. Sons followed fathers as hereditary burgesses; the same men ran the burgh council year after year and their friends and relatives enriched themselves from town contracts and through the influence of their contacts on the councils. Those who were well off were 'elected' as magistrates (bailies) and councillors; they often had no other qualifications for their appointment. These men literally elected themselves into what had become an exclusive tier of society; they ran their communities for their own self-interest and that of their families. They were held in considerable awe by the common folk. Over at least two centuries, their ships and trade interests extended to the delta of the river Scheldt, the Baltic ports, the Norwegian fjords, the Danish Sound, Greenland, the important Scottish Staple at Veere in the Netherlands and in some cases like the Fall family, the Americas. In the organisation of foreign trade, the Scottish Staple at Veere was an institution whose monopoly in trade managed to survive the Act of Union well into the next century. The Convention of Royal Burghs also survived the union, becoming one of the oldest representative governing bodies in the whole of Europe, arbiters in all matters of trade and commerce, directing - and reprimanding - the royal burghs when required. Through such organisations, the burgesses and merchants made - and occasionally lost - small fortunes; they enjoyed a lifestyle unprecedented among low-born men, especially during the Middle Ages. Their modern day equivalent, the local traders with their Association exercised considerable power in Dunbar and elsewhere, often influencing the burgh council's decisions - not always for the good of the community as a whole. It can be said without fear of contradiction that David II's charter of 1370 bestowed an enviable lifestyle for generations of Dunbar merchant-burgesses for six centuries.

Royal burghs were already an anachronism long before national income tax was introduced by Pitt the Younger in 1798; they were reactionary units of administration which belonged to the Middle Ages rather than the nineteenth century. These unique organisations had blocked progress for centuries, being largely concerned with the self-interests of the few men who held power and influence. The powers of the royal burghs were gradually eroded as central government began to assume responsibility for economic regulation and abolish the restrictive practices which they had jealously defended. The death-knell of the royal burghs was preceeded by the Reform (Scotland) Act of 1832 which extended the vote from 1 in 125 males to 1 in 8 who paid at least £10 a year in rent; this was closely followed by the Royal Burghs (Scotland) Act 1833, a measure which brought them in line with the rules on local elections introduced by the Act of 1832. Despite these moves, Dunbar burgh council - perhaps now accepting that the sea change of reform was unstoppable - presented an address to William IV in support of Earl Grey's reform legislation of 1832 and 1833. Grey, then Prime Minister, had asked the king to force his Reform Bill through by creating 100 Whig Peers to vote against the Opposition, led by the Duke of Wellington. The king refused although the Bill was enacted. The reform legislation led to public demands for its speedy implementation and William IV, alarmed by the raft of reforming measures being pushed through the muddy waters of enfranchisement, took advantage of a chance defeat of the Whig administration to call for its resignation. On 24th November 1834, Dunbar burgh council respectfully suggested that the king should listen to wiser council; their letter was acknowledged by the Duke of Wellington, back in power and strongly opposed to reform. King William asked Sir Robert Peel to form an administration committed to reform but in the usual leisurely fashion of Tory governments, nothing was done. When William dissolved parliament, Peel was forced to resign when the voters returned the Whigs with almost the same majority they had enjoyed in 1832.

The reform legislation not only abolished the 'rotten' methods of election of councillors but overhauled the constitution of every Scottish and English burgh council. In Scotland, the distinction between royal and ordinary burghs disappeared overnight, when all were reconstituted as parliamentary, then police burghs. However, there was still some fight left in the royal burghs whose special position was again weakened by the Royal Burghs (Scotland) Bill of 1840. On 8th June that year, Dunbar burgh council studied the Bill's provisions which were designed 'to provide for the better regulation of municipal corporations in Royal Burghs in Scotland.' The burgh petitioned against the Bill since in its opinion, it wouldn't lead to improvement in the government of the time and also because the Bill reduced the number of magistrates in every royal burgh which the Dunbar administration considered 'a serious evil'. The Bill also proposed the election of non-burgesses as councillors - clearly the intention was to break the strangle-hold of what was a closed shop arrangement in the election of councillors - something which Dunbar felt would weaken the administration as such councillors would have no control over burgesses' property. The final straw was the provision which required every magistrate to be personally responsible for acts of the council; the burgh council felt this was a bad move as it would deter 'respectable persons from accepting office.' They didn't like the cold wind of change.

It was long overdue. While there had been too much of *laissez faire* politics and administration in many royal burghs, some had genuinely struggled to cope with the problems of bad housing, poor sanitation and lack of public health measures, failing simply because they were ill-equipped and inadequately funded to deal with these massive problems. And there were also the ubiquitous and deserving poor at the bottom of the heap in every burgh - royally chartered or not. Despite national legislation to put matters right and improve standards, examples of the bad old days lingered on until the twentieth century. At Dunbar, a classic example was the continued existence of the Cat's Row, a veritable Hell's Kitchen in Victoria Street - less than a stone's throw from where I live today - until it was demolished in 1935. The decayed hovels were a breeding ground for vermin and disease; dampness brought tuberculosis - consumption as it was known then - to the families of men who made their living at sea, themselves suffering from the effects of constant soakings and consequential poor health caused by a strenuous and dangerous occupation. The Cat's Row was demolished in 1935, as we are informed by an illustrated signboard on the wall of Castle Gate, branching left off Victoria Street. New housing estates were created between 1922 and 1935; council house building continued until the very eve of the Second World War which interrupted the programme. After the war, new houses were built on the site of Cat's Row, then a major new estate was created at Riggs and Floors near Belhaven Church for Glasgow overspill in the 1960s. Gradually, old property was condemned or upgraded, health improved dramatically and a better lifestyle was enjoyed by more people than ever before - largely through central government initiatives administered by the Secretary of State for Scotland's Scottish Office at St Andrew's House, Edinburgh.

Dunbar has known steady decline since the late 1960s. Although burgh councils ceased to exist after 16th May 1975 under local government reorganisation, Dunbar is still rightly proud of its town seal struck in 1370; its earlier version (c.1357) is one of the oldest recorded in Scotland, depicting a three-towered castle on rocks - all silver-coloured - superimposed on a red background, (red and silver being the heraldic colours of the old earldom of Dunbar). The 1357 version was surmounted by a coronet and enclosed by a shield bordered by eight roses, part of the Earls of Dunbar coat-of-arms which is thought to signify the proximity of the earldom of Dunbar to England.[26] Throughout successive centuries, the burgh took considerable pride in its status and expressed its loyalty directly to kings of Scotland and England as any royal burgh should; the burgh council minutes repeatedly record the celebration of various monarchs' birthdays.[27] In 1840, the serving provost wrote a letter of congratulation to Victoria on her marriage to Albert, sending congratulations on the birth of their first child - the future Empress Frederick - in November the same year. The burgh council also expressed their relief in a letter to the royal couple when they survived an assassination attempt in the autumn of 1840.

In his biography *Cromwell*, Thomas Carlyle described Dunbar as

> 'high and windy, looking down over the herring boats, over its grim old castle, now much honey-combed, on one of those projecting rock formations with which the shore is vandyked [lacy bordering?] as far as the eye can reach....close by is the deep bay and fishy little village of Belhaven....Here rises, some short mile off, a dusky continent of barren heath hills, the Lammermuirs, where only mountain sheep can be at home.'

The purple prose apart, this is a somewhat condensed and superficial description of Dunbar a century ago; there was much more to it than that. But then Carlyle was more interested in its battle of 1650, an event which brought him here to attend the dedication ceremony commemorating - commiserating is perhaps more apt- Cromwell's famous victory. The town also doesn't deserve the rather jaundiced view in John Murray's *Handbook of Travellers in Scotland* (1898) which describes it as

> 'a lifeless town....Notwithstanding its antiquity, there are no buildings of any age or beauty in the town.....Excellent golf links are its principal attraction nowadays...'

Whoever did the research for Murray's *Guide* must have walked through Dunbar with his eyes shut. How could he possibly miss the Town House, Lauderdale House and the Parish Church? Perhaps he had sampled the town's excellent ale the night before!

Fig. 12 Commissioners to the Convention of Royal Burghs, Provosts, some Honorary Burgesses and Freemen

Representatives from the royal burghs did not take their seats in parliament until some time between 1357 and 1370. Although David II created Dunbar a free burgh in 1369-70, it would have been represented by the Earls of Dunbar and their successors after 1435 until 1455, the year it was elevated to a royal burgh by James II. Thereafter, when the Convention of Royal Burghs was created and royal burgh commissioners were appointed, they were automatically assured of a voice in parlaiment, although not in the same way as a modern MP. Dunbar was represented at the first recorded meeting of the Convention in 1552. The following information derives largely from the *Acts of the Parliaments of Scotland vol xii Part I Index A-H* and the *Records of the Convention of Royal Burghs* vols i - vii

1552	William Achesone, [Aitchison]
	Ionhe [John] Kelly
1555	William Leirmonth,
	William Bonkill [Boncle]
1574	Moreis [Maurice] Lawder 'baillie of Dumbar'
	(Dunbar is also spelt Dumber, Dvmber)
1575	Cuthbert Kelly
1577	William Bonkill,
	Richert Fyscher [Richard Fisher]
1578	William Bonkill,
	William Kellie, Maureis Lawder
1579	William Boncle(He was given an acreage of
	land near Dunbar Castle in 1581 to compensate
	for money he spent out of his own pocket on the
	castle's demolition in 1568 (*RMS vol v* No 1873.
	He owned land in West Barns (*RMS vol v* No 259)
1583-84	John Aitchison (He may have been the father of
	John Aitchison (see entry for 1613)
	(*RMS vol vi* No 2085)
1585	Maurice Lauder
1587	Hugo Lauder
1588	Robert Craige
1589-92	Maister Alexander Kellye [Kellie] [The title signifies
	Kellie was a landlord or feudal superior]
1594	William Kellie
1595-96	Exemption
1597	Maister Eduard Aickyne [Edward Aitken]
1598-99	Maister Alexander Kellie
1600	" " "
1601	William Lawder
1602-04	Maister Eduard Aikyne (A wealthy landowner of
	Underedge (*RCRB vol i No 309*)
1605	Nicoll Kellie
1606	Henrie Lawder
1607	Exemption
1608-09	Maister Eduard Aikyne
1610	Ionhe Mure [John Muir]
1611-12	Maister Eduard Aikyne (Baillie)
1613	Provost Ionhe Achesone [John Aitchison] (In 1616,
	the Privy Council ordered him to 'haif a caire that no
	hering be foirspoken nor boght afoir they be tane and
	brocht to land [have a care that no herring be
	promised or bought before they are caught and
	landed]; the Convention made the same complaint on
	several occasions between 1606 and 1616. Selling
	fish to 'unfreemen' ie unauthorised merchants

1614	No name
1615	George Purves
1616	William Lawder
1617	Maister Johne Achiesone,
	William Lawder
1618-20	George Purves
1621	Exemption
1622-29	George Purves
1630-49	Gap in records
1649-52	Thomas Purves
1653	James Lauder
1654	George Forrest
1655	James Lauder
1656-57	No name
1658	James Kellie
1659	No name
1660	James Lauder,
	Thomas Purves
1661	James Lauder
1662	William Wood,
	James Lauder
1663	James Lauder
1664	Maister George Purves
1665	James Lauder
1666	James Kellie
1667	No name
1668	James Lauder
1669-70	Robert Pringle
1671	James Hamiltoun
1672	No attendance
1673	Robert Pringle
1674-78	James Kello [Kellie?]
1679	No name
1680	James Smith
1681-83	James Kellie
1684-85	James Smith
1686	William Kirkwood,
	James Smith
1687-88	Sir Adam Blair
1689	William Kirkwood
1690-92	Robert Kellie
1708	James Faa,
	William Faa
1709-20	William Faa
1721	Charles Fall,
	William Fall

	deprived the king of income from the tax levied on herring
1693	James Smith (Ordered by the magistrates of Dunbar to explain his absence from parliament, Smith confessed he was unable to swear an oath of allegiance to William of Orange on grounds of conscience
1694	Robert Kellie [In this year, Sir John Hall of Dunglass became provost of Edinburgh]
1695	Robert Faa [Fall] (Founder of the Fall empire in Dunbar?)
1696-97	Robert Kelly
1698	Robert Kelly, Robert Faa
1699	Robert Faa
1700	Robert Fae [Fall]
1701	Robert Kirkwood
1702-07	Robert Kellie, William Faa (1707)
1708	James Faa, William Faa
1709-20	William Fall
1721	Charles Fall, William Fall
1722	William Fall
1723	James Fall, William Fall

1722	William Fall
1723	James Fall, William Fall
1724-25	William Fall
1726-27	James Fall
1728	Captain James Fall
1729	No attendance
1730-31	James Fall, Captain James Fall (1731)
1732-36	James Fall, Captain James Fall (1733)
1732-36	James Fall, Captain James Fall (1736) Charles Fall

Provosts of Dunbar (terms in office are indicative and approximate)

1601-14 ?	Sir George Home of Spott (Earl of Dunbar 1605-1611)
1613 and 1616	Iohne Achesone (John Aitchison)
1622 -24	Sir James Baillie of Lochend
1721-26	Illegible in records
1678	James Lawder may have been provost although he is not named as such
1679	James Collie " " " "
1693-1701?	Robert Faa [Fall]
1721-26	Captain James Fall (In 1734, Captain Fall became MP for Haddingtonshire)
1721-27	Post vacant. Bailie William Fall is prominent amongst council members
1721-28	Captain James Fall?
1726-36	William Fall
1738-1744	Charles Fall
1745-65	?
1766 -?	Charles Fall (son of William above)
1781-89?	Robert Fall (son of Captain James above)
1793-94	Charles Hay
1794-1804	Major Christopher Middlemas; a former employee of Fall, Melville and Company
1811-14?	" " "
1833-1836	Simon Sawers
1836-1847	Christopher Middlemas; between 1794 and 1847, Middlemass served as provost for 26 years
1847-1849	Simon Sawers
1849-1855	John Kelly
1855-1861	William Combe
1861	Charles Lorimer Sawers
1862-1872	William Purves
1872	Lockhart Dobie
1873-1875	Thomas Inglis Gardner
1875-1896	James Brand
1896-1899	John Kelly Keir
1899-1905	John Gibb (the annex to the Town Library in Castellau House is named for him)
1905-1911	Daniel Smith (owner of a tailor's shop and gentleman's outfitters in the High Street from the nineteenth century, the last owner of the shop trading in clothes was Dan Cairney, currently serving on the Community Council and member of the Dunbar John Muir Association)
1911-1913	George Low (another local trader whose business was taken over by Fairbairn of Berwickshire in recent years)
1913-1919	Alexander Simpson (Great War provost)
1919-1925	Robert Aitken (a local trader and manufacturer of soft drinks)
1925-1937	Alexander Sinton (a local grocer whose premises were later occupied by Cooper's and is now the local delicatessen)

1937-1947	Phipps Oswald Turnbull (Second World War provost)
1947	John R Hannan (caretaker provost)
1947-1957	Alexander J Manderson (a local joiner and owner of Woodbush, traditionally the wood store in Dunbar; Alexander was my mother's cousin and his family may descend from Sir George Home of Manderston, last Earl of Dunbar)
1957-1963	W G R Findlay
1963-1966	Harry O More (former proprietor of the Hillside Hotel which in his time was the YMCA Hostel)
1966-1969	Mrs Violet B Kirkwood
1969-1975	R H James (history teacher at Dunbar Grammar School, then Rector of Dalkeith Academy, he was the last provost of Dunbar, when the Local Government Act of 1974 abolished burgh councils)

Some Honorary Burgesses and Freemen from 1680 to 1914

1680	Earl of Tweeddale and his son
1688	Earl [Duke] of Roxburghe
1789	James, 7th Earl of Lauderdale
1807	James, Viscount Maitland
1819	James Hogg, the 'Ettrick Shepherd'
1819	Field-Marshall the Marquis of Tweeddale
1819	HRH George Frederick, Prince of Coburg, later king of Belgium
1820	Captain James Hay of Belton
1826	Sir John Warrender of Lochend
1827	The Hon. Captain Anthony Maitland
1831	Lieutenant Charles Shaw, RN
1840	Sir George Warrender Bart. of Lochend
1842	Captain Andrew Ramsay, Earl of Dalhousie
1843	Captain James Hay of Belton, RN
1848	Sir R Ferguson Davie, Bart.
1893	Field-Marshall Lord Roberts - the Right Hon. Frederick Sleigh Roberts, Baron Roberts of Kandahar in Afganistan and of the city of Waterford KGB (known affectionally as 'Bobs')
1894	Captain Baird Hay and Mrs Baird of Cambusdoon #
1900	Sir Reginald Wingate (of the Sudan)
1914	Major Reginald Seager Hunt +

@ Most of these names are taken from the List of Honorary Burgesses from September 1789 to August 1893: Gentlemen who received the Freedom of the Royal Burgh of Dunbar (SRO ref. B 18/21/1)

For gifting the West Promenade to the people of Dunbar

+ Major Hunt, 1st King's Dragoon Guards commanding No 6 (Scotland) Cavalry Depot received the freedom of the burgh in recognition of the town's appreciation of having been chosen for the depot, he being its first commanding-officer. Major - later Colonel Hunt - never forgot the gesture; when he died in 1942, his solicitors sent items of his military uniform to Dunbar as provided in his will

ALFRED HORNE, St George Stables, DUNBAR.

First-class Stabling and Coach-Houses for Liveries. Horses by the Week, Month, or Year.

Posting in all its Branches. Saddle Horses, &c.

Charges for Carriages, Saddle Horses, &c.

	One Horse. s. d.	*Driver.* s. d.	*Pair Horses.* s. d.	*Driver* s. d.
Airing per Hour	3 0	1 0	—	—
To Broxmouth Grounds	3 0	1 0	—	—
,, Spott and back	4 0	1 0	6 0	1 6
,, Innerwick and Eastbarns and back	6 0	1 6	—	—
,, Drive through Biel Grounds	6 0	1 6	9 0	2 0
,, Drive through Tynninghame Village and East Linton	8 0	2 0	12 0	3 0
,, Thurston and back	6 0	1 6	9 0	2 0
,, Biel and Pressmennan	8 0	2 0	12 0	3 0
,, Biel Stenton, and Whittinghame	8 0	2 0	12 0	3 0
,, Boarhouse, Little Spott, Pitcox, Stenton, and back by East Linton	9 0	2 0	12 6	3 0
,, Pressmennan and back	7 0	2 0	10 6	2 6
,, Whitekirk and return by Newbyth and Prestonkirk	9 0	2 0	12 6	3 0
,, Dunglass Bridge and back	7 0	2 0	10 6	2 6
,, Cockburnspath and back	8 0	2 0	12 0	3 0
,, Pease Bridge and back	10 0	2 6	15 0	3 6
,, Tantallon Castle, Canty Bay	10 0	2 6	15 0	3 6
,, North Berwick	12 0	3 0	18 0	4 0
,, Dirleton Castle and Gardens	14 0	3 6	25 0	5 6
,, Fast Castle	14 0	3 6	25 0	5 0
Large Brake for Picnics, &c., per day	—	—	30 0	5 0
Any other Carriage	—	—	25 0	5 0

Half an Hour Waiting Free. Pony and Phaeton, 2s. 6d. per hour, 10s. per day.

PRINCIPAL PLACES OF INTEREST NEAR DUNBAR.

1. Biel Grounds, the Seat of Mrs Hamilton Ogilvy, noted for its picturesque scenery—open to Visitors. 6 miles
2. Tynninghame Grounds, the Seat of the Earl of Haddington—open on Saturdays during the season. 6 miles
3. Pressmennan Lake, pleasant place for Picnic Parties 7 ,,
4. Pease Bridge, favourite trip for Visitors. 10 ,,
5. Tantallon Castle, famous old ruin, once the Seat of the Earls of Douglas, and visited by Queen Victoria 10 miles
6. Canty Bay, for the Bass Rock. 10 ,,
7. North Berwick, pleasant drive through Binning Woods, and return by Canty Bay. 12 miles
8. Dirleton Castle and Archerfield—open to the Public on Thursdays. 15 miles

9

Agriculture and Fishing

In many respects, this chapter is a continuation of Chapter 8, as Dunbar's economy was directly related to its status as a royal burgh until well into the twentieth century. While the early years of Dunbar's socio-economic state are difficult to determine, given the lack of reliable source material prior to the thirteenth century, it is safe to assume that the local economy and the lives of the people developed along similar lines to other burghs under the feudal system introduced in Scotland in the twelfth century. The impact on the social and economic structures of the country was all-inclusive and Dunbar probably conformed to the national pattern. At the outset of the Middle Ages, the country as a whole experienced a period of intense change unparalleled since the Roman occupation, although that amounted to little as far as Scotland was concerned.

The first major step was the introduction of parishes, then burghs; these units of administration were universal and brought about change for the better - at least in the beginning. The upheaval caused by the Wars of Independence from 1296 had a profound and detrimental effect on Scotland's economic growth. Before then however, the introduction of parishes in the twelfth century which along with royal burghs, burghs of regality and burghs of barony created by royal charter were the basis of local government, bringing not only law and order to isolated communities but encouraging economic stability and progress while providing the monarch with much-needed income.

In the previous chapter, we saw that royal burghs were the brain-child of David I (1124-53). From the tenth century to the medieval period and beyond, little changed in the lives of the humble folk who lived on and worked the land; the towns which sprang up or developed into sizeable communities were a new concept in twelfth century Scotland. Many were founded on existing religious establishments or castles, while others were determined by their geographical position ie those near a fordable river or a natural coastal inlet which provided a safe haven for vessels. Royal burghs were vital to the economy, created by the king for his financial gain, an integral part of David I's policy and those of his descendants to boost the national economy and encourage the growth of industry - even if the latter was based almost exclusively on animal husbandry and animal products. It wasn't until the eighteenth century that Scotland experienced an industrial 'revolution' so that up till then, the burghs with their locally-based, low output industries were the mainstay of progress which rested in the hands of merchants, burgesses and craftsmen.

In its raw state, economics is a dry subject. In the early centuries the concept of an economy would have been lost on the average working man since he was wholly preoccupied with producing enough food for his family. Even among his betters, farming was pursued at subsistence level so there was no incentive to trade with other communities let alone other countries. That changed after parishes were created but even so, it wasn't until the mid-thirteenth century that we have an indication of the state of Scotland's economy, recorded in the *Exchequer Rolls* (*ERs*) between 1264 and 1600. Even so, it is sometimes difficult to obtain a clear picture of the contribution made to the economy as a whole by a single small community such as Dunbar.

In economic terms, the fabric of Scottish society in general and Dunbar in particular remained static for several centuries. Most men and women were tied to the land they worked; freedom was largely an abstract concept, much in the same vein as were the 'free' and 'unfree' men - terms which related to status within the burghs rather than to freedom in the political sense. All were subject to the authority of their superior, be he lord, senior churchman or the king, paying food-rents for the land they worked. Food-rents were the norm until about the twelfth century, when any surplus produce was turned into cash which led to the gradual introduction of money-rents. Agricultural surpluses were traded in the burgh markets which brought about the beginnings of a cash economy. There were markets and fairs at Dunbar even before it was granted 'free' burgh status by David II in 1370. After that, the freemen - merchants and craftsmen - predominated in the same fashion as had feudal overlords. Agriculture and the economy were interdependent; the twelfth and thirteenth centuries were the era of the cloth merchant, while the late fourteenth and fifteenth centuries gave status to the farm husbandman and the urban craftsman. But the majority of the labour force led lives which differed very little over the period, continuing virtually unchanged until the twentieth century

It would be a fallacy to presume that development in early medieval Scotland was hampered by a stagnant economy; in fact there was modest prosperity until the middle to late medieval period, when the economy was destabilised by war and internal conflict, in much the same way as the Stock Market today is subject to fluctuations in times of crisis. The untimely and tragic death of Alexander III in 1286 had a marked effect on the economy; with no heir to the throne, the fragile stability of the feudal system was threatened as never before.

In the thirteenth century, the important trading centres at Berwick, Roxburgh and Perth were thriving communities; Berwick was however occupied periodically by the English after 1296 and significantly after 1333, when Dunbar began to assume a new importance due to English occupation of Berwick - a focal town for Scottish, English and Continental traders. Cloth manufacture there was in the hands of Flemish and German craftsmen which brought the town a valuable income from its sale as well as from the raw materials used - wool and flax. Berwick, with its rich hinterland and the great wool-producing abbeys at Melrose, Kelso, Jedburgh and Dryburgh was literally the jewel in the Scottish crown. Melrose Abbey owned 15,000 sheep at the end of the fourteenth century, the largest flock of all the religious houses; most Border abbeys owned property in Berwick because of the trade in wool and the cloth trade. But these trades declined rapidly as a result of the Wars of Independence coupled with the loss of Berwick in 1333.

In the thirteenth and fourteenth centuries, Scotland's main wealth derived from wool, woolfells - the skins of sheep with the fleece remaining - and other animal skins or hides, although there was some trade in grain. As noted earlier, the chief source of information is contained in *ERs* which provide a detailed breakdown of the extent of trading activity and the amounts paid as Great Customs to the king. Like other communities, Dunbar relied on wool and leather products for its income, although when it became a royal burgh in the mid-fifteenth century, its wealth shifted from these basic commodities to a market economy based on agricultural produce and fishing; these remained the basis of the local economy until the first half of the twentieth century. In the final decades of the nineteenth century, Dunbar's wealth shifted from trade to tourism; its reputation as a popular east coast watering hole would last for about seventy years until cheap package holidays abroad became more attractive. How all this came about is examined below.

Not surprisingly, trade between Scotland and England was limited, largely centred on Berwick. The Great Customs show that the trade in wool and hides amounted to £7,040 (wool) and £600 (skins) for the whole of Scotland in 1378-79; at that time, Dunbar accounted for £180, just over 2.6% of the national total (See Fig. 13, chapter 10). In 1328, the royal income from the burghs was slightly less than £4,000; by David II's reign (1329-71) it had almost quadrupled to over £15,000. While the burghs were the mainstay of the royal finances, there are fluctuations which are not easily explained. For example, by 1410, the royal income was less than half of the average for the 1380s; by 1492, the king's income had shrunk to something in the region of £2,600, Dunbar accounting for less than £10, about 0.4% of the national total. Much of the fluctuation was due to uncertainty in the country brought about largely by the weak Stewart dynasty, although it is difficult to pinpoint specific instances to support this view. While an increase in trading activity - exports in particular - was automatically reflected in the royal income, it was £4,500 in 1535, Dunbar's contribution being £2; devalued by inflation, this precipitated a sharp rise in customs duty. It is this rather than an increase in the volume of trading which significantly boosted the king's income in 1578, when it was nearly £12,000. What growth there was derived chiefly from the export of cloth and grain; while these economic 'facts' cannot be interpreted too literally, they provide a valuable snapshot of the state of the medieval economy. It would also be wrong to assume that the state of the royal finances was directly linked to Dunbar's prosperity or that its economy was depressed; on the contrary, at the end of the sixteenth century, Dunbar was poised on the brink of one of its most prosperous periods.

We shall now examine in detail the state of the three main money-producing activities in and around Dunbar - agriculture, fishing and local and international trade - taking account of small local industries. We will also look at the social conditions from the Middle Ages to the present day.

While many today maintain that Dunbar's wealth derived from fishing - it would be irresponsible to deny the extent of the contribution made by that industry - the facts prove that the real producers of wealth were those who owned and worked the land. Take for example figures appearing in the *New Statistical Account* in 1844:

'turnips, wheat, grass, oats and beans	£56,700
lime (10,800 tons)	1,300
fish and lobsters	950

These figures speak for themselves, even if they are only a snapshot for a single year. For most of the nineteenth century and certainly by 1844, fishing at Dunbar was in decline due to the shift of the herring shoals and because there was insufficient investment in larger deep-sea vessels such as those used by the Dutch who had literally cornered the market. We now examine the main industries from which a significant proportion of Dunbar's wealth derived

Agriculture

We have already seen that Dunbar was settled by Neolithic, Bronze and Iron Age farmers but it wasn't until the beginning of the Middle Ages that farming developed beyond bare subsistence level. We know also that the early farmers were able to cultivate higher levels than today because of a gentler climate. In some areas of the Lammermuir Hills, there is evidence of this in the irregular ridge-pattern furrows made by primitive ploughs often higher than 750 feet above sea-level.

The early Dark Age peasants of East Lothian lived mostly in isolated farms until the seventh century, when the Angles of Northumbria annexed East Lothian and created nucleated villages. These villages are identified easily by at least one feature which originated in England - the village green, sometimes called 'loans' in Scotland eg Spott Loan. Examples exist at Stenton, Dirleton and less obviously due to modern development, at Whittingehame, Tyninghame, Oldhamstocks and Innerwick - villages whose names are basically Anglian.

In the eleventh century, Scotland was a wild country with unbridged rivers, gloomy woods, mosses and bogs; animals such as the beaver, the wolf and the wild boar roamed the countryside. Agriculture was patchy, with only the Merse, the Lothians, certain areas of Fife and Angus in the east and Ayrshire and Dumfries and Galloway in the west producing significant returns on account of their fertile soils. In the predominantly arable district of Dunbar, hamlets could survive and even prosper on what was grown; elsewhere, agriculture was largely pastoral which meant that farms were isolated, particularly where there was a scarcity of extensive and reasonably well-drained ploughing land. In the Lowlands, the hamlets were called *ferm-touns* or farm towns; many would evolve into proper villages and towns which make East Lothian and the Merse unique with their nucleus of villages created on Anglian design. Despite this, Dunbar differed little from any other low-lying settlement; beyond its cultivated areas and meadows, there were large tracts of unproductive land - heaths, moors, bracken commons and wooded areas - and only modest attempts were made to improve and extend their use from animal grazing to cereal production. These early medieval farm-towns must have looked like small islands floating in a sea of green. As for the community of Dunbar, it was little more than a huddle of smoky huts huddled round a stockade-type fortification on the promontory fronting the Castle Rock on which the later stone castles were built.

The landscape around Dunbar may not have changed dramatically over the centuries but in the seventh century, it would have been unfamiliar to modern eyes. The post-glacial loch at Lochend remained undrained for centuries, the countryside was still clothed in extensive woodlands, although these were disappearing gradually - not so much out of a need to cultivate land but for fuel. By the time Earl Gospatric arrived from Northumberland in 1072, there were fewer woods or belts of sheltering copses. The land wasn't enclosed until the seventeenth century; fields sprawled haphazardly from the very edge of the community to the Lammermuir Hills whose gentle slopes were covered with sheep. Even in 1830, the town plan of that year indicates that there were fields adjacent to Lauderdale House, the West Port and the Parish Church. The landscape we know today is man-made and dates back no further than the sixteenth century but even then, little changed. The serfs and bondsmen and their descendants, the cottars, hinds and labourers lived in isolated farms, each family cultivating plots of land beside those of their neighbours. As in the eastern counties of England, land was allocated in a mixture of runrig strips which consisted of the sunny south-east and the shadowy north-west so that all benefited equally from some good land and had to make do with some bad. Medieval land-use was very inefficient; the infield runrig system meant that the outfield of poorer, uncultivated land could only be used for grazing. No attempt was made to improve these acres by the introduction of manure. Despite this wasteful practice, Fife, the Lothians and the Merse produced a more diverse range of crops than elsewhere in Scotland, the staple crops being oats, barley and meal. In Dunbar, while these standard crops were grown, others such as wheat, rye, peas and beans flourished along with flax and hemp for linen and rope-making. Dunbar's economy was almost exclusively agriculture-based, fishing making a significant contribution to diet, if not to wealth. There is virtually no evidence of heavy industries such as coal-mining, although coal did exist in small seams which were worked for domestic use; the entrances to two small mines survive at the Cove Shore, near Cockburnspath, where coal was extracted for the fires at Dunglass House.

The humble folk lived on the produce they grew on the small strips of land rented to them by their superiors; they paid their dues in food to the local baron who in return gave them protection and administered justice. In addition to their food-rents, the strip-holders were required to set aside a certain number of days each year to work for their feudal superior, particularly during the labour-intensive seasons of spring and autumn. The local lord exercised considerable control over his inferiors in more ways than purely agricultural activity. (Men were forbidden to leave the district or marry without his permission; when a man died, his son might succeed to the tenancy but only on payment of appropriate death-dues and by consenting to work on his superior's land). A typical example of labour due to a lord - known as *dawark* - almost certainly applied in the Dunbar district follows:

reaping at harvest by the whole family	4 days
reaping by husbandmen and two men carting peats	1 day
ploughing one and a half acres	2 days
harrowing fields	1 day
working with wagon at harvest	1 day
sheep washing	1 day
one man and horse to Berwick once a year with a load of 3 bolls[1] of corn or 2 bolls of salt or one and a half bolls of coal	2 days

In the above example which appears in *Liber Sancti Marie de Calchou* (*Kelso Liber* or chartulary), the husbandman was also charged an annual rent of six shillings and eightpence (33p) or its equivalent in food for his land.

Land held by 'freemen' was let on *tack* or lease which could be for 3, 5, 7, or 9 years; a husbandman was also required to pay a *grassum* or lump sum for entry to a lease or when it was due for renewal. Rents were in kind - invariably oats, wheat, barley, cheese, butter, fowls and eggs until gradually, money payments became more common. All the corn grown by Dunbar tenant farmers - free or unfree - had to be ground at the Earl of Dunbar's mills at West Barns and Beltonford; in time, the royal burgh took these over, often renting them out to a tacksman who exacted his dues and paid rent to the burgh council. *Thirlage* [2] was due to the lord, a form of early taxation - usually a stipulated weight of corn ground or flour milled - for the privilege of using the mill, known as a *multure*. The Dunbar earls had their own farms but a large proportion of the food they ate was provided as rent from their tenants. Also, all landowners and tenants were required to pay church *teinds* or tithes - a tenth of all they produced. An earldom such as Dunbar was rich in produce; when money payments replaced perishable food-rents, the earls grew rich and were wealthy enough to build a stone castle in the mid-thirteenth century. In the parish of Dunbar, there were at least 20 farm-towns. The growth in size of the Dunbar farm-towns led them to be sub-divided every now and then by the Earls of Dunbar to provide income for their heirs; this accounts for the similarity in names of some of the local farms today - Pinkerton, Little Pinkerton, Meikle Pinkerton, Easter and Wester Broomhouse, Spott and Little Spott. The practice of sub-dividing farms was common on both sides of the Border.

When the Black Death took one in every six of the working population in 1349-50, the reduction in the labour force brought freedom to the bonded serfs; husbandmen were also able to farm larger areas of about 50 acres with their subservient cottars and sub-tenants working between 5 and 10 acres. As the population recovered from the ravages of the plague, then increased, there was more intensive use of land. Arable farming continued to meet the needs of an expanding population but it was still largely sheep and cattle which formed the basis of Scotland's trade with the Low Countries, the Baltic, France and to a lesser extent, England from the twelfth to the sixteenth century.

Agricultural life was hard, unremitting and monotonous, with fluctuating rewards and on occasion starvation; because farming methods were rigid, crop yields were erratic, the soil became exhausted and despite some improvement, land was poorly used even in fertile East Lothian until the late seventeenth century. Sheep husbandry in the Lammermuir Hills, a more relaxed and rewarding occupation, made a significant contribution to the national economy. In summer, the shepherds and their families took the flocks to the high pastures, living in temporary huts or *sheilings*, making butter and cheese from ewe's milk, a diet on which they existed for half of the year. There are several places near Dunbar whose names end in *-shiel*, testifying to their use as summer pastures - Penmanshiel and Mayshiel for example. When Melrose Abbey was founded in the twelfth century, the Cistercian monks became expert agriculturalists and sheep-breeders, possessing lands granted by charter from nobles as far afield as Haddington which allowed them to graze their sheep in out of the way places that didn't interfere with hunting and hawking, the sports of kings and nobility.

Thus agriculture remained largely at subsistence level until at least the late fourteenth century when surpluses became available after the plague thinned out the population. Surplus meant trade and the markets in the royal burghs grew wealthy on the produce sold there. The burgh grain markets probably began after the Black Death had passed on. As Berwick see-sawed between England and Scotland and finally became English in 1482, the merchants looked about for other outlets for their goods. Until David II's charter making Dunbar a free burgh, Berwick and Roxburgh were the main market towns in the area. Markets and fairs at Dunbar brought trade, as did its natural harbour at Belhaven.

We know from fourteenth century charters that grazing land was measured by the simple expedient of the number of cattle and sheep it could support. The ancient Celtic units of measurement were superseded by the *davoch* or *ploughgate* and the *oxgang* [3] In 1497,[4] we learn that there were four mill-quarriers at Dunbar - men who made the millstones - which gives some indication of the extent of grain-production at the time. By the Reformation, nine out of ten people still made their living from the land. Even so, farms were poorly managed; large tracts of land were untended, given over to thickets of broom and gorse and if cultivated at all, only in small plots.

Little changed until the seventeenth century. By then, farms of reasonable size were run by a hierarchy from the proprietor downwards. After him came the steward - usually a major tenant who presided over the local baron courts which settled disputes in agricultural matters; next came the chamberlain who collected his master's rents, then the humbler members of the workforce. Later on, there were factors, grieves, husbandmen, cottars and at the bottom, the landless peasants and servants who worked in the farmhouses. Working life in the outlying farms near Dunbar is not too difficult to imagine before the eighteenth century. Most of what we know derives from the rural or baron courts. These courts were presided over by the landowner or his steward or factor; they heard local disputes and tried petty criminals not referred to the sheriff court. There were also less formal meetings of what were known as *birlaw* or *birlay* courts[5] which consisted of between four and 14 chosen men of good character whose task it was to keep 'good neighbourhood', settle minor arguments and report decisions taken on agricultural matters at the baron court to the workforce. The *birlaymen* also reported tenants and workers who ignored or were in contempt of baron court rulings to the proprietor. We know there were open air birlay courts held at Little Spott where the traditional meeting-place was marked by a long-since vanished ash tree near the Witch's Stone.[6]

Although modern economists no longer accept there was an agricultural 'revolution' in Scotland, there was a marked change in the attitudes of some gentlemen farmers towards the end of the seventeenth century, particularly in East Lothian. These men were far-seeing, looking beyond next year's harvest; the more perceptive were conscious of the need for improvements in husbandry and soil use. The clumsy, inefficient methods of farming in the past combined with poor soil management meant that much of the potential gain from cereal production - the mainstay of the national diet - was lost. Dunbar managed to supply some of the home markets with grain but overseas trade was hardly worth the risk; although cargoes were sent to England in the late seventeenth century, most were returned unsold or undelivered because of the rigid application of the English Navigation Acts which precluded merchants buying from vessels not registered in England. There had to be change and change certainly came about, albeit slowly, thus diluting the impact of the so-called 'revolution' in agricultural improvements.

One of the first improvers was John Hamilton, 2nd Lord Belhaven, who owned the rich and productive cornfields of Bielside, near Beltonford. As with all improvers in the conservative world of agriculture, Belhaven had an uphill struggle to persuade his fellow farmers to adopt his suggestions. His approach was patient and realistic however; his writings show that he appreciated the pitfalls in introducing change too quickly, bearing in mind the initial outlay of money with poor prospect of immediate rewards. Husbandry was Belhaven's specialty; in 1699, his pamphlet, *The Countrey Man's Rudiments; or An Advice to the Farmers in East Lothian to Labour and Improve Their Ground* ran to three editions which is indicative of its worth. In his *Rudiments*, Belhaven outlined his views on the layout of farm buildings which ultimately led to the replacement of the old farm-towns by steadings kept some distance away from the main farmhouse, which he recommended should be built of stone. Belhaven's blueprint envisaged a group of barns, byres and stables arranged round a central courtyard; he recommended that barns for storing hay should be built on the west side of the farm, preferably on raised ground so that the prevailing west winds would dry the hay quicker. While also suggested a three-year cycle of crop rotation - wheat, bere, oats - he wasn't the first to realise the benefits from it. He was also concerned about the need to introduce fertilisers and proper tillage to improve the soil quality and therefore crop-yield. Like Andrew Fletcher of Saltoun, Belhaven highlighted the serious shortage of winter fodder for livestock which meant that most of the fatstock had to be slaughtered and salted in November (Martinmas).

Belhaven enthused about the need to remove stones from fields, recommending they be used to build dry stone dykes; he was also a keen planter of trees to provide shelter from the elements in open fields. Incredible though it may seem today, there was resistance to tree and hedge planting; farm labourers regarded both as a nuisance as in their opinion, the roots spoiled the ground, the shade prevented grain from ripening, the hedges and trees provided breeding areas for birds which ate the crops. Most farmers of the time considered trees unnecessary and often sent their labourers out at night to uproot newly-planted saplings and damage mature trees in the fields owned by their neighbours. A change in attitude came in the mid-eighteenth century when it was conceded that trees and hedges not only had an aesthetic effect on the general landscape but offered protection from the effects of bad weather on young crops but more importantly, prevented topsoil from blowing away. Belhaven's enthusiasm for trees was shared by the 6th Earl of Haddington whose Countess was so unhappy with their treeless estate at Tyninghame that she persuaded her husband to plant 500 acres down to the seashore. Binning Wood became a famous landmark, sheltering fields and providing income from the sale of wood for fuel until the trees were cut down during the Second World War.

Belhaven's preference for enclosed land brought him into conflict with his neighbour, David, Lord Hay of Belton in 1703.[7] Belhaven considered that a recent act of parliament gave him a statutory right to straighten his boundary line; in the process, he annexed some of Lord Hay's land. The dispute was settled in Belhaven's favour, although Hay received some Belhaven land by way of compensation. Provision for straightening and fencing boundaries had been made in legislation passed in 1661, 1669 and 1685. Belhaven had no doubt cited the act of 1685; it was a poorly drafted piece of legislation, the cause of several similar lawsuits.

Despite pioneering spirits like Lord Belhaven, Fletcher of Saltoun and Cockburn of Ormiston, much of the landscape remained unchanged during the first four decades of the eighteenth century. Bogs were left unattended and what drainage there was amounted to little more than the natural slope of the land to carry away excess water; there was no incentive to improve, no government-grant schemes to assist the farmers. Even famine didn't act as a fulcrum; while there were years of dearth in every century, famine proper appeared at roughly 25-year intervals - in 1623, 1658, 1673 and 1699. The first English leisure travellers to venture north floundered about on horseback over poorly-made roads and tracks, finding Scotland a depressing, water-logged country; they were relieved when they encountered even humble communities such as Dunbar with its church and inns for solace. To most southerners, Scotland remained a terrifying place until Thomas Pennant published his famous *Tours of Scotland* and allayed their fears.

As noted earlier, modern economists discount the idea of revolution in agriculture; the word is political and implies swift and ground-breaking action - no pun intended - to remedy a drastic situation. The development of agriculture didn't occur in that fashion, especially in East Lothian. It was more a case of farming beginning to adjust to increased demand and leaving behind the dark, impoverished centuries, matters put right by only a few dedicated individuals. That development began in the Lothians and the Merse should come as no surprise as not only were these counties fertile, their farmers knew by instinct that production could be improved; the first step towards this end occurred in these counties, the first to recognise and abolish the inefficient runrig system which had long hindered improvement. Under men like Lord Belhaven, what was uneven was made straight; what had been barren was fertilised; what had been waterlogged was drained and what had been pastured was cultivated. Thus a not inconsiderable element of estate management was pioneered in the Dunbar area, the landscape beginning to show the visible effects. The population boom of the seventeenth century provided the improvers with the impetus they needed. Prices of agricultural produce remained stable as long as production kept pace with demand; however, the exhaustion of the land, a series of wet summers and poor harvests pushed prices beyond the ordinary man's pocket and starvation stared many in the face. Something had to be done.

In addition to men like Belhaven, Cockburn and Fletcher, the Lords Kaimes and Monboddo were keen agriculturalists, encouraging innovation and supporting those who wanted change. Such men were the first to practise new techniques like crop rotation and the introduction of new crops. Farming made a great leap forward in the Lothians and the Merse in 1765 with the replacement of the clumsy plough which had needed a team of oxen to draw it; the new two-horse iron or Scotch plough invented by the Merse farmer John Small of Ford, a native of East Lothian; Small's plough made a difference to spring planting, speeding up the process considerably. Next came the reaping machine introduced by Patrick Bell, a contraption which replaced the tedious hand-flail which created a bottleneck in harvesting crops and consequently the late delivery of grain to the markets. Andrew Meikle of Houston Mill near Prestonkirk - one of a dynasty of East Lothian millwrights[8] and agricultural engineers - began to experiment with different types of threshing mills and finally perfected his efficient version in 1785. Meikle's first mill was installed at Clackmannan, his second at Phantassie, East Linton, a farm owned by George Rennie, father of the famous civil engineer John Rennie. George Rennie bred cattle which excelled in size, weight and quality, fetching good prices at local fatstock markets. He established the Linton distillery, with offshoots at West Barns and Haddington, thus creating conveniently near outlets for his grain. At one point, East Lothian possessed nine distilleries of which only Glenkinchie at Pencaitland has survived. Andrew Meikle's mill greatly improved the output of grain to supply these heavy consumers. A fine example of a mill has been preserved by the National Trust at Preston Mill, East Linton (**ill 79**).

Andrew Meikle (1719-1811) was the son of James Meikle who introduced machine fanners and barley mills.[9] Bringing to an end the slow processing of grain in the previous centuries seems to have been a personal crusade of the Meikles; however, it must be said that East Lothian never experienced a 'revolution' since change was gradual over the whole of the eighteenth century. Andrew Meikle's design for a threshing mill in

Illus 79: *Preston Mill, East Linton* HM

1786 was soon widely adopted but he failed to patent his idea until 1788 which meant that he personally profited little from his invention. In the relatively short space of twenty years - a generation in fact - there were no fewer than 350 threshing mills in East Lothian alone. In his last years, Meikle must have ruefully reflected on how rich he might have become. However, Sir John Sinclair (1754-1835) the great agricultural improver [10] and statistician raised £1,428 for Meikle in his old age; sadly, the poor man died before he could enjoy the gift which was passed to his son and daughter. Sinclair is better known for his compilation of the *Old Statistical Account*, so-named to distinguish it from the two following it in the nineteenth and twentieth centuries. Sinclair's account was a major social survey of Scotland at the outset of agricultural and industrial progress and like the modern census, was an invaluable source for historian and social reformer alike. Sinclair was the MP for Thurso.

Meikle used various power sources, the most amenable being the horse. His polygonal horse-gin or horse-mill was cheap to run, its sides were open so that the horses could keep cool as they plodded in a circle turning the milling equipment. An example of this type survives in Roxburghe Terrace, at the south end of Dunbar; there was another at Friarscroft but it has been renovated and forms part of a modern dwelling-house today, its distinctive squat shape with pantiled roof faithfully imitated. Other forms of mill were those driven by water and wind. Where insufficient force of water precluded the use of that type of mill, Meikle built windmills to augment that source rather than to directly power the mill. In the eighteenth century, Oxwellmains Farm had a fifteen-foot windmill to pump water; an example of this type of windmill survives in the grounds of the former Knockenhair House which although dating from the seventeenth century, was rebuilt to its present seventeen feet in 1855 and given a conical roof in 1907. The thirty-foot water-mill at Bielside in the eighteenth century was used chiefly for grinding corn. Meikle did however experiment with windmills proper and devised a system for reefing the sails quickly at the onset of a storm. When he died in 1811 aged 92, his achievement was recorded with appropriate pomp on his gravestone in Prestonkirk Parish Church cemetery in East Linton.

A clear example of the difference between Lowland and Highland agricultural development can be seen in the time of the '45 rebellion. In 1745, Cameron of Lochiel succeeded in building one or two water-mills to grind corn but they were both under-used; at that late period, the Camerons plucked corn out by the roots, burnt the straw and ground the corn in querns or hand mills. It was labour-intensive but the labourers were slow to embrace change in that traditionally-minded, conservative area. In Lothian and the Merse some 500 years earlier, the monks at Melrose and Kelso Abbeys had achieved what Cameron of Lochiel was attempting to introduce in his clan. In East Lothian, the steam threshing mill followed closely on Meikle's invention, although these mills could be dangerous if not properly maintained; the *Haddingtonshire Courier* for 7th July 1899 reported the explosion of the steam mill boiler at Pinkerton Farm, fortunately without loss of life. By 1845, there were 386 farms of 60 acres or more in East Lothian of which 80 had steam-powered mills, 7 powered by wind, 30 by water [11] and 259 by horse; by 1840 however, the horse-gin went into decline and was made completely obsolete in 1890 by the steam-mill. In almost every part of East Lothian there is ample evidence of the extensive use of the steam mill, identified by its tall brick chimney which is often mistaken for an industrial factory.

East Lothian farmers quickly adopted Jethro Tull's horse-drawn seed drill; other mechanical appliances were soon introduced which improved output but reduced the workforce considerably. Also making an early appearance in East Lothian was the humble turnip, originally used exclusively as winter fodder for sheep and cattle, thus avoiding the need for mass slaughter of animals at Martinmas for salting as winter food. There are conflicting claims about the first Scottish farmer to introduce turnips as a crop; the vegetable came to Scotland via Holland and England in 1716 but it wasn't universally grown until about 1739. Credit for its introduction goes variously to the Earl of Rothes in 1716, Cockburn of Ormiston in 1725[12] and Sir Archibald Grant of Monymusk in 1726. Dr Hamilton who farmed at Hallhill near Lochend, Dunbar was reputedly the first to grow turnips in the vicinity in 1784 which seems rather late for this important addition to the diet of cattle in a significantly productive cattle-rearing district. In 1793, Swedish turnips, known by their Latin name *ruta baga* - hence their local name of *baigies* or *bagies* by which they are still known today rather than the more English *swede*. Hallhill was extremely fertile like its Warrender proprietors' farm at Lochend, being on the site of the Great Loch of Dunbar. (It is interesting to learn from Captain Edward Topham, visiting Scotland in 1770, that turnips were served as the dessert course at one fashionable Edinburgh dinner table![13])

Despite the improvements, farming was still a precarious business and occupation. The *Old Statistical Account* abounds with anecdotes about bad harvests and the uncertain climate with its frequent and sudden changes from mild to cold, dry to wet and with frosts arriving as early as August and lasting until March and April, thus preventing the sowing of crops. May is often described as a cold month, July and August are wet; one year a hard frost arrived in August, followed by violent storms which flattened the almost-ripe grain. In 1771, the Year of the Black Spring, sowing was impossible and food prices rose sharply. In 1782, snow lay until late February with the previous autumn's harvest rotting beneath it. Even when a good crop was lifted, the want of decent roads was a drawback since those that existed were unsuitable for heavily laden carts, often making it necessary to transport small quantities of grain, coal and lime on horseback which affected prices. Until the new threshing methods arrived, grain was rarely delivered to its destination earlier than Christmas and sometimes as late as Candlemas in February. Far-seeing proprietors like Sir John Nisbet of Dirleton, Lord Advocate of Scotland decided to rent a *girnel* or granary near the Old Harbour where his Innerwick and Thorntonloch tenants had to deliver the grain by cart and store it in the grim Spot's Girnal - now demolished - until it could be transported to its destination by sea.

Dunbar and district grain production was considerable; in addition to Spot's Girnal, Christopher Middlemass, the enterprising merchant and provost bought most of a row of dwelling houses in Lamer Street near the Old Harbour, where he lived in the prestigious Cromwell House, now sadly demolished. Middlemas proposed to demolish the houses save one at each end of the row. His proposal didn't go unchallenged however; a Mr Stewart living at one end - possibly supported by Mr Muirhead at the other - required Middlemas to produce a before-and-after sketch, an early form of planning permission. The granary was built in 1817 and had many subsequent changes of use; known within living memory as The *Dreadnought*, it housed various businesses including Martin Riley's Guest House, a cinema in the early part of the twentieth century and Alec (Eck) Waite's warehouse for storing second-hand furniture. Today, the building is enjoying a phoenix-like and tasteful conversion by W A Gillespie and Son, local builders. A further testament to the success of the grain trade was the Corn Exchange, built in 1855 to accommodate the weekly grain market.

However, as machinery was invented and roads improved, grain was available sooner for the markets at places like Dunbar although at the end of the eighteenth century Britain had to import foreign grain to feed a rapidly-expanding industrial population. The strong corn lobby in parliament-the rich landowners-made sure that imported grain was subject to prohibitive duty, enshrined in the Corn Laws. In 1813, Dunbar burgh council petitioned parliament against the repeal of these laws, arguing that price of corn would fall and the wages of agricultural workers would suffer. It is more likely the council was protecting the burgh's interest and that of the local landowners in an above-average cereal-producing district.

Those farmers who resisted change soon found themselves in the minority; gradually they were converted by the evidence of their eyes. Increased production brought with it specialisation in the labourforce. In the Lowlands, the tenant farmer - husbandman or *gudeman* - usually engaged a sub-tenant as hind or ploughman in exchange for a plot of land. In the hierarchy of the agricultural workforce, the ploughman came first, then the hind or thresher; next was the cottar who often doubled as weaver, tailor, cobbler or shoemaker. At the very bottom were the farm servants and labourers; the former might work either in or out of doors in specified jobs. There were few outward signs of difference in their lives; most lived in cold, damp and draughty cottages or huts clustered round the farmhouse. Those slightly higher up the pecking-order were allowed a kailyard or small parcel of land on which to grow crops, vegetables or even keep a few sheep and a cow or pig for their food.

Men were *fee'd* – hired - for a term; these varied depending on marital status. Married men were hired for a twelvemonth, bachelors for six months. Terms ended at Whitsuntide (May) or Martinmas (November); feeing fairs were held twice a year, the most well-attended occurring in February. Men seeking a fee congregated at places like Dunbar, never speaking a word to the farmers who inspected them; the farmer made the initial approach, striking a bargain with a token payment of one shilling (5p), known as the *arles*. Dismissal was also tacit, never stated; if a farmer stopped speaking to a worker, or didn't ask him to *bide* [stay on]as the months of

SLA

Illus 80: *Dancing Bear, Dunbar High St. c.1900*

May and November grew close, it was a sign for the man to move on. At Dunbar, the February feeing fair took place on the first Tuesday in the month, followed by the Haddington fair, two days later; this gave the unsuccessful job-seekers a second chance. The Martinmas or November feeing fair was held at Dunbar in the first week of the month, occurring on 8th November in 1864, as reported in the *Haddingtonshire Courier.* Feeing fairs continued until well into the twentieth century in East Lothian; these were held not only for men seeking employment but became annual holidays enjoyed by the people at large. They were red-letter days infused with a carnival atmosphere. It was an occasion for merriment; stalls and sideshows were set up on the east side of the High Street from the head of Victoria Street to the Town House; there were swing-boats, chair-o-planes, hobby-horse rides, merry-go-rounds and rifle booths. The dancing bear shown above may well have been part of the day's entertainment. The pubs did a brisk trade, attracting the censure of the godly moralising minority who deprecated the drunken and licentious behaviour of young men and women; drink and the natural urge of hormones were powerful driving forces on feeing days.

The lot of the farm labourer changed little between the eighteenth century and the First World War. The horse was the single effective means of traction and in the rural hierarchy of worker, the horseman ranked beside the ploughman, who often undertook both jobs on the smaller farms. It is said that of all farmworkers, the ploughman was the least intelligent and communicative because he spent most of his time with horses, often preferring them to his fellow human beings. The first accusation is biased and unfair but the second is probably true. Because the horse was valuable, it was often better treated than some farm workers. In 1845, the instructions to farm servants contained an exhortation to be

'patient and kind with horses, never overload them.'[14]

Just outside Innerwick there is an ornamental horse trough which expresses much the same sentiments in an inscription above the trough (**ill 81**). The ploughman was king in his day, spending more time with his horses than his co-workers, looking after these noble creatures as lovingly as if they were his own (**ill 82**).

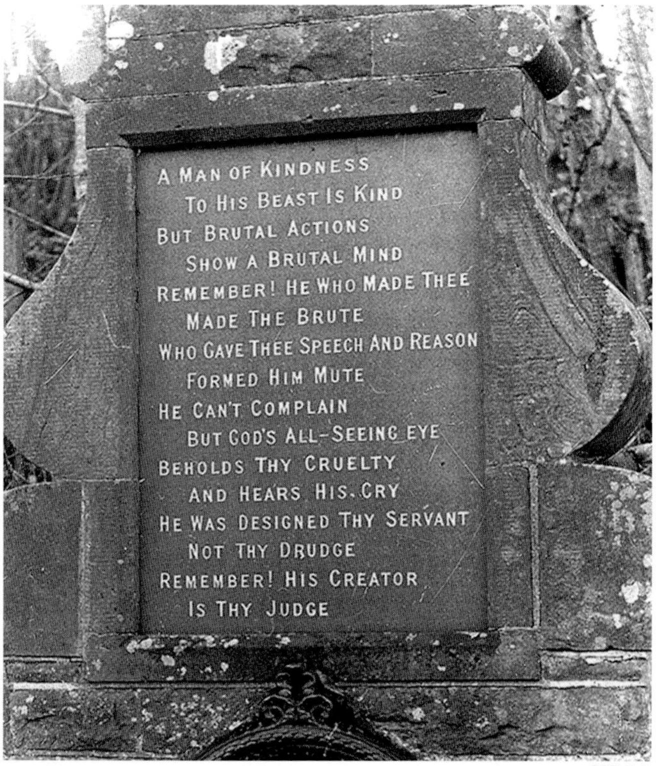

KRM

Illus 81: *Horse trough near Innerwick*

Although mechanisation and specialisation brought much-needed improvements both for farmer and the male members of the workforce, women also made a significant contribution. Agricultural work required physical strength and stamina which made it a predominantly male occupation. In Scotland, this was never the case; in the Lothians and the Merse for example, every married farm labourer and hind was expected to provide the services of a female - wife, daugh-

Illus 82: *Abe Darling with a fine pair of Clydesdales, West Barns 1931* SLA

ter or sister - for employment as servants in the farmhouse or as *bondagers* (**ill 83**) in the fields. The name has a feudal ring to it. Women with their deft fingers making up for their lack of physical strength could work wool and flax, sort seed potatoes, single young leeks for planting out, weed the drills of young plants and of course, *tattie-howkin'* (gathering potatoes). Even so, they were expected to do much harder work than might be imagined - and back-breaking work at that. In nineteenth century East Lothian, 46% of the workers were bondager women or casual labourers from the towns; they milked cows, hoed, weeded and pulled turnips, forked sheaves of corn - a particularly strenuous task - cleared fields of stones, spread dung and lifted potatoes. These were all classed as light jobs. Bondagers worked between 20 and 160 days every year depending on the farmer's needs, especially at seed and harvest times. (**ill 84** Harvesting oats at East Barns). The bondager's wages were poor; they perhaps paid for the rented cottage and provided some of the family's food. At harvest, farmers hired additional women and children from nearby villages and towns as well as Highland and Irish immigrant workers, housing the latter in *bothies* or communal huts with practically no amenities other than a fireplace to cook food. Although the bothy system for housing young unmarried men was common throughout Scotland, it was used sparingly in East Lothian, usually only at harvest time or on remote farms where there were few farm cottages available. Bothies were largely used for shelter during bad weather and for eating meals - the ubiquitous *piece* or sandwich washed down with cold tea or milk at noon. Residential bothies were brutish places with no facilities; they lacked privacy, companionship, coarse humour and whisky compensating for the lack of amenities. Even in the mid-twentieth century, the bothy was an awesome place, even for simply eating food. I spent one or two summers working on farms round Dunbar during the 1950s; the work was monotonous and back-breaking even then and we looked forward to *lousing* or finishing time which never seemed to come. The bothy was where we took our *piece* - unless driven into hiding places when we were tormented by the women whose humour and behaviour were, to say the least, crude and physical. In the previous century, bothy life was primitive, with few concessions to comfort. The horses were more grandly housed and cared for; the stables I recall seeing at East Barns in the 1950s had ornate carvings based on classical motifs.

The workforce in the twentieth century was comprised unequally of males and females; jobs like weeding and singling seedlings were usually undertaken by the older women, young girls and boys. A century before, women were expected to work alongside the men and undertake tasks which taxed a man of average strength. Although the hinds resented the bondager system - unique to Scotland - they failed to persuade their employers to

Illus 83: *Bondagers at the tattie-howkin* DDHS

Illus 84: *Harvesting oats at East Barns* SLA

end it and the custom lingered on until the very eve of the First World War. Wages of both men and women were poor, work was hard and males and females aged prematurely. Eventually the bondager system was challenged by the Farm Servants' Protection Society which campaigned vigorously for its abolition. The reason why a high percentage of women in and around Dunbar worked in the fields was because there was simply no alternative; there was no significant manufacturing base, villages were remote and women were cheaper to hire than men. Thankfully, the bondager system had all but died out in Dunbar by 1875, when the seasonal employment of Highlanders and Irish families brought large numbers to the district. Dunbar women were hardy creatures; when not employed in the fields, many worked at the harbour, gutting and cleaning herring - a dirty, cold job.[15] By 1914, other employment was created by the war and while the days of cheap labout were almost over, female farm workers' wages remained low.

Vestiges of the bondager system remained however - particularly in the way female field workers were dressed. They wore what was known as the *ugly* - in some areas, little more than a cape worn round the neck with the folds of cloth drawn over the head with tucks and stiffened, making it look like a beehive. More common in East Lothian generally and Dunbar in particular was the basket-shaped hat or bonnet made of calico, gingham or coloured cotton cloth stretched over a high cane or wire framework, which allowed an extended brim and drape over the face and neck for protection against sun and wind (**ill 85**). An alternative was the *hankie* or headscarf which was wrapped round the head and neck for protection against the dust and the weather. Most women wore a blouse of coarse material, a *drugget* skirt - tough material like modern jeans - and side-buttoned boots which often had straw ropes twisted round the legs as leggings, still in use around the time of the Great War. Wellington boots became popular much later. In living memory, women worked in the fields all the year round, taken to and from the farms in tractor-drawn trailers often without sides or soft-skinned lorries. I can remember sitting beside the farm women in the tractor which took us home at the end of the day's work, our legs dangling over the edge of the trailer; the women jumped off at their stop as nimbly as the boys. (I thought the *ugly* was like a miniature version of the covered wagons I saw in Westerns shown at the local cinemas!) In the bad old days, a bondager earned about fourpence a day (less than 2p) the price of a pound of sugar or slightly less than an ounce of tea. In 1910, a female farm worker earned ten shillings a week (50p) which rose to sixteen shillings (80p) in 1912 then thirty shillings (£1.50) a week in 1919. A ploughman's wife milking cows early in the morning seven days a week in the 1930s earned just over five shillings (26p)

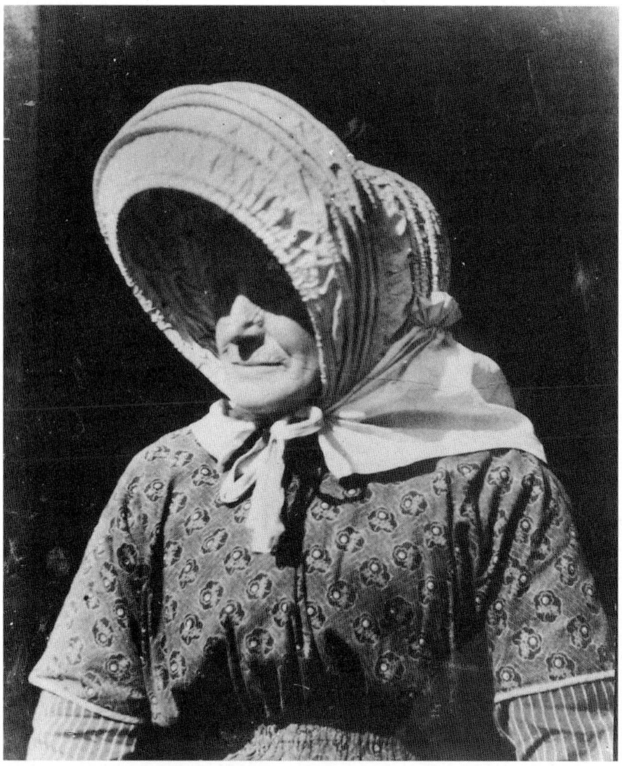

Illus 85: *Traditional bondager headgear - the 'Ugly' c.1920* SLA

By comparison, men were paid only marginally better. In 1843, one East Lothian farmer submitting evidence to the Poor Law Commission said that a ploughman's most valuable possessions were a good wife, a good cow and a good razor. In that year, a Dunbar ploughman could expect to receive the equivalent of £26 a year compared with half that in Inverness. At Dunbar, the typical ploughman's wage was largely in goods - 66 bushels of oats, 18 of barley, 8 of beans, 4 bolls (48 hundredweights) of coal, grass and winter keep for his cow, 1,500 yards of land for growing potatoes, a month's free meat at harvest, a free house and garden and £2 a year. A female at that time earned about £6:10:0 (£6.50) a year, a day worker tenpence (4p) a day, a labourer nine shillings (45p) a week, a carpenter two shillings and sixpence (about 12p) a day and stone masons slightly more than that at two shillings and ninepence a day. In 1862, a ploughman could expect to be paid £30-£50 a year in cash, with perquisites added - in theory at least. A survey undertaken at the time confirmed that wages varied considerably and were nearer between £17-£23 a year. Seventy years on, a ploughman was paid £84 a year, female workers £57; after the Second World War, the ploughman lost his skilled status with the arrival of the Ferguson tractor - the *Wee Fergie* - although Clydesdale horses were still drawing the ploughs near Dunbar in the 1950s. Twenty years before that, feeing fairs had been consigned to history.

Thus with mechanisation, the farm labourer's working conditions became less onerous but his quality of life - or more accurately, his standard of living - barely improved. There is an excellent account of farm life at the sharp end near Dunbar around 1830 in Alexander Somerville's *Autibiography of a Working Man Who Has Whistled Behind the Plough;* published in 1848, the style is remarkably modern and very readable for a man who had only the most basic school education available at the time. Somerville's account of mid-nineteenth century life is a little gem of a book; sadly, it has been out of print for many years.

Somerville's father was born in the parish of Muckart in 1760; his mother, who came from Ayton, Berwickshire, had the unusual name of Orkney. An ancestor Etty or Etta Orkney was, according to Somerville, a witch although in my earlier book, *The Deil's Ain,* there is no mention of her, probably because she managed to escape the attentions of the authorities. (The surname can be found on headstones in Ayton Churchyard today). Alexander's family lived and worked at the Cove, near Cockburnspath, then Thorntonloch, Thurston Mains, Springfield and Branxton. Clearly, the father regularly moved on at feeing times, although remaining largely in the same area, which tells us something about his standard of work. Somerville senior was a barn man or thresher; his children worked on farms for most of their lives. Alexander was born at Oldhamstocks in 1811 and subsequently worked on most of the farms mentioned above. He tried other occupations and wanted to be a forester; however, he seemed not to have possessed the relevant qualifications and eventually he joined the Royal North British Dragoons, or Scots Greys. He served briefly as a cavalry trooper until he fell foul of army discipline and emigrated to Dublin, then Canada, where he died in poverty.

Somerville's book is a catalogue of his life as farm labourer, timber-feller, ditch-digger and saw-miller; he also worked on the construction of Cove Harbour and at the Skateraw limekiln, the latter a dirty, smoky and back-breaking job. The record of his life up to 1832 illustrates the hardships faced by young men with no formal education, no money and little prospect of steady employment. The poet James Hogg - the *Ettrick Shepherd* - protested in 1832 about the poor lot of the farm labourer who had declined into

'a state of absolute slavery with only one amelioration, namely the liberty
at each term of selling themselves to the highest bidder.'

In the same year, William Cobbett, the radical reformer visited East Lothian, drawing attention to what he saw was a miserable peasant existence which the labourer accepted without protest. Horrified by the wholesale enclosure which had forced farm workers off the land, he wrote:

'Everything here is abundant here but people, who have been studiously swept from the land.'

The reason for this passive acceptance was simply because men without education believed it was their destiny to labour for the common good and because they knew of the considerably more harsh lives their grandparents had known. The new machines and farm methods were beginning to ease the country folk's toil even if that meant fewer were able to earn their living from the land. Perhaps something of folk memory remained; in 1690, it had been considered demeaning to ask for cash wages for working the land since that and its produce were ample rewards. The emphasis on money for labour was alien to the farm worker even in the early eighteenth century. Only the deserving poor accepted money payments for their efforts - often as little as £1 Scots a year (about 30p) since 'wages' largely consisted of food, shelter and a small plot of land to grow vegetables for the table or rear livestock and chickens. Having said that, until fairly recently, vegetables rarely appeared at mealtimes.

When other workers took the lead from the craftsmen with their guilds and societies, why did the farm workers who contributed so much to the wealth of the country take so long to organise themselves in order to improve their standard of living and lifestyle? The answer is that they were conservative with a small c. In the early 1800s, English farmers were willing to pay East Lothian ploughmen £6 or £7 a year in cash in addition to generous wages in kind - such was the quality of their work. Why were wages depressed in Scotland? The farmers themselves certainly made no secret of their debt to the workforce even if they rarely supported any attempts to improve their lot with cash. They put their men's loyalty down to the paternalistic attitude prevalent at the time. The tied cottage and wages in kind trapped the family man in the system. In 1860, there was a short-lived Farm Servants' Union, closely followed by the Farm Workers' Protection Society; the latter sought a basic wage of fifteen shillings (75p) a week, a free cottage, coal and a month's food at harvest for every farm worker. The Society had some success in the Lothians and Berwickshire but it gave way to a second Farm Servants' Union in 1912 which finally united the workforce although it's success was limited except during the two World Wars. By 1939, fewer than 100,000 people - a large proportion being women - were engaged full-time in agricultural labour. The figure has declined rapidly in the past fifty years.

No account of Dunbar's agricultural success would be complete without mention of the one vegetable for which it is rightly famous - the 'red soil' potato. (There is of course no such species of seed potato - red soil merely describes the rich fertile ground around Dunbar which is especially suited to growing named varieties like *Epicure*, *King Edward* and other well-known types). The potato was introduced to Scotland in the eighteenth century and by 1750 had become a kitchen garden vegetable. At first, potatoes weren't grown commercially in East Lothian, the crop of small farms around Dunbar, Haddington and North Berwick being sold for local domestic use. Used to 'clean' rough ground for cultivation, the potato also thrived on old pastureland and even wet fields. By 1794, potatoes made up 30% of the diet of the poor and they were used as fodder for livestock and poultry. In 1805, landowners were renting land at £5-10 an acre for growing potatoes.

Illus 86: *Potato planting at East Barns c.1939* SP

From the late nineteenth to the mid-twentieth centuries, the fields around Dunbar were thronged first in spring with women planting potatoes (**ill 86**), then in the autumn, when gangs of *tattie-howkers* - mainly women and children - were employed for about 4-6 weeks lifting potatoes by hand, a back-breaking job if ever there was one. The money was good however. At East Barns - now a decayed community - potatoes were grown on 335 acres; the farm population was 150, swollen by 100 or so seasonal potato-pickers. I recall one frosty autumn I spent on the farms at Pitcox and Tynefield owned by two local farmers, father and son by the name of Spence. There was always a sense of urgency about the lift before the 4-week leave from school expired, a throwback to the war years when most schoolchildren were expected to do their 'bit'. It was hard work but the wage in 1954 for boy or girl was £4:13:0 (about £4.65) for five and a half days' work - sometimes increased by £1 when required to work on Saturday afternoons. This was a small fortune to children who were accustomed to receiving sixpence a week pocket-money. At that time, the wages of a grown man averaged about £14. Potato-lifting was labour-intensive, giving work to 12,000 women and schoolchildren until mechanisation was introduced. In living memory however, mechanisation thwarted James Hope of East Barns, a well-known farmer who had to resort to the horse again when his steam-driven plough failed to negotiate the steep field he had planted that year. For over a century, public opinion has been loyal to the quality of Dunbar potatoes. A G Bradley, writing in his *Gateway to Scotland* refers to Dunbar's red soil as 'the cream of the country, probably the cream of the earth' which produced heavy croppings. Dunbar's heyday as a major supplier of potatoes by boat to England lasted from 1850 to 1914, after which the Great War induced the Lincolnshire farmers to grow their own. Even so, within living memory, potatoes were brought to Beeson's Store which stood on the site now occupied by the flats at Cromwell Quay and Cromwell Cottage at the Old Harbour. The sea-trade never recovered.

It is perhaps appropriate here to briefly mention the prime activity of the agricultural year - the harvest.

From earliest times, no season has captured man's imagination so much as the harvest. It has moved many poets. The significance of harvest was religious as well as social and economic. Not only was it the culmination of the year's hard labour but the bounty of a benevolent god, recognised by Christian Church and the state alike. The *hairst* or harvest had a special place in the rural - and cultural -calendar; it fed farmers' and workers' families and if the crop had been especially prolific, allowed the farmer to 'put by' spare cash - today, that term ironically means 'to leave fallow'. For the labourer, it was a time of heavy work for long hours; in the last two centuries, work continued after dusk and even today, the large combine harvesters are able to work in the dark with their powerful lights. In the nineteenth century, the intense activity meant high wages and free food to keep men and women working. Even those who didn't earn their living from the land, the harvest was viewed with a sense of accomplishment and pride; a good harvest was celebrated for the reassurance it brought and for the honest sweat of the workers. Services in churches - Harvest Homes - were always well-attended by young and old whether regular churchgoers or not. It was a community ideal. For me, the sight of tables in Belhaven Church covered with vegetables, sheaves of corn and fruit tastefully arranged and cleaned for the occasion is among those memories which will outlast any others of the church in the twentieth century. *Hairst* picnics (**ill 87**) were followed by *kirns* or supper dances at the end of the season.

Weather permitting, the harvest traditionally began in mid-August. Before the days of mechanical reapers, Lothian farmers hired Irish immigrant labour and Highlanders - usually reapers - to gather in the grain. The Highland reapers formed themselves into *bandwins* or squads, beginning with the *Lowden Hairst* (Lothian and Berwickshire Harvest); they then followed the ripening corn through Fife and central Scotland to the Tay estuary, then they crossed to the west. In the 1660s, there were shearing markets held in the Lothians where men were hired for wages only, cutting the corn with the *heuk* or hand-held sickle. The following two centuries saw an annual invasion of Irish workers which led to the introduction of the bothy system. Some Highland shearers and Irish laboureres stayed behind to work in the Lowlands after the harvest. One such man who rented a small croft in Vaternish, Skye for £5 a year came to Dunbar to work for Dudgeon of Easter Broomhouse from 1830 to 1850. He paid part of his croft rent from his wages and received seed corn from Dudgeon to make up the rest. He would work for six months at Easter Broomhouse, then return to his family in Skye, enjoying his croft in relative idleness for the winter months.

Illus 87: *A picnic at Woodhall* HM

Harvesting corn was hard work before horse, then tractor-drawn reaping machines. In a typical team, the scytheman cut the stalks, a girl would gather them into sheaf-sized bundles and the third member of the team would bind, then *stook* or stack the sheaves together to let the sun dry them. Thereafter, they were pitchforked on to a cart and taken to be threshed. The straw was stacked into hayricks for winter fodder for the cattle. By 1860, East Lothian had 160 horse-drawn reaping machines at work and the labour force was consequently reduced. As mentioned earlier, Dunbar had a Corn Exchange in 1855. The burgh council was entitled to charge tax on the sale of corn in Dunbar just as it did on the sale of cattle and sheep at the monthly market introduced in 1838. The council declared then that it would receive half of the customs due on the sale of beasts 'as for the corn market.'

Before the arrival of the tractor, cartwrighting was an important trade, carried on at Broxburn (**ill 88**) which also had a forge or *smiddy*. The smiddy has been converted into a modern dwelling house like the adjacent Anvil Cafe, both commemorated by name plaques on the walls. (There was another smiddy and garage at Beltonford - also long-since disappeared; the dwelling house survives although it and the outbuildings were moved from their previous site now occupied by the roundabout for the AI Bypass).

The old ways were changing fast. At one time, farmers worked alongside their men but after 1860, they became remote figures who simply supervised their workers. The last vestige of the old peasant-farmer bond lingered on at the harvest *kirns* or supper dances; versions of these are still held near Dunbar, usually combined

Illus 88: *Cartwrighting at Broxburn, c.1890-1900* SLA

with village flower shows and evening dances in places like Innerwick and Stenton.

The prosperous Hope brothers Robert and James were well-known figures of their day. Robert - the more eccentric of the pair - lived through most of the twentieth century. Robert Hope, born in 1910, was highly successful at Oxwellmains and Barney Hill, near East Barns. His grandfather came from Duddingston, Edinburgh; he bought East Barns in 1870, then the Hopes became tenants at Oxwellmains, which Robert and his brother James developed into an efficient and well-managed farm. Robert married the daughter of Marshall B Lang, the minister at Whittingehame and author of a history of the parish. The Hopes moved with the times, progressing from horse to tractor, binder to combine harvester and from hoeing weeds to chemical spraying. I worked at Oxwellmains in the 1950s, during summer holidays; the hours were long and spent singling young leeks for planting out, weeding and thinning turnip, carrot and beetroot seedlings, then picking strawberries and peas. When Oxwellmains was sold by its owner the Duke of Roxburghe to the Portland Cement Company in 1962, Robert Hope continued to farm East Barns. He was a traditionalist in that he was ordained as a kirk elder in Dunbar Parish Church in 1930. He died in 1995.

It is all gone now - or very nearly so. The great haystacks secured by ropes and weighted down with stones, towering above the landscape....the fields of turnips which in late autumn had to be prised out of the frozen drills using *cleeks* or special iron hooks, their green tops and roots 'docked' with knives.....the dependable pairs of Clydesdales, gentle, obedient, their heads nodding in a rhythm that was determined by the ploughman, harnesses jingling and gleaming in the sun, the distinctive smell of horse-leather and horse-sweat carried on the wind. Whether he had a mind to put it into words or not, the farm labourer's life was ruled by the seasons; it was once said of Spain that there were two kinds of aristocrat - the noble and the peasant - and perhaps this is true of all rural economies. The plough was a strong, appropriate metaphor, turning the earth and the farmworker's life. Perhaps Lewis Grassic Gibbon expresses best the emotional pull of the earth and the ambivalence of mens' feelings about it in a style that has never been excelled by other writers before or after him. We are unlikely to have any better. In *Sunset Song,* the first book of his memorable *Scots Quair*, he wrote movingly about his part of Scotland and spoke for the last of the old rural folk, the ploughmen and cottars who never returned from the Great War. Many of these men had their last glimpse of

Illus 89: *Haystack building* KA

SLA

Illus 90: *A rare image of a work ox.*

their beloved enemy, the earth, on the killing fields of the Somme. Gibbon knew only too well that the earth's was a dour, harsh and unforgiving love which left its scars on those who worked it. They were a different breed of men and women in the Mearns as elsewhere in Scotland; these quiet, shy folk who made their living from the farms around Dunbar are largely gone now, part of social history. They spoke slowly and sparingly, coming into town on Saturday afternoons to shop and visit the local cinemas and pubs, their only recreation of the week. The men walked with the slow, rhythmic pace of those who spent their days in the open with animals and ranged the ploughed fields. Their conversations were usually about the weather, a subject that to a great extent controlled and directed their lives. They were quietly proud of their existence, knowing that until fairly recently, a high proportion of the food they grew was consumed locally so that theirs was a vital contribution. They would have been acutely embarrassed to have read this or if anyone had troubled to ask them about their feelings for the land. Gibbon spoke best and truthfully on their behalf. There is no need to say more.

The men, women and horses have disappeared from the fields; even the sound of the harvest is different, dominated by the great monotonous whine of giant insects, the combine harvesters that work late into the night, illuminating the landscape with their white light. The old folk culture is all but extinguished; harsh words and times these men and women knew but theirs was a deep and lasting satisfaction, sustained by the customs and rituals of the seasons. The age-old compact between men, women, animals and the land is over, the sunset song but a dim echo. The calendar of the year, the rhythms of the seasons, the haunting voice of the earth no longer speaks to us as it once did. Without doubt, our lives are the poorer for that silence

Fishing and Sea Trade

We know from the remains of prehistoric middens that early man hunted for his food and that fishing predates his attempts at animal husbandry and cereal production. The early fishermen used spear, hook and trap, then line and net over 4,000 years ago. Sea-fishing is well-recorded in the sixth century AD but it is much older than that, probably as old as man himself. It became a way of life for many men and women on the east coast of Scotland for centuries; fish were caught not only for local consumption but for barter, as is confirmed by the monastic chronicles.

In Chapter 8, we learnt how Dunbar progressed from a free to a royal burgh in the space of 75 years, its elevated status allowing it to trade abroad. It is often said however that Dunbar became wealthy and famous because of fishing and its harbours. Of course this is true to some extent but we should remember that Dunbar first gained its reputation as an important Anglian shire centre in the seventh century AD, its economy probably being based on a mixture of agriculture and fishing. The anchorage at Belhaven is mentioned in the twelfth century as is confirmed by the archives. There is no mention of a harbour at Dunbar until James II's charter of 1445, which refers to Lamercraig and Lamerhaven; the former was the site occupied by the Battery, the latter the inlet later known as Broadhaven, probably the first 'harbour' in Dunbar. Fishermen would have used this natural haven during the Middle Ages but it was hardly a harbour in the sense we recognise today; most 'harbours' were little more than a muddy slope on a shore which had a small jetty or anchorage nearby.

Having said that, the men of Dunbar have fished the North Sea as far back as the Dark Ages and earlier. Their success in the Middle Ages certainly made the community a major centre for the herring-processing industry. Fresh herrings were not only a valuable source of protein, they could be salted or cured for use in the long winter months after the last fresh meat was slaughtered and salted at Martinmas. The Old Herring Road from Dunbar across the Whitadder Valley to Lauder is testimony to the use of fish as an important dietary item in winter; today, the road used by generations of monks and country folk to cart their 'silver darlings' from Dunbar to the Borders is traceable only in parts, identified by the deep v-shapes made by horse-drawn sledges.

The coming of the Industrial Revolution ensured there was an expanding market for Dunbar fish well into the nineteenth century; in the twentieth century, deep sea steam-powered vessels took the local fishermen further afield. Before that, the arrival of the railway in 1846 meant expansion of the market as catches could be sent all over Britain. In the boom years of the herring drave, Dunbar became a household word until the shoals moved elsewhere and local catches were restricted to shellfish - crabs, lobsters and prawns - and some whitefish like cod and haddock. That fishing contributed to the wealth and development of the burgh is indisputable; it made possible the creation of its two harbours and a fairly successful - if short-lived - coastal and overseas shipping trade.

It was Belhaven rather than Dunbar which provided Dark Age and Middle Age fishermen and sailors with a safe, natural haven. *Bielhaven* - from the Biel Burn which empties into the broad sandy bay - wasn't a man-made harbour. Its origins are obscure; it appears first in a charter of 1153 granted by Gospatric III in favour of the Cluniac monks on the May Island and again in David II's charter of 1369-70. We also know from a thirteenth century law book that a ship arriving at Belhaven laden with peas, beans and salt was required to pay dues of twelve pence (5p) and 2 bolls of each commodity to the town of Dunbar, an early form of customs duty. Surprising though it may seem, Belhaven was still being used by shipping in 1814, the year the burgh council levied tax on cargoes under a charter of 1618 [16] which is an indication of the lengths to which royal burghs went to enforce their rights. Perhaps the shipmaster had hoped to avoid paying dues at the Old or Cromwell Harbour. That Belhaven served as a port was confirmed when remains of masonry were found at Belhaven Toll (Benston Cottage) at the beginning of the twentieth century which included a stone block with an iron ring inserted, thought to have been used for mooring small boats. In 1841, local residents remembered the remains of a pier[17] and a line of posts were found that year by John Mason, the Belhaven surveyor who drew up the plan of the Victoria Harbour in 1837. It is more than likely however that Belhaven had silted up by the sixteenth century - hence the need to create the Old Harbour; we know however that the sea came very close to the main road in those days as much of what is now known as Seafield was reclaimed land.

Fish was a useful variation in the diet of the Middle Ages, as we know from John Mair or Major, whose account *A History of Greater Britain* was published in 1517. Major describes how

> 'in Lent and in summer, at the winter and summer solstice, people go early in the morning from my own Cleghornie [a hamlet near North Berwick] and surrounding parts to the shore, drag out the polypods [lobsters] and crabs with hooks and return with well-filled sacks.'

This was because at these times of year, the tides were at their highest and lowest and the crustaceans were trapped in rock pools near the shore. The practice was undoubtedly followed at Dunbar and elsewhere along the east coast. Because the Roman Catholic Church forbade the eating of meat on Fridays and during Lent, fishing was a profitable business for fisherman and church alike - tithes being due on catches - provided stocks were plentiful and reasonably close to the shore.

The beginnings of the Old or Cromwell Harbour can be detected in a charter of 1555[18] which refers to Lamerhaven, a natural tidal anchorage sheltered by Lamer Island. We know that Dunbar didn't have a harbour in 1548-49 from the writings of Jean de Beaugue who came to Scotland with the French army sent to besiege Haddington, occupied that year by English troops during the *Rough Wooing*. De Beaugue lamented the lack of a harbour which he considered could be built at minimal cost.[19] It wasn't long in coming, possibly as a result of French pressure. We learn from a Privy Council *Register* that Dunbar was authorised to levy customs in 1574,[20] the proceeds to be earmarked to cover the cost of building a haven

> 'under the toun and be east the Castell thairof.'

Thus we have proof that the Old Harbour wasn't built until after that year. It must surely put an end to the long-held local belief that Dunbar grew from its harbour area; as with other royal burghs, it developed along the main thoroughfare from castle to parish church, although this does not mean that the lower or harbour area wasn't populated before the harbours were created.

A harbour was needed to accommodate the increasing number of small boats engaged in the herring fishing some time after 1574 and certainly by 1579, when disaster struck the fleet in a storm just off Belhaven Bay, a disaster which James Miller records in his poem *The Luckless Drave*. The harbour was probably extended at some point between 1574 and 1591.[21] It accommodated local and visiting herring boats, a customs house with a gauger [customs and excise officer] to prevent smuggling and facilitated the collection of seaweed for use as fertiliser in the outlying farms, as noted by Brereton in 1636 (see Chapter 3).[22] At that time, there wouldn't have been significant sea-going trade. However, in addition to herring fishing, the curing of fish was carried on at Dunbar in the sixteenth century and probably long before then. In a letter of 1616 to James VI and I, the Privy Council refers to a patent for curing herrings by a method introduced to Scotland by Sir George Hay - the patent being granted to one Robert Hay for the manufacture of 'rid [red] herring.' Certain Edinburgh merchants who had started a factory for the cure of herring at Dunbar in 1609 lodged a complaint with the Privy

Council to the effect that an Archibald Campbell - probably one of the city merchants - had been granted the monopoly for curing herring and the grant of 1616 was an infringement of their franchise.[23] This is yet another example of how the royal burghs and their trader-merchants jealously protected their exclusive rights and privileges. It appears that during the period 1609-16, several 'monopolies' were granted for the manufacture of red herring, the king benefiting from sales which increased his share of the revenue - the Great Customs. In 1616, Dunbar sent a large percentage of its cured herring to Newhaven in Edinburgh for export abroad - another indication that overseas sea trade from Dunbar was still not possible because it lacked sea-going vessels of adequate tonnage.

It wasn't until about 1618 that the Old Harbour's bulwarks were extended to their present location; after that year, there are numerous references in the local records to repairs needed to the harbour walls. That Cromwell donated £300 for repairs in 1650 is unlikely; he had far more pressing problems that year, as we know. The *Old Statistical Account* states that

> 'the east pier of the present harbour was begun in the time of Cromwell's protectorship, to the extent of which Oliver granted £300 as appears by a letter of General Monck from Dalkeith'

This surely puts the date of the grant after 1650 and before March 1652, as Monck left Dalkeith at that time.

While Dunbar derived comparative wealth from its herring industry for a few centuries, fishing was precarious and unpredictable. During the Cromwellian Protectorate, a petition was presented to the Council of State in Whitehall regarding the repairs needed to the harbour.[24] In May 1657, the Committee for Scottish Affairs considered the Dunbar petition

> 'shewing how the demolishing of their harbour [by storm] had injured the town.......and that since the storm of December 1655 there has been no shelter for the herring industry there, which yields employment to most [sic] of the inhabitants round about.'

The petition struck the right note; the local councillors later expressed their gratitude for the low tax assessment levied on Dunbar which gave them the necessary breathing space to undertake the necessary repairs although they were unable to meet the full costs. The Council of State was empowered to make the necessary arrangements for the work to be done and it is possible the £300 grant in aid referred to above was paid at that time. The payment may also have been made as a result of Thomas Tucker's report at about this time;[25] as noted in Chapter 3, Tucker was a civil servant sent to Scotland in 1656 to assess the state of the economy for levying customs and excise duties. Tucker came to Dunbar that year and noted the success of the herring fishing, the only other trade being in salt which was imported and sold for preserving the fish in the winter months.[26] Perhaps Tucker's recommendations influenced the English civil authorities who were keen to improve Scotland's economy after 1650-51. Dunbar was fortunate to escape the devastation suffered by other east coast seaports during the Civil Wars; several had been raided by Montrose's royalist forces between 1644 and 1646 to prevent provisions falling into enemy hands. In addition to the English grant, the Convention of Royal Burghs made additional funds available in 1666 for harbour repairs at Dunbar.

It is thought that most of what survives of the Old Harbour today dates back no further than the first half of the eighteenth century when it was rebuilt between 1710 and 1730; a stone slipway was also added later to allow the unloading of coal. Perhaps the chiselled markings denoting depths on the left hand side of the entrance date from this period. Experts believe that the stone for the east pier was spoil from the ruined castle, which is extremely likely. The *New Statistical Account* states that the Convention of Royal Burghs provided £600 for repairs in 1785 and the burgh minute book frequently refers to alterations to the entrance and the considerable costs involved. The problem was that Dunbar, being exposed to violent storms, suffered continuous damage as a result; for example, on 1st February 1806, the burgh minutes record that a section of the Old Pier fell down during the night and took more than a year to repair. Between 1806 and 1810, no less than £2,888 was spent on repairs, a considerable sum for the time. It was considered well-spent however since although the fishing industry was in decline, sea-going trade was flourishing to such an extent that a *girnel* or granary and several warehouses were built near the harbour.

Dunbar's geographical location had an important bearing on its prosperity; it lies exactly midway between the productive hinterland of the Central or Midland Valley Fault and the Southern Uplands Fault. It was ideally placed for cargoes of grain and wool to be shipped to England, the Continent and the Baltic. If sea-trade was improving, the state of fishing left much to be desired; its decline was perhaps predictable given that there was much wrong with the way the industry was run in addition to the constantly shifting of the herring shoals.

In James III's reign, the herring fishing and cure and export of fish were well established. However, in the fourteenth century, Dutch, Flemish and German vessels competed with Scottish boats during the annual *drave* or harvest off the east coast. James III and James IV encouraged fishing and took steps to deal with foreign competition, albeit with limited success; gradually, the Dutch fleets gained a supremacy which wouldn't be seriously challenged until the eighteenth century. As early as 1423, herring was cured, salted and barrelled at Dunbar. Because it was a thriving industry, the proper securing and preparing of herring was a subject close to the Scottish parliament's heart. As a result, James IV taxed the catches, thus increasing his share of the customs.

Great care was taken over the control and management of the fishing industry. For example, in 1519, an act of parliament stipulated that barrels should bear the name of the skipper from whose boat the fish had been packed so that those who sold bad fish-herring deteriorate quickly out of sea water-could be identified and fined. Inspectors were appointed to oversee the herring drave at Dunbar every August and to ensure that all was done in accordance with the law. In the previous century, a series of acts regulated the size of barrels which also had to display the name of the cooper who'd made them. Only a certain type of salt was allowed for preserving the catch and the size of the boats and the nets they used were subject to regulation. The Convention of Royal Burghs stringently regulated the trade in fish; in 1570, it decreed that each barrel of herring should contain ten gallons of fish and that every cooper 'mark his barrel with his awn birning yrng' [his own burning iron]. The Convention imposed this rule so that it could trace merchants who sold underweight and thus be prosecuted. Herring - a staple of the winter diet - were among those goods which could only be exported from royal burghs with their exclusive trading and tax-raising rights. Acts passed between 1657 and 1673 also stipulated that catches were to be sold to 'free' merchants - meaning those resident in royal burghs. In 1587, yet another act required Scottish boats to land at least one-third of their catch in Scotland so that there was an adequate supply of preserved fish was available for domestic consumption during the winter months.

As mentioned earlier, herring is a fish which rapidly deteriorates when taken from the sea, so it had to be cured within a few hours; while there were ready markets for fresh fish locally, the bulk of the catch at Dunbar had to be 'reddened' - hung in curing houses and smoked or salted for the markets at Newhaven, Leith and Edinburgh. The Privy Council *Register* for 1616 shows that Dunbar red herring was exported to Dieppe and Bordeaux out of Newhaven. As we saw earlier, Dunbar had been granted the monopoly for the curing process, other areas such as Fife were given the same right, which not surprisingly caused a good deal of confusion, rivalry and bad feeling. In the earlier centuries, Scottish kings claimed a quota of the herrings caught off the Scottish coasts for the royal kitchens, later commuted to a tax of ten shillings (50p) on every boat. The duty was payable to the High Admiral of Scotland whose duty it was to protect Scottish boats at the herring drave. By 1853,[27] the royal tax was no longer levied, although the burgh of Dunbar exacted one-fifteenth of the value of all catches as 'herring teinds.'

The Convention of Royal Burghs worked ceaselessly to regulate and promote this important industry, protecting the fishermen's interests at the same time. Burghs trading in fish had to ensure that the appropriate measures of fish were barrelled, identified and sold only to 'freemen' or men belonging to the burgh. In 1606, Dunbar was warned that failure to abide by the rigid rules imposed by the Convention on herring fishing would mean a fine of £100 Scots (about £8 sterling). In that year, the magistrates had failed to superintend the herring drave properly by allowing ' unfreemen to tak and peill hering' [curing and preparing herring for sale to unauthorised merchants who did not pay the appropriate tax]. The burgh magistrates were ordered to take the names of offenders and punish anyone who removed 'dowlit hering' [herring subject to duty]. For the next seven years, commissioners appointed by the Convention from other royal burghs were ordered to Dunbar to attend the herring drave in August to ensure that the local magistrates enforced the rules. In 1611, the Convention also drew to Dunbar's attention that their own and visiting fishermen were using stones for ballast until they made a catch, whereupon the stones were cast overboard 'so that the fishing of the hering suffers and the ground was fylet [defiled]'. The Convention ordered that in future, fishermen would use sand for ballast. Dunbar burgh was ordered to write to several Fife fishing ports, warning them that failure to comply with the rules on ballast would attract a fine. Dunbar was again warned that if it didn't clear up its act on sales by 'unfreemen' and monitoring of the proper measure of fish contained in each barrel, the burgh would be fined £100 Scots. The Dunbar magistrates had to ensure that no man boarded a boat outside the harbour and that no fish was sold before the boats returned to port.

In July 1613, the Convention held its general meeting in Dunbar, probably to reinforce its message about the proper control of the herring drave. At that meeting (6th-9th July), Dunbar was authorised to inform the superiors of the burghs of barony in Fife that failure to comply with the regulations on the sale of fish, on ballast and on weights and measures, the burgh would fine offenders. In the same year, the Admiral Depute recommended that every fishing burgh should maintain an armed flyboat or cutter to apprehend

> 'sik [such] as steilis [steals] thair nightbours' [neighbours'] geir, scaks [casks?], thair
> netts, make quarrells and fechts [fights] and dois uther [do other] injuries.'

In 1614, Dunbar was authorised to levy a duty of six shillings and eightpence (38p) on each 'last' of herring [a last = 12 barrels each containing ten gallons of fish]. The following year, commissioners from Edinburgh, Anstruther Eister [Easter] and Dysart were sent to Dunbar to supervise the drave, taking particular care to ensure that the Convention's rules on 'balasting of boats, measures of hering and barrells of hering' were strictly observed.

Inevitably, there were times of dearth, even during the herring harvest, when the boats couldn't leave the harbour because of summer storms, as is recorded in the kirk session minutes. The Tyninghame Parish Kirk session minutes record that the period from 1621 to 1623 was a time of famine. Repeated shortages probably led to the passing of an act in 1663 which prevented the export of oysters to foreign ports; the Privy Council *Register* for 1661-64 records a petition received from the families of 'oyster dreggars' [dredgers] on the coasts of Lothian and Fife who made their living from the herring fishing at Dunbar. The petitioners offered to sell part of their catch to Edinburgh at three shillings (15p) per 100 shells if they were allowed to export the rest. The Privy Council refused their request.

The sea is a dangerous place. In the sixteenth century, the Dunbar *Draife* or drave[28] was carried on during the Sabbath by both Dunbar and North Berwick fishermen which the church of course denounced. As mentioned above, James Miller's poem *The Luckless Drave* describes the tragedy which occurred at Belhaven Bay in 1579, also recorded in the kirk session minutes and quoted in Scott's *Fasti Ecclesiae Scoticanae (Fasti).* On Sunday, 17th August 1579 about 1,000 boats - cobbles rowed by four or six men - put out to sea and cast their nets in the Bay. The anxious womenfolk reputedly watched their men from Knockenhair Hill. A sudden storm arose around midnight, catching the fleet of heavily-laden boats. Miller freezes the tableau for all time in his poem. The women saw boat after boat go under, tearing their hair in anguish - legend has it that Knockenhair is named for this tragedy; the word is Gaelic for *the watch hill* and has nothing to do with hair. *Domestic Annals of Scotland* records that three score boats and 300 men were lost. According to the kirk session minutes, the tragedy occurred 'about the year 1577' on the authority of Simson, minister at Dalkeith whose father Andrew Simson then held the incumbency at Dunbar. Simson junior's memory wasn't quite accurate in terms of the year as we know from the almost contemporary account which is contained in Moysie's *Memoirs of the Affairs of Scotland*:

> 'The hearing dreav [herring drave] of Dunbar - 17 August 1579, "Vpone [upon] the feventein [seventeenth] day in the nicht [night], an xviij [at 1800 hours but actually 6am], thair [there] blew fich [such] ane tempeft [a tempest] at the hearing dreav of Dunbar that perifchit [perished] iij^{xx} fifcher botis an htie hundrette [60 fishing boats and three hundred] men."'

Not unexpectedly, the church regarded the disaster as divine judgement for breaking the Lord's Day.

Repairs at the Old or Cromwell Harbour were a constant drain on the burgh's resources. In July 1666, the Convention of Royal Burghs noted that Dunbar had obtained permission from the Privy Council to apply to other burghs using the harbour to make a contribution to these repairs. Several burghs failed to do so and the Convention ordered the defaulting burghs to comply.

In 1692, the Convention ordered an investigation into the state of every burgh in Scotland in relation to trade. The commissioners sent to Dunbar to report on the financial health of the burgh made their assessment. Their report makes gloomy reading. They found that that inland and foreign [sea-going] trade had been negligible for the past three years. The harbour vessels numbered only two small barks; the *Margaret* (18 tonnes valued at 1,000 merks [£600 Scots or £50 sterling], master James Osbourne and the unnamed bark mastered by Alexander McLeish (12 tonnes valued at 300 merks [£180 Scots or £15 sterling] were engaged solely in carrying coals from the Forth coastal area. At that time, there were only 16 or 17 herring boats, described as ' extraordinalie unprofeitable' due to the decay of the herring fishing. A local burgess (possibly one of the Fall family) owned a sixth part of a Kirkcaldy-based cargo ship which had been 'amissing these three years'- probably because it sank in a storm.

Even so, for several centuries, Dunbar was Scotland's main herring port until 1725 when the shoals stopped coming to the Firth of Forth for several years. Trade in curing the fish continued however. The Dutch were increasingly active in the North Sea where the herring were plentiful but out of reach of the small Scottish boats. Dutch vessels were so efficient that the government of the day tried to encourage skippers to buy deep-water boats through the newly-formed Board of Trustees for Fisheries and Manufacture (1727). Bounties and grants were available to skippers who fitted out vessels for offshore boats but the initiative failed because the tax on salt used to pickle the herring for export was prohibitive and legislated against any improvement in the fishing fleet. Frequently, Scottish salt made from seawater was unsuitable because of the type of process used. (Sodium chloride, or common salt, is a major compound in brine but there are also several other soluble compounds, the presence of which reduces the ability to preserve. Scots salt was often boiled too quickly or too long and these undesirable compounds remained in the batch). Consequently, foreign salt of the right kind was often imported until far-seeing men like Robert Fall and his sister Janet's husband, Sir John Anstruther, a coalmine owner in St Monans, Fife financed the creation of saltpans there and manufactured the proper kind of sea-salt for pickling herring.

Although the Act of Union in 1707 allowed the Scots to import salt free of excise duty, it was still subject to customs duty of seven shillings and sixpence (37p) per 50 bushels and was to be used exclusively for the cure of fish for export. Because it was difficult to prevent foreign salt from being diverted for other purposes eg the cure of herring for the domestic market, intricate controls were set up requiring the salt to be delivered to the customs houses where a bond was granted for the excise duty and a guarantee was needed certifying its use for export purposes only. The document cost seven shillings and sixpence - the precise sum which otherwise attracted duty. At Dunbar, the fishermen were under the watchful eye of the local customs and excise officer; they offered to pay the excise duty simply to avoid going through the intricate and complicated procedures for movement and use of the salt. Herrings sold at very low prices which meant that even the poorest people could afford to buy them; at the end of the eighteenth century, the fish could be bought at twopence (less than 1p) per 100.

The Dutch monopoly in the North Sea caused great concern to the Dunbar fishermen who along with other east coast men regarded this as an insult to national pride as well as a loss of income. Dutch success was largely due to the large capital investment they were prepared to make in their faster, sturdier vessels. The herring shoals swept around the coasts every year but both numbers and appearances could be unpredictable although at Dunbar, they seem to have made a regular appearance every August for many years. Dunbar certainly accounted for 5,000 of the 7,000 barrels of salted herring exported from Scotland; in 1798, 134,572 barrels of herring were caught, Dunbar contributing to this astounding catch along with the other main east coast ports like Bo'Ness, Kirkcaldy and Leith. Caught in such great quantities, unsold fish were used to manure the fields. In 1853, 35,000 barrels of herring were landed at Dunbar but it is likely that the bulk of the catch ended up as fertiliser.

While it is difficult to accept today, in 1788 Dunbar was second only to Leith as a whaling port. Its greatly improved harbour made it popular with the sea-going traders especially since places like North Berwick had little more than a pier and a muddy shore allowing access only to shallow draft boats. It is difficult to understand therefore why the Falls of Dunbar - described as merchant princes - failed so disastrously in 1789. (Their bankruptcy was put down to high living in their grandiose Dunbar House - now Lauderdale House). The Falls tried their hand at everything; they were grain merchants and fish curers and when times were lean in the latter trade, they bought up quantities of herring at their Caithness premises, shipping them to their Dunbar curing station. It appears that between 1770 and 1794, the herring shoals failed to appear off Dunbar in sufficient numbers and the boats had to sail to Caithness and the Moray Firth for their livelihood.

At the start of the nineteenth century, the Old Harbour was enlarged and deepened by digging into the solid rock to a depth of eight feet. The *Old Statistical Account* also recorded that extensive new quays had been made a few years before. Nevertheless, the burgh council was constantly bedevilled with complaints from harbour users about its defects so that the burgh was obliged to spend considerable sums on improvements. The following is a typical complaint in 1810:

> ' The Provost read a memorial by the Ship Owners and Shipmasters belonging to and trading to this Harbour which is of the following tenor. "We Subscribers, carriers and Masters of vessels belonging to the port of Dunbar do hereby certify that we have for several years observed that the old pier....has been much injured by the heavy sea that runs into the mouth of the Harbour and that that part of the pier called the round head is at present in great danger of tumbling down, and if not immediately repaired, it is our opinion it may choke up the Harbour altogether. We further declare....that it is entirely owing to the length of the new pier upon the Island [Lamer Island opposite the harbour mouth] which confines the heavy seas betwixt the pier heads that has repeatedly occasioned the damage sustained by the old pier, and that neither vessels nor boats of any description can take the harbour mouth with the same safety as if there was only a jetty head upon the outer point of the Island, by which means the sea could expand itself upon the Island rock after it came round the jetty, and become smooth as it approached the old pier."'

This rather convoluted way of expressing the need to lessen the force of the tide by adjusting the breakwater pier at Lamer Island ends with a plea for its pier to be shortened, the redundant stones being used to rebuild the old pier with moveable booms placed across the harbour mouth to lessen the effects of rough seas. The burgh council agreed to meet the cost of this work in due course. George Bruce, the parish minister had earlier written of the new pier at Lamer Island in his contribution to the *Old Statistical Account* in 1793. In his considered opinion, it had made the harbour difficult to enter:

'There was lately a new pier built on the rocks, and from the west side of the entry
to the expence [sic] of which the Convention of Royal Burghs gave L600 sterling [£600].'

At the time, the Old Harbour was a good investment. Today, the stones from the former pier at Lamer Island lie jumbled about on the west side of the harbour whose entrance has long since been sealed with large stone blocks.

Even if by 1750 the Dutch had monopolised the herring industry, some 500-600 boats continued to gather at Dunbar every August. Scottish fishermen either couldn't or wouldn't enter capital investment schemes with their prohibitive interest payments to obtain sturdier vessels to compete with the Dutch whose fleet was protected by their navy. The *Old Statistical Account* again:

'The herring fishery was formerly more considerable and regular. It is often of
great benefit to the town, and to all the country round; but, for several years past,
it has become very precarious and uncertain.'

The writer might have added that government help was needed to finance an already ailing industry.

At least in other respects, Dunbar continued to thrive. Because its harbour was constantly improved, it had an edge on other similar-sized ports in the coastal and overseas shipping trade. Also, the demand for oil made whaling a lucrative business. In 1750, Leith's first whaler set sail. Robert and Charles Fall of Dunbar followed this initiative; two years later, they formed the *East Lothian and Merse Whale Fishing Company*, fitting out their first whaling ship which left Dunbar for Greenland in 1752. The largest catch landed at Dunbar occurred in 1781, when the oil from 21 whales was brought into port. In 1788, Leith led the industry with its six whalers; Dunbar came next with five employing 238 seamen, then Dundee with three boats. Yet only three years later, the Dunbar fleet had been reduced to two ships employing only 50 men, although the East Lothian and Merse Fishing Company owned 8 other vessels engaged in foreign trade, employing 67 men.[29] (The remains of the round head pier where the Company berthed its vessels survive at the side and rear of the Battery facing north-east). There were also 12 small boats employing 40 men in fishing for lobsters, cod, ling, turbot and whiting. As to trade, it was said that Dunbar skippers were usually last to leave for the Baltic port of Danzig (modern Gdansk) before the winter storms set in. Whaling ceased in 1804[30] and by the 1840s, only 300 small boats were able to participate in the herring fishing, half the number of a century before.[31] Even so, a new fish market opened in what was formerly known as the Davel Brae (modern Victoria Street) and was rented to the local fishermen by the burgh council.

The decline of the herring industry was bad enough but things got much worse when the import-export trade grew ever more erratic. Despite this decline, in 1822, the Old or Cromwell Harbour (**ill 91**) was considered inadequate for the fishing and sea trade industries. Moving cargoes by sea was more economical than using the turnpike roads with their toll charges; however, balancing that was the element of risk of shipwreck. Dunbar failed to make the best use of her port facilities until virtually the eve of the arrival of the railways in 1846 which of course sounded the death knell of the sea trade. The Board of White Fisheries for Scotland, hoping to benefit from an anticipated increase in coastal and overseas trade, embarked on a programme of harbour improvement which unfortunately came too late. Dunbar burgh council had been arguing for a new harbour for some years; a site was identified and surveyed in 1837 by John Mason, the Belhaven surveyor and on 24th September 1840, the council agreed that a second harbour was needed to accommodate the herring fleet. They argued - perhaps rather desperately as it turned out - that with the imminence of the railway from Edinburgh to Newcastle would bring a new initiative in trade opportunities. The burgh council may have thought they were seeing

DDHS

Illus 91: *The old harbour entrance from the battery, 1822*

far into the future; they were in fact looking back to the past.

The burgh council decided to approach the Board of White Fisheries for Scotland in 1840, seeking funds for the construction of a new harbour. The Board's minutes of 29 October 1840[32] record that William Ritchie, Town Clerk of Dunbar had made a formal approach to it, outlining the need for a second harbour. The Board's minutes of 5th January 1841 contain a report by its engineer, Mr Mitchell, who'd visited Dunbar in the intervening months. In his view

'.....the capabilities for improvement [were] very considerable.'

At the end of the month, Mitchell reported to the Board that he'd informed Provost Middlemass that the Commissioners of the Board would probably offer £6,000-6,500 to meet part of the coat of the proposed harbour, the burgh council having to make up the balance of the total cost, which he estimated at not less than £10,000. Mitchell said that Middlemass had informed him

'....that he had no doubt they [the burgh council] would be able to make up the difference between the Town and the neighbouring proprietors.'

Later that year, Mitchell revised his original estimate to £10,933.

At this juncture, an important matter under discussion was the siting of the harbour entrance. The Board's minutes of 16th February 1841 indicate that two possible sites had been identified - the Blue Stone Passage - the present entrance - and the King or Prince Edward Passage which would allow access through a channel formed between the Blockhouse and the castle forework. It was said that the local fishermen were consulted about the possible entrance and that they chose the Blue Stone Passage (see Appendix K). This may have been the case but my own view is that the Earl of Lauderdale's preferred choice influenced the Board in its decision. Lauderdale owned the land which fronted the castle forework; he was also one of the 'proprietors' referred to by Provost Middlemass from whom funds would be requested to meet Dunbar's share of the expense incurred in building the harbour. Middlemass wrote to the Board, recommending the community's preference for the Blue Stone Passage. It was accepted. He also informed the Board that he had secured a loan of £4,500 from Mr James Balfour of Whittingehame - the father of A J Balfour, the future Prime Minister - to meet the Dunbar share of the project.

A subsequent approach to the Lords of the Admiralty seeking approval for a 'harbour of refuge' at Dunbar was granted; the way was now clear for the Board to apply to HM Treasury for the necessary funding. In a letter to the board dated 8th December 1841, C E Trevelyan, Assistant Secretary to the Treasury, offered a grant of £5,000, provided the Dunbar share of the whole was deposited forthwith in the Board's bank. (Trevelyan, later Sir Charles, has in recent years been accused of administrative and financial callousness during the Irish Famine years of 1847-1848 but he cannot be faulted as far as Dunbar was concerned in 1841).

At the Board's meeting on 12th April 1842, ten tenders for the work were considered. The lowest of £12,990 was submitted by David Lyon and Co., a Glasgow contractor. The highest of £24,245 came from Alexander Wilson of Edinburgh. Six of the ten tenders were submitted by Scottish-based firms. What emerged later was that the Board's engineer Mitchell had 'much under calculated the quantity of Rock Excavation [to widen the Blue Stone Passage] in stating it at 33,778 cubic yards' the truer figure being in the region of 45,000-50,000 cubic yards. This brought the total cost to £12,206 which the Board considered beyond their means unless Dunbar could come up with a further £1,500. After a period of anxious negotiation, the contract went to David Lyon of Glasgow, who reduced his tender to £12,840.

On 16th September 1842, work on the harbour had begun. Mitchell reported that Lyon had opened 'an excellent quarry on the eastside of the town' and was employing 120 men. The quarry was probably on Broxmouth Estate, where the black granite on the shore provided stone for the quays. *Miller,* Dunbar informs us that on 27th September 1842, the foundation stone was laid with due ceremony, a hermetically-sealed container being placed under the stone; the jar contained newspapers, coins and other contemporary artefacts. Though the work proceeded on schedule, the project was not without problems, largely caused by the severity of storms during the course of construction.. In June 1843, Lyon informed the Board that 60 lineal feet of the main pier had given way ' the inner Wall first, and [it] fell in a Mass inside the Harbour, and the packing Sea Wall as a matter of course followed.' This was in fact the third time the wall had collapsed through the impact of high seas. However, work proceeded until November 1843, when all activity was suspended for the winter. By May 1844, Lyon had exhausted the supply of local stone and was obliged to bring stone from Fife. The work was finished in November 1844; the Secretary to the Board of Fisheries had visited the site in May that year and described the new harbour as 'quite magnificent.'

There is an interesting postcript to the construction. In December 1844, Mitchell, the Board's engineer reported this:

'....the Old Harbour, when opened up and Connected, would form the *real Commercial Harbour* [my italics]...and that the new Harbour should be an Outer Basin for the Fishing Craft entering or going to sea....and lie in perfect safety in the Inner Harbour.'

What had Dunbar got for its money? The fishermen were in no doubt. They sent an address to the Board of Fisheries in which they expressed 'the blessing conferred on them and their Families'. The final cost of the five-acre harbour was £15,657. In 1841, Dunbar was granted permission by Prime Minister Sir Robert Peel to name it the Victoria Harbour in honour of the queen. Dunbar was having problems meeting its share as late as November 1844, when James Balfour of Whittingehame had to remind the burgh council they'd agreed to repay him £4,500 with interest in two years; he received £166 on account. Dunbar was never bankrupted by the venture but it came perilously close to insolvency.

Only two years before the North British Railway Company brought trains to Haddington, Dunbar and the south, the Victoria Harbour was formally opened by the Earl of Dalhousie. The proposal to build a rail link serving Dunbar and the south was already known to the burgh council as well as the Fisheries Board but both hoped that transport of goods first by sea, then by rail would be attractive to merchant and fish trader alike. In their view, the harbour was justified. It would be wrong to lay the decline of the sea-going trade or the fishing industry entirely on the railways however; sea-trade was almost non-existent by the end of the nineteenth century simply because the port of Leith had become more efficient and effective. The decline of the fishing industry was a mixture of poor catches - the capricious herring shoals often failed to appear - the short-sightedness of fish traders and the fishermen who were content to leave the repair and fitting of boats to the retailers who demanded more shares in the catches while offering lower prices for them

The Victoria Harbour may have earned revenue for the town at the outset but the investment did not realise the expected return. The harbour has always suffered from one major defect - its entrance. Many consider it was built at the wrong end; it is difficult to access in bad weather and has on occasion been blocked by masonry falling from the castle or unstable stone from the Castle Rock itself.

Even if the herring fishing off the east coast of Scotland was still the largest in Europe in the 1850s, the Victoria Harbour was something of a white elephant, used only by boats seeking shelter in bad weather between Leith and Newcastle. Added to that was the improvements at Eyemouth Harbour which in time superseded Dunbar with its deep-sea trawlers. Victoria Harbour was in perpetual need of maintenance; the Fisheries Board had to dip into its coffers again in 1849 to meet part of the cost of a new sea wall - only five years after its completion. Dunbar was obliged to meet part of the cost and it was running out of resources.

The burgh council had sold off a good deal of burgh land by 1800; in that year, the council minutes record that as the town was deep in debt and had little prospect of meeting its liabilities, Provost Charles Hay recommended the sale of common land as it was a favourable time to do so. It was agreed to dispose of the Latch Park, the West Common and other parcels of land along with the West Barns Bleachfield. The Latch Park fetched £900, the West Common and other land realised £1,470 and the Bleachfield was sold to the late Provost Robert Fall's widow Magdalen for £210, making a total of £2,588. More of the commonty was sold in 1837 when on 24th May, the burgh council minutes record the following items up for sale; the burgh feus, the Outer Common, Belhaven Saltgreens, Gala Green, the Grass Park at Belhaven, Sisters Granary, Broadhaven, a garden off Silver Street, the Old Mathematical School and the Flesh Market. The town expected to realise about £5,000 to clear its debts. By 1838, town property was valued at £10,740 with debts amounting to £5,640; by 1845, property was valued at £12,940 with debts amounting to £9,537 although by 1857, the town had recovered to some extent with its property valued at £6,350 and debts of only £2,644.

The Victoria Harbour may have earned the town revenue at the outset but the investment did not realise as much return as had been envisaged. It has always suffered from one main defect-its entrance. Despite being well-constructed, many consider the entrance at the wrong end; it is difficult to access in bad weather and has on occasions been blocked by masonry falling from the castle. By its completion in 1844, the harbour was a white elephant although having said that, within living memory, it could have been crossed by stepping on the boats anchored in it.

Even if the herring fishing off the east coast was still the largest in Europe in the 1850s, it was the new railway which killed off the coastal shipping trade; Dunbar's overseas trade had also gone into decline so that in time, the prestigious harbour was used only by boats seeking shelter in bad weather between Leith and Newcastle. Added to the impact of the railway were the vastly superior facilities at Leith which killed off the trade in many small east coast ports like Dunbar. Even so, the commissioners for the British Fisheries helped to finance a new sea wall at Dunbar in 1849 - only five years after construction. Harbour repairs amounted to £6,000 in 1855, by which year the town debt amounted to £3,150 with assets valued at £6,590 which left very little for any future repairs. As early as 1850, the burgh council had informed the Board of Fisheries that the harbour was of no use to coasters and was only used by herring boats in the summer months, the harbour being 'deficient and of no use for coasting purposes until its construction be altered.'

The council also indicated that it had no money

'to expend on the constant repairs which seemed to be required........the resources of the port are not sufficient to give hope that any further outlay can be made by the Town of Dunbar for many years to come.'

In 1856, the sea wall was extensively breached and a deputation was sent by the council to London to seek government support. The deputation argued that if funds were not forthcoming for the wall, the future of the harbour was doubtful. On 27th March 1857, the burgh minutes indicate that the deputation sent to Whitehall a month earlier had managed to convince the Treasury - already hard-pressed with expenditure resulting from the Crimean War - that Dunbar required its harbour to survive. The Dunbar deputation was supported by a handful of MPs including Sir Henry Davie, Sir Graham Montgomery, Mr Blackburn, Mr Wells (acting for Lord Elcho), Mr Cowan, Mr Adam Black, Lord Gifford, Mr Bailie Cochrane, Mr Nisbet Hamilton and Sir Islay Campbell. Also atending from East Lothian were Sir John Hall of Dunglass, Sir John Warrender from Dunbar and Provost Roughhead from Haddington. The meeting unanimously agreed that Dunbar should have its harbour repaired; Sir Henry Davie and the others were supported and joined by the Earl of Dalkeith and three others who met with the Chancellor of the Exchequer on 15th February. Various petitions were presented including one surprisingly signed by the Lord Mayor of London, Alderman Sydney. The Chancellor of the Exchequer said he would give Dunbar's request for £15,000 his 'early and favourable consideration.' On a subsequent visit to London and the Treasury, an official gave the Dunbar deputation the news they had hoped for; the sea wall would be repaired immediately. Work began in April.

Eventually, HM Treasury granted Dunbar burgh council £10,000 free of interest and a further £20,000 at 3% interest, the whole sum to be paid from the income from the two harbours except for £100 a year allowed for repairs to the Old Harbour. The Treasury minute of 18th June 1857 stated that the outlay would provide berths for 500 boats and help with the landing and dispatching of catches. These protracted negotiations were completed by 24th November 1858; the money was paid into the local branch of the Commercial Bank. The burgh council and the fishermen regarded this only as a reprieve; however, the uncertainty didn't prevent the town celebrating the event with a firework display, free ale from Belhaven Brewery and the inevitable - and expensive - dinner held in honour of the burgh council and the local notables. The government loan had to be written off as bad debt even if the money was put to good use. The harbour was deepened, a new wharf was created and the sea wall was strengthened. In 1859, minor alterations included squaring the corner of the harbour abutting the east wall of the castle and creating a site to house the Harbourmaster's Office, which according to the survey plan was built on the site of the Castle dungeon. (It is clear today from the surviving stonework that a wall of some sorts had existed, possible the rear wall of the so-called dungeon). In 1883, further improvements cost the Fisheries Board £35,000 but still left unresolved the problem of safe access as the entrance wasn't deep enough to allow boats to enter and leave at all states of the tide. Worse still, the upgraded harbour didn't result in a significant increase in the fishing industry, nor did it guarantee Dunbar's future as a small trading port.

Illus 92: *A herring catch c.1900* KM

Dunbar was among the few east coast ports which managed to carry on fishing until about the middle of the twentieth century. The rate of decline may be measured between 1830 and 1899 by reference to the numbers of boats registered for Dunbar and the men they employed. In 1830, there were 28 boats as well as upwards of 300 herring boats employing perhaps around 700 men; by 1855, there were 41 boats giving work to 120 men and boys which with coopers, net makers, fish curers and vendors employed about the same number-about 20% of the population. The year 1881 saw a peak with 68 boats giving work to 125 men and boys. The decline becomes marked thereafter due to a combination of poor investment and competition from Eyemouth in Berwickshire, Port Seton, Granton and

Illus 93: *Herring landing* DDHS

Leith. By 1899, the coastal shipping which had been carried out by 17 Dunbar vessels was over, although potatoes were transported by sea until 1923. And yet herring catches were still plentiful at the turn of the twentieth century, as can be seen from the photographs of that time (**ill 92 and 93**). But in 1928, only 12 boats gave work to 49 men; many of the boats were still powered by sail and couldn't compete with the 55 motorised vessels out of Eyemouth. There was a brief upsurge in 1948, when 26 boats and 250 men were engaged in whitefish netting and shell fishing. Today, the Victoria Harbour is virtually empty of working boats, its main purpose being to provide berths for the lifeboat and the pleasure yachts which outnumber the working boats. The present generation of fishermen's sons aren't interested in the family employment, preferring to seek their living in safer and more lucrative occupations. To this might be added the belief of other east coast fishing ports that Dunbar fishermen lost their living because of their habit of fishing on Sundays - in the recent past a cardinal sin in the view of many fishermen.

In 1914, Dunbar's importance lay in its shore batteries, the first in a line of coastal defences stretching to Burntisland to protect the Firth of Forth. In 1915, the port had the only fish curing station in East Lothian; by then, crabs and lobsters formed the bulk of the catch although some haddock and cod were landed. Forty years later, although the government of the day financed a programme of repairs and development from which Dunbar marginally benefited, the most successful enterprise was at Eyemouth, now a thriving harbour and fish market. Some fishermen work at Dunbar today, persevering with their lobster pots, prawn nets and mackerel lines. It is unlikely that fishing will die out completely but there is no prospect of a return to the boom days, with stocks dwindling and European Commission restrictions on catches in the interests of conservation. As this book is being completed, the embattled fishermen are making their views known to the government but as with the farm industry and the moves already introduced to restrict harvests on land and at sea, it is certain that skippers will be paid to lay up their boats for longer periods every year.

Illus 94: *Storm warning (Fishermens' monument also known as the Barometer)* DDHS

In their heyday, the fishermen of Dunbar were paid a tribute by a local businessman, William Brodie, the proprietor of the long-vanished Seafield Brickworks at West Barns. Brodie organised a public subscription to erect a Fishermen's Monument in the Old Harbour - known latterly as the Barometer (**ill 94**) which was unveiled at the harbour on 24th May 1856. Restored in 1998, it bears the following inscription:

'Presented to the Fishermen of Dunbar to Whose Perilous Industry the Burgh
Owes so much of its Prosperity.'

On the base is a couplet from the poem *The Boatie Rows* by John Ewen (1741-1821):

O, weel may the Boatie row
That wins the Bairnie's bread!

Fair and justified praise of men who were not only hardworking but gave their lives on occasions. We are fortunate to have photographs of some of these men and their boats (**ill 95, ill 96**) and harbour scenes then and now (**ill 97, 98**).

Illus 95: *Some local worthies c.1900* KM

Praise is also due to the women of Dunbar. As in agriculture, women had a crucial role; they baited the lines, then gutted the fish their husbands and sons caught as well as selling the catches on the streets and round the doors. There are many photographs in the archive of the Dunbar and District History Society which show women at work on the quayside at Victoria Harbour (**ill 99, 100 and 101**). Responsibility for the two harbours was passed from local government to the Harbour Trust formed in 1999; among its responsibilities is the castle ruin which I hope will be made safe enough for access by the public.

Mention should be made here of the other harbours near Dunbar. Skateraw, itself once a fishing village had a small harbour which was built between 1799 and 1825 to allow shipments of coal to be landed for the Skateraw limekiln. It also gave shelter to the few fishermen caught in bad weather making for Dunbar. The harbour was built by two local farmers, Brodie of Thorntonloch and Lee of Skateraw who worked the lime quarry and supplied the Devon Ironworks at Alloa with lime which was used in the fluxing process in iron-smelting. Skateraw lime was also used by farmers as a soil dressing in East Lothian and Berwickshire. Skateraw Harbour never amounted to much, providing only two berths; remains of the quay can still be seen below the Torness nuclear power station. The next harbour is at the Cove, near Cockburnspath. It was built by Sir John Hall of Dunglass between 1770 and 1831. To accommodate the carts which took the fish catches from the quayside, a tunnel 180 feet long was blasted out of the rock; from this at least one man-made cellar was hewn out of the tunnel at a right angles to store rope and barrels. Other 'caves' occur on the seashore, resulting from the small coalworkings which supplied Dunglass House with its domestic supply. In the 1850s, as many as 100 boats landed their catches of herring at the Cove. Cove-caught lobsters and crabs were taken by sea from Dunbar to London for many years. The harbour declined after 1850, when only 25 boats gave work to 100 men until 1950, when there were but 5 boats employing 12 men.

Illus 96: *Fishing boats in the Broadhaven c.1900* RJP

Boat-building on a small scale was carried out at Dunbar for over a century. It is claimed that a Dunbar marine engineer, Robert Wilson (1803-82) invented the screw-propeller for ships; he was only one of many engineers involved in its development, although he built a working model at the age of 24 in 1827. Wilson

DDHS
Illus 97: *Dunbar from the sea before 1819*

wasn't a sea-going man - his fisherman father was a member of the lifeboat crew and was drowned in 1810 attempting to rescue men from *HMS Pallas*, one of two naval frigates that foundered off the coast near Broxmouth. Wilson had no desire to make his living from the sea, so he was first apprenticed to a local joiner, serving his apprenticeship as joiner and cabinetmaker. He built a three-foot scale model of a propeller-driven boat in 1826 but wasn't able to interest the Admiralty in his design. (The model can be seen in the National Museum of Scotland in Edinburgh) In 1834, Wilson was awarded the Silver Medal of the Royal Society of Arts for his design of the propeller, which the Society referred to the Admiralty. True to fashion, the Admiralty appointed a committee to consider Wilson's invention. However, perhaps it was the problem of patenting which tipped the scales against poor Wilson. As early as 1794, nine years before Wilson was born, an Englishman by the name of Lyttleton produced what he called his 'aquatic propeller'. Credit for the application of the method - if not the invention itself- went to Sir Francis Pettit Smith and a Swedish engineer called Ericsson, both of whom took out patents for their propeller in 1836. The Admiralty adopted Pettit Smith's propeller in 1840. Perhaps Wilson was unlucky in having been born in a small, obscure Scottish seaport. Underrated as an inventor, he found his niche in England, when in 1838, he joined Naysmith's Foundry in Manchester, making several improvements to Naysmith's steam hammer. Wilson was nothing if not industrious; between 1842 and 1880, he took out no fewer than 24 patents for locomotives and other steam-driven engines, textile and hydraulic equipment, valves, pistons, propellers and other devices. Eventually, his move to England paid off; in 1856, he was made a partner in the foundry and in the same year, Naysmith, Wilson and Co. built an improved steam hammer for Woolwich Arsenal, patented by Wilson in 1861. The year before, he published his pamphlet *The Screw Propellor-Who Invented It?* In 1880, he was awarded £500 by the War Department for the use of his screw propeller in their torpedoes. Although Wilson wasn't a man of the sea, it certainly gave him many ideas about marine engineering.[33] Robert Wilson died in 1882, in Derbyshire. The bicentenary of his birth is to be celebrated in Dunbar in September 2003. It is proposed that a ceremony organised by Dunbar Community Council will honour their famous son in an imaginative way; it is proposed to unveil a memorial which will consist of a stone plinth on which will be mounted a propellor from a Clyde tug.

KRM
Illus 98: *The Old Harbour entrance in early 2003*

It is appropriate here to mention the local lighthouses; a coast in utter darkness is unimaginable today but it wasn't always so. While the east coast isn't extensively indented, Leith Roads and the Forth Estuary presented a hazard to shipping in the earlier centuries, so much so that in 1625, the Convention of Royal Burghs received the first proposal for a light in the Forth. At first, Scottish ship owners were lukewarm about the idea since they knew they would have to pay tolls similar to those levied in English waters by lighthouse authorities. Alexander Cunningham of the Bass who held a crown charter for lands in West Barns had first proposed in 1616 that a light or beacon should be placed on the May Island. Cunningham rightly believed that not only would it reduce the number of shipwrecks, it would also act as a navigational aid for fishermen on both coasts of the Firth of Forth as well as foreign vessels sailing to Leith. Even so, the burghs were not enthusiastic until Cunningham petitioned the Privy Council. The promoters of the light were joined by James Maxwell of Innerwick, the future Earl of Dirleton and Charles II's Gentleman of the Bedchamber. Under Maxwell's influence, a crown charter was issued on 23rd April 1636[34] in his, Cunningham's and his son's favour. Scotland's first lighthouse was no more than a coal fire burning in a brazier on top of a crenellated stone building until 1816 when a conventional light was erected. In my earlier book, *The Deil's Ain,* it was claimed that Cunningham of the Bass was drowned by a storm raised by Fife witches because his intention was to save life by bringing light to the dark coast, thus interfering with their night-time activities.

Illus 99: *Baiting the lines* KM

The right to collect dues from the ship owners for the upkeep of the Old Light remained in the Cunningham family until the May was sold in 1714 along with parts of West Barns to David Scot of Scotstarvit whose grandfather wrote *The Staggering State of the Scots Statesman.* Several famous people visited the May to inspect its light, a wonder of the time. Among them was the poet Robert Fergusson who sailed there in a utility boat out of Dunbar in the 1770s. The May light was also revolutionary in another sense in that it was the first lighthouse to be converted to electricity. Other lights followed; St Abbs and the South Carr Beacon (1844), Barns Ness (1901) and the Bass Rock (1903). These lights now operate automatically. Some of the inshore rocks at Dunbar have iron poles embedded in them from which it is believed lanterns were hung as a warning to boats unfamiliar with the waters. The rocks off Dunbar have interesting and fanciful names whose origins are obscure or can only be guessed at. Staring with Long Craigs off the West Promenade, we come to the impressive Pincod or Pincushion which once formed part of the cliffs; next to it is the Delves, a plateau of rock which offers vantage points at low tide for rod and line fishermen; towards the harbour entrance is the Doo [Dove], Oliver's Ship, Wallace's Head - on which a beacon light was installed to guide ships into the harbour - Scart Rock - probably named for the cormorants which roost there - Castlefoot Rock - no guesswork needed in this case - and the Gripes [modern spelling The Gripps] which enclose Johnstone's Hole, a shingle beach; after that come Mackerel Buss, Long Steeple, Round Steeple, the Yetts [near the Battery] and the eastmost rocks known as Little Spicer - also near the Battery - and finally, Meikle Spicer before the Old Harbour entrance.

Illus 100: *A successful haul (herring) c.1900* RJP

Many ships foundered off Dunbar before and after the lighthouses came into being; more loss of life would have occurred had it not been for George Miller's success in obtaining a Henry Greathead type lifeboat through public subscription at Dunbar in 1808 (see Chapter 7). The *Zetland* (**ill 102**) is an example of Greathead's lifeboat). Before that however, wrecks were an almost annual tragedy during the winter months, notably *HMS Fox*, a man o' war which was reputedly loaded with firearms belonging to Dunbar and the valuables of several local landowners fleeing from the advancing English after the battle of Prestonpans in 1745. The *Fox* was lost with all hands on 14th November 1745 after it struck the May Island and drifted out of control on to the Tyne's treacherous sand basin near West Barns Links. Most of the corpses were found along the Links and behind Dunbar Castle. At least two cannon were salvaged from the wreck and reputedly placed on the castle ruins, presumably to discourage any hostile vessels from attacking the Old Harbour. (We know that in 1795, it was recommended that two of the guns from the Battery built in 1782 should be placed on the castle - see Chapter 11). As mentioned earlier, the shipwreck of two navy frigates claimed the life of one of the crewmen of the Dunbar lifeboat, Benjamin Wilson, the father of Robert Wilson. The wrecks occurred on 18th December 1810, when *HMS Pallas* - once captained by the famous Fife sailor, Admiral Cochrane, Lord Dundonald - and *HMS Nymph* foundered near Broxmouth; apparently their captains had confused the fires at the Skateraw limekiln with the Bell Rock and May lighthouses. About half of the 300 men aboard the *Pallas* perished; the crew of the *Nymph* were more fortunate as they were able to crawl to land along the rigging and masts of their ship which lay on its side. Then a Newcastle sloop the *John and Agnes* - subject of a poem by James Miller - went aground on 9th November 1816, although most of her crew was saved. The schooner *Caroline* out of Hull sank on 30th August 1830 with no loss of life. Between 1810 and 1822, 28 vessels were wrecked off Dunbar and a further 33 were lost between 1830 and 1920 (**See Fig. 14** at the end of this chapter). In August 1845, a tragic shipwreck occurred outside the harbourmouth when the *Red Rover*, a Buckhaven fishing boat lost 4 of its 5 crew. Six men were drowned attempting to save a survivor; those who lost their lives in the attempted rescue are commorated in the kirkyard (see Chapter 5). James Miller recorded the tragedy in his poem *Verses on the Late Melancholy Boat Wrecked at Dunbar*; I found a copy of his poem pasted in the flyleaf of the burgh council minute book for 1841-1857. Despite a dedicated rescue service, Dunbar's rocky coastline continued to claim lives and vessels; a dramatic view of one appears below (**ill 103**). Between October 1808 and December 2002, Dunbar lifeboats including inshore boats have been launched on [448] occasions and [346] people have been saved. The lifeboat crews were ably assisted by the Rocket Brigade which used the Manby apparatus, firing lines by

Illus 101: *Mary MacFarlane, 1878* DDHS

Illus 102: *Greathead type lifeboat 'Zetland'* RCM

Illus 103: *After the storm, a late 19th century wreck at Dunbar* HLHC

means of a mortar from shore to ship which George Miller had proposed several years before Manby patented it (see Chapter 7).

The first RNLI boat stationed at Dunbar was the *Wallace*, gift of Lady Cunningham Fairlie of Dumfries in 1865; it capsized on a training exercise on 13th October 1877, drowning its coxswain Robert Herkes and former coxswain Robert Clements. Next came the *Sarah Pickard* (1893-1901) gifted by Andrew Pickard of Leeds which cost £405; it was succeeded by the *William Arthur Millward* (1901-31), the legacy of W A Millward of Derby which cost £879 (illustrations of the crew and the boat proceeding to the assistance of the *King Ja Ja* appear below (**ill 104 and 105**). After it came *George and Sarah Strachan* (1931-59), the first motorised lifeboat, the legacy of George Strachan of Pollockshields costing an astronomical £7,680. It was followed by the *Margaret* in 1959, the legacy of A Black of Edinburgh and J Taylor of Sheffield, a boat which cost £35,000. In 1986 came the *Joseph Soar* purchased by the Civil Service at a cost of £41,106; then in 1988 came *Hugh William, Viscount Gough* the former Barra lifeboat gifted by the Dowager Viscountess Gough and Vicount Gough costing £75,000. It was replaced in 1993 by the *Thomas James King,* the former St Helier lifeboat and funded by local appeal in Jersey at a cost of £68,000. The present lifeboat, *Sir Ronald Pechell* began operating in 1996; in addition, a high-speed inflatable operates from Skateraw, used for inshore work. The names of the lifeboats, their coxswains and statistical information on mercy missions and lives saved up to 31st December 2002 are shown in **Fig. 15** at the end of this chapter.

Illus 104: *Dunbar lifeboat 'William Arthur Millward' going to the rescue of the 'King Ja Ja' in 1905* DDHS

Before we examine the extent of smuggling on the east coast, it should come as no surprise that the local population wasn't averse to the occasional plundering of boats which ran aground. In 1636 a Dutch ship was wrecked off Thorntonloch; most of its cargo was carried off in carts and sledges. Those responsible are named in the Privy Council *Register* for 1635-37. The majority were from Cockburnspath, Innerwick, East Barns, Broxburn, Dunbar and Belhaven. Even in the days of poor communications, news, bad - or good, depending on your sentiments - travelled fast. The cargo was rich indeed - 650 merks of gold and silver, taffeta, silks, nutmegs, raisins and 1,000 pounds of tobacco. Most of the 103 people involved were found guilty and ordered to return the goods or pay their cash value to the owners.

That smuggling was rife in and near Dunbar is without doubt-hence the need in 1793 to have a customs boat with a seven-man crew.[35] In the eighteenth century, smuggling was as popular as witch burning had been in the previous one. In August 1744, the Dunbar magistrates framed a resolution against smuggling and undertook to give

'all due assistance to the oficers [sic] of the revenue' as well as 'discouraging the immoderate use of Brandy,

Tea and other Smugled [sic] goods.'

The resolution was published in the newspapers.

The coastline between Berwick and Musselburgh provided many discreet and safe landing places for contraband; the smugglers considering themselves socially motivated by reducing the cost of creature comforts for their fellow Scots at the expense of an unpopular Act of Union with England. In 1793, national revenue was seriously reduced by smuggling. At one time, there was an unbroken chain of smugglers from Berwick to Prestonpans. Some vessels also made 'pretended' voyages from east coast Scottish ports. In October 1754, the *Elizabeth* of Dundee, bound officially for Bergen with a cargo of exciseable goods put into Whitby because of bad weather. The Customs Board directed the collector at Dunbar to be vigilant as

> 'there is cause to suspect the cargo is designed to be run upon this coast, we direct you to put all the officers in your district on their guard.'

Then again in 1760, the Dunbar collector was warned about the *Margaret* of Dundee which was reputed to be returning from Norway with a cargo of wines and spirits.[36]

Illus 105: *The crew of the 'William Arthur Millward' in 1903, observe the cork lifejackets.* KM

The goods smuggled from the Continent were predominantly French brandy, Dutch gin, tobacco and tea. The men who ran their boats ashore on dark nights hid their booty in the Lammermuir Hills and were regarded as heroic traders; to 'jouk the gaugers' [avoid the customs men] was an honourable pursuit. Cartloads of kegs containing excisable spirits were landed at out of the way places such as the Cove, Redheugh, Coldingham, Eyemouth, Dunbar and North Berwick to be hidden and carted off to Edinburgh when the opportunity arose. Many Dutch and French luggers made Gullane Point their rendezvous with those whom they had arranged to trade; often, the two sides disagreed over prices and fights between the smugglers were only exceeded by those between the smugglers and the gaugers.

In 1713, the British government announced its intention to levy a duty on malt in both Scotland and England which rattled the Scots on three counts; the first was that the Act of Union in 1707 had exempted Scotland from taxes raised to finance the English war with Holland; also, the Treaty of Utrecht (1712-13) which gave Gibraltar to England and ended the War of Spanish Succession specifically excluded the Scots from taxes levied in England. The third reason was that the Act of Union had stipulated that while future taxes should be fairly apportioned, application of an 'equal' tax on malt would be unfair as the Scottish barley crop was a fraction of that over the Border. To tax Scotland at the same level as England was therefore unconstitutional. The Malt Tax Act was enacted but the Malt Tax riots of 1725 forced the government to amend the act to

Illus 106: *Gypsy encampment at the Victoria Harbour c.1899* RJP

Illus 107: *Captain James Fall* LRM

exclude Scotland. (Scottish merchants and burgh councils like Dunbar urged their parliamentary representatives to vote against the act as it threatened to set a dangerous precedent.

The Act of Union increased sea-going trade, developed in Dunbar by the Falls mentioned earlier. The Falls brought prosperity to the burgh which they ran almost exclusively for most of the eighteenth century. Who were they and when did they come to Dunbar? Some sources imply, other strongly assert, that the Falls were descendants of the gypsy Faas of Kirk Yetholm although this is difficult to prove conclusively. Gypsies certainly visited Dunbar regularly, especially at the time of the herring drave.(**ill 106**) They were also frequent visitors to Lochend, enjoying the patronage of the Baillies, the Sinclairs and at first the Warrenders, one of whom decided he no longer wanted them to exercise their ponies on his land. (Local legend has it that the head of the tribe cursed the Warrenders, saying their house would be burnt down three times. After the second fire in 1859, the family decided not to take any chances and returned to Edinburgh). There are references to Faas and Falls from the reign of Robert III (1390-1406), when a Thomas Fall was a Dunbar burgess; a James Faw is mentioned in *Registrum Magni Sigili Regum Scotorum (RMS)* or the Register of the Great Seal of Scotland on 25th January 1507. Local records also indicate that a John Fall, constable of Haddington, lived at Stenton in 1598. Bailie Faa reputedly sheltered the fugitive Covenanter minister John Blackadder, the most well-known in the Martyrology of the Killing Times in the 1680s; Blackadder ended his days as one of the Bass Rock Martyrs. A George Fall was yet another Dunbar burgess during the seventeenth century, a James Fall was principal of Glasgow University in 1684 and Provost Robert Faa was a Dunbar commissioner to the Scottish parliament between 1693 and 1701, continuing as provost until the first decade of the eighteenth century. Whether all these Falls were related is not known but it seems likely; it also quite possible that they had originated in Kirk Yetholm as gypsies who made their living from barter.

The eighteenth century Falls (see **Fig. 13**) who amassed and lost a fortune included Captain James Fall (**ill 107**), Provost of Dunbar for several years afterwards, then MP for Haddington, Dunbar, North Berwick, Lauder and Jedburgh (1734-41). Captain James, a staunch Whig was Provost in 1706, as we know from the Court of Session records for that year. (Fall and Sir James Suttie of Balgowan were appointed bondsmen for the heirs to the estate of James, 6th Earl of Dunfermline who had been forfeited in 1690 for his support for the Jacobite James Vii and II. James Fall was appointed tacksman and factor of the estates of Urquhart and Fyvie and the associated fishing rights on the Spey. He served in these capacities until 1733, when he and Suttie arranged the sale of these estates and fishings to the rightful heir. Perhaps from the proceeds of his fees for these functions, he was able to build the prestigious Dunbar - later Lauderdale - House in 1734).

The Falls ***were*** Dunbar for most of the eighteenth century. They formed businesses with premises at Dunbar, Caithness and Sutherland; they bought land in and around Dunbar, they cured fish, established a thriving whaling business, were grain merchants and engaged in overseas and coastal trade. From 1694, brothers William, Robert, James and Charles, along with William's son Charles, James' son Robert and another relative called John - possibly Charles Senior's son - all served on the burgh council as provosts, bailies and councillors. Most of the Falls were commissioners to the Convention of Royal Burghs, which entitled them to sit in the Scottish parliament until 1707. The first mention of the family occurs in 1693, when Robert Faa was appointed provost of Dunbar; in 1695, he became the Dunbar commissioner to the Convention of Royal Burghs. Captain James was provost in the early seventeenth century, the MP for the county of Haddingtonshire; brother William Fall became provost in 1726 and served in that capacity until his death in 1736; brother Charles followed him as provost and died in 1744, then William's son Charles became provost in 1766. (See **Fig. 12** in Chapter 8 for further information). Charles Fall was instrumental in providing an improved water supply to the town from

Spott. Perhaps the most celebrated of all were Robert and Janet, son and daughter of James, the MP. Janet married Sir John Anstruther of St Monans; of Robert we shall hear more in due course.

The Falls owned two companies, the main being the *East Lothian and Merse Fishing Company* - more accurately *the East Lothian and Merse Whale Fishing Company,* as for a few years, it sent two whalers to Greenland, off the north-east coast of North America. The other company, *Messrs. Fall, Melville and Company,* Robert Melville being a brother-in-law, traded chiefly in the herring it cured and import-export; this is amply illustrated by an extract from the Custom House Port Book of 1765 (see **Appendix L**) when the Falls were at the peak of their success. Probably their extravagant lifestyle together with poor herring catches brought about their demise. Charles and Robert Fall were declared bankrupt in 1788, their companies going into liquidation. Even so, Robert who became provost of Dunbar, no doubt ably assisted by his beautiful wife Magdalen Stephen (**ill 108**) was an astute businessman who correctly identified the solution to the east coast fishing problem. He argued that it should be developed along the lines of the Dutch fishery, using larger vessels on deep-sea trips although he conceded that success wouldn't come overnight. At the time his sister Jenny married Sir John Anstruther, Robert entered into partnership with Anstruther in the production of salt distilled from sea water at St Monans. Anstruther, a coalmine owner put his otherwise unsaleable small coal to good use, creating the saltpans at St Monans which provided Robert with a cheap source of salt for curing herring. (A major part of the archaeological excavations carried out at these salt pans in the mid 1990s, was directed by Robin Murdoch whose company, Harlaw Heritage, published this book)). As for Jenny Fall - a very attractive lady by all accounts - she probably persuaded her husband to go into business with her brother, no doubt using her charms. (It is said that the Lady Tower which stands at the beach near Elie, just along the coast from St Monans, was built for her by Sir John so that people wouldn't see her undressing for her swims in the sea!)

Illus 108: *Magdalen Stephen, wife of Robert Fall* LRM

Robert Fall also saw how improvements to the Old Harbour would benefit the town as well as himself. On 13th May 1785, the burgh council minutes record that he petitioned the council as a businessman, recommending that a dry dock be created at the harbour for cleaning and repairing vessels, arguing that this would lead to

> 'the increase of Trade and advantage of the Town as well as his private interests.'

The dock was built, although perhaps by then, he knew the Fall empire was in danger since in the same year, the Fall fishing company failed to pay dividends to its shareholders. Then at the start of 1788, Robert, a leading grain merchant in the district was discovered to be heavily in debt to his bankers, Sir William Forbes, James Hunter and Co, successors to Coutts and Co. of Edinburgh, a merchant house which offered banking facilities. There was considerable panic among the East Lothian and Merse farmers which caused a run on the bank. Matters went from bad to worse. In January 1788, the Falls were in serious financial difficulties; the sequestration papers dated 24th January 1788 [37] contain the names of over 50 creditors who together were owed over £17,000, a frightening sum for the time. The creditors were mainly local merchants - Christopher Middlemass, merchant, was owed £1,000-along with tenants, shipmasters and others from Edinburgh, Fife, London and even the East Indies. Robert was forced to sell Dunbar House to Captain James Maitland, the future 8th Earl of Lauderdale. In 1790, trustees were appointed in the sequestration of Charles and Robert Fall for the fishing company and Robert Fall and Robert Melville for the trading company. With their demise, the sea-trade virtually came to an end and the family faded from business and public life. Their fine town house is their only monument. Robert, last of the issue of the'Four Eminent Brothers' died on 18th December 1796 survived by his widow Magdalen who continued to live in Dunbar, owning property and some land in the burgh. Unaccountably, none of the family appears to have been interred in the local cemetery, although there is a grave containing the remains of a Robert Fall Drysdale, son of Elizabeth Castellau and Alexander Drysdale who may have been a relative of the Falls. In 1883, a Fall family living in York claimed descent from the Romany race; perhaps they were related to the Dunbar Falls, thus confirming the link with the Gypsy Faas of Kirk Yetholm.

There is an interesting but equally harrowing postscript to the Fall story. Thomas Melville, Robert Fall's nephew-in-law and son of his business partner Robert Melville went north in 1788 to establish the fishing port of Ullapool. Thomas had organised Robert Fall's Caithness and Sutherland interests and when these went bankrupt, he approached the British Fisheries Society (1786-1893) and persuaded them to enter a contract aimed at developing the Society's 1,500 acres at Loch Broom, on the west coast of Scotland. The Society, an ambitious enterprise established in 1786 to stimulate development in the West Highlands had as its main objective the creation of small towns and villages to act as depots for the fishing industry; it argued that by doing so, this would generate specialised employment and income, perhaps managing to reverse the growing tide of the Highland Clearances. Melville, a man of undoubted experience and resourcefulness, undertook to develop a fishing port and village at Ullapool. He fitted out the sloop *Gilmartin* and sailed out of Dunbar on 5th June 1788 with a cargo of bricks, timber, tiles, lime, furniture and farm implements; the passengers and crew numbered 55, including a blacksmith, a cooper, a netmaker, builders and fishermen with their families, most of whom were from Dunbar. It was almost a Darien Scheme in microcosm; like many attempts to create a Utopia, it was destined to suffer the same end as that ill-fated venture.

At first it looked like Ullapool would be a success. Melville's hard-working, enthusiastic nature produced rapid results but he was temperamental and easily offended by even well-meant criticism, a common fault among Dunbar men - myself included! Initially, the community thrived but from 1801 to 1809, there were poor catches of herring and indifferent harvests; the community declined to such an extent that the British Fisheries Society was obliged to ship oatmeal, potatoes and seed to the starving settlers. In 1804, Melville was in debt, his assets were sequestrated and he was declared bankrupt in 1808. The Fall bad luck had come with him from Dunbar.By 1847, the Fisheries Society had sold Ullapool as a bad investment; its failure was a combination of bad luck, poor judgement, the elusive herring shoals - and it must be said - the indolence of the west coast fishermen. Others who came after Thomas Melville no better and more by luck than design, Ullapool survived to become a holiday resort and war-time signal station. Fishing is still the main occupation. Melville's dream colony survives today in cottages and outbuildings he created over two centuries ago.

As Chapter 9 is chiefly concerned with the state of the fishing industry, it is right that it should end with it. Apart from two high yield years in 1894 and 1914, the herring catches went into steep decline. Steam-powered ships were gradually replaced by diesel vessels which allowed some local families to invest their futures in long-distance, deep water fishing. But today, the sons of the few fishermen no longer want to follow in their fathers' footsteps. Fishing has become an expensive business with little return on capital investment; it is wholly controlled from Brussels and it makes depressing news to read of the restrictions which have been imposed by the bureaucracy of civil servants who believe they are legislating for the survival of the industry in Britain. The great era of the herring draves is long past; the days when the local people - myself included - would gather at the harbour to watch the boats returning home are fast fading from memory. Fishing as a way of life has become social history.

This story would be incomplete without mentioning some of the famous local fishing families. The most common fisherfolk names include Brunton, Cockburn, Craig, Easingwood, Fairbairn, Herkes, Johnston, Johnstone, Main, Marr, Paxton, Runciman, Smith, Tear, Thomson and Turnbull; many of the men from these families also served - and gave their lives - as coxwains and crews of the local lifeboats. Some of them had colourful nicknames which even now are fading from memory as the generations that knew them die out - Arry, Aipple, Boups, Callacher, Cud, Elicky, Gee Gee, Hillsixty [named for the bloody battle for a small pimple on the landscape of Flanders during the Great War?], Paidler, Shie, Tampat, Topsey, Traiveller, Whitecraw - and perhaps the most physically evocative of the breed, The Masher, probably so-called because of his strength; the tradition survives in contemporary nicknames such as Caesar, Fuzz and Spider. The women in the time of Shie, Tampat and Traiveller weren't to be outdone however - nicknames like the Duchess, Lizzie Tattie Soup and the Sandshoe Queen were well-known figures in the High Street. (The last-named was so-called on account of her preferred footwear by the soldiers at the Castle Park Barracks between the two world wars; an alternative name for her was Chinstrap because she often wore a straw hat clamped down on her head by a large elasticated band under her chin to keep the hat in place during the notoriously fierce local winds!). The fishing families were collectively known as *The Channel Fleet* - but never in their hearing and certainly not on a Saturday night when the ale flowed!

Fig 13 The Falls of Dunbar (18th Century)

George Fall
(Burgess, Dunbar)

- William [1] m. Jean Suttie
  - Robert George (1717) (1718
  - Charles [7] (1720?)
  - James (1724) m. Ann Ferguson
    - David James
  - William (1726)
  - Marion (1728)
- Robert [2] m. Mary Melville
- James [3] m. Jean Murray
  - Robert [5] (1724) m. Magdalen Stephen
  - Janet [6] 1725 m. Sir John Anstruther
    - John (1753)
    - Margaret (1759)
  - Jean m. John Melville (1748)
- Charles [4]
  - John m. Elizabeth Wallace (1710)
    - William (1711)
    - Marie (1714)
- Margaret m. William Kelly (1706)
- Mary (1725)
- Janet (1726)

1 Councillor in 1725, then provost until his death in 1736

2 Probably provost Robert Faa. Mary Melville's brother Robert was a partner in Fall, Melville and Company, Dunbar. Robert Melville's son Thomas was also employed by the company, working in the north of Scotland; it was he who attempted to develop Ullapool as a fishing port

3 Councillor, provost, then MP for the Haddingtonshire burghs from 1734-41. His wife was the daughter of Patrick Murray of Pennyland. James was an unreconstructed Jacobite; he died before the '45. It is not known why he called himself Captain

4 Counciller, then provost until his death in 1744

5 Perhaps the most famous of the Falls, Robert was born in 1724. Bailie, then provost, he served in the latter capacity during the farcical raids on Dunbar by John Paul Jones and Captain G Fall. He had two other sisters Isabel (1727) and Catherine (1728) but nothing is known of them. Robert died in 1796

6 Alexander 'Jupiter' Carlyle, minister and socialite, referred to Janet as Jenny, calling her 'a coquette and a beauty....lively and clever, no less than beautiful' Sir John was 2nd Baronet of Anstruther and lived at Elie, Fife. It is said that the Lady Tower near Elie was used by Jenny to allow her to change into her bathing dress in private, as Sir John was very jealous!

7 Provost in 1766, his administration was responsible for the fresh water supply piped to Dunbar from Spott. In 1764, he was granted a coat-of-arms which proved descent from Thomas Fall in the reign of Robert III (1390-1406 and Alexander Fall in the reign of James I (1406-37)

Main sources *TELAS vol iii* 1938; Parochial Register for East Lothian (Edinburgh Public Library)

.

Fig 14 A list of vessels wrecked off Dunbar between 1745 and 1920

Date	**Name of Vessel**	**Home Port**	**Value £ (where known)**
November 1745	*HMS Fox*	*Leith*	
1806	*Mercurius*		
	Jenny		
	Susannah	Newcastle	
1807	*Betsy Lyal*		
	Barbara		
October 1808	*HMS Cygnet*		
December 1810	*HMS Nymph, HMS Pallas*		60,000
	Goodwill		2,000
	Joan	Cadiz	8,200
January 1811	*Hope*	Yarmouth	1,000
	Lovely Ann		800
	Ranger	Leith	2,900
December 1812	*Nancy*	Kincardine	1,000
1812	*Jessie and Nancy*	Leith	1,200
1813	*Ravispure*	France	1,200
1814	Unnamed vessel	Leith	2,900

1816	*Ann and Elizabeth*	Alloa	
May	*Diana*	London	3,048
November	*John and Agnes*	Leith	1,612
December	*Thebes*		700
1817	*Amelia*	Banff	
1818	*John*		
October	*Signet*	North Shields	
1819			
February	*Comora*	Arbroath	1,500
October	*Nancy*	Kincardine	1,100
October	*Lady Grant*		800
November	*Fortune*	Arbroath	2,848
December	*Fortune*		2,500
	Elspeth and Betsy		670
November 1820	*Henry*	Yarmouth	1,200
1821	*Adelaide*	Yarmouth	1,000
February	*Yeoman*		900
November	*Lady Anne Murray*	Gatehouse-of-Fleet	1,500
December	*Nancy*		1,200
1822			
January	*Isabella and Jane*		1,800
May	*John*	Grangemouth	1,356
1824	*Friendship*	Leith	
1827	*Elizabeth and Ann*	Newcastle	
	James and Mary		
	Euphie	Alloa	
1828	*Five Brothers*	Alloa	
1830	*Union*	Aberdeen	
August	*Carolina*	Hull	
February 1831	*Czar*	Leith	
1832	*Forfarshire*		
1834	*George*		
	Albion	Dundee	
	Yeoman	Dunbar	
January 1835	*William Davidson*	Thurso	
	Bell		
	Diana		
	Barbara		
1841	*Hythe*		
1842	*Betsy and Mary*	Aberystwyth	
1843	*Cleveland*	Rostock, Germany	
	Vistula	Inverness	
January	*Isabella Black*		
October	*Maria Emilia*	Aberdeen	
August 1845	*Red Rover*	Buckhaven	
1864	*Chevrette*		
	Catherina	Berwick	
1847	*Brothers*		
	*Northumberland**	Alloa	
	*Agenoria**	Berwick	
	*Johns**	Limekilns	
	*Le Rodeur**	Bruges, Belgium	
	*Blackets**	Berwick	
* All on one December night of severe storm			
1849	*Tay*	Berwick	
1852	*Frankfurt Packet*		
January	*Susan*	Fraserburgh	
1853	*Ariel*	Boston	
	Sibella	Newcastle	
	Collins		
February 1854	*Brilliant*		
April 1855	*Early*	Newcastle	
1856	*Sisters*	Sunderland	
	Valentine	Rostock	
1857	*Shelagh*	Sunderland	
	Cromarty	Denmark	
	Sisters	Faversham	
	Hebe	Inverness	
1859	*Ora*	Sunderland	

1860	*Elizabeth*	
	London	Dundee
1861	*Liverpool*	
	Mary	North Shields
1863	*David Key*	Shoreham
1864	*Strand*	
1865	*Ocean*	Montrose
	Lord Adolphus	London
October	*Patrios*	Prussia
1866	*Osbourne*	Rostock
1867	*Corsair*	Aberdeen
	Polar Star	
	Alpha	Cowes
1869	*Josephine*	
	Concord	London
	Ludovic William	Newcastle
1871	*Hannah*	Leith
1872	*Elise*	
1874	*Perseverance*	Buckhaven
1877	*James*	Greenock
1881	*Concord*	
	Tiara	
	Transcendant	
	Margaret and Catherine	
	Beautiful Star	
	Sunshine	
	Alice	Berwick
	Six Brothers	"
	Mary and Margaret	"
	Lass of Gowrie	"
	Florida	"
	Guiding Star	"
	Fiery Cross	"
	Industry	"
1888	*Nile*	Lossiemouth
	Heroine	Exeter
1889	*Helen Elisabeth*	
1892	*Charlotte Stringer*	Finland
1893	*River Garry*	
1895	*Wave*	Montrose
1896	*Poderosa*	Grimsby
1900	*Ecclefechan*	
1904	*Lavinia*	Eyemouth
1905	*Riso*	Germany
1906	*King Ja Ja*	
1907	*Alfred Erlandsen*	Denmark
1908	*Prosum*	Christiana (now Oslo) Norway
1914	*Norway*	
1915	*Barge 132*	
	Spartan	
1920	*Malabar*	

(This is not an exhaustive list. However, between 1810 and 1822, 26 vessels whose recorded value amounted to about £105, 000 were lost off Dunbar)

Sources: SRO (ref. B 18/42/10); *Miller, Hist. Dunbar;The Dunbar Lifeboat History*; *Off Scotland: A Comprehensive Record of Maritime and Aviation Losses in Scottish Waters* (I Whittaker, Edinburgh, 1998)

Fig 15 Lifeboats and coxswains at Dunbar from 1808 to the present day

Period of Service	Lifeboat	Cost	Coxswain	Services	Lives saved
1808-1816	Unnamed*	£150	David Laing	2 or more	45
1865-1893	*Wallace@*	£250	Robert Clements (1865-1872) Robert Clements (1872-1877) Thomas Herkes (1877-1893)	11	42

1893-1901	*Sarah Pickard*	£405	Thomas Herkes (1893-1897) Walter Fairbairn (1897-1901)	9	24
1901-1931	*William Arthur Millward*	£879	Walter Fairbairn (1901-1931)	30	34
1907-1943 (Dunbar No 2)	*Sarah Kay* # (1931-1944)	£300	George Brunton Walter Fairbairn (1907-1931)	16	57
1931-1959	*George and Sarah Strachan* +	£7,680	George Brunton (1931-1944) David Brunton (1944-1954) Peter Johnston (1954-1959)	74	16
1959-1986	*Margaret*	£3,500	Peter Johnston (1959-1964) Robert George Brunton (1964-1979) Robert Marr Davies (1979-1981) Robert Noel Wight (1980-1986)	72	29
1986-1988	*Joseph Soar* (Civil Service No 34)	£41,106	Robert Noel Wight	6	0
1988-1993	*Hugh William, Viscount Gough*	£75,000	Robert Noel Wight	32	8
1993-1995	*Thomas James King* (Funded by local appeal in Jersey: formerly St Helier lifeboat)	£68,000	Robert Noel Wight Alan Bird (1993-1994) Robert Noel Wight	21	0
1995-2002	*Sir Ronald Pechell*	£1.025m	Robert Noel Wight until 2003 Gary Fairbairn 2003-	128	7
Temporary and Relief Lifeboats					
1931-1959				6	0
1959-1986				13	4
1986-1995				20	24
Inshore Lifeboats				141	63
Totals		£1.222m		581	333

Notes

* This lifeboat (sometimes confused with the *Lady Anne Murray*, a cargo ship wrecked in 1821), was purchased by public subscription following the initiative by George Miller of Dunbar (see Chapter 7). It was never formally named and is referred to variously in *Miller, Hist.* as 'The Lifeboat','The Dunbar Lifeboat' or 'The Lifeboat for the County of East Lothian.' The lifeboat was built by Henry Greathead of Newcastle, its originating port; the *Lady Anne Murray's* home port was Gatehouse-of-Fleet, Kirkudbrightshire

@ The first Royal National Lifeboat Institution (RNLI) lifeboat at Dunbar, *Wallace* capsized on a training exercise in 1877, tragically drowing coxswain Robert Herkes and former coxswain Robert Clements

The last of the sail powered and horse-drawn or pulled lifeboats in Scotland

+ The first motorised RNLI lifeboat at Dunbar

~ Great-grandson of Walter Fairbairn

Sources: *Miller,Dunbar;The Dunbar Lifeboat History*

Chapter 10

Trade, Industry, Commerce and Social

Scotland was slow to manufacture goods for export on a significant basis because until the creation of royal burghs, there was no incentive for the artisan class. Until the late twelfth century, trade was restricted to raw materials - wool, hides, furs and salted fish, the last being sought by Europe. The imported goods - silks, velvet, feather beds, pillows, fine wines, spices and cooking materials - were for the exclusive use of the nobility, the richest churchmen and the merchant class who could afford luxury items. In economic terms, Scotland remained medieval in outlook until the eighteenth century - or so it seems. The economy was fairly static as there was no money to stimulate activity; for centuries, the bulk of the population survived on a poor or at least monotonous diet and occasionally faced starvation. Until surplus food was grown, trade was hardly possible, restricted to leather goods and those made from wool.

Trade may have been conducted on a modest scale prior to David II's charter of 1370. The main exports after that were wool and animal hides; there were also thriving markets and fairs which sold agricultural produce and manufactured goods of leather. As we have seen in Chapter 8, all goods entering and leaving Dunbar by road or by sea - were subject to tax, the king receiving his share, the Great Customs.[1] An example of these customs is shown in **Fig. 16**.[2] The amounts paid over a century and a half weren't great, especially when a significant proportion was diverted to the Earls of Dunbar and their families which reflected the policy of several Stewart kings from Robert II onwards who secured their services by making cash payments. The figures for Dunbar indicate an underlying decline in the royal revenue from about the beginning of the fifteenth century, less than forty years after Dunbar became a royal burgh; by then, the king's income was virtually at an end, hardly worth the trouble of collecting.

And yet for centuries, the Lothians in general and Dunbar in particular were great cereal-producing districts comparing favourably with others in England and France. The merchants were quick to realise that commerce rather than land ownership was the key to wealth since there were practically no overheads and income was less subject to fluctuation caused by the uncertainty of the weather and the quality of the harvest. As in all economies, poor harvests meant high prices; however, the merchants rarely suffered whatever the state of the market. Also, within the royal burgh boundary, materials brought there to make goods were exempt from burgh taxes, becoming liable only on sale to 'unfree' merchants ie those who didn't reside in the burgh.

Like most royal burghs, Dunbar contained a number of burgess-craftsmen who enriched themselves as well as the burgh itself. Among these were the fleshers (butchers), fishmongers, baxters (bakers), skinners, lorimers (sadlers), tanners, hammermen (armourers and metal workers), cordiners (shoemakers), lacemakers, weavers, listers (dyers), fullers (clothmakers), cardmakers (for carding wool and flax), potters, poulterers, cheesemongers, basket weavers, cornmongers and haymongers, brewers, fishermen, sailors and last but not least, the blacksmith. Many of these occupations are the source of Scottish surnames; note how many are connected with the production of cloth, probably the main export from Dunbar along with leather goods, fish and grain.

The power of the burgess-craftsmen grew in proportion to the amount of local and international trade conducted in the burgh. At first the burgesses were responsible for running the town then gradually, town councils began to take shape. An act of parliament in 1469 stipulated that members of a town council were chosen by the retiring members - inevitably, fathers elected sons or sons-in-law which gave the same families a continuous monopoly in the way the town was run; names such as Fall; Kellie and Purves appear often in the town records from the sixteenth century onwards. Nepotism was rife; not only was it practised, it was enforced by the law and little would change until the reform legislation of 1832 and 1833 swept away the worst of these practices.

Gradually, the range of goods exported from Dunbar expanded from wool and hides to fish, grain, textiles, woollen goods and those made from linen and cotton grown locally. From the seventeenth century, Dunbar also traded in salt, an essential commodity used for preserving fish and meat in the winter months. However, even then, overseas trade was minimal; in 1692, commissioners appointed by the Convention of Royal Burghs found that Dunbar had no vessel of sufficient tonnage to engage in local coastal let alone overseas trade apart from two barques of 12 and 18 tons respectively - used mainly to transport coal - and only

> '16 or 17 herring boats which proves [sic] extraordinarie unprofiteable [sic] by thedecaying of the herring industry.'

Fig 16 Extract of Great Customs collected at Dunbar from 1370 to 1535

The loss in 1333 of Berwick and Roxburgh to England diverted some of the Cheviot wool production to the English customs; this explains in part why Dunbar was created a free burgh in 1370. Even so, the Great Customs collected there constituted a very small proportion of the royal income, as will be seen.

'Great Customs of Dunbar at the Port of Belhevyne'*

1370 According to *TELAS* 1929-30, the sum of £2097:9:8 (£2097.49) was collected at Dunbar; this must be an error as the amount for the whole of Scotland was £5000. The true account was more likely to have been £209. The undernoted sums were collected between 1379 and 1535 but the figures are not meaningful inrespect of amounts paid to the kings of the time. For example, Robert II (1371-90) had a habit of authorising payments from his Great Customs to pay for services of his vassals despite their feudal obligations to him.[42] We learn that in 1389# the 10th Earl of Dunbar received £250 from the Great Customs and money was diverted to others; the amounts ultimately handed over to the king's Great Chamberlain is net of these payments. Minor amounts were deducted as fees to the custumar and tron operator who weighed the goods, with an occasional few shillings paid for the upkeep of the tron itself.

.	Wool, woolfells, hides			Expenses and Grants			Paid to Chamberlain		
	£	s	d	£	s	d	£	s	d
1379-1380	227	14	5	38	10	11	180	0	0
1380-1381	309	13	2	236	11	9	73	1	5
1393-1395	78	9	8	168	6	0	10	3	8
	100	0	0 (arrears)						
1396-1398	349	7	2	404	2	10	16	9	6
	71	5	2 (arrears)						
1399-1400	229	9	9	197	9	10	40	0	0
	88	0	1 (arrears)						
1402-1405	(Nothing was customed at Dunbar because of the war with England, during the period of the 10th Earl of Dunbar's defection to Henry IV)								
1407-1409	124	12	0						
	310	0	11 (arrears)	434	13	0	0	0	0
1411-1412	427	5	5	427	5	5	0	0	0
1416-1417	160	5	5	124	18	11	35 (Balance)	6	6
	(In the next twenty years, the customs decreased dramatically)								
1438-1440	47	4	5	23	4	1	24 (Balance)	0	4
1448-1449	43	9	2	22	6	1	21 (Balance)	3	1
1453-1454	14	19	3	14	19	3	0	0	0
1477-1480	(The Customs amounted to only £7:16:7 of which all but two shillings and sevenpence went to the Receiver)								
1491-1492	(Only £9:8:11 was collected, including arrears of £3:14:11: £9:7:0 was paid to the Comptroller of the royal household)								
1495-1496	(Only £31:16:5 was collected of which £29 was paid to the Comptroller of the royal household)								

* Source = *ERs*

In August 1389, three shillings (15p) were levied on each tun of wine, 12 pennies (5p) in the pound on all foreign merchandise. The custumar for the East March collected £28:14:2 (£28.70) in tax on merchandise valued at £574:2:6 (£574.12), or about 5%; the goods included red herrings, salmon, otter skins, shoes and malt for the 9th Earl of Dunbar and others (*CDS vol v* No 864).

@ Rarely more than £20 in all

In 1530, Dunbar contributed £17:6:8 (£17.33) to the Great Customs; this was made up of £4 in *feu-ferme,* or fermes by feu-chart as the quitclaim of any customs, together with £13:6:8 (£13.33) from the town mills at West Barns. In the following year, the same amount was paid; by 1534, this had diminished to £4 and in 1535, the amount was a paltry £1:6:8 (£1.33). As the customs collected reflected the extent of trade, Dunbar had become a depressed area.

The yearly fair which lasted two days brought the burgh only £19 Scots in petty customs; a third of the houses in the burgh were described as being in a ruinous state.

Something had to be done to change this. We know that famine visited Scotland in 1644-45 and again at the end of the century. Trade with her nearest neighbour England was virtually non-existent because of the discriminatory policy south of the Border. The English Navigation Acts of 1660 and 1663 treated Scotland as a foreign country and because of this, her merchants were technically excluded from trade with the American Plantations The legislation was difficult to enforce however and the Glasgow merchants benefited from trade with the colonies by underselling their English rivals because while Scottish goods were of poorer finished quality, they suited the basic needs - and pockets - of the pioneering colonists, many of whom were of Scottish descent. However, on the eastern seaboard, trade was predominantly with Europe, although until the eighteenth century, Dunbar's trade was limited to coastal waters including England, with its heavy tariff barriers. By 1692, like many other royal burghs, Dunbar's economy was showing distinct signs of economic flabbiness. After the failure of the Darien Scheme in 1698, many Scottish landowners were bankrupted and sought to restore their fortunes by a closer relationship with England. Eventually, the talk turned to union with England, as many believed it would cure Scotland's economic ills by providing a ready market for cattle, cloth, fish and grain. By the crude economic standards of the day, Scottish landowner and merchant alike envisaged the country awash with English gold which would allow existing industries to develop - fishing, mining, agriculture and timber. The union certainly made economic sense; while trade with Europe continued, it tended to fluctuate and trade with England was increasing. East coast burghs like Dunbar were set to make - and did make - money out of the Act of Union in 1707. As we have seen, the merchant Falls of Dunbar prospered for a considerable part of the century as the economic climate improved.

The events preceding union illustrate a disturbing divergence of views. In 1703, the Scottish parliament passed an act of security which stated that when queen Anne died, the Scots wouldn't accept the same monarch as England unless they were guaranteed equal access to English markets. England responded to this act of brio by passing the Alien Act of 1705 which disqualified Scotsmen from inheriting English land or property - basically an attack on the nobility who practically ran Scotland. The act also stipulated that English merchants would cease buying Scottish goods after 25th December 1705 if by then the Scots hadn't accepted the Act of Settlement of 1701 on which was founded the Hanoverian succession to the throne. This tit-for-tat diplomacy finally worked in England's favour; faced with the prospect of a fall in trade, the nobility and merchants alike were forced to accept the reality of the situation.

As we know, the two most vociferous opponents of union were Andrew Fletcher of Saltoun and 2nd Lord Belhaven at Biel. While Fletcher is regarded as the more able and persuasive of the two, unlike Belhaven, he wasn't always in favour of Scotland remaining independent. On 8th January 1689, he commented in a letter that

> 'We can never come to any trew setelment [true settlement] but by uniting with England in Parliament and Trade.'

In mitigation however, Fletcher was writing at a time when it seemed that the English constitution was about to be overhauled and the powers of the monarchy limited, these being his chief aims as far as Scotland was concerned. As described elsewhere, the union of 1707 wasn't the first attempt to bring the two countries together. The first peaceful attempt after Protector Somerset dreamed of an Emperor of Great Britain imposed on Scotland at sword point in 1547 was the brainchild of James VI, then Charles I and the Cromwellian Commonwealth which followed. If there was no ineluctable drift towards union after Cromwell's death in 1658, there were certainly mutterings in its favour long before 1707. Had union occurred at any time before 1707, different social, economic and political considerations would have obtained. When union did come, to describe it a democratic outcome would be a misuse of language; the vigorous denials of bribery then are equalled by the vitriolic accusations of today. The truth lies somewhere in between. In the absence of a modern political party system, inducements and favours in the form of money payments sadly were the way things got done. There were initial benefits to Scotland, particularly when the English Navigation Acts were extended to Scotland, thus allowing legal trading with America.

By the end of the eighteenth century, other than fish, Dunbar's main export was grain. The granaries have long-since disappeared, although the Corn Exchange and the great storage barns in the outlying district survive as testimony to the success of the grain trade. The main imports were coal, timber and iron. In 1793, the Dunbar contributor to the *Old Statistical Account* indicated that 6,000 tons of each were landed at the Old Harbour. Linen was manufactured in the eighteenth century and a result, a Bleachfield was created at Countess Park in 1756, with a second field at West Barns. The British Linen Bank was established in 1747 to finance the production of linen; in 1788, a branch of the bank opened in Dunbar in what today is Croft House, in Delisle Street, near the West Port. Sadly, the linen industry in Dunbar did not survive long. There was also a ropeworks, two starch factories and a soap factory but these were minor industries employing a few men and women. For about 40 years, cotton was manufactured, first at West Barns in 1792, then at Belhaven in 1815. In the latter case, the burgh council minutes record a petition received on 11th January 1815 from Messrs Goudie and Borthwick, cotton manufacturers, proposing to convert the former Belhaven cavalry barracks set up during the Napoleonic Wars into a factory. They offered a rent of £400 a year for a lease of 20 years and a *grassum* [token payment] of £50 for the renewal of the lease every ten years thereafter. The company also offered to buy the empty huts on the site for £1,200, at £900 after 10 years and £500 after 20 years. The offer of immediate purchase was accepted; when the lease was granted, Bruce Borthwick successfully applied to become a burgess for life on payment of the usual £5 fee.

The Belhaven factory lasted 16 years and failed about the same time as that at West Barns. The remains of a flax mill in the grounds of Bielside House -formerly Distillery House - on the outskirts of West Barns may well be that described in the *New Statistical Account* as having closed by 1831. Attempts to establish a major manufacturing base at Dunbar were repeated in many Scottish towns, part of a search for a new Scottish identity; such projects were short-lived. There was also a waukmill [clothmill] at Beltonford, on the Cleikimin Road, now the A1 bypass and near the modern trout farm. The waukmill sluice at the railway bridge was drained off by a small channel that still runs into West Barns. There was a quarry at Bowerhouse which supplied the red sandstone for the modern parish church and another smaller quarry beside Knockenhair Lodge. By 1835, most of the small industries had collapsed or shrunk; even the manufacture of steam engines at Dunbar ceased later in the century. The satellite village of West Barns continued to thrive however. In 1862, Alexander Annandale, a paper manufacturer in Lasswade, Midlothian purchased the Dunbar corn or flour mill on the outskirts of West Barns. Annandale built his paper mill using bricks bought from William Brodie of Battleblent's Seafield Brick and Tile Works. Beltonford Paper Mill opened in 1866. On 2nd April 1892, a disastrous fire gutted the buildings, ending the paper-making business. In 1894, Alexander Hunter of Belhaven Brewery bought the site and converted the surviving buildings into a maltings which were subsequently sold to British Malt Products Co Ltd. The site was unlucky; in the 1940s, another fire destroyed the Maltings and the site was next occupied by Associated British Malsters Co until the 1970s, when a third fire destroyed the buildings. The area is now a lorry park. In addition to making bricks, Brodie's Seafield Brickworks exported drainage pipes to Holland in the appropriately-named vessel *Firebrick*; the return cargo was red pantiles for ballast which explains why many farm buildings around Dunbar have pantiled roofs. From the start of the nineteenth century, Sked's Foundry at Edenholme beside the Eden Hotel was engaged in supplying steam engines and threshing mill equipment to the farming community; Sked's initiative was taken up by Thomas Sheriff and Sons at West Barns, manufacturers of agricultural implements which continues to trade to this day. (Sheriff 's occupies the site of the former flour mill). At one time, there was probably a glue factory in Duke Street, Belhaven which is thought to have also tanned leather. In 1841, R Forsyth wrote in the reprint of his *Beauties of Scotland* that the chief trade at Dunbar was in wheat, oats, barley, hulled barley, peas, beans and malt; soap and starch were also produced. The burgh shipping amounted to 2,300 tons.

Dunbar was touched only marginally by the Industrial Revolution. However, no account of its economic state dare ignore one of its most successful enterprises, the brewery at Belhaven. The story of ale-brewing in Scotland is well-documented and need only be touched upon in the local context. Ale was brewed at Belhaven from the twelfth century, when Earl Gospatric III (1138x39-1166) made a gift of a toft at Belhaven to the Cluniac monks whose monastery was established on the Isle of May in 1150. The lay Brothers at Monkscroft, Belhaven grew vegetables and brewed ale for those on the island; the potable well water and top quality barley of the district proved a winning combination even in those days.

In the sixteenth century, records confirm that Belhaven ale was supplied to the French expeditionary force commanded by Mary of Guise, a large part of which was garrisoned at Dunbar Castle. Mary, the spirited widow of James V and mother of Mary, Queen of Scots, no doubt encouraged her soldiers to partake of the local ale. By 1719, ownership of the small family business was in the hands of John Johnstone; it remained in the Johnstone family until 1815, when the business passed from George Johnstone to his son-in-law, Ellis Dudgeon. Before that however, there were five local breweries - John Brown at Shore Street, John Dod at Davel Brae (now Victoria Street), Harry and William Knox and A M Bruce in the High Street and the Johnstones at Belhaven. Harry Knox - we encountered him in another context in Chapter 5 and A M Bruce restricted their sales to the town of Dunbar; the former ceased trading in about 1770, the latter in 1825. The early nineteenth century witnessed a peak in country brewing, although fluctuations in the prices of grain and barley were obviously reflected in the cost of malt and ale production, forcing many of the small breweries like Brown's and Dod's out of business. However, Belhaven survived, using the best malt barley which was grown around Haddington, East Linton and Dunbar; in 1793, Dunbar malt was of such quality that it supplanted Elgin as the main supplier to Norway. The maltings of the day processed some 9,200 tonnes of malt barley.

For long, brewing was conducted on a purely domestic consumption level. In modest country breweries like Belhaven, the accounts and book-keeping were undertaken by members of the family. However, Dudgeon of Belhaven had ambitious plans to expand the business. In 1830, he bought Belhaven Mill from Dunbar burgh council and incorporated it into the brewery. In 1837, the *London Morning Chronicle* advertised Belhaven ales for sale:

'....such is their quality that the Emperor of Austria selected them.....on which occasion the Emperor declared that Belhaven ale "was the Burgundy of Scotland; and famed as Bavaria is for its strong beer, it cannot produce the like...."'

Fair praise indeed. But even before that, in the previous century, James Boswell, the biographer of Dr Samuel Johnson who visited Dunbar in 1773 (see Chapter 3) declared the local ale was "the best small beer I ever had."

By 1850, Ellis Dudgeon was selling 150 barrels of beer and ale to the inns of Dunbar and surrounding villages, extending well into Berwickshire. The brewery suffered two damaging fires - one in 1814, the year when the impressive Monkscroft House was built - the second in 1887. By the latter year, most of the other small local breweries had closed but Belhaven continued to expand and flourish. A new well was bored in 1890 and new maltings were built at West Barns in 1894. Belhaven went from strength to strength in the following century, expanding its markets while retaining its distinctive character. During both World Wars, Belhaven supplied ale to the troops despite the severe rationing of the ingredients used to make ale. By the middle of the twentieth century, only Dudgeon of Belhaven and Younger's of Alloa survived as independents, the rest having been taken over by the brewing giants. The reason why these two companies managed to remain independent was that they continued to use traditional brewing methods, producing a range of superior and distinctive ales and beers.

In 1944, Belhaven became a private brewing company, trading under the name of Dudgeon and Co. Ltd. In 1946, Alexander (Sandy) Hunter joined the company; it was he who created the now familiar *Belhaven Bill* in 1951, the fat, jolly, bucolic seaman and the company's trademark for over half a century. Framed by Dunbar Harbour, the pot-bellied, avuncular character was soon to be found on beer mats in bars and tables of pubs throughout Scotland. Not unsurprisingly, Belhaven figured prominently in the Campaign for Real Ale, a movement which has furthered the quality of its products - and rightly so.

Ellis Dudgeon Hunter, Ellis Dudgeon's grandson who had been appointed manager in 1898 died in 1964 aged 87. He was succeeded by his son Alexander (Sandy) Hunter who became managing director, then chairman of the brewery until his retirement in 1982. Before that, a new well was sunk in 1973 which today supplies the water for brewing rather than the town supply. In recent years, Belhaven has survived many attempts by big business to depersonalise its character. In April 1994, Belhaven won the Overall Scottish Marketing Award for outstanding performance in what has become a very competitive industry. Two years later, the company was floated on the Stock Market, when its sales grossed £17 million with an operating profit of £2.5 million. Today, the brewery produces 70,000 kegs of ale per annum and a further 30,000 barrels of contract bottling; it owns 70 public houses in Scotland. Long may it flourish.

Another local success story is the cement industry. Dunbar had a thriving lime industry long before Blue Circle Industries began to extract limestone from 1963 on an impressive scale; the factory altered the surrounding countryside for ever but the company (now Lafarge Cement Co. UK) deserves to be congratulated on its concern for and care of the environment. Lime was produced in Fife and the Lothians from the Middle Ages, providing not only the mortar to build church and castle but also the distemper finish which lightened their gloomy interiors. By the eighteenth century, locally-produced lime was chiefly used on fields, when the soil had a higher level of acidity than desirable; liming the land improved crop yields and made previously untilled land productive. Liming of the soil was introduced in East Lothian by Cockburn of Ormiston, the Earl of Haddington and Lord Belhaven of Bielside, near Dunbar; these men realised the importance of crop rotation, when to lime the land and when to leave it fallow.

The earliest extraction of lime probably dates from the mid to late thirteenth century, when Scotland experienced an unprecedented building programme of stone-and-mortar castles. After that, stone buildings were regularly lime-washed for aesthetic and hygienic reasons. It was indeed fortunate that rich lime deposits were available near Dunbar; it may also account for the fact that East Lothian and Berwickshire were among the first - if not the first - counties to add lime dressings to the soil. The only other mining - of coal - was conducted on a very modest scale at the Cove, as mentioned earlier.

The remains of eighteenth century limekilns can be found throughout the central belt of Scotland, particularly at Limekilns, Fife. Two good examples of draw kilns survive at Catcraig and Skateraw; the Oxwellmains kiln has long-since been obliterated by commercial mining.. The kilns used by the medieval builders were usually temporary affairs - small turf, earth and stone structures which could be built easily. Lime was quarried commercially at Dunbar from the seventeenth century; as agriculture and industry developed, production increased. Lime was a vital fluxing agent in the iron-smelting process in the iron smelting process which dates from the Napoleonic Wars; local kilns supplied the Devon Iron Works at Clackmannan from then until the twentieth century. The stone-built vertical kilns at Catcraig, near Barns Ness Lighthouse restored by the Associated Portland Cement Co. in 1966 and Skateraw at Torness Point restored by Scottish Power give us an impression of their size and capacity. Catcraig operated until 1821; a smaller kiln at East Barns, now obscured by the operations of the modern cement company ceased production in 1860. Skateraw was created by Brodie of Thorntonloch and Lee of Skateraw; Lee entertained Burns to dinner on 12th May 1787 during the poet's Border Tour. The kiln at Skateraw/Torness (**ill 109**) operated during the nineteenth century and as previously mentioned, had a small harbour for unloading coal and loading the finished lime. Alexander Somerville was employed there in 1830; in his autobiography,[4] he describes the working conditions of the time. He was put to work at the kilnhead, shovelling alternate layers of coal and limestone into the kiln, a dirty, smoky and unhealthy job that covered him in lime and coal dust. His day began at 3 or 4am and he rarely got home before 5 or 6pm. His wage was about nine shillings (45p) a week - poor by comparison with a collier (27 shillings or £1.35) or miner (12 shillings or 60p).

KRM

Illus 109: *Limekiln at Skateraw/Torness*

Most kilns were built into a natural slope so that coal and limestone could be loaded from the top; as the stone crumbled in the heat, the lime fell to the bottom and was extracted from a draw hole at the kiln's base. The landscape behind the ruin at Catcraig is pitted with holes and depressions caused by limestone extraction. Thus Dunbar's early attempts at lime production evolved into what is now a major enterprise which brought much-needed employment to the town in 1966. The OS map for 1907 identifies an area at the base of the Winterfield Golf Clubhouse where cement was produced, probably in small premises rented from Winterfield Mains Farm which was situated near the present day chalet holiday homes at Belhaven.

Fig 17 Lime Production in 1837 and 2002

The following is a snapshot figure of lime production in East Lothian in the year 1837

Parish	Lime (bushels)	Sale Price per bushel	Gross Value £
Saltoun	139,392	3 3/4d	2,178
Crichton Dean	139,392	3 1/2d	2,032
Skateraw	71,568	4 1/2d	1,342 +
East Barns	27,832	4 3/4d	551

The cost of the coal used to produce the lime had to be offset against the return; coal varied in price in the above parishes

+ Thus at Skateraw, near Dunbar, the lime industry was worth £1,893; by 1844, the value had dropped to £1,300 (*New Statistical Account*).

Cement production continued on a relatively minor scale until 1961, when Blue Circle Cement Co. established a major plant; its first two kilns went into operation in 1963, a further kiln was brought into operation in 1966, by which time the workforce exceeded 500. In 2000, the company was taken over by Lafarge Cement Co. UK. In the financial year ended 5 April 2002, the factory's output was one million tonnes, an exceptionally good year, as normal production is about 930 thousand tonnes.

In addition to Catcraig, Skateraw, East Barns and Oxwellmains, kilns existed at Thorntonloch and

Oldhamstocks. In 1950, the Coltness Iron and Steel Company at Oxwellmains was mining limestone for New Mains, a cement factory in Lanarkshire; in 1955, I recall picking peas at Oxwellmains farm, near which was a small single-gauge railway line used to transport the limestone to a goods loading point on the main London and North East Railway line (now GNER). In the nineteenth century, France's Seafield New Cement Company at West Barns (near the West Barns Inn) probably used small quantities of locally quarried lime. In 1951, investigation of Oxwellmains proved that there were significant yields to be had from the area - much more than the Coltness Company could extract. Figures for lime production in the nineteenth century are given in J Carmichael's publication of 1837;[5] the output for East Lothian and Skateraw in 1837 and 2002 is shown in **Fig. 17**. Apart from the restored kilns, the others have either been demolished or in-filled.

No study of Dunbar's economic history would be complete without reference to the local transport systems. For centuries, there were no roads other than three main paths beaten through the Borders from England; one was in the West March and passed through Annandale; the second came through the Middle March via Lauderdale - the most favoured by the English invading armies - and the last roughly followed the A1 road. Roads were little more than cart tracks, difficult to negotiate even on horseback; most use of these was by farm carts, sledges and packhorses. In the seventeenth century, the main roads were haphazard affairs, so much so that in 1699, the Scottish parliament passed an act which instituted a system of statute labour for road maintenance and comparable with arrangements in England which dated as far back as 1555. Sheriffs and justices of the peace were constituted as local road authorities, meeting annually to report on the repairs needed to the roads and bridges in their districts. These road committees were empowered to call out the local population for six days a year - in June and July - to fill in potholes and redefine verges; the committees were also able to raise money from landowners on their income from renting land and by charging tolls. The Scottish road network was better developed than England's in one respect; it was organised on a county rather than a parish basis but it was still poor grade. Dunbar was fortunate enough to lie astride the Great Post Road from England even it was of doubtful quality, requiring constant repair because of heavy traffic. Sometimes, overbearing landowners attempted to interfere with the local road systems, as occurred near Dunbar in 1711. The burgh council was moved to submit a petition to the Convention of Royal Burghs, complaining that the Duke of Roxburghe intended to enclose

> 'ane highway leading to and from the burgh of Dunbar through the links of Broxmouth, of which road the said burgh has been in possesssione past all memory of man, and that the inclosing thereof will be very preduciall to the fishing of that place and all round about.'

The burgh appears to have successfully defended its rights and obtained a grant of £100 Scots (about £8 sterling) to assist with the costs of their legal defence - even if the burgh had to wait until 1715 to secure the grant. In 1750, the roads were in an appalling state. A stagecoach from Edinburgh to London went only once a month and took twelve to sixteen days to complete the journey. Roads weren't substantially improved until the latter half of the eighteenth century, when the Turnpike Road Act of 1751 was passed. This measure was implemented by the Commissioners for East Lothian ahead of any other county in Scotland. The 'voluntary'statute labour was abolished as income from the new tolls enabled the roads committees to hire semi-skilled labourers as full-time road menders. In 1760, the Great Post Road was much-improved and daily stagecoaches changed horses at Cossar's [later the St George] Hotel. The late eighteenth century witnessed a revolution in road building in the Lowlands with the introduction of the turnpike system - an English initiative which Scotland quickly followed. The new roads were managed by Turnpike Trustees authorised to raise money by various means - chiefly toll charges - to finance further road building and improvement.

The first turnpike road from Dunbar was completed some time after 1751, connecting Dunglass and Ravensheugh. In 1755, Dunbar sent burgh officials to Haddington to establish a turnpike road from Beltonford. By 1793, the Post Road ran from east to west along the route of the present A1; there were three toll bars; Kirkhill, adjacent to the Parish Kirk; Belhaven, where the tollkeeper lived in Benston Cottage, still in existence and Cleikimin at the modern Spott road-end roundabout- aptly named, as the old Scots word *cleik* means to lay hold of or catch. There were four bridges which had to be maintained by the county as well as the cross or minor roads; not being main or turnpike roads, they had to be

> 'kept in good order by the statute labour'[6]

To save money, landowners expected their tenants to carry produce by cart over poor roads to their premises or to the granary at Dunbar. For example, Lord Hay of Belton made his tenants bring coals to his house by cart from Tranent, nearly fifteen miles away. And Sir John Nisbet of Dirleton who owned land in Innerwick and Thorntonloch had his tenants deliver their grain to the harbour granary, as we have seen. However, the poor roads were a boon to the coastal shipping trade, particularly in the transportation of heavy raw materials such as coal, timber, stone and iron. Sea transport also avoided turnpike tolls. Bridges were a great problem, needing almost continuous repair; in 1595, the Privy Council recorded that the bridge at East Linton was in danger of collapsing and ordered tolls to be collected there from 1595 to 1598. Charges were a penny per adult pedestrians and two pennies per horseman, horse load, ten sheep and one cow or ox.

The stagecoaches which plied between London and Edinburgh which stopped to change horses at Lorimer's, then Cossar's Hotel weren't the first 'public' wheeled transport between Dunbar and Edinburgh. Duncan McCulloch, a Dunbar vintner started his business in 1781; more of a covered wagon than stagecoach, the vehicle took a whole day to get to Edinburgh. The first stagecoach proper was run by Henry Laidlaw in 1804; Laidlaw reduced the journey to Edinburgh to five hours, a considerable feat for the time. Stagecoaches were familiar sights in East Lothian from about 1678, plying mainly between Edinburgh and Haddington. It was well into the next century before a network of reasonably passable roads was created, allowing more commercial and public transport. The horse was of course king of the road, even if it could carry only small loads. Although he contributed little to road making and bridge building in East Lothian, the East Linton born civil engineer John Rennie (1761-1821) deserves mention here. Rennie was born at Phantassie, East Linton and attended the grammar school at Dunbar. He worked with Andrew Meikle the millwright until he started his own business, designing and building mills. His works in Scotland include the Clyde Navigation and Glasgow Docks, the Crinan Canal, harbours at Saltcoats, Stranraer, Montrose, Queensferry and Berwick. He built bridges at Kelso, Musselburgh, Newton Stewart and New Galloway and the docks at Leith and Greenock. He went to England where he built the Southwark, Waterloo and London Bridges across the Thames, the London Docks, the East and West India Docks as well as docks at Hull, Liverpool, Chatham, Portsmouth and Plymouth.[7] He also assisted Robert Louis Stevenson's grandfather in the planning of the Bell Rock Lighthouse, the impressive light off the coast of Angus.

But the most revolutionary form of transport was the railway. Although the line which passed through Dunbar didn't open until June 1846, an earlier attempt had been made in 1825, the intention being to freight grain, coal and lime. Robert Stevenson, who built twenty lighthouses round the Scottish coast, conducted a feasibility study into a line from Edinburgh to Tranent, then southwards to Winton Gate and Haddington, from where it was to follow the river Tyne and culminate at Dunbar - a distance of 40 miles. The sponsors reputedly met in Edinburgh in 1825; what became of Stevenson's scheme remains shrouded in mystery to this day. There is no reference to the East Lothian Railway in the House of Commons Journal for 1826-27; it is thought that the scheme was abandoned as it lacked the support of local landowners. It was left to the North British Railway Company (NBRC), formed in 1843, to bring trains to Dunbar based in part on Stevenson's plan. In 1841, parliamentary commissioners Smith and Barlow identified two possible rail routes across the Border; they increased this to three, one of which was the east coast route. Parliament approved the new line in 1844, the year when Dunbar's Victoria Harbour was completed. The NBRC hastily opened a poorly-constructed line from Edinburgh to Berwick Castle via Dunbar in June 1846; the line couldn't go beyond Berwick as the river Tweed didn't then possess a bridge strong enough to support heavy rolling stock, although by 1848, it linked Edinburgh and London. In 1946, the LNER intended to produce a book commemorating the centennial of the opening of the line and contacted the town council to obtain any photographs of the original railway station at Dunbar. Unfortunately, none seems to have survived.[8] However, one was taken in the winter of 1945-46 to celebrate the centenary of the line (**ill 110**). The railway has served Dunbar well for the past 150 years and it is hoped that trains will continue to stop there in the present century.

RJP

Illus 110: *Dunbar Railway Station 1945-46*

Now there is the ubiquitous - iniquitous - car, insatiably devouring space for parking and obstructing views and even obliterating historic sites. The leisurely pace of horse-drawn vehicles continued until the turn of the twentieth century, when the early version of the motor car changed the world forever. The first cars appeared on the roads at Dunbar in 1904, when burgh council minutes of 9th November record concern about the dangers they brought. The council suggested - they had to proceed with caution, as only the rich could afford cars - that danger signals be erected at the West Port and the Station Road. A classic love-hate relationship began nearly a century ago. Today, the High Street has been narrowed to make the streets more pedestrian-friendly. It has come too late and leaves much to be desired. Visit Dunbar but cross the street with caution at the designated places; few drivers can be blamed for not observing these pedestrian 'crossings' because they aren't identified. At least there is a traffic warden....

The last word on roads. As this book is being completed, the long-awaited expressway from Haddington to Dunbar is at last under construction, it could however reduce Dunbar to little more than a dormitory or commuter town conveniently close to Edinburgh. Whether the new road will benefit the town and its economy remains to be seen. One hopes that it will.

Education

The Scots have always set great store by learning. Despite its relative poverty, Scotland opened its first university before England and for centuries, educational provision outstripped and was superior in quality to that south of the Border. In medieval times, Scottish scholars attended the great seats of learning on the Continent - in Paris for example. They were more cosmopolitan than their supposedly better developed neighbour. Education was largely provided by the Catholic Church until the Reformation, when a serious attempt was made to provide a school in every parish. The reforming fathers were keen on education and made exaggerated claims about their success in providing it. However, it was their declared aim that every parish should have its own school.

At the time of the Reformation, more than half of the 1,000 or so parishes in Scotland already had a school of sorts; by the early seventeenth century, 700 schools were spread unevenly across the country. Parochial schools catered for every pupil - boy and girl - from all walks of life; a few were fortunate enough to have parents who could afford to pay for extra tuition. While the curriculum was limited to Latin, English, Mathematics, the Catechisms and religious studies, the parish school offered a sound, if basic, education to the sons and to a lesser extent the daughters - girls learnt to spin, sew and knit - of even the most humble folk. Education was promoted in Dunbar as elsewhere. The first mention of a school in Dunbar occurs in 1564, when its schoolmaster Andrew Simson noted that ' the people have a real desire for education.'

In 1679, an unusually liberal burgh council introduced regulations or bylaws governing the conduct of Dunbar's school pupils.[9] One of the measures was well ahead of its time and apparently didn't happen until much later elsewhere in Scotland. The Dunbar council stipulated that there should be a fair proportion of work and play so that

> 'the Children be nor ufed [used]as flaves [slaves] but as freeborne and that their labour may be fweetened [sweetened] unto them every Tuefday and Thurfday'

these being the days they were allowed to play outside for thirty minutes - weather permitting - returning to their schoolbooks until 6pm. However, the same regulations ruled that scholars who broke windows, desks or locks would be liable for the damage and if the culprit wasn't identified, every schoolboy in the class would share responsibility for the damage, which of course meant that their parents would have to pay for it. Those playing truant or, in the quaint language of the age 'turne fugitive' would be hauled back to school and punished. Any schoolboy who refused to submit to discipline had to be made an example of *pour encourager les autres* and

> 'if the ftubborne partie be too strong, [the master was] then to call for help from the Magiftrates.'

However, whatever the type of punishment meted out, the masters were enjoined not to chastise children

> 'for every trifle and ftupefie ym wt [stupefy them with] stroakes'

meaning of course the cane or tawse. So much for the legendary tales about excessive and unnecessary corporal punishment in Scottish schools although perhaps Dunbar was ahead of its time. In the eighteenth century, as soon as boys were old enough, they went to the parish school. In that century, it wasn't uncommon for boys to walk several miles to and from school, starting out at 5 or 6am and not returning home until about 7pm. School hours were long. Classes started at 6am in summer, 7am in winter, with breaks to

> 'keep punctual diets at ten after breakfast and one after dinner.'[10]

School ended at 6pm, holidays were few, restricted to a month at harvest time for obvious reasons. Things had improved slightly by 1727, when lessons were taught at Dunbar Grammar School from 7 to 9am, 10am until noon and 2 to 6pm; on Saturdays, the school closed at noon.

Discipline was never far from the surface. The magistrates were at pains to impress upon parents the need to report any acts of wilful disobedience in the home; the parents were urged to admonish their children first, then if bad behaviour persisted, they were advised to flog the little darlings. Perhaps today's liberal reformers may wish to take notice.

Not unexpectedly, great emphasis was placed on religious education. In 1679, the masters at Dunbar were obliged to recommend the children to god by prayer in the morning and

'as they began, let them close the day with prayers'.

The masters were also required to instruct their charges in the principles of Christianity; on Sundays, the children were quizzed on what they had learnt at the Sabbath morning service.

To a certain extent, rural parochial schools were mirrored in the burghs like Dunbar which under the Act of Settling Schools in 1696 had a statutory obligation to provide a school and schoolmaster. Where burgh schools differed was that the magistrates appointed the masters and paid their salaries. Thankfully, the Kirk had less say in the way burgh schools were run. At the beginning of the eighteenth century, all burgh schools were grammar schools, teaching Latin; the curriculum also included reading, writing, arithmetic and in sea ports like Dunbar, navigation. In addition, Dunbar Grammar School provided tuition in Greek, geography and book-keeping.

A James Kirkwood, schoolmaster at Dunbar produced *Grammatica Facilis* in the seventeenth century, a treatise which tortured generations of schoolboys well into the next century. Before that, two other Dunbar schoolmasters attempted to have their own Latin crammers adopted throughout Scotland. The first to do so was Andrew Simson, minister and schoolmaster who published his version in 1564. Simson was one of six people appointed by the Privy Council in 1575 charged with the task of advising on the form of Latin grammar which should be used in every Scottish school. After due deliberation, the committee recommended not one but two grammars.[11] Next came Andrew Home, master of the school at Dunbar in 1615, who five years earlier had applied to the Privy Council for permission to have his *Latin Rudiments and Grammar* adopted throughout Scotland. After the six-man committee of 1575 was disbanded, the Council had finally agreed that there should be a single Latin grammar and naturally, Home believed his was superior to the two which had preceded it. In 1612, the Privy Council adopted Home's version for universal use; any schoolmaster who didn't use it was fined £100 Scots and dismissed from his post. However, Home's grammar proved so unpopular that many schoolmasters were never fined or sacked. By 1623, Home had produced a revised and simplified version but the Privy Council rejected it. By 1630, Home faced the challenges of three rivals, among them David Wedderburn, master of Aberdeen's Grammar School who was given the monopoly although he was required to pay Home a sum of money by way of compensation. James Kirkwood compiled and introduced his *Grammatica Facilis* in Scottish schools some years later.

As already noted, masters of burgh schools were appointed by the local magistrates. Although there were several schools in East Lothian before 1696 'supported by the labourers of the ground',[12] the Education Act of 1696 required every parish to employ a *dominie* [schoolmaster] appointed by the church heritors and to provide a 'commodious house' to be designated as the school; 50% of the costs were to be met by tenant farmers and other people of means, the remainder being borne by the heritors, or major landowners. Before that, John Turnbull was appointed master of the common or Scots school at Dunbar, teaching children to read, write and count. The Scots school offered a basic education and was less prestigious than the English and Grammar Schools and this was reflected in Turnbull's stipend of £50 Scots (about £8 sterling) per annum, although he could charge parents who could afford it a further 14 shillings (about 12p) per pupil per quarter. By 1697, his salary had risen to £100 Scots (£16). In that year, James Douglas, master of the Grammar School was paid £200 Scots (£33). In 1721, two masters teaching English and Latin received £200 Scots each; the master who taught navigation, writing, arithmetic and book-keeping was paid £180 Scots (£30). By 1822, the burgh council minutes record that the master of the Mathematical School was paid £36 sterling and the master of the Grammar School received £42 sterling.

In 1706, the burgh records refer to an act of 18th January 1677 which compelled local inhabitants to send their children to school; the magistrates at Dunbar published the act's provisions so that

'none pretend ignorance'.

In 1714, a local bylaw levied two pennies Scots on every pint of ale or beer sold in Dunbar; the proceeds went towards maintaining the harbour, repairing the Town House, building a new school and meeting the cost of repairs to other public buildings and supplying fresh water to the town. Who said that drink and learning are uneasy companions! In 1727, new masters were appointed to the local schools and the town drummer was ordered to announce these appointments in the streets. The magistrates had sacked their predecessors on 12th December 1726 as they had let the English and Grammar Schools fall into decay. By 1792, Dunbar had an English and Grammar School teaching Latin, English and Mathematics and a Mathematical School offering navigation and book-keeping. To avoid confusion, the magistrates might have called the latter a Navigation school but this detail appears to have escaped their notice at the time, although remedied later. In addition to these schools, West Barns with a population of 800 had opened a parochial school and a private school had been established at East Barns. By the late eighteenth century, the children of the poor could expect to be taught to read but not write; every school child had to be able to read in order to learn the Scriptures and the Shorter Catechisms.

Provision was also made for the very young. At one time, the infants' school was situated at the foot of Davel Brae as we know from John Muir who attended Mungo Suddon's school there in 1843. Prior to 1824, the main burgh schools were situated behind the Town House in Silver Street. In 1824, two new school buildings were erected close by the sea as *Miller, Dunbar* tells us. These schools taught Latin, English and Mathematics and were known as Lyon's School which ultimately became the main burgh Grammar School at Woodbush. David White's grave in the parish kirkyard informs us that he was the rector of Dunbar Grammar School for 40 years, dying in 1822. David Lyon ran the Grammar and English School from 1823 to 1851 and a Mr Morton was in charge of the Mathematical and Navigational School, both at Woodbush. By 1845, there were also three unendowed schools (see below) and parochial schools at East and West Barns. In 1845, the masters of the English and Grammar School and Mathematical Schools were housed free and paid respectively £40 guineas (£42) and £20 a year. William Dick was rector of the combined burgh and endowed schools in 1859; the Castle Street charity school and Lamer Street public school were housed in a single building in Lamer Street under the care of Arthur Folkarde (1871-1897). Successors to William Dick who took charge of all the schools which were housed in Woodbush were Andrew Comrie (1897-1927), Robert Macauley (1927-53), Hugh Cowan (1953-61), men who inculcated the spirit of not only the three Rs but the three Ds - discipline, dedication and determination among the students, the last two of whom were ably assisted by the eccentric, scholarly and lovable classics master, J I W Milne. After Hugh Cowan came John Muir (1961-70), Norman Macphie (1970-83), Will Collin (1983-97). The present headteacher is Don Ledingham. (However, in my opinion, the best Headteacher Dunbar Grammar School never had was the late, memorable J I W Milne. Jack Milne (pronounced Mill) was a human man with incorruptable, high principles, a brilliant conversationalist, wit and entertaining raconteur, poet, storyteller and amateur dramatics enthusiast.

On 4th September 1834, the burgh council fixed the hours of attendance at the various schools. The Grammar School hours were from 9am to noon and from 2 to 5pm in summer, to sunset in winter. The English school opened its doors at the same time but broke for lunch at 1pm, while the Mathematical School didn't start classes until 10am. In 1837, the burgh records indicate there were 68 scholars attending the English and Grammar Schools, arranged in 27 classes which must be a misprint!

A major change in the education system took place in 1872 with the passing of the Education (Scotland) Act, a more modern piece of legislation which established a School Board in every parish and burgh; these Boards had a duty to provide

> 'a sufficient amount of accommodation in public schools available for all persons resident in such parish or burgh, for whose education efficient and suitable provision has not otherwise been made.'

Apart from the vagueness of the legislative drafting, the act was important as it removed education from the hands of both church and burgh authorities, although inevitably, both were represented on the school boards. The financing of schools came out of a school fund managed by the Boards themselves; its income derived from a mixture of national taxation, local rates and school fees. In addition, burghs which had hitherto made contributions to the local burgh schools prior to the act of 1872 were required to continue doing so at the same level of grant. This gave rise to some controversy, especially at Dunbar. In 1876, the Court of Session considered the case of *School Board of Dunbar v Magistrates and Town Council of Dunbar* (18th March 1876, ref. 3R 631). Prior to 1872, the burgh magistrates had paid £102 to the school but in 1876 declined to pay the School Board more than £60 as they had paid £42 as a lump sum allowance to a retiring teacher. The Court of Session ruled that this had been exceptional-the sum being the teacher's full salary during employment-and by way of compromise, ordered the magistrates to pay the Board £80.

As noted earlier, the main schools were concentrated at Woodbush in 1824; they were amalgamated in 1859. After the Education Act of 1872, a survey of all schools in the burgh in 1873 recorded the existence of three unendowed schools - Castle Street Charity School (1823), a girls' Sewing Seminary sited possibly in West Gate Road near the castle (1832) and the Free Church School (1845-76). The first two were amalgamated in 1878 and became known as Lamer Public School. In the same year, extensions were made to the Woodbush school; further accommodation was built in 1895 and in 1897, the burgh school and Lamer Public School were amalgamated to become Woodbush Grammar. In 1906, the centre portion of the school was rebuilt to form classrooms where the headmaster's house had been situated. By the 1950s, the school at Woodbush was known as Dunbar Grammar School; it closed its gates in 1961 when a new purpose-built grammar school was opened in Summerfield Road. The old school at Woodbush was demolished shortly afterwards; the site is now occupied by modern flats although the buttresses attached the old school boundary wall can still be seen. A separate primary school was built in Lammermuir Crescent in 1951; as this book goes to print, the primary school is being extended to cope with a projected expansion in the junior school population.

Some of Dunbar's pupils in the last two centuries made considerable reputations for themselves. The most well-known is John Rennie, the civil engineer born at East Linton. A less well-known but colourful character was Alexander Dow. In the eighteenth century, Dow's father was a customs and excise officer at Dunbar. When Dow junior left school to begin an apprenticeship in Edinburgh, he ran away - reputedly for duelling - and subsequently joined the army, an occupation better suited to his temperament and talents. Posted to India, he was soon in command of a regiment of Sepoys and he became something of a writer, the author of a play *Zingis* and a *History of Hindustan.* At one stage in his career, he was personally responsible for the safety of the Great Mogul, or leader of India; at that time, Dow commanded two regiments at Delhi so he probably held the rank of brigadier. He later confessed to a friend that he had been tempted to dethrone the Mogul and rule India himself which he certainly could have done without too much difficulty. It is to be wondered whether Dow was the inspiration for Rudyard Kipling's story *The Man Who Would Be King.* According to Alexander Carlyle, Dow later confessed that he had resisted the temptation as he'd reflected

'on what his old schoolfellows at Dunbar would think of him for being guilty of such an action.'

Dow died in 1799. Other students who went on from Dunbar to make names for themselves in one way or another were James Miller, the local historian and John Muir, the father of conservation. In the twentieth century, one of the school's most brilliant students was Douglas Vickers of West Barns who mastered Greek with disgusting ease and became an Oxford Don.

The first attempt to separate the primary and secondary schools in Woodbush occurred in 1936, when the burgh council decided that the senior school should move to the Sailors' Park, off Summerfield Road to the right. On 30th June that year, the council minutes record that approval was sought for the new school from the Secretary of State for Scotland, the Department of Health and later, the Scottish Education Department. The modern school stands on ground occupied by Summerfield Mains Farm adjacent to Summerfield Dairy, which I remember vaguely from childhood. The land was sold to the county council for £1,100 which was held by the trustees of the Dunbar Sailors' Society which had owned the Sailors' Park. (The Society had been formed for the benefit of superannuated seamen and their widows' and children; its funds originally derived from a duty of eight pennies (1p) levied on every £1 Scots paid in wages to every shipmaster, mate and seaman frequenting the port of Dunbar. The Society's trustees were the magistrates of Dunbar and the money deriving from the sale of the Park was to be invested and income deriving therefrom was to be used for recreational purposes.)

The old grammar school had character, dignity and style; it featured an attractive sunken quadrangle where the entire school would gather on Armistice Day to honour its glorious dead - former pupils of two World Wars whose names were engraved on a plaque above the drinking fountain on the east wall. The school also had a bell tower and the bell was rung at the start of every day. Being situated at the seashore, biology was sometimes taught out of doors during the summer term. The school always had a larger pupil roll than it could accommodate (750-800) and it had to farm out at least one class to the Parish Church premises just off the High Street. Unfortunately the poorly-planned site near the East or Coastguards' Beach allowed no room for expansion. Thus the old school was vacated and demolished; neither of its successors has any charm whatsoever.

To celebrate the centenary of Dunbar Grammar School, an attractive and highly informative book was published in 1997. *From Slate to Disk* is a veritable treasure trove of anecdotes that are also telling social comments. The book is still in print and is recommended reading.

While each generation considers its educational achievements better than those of its predecessors, the standard of education still seems superior to that of today. Education is constantly evolving and fashions change more quickly than in the past. New technology has revolutionised teaching methods so that the acquiral of knowledge has become almost a leisure pastime. The standard of spelling has suffered and there are few who can calculate mental arithmetic or work out percentages and fractions. Perhaps they no longer need to. Those who were fortunate enough to be taught at Dunbar Grammar School until 1961 are a special breed with special memories and pride in a school which gave so many of us a solid start in life; we didn't have the benefit of counselling and perhaps we suffered because of that. But we gained a sense of independence and the ability to work things out for ourselves because we had to. Such qualities cannot be taught by formal education; they come from within.

Social

The social history of any community is often a study in microcosm of that of the nation. For centuries, the majority of men, women and children lived short, brutish and unhealthy lives in the Dark Ages, the Early Middle and Late Middle Ages and up to the end of the nineteenth century; living conditions in Scotland were little better than those of modern African tribesmen and in a less hospitable climate. Despite the lack of hard evidence, we may conclude that life expectancy fell far short of that in the last century. The population aged prematurely through hard work, food shortages, poor health and unsanitary housing. Medieval man in particular experienced indifferent health and many people were sick for a large part of their lives. The minor illnesses of today laid people low and killed them five centuries ago. Even when food wasn't scarce, imbalances in nutritional value lowered resistance to many diseases although modern dietitians consider the diet prevalent in the Middle Ages was superior in many ways to our own. When harvests were poor or failed, prices and the death rate soared. And there were frequent visitations of plagues against which the crude and rudimentary medicine of the day was ineffective. Of the several plagues which ravaged Scotland, the most well-documented was the Black Death (1349-50), thought to have carried off one third of Scotland's working population. There was some benefit in its aftermath however; the reduced workforce was given more land to work which increased prosperity and allowed the last of the slave workers to gain their freedom - much earlier than their counterparts in England.

As we have seen elsewhere, Dunbar experienced several periods of cultural change from the time of the Anglian occupation until 1018 when, with the rest of East Lothian and the Merse it became permanently Scottish. Perhaps the greatest change of all was the introduction of the Norman feudal system by David I and his immediate successors. The Celtic-British-Anglian culture which Dunbar had known for several centuries was a form of tribalism; it didn't disappear overnight but gradually, feudalism brought change first to the Lowlands, then ultimately to the north. Feudalism was a refined form of tribalism; all-inclusive, it supported a single tribe - the people of Scotland. All land was royal land which the king granted to his vassals and was solemnised by an act of homage. In turn, a vassal became a feudal superior by granting land to his sub-vassals or tenants, the process continuing down the strata of society to the humble peasant who might cultivate land but couldn't own it.

Were the Dunbar folk inconvenienced by these changes? It is doubtful whether their working lives altered significantly from the Anglian occupation until the later Middle Ages. After the introduction of Norman feudalism, all men and women, whether high or low born were entitled to a seigneur's protection in return for certain obligations of vassalage. The feudalisation of Scotland was completed by the reign of William I 'the Lion' (1161-1214); the system would eventually die out by the seventeenth century, with the rise of the merchant and craft classes, although vestiges of the system persist to this day.

Under the feudal system, the king owned all land, investing it in those who served him; in effect, land was on loan to a vassal but in time, sons inherited or more accurately were re-invested with their fathers' fiefs or landholdings. In time, land became heritable among the great families and freemen - noble and commoner alike - passed on their lands to their descendants. At the bottom of the hierarchy were the peasants who could neither own or inherit land. They were called bondsmen, tied to the land of their lord and passed on with it to the next generation of owners. This state of serfdom was slavery under another name. There were various classes of peasant in the hierarchy however; after the freemen came the *villein*, who was fortunate enough to possess a small allotment of land for his personal use but liable for certain services to his lord for the privilege; next were the *bordar* or poultry husbandman and the *cottar* which literally means cottage-owner. At the very bottom was the *serf* or menial labourer, known variously in Scotland as *neyfs, bondi, cumlaws* or *nativi* - perhaps the modern slang word *nyaff* [Scots for a worthless individual, or runt] derives from the lowly *neyf.* Woodcuts depicting rural and provincial scenes in England are equally representative of Scottish peasant life, although Scottish serfs enjoyed fewer rights than their English counterparts. Nonetheless, a serf in East Lothian enjoyed comparative freedom from slavery some two hundred years before English serfs, largely because of the depopulation caused by the Black Death. However, from about 1130 until the mid-fourteenth century, serfs were bought and sold as slaves throughout Scotland as is confirmed by many contemporary charters. For example, in 1170, Waldeve, 4th Earl of Dunbar gave an entire family of *nativi* to the Abbot of Kelso in the following deed, whose brevity is typical for the time:

> 'I give and confirm to the abbot and monks of Kelso, Halden and his brother William
> and all their children and all their descendants.'[13]

In the early thirteenth century, the 5th Earl of Dunbar ordered *neyfs* who had escaped from Coldingham Priory[14] to be returned there. The Church saw nothing reprehensible in this, accepting the reality of the prevailing social conditions of the day. It wasn't all gloom however; *Kelso Liber* records that in 1160, serfs were made freemen who thus became rent-paying tenants of the abbey. By the mid-fourteenth century however, both serf and *neyf* had virtually disappeared even if aspects of serfdom survived.

Until the late Middle Ages, the fabric of society remained static; we know practically nothing about the activities which occupied the people's daily lives other than work. Very little concerned them beyond the parish boundary - the doings of kings, the application of domestic law and foreign affairs affected them only peripherally except in time of war. The people of medieval Dunbar were no strangers to the whims of national politics however; living close to the Border, they constantly experienced the desolation of war, plunder and burning until the sixteenth century was well advanced. Every citizen - free or unfree - had a relationship of one kind or another with and was under obligations of varying degrees to a local lord. The *neyf* grubbing for a meagre existence from the soil, the merchant preoccupied with profit and loss, the cleric fussing over his benefice and flock; all had to pay their repects - and taxes - to their overlords, the Earls of Dunbar.

By the time Dunbar became a free burgh, the bourgeoisie had grown in number and therefore influence. This class included merchants, burgesses, craftsmen, advocates, notaries, Writers to the Signet, surgeons, tenant farmers and ship owners. The working class was almost exclusively employed on the land or at sea, although a few lucky men found work as burgh officials – those in the local watch, or early police force, inspectors of food and weight, tollkeepers and tax collectors, the town drummer and piper, the executioner who often doubled-up as the burgh scavenger or street sweeper. Men and women born to servitude as labourers, farm servants, journeymen, carters, shepherds and drovers rarely ever escaped their lot. Until the late eighteenth century, Dunbar's population lived largely from the land; their lives hardly changed from generation to generation.

Modern society is showing an increasing interest in the lifestyle of medieval man - what he ate, how he earned his living, the state of his health and the conditions under which he lived. For the most part, the majority of the population lived a life of drudgery, struggling against the elements, the environment, the fortunes of war and the visitations of famine, disease and pestilence. As a consequence, medieval man was an enthusiastic Christian, having little else but faith to sustain him. The highlights of his life were marriage and the birth of his children; his existence was irretrievably yoked to the Church from the day he was born to the day he died. The Church gave him solace and provided colour and entertainment, with its festivals of Yule (Christmas) or Pasche (Easter) and other seasonal events such as the celebration of the lives of the saints, religious plays and carnivals presided over by the Lord of Misrule at Christmas, the forerunner of what today would be pantomime. The periodic fairs and markets at Dunbar also helped to relieve the harshness of their lives, such occasions giving some meaning to the passage of time.

After 1370, the burgh built its reputation on trade and commerce. The people accepted the mixed blessing of living in the shadow of a strong stone castle, knowing it would - and did - attract the unwelcome attentions of invading English armies which, when they couldn't capture it, vented their spleen on the local population, destroying property and stealing animals. And yet Froissart, writing in the second half of the fourteenth century describes the typical response of the Lothian population to an English raid:

'the people....made light of it, saying that with six or eight stakes they could soon have new houses.'

The burning of the wood and wattle thatched cottages in Dunbar was more an inconvenience than a loss, as raids usually took place in the campaigning season before or after winter. With the right materials to hand, these simple dwellings could be 'bigged' [built] in a couple of days. What was important was that the common people trusted their lord to protect them even if at times such protection was ineffective. The prevalent attitude at the time was expressed by a medieval poet who wrote that

'Men without a lord are ill-provided for.'

The peasants of the Middle Ages strike us as remarkably resilient and resourceful; they accepted their dull, brutish lives yet still found time to be optimistic about life, sustained by the comfort of religion and finding solace and companionship in their families.

In the Middle Ages, the population of Dunbar was probably no more than a few hundred souls.[15] The quality of life of rich and poor alike was of course dramatically different, even if neither enjoyed much luxury and comfort in the sense that prevails nowadays. We know more about those who lived in castles than in cottages since castles were administrative centres employing scribes to draft petitions, charters and writs of which the bulk of surviving public archives consist. The castle was a landmark in a sea of cultivated fields; it gave a village status, attracted important visitors and dominated the district. The common folk lived in their limited world, rarely ever leaving the community. Other than the nobility, churchmen, merchants and pilgrims travelling in groups for safety ventured into the wider world; along with visitors to the castle, they were the main source of gossip and news. Thus castle, church and marketplace dominated the lives of the majority.

The castle hall was the place low-born and commercial classes alike aspired to. Medieval dinners were the highlight of the day. The earl and his family sat with their guests at the 'hie burde' [high board or table]. Furnishings were scant and functional - trestle tables, a few chairs and chests. The earl, his family and guests were seated on high-backed chairs attended by two boys - one with a basin and napkin, the other with a ewer so that the prominent diners could wash their hands after each course, as food was eaten with the fingers. The important people kept on their headgear at table - not out of eccentricity or to denote status but to prevent 'flies and other filthe' falling from the head to the food - an interesting comment on the hygiene of the day! The salt cellar was the most important table vessel; of almost ceremonial significance and reserved for the head of the house and his family and guests, it explains the saying 'to sit above the salt' - meaning the privileged. At the end of each day, a light meal was served between 4 and 6pm. The earl and his steward usually discussed the day's business while they ate. At night, the household bedded down in the hall sleeping on pallets or straw and rushes on the floor. The earl and his countess occupied a small private chamber with a proper bed and feather mattress; sons, daughters and senior household officials - the steward, the constable and the bailiff - slept in truckle beds in barely furnished cell-like apartments. The earl's bedroom might have had the luxury of a carpet or tapestry hanging on the wall; there would have been a wardrobe or small room leading of the bedchamber where the earl and countess hung their clothes on wooden pegs which sometimes doubled as sleeping perches for his falcons - another comment on hygiene.

Dunbar Castle was fortunate in having an effective system for the disposal of human waste - the *garderobe*. These crude privvies were no more than holes with wooden seats, set in convenient places in the castle towers; the *garderobe* chutes at Dunbar emptied into the sea so the occupants were spared the unpleasant odours which prevailed in land-locked castles.

It is naive to assume that the nobility spent the bulk of their lives glowering at their enemies from their castle walls. Castles were fortified houses where the nobility conducted their business. In their role as law enforcement officer, the earls of Dunbar held baron courts at Whittingehame. These courts were largely concerned with agricultural matters but occasionally criminal cases were heard and executions ordered. In the fourteenth century, the 9th Earl of Dunbar employed Alexander Ryklynton,[16] a manorial constable whose duty it was to ensure his master's lands weren't damaged or his livestock stolen. Earls had judicial powers held of the king; they could command the local sheriff to surrender a prisoner who was a native of the parish even if his crime had been committed outwith it. A guilty verdict could mean a fine, mutilation, banishment or death. The local population expected swift and unequivocal justice even if truth was often casualty. Medieval justice could be capricious - an innocent but unpopular man declared guilty was of little consequence. Convictions were obtained by a crude form of jury system; a defendant who could muster sufficient supporters to voice oaths in his favour was declared innocent. Thereafter, the lord's decision either confirmed or rejected the consensus vote and his decision was final.

Sanitary conditions were primitive until well into the nineteenth century and sickness and premature death were ever present. As urban life developed, streets were filthy, disease-ridden rubbish piled up and people washed infrequently. The Black Death and other plagues came to Scotland in 1349, 1580, 1584 and 1636. The Privy Council ordered burghs like Dunbar to publicly warn their inhabitants of the danger. In 1584, fairs in Dunbar and elsewhere were suspended by the Privy Council because of plague. [17]

And yet despite these appalling conditions, the population of Scotland increased in the sixteenth century for the first time in three centuries, both in rural parishes and major towns. However, a steep rise in food prices together with a draconian devaluation of the currency widened the gulf between rich and poor. The Reformation did little to alter the situation, even if it removed the exploitation of the poor by a Roman Catholic Church which had grown corrupt and greedy, charging for every service its priests and friars provided and imposing the infamous *Peter-pence*, or annual tribute of one penny levied on every family and paid to the see of Rome on the festival of St Peter. The poor increased in number and lived a harsher existence although one of the side effects of the Reformation was to introduce a form of poor relief in Scotland. In 1574, parliament made provision for the legal assessment of the deserving poor, support being the responsibility of local parish churches from the weekly collection plate and hire of mortcloths and hearses.

Thus if life was hard for the Dunbar peasants in the Middle Ages, their descendants fared only marginally better. The Poor Laws of 1575 and 1845 failed to make provision for the able-bodied unemployed and at Dunbar, the seasonal occupation of fishing meant that in the winter months, many families went without adequate food and lived in mean hovels near the shore. An act of 1661 defined the poor as

> 'aged, sick, lame and impotent [ie unable to work] inhabitants.....who (of themselves) have not [relatives] to maintain them....orphans and other poor children....left destitute of all help.'

The long-term poor were sometimes given a one-off payment or were encouraged to beg. Those thrown out of work had to beg illegally or steal to survive.

In the eighteenth and nineteenth centuries, living conditions for common labourers and fishermen alike remained primitive; the majority lived in rectangular-shaped houses with timber frames filled with turf, clay or mud. The roof had no ceiling and was thatched with turf or reeds and the fire in the centre of the dirt floor had only a hole in the roof to allow smoke to escape. Agricultural workers often shared the building with their stock, animals at one end, family at the other, the original 'But and Ben'. Glazed windows were unheard of, many houses did not even have window apertures (black houses) and those that did used boards or rags to stop the draughts particularly in the cold winter months. Interiors were sparsely furnished and many considered themselves fortunate to possess a table, some chairs, a bed and a few cooking pots, wooden platters and a mug or two. In places like Dunbar, these mean huts were separated by vennels or dark closes with some ground at the side, enabling the inhabitants to grow a few cabbages, onions and leeks.

Ordinary town and country people dressed in similar fashions; the men wore plaids, trousers and shoes, the women dressed in linen shifts with a plaid drawn over their heads and pinned across their chests, falling to about knee-length. Women and children generally went barefoot except on Sundays when they carried their shoes to church, putting them on in the porch. In 1750, we know that men wore knee-breeches and long stockings with full jacket or frock coat which reached below the backs of the knees. By the late eighteenth century, while the rich could afford velvets and silks, these weren't seen much in the rural areas where even gentlemen farmers wore rough durable tweeds and workmanlike clothing except on special occasions.

The traditional diet in Dunbar was common throughout Scotland - peasemeal, oatmeal, barley bannocks, sowens (an oatmeal dish) - until these gave way to wheaten bread produced by local baxters or bakers. Potatoes figured prominently in the diet after 1750; home brewed ale or beer was superseded by spirits smuggled from the Continent because of the Malt Tax created after the Treaty of Union in 1707. Tea was becoming popular as a beverage and due to the cultivation of turnips which provided winter fodder for beef cattle and sheep, the Martinmas slaughter of fresh meat for salting was made obsolete as fresh meat was available from the wintered beasts.

At the end of the eighteenth century, the *Old Statistical Account* attributed the incidence of disease to a moist climate, impoverished diet, inadequate clothing and bad housing. Smallpox was rife, particularly among the young, who invariably succumbed. Some of the conclusions reached by the parish ministers who contributed to the statistical account are quaint and unscientific but then it was an unscientific age. For example, children who lived

> 'on the sea coast, where the inhabitants feed much on fish'

were more susceptible to smallpox because

> 'fish, unless perfectly fresh, is not a wholesome diet; but it often has a tendency to corrupt the blood, and to aggravate the majority of putrid disorder.'

Even so, the account concludes that on the whole, the health of the nation was reasonable; in Dunbar, the people were

> 'more attentive to cleanliness in their persons - are better lodged - [because] - they consume greater quanti ties of animal food in a fresh instead of salted state - they have the means of escaping smallpox.'

The disease is caused by a virus and is prevented by vaccination. A century after the *Old Statistical Account* was published, the Battery at the Victoria Harbour housed an isolation hospital (**ill 111 and 112**) or Casual Sick House for those suffering from infectious diseases. The burgh council experienced difficulty in introducing it; on 1st August 1899, the Local Government Board informed the burgh council that the hospital had to make provision for at least two infectious diseases, the patients being treated in separate units, with segregation of the sexes. The burgh council argued that these requirements were in place and that in the preceding three months, eight cases of scarlet fever had been treated successfully. On 6th February 1900, the Local Government Board informed the burgh authorities that it

DDHS

Illus 111: *Isolation Hospital at the Battery*

DDHS

Illus 112: *Isolation Hospital and the outer pier*

wouldn't approve the use of the Battery hospital until it satisfied the requirements of the Public Health (Scotland) Act 1897. The burgh council spent £600 on repairs and upgrading in August 1900 to comply with the 1897 legislation.[18] The improvements were accepted. During the Great War, the hospital accommodated wounded soldiers and continued to treat patients until 1926, when it was closed down and replaced by the East Links Cottage Hospital in 1927 which operated until 1973.

Much of the disease was caused by poor sanitary conditions and bad housing. The infamous group of houses at the Cat's Row (**ill 114**) in Victoria Street were demolished and replaced in 1935 Gradually, the rented housing accommodation was improved as successive modernisation programmes were brought into effect; one of the major developments occurred at the time of the Cat's Row demolition; in 1932-33, new housing schemes were created at Boroughdales, Countess Road, Doon Avenue, Summerfield Road and Lammermuir Crescent, where many families from the harbour area were rehoused. (As a boy, I lived in Lammermuir Crescent, where the scheme ended at Summerfield Road and gave way to cornfields, later developed in a second major housing scheme in the 1950s, a suburb known as the Tree Scheme as its streets are named after trees eg Plane and Pine Streets. Other developments took place at Ashfield and Floors. As this book is being written, probably the largest single development ever in Dunbar's history is in progress on the south side of the town.

DDHS

Illus 113: *East Links, Dunbar*

Although much of published social history in the eighteenth and nineteenth centuries is restricted to the four main towns of Edinburgh, Glasgow, Dundee and Aberdeen, the history of social conditions in the smaller burghs is now receiving more attention. The thriving middle class in Dunbar concerned itself more and more with progress and efficiency, the burgh council introducing a pure water supply, street paving and lighting. New schools were built, a subscription library and reading room were made available by George Miller whose printing presses provided the local population with reading material that was both social and educa-

DDHS

Illus 114: *The infamous Cat's Row with Rock House*

tional. Miller's initiative as far as a public library was concerned wasn't followed by the burgh until 1946 which is incredible, but in his day, it was left to commerce to provide such luxuries, albeit at a small cost to the individual. Even so, people tried to save a few pennies every week to tide them over on rainy days; a friendly society and savings bank opened to cater for the modest savers who deposited what they could, expecting 3 or 4% interest. More attention was paid to the deserving poor, orphans and young apprentices, particularly with regard to their education. Dunbar's municipal institutions, for long wedded to the old feudal system, would finally change in the face of a growing philanthropic liberalism.

Dunbar's working population was housed almost entirely in the High Street and in the areas at the harbours. The poorer families lived in single-roomed flats, tenants of local property owners. Despite the advances which had been made, life was far from easy. Water had to be drawn and carried in pails from public wells; it became contaminated with sewage which spread disease. The enclosed backyards housed communal wash-houses but these often became unofficial dumps for rubbish so that the burgh council had to monitor this dangerous practice as it spread disease. The constant struggle for cleanliness was difficult but not impossible; however, many of the poorest families simply gave up, particularly those who made their living from the sea.

Cholera came to Haddington and Dunbar in 1832; medical opinion was divided on how best to treat, let alone prevent it. Rumours abounded that cholera victims ended up on the dissecting table and even worse - Catholics were being buried in Protestant cemeteries. However, disease apart, many of the major national events of the time seem to have attracted little attention in the burgh records of the time. Even the great Reform Bill of 1832 failed to stir the imaginations of the townspeople although it exercised the minds of town council members fearful about their futures in public office. Local concern was about improved housing, better roads and the constant repairs needed for the harbour-concerns which the new legislation would help to resolve in time. Despite the emphasis on education, the authorities at Dunbar excused up to 40% of local schoolchildren from their classes to work in the fields in 1870. For all the fuss about gaining knowledge, literacy was poorest in the major towns and cities where child labour was cheap and plentiful; many a town schoolmaster must have asked himself whether it was all worth the candle.

To get a glimpse of life in the vicinity of Dunbar in the 1830s, we turn again to the graphic autobiography of Alexander Somerville of Branxton Cottages. Somerville and his family lived in a succession of mean, tiled sheds - by no stretch of the imagination could they be described as cottages - with an entrance so low that even people of average height had to stoop to enter. The windows were unglazed, the floor was earthen and there was no ceiling to cover the rafters. Somerville was one of eight brothers and sisters, three of whom died young and were buried in Ayton Churchyard. As farm workers moved at the end of a term of six or twelve months, Somerville's siblings were born in different places. Usually hiring or fee'ing fairs in February and November would determine a man's workplace for the next six months, the farmer providing an open cart to move his employee and family with their meagre possessions which included the all-important kitchen grate.

We know the birthplaces of Alexander's brothers and sisters except William. James was born at Thortonloch, Janet at Woodhall and May at Thornton Mains. When Alexander was born at Springfield on 15th March 1810, his father John Somerville was too poor to pay the shilling fee (5p) required by the parish clerk of Oldhamstocks to register the birth. Alexander's brother James appears to have been the most successful in the family; apprenticed as a cooper in Leith, he built up a thriving business at Innerwick and was instrumental in organising benefit socials and singing classes in that village. He also organised the watch at the local cemetery to prevent the removal of fresh corpses by the resurrectionists. William became a forester on a Yorkshire estate and Janet and May married local men. At the age of fifteen, Alexander was briefly a ploughboy at Branxton Farms; being too inexperienced for this work, he was set to hoeing turnips and at harvest, he sheared and stacked corn sheaves, loaded carts and drove the horses although the farmer had to engage a man to carry the sacks of wheat. In winter, Alexander dug drains, earning 7 to 9 shillings (35-45p) per week; he broke stones for road-mending at a farthing (0.1p) a cartload and he looked after his master's garden, renting a plot of ground for 6 shillings (30p) a year to grow potatoes and keep a pig. In 1825 the weather was so dry that he hardly harvested enough potatoes to meet the rental so the family ate them. In May 1826, he became a tree-feller near Cockburnspath and was paid one shilling and sixpence (about 8p) per day for this hard work, constantly in danger of being bitten by adders. In June that year, he found work at the Skateraw Limekiln which meant he had to be out of bed at 2am and walk to Skateraw to be able to start his day's work at 4am; he rarely returned home before 7pm, had supper and went to bed. For this work, he was paid 9 shillings (45p) a week. Many Lothian and Merse farmers used lime to reduce the acidity of their fields and trade was brisk; Alexander remembered seeing as many as 300 carts queuing up for lime in the autumn.

His dirty, smoky employment at the kiln sickened him so he returned to Branxton Farm pulling oats, barley, peas, beans, shearing sheep, digging drains, ploughing, gardening and pruning hedges for 6 shillings (30p) a week. He decided to try a new hire and went to Duns to the fee'ing market

'with a piece of whipcord and a piece of straw in my mouth, as signals that I wanted to be hired.'

Unsuccessful, he tramped the sixteen miles back home and tried to get work at the Dunbar Hiring Fair which occurred on the first Tuesday in February, again without success there or two days later at Haddington. At age seventeen, he was competing with men who were older, stronger and more experienced for such jobs as were available.

Young Somerville was nothing if not a trier. It ran in the family. His father had worked once at Dunglass House as a mason's labourer, helping to restore the old house; for this, he received the almost princely sum of 15 shillings a week (75p), the best wage he would earn in his entire life. His employer was Sir James Hall, father of Captain Basil Hall, RN. Old Somerville's only vice seems to have been chewing tobacco which he could buy only in Dunbar, so he rationed himself by chewing, smoking only on Sundays - frowned upon by the Kirk - and listening to sermons read from the family bible by one or other of the children. He then worked and lived at Springfield, where Mrs Somerville worked as a bondager, carrying sheaves to the barn and shearing corn at harvest from sunrise to sunset - back-breaking jobs which paid tenpence (about 4p) a day.

Alexander gives us a brief glimpse of the living conditions common at Springfield and elsewhere at the time. The family shack was without a ceiling, cold and draughty with a makeshift grate, no cupboards or even recesses, no partitions except those which the beds made and only four small paned windows. After his day's work, Alexander's brother William cobbled the family's shoes until midnight and Mrs Somerville spun yarn from lint for the local weaver to make into shirts for her menfolk or spun wool to knit their stockings.

At Whitsuntide in 1813, the family had moved to Thriepland Hill near Branxton, then part of the Thurston estate. Alexander's father died there in 1834. As soon as he was able, young Alexander herded cows, then drove the horse harrows and held the plough; at age six or seven, he remembered the year 1816-17 as very hard when 'potatoes were bad and few' and salted herrings bought at Dunbar had to feed a family of six. At that time, John Somerville had found work at the Skateraw Limekiln, regarded as one of the best quarrymen; his friend Robert Wallace - also a quarryman until he grew too old for the heavy work - had to resort to poorer paid work raking muck from the turnpike road to Dunbar.

Alexander went to school at Birnyknowes, a hamlet of 20 houses which formed a square within which were

'pigsties, dunghills, stagnant pools and stacks of firewood'.

Near the houses were the slightly superior cottages of the local weavers; the meanest hovel of all housed the school and its *dominie*, a lonely man who had taken up the teaching profession as he wasn't able for manual work. The man used the tawse freely, young Somerville being a frequent recipient of the heavy leather strap. In his childhood games, the boy casts himself in the role of underdog, marked by the raggedness of his clothes. The boys would play games of Radicals versus Soldiers - a comment on the political scene of the day. Radicals were regarded in the same way as Communists were in the early twentieth century, being concerned with political reform and therefore troublemakers. The Soldiers were the sons of the better-off farmers; they called Alexander a 'ragged radical' thus adding insult to injury. He was the scapegoat of at least one fight after which he was soundly flogged by the *dominie* and made to sit apart from the rest of the class. His torment lessened after he went to Oldhamstocks village school later in the year.

On one occasion, Alexander ran away from home because he was accused of stealing three bottles of whisky provided by the farmer for his harvest workers. His version is that he took one bottle to give to some Antrim men whom he knew would get none of the drink because they were Irish immigrants. A local man who'd stolen the other two bottles for himself accused Alexander of the theft of all three bottles. Alexander compounded his apparent guilt by putting 52 miles between himself and the farm but he had to return home to face his father.

After leaving school, Alexander's work at Thriepland Hill brought only a pittance wage and he decided to seek his fortune in Edinburgh. He left home after Old Hansel Monday - the first Monday in January 1828 - walking to a relative's house in Stenton, where his uncle, Mr Doughty, worked as a storeman on the Biel estate. Alexander stayed one night at Stenton, then was accompanied by his uncle almost as far as Haddington. The two men trudged through snow almost three feet deep in places. Arriving in Edinburgh a day or so later, Alexander wasn't too exhausted to marvel at the gaslit streets of the city, which he described as long chains of fiery lights. His brother James was then employed in a sawmill in the city and managed to get him work; this made him unpopular with the other workmen who had relatives and friends out of work in the depression which lasted until about 1844. While in Edinburgh, Alexander managed to attend several theatres, enjoying plays and a performance of the pantomime *Mother Goose*. When the timber trade declined later in the year, Alexander and Adam Skeldon - former overseer of the parish road squad - managed to obtain work at a farm close to Arthur's Seat during the harvest; the pair earned three shillings and sixpence (about 18p) per acre of corn harvested. From there, they went to work on other farms at Duddingston, Dreghorn and Blinkbonny, the latter near Currie in Midlothian. The two men then walked 34 miles back to Thriepland Hill, where the harvest was in progress; there first put to work in the fields cutting corn, then ploughing and carting work. Alexander next managed to obtain work in the Lammermuir Hills with a country wright, David Whitehead, who made gates for farms on the Renton estate. He pruned oak trees for 9 shillings (45p) a week, receiving free lodgings and

'as many potatoes for supper at night, cooked in any way I wanted them, as I could use'.

He appears to have worked for Whitehead from 1828 until January 1830, during which time he also dug drains on farms, work which he detested.

In April 1830, he learnt that the harbour at Cove, Cockburnspath was being improved and got work there as a labourer earning 9 shillings a week. As the quay had to be laid at ebb tide, the men could work only according to the tides. Alexander was considered a good worker and was soon earning higher wages; the other men were less effective, probably because they spent most of their earnings on whisky, which Alexander 'loathed and hated.' In the autumn of 1830, he worked again at the harvest on the farms at Thorntonloch, Branxton and Pathhead, near Little Spott. In winter, he was back at the Cove, quarrying stone. Late in that year, he helped to rescue nine men whose brig foundered at Bilsdean Burnfoot, not far from the Cove.

In 1831, Alexander knew of the Reform Bill which would become law the following year; he describes how the majority of one *Aye* over the *Noes* in parliament during the Bill's Second Reading was an occasion marked by the ringing of church bells, so great was popular support for the Bill. At this time, fired with the idealism of his years, he had a letter published in an Edinburgh newspaper in which he drew attention to Dunbar Kirk session's less than effective provision for the parish poor. Out of work once more, he decided to enlist in the Royal North British Dragoons - the Scots Greys - along with some of his Cove Harbour workmates. Sir James Hall of Dunglass had earlier recruited a troop of Greys from Cockburnspath and Innerwick; it was present on the field of Waterloo, participating in the famous but fatuous charge of the Heavy Brigade against the French guns when Ensign Charles Ewart captured the Eagle of the 45th French Regiment. Of the Greys, Napoleon remarked

'Qu'ils sont terribles, ces Chevaux Gris' [how awesome are these grey horses].

Out of its complement of 396 Greys who took part in the Union Brigade's glorious but tactically worthless charge, losses were 14 officers and 185 other ranks, nearly 50% of the regiment's strength. At Dunglass Collegiate Church there is a memorial to Sir William de Lancy, Wellington's Quartermaster General who was married to one of Hall's daughters and who fell at Waterloo.

It was perhaps inevitable that Alexander should enlist in the Greys - not just because the life was better but because Dunbar was the regiment's depot for many years. While most of his post-military life was spent outside Scotland, his story is of interest. He was posted to England, enjoying for the first time in his life roast goose and roast beef and Yorkshire puddings. Army life didn't suit his individualistic temperament however; with his intuitive sense of fairness, he couldn't reconcile social justice and democracy with what was to him the stupid and meaningless discipline of the army, with his strong sense of fairness and social justice. His was a bad career move; he fell foul of the army because he dared to criticise it.

The raw recruit was shipped from Leith to London in a barque called the *Eagle* whose crew included Geordie Punton from Dunbar; Punton later became skipper of a Leith trader and was tragically drowned in the Thames. In 1831, Alexander probably enjoyed a better standard of living than he had ever known. Cavalrymen were paid one shilling and threepence a day (6p); in reality however, each man received only twopence (less than 1p) a day after deductions for victuals and equipment. On the march, full pay was given and the men were entitled to an extra tenpence (about 4p) as subsistence money which the billeting sergeants paid to the innkeepers of the inns where they lodged.

In his remarkable book, Alexander Somerville who cared about his fellow men - particularly the poor - is occasionally smug and self-satisfied. Even so, his championing of justice was sincere and he paid a stiff price for it. He was stationed in Birmingham where rioting was an almost daily occurrence, encouraged by those who were opposed to the Reform Bill. There were several reforming measures passed at this time but that of 1832 contained sweeping reforms; it proposed to abolish 56 'rotten' boroughs - those run by local families or magistrates who purchased their appointments - and increased the parliamentary representation of cities like Birmingham. The 1832 Bill proposed to enfranchise about 500,000 people from the lower middle classes, even if it did little for the ordinary working man; it would take 50 years before the reforms of 1832 were extended to all men and more for women (1918). However, in 1832, the privileged upper and middle classes were apprehensive about the reforming measure, none more so than the Duke of Wellington during his term of office as Prime Minister from 1828-30. In 1832, Wellington advised his fellow Opposition peers to absent themselves from the Lords when the Bill was debated there; this didn't prevent the mob from attacking his London residence, Apsley House which had to be fitted with iron shutters to prevent the windows being shattered. The epithet of *Iron Duke* had nothing whatsoever to do with his Waterloo victory

With other units of regular cavalry, the Scots Greys were ordered to disperse the mobs gathering to demonstrate for or against the new law. The Greys were put on alert in May 1832 and ordered to rough-sharpen their swords to inflict ragged wounds on any rioters who got out of hand. Alexander had read a mischievous article in a Birmingham newspaper which implied that the Greys' alleged support for the reform measure was a fabrication concocted by the pro-reform press. Indignant at this attempt to discredit the regiment, he rather foolishly decided to write to the paper, the *Weekly Dispatch*, which was his first mistake. The army like the Civil Service then and now serve the government, whatever its shape or colour; both insist on loyalty and enforce it with law.

Alexander's letter was published by the *Dispatch.* He wrote that while some troopers had sent in their names in support of the Reform Bill, no one should think that

> 'those who refrained from doing so cared less for the interests of their country. I, for one, with no such public avowal of my opinions, for I know it to be an infringement of military law.'

Knowing it, he was unwise to admit it as he had effectively damned himself. He took pains not to compromise the army's position but it was obvious that he personally supported reform. His letter continued by drawing attention to his own and the regiment's growing unease about the ugly mood of the Birmingham mobs and ended on a particularly damning note that made it abundantly clear where he personally stood. The Greys

> 'would be the last to degrade themselves below the dignity of British soldiers, in acting as the tool of a tyrant. The Duke of Wellington, if he sees or hears of this, may assure himself that military government shall never again be set up in this country.'

The last is of course a reference to the Cromwellian republic of 1649-60.

The hot-headed young Scot had committed his second error; not only had he published a letter without the permission of his commanding officer, he had dared to criticise the Establishment.

It wasn't long before Trooper Somerville was brought before his commanding officer, a veteran of Waterloo who probably regarded Wellington in the same light as later generations would venerate Charles Gordon of Khartoum or Winston Churchill. Alexander made no attempt to conceal the fact of his letter: His Commanding Officer's response was cold and unfeeling:

> 'You are fond of writing letters'

In the eyes of the army, Alexander Somerville had wilfully breached King's regulations, his public statement considered almost treasonable. When asked to name the troopers who supported the Reform Bill, Alexander refused to inform on them. Again, his CO censured him:

> 'My lad, you will repent of that'.

Alexander was court-martialled; at the hearing he explained his actions by stating quite categorically that the Scots Greys would act against any mob but never against the people - a somewhat ambiguous if spirited line of defence. To make sure he was found guilty, the court martial linked his name with an earlier, minor breach of discipline to discredit him as a grumbler, a barrack room lawyer.

Alexander Somerville was found guilty of dishonouring the regiment and sentenced to 200 lashes to be administered before the entire regiment on 29th May 1832. The punishment was delivered by a farrier and a trumpeter who were ordered to lay on 25 strokes of the cat o' nine tails, in two separate lots of 200. Alexander refused the half pint of rum which was his right before the flogging. During his ordeal, he admonished the trumpeter to

> 'Come quicker Simpson, and let it be done; you are very slow.'

After the first 100 strokes were administered, Alexander was dragged away, muttering that he would make his punishment as public as the newspapers would allow. He carried out his threat. A Court of Inquiry was held in July that year, Alexander characteristically cross-examining witnesses personally. He wrote to the *Weekly Dispatch* and the *Birmingham Journal* as well as an Edinburgh newspaper which his brother James read. Radicals up and down the country adopted the unlikely hero from an obscure country village in Scotland and, much to his embarrassment Alexander became a *cause celebre* overnight.

Alexander Somerville's flogging was only one of many cases which were censured by the press. When the Whigs were in opposition, they demanded the abolition of physical punishment but now back in power, they argued that the army couldn't discipline the troops without it. In point of fact, ineffectual officers used the lash to cover their own shortcomings; it was used indiscriminately, often for petty offences. Corporal punishment wasn't outlawed in the British army until 1881.

With the support of several newspapers and liberal-minded friends, Alexander obtained his discharge from the Greys; a collection on his behalf raised £320 of which he used £30 to buy himself out with £40 for legal expenses. He never had so much money in his life. He was feted in Birmingham and elsewhere, a common man from an obscure background who had challenged the mighty military machine and won. *Madame Tussaud's* wanted to make a wax model of him for which he was to be paid £50; some radicals offered to organise a 'benefit' for him at a London theatre which would have earned him £150. However, Alexander turned such offers down; he was weary of being in the public eye and refused to become part of the propaganda campaign mounted by the supporters of the Reform Bill - even if his protests came rather late in the day. Perhaps he knew that at first, martyrs are venerated, then they become the butt of jokes and finally as embarrassments.

Alexander Somerville returned to his family at Threipland Hill. For a time he worked as a wood-sawyer in Edinburgh, losing his money on unwise investments, which may have been intentional; for example, he started a newspaper in Edinburgh and it failed. He was possibly ashamed of the way he'd obtained his small fortune and he appears to have been genuinely relieved when it was gone. He returned to England in 1837, writing about social and economic reform and against the use of violence in his salutary warning to the people on street warfare. His many newspaper articles denouncing the Corn Laws found favour with the Anti-Corn Law Leaguer Richard Cobden, known as the apostle of free trade; Somerville helped him to gather information on the way these laws operated in some parts of England. He published his *History of the British Legion and the War in Spain* in London in 1839; in the same year, he wrote and published *Public and Personal Affairs: An Enquiry.* He worked as a correspondent for the *Manchester Examiner* in 1844 and published his *Autobiography of a Working Man* in 1848; subsequent publications were *The Whistler at the Plough, Free Trade and the League* (1852) and the *Life of Roger Mowbray: A Tale* (1853). In 1841, he married the daughter of Francis Binks of Gretna Bridge, Yorkshill; by 1853, he was in dire poverty, mainly at the hands of exploiting literary agents. His health was poor, so he decided to emigrate to Canada with his wife. Friends collected money to finance their voyage. On arrival in Canada, his wife died shortly afterwards, which must have bruised his spirit. Even so, he managed to secure work as editor of the *Canadian Illustrated News.* When he retired from active life, poverty again overtook him. Alexander Somerville was found dead in a shed in Toronto in 1885, homeless and penniless. He was survived by one child.

Alexander Somerville's *Autobiography of a Working Man* should be required reading in the school curriculum; not only is it a valuable source of local history, it makes informed comments on the wider world in which he lived. Although he wasn't trained as a journalist, he had a way with words that are refreshing to read over a century and a half after they were written.

Life in the rural communities was still hard although working conditions gradually improved as the century progressed. Starvation was never far away however; in 1867, adverse weather prevented many people earning a living on the land. Several influential residents in Dunbar persuaded the provost and the burgh council to set up a soup kitchen for the relief

> 'of the labouring classes out of employment during the present storm under
> the Management of the Magistrates and Council.'

Subscriptions for the soup kitchen realised £24:6:0 (£24.30) [19]

Social evenings were the prerogative of the well off, although the man in the street might choose to join the *Dunbar Castle Lodge of Freemasons* founded in 1758; three of its earliest members were James Kilgour (1758), Philip Delisle (1762) and Robert Castellau (1766), names immortalised respectively by the close next to the Eagle Inn, a street in the West Port and the building which now houses the local library. Other than the regular weekly markets and periodic fairs, major social events which even the humble could attend were few and far between. At the six-monthly fee'ing fairs, merry-go-rounds were permitted in the High Street in 1894. In 1901, Lady Grizell Baillie successfully petitioned the magistrates to heat and make available the Corn Exchange to give shelter to the country people visiting Dunbar.

The majority enjoyed dancing and even if the poor couldn't afford the suppers and musical evenings in the town's Assembly Rooms; they gathered round the fireside or in the hostelries to sing or play cards while supping Dunbar's famous Belhaven Ale. Drink was of course a great curse, a constant refrain in the statistical accounts of 1793 and 1845. In the nineteenth century, Dunbar had 55 public houses - one for every 83 inhabitants and a 'number by far too great' in the opinion of George Bruce, the parish minister who contributed to the account of 1793. However, the farmworkers and fishermen couldn't afford to get drunk too often and opportunities arose only at hiring fairs, markets and harvest homes. The better-off tended to drink in their own homes, in comfort. The century saw the emergence of a strong temperance movement; the Forbes Mackenzie Act of 1853 was a great victory for the teetotallers as it closed the pubs to all but *bona fide* travellers on Sundays and restricted the licensing hours to ensure that all pubs were shut by 11pm on weekdays. Certainly, something needed to be done about licensing hours; in 1853, hotels in Dunbar were licensed to sell alcohol between 8am and 11pm, the pubs opening a full hour earlier and closing at the same time. In 1894, the magistrates refused an application for pubs to open at 6am during the herring fishing season, although two years later, they relaxed this ban by extending the hours in the pubs at the harbours on condition that they closed an hour earlier on every evening except Saturday.

Dunbar's police records for 1849-61 are almost exclusively about cases of drunkenness, brawling and the use of foul language, licencees selling liquor outwith permitted hours or on the Sabbath. In the previous century, drinking was an occupational hazard for the publican and pubs could be dangerous places for the reforming ministers, particularly in rural areas. Men often carried *whingers* - short cutlasses - when they caroused in Tyninghame and Kirklandhill's Muttonhole pub, now long gone. Most petty crimes committed in nineteenth century Dunbar were probably drink-related; thefts of food and items of clothing were common, probably because the thieves had spent their money on drink or were too poor to buy clothes. A fair proportion of incidents in which drink was a factor occurred in Davel Brae, often between fishermen and their wives.[20] However, inns like Cossar's (the St George) were necessary for the weary stagecoach travellers of the day; writing in 1841, Robert Forsyth noted that

> 'As Dunbar is on the principal road from London to Edinburgh, there are good inns here, as well as at Haddington, for the accommodation of travellers.'

Forsyth also remarked on the leisure facilities and amenities:

> 'At some distance among the rocks, is a retired place for sea-bathing with a room to undress.....The town is supplied with an abundance of pure water, conveyed from St John's Well near the village of Spott, at the distance of two miles. It is brought in leaden pipes. This work was accomplished in 1766 by the magistrates, assisted by the contributions of the inhabitants. On the same occasion, the streets were new paved.'[21]

Illus 115: *The Ladies only swimming pool at the Glebe, pre 1905* DDHS

Dunbar was of course famous for its safe and clean beaches which allowed sea-bathing as many old photographs testify. An amateur photographer, W F Jackson, general manager of the North British Railway Company frequently visited East Lothian. In 1899, he took almost 100 photographs of local scenes; in 1912, Jackson captured on film the Ladies' Bathing Pool at Bayswell Cove, a site later developed to accommodate the prestigious modern swimming pool which was based on the design of the swimming pool at Scarborough. To the west and screened from the Ladies' Pool (**ill 115**) was the Gentlemen's Pool (**ill 116**) or *Old Bathe*, beside the *Bathe Rock,* below Bayswell Park (**ill 117**). Another pool for males was *The Kettle*, situated off the East Promenade, near the East Links Golf Course. Until the end of the Great War, mixed bathing was frowned upon; a morally outraged *Edinburgh Evening Dispatch* reported on 15th September 1912 that

Illus 116: *The Old Bathe or Gentlemen only swimming pool, Bayswell* DDHS

> 'the first instance of mixed bathing took place at Dunbar gentlemen's swimming pool today.... several

strangers who were on the hill at the time appeared to be quite aghast at the presence of a lady in the pond'. Times thankfully changed. By 1923, the *Old Bathe* had been enlarged and mixed bathing was permitted. In 1927, the burgh council decided to develop Bayswell Beach, the site of the Ladies' Only Pool since 1886. First came a childrens' paddling and boating pond in June 1928, followed by the Safety Swimming Pool which opened on 15th June 1929 (**ill 118**); one of Dunbar's most popular and attractive amenities, it was used until 1981, demolished in 1985 and eventually replaced by the indoor pool situated in Castle Park.

Illus 117: *Bayswell* DDHS

Bathing in the sea has been a custom in Dunbar and Belhaven for as long as anyone can remember. Belhaven was once a very popular village which briefly had a spa (**ill 119**). When the spa was discovered, the burgh council showed some interest, minuting on 4th December 1837 that it was thought to be similar to the spa at Harrogate. However, on 7th April 1838, those who petitioned for its development complained to the council that the £100 it had offered was inadequate, urging the council to think again as similar waters had brought wealth from 'much more slender beginnings.' The council turned down the request for more cash although the spa went ahead and was in use until the 1850s when for some reason it went into decline. *The Haddingtonshire Courier* of 6th October 1899 reported the unsuccessful attempt by the owner of Winterfield Mains Farm to find the source of the spa. The small building which contained it was a cylindrical tower built of yellow brick which could be reached by means of a plank bridge from the beach. In time, storms destroyed the structure, some of its bricks were removed to build a wall and for many years, all that remained was a low circle of brick barely visible near Seafield Bridge. The OS map of 1907 indicates the spa's position, near the banking where stone cists were found in 1891 and 1906. The area is described as a rifle range with butts or targets on what is now the 15th hole at Winterfield Golf Course. Today, the site is enclosed with a concrete cylindrical structure which suggests that the spa has become polluted. Seafield Bridge - the Bridge to Nowhere - (**ill 120**) was built in 1886 and opened by a Mrs Anderson of Bowerhouse; it allowed visitors to cross the Biel Burn at low tide. The casual visitor seeing the bridge at high tide can be forgiven for thinking it eccentric; its surrealism would not be out of place in a Roman Polanski film.

Illus 118 : *The safety swimming pool in its heyday* DDHS

Even the price of a short holiday was beyond the pocket of most Dunbar families; few could afford such luxuries and made do with facilities on the doorstep. However, to help the less well-off save for red-letter occasions such as Christmas and New Year, a Mutual Assistance and Savings Society was founded on 28th January 1828 and was still operating in the middle of the twentieth century as I recall well. One of the committee members in 1859 was Mungo Suddon, the schoolmaster who taught John Muir; within living memory, the money and interest deriving therefrom was known locally as the *Siddonses* (after Mungo Suddon who ran

Illus 119: *Belhaven Spa* DDHS

the Davel Brae school and taught John Muir) which paid twice-yearly dividends to its shareholders, payments I recollect queuing for as a boy at the Corn Exchange in June and December

Unlike Musselburgh and some Border towns, Dunbar long ago ceased Riding the Marches. The local magistrates and bailies used to ride the marches to the Outer or Dunbar Common every seven years; in 1805, R Somerville, a surgeon in Haddington and author of a report on the state of agriculture wrote that the greatest expanse of waste land in East Lothian was 4,000 acres in the Lammermuir Hills known as Dunbar Common. In Somerville's opinion, the Common brought no advantage whatsoever to the community of Dunbar other to give the local burgesses 'a holiday ride....every seven years'. The last perambulation - as it is described in the burgh minute-book - took place in 1829. The Inner Common was a different matter; extending from the Bleachfield to West Barns, it was productive, being used to graze cattle. It was customary to walk the Inner Common on the king's birthday. How many local people remember that the local Lovers' Lane began at the Bleachfield and proceeded to Lochend Woods, via the underace or railway tunnel? Also, are there any who have mementoes of the annual Carters' Play when high and low raced their horses for prizes of a silver whip or small bell at the Gallows' Green [Gala Green]? This occasion was usually preceded by a procession of the horses decorated with plumes, their riders stopping before a local civic dignitary's house for 'something to wet their mou[th]' The event ended with a ball held in the Assembly Rooms in the evening.

Illus 120: *Seafield Bridge, 'the bridge to nowhere' , Belhaven* KRM

From the sixteenth century onwards, Dunbar's civic authorities wrote to monarchs congratulating them on their succession to the throne; these 'illuminated' addresses were sent to the king's private secretary, then after the restoration of the office in 1885, the Secretary of State for Scotland. The provost and bailies sent carefully and respectfully worded letters re-affirming the burgh's loyalty to a new monarch and expressing its condolences on the death of one, a practice which continued well into the twentieth century. Letters of this kind are recorded during the reign of George III and occurred long before it. George V was a particular favourite with the British people as he reigned through the First World War. His jubilee was celebrated enthusiastically in Dunbar in 1935. On the death of the king in January 1936, Dunbar council conveyed the burgh's sympathy to the Secretary of State for Scotland and intimated that proclamation of Edward VIII's accession would be delivered at the mercat cross - which didn't exist - and the Old Harbour pier head on 24th January. On 28th January, George V's funeral was commemorated by the entire nation; shops and offices closed between the hours of 11am and 3pm and the population observed two minutes' silence. At the appointed time, about 1,000 people gathered at Dunbar Town House to observe the silence which was announced by artillery fire from the Castle Park Barracks. A united church service followed. A movement to commemorate the old king began almost immediately; every burgh was invited to create King George V Playing Fields - established in Dunbar's

Countess Park in 1938. The council next sent the burgh's good wishes to George VI who succeeded the quickly abdicating Edward VIII. To celebrate his coronation in 1937, a holiday was declared and the local schoolchildren were given the following:

ages 3 to 5: a metal case containing a block of Rowntree's chocolate
" 5 to 14: a pottery mug modelled and designed by Dame Laura Knight
aged over 14: a book entitled *George VI*

Illus 121: *West Promenade with War Memorial in its original position* DDHS

Those on the Poor Roll were given two shillings and sixpence (about 13p) and the patients at the Yorke House Cottage Hospital enjoyed 'treats'. A sports day was held and the children were treated to a free tea. The elderly were given a free lunch in the Corn Exchange. The evening was marked by a bonfire and firework display at the Victoria Harbour; probably at the battery where bonfire night is still celebrated today. Similar arrangements were made for the coronation of queen Elizabeth II and I in June 1953; before that, her marriage to the Duke of Edinburgh on 20th November 1947 was marked by a firework display which cost £26 as is recorded in the burgh minutes of 25th September. On 3rd June 1953, the Town House was floodlit and decorated with bunting and floral arrangements which incorporated a five-foot photograph of the queen. The local and district schools held a special sports day with prizes of vouchers for sweets which had only recently come off war-time rationing. The old people were given a free dinner. At midnight on 2nd-3rd June 1953, a bonfire was lit on Doon Hill, the men tending it being given a free barrel of beer by Belhaven Brewery. A simultaneous fireworks display costing £100 was staged and there was dancing in the Castle Park Barracks Gymnasium, the Gym, later known as the Victoria Ballroom, now long-demolished. These celebrations reflected Dunbar's royal burgh status and special relationship with the monarch, if on a superficial and anachronistic level.

Illus 122: *Golf on the East LInks c.1899* RJP

Men of some vision saw that the decline of the fishing industry meant that Dunbar needed to change direction - they realised Dunbar's worth as a holiday resort. In the mid-nineteenth century, Dunbar was considered an 'agreeable' east coast watering hole; four decades later, it had advanced its reputation from being merely agreeable to fashionable. This brought about the building of impressive houses in the West End which provided summer houses for the well-to-do businessmen from Edinburgh and Glasgow seeking diversion from their busy lives on the golf course or in the bathing places provided. One of the summer visitors was Sir Reginald Wingate and his family. For some years, Wingate rented the prestigious Stafford House with its gardens overlooking the Old Bathe at Bayswell until he built his permanent residence at Knockenhair in 1907. Between the two World Wars, a publicity officer was appointed to ensure Dunbar attracted its share of visitors. Apart from golf, the main holiday sport, tennis, bowling and cycling were popular. There was also a curling pond for use in winter by the locals although it only lasted from 1899 until February 1938.[22] In September 1899, the *Haddingtonshire Courier* announced that the Latch Park Curling Pond would open for business the following month; the remains of the pond can still be seen on the edge of Lochend Wood. There was also a gun club at West Barns from 1902 to 1931 although in the light of present concern about such clubs, the less said about it the better.

Illus 123: *Zenith Entertainers, 1928* KM

In the early part of the twentieth century, trains were more frequent, bringing hordes of summer visitors to North Berwick and Dunbar. The Lothian Coach Express plied between Glasgow and Dunbar from June to September between 1912 and 1934 - war years excepted. The fast train left Glasgow every day at 3.55pm, arriving at Dunbar at 5.43pm with coaches detached at Drem to go to Gullane and North Berwick. This allowed a businessmen from Glasgow to install his family in a summer cottage at Dunbar while he was at work until he joined them in the evening, often managing to get in a round of golf before supper. A train left Dunbar every morning at 7.55am to take them to their desks in Glasgow for 10.00am. In 1914, Dunbar was described somewhat poetically - and gloomily - as being in decay; to the writer, it had become a place noted for

> '.... windswept streets....everywhere weathered and scarred as if the town had become worn and exhausted by the continuous struggle against the elements.' [23]

Despite this pessimistic view, the burgh council was in no doubt about the burgh's attractiveness and they made sure no one else was. From about 1895, annual guides[24] were published to extol Dunbar's undoubted virtues; these also contained a remarkably accurate - if brief - history of the burgh, covering signal events such as the siege of Dunbar Castle in 1338 and the Cromwellian victory in 1650. The guide took pains to emphasise the town's clean and tidy appearance and that it was

> 'well supplied with excellent Hotels, and Tourists, Holiday Makers, Golfers and Cyclists will find Dunbar an excellent centre, whether for a long or short holiday.'

Indeed it was - then. Well served by public transport with safe and clean beaches and many places of interest in and around it, the boarding houses and hotels were invariably full to capacity in the peak months of July and August. Dunbar had much to offer until 1965, when cheap package holidays abroad all but killed off the seaside holiday trade in Britain. There were swimming pools, tennis courts, two golf courses - the East Links opened in 1856 and was popular with Edwardian fanatics (**ill 122**), with Winterfield Course established in 1935, bowling and putting greens, parks, a reading room, a billiard hall, two cinemas, a theatre, several pubs and perhaps one of its best attractions, the West Promenade at the Heugh Heads, or Winterfield Cliffs (**ill 121**) - the modern clifftop walk - gifted in 1896 by Mrs

Illus 124: *Roxburghe Marine Hotel* DDHS

Illus 125: *Bellevue Hotel* DDHS

James Baird, daughter of Rear-Admiral Hay of Belton.[25] Pierrot troupes performed first at the harbour, then in Winterfield Pavilion which opened in 1925 and finally in the Corn Exchange. Song-and-dance groups like the Zenith Concert Party dressed up in a variety of costumes, most famously those of clowns; their arrival in Dunbar marked the official start of summer, an attraction much loved by locals and visitors alike. The troupe in more sophisticated attire appears in **ill 123**.

Illus 126: *The Eagle Inn* MD

Prestigious hotels like the Roxburghe Marine Hotel (**ill 124**) and the Hotel Bellevue (**ill 125**) before it was destroyed by fire about a decade ago were well patronised. The Roxburghe began life as Roxburghe Lodge, built in c.1885 at the extreme end of what was once known as Kirkhill Braes; it was extended in the twentieth century and became an extremely well-appointed hotel. Towards the town and opposite the modern Goldenstones Hotel - formerly the Albert Temperance Hotel - is Bowmont, a row of impressive terraced houses, probably also used as holiday homes until the Great War. The street is named for J H Bowe, a local farmer; No 1 bears a plaque which is inscribed 'Bowmont JHB [Bowe's monogram]1884.' (The monogram was also incorporated on the East Links Cottage Hospital which was opened in 1927 by the Duchess of York; as indicated above, the hospital was known as Yorke House and Bowe was probably one of its governors. Also present at the inauguration ceremony were Sir Reginald and Lady Wingate and their daughter). Today, only Belhaven Cottage Hospital survives

Near the *Goldenstones Hotel* are the *Hillside Hotel,* the *Dolphin Public House* incorporating the former *Railway Hotel* and the *Barns Ness* (formerly the *Royal Mackintosh)*(**ill 127**). In the High Street are the *Lothian*, the *Black Bull* and the *Eagle Inn* (**ill 126**); the *Castle* on the corner of High Street/Victoria Street has subsumed what was *Folkarde's Grocery Store* in its lounge bar. At No 134 once existed the Lorne Temperance Hotel (the home of John Muir from the age of three and now a locksmith's). Of several pubs which once existed near the harbour, only the *Volunteer Arms* has survived, its recently-refurbished dining-room a welcome addition to the nearby *Creel* and *Cuckoo-Wrasse* restaurants. An initiative which met with considerable success was the introduction of the cinema. Dunbar's first cinema was housed in *The Dreadnought,* around 1916, then the Corn Exchange a year or two later. In 1923, the first proper cinema was opened in the High Street; *The Empire* proved so popular that Caledonian Cinemas built their prestigious *Playhouse* at the top of the Station Road in 1937. Sadly, the advent of TV had closed both by 1984.

Later on, when caravan holidays became popular, Dunbar created its first caravan park in 1947 at Winterfield Mains which had been requisitioned by the army during the war; the War Office sold it to the burgh council for £7,710. After the war, the holiday trade resumed and was in full swing, with Dunbar's East or Coastguard

Illus 127: *These two views of the east end of Dunbar around 1900 are interesting, showing the addition of the Dolphin pub to the former Railway Hotel and structural additions to the Hillside Hotel. Note also the change from gardens to tennis courts in the left foreground.* HH

HH

Beach (**ill 128**) proving extremely popular until 1963, by which year the writing was on the wall for bucket-and-spade holidays in Scotland. It is interesting to note a survey conducted in 1938 which shows the holiday population at Dunbar was a staggering 18,000 between April and September that year[26]:

April	1,000
May	2,000
June	3,000
July	6,000
August	4,000
September	2,000

Thus in July 1938, the holiday population outstripped the town's resident population by 1,000.

We have already noted that on hiring or fee'ing days in the previous century, there were merry-go-rounds permitted in the High Street. In the next century, Countess Park became the venue for fairgrounds and circuses such as Madame Fossett's and the popular Robert Brothers. Some people remember the elephants being led to the East Beach to have a bath! There were donkey rides on the sands and during the Second World War, one enterprising local gentleman from Belhaven applied for permission to give local children pony rides for threepence a time. The burgh council refused him a licence but that didn't deter Mr Rutherford - known as *Aye-Aye-* from doing it anyway.

Despite the abundance of hotels and boarding houses in Dunbar, the summer invasion of visitors during the Edinburgh and Glasgow Trades Fortnights was so great that the burgh council permitted its tenants to 'let' a room or rooms during the holiday season. Letting came at three levels; the most expensive let was 'with full board' which meant that the landlady bought and cooked the food for her guests, cleaning the rooms, making the beds and offering her sitting room to her 'visitors';

Illus 128 : *The East Beach in the 1950s* DDHS

the next level was 'half-board' where the landlady bought and cooked the food for one meal, usually at evening; the cheapest and most popular arrangement was 'with attendance', where the visitors bought their own food, cooked it and kept their own rooms clean. (My mother always welcomed 'with attendance' visitors for obvious reasons, marking them with an asterisk in her 'letting' book!)

One of the signal events of the twentieth century occurred in 1970, when Dunbar celebrated 600 years of its free burgh status under David II's charter of 8th February 1369-70. *Anniversary Week* was held on 20th-27th July and the burgh's Centennial Committee organised a series of events[27] to mark this important date in the town's history. There were the inevitable sports fixtures, fancy dress parades, barbecues, official dinners and exhibitions. One of the exhibitions featured the early burgh records, on loan from the Scottish Record Office for the occasion. The earliest of these is a legal transaction about West Barns Mill and is dated 1576. Two events were memorable. The first was *Dunbar Through the Ages*, a parade which incorporated tableaux depicting famous scenes and staged by the children and students of the local schools. Tableaux which remain uppermost in memory are those depicting David II's charter, Black Agnes' defence of Dunbar Castle in 1338 and Mary, Queen of Scots' escape from Riccio's assassins in 1566; the latter tableaux indulged in a little poetic licence by including the queen's Four Maries who weren't of course present on that occasion. Another well-depicted scene was the 1650 battle with Roundheads and Cavaliers engaged in their conflict. Other scenes showed the Old Herring Road Market, Burns' visit in 1787, Boswell's in the eighteenth century to the St George Hotel and Victoria's sojourn in 1842, after which they named the new harbour in her honour.

The other memorable event was the roasting on a spit of a whole ox in the Castle Park Barracks; the oxburgers were washed down with a free pint of ale provided by Belhaven Brewery. *Anniversary Week* proved such a success that the Centennial Committee continued to meet and from that developed Dunbar's *Civic Week* held in June every year.

Dunbar has had its fair share of tragedy over the centuries - loss of life at sea even in recent years despite the efforts of the local lifeboat crews. On one or two occasions it was marine life which suffered; in 1914, three whales were stranded at Thortonloch's White Sands, where an even more tragic ecological disaster occurred nearly forty years later, on the same beach. A school of about 150 whales came inshore in 1951, possibly disoriented and finding themselves in shallow waters because of sickness - whales are very loyal to each other and when one is in distress, the entire school will not leave a stricken member. Despite several attempts to take them out to sea, the entire school wouldn't leave and had to be humanely destroyed.

And there were dramas caused by freak weather. The most memorable was the dreadful winter of 1947 when Dunbar, like the rest of Britain, experienced its worst and longest snowstorm in living memory. Snow fell at the end of January and lay until the third week in March. Outlying farms near Spott and other places were cut off for weeks and food had to be taken to the beleaguered villagers by horse or as at Garvald, on sledges hauled by the Cistercian monks at Nunraw Abbey, then under construction. In the following year, a great flood devastated East Lothian on the night of 12th-3th August and although a good deal of livestock was lost, fortunately no one was drowned. According to the burgh council minutes, 29 families had their houses damaged and the council set up a Flood Disaster Fund which collected £930. The flood was comparable to those which have occurred in recent years in England, where in some areas, people have been forced out of their house twice and even three times.

Today, Dunbar's social life is showing signs of recovery; several recent initiatives by East Lothian Council and the Community Council may relieve the depression which has bedevilled the town for many years. It is of course clear that the community will never again enjoy a reputation as a holiday resort; these days are gone forever. However, the Town House Museum may be on course to expand in the future. Also the forthcoming John Muir Interpretive Centre is already attracting considerable interest; although I in no way wish to diminish the importance of this enterprise, there is a danger that the Muir initiative may divert attention from the rest of Dunbar's long and colourful history. It would not be difficult to suggest a number of initiatives which would enhance and promote the community.

11

The Prophet

At the dawning of the twenty-first century, when we look back on the achievements of the Second Millenium - its triumphs and tragedies - we should be thankful that the planet has survived, albeit in an occasionally parlous state. The environment has rarely been writ large in the book of human experience, not to mention that of economics and commerce. This is now changing, thanks to such organisations as Greenpeace and Friends of the Earth who have taken the initiative to conserve what I consider to be vital to the survival of our species. The world has finally recognised that Cockpit Earth will sicken and wither if we do not check the growth of pollution, the destruction of natural habitats of wildlife and the sacrifice of the countryside on the altars of commerce and industry. Most developed countries now accept that without a healthy environment, the future won't happen. More than any other century, the twentieth threatened the very survival of the planet; it is by luck rather by design that major ecological disasters have been averted. We can't afford to be complacent however; the world is at risk and we should be grateful to those dedicated organisations which have already courageously taken on the corporate giants and made them think again. I am not an unqualified supporter of these organisations however; on some occasions, they have overstepped their remit and I deplore any who hold the world to ransom or senselessly obstruct developers who genuinely care about the environment.

Scotland is rightly proud to be able to boast of one of her sons, a man for all seasons, a giant of a man who in his lifetime saw into the future and began to ring alarm bells long before anyone thought of or cared about the environment. He believed his cause was not only just but vital to the survival of his own and future generations. While he could not have foreseen the coming of the Atomic Age or its dreadful consequences, he wouldn't have been surprised by it. He was acutely aware that progress is always achieved at the expense of something else. For him, the environment was too important to be left to its own - or rather man's - devices and he refused to accept that it should be sacrificed on the altar of big business. But he also believed that disaster wasn't inevitable, that man could intervene and change things by positive intervention, learning the lessons of changes he had wrought in earlier centuries. He wasn't the first to recognise the pitfalls - the poet William Blake and others like him had warned about England's 'dark, satanic mills'- and while we do not know if he had read Blake's philosophy, he began a personal crusade to preserve and conserve what he rightly believed to be vital to the future of mankind. Today, others continue that crusade in his name.

The man I write of was John Muir, father of the modern environment movement. He was born in Dunbar in 1838, but emigrated with his family to America a few years later. Like many other Scotsmen before and since, he wasn't acknowledged by his native country until many years after his death. John Muir has been variously called the prophet of the wilderness, an eccentric, fire-and-brimstone crank and perhaps by way of consolation among those who cannot understand those obsessed by their ideals - a genius. Muir's greatest and lasting achievement was the creation of the American National Parks. And yet until about 1960, hardly anyone in Scotland knew of him, although he had long been famous in America. Scotland is often slow to acknowledge her famous sons and Dunbar is no exception; it appears to be a national trait. Even then, official recognition was patchy, although in 1997, a statue was placed in the High Street in his memory; since then, a new housing development currently being constructed near Lochend Woods has been named Muirfield, an estate which contains streets called John Muir Park, John Muir Avenue and so on. The developers perhaps miss the irony of this; while wishing to acknowledge the great man, they are in fact acting against his philosophy; for centuries, Lochend was a natural habitat for wildlife and flora. The housing development will destroy that habitat. It is a comment on our times, the facetiousness which is lost on the minds of accountants and the other living dead that fail to understand what Muir was about.

Nothing was taught about John Muir in the local schools until the second half of the twentieth century. In 1976, the East Lothian District Council finally managed to acquire some unused land near the West Barns links, fenced it off, built an ugly toilet block and swings for children and called it the John Muir Country Park. At least it was a start. It has improved since then, reflecting more of what John Muir was about. However, the 1,700 acres which begin at Dunbar Castle and end at Tyninghame Bay have been designated as a park and wild life reserve, home of rare birds such as shell duck, curlew, little terns, oyster catchers and eider duck. The Muir Movement was kick-started by Frank Tindall, the former East Lothian County Planning Officer who deserves credit for his dedication.

In America, John Muir was famous long before he died in 1914. In Dunbar let alone the rest of Scotland, little was known of him, although in the burgh council minutes of April 1938,[1] the provost of the day eulogised over the fact that the centennial of Muir's birth would occur on 21st April. He informed the council that Muir had written regularly to his Dunbar cousin - Mrs Margaret Hay Lunam of Westfield and her daughter, Margaret Rae Lunam. He also intimated that Muir had sent money every Christmas for the relief of the Dunbar poor. So why did officialdom ignore him for so long? The answer is simple - like so many others, he was a prophet not honoured in his own country.

The best the provost and councillors could come up with was to register their appreciation of his career and their regard for a distinguished man

> 'who although his life was spent and his fame earned in a far country.........[he] never forgot his nativity of this old Town.'

The irony of this was lost on the councillors of the day. Five months later,[2] the council minutes refer to a request received by the provost from Kenneth E Selby, Seattle Public Schools, who raised the subject of Muir's centenary. He wrote that the pupils of Seattle were intending to publish a pictorial biography 'of this great naturalist' and asked if there were any photographs of Muir's birthplace, school, or family they could use in their project. It is not beyond the realms of possibility that the good men on the burgh council asked themselves why on earth Seattle was interested? More important, they hadn't a clue where John Muir had drawn his first breath - the house that is, as by now, they were certain he'd been born in Dunbar. Reading the minutes, one gets the impression that the men serving on the burgh council of that time were completely underwhelmed by Selby's request; apathy was always an essential ingredient in the inkwells of the Town Clerks who compiled the burgh council records up and down the land. (Even with the advent of new technology and county councils since 1975, little has changed).

The minutes record that the Town Clerk had responded to Kenneth Selby informing him that the house where John Muir had been born had been demolished![3] He also said that the school he'd attended - Lyon's school, that at Woodbush - was 'no longer recognisable' which was of course the case.. All that the Seattle kids got were photographs of the High Street, the Swimming Pool and the old Cat's Row which housed fishermen then as well as in Muir's day. As so often happened in Dunbar, the council's lack of imagination had surpassed itself, as it has before and since.

Thus John Muir's centenary passed without any public celebration in Dunbar on 21st April 1938. Almost 30 years later, the US Mail Service issued a five-cent stamp in recognition of the fiftieth anniversary of Muir's death. Dunbar managed to miss that by a whole year. On 15th September 1965, the American Consul in Edinburgh opened a John Muir exhibition in the Corn Exchange. Thus began the rediscovery of John Muir from Dunbar, Scotland. In 1967, Muir's biographers Bill and Maimie Kimes came to Dunbar on a personal pilgrimage, managing to embarrass the lady provost of the day by seeking a tour of the places John had held special in his childhood. The provost frantically searched for information about Muir, finding nothing written by or about him in the local or county libraries. As a result of her endeavours and prompted by the Kimes, the town finally acknowledged Muir's birthplace at No 128 High Street by a plaque inscribed 'Birthplace of John Muir, American Naturalist, 1838-1914.' The ambiguity of this seems to have escaped the authorities' attention; nor did they fully understand what Muir had been about. Worse was to come; in 1978, it was found that the National Library of Scotland hadn't a single book on or about Muir or his achievements, which thankfully was soon put right. In 1981, Muir's birthplace at Nos 126-128 High Street was converted into a museum and opened to the public. The John Muir Trust was then established in 1983 by several well-known personalities including Chris Brasher, with the Prince of Wales as its patron. One of the Trust's main objectives is to acquire wild land in Britain for conservation.

Meanwhile, across the Pond, the Americans were going from strength to strength. The State of California designated 21st April 1988 - the 150th anniversary of Muir's birth - as John Muir Day. With the exception of the *Glasgow Herald,* the occasion successfully evaded the interest of other Scottish newspapers and television channels alike; even the *East Lothian Courier* was silent about this important tribute to one of the county's famous sons; no doubt it was preoccupied with other signal events. However, those who didn't let the day pass unnoticed included the National Memorial Fund and the Sierra Club in California, the latter donating cash to purchase a mountain in the West Highlands of Scotland for conservation, celebrating the day in a way the man himself would have applauded. Dunbar eventually got round to planting 150 trees in Muir's memory and the local schoolchildren were encouraged to write to the heads of every state in the world, urging them in Muir's name to protect their environment.

The Dunbar John Muir Association (DJMA) was formed in 1994, chiefly to challenge East Lothian Council's proposal to set up a John Muir World Environmental 'theme park' in the John Muir Country Park. The issue was debated at length; one faction felt that the Environmental Centre should rightly be based in the town itself, the opposing faction favouring the Country Park. A basic fact seems to have escaped the latter group - the John Muir World Environment Centre had to be situated where it wouldn't pose a threat to the environment; the Country Park is unsuitable for a variety of reasons, not the least being that visitors to the centre would put in jeopardy an area where rare birds such as the little tern make their nests, contrary to everything John Muir stands for. Thankfully, the DJMA has won the argument

Who was John Muir? Who or what stirred his imagination and his determination to convince the people of America that they were in danger of losing much of their natural heritage - the wild and beautiful places in their country? The answer lies in Muir's humble origins.

John Muir was born in Dunbar on 21st April 1838, one of eight children born to Daniel and Anne Muir, the eighth being born in Wisconsin. Daniel was the son of an army recruiting sergeant whose profession he followed. Born in 1804, Daniel Muir was raised by relatives on a farm at Crawfordjohn in Lanarkshire. A strict Calvinist, anti-intellectual and as often goes hand-in-hand with these characteristics of personality, a brutal disciplinarian, he came to Dunbar in 1829, marrying a relatively well-off woman. She brought him money which allowed him to buy himself out of the army and purchase a grain-store in Dunbar. When she died leaving him with a child who followed its mother to the grave in infancy, he married Anne Gilrye in 1833; Anne was the daughter of a local butcher. At that time, Daniel Muir was described in the parish register as a shopkeeper. Anne's father and mother, David and Margaret Gilrye were solid and respectable, Gilrye being a kirk elder. They lived at No 109 High Street, identified today by its cornerstone as Gilrye Place, adjacent to the Royal Bank of Scotland. David Gilrye died in 1855; the family grave in the kirkyard contains his remains, those of his wife who predeceased him in 1852 and six of their children.

Illus 129: *John Muir Museum before renovation in 2003* KRM

Daniel Muir bought No 128 High Street (**ill 129**); three years after John was born, the family moved to a nearby house, No 134, which Daniel Muir bought from a Dr Wightman in 1841, then sold to a Dr Lorn in 1849, the year he and his family emigrated to America. The building was later converted into a Temperance hotel known as the Lorne (who added the 'e'?); the building is thought to have been smaller than it is today, an additional storey being added later. In the deed of sale of No 128, Daniel Muir is described as a corn dealer; he conducted his business at street level, living above his shop. John was the eldest of the boys but third in a succession of five daughters and three sons. Daniel Muir was a sadistic disciplinarian whose religious beliefs permeated his and his children's lives; they were obliged to memorise several verses from the King James Bible every day, defaulters being thrashed. The savage beatings inflicted on the young Muir by his puritanical father were bound to have a lasting effect on his character. They probably explain why to re-make himself, to recover his loss of self-esteem, he was driven to undertake punishing hikes alone in the wilderness. The same may explain why he was never much of a family man, leaving his wife and daughters for long periods, preferring lengthy expeditions into the forests of America. Despite his many beatings, John Muir bore no grudge against his father; they were on good terms when Daniel Muir died in 1885, when John wrote:

'in all our devious ways and wanderings, we have loved one another.'

John was educated up to his eleventh year in Dunbar schools where he was taught Latin, French, English and other subjects. His first school, Mungo Suddon's, was situated in the Davel Brae, now Victoria Street, beside the Methodist Church. John recalled sliding down the icy hill on winter mornings. He next attended what was known as Lyon's or Woodbush school, later to become Dunbar Grammar School[4] which was attended by many generations of local children until 1961.

The atmosphere of a small east coast fishing community is captured beautifully in John Muir's unfinished autobiography *The Story of My Boyhood and Youth*, a lively little book which is sprinkled with examples of pawky Scots' humour; it contains such gems as

'Scotch boys are seldom spoiled by money.'

Education was important in his day. Before he attended school, John learnt his letters from grandfather Gilrye, a proud old man of Highland stock; he taught the boy to read by deciphering shop signs in the High Street. From John's unfinished autobiography, we learn that his father had bought No.128 High Street from a doctor[5] whose servant frightened the Muir children by informing them that the ghost of the doctor's father - also a doctor - haunted the premises. One room on the second floor through the wall from John's bedroom contained the paraphernalia of the dead man's profession - phials, flasks, test-tubes - which fired the boy's imagination. The mystique which was medicine was greater then than today and the medical apparatus inspired John to invent games he called 'scootchers'; the aim was to test resolve by standing alone in the room which was completely darkened by windows blocked-up to avoid paying the window tax levied at that time.[6] One of John's phrases whose meaning and derivation is lost to us but which was intended to send shivers down the spine was 'sookin'-in-goats' - his name for the rock channels at the foot of the West Promenade from the rock formation known as the Delves and beyond the Pincod (Pincushion) Rock which contained miniature whirlpools that could suck or drag a body under. These gullies have claimed a few lives in modern times.

The house where John was born was bought by the John Muir Birthplace Trust as a museum; now it is scheduled to become an environmental/interpretative centre. The upper floor consisted of two rooms, a kitchen and bedroom which gave us a glimpse of the living conditions of the time (**ill 130**). The focal point of the household was the kitchen with its range for cooking and heating water; the fire was kept going all day and a bunker or box on the stairs meant there was always a ready supply of coal and logs near at hand. The room contained examples of contemporary cooking utensils, including the heavy irons which were heated on the fire to press clothes, girdles for making scones and a tin bath for washing by the fire. There was a sampler on the wall to the left of the range which John's mother had made when she was a young girl; no doubt it has been removed for safe-keeping. The main bedroom with the best bed would have been occupied by the parents, although this is speculative. When the new centre opens - hopefully in 2003 - the character of the interior will have disappeared. For those who enjoy social history - the display of artefacts - the change of use has already created bitter divisions between those who wish to conserve Muir's birthplace and those who feel that promoting John Muir's message is more important. (The museum faction should bear in mind that the artefacts on display didn't belong to the Muir family, nor were they contemporary. And yet, people like to view the living conditions of their heroes. I ask the question; couldn't the revamped centre have catered for both interests? The answer will be in the negative by those who are determined to succeed. I am saddened by that but bow to the wisdom of others involved in the refurbishment....)

RJP

Illus 130: *Kitchen in John Muir birthplace before renovation*

Like most boys - and some girls - John and his two brothers felt they had to test scientifically the theory that cats always land on their four paws when they fall. This induced young Muir to take one poor animal to the top storey of the house and heave it out of the window. John ruefully recounts that the experiment was a complete success although the cat's chin was bruised and swollen, adding that it was a cruel thing to do. Perhaps this was one of his earliest lessons; that we should take care to temper scientific discovery with humanitarian concern where life is involved! However, the boy's tender nature is revealed by another incident which occurred behind the house at No. 134 High Street. He watched a Scots Grey trooper remove some fledgling robins from a nest in an elm tree in the back garden; his mother told him that the baby birds would be sold as song birds for ale money which upset him and his brothers and sisters. The memory never left him. (Was his memory accurate? Robins are not in the habit of nesting in trees - they tend to nest in holes or walls, or things discarded by man such as tin cans, pots and kettles. Was he thinking about the trooper 'robbing' [robin?] the nest?)

The main event of the six year-old's life came in July, when Mungo Suddon's school closed for the summer holidays, leaving John free to roam the fields and beaches. John mentions that one of his favourite playing areas was the old castle; he wrote that he and his friends

> 'firmly believed that every bone we found in the ruins belonged to some ancient warrior.'

Of his boyhood years in Dunbar, he would later remember that he liked best of all

> 'to watch the waves in awful storms thundering on the black headlands and craggy ruins of the old Dunbar Castle.'

John left the common school at age seven or eight to go to the 'big' school at Woodbush where he learnt Latin, French, English, History, Geography, Arithmetic and Spelling - the broadly standard curriculum which would continue well into the twentieth century. Teaching methods were basic; pupils were expected to learn their Latin primers and grammars by heart, much in the same way as John's disciplinarian father insisted that he memorised parts of the Bible on Saturday nights for the Sabbath School. By the age of eleven, the boy could recite 75% of the *Old Testament* and from *Matthew* to *Revelation* in the *New Testament* without a pause. If this is true - and he admits he received many beatings in and out of school to improve his memory - it is no mean feat. John Muir described his teachers as old-fashioned, with no time for short cuts or innovative, psychological teaching methods. In his laconic words

> 'We were simply driven point-blank against our books like soldiers against the enemy, and sternly ordered, "Up and at 'em. Commit your lessons to memory! " '

Thankfully, such crude methods are no longer in favour although they were still being employed during my education between 1946 and 1958. John's wry comments on his thrashings weren't unfamiliar to my generation either.

> 'If we failed in any part, however slight, we were whipped; for the grand, simple, all-suffering Scotch discovery had been made that there was a close connection between the skin and the memory; and that irritating the skin excited the memory to any required degree.'

It is of course true that the John Muirs of this world will always succeed in what they do despite their education - or lack of it. Education cannot in itself build or create character; it can train and inform the mind but seldom does it make the man or woman. Only experience of life and self-examination can achieve that. Systems are necessary - nature itself teaches us that lesson - but they must be flexible to accommodate individualism and imagination. John Muir succeeded despite rather than because of the educational system of his day because he was able to see beyond its limited horizons. To put it another way, he learnt valuable lessons out of the classroom simply by using his eyes.

Young Muir was no prig however. He joined in the rough-and-tumble of the playground, accepting that fighting was man's nature. He wrote of single combat or 'wars' fought between rival gangs on the seashore. One test of endurance involved two boys whipping each other's bare legs until one succumbed to the pain and asked for quarter. The group battles usually ended in a draw with one side declaring

> 'if ye'll let us alane we'll let ye alane.'

In 1893, John Muir returned to Dunbar and had dinner with the local minister and William Dick, the former headmaster of the Grammar School. During the meal, the minister asked Dick whether he would have liked to have taught in the 1840s and had the

> 'the immortal glory of having whipped John Muir.'

Muir doesn't inform us of the response, commenting only that the minister had also been a fighter in his youth.

A typical day for the Muir children would begin with a breakfast of oatmeal porridge and a little milk or treacle, served in wooden dishes John called *luggies*; then it was school all morning until noon, when a dinner of vegetable broth and boiled mutton - probably from the soup - were served with barley-meal scones which none of the children liked. Afternoon school was followed by tea, consisting of half a slice of white bread without butter, barley scones and warm water with a little sugar and milk added, a drink John called *content.* After that, the boy usually visited Grandfather Gilrye across the street, reciting his lessons to the old man. At the very end of the day, a supper of boiled potatoes and the inevitable barley scones was dished up, followed by family prayers, then bed.

Like most young boys, John delighted in what Americans today call quality time - Saturday afternoons and school holidays - when he could escape the drudgery of lessons and revel in adventures in the countryside or by the seashore. There was keen competition among the boys as to how many species of birds they could identify and how many eggs they could find. John derived immense pleasure from the skylark's song which he maintained no Scottish boy could fail to appreciate for its fluid outpouring. However, he admitted that it was common practice to remove young larks from the nest before they could fly and put them in cages. John confessed he too was guilty of this but added that it was heart-breaking to watch the little birds frustrated in their instinctive attempts to fly skywards. Empathy and perhaps the incident of the baby robins made him set the little birds free in the meadow where they'd been born; he was beginning to learn that the freedom nature gives is beyond price.

It would have been unnatural for any child living in Dunbar, with its rich landscapes and long stretches of beaches not to want to stay out of doors for as long as possible, even risking parental floggings for coming home late. As John wrote:

'no punishment...was of any avail against the attractions of the fields and woods....wildness was always sounding in our ears and Nature saw to it that besides school lessons and church lessons, some of her own lessons should be learned.'

The sense of wildness and beauty of hill and shore never left him:

'Kings may be blessed; we were glorious, we were free,'

John's departure for the USA in 1849 came as a complete surprise. He wrote how one evening, he and one of his brothers were busy with homework at their grandfather's house when Daniel Muir walked in to announce that they needn't finish their lessons as they were emigrating the next day. After what must have been a few emotional moments, Grandfather Gilrye handed each boy a gold sovereign as a keepsake, looking

'very serious for he was about to be deserted in his lonely old age.'

The boys couldn't contain themselves however; they rushed out into the High Street shouting to their classmates

'I'm gan to Amaraka the morn!'

To the Doubting Thomases he simply said:

"Weel, just you see if I am at the skule [school] the morn! [tomorrow]"

Daniel Muir probably surprised his wife Anne as much as her father; he was that kind of man, demanding his right as head of the family. He set off the next day with Sarah, the oldest girl, John and David; the other girls Margaret, Mary and Anna and the youngest boy, Daniel, and their mother would follow once the pioneers had settled in their new home in Fountain Lake Farm, near Portage in the wilds of Wisconsin. John vividly recounts his early impressions of life on the lonely farm where he lived until he reached the age of 21. At age 12, he was put behind the plough, working 17-18 hours a day; his other chores included rail-splitting, fence-making, hoeing the maize crop and mowing with a hand-held scythe. He was once made to quarry out a 90-foot well and almost died from asphyxiation in the process. His disciplinarian father forbade him to read any books other than the Bible in the evenings. This irked the young man so much that he got round the problem by rigging up the first of several outlandish inventions; he made an early-rising machine which consisted of a wooden block hitched to apparatus which tilted his bed forward and set him on his feet. He usually timed the machine to wake him at 1am so that he could enjoy his books before his day's chore. Other early inventions included a self-setting sawmill, water wheels, an automatic horse-feeder and lamp-lighting and fire-lighting devices. In 1860, he took two of his clocks and a thermometer he had made of wood to the Wisconsin State Fair in Madison which brought him into contact with the university authorities. The young man decided to continue his studies; he left home with his grandfather's sovereign and 10 dollars in his pocket. He was forced to take several jobs to pay for tuition and food at Wisconsin University; while there, he invented yet another machine which consisted of a desk which arranged in order the books he needed for study at each term start. He also made a bed which set him on his feet and lit a lamp. His book-selecting machine would then produce the first book he had to read from a rack below the desk, opening it at the first page. The contraption also closed the book and returned it to its proper place on the rack.

Not unexpectedly, John studied botany at Wisconsin. His student days were limited however. Typically, he left university in 1863 without having obtained a degree as he preferred to choose his own subjects for study; in addition to botany, he read geology, chemistry, physics, mathematics and a little Greek and Latin. While attending university, the American Civil War broke out and for two years, he worked in Canada; some accounts maintain he went there to dodge the draft for the Union Army, although recent research indicates that his name was omitted from the first and second draft lists issued in the early stages of the war and that it was one of his brothers who went to Canada to avoid the war. Whatever the truth of it, when the war ended, John was working in a wagon factory in Indianapolis, Indiana, which tends to support the modern view. Sadly, at Indianapolis, he sustained an injury to one eye which forced him

> 'bade adieu to mechanical inventions'.

He decided that from then on, he would devote the rest of his life

> 'to the study of the inventions of God.'

Thus he began a foot-tour of Wisconsin, Iowa, Illinois, Indiana and Canada. It turned out to be a 50-year lesson in botany and geology. The University of Wisconsin had given way to the university of the Wilderness, a learning curve that John Muir instinctively knew would end only when he died.

So, two years after Robert E Lee surrendered to Ulysses S Grant at Appomattox Court House, Virginia, John began his 1,000-mile walk to the Gulf of Mexico. His tour took him through some of the worst devastated lands of the Confederacy, the Old South. On the principle that he who travels lightest travels fast, John's only luggage were a plant press, a brush, towel, soap, change of underwear, a *New Testament*, Burns' poems and Milton's sonnets.

John kept a diary or daily journal, recording his impressions of and observations on the *flora, fauna* and topography of the country as well as some of its inhabitants. There is a touch of rustic, childlike simplicity about his first journal; he entered his name in the fly-leaf, giving his address as *The Earth planet, the Universe* - the kind of entry used by generations of schoolchildren to personalise their exercise books. The journals contain John Muir's spontaneous reflections on man's attitude to and relationship with nature, the animal world and the life-death cycle. From these jottings grew his book *A Thousand Mile Walk to the Gulf*; it is beautifully written, filled with sharp, vivid impressions of the plants and animals he encountered in the Southern States of America. He writes of how he 'met' certain plants - a more prosaic writer would have said 'discovered' but then, like America itself which Columbus had 'discovered' he knew that the plants, like the continent, had never been 'lost'. His poetic descriptions give the impression of a man making new friends, which of course he was. The book was published posthumously in 1916; it encapsulates John Muir's philosophy and conveys his message in a delightfully refreshing style.

The young man had planned to visit South America after crossing to Cubs but instead ended his walk at the Gulf of Mexico. When he reached Florida, he smelt the sea for the first time since leaving Dunbar in 1849; it conjured up images of

> 'rocky coast, winds and waves; and my whole childhood, that seemed to have utterly vanished in the New World, was now restored amid the Florida woods by that one breath from the sea.....I could see only dulse and tangle, long-winged gulls, the Bass Rock in the Firth of Forth, and the old castle, schools, churches, and long country rambles in search of birds' nests....'
>
> (*A Thousand Mile Walk to the Gulf*)

En route, Muir had encountered California and the Yosemite Valley in 1868 which he would explore over the next six years. Although he found the Yosemite already popular with tourists, his visit proved to be an experience which altered the entire course of his life. In his book *My First Summer in the Sierra*, he wrote that the Sierra Nevada mountain range

> 'seemed not clothed with light, but wholly composed of it, like the wall of some celestial city. Well may the Sierra be named not the Snowy Range but the Range of Light.'

That summer of geophysical discovery was also one of self-discovery. John Muir worked as a shepherd in the foothills, filling his journals with impressions and descriptive narrative that are little short of poetry; about 70 of these journals have thankfully survived. Although he earned his daily bread - and modest bread at that - tending sheep, he regarded them as a menace. They destroyed seedling trees, stripped vast areas of vegetation and ruined the forest trails so much so that he was moved to describe them as 'woolly locusts'. His early observations on the effects of sheep on the landscape convinced him of the need for conservation and control of the environment. He also deplored the logging of the beautiful 3,000 year-old giant redwood trees for roofing timber. He wanted to stay in the Yosemite for the rest of his life and he took several jobs there to give him time to explore the entire area.

In John Muir's view, neither words nor images could do justice to the grandeur of the Yosemite and other places like Nevada, Utah, the Northwest and Alaska:

> 'When I am free in the world, I discover some rare beauty in lake or cataract or mountain form and instantly seek to sketch it....but the drawing is always enormously unlike reality. So also in word sketches.... The few hard words make but a skeleton, fleshless, heartless and when you read, the dead boney words rattle in one's teeth.'
>
> (*The Mountains of California*)

It was Muir's theory - now accepted - that the Yosemite (**ill 131**) had been formed by glacial action over thousands of years, not the result of an earthquake as propounded by Josiah Whitney, the California State geologist. Muir's theory was published in the *New York Tribune* in 1871; he reinforced that theory by going to Alaska to study glaciers and how they affected the landscape. In 1879, an Alaskan Indian tribe adopted him, giving him the honorary title *Great Ice Chief*; a glacier in Alaska is named for him. From 1871, Muir attracted public attention; one of his supporters was Ralph Waldo Emerson, the poet and philosopher. After meeting the Scotsman, Emerson admitted that Muir was one of the men who had most influenced his life.

Despite his many and wide wanderings, John Muir found time to get married. He fell in love with Louie Wanda Strentzel, marrying her on 14th April 1880, a week before his forty-second birthday. Louie was the daughter of Dr John Strentzel, a Polish entrepreneur who established the California wine trade. After the unsuccessful revolution of 1830 when Poland tried to break away from Imperial Russia, Strentzel had emigrated to America, married Lousiana Erwin of Tennessee and joined a Clarksville wagon train bound for California in 1849 where he settled and became a well-respected horticulturalist. Muir later bought part of his father-in-law's fruit farm and mastered the technique of vine horticulture; he 'settled' in San Francisco but spent his summers in the Sierra. During 1880-81, he travelled and wrote little as he was busy trying to gather enough money to provide for his wife so that he could resume what he knew was his true vocation. Finding the responsibility of the farm he owned irksome, he sold part of it for capital and leased the rest to provide a regular income for his family's needs. From then on, he devoted the remainder of his life to travel and study.

KRM

Illus 131: *Yosemite*

Muir's fascination with the phenomena of the natural world was limitless and he devoted his years to study the glaciers and forests of America. In addition to defining the origins of Yosemite and disproving the orthodox earthquake theory, he was the first to use the generic term *Yosemite* to describe a type of valley formed by glacial action. In his study of trees, a particular passion was the giant sequoia; his knowledge of different species of trees would be extended by trips to Australia, Africa and South America where he became a noted authority on the most exotic species in these countries.

Muir's feelings about the natural world and the wilderness went deep and were religious; he saw nature as a higher spiritual reality which transcended orthodox religion. In many ways, he compares favourably with D H Lawrence, a writer he never met and whose work he probably never read. Lawrence was another disciple of a world which he hoped would be freed from Blake's 'dark, satanic mills' which he knew from his life in Nottinghamshire, particularly the coal pits where his father worked. Muir's description of a Douglas squirrel he encountered in the pine woods ranks alongside Lawrence's most vivid writings about animals:

> 'The Douglas is the squirrel of squirrels, flashing from branch to branch....One never tires of this bright chip of nature - this brave little voice crying in the wilderness.'
>
> (*The Mountains of California*)

Lawrence would have described the little creature as a 'spark' rather than a chip but if the two men had met, I doubt they would have fallen out over their respective descriptions. In my view, Muir's adjective hits the spot, a little creature flying among the trees like a woodchip from an axe. Lawrence would have strongly endorsed his sentiment that

'Most people are on the world, not in it - [they] have no consciousness, sympathy or relationship to anything about them.'

The message was not simply that nature should be protected from man's depredations but to encourage him to develop a balanced - and spiritual - relationship with it, a fundamental Lawrentian concept.. Perhaps the two men, separated by almost half a century in their ages but with not very different religious upbringings wrote in the style they did because of the latter. Their forms of expression are uncannily similar.

Muir's first encounter with the majestic Redwood (sequoia) trees overwhelmed him; he wrote of the grandeur of the beautiful California Redwood in his familiar Biblical style:

'I wish I were....descending from...this divine wilderness like John the Baptist....crying 'Repent, for the Kingdom of the Sequoia is at Hand.'

(*The Mountains of California*)

In 1876, Muir had begun to broadcast his ecological theories; in a letter to the editor of a Savannah newspaper, he asked how the American forests were to be preserved. It was no rhetorical question; he had the answer. This was the opening shot of a campaign which not only concentrated on conservation on aesthetic grounds but predates the modern ecology movement by a century, highlighting the inter-relationship between trees, soil, climate and people's lives. From then on, a steady stream of articles and letters flowed from his pen. By 1894, he had published his first book, *The Mountains of California*; as a result, he was soon acknowledged as the main and often fiery spokesman for a growing conservation lobby.

In 1889, John Muir persuaded Robert Underwood Johnson, one of the editors of *Century Magazine* to accompany him on a camping tour of the Yosemite Valley region, pointing out the destruction caused by flocks of sheep over the years. At Johnson's suggestion, the pair launched a campaign which would lead to the creation of Yosemite National Park. During the previous decade, *Scribner's Monthly* and the *Century* had published a series of Muir's robust articles on the western forests and landscapes which had fired popular American imagination. Public-spirited people across the whole country responded to the Muir-Johnson movement and the campaign was directly responsible for the enactment of the Yosemite National Park Bill by Congress in October 1890. In time, Muir's political lobbying would lead to the creation of two others-the General Grant and the Sequoia National Parks. In 1891, Congress passed another act which empowered the President of the United States to create forest reserves.

In 1892, Muir played a vital part in founding the Sierra Club which was dedicated to conservation; as its first president, Muir was able to extend the protected boundaries of the Yosemite as America's second National Park. The movement went from strength to strength; as early as 1876, Muir had advocated the formation of a National Parks Commission to investigate the wasting of forests and to plan for their conservation. The Commission finally came into being in 1896, Charles Sargent, director of the Arnold Arboretum being appointed chairman. Sargent wrote several books on *coniferae*, one of which was dedicated to John Muir.

Sargent invited Muir to join the tour of inspection of several forests; in 1897, as a result of the Commission's - and doubtless Muir's - recommendations, President Cleveland created 13 forest reserves of 21 million acres. This didn't go unopposed however; those with vested commercial interests considered conservation as interference in their right to capitalise on natural resources in pursuit of the mighty dollar. Never a defeatist, Muir kept up the pressure, writing several articles for *Harper's Weekly* and the *Atlantic Monthly Review* to keep the issue fresh in the public mind. Muir's style was eminently suited to his task; he borrowed from the Hebrew prophets, language which would have delighted and inspired D H Lawrence. Muir denounced the big business corporations whose governing boards thrived on 'wickedness in high places' allowing the country to be ravished by greed and selfishness. Like Lawrence, Muir believed that on earth, all things are connected even if they aren't always in harmony:

'When we try to pick out anything by itself, we find it hitched to everything else in the universe'.

(*My First Summer in the Sierra*)

Lawrence could scarcely have put it better himself.

The persistent voice which advocated that the landscape and all its rich and wild beauty should be passed on intact to future generations found a willing ear in America's next president, Theodore Roosevelt. In his first term of office in 1903, Roosevelt accompanied Muir on a four-day camping trip and was impressed by the Scot's impassioned views on the need to conserve and preserve more tracts of land and forest by creating more national parks. This trip led directly to Roosevelt's support for Muir; 16 national movements were formed between 1903 and 1909 and the president doubled the number of parks, setting aside 148 million acres of additional woodland reserves. Roosevelt may well have had Muir in mind when he wrote

'We are not building this country of ours for a day. It is to last for posterity.'

It was at this high point in his life, when he had achieved his dream that Muir suffered his worst defeat. In

San Francisco, the city fathers had sought the federal government's permission to dam the beautiful Het-Hetchi Valley in Yosemite, thus creating a reservoir for the city's water supply. Despite vigorous campaigning by Muir, his Sierra Club and even reports by army engineers that there were several alternative sites suitable for the dam, public opinion was swayed in favour of the city fathers' proposal. This probably stemmed from sympathy for the San Francisco population whose city had been wiped out by the earthquake and fires of 1906. Emotional appeal and a considerable degree of political intrigue and commercial muscle ensured the success of the city's second application to dam Het-Hetchi in 1913.

Muir rounded bitterly on big business and the local authorities like an *Old Testament* prophet, decrying their short sightedness with an appropriate pun:

> 'Dam Het-Hetchy [sic]! As well dam for water tanks the people's cathedrals and churches, for no holier temple has ever been desecrated by the hand of man.'

The Bill consenting to the project was passed by Congress in 1913. It was Muir's greatest disappointment and many believed it brought his death the following year. The struggle wasn't in vain however; such were Muir's persuasive arguments that public opinion turned against further developments of this kind. Muir's greatest achievements were however behind him.

John Muir, prophet of the Wilderness, botanist, geologist and polemicist was a man of medium height and spare frame but he possessed impressive powers of physical endurance. His auburn hair turned white, his inquisitive blue eyes - why do so many men and women of conviction and vision have blue eyes? - complimented his engaging personality. In his photographs, he resembles an ancient prophet (**ill 132**). His conversation was easy on the ear, vivid and entertaining, with flashes of well-directed humour; good in argument, his delivery was quick and to the point, speaking in his native Scots tongue. Some of his enthusiasts consider that his thundering *Old Testament* prophet style outbursts were delivered with a certain degree of tongue-in-cheek, a style he deliberately adopted to stir the minds of his audiences. I am not convinced. It may have been an affectation, pure kitsch media-grabbing but as his childhood was steeped in the Bible, it is unsurprising that he employed the style to attract attention.

John Muir never forgot his origins or his home town. He was a theist with leanings towards the philosophies of Emerson and his friend Thoreau but he was unlike either. In time he became a Fellow of the American Academy of Arts and Sciences and received honorary degrees from Harvard, Wisconsin, Yale and California Universities. Not a bad score for a small boy from Dunbar.

In 1913, John Muir wrote prophetically:

Illus 132: *John Muir in late life* RJP

> 'Everybody needs beauty as well as bread, places to play in and pray in, where nations may heal.... and give strength to body and soul alike.'

Perhaps he foresaw the imminence of the Great War and the destruction that lay ahead. A love of nature was indelibly written on his heart during his Dunbar childhood. He returned home only once, in 1893, to remind himself of his early years of which he had once written\:

> 'When I was a boy in Scotland, I was fond of everything that was wild....and all my life, I've been growing fonder and fonder of wild places and wild creatures. Fortunately, around my native town of Dunbar, by the stormy North Sea, there was no lack of wildness....with red-blooded playmates, wild as myself I loved to wander in the fields, to hear the birds sing, and along the seashore to gaze and wonder at the shells and seaweeds, eels and crabs in the pools among the rocks when the tide was low; and best of all to watch the waves in awful storms thundering on the black headlands and craggy ruins of old Dunbar castle where the sea and the sky, the waves and the clouds [were] together as one.'

(*The Story of My Boyhood and Youth*)

In that brief holiday, he walked his beloved shores,

visiting the scenes of his childhood. Dunbar shaped him. He never forgot that, nor did he ever hesitate to admit it. Why should he?

John Muir liked to think of himself as a philosopher-tramp, perhaps some kind of ragged-trousered philanthropist. He became an American hero. His vision of nature, shared with the dwindling Indian tribes was that the land was 'instinct with deity' - yet another phrase of which D H Lawrence would have approved. Muir was certainly ahead of his time; everywhere, he saw the greed of economics in the mining, logging, trapping and ranching and he fought to persuade the American people of their right to enjoy nature, warning them of the need to protect an irreplaceable heritage. Well might he write that

> 'Any fool can destroy trees. They [the trees] cannot run away; and if they could, they would still be destroyed.......'

Through the centuries before the coming of the whites God had cared for these trees and saved them from all manner of natural disasters but

> 'he cannot save them from fools - only Uncle Sam can do that.'

John Muir died on Christmas Eve 1914, eight years after the death of his wife, survived by his two daughters. His life came to an end when the bloodiest war in history was in its early stages. Almost at the same time as his death, the first aerial bombardment of England was carried out by a lone German plane on 21st December; the second raid from the air on Dover occurred on the very day he died. He left a world poised on the brink of an unimaginable disaster, a war that caused unprecedented loss of life and devastated the landscape of Europe. Muir was better off not knowing about it.

A small sapling from Dunbar grew into a great tree in America. Some 200+ sites in that continent are named in John Muir's memory and honour. They include Muir Peak, Muir Crest, Muir Grove, Muir Meadows, the John Muir Memorial Park and Muir Lake Scientific Area (Wisconsin); Mount Muir, Muir Glacier and Muir Inlet (Alaska); Muir Wood and Muir Beach (San Francisco) and the John Muir Wilderness and John Muir Trail (High Sierra, California). Several schools are named for him and he has been immortalised in *flora* and *fauna* - the species of *iversia* muiri - the mousetail plant - and the Sierra butterfly *thecla muiri*. Forgotten in Scotland until 1970 when the Countryside Campaign restored his name to the Scottish people, he was also the subject - at last - of an exhibition organised by the National Library of Scotland in 1979, more than half a century after his death. As yet there are no national parks in Scotland although the John Muir Country Park was formed in 1976 at Dunbar. In 1987, the John Muir Trust purchased a 3,000 acre site in Knoydart to protect and conserve the wild area there. The John Muir Birthplace Trust was formed in 1995 at the instigation of Dunbar's John Muir Association (DJMA), its trustees drawn from the DJMA, Dunbar Community Council and East Lothian Council. Its aim was to raise funds to purchase the house where Muir was born, achieved by 1999. Despite some acrimonious disagreement as to its use, the site is presently being developed as a cultural and heritage centre, devoted to John Muir's aims and beliefs

John Muir shared William Blake's and D H Lawrence's horror of industry and intensive farming; even in his own time, California had a face 'ravaged by disease'. He once wrote

> 'Few in these hot, dim times are quite sane or free, choked with care, doing so much good, making so much money - or so little - they are no longer good for themselves.'

These words apply equally to the stressful world in which we live today. For Muir, man was half-human, half-angel; to preserve and recreate himself, man needed the beauty of the Wilderness . Such Lawrentian philosphy is as true today as it was then. Society needs clean, cool winds blowing over uncorrupted fields and woodlands, hills and beaches to keep its sanity in a world of shifting and ephemeral values. The wild places heal the sick mind, the tired spirit - much more effective in my opinion than what the churches have on offer.

It is to be regretted that for years, ducation authorities in East Lothian kept its children in ignorance of a great local man. We need to approach John Muir with the heart as well as the head; like him, I was never taught to swim but learnt by watching a frog. And I share his belief that animals and birds have souls, a heretical view which had me expelled from the Church of Scotland many years ago, while acting as a Sunday School teacher. For spirits like John Muir, all life is holy; the countryside and the seashore are simply larger classrooms as well as playgrounds, facts which the lovely place of Dunbar teaches so well. Not for nothing did the 23rd Psalm exhort us to lift up our eyes to the hills, where rewards lie. I am a devout atheist and will die one; but that doesn't mean I don't have a soul.

At last, we are beginning to honour our prophet in his own country. And yet, incredibly, a minority in Dunbar voiced their opposition to John Muir's statue - well at least to the site chosen for it - in Dunbar High Street. Where else could it go but within a few yards of the house where he was born? It would have been difficult to site the statue in front of No 128 High Street for a whole variety of reasons, not least the obstruction of the pavement. From a purely nationalistic point of view, perhaps a measure of the opposition stemmed from the fact that the bronze statue which cost £25,000 was the work of a Ukrainian artist, not a Scot. I believe that to be a fatuous arguement, a smokescreen by local nit-pickers. The controversy would have been distasteful to Muir himself; his message was for all people, all countries of the world, not just Scotland or the Scots. About 250 people signed a petition to the Secretary of State for Scotland protesting about the proposed statue.[7] Fortunately, they were unable to fulfil Henrik Ibsen's contention that the minority is always right. As for the statue itself, it is naive, pure Peter Pan - but at least it is here in Dunbar, where the boy laid the foundations for the man he became, never forgetting his love for the town where he was born and which has largely ignored him for too long. Although Dunbar isn't John Muir, John Muir is Dunbar.........

Scotland has her share of writers and John Muir ranks among the best. When he visited his cousin Margaret Lunam in the Lammermuir Hills in 1893, he wasn't only seeing family but revisiting the places of his heart. Writing to his daughter Wanda that year, he described the sea at Dunbar whose waves

> 'made a grand show breaking in sheets and sheaves of foam, and [sang] grand songs, the same old songs they sang to me in my childhood, and I seemed a boy again and all the long years in America were forgotten while I was filled with that glorious ocean psalm.'

In truth, he had never left the place of his birth; it remained uppermost in his mind until he died.

John Muir lies buried on his ranch in Martinez, California, now known by the prosaic name of The John Muir Historical Site. His headstone is decorated with a simple Scots thistle, his choice of design. I envy a man who could write the following words, sharing as I do his sentiments but unskilled enough to express them so well:

> 'A man in his books may be said to walk the earth long after he has gone'

And best of all

> 'I only went out for a walk, and finally concluded to stay out till sundown. For going out, I found I was really going in.'

What better epitaph can there be for the prophet of nature who lies under the Californian earth?

12

Military Annals

Over the past thirteen centuries, Dunbar has lived under the shadow of war. In the last three centuries, its streets have known the braying of bugles, the clatter of horses' hooves and the tramp of feet marching to fife, drum and bagpipes. We know that the community was established around 75AD, occupied at that time by the Votadini, then the Angles; from excavations made in the last decade of the twentieth century, we know that a fortified site had been established around 75AD (see *Castle Park*: Two Thousand Years of a Fortified Headland). When the Angles invaded Lothian in the early seventh century and took Dunbar from the Votadini, they no doubt strengthened the existing fortifications. We know that a wooden fort existed in the ninth century as it was burnt by king Kenneth mac alpin in 856. When Gospatric, Earl of Northumberland arrived in 1072 to found the dynasty of the Dunbars, he would have found a thriving community protected by a palisaded fort, possibly built on the Castle Rock. Thus from earliest times, Dunbar was no stranger to a military presence which continued until the mid-twentieth century. We have already discussed the battles of 1296 and 1650; this chapter will concentrate on the military annals from the post-Cromwellian period, when the comings and goings of militia and territorial units, then regular soldiers of the British Army were a familiar sight on the streets. In turn, the promontory provided accommodation for militia artillery, then it became a cavalry depot, a regular infantry barracks, an Officer Cadet Training Unit with separate accommodation and finally housing mechanised units of the British Army after the Second World War. In the late nineteenth century, artillery practice was conducted from the site now occupied by the Leisure Centre; in the following century, practice ranges for tanks and small arms were established at Hedderwick Links, West Barns Links and the Butts at Belhaven.

During the Middle Ages, like any other burgh, Dunbar was required to hold *wapinschaws* - literally weapon-showings. These military musters were established by Edward I of England under the Statute of Westminster, a measure adopted by Scottish kings, as neither country could afford to maintain a standing army. In times of war, all able-bodied men between the ages of 16 and 60 were required to answer the royal summons to arms at the mercat cross; in peacetime, periodic *wapinschaws* were held to ensure that each man possessed the appropriate arms and accoutrements according to his station in life. For example, nobles, merchants and burgesses were expected to provide themselves with swords and dress in full or partial body armour; the common man equipped himself with bow and arrows, pike or spear and a dagger. By the seventeenth century however, regular army units or companies were being raised by local landowners who usually gave their name to the unit. This practice began during the English Civil Wars and soon spread to Scotland.

The logistics of feeding, equipping and accommodating a standing army didn't begin in the 1640s although it was predominant from then onwards. It is during this period that we learn of Dunbar's statutory obligation as a royal burgh to meet the cost of quartering troops. This seems to have first occurred in 1645, when the local magistrates were ordered to meet the cost of quartering 12 soldiers at a cost of £108 Scots (£18 sterling) a month from 1st March to 31st August and for a further six months in 1646. By 1647, the rate had increased to £180 Scots (£30) a month, the soldiers being quartered for nine months, then a further five in 1648 and so on.[1]

After the defeat of the Army of the Covenant at Dunbar in 1650, the town was obliged to provide quarters and food for the Roundhead regiments stationed there, although Cromwell paid compensation to those who provided it (see Chapter 6). As Governor of Scotland, General Monck later billeted 70 foot and 40 horse at Innerwick and Duns respectively, the cost being met by the English Exchequer. After the Commonwealth ended in 1660, Dunbar settled down to a period of relative peace and a military presence wasn't needed for the next few years. However, the Privy Council ordered every seaport to provide quotas of men for service in the king's navy; in 1664, Dunbar and Belhaven provided 10 men[2] and 4 in 1672.[3] This practice continued for some years until acute shortages in ship's companies were made good by the iniquitous press-gangs which roamed the streets of many seaports seeking 'recruits'.

Covenanters and Jacobites

Meeting the cost of small detachments was one thing but quartering troops on a large scale was beyond the resources of small burghs like Dunbar. The Restoration government of the 1660s expected local landowners to bear the cost of accommodating troops who not unnaturally resented the imposition; the problem was solved by creating militia who also doubled as constables before municipal police forces were established in the nineteenth century. In 1677, the Privy Council ordered half a company of the Earl of Linlithgow's regiment to be quartered at Dunbar to discourage the Covenanter conventicles - gatherings for religious worship in the open air or in barns - within the parish boundary. The troops had orders to apprehend any Covenanters they discovered in the vicinity;[4] their presence seems to have had some effect as the company was recalled shortly afterwards. However, in the following year, conventicles were again reported in the area, especially in the vicinities of East Barns and West Barns.

The period from the Restoration of Charles II in 1660 until the mid-1680s was a time when the government was concerned with the rise of political exiles in Holland; it was feared that these exiles were in league with the Dutch during the Second Anglo-Dutch war of 1665-67. All those who had refused to rescind their oath to the National Covenant were regarded as traitors and a period of repression began almost from the outset of Charles II's reign. Extreme differences of opinion existed in the Privy Council and among the bishops in Scotland as to the treatment of religious non-conformists. When the predominant recusants, the Covenanters, were suppressed in one part of Scotland, they re-appeared somewhere else. Despite harsh measures to suppress the Covenanters, conventicles increased in the Dunbar area between 1676 and 1678. Any who were caught in the periodic sweeps in East Lothian were imprisoned and transported to the Plantations of North America. To maintain order, the government allowed the formation of militia companies by act of parliament in 1663.

Matters came to a head in 1666, with the first of the Covenanter uprisings. Known as the Pentland Rising - something of a misnomer, as the rebellion originated in the south-west of Scotland - the government reacted hysterically, panicked into believing it was connected with the Anglo-Dutch war. The Covenanter 'army' was neither led by any prominent figure, nor was it ever more than 3,000 strong; by November 1666, it had shrunk to about 900 wet, cold, half-starved men disappointed by the lack of sympathy for their cause in the south-east of Scotland. These 'irreconcilables', as they were known by church and state, camped in the Pentland Hills, refusing to negotiate with government-appointed ministers of the Church of Scotland, electing to petition the Privy Council direct to seek religious tolerance. On 28th November, they were caught at Rullion Green in the Pentland mosses by government troops led by General Tam Dalyell, known as the *Muscovite Beast*;[5] after the skirmish, fifty lay dead and 21 of the 80 taken prisoner were executed, the remainder being banished to Barbados. The dead were buried where they fell; the site is marked by the Martyrs' Monument at Rullion Green.

Despite - or perhaps because of - this setback, conventicles were on the increase again, particularly in East Lothian. Then in 1679 a second rising occurred after the murder of Archbishop Sharp near St Andrews. To the Covenanters, Sharp was regarded as something of a Judas, being one of four bishops appointed by the government to forbid meetings of presbyteries or synods without permission. The final act in the Covenanters' bid for religious tolerance took place at Drumclog on 1st June 1679, when the nonconformists won a minor victory over the government forces led by John Graham of Claverhouse. Drumclog raised the Covenanters' hopes; three weeks later, these were dashed at Bothwell Brig, where they were defeated by the Duke of Monmouth, the illegitimate son of Charles II. The fiasco at Bothwell Brig resulted in 30 fatal casualties and many were taken prisoner; this led to the execution of 16 dissenters; in all, about 100 Covenanters were executed and 80 fell in the field; a further 258 were transported. It was hardly justification for dubbing the 1680s as the Killing Time[6] and branding the Lord Advocate, Sir George Mackenzie as 'Bluidy Mackenzie'. After all, the Covenanter Church had executed far greater numbers of women for alleged witchcraft, their victims running into several hundreds between 1644 and 1663.[6] 'Bluidy' Mackenzie is on record as having deplored their hysterical reaction to the supposed existence of so-called witches over that period; the Covenanter Church was entirely responsible for the epidemics of 1644-1650 and 1660-1663

The flag carried at Bothwell Bridge on 22nd July 1679 came into the possession of an old woman in Dunbar by a circuitous route. In his *Lamp of Lothian,* James Miller recounts how he saw the flag on one occasion; it was of blue silk and inscribed in gilt lettering which proclaimed the cause was *For Christ and the Truth*; beneath was the legend *No Quarter for Ye Active Enemies of the Covenant.* Brave words, they instilled little inspiration at Bothwell Bridge. In 1817, James Hogg, the Ettrick Shepherd visited Dunbar and tried to coax the old lady to bequeath the flag to an antiquarian society but she refused, saying she couldn't part with the honours of her family. Apparently, some time after the battle, the flag was passed to James Raeburn, a cabinetmaker in Dunbar. It had first been in the possession of Henry Hall of Heughhead, a Covenanter present at Bothwell Brig. Hall then gave it to his son who passed it to James Cochran, a shoemaker in Greenlaw. Cochran subsequently gave it to Michael Naismyth, who in turn passed it to Cochran's son-in-law James Raeburn in Dunbar. One can but speculate where the flag is today.

In 1689, parliament's Committee of Estates ordered Sir John Sinclair of Longformacus - then owner of Lochend Estate in Dunbar - the Laird of Spott and Robert Lauder of the Bass to 'concur with the magistrates of Dunbar for taking care of his Majesteis forces [ie those of William of Orange], horfe [horse] or Dragoons which fhall [shall] happen to be within the presbyteries of Durnbar [sic] and to provyde them with Oats, Hay and Straw.'[7]

It is probable that the army was then operating in the vicinity to discourage supporters of the recently-deposed James VII and II from taking any punitive action, although James' flight on 23rd December 1688 and the arrival of William of Orange to take the throne were aspects of a predominantly English crisis, one whose effects are not easily traceable in Scotland.

NMS

Illus 133: *The Bass Rock*

The first stirrings of Jacobite rebellion came in 1691, when 20 determined men captured the Bass Rock (**ill 133**) in James VII's name and defended it until 1694, when they surrendered on honourable terms. Before that however, on 10th December 1691, the Privy Council ordered Colonel Lawder to march his own and Colonel Beveridge's regiments to Dunbar and Prestonpans to monitor the activities of a French man-o'-war delivering supplies to the Bass Rock.

In 1694, a party of Bass Rock Jacobites managed to board a vessel which was becalmed off the Rock. The ship had been commissioned by Bailie William Kirkwood of Dunbar to transport his cargo of grain to Leith. The Jacobites took command of the vessel, intent on providing their colleagues with bread but a sudden storm rose, carrying the vessel to the coast off St Andrews. Sense prevailed; the Jacobite pirates sought to be set on land and they escaped into the wilds of Angus, no doubt glad to be back on land (*TELAS,*1979).

In 1696, the 2nd Lord Belhaven commanded the Haddingtonshire Foot Militia, thus proving that he was no Jacobite sympathiser and was loyal to William III, even if ten years later, he was one of the few opponents of union with England. A greater threat came in 1708 when James VIII, known to history as the Old Pretender, mounted an unsuccessful invasion of Scotland to reclaim the throne from William III. Unfortunately for James, the French fleet carrying an army of 6,000 ran into a storm and was forced to limp back to Dunkirk with some loss of life. James later distinguished himself on the fields of Oudenarde and Malplaquet (1708-09) fighting alongside the French against the Duke of Marlborough, Lord Churchill of Eyemouth. However, during the emergency of 1708, the Dunbar magistrates ordered Bailie Fall to apply to the Privy Council for

'100 stands of fyre armes [firearms] out of the magazine of Edinburgh Castle.....and
200 lbs weight of lead and musket balls'

from Newcastle so that at least some of the population could be armed to meet any threat to the burgh; the armed men were in effect an early form of the Home Guard of 1939-1945.

In 1715, when James VIII and III (the Old Pretender) landed his forces on the Scottish coast to precipitate the first of two major Jacobite rebellions, the burgh council minutes of 30th December record that Dunbar was required to provide a quota of 21 mobile militiamen; in addition, a small squad of 20 men, a sergeant and a captain were appointed for local defence. The same minute records that intimation was to be given to all able-bodied men in the burgh to enlist as volunteers; by way of inducement, they were to receive their Burgess Ticket, a shilling sterling for enlisting and sixpence a day for the duration (5p and 3p respectively). In 1715, Sir George Warrender of Lochend, the Whig politician and late provost of Edinburgh - he had given up his appointment to become an MP - wrote to the city fathers advising them how to keep control in Edinburgh; an attempt by local Jacobites to take Edinburgh Castle in September failed but it caused sufficient alarm to prompt Sir George to ask Westminster for regular troops to be stationed in the capital during the emergency. It is interesting - and somewhat ironic - that the 3rd Lord Belhaven commanded the East Lothian troop of Horse on the government side at the indecisive battle of Sheriffmuir on 13th November 1715; his father had been arrested on suspicion of Jacobite sympathies only seven years earlier.

KRM

Illus 134: *Bonnie Prince Charlie*

If the '15 was short-lived and somewhat farcical, the '45 was equally brief but tragic, mainly because of its youthful, impetuous and militarily inexperienced leader Charles Edward Stuart *aka* Bonnie Prince Charlie (**ill 134**). There was little that was bonnie about Charlie apart from his looks; idealistic, vain and wilful, he refused to listen to the sound advice of his aides - experienced military men like Lord George Murray. Time has given the '45 a patina of romance and the mists of the years have softened its sad and tragic outcome; a romantic Scotland, obsessed with lost causes, allows her to overlook Charles' less attractive character and celebrate his failure in sweet-sad songs and poems. Those with a more practical approach readily admit that he would have been a disaster as a king and the restoration of the Stuart dynasty perhaps calamitous.

The cards were stacked against Charles from the outset. By 1745, Britain maintained a standing army so the Jacobites were obliged to seek seasoned troops as well as arms from abroad while conveniently ignoring the British government's propaganda that they were pawns of foreign - Catholic - powers. Having said that, the mainstay of the Jacobite cause in Scotland were the Episcopalian rather than the Catholic Highland Clans. Webster's remarkably accurate census of 1755 gives only 16,490 Roman Catholics in a population of 1.2 million Scots; even discounting women and children, the number of Catholic males who followed the Jacobite flag raised at Glenfinnan was disproportionate to the non-Catholics who supported Charles.

KRM

Illus 135: *Battlefield of Prestonpans in the mid 19th century*

Enough has already been written of the '45 rebellion and there is little purpose in revisiting the conflict other than to examine its peripheral effects on Dunbar. The young prince's initial tactics were blessed by success, more by the inexperience of the English army sent against him than by sound judgement. Lieutenant-General Sir John Cope had flagrantly disobeyed his orders, eschewing a confrontation with the Jacobites at the Great Glen in Inverness-shire, thus allowing Charles to march south and take Edinburgh with ease, although the castle held out against him. Cope, having thrown away his opportunity in the north, shipped his 2,000 raw recruits from Inverness to Dunbar, landing there on 17th September. (The remains of a set of steps in the Old Harbour are known locally as Cope's Steps). Cope 'borrowed' the 'stand of armes' which Bailie Fall had obtained to meet the threat in 1708. At Dunbar, Cope was joined by Brigadier Fowkes and two regiments of Dragoons led by Colonels Gardiner and Hamilton who had retreated from Edinburgh on the approach of the Highland army. Gardiner had dinner with the Reverend Pyott of Dunbar Parish Kirk the night before Cope left for Edinburgh. A few of the nobility joined the army on its march to Prestonpans but left it as soon as the prospect of an engagement drew near; among them were William, 8th Earl of Home, then holding a commission as general in the British Army, Francis Scott, 6th Lord Napier of Merchiston, Andrew Fletcher and Lord Milton. On 21st September, the day of Cope's defeat at Prestonpans (**ill 135 and 136**), the frantic Dunbar magistrates wrote to the Lord Advocate in Edinburgh, informing him they had weapons which they didn't want to fall into rebel hands; the armoury contained 101 muskets, 95 bayonets and 35 pistols. The burgh council minutes ruefully record the requistion of 100 muskets by Cope, who had lost them

'on the bloody field of Prestonpans.'

Cope's appropriated weapons weren't replaced until 1747.[8]

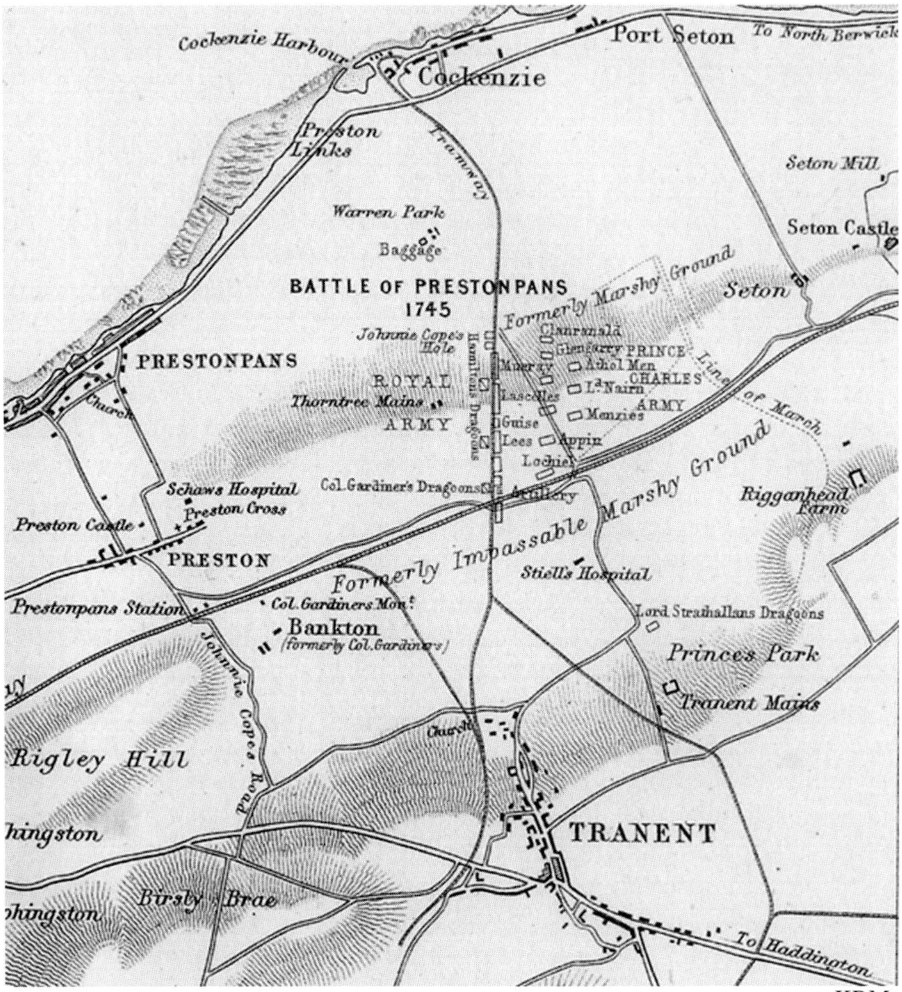

KRM

Illus 136: *Plan of the battle of Prestonpans*

Prestonpans sent shockwaves throughout the Establishment in England; in London, George II was preparing to flee the country when the rebels, disappointed by the lack of support from Jacobite sympathisers in Lowland Scotland and in the North of England, halted at Derby to take stock of their position. The Jacobite council of war's decision to march into England had been carried by a majority of only one; most of the Highland chiefs opposed the decision and at Derby - only 127 miles from London - the ablest of the military strategists, Lord George Murray, voted to retreat northwards, only one Highland chief supporting Charles' plan to march on the capital. Charles reluctantly agreed and sullenly led his troops back across the Border. The small army had nonetheless made outstanding progress in six weeks; and Prince's disappointment was all the more bitter for that. He never forgave Lord George Murray. Retreating in good order, the Highlanders were still a formidable force; on 28th January 1746, they inflicted another defeat on the government army at Falkirk, routing General Hawley's troops who had passed through Dunbar, cheered by supporters of the Hanoverian monarchy. However, one thing was clear to the Hanoverian generals; there was now no question of an invasion by the French in the south so two fresh armies were sent after the Prince, the main led by William, Duke of Cumberland, the king's second son. Cumberland rested at Dunbar and was lavishly entertained by the magistrates before proceeding to his destiny at Culloden.

Dunbar was predominantly Whig in its political sympathies; it was also a royal burgh in a Hanoverian reign which had been marked by booming trade and years of peace that convinced Lowland noble and merchant alike that rebellion was the last thing they or the country needed. The Dunbar magistrates sent a letter of congratulation to George II on the successful suppression of the rebellion on 26th April - exactly 10 days after Culloden. Parts of the letter are quoted below to demonstrate the extent of the burgh's loyalty to the Hanoverian succession. To modern eyes, the letter is sycophantic but at the time it was written, it was prompted by a sense of genuine relief on the magistrates' part:

' ....the many blefsings [blessings] we have enjoyed under your Majestie's mild and auspicious

> Government Do with the Greatest Sincerity declare the vile abhorrance We have ever had against the wicked and unnatural Rebellion which was raised and promoted in this Kingdom in favour of a Popish Pretender, a meer [sic] Tool and minion of the French King. We have ever looked upon the Support of your Majestie's Government to be the only Interest of these Kingdoms and the authores and abettors of this Monstrous Rebellion to be a Sett of men destitute of all Regard to their country who wanted to introduce Tyranny and Popery in Exchange for our Noble liberties civil and religious [at] the expence [sic] of so much blood and treasure Secured to us by the Happy Revolution and of which we have had the Most Ample enjoyment under your August House......and Your sending down His Royal Highness the Duke [of Cumberland] to command the army, was such an instance of your Paternal Goodnefs [Goodness]as we hope will never be forgot by our later Posterity.......and we highly felicitate your Majestie on the Joyfull event A Glorious and Compleat Victory gained over the Rebells by your Arms under the command of this illustrious Hero [Cumberland], who we shall always look upon under your Majestie as the Deliverer of our Country.'

The magistrates ended by offering a rather lame excuse for their part - or more accurately, the lack of it - in helping to suppress the rebellion:

> 'It was owing to the Inconsidreablenefs [small size] of our community that we did not Manifest what our Royalty [ie the royal burgh] dictated towards the Suppression of this Unnaturall Rebellion.'[9]

An interesting footnote to the Jacobite rebellions is that in 1725, the Old Pretender had resuscitated the honorific Earl of Dunbar, granting the title to James Murray, second son of Viscount Stormont, who had acted as the Prince's tutor. Yet another footnote is that for years afterwards, the Dunbar magistrates were censured by pro- and anti-Jacobite alike for its perhaps too lavish hospitality towards the Scottish and English officers in Cumberland's army.

With memories of the '45 still fresh in the government's mind, troops of cavalry and dragoons were thereafter regularly stationed at Dunbar, certainly in 1757, when 'stables for the dragoons' are mentioned in the burgh council minutes in May that year, then again in 1758.[10] Even if economic and social change led to the complete reduction of the Stuart cause after Culloden, there was sufficient life in the movement to make yet another attempt on the British throne. As late as 1759, Sir Alexander McKenzie Douglas of Kildin, an advisor to James VIII, proposed a landing at Bristol where he hoped to attract thousands of Welsh Jacobites to the cause. At the same time, he proposed diversionary landings at Glasgow and either Dunbar or Newcastle. The English navy put paid to these last feeble flickerings; by the end of that year, the Jacobite candle was finally extinguished, although unrealistic plotting continued during the remaining years of the eighteenth century.

In 1762, a yeomanry volunteer unit was embodied at Dunbar, its members drawn from respectable elements in the burgh and gentlemen farmers in the parish. Being volunteers, the unit wasn't recognised by the government as Scotland was forbidden to raise militia battalions because of a residual fear of Jacobite resurgence. While it was all very well to include Scottish regiments in the regular army, the idea of armed militia roaming the countryside unsupervised by regular officers was a nightmarish prospect in Whitehall. The Whig government of 1760 had passed an act to prevent the enrolling of militia, a measure by no means unpopular in Scotland. In 1762, the Earl of Haddington chaired a committee which sought the views of various counties and royal burghs on the question of militia and recommended the need to have such companies. *Miller, Dunbar* records that Haddington burgh opposed the measure though the county and the burghs of Dunbar and North Berwick supported it. Perhaps some gentlemen farmers disliked the idea because it deprived them of their workforce. However, the middle-class in Dunbar went ahead with their own volunteer force, taking care not to call themselves militia.

On 29th January 1772, Dr James Hamilton, physician in Dunbar and tenant of Hallhill Farm adjacent to Lochend Estate - reputedly the first Dunbar farmer to grow turnips for cattle fodder - successfully petitioned parliament for the feu of ground at West Barns to build stables for quartering the King's Dragoon Regiment whenever it passed through Dunbar. Dr Hamilton had an eye for business; he also sold fodder to the regiment! Thus began Dunbar's long association with the military, a link which would continue until after the Second World War. In 1778,[11] the magistrates received a letter dated 3rd September from Captain Charles Napier at Leith, warning them that two French frigates and a cutter had left Dunkirk and were bound for the east coast. After some discussions with the Falls - owners of the *East Lothian and Merse Fishing Company* - it was suggested that a coastal battery should be built to defend the entrance to the Old Harbour, a suggestion eagerly accepted by Provost Robert Fall. A committee was formed to consider the proposal, the fishing company agreeing to share the cost with the burgh council. Delays occurred however and the Battery wasn't built until the second half of 1781, after attacks by John Paul Jones and Captain G Fall (see Chapter 3). We cannot say for certain that Captain Fall was any relation to the provost but it seems suspiciously too much of a coincidence -

did Robert orchestrate the incident to justify the burgh's expense on the Battery? Certainly, he had a vested interest in its construction, as his own vessels would be protected by it. Even before the Battery was built, the site on Lamer Island was used to repel Fall the freebooter in 1781. Both he and the guns on shore exchanged three shots apiece without inflicting damage, although one of the shore shots directed by Geordie Spiers, an old seaman, nearly carried away the mast of Fall's ship.[12] This incident precipitated action on the part of the burgh council; the contract for erecting the Lamer Island Battery was agreed in June 1781,[13] when Provost Robert Fall wrote to William Nisbet of Dirleton, landlord of Skateraw, requesting stone from his quarry there to build the Battery's platform. At the time, it was agreed to mount six guns to keep costs to a minimum. Nisbet responded on 11th June, indicating he would supply the stone for both platform and coping. In the same year, the Battery militia complement included Robert Melville, Charles Lorimer and Robert Macklish [MacLeish?]- all members of Dunbar Castle Lodge. By 1782, the Battery accommodated 12 guns -9, 12 and 18 pounders - increased to 16 guns by the time of the Napoleonic Wars. (There is a cannon embedded in the quayside at the Old Harbour which serves as a bollard; did it come from the Battery, or as some maintain, was it rescued from the wreck of the *Pallas* in 1810? Another small cannon on the wall of a house at the Victoria Harbour appears to be a naval signal gun rather than a piece of ordinance, although this is conjectural). On 30th May 1782, the burgh council invited the local farmers to an evening's entertainment by way of thanking them for carting stones for the Battery from Skateraw. The carting operation wasn't without incident however; in 1783, the council was moved to respond indignantly to a demand from the tacksman [tollkeeper] at the east tollgate for unpaid toll charges amounting to £9:18:6 (£9.92) for the use of the turnpike road in transporting the stone! The magistrates duly informed the tollkeeper that they'd obtained an exemption from the trustees for the road, probably reminding the troublesome bureaucrat that the Battery had been built in the interests of local - if not national - security.

By the time of the Napoleonic Wars, the Battery had furnaces for heating roundshot to set fire to enemy vessels. In February 1793 however, the building had fallen into disrepair and it had to be restored the following month with a guard mounted at night.[14] When the Battery was inspected in 1795 by a lieutenant of Royal Engineers, he recommended that two of its guns be placed on the old castle in order to

'assist the effect of the guns in the battery or.....command the bay to the westward.'[15]

At the end of the war with France in 1815, the Battery's ordnance was removed to Edinburgh Castle. In time, the Battery served as an isolation or infectious disease hospital, then as a hospital/convalescent home for soldiers wounded in the First World War. At the end of that war, it was closed, its patients being transferred to Yorke House Cottage Hospital at the East Links, a site now occupied by sheltered houses known as Broadhaven and Lammermuir House, a private nursing home. The Battery's residual buildings were accidentally set on fire by a bonfire lit to celebrate the coronation of Edward VIII in 1936 - a veritable bonfire of the vanities, given the brief reign of that unhappy, love-smitten man.

Perhaps because of the visits from Captains John Paul Jones and George Fall, the South Fencibles under the command of the Duke of Buccleuch were sent to Dunbar and quartered at West Barns Links, joining the 21st Regiment of Foot. These units were relieved in 1783 by the Essex Light Dragoons and a ' regiment of Black Horse' [the 7th (Princess Royal) Dragoon Guards].

Napoleonic Wars

When France was declared a republic in 1792 and Louis XVI was beheaded the following year, Europe was shocked; several countries began to re-arm for the inevitable conflict that would follow. Britain had already declared war on the republic in 1792; a year later, Dunbar was in a state of readiness, its Battery repaired and operational. In subsequent years, the burgh council offered to help with the costs of providing barrack accommodation for use during the emergency.[16] At the same time, the provost of the day proposed to raise a corps of volunteers to man the Battery's guns and to train in the use of small arms. Perhaps these were the 100 men later known as the Dunbar Defensive Company formed in 1793 by Major George Hay; after Hay was appointed to a militia unit, the Company was commanded by Christopher Middlemass. The burgh asked the government to provide *cartouches* - small wooden ammunition boxes attached to a militiaman's waist belt - and other items of equipment to make the men more comfortable while on duty. The council itself donated 50 guineas to the Company for new equipment.

The first substantial armed camp was built in 1794 at West Barns and was occupied by the Scots Brigade - the future 94th Regiment of Foot and the 4th Regiment of Dragoons - commanded by General Francis Dundas. One of Dunbar's prominent residents, Philip Delisle - for whom a street was named in the West Port - was at that time serving in the 13th Regiment of Dragoons and he may have been stationed at Dunbar. The camp was next occupied by the Dumbarton, Lanark and Dumfries Fencibles. In 1797, the anonymous author of *A Journey to the Northern Parts of Greater Britain*[17] refers to the New Inn Barracks in the High Street, a property occupied exclusively by officers; he mentions regiments he saw on the sands at Belhaven and West Barns - the Cambridge Fencibles, the Windsor Foresters, the East Lothian Yeomanry Cavalry - formed according to *Miller, Dunbar* in 1797 - and a fourth which the writer was unable to identify.

In some respects, the initial years of the Napoleonic Wars were not dissimilar to the 'phoney' war of 1939-40. By 1797, the war had progressed in a patchy, ill-managed way and only Britain's navy prevented a French invasion. A contemporary description of the war was that it was a conflict between a whale and an elephant as neither power was able to attack the other. Napoleon resolved the stalemate by undertaking a conquest of the Turkish possession of Egypt, the stepping-stone to India, jewel in the British crown. The 1801 campaign was a disaster for the French largely due to Nelson's brilliant naval victory at Aboukir Bay and the land engagement fought and won at Alexandria by Sir Ralph Abercrombie, who was fatally wounded; one of the officers who took part in the battle was Major General George Don who was also wounded but survived to become second-in-command of the Scottish-based forces in 1803. We shall learn more of George Don presently.

Before these significant successes however, the worsening military position produced a change of heart in a government desperate for manpower; in 1797, an unwanted Militia Act was passed, largely the work of Lord Advocate Henry Dundas, known as 'Harry the Ninth, uncrowned king of Scotland', a surrogate Secretary of State for Scotland when the post was abolished after Culloden; his family descended from the Earls of Dunbar. Highly unpopular for his skilful manipulation of a corrupt electoral system, Dundas had made an earlier attempt to introduce a Scottish Militia Bill in 1792 which failed because of the government's continuing nervousness about Jacobite resurgence. However, five years on, the situation had changed; a French invasion was expected at any time on the east coast of Scotland. French men o' war were increasingly seen in the eastern seas, close to the shore and intent on identifying likely invasion sites. On 7th March 1797, Henry Dundas, the future Viscount Melville, outlined to parliament his ideas about the defence of the country;[18] he proposed to raise an additional 1,500 regular troops, 2-2,500 militiamen and 3-4,000 cavalry with a due proportion of artillery

'either encamped or cantoned at Dunbar, or some other place about the south of the Firth of Forth'

to defend Edinburgh. In June 1797, the Militia Bill became law and provided for the raising of 6,000 militiamen for service in Scotland. Schoolmasters in every parish were required to compile a list of every able-bodied man between the ages of 19 and 23, the list to be posted on church doors on the Sunday preceding meetings of the Deputy Lord Lieutenants in every shire, when requests for exemptions would be heard. Married men with more than two children were automatically exempt from service but this didn't prevent demonstrations against the Militia Act. The pay was reasonably attractive however; a militiaman received one shilling a penny and a half (6p) a day at a time when men were fortunate to earn six or seven shillings (30-35p) a week for heavy farm work.

Enforcing the Militia Act brought riots in Eccles (Berwickshire), Tranent (East Lothian), Galloway, Central Scotland, Fife, Perthshire and Aberdeenshire; there were also peaceful demonstrations at Gifford, Haddington and Dunbar on 28th and 29th August 1797. One of the worst riots was severely put down at Tranent on 29th August. The *Cinque Portes* [Sussex]Dragoons shot or sabred 11 people, a twelfth victim later dying of wounds. Nevertheless, militia units were embodied in the autumn, after the harvest was brought in.

To avoid confusion, it may be helpful here to define the various types of military units which existed at the time:

Fencibles:	units raised by individuals - usually major landowners; permanent forces paid by the government
Militia:	conscripted men who could avoid service if married with three or more children or were already volunteers or who could provide a substitute on payment of a fine which was used to buy the substitute; militia could be summoned at short notice for serviceanywhere in Britain although the Militia Act of 1797 stipulated that while men had to serve for the duration plus one month, they only served in Scotland; they were in effect the forerunners of the Territorial Army; pay and equipment was provided by the government
Volunteers:	civilian, part-time soldiers supplied with government arms, usually meeting to drill twice-weekly; they were the equivalent of the Home Guard; volunteer units had artillery companies in coastal town like Dunbar, with infantry and cavalry units in the rural areas; the men provided their own uniforms and served only in the district where they were raised.[19]

The commander-in-chief of all military personnel in Scotland was the unlikely-named Earl of Moira, later

Marquis of Hastings; from 1803, his second-in-command was Major General Sir George Don who had fought the French at Alexandria.

In 1797, Robert Hay of Spott established the 75-man strong 4th Dunbar Troop of the East Lothian Yeomanry, a volunteer cavalry unit which contained three other troops of 50 men from towns like Haddington. The Yeomanry were later amalgamated with a Border cavalry unit, becoming the East Lothian and Berwickshire Yeomanry, ultimately the Lothian and Border Horse. We have already noted the formation of the Dunbar Defensive Company of volunteer artillerymen in 1793. Then in 1803, the Dunbar Loyal Volunteers were formed; they were an infantry unit numbering 320 men and like other volunteer outfits, the Dunbar men were determined to cut a dash with their uniforms. At that time, the regular soldier's uniform was smarter, more comfortable and colourful than it would ever be again. The Dunbar Volunteers wore the regular army scarlet tunic but adopted green facings - collars and cuffs - with white lace across the chest, white breeches and black, knee-length gaiters. They wore the French-style 'stovepipe' shako headgear - rather like a top-hat - of the regular army, later replaced by the more attractive and serviceable 'Belgic' shako of 1812.

The main difference between the uniform worn by the Volunteers and regular army regiments was in the quality of the cloth; as the Volunteers paid for their own uniforms, the material was generally superior in quality to government issue. The Dunbar Volunteers were organised on the same basis as regular infantry regiments; these consisted of 6 battalion companies, identified by a white-over-red shako plume, a grenadier company with an all-white shako plume and a light company with an all-green plume. Each company contained 40 men, although some sources indicate that the Dunbar Volunteers consisted of only 4 companies of 80 men. The eight-company formation was standard for the time and it was probably used by the Dunbar Volunteers. The unit was commanded by Major Christopher Middlemass. In November 1803, General Sir George Don wrote[20] to Major Middlemass suggesting improvements in the Volunteers' equipment to make the men more efficient soldiers. Again, Dunbar burgh council chipped in, paying 50 guineas for this purpose.

Thus Dunbar was well prepared for and made a considerable contribution in manpower to meet the threatened invasion of the east coast; 500 local men were in uniform - more than 10% of the burgh 's population - and they were supported by a formidable battery of 16 cannon. In addition., local men served in the regular army as we know that a troop of Scots Greys - about 80 men - from Dunbar and district took part in the Union Brigade cavalry charge at Waterloo. A local gentleman farmer, Major Anderson of Winterfield was present on the field, serving in the Royal Artillery on that decisive day of 18th June 1815.

War generates its own distinctive brand of bureaucracy and injustice, as can be seen in the following incident which occurred in 1800. Peter Runciman of Dunbar - one of a family whose name appeared frequently in the burgh police records of that century - usually for being drunk, but let us not dwell on that - was a seaman on the *Duke of Gordon*, a ship owned by Christopher Middlemas. Peter Runciman had been taken prisoner by the French when his ship was captured en route to Naples in trade. The entire ship's crew had their clothing impounded to prevent their escape, then they were exchanged for French prisoners-of-war. Runciman's ship berthed in London and he sailed to Leith in a fishing smack; walking to Dunbar, he was

> 'overhauled by the Press Gang belonging to Fisherow [Musselburgh] who said he had ran from a King's Cutter but he informed them he was exchange for French prisoners and was on his way home, but they would not believe him and took all his clothes from him which he had on his back packed up in his Trousers,'

He was told to write to the Regulating Captain at Leith by decree of Mr Middlemas, his employer, to claim

> 'a hat, jacket, vest, handkerchief, shirt, pair of trousers and a pair of stockings, all packed up in the Trousers, except the hat.'[21]

Poor Peter Runciman. One hopes he retrieved his belongings. A century later, one of his descendants was among the crew of the *William Arthur Millward*, the Dunbar lifeboat of the time.

Perhaps Dunbar's merchants and local businessmen like George Miller were privately grateful to Napoleon. With an expanding military presence, the local traders made small fortunes from army contracts for the supply of meat, bread and other commodities. For example, in 1804, a loaf of bread cost ninepence (4p); with the town's population boosted by 1,500 militiamen - 35% of the peacetime population - local bakers were grossing about £1,000-1,500 a year in added business. The butchers, brewers, grain sellers and blacksmiths certainly benefited from the war, supplying the army with beef, ale, hay and horseshoes. The Napoleonic Wars brought about a military presence in Dunbar for the next 150 years; fortunes made in 1797-1815 enriched families whose descendants continued to trade - and prosper - until the twentieth century.

By 1802, the Dunbar Defensive Company had been disbanded. In the following year, the threat of invasion had reached panic proportions. That year of 1803, General Don was appointed second-in-command to the Earl of Moira for all military forces stationed in Scotland. Don regularly visited the camps at Dunbar - the Heugh

Heads, Gala Green/Belhaven (cavalry barracks) and West Barns - accommodating 300 artillerymen, 300 cavalrymen and 1,200 infantry.

A brief biographical note about George Don is appropriate here. The younger son of Sir Alexander Don of Newton in the parish of Nenthorn, near Kelso, the Dons held a baronetcy from 1667 until 1862, when the last male in the family became an actor and sold his land and property to Charles Balfour of Whittingehame. George Don joined the army in 1780 aged 14, becoming ensign, then brevet-major in the 31st Foot Regiment in 1785. He was stationed at Gibraltar from 1784 until 1792 and bought the colonelcy of the 31st Foot in 1789. His next major posting came in 1795, when he joined the Duke of York's army in the first of two disastrous expeditions to the Netherlands. Promoted Major-General in 1798, Don was given command of the troops on the Isle of Wight, then he commanded a brigade in the second Netherlands expedition in 1799. In that year, the Duke of York was forced to seek an armistice; Don was sent to the French lines under a flag of truce but was taken prisoner until he was exchanged the following year-possibly along with Peter Runciman, the debagged Dunbar sailor. As noted earlier, Don was present on the field of Alexandria with Abercrombie. In 1803, he was promoted to Lieutenant General and became the Earl of Moira's deputy. In this capacity, he came to Dunbar many times, issuing standing orders to ensure the camp at West Barns was in constant readiness. For example, every soldier was required to carry 60 rounds of ball cartridge and two days' provisions at all times. Don also advised the troops to dip their legs in the sea - he believed it would strengthen them - and he ordered his men to meet the French with the bayonet in the Belhaven surf, as he rightly contended that the great mistake the French made in Egypt in 1801 was to allow British troops to get ashore.

The barracks at Dunbar, Belhaven and West Barns were built quickly and at considerable expense to the government. The artillerymen and some infantry were accommodated west of Dunbar Castle in what was known as the Heugh Heads [the West Promenade]; 300 cavalrymen were housed and stabled in the area from Gala Green to Summerfield House[22] with the bulk of the infantry camped at Belhaven and West Barns. Although the Treaty of Amiens concluded by Prussia, Britain and Spain on 27th March 1802 ended hostilities for a time, war was resumed the following year and invasion remained a key part of Napoleon's plans for Britain. He assembled a Grand Army of 150,000 at Boulogne, where it remained for the next two years. Coincidentally in 1803, a French officer, General Charles Demouriez defected to Britain as he detested Napoleon and was sceptical of his invasion plans. Perhaps British intelligence considered him a spy as he meticulously analysed possible invasion sites but considered the east coast of Scotland an unlikely one.[23] The military thinking at the time was that Napoleon would come by way of the Channel and land somewhere in southern England, where in Sussex the Royal Military Canal was created and several Martello Towers were built as strong points. Nonetheless, the camps at Dunbar and West Barns were kept up to strength and on constant alert.

Camp life was comfortable at Dunbar. The soldiers' accommodation consisted of stout wooden huts, roofed with the inevitable red pantiles, with cooking stoves for every hut's 20-30 occupants. Be that as it may, the easy life was also monotonous although there were brief interludes of excitement. Rumours of invasion in 1803 grew to fever pitch, prompting General Don to issue orders from West Barns to the effect that the militia in North Berwick, Aberlady and Dirleton should occupy the Garleton Heights at the first signs of trouble. In addition, three troops of the East Lothian Yeomanry were ordered to a new position in Haddington, the fourth (Dunbar) troop proceeding to Dunbar to join the cavalry units already there. Such periods of flurried activity were few and far between however and the men, like soldiers in any war, relied on their sense of humour for relief or drowned their boredom in the local alehouses.

A humorous - and timeless - incident is recorded in Martine's *Reminiscences of the Royal Burgh of Haddington*; it is a typical *Dad's Army* episode. At the height of the invasion scare in 1803-04, Martine wrote of George Wood, a Haddingtonshire volunteer known for obvious reasons to his comrades as *Crackie-Fartie*. One night, Wood was on sentry duty at the shore and hearing a loud noise, thought the French had landed. He discharged his musket into the darkness and ran back to the camp to raise the alarm. The 'French' turned out to be a gaggle of wild geese cackling on Belhaven Beach!

It is perhaps worth pausing here to examine the steps taken to fortify the east coast and also compare the threatened French invasion with that of Germany a century and a half later. An observation point was created on Blackcastle Hill in 1800; it was a logical place for it followed in the footsteps of two 6th century Votadini forts. The local people were prepared to sell their lives dearly, hopefully stopping the invaders on the seashore. Unfortunately, like their descendants in 1940, they possessed neither weapons, adequate fortifications or training to do more than delay a determined - and in 1940 - a vastly superior enemy. The men of the Napoleonic period were undoubtedly brave and felt soldierly in their fine uniforms of scarlet, laughing at each other's awkwardness and mistakes in drilling and marching like any other citizen army before or since. The coastline from Belhaven to the Tyne basin was particularly vulnerable with its long stretches of flat beaches, an ideal landing place in 1803 and 1940. Although there appears to be no contemporary records of the local fortifications other than the Battery at the harbour, there would have been *chevaux de frises* - long timber poles sharpened at the business end and placed in front of the trenchworks. There was no barbed wire in that period - only short-range muskets and cold steel. In 1940, the coastline was edged with double and treble rows of concrete anti-tank blocks arranged in zig-zag patterns to shelter riflemen and hopefully prevent tanks from breaking out of the beach-head. Britain could never be sure that Napoleon would abandon his planned invasion until Nelson's victory at Trafalgar in 1805 gave Britain command of the seas; in the same way, Hitler knew he had to gain mastery of the skies before he could proceed with his invasion plans. History does indeed repeat itself.

Then in 1804 came the famous False Alarm. The French had been expected daily since the previous summer and every armed camp on the east coast was on full - and nervous - alert. The nervousness was relieved on the night of 31st January 1804. The watchers at Home Castle in the Borders saw what they later claimed to be the long-awaited signal that the French were coming. They lit their beacon fire. It was answered from every warning station throughout Teviotdale, Liddesdale, Tweeddale and at Habchester, near Ayton. In East Lothian, the alarm signal was based on a system of beacons to be lit on Knockenhair, Blackcastle, Pencraig, North Berwick Law and the Garleton Hills. The system worked perfectly. The farmers of the yeomanry units were in the saddle immediately and within a few hours, the entire south-east of Scotland was on the move, gallopers making for the designated rallying places. In Jedburgh, the authorities were convinced that the French had landed somewhere on the coast. Mobilisation was swift, effective and efficient; the whole business went like clockwork. The only problem was - where were the French?

By dawn on 1st February, all units were at their designated stations. It proved the effectiveness of the defensive arrangements as well as the men's readiness. But that was all it was. It transpired that the fire seen by the lookouts at Home Castle were caused by the burning of charcoal across the Tweed in Northumberland.[24] The sentinel at St Abb's Head was rightly sceptical and cautious; he suspected something wasn't quite right since the alarm had originated inland rather than on the coast and he refused to light his beacon. He said he would do so only when he saw a fleet of French ships. A cool-headed man he was; the temptation to raise the alarm must have been great, with a nerve-wracking few hours' wait until dawn. The Merse volunteers had however headed for their rendezvous at Dunbar and Dalkeith; the alarm was raised in Edinburgh by gallopers despatched from the Borders. One of the Selkirk volunteers named Chisholm was married on 31st January. There was no question of his remaining with his new bride that night. "Weel, Peggy, if I'm killed, ye'll hear tell o't. And if I'm no killed, I'll come back as sune [soon] as I can." When the truth emerged, the militia and volunteers returned sheepishly home; no doubt General Don was privately satisfied with the swift implementation of his defence plan. A century later, the Border associations of Edinburgh and Glasgow celebrated the night of the False Alarm on 31st January 1904 in Edinburgh's North British (now the Balmoral) Hotel; the Dunbar magistrates declined an invitation to attend.[25]

After the clamour subsided, the troops resumed their boring life of endless drilling and guard duty. On 7th May, the Haddingtonshire Volunteers did a spell of duty at West Barns and together with the other regiments - about 5,000 men - twelve days later, they were reviewed on West Barns Links by their commander-in-chief, the Earl of Moira. The year progressed with little else to relieve the boredom. Napoleon knew that his only chance of success was to ensure a safe passage through the English Channel for his flat-bottomed invasion craft-out of the question after Nelson's resounding victory at Trafalgar on 21st October 1805. Before that however, there seems to have another invasion scare as the Lord Lieutenant of Haddingtonshire, the Earl of Haddington issued a proclamation on 7th July advising the local tenant farmers to remove all the horses, cattle, meal and flour to safe places. Even if Trafalgar ended Napoleon's hope of conquering and occupying Britain, the war dragged on for a further ten years.

As for General Don, his appointment in Scotland ended after Trafalgar. The threat of invasion now averted, he was transferred to the vulnerable area of the Channel Islands, where he was appointed military governor of Jersey, his second posting there. In his usual efficient fashion, Don organised the island's defences, creating 18 military roads to link all parts of the island. This made him highly unpopular with the Jersey farmers and he had to be escorted by a troop of soldiers wherever he went. The townspeople liked him however. Although Trafalgar had made Jersey easier to defend, Don formed a military corps and devised a signal system to alert the British fleet at nearby Guernsey of approaching hostile ships. He also built Fort Regent at St Helen's; the fort bears a plaque with his name and that of Colonel John Humphreys of the Royal Engineers, intimating they had laid the foundation stone. His popularity in Jersey far outlived the hostility of the farmers; there are several places named for him on the island - Don Street, Don Road, Don Bridge. His term of office as military governor was commemorated by an impressive Nelson's Column-style memorial which was unveiled in 1805 in the parade at St Helen's. Don's statue surmounts the plinth, which is flanked by figures representing Commerce and Industry, the whole being guarded by large cannon. On 21st May 1810, the local militia presented him with a gold-hilted sword, now in the Scottish United Services Museum at Edinburgh Castle. General Don left Jersey in 1814 to become governor of Gibraltar, where he died in 1832; his remains lie in the garrison church.

Several men in Dunbar saw action in the Napoleonic Wars; Rear-Admiral Hay of Belton served in *HMS Defiance* at Trafalgar and Sir George Warrender of Lochend was with Wellington in the Peninsular War (1808-14) suffering wounds at the battles of Busaco (1810) and Vittoria (1813). After Napoleon's abdication came the *Hundred Days* which culminated with his defeat at Waterloo. With Wellington that day was Colonel Sir William de Lancey, Acting Quartermaster General who died of wounds and was buried in Brussels; de Lancey was married to Magdalen, daughter of Sir James Hall of Dunglass; a plaque to his memory can be seen today in Dunglass Collegiate Church. The war with France finally at an end, the regiments came back. In 1816, the 43rd Regiment of Foot (Black Watch) marched through Dunbar, its ranks greatly depleted by casualties sustained at Quatre Bras which preceded Waterloo. By then the vast encampment at West Barns had been dismantled, the cannons at the Battery removed to Edinburgh Castle and the local traders had lost a good deal of income from army contracts.

It is a tradition in Dunbar that French prisoners-of-war incarcerated in the Borders were brought here to build the boundary walls of Lochend and Belhaven Brewery at some point between 1812 and 1814. This cannot be established with certainty, although it may not be without foundation. Several Border towns, notably Selkirk, were hosts to these unfortunate men; so far however, my researches have been unable to confirm that French prisoners came to Dunbar to build or repair walls. However, the fact that Sir George Warrender fought in the Peninsular War gives some credence to the tale; he may have requested a prisoner workforce to put up walls at Lochend to compensate for the wounds he had suffered at Busaco and Vittoria.

It took almost 22 years to defeat Napoleon. The government's demands for food, clothing and munitions came to an end and foreign trade declined as many European countries were so impoverished by the war that they couldn't afford British goods. The domestic labour markets were swollen with demobilised soldiers and sailors, keeping wages down and causing widespread unemployment. The same happened after the First World War a century later. Even so, Dunbar seems to have weathered the economic crisis that followed, although men like George Miller ultimately went bankrupt either directly or indirectly because of the French war. In 1827, three troops of the East Lothian Yeomanry were disbanded; only the Dunbar troop remained, serving without pay. Two troops were reinstated in 1846 however and a third from Berwickshire was added in 1848. At some point before 1846, Dunbar became the depot for the Scots Greys, as we know from John Muir's autobiography *The Story of My Boyhood and Youth.*

In 1840, a national movement was formed with the aim of creating a monument to commemorate the Duke of Wellington's victory. Wellington was deeply unpopular as a Prime Minister, then at the time of the reform Bill of 1832 which he opposed. After the Bill became law and the shouting died down, subscription lists were issued in Scotland for a monument; today, Edinburgh not only possesses a splendid if somewhat romanticised equestrian statue in front of the Scottish Record Office; nearby Waterloo Place was named in Wellington's honour. The statue cost £10,000; East Lothian contributed £1,553 - more than 10% - but this may have been due to the influence of the Duchess of Wellington, Lady Elizabeth Hay, daughter of the 8th Marquis of Tweeddale. Rather petulantly, Wellington declined an invitation to review the East Lothian Yeomanry in 1850, pleading pressing business elsewhere - the usual excuse of politicians then and now.

Until the First World War, Waterloo Day was celebrated every 18th June, an event commemorated longer than any previous military success save for Trafalgar. Little of moment happened at Dunbar during the next major conflict, the Crimean War (1854-56) although again the town had militia units in its midst once more, verified by the burgh police records. On 18th July 1855, two militiamen from the 4th Company, Haddington Volunteers were in court for assaulting a local man; one of them received ten days' imprisonment.[26] In 1856, cases of drunkenness among the militia attracted fines or a short spell in jail.[27] In the previous year, the burgh council offered to hand over the Lamer Island Battery to the army free of rent provided they kept it in good repair.[28]

Crimean War

The Crimean War between Britain and France in support of Turkey against Russia lasted from 1854 to 1856. It touched Dunbar only marginally. The Burgh Council, ever hopeful of reducing its financial liabilities - especially expenditure on its periodic white elephants - approached the War Office to ascertain whether it would be prepared to take over the manning and repair of the Battery on Lamer Island. The War Office wisely declined. After all, it was highly improbable that Russian warships would be able to make a serious attack on Britain, let alone Dunbar.

However, a few local men were involved in the Crimean War; one of these was an artilleryman, Alexander Goodall, from Woodbush, the future site of the local Grammar School; Goodall survived the conflict. Other survivors were Lieutenant Julian Hall (1837-1911), Coldstream Guards, who was present during the siege of Sebastopol; another was Commander Edward Hay RN who served in *HMS Agamemnon,* also at Sebastopol. But the most famous - and whose health was toasted among the common folk - was Sergeant John Penn, one of the survivors of the Charge of the Light Brigade at Balaclava on 25th October 1854. Although not born or bred in Dunbar, Penn came to the town at some point between 1864 and 1869, residing at No 41 High Street (adjacent to the *Crunchy Carrot*) until his death in 1886; his grave in the churchyard is described in Chapter 5.

John Penn was English, the son of farrier-major Penn who served in the 14th Light Dragoons. The army was in young Penn's blood from the outset. Born on the last day of 1820, John Penn enlisted with the 3rd Light Dragoons; his first engagement was in India, or to be precise, Afghanistan, where he took part in the First Afghan War, then the First and Second Punjab Wars. In the latter conflicts, he was present on the fields of Mudki and Sobraon, then at the final defeat of the Sikhs at Gujerat which led to the annexation of the Punjab into British India. In February 1854, Penn transferred to the 17th Lancers as a trooper; on 4th October that year, he was promoted to the rank of corporal. To the men of the 17th, he was known as 'Old Jack Penn'.

On 25th October 1854, he was among the 673 officers and men who paraded that fateful morning to take part in the disastrous Charge of the Light Brigade. He left no record of his views on the misinterpreted order conveyed to Lord Raglan by Charles Nolan, an impetuous Irishman serving with one of the dashing Hussar regiments that day. Among those who took part in the charge, 113 officers and other ranks were killed, 165 were wounded and 25 were taken prisoner; 15 of the prisoners served with the 17th Lancers which proves that the regiment was positioned in the van of the attack and reached the Russian guns. Even so, apart from those taken prisoner, the 17th lost only 24 killed with 37 wounded. John Penn was among the survivors who limped back to the British lines.

Penn was probably over-fond of toasts in the mess. In January 1855, he was promoted to Sergeant, then in July, demoted to Private in July 1855. His name appeared in the Regimental Defaulters' Book no less than 14 times and he was court-martialled at least thrice, probably for drunkenness. At some point after July 1855, he was invalided out of the army to England. On his breast were several medals; the Crimean Medal (ABIS which signified he had been present on the fields of Alma, Balaclava, Inkerman and Sebastopol), the Turkish Medal and the Distinguished Conduct Medal. How could such a brave man be sent down? The answer has to be the drink. At some point between 1855 and 1864, he came to Scotland; he was living in Dunbar in 1869 as we know from the registering of the birth of one of his children. He joined the East Lothian and Border Yeomanry Cavalry at some point, teaching raw recruits how to remain in the saddle. *Honour the Light Brigade* (ed. W M Lummis and K G Wynn, 1973) informs us that Penn attended the first 'Survivors' dinner of the Light Brigade held at Alexandria Palace, London, in 1875 and he became a member of the Balaclava Association formed in 1879. No doubt he continued to attend these annual dinners until October 1885, as he died on 31 January 1886. The last survivor of the Charge of the Light Brigade died in May, 1927.

The next conflict was relatively minor although considered serious at the time. The Indian Mutiny (1856-57) took Dunbar men to India, notably Surgeon-General Sir Anthony Dickson Hume, VC, KCB, MD, MRS. Born in Dunbar on 30th November 1826, he joined the Army Medical Department in 1848 as an Assistant Surgeon. From 1855 to 1858, he served as medical officer to the 90th Regiment of Foot in India. During the Mutiny, he was awarded the Victoria Cross - one of the first - for his part in the siege of Lucknow on 20th September 1857; the citation reads as follows:

'For persevering bravery and admirable conduct in charge of the men left behind the column, when the troops under the late Major-General Havelock forced their way into the Residency at Lucknow, on 26th September 1857.'

Illus 137: *The Relief of Lucknow* KRM

Illus 138: *Artillery volunteers 1867* HLHC

Although Havelock relieved Lucknow (**ill 137**), the siege lasted a further six months. Hume was knighted in 1875 and promoted to the rank of Surgeon-General; he died on 10th August 1914 aged 88. Edward and David Hay of Dunbar also saw action in the Mutiny - the former in the Naval Brigade from *HMS Shannon*, the latter defending the Residency at Lucknow, dying on his way home of war-fatigue.

In 1859, war clouds were again gathering in Europe, largely due to the aggressive foreign policy pursued by the French, fresh from their achievements in the Crimea. The government in Britain felt that the national defences were inadequate. In Scotland, the volunteers raised in 1803 were but a memory. In May 1859, the War Office issued a circular to the Lord Lieutenants in every shire asking them to submit proposals for forming volunteer rifle companies and artillery corps, the latter to be stationed in maritime towns where forts or shore batteries already existed. Haddingtonshire subsequently formed an artillery unit, its main aim being the defence of the Battery at Dunbar. The basic organisation was a complement of 10-12 men per gun. In 1855, the War Office had bought Lauderdale House from the Earl of Lauderdale, converting it into barrack accommodation. On 20th December 1860, the 1st Haddingtonshire Artillery Volunteers - a corps of a single battery at Dunbar - was raised; it merged with the 1st Linlithgow Artillery[29] in 1897. A team of Dunbar Artillery Volunteers were the winning squad at a rifle shoot at East Barns in 1867(**ill 138**).

The annual East Lothian Yeomanry review - known as Yeomanry Week - was held at Belhaven Sands in July, when a Race Day was held (**ill 139**)from at least 1866. A local poet, James Lumsden, or 'Samuel Mucklebackit' of Nether Hailes near East Linton mentions the yearly occasion in his *Rural Rhymes and Sketches* which contain his poem *Belhaven Races* viz.

'At Yule's heels, Hansel Monday reels
    Then baith the Hiring chases, O!
But simmer [summer] brings on golden wing
    Belhaven's glorious races, O!

(The first two of these red letter days occurred in January and February; Hansel Monday was the first after New Year and the hiring or *fee'ing* Fair occurred on the second Tuesday in February, when married and single farm labourers were hired from Whitsun, the latter only for six months. The second hiring day for batchelors only was held in November).

By the end of the nineteenth century, Lauderdale House - or Castle Park Barracks as it was known then - had fallen into disrepair, largely due to a fire which made part of the building uninhabitable. At the turn of the century, the Castle Park was used for gun drill (**ill 140 and 141**); before that, two large mounds, thought to contain prehistoric relics was levelled to make a parade ground for drilling the Haddington Militia. Castle Park Barracks became the headquarters of the East Lothian and Berwickshire Yeomanry, whose volunteers were trained for service in the Boer War. By 1914, the Barracks had become a cavalry depot for the regular army; in the Second World War, it housed an Officer Cadet Training Unit (OCTU).

In 1881, Scottish artillery units were grouped into regimental districts for organisational purposes; the Haddingtonshire Militia formed part of regimental District No 1, Glencorse, near Penicuik. That District consisted of the 1st and 2nd Battalions, Royal Scots, the 1st Foot and the Edinburgh Light Infantry, with the volunteer battalions of the 1st and 2nd Edinburgh, 1st and 2nd Midlothian, 1st Haddington (Artillery) and the

Illus 139: *East Lothian and Berwickshire Yeomanry on Belhaven Beach* RA

1st Linlithgow (Artillery). The Haddington Artillery then had a complement of two officers and 56 men under the command of Captain J Reilly. The following year, the artillerymen were incorporated into the Royal Artillery, Southern District. Undoubtedly, Dunbar men served in the regiment.

That there were annual rifle shooting competitions among the volunteers is borne out by a leaflet I have seen which advertised such a competition in 1882. Prizes were donated by the Earl of Haddington (£25), Sir George Warrender of Lochend (£5) and the Marquis of Tweeddale (£5). The leaflet was discovered under the floorboards of a house being modernised in Tranent in 1992; among the papers found were the rules of the Haddingtonshire Rifle Volunteer Corps embodied under the Volunteer Acts of 1863 and 1869.

Illus 140: *Castle Park, big gun drill c.1899* RJP

By 1895, the Castle Park Barracks were used as offices for the Haddington,Berwick, Linlithgow and Peebles Artillery Militia, known then as the South-East of Scotland, Southern Division Royal Artillery which had full-time staff accommodated at Dunbar. By that year, the regiment had a complement of 450 men who assembled at Dunbar every summer to practise 'big gun' drill. In 1901, the artillery were re-named the 5th Company, 1st Militia Royal Garrison Artillery, a title it used until 1907, when a major reorganisation of the militia and yeomanry regiments resulted in the formation of the Territorial Army, a second-line force of reservists which in theory would serve only in the UK although the enabling legislation provided for service abroad. Before 1907 however, the 5th Company of the Royal Garrison Militia used 64-pounder naval guns which remained permanently at Dunbar with their associated powder magazine and grain store for the horses which pulled the guns. The company had its own band and was a familiar sight on the High Street in summertime (**ill 142**). By the turn of the century, Castle Park Barracks had become the HQ of the East Lothian and Berwickshire Yeomanry (**ill 143**).

Dunbar men were nothing if not far-flung throughout the British Empire. During the Boer War, Sir George Warrender of Lochend commanded the Second Squadron of the British fleet; since joining the navy in 1873, Warrender was involved in the Zulu Wars of 1879, then the Boxer Rebellion in China in 1900, when an

Illus 141: *Castle Park, big gun practice c.1899* RJP

international relief force of 2,000 men was despatched from Tientsin on 10th June but failed to reach Peking, the Forbidden City where the European legations there were under siege. The legations had only token forces; these small groups held out against the Boxers and units of the regular Chinese army for 55 days, from 20th June to 14th August.[30] Sir George Warrender had brought the first British relief force to Tientsin in his squadron; a second attempt to relieve Peking with 22,000 troops of mixed nationalities[31] was successful on 14th August. China was forced to pay £64 million by way of compensation; the Boxer Rebellion proved there was a need for reform in China, where the Empress, last of the Manchu dynasty abdicated in 1911. Thereafter, the country became a republic, instituting modern policies.

Illus 142: *Artillery militia leaving the Castle Park c.1899* RJP

After the major Napoleonic and Crimean conflicts came the 'little' Victorian wars instigated by men like Cecil Rhodes who were instilled with the ruthless empire-building policies pursued by England. While the famous stand against the Zulu *impis* at Rorke's Drift saved British face after the battle of Isandhlwana in July 1879, the Boers who fought and defeated the Matabele and Zulus felt strong enough to challenge the might of Britain. Much has been written of the Boer Wars and need not be revisited here; this account is concerned only with incidents which involved the community of Dunbar - directly or indirectly. Prior to the outbreak of the second Boer War in 1900, the War Office decided to train the local artillery militia at Dunbar rather than on the Isle of Wight. On 10th March 1899,[32] batteries at the Castle Park resumed target practice. Local traders sent a petition to the War Office seeking assurance that the local militia would remain at Dunbar; the local businessmen were clearly concerned that a lucrative source of income would be lost if the resident East Lothian and Berwickshire Yeomanry were moved to Edinburgh. By September, the Scots Greys were back; a month later, the Boer War began. The traders were in business again.

An anecdote of interest to the community occurred in the early stages of the war. On 27th October 1899, the *Haddingtonshire Courier* reported that Lady Sarah Wilson, sister to the Duke of Roxburghe was at Mafeking with her husband, an officer in the British Army. Somehow, the Boers captured Lady Sarah; she remained their prisoner until exchanged in December for a Boer - described no doubt for propaganda purposes by the *Haddingtonshire Courier* as 'a notorious horse-thief and convict.' Weren't they all horse thieves and criminals in the eyes of queen Victoria's government?

In the course of the Boer War, the *Courier* reported troop movements, something which wouldn't be permitted during the World Wars. The Duke of Roxburghe, perhaps smarting from bruised family honour, joined the

RJP

Illus 143: *Lothian and Berwickshire Yeomanry c 1899*

Household Cavalry which was about to disembark from London for the Transvaal. By November 1899,[33] Roxburghe had joined 30-40 Dunbar men on active service in South Africa; in that month, three local men were wounded in the fighting at Elandslaagte. In November, the British had some success between Ladysmith and Colenso, although the latter town was abandoned; during the evacuation, Lieutenant Roberts, son of Field Marshal Lord Roberts, was killed and awarded a posthumous VC for attempting to save a battery of guns. His death was recorded in the Dunbar Provost and Magistrates Committee minutes on 21st December 1899, probably because his father, known affectionately as 'Bobs' had been made an honorary burgess of Dunbar in 1893.

Casualties were mounting daily. The death on 16th November 1899 at Wimbledon, South Africa, of Trooper Tom Goodall from Woodbush, Dunbar, was reported by the *Courier*.[34] He had been home on leave only two months previously. (In his case, there seems to have been some incorrect reporting - see note 34 to chapter). Casualties were causing concern in Britain; on 15th December, losses were 578 killed, 2,071 wounded and 2,048 missing, with an additional 838 killed and wounded at Maggersfontein, a total of 5,530. A week later, the figure had risen to 7,630. Another Dunbar man was among the casualties - Sergeant H Wellington, a Royal Artilleryman wounded in action at the battle of Tugela River.[35] The Boer War continued for another two years until military pressure forced the Boer leaders to the negotiating table.

HLHC

Illus 144: *Imperial Yeomanry*

I am not sure whether today's schoolchildren are taught about the Boer War; however, at the time, the relief of Ladysmith in February 1900 and that of Mafeking on 17th May 1900 were events celebrated throughout Britain. The Dunbar burgh council minutes record[36] that the news of Ladysmith was announced by ringing the town bell for thirty minutes, with a firework display hastily arranged by the provost. In March,[37] two Dunbar volunteers, William Leckie and Alexander Goodall - probably a brother of the late Tom Goodall - enlisted as sharpshooters; increasingly, volunteer units were being called to South Africa to reinforce the regular army, depleted by the recent fighting.

Several of the men of the East Lothian and Berwickshire Yeomanry never returned from South Africa. An impressive memorial to the fallen executed by W Grant Steven in 1902 was placed near the entrance gate at the Parish Church but not before some insensitive and unseemly squabbling between the burgh council and the kirk session. The burgh council had agreed the site with the regimental authorities without first discussing their intentions with the kirk session, probably because the site belonged to the town. The session contended that the council had no right to offer the site to the regiment and that its presence would cause 'great inconvenience' to the congregation leaving the church on Sundays.[38] (Perhaps those who had given their lives in a colonial conflict might have thought their deaths somewhat 'inconvenient' if they could have voiced their opinion. An alternative site within the kirkyard was suggested but in the end, the memorial went ahead on the site originally agreed. The East Lothian and Berwickshire Yeomanry existed until 1908, when they were re-embodied as the Lothian and Border Horse, a Territorial Army unit. The Imperial Yeomanry as they were called before 1908 were an impressively uniformed - if archaic - unit (**ill 144**)

The Great War

Britain's poor military performance during the Boer War didn't pass unnoticed by the international community in Europe, particularly Germany. At one point, the Kaiser had contemplated offering the Boers military support. Britain's less than honourable prosecution of the war - the British were first to use concentration camps to house the wives and children of the Boer guerrillas, many of whom succumbed to sickness, disease and starvation - had attracted the censure of many European countries.

In 1914, Dunbar's strategic importance lay in its Battery which was included in the line of fortified sites from Berwick to Burntisland and Dalmeny in Fife to protect the Firth of Forth against naval attack. At the outset of the twentieth century, Germany's trade and industry had developed at such a rate that its navy was second only to Britain's and the size of its army caused great concern in Europe. When it came, the Great War involved nearly every country in the world; for most thinking people, it remains the greatest human tragedy ever known to mankind. Few countries escaped its devastation; given its small population, Scotland paid a heavy and disproportionate price in terms of human loss in the wasteful and badly-planned battles of 1916-18, particularly the Somme. As for Dunbar, the burgh records are deficient in references to the war and its effects on the community, although it has to be said that this was probably due to restrictions in wartime reporting.

The declaration of war on 4th August 1914 brought an immediate and universal response from the young men all over the country and Dunbar was no exception. Men in the grip of what later historians refer to as war fever enlisted in their thousands. So many signed up that there weren't enough uniforms or weapons to go round. By the end of the war, the butcher's bill in Scotland totalled 110,000, accounting for just under a fifth of the British war dead - the population was then 10% of the rest of Britain - few countries in Europe suffered so heavily. Some historians maintain that Britain never fully recovered from the terrible attrition of the trenches, referring to those who never came back as the *Lost Generation*. It certainly took several decades for the post-war generation to revive; one consequence was the failure of the Scottish economy and industry between the two world wars; some believed that the best blood in Britain had been sacrificed, thus weakening the moral and intellectual fibre of the country for all time.

The Great War changed the fabric of British society forever. One of its many consequences was the long-overdue enfranchisement of women in 1918. Before the war, the Suffragette movement was active in Scotland; clamour for votes for women increased dramatically during the course of the war and several incidents gave the movement publicity which, as inevitably happens in such emotive issues, discredited it. One incident took place near Dunbar on 26th February 1914; the destruction of several important historical articles at Whitekirk Church was an unnecessary act of vandalism (see Chapter 5). The local minister published his censure in the *Haddingtonshire Courier* of 6th March; the police offered a reward of £100 to anyone who could provide information about the car which had taken the suffragettes to the church. On 11th March, the Dunbar burgh council minutes refer to the incident in suitable language; it was a 'dastardly outrage.' The council was moved to send a letter of sympathy to Lord Haddington and the other Whitekirk church heritors. Soon there would be other conflagrations and destruction on a global scale.

The Royal North British Dragoons - the Scots Greys - periodically stationed at Dunbar, returned there at the outbreak of the Great War. They received special mention in a letter to Herbert, Lord Kitchener from Czar Nicholas of Russia. The Russians had a special regard for the Greys because the founder of the regiment, General Tam Dalyell - who had persecuted the Covenanters - had been in exile in Russia after the defeat of the Royalist army of Charles II at Worcester in 1651. General Tam served in Czar Alexei's army until he returned to Scotland after the Restoration. The Greys were mounted troops in 1678, formally embodied by Dalyell as the first British Dragoon regiment in the service of Charles II in Scotland in 1681. Tradition has it they received their nickname from their grey chargers; the Dalyell family insist today that this is a myth and that the name derives from their habit of wearing Russian grey overcoats. The myth is perhaps more appealing, as myths usually are. Be that as it may, Czar Nicholas was moved to write to Kitchener in 1914 as follows:

> '[I] am happy that my gallant regiment, the Royal Scots Greys are fighting the enemy, convinced they will uphold the glorious traditions of the past.'[39]

The Greys served as dismounted troops in the Great War and would in 1915 add Ypres to their impressive list of battle honours.

Dunbar thus had a substantial military population again; in June 1914, Castle Park Barracks was designated No 6 (Scottish) Cavalry Depot under the command of Major Reginald Seager Hunt, 1st King's Dragoon Guards. The burgh council had been clamouring for the depot - no doubt under pressure from the local traders, some of whom were council members. On 23rd June 1914, Major Hunt was made a freeman of the burgh as a token of the residents' appreciation. When Major - then Colonel - Hunt died in 1942, he bequeathed certain items of his uniform to the town

> 'in remembrance of and grateful thanks for the great honour they conferred on me.'

Other units stationed at Dunbar during the Great War included the 17th Lancers - re-embodied after the disastrous Charge of the Light Brigade in 1854 - the Dragoon Guards, the Lanarkshire Yeomanry, the Lothian and Border Horse [formerly the East Lothian and Berwickshire Yeomanry], the Royal Dragoons, the Royal Scots and the King's Own Scottish Borderers.

In July 1914 - a month before the outbreak of war - there were planes seen above Dunbar, thought to be German. In that month, the East Coast Fisheries Association complained to the Admiralty that Royal Navy battleships firing their guns in target practice were interfering with their members' livelihood. The *Haddingtonshire Courier* avidly reported the movements of Sir Reginald Wingate (**ill 145**), on summer leave at Knockenhair. Wingate of the Sudan, Sirdar (commander-in-chief) of the Egyptian army in the closing years of the nineteenth century was a Grand Old Man, a Victorian who had accompanied General Charles 'Chinese' Gordon to Cairo Railway Station from where he went to gain immortality at Khartoum. He was also present on the field of Omdurman with Kitchener who broke the army of the late Mahdi's Dervishes under the leadership of his successor the Khalifi who ruthlessly subjugated and devastated the Sudan for many years. Born in 1861, Wingate began his military career at Khandahar during the Second Afghanistan War. From there, he went to Cairo, where he was appointed commander of the local cholera hospital. He then joined Herbert Kitchener's staff as intelligence officer, gathering information about Dervish policies and movements in the Sudan. After Omdurman, he helped in the mopping-up arrangements, pursuing one of the Dervish leaders for a year before killing him in the Nile marshes. At the end of 1899, Wingate was appointed Governor of the Sudan and Sirdar of the Egyptian army. During the First World War, he encouraged the Arab Revolt against the Turks, befriending Lawrence of Arabia and became his paymaster. Lawrence later paid tribute to him in *Seven Pillars of Wisdom*, his account of the revolt in the desert. After a distinguished military career, Wingate retired to Dunbar and his favourite pastime, golf. He died on 28th January 1953, mourned by many in the community. However, in 1914, Wingate had lately returned from Khartoum, fuelling talk that he had given up his appointment as Governor-General of the Sudan. The rumours were proved groundless when he returned to Egypt on 2nd August 1914.

Illus 145: *Sir Reginald Wingate* HLHC

When war was declared on 4th August, many Dunbar men rushed to join the colours. Popular opinion was that the war would be over by Christmas. On 7th August, the *Courier* reported that prayers were offered up in

Illus146: *Draft leaving for the Western Front* HLHC

churches throughout the country. In that month, 800 Scots Grey reservists left Dunbar for the Western Front,[40] followed shortly afterwards by the 8th Battalion Royal Scots, billeted in Haddington; this battalion was among the first territorial infantry regiments to enter the front line in November 1914. The *Courier* reported that a great assembly - about 1,200 reservists - had mustered at the Castle Park Barracks from London, Edinburgh, Glasgow and the north of Scotland to join the various regiments there - the 1st King's Dragoon Guards, the 1st Royal Dragoons and the Scots Greys - to receive their uniforms and equipment. On 6th August, about 300 left Dunbar to report to base camps in York and Aldershot. The *Courier* reported in true patriotic style that

'The trained manhood of the nation is in arms.'

In somewhat lighter mood, the same issue quoted the comments of a Haddington lady on the business:

'Nae [no] need for a war, nae wonder there's a war - wi' sugar at seventeen pence a pund [pound].'[41]

Food prices rose sharply at the outset but these soon returned to their pre-war level except for sugar and butter.

During September, recruits were volunteering at the rate of 120 a day; reporting to the Castle Park Barracks Cavalry Depot, they were given uniforms (**ill 146**). After only five weeks of warfare, the first casualties were reported.[42] Bombardier A E Smith, a native of Dunbar residing in Edinburgh wrote home from the Front that the German battalions advancing *en masse* and firing from the hip presented

'splendid targets for our guns. As soon as one lot gets mown down, the gaps are as soon filled up with fresh men....'

Little did Bombardier Smith realise these tactics would lead to static trench warfare, when a few yards of mud gained in No Man's Land was bought at the terrible cost of human life.

On 5th September,[43] the destroyer *HMS Pathfinder,* the first warship to be sunk by a torpedo from a submarine went down in four minutes off St Abb's Head with all but nine of her 268 crew. *Pathfinder* had been searching for an unidentified enemy fishing trawler suspected of sowing mines in the Forth. An unidentified seaman from the vessel was washed up on the shore at Dunbar; his remains were interred in the kirkyard, the headstone inscribed 'known only unto God'. In the same month, Lord Arthur Hay, brother of the Marquis of Tweeddale was killed on the Western Front;[44] his grandfather had been present on the field of Waterloo. By the middle of the month it was reported that 8,000 Scots Greys recruited at Dunbar had been sent to boot camps in England. The war was gathering momentum.

In October, the steamship *Rohilla* was sunk by a mine off Dunbar; in November, mines were increasingly being laid in the North Sea by vessels flying the Dutch flag; the Admiralty warned the east coast ports to be vigilant when Dutch vessels entered harbour. Not unexpectedly, the herring fishing was suspended for the duration. On 25th November, the burgh council debated the likelihood of invasion and decided to divide the burgh into 8 districts so that the inhabitants could be warned quickly by one of the 56 special constables sworn in for the duration.

In March 1915, the *Courier* reported that Sir Reginald Wingate's son Roy had received the MC for conspicuous bravery at Givenchy, in the First battle of Ypres.[45] In the same month, the war-wounded were arriving at the Castle Park Barracks and the Battery hospital - the latter being the isolation hospital for those suffering from tuberculosis and infectious diseases.[46] On 7th May, the Cunard steamship *Lusitania* was sunk off Ireland by a German submarine; among the survivors was a Mrs Gwyfer, daughter of a Dunbar farmer called Cairns.[47] In the same month, it was reported that a nephew of a Broxmouth man had been tragically killed in the railway accident at Gretna Green when two troop trains collided, with much loss of life, particularly among a battalion of the Royal Scots.[48] In June, a poignant ceremony took place in the parish kirkyard. The cemetery contains the grave of a Royal Artillery officer who had been present at Waterloo; on 18th June 1915, the centenary of the battle, serving officers of the Royal Artillery arranged for a wreath to be laid on the grave of Major General William Cochran Anderson.[49] At the same time, men with Dunbar connections were receiving their share of military honours; an MC was awarded to Lieutenant Alexander Drysdale - grandson of the owner of Castellau House in Dunbar - for his conspicuous gallantry in the First battle of Ypres, during which Roy Malcolm Wingate also distinguished himself.[50]

Regrettably from the local historian's point of view, the burgh council and kirk session minutes contain very little about social conditions during the war. However, the session recorded that the serving minister, James Kirk gave his life in the last year of the conflict. Captain Kirk - he baptised my mother in 1914 - was appointed military chaplain to the 7th Argyll and Sutherland Highlanders in April 1915. In July, a soldier at the Front wrote to a friend in the Lothian and Border Horse to inform him he'd met Kirk, who regularly visited the support trenches with food and cigarettes for the men and that

'when under shell fire, he is about the coolest man we've seen.'[51]

Illus 147: *Detachment Royal Garrison Artillery, Castle Park (George Dann, Dunbar, front row right)* MD

Kirk returned to his ministry at Dunbar in September 1917, having been awarded the MC. Chaplains were regarded with cynicism by the Front line troops; they called them 'Woodbine Willies' who stayed well to the rear, offering the wounded consolation and cigarettes. In contrast, Roman Catholic priests were usually seen in the thick of the fighting, administering the last rites to the fallen. Captain Kirk appears to be among the few Church of Scotland ministers who regularly visited the front line trenches. He was asked to return to France in February 1918 and died on 1st April of wounds sustained on 27th March in Ludendorff's final desperate offensive launched a week earlier. A memorial pulpit in his name was unveiled on 3rd April 1921 and the Parish Church still possesses Kirk's communion vessels which were donated to it after the war. An ornate headstone in the churchyard dedicated to Kirk's memory and containing the remains of his wife Elizabeth is inscribed *Dulce et Decorum Est Pro Patria Mori* (It is sweet and becoming to die for one's country' - a line in one of Wilfrid Owen's bitterest poems about the futility and waste of war). Captain Kirk's remains were interred in Wimereux Cemetery, Belgium.

By July 1915, Dunbar men were serving at Gallipoli in the Dardanelles. In October the same year, Haddingtonshire was declared a prohibited area because of spy activity. On 18th December, the *Courier* reported that Slatin Pasha - Baron Rudolf von Slatin, the Anglo-Austrian friend of Sir Reginald Wingate from his Sudan days - had renounced his British appointments and decorations. (Slatin became head of the Austrian Red Cross and was known for his humanity towards Allied prisoners.) At the end of the first year of war, casualties convalesced in Castle Barracks Hospital and the former Isolation Hospital at the Battery under the care of Dr David MacDonald, the military medical officer and his team of Voluntary Aid Detachment (VAD) nurses.

The kirk session minutes contain intermittent references to local fund-raising campaigns, mainly in aid of the Red Cross Society, whose president, the Dowager Duchess of Roxburghe regularly entertained the wounded in the grounds of Broxmouth House. The other main charity supported in Dunbar was the Royal Scots' Prisoner of War Committee; Dunbar Parish Church initially contributed £2 a month for every Royal Scot prisoner, later increased to £3 a month. Unlike in the Second World War, there are no anecdotes or mention of local men who fought and died in the Great War. Perhaps this was because there were so many. I have a badly damaged 1916

(Photo by W. Black, Dunbar.)
Sergeant W. LINDSAY ("Jock"), 5th Dragoon Guards, a most popular member of the Sergeants' Mess of Dunbar Cavalry Depot, who was killed in the trenches.

Private THOMAS BOYLE, 1st Royal Dragoons, formerly of the Scots Greys, who was killed in action in France on 13th May. He was the son of Mr Thomas Boyle, Dunbar, and four of his brothers and a brother-in-law are serving with the colours.

(Photo by W. Black, Dunbar.)
Sergeant J. PEARSON, Scots Greys, killed in the firing line in France. When in the Dunbar Depot he was Gymnastic Instructor, and was well-known as a boxer, having held the Amateur Championship of Scotland for some years.

RJP

Illus 148: *Three Dunbar casualties of the Great War*

supplement to the *Haddingtonshire and East Lothian Journal* (1881-1923) which describes itself as the 'Only Illustrated Newspaper in the County'. The supplement contains photographs and brief biographical details of 25 East Lothian men, 19 of whom were killed in action or died of wounds. The most poignant of these are the three Lyons brothers from North Berwick, all young lieutenants who fell in action, probably on the Somme. One of the three Dunbar men killed that year was Thomas Boyle (**ill 148**) whose brother James also fell in action.

From 1918 onwards, the weekly *Roll of Honour* - those killed or wounded - in the *Courier* contains more names than in the first three years of the war. In May 1916, two Dunbar men were reported killed during the inconclusive battle of Jutland in the North Sea, the sole engagement between the British and German fleets. Then came the Somme. On 1st July 1916, the first day of that terrible battle, the casualties numbered almost 60,000; these continued to mount and remained high until the battle ended in November. The *Courier*, like other newspapers published misleading reports of success on the Somme, giving the impression of a great victory in the making. It was indeed a triumph. For Death.

In the graveyard is a monument to one Dunbar man who fell on the first day of the Somme. Charles Edward (Chugs) Vassie, a 2nd Lieutenant in the King's Own Yorkshire Light Infantry; he was only 21. The inscription on his grave bears the mispelling 'Leiut.'; perhaps the stonemason was distracted by his emotion....(**Ill 149**).

From November 1916, there was a marked increase in the cases heard by the Berwickshire Military Tribunal for exemption from military service; clearly, the butcher's bill on the Somme was having an effect on recruitment drives and men were no longer quite so eager to join the colours. While local men continued to win honours, the casualty lists were exceptionally high; even out of the trenches, some men couldn't stand it any more. In May 1917, a soldier described as being in poor health - he was probably suffering from shell-shock - was found dead in Lochend Woods. He had shot himself.[52]

Not listed among the Dunbar war dead on the local war memorial but whose family had lived in Dunbar was Charles Hamilton Sorley, a relatively unknown war poet who has recently been belatedly recognised for his few war poems. Charles Sorley's grandfather William was minister of Belhaven Church in 1840; William Sorley married Anne, daughter of William Hamilton Ritchie, solicitor and Town Clerk of Dunbar who was involved in the preliminary discussions to create the Victoria Harbour (see Chapter 9). William and Anne's son, Professor William Ritchie Sorley was the father of Charles who fell in France in October 1915. Charles Sorley's output of poems was meagre - he was only 20 when he was killed - but the surviving 45 include six about the Great War. The war poems show considerable in one so young and inexperienced. His finest poem, Poem No 2 - *The Pale Battalions* - possibly the last he wrote - contains lines worthy of Siegfried Sassoon and Wilfrid Owen. The following lines occur at the beginning of the poem, which tell us of the young man's anguish:

When you see millions of the mouthless dead

Across your dreams in pale battalions go
Say not soft things as other men have said
That you'll remember. For you need not so

Charles Sorley took a mature, objective view of the war, criticising Rupert Brooke for his misplaced sentimentality. In Sorley's view, a poet should write the truth. He was proved awesomely, terribly right. As for his half dozen war poems, they indicate a fine talent in the making. The realist in him as to war was reflected in his poetry; he knew that birds do not 'stir,' nor do trees 'whisper,' nor is heaven 'bright.'

There were a few odd little anecdotes reported in the *Courier* from time to time.[53] One can but speculate about the story behind the discovery by a Chirnside woman of an enamelled brooch she found in the belly of a fish she'd bought in Eyemouth. The brooch bore the inscription *I promise you*; on the reverse was *In memory of those who have died for me, never to trade with Germany or a German as long as I live.* Was its owner a bereaved mother, sweetheart or wife? And how did the brooch end up in the belly of a fish?

KRM

Illus 149: *Charles Vassie's grave-*

In the final and almost successful German offensive mounted by Ludendorff on 21st March 1918, several men from Dunbar or connected with it were killed; among them were Captain James Kirk and Major Roy Wingate, Royal Engineers.[54, 55] By 1918, Wingate had added the French *Croix de Guerre* to the MC he had won earlier; ironically, he was killed on 27th March, the same day Captain Kirk was fatally wounded. In June 1917, it was reported that 74 officers and other ranks from Dunbar had lost their lives up to that point in the war; however, this doesn't mean that the other 47 whose names are inscribed on the war memorial at Bayswell Park died between then and Armistice only five months later. Many had been posted missing or subsequently died of wounds.

A surprising story with not a little whiff of *Boys' Own* or *The Magnet* - comics for boys extolling the virtues of good, clean-living and upstanding lads - appeared in the *Courier* of 21st June 1918[56]. Well, at least it was heroic from the German point of view. The local paper reported that a book entitled *Amazing Confessions* had been published by Colonel Otto von Heynitz, the Aide-de-Camp to the Crown Prince of Germany. The *Courier* quoted a few lines from the book:

'Oh, how you dear British have been bluffed, Before the war, the Count [Colonel Count von Neumann Cosel, the author's friend] lived as a gentleman of independent means in your country in a fine house near Dunbar, in Scotland, and, under an assumed name, secretly directed the German military survey of your country.'

MD

Illus 150: *German cannon of 1914-15*

Was Otto von Heynitz writing the truth? Was his admission simply propaganda designed to undermine British morale at a bad time for Germany, when the USA entered the war? We will never know.

A little known fact until recent years was the use of Belhaven Sands for airborne torpedo trials in the final stages of the war. East Fortune aerodrome was the base for a prototype aircraft-carrying torpedo. With its firm sands, Belhaven was an ideal training area; the Sopwith T1 - later known as the Sopwith Cuckoo - flew over Belhaven for 230 of the 270 trials carried out in Britain. Airborne torpedoes were never used in the war, no doubt much to the relief of the pilots who flew the Sopwiths; apart from their single torpedo, the flimsy aircraft carried no defensive armament, relying on manoeuvrability for getting out of trouble.

When the Great War ended, a fund was set up to honour the Glorious Dead - or rather, to comfort their relatives. Like every other sorrowing parish in Scotland, Dunbar erected a war memorial; in January 1919, the burgh council outlined its intention and a subscription list was issued in April. A dedication ceremony was held on 3rd July 1921, the address read by Sir Reginald Wingate. The memorial contains the names of 12 officers, 108 other ranks and Sister Violet Fraser, a nurse from the parish. Their names appear in **Fig 19**. Among them is my uncle George Henderson, Royal Artillery; he reputedly served throughout the war unscathed until its closing stages. In 1924, the British Legion organised a War Graves Pilgrimage to Flanders and invited the bereaved in every community to join the pilgrimage. Most widows and other relatives in Dunbar declined the invitation as they felt it would re-open old wounds. Only six went from the town.[57] As far as I know, no official death roll of Scots has hitherto been published, Scotland lost about 110,000 dead, a fifth of the UK fatal casualties (573,000); Scotland's population was about a tenth of the whole, making her sacrifice double the proportion of her population.

World War II

As the 1930s progressed, war clouds again gathered over Europe, heralded by the Spanish Civil War. A Dunbar man called McCluskie volunteered to join the Republican International Brigades against the Nationalists under Franco. He returned home and wore his Spanish beret proudly for the rest of his life. A committed Communist, he had his own seat in local pub and woe betide anyone who used it. It is said that when he died, his few comrades wanted to give him a military salute at his funeral but as guns were not allowed in the graveyard, his pals had to content themselves with singing the *International.* Few who remember McCluskie today gave his unselfish gesture much thought in the 1930s; he was astute enough to realise that the Spanish conflict was a prelude to the Second World War and that those who mocked his beliefs would soon be in uniform themselves.

Increasingly, the talk turned to the likelihood of war with Germany. Despite the efforts of those who hoped to appease Hitler, the government began to prepare - just in case. As early as 1937, local authorities were given special powers under the Air Raid Precautions Act of that year, followed by the Civil Defence Act of 1939. These powers were exercised at county or large burgh level; counties were empowered to direct the small burghs within their boundaries to take any necessary steps for a war which was expected to be fought mainly in the air. Burghs like Dunbar were requested to recruit Air Raid Precautions (ARP) personnel in 1937; the burgh council appointed nine air wardens, six decontaminant (gas) squads and five cyclists and runners. Until well into 1940, the burgh council and the provost and magistrates' committee minutes are preoccupied with purely precautionary measures, largely centred on Castellau House, for long a derelict mansion at the foot of the West Port. In 1938, Castellau became a first-aid post and was used to instruct volunteers in anti-gas attack measures.[58] The burgh council busied itself complying with ARP circulars issued from the Scottish Office in St Andrew's House, Edinburgh, allocating child evacuees from Edinburgh to local families and organising temporary shelter for those made homeless by enemy action. Blackout enforcement - the removal of street lighting and painting the High Street kerbstones white - fire watching and liasing with the local Home Guard platoon were uppermost on the council's agenda.

By 1939, the Castle Park Barracks had gained a new significance; the building became the HQ of the 165th Officer Cadet Training Unit (OCTU). The council minutes of the time contain references to the billeting of officers and cadets in the Hillside and Craig-en-gelt Hotels and private homes, including my mother's. Preparations were made for the safety of civilian population and military personnel alike. The former were provided with somewhat ineffective above ground air raid shelters, initially in the High Street and then in the conurbations; there were however some deep underground shelters in the High Street as it was considered a prime target because of its proximity to the railway line. The military set about doing what their fathers had done 25 years earlier; they dug slit trenches everywhere, particularly at Bayswell Park, Belhaven Shore and West Barns Links, the last two being protected by lines of anti-tank concrete blocks which eventually ran the entire length of the coast. There are surviving examples at Tyninghame and Gullane foreshores; most of those at Dunbar were used after the war to shore up the eroding bank at Winterfield Golf Course, near the fifteenth tee. Belhaven Bay was also sown with anti-glider poles embedded in concrete and sunk into the sand to forestall a glider-borne invasion. Another anti-invasion measure was a concrete hut placed at the Victoria Harbour mouth, opposite the harbourmaster's office; described somewhat erroneously as a 'flame control' building, in the event of a German vessel entering the harbour, the occupants would spray petrol on the sea, then set it and the invader alight. In your dreams....

Mention of the local golf course brings to mind an apocryphal story told of Sir Reginald Wingate during the early years of the war. It isn't a golfing tale, although Wingate was keen on the game. In the 1990s, a former cadet-officer stationed at Dunbar took part in a documentary about Thomas Cook's Tours, which had begun at the time of the Mahdi uprising in the Sudan, Cook's had provided the boats to take Kitchener's forces up the Nile in an attempt to relieve Khartoum and save General Gordon. The retired army officer was retelling this tale of Cook's and mentioned Wingate, who had accompanied the relief force. He said that as a young cadet-officer at Dunbar, he and some colleagues had been invited to Wingate's house at Knockenhair for drinks one evening, The Grand Old Man began to regale the company with anecdotes of the Sudanese wars when the cadet noticed a skull in a glass cabinet. He asked Wingate whose it was. The old man informed him that it was the head of the Dervish chief he had chased through the Nile marshes in 1899. When asked the reason for the silver plate or cup embedded in the skull, Wingate told the young man that he drank his claret from the grisly memento! One wonders whether Evelyn Waugh had heard this story as Brigadier General Ritchie Hook - one of his characters in his World War 2 novel *Officers and Gentlemen* - had similar alarming tendencies.

Without in any way minimising the ultimate sacrifice made by those from Dunbar who never came back, the war interfered with rather than threatened the lives of those who were fortunate enough to stay at home. The war was, in short, an inconvenience. The farmer was primarily concerned with the harvest, the fisherman with his catch, the local trader with his sales - made more difficult by the imposition of rationing. Due to enemy submarine warfare, imports of food were restricted; as a consequence, there was a pressing need to grow more food and the authorities urged the civilian population to 'dig for victory.' (Many of my parents' generation will recall the famous poster of the apparently one-legged man with foot on spade!). In Dunbar as elsewhere, every public park, every private and council house lawn and flower garden became kitchen gardens almost overnight. The burgh authorities put the Winterfield Public Park to crops, organised allotments at Lauderdale Park and created a municipal farm at Seafield, West Barns, where pigs and chickens were reared and grain and potatoes were grown. Shortages of raw materials became acute - timber, coal, iron and steel - so the parks and gardens were stripped of their iron railings. The public were repeatedly encouraged to save everything - waste paper and string for example - and to hand over their aluminium pots and pans for the production of Spitfires - the latter a piece of pure propaganda. Most of these campaigns were aimed at raising civilian morale, the public thereby believing that by their small sacrifices, they were 'doing their bit'. As in the Great War, there were periodic drives for funds; flag days for the Red Cross and other charities, Battleship Week, Wings for Victory Week, Jock's Box - a war comforts fund for faraway soldiers - and the War Entertainment Committee which put on shows to raise cash in aid of prisoners-of-war. Throughout the duration, the burgh council minutes are written in a style which exudes solid dependability, courage and stoicism. And on occasion, little less than unintentional farce.

Dunbar was prepared for anything Herr Hitler might throw at it. This message comes across in the council minutes of 4th September 1939, the day after war was declared. On that momentous occasion, the burgh councillors boldly and imaginatively spent a considerable part of the meeting discussing matters such as how early shops should close, finally agreeing to leave the matter on the table. (In any event, the Blackout Regulations would resolve the problem as darkness comes earlier in autumn). This may be slightly unfair to the no doubt worried councillors of the day, led by their embattled provost, Phipps Oswald Turnbull - a name which would not have been out of place in a novel by H G Wells, the initials being mildly amusing. However on that figuratively dark September day, the council minutes leave us in no doubt as to the sentiments of these determined men:

> 'On Sunday, 3rd September, Great Britain and France declared war on Germany. Today, the Town Council met to consider taking any emergency measures which might be necessary. Most arrangements, however, had been well thought-out beforehand and the community was in a prepared state.'

They might have mentioned that kerbstones had been painted white, for that was the extent of the community's 'prepared state'. The plain fact is that these imagination-challenged men hadn't a clue what to do. How could Hitler have known what he was up against? How on earth did he believe he could win the war?

There were more subtle and clandestine measures in preparation, if not already in place. These measures have only recently come to light. It may be conjectural but with hindsight, was there a more sinister reason behind the innocent application submitted by the governors of Belhaven Hill School to the local Dean of Guild for a warrant to erect an additional building containing a bathroom, classroom and bedroom on 2nd September 1939? In 1995, it was revealed[59] that the school had in fact housed personnel of the Special Operations Executive (SOE), Britain's top level spy organisation, a fact made known in the release of wartime papers under the fifty-year rule. Female SOE operatives were ostensibly members of the First Aid Nursing Yeomanry

(FANY) to cover their clandestine work. The SOE was made famous by the exploits of special agents like Violette Szabo and Odette Churchill; fluent in French, they were parachuted behind enemy lines in France to report troop movements. In June 1943, Belhaven Hill School became a Special Training School (STS No 54B) and communications post for SOE operatives in occupied France. Its operatives who departed on dangerous missions which often ended in capture, torture and death were taught their codes by the Belhaven Unit, maintaining their contact with Belhaven from France and Norway. This was one of the best-kept secrets of the war. The military personnel at Belhaven were sworn to secrecy. On the staff were twins Margaret and Jean Hunter from Aberdeen; in their own words

> 'We were taught [ordered?] not to socialise with the people of Dunbar. We ate and slept in Belhaven. Everyone just thought we were drivers. Little did they realise what we were doing.'[60]

The twins worked for a small team of six operators who decoded messages sent by morse code from France and sent them on to senior military staff in England. Many agents were probably trained at Dunbar. Violette Szabo never came back; she was captured and shot in Ravensbruck conentration camp early in 1945. Odette Churchill was severely tortured but survived; she was awarded the George Cross, posthumously awarded to Violette Szabo. Every operative was identified by the way he or she tapped morse code messages; any change in the pattern meant that the Germans had captured the operative. Were operations directed from the bogus schoolroom for which permission was sought from the Dean of Guild? It seems so. The bedroom/bathroom was clearly for the use of the six operators working in pairs three shifts of eight hours non-stop every day so that surveillance was round the clock. The unit played a vital role in intelligence gathering and the deception plans which achieved the successful landings on the Normandy beachhead in June 1944. The SOE unit at Belhaven was closed down in July 1945.

Relations between the military and the burgh council appear to have been relatively amicable although on occasion, the council minutes betray the councillors' naivety and utter lack of reality. For example, a sense of public decency and morality prompted the Town Clerk to complain to the military commandant at the Barracks about the placing of latrines in the Kirkhill for use by the army personnel billeted in the Hillside Hotel. The presence of these 'necessaries' in full view of the general public using the road was considered 'most objectionable.' The minutes are silent about who won the argument but it is likely that the latrines remained in situ.

The Kirk didn't let interference by the military go unrecorded either. At about the same time, there is a tacit sense of ruffled feathers in the session minutes of 28th September 1939 which record that the local Sunday School would have to meet in the church as the military had requisitioned the church hall. Shades of *Dad's Army* indeed. The same minutes record that the Reverend A Sawyer had been accepted for chaplaincy duty; when he returned from active service in 1941, the session minutes of 16th December intimated his invitation to the session to consider the Kirk's position in relation to the war and what it meant to the pacifist and the wider community. He outlined a Three Year Mission in Dunbar to assess the aims of the church. He believed that emphasis should be on worship:

> 'The need for this is urgent, for there will be great changes after the war and we must be ready to give a Christian lead to the community or else they [sic] will be lost. This is especially true if, as seems likely, the Russian Communism [sic] is going to be the first power to halt Hitler. Therefore we must prepare and have our plans laid.'

His warning to the kirk session in 1941 was followed about a week later by the arrival of a publication which to modern eyes has a disturbingly Orwellian ring to it. On 24th December 1941, the session minutes refer to a circular letter from the National Committee of the Religious Instruction of Youth's circular letter enclosing a leaflet entitled *The Call of Youth, Tomorrow's Builders of a New World Order.'* Wasn't that what Nazi Germany was trying to establish? There is a distinctly menacing tone about it all, shades of Orwell's *1984.*

There is a slight whiff of Churchillian rhetoric in Sawyer's mildly alarmist speech; the fear of communism sorely afflicted the Church, much more then than today. The prospect of Britain achieving freedom from Nazi tyranny at the expense of its state religion was quite frankly terrifying the Church, just as the fear of witches had driven it to acts caused by superstitious hysteria three centuries earlier. The Nazis were anti-Christ but the Church wasn't prepared to throw the baby out with the bathwater. It had to survive as it - and only it - possessed the right degree of moral rectitude and defence against the Ungodly. Having said that, Sawyer's personal contribution to the war effort wasn't in doubt; he was awarded the MC and given the rank of Major in March 1945 on his appointment as Chief Chaplain to the British Army.

The first enemy aircraft attack on Scotland occurred on 16th October, when a Heinkel 111 on a reconnaissance flight was brought down in the sea off St Abb's Head. On 28th October, the Scottish air ace Archie McKellar brought down another Heinkel 111 which landed intact at Humbie, six miles from Haddington. About this time, Junkers 88 bombers attacked Royal Navy vessels in the Forth and at Rosyth. Two enemy aircraft were shot down. On 30th October, a lone German aircraft circled over Dunbar and according to the council minutes[61]

> 'a subsequent broadcast from Hamburg......stated that Dunbar was a centre for training officers and a military centre and also at Fentonbarns there was a large aerodrome.'

Provost Turnbull was moved to inform the council that because of this - he clearly associated the Hamburg broadcast with the recent appearance of what he believed was a spy plane - he had written to the county council to protest against the ineffectiveness of the warning arrangements and requested that the defences be tightened. In all probability the plane had been on a reconnaissance mission; however the Germans probably knew that Dunbar was a military training centre as implied in the memoirs of a First World War German officer (see above). Reconnaissance sorties had already been made on Rosyth only two weeks before, when German raiders tried to bomb the Forth Rail Bridge in what was the first attack on the British Isles. Following this, a series of three waves of bombers flew up the Forth estuary, one of the targets being the battle-cruiser *HMS Hood*. The third of these enemy sorties crossed the coast at Dunbar at 2.45pm and was intercepted by Spitfires from 602 (City of Glasgow) Squadron out of Drem and 603 (City of Edinburgh) Squadron from Turnhouse. The defenders claimed one Heinkel, one Dornier and a third unidentified aircraft; a fourth plane was seen flying out to sea with one of its engines out of action.

During what was known as the 'phoney' war of 1939-40, a touch of irony appears in the burgh council minutes of 10th January 1940, four months before the evacuation at Dunkirk:

> 'It was agreed that the military authorities have the use of the swimming pool for the purpose of trying out paddle boats in connection with military training.'

Paddle-boats was about all they had in May that year, though the training was put to good use. (Dunbar and District History Society has in its possession rare film footage of probationer officers from OCTU furiously paddling - and clowning - in the swimming pool. It was the behaviour of the desperate).

News in 1940-42 was almost always depressing, broadcast over the BBC Home Service by Alvar Liddell in his stark, unrelieved tone disseminating usually bleak and ominous information. The one high moment was the euphoria - some would say miracle - of Dunkirk, a defeat which only the British could have snatched from the jaws of victory but called it one anyway. On 28th June 1940 - a Sunday - an anti-invasion meeting was held in Dunbar's Playhouse Cinema; the talk was entitled 'If the Nazis Come.' Before that, there was an incident which boosted Dunbar's morale during the evacuation of the British Expeditionary force in June 1940. Six months afterwards, on 8th January 1941, Provost Turnbull received a letter written by the Engineering Officer to the Commanding Officer, *HMS Saltash*, describing the distinguished conduct of Stoker First Class Brian Gaughan of Dunbar who

> 'displayed considerable initiative, courage and resource during the rescue of men from the *SS Brighton* and *SS Scotia* [merchantmen taking troops off the beaches] on the 1st of June. Observing two men in the water at least a quarter of a mile away from the ship [the *Saltash]* Gaughan stripped naked, fashioned [sic] a light line to himself and commenced his swim to the drowning men. At the end of a hundred yards Gaughan abandoned the life line as an encumbrance and swam on unaided. He succeeded in bringing both men back to the ship. After a brief respite, Gaughan continued to swim a life line to men struggling in the water within a couple of hundred yards of the ship. During his rescue operation, Gaughan was both bombed and machine-gunned by a German aircraft.'

This act of heroism earned Stoker Gaughan the DSM which was presented by king George VI on 8th April at Buckingham Palace. Before that, the town council congratulated Brian Gaughan; he acknowledged their praise at a council meeting on 3rd January 1941, modestly professing that

> 'any Dunbar boy would have done the same.'

The council minutes of 17th January[62] record that Stoker Gaughan attended the meeting to receive a silver wristlet watch awarded as a token of the town's esteem. The inscription read as follows:

Presented by the Town Council of Dunbar
to
Brian Gaughan, Stoker, First Class
in recognition of
Distinguished Conduct at Dunkirk, 1st June 1940

Although Dunkirk was a miracle that snatched victory from the jaws of defeat, many men were left behind, notably the 51st Highland Division at St Valery en Caux, where the Division covered the retreat of the 1st Armoured Division and other elements. While the fate of that famous Division is well-documented in regimental histories, I was fortunate recently to be gifted an unusual publication by the relatives of the late Margaret Dann whose brother Ted was among the prisoners. The book, *The Prisoners' Progress,* is hardly a war diary; it contains seven maps showing the march of the prisoners from St Valery to Germany, compiled by 2nd Lieutenant Leslie C Hunt of the East Surrey Regiment. It is a remarkable odyssey and bears some comparison with the treatment of prisoners who were forced to march from Dunbar to Durham after Cromwell's victory at Dunbar in 1650. I have inserted some extracts to illustrate the privations of men like Edward (Ted) Dann and another East Lothian man, the late David (Dave) McLeish of Elphinstone and Macmerry.

The march began at St Valery on 11th June 1940. The battle-weary men marched 220 miles in 14 days, travelling another 130 miles by water, followed by an uncomfortable train journey of 500 miles to Laufen, near Munich, where Oflag VIIC, a prisoner-of-war camp had been established for British and French officers. At some point, Ted Dann and Dave McLeish were syphoned off to Danzig (modern Gdansk) to POW camps in Thorn and Gold in East Poland. The following extracts written by Lieutenant Hunt who like other British officers were housed separately from their men -the first comparison with Cromwell's tactics in 1650 - was a source of bitterness. The second is the want of-food provided in the early stages of the march, as these extracts wuill indicate, although Lieutenant Hunt is at pains to excuse his German captors who had little food themselves.

June 11: [Formerie, France] 'Marched 12 miles. By lorry from Buchy. Slept in a field....desperately cold and miserable. Took coats off men killed in action a few days ago. Bowl of pea soup was our only meal'.

June 15: [Domart St Leger] 'Marched 16 miles. Rested one day. Had only one ladle of soup in two days, so ate dandelions [at Morpeth in 1650, the Dunbar captives ate raw cabbages, twigs and leaves] and tinned potatoes carried from St Valery. Column about 2,500 strong.'

June 17: [Doullens] 'Marched 12 miles. German rations increased, also made stew from mangolds [beet used to feed cattle]. Explored rubbish heap, found tin of salmon; ate it!....France asked for armistice today.'

June 18: [St Pol] 'Marched 17 miles. First camp for officers only. Meat and soup from Germans, ample supply of biscuits from a B[ritish] E[expeditionary] F[orce] store. Bought butter, chocolates and wine from villagers....Getting used to marching 20 odd miles a day on a breakfast cup of "acorn" coffee; only one meal always at the end of the day's march.'

June 19: [Bethune] 'Marched 18 miles. About 3,000 prisoners here. Cooked eggs bought on march, while little girls brought us bottles of tea, and asked for a kiss. Town provided us with two meals of really good vegetable soup.'

June 26: [Aalst, Belgium] 'Marched 9 miles. Belgian people ignored us....Many reunions between officers and men who were thought to have been killed. [In the French mining town of Domart and elsewhere in the mining district of France, farmers' wives and their daughters ran errands for the prisoners, buying their food and bringing back their change. Towns north of Brussels received the prisoners more sympathetically, while in Holland they were positively welcomed].

June 27: [St Nicholas, Belgium] ' Marched 16 miles. First arrivals [here] greeted with ice cream. Haircut, shave and shampoo by Belgian barber. Good rations. Civilians set up stalls for the sale of custard pies, fruit, etc....guards very strict; author was shot at while shutting a window at night.'

June 28: [Holland] 'Marched 18 miles to the long-promised rail-head at Hulst. Dutch very kind to us.'

June 29: 'Crossed River Scheldt and entered canal....No food and hardly any water.'

July 1: 'Germany....People received us, without hostility, in silence....Two meals of bread, cheese and coffee.....No mor marching.'

July 2: [Limer] 'Weary day on crowded train. French still with us......Quite well fed by Polish cooks. Again searched. [The men had been searched earlier and any military equipment had been confiscated, even knives and forks].

July 7: [Laufen, near Munich, Oflag VIIC] 'Arrived Laufen after 2 1/2 days' awful train journey, during which hardly any food or sleep. Journey's end - for the present.'

At some point en route to Laufen, Ted Dann, Dave McLeish and others were syphoned off to various Stalags, or POW camps. They were destined for Danzig. Ted Dann was imprisoned in a camp at Thorn, where he died. The late Dave McLeish was probably there also, although I recollect him mentioning a place called Gold where in the harsh winters of captivity, he was put to work prising turnips from the frozen fields; he was among those who survived captivity and were liberated by the Allies in 1945. He was a fine man, though he was bitter about the sacrifice of the 51st at St Valery.

Lieutenant Hunt ends his preamble thus:

"Some day the story of "the march" may be written - perhaps it never will be - in any case it will not be forgotten by those of us who were there."

When Churchill delivered his stirring speech about fighting on the beaches, the words had particular significance for the people of Dunbar, especially when Norway was occupied. That brought the war much closer.

Dunbar had lived with the threat of invasion in 1803-04; did Hitler know his history and would the invasion force land there? The spirit of 1804 had been different, for at that time, there had been no weapons of mass destruction; it was man against man. Not surprisingly, by 6th September 1940, the army had been given exclusive rights over all the beaches at Belhaven and West Barns north of the A1 road and between the road and the foreshore. History was repeating itself yet again.[63]

On 25th June 1940,[64] 15 Heinkels attacked Fife, Midlothian and East Lothian. A single plane detached from the flight and went on to Ayrshire, intent on bombing the ICI factory there but it had to abort the mission due to poor visibility. Returning to the east, it flew over Edinburgh and was damaged by steady fire from the West Pilton AA Battery; it then crossed East Lothian, pursued by a Spitfire from 603 Squadron which attacked it three times. The Heinkel began to lose altitude and finally crashed into the sea off Barns Ness lighthouse, four of its crew being taken prisoner. On 1st July two Junkers 88 on a reconnaissance mission were intercepted by a flight from 602 Squadron; one of the Junkers was chased by two Spitfires and had to jettison its bombload on Belhaven foreshore; it eventually crashed in France.

On the ground, the burgh council had matters well in hand by 5th July 1940, when it was minuted that the installation of underground air raid shelters at Nos 48 and 97 High Street had been completed, followed by surface shelters on the grass plot fronting the Railway Inn (now the Dolphin), the Countess Park and the Glebe, Bayswell Park. However, human nature being what it is, the authorities soon discovered that the children and others who should have known better were using the surface shelters as unofficial toilets so they had to be locked. One can imagine what would have happened if an enemy air raid had Dunbar as its objective.

In 1941, a further 10 sites were earmarked for shelters in the High Street and at the town farm at Seafield. Unaccountably, the county authorities failed to provide shelters for the schoolchildren at Woodbush; in fact the local education authority had decided that the pupils should remain within the school precincts and buildings in the event of an air raid! The burgh council rightly protested that this was inadequate provision for those who had recently been described in a quasi-religious pamphlet as 'Tomorrow's Builders of a New World Order.' The school got its shelters, although in 1942, the roofs had to be coated with bitumen to dull the glare from the concrete which made them obvious targets from the air.

The war in the air intensified. On 26th October 1940, a lone German aircraft dropped four bombs on East Linton, all of which failed to explode; from the positions of the bombs, the target had been East Linton Bridge. On 2nd November, minor hit-and-run raids were made on Dunbar and seaports in Fife. On the morning of 4th November, two bombs were dropped on South Belton Farm, severing electrical cables providing mainly commercial supplies; the majority of homes were still lit by gas. Then in March 1941, the Luftwaffe switched targets from the Forth to the Clyde Valley and bombers flew over Dunbar on several nights to inflict severe damage on Clydeside. On the night of 13th March, the crack Luftwaffe Pathfinder unit, Kampf Gruppe 100 which had led the devastating attack on Coventry guided 236 bombers to Clydeside; Clydebank was bombed the following night and again on 7th April and 5th/6th May, part of Germany's *Baedeker* raids on Britain's large industrial cities and ports. On 16th August, Innerwick Railway Station was bombed but the missiles failed to detonate; one bomb went through the parapet of the station bridge, the other two landed in a nearby potato field. There was loss of life however; one railwayman was killed and five others were wounded by machine-gun fire. The same aircraft proceeded to strafe Dunbar but it appears to have inflicted only superficial damage.[65]

On the night of 7th November 1941, Dunbar sustained superficial damage when four bombs were dropped in Blair's field at Summerfield Mains

> 'in the hollow between the railway and Summerfield [Road]'[66]

Damage was limited to broken and cracked window panes and cracked plasterwork, although one of the bomb fragments fell within twenty feet of one of the town's gasholders in the Sailor's Park. The town was bombed again on 2nd March 1942[67] when council records indicate that

> 'war damage was sustained....and 18 houses were slightly damaged.'

(My mother's bedroom window facing the Sailor's Park was cracked and not repaired until twenty years later, as I well remember her informing the Burgh Surveyor of the day who had called to make an inventory of repairs needed in houses in Lammermuir Crescent. He enquired if the crack in the pane was the result of children playing golf or football in the playing field over the garden wall. My mother, rarely ever heard to swear, left him in no doubt;

> 'That bloody Hitler did it, only four weeks before my twenty-eighth birthday. You took your time coming to fix it.'

On the evening of 3rd March 1942, three bombs were dropped on Dunbar, according to *East Lothian at War* (vol. 2), two exploded in the vicinity of Countess Road and a third proved dud, falling on Eweford Farm.

According to residents of the day, only one of the bombs exploded at Countess Road, near the railway; the other failed to explode and lay buried in the cornfield beside the railway until it was disarmed and removed in the 1960s, as I recall from a report in the *Courier*.

Britain was alone in 1941, only just holding her own against the enemy, particularly in Africa, where General Erwin Rommel and his crack Afrika Corps besieged the key British base at Tobruk from 1941 to 1942. It wasn't all bad news however; in June 1941, Hitler invaded Russia, giving Britain an unexpected ally. In addition, the Americans were supplying Britain with arms and equipment under the lend-lease agreement. In the wake of this came the American Namesake Towns Aid movement, whose British HQ at Bishop Stortford was known as American Namesake Towns Committee. The aim was to establish links between the mayors of USA and British cities with the same name - in the same way as modern town-twinning. The Committee informed Dunbar burgh council[68] that there were nine Dunbars in the States, most of them small communities. These were in the states of Georgia, Iowa, Louisiana, Mississippi, Minnesota, Carolina, Virginia, West Virginia and Wisconsin - was the latter named for John Muir who lived there for a few years? (It is interesting that six of the nine Dunbar communities occur in the Confederate States of the American Civil War; perhaps many emigrants from Scotland settled in these states).

It transpired that Dunbar, West Virginia, was the largest of the nine communities and Provost Phipps Turnbull wrote to his counterpart there; the mayor responded in August 1941. He said he hadn't known of a town called Dunbar in Scotland! He wrote to Provost Turnbull, informing him that Dunbar, West Virginia had been chartered only 20 years earlier; in 1941, it had a population of about 6,000 which was expected to increase. The provost replied with an account of Dunbar Ancient and Modern;[69] part of his letter contained a description of Dunbar in the sixteenth century, attributed to 'an officer commanding the French garrison at Dunbar Castle,' a fact which must have confused his American counterpart. French soldiers in a Scottish town? Phipps' account is remarkably similar to that of Jean de Beaugue in 1548 (see Chapter 3); while attempts to trace the source of the extract, the so-called French soldier's version is quoted from the burgh council minutes:

> '[Dunbar] is a town that stands upon the brink of the sea about ten leagues from Edinburgh, upon the skirts of Lothian in a very good country and accommodated with all these advantages that conduce both to the pleasure and support of life. If the place were fortified [sic] and a good harbour contrived, which might be done with very inconsiderable charges, it would unquestionably claim a precedence among the goodliest towns which are anywhere to be seen in these islands. It has already a very strong and beautiful castle, built upon a high rock, on the edge of the sea; the avenues that lead to it are not to be forced but with vast danger and difficulty; and art here has seconded nature so admirably well that there are few places in the universe that can vie with those conveniences the Castle of Dunbar affords for defence against batteries of any warlike engines or invention whatever.'

This is virtually de Beague's account; as we know, he was an historian, not a soldier. This apart, was the passage chosen deliberately to impress the Americans? Like war, propaganda brings strange bedfellows. Scotland had resisted English invaders in the past; a united Britain was now resisting a formidable enemy, even if molished in the late 1960s to make way for modern housing. 'A' Company served from 1940 until they were stood down at their final parade on 3rd August 1944. Many tales are told - no doubt exaggerated - of these bucolic 'teeth and stomach' battalions which inspired the popular and endearing TV series *Dad's Army* which gently mocked these volunteer units and their activities. Beneath the humour was pathos; these superannuated men and young boys were determined to 'do their bit' and engage the enemy if and when he invaded Britain. The Home Guard in fact played a vital role in releasing regular soldiers from guard and lookout duties. Its members swore to fight and give their lives if necessary. By 1943, the Home Guard was improved and efficient. There is an apocryphal story told in Dunbar - and elsewhere, which makes its authenticity suspect - that on one occasion, the platoon was marching dangerously close to the cliff edge at the West Promenade. Lieutenant Barlas apparently forgot the recognised command words to change direction and had to be prompted by a veteran NCO, who stopped the men marching over the cliffs! So the story goes. It might be true and wouldn't be out of character in *Dad's Army.* No photograph of the Dunbar platoon has so far turned up but there is one of the Broxmouth platoon (**ill 151**).

The war had much to answer for; it brought out the best and the worst in people. It was certainly responsible for encouraging the latent arrogance in many small-minded men and perhaps some women who were placed in positions of authority in the ARP and Civil Defence Services. Their boiler suits and tin helmets gave them an air of authority and a sense of importance they had never enjoyed in peace-time. One suspects that the ARP warden in *Dad's Army* was typical of the breed - the small town greengrocer suddenly given power beyond his imagining and capability. Such people dominated the lives of the civilian population to a degree which would never be tolerated in peace-time. In theory, they made no distinction between the great and the rich, the humble and the poor; the truth is that they deferred sycophantly to the former and vented their spleen on the latter. Attempts to argue with them or complaints about their overbearing attitude would be met with the stock response:

'There's a war on, you know.'

The war was a great gift to the small man, the bureaucrat and the snooping meddler. Little people thrown into positions of authority are remarkably quick to grasp pretensions of grandeur; invariably, they succumb to fatuous pedantry, which is always a dead giveaway to their true nature.

Illus 151: *Broxmouth Platoon, Home Guard* DDHS

The town's embattled Provost Phipps Oswald Turnbull (1937-47) had many discussions with the local military in his municipal role; on the whole, relations were cordial but goodwill became stretched occasionally.

The burgh council complained about the damage being done to the road surfaces by tanks and bren gun carriers; the latter were particular nuisances since being light vehicles, their drivers liked to race through the streets, probably to impress the local girls. Their dangerous driving led the council to voice its concern about danger to life and limb. There were also problems with the young cadet officers from OCTU who used local roads for their driving lessons until these roads were declared off limits.

Despite Britain's poor military performance in 1941, brighter days appeared on the horizon. On 7th December 1941, the Japanese attacked Pearl Harbour without warning, thus precipitating America's entry into the war. Early in 1942, [70] the Admiralty suggested that the county of East Lothian should adopt the minesweeper *HMS Dunbar* which had been built at a cost of £250,000; Dunbar agreed to meet £15,000 of this through war savings schemes. The ship's First Officer, Lieutenant L M Trevor later wrote to the burgh council intimating that as this was the first ship to be named for the town, the officers wanted to buy a ship's crest for the foredeck of the bridge. The council agreed to provide a bronze plaque bearing the municipal coat-of-arms and which had lately adorned the gates of Winterfield Public Park. This wasn't as straightforward as had been assumed; the plaque had first to be matriculated - registered - by Lyon, King-at-Arms, the heraldic officer who presides over the Lyon Court and records pedigrees and authorises armorial bearings. The plaque was registered on 20th October 1942. A presentation ceremony was held in the County Buildings, Haddington on 13th February 1943 - clearly no one was superstitious - and the plaque was inscribed as follows:

'This plaque is presented to HMS Dunbar to commemorate her adoption by the county of East Lothian during Warship Week from 28th February to 7th March inclusive.'

They might have been a bit more lavish in their enthusiasm. A photograph of the plaque was hung in the burgh chambers at Dunbar. *HMS Dunbar* was engaged in minesweeping operations off the Normandy coast on D-Day.

Activities such as Warship Week were measures intended to boost civilian morale. At about the same time as the above event, another of Dunbar's young men was honoured by the burgh council. Dr Luigi Togneri received the MBE from the king at Buckingham Palace on 10th March 1942 for gallant conduct when the ship on which he was serving as medical officer was torpedoed on 19th September 1940 in the Atlantic. The crew took to the lifeboats but the captain, mate and Dr Togneri remained on board

'and by their determined and heroic efforts, kept the ship afloat until rescue arrived.' [71]

The burgh council presented Dr Togneri with a silver wristlet watch at their meeting on 3rd April 1942. Luigi, or Louie, as he was known locally, was torpedoed a second time and the council met the cost of repairing his watch which had been damaged by salt water. Tragically, Louie Togneri MBE, whose family still lives in Dunbar, didn't survive a third sinking. His incredible luck ran out in 1944, when he was drowned aged only 31. His father Joseph was also lost at sea in 1940 aged 54.

Although the war began to turn in the Allies' favour, the threat of invasion was never far away. In 1942, Dunbar's Invasion Committee - they had a committee for everything in that war - busied itself with plans for evacuating the general population, provision of medical and nursing services and, ominously, the training of National Fire and Civil Defence personnel in small arms training. On 13th May 1942, the burgh council was informed by the Scottish Home Department that because of renewed activity by enemy aircraft, it was possible that the Luftwaffe might seek to exploit opportunities in the next six weeks, turning attention to places of historical interest and that as a consequence, Fire Guard personnel were to be put on full alert.

Then came the best news of the war to date. In November 1942,[72] the town learnt of the victory at El Alamein. The burgh council minutes refer to

> 'the good news which had been received that morning of the success which has attended our arms in Egypt. This is a glorious achievement and augurs well for our ultimate victory over the Axis powers.
> It was agreed to record the Council's sense of pride and satisfaction with the military situation in Egypt.'

During Wings for Victory Week (12th-19th June 1943), Dunbar witnessed what the burgh council minutes describe as the most complete parade and opening ceremony the town had known in modern times. The parade took two minutes to pass the saluting base at the Town House, where the salute was taken by the Earl of Haddington. Wings for Victory Week was a resounding success throughout Britain; East Lothian's target was £400,000, Dunbar offering to raise £42,500. The total contributions from war and defence bonds and savings schemes amounted to £532,129 for the county, £52,624 raised in Dunbar. The Dunbar contribution purchased a Lancaster bomber, a Hotspur and two Spitfires.

In September 1943,[73] another Dunbar man was praised for an act of gallantry although his achievement didn't attract much official recognition. The council minutes paid tribute to the bravery of Robert Marr, fisherman of Castle Cottage for putting to sea

> 'at a moment's notice and affecting the rescue of an Airman who had come down in the sea on Monday, 6th inst. The Chairman recalled that it was only one of the many cases of rescue work in which this man has been concerned.'

Fair if somewhat muted praise. Bob Marr was a well-known and much-loved fisherman at the Victoria Harbour for many years.

As the war progressed, there appears to have been a degree of relaxation in the prescriptive measures introduced at the beginning. The council minuted become more concerned with implementing Scottish Office circulars on ARP and other related matters. There are also many references to the town farm at Seafield, West Barns which throughout the war years produced much-needed produce - oats, barley, potatoes, turnips, pigs and chickens. The local public park was sown with oats, barley and potatoes for most of the duration and local men were enjoined to cultivate town allotments in Lauderdale Park. All these measures were part of the Dig for Victory campaign which urged both local authorities and private individuals alike to convert their parks and gardens into vegetable plots.

One of the regiments which took part in the Sicily landings in 1943 was based at Dunbar; 227 Battery, 66th Medium Regiment, Royal Artillery (Territorial Army) which recruited in Edinburgh and East Lothian had the distinction of being the first medium Royal Artillery unit to engage the Germans since the fall of France in 1940. There were probably Dunbar men in the regiment as it held a reunion in the town on 31st July 1966.[74] Surprisingly, there are no references to the D-Day landings in the local records, perhaps because of war-time restrictions. Without doubt, Castle Park Barracks trained men for that great invasion on 6th June 1944. About four months after D-Day, we know that a derelict house in Victoria Street was used to train men in street fighting, as the Town Clerk was obliged to complain to the Officer Commanding at Castle Park about the state of the roadway after these training exercises. He describes the road as 'untidy and dangerous' with coping stones, bricks and other material left strewn about the street, making it a public nuisance. The Town Clerk stood his ground and respectfully requested that

> 'the roadway should be cleared at the close of practice.'[75]

No doubt those being trained in a type of fighting intended to slow down the Allied advance in Europe were suitably chastened by an attack of a milder nature.

Perhaps after D-Day, I dimly recall thinking there was something not quite right in the small idyllic world of Dunbar, yet I enjoyed the experience. At the age of three and a half, I have a vivid memory of being led along the Edinburgh Road clutching a loaf of bread to feed men who clamoured behind the wall of a field known as Riggs and Floors, now the site of a modern housing estate. These men spoke in funny voices and they laughed and smiled a lot. They were probably happy to be prisoners of war and they eagerly grasped the bits of bread I held up to them. One man showed his gratitude by giving me a beautiful hand-carved brown wooden horse on wheels; another handed over a small ring made from a teaspoon as I was later told. Much to my eternal regret, my war trophies were lost in some domestic clear-out in the 1950s. (One of these men - an Austrian by birth - stayed behind after the war to work on a farm at East Barns, marrying my mother's niece, then leaving to become a miner in Doncaster).

MD

Illus 152: *Poppy laying ceremony at the Parish Church between the wars*

Perhaps the lack of a celebration to mark D-Day was a sign of the war-weariness in Dunbar. However, in the autumn of 1944, the town along with the rest of the UK celebrated Battle of Britain Sunday on 17th September

> 'to commemorate......not only the air engagement of 1940 but also the work of the Civil Defence Services and of all others who rendered service during the period of intense air attacks aimed first at the invasion of this country and later at the destruction of the morale of the civilian population.'

Dunbar held its united church service in the *Playhouse Cinema* at 3pm that Sunday. One of the airmen, local man Flight Lieutenant J E 'Chit'Dann was awarded the DFC in April 1945 for gallantry and meritorious service.[76]

Then suddenly, it was all over. With a few notable exceptions, Scotland had been relatively untouched by the bombing raids compared with other areas of Britain. Dunbar escaped with only minor damage and as far as can be ascertained, there were only two fatal civilian casualties, both at Innerwick. On 11th May 1945, the *Haddingtonshire Courier* reported that VE Day was received with mixed feelings in Dunbar and there were no noisy celebrations. On 15th June, the *Courier* noted the return of the first prisoners-of-war to their homes in Dunbar. On 24th August, after the Japanese surrendered, VJ Day wasn't recognised by any official formalities. The burgh council was preoccupied with the resumption of summer holidays in the spring of 1945.[77] The Town Clerk wrote to the Officer Commanding, Castle Park Barracks requesting that the trenches in the Bayswell be in-filled and re-turfed as visitors coming to the town for their holidays would be anticipating their games of putting! The irritation of war had been inconvenient, interrupting the life of a holiday resort.

It took much longer to remove the larger but somehow less intrusive obstacles such as the serpent-like wall of concrete blocks set up as tank traps along the Belhaven and West Barns foreshores. They were the delight of many a schoolboy playing on Saturday afternoons; at least two generations after the war used them and the surviving trenches in their re-enactment of the war. Most were removed in or around the 1960s,[78] used to shore up eroding banks at Belhaven's Winterfield Golf Course; a few survive at Tyninghame, where they have been covered by moss, tamed by nature, mute testimonies to a once hostile time.

More obvious - but not detrimental to the holiday trade - were the tall wooden poles embedded in concrete bases along Belhaven sands, intended to deny the hard, flat beach to enemy gliders in the event of invasion. Not surprisingly, the War Office's cavalier request that the local council meet the cost of removing these poles in September 1945 was met with stony silence particularly as the council had to pay one shilling (5p) for every pole erected at the start of the war. (The stumps of some of the poles survive today, on the foreshore fronting the John Muir Country Park). In September 1945, the air raid shelters in front of the Railway Hotel, the Glebe and Bayswell Park were dismantled. Life was getting back to normal. Even so, the nondescript brick-built shelters elsewhere in Dunbar were still around 10 years later, used mainly as gang huts, unofficial toilets or for firewood and waste paper hoarded for Guy Fawkes Night bonfires.

As elsewhere, the fatal casualties suffered in the community were considerably less than those in the Great War; even so, Dunbar's sacrifice was not inconsiderable. Sixty-four men and a woman lost their lives, compared with 120 men and one woman in the Great War; their names appear in **Fig 18.**

Although civilian Scotland had escaped the worst of the war, its first and final actions took place in the Firth of Forth. The first shots had been fired in the Forth Estuary in 1940, the last off the May Island on 7th May 1945. A German U-boat sank two ships in convoy off the island then sailed home to surrender. Nine men needlessly lost their lives in this pointless action. After the hostilities ended in Japan in August 1945, the process of rebuilding the country began slowly; it would be many years before cities like London, Coventry and areas like Clydeside would fully recover. Rationing of several items such as sweets continued into the 1950s, noted as years of austerity. Sadly, the war Provost of Dunbar, avuncular Phipps Oswald Turnbull died on 23rd February 1947; at least he lived long enough to see peace restored. The town gave him an impressive funeral in honour of his stewardship of the burgh during the crisis.

A year after the war ended, the government requested that all local authorities provide a victory celebration for their schoolchildren; at first, Dunbar began to prepare for the event, then for some reason postponed its celebrations. Eventually, the Victory Day Celebrations went ahead at Winterfield Sports Ground on 8th June 1946, an event attended by children from the town schools and those in the rural areas.[79] After the war, the tanks of the Lothian and Border Horse were based at Castle Park Barracks, their training ground being at Hedderwick Sands for the next ten years. They remained there until 1954-55, after which the Barracks were vacated. Swords turned quickly into ploughshares. The Barrack accommodation served as a venue for various clubs well into the 1960s; its Gymnasium or Gym was transformed into the Victoria Ballroom, where dances were held and obscure pop groups such as Lulu and the Luvvers entertained the local population on occasions. Lulu has probably forgotten her appearances in Dunbar....

In May 1964, Dunbar organised a Bygone Days Exhibition which featured mainly old photographs of the town; however, the display included items of equipment, weapons and uniforms worn by the East Lothian and Berwickshire Yeomanry, re-constituted as the Lothian and Border Horse.[80] In September 1995 the *Edinburgh Evening News*[81] organised a special show entitled *East Lothian at War* which toured the county, illustrating through live sketches and historical anecdotes how the war had affected the area.

After two world conflicts, the decline of Britain's empire was in its final stages which gave rise to what may be termed end of empire fever rather than war. One such incident involved Malaya where communist elements who had fought the Japanese demanded independence from Britain. I lost a cousin in that conflict, Private Dennis Moore, in 1949, killed along with an officer and a sergeant on burial detail in the jungle. The incident was reported in the national press. Communist 'bandits' had booby-trapped the body of a dead British soldier and as the burial party lifted the corpse on to the stretcher, the grenades detonated. Dennis Wood was one of 600 British soldiers - mainly National Servicemen - who lost their lives between 1949 and 1964 in what was described as a police action. It is ironic that the Second World War, known as The Emergency officially ended on 31st March 1949 by Order in Council of parliament. Inexplicably however, the War Graves Commission declared that those killed in action after 1947 wouldn't be treated as casualties of the Second World War. Such is the stuff of bureaucracy,

After Malaya came Korea, then Suez. None of these affected Dunbar in any sense although in the summer of 1956, I recall the announcement which came over the tannoy at the swimming pool that far off summer requesting all Class A reservists to report to the local police station for registration. Several men rose out of the summer crowd, left their families and went off to war again, this time in Suez.

In the early 1950s, the army finally left Dunbar for good. After a century of occupation by the military, the War Department informed the burgh council in 1955[82] that portions of the Castle Park Barracks and the entire New Inn Barracks had been placed on the redundant lands and buildings list and were available for sale; central government asked the council if it might be interested in these properties. The council expressed their interest in Castle Park but financial constraints prevented them from tendering for the New Inn Barracks. After some deliberation, the War Department sold Lauderdale House to East Lothian County Council for £9,775 in 1962. The property fell into decay although some of it was serviceable and used by various organisations periodically. A friend and I used the basement for the *Doone Art Gallery* in 1965-66, selling paintings by local and other artists and arts and crafts. Unfortunately, Dunbar wasn't ready for such amenities and the gallery closed due to lack of interest. Lauderdale House was finally refurbished to go the way of many fine building these days; converted into flats in 1995, its exterior features have been preserved.

After more than three centuries, Dunbar's love affair with the military finally came to an end in 1955. The presence of troops in the community were not only a valuable source of income for the local traders; many local women married soldiers from other parts of Britain which accounts for the presence of 'foreign' surnames in Dunbar today - my own included. The army brought music and colour to Dunbar - all the world loves a parade, as they say.

Fig 18 Casualties of War 1899-1945

There are two war memorials in Dunbar; the first is dedicated to the men of the Lothians and Border Imperial Yeomanry who fell in the Boer War and to those of the Lothians and Border Horse in the two World Wars. Only the names of the Yeomanry casualties appear on the monument, which is situated outside the Parish Church.

The second monument is at Bayswell Park, dedicated to the men and women who gave their lives in the two World Wars. These are named below, along with the names of men who had some connection with Dunbar and whose graves or memorials are in the Parish Church cemetery but whose names do not appear on the Bayswell Memorial.

I Monument dedicated to Dunbar men of the19th Company of the Lothian and Border Imperial Yeomanry; these are listed below in alphabetical order, not in the order in which they occur on the monument:

Corporal G M Addie, October 1900 at Frederickstad
Lieutenant Alfred Cochran- Campbell, shot at Nooltgedach 13th December 1900
Trooper A A Cowan, April 1901 at Brandfort
Trooper Ian Fletcher, May 1901, Winburg
Corporal G R McGibbon, October 1900 at Velverdiend
Trooper J McGuire, Colt-Gun Section, April 1900 Stellenbosch
Corporal J McLaughlan, April 1902 at Steinkop
Trooper C R Peddie-Waddell, February 1901 at Johannesburg
Sergeant W W Romanel, February 1901 at Johannesburg
Trooper G Stobo, October 1900 at Krugersdorp
Trooper D Turnbull, 1901, Pretoria.

'DULCE ET DECORUM EST PRO PATRIA MORI'

2 War Memorial Bayswell Park. Information in square brackets derives from headstones in Dunbar Parish Churchyard.

'In Memory of Those from the Burgh and Parish of Dunbar who gave their
lives in the Great War 1914-1918'

'Their Name Liveth for Evermore'

A[ndrew] Stewart Anderson [Major, 10th Battalion Royal King's Liverpool Regiment (Liverpool-Scottish):
fell leading his men in the charge at Hooge on 16th June 1915]
Duncan Anderson [killed in action at sea 4th May 1918 aged 39]
Edward Anderson
George Anderson [Scots Guards, died of wounds in France 19th June 1915 aged 21]
Robert Anderson [Captain 8th Battalion Royal Scots, killed 5th March 1916]
James Angus
John Bald
William J Black
James M[orrison] Borthwick [France, 7th June 1919 aged 28]
Thomas Boyle [see illustration 148]
James Boyle
William Brims
James Browning
Robert L Bruce
Alexander J Budge
James Buglass
Charles M Burgoyne
George [Edward] Burton [killed in action in France 1st August 1916 aged 21]
Alexander Campbell
William Chapman
Hugh Christie
William Coe
William Colborne
John Y Collins
James Collins [this is the order of listing on the Memorial]
George H Combe

George E Crooke
John Cross
William Cunningham
Thomas Curr
James W Davis
Kenneth Dickson
William S Dickson
John Donaldson
Thomas Edington
John Edmonds
Alex McK Elrick
John Esson
Gavin Fairbairn [killed 2nd April 1918 aged 33]
John Fairbairn [killed 13th April 1918 aged 21]
Peter Fairbairn
John Farquhar
George Farquhar [this is the order of listing on the Memorial]
John A Farrell
Adam Fleming
Robert K Galloway
Robert Gardner
Thomas Gardner
James Gaughan
John Gaughan
Thomas Gilhooly
James Gillan
John Gillan
James W[ilson] Good [1st/4th Royal Scots drowned Suez Canal, 8th March 1916]
William Gordon [Private, Machinegun Corps (Infantry) killed 17th September 1918 aged 35]
George Hannan
Andrew C Henderson [Lance-Corporal, killed 20th April 1917 aged 20]
George Henderson [my Aunt's first husband].
James Hepburn
James Herkes [killed on the Western Front - probably at Mons - in 1914 aged 24]
William Hill
Peter Hogg
Alexander Hunter
Walter Jardine
James R Jeffrey
B Jenkins
Charles Kerse
John Kerr [this is the order of listing on the Memorial]
Rev James Kirk [MC]
James R Knox [Sergeant, Royal Garrison Artillery, died 25th November 1918 aged 44]
William Lough [Private, Royal Army Medical Corps, died 24th November 1918]
John P Mason [Sapper, Royal Engineers killed 21st February 1915]
Robert Mason
Thomas Mason
George Mercer
Richard Mercer
Alexander Millar
Alexander Miller
David T Marr
Hugh Marr
Robert Marr
Edward A Marrow
James Moncrieff
John Moncrieff
William J Mustarde
Andrew Moody
James Moody
John E Myles
George MacDonald
David J MacLeod
John C McIntosh
Alexander Nisbet [fell in action in France 29th June 1917 aged 25]
James O'Brien
John O'Brien

William Paxton
Robert Penney
Martin Pott [Corporal, 1st/4th Battalion Royal Scots, died of wounds received in action in France 23rd August 1918 aged 24]
Robert Pow
G C Prescott
Robert S Prescott
John Punton
John Pritchard
Angus Ramage
W B Robertson
Ralph S[cott] Russell [16th Royal Scots killed on the Somme 1st July 1916 aged 29]
Sinclair B Rutherford
George A Scott
Robert Shiell
James H Smith
Robert Smith
Thomas Smith
William Smith
John Stewart
Peter Stewart
Alex[ander] J Tait [Lancashire Fusiliers killed 29th March 1918 aged 19]
David S Thomson
James Turnbull [Private, Lothians and Border Horse, died 26th February 1919]
Alex M[arcus] Vassie [Heavy Battery, Royal Garrison Artillery died of wounds at Basra, Mesopotamia 21st March 1917 aged 31]
Charles E[dward 'Chugs'] Vassie
James Veitch
George W Warren
Sir George John Scott Warrender Bart.
William Watson
William Watt
Malcolm R[oy] Wingate 'MC, Croix de Guerre'
Thomas Young [prisoner-of-war in Germany, died in 1919 aged 22]
Sister Violet [T M] Fraser [died at Predejane, Serbia 5th March 1919 aged 34]

2B Memorials in the Parish Church graveyard whose names are not recorded on the Bayswell Park Memorial; presumably they are recorded elsewhere.

Lance-Corporal J Aitken, Argyll and Sutherland Highlanders, killed 25th October 1918
Lieutenant Adrian Espinalsson Barbe [5th Highland Light Infantry attached to RAF; lost in the Mediterranean through enemy action on 20th May 1918; his father was Louis Auguste Barbe of Dunbar, author and one of the first members of the East Lothian Antiquarian and Field Naturalists' Society]
Private Alexander Briggs, died in a prisoner-of-war camp in Germany 20th October 1919]
Robert Brown, 1st Highland Light Infantry died on his way home from Mesopotamia and was buried at sea on 24th May 1916 aged 36]
Henry George Congdon killed in France 20th May 1918
Sergeant 'Jock' W Lindsay (no memorial in cemetery)
Captain John M McDonald, Cameronian Regiment (Scottish Rifles) killed at High Wood (The Somme) 20th July 1916 aged 22
Sergeant C McGuire, Argyll and Sutherland Highlanders killed on 28th April 1915 aged 47
Captain Frederick Reid, 3rd/7th Argyl and Sutherland Highlanders killed on 28th April 1915
Lieutenant James M Robinson, died of wounds received during the Great War, 27th September 1922 aged 48 [by then, the War Memorial had been in place for some months, so it is not surprising that his name is not included]
Lieutenant Oswald Robinson, Royal Navy Voluntary Reserve, killed in action at Zeebrugge 23rd April 1918
P Sudworth DCM, Royal Scots Greys, 16th January 1919 aged 49
Sergeant George Murray Tinto, killed in Belgium, 4th October 1917
Alfred Edward Turnbull, lost in action while acting Surgeon on HMS Cressy, 22nd September 1914 [Brother of Phipps Oswald Turnbull, Provost of Dunbar during World War 2]
Andrew Yorston, 2nd Highland Light Infantry, killed 1916
Willliam Yorston, 8th Seaforth Highlanders, killed 1916

(The above list cannot be exhaustive as many gravestones have been thrown face down or are badly weather-worn). In addition to the above and shown in Illus 148 are Sergeant W Lindsay and Sergeant J Pearson

3 War Memorial Bayswell Park 1939-1945

Robert G Amos
William Archibald [Private, Royal Scots, 4th July 1944 aged 18]
Richard Barber
Edgar S Beevers [Glider Pilot, Regiment of Army Air Corps, 17th August 1942 aged 26]
George [C] Brunton [lost at sea]
William Burns
Colin Campbell
John G[eorge] Cook [Gunner, 11th Regiment Royal Horse Artillery, 27th August 1945 aged 33]
William Crarer
Edward [Ted] Dann [surviving relatives have informed me that Ted Dann of the Royal Horse Artillery was among the prisoners of the 51st Highland Division from St Valery and that he died a prisoner-of-war in East Poland]
Stewart McI Donaldson [died of wounds in the Middle East 14th January 1943]
Andrew H Dores
William McL Dores [Merchant Navy 1943]
William J Fairbairn
Philip L Gullane [died of wounds 28th January 1942 aged 27]
James Gullen
James Hastie
Rupert A Hendy [died in a Japanese prisoner-of-war camp: interred in St Luke Cemetery, Thailand]
James B Herbert
Alexander Herkess
James Herkes [Royal Marines, drowned in the sinking of *HMS Repulse* on 10th December 1941]
Robert Heugh
William Hewat [Sergeant, REME, 30th October 1943 aged 34]
James F Hughes
Hugh Hume
James G Johnston
William Jowitt [Trooper, Royal Scots Greys killed 10th April 1945]
Murdoch MacPherson
George Main
Robert A Malcolm
Robert B Marr
William McDonald
Angus F McPherson
William A Murray
James Nairn
Arthur Paxton
Henry Paxton
Adam Peffers
John A Rennie
Ian J Robertson
James Robertson
Peter Robertson
William Robertson
Arthur G Sergeant
John Smail [killed through enemy action 11th June 1941]
Alexander [Ross] Smith [killed in action 10th December 1941]
Hugh Smith [Sergeant, Royal Artillery, killed 22nd April 1942 aged 33]
Thomas [E] Smith [Air gunner RAF, killed when his aircraft crashed 2nd March 1940 aged 18]
Thomas S Songhurst
George F Thomson
Robert E Tofts [Sergeant, killed in air operations 15th June 1943]
[Dr] Luigi Togneri MBE
Peter P Watson [Sergeant, Royal Artillery, 8th December 1939 aged 40]
Robert D Watson
Allan H White
James H Williams
Albert Wilson
Joseph M Wilson
John Wood [Lance-Corporal, died of wounds 1945]
David C Young
Robert Young [Private, Royal Army Service Corps, killed 11th October 1940]
Agnes [C] Johnston [Auxiliary Territorial Service, thought to have died of tuberculosis contracted while on active service aged 25]

Names added later:

Colin A Malcolm
Dennis Moore died 25th September 1949

3A Memorials in Parish Church cemetery whose names are not recorded on the War Memorial possibly because most were not resident in Dunbar.

John Minto Clarke, killed 10th April 1942 aged 36: interred at Pieta Cemetery, Malta
M L Davis, Officer Cadet, Gordon Highlanders killed 23rd November 1940 aged 33
Robert Duncan, Sergeant, Wireless Operator RAF Voluntary Reserve reported missing on 13tth March 1941
I D Wallace, Officer Cadet, Royal Army Pay Corps killed 12th August 1942
E H Wells, Officer Cadet, Lincolnshire Regiment killed 5th February 1942 aged 28
J H E Wright, Royal Artillery killed 13th April 1943 aged 27.

13

The Hills

No history of Dunbar would be complete without mentioning its hills, the Lammermuirs. Most of the hills of Scotland were occupied at one time or another in history and the Lammermuirs are no exception. We know that human occupation goes back at least to the Neolithic Age around 3,000BC and possibly predating that period. However, thus far, the hills have been reluctant to part with their earliest secrets.

East Lothian is divided roughly into three parts; the coastal fringe from Musselburgh to Dunbar, the flatlands of the river Tyne and the sheep pastures of the Lammermuir Hills. The Moorfoot and Lammermuir Hills escarpment forms a long blue line south of Edinburgh to the Border ranges which effectively separate the Lowlands from Berwickshire; the Merse, or plain of the lower Tweed is however a continuation of East Lothian, parts of both shires having formed the old earldom of Dunbar.

The Lammermuirs are typified by meltwater channels created after the Ice Age, notably from Gifford to St Abb's Head. They are bounded by soft, round protuberances, occasionally steep but not high; contained within them are deep, winding *cleughs* or glens and countless small streams which make the area attractive for hill walkers. Largely pastoral, there is evidence of crop cultivation dating from the Middle Ages, when conditions were more favourable for growing cereals at higher altitudes than today's climate allows.

Millions of years ago, Scotland's south-eastern coastline was shaken by violent volcanic activity which threw up cliffs hundreds of feet above the sea. Further inland, this seismic activity created steep, sharply-defined hills whose surfaces were gradually worn down over the millenia; the attrition of wind and rain produced the Lammermuir Hills familiar to us today. It is a picturesque landscape of soft shapes and easy inclines, although in some parts, a single hill rises starkly above its neighbours, reminding us that much higher mountains once existed. Few of the Lammermuirs are high by Scottish standards; highest is Meikle Says Law 533 metres (1750') near Cranshaws, followed by Lammer Law 528m (1733') at Humbie, Little Says Law 478m (1569'), Redstone Rig 427m (1382') and Clints Dod 398m (1307'). Dunbar's Doon Hill 279m (917') pales into insignificance by comparison but its historical importance more than compensates for its lack of grandeur. While the Lammermuirs possess none of the drama of the Highlands or even other impressive hills in the Lowlands, they have a quiet loneliness that is particularly their own. In some parts, the hills will shout your name back at you but on most days, the upland silence is broken only by the bleating of sheep, the wind sifting through the grass and the muted gabble of small streams.

Although there is scant evidence to substantiate it, the Lammermuirs were probably inhabited by early colonists from Europe. The Pentland Hills have their Pictish ghosts but the feet of the Lammermuirs contain earlier shadows - those of Mesolithic Man. The later Bronze and Iron Age tribes settled for longer periods, the local Iron Age tribe being the British Otadini or Votadini who have left tantalisingly few traces of their presence. Doon Hill and its eastward-facing valley are famous because of more recent history - the victories gained by Edward I in 1296 and that of Cromwell in 1650 - but during the Iron Age, the hill was one of the Votadini's key strongholds, a dependency of their capital on Traprain Law five miles to the west.

It is difficult to prove earlier occupation although it is certain that Neolithic and Bronze Age Man settled the area, erecting the few surviving standing stones in the vicinity; he also built cairns and stone huts in circles which are scattered throughout the area, although the hills have guarded their secrets well. Evidence of human occupation in pre-history can be detected only with difficulty. Archaeologists speculate on the nameless Neolithic tribes and sub-tribes which gathered food, hunted and farmed in the Lammermuirs; finds of artefacts have been scant, consisting mainly of spear and arrow heads of flint, shaped bones, scrapers and stone axe-heads. An accessory cup was found near Dunbar; at Skateraw in c.1806, one of several cists yielded not only a human skeleton but a finely-crafted dagger with a gold pommel. Beakers dating from 1,800-1,500BC have also been discovered in the area. These artefacts are now in the National Museum of Scotland in Edinburgh.

The occupation by early colonists is corroborated by several hill-forts and camps at Penshiel, Priestlaw and Garvald the oval-shaped camp at Priestlaw was probably an important settlement as it measures 2,000 feet in circumference. Built on hilltops, these encampments featured *circumvallations* - concentric rings of earth and turf banks separated by ditches. Perhaps they were defended against the Votadini who came from Brittany/Gaul to establish their 'kingdom' in East Lothian, with its capital at Dunpender - Celtic for *the fort of the stockades* - or Traprain Law as it is known today. At its peak, the Votadini kingdom stretched from Northumberland to Stirling until the Angles of Northern England and the Picts of Northern Scotland between them reduced their lands and conquered them.

Traprain Law has provided rich pickings for archaeologist and historian - axe and arrow heads from the Neolithic and Bronze Ages, bronze, glass and jet ornaments, pins, moulds for casting spearheads and swords, farm implements and Roman coins of the fifth and sixth centuries. The most exciting find was the so-called Traprain Treasure, a hoard of hammered silver weighing 770 ounces Troy-weight which was excavated in 1919. A report by the *Society of Antiquaries* of the time of the dig listed

> 'bowls, cups, spoons, and a miscellaneous collection of pieces of plate, tarnished and soiled, but obviously silver....in some cases the silver had so rotted away that it crumbled when touched, though with exposure to air, it hardened somewhat.'

Mystery surrounds the reason for the treasure being there, how it came to be there. It appears to have been hurriedly buried; the *Society* ventured to say that it was from Gaul, possibly from some religious house and brought to Traprain by pirates - possibly Vikings or Anglo-Saxons. Some archaeologists believe it to be a bribe from the Romans with whom the Votadini had formed a treaty of mutual peace but both theories have been challenged in recent years. Modern historians consider it was more likely to have been a form of subsidy. The hoard is on display in the National Museum of Scotland, Edinburgh.

Illus 153: *Standing stone, Easter Broomhouse* KRM

Neolithic burial cairns occur at Spartleton Edge and Priestlaw; *tumuli* of later periods are scattered throughout the hills. Standing stones have survived at Pencraig Hill Cairndinnie near Traprain Law, Kirklandhill to the left of the A1 to Dunbar and at Easter Broomhouse, near Doon Hill (**ill 153**). The latter bears three enigmatic cup and ring marks which occur in other stones throughout Scotland; these are thought to have some religious significance. Of the seven stone circles which occur in East Lothian, six are in the Lammermuir Hills - four in the parish of Whittingehame and one each in the parishes of Stenton and Spott. The largest, at Kingside Hill, consists of 30 small stones in a circle less than 40' in diameter; a small mound, probably a burial cairn, is contained within the circle. Traces of Bronze Age burials have been found near Priestlaw, Penshiel and in 2001-2, Neolithic and Bronze Age sites at Eweford, on the A1 Bypass. Stone circles have been identified at Crystal Riggs (Friar Dykes). The largest find of human remains occurred in the nineteenth century at Kirklands, Whittingehame on what was thought to have been the site of an early Celtic church. About 200 stone cists were discovered; unfortunately the stones were used by workmen before they could be examined by experts. More recent finds are those at Castle Park (1993-97), where at least 150 skeletons were uncovered dating between the seventh and tenth centuries.

The most exciting find recently was that of a Mesolithic settlement near Oxwellmains, on the site owned by the Lafarge Cement Company. No more than a scoop in the ground, the post holes indicated that a reasonably-sized family dwelling place had been occupied for many years or seasons. Mesolithic tribes or families were hunter-gatherers who moved from place to place to obtain food in season. At Oxwellmains, the site was marked by finds of great quantities of hazelnut shells, roasted to provide food in winter. Thus we know that the area which is treeless today had at least a grove of hazelnut trees. The site is thought to have existed between 9,000 and 8,000 BC and, while radio-carbon dates are still awaited, it could be one of the oldest sites so far recorded in Scotland (**ill 154**). Discussing the site with the archaeologist in charge, he informed me that not only was Dunbar's Mesolithic site important - one of about six so far discovered in Britain - it was not far from, and closely resembled, another site just inside the Northumbrian border, at a place called Howick. Could there have been a tribal/family link? The Dunbar site was constructed in a natural hollow, with the post holes of its

Illus 154: *Mesolithic house at Oxwellmains* MB

wooden structure formed in a roughly circular pattern. The wooden framework inclined to a central point, creating a dome-shaped structure which may have been roofed with animal skins or turf. The round-house - for that is what it was - probably served as a seasonal dwelling; the experts consider that while it was not occupied permanently, it was visited for many years. More than 25,000 flint fragments and objects were found scattered about the site; the gap at floor level between the ground and the wooden walls is thought to have been turfed to keep out the stiff winds.

Iron Age/Votadini occupation was confirmed by the discovery of defensive hill forts at Blackcastle, near Innerwick and the summit of Doon Hill. The Doon Hill fort (now obliterated) was discovered during excavations of a sixth century British/Votadini hall on which was superimposed a seventh century Anglian pended hall, after the Votadini were conquered or expelled from the hill. A series of forts continues beyond Doon Hill, the next occurring at Chesters (Spott), Spott Home farm - traces of the latter have been long since obliterated although the site is identified on the Ordnance Survey map - and of course, Traprain. Traces of forts further inland have been found at Friar's Nose (Priestlaw), White Castle and Garvald Mains and hut circles are scattered from Dunbar Common down the valley of Spartleton Edge to Killpallet; these are difficult to locate in the dense bracken and heather. In the latter centuries of Dark Age Scotland, the missionary St Cuthbert who was reputedly born in or near Lauder and tended sheep in the Lammermuirs as a boy, returned there to evangelise

> 'villages which were remotely situated among steep and rugged hills, places where others feared to visit.'

During the early medieval period, the Lammermuirs became a royal or baronial hunting ground until they were deforested and divided up into pastoral holdings let to the tenants of the Earls of Dunbar. The upper and lower slopes still bear traces of medieval farming which are easily identified after a light dusting of snow or in autumn evenings when they are revealed by that season's long shadows. We know there was a minor Ice Age between the fourteenth and eighteenth centuries, when the climate grew colder and wetter and forced the medieval farmers to abandon the higher pastures. Even so, the ancient rigs remain like wrinkles on the brows of hills; aerial photography has pinpointed the old field systems which appear as long reversed *S* shapes made by the early and cumbersome Scots plough of the time. Traces of these fields have been found as high as 1,000 to 1,300 feet above sea level, altitudes which wouldn't allow today's corn to ripen.

When farming was restricted to the lower slopes and the flat fields, the hills still provided excellent grazing for flocks of sheep - Lammermuir is said to derive from the Celtic *lambermhore* or great sheep pastures - particularly round the Stenton area, where the monks of Melrose Abbey were granted grazing rights by the Earls of Dunbar and other major landowners in the vicinity. The monks were expressly forbidden to build cottages or other permanent dwelling houses which would have interfered with hunting; in the twelfth century, Waltheof, 4th Earl of Dunbar stipulated that

> 'moveable folds and lodges for the shepherds should accompany the flocks of the abbey, so as to avoid any permanent building or settlement within the forest.'

Melrose Abbey had the largest flocks in the district so that Dunbar Common was grazed throughout the spring and summer by their sheep which produced the best quality wool for export to the Low Countries during the Middle Ages. As a tax was levied on wool, woofells, skins and hides exported from Scotland, any wool leaving

Dunbar by ship after 1370 - the year it was created a free burgh - was subject to the king's Great Customs (see Chapter 8). In later centuries, stone sheilings were built in the hills and whole communities moved their sheep and cattle to the summer pastures, living in the hills until autumn. The ruins of these summer dwellings are scattered throughout the Lammermuir Hills; East Lothian farmers were probably among the last to abandon the sheiling system and many place-names bear testimony to their main occupation eg Penshiel, Mayshiel and Gamelshiel.

Traces of old roads which began in the coastal plain and criss-crossed through the hills can still be detected today. The best well-known and used was the Old Herring Road from Spott by way of Spartleton Edge south of Johnscleugh to the river Whitadder, from where it continued south-eastwards via the head of the Dye Water to Lauder. The road was vital for the transport of Dunbar salted herrings - a staple item in the winter diet - and it was used by the monks travelling to Dunbar from Melrose Abbey. Many of the hamlets where the Cistercian brothers may have sought a *stoup* [flagon]of water or ale have long vanished. Several of these roads - cart tracks in reality - ran from Lothian Edge but these are barely visible today; formed by use rather than design, their width expanded and contracted according to the terrain as horses and carts struggled to negotiate boggy ground or difficult slopes.

In later centuries, cultivation of the lower slopes and sheltered areas of the Lammermuir Hills undoubtedly obliterated many Neolithic and Bronze Age stone hut circles and settlements; only those built on the higher slopes have survived but these are difficult to find today. After the Dark Ages, the major events in Scottish history bypassed the Lammermuirs, leaving them to drowse away for centuries, their small hamlets untouched by outside events. In the less accessible areas, people were left to themselves, rearing children, escaping the ravages of plague and dying in fairly advanced years. Medieval man rarely ventured outside his parish; life in the Lammermuirs must have been calm and even rewarding. The hill folk visited Dunbar only on market days and at fairs and carnivals. However, history inevitably intruded on their lives, as the defensive stone towers at Penshiel, Stoneypath, Whittingehame and Cockburnspath testify.

The Lammermuir Hills may not figure greatly in Scotland's history but they played their part in the economy of East Lothian. They have been variously described as gentle, rolling, pleasant, bleak, featureless and even nondescript - all of which is true. Visiting Dunbar in 1787, Robert Burns had mixed feelings about them:

'Left Edinburgh May 6, 1787. Lammermuirs miserably dreary, but at times very picturesque.
Langton Edge [offers] a glorious view of the Merse.'

If East Lothian deserves a place among the Gardens of Scotland, it owes something to the shelter of its hills. Like any other hills on wet, windy winter days, the Lammermuirs are uninteresting; when the weather is fair, they are never boring or dull. Stretching from the vale of the Gala Water, they were once clothed in forests of oak, ash and birch; pockets of trees still survive. The soil is mostly a light peat mould interspersed here and there with belts of fertile earth which allowed cultivation. The bare, high-lying valleys have no alpine pretensions but they nevertheless inspire the solitary walker. Many of the names of the small dwelling-places derive from the animals which once thrived there - Hartshill, Hartside, Heart (meaning deer) Law and Harelaw.

All hills have a special light of their own. Every kind of sky has passed over the Lammermuirs and they are noted for their moving cloudscapes and shadow patterns of summer; the smoky, blue horizon they offer before the onset of a storm defines them with their distinctive sharpness. Colour and sun, light and shadow compliment each other. When the early morning mists disperse, the hills emerge like icebergs drifting in a milky sea. The colours of harebell and heather are almost a source of light themselves. The seasons bring their special effects; in spring, the *cleughs* move like the sea under the wind, the grass shines in the sun, the streams in spate turn the colour of generously milked coffee. The hills are softer until they are transformed by a blaze of colour when the gorse blossoms. But perhaps the hills come into their own in autumn, when their long shadows create a special blue of their own, their contours sharpening, their sunsets muted like light from a half-shut door. Winter often arrives unnoticed as autumn slips away under cover of a North Sea haar which can make the hills dangerous for the unsuspecting hill walker suddenly plunged into a wet, clinging mist, losing visibility within minutes. Often it is New Year before the gruff, scowling winds arrive to tear at the ridges and turn pools of water into glass. Spring and summer, autumn and winter merge imperceptibly under moons that cast their light on an eerie, silent, pre-historic landscape.

There are only two seasons in the Lammermuirs - when the sheep are there and when they aren't. The panorama is one of sweeping, rolling moorland punctuated by dry-stone dykes built in previous centuries to enclose sheep pastures. Of the many streams which chatter and gurgle through the bracken, Spott Burn is perhaps one of the best examples; flowing through Spott Glen, an Ice Age valley, the burn changes its name to the Brock or Brox Burn as it approaches the sea. Even the valley is known by a different name as it winds at the foot of Doon Hill; it changes from Spott Glen to Oswald Dean - perhaps the name comes from the Anglian king

Oswald who may have built the wooden hall on the summit of the hill. This small burn has flowed with the blood of Scottish soldiers on at least two occasions in the last seven hundred years.

Lammermuir Hill folk are sturdily independent, resourceful and trust their instincts; like fishermen, they are preoccupied with bad weather, in their case at lambing time. If the older generation is economical with words, it is because they have little use for them after years of working on remote farms. They speak to each other in the vernacular, sometimes 'forgetting' themselves in front of strangers; when they feel obliged to speak 'proper' English, they pronounce their words slowly, loud and precisely - mainly for the benefit of their audience. If they know you belong to the district - the East Lothian accent is quite distinctive - they revert to their own tongue which is broad and sometimes difficult to understand, especially when they know they are speaking to their own and thus feel comfortable to speak quickly in the vernacular. Once when asking directions to a small hamlet near Innerwick, the place I was looking for was referred to as *Widdle* and *Widdaw* by two of the locals who lived only a few miles apart. For all that, the road to Woodhall is pleasant no matter how they pronounce its name. Recently, I discovered that near Woodhall is a *Tinker's Loup* or jump; local tradition has it that the tinker was fleeing from pursuing English Redcoats and managed to outsmart them by jumping across a fifteen foot gully.

The Lammermuirs were once famed for a fairly comon Scottish ploy - the distillation of illicit alcohol. Although rarely talked about today, there were whisky *stells* or stills in the more remote areas. These *stells* were little more than circular dry-stone enclosures built, it is said, as shelters for shepherds. About five feet high, the stones were so well-knitted together that they resembled stacks of baker's rolls. The distilling equipment could be moved at short notice, the enclosure reverting to its primary role when the gaugers got too close. Many a gallon of *Lammermuir Dew* was made on the steep side of a burn chosen for the quality of its water. As noted in Chapter 10, smuggling was rife in the eighteenth and early nineteenth centuries; goods landed at the Cove, near Cockburnspath were quickly dispersed in the nearby hills. Many a cask of French brandy buried in the sands at Cove Shore found its way to minister's manse and remote farmhouse to cheer the long winter evenings. Local farmers kept a watch for the Dutch or French luggers slipping into the Cove, Coldingham Bay or Eyemouth. It was fairly easy to *jouk the gaugers*, or avoid the customs men; only two were based in eighteenth century Dunbar to patrol the coastline from Musselburgh to Berwick. All that is past although, within living memory, a Russian ship anchored off the Cove offering crates of vodka for Galashiels-made woollen sweaters!

In remote places in Dunbar's hinterland, nestling in hidden valleys and rarely used roads, time has literally stood still. Some landmarks of living memory, such as the old Broomhouse Mill, a ruin in Oswaldean until the latter half of the last century have been obliterated by modern housing. However, isolated houses still survive. West of Bowerhouse are the Standard - reminiscent perhaps of the battle of 1296 - The Pleasants, Chesters - obviously a Roman camp and once the site of a quarry. - and The Halls near Spott, with its ford and three cottages. The road from The Halls wins uphill, bordered by well kept, thick thorn hedges that enclose the tidy pattern of fields and parks. Today, such out of the way placesbarely hint of of cold, windswept days of back breaking work. The past is a fading memory, the present a strange, almost unfamiliar country. Three, perhaps even two generations ago, there were more people but now the fields and hills no longer echo with the piercing whistles of shepherd or ploughman. (Today the shepherd races round on quad bikes with fodder for the sheep, the dogs invariably hitching a ride). Many of the fields lie fallow and the horse drawn ploughs are seen only in competitions. The landscape is man made with dry stane dykes and hedge rows, most no more than two centuries old, when the last vetiges of the medieval farming sytems wre swept away by the improvemnts of the so called Agricultural Revolution.

There are many intriguing place names on the 1799 map of Haddingtonshire printed in 1802. Among them is the Old Broomhouse Mill, Oswald Dean, a ruin for many years and now obliterated in favour of a modern house. Beyond The Halls is an access road which ends at Pathhead, virtually deserted; nearby are East and West Heartside (originally Hartside, a deer park for the medieval nobles' hunting parties). Near the hamlet of Woodhall is the Priest's Pulpit - possibly named in the early years of the Reformation, when outlawed Catholic priests were forced to celebrate Masses in the fields. Not so easy to explain are Maiden Step, Croft Angry, Sneep [Snipe?] and Hookerslaw, a traditional meeting place of farm folk intent on barter and where deals were struck.

Nearer Dunbar itself, places south of the railway line are fast dissappearing as this book goes to print. Already a casualty of housing development, the once attractive Latch Park - haunt of lovers and children gathering wild brambles in season - is now marked only by a bank of trees. The Latch Park road is now Spott Road; the name survives only in the Latch Park Curling Pond - also possibly threatened - and the area known as St. John's Croft, once owned by the Knights Hospitaller of St John and later by an Edinburgh Burgess, has been developed. On the plus side, the once forbidden Lochend Woods have been made accessible to the public, a measure of consolation to those who in living memory used the Latch Park for recreation.

Nowadays the drift from the land is almost complete and few Lammermuir Hill folk make their living from it. Many of the farm cottages and entire villages have been taken over by city folk who give their houses pretentious names and wear green wellington boots. They form committees to 'run'communities which less than fifty years ago 'ran' themselves because an ageless community spirit existed. The children of these incomers - universally known as white settlers – may think they are better informed and more sophisticated than those whom they replaced; they may also be able to identify the sights, sounds and smells of the earth but they are less captivated by them, nor I fear do many really understand them. Those who were born and bred in the hills and in Dunbar and who went to work in the cities cannot escape their childhood, no matter how they may try; it is ingrained like dirt in the skin. Some may try to forget it or speak disparagingly of it but few can resist coming back. I am proud of my roots and will never turn my back on them. Though there were few material distractions and attractions, I among so many of the town felt the comings and goings of the seasons more acutely and loved each in its turn. Even the dead never disappeared completely or as quickly as they do in the cities and the towns; they remained part of the parish, talked about as if they were still there many years after their deaths. Why not? After all, they were. The existence of their graves prove it. The memories of their families and their friends outlived them.

Traditional rural life is fast disappearing. Vestiges of old customs and ways linger on here and there but by the end of this new century, they will be gone, like the characters talked about in the pubs and clubs or wherever people meet. They too will be forgotten. If the past century has taught us anything, it is that life is ephemeral; change is constant and nothing stays the same for long. Perhaps in this new century, the Lammermuir Hills will successfully resist attempts to develop them and thereby destroy their quiet beauty. Perhaps some John Muir of the future will ensure that they remain inviolate; had Muir remained in Dunbar, I am sure he would have described them as cathedrals of grass, cloud and sky. Those who live in Dunbar today should never forget that the community began in those hills, where history was made. The blue, rolling hills formed the character of countless generations of forgotten folk who lived and worked in their shadow and made their contribution to the town of Dunbar.

Postcript

The history of Dunbar is easier to trace than that of its people. This is simply because there are documents to inform us about the past - local burgh and church records, national archives, government reports and contemporary chronicles and histories. However, documentary information about the lives of the ordinary people - how they lived, the work they did and what they thought of the society in which they lived - is practically non-existent. Archaeological finds offer us a glimpse of living conditions at various periods in time - what was important or significant to them, the tools they used, what they ate - but their emotions and thoughts about the world in which they lived remains a closed book.

It isn't until relatively recent times that we obtain snapshots of the lives of the ordinary people. Most of human history is about the struggle to survive in a frequently hostile environment. It is only when we draw closer to our own time that we are able to appreciate the conditions in which the majority of the population lived and worked. Records of famine, plague and environmental disasters give us some clues; the most reliable and informative records about local social history exist in four important informative publications. These are the First (Old) Statistical Account, the Second (New) Statistical Account and the Third Statistical Account, compiled for every parish in Scotland by the local minister between 1795 and 1951. The fourth source is the report of the Poor Law Commission published in 1844. These major archival records give us tantalising glimpses of the occupants of farm cottage and town tenement, even if what is written does not come from the mouths of the people written about. Other sources are of course church records and disciplinary cases which although of value in the latter aspect, are slanted since their objective was biased in the interests of improving the moral climate. But the majority of people remain faceless and featureless, anonymous individuals who wrote down very little and what little they did hasn't survived. Often we only have the briefest epitaphs on a badly weathered tombstone to acknowledge their existence. In the last two centuries, all that we have to offer some understanding of the common man are folk memories and oral traditions handed down from generation to generation. These can and do suffer from distortion or exaggeration, so we must rely on the history of the community to gain a degree of knowledge about the way the majority of the population lived. That is why this book is relevant.

It is no easy task, writing history, especially that of a small community such as Dunbar. (In the 1920s, one of the first members of the *East Lothian Antiquarian and Field Naturalist Society,* Louis Barbe, a resident in

Dunbar and himself a published writer, ruefully confessed that he had attempted to write a comprehensive history but gave it up as an impossible task. I think he was over-harsh on himself; advanced years and state of health were probably the real reasons for his defeatist attitude. I sympathise with Louis Barbe, as I began this book at the mentally active age of 48, some fourteen years ago.... Despite the impressive body of archival material and written documentation - be it national government, local burgh or the estate and private papers of the landed gentry - the evidence requires to be critically examined to remove political bias, distortion and omission, since those with axes to grind will inevitably record their personal views in the most favourable light. However, having recognised this, it is better to have too much than too little; the historian is fortunate enough to be blessed by the benefit of hindsight and the passage of time to draw balanced conclusions from the often conflicting evidence which survives.

For centuries, the majority of Dunbar people lived in abject poverty, often in the shadow of starvation and disease and generally suffering poor health, leading short, brutish lives. That they lived in conditions of penury and squalor does not require volumes of archival material to describe their lot. Until fairly recently, we know that landlords and landowners - often the same men - dominated the working and social lives of the people, using their positions as church heritors to control their behaviour, employing kirk discipline to chastise those who deviated from the accepted moral climate and strayed from the paths of righteousness. (Hypocrisy was never far away among such men who thought nothing of indulging their own appetites, behaving as they pleased in private while publicly appearing to set an example to those whom they undoubtedly considered weak vessels). In mitigation, there were some landlords who did make an attempt to improve the lot of their tenants and employees provided there were gains to be had from their munificence and they weren't financially disadvantaged. In the society of the time, that was as near to benevolence as many landlords got.

The life of every community ebbs and flows according to the state of its economy, a process which is repeated again and again throughout its history. In the early centuries, man struggled to survive, first as a nomadic hunter-gatherer, then settled in fertile districts to farm, although existence was often at a bare subsistence level. Man's fear of his own species compelled him to expend a good deal of his energy in defensive activities - building and maintaining turf and earth forts, then wooden stockades and finally, the great stone castles of the thirteenth century. During these centuries, economic progress - agriculture and fishing - was erratic, subject to the uncertainty of the weather and the capricious movements of the herring shoals. Up to the twentieth century, Dunbar moved to a rhythm and pattern dictated by the seasons, its working and social life regulated by the calendar. It wasn't until about the eighteenth century that the economy began to show signs of recovery - or at least a positive trend - and even then, poor harvests occurred with alarming frequency. In the farming world, improvements were resisted by landlord and farmworker alike, although men of vision persevered with their attempts to make the land more productive - men like Lord Belhaven of Biel, John Cockburn of Ormiston, Sir Archibald Grant of Monymusk and Sir John Sinclair ('Agricultural Sir John'), better known as the instigator of the First (Old) Statistical Account. Despite their efforts, the standard of living of the majority changed little however, remaining virtually static until the last century.

As Dunbar's economy was almost exclusively based on agriculture and fishing, people worked in close proximity to each other which engendered a community spirit to a degree unknown today; modern society is unable to capture that spirit without some committee or council to make it work. People shared a common lot; what little they had, they shared or at least it didn't cause the envy and divisiveness which materialism has introduced in modern times. For centuries, the social structure was founded on an integrated network of families linked by blood, marriage and work. The people of Dunbar didn't experience the sharp end of the Industrial Revolution, nor was there dramatic evidence of the drastic surgery of the Highland Clearances. There were no dark, satanic mills, no coalfields in the vicinity, but the people did suffer the consequences of the Agricultural Revolution; agriculture was a labour intensive industry and the new labour-saving machines and farming methods merely reduced the workforce. This was only marginally offset by the arrival of the military, when Lauderdale House was purchased by the War Office in the mid-nineteenth century and turned into a barracks. (Many soldiers stationed here married local women which accounts for the unlikely names to be found in the Voters' Roll - my own included). As there were few alternative work opportunities, Dunbar like many another rural town experienced a subtle and gradual emigration of its people to Scottish and English towns and cities, where jobs were more plentiful. It was only in the second half of the last century that new jobs were created to reverse the population decline; first was the development of the lime/cement industry, then the expansion of the local brewery and finally, the creation of Torness Nuclear Power Station, regarded by many as a mixed blessing. Minor 'invasions' of new people came in the 1960s, when Dunbar accommodated several hundred families ignominiously described as Glasgow Overspill. (What an insulting way to descibe these people; it suggests they were surplus to somebody's requirements). While the prevalence and incidence of modern migration is not solely dictated by economics, it is indicative of a community's inability to offer its population alternatives. Migration need not be irreversible. Modern society no longer thirsts after land as a source of wealth. Increased mobility means that people have a certain degree of choice as to where they work and where they live, not necessarily in the same place. The fact that Dunbar is poised to receive a boost in its resident population proves that people in employment are keen to live - if not work - in attractive surroundings. The emphasis today is not only on steady and sustained employment but on quality of life. The latest influx of people will come from Edinburgh, to the new estates at King's Meadows, Poppyfields - who thinks up these names? - and of course Muirfield, the last-named paying a somewhat ironic tribute to our emigrant conservationist by removing a considerable acreage of Green Belt land.

So what does the future hold for a small community like Dunbar? What will happen to it in this new century, the Third Millenium? One thing is certain; it has to change direction. The lives of the majority are no longer tied to the land or to the sea which is no bad thing. But by no stretch of the imagination may Dunbar be described as a dynamic or even modestly thriving community. The lives of the majority of working people are no longer tied to the land or the sea which is perhaps not all bad news. No one is in any doubt that there will never be a rejuvenation of the summer visitor trade or the resurgence of bucket-and-spade holidays; these days are long gone. Not too long ago, the now-defunct Lothian and Edinburgh Enterprises Ltd (LEEL) was promoting what it termed the *Dunbar Initiative*; it promised much by assuring us that

> '....new horizons are opening for Dunbar. The process of regeneration is in full
> flow and we are pursuing every opportunity to enrich the quality of life in the town.'

Oh, really? I am glad I did not hold my breath waiting for these lofty sentiments to bear fruit. The exact opposite has been the case. Perhaps the extension of the Edinburgh to Haddington dual carriageway to Dunbar will have some positive effect but I doubt that it will materially affect the local economy. Leisure and cultural activities seem to be the likeliest inducements to attract visitors to Dunbar; leisure amenities have never been better, with considerable resources already invested in sports facilities - the Healthy Living Centre at Hallhill with its football and rugby pitches, running track and indoor sports and the Splash leisure swimming pool at Victoria Harbour are sufficient for even an expanded population. It should be abundantly clear that we need to invest resources aimed at promoting, developing and expanding existing facilities to maximise the attractions offered by our local heritage; perhaps the refurbishment of the John Muir Birthplace Museum is a start in the right direction. Dunbar has a golden opportunity to capitalise on its remaining - perhaps most important – asset, its rich and colourful history. Dunbar has missed such opportunities in the recent past; the fear is that it will do so yet again. Let me illustrate this by reference to the period 1965 - the start of Dunbar's decline as a holiday resort - and 1985, by which time it had lost one of its most attractive features now but a fond memory among generations of visitors who came here every summer - the open-air swimming pool.

In 1965, to add a different dimension to the local leisure activities, a friend and I pooled our spare capital to open the *Doone Art Gallery* in the basement of Lauderdale House, then virtually empty. We received no financial or even token support from any organisations - local government or commercial - although the then Entertainments Officer at least visited us on two occasions, more I am sad to say to gain experience of how to organise an art exhibition, which he did the following year. After two summers, the gallery had to close due to lack of interest. In vain, we attempted to convince the local authority that we were spearheading what we thought would be a concentration of amenities in Lauderdale House. We suggested that the local library be moved from its cramped quarters to the rear of the Town House; we suggested that there could be a heritage/history/agricultural/fishing/military museum sited on the premises, which would also serve as a community centre for young and old alike. What better use for an historic building which was crumbling rapidly. Our efforts came to nothing.

Next was the closure of the outdoor swimming pool; another golden opportunity. Local building contractor W A Gillespie and Son offered to purchase the site, create a yachting marina, roof the pool and heat it and build a luxury hotel on the Glebe, with facilities for indoor sports - all enclosed. There was also the possibility of a cable car from the Glebe to the castle and harbours, thus allowing visitors to view these attractions in comfort and whatever the state of the weather. Mr Gillespie's efforts came to nothing. (The subsequent indoor swimming pool at Castle Park had at least one vital spin-off; preliminary excavations revealed an extremely valuable historical site which proved that Dunbar had been occupied for at least two thousand years). I have to admit to personal prejudice about the indoor pool; it is neither in keeping with nor adequate for the town of Dunbar. I have been known to describe its architectural style as Late Modern Perpendicular B&Q; in less than a decade of existence, it is showing signs of wear and already extensive external work has been necessary, with evidence of further attention required.

Now the latest initiative is to refurbish the Free or Abbey Church in the High Street. In the spirit - if ultimately not the letter - of democracy, the people have been invited to submit proposals for its future use; it is the usual cosmetic approach of the bureaucrat. And it is *deja vue* in tyhe light of my experience of Lauderdale House, a far older and more architecturally attractive building which had endless possibilities. I cannot therefore raise much enthusiasm, although I applaud those who wish to make an historic building wind and water proof, then become a working building. But I ask the important question. Whatever its future use - as cinema, heritage museum, history museum, art gallery etc - who will provide the resources to staff and maintain it? One supposes that the East Lothian Council Museum Service will form a composite steering committee representative of the Council, the Community Council, the Dunbar and District History Society, the Harbour Trust and the local traders. If we do not pull together, we will fall together....

There is so much waiting for someone with imagination and determination to develop. We need not stop at museums and pictorial exhibitions. Why not resuscitate Dunbar's medieval fair and market on one or two occasions in season? Culross in Fife holds an annual medieval fair according to its founding charter of the late fifteenth century. There are stalls whose owners dress in period costume; a troop of Lord Lumsden's Foot raised to fight Cromwell parades in their period uniform and demonstrates its skill with the musket. The event is run in conjunction with the National Trust, who admit visitors free to Culross Palace that day. It is a lively, colourful occasion, with children dressing up in the clothes of the time, playing contemporary games and dancing. Over to you, Dunbar Trades and Business Association....you have a vital role to play.

It is perhaps naive of me to suggest that business property developmers will in themselves give Dunbar a Great Leap [Frog?] Forward; it is a forlorn hope if these developments do not bring much-needed jobs to the community, thus keeping our young people at home. Also, my cynicism about 'development' is informed by nearly forty years in public service. Development is often a euphemism for removing buildings and open spaces which have for centuries been part of a community. (I don't mean the slums which are best left to photographic record). It is often a knee-jerk response to progress, gained at the expense of a community's identity and sense of history. 'Much-needed development' is often a euphemism for hasty, ill-conceived short-term decisions about what is good for us - or perhaps someone else!

Despite appearances in this particular part of the book I did not write it to sermonise; I leave that to others better qualified than myself. My overriding interest is in Dunbar's past and how it may be used to give the town a sense of identity and attract visitors interested in its history.

Whatever future Dunbar may have, I would hope that the generations born after 1950 will enjoy Dunbar as much as mine did. Indeed, those born between 1870 and 1950 knew a different Dunbar, when it was a vibrant and lovely place for holidays. Today's children have never known a world without instant entertainment such as television; perhaps they are missing out on more natural activities. They have lost a little of the magical world that offered innocent and gentle pleasures which were also instructive.

It is probably true that we only begin to understand a century until it is past - like the 'owl of Minerva [which] only spreads its wings with the falling of dusk'. Now that we have left the twentieth century behind, it is vital that we don't repeat the mistakes we made in it. There are ideal opportunities still for Dunbar; it can become a good, clean and safe place to live; however, bureaucracy cannot be relied upon to achieve that, as it has disastrously demonstrated in the past fifty years. The people themselves must work hard for that - especially the young. I am fully aware that here I ***am*** sermonising, but I know that many who live in Dunbar and have lived here all their lives will agree.

My motivation for this book came from James Miller, who wrote the first history of Dunbar. Miller cared about the town in which he lived and wanted others to learn about its rich and colourful past. I share that with him. I wrote this book to take account of what we have learnt since his day; to expand on or introduce aspects which he chose not to cover; to confirm wherever possible his several theories, using modern archaeological findings and reports; and lastly, to correct his errors which have been perpetuated by later writers using him as a source.

In common with many other Scottish communities. Dunbar not only has a history, it has also made history in so many diverse ways disproportionate to its size. In recent years, history has undergone a type of plastic surgery which has transformed it into heritage. Heritage is an expression used by tourist agencies. A rose by any other name? If, as someone once wrote, the historian is a failed novelist or storyteller, then I am unashamedly both. For me the last two thousand years are history, not heritage

Part of Dunbar's future is in its past; people made aware of it will come here to learn more about it and the role the community played in Scotland's history. I wish every success for the now well-established and thriving Dunbar and District History Society, the Harbour Trust and East Lothian Council Museum Service for opening and maintaining the Town Museum; they give me much hope for the future. I also wish to applaud the efforts made by Grahame Smith of Lothian Computers, Dunbar who has created a Dunbar website on the Internet and who makes every attempt to answer the many thousands of enquiries he receives about Dunbar from every corner of the globe - the majority of which are interested in the town's heritage and history. In 2002, East Lothian Council appointed a Heritage Officer with a wide remit which includes co-ordinating rescue/archaeological excavations in advance of commercial developments eg road and other improvements. She also encourages research and community projects, promotes East Lothian's heritage by leaflets and through the Internet.

Evidence of Dunbar's rich historical past was highlighted by the major excavation of Castle Park between 1989-1993. In the summer of 2002, excavation of a small area to the rear of The John Muir Birthplace at No 128 High Street revealed what is thought to be a medieval cobbled street with a gutter or water channel beside a contemporary wall - perhaps a building, which proves that stone-built houses existed in Dunbar much earlier than we had supposed.

As this book was being prepared for publication, the local press announced the find of one of the oldest human habitations hitherto found in Scotland. During quarry excavations in 2002, Lafarge Cement Co Ltd uncovered a site in August which brought in the archaeologists. Subsequent investigative work confirmed that the area had been occupied by a family of Mesolithic hunter-gatherers. It is the first example of a Mesolithic house to be discovered in Scotland. Constructed in a natural hollow in the ground, the post-holes were formed in a roughly circular pattern and positioned so that a wooden framework inclined to the centre, forming a dome-shaped structure which was probably roofed with turf or animal skins. Given the efforts which went into the erection of what may be termed a round-house, the experts believe that the occupants spent some time on the site, revisiting it in seasonal periods when food was plentiful. More than 25,000 fragments of flint were found in and around the house, along with vast quantities of burnt hazelnut shells, used for food or food-flavouring at the time. (This proves that Oxwellmains probably was extensively wooded). Carbonised hazelnut shells are an excellent source for radio-carbon dates. The site is similar to one found at Howick, Northumberland, about 60 miles to the south. The ancient finds between St Abbs and North Berwick - and Dunbar in particular - proves that the twenty-five mile coastline was well-populated by early peoples seeking food which was at hand rather than food they had to plant and harvest.

In the autumn of 2002, a child's skeleton dating from 3,500BC was found near Dunbar in which the presence of leprosy was detected, raising questions about the first appearance of the disease in Scotland.

At the time of publication of this book, Dunbar and District History Society is engaged in a comprehensive survey of the graves in the local cemetery which will be of interest to those keen to learn of their genealogy. Future activities planned for Dunbar are the excavation of an area near the fishermen's huts that front the castle; the site is under the modern car park and is possibly the cellar of a house that once stood there. Some hope that it will prove the existence of an underground tunnel from the castle to 125 High Street, thus proving a long-held hypothesis. Other activities are the restoration of McArthur's Store, an eighteenth century building near the entrance of the Old Harbour. It is also hoped to excavate the Lochend Ruin, home of the Baillie family in the seventeenth century. A Burgh Survey of Dunbar will be published soon.

Writing this book has been a labour of love which enriched my life as I discovered more and more about the community from which I sprang. Someone wrote recently that history is real. He or she was a wise person. After all, you can't and wouldn't want to make it up. It is interesting in its own right. And it will continue as long as there are people to make it happen.

Balerno, Midlothian (Autumn 1990 - 2000)
Dunbar, East Lothian (2000 - Spring 2003)

APPENDIX A

Owners or governors of Dunbar Castle 869-1936*

*Sources consulted: *RMS, RSS* and *TA*

869-late tenth century	Thanes of Dunbar - possibly cadets of the Anglian Eadwulfings
Late tenth century-1005	Patrick, Thane of Dunbar (or Lothian)
1005-1072	Crown possession
1072x1120x1130?	Gospatric I (although never styled Earl of Dunbar, he is regarded as the 1st Earl)
1120x1130-1138x1139	Gospatric II (styled 'Earl Gospatric, brother of Dolphin', then Earl of Dunbar)
1138x1139-1166	Gospatric III (styled 'Earl of Dunbar')
1166-1182	Earl Waltheof of Dunbar (known as 'Earl Waldeve')
1182-1232	Patrick, 5th Earl of Dunbar
1232-1248	Patrick, 6th Earl of Dunbar
1248-1289	Patrick, 7th Earl of Dunbar
12891308	Patrick, 8th Earl of Dunbar
1308-1369	Patrick, 9th Earl of Dunbar
1369-1416x1424	George, 10th Earl of Dunbar, Sir Richard Maitland 1400, then Archibald Douglas to 1407
1416x1424-1435	George, 11th Earl of Dunbar
1435-1445	Adam Hepburn of Hailes, Walter Haliburton of Dirleton
1446	Patrick Hepburn of Hailes
1446-1452	Adam Hepburn of Hailes (also Dean of the Collegiate Church in 1448)
1452-1454	Robert Ledale [Liddle?] for the Crown [James II]
1454	James, Earl of Moray for the Crown (keeper James Crichton)
1454-1460	Robert Ledale for the Crown [James II]
1460-1462	Lord Hailes for the Crown [James III]
1462-1479	Alexander, 3rd Duke of Albany, James III's brother: in 1467, Archibald Boyd was captain of the castle
1479-1482	James III; John Ellem of Butterdean
1482-1483	Alexander, 3rd Duke of Albany
1483-1484	English garrison
1485-1488	John of Moray (1486), John Ramsey (1487-1488) for the Crown (James III)
1488	Castle dismantled by order of James III
1497-1501	Castle rebuilt by James IV and governed by Sir Andrew Wood of Largo for the Crown until 1503
1503-1510	Andrew, Bishop of Moray for the Crown (James IV)
1510-1513	James IV
1514	Robert Forman, Dean of Glasgow
1514-1517	Sieur de la Bastie for John, 4th Duke of Albany, regent of Scotland after the death of James IV at Flodden
1517-1536	Under French command with a French garrison
1536-1546	James V; in 1542, William or Patrick Wemyss of Raith was the castle's keeper, followed in 1543 by Robert Hamilton of the Briggs until 1546
1546-	Sir John Melville of Raith for the Crown (James V)
1547-1561	French occupation, first under the jurisdiction of James Hamilton, 2nd Earl of Arran, then Mary of Guise-Lorraine, queen regent after James V's death; Sieur La Chapelle was captain in c. 1548, followed by Captain Corronant in 1553; the last French officer in command was Captain Sieur la Bois [Sarlabos] in 1561
1561-1565	John, Commendator of Coldingham Priory for the Crown [Mary, Queen of Scots]
1565-1566	Simon Preston of Craigmillar for the Crown [Mary, Queen of Scots]
1565-1567	James Hepburn, 4th Earl of Bothwell for the Crown [Mary, Queen of Scots]
1567	Patrick Whitelaw for James, 4th Earl of Bothwell
1567-1568	James Stewart, Earl of Moray, Regent of Scotland; it was occupied by a token garrison until parlia ment ordered it to be dismantled in 1568.
1573	James VI gave the site and policies to William Boncle, burgess of Dunbar
1597	James VI's proposal to reinstate the castle came to nothing
1605-1611	Site owned by George Home, Baron Berwick and Earl of Dunbar
1613-1617	Site owned by Lady Anne Home, daughter of above
1617-?	Site owned by Sir James Baillie of Lochend
1789-1855	Site owned by the Earls of Lauderdale
1855-1927?	?
1927?-1936	Site owned by the Earls of Home
1936-1998	Site owned by Dunbar burgh council, then East Lothian Council from 1975
1999-	Dunbar Harbour Trust

APPENDIX B

An English Letter of Gospatric I

'Gospatrik greets all my dependants and each man, free and dreng,[1] that dwell in all the lands of the Cumbrians, and all my kindred friendlily: and I make known to you that my mind and full leave is that Thorfynn Mac Thore [2] be as free in all things that are mine in Alnerdall [3] as any man is, whether I or any of my dependents, in wood, in heath, in enclosures, and as to all things that are existing on the earth and under it, at Shauk [4] and at Wafyr and at Pollwathoen and at bek Troyte [5] and the wood at Caldebeck; [6] and I desire that the men abiding with Thorfynn at Cartheu [7] and Combetheyfoch be as free with him as Melmor [8] and Thore [9] and Sygulf were in Eadred's days,[10] and that [there] be no man be so bold that he - with what I have given to him cause to break the peace such as Earl Syward [11] and I have granted to them for ever as any man living under the sky; and whosoever is there abiding, let him be geld [12] free as I am and in like manner as Walltheof [13] and Wygande and Wyberth and Gamell and Kunyth and all my kindred and dependants; and I will that Thorfynn have soc and sac, toll and theam [14] over all the lands of Cartheu and Combetheyfoch that were given to Thore in Moryn's days [15] free with bode and witnessman [16] in the same place.' [17]

This undated writ was supposedly engrossed after 1045 (c. 1055-1092[18]), when Maldred, then influential in Scottish Cumbria, was killed fighting Macbeth. The writ was discovered in Lowther Castle among the private papers of the Earl of Lonsdale (the *Lowther Muniments*) at the turn of the nineteenth century. Published in the *Scottish Historical Review (SHR)* [19] it gave rise to much speculation as to the identity of its author. An enigmatic writ it certainly is. It has been attributed to Gospatric, son of Uhtred, Earl of Northumberland (1006-1016) and also to Gospatric, son of Maldred of Cumbria who was Earl of Northumberland (1067-1072) and who later settled in Dunbar. The writ could have been engrossed at any time between 1055 and 1092, particularly in the years 1067 to 1072, after which latter year, Gospatric was deprived of his Northumberland earldom and founded the dynasty of Dunbar earls. To avoid confusion with his half-uncle Gospatric mentioned above, he is referred to here as Gospatric I.

Historians enjoy differing on questions of identity and this writ is no exception; Stenton [20] and Barlow [21] agree with the *English Historical Review (EHR) vol xx* (1905) that the writ was by Gospatric, murdered in 1064. Ritchie [23] maintains the granter was Gospatric I 'who ruled alternatively or concurrently in Cumbria at Carlisle, in Lothian at Dunbar and in England at Durham.' Considerable support for this view comes from Anderson.[22]

Let us examine the arguments for and against Gospatric I. His father Maldred ruled or was prince of Scottish Cumbria until 1045, when he was killed along with his father Crinan the Thane fighting Macbeth. Gospatric I was Maldred's eldest son and would have inherited his possessions although not necessarily his titles. His half-uncle Gospatric had a dubious claim on his father Maldred's Cumbrian possessions, but he seems not to have enforced the claim before his murder in 1064. From Maldred sprang several noble families in Cumbria; the family presence there was still secure even after William Rufus expelled Dolphin, Gospatric I's son from Carlisle in 1092. Gospatric's other son Waltheof and his descendants remained in Cumbria until after the twelfth century. While the writ refers to Waltheof as being one of the granter's kinsmen, this in itself does not resolve the difficulty; Waltheof was a common name in northern England and Earl Siward, also mentioned in the writ, had a son who became Earl of Northumberland in 1072. Anderson considers that the Waltheof in question was Gospatric I's son.

Charters and writs provide us with clues about the workings of the feudal system; among the earliest historical sources, they can be frustrating in their ambiguity and obscurity. Gospatric I's writ - or letter - is no exception. It bestows a grant of land on the obscure, unidentified Thorfinn MacThore and refers to other men whose identities are either unknown or are open to speculation. It mentions men of whom Gospatric I had personal knowledge or with whom he was acquainted. For the historian of whatever shade of opinion as to the author, the letter's true value lies in the light it sheds on the political history of Cumbria at a time when little is known about the province until William Rufus annexed it to England in 1092. Among the very few documents relating to Cumbria which has survived, the letter conveys a sense of unquestionable authority on the part of the writer; he speaks with the voice of one who enjoyed high rank and status. He is not simply a landowner. Gospatric I addresses the men of Cumbria as their lord - probably the Lord of Allerdale, as he refers to settlements in the district, places he knew intimately. Given his father's standing in Cumbria, Gospatric I is almost certainly the author. He exercised authority in the area south of the Solway Firth to the Derwent as vassal of Malcolm III, his cousin. That part of Cumbria belonged to the ancient British kingdom of Strathclyde and it was subject to Scottish jurisdiction until 1092.

The letter contains information which places in doubt the view that the granter was Gospatric I's half-uncle who was dead by 1064. It also challenges the view that William the Conqueror gave Cumbria to Gospatric I, although the source for this argument [24] concedes that the letter might have been written by another hand. There is still room for niggling doubt - the letter refers to 'Eadred's days' [this could have been a scribe's error for Ealdred who ruled Northumberland from 913 until c.927; it could have also refer to Ealdred II, Lord of Northumberland from c.1019 to 1038]. The reference to Siward, Earl of Northumberland from 1041 to 1055 is also significant. However, these facts do not provide cast-iron proof that the author was Gospatric I of Dunbar.

The Reverend James Wilson's article on the letter for *SHR* (1903-04) makes a strong case for Gospatric I. Graham, Cumberland and Westmoreland Antiquarian and Archaeological Society *(CWAAS) vol xxv* ventures that the writ dates from 1072, after Gospatric I was deprived of his Northumbrian earldom ie when he was reduced to being

> 'only the ruler of Cumbria south of the Solway'

Graham also insists *(CWAAS vol xxxii)* that Gospatric I, ejected from his earldom fired a parting shot at the new Norman regime in what he considers to be a

> 'bombastic charter addressed to his men in Caldbeck and elsewhere in Allerdale, at the same time warning them of an impending re-imposition of the ancient tax of cornage' [perhaps the forerunner of the *multure* or fee charged by a lord for grinding corn at his mill]

by William the Conqueror. (This interpretation may explain Gospatric I's empty promise to Thorfinn MacThore, the beneficiary, that he is to live 'geld free' as Gospatric himself did.). Graham's is perhaps a somewhat shaky conclusion, although it is not without foundation.

If the letter is indeed a defiant gesture aimed at William - in character for Gospatric I - it puts it beyond doubt that the granter was none other than himself as his half-uncle was dead before the Conquest took place. That defiance is all the more understandable when we take account of the fact that when Gospatric I was deposed, he was among the very last of the Eadwulfing dynasty which had ruled Northumberland almost without interruption since the tenth century.

Notes to Appendix B

1 Feudal term for a landowning person with modest wealth but not of the peasant class
2 Thorfynn or Thorfinn may have been ruler of Strathclyde in 1045 which at that time included Carlisle and Allerdale. The name possibly survives in a hill called Torkin, near the village of Thursby. The use of Mac - son of - indicates the Celtic origin of the beneficiary - very unusual and rare in the locality
3 Allerdale
4 Showk, Waver and Wampool are three boundary streams in north and north-west Allerdale
5 Troutbeck. This may not be the village near Keswick/Penrith since the name simply means a small stream and probably has no connection with the popular lakeland beauty spot.
6 Caldbeck in eastern Allerdale was the birthplace of John Peel, the huntsman. Gospatric I reputedly founded a hospital there (*CWAAS, vol xxv*)
7 Cardew and Cumdivock, two vills in the parish of Dalston, near Thursby. Cardew Hall still exists and Cumdivock is a thriving village. Thursby is the birthplace of Sir Thomas Bouch, the engineer who built the Tay Bridge which collapsed in 1879
8 Maelmhure or Melmor was also the name of Duncan I's third son and Gospatric I's uncle. It is possible that like Malcolm III, he lived in temporary exile with Earl Siward or in Cumbria during the conflict with Macbeth. J Wilson believed he was the landowner from which the parish of Malmerbury in east Cumberland took its name
9 Thorfynn MacThore's father; Sygulf may have been the owner of Greystoke, in the vicinity
10 Anderson, *Early Sources of Scottish History* (*ES Scot His)* ventures that Eadred was an Allerdale tenant. This could be a mispelling of Ealdred, Earl of Northumberland from c.1019 to 1036; his daughter married Siward, the Danish-born Earl of Northumberland from 1041 to 1055.
11 Siward assisted Malcolm III against Macbeth; both Gospatric I and his half-uncle Gospatric would have known him.
12 Geld free - exemption from land tax; *geld* was assessed on the *hide*, a unit of land in Anglo-Saxon law which the Normans continued to enforce after the Conquest. Geld exemptions were given as poltical favours or patronage
13 Waltheof may have been Earl Siward's son. He became Earl of Northumberland in 1072, after Gospatric I was deprived of the earldom. He was executed for treason by William the Conqueror in 1076. Anderson, *ES Scot Hist* believes this Waltheof to have been the Lord of Allerdale, Gospatric I's son. Wygande probably owned Wiggonby which is noth-west of Thursby, in the parish of Aikton. Gamell may have beeen the owner of Gamelsby in Aikton parish; he may also have been the son of Orm who married Gunnilda, Gospatric I's daughter. Kunyth is probably a form of Kenneth. Ragg, *CWAAS vol v* believes these were thanes.
14 Feudal terms for rights of ownership and exercise of authority; *soc* and *sac* were powers of jurisdiction; *toll* was right to impose sales taxes; *t[h]eam* was the right to hold courts to establish rights of property ownership.
15 Morin may have been the proprietor of Dalston (Ragg, *CWAAS vol v*)
16 These were well-known institutions, the precise nature of which are obscure; they belong to the culture of ancient Cumberland.
17 Thus the area granted to Thorfynn appears to have been about 4 miles south of Carlisle from Thursby-Dalton to Caldbeck, 7 or 8 miles further south of Mungrisdale (St Mungo's Dale) and near the A66 from Penrith to Keswick
18 Ragg (*CWAAS vol v*); Ragg believes that Gospatric I granted the writ some time in 1072; Anderson (*ES Scot Hist*) gives betwen 1055 and 1072; Wilson (*SHR vol I*) gives 1067x1072.
19 *An English Letter of Gospatric,* Reverend J Wilson (*SHR vol I* 1903-04)
20 Frank Stenton, *Anglo-Saxon England*
21 G Barrow, *Edward the Confessor*
22 Ritchie, *The Normans in Scotland: The County History of Northumberland vol vii* refers to Gospatric I as Lord of Allerdale.
23 Anderson's *Earliest Sources of Scottish History 500 to 1286 (ESC Scot Hist.)*
24 'King William the Conqueror [took] the county of Cumberland from Gospatric, to whom he had first given it.' (*History of the County of Cumberland* vol ii).

Appendix C

The Northumbrian Possesssions of the Earls of Dunbar *

The following are the vills and manors which Gospatric II inherited from 'Edmund' - his unidentified wife's uncle - in Northumberland, along with manors which had belonged to 'Winnock', who may have ben a relative. These properties came into Gospatric II's possession some time between c.1093 and 1110; other properties followed as a result of a special arrangement with Henry I of England.. This arrangement was that Gospatric II and his descendants agreed to act as Henry's special constable to ensure the safe passage of English official coming to Scotland on state business. The vills of Bewick and Eglingham were granted to the Dunbars by the Abbot of St Albans on behalf of the daughter house at Tynemouth in 1138, under threat by David I when he invaded England that year.

The original properties - most in the Morpeth-Wooler district - in c.1100 were as follows:

Brandon, Branton, Beanley, Harehope, Hedgeley, Horseley, Long Wotton, the three Middletons (possibly Upper, Long and Nether), Nether Witton, Rittam, Roddam, Stanton, Tittlington and Windygates.

Later additions were

Bewick and Eglingham (given to Gospatric II or III in return for protecting the cell of St Albans at Tynemouth; when David I invaded England in 1138, he guaranteed Tynemouth's safety in a charter witnessed by Gospatric II), Edlingham, Lemoutone (Lemmington), Leverchilde and Shipley.

These 22 properties were sub-infued to Gospatric's issue at first, then over the next two centuries, passed to other tenanats who paid rent for them. On 11th April 1247, at the height of a dispute between the 6th Earl of Dunbar and the monks of Tynemouth as to the ownership of Bewick and Eglingham - on-going since 1201 (*Calendar of Documents Relating to Scotland* or *CDS vol I Nos 456 and 1343*) Henry III of England was asked by Matthew Paris, monk at St Albans, to enquire into the Earl's possessions in Northumberland in general and these two vills in particular (see Chapter 2).

Outwardly, the dispute arose through the 6th Earl's alleged blasphemy - he had mocked the relics of the Christian martyr St Oswin at Tynemouth, declaring them bogus. Matthew Paris, the St Albans chronicler was a personal friend of Henry III and interceded on Tynemouth's behalf in the dispute. Paris persuaded the king to prepare an inventory of Dunbar possessions in the north of England; these were listed as follows:

Beanley, Brandon, Branton, Edlingham, Harehope, Hedgeley, Horseley, Lemmington, Leverchilde, [the three Middletons were omitted for some reason] Ritton, Shipley, Stanton, Windygates, Witton and Wotton

Thus the 6th Earl of Dunbar lost Berwick and Eglingham to the monks of Tynemouth on the orders of the English king. It will be seen that of the 22 properties identified above, the 6th Earl or his antecedents had disposed of a further two - probably as wedding gifts to members of his family. After the Tynemouth incident, the 6th Earl apologised to Tynemouth and went on Crusade to show good faith for his contumacy; he died before reaching the Holy Land. At that time, he personally owned only Edlingham and Hedgeley, the remaining 4 properties being rented.

A later enquiry into Dunbar holdings in Northumberland was held in 1309, after on the death of the 8th Earl of Dunbar the previous year. The enquiry indicated that the Dunbars were due rents to the English Exchequer for the following properties:-

Beanley (£8), Edlingham (12 pennies (5p) or a sparrowhawk, Middleton (5 marks) and Shipley (six shillings and eight pennies (34p). In addition, there was a 'tenagium' of twenty shillings and ten pennies (£1.5) due to the Exchequer for each of the vills of Beanley, Brandon, Branton, Edlingham, Harehope, Hedgeley, Lemmington, the 3 Middletons, Roddam (Ritton?) and Wotton.

Windygates and several other properties had been given to Juliana, daughter of Gospatric I as wedding gifts, although only as a sub-tenant. Windygates seems to have passed to another owner at some point between 1248 and 1308. The amounts of £12 and 12 shillings (£12.60) and 30 shillings (£1.50) for

'St Cuthbert's Farm' at Middleton and Roddam/Ritton were paid to the Exchequer in Newcastle.

These facts bring into question any argument that from 1292 to 1314, the Dunbars were unduly anxious to protect their English possessions by adherence to Edward I and Edward II. By 1314, these possessions were token properties from which the Dunbars were unlikely to receive any significant financial gain although under the feudal system, they were entitled to knight-service from their tenants. In 1363, the Dunbars lost Shipley so that by then, their properties were minor holdings, hardly worth the trouble of collecting rent.

Many of the above possessions survive today in the Wooler-Alnwick area eg Beanley, Bewick, Brandon, Branton, Edlingham, Eglingham, Embleton, Harehope, Leamington and Roddam (see OS map of Nothumberland).

* Sources: *The County History o f Northumberland, vol viii; CDS vol I No 1712, vol iii No 77 and vol iv No 83*

APPENDIX D

The Great Cause. The Thirteen Competitors for the throne of Scotland as recorded in the Great Roll of Scotland, 3rd August 1291 (*CDS vol ii* No 507)

1 Florent [Florence] V, Comte de Hollande; claimed as great-grandson of Ada, eldest daughter of Henry, prince of Scotland [son of David I] and sister of William the Lion.
2 Patrick de Dunbar, 8th Earl of Dunbar and 1st of March: claimed as great-grandson of Ada,* daughter of William the Lion.
3 William de Vesci: claimed as grandson of Margaret or Marjory, daughter of William the Lion.
4 William de Ros [Ross]: claimed as great-grandson of Isabella * said to have been the eldest daughter of William the Lion.
5 Robert de Pinkeney [Flemish=Piquiny?]: claimed as great-grandson of Marjory, daughter of Henry, prince of Scotland and sister of William the Lion.
6 Nicholas de Soules: claimed as grandson of Marjory, daughter of Alexander II.
7 Patrick Galithly [Golightly]: son of Henry Galithly and, as he contended, claimed as lawful grandson * of William the Lion.
8 Roger de Mandeville: claimed as great-great-grandson of Aufrica * daughter of William the Lion.
9 John Comyn, Lord of Badenoch: claimed as great-great-grandson of Hextilda or Histilla, grand- daughter of Donald Bane. [John Comyn was the Red Comyn's father]
10 John de Hastyngs of Abergavenny: claimed as grandson of Ada, third daughter of David, Earl of Huntingdon.
11 John Balliol: claimed as grandson of Margaret, first daughter of David, Earl of Huntingdon.
12 Robert de Brus [Bruce], Lord of Annandale: claimed as son of Isabella, second daughter of David, Earl of Huntingdon.
13 Eric II, king of Norway, representing his late daughter, the Maid of Norway, grand-daughter of Alexander III.

* illegitimate

The final three competitors showing their relationship to David of Huntingdon, grandson of David I

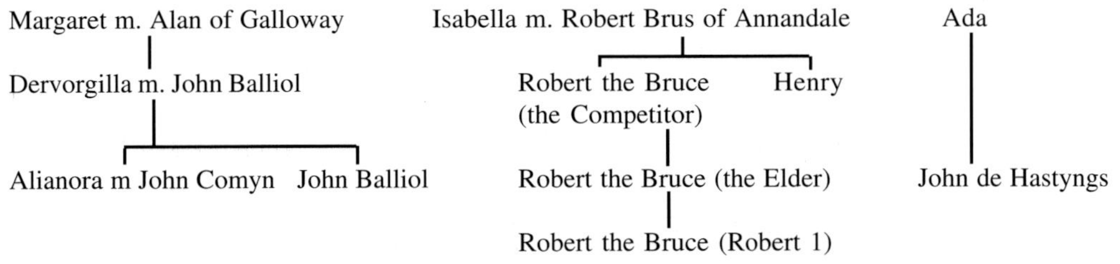

APPENDIX E

1296, March 25-Extracts from a Journal of the Movements of King Edward [I] in Scotland *

'On the day of St George, 24th April, news came to the king that they of Scotland had besieged the Castle of Dunbar, which belonged to the earl Patrick, who held strongly with the king of England. It was upon a Monday [23rd April] that the king sent his troops to raise the siege. Before they came there the castle had surrendered, and they of Scotland were within. When the troops of the king of England came there, they besieged the castle with three hosts on the Tuesday [24th April] that they arrived before it. On the Wednesday [25th April], they who were within sent out privately, and on Thursday and Friday [26th and 27th April] came the host of Scotland all the afternoon to have raised the siege of the Englishmen. And when the Englishmen saw the Scotchmen, they fell upon them and discomfited the Scotchmen, and the chase continued more than five leagues of way, and until the hours of vespers [evening]. And there died sir Patrick de Graham, a great lord, and 10,055 by right reckoning. On the same Friday by night, the king came from Berwick to go to Dunbar, and lay that night at Coldingham, and on the Saturday [28th April] at Dunbar, and on the same day they of the castle surrendered themselves to the king's pleasure. And there were the earl of Atholl, the earl of Ross, the earl of Menteith, sir John Comyn of Badenoch the son [ie the Red Comyn whom Bruce murdered in 1306], sir Richard Suart [Siward], sir William de Saintler [Sinclair] and as many as fourscore men-at-arms and sevenscore footmen. There tarried the king three days.'

* From an *MS* of the fourteenth century in the Imperial Library at Paris, Fonds Lat., 6049, fol. 30, b (See also Stevenson, *Historical Documents of Scotland* 1286-1306).

APPENDIX F

Incumbents of Dunbar Parish Church from 1342 to 1584 and 1560 and some ministers of local churches from 1560 [1]

(A) = Archpriest [2] (C) = Canon (D) = Dean

1342-1343	'Laurence' (D)
1343-1368	? (D); Thomas de Harcars [Harkess?] was (C) in 1353
1369	'David' (D)
1370-1403	Thomas de Merton (D)
1404-1408	William Stephani or Stephens (D); he wasn't elected
1409-1423	Columba de Dunbar (D). He is described in 1394 as 'student in the arts for several years at Oxford, legitimate son of George de Dunbar, earl of March' [3]Aged 14 in 1394, Columba's studies at Oxford began earlier than in modern times. His father petitioned the pope to allow him to hold a benefice without cure of souls; in 1413, Columba was permitted to retain the Deanery, canonry and prebend.of Dunbar, thus enriching himself. Columba was one of the witnesses to the Bishop of St Andrews' charter bestowing privileges, liberties and immunities on St Andrews University when it was founded in 1411. (*Calendar of Papal Letters to Scotland of Benedict XIII of Avignon* 1394 - 1418, *CPL Benedict XIII*)
1412-1422	Robert Young (A) [4]
1422-?	Ingram de Lindsay (D); his incumbency was possibly in tandem with Columba in 1422
1423-1433	Robert Young (D) [5] whose incumbency probably continued until 1440'
1424-1426	Donald Post (A) (*Calendar of Scottish Supplications to Rome vol ii* 1423-28, *CSSR ii*)
1430-?	Laurence de Abernethy (A).
1430-?	Thomas de Mireton (C); Patrick de Crumby [6]
1432-?	Thomas de Lawedre [Lawder] (C) [7]
1440-1453	Adam Hepburn of Hailes (D) who was also in charge of Dunbar Castle between 1446 and 1452
1454-1466	?
1467-1471	Archibald Whitelaw
1477-1499	Alexander Giffert [Gifford]; Malcolm Drummond was Rector
1500-1506	? One of the Canons was Robert Ross in 1503
1506-1513?	Alexander Stewart (D) who was half-brother of the 1st Duke of Albany (*TA vol iii*)
1516-1543	James Salmond
1524-1542	Thomas Hay of Yester [8]
1529-1540	George Hay of Yester
1542-1543	Thomas Hay of Yester (A); *Yester Writs* No 605 states that he received permission from Pope Paul III to retain the Archpresbytery of Dunbar on payment of £20 to his predecessor, James Salmond. He was one of the first members of the Edinburgh Court of Session in 1532.
1544-1552	?
1553-1568	John Row (D) but also known as the Provost
1556-1568	Claud Hamilton; forfeited probably because he refused to renounce the Catholic faith at the time of the Reformation; John Manderston (C)
1569-1572	?
1573-?	Sir Thomas MacGill (*Yester Writs,* No 771) [9]
1584-?	John Reid (D) (*RSS vol viii* No 1774)

Notes to Appendix F

Appendices

1 From Watt, *Fasti Ecclesiae Scoticanae Medii Aevi ad Annum 1638,(Watt, Fasti)* (1342-1584); Scott, *Fasti Ecclesiae Scoticanae,* Scott, *Fasti* (1560-present day)

2 Usually the head of a Collegiate Church was known as the Provost but at Dunbar, the title Dean was used; next in the hierarchy was the Archpriest, then a number of prebends, canons or chaplains, the number varying according to the size and wealth of the foundation

3 In addition to Dunbar, Columba held many other benefices under the system known as *pluralism* ie those churchmen who were fortunate enough to earn additional income from holding offices in other churches. In a letter dated 4th March 1415, Pope Benedict XIII collated 'Columba de Dunbar, secular dean of the Collegiate Church of St Beya de Dunbar, St Andrews diocese, kinsman of James [I], king of Scots, son of George, earl of March "to the benefice of Ruthven, Aberdeen," ' *(CPL Benedict XIII)*. Another example of pluralism was the installation on 8th January 1412 of Alexander de Carnis, secular provost [dean] of the Collegiate Church of Lincluden, Glasgow into the canonry and prebend of Linton [Prestonkirk], a secular prebend of Dunbar Collegiate Church. Carnis [Cairns?] held the position in 1417

4 Young was the archpriest and personal confessor of George, 10th Earl of March and his son-reputedly in 1419, which means that George Dunbar was still alive that year (see note 9 to fig 4). In January 1419, Young was given papal authority to absolve all Scots

> 'who shall go to war against the English while they remain schismatics and to grant full remission of sins to those Scots *in mortis articulo* [confession at death] because of the war.'

The Great Schism came in 1378, when there were popes in both Rome and Avignon. Scotland, being pro-France under the *Auld Alliance* looked to the pope at Avignon for spiritual guidance; Benedict XIII was one of the Avignon popes (1394-c1418).

5 *CSSR vol ii*

6 Because of the widespread practice of pluralism, it is almost impossible to identify the various canons at Dunbar. Thomas de Mireton [Merton?] was a canon of Spott in 1430, treasurer to James I and vicar of Haddington. *(Calendar of Scottish Suppli cations to Rome vol vii* 1428-32 *(CSSR vii)* Patrick de Crumby [Crombie?] was allowed to hold two benefices despite his being the son of an unmarried man and woman *(CSSR ii)*

7 Lauder was yet another pluralist who in 1432 held no fewer than 5 benefices including the 'canonry and prebend of Petrokis [Pitcox] in the Collegiate Church of Dunbar notwithstanding defect of his birth of an unmarried man and an unmarried woman.' The chapel of Pitcox fell into disuse and was moved to nearby Stenton

8 At the Reformation, Dunbar Collegiate Church remained as originally constituted with provosts [deans] holding office until 1580 (*RMS vi* No 1773 and Watt, *Fasti*)

Some Ministers of Dunbar Parish Church from 1560 to the present day

1560-1563	John Manderston - more correctly John Home of Manderston - canon at the time of the Reformation. Among those who were appointed to hear Lady Jean Gordon's suit for divorce from James Hepburn, 4th Earl of Bothwell in 1567 to allow him to marry Mary, Queen of Scots
1563	George Home of Broxmouth, formerly of Pinkerton
1563-1564	Jasper Home of Lawfield 'rector of Dunbar' according to *Miller, Dunbar*
1564-1567	Andrew Simson. According to the session minutes, he was the incumbent who witnessed the tragic fishing disaster at Dunbar in 1579 (see Chapter 10). *Scott, Fasti* records the following: 'The catastrophe known as the Lost Drave of Dunbar occurred during his ministry here.' An extract from the session minutes follows; the words are those of Simson's son, minister at Dalkeith: Simson also accused Rev John Kello of murder, (see Spott). ' "A fearful judgement of God fell forth about the year 1577 [sic], whereof I [Simson senior] was an eyewitness" My father of good memory, being minister thereof, when going to the church, saw a thousand boats setting their nets on the Sabbath. He weeped and feared that God would not suffer such contempt. It being a most calm day as ever was seen at that season - at midnight, when they went forth to draw their nets, the wind arose so fearfully that it drowned eight score and ten boats, so that there was reckoned in the coast side fourteen score of widows,' In point of fact, the disaster occurred on 17th August 1579 as indicated in Moysie, *Affairs of Scotland.* While correcting the error in the date, Moysie disagrees with the number of boats destroyed - he gives 60 - and states that 300 men were drowned leaving 280 widows; most of these being local women which would have imposed an intolerable burden on the poor relief fund
1599-1635 *	James Home, brother of George Home of Lawfield and related to Jasper Home above. Summoned before the Court of High Commission on 26th June 1620 for failing to observe holy days and for not celebrating communion in accordance with the Five Articles of Perth introduced by James VI. James Home must have complied as he remained at Dunbar until his death in 1635. He was buried at Tyninghame.
1635-1639	William Maxwell. Deprived of his living by the Commission of Assembly on 3rd January 1639 for 'erroneous doctrine, meddling with [stealing from] the poor's box, for tyrannical behaviour towards his parishioners, in urging their conformity to the Articles of Perth [by then rejected by those who signed the National Covenant in 1638], declining [ignoring] both the Assembly and Presbytery and appealing to His Majestie [Charles I]'.
1639-1644	Andrew Stevenson. Rejected the Articles of Perth and was thus acceptable to the General Assembly.
1644-1652*	David Robertson. Rebuked in 1647 for pre-nuptial fornication with a woman he subsequently married
1657-1658*	Richard Waddell who subsequently moved to Stenton
1665-1675*	Andrew Wood, first as minister at Spott in 1643, then Dunbar in 1665. After the Restoration in 1660, he became Bishop of the Isles, then Caithness in 1680. Died at Dunbar aged 76 in 1695
1681-1688*	Thomas Wood, son of Andrew Wood above
1733-1765	Alexander Pyott or Pyot. His appointment by John, Duke of Roxburghe, heritor, was opposed by the congregation at Dunbar, so much so that on the day of his induction, the kirk doors were closed against him and he had to climb into the church through the vestry window! On the two nights preceding the battle of Prestonpans in 1745, he acted host to Colonel Gardiner in Cope's army. Pyot was the butt of a satirical piece, *Memoirs of Magipico*, written by

Samuel Haliburton, chaplain to the First Regiment of Foot [the Scots Guards]. One of Pyot's sons became the deputy governor of Georgia, USA

1766-1795 George Bruce. He wrote the account of Dunbar parish for Sinclair's *Old Statistical Account*. When he died in 1795, he bequeathed £50 to the school at East Barns

1795-1819 Professor Patrick Carfrae of Garvald. Known locally as 'Paper Pate' [paper head] from his practice of reading sermons instead of memorising them. The General Assembly of the Church of Scotland ruled that the reading of sermons was 'displeasing to God's people'. He published *Letter to a Scot's Bard* which elicited a response from Burns. (Burns' *Works,* Wallace Edition). Carfrae retired to Bourhouse, near Dunbar where he died on 5th March 1822. He was the last incumbent of the old Collegiate Church which was demolished in 1819

1821-1862 John Jaffray, first incumbent of the new Parish Kirk which was designed by Gillespie Graham and opened its doors in 1821. Jaffray wrote the account of Dunbar parish for the *New Statistical Account.* He had a reputation as an authority on agriculture and soil improvement; he was the author of *An Account of an Experiment in Deep Ploughing.* One of his sons was a Dunbar banker. John Jaffray was a well-loved minister; he was buried at Dunbar.

1862 - 1901 Robert Buchanan

1901 - 1912 William Borland

1913 - 1917 James Kirk, who was appointed chaplain to the 7th Argyll and Sutherland Highlanders (1915), then the Seaforth Highlanders (1918); he died of battle wounds on 1st April, 1918

1918 - 1938 William Brown

1938 - 1955 Alex William Sawyer

1956 - 1965 Harold C M Eggo

1965 - 1992 William Chalmers; during his incumbency, the Parish Church was gutted by fire (1987)

1993 - 1999 Alexander B Noble

1999 - Eric Foggitt

Some Ministers of Belhaven Parish Church from 1840. Built in 1838, it was a Free Church for a time, then Church of Scotland again

1840-1858 William Sorley who left the Church of Scotland at the Disruption of 1843 and was active in founding the Free Church. Married Anna Ritchie, daughter of William Hamilton Ritchie, banker and Town Clerk at Dunbar. Their son William became Professor of Moral Philosophy at Cambridge University. Their grandson, Charles Hamilton Sorley who wrote poetry was killed at the battle of Loos in 1915 after only six months in the trenches. He is now receiving acclaim as a war poet; unlike Rupert Brooke, his contemporary, Sorley was greatly disillusioned by the war from the outset.

1948-1974 John Stein McMartin, MC. Mentioned in Dispatches during World War II. He was well-versed in local history

Some Ministers of Spott Parish Church between 1554-1945

?-1554 Robert Galbraith, also Senator of the College of Justice in Edinburgh. Stabbed to death in a brawl with a burgess in Edinburgh's High Street.

1559-1570 John Hamilton, illegitimate son of James, 1st Earl of Arran. He became Archbishop of St Andrews and was hanged at Stirling in 1571 for his alleged complicity in the assassination of James Stewart, Regent Moray in 1570

1567-1570 John Kello. He strangled his wife on Sunday morning, 24th September 1570 as he wanted rid of her to marry the daughter of a rich man. After the deed, Kello went into the pulpit and preached a more than usually eloquent sermon. Tortured by guilt, he narrated a dream he claimed to have had to Andrew Simson, minister at Dunbar. A few days later, Simson reminded him of the dream accusing him thus:

> 'Ye are, I fear, the author yourself of that cruel murder.'

No account of Kello's trial appears to have survived but the sentence passed on him was recorded on 4th October 1570:

> 'John Kello....to be hanged to the deid, and thaireftir his body to be cassin [cast] in ane fyre, and brint [burnt] to assis [ashes], and his gudis [goods] and gear to be confiscat [confiscated].'

This was the usual sentence for women found guilty of practising witchcraft.

1627-1631* John Sinclair

1631-1642 William Douglas, brother of Sir Archibald Douglas of Whittingehame.

1643-1665* Andrew Wood who moved to Dunbar in 1665

1683-1689 Archibald Buchan, on 27th February 1689, he was 'roughly handled' by some of his parishioners who early one morning dragged him from his bed and carried him half-naked to the church and dared him to officiate any longer as their minister. He was subsequently deprived of his living by the Privy Council in September 1689 for failing to read the *Proclamation of Estates* and praying for William of Orange who became king in 1689. He was clearly an adherent of the deposed James VII

1698-1726* Andrew Brown

1790-1798 John Martin who wrote the Spott Parish account for the *Old Statistical Account*

1799-1836 Alexander Graham. He had 14 children, one of whom was lost at sea in November 1828 from his ship, *HMS Ariel*

1836-1880 Robert Burns Thomson, son of Captain Andrew Thomson who served with Nelson

1889-1945 Lothian Gray who died after an incumbency of 56 years

Some Ministers of Stenton (formerly Pitcox) between 1578-1689

1578-1586	Thomas Daill [Dale?]; he was 'Callit from Papistry to the true profession of the Gospel.'
1606-1612	William Carkettill whom the presbytery thought 'over young in years.'
1641-1657*	Robert Davidson
1658-1660*	Richard Waddell from Dunbar
1661-1679*	John Pollok
1683-1689	Alexander Hamilton. He was deprived of his living in 1689 for refusing to pray for William of Orange who became king in that year and for making hostile remarks about the king's honour

Some Ministers of Innerwick Parish Church between 1608-1666

1608-1640*	Patrick Hamilton the illegitimate son of Thomas, 1st Earl of Haddington
1663-1666*	James Wood
1899-1906	Robert Gray, dismissed after a church court found him guilty of intemperance, Robert Gray returned to Innerwick in the 1930s and preached to a packed church, clearly his parishioners loved him

Ministers of Prestonkirk and Tyninghame Parish Churches between 1613-1662

Prestonkirk

1619-1649	John Dalzell

Tyninghame

1613-1662	John Lauder. He was chaplain to a regiment in the Army of the Covenant which fought on the parliamentary forces' side during the English Civil War. He was a witness to the execution of ten 'witches ' in Dunbar in 1650

Some Ministers of Whitingehame Parish Church between 1602-1918

1602-1611	John Mannuell; he may also have been a schoolmaster at Dunbar
1662-1694	Archibald Millar, who demitted office as Episcopal minister in favour of John Watson (After 1661and the Restoration of Charles II, Presbyterian ministers were ejected from their livings by those who favoured the Episcopalian form of church government. Presbyterians weren't restored until the reign of William I (of Orange)
1734-	Thomas Sinclair who was ordained on 4th September 1734 and died 13 days later, never having preached a ser mon.
1769-1776	Adam Dickson who was killed by a fall from his horse when returning home on 25th March
1918	Marshall B Lang who wrote a history: *Whittingehame: The Seven Ages of an East Lothian Parish*

Some Ministers of Oldhamstocks Parish Church between 1547-1690

1547-1568	Thomas Hepburn. He proclaimed Mary, Queen of Scots' marriage to James Hepburn, 4th Earl of Bothwell and witnessed their marriage contracts at Dunbar Castle in 1567. He made an unsuccessful attempt to retrieve the so-called *Casket Letters* which were doctored to implicate Bothwell and the queen in the murder of her husband, Henry, Lord Darnley. When Mary escaped from Leven in 1568, Thomas Hepburn attempted to recapture Dunbar Castle in her name. He was forfeited for heresy in 1568 (but see below)
1568-	John Hepburn
1578-1585	Thomas Hepburn. He was reinstated and died at Oldhamstocks in 1585
1586-1599	Thomas Hepburn, son of the above who was removed in 1568; the son was also removed in 1599 and reinstated two years later
1601-1629	Thomas Hepburn, reinstated; he may have been involved in the single recorded witchcraft case at Cockburnspath, then a dependency of Oldhamstocks
1672-1690	John Gibson who was deprived, possibly because he had Episcopalian sympathies

* Identifies ministers who were probably involved in bringing suspected witches to trial

APPENDIX G

Scottish Regiments at Dunbar, 1650.

In September 1650, Lieutenant-General David Leslie commanded a force of 16,000 foot and 7,000 horse, with an artillery train of 32 guns. The Covenanter army carried banners - usually a saltire or white St Andrew's Cross on a blue field with a variety of mottos on the common theme of the Scottish religion ie *For Religion, King and Kingdom* or *For Covenant, Religion, King and Kingdoms.*

The regiments which took part in the battle are listed in Furgol, *A Regimental History of the Covenanting Armies 1639-51*. The list which appears in that publication is virtually identical to that contained in the *Harleian MS,* [1] an English compilation quoted in Miller, *Lamp of Lothian.*

Regiment	Commanding Officer (s)	Number of Men	Shire
Arnot's Horse	Colonel Charles Arnott Major William Johnston	Not known	Lanark, Renfrew Ayr
Artillery train [2]	General of Artillery, James Wemyss of Caskieburn	Not known	Various
Brechin's Horse	Colonel George, Lord Brechin	400?	Angus Perth
Brown's Horse	Major-General Sir John Brown of Fordell [3] Colonel Sir Arthur Forbes Lieutenant-Colonel William Bruce	230	Perth
Brymer's Foot [4]	Colonel Brymer	Not known	Edinburgh
Buchanan's Foot	Colonel George Buchanan of Buchanan Lieutenant-Colonel Sir James Douglas	1000?	Linlithgow Clackmannan Stirling
Earl of Cassillis' Foot [5]	Colonel John, 6th Earl of Cassillis	870	Ayr Renfrew
Castle Stewart's Horse [6]	Quartermaster General William of Castle Lieutenant John Bannatyne of Corhouse	260?	Galloway Wigton Stewartry of Kirkcudbright
Darroch's Foot [7]	Colonel Archibald Douglas Lieutenant-Colonel John Crichton of Crawford	900?	Dumfries
Edzell's Foot [8]	Colonel John Lindsay of Edzell	Not known	Angus
Master of Forbes' Horse	Colonel William, Master of Forbes Lieutenant-Colonel Arthur Forbes of Echt	120?	Aberdeen Banff
General of Artillery's Foot	General of Artillery. James Wemyss of Caskieburn	Not known	?
Gleneagles ' Foot [9]	Colonel Sir John Haldane of Gleneagles Major John Cockburn	920	Perth
Greenhead's Foot	Colonel Andrew Ker of Greenhead [10]	200	Teviotdale Selkirk
Hackett's Horse [11]	Colonel Sir John Hackett Lieutenant-Colonel Robert Hackett	200	Dunbarton Galloway Linlithgow
Robert Hackett's Horse	Colonel Robert Hackett [12]	137	Nairn Elgin Inverness
Hartwoodburn's Horse	Colonel Walter Scott of Hartwoodburrn Lieutenant-Colonel William Ker of Newton	225	Teviotdale Selkirk
His Majesty's Life Guard of Foot [13]	Colonel Archibald, Lord Lorne Lieutenant-Colonel James Wallace of Achens Colonel Sir Alexander Stewart	400	Mainly Ulstermen

Holborn's Foot [14]	Colonel Major-General Sir James Holborn	500	Stirling Clackmannan
Ker's Horse [15]	Colonel Gilbert Ker Lieutenant-Colonel Archibald Strachan	280?	Dumfries
Kinhilt's Horse Troop	Colonel Sir Robert Adair of Kinhilt	80?	Ulster
Lawers' Foot	Colonel Sir James Campbell of Lawers [16] Lieutenant-Colonel Colin Campbell [17]	600?	Linlithgow
Kirkcudbright's Foot Dragoons [18]	Colonel John, 3rd Lord of Kirkcudbright	900	Galloway Ayr Renfrew
Kirkness' Foot Leslie's Horse	Colonel Sir William Douglas of Kirkness [19] Lieutenanat-General David Leslie [20]	2700 400?	Fife & Kinross Lanark, Renfrew Ayr
Earl of Leven's Horse	Colonel Lord General Alexander, 1st Earl of Leven [21]	174?	Berwick Haddington
Lovat's Foot	Colonel Sir James Fraser of Brea [22] Colonel Alexander, Master and Tutor of Lovat Major Hugh Fraser of Struy	750?	Inverness
Lumsden's Foot	Colonel Lieutenant-General Sir James Lumsden of Innergelly [23]	Not known	Fife
Lord Mauchline's Horse	Colonel James, Lord Mauchline	900	Lanark
Menzies' Dragoons	Colonel William Menzies [24]	Not known	Fife
Ministers' Horse	Colonel Archibald Strachan [25] Lieutenant-Colonel William Ralston of Ralston Major Govan	500?	Not known
Montgomery's Horse	Major-General Robert Montgomery Lieutenant-Colonel James Chalmers of Gadgirth	400?	Ayr, Renfrew
Mouswall's Foot Dragoons	Colonel Sir James Douglas of Mouswall [26]	600?	Dunfermline
Pitscottie's Foot	Major-General Colin Pitscottie [27]	400?	Fife & Kinross
Riccarton's Horse [28]	Colonel Adjutant-General Thomas Craig of Riccarton Lieutenant-Colonel Alexander Inglis of Ingliston	133?	Midlothian
Scottscraig's Horse [29]	Colonel Sir Arthur Erskine of Scottscraig	233?	Stirling Clackmannan
Valleyfield's Foot [30]	Colonel Sir George Preston of Valleyfield Major James Stewart	900	Perth
Wedderburn's Foot [31]	Colonel Sir David Home of Wedderburn Lieutenant-Colonel George Home of Wedderburn the Younger	300?	Berwick

A comparison between Furgol's list and the *Harleian MS* shows only minor discrepancies in the composition of the Scottish army ie

Furgol		*Harleian MS*	
Regiments of Foot Dragoons	= 2	Brigades of Foot	= 5*

Regiments of Foot	=17	Regiments of Foot	= 9
Regiments of Horse	=18	Regiments of Horse	= 18 or 19
Artillery Train	= 1	Artillery Train	= 1
Total	=38		= 37/38

* It is likely that each brigade contained two regiments

It is difficult to provide accurate numbers of Scottish casualties, far less to estimate to estimate precisely the size of Leslie's army because of the purges which were still taking place on the eve of the battle. It is generally accepted that Leslie's force at the outset was 16,000 foot and 7,000 horse facing Cromwell's 10-11,000. Furgol's estimated numbers (where provided) account for about 15,600 in Leslie's force. If the total was indeed 23,000, each foot regiment would have had to average about 850 men and each horse regiment about 400 troopers - if up to strength that is. Foot and horse regiments in 1650 numbered about 900 and 3-400 respectively, so these figures are about right. There is no evidence to confirm whether the Presbytery of Dunbar provided men for any of the Lowland regiments although Wedderburn's Foot and Leven's Horse may have included some local men

NB Of the 500 or so Ulstermen who took part in the battle, most were those who had escaped the upheaval in Ulster brought about by Scots in Ireland who were sympathetic to the Engagement or had Royalist sympathies - regarded as Malignants by the Covenanter Kirk Party. The Ulstermen were thus acceptable to the Kirk Party.

Casualties

It is generally accepted there were 4,000 dead and 10,000 prisoners at Dunbar - about 61% of the strength of Leslie's army. Not unexpectedly, the foot regiments suffered the highest casualties; the worst were the regiments of Gleneagles, Lawers, Cassillis, Brymer, Darroch, Pitscottie, Valleyfield, Wedderburn and Kirkudbright

Notes to Appendix G

1 *Harleian MS* No 6844 fo. 123, British Museum
2 Because of the sudden and unexpected English attack, the artillery were never used at Dunbar. The entire artillery train was taken.
3 On 2nd September, Brown added his voice to those of Ker and Strachan, urging Leslie to come off Doon Hill and fight Cromwell. Brown's troopers escaped and reached Stirling
4 Also known as the Town of Edinburgh regiment; it was almost certainly destroyed at Dunbar
5 This regiment is shown as a horse unit in the *Harleian MS*; it was probably destroyed at Dunbar
6 Posted on the left flank away from the initial English attack, this regiment probably saw very little action, although Castle Stewart barely escaped with his life
7 This regiment was probably destroyed
8 This regiment suffered some losses as a company of 90 men had to be recruited to it a month later
9 All three officers were killed. It may have been the other 'Highland ' regiment which fought well alongside Lawers' Foot. Both regiments were virtually annihilated
10 Ker was incorrectly reported killed in action
11 Part of this regiment managed to escape
12 Also nominally Lieutenant-Colonel of J Hackett's Horse; most of the regiment escaped
13 Suffered heavy losses; Colonel Stewart was killed and Lieutenant-Colonel Wallace was taken prisoner
14 Holborn acted as a brigade commander; it was he who ordered all but a few men to extinguish the matches for their muskets, thus rendering them almost useless in the sudden English attack. About 300 of his men were either casualties or prisoners
15 Although Ker was an ineffective commander, his regiment managed to escape from Dunbar with minimum losses
16 In 1649, Dunbar, Haddington, North Berwick and Queensferry were required to contribute towards the £639 needed to pay Lawers' Foot and three horse troops. At Dunbar, Lawers was a brigade commander on the right flank; although he appears not to have been present at the battle, his regiment resisted with great courage together with another - probably Preston of Valleyfield's. An English report stated that

> 'Only Lawers his Regiment of Highlanders made a good defence, a Lieutenant-Colonel [Colin Campbell] being slain by one of the Generals [Monck's] Servants, the Colonel was absent of the name of the Campbells [ie Campbell of Lawers], they stood to the push of the pike, and were all cut in pieces those were all the Foot that ingaged [sic] '. (Furgol, p93)

Lawers' men were most likely armed with flintlocks which meant they were well prepared fromthe outset. It is thought that his regiment lost over 200 men, about a third of his strength
17 As mentioned in note 16, Colin Campbell was killed. Miller, *Lamp of Lothian* refers to him as Captain Campbell of 'Towers'' Regiment - clearly a misprint.
18 Engaged with some losses
19 Kirkness was taken prisoner and later died of his wounds. Miller, *Lamp of Lothian* implies that Douglas of Kirkness was mortally wounded as

> 'a plain stone, bearing his name, lies in the shrubbery south-east from the house [ie Broxmouth House].'

20 David Leslie of course escaped
21 Alexander Leslie was too old to take part in the battle or indeed the entire campaign
22 Fraser survived Dunbar but is thought to have died of wounds
23 Lumsden served as a brigade commander; his regiment was entirely destroyed and he was taken prisoner

24 Menzies escaped from the field on a horse loaned to him by Sir James Douglas of Mouswall; the horse still hadn't been returned nine months after the battle!

25 Strachan, a committed Republican, played a prominent part at Dunbar - for good or ill. Along with Ker, he engaged in clandes tine talks with Cromwell's staff early on in the campaign - more it should be said because he was anti-Royalist rather than pro-Cromwell. Both he and Ker strongly urged Leslie to fight at Dunbar in the battle, Strachan's horse were positioned on the right flank, the first line consisting of lancers with long Spanish lances. The regiment repulsed the English cavalry under Lambert and to his credit, Strachan fought a stiff fight, managing to extricate his men and reach the safety of Stirling

26 Mouswall, who had lent his horse to William Menzies (see note 24) also managed to reach Stirling

27 Pitscottie served as a brigade commander; his regiment lost about 170 men

28 Riccarton's Horse served with Leslie throughout the summer of 1650

29 This regiment managed to reach Stirling

30 Although of a well-known Fife family, Preston of Valleyfield's regiment was recruited from Perthshire. The regiment suffered very heavy losses

31 This regiment was destroyed at Dunbar and both Homes were killed.

APPENDIX H

Sir Arthur Hesilrig's Letter to the English Parliament dated 31st October 1650

'*Gentlemen,* - I received your Letter, dated the 26th of October. In that you desire me that 2,300 of the *Scots* Prisoners, now at *Durham* or elsewhere, able and fit for Foot Service, be selected and marched thence to *Chester* and *Liverpool, to be shipp'd* for the South and West of *Ireland;* and that I should take special Care not to send any Highlanders: I am necessitated, upon the Receipt of this, to give you a full Account concerning the Prisoners.

After the Battle of *Dunbar*, in *Scotland,* my Lord-General wrote to me, that there were about 9000 Prisoners, and that of them he had set at Liberty all those that were wounded, and, as Mr. *Downing* wrote, 5100. The rest the General sent to *Newcastle,* conducted to *Berwick* by Major *Hopson* [Hobson], and from *Berwick* to *Newcastle* by some Foot out of that Garrison, and a Troop of Horse.

When they came to *Morpeth*, the Prisoners being put into a large wall'd Garden, they eat up raw Cabbages, Leaves and Roots, so many, as the very Seed and Labour , at 4 *d* (2p) a day, was valued at 9 *l* (£9), which Cabbage (they having fasted, as they themselves said, near eight Days) poison'd their Bodies; for as they were coming from thence to *Newcastle, some died by the Way-Side; when they came to* Newcastle, I put them in the greatest Church in the Town [St Nicholas]; and the next morning when I sent them to *Durham*, about 140 were sick, and not able to march; three died that Night, and some fell down in their march from *Newcastle* to *Durham* and died. I having sent my Lieutenant-Colonel and my Major with a strong Guard both of Horse and Foot, they being there told [counted] into the great Cathedral Church [Durham], were counted to no more than 3000; although Col. *Fenwick* wrote me, there were about 3500: But I believe they were not told at *Berwick,* and as to most of those that were lost, it was in *Scotland;* for I heard that the Officers who march'd with them to *Berwick,* were necessitated to kill about 30, fearing the Loss of them all, for they fell down in great Numbers, and said they were not able to march, and they brought them far in the Night, so that doubtless many ran away. When I sent them first to *Durham*, I wrote to the Mayor, and desired him to take Care that they wanted for nothing that was fit for Prisoners; and what he should disburse for them I would repay it. I also sent them a daily Supply of Bread from *Newcastle*, and an Allowance equal to what had been given to former Prisoners; but their Bodies being infected, the Flux increased among them. I sent many Officers to look to them, and ordered those who were sick to be removed out of the Cathedral Church into the Bishop's Castle, which belongs to Mrs. *Blackiston.* Cooks were provided, and they had Pottage made with Oatmeal, Beef and Cabbage, a full Quart at a Meal for every Prisoner: They had also Coals daily brought them, as many as made about 100 Fires both Night and Day, and Straw to lie upon. I appointed the Marshall to see all these Things orderly done, and he was allowed eight Men help him to divide the Coals, Meat, Bread and Pottage equally: They [the Scots] were so unruly, sluttish, and nasty, that it is not to be believed; they acted rather like beasts than Men; so that the Marshall was allowed 40 Men of the lustiest Prisoners to cleanse and sweep them every Day, who had some small Thing given them extraordinary. The above Provisions were for those in Health; as to those that were sick, and in the Castle, they had very good Mutton Broth, and sometimes Veal Broth, and Beef and Mutton boiled together; and old Women appointed to look to them in the several Rooms: There were also a Physician to let them Blood, and dress such as were wounded, and give the Sick Physic; and I dare confidently say, there was never the like Care taken for any such Number of Prisoners in *England*

Notwithstanding all this many of them died, and few of any other Disease then the Flux; some were kill'd by themselves, for they were exceedingly cruel one towards another. If any Man were perceived to have any Money, it was two to one but he was kill'd before Morning, and robb'd; and if any had good Cloaths, he that wanted, if he was able, would strangle the other and put on his Cloaths.

The Disease of the Flux still increasing among them, I was then forced, for their Preservation, if possible it might be, to send to all the next Towns in *Durham*, within four or five Miles, to command them to bring in their Milk, for that was conceived to be the best Remedy for stopping of their Flux; and I promised them what Rates they usually sold it for at the Markets, which was accordingly performed by about 60 Towns and Places. Twenty of the next towns to *Durham* continue to send daily in their Milk which is boiled, some with Water, some with Bean Flower [flour], the Physicians holding it exceeding good for the Recovery of their Health.

Gentlemen, you cannot but think strange of this long Preamble; and wonder what the Matter will be. In short it is this; out of the 3000 Prisoners that my Officers told into the Cathedral Church at *Durham*, 300 of them, and 50 from *Newcastle* of the 140 left behind, were delivered to Major *Clarke*, by Order of the Council; there are about 500 Sick in the Castle, and about 600 yet in Health in the Cathedral, the most of which are, in all probability, Highlanders, they being hardier than the rest; and we have no other Means to distinguish them. About 1600 are dead and buried, and about 60 Officers are at the Marshall's in *Newcastle,*

My Lord-General having released the rest of the Officers, and the Council having given me the Power to take what Men I thought fit, I have granted to several well-affected Persons that have Salt-Works at *Shields* [South Shields], and want servants, 40; they have engaged to keep them at Work at their Salt-Pans, and I have taken out about 12 more, Weavers, to begin a trade of Linen Cloth, like the *Scots* Cloth, and about 40 Labourers.

I can not give you, on a sudden, a more exact Account of the Prisoners, neither can any Account hold true long, because they still die daily, and doubtless so they will, so long as any remain in Prison. And for those that are well, if Major *Clarke* could have believed that they had been able to have marched on Foot, he would have marched them by Land; but we perceive that divers that are seemingly healthy, and have not at all been sick, suddenly die; and we cannot give any Reason for it, only we apprehend they are all infected; and that the strength of some holds out till it reaches their very Hearts.
Now you fully understand the Condition and Number of the Prisoners. What you please to direct I shall observe, and intend not to proceed further upon this Letter, until I have your Answer upon what I have now written. I am, Your most Affectionate Servant,
Ar. Haselrigge.'

NB Comment on this letter appears in the text. That 1600 men died within a period of two months - nearly 30 a day - is scandalous. The men picked by Cromwell to go south were described as not wounded, sound and fit to travel. Why was it necessary for a doctor to 'dress such as were wounded' at Durham?

APPENDIX I Medieval Currency and Scottish Coinage

Scotland did not mint its own coinage until the mid-twelfth century. For the first seven centuries of the Christian era, occasional finds of British-Celtic coins, then money hoards and random finds of Roman coins indicate the need for coin in the more settled Lowlands up to the fifth century.
David I was the first Scottish king to issue coins; his capture of Carlisle and its mint in 1136, with nearby silver mines, paved the way for the introduction of Scottish coinage. For the first two centuries of Scottish coins, the model type was the English penny and the 'Carolingian' system of account was used ie the pound [*libre or lb*] of silver; the shilling [*solidus*] or twentieth part of a pound and the penny [*denarius*], the twentieth part of a shilling. * Thus there was LSD which remained in force until decimalisation in February 1971. (Those who argue for the *ecu* in modern times should remember that the pound, the shilling and the penny were adopted across Europe from the early Middle Ages).
The coin of Scotland current in the Middle Ages was the silver penny, or sterling. It should be stressed however that neither the pound or the shilling were struck until the reign of James VI (1567-1625) and LSD was purely a system of account. Until 1390, when Robert III ascended the throne, the coinage was virtually exclusively silver but from that year onwards, gold became a regular feature of the currency.
In addition to the Carolingian system of account, the Germanic system favoured by the Scandinavian and Low Countries - from which Scotland derived a substantial mercantile income in the early to high Middle Ages - was used as a system of account; under this system, precious metal was weighed by the *mark* or *merk*, as it was known in Scotland; the Scottish *merk* contained 8 ounces each of twenty pennies so that one *merk* was equal to 2/3 of a pound (76p). To understand medieval monetary values, it is necessary to know that while Scottish and English silver pennies were of equal value at the outset, devaluation occurred in the course of time. The following table illustrates the extent of devaluation in Scotland:

1350	£1 English	=£2 Scots
1450		=£3 Scots
1500		=£4 Scots
1560		=£5 Scots
1565		=£6 Scots
1600		=£12 Scots until the Act of Union in 1707 brought the currency into line

A *merk* in 1689 was worth 2/3 of £1 Scots or about one English shilling (5p)
Minting of coin from 1136 to 1603 took place all over Scotland but chiefly in towns such as Edinburgh, Berwick and Roxburgh; the peak years of minting occurred during the period 1249-80, when there were no fewer than 18 centres including, it is thought, Dunbar. Throughout the period 1136 to 1603, coins were minted at Edinburgh except in 1320-29, when Bruce minted only at Berwick. After 1603, Edinburgh became the sole mint in Scotland. Coins were not in great supply however. For example, even up to the eighteenth century, the Duke of Roxburghe, Secretary of State for Scotland in 1720 was obliged to have £100 sent to him in London by waggon from Dunbar every month (Somerville, *My Own Life and Times*). Until about 1750, foreign coins were in circulation in Scotland and were acceptable tender; these coins came from Holland, France and Spain and included what were known as *leg-dollars, rix-dollars, guilders*{still in use in Holland] and *ducatoons* but even these became scarce as they were drawn to England during the Continental Wars. Although the two Scottish banks issued £1 notes from 1727 onwards as a respectable amount for the use of merchants, changing a £10 note could take days; the owner often had to visit half a dozen towns to find a merchant with enough silver to cash his note!

* In theory, 240 pennies weighed a pound

APPENDIX J

Convention of Royal Burghs

As indicated in Chapter 8, royal burghs were regulated by the Convention of Royal Burghs. Royal burghs were also known as 'kyngis burges' [king's burghs] and they provided the sovereign with much-needed income, known as 'the Kingis Maiestes Customes' or Great Customs; this derived from taxes levied on a whole range of items too numerous to list here. These taxes were raised on imports and exports carried by sea. The burgh raised its own income, known as 'Pittie-Customes' or Petty Customs levied on goods entering or leaving the burgh by road.
Royal burghs were regulated by the *Leges Quator Burgorum* [Code of Burghal Regulations] which stemed from the *Leges Burgorum Scocie* [Laws of Scottish Burghs] of which there were no fewer than 119.
Each royal burgh appointed one or more baillie to represent it as a commissioner to the Convention, which automatically allowed the

commissioner a seat in the Scottish parliament until 1707, when the Scottish and English parliaments became one. Failure to attend a Convention meeting meant a fine of £20, although occasionally, burghs were given permission to exempt themselves from attendance; this possibly occurred during times of financial strain or when some major development required the commissioner to remain in the burgh. The Convention took great pains to satisfy itself that every commissioner was qualified to represent a burgh and that its rules weren't flaunted. (For example, Dunbar was considered improperly represented in 1600 by William Lauder; the Convention ruled that he didn't possess the proper qualities of a commissioner and warned the burgh to comply with the regulations in future. The burgh was fined £40 the following year for non-compliance).
Every baillie was required to swear an oath on his appointment to the burgh or town council; this took the following form and it was usually sworn in Latin:

> ' In the first place, they shall swear that they will be loyal and true to our Lord the King and to the community of the burgh; and they shall swear faithfully the laws of the burgh to preserve, and its customs to hold and administer, and that they will do justice to rich and poor equally according to their judgement, and that they will spare no one for favour or fear nor for the taking of gifts.'

Fine words. If they were upheld. Every burgess was also required to swear a general oath to the effect

> 'that he will be leel and feel [loyal and faithful] to our Lord the King and to the community.....and that he will give to the King faithfully, rent for the lands which he defends.'

There were specific oaths for aletasters who were required to

> 'swear faithfully to taste the ale, and lawfully apprise [sell] same according to the price of malt.'

Fleschers [butchers] were required to swear that they would sell meat

> 'according to the price at which beasts are sold in the country'.

As indicated above, it would be a mammoth task to provide an exhaustive list of the goods subject to tax but the following gives an idea of these:

> bread, corn, salt, malt, beans, onions, leeks, butter, cheese, fish (fresh and cured); cloth (cut and uncut), madder [dye], hides, skins, wool and leather; pots, pans, iron goods; oxen, cows, horses, sheep, goats and pigs.

Other general taxes imposed by the burgh were as follows:

Shop tax
Commutation tax (possibly paid on bills of exchange)
Wheel-carriage tax
Female servants tax
Male servant tax
Carriage and horse tax
Inhabited houses tax
Cart tax
Dog tax
Draught horse tax

A list of commissioners from Dunbar appears in fig.13

APPENDIX K - Harbour development

The plan (**ill 155**) shown overleaf is of interest; although it depicts a plan for the new harbour at Dunbar in 1841 it was never actioned. The early 19th century saw the production of quite a number of plans of this type which never came to fruition. For instance there are quite a number for the then no-mans land between Edinburgh and Leith. Grandiose schemes for a new 'new town' show fine geometric layouts of streets etc, many of them even named. The unwary historical researcher could easily be caught out by these plans which never progressed beyond the drawing board.

Having said that, this 1841 plan of Dunbar nevertheless has considerable value because it shows quite a number of the real features of the harbour area alongside the aborted proposals and perhaps most importantly, pre-dates the partial demolition of the castle to create the new harbour entrance. The granaries and Custom House are clearly marked as is the dock in the Old Harbour and a ship-building yard at the head of Broadhaven. Many people may be unaware that a substantial part of the north end of the castle was blasted away to create the new entrance for what was to become the Victoria Harbour. What is also interesting is that what was perhaps the most obvious route was not taken.

Originally there was a debate on which of two possible routes the new entrance might take, The Blue Stone Passage to the north of the castle or the King Edward Passage to the south. Both of these options would have required the removal of a considerable amount of rock and after consultation, the northern one was chosen. Referring back to the plan overleaf, one would imagine that the obvious solution would have been to simply widen and deepen the Blue Stone Passage, exactly what the plan shows. However, what actually happened is that the new entrance followed the line of the Blue Stone passage for about one third of the way in from the west, then it was turned south east to meet up with an apparent inlet facing into the current harbour basin. This meant that the NE tower of the castle and the rock on which it stood was blasted or quarried away. The most likely reason for this was to use bedrock wherever possible to provide good foundations for the new quay and breakwater. The free-standing stone stack which can be seen in the plan and on Miller's engraving (**ill 3**) still survives today. Compare the 1841 plan with a detail of the 1977 RCAHMS survey (**ill 156**) and the clever use of bedrock becomes evident.

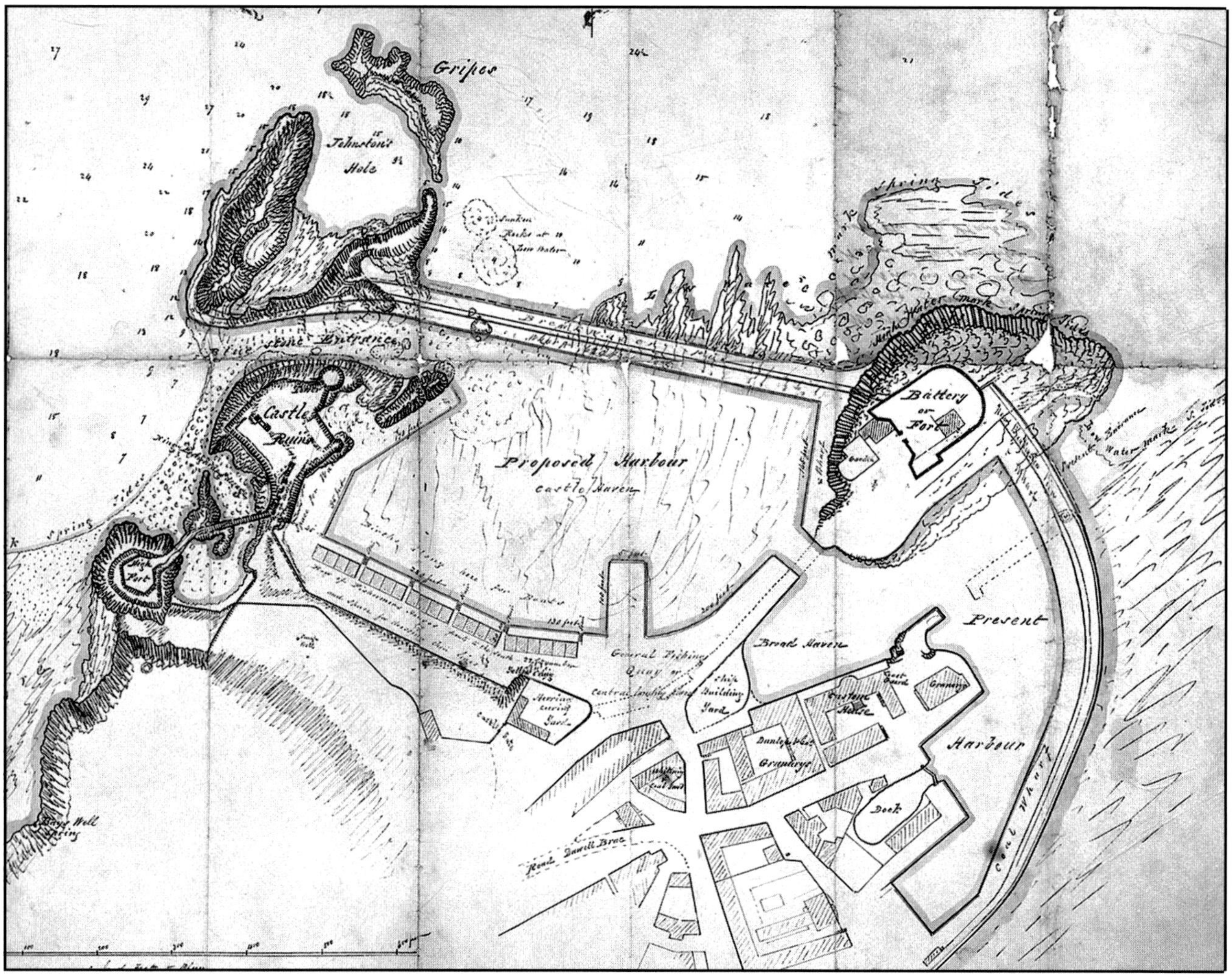

Illus 155: *Plan proposed, but never actioned, for new harbour, 1841* RCAHMS

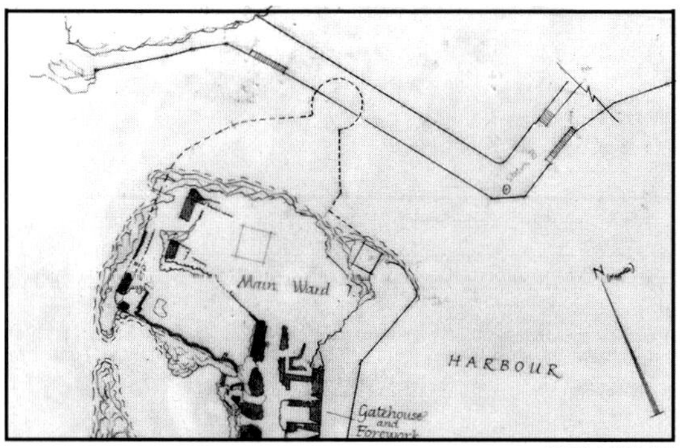

Illus 156: *Detail from RCAHMS plan of 1977* RCAHMS

Appendix L: Dunbar Shipping: Arrivals and Sailings in 1765

Departed	**Returned**
26th March *North Star*, a whaler of 295 tons Thomas Dawson, master, with 40 crew and a surgeon bound for Greenland	24 th July cargo of whale blubber and fin
Endeavour, a whaler of 316 tons: Alexander Roxburgh, master, with 42 crew and a surgeon bound for Greenland	" " " "

Princess of Wales, a whaler of 344 tons: Robert Beattie, master, with 42 crew and a surgeon, bound for Greenland	12th August 3-and-a -half barrels of blubber
1st June *Submission* Adam Lourie, master, bound for St Petersburg with 253 gallons of wine	28th September 19 tons iron, 38 tons hemp, 17 and three-quarters flax
1st August *Jean of Elie* * John Smith, master, bound for Bremen with 108 tons of Carolina rice for Charles and Robert Fall	
31st August *Magdalen* # Robert Beattie, master, with 10 crew bound for Charleston, South Carolina carrying coal, wine, metal, barley, butter, parmesan cheese, linen and 41 barrels of British ale	Not returned by 23rd December

In 1791, the *Old Statistical Account* shows that the tonnage of the whaling ships was less, although there appears to have been more vessels engaged in trade ie 8 ships amounting to 408 tons engaged in the coasting trade and employing 33 men; 8 others amounting to 1097 tons engaged in foreign trade employed 67 men; and two vessels amounting to 675 tons (955 tons in 1765) employed 50 men in whaling.
Just over half a century later, imports and exports at Dunbar were in fairly typical commodities; *Miller, Dunbar* gives a snapshot of these in 1830:

Imports	**Exports**
Coal	Wheat
Timber	Barley
Corn	Oats
Barley	Beans and Pease
Oats	Malt
Wheat flour	Wheat flour
Buck wheat	Whisky (203276 gallons)

* The ship had returned from Carolina with a cargo of rice, pitch, tar, mahogany, rum and cotton wool
# No doubt named for Robert Fall's wife

In 1844, the *New Statistical Account* states that in the year ending 5th July 1835, 23 vessels of 2,310 tons in all entered Dunbar Harbour, paying duties on cargoes valued at £2,942; the harbour was also used by 393 smaller vessels engaged in the coasting trade. In 1859, Dunbar's chief exports were potatoes, grain and herrings; imports were timber, rape-cake, coal and agricultural manure. The ships belonging to the port in that year were as follows:

Black Agnes:	William Smith, master: 58 tons, employed in foreign and coasting trade
Sisters:	William Richardson, master: 47 tons, employed in coasting trade
Margaret Lang:	J Mackintosh, master: 43 tons employed in coasting trade
Stephens:	Robert Fraser, master: 36 tons employed in coasting trade

By 1886, the chief industries at Dunbar were brewing, malting, fish-curing, boat-building, brick- and paper-making, rope-spinning, iron foundry manufacturing agricultural implements, sailcloth and artificial manure. Between 1876 and 1923, coasting vessels brought imports of coal, china clay, oilcake, wheat and barley, wood. stone and manure; by 1923, most vessels entered Dunbar empty, possibly only to shelter from adverse weather. By that year, Dunbar's days as a trading port were over. In the same period, exports in the coasting trade were potatoes, turnips, tiles and bricks, wood and wheat. The main ports for which these were destined were Burntisland, Methil, Kirkcaldy and Arbroath. By 1904, vessels were carrying only potatoes to London, a trade interrupted by the Great War and which declined after 1923. *

+ *Dunbar Harbour Arrivals Book* 1876-1923 (SRO ref. B 18/18/21)
* *Dunbar Harbour Sailings Book* 1876-1923 (SRO ref. B 18/18/22)

NOTES TO CHAPTERS ONE TO TWELVE

Chapter 1: The Castle

1 The site is now occupied by an indoor swimming pool/ leisure centre
2 Tradition has it that Bernicia was founded in 547 by Ida, a pirate-chief from whom the royal house of Northumbria descended. At one time, Bernicia included Northumbria, Teviotdale, Lothian, Abercorn near the Firth of Forth in the east and Whithorn in the west (Bede, *Historia*)
3 Stephanus, *Vita S. Wilfridi*; Vitalis, *Historia Ecclesiastica*; Ordericus Vitalis was an eleventh century monk
4 More probable is that Egfrid took revenge on Wilfrid for encouraging his first wife to leave him and take the veil at Coldingham Priory.
5 'And when Kenneth had done him homage, king Edgar gave him Lothian.' (*Symeon of Durham, Scottish Annals from English Chronicles 500-1286 (SAEC)*
6 Holinshed, on the authority of Boece, *Scotorum Historiae (Boece, Hist.)* states that Captains Dunbar and Grahame helped to defeat the Danes. According to Shaw, *History of the Province of Moray*, Thane Dunbar of Lothian fought at Cullen Fields in 961 and at Mortlake in 1010; Mortlake was fought in 1005. Shaw identifies Dunbar as a commander and writes as if he were alive in 1061, giving Buchanan, *History of Scotland (Buchanan, Hist.)* as his source. However, *Boece, Hist.* says that Thanes Patrick de Dunbar, Grim of Strathearn and Kenneth of the Isles perished at Mortlake in 1005
7 *Encyclopedia Britannica*
8 The influence of the post-Conquest incomers resulted in the building of stone castles in Scotland in the mid-thirteenth century
9 The *castellum de Dyrleton* is referred to in 1225 but it is thought this was a motte-and-bailey which the de Vaux family replaced later with a stone castle. Yester wasn't built until 1257-1267 (*TELAS vol v* 1952); Hailes was a Dunbar vassalage and therefore unlikely to have been built before Dunbar. Tantallon was built in 1350
10 "Is there no Department whose duty it is to preserve such old historic places? " (*Haddingtonshire Courier,* 1st September 1899)
11 This letter is preserved in Durham Cathedral
12 The family reputedly came from Hebburn in the parish of Chillingham, Northumberland. In David II's reign (1329-1371) the founder of the Scottish branch of the family was taken prisoner and brought to Scotland; apparently, he rescued the 9th Earl of Dunbar from a savage horse which earned him his freedom and lands near East Linton (*Chron. Auchinleck*). The Hepburn coat-of-arms incorporate a horse's head
13 The Hepburns were ambitious, casting their eyes on the Scottish throne in 1567-1594 in the persons of James and Francis, 4th and 5th Earls of Bothwell respectively
14 *Chron. Auchinleck*
15 Mary reputedly took Adam Hepburn as her lover; he was the son of Patrick, Lord Hailes. The story is discounted by modern historians as there is no evidence to support it. It is thought that Joan Beaufort, widow of James I (1406-1437) may have taken Lord Hailes as her lover in 1445 and that the chroniclers confused the two queens
16 In 1467, Archibald Boyd was captain of Dunbar Castle (*ER vol vii* p494)
17 The first reference to gunpowder occurs in 1382, when consignments were delivered to Berwick and Roxburgh Castles (*CDS vol iv* No 323)
18 A farm near Coldingham. Albany appropriated Belton in the barony of Dunbar in a charter made in his favour at the castle on 3rd November 1478, witnessed by Ellem of Butterdean (*Yester Writs* No 191)
19 *CDS vol iv* Nos 1475 and 1476
20 *Ibid* No 1486
21 *APS vol xii* Part I, pp31-33
22 *CDS vol iv* Nos 1505 and 1506
23 *Ibid* No 1508
24 His descendant George, Baron Home of Berwick, was created Earl of Dunbar in 1605
25 James had recently signed a seven-year truce with Henry VII at Ayton, Berwickshire
26 Wood gained fame by capturing 5 English ships attacking the Scottish coast; he defeated a smaller force under the English captain Stephen Bull off the May Island in 1490 with his two ships *Yellow Carvel* and *Flower*
27 *TA vol I* 1473-98; *ibid vol ii* 1500-04
28 Merlioune was French; he built a turreted wing at Holyroodhouse just before Flodden in 1513
29 'Hans' is mentioned in *TA vol I* 1473-98; there are several references to Hans or Hannis in *TA*
30 *TA vol i* gives details of these payments
31 Reputedly the grandson of Sir Patrick Dunbar of Biel. The poet is thought to have been born in the Garleton Hills, near Haddington; he became a Franciscan monk, then James V's ambassador in Europe. His poem *Lament for the Makars* is considered the most memorable inany language, with its repetitive line *timor mortis conturbat me* (the fear of death disturbs me). Born c.1460, died c.1520
32 *CDS vol iv* Nos 1706 and 1709; Carr, *History of Coldingham Priory*
33 McDonald, *Burgh Register and Guide to Dunbar* gives MacDonald; Pitcairn, *Criminal Trials* says McIntosh. Highland prisoners were often kept at Dunbar (see *TA vol vii*)
34 *ADCP* 1501-54
35 The Blockhouse may have existed prior to 1523. *TA vol v 1515-31* p15 records the delivery of boards, lead, iron bands and great nails, wood, 30 stone of lead and about 7 stone of iron bands in August and September 1515, then 12 stone of iron for making 'an iron wall' in December. (*TA vol v*). The castle's garrison included gunners in 1518 - not in itself proof that the Blockhouse existed then - but payments to the gunners begin to appear in *TA* from this time onwards [eg to Master-gunner Wolf and gunners Rowan, Combat - father and son - Bestiane and Maryen].

36 'The castel of Dunbar; quhilk be nature and crafty industre of man, is the strenthiest hous, this day, of Albion.' (*Boece, Hist.*). Surely he means *Alba*, the ancient name for Scotland
37 Pevsner, *The Buildings of Scotland: East Lothian*
38 Robert Forman, Dean of Glasgow was ordered by the Lords of Council to hand over the castle (*ADCP* 1501-54)
39 The *New Statistical Account for Berwickshire* describes this incident as having occurred at Langton on 13th October 1517
40 Hume decapitated his victim and carried off the head with its lovelocks; the grisly trophy remained in the family until 1860, when a woman in the household finally burnt the remains
41 *TA vol vi 1531-38* p136
42 Pitscottie, *The Historie and Chronicles of Scotland 1437-1575 (Pitscottie, Hist)* gives the words as 'it come with ane lass, it will pas [sic] with ane lass.'
43 Queen Anne, the last Stewart monarch died in 1714; leaving no heir, the throne went to the Elector of Hanover who became George I
44 British Library, *BM Add. 24965 fo. 161; Pittscottie, Hist*
45 *Hamilton Papers, vol ii* 1543-90 p108; *TA vol viii* and *ix* indicate that Robert Hamilton was in command at Dunbar from 1543 to 1550; other sources give 1543-46
46 On 12th August, the lairds of Innerwick and Pilrig and 12 Dunbar burgesses were slain (*Diurnal of Occurrents That Have Passed Within the Country of Scotland 1513-75 (Diurnal Occurrents)*
47 *Hamilton Papers vol ii* p379
48 *Diurnal Occurrents*
49 Hume, *Douglas and Angus*
50 So termed as the Scots repudiated the Treaty of Greenwich of 1543 which had made provision for the marriage - hence 'the wooing'
51 Somerset eventually fell victim of a power struggle in England; he was executed for alleged treason in 1552
52 Even after 1547, Arran vacillated towards France and was bribed with the Dukedom of Chatelherault to win him over
53 Miller, *Lamp of Lothian.* Dunglass surrendered readily but Home's vassal at Thornton, Tom Trotter and the captain of the Hamilton stronghold at Innerwick put up a spirited defence
54 Patton, *Expedicioune into Scotland etc*
55 Some contemporary accounts put the figure higher
56 In 1546, Dunbar was commanded by Sir John Melville of Raith (Percy, *John Knox*)
57 *Calendar of State Papers of Scotland (CSP Scot) vol I* 1547-63 No 86
58 Dunbar was burnt in June and August; Grey wrote to Somerset on 12th June that 'departing from Haddington early this morning, I saw Dunbar "burne hansomely" as I had ordered.' He also reported sighting 120 French ships off Dunbar en route to Leith (*CSP Scot, vol I No 242*)
59 Forbes Gray, *A Short History of Haddington*
60 John Brende, one of Somerset's spies, reported that on 17th January 1549, 500 French troops with scaling ladders had arrived at Dunbar by sea, possibly intent on besieging Dunglass (*Hamilton Papers vol ii* p623
61 *Scottish Correspondence of Mary of Lorraine (Mary of Lorraine Corres.)* p355
62 The Scots had re-occupied Haddington by 20th September. (*TA vol ix*); *RCAHMS* gives 27th September. A note of 15th September in Thomas, *Lauder and Lauderdale* states that the English 'passed out of Haddington and burnt it and Leddington [Lethington] and passed away without any battel, for the pest [plague] and hunger was richt evil amangst them.'
63 Beaugue, *Histoire de la Guerre d'Ecosse pendant les Campagnes* 1548 et 1549 *(Beaugu, Hist.)*
64 Home Castle fell in December and the others early in 1550
65 'Whoever is stronger on land could batter it with 10 or 12 [artillery] pieces' in 1558 (*CSP Scot. vol I* 1547-63 No 437)
66 The muster roll of the 100-strong French garrison at Dunbar in 1553 appears in the *Miscellany of the Scottish History Society vol ii* 1904. The castle was commanded by Captain Carronant, which may be a corruption of de Beaugue's Corroman who harried the English at Dunbar in their retreat from Haddington in September 1549
67 Knox, *History of the Reformation in Scotland*
68 Percy, *John Knox*
69 *Ibid*
70 The ruins were visible in James Miller's time and were excavated recently (*TELAS vol xxii* 1993)
71 Save for 60 men each at Dunbar and Inchkeith. Inchkeith, known as *L'Isle des Chevaux* as the French grazed their horses on it during the siege of Leith. When Randolph wrote to Secretary Cecil, Lord Burghley on 23rd September 1560, he allowed himself a moment of light relief on the subject of Inchkeith:

> 'It is said there are more women than men in it; and the merrie* men
> call it "Lisle des femmes, and not des chevaux,' (*CSP Scot. vol I* No 906)

72 Robert Hamilton visited the fort on 2nd August 1560 and found it could hold at least 500 men (*CSP Scot. vol I* No 862)
73 *Ibid* No 875
74 *Ibid* No 875 which lists their names
75 *Ibid* No 873
76 Mitchell, *Travels and Tours Relating to Scotland, 1200-1900;* he refers to a book published in Paris in 1897 about a Captain Sarlabous 'Maistre de Camp, Gouvernour de Dunbar (Ecosse),'
Sieur Labois married one of Marie of Guise's ladies-in-waiting, an Elizabeth Henderson or Anderson by whom he had two children. At Dunbar, he received a payment of £54:8:0 (£54.40) and two deliveries of foodstuffs for the castle in 1560-61 (*ER vol xix*)
77 *CSP Scot. vol I* No 96
78 Marie of Guise's remains weren't allowed to leave Scotland until October 1560 (Antonia Fraser, *Mary, Queen of Scots*)

* In the Elizebethan age *merrie* meant bawdy or riotious (sexual) behaviour

79 *CSP Scot. vol ii* 1563-69 No 183. Nicholas Throckmorton was one one of Elizabeth I's chief political advisors; Maitland of Lethington was Secretary of State for Scotland in 1558 and 1561; at first a devoted servant of the queen, they later quarrelled. Maitland was the real ruler of Scotland in the early years of Mary's short reign
80 Stewart, *Sir James Melville of Halhill; Memoirs of His Own Life*
81 Lang, *The Queen's Scotland; Edinburgh and the Lothians*
82 Martine, *Reminiscences of the Royal Burgh of Haddington*
83 It is impossible to ascertain the exact purpose of the meeting at Whittingehame as other nobles present were later on opposing sides and accused each other. In 1582, Morton claimed it was Bothwell who suggested Darnley's murder; his comments are considered suspect however as he and Bothwell were bitter enemies for many years
84 *CSP Scot. vol ii* No 393 quotes Randolph:
'Bothwell has the whole inheritance of Dunbar given him, the castle reserved to the Queen.'
Knox, *Hisory of the Reformation* states that Bothwell was also given the castle
85 Sir William Drury wrote to Secretary of State Cecil in England from Berwick that 'There is one of Edinburgh that affirms how Sir James Balfour bought of him, powder, as much as he should have paid three score pounds Scottish.' (PRO, *State Papers Border vol xii* p207)
86 'There shall not fail to be noses and lugges cut and far greater displeasure.' (*Calendar of Manuscripts at Hatfield House*)
87 Melville informed Cecil that Bothwell had carried off the queen 'violently'. On 8th May, Kirkcaldy of the Grange wrote to Bedford in England that the Scottish lords wanted to
'get Bothwell out of Dunbar or Edinburgh, not for fear of him in the field - but besides these two strengths, he has all the munition.' (*CSP Scot. vol ii;* No 502; *Diurnal Occurrents*)
88 *CSP Scot. vol ii* No 523
89 '....the laird of Whytelaughe the governor who will render it to none but the Queen.' (*Ibid* No 581)
90 *Register of the Privy Council vol I* 1545-69 (*RPC*) p524
91 *Ibid.* On 10th September 1567, Whitelaw was denounced as a traitor at Edinburgh's mercat cross
92 *Diurnal Occurrents*
93 Miller, *Lamp of Lothian*
94 *RPC vol I p576*
95 *Ibid* p576
96 The lords had all the artillery 'save a little at Dunbar'. (*CSP Scot. vol ii* No 527)
97 Hepburn was accused of heresy in 1567 and was removed from his ministry the following year; he was reinstated in 1578 and died at Oldhamstocks in 1585. (Scott, *Fasti*)
98 Armstrong Davison, *The Casket Letters*
99 Apparently, visitors were charged sixpence (about 3p) to view the remains until the queen of Denmark ended the gruesome practice in 1978
100 *APS vol iii* 1567-92
101 Boncle is identified as a tenant of West Barns in 1583 (*ER vol xxi* p557). James VI granted him some of the castle's policies in 1573 (*RMS vol iv* No 1873); in June 1576, other areas were leased to William Maislet, burgess of Dunbar who was given 'the landis, yairdis and boundis foranent and about the sumtyme castell' (*RSS vol vii* No 639)
102 *APS vol iii* 1567-92
103 Letter of 28th July 1597 (*Calendar of Border Papers vol ii* 1595-1603 No 705 (*CBP*)
104 *RMS vii* Nos 1499 and 1808
105 *RMS vol xi* 1660-68 No 50
106 *TELAS vol ii* 1929-33
107 The late Alec Gospatrick Douglas-Home, the former Prime Minister for example

Chapter 2 : The Earls (1072-1289)

1 *Miller, Dunbar*
2 Croal, *Sketches of East Lothian from the Haddingtonshire Courier*
3 The battle of Cullen Fields, 961. Cramond, *The Annals of Cullen* 961-1904 indicates that two nobles, Graeme and Dunbar, Thane of Lothian were present at Cullen and at Mortlach in 1005; sources are Shaw, *The History of the Province of Moray* and Anderson, *The Scottish Nation*
4 *Miller, Dunbar* states that Patrick de Dunbar died serving in the army of Malcolm II (1005-34) when he fell at Mortlach. *The History of the Province of Moray* states that due to their impetuosity, Thanes Dunbar, Strathearn and Kenneth of the Isles were slain. It is improbable but not impossible that Dunbar was present at both battles, which were fifty years apart. There is no foundation for the legend quoted by *Miller, Dunbar et al* that a soldier named Bar was the progenitor of the surname Dunbar or that the town was named for him (see also note 6, chapter 1)
5 Anderson, *SAEC* states that Crinan was reputedly related to St Columba and was lay Abbot of Dunkeld. One of the most powerful among the warrior-nobles, the Norsemen called Crinan *Jarl Hundi* - the Hound Earl. Crinan was of the House of mac Alpin and chief rival of Moray; he claimed descent from the kings of Dalriada and styled himself *mormaer* [chief] of the Isles.
Killed with his son Maldred by Macbeth in 1045 attempting to avenge the death of his son Duncan I whom Macbeth had killed in 1040 to take the throne. Crinan's death is recorded in *The Annals of Ulster:*
'Cronan [sic], abbot of Duncaillon [Dunkeld] fell in battle.'
The Annals of Tigernach state he was slain with 'nine times twenty heroes' in 1045. Despite Shakespeare, Macbeth of Moray was a more popular king than Duncan I until 1050, when he became cruel and vindictive.
6 Elfgiva, daughter of king Aethelread or Ethelred, known as 'Unready' which is a corrupt translation of the Anglo-Saxon word *unraed* meaning 'lacking in counsel'
7 *SP* ventures no more than that she was sister to 'Edmund' who owned land in Northumberland. *CWAAS vol xiv* gives her name as Christiana; Dunbar *Scot Kings* suggests she was the sister of 'Eadmund' and reputed to be Gunhilda, daughter of Harold II

[of Hastings]. Gunhilda in fact became a nun, then renounced her vows to marry a Breton Count (Adams, *A Conquest of England*).

8 *CWAAS vol xlvi*

9 *EHR vol xx* claims that the Gospatric of the Writ (see Appendix B) was Maldred's half-brother; not unexpectedly *SHR vol I* contends he was Gospatric I of Dunbar

10 Stenton, *Anglo-Saxon England* contends that Cnut invaded Scotland to preserve security in the north of England

11 Dunbar, *Scot. Kings* suggests that Maldred was probably Lord of Cumbria when his brother became Duncan I. According to *CWAAS vol xxxii* and *Prs Henry II,* Gospatric held 'the lands of Carlisle from Solway to Allerdale.'

12 Carlisle Cathedral reputedly has a runic inscription which translates as 'Dolphin saw these walls.'

13 Fordyce, *Historical Records of Remarkable Events in Northumberland suggest*s that the rebellion failed because of the treach ery of Edwin of Mercia and his brother Morcar; this is unlikely as Morcar accompanied Gospatric to Scotland after the rebellion

14 *ASC* which says

> 'And Earl Gospatric and the best men went to Scotland'.

Northumberland County Hist. vol vii states that the other men were Arkill the Thegn [Thane] and Merlesweyn

15 Christina became a Benedictine nun in Romsey Abbey in 1086 (*ASC, Chron. Florence of Worcester*)

16 Nagy, *St Margaret of Scotland and Hungary*

17 *Domesday Book* (1086) indicates that even 20 years after the Conquest, the Normans hadn't consolidated their hold over northern England

18 Raine, *North Durham* states that the peasants torched the town and slaughtered every Norman. There is no mention of Gospatric or any part he played in the massacre; he may have encouraged it however, as he had considerable influence in the district and was popular in Durham (but see note 22)

19 According to Ordericus Vitalis, *Historia Ecclesiastica vol ii,* Gospatric was declared absent from the king's court. Vitalis was an Anglo- Norman monk whose history begins with the birth of Christ and ends in the eleventh century

20 *Northumberland County Hist. vol i*

21 Duncan remained in the English court until 1094

22 *SP; Symeon of Durham* indicates that 'by his counsel and aid he [Gospatric I] had been among those who had slain the earl [Comines].....although he had not in person been present there.'
[Words attrib. to William the Conqueror]

23 Malcolm III invaded England five times

24 De Meschin's daughter married Robert de Romly whose daughter Alice married William Fitzduncan, son of Duncan II and E thelreda of Dunbar. Through his marriage, Fitzduncan acquired the honours of Skipton and Egremont

25 *Boece, Hist.* tells us that Gospatric slew 600 thieves and hanged another 40; chronicles are notoriously inaccurate in numbers and Boece is prone to exageration. A note in Buchanan, *Hist.* contends that the story is fictitious. However, Boece continues:

> 'Under this condition [under which the earldom was granted], in tymes cuming,
> the Erlis of Marche sal purge Merse and Louthian of all thevis.'

26 Attempts to identify this poem, quoted in Thomson, *Coldingham; Parish and Priory*, have been unsuccessful

27 Other than the Anglian settlement discovered in 1989 along with traces of Marie of Guise's fort (see Chapter 1)

28 Undated, Duncan II's charter is in favour of the monks of St Cuthbert at Durham, possibly by way of thanks for his victory over Donald Ban. It granted the vills of Tyninghame, Auldhame, Scougal, Knowes, Hedderwick and Broxburn to Durham - all lands near Dunbar which he hadprobably received by way of dowry from Gospatric 1, Ethelreda's father. It is doubtful if the charter was ever enforced; the original is in Durham Cathedral (Charter No 554 and Lawrie, *ESC,* Charter No xii)

29 *ASC;* Dunbar, *Scot. Kings*

30 *Symeon of Durham* is written as if Gospatric I were still alive between 1120 and 1130; perhaps this is a confusion of father and son, although Symeon was well-placed to observe the events and people of his time

31 *Miller, Dunbar* states he died at the end of the eleventh century; *Northumberland County Hist. vol iii* states that Gospatric was shriven in 1074 by Turgot and Aldwyn, monks of Melrose Abbey, that he died in 1075 and was buried in Norham Church - all of which appears to derive from *Chron. Roger Hoveden* ie

> 'But after a short time had passed [Gospatric] being in extreme ill-health summoned to him the monks Ealdwine and Turgot who were at that time living for Christ's sake in poverty of goods and spirit at Melrose. And after a thorough confession of sins and lamentations of penitence, he ended his life at Ubbanford [Norham] and was buried there in the exit of the church. He had given them two noble dossals [altar drapes] so that in whatever place they should receive a seat in which to remain, they might keep them there in memory of him. They are still preserved in the church of Durham.'

Conclusive as far as it goes, this is dated between 1073 and 1074. If *Chron. Roger Hoveden* is correct, the Gospatric who is mentioned in Domesday Book (1086) may have been Gospatric II who died of wounds after the battle of the Standard in 1138. However, other sources such as *Symeon of Durham* and Dunbar, *Scot. Kings* indicate that Gospatric I was alive in at least 1107 and possibly later than that

32 Anderson, *ESC Scot. Hist.*

33 If Gospatric I was shriven - the word only implies that confession was heard - by Turgot - this could have occurred before 1087 but does not necessarily mean he died in that year

34 *Miller, Dunbar* gives the dates as 1115 and 1116 but see Lawrie, *ESC* (Scone, Charter No xxxvi Glasgow No 1 and Govan No civ)

35 The Holyrood Charter (Lawrie, *ESC* No cliii) dates from 1129 to 1138 and it is thought that different parts were witnessed on various dates by several individuals - not always the same persons

36 In 1286 there were 8 Earls ie Dunbar, Caithness, Ross, Mar, Atholl, Strathearn, Lennox and Fife. Norman-French families occupied Sutherland, Buchan (the Comyns), Angus (de Umfraville), Menteith (Stewart) and Carrick (Bruce)

37 Gospatric II witnessed David I's charter giving special protection to the Church of St Mary and St Oswin the Martyr at Tynemouth during the Scottish invasion of 1138 which culminated in the battle of the Standard. Gospatric's descendant, the 6th Earl was in dispute with the same church in 1247 which had begun in c.1201

38 *Kelso Liber* No 288; Barrow, *Acts of Malcolm IV (RRS vol. I* p90)

39 *National MSS of Scotland,* No 25; Coldingham was founded - or dedicated a second time - in 1098 but no Scottish diocese was responsible for it. The monks depended on the Earls of Dunbar and their vassals for protection
40 Buchanan, *Hist. vol. I*
41 David I's army was predominantly Scottish, with some Norman and Cumbrian elements; the English army under Baliol was Norman, as is confirmed by several contemporary chronicles
42 *Chron. Henry of Huntingdon;* Anderson, *SAEC*
43 *Miller, Dunbar* gives 16th August 1138 as the date of Gospatric II's death and also coincidentally the date David confirmed Gospatric's charter of 1138x1139 (but see note 44). Lawrie, *ESC* (Charter No cxxi) shows the charter dated xvij KL Sep. anno mcxxix - the Kalends of September, or 11 September 1139
44 Anderson, *ES Scot Hist.* suggests that the hostage-giver may have been Gospatric II which would be feasible if he died in August 1139; Anderson admits he is unsure of the year of his death however. We note that the confirmation of the charter by David I was indeed 11 September 1139 and that it was witnessed by among others Alan, son of Waltheof and Alan's brother Gospatric - nephews of Gospatric II. There is no reference to Gospatric III who surely would have witnessed his father's charter had he been available to do so. Was he already a hostage in England?
45 Lawrie, *Annals* states he was probably Waltheof who succeeded to the earldom in 1166.*Northumberland County Hist.vol.iii* accepts this theory. Richard of Hexham, *Chronicles of the Reigns of Stephen, Henry II and Richard I vol. I* refers to the 'son of Gospatric'. It is tempting to believe the hostage was Gospatric III, even if his father was dead by 1139.
46 Thomson, *Coldingham Parish and Priory* contains a genealogy indicating that there was another Gospatric, indicated obliquely, which denotes illegitimacy; Gibson, *An Old Berwickshire Town* states that Gospatric III gave the church of Greenlaw and the chapel of Lambden to Kelso Abbey in 1147 'in which year he died' There may have been another Gospatric but perhaps he was never referred to as Gospatric IV
47 Quoted from records referred to in *Northumberland County Hist. vol. vii*
48 Waldeve or Waltheof, 4th Earl of Dunbar, was due half a knight's fee for service to William the Lion each year for 300 acres; he gave the lands of Dundas to Helias, son of Huctred for the service of half a knight (Innes, *Scotland in the Middle Ages* and *APS,* 1124-1423 *vol. I* p92. The Dundas family descends from the House of Dunbar (*British Encyclopedia*)
49 *RRS vol. I, Acts of Malcolm IV* No 85; Malcolm reserved some of the Drem lands for himself
50 Lawrie, *Annals* quotes from *The House of Gospatric* by Canon Greenwell in *Northumberland County Hist. vol. vii* which states that Gospatric 'is said to have founded the nunnery at Eccles.'
51 Waldeve is styled Earl by *Chron. Melrose* and also in a footnote to Malcolm IV's Charter No 292 (Barrow, *Acts of Malcolm IV*), both indicating that he became earl in 1165; Barrow suggests his title was proleptic as his father was still alive in 1165.
52 *PRs Henry II*; in 1160-61, Gospatric III paid 12 silver merks to the English king for his lands in Northumberland; his grandson, the 5th Earl also paid this amount which was the equivalent of six knights' fees. This gives some indication of the size of the lands the Dunbars held in Northumberland. If the same scale applied on both sides of the Border, these estates may have amounted to 3600 acres (see note 48 above)
53 *Coldingham Charters;* Raine, *North Durham.* The lands were situated between Fogo and Swinton and included parts of Billie, between Reston and Auchencraw along with the Lordship of Swinewood, a village which no longer exists. Waldeve's son Patrick, the future 5th Earl, reputedly gave Swinton to Coldingham Priory for 100 silver merks in 1231, the year in which he formally renounced any right to it (*APS vol. xii* Part I, Index A-H)
54 Noted in Lawrie, *Annals* p49
55 *Ibid* p116
56 Dunbar, *Scot. Kings*
57 These earls were also sworn to support Henry II if William broke the Treaty of Falaise (Lawrie, *Annals* pp201-203). The treaty is among the earliest examples of Anglo-Scottish agreements (*AR* 1174-1328)
58 *Chron. Melrose*
59 *Ibid*
60 Patrick is one of two earls whose armorial bearings are the oldest examples in Scotland; the seal of Alan, High Steward of Scotland dates from 1177 and that of Patrick Dunbar from 1182 (Innes of Learney, *Scottish Heraldry*)
61 There were three justiciar appointments, the other two being for Dumfries and Galloway and the north of Scotland. Patrick was the king's chief administrator and circuit judge for Lothian, trying cases referred to him by local sheriffs. *Chron. Roger Hoveden* describes Earl Patrick as *summus justiciarum totius regni Scotia* - justiciar for all Scotland. It is believed that he shared the Lothian appointment with David de Lindesay from 1195
62 As Chief Justiciar for Scotland, Dunbar witnessed William's declaration of homage to king John at Lincoln on 21st November 1200
63 *Chron. Roger Hoveden*
64 *Ibid.* Otto of Saxony was Richard the Lionheart's nephew
65 *Ibid; SHR vol xxxiii* contains an article on the early Tweed bridges at Berwick and states that the first stone version was built in c1272 and was washed away in 1294. It is perhaps one of history's many coincidences that Patrick built a wooden bridge in 1199 and the last holder of the title Earl ofDunbar - George Home - built one in the early part of the seventeenth century
66 The ancient name for Stow near Selkirk. It is referred to in charters as the Stow of Wedale - the Vale of Woe. The disputed land appears to have been the boundary of the east section and its configuration with land already owned by the monks and the de Morvilles in the south-east aspect
67 Barrow, *RRS, William I,* Charter Nos 482 and 483. The grant was an arable acreage known as Sorrowlessfield, beyond the river Leader; it was named for its owner, William Soroules. Charter No 483 was engrossed by Patrick's son and heir rather than himself - an indication of his bad grace as to the result
68 Also said to have been founded by Patrick's second wife, Christian Bruce, which is unlikely. The convent owned land in East Lothian
69 *Chron. Roger Hoveden*
70 Lawrie, *Annals,* p323
71 *Ibid.,* p380. William was to be John's liegeman or vassal and his son Alexander was to be John's son's vassal

72 *CDS vol I* No 574

73 Some historians maintain it is unlikely that John personally led the English army; however, Michel, *Histoire de Ducs de Normandie et les Rois d'Angleterre* states that John himself destroyed Dunbar and took its castle 'which belonged to earl Patrick, an earl of the king of Scotland's land. Then he rode forward, pillaging the land as far as the town that is called Haddington. He could go no further but turned back; and he burned and destroyed the town of Berwick'

74 Easson, *Religious Houses Scotland* implies that the settlement was separate from the *maison de dieu* founded by Christian Bruce in 1240-1248. *Scoti-monastichon* strates that the earl founded the house in recognition of the efforts of a George Cummings [Comyn?] who went to Algiers on the earl's behalf to redeem captives of the Turks 'in compliance with a dream the earl had about his cousin who had been slain in battle. The property passed to George Home of Friars' Lands. The house was burnt by the fanatics [Protestants].' Dunbar's cousin had joined the Fifth Crusade which succeeded in capturing the important seaport of Damietta in Egypt in 1219, only to lose it to the Saracens again. Patrick 6th earl of Dunbar died in Marseilles, en route to the Seventh Crusade in 1248; led by the 'Blessed St Louis' - Louis IX of France - it enjoyed brief success. Louis took Damietta in 1249, only to lose it again shortly afterwards

75 The foundation charter is dated 21st September 1342 (Cowan, *SHS Misc. vol vi*)

76 *CDS vol I* No 808

77 *Kelso Liber,* Charter Nos 76 and 80

78 Ada married William Home, son of Patrick Dunbar of Greenlaw from whom descended the Homes

79 *Chron. Melrose*; thus

> 'And bidding a last farewell to all, he closed his last day of St Silvester [31st December] in the fiftieth year of his earldom. And he was buried in the church of St Mary at Eccles. He was succeeded by Patrick, his son, a strenuous knight, and nephew of the king.'

80 *Northumberland County Hist. vol viii*

81 *CDS vol I* No 1179

82 ' "In fee and heritage" and " in free forest" for the service of one third of a knight.' (Soutar, *Handlist of Acts of Alexander II* No 202)

83 Robertson, *Scotland Under Her Early Kings*

84 *CDS vol I* No 1654 dated 19th November 1244

85 *PRs* No 477; Anderson, *ES Scot. Hist* p538

86 *CDS vol I* gives the date as 13th October 1222 but this is incorrect; the date is 1245, as in Hugh de Bolbec's letter to Henry III and quoted in *AR,* 1174-1328. Also, David de Lindesay was not Justiciar of Lothian in 1222

87 *CDS vol I* No 1699 dated December 1246; it is thought that Dunbar was absent on that occasion although he may have been represented by his brother Robert

88 *CDS vol I* No 1712

89 *Northumberland County Hist. vol viii* states that in 1174, Edlingham passed to Durham Cathedral; we know that in that year, it was forfeited by Edgar, son of Gospatric II

90 Patrick was sparing with generosity to religious houses; between 1239 and 1248, he and his Countess founded a house for Augustinian Friars at Blantyre (*CEPR*) The Tynemouth incident is well-documented in *Chron. Matthew Paris vol iv.* Paris calls Dunbar 'the mocking disturber of the Church of St Albans' - understandable as he was a brother at St Albans and in sympathy with the monks of Tynemouth, a cell of the same Convent. (See also *Northumberland County Hist.vol iii* for the Parish of Tynemouth, which identifies the true reason for the dispute; Dunbar had contested the ownership of the manors of Bewick and Eglingham)

91 Bower, *Scotichronicon* states that 240 Scottish and French knights met their deaths on this Crusade; Cockayne, *CP* states that Dunbar died between May and December 1248. MacQuarrie, *Scotland in the Crusades* 1095-1560 quotes from *Boece Hist vol i* which indicates that Dunbar took with him 'David Lyndsaye of Glenesk and Walter Steuart of Dundonald with ane grate novmber [number] of chosin men to support King Lewis.' These men were probably part of Dunbar's retinue

92 St Louis returned to France in 1254; in 1270, he led the Eighth Crusade, an even greater disaster than its predecessor

93 *Chron. Lanercost*

94 *Northumberland County Hist. vol viii*; *CDS vol I* No 1750

95 The lands were reputedly in Halsingtune [?] according to Soutar, *Handlist of the Acts ofAlexander II*

96 'He died signed by the Cross on pilgrimage in the company of the lord king of the French.'

97 Some sources including Miller, *Dunbar*, Keith, *Bishops* and others consider it was granted to the Carmelites in 1263. Bower, *Scotichronicon,* a reliable source written in the fifteenth century lists every Carmelite and Trinitarian establishment in his time; he makes it abundantly clear that there was no Carmelite house at Dunbar, only Trinitarian. Easson, *Religious Houses* agrees with Bower.

> The earliest reference to a minor Carmelite presence in the area occurs in the mid-sixteenth century (*RSS vol vi* 1567-74 No 161 dated 22nd February 1568 refers to the 'waird [ward] of the Freiris Carmeleittis' near Newtonlees; a reference also occurs in *RMS vol iv* 1546-80 dated 1st April 1576 to land 'inter wardum Fratrum Carmelitarum' - between the ward of the Carmelite Brothers [at Newtonlees]

98 *Yester Writs* No 14

99 *SP*; perhaps the 7th Earl grudged her the 'widow's portion' which was then customary.

100 *Chron. Melrose*

101 Alexander married Henry's daughter Margaret

102 Grandfather of Robert the Bruce

103 In Henry's letter of 20th September to Alexander III, he mentions that Dunbar would risk papal displeasure if he failed to comply with Alexander's wishes (*AR* 1174-1328)

104 The young queen spent her lying-in time with her mother in England. (*CDS vol I* No 2229).

105 See note 97 above

106 *Yester Writ* No 14 1240x1248

107 Edward I and Cromwell won signal victories at Dunbar and both plundered the state archive
108 The Lanercost chronicler of the day admits he couldn't face the wind, rain and snow on that day; he also accuses Alexander of habitually visiting women at night and hints that his death was a divine judgement on his conduct
109 Bower, *Scotichronicon vol vi* p429
110 Learmonth wrote the romance *Sir Tristrem*; he was supposed to have been spirited away to fairyland where the Queen of Elfland taught him his poetic skills
111 Bower, *Scotichronicon, vol iv*
112 *CDS vol I* Nos 1969, 1971, 2031 and 2244
113 *Ibid* No 2342; the properties were Witton, Stanton, Windygates, Horseley, Ritton and Leverchild, given to de Merlay as dowry for marriage to Dunbar's daughter Juliana
114 *Chron. Lanercost* tells us that he died at Whittingehame
'a man whom we have seen to be addicted to many vices, but who was mercifully forgiven by God on his deathbed.'
For all his alleged vices, Dunbar granted the monks on the May Island five acres of land at Belhaven, feued as 'Belhevyne Croft' or the Monks' Croft, a site now occupied by the modern Belhaven Brewery (*TELAS*). It is also stated in *Scotimonastichon* that he founded a Trinitarian or Red Friars settlement at Luffness, near North Berwick. The settlement was however Carmelite, one of many instances where the two Orders have been confused

Chapter 3: Indwellers and Visitors

1 I am indebted to Mr Peter Aitchison of West Barns who showed me the remains of a skeleton he found in a stone cist at Auldhame many years ago. The remains were examined professionally and radiocarbon-dated to c.2000BC
2 Now in the National Museum of Scotland, Edinburgh
3 *PSAS vol 98* (1964-66) and *vol 99* (1966-67).
4 *Ibid vol 99.* The late Major Tweedie, the farm's proprietor, gave every assistance to the archaeologists who dug the site in extremely adverse weather in the spring of 1962
5 Excavations at the summit of Doon Hill revealed the existence of a British sixth century fort (*RCAHMS Report:East Lothian* 1924)
6 *TELAS vol xxii*: Excavations at Dunbar, P Holdsworth
7 Ebba may have also founded a convent at St Abbs
8 Bede, *Opera Historia*
9 Eddius Stephanus, *Vita S. Wilfridi*
10 The Eadwulfing dynasty is shown in fig. 1, Chapter 2
11 A wooden fort of the Angles, possibly not a structure on the Castle Rock, was burnt in 856AD
12 De Beaugue, *Histoire de la Guerre d'Ecosses pendant les Campagnes 1548 et 1549*
13 *Descriptions des Royaulmes d' Angleterre et d' Ecosse* (c1558)
14 *A List of Travels and Tours in Scotland 1296-1900, PSAS vol 35* (1900-01)
15 Known as 'deid bells'; there may be one dated 1630 at Cockburnspath Church as noted in *TELAS vol I* (1928-29)
16 In 1949, the Society of Antiquaries reported that at Nos 24 and 25 High Street, excavations revealed a section of the town wall (*PSAS vol 85*). *Miller, Dunbar* indicates that Bamburgh Close adjacent to the site is traditionally regarded as the exit from an underground passage from the castle; to date, no such passage has been discovered. The land belonged to the Knights Templars, then the Knights Hospitallers of St John
17 Miller, *Lamp of Lothian* indicates that a William Valey of Dunbar received £15:17:4 (£15.86) for providing forage for the horses of Gardiner's and Hamilton's Dragoons
18 For example, Pococke has the Scots defeating the English at Pinkie in 1547!
19 The site where an unidentified lead coffin was discovered in 1987; a recent investigation (see Chapter 5) revealed a possible identity for the female occupant
20 *Boece, Hist.* has Gospatric I rooting out robbers in the Merse; Home was also known to have hanged a number of thieves there, dispensing what was known as *Jeddart Justice* (Jedburgh Justice ie hanging without trial by jury)
21 Pococke is describing Friarscroft, the site of the Red Friars' church
22 The Dunbar arms
23 The Blockhouse or Magazine
24 *New Statistical Account vol ii* entry for Innerwick parish
25 Computed miles seem to have been the Scottish 'long miles' which were one-and-a-half times the statutory or measured mile
26 Pennant is here referring to the undercroft which still exists; it would have been at sea level in his day
27 Keith, *Bishops*
28 *Haddingtonshire Courier,* 22nd October 1965
29 McDonald, *Burgh Register and Guide to Dunbar; Descriptive History of the Burgh, Castle and Battle. Miller, Dunbar* says no shots were fired
30 Lang, *The Queen's Scotland: Edinburgh and the Lothians*

Main sources quoted in Chapter 3:-

Hume Brown, *Early Travellers in Scotland*
Macky, *A Journey Through Scotland*
Mitchell, *Travels and Tours in Scotland 1296-1900 (PSAS)*
Pennant, *Tours in Scotland*
Pococke, *Tours in Scotland*

Notes and Bibliography

Chapter 4: The Earls (1289-1611)

1 The signatories were Bruce the Competitor, James the Steward, Dunbar, the Ulstermen de Burgh and de Clare and two other Ulster nobles. The 7th Earl of Dunbar was clearly protecting his lands in the vulnerable south-east. The fact that Irish nobles were involved suggests that the Bond represented a tacit agreement to provide mutually beneficial military aid as Bruce was then married to Elizabeth de Burgh. The document is described in *Historical Documents of Scotland 1286-1706* as a 'Bond of Certain Nobles of Scotland and England [sic] for Mutual Defence.'

2 To avoid confusion, the three Bruces are identified in the text as Bruce the Competitor (1214?-95), Bruce the Elder (1253-1304) and Robert Bruce (1274-1329)

3 *Calendar of Fine Rolls, Edward I* (1272-1307)

4 *National MSS of Scotland vol iii* No 1; the Treaty of Birgham, *APS vol I* Nos 85 and 86

5 Brigham, later re-named Birgham; the original name derived from a bridge over the Tweed. Birgham was within the Dunbar earldom

6 Bishop Fraser, St Andrews (Balliol) and Bishop Wishart, Glasgow (Bruce); the Earl of Fife and James the Steward (Bruce); the Earl of Buchan and the Lord of Badenoch (Balliol)

7 There is however a letter dated 7th October 1290 from Bishop Fraser, a Balliol supporter. The letter appeals to Edward I as the brother-in-law of Alexander III to intervene in Scotland's domestic affairs. Fraser graphically describes the unrest in the country, identifying the cause as rivalry between Bruce the Competitor and Balliol; not unexpectedly, he lays the blame at Bruce's feet. Fraser asks Edward to negotiate with Balliol and warns him of impending civil war:

> 'There is fear of general war and a great slaughter of men unless the Highest, by means of your identity and good services apply a speedy remedy.'

(*National MSS of Scotland vol I* No 70) The letter also reports the rumoured death of the Maid of Norway. *CDS vol ii* No 459 does not quote the letter in its entirety but the abridged version urges Edward to

> 'come to the [Scottish] march without delay to prevent bloodshed.'

8 For all his political aggression and military strength, Edward was never able to coerce the majority of the Scottish nobles to bend their knees to him for any meaningful length of time

9 According to Pickering, *A History of Noble British Families*, the Seven Earls of Scotland have been largely ignored by modern historians; they were reputedly distinct from the others, a political group which represented the seven ancient earldoms of Scotland

10 *ASR vol. ii*

11 *CDS vol ii* No 483; the Competitors are not named but Dunbar was present

12 *Ibid* Nos 485 and 492

13 *Ibid* Nos 488 and 489

14 *Ibid* Nos 492 and 496

15 *Ibid* No 498

16 *Ibid* No 499

17 *Ibid* Nos 506 and 507; on the same day, 3rd August, Edward demanded that he and future kings of England should be at liberty to decide the succession to the Scottish throne (No 506); 104 auditors received the claims of 12 of the 13 Competitors (No 507)

18 *ASR vol ii*

19 These incidents are described in *Historical Documents of Scotland vol I* No cccxii and *vol ii,* No ccccxi

20 This was however the first formal treaty between Scotland and France; signed by Balliol and Philip 'Le Bel'; ratified by parliament on 23rd October 1295, it would last for the next three centuries

21 Literally a weapon-showing, or military muster

22 Bruce the Elder's lands in Annandale were placed under the control of the Earl of Buchan, the Black Comyn, who was Dunbar's son-in-law. Curiously, Dunbar's lands were never confiscated

23 *ASR*

24 According to *Chron. Fordun*

25 *Chron. Lanercost*

26 The *diffidato* was an essential element of Continental feudalism; its withdrawal constituted a formal renunciation of homage to a feudal superior

27 *Chron. Lanercost*

28 *Scalacronica* (1356)

29 In addition to Cromwell's battle in 1650, William Wallace reputedly engaged Bruce the Elder, Antony Bek, Bishop of Durham and Dunbar at 'Spottsmuir' in 1297-98 according to Blind Harry's epic - if occasionally exaggerated - poem. The site of the 1296 battle is given as Oswald Dean in C E Grant, *East Lothian*; Ridpath, *Border History* states that one of Fordun's Mss places the battle near Spott which *Miller, Dunbar* assumes was Oswald Dean. The OS map identifies the site to the west of Spott

30 Hartshone, *Feudal and Military Antiquities of Northumberland and the Scottish Borders*

31 *Chron. Lanercost* gives 10,000 and mentions that among the dead were several tonsured priests. Only one English knight is said to have fallen. Cotton, *Historia Anglicana,* states that Sir John Benstead in the English army counted a total of 10,652 corpses which suggests that the English dead numbered 647 - if the figure of 10,005 Scottish losses is correct

32 A traditional jibe used at Dunbar in 1296 and Berwick 1333 was

> 'Come on ye long-tailed hounds and we will cut off your tails for you.'

33 See Appendix E which is an eye-witness account of Edward's campaign. Some accounts give between 29 and 70 knights and esquires with between 80 and 100 men-at-arms; the higher figures are usually quoted in English chronicles. *CDS vol ii* No 744 gives 131 earls, knights and esquires; *Chron. Lanercost* states there were 437 prisoners including several barons, 20 knights, 80 esquires and 300 men-at-arms, the latter being freed on giving their parole not to fight against England in the future

34 Some of these were William de St Clair whose son Thomas was killed carrying Balliol's standard at Spott; Fitzgeoffrey, Alexander de Moray, Edward Comyn of Kilside, Menzies, Richard Siward, David, son of Patrick de Grantown, Nicholas, son of Thomas Randolph who was a Merse landowner until he was forfeited and Bruce created him 1st Earl of Moray; John Mowbray,

Malcolm of Haddington, Hubert of Morham, Walter of Edington, Andrew of Synton, Maitland of Ayton, John of [East] Fortune, Roland of Perisby [?], William of Nenthorn and John of Inchmartin (*CDS vol ii* Nos 720, 960,1114 and 1156)

35 *Ibid* No 742 lists the prisoners and their prisons

36 *Ibid*

37 See Chapter 5

38 An example of this occurred in 1304, when Edward wrote from Inverkeithing admonishing Dunbar for failing to prevent the escape of several Scottish nobles whom he could have easily captured

39 *CDS vol ii* No 862; *Historical Documents of Scotland* No ccclxi

40 *Verbatim, Liber Pluscarden.* According to Bower, *Scotichronicon*, Edward I promised the crown to Bruce the Competitor which is an error as he died in 1295; it was Bruce the Elder who was asked to recruit all his friends and allies against the nationalist nobles

41 Literally 'Empty Jacket'. Some sources argue that Balliol had earned this epithet before his surrender to Edward as the *tabard* - the knight's garment worn over armour - which Balliol wore bore a shield without any heraldic device within it (Lang, *A History of Scotland* and *SP*)

42 *CDS vol v* p446; *The Wardrobe Accounts of Edward I,* March 1297

43 A *blanche* or empty *ferme* reminded the parties to it and outsiders that both title and grant of ownership existed between the superior and the vassal. A typical example of *blanche ferme* is that of Patrick, 9th Earl of Dunbar who granted the lands of Traprain and Dunpender 'to be hald [held] in blanche for ane paire of gilt spurris [spurs] (*Acts of David II,* 1343)

44 Lothian and the Merse have been singled out by several historians for lack of patriotism in 1296-97. However, about 60 freeholders from Coldingham - an area particularly vulnerable to English attack - joined Wallace in 1297. Coldingham was a dependency of Durham, so it is significant that these men defied both church and feudal superior

45 *Rot. Scot vol I* p49

46 Blind Harry. According to Thomson, *Lauder and Lauderdale,* the ensuing skirmish took place near Yester in 1298; the site may be correct but not the year

47 Blind Harry calls the outcome as a Pyrrhic victory for Dunbar who lost 7,000 to Wallace's 500; both figures are suspect

48 This operation could only have occurred between 25th September and 18th October 1297 as Wallace invaded the north of England some time between 18th October and 11th November. Some authorities question whether Spott Muir took place since Blind Harry's account - the only known source - is much given to reinforcing Wallace's legend at the expense of truth. When history and legend are in conflict, legend will usually come to the fore. Wallace's story is one of heroic action and it has no need of a minor battle at Dunbar to enhance his reputation. For that reason, I accept Blind Harry. There is one glaring inaccuracy however; if the fight took place between 25th September and 18th October 1297, Bishop Antony Bek couldn't have been present as he was in Flanders from 22nd April 1297 to 21st February 1298 (Fraser, *A History of Antony Bek, Bishop of Durham*). Some accounts have Wallace besieging Dunbar Castle before Stirling Bridge which is more than likely since Wallace had to retreat from East Lothian on the approach of the English army of Cressingham and Warenne. Blind Harry's account may have confused aspects of the English approach prior to Stirling Bridge with a local skirmish

49 Wallace's invasion of England appears in several accounts, notably Tytler, *A History of Scotland.* The properties Wallace destroyed are listed in the *Calendar of Inquisitions Post Mortem Edward I vol iii* No 423

50 *CDS vol v* No 396. The letter does not bear a date and it is ventured that it was written between 1297 and 1304. However, there is a note in *Historical Documents of Scotland* (No ccccxxix dated 24th May 1297) which indicates that the writer was Patrick 'son of the Earl of Dunbar' and others regarding a proposed expedition to Flanders to reinforce Edward I. The 8th Earl of Dunbar was with Edward in France 1297 but he returned to Scotland in the autumn of that year

51 Conveyed by a young man in Dunbar's service

52 Lang contends that neither noble should be considered a traitor for supplying Edward with military intelligence about Wallace's army at Falkirk as both were in English service and under feudal law were obliged to act as they did. A more modern historian might have taken the view that the two could have withheld the information without fear of detection

53 *ASR* 1174-1328

54 For example, on 16th July 1299, to discuss the garrisons of Scottish castles (*Historical Documents of Scotland vol ii* No dlxxii)

55 *Ibid* No dxv

56 *Ibid* No dxl which describes him as 'Governor of Scotland south of the Forth.'

57 *CDS vol ii* No 1066

58 *Calendar of the Close Rolls, Edward I vol iv* 1296-1302

59 Confirmed by the *Wardrobe Account* for 1300. Among 87 Scots vassals present were the 8th Earl and his son Patrick - then aged 18 - and Alexander de Balliol, John Balliol's brother

60 *CDS vol iv* p450

61 *Ibid vol v* No 273

62 *Ibid vol ii* No 1236 dated 3rd October 1301

63 *Ibid vol ii* Nos 1286, 1293, 1321 and 1326 dated between 2nd February and 20th September 1302

64 *Ibid vol ii* No 1360

65 *Ibid vol ii* No 1356

66 *Historical Documents of Scotland vol ii* No dccxxxii

67 *CDS vol ii* No 1549 dated 26th June 1304

68 History has so far failed to identify this lady's identity. Dunbar, *Scottish Kings* wrote a short pamphlet entitled *Who Was the Lady Ermigarda?* According to *Northumberland County Hist. vol vii,* Patrick married Ermigarda in 1303; the following year she was pregnant when her husband was aged 19. The future 9th Earl subsequently married Agnes Randolph but his issue was from Lady Ermigarda

69 *CDS vol iv* No 1815

70 *ASR* 1173-1328

71 *APS vol I* pii9

72 The role was undertaken by Fife's aunt Isobel, the wife of John Comyn of Buchan, brother-in-law to Bruce and the 8th Earl of Dunbar
73 *ASR* 1173-1328
74 *CDS vol iv* No 492 dated August 1306; this was probably a wise precaution as Bruce's supporters foraged repeatedly in East Lothian for supplies
75 After Methven, an ailing Edward I hanged 12 Scottish knights on the battlefield and executed others in London. Three of Bruce's brothers were put to death; his sister Mary was imprisoned in a wooden cage at Roxburgh castle as 'the guest of the Earl of Dunbar' and Isobel, Countess of Buchan was similarly imprisoned at Berwick Castle
76 Barrow, *Robert the Bruce*
77 *CDS vol iv* No 527; £26:13:4 (£26.66) for the year July 1308-09 'for staying in that [the East] March for the keeping of the truce between the king and Robert de Brous.'
78 A truce was however given by Robert Bruce on behalf of the 'County of Dunbar next to Berwick' (*Chron. Lanercost*). This meant that East Lothian was considered enemy territory, being 'in the [English] king's peace,' The truce was dearly bought
79 *CDS vol v* No 552
80 Lothian had to pay Bruce's forces not to molest the inhabitants - blackmail in effect - but even this didn't ensure protection. In 1313, the men of Dunbar were saved from fire and sword only by handing over 1,000 quarters of corn, as indicated in Dunbar's letter to Edward II (*CDS vol iii* No 337
81 *CDS vol iii* No 337 dated October/November 1313
82 *Rot. Scot. vol I* No 1146
83 'Many say openly victory will go to Bruce' (*CDS vol ii* No 1923)
84 Barbour, *Bruce*
85 The garrison probably contained English troops (*PRO E 372/160 m 50*).
86 Gray, *Scalacronica*
87 *Chron. Walsingham*
88 Dunbar was deemed to have forfeited his lands in Beanley from 25th June 1314. About three years later, Edward II issued a presentation in favour of Stephen de Blount, his clerk; Dunbar Church was his gift 'by rebellion of Patrick de Dunbar, a Scotsman.' (*CDS vol iii* No 536 dated 2nd February 1317). Blount of course stood little chance of realising the income from his 'gift' until Scotland was subjugated
89 *APS vol I* p464
90 Gray, *Scalacronica.* Spalding was an English burgess married to a Scottish woman; he was disillusioned with the way the governor of Berwick dealt with Scottish prisoners and helped the attacking forces to place their scaling ladders against the walls while on sentry duty
91 After the Great Schism, there were two popes - one in Rome and one in Avignon. The Scots supported the Avignon popes because of the *Auld Alliance.* The copy sent to Avignon was lost in the ensuing centuries but a fair facsimile was kept in Scot land. A further copy was said to have been kept at Tyninghame House for two centuries
92 *CDS vol iii* No 1024
93 Balliol had English knights in his force - men like Henry de Beaumont, Gilbert de Umfraville, Talbot, Ferrers and de la Zouche - all of whom had lost estates in Scotland. David de Strathbogie, Earl of Atholl, was prominent among these men, later becoming Balliol's representative in Scotland
94 Known as the Good Regent during David II's minority, Randolph, Earl of Moray, spent the last years of his life governing Scotland
95 *Chron. Wyntoun.* Initially £40 was spent on repairs to which Dunbar added a further £110:7:2 (£110. 35) of his own money, a considerable sum for the time and surely proof of his intentions (*ER vol I* pp410-411)
96 English chroniclers give 70 lords, 500 knights and 30,000-65,000 foot. Fordun admits he gave up listing the dead as a pointless exercise. English losses were one knight, one footsoldier and a body of men from Newcastle who joined the battle later. These figures are suspect
97 On 15th July, an indenture was concluded by Dunbar and Edward III regarding the surrender of Berwick. The letter of protection of 26th July gives assurances for Dunbar's safety, his followers,
lands, rents and possessions; nothing belonging to him was to be requisitioned for the king's use. All who were dependant on or followed Dunbar had to swear allegiance to Edward or leave Berwick within 40 days (Walsingham, *Historia Anglicana; Rot. Scot. vol I* p155; *CDS vol iii* Nos 1081 and 1982)
98 According to Lang, *A History of Scotland*; this may have been based on *Scalacronica* which simply states that Dunbar 'became English'. However, one realistic English chronicler wrote that even when Scottish nobles supported England, they weren't with them 'sincerely.....their hearts if not their bodies were always with their own people.'
99 Holinshed, *Chronicle of Englande, Scotlande and Irelande vol I* p471
100 Henry de Beaumont became Earl of Buchan, Strathbogie was made Earl of Atholl, Robert Talbot was appointed Earl of Mar, Percy of Northumberland was given Annandale and John de Warenne received the earldom of Strathearn
101 *CDS vol iii* No 1115 shows that Edward III allowed Dunbar to retain his rent of £30 for lands in Berwickshire due to Berwick Castle until the ' King's debt of 100 merks to him is satisfied.' On 13th May, Dunbar acknowledged receipt of the 100 marks sterling in part payment of 600 marks sterling still owed to him by Edward (*CDS vol iii* No 1126)
102 *CDS vol iii* No 1121
103 Five of these were former Disinherited nobles; the other two were Dunbar and Sir Robert Lauder
104 His esquire, Adam Nicholson received 100 marks on his behalf (British Museum *NERO c. viii*)
105 Included among these fees were 12 marks rent due from Beanley (*CDS vol iii* No 1142; No 1145 lists each knight from whom fees were due 'forfeited by Earl Patrick's enmity and rebellion.')
106 *CDS vol iii* Nos 1142 and 1146; *Rot. Scot. vol I.* The manors were given to Thomas de Bradestan for a *blanche ferme* of one sword a year to Edward
107 Namur was Edward Balliol's cousin
108 *Chron. Lanercost* suggests they attacked Namur twice or thrice

109 In 1867, a large quantity of human bones was uncovered about five feet below ground at the northern end of the Burghmuir; Edinburgh City Council had the remains re-interred in consecrated ground (Grant, *Cassell's Old and New Edinburgh*)

110 Tytler, *History of Scotland; Chron. Lanercost* states that Moray attacked the English rather than they him and that Notting ham Castle was his first prison, then Windsor on 13th July 1336 (see also *Rot. Scot. vol I* p393)

111 See note 106. On 20th March 1336, Dunbar's Northumberland possessions were given to Percy, Dunbar being described as'the king's rebel.' (*CDS vol iii* Nos 1181 and 1200). Scottish possessions forfeited were Dunbar's manor at Earlston, his vill - probably the tower - at Cockburnspath, Whittingehame, Over and Nether Markle, Traprain and Ruchlaw

112 David II residing in Normandy was still not universally accepted as rightful king; *Chron, Wyntoun* states that only children in their games dared to call him king

113 In his acount of the battle of Culblean, Dr W D Simpson states that the figure of 800 is absurdly small; he considers this figure relates to the men of chivalry - the knights - and that the total force was nearer 4,000. Strathbogie had 3,000 men at his disposal when he besieged Kildrummy Castle (*PSAS vol 64* p205)

114 *Chron. Lanercost; Rot. Scot. vol I* p488

115 *Chron. Fordun*

116 'Be resone she was blak skynit.' (Pitscottie, *Hist.*)

117 Ridpath, *Border History*

118 Many accounts are widely inaccurate in dating the siege; even allowing for the Old Style calendar, according to which the siege started on 13th January 1337; years range from 1336 to 1339. The duration is also often inaccurate; papers in the *PRO,* Pitscottie, *Hist.*and *Chron. Lanercost* all agree that the siege began on 13th January; *SP* gives 28th January. According to *Chron. Lanercost,* the siege ended on 16th June

119 *CDS vol iii* No 1233 dated 3rd June 1338

120 Crabb was paid about £24 on 13th February 1338, this being his fee and expenses for assembling siege equipment (*CDS vol iii* No 1302)

121 Johnson, *National Trust Book of Castles*

122 Tytler, *History of Scotland vol i* states that a similar taunt was made at Berwick in 1318 and perhaps Agnes was familiar with it through her husband who was present at that siege. Tytler quotes Barbour as his source for the Berwick incident:

'the Scots, raising a shout, cried out that the English sow had farrowed her pigs.'

The defenders destroyed the machine by dropping a large boulder on it, then set fire to the timber

123 Anderson, *The Scottish Nation*

124 *Chron. Lanercost:* 'If you do this, I shall be heir to the earldom of Moray,'

125 He may have been the same John Coupland or Copeland who captured David II at Neville's Cross in 1346

126 *Miller, Dunbar*

127 Tytler, *History of Scotland vol i*

128 *Chron. Lanercost*

129 In Dunbar, Percy wrote to the Bishop of Chichester on 28th April asking for protection for his companion 'Monsire William Brous.' (*CDS vol iii* No 1268)

130 Holinshed would have us believe that Edward III was present at the end of the siege; the king was certainly at Berwick, confirmed by *Chron. Lanercost* but he reputedly avoided Dunbar, going to Whitekirk, possibly because it was a holy shrine. However, *Chron. Pluscarden* states that

'Having seen the letters [of Edward] bidding him [Montague] leave all and return to England, he withdrew without ceremony, taking no leave of his hostess' (*Chron. Pluscarden vol ix* p36)

131 Even Stirling Castle housed only about 100 men; more would have posed a supply problem during a long siege

132 *Buchanan, Hist.* states that Dalhousie with his 40 men and some of the garrison rushed out of the castle at midnight with 'a great noise in the English and made terible slaughter among them.'

133 *Chron. Wyntoun* reads:

'Came I aire [early], came I late
I fand Annot [Agnes] at the yate [gate].'

134 Gray, *Scalacronica*

135 *PRO ref E101, 20/25*

136 *Chron. Lanercost; Rot. Scot. vol I* p540

137 *Chron. Walsingham vol I* p200

138 *RMS vol I*

139 Tytler, *History of Scotland vol ii* informs us that the mid-nineteenth excavations at Hermitage - a gloomy Border keep - revealed a stone vault; in it lay the skeleton of a man beside a pile of chaff, a bridle-bit and an old sword. Dalhousie's prison was under a grain store and he supposedly survived for some time on the ears of corn that trickled through the wooden floorboards above him. The remains were almost certainly his

140 Was she black-skinned? Pitscottie says so but he may have meant suntanned or weatherbeaten. Also the colour black signi fied wildness, untamed nature and perseverance in medieval society so perhaps Pitscottie was using poetic licence to make her a worthy opponent of the chivalrous Salisbury

141 *CDS vol v* No 809

142 The first was St Mary-of-the-Rocks, St Andrews in c1250; the second was founded at Abernethy between 1325 and 1345 (*Misc.of the SHS vol vi Third Series* (1939) although Easson, *Religious Houses* gives 1328x1331. After Dunbar in 1342 came Bothans (Yester) in 1421, Dunglass (1443), Dirleton (1444), Seton (1493) and Haddington (c1540). Many of the 42 Collegiate Churches survive today. After the Reformation, Collegiate establishments were converted into parish kirks; in Dunbar's case, the revenues were given to the bailies and community of Dunbar on 31st March 1567, the money being used chiefly for bursaries for local students attending university (*TELAS vol I* (1927-28) and *vol iv* (1948); *RSS vol v* No 3386). Dunbar Collegiate Church was financed by its associated chapels at Whittingehame, Spott, Pitcox (Stenton) Penshiel, Belton (Hedderwick), the parish church of Linton (Prestonkirk) and secular revenues due from the communities of Dunbar, Duns and Chirnside

143 *Misc. of the SHS vol vi Third Series* (1939)
144 *CDS vol iii* No 1379 dated 20th March 1342 and No 1386 dated 29th April 1342. The first letter gave safe conduct to 100 horse and 200 persons including William and Adam, respectively the Bishops of St Andrews and Brechin
145 Lang, *History of Scotland*
146 *Chron. Fordun*
147 *Scotichronicon,* Book II p347
148 The Scots called the plague 'the foul death of England'
149 *CDS vol iii* No 1576 dated 13th July 1354
150 *Rot. Scot. vol I* p779
151 Two important aspects in heraldry relate to this period. The coat-of-arms of Patrick Dunbar of Biel and his wife Isabella de Dunbar (Randolph) is the earliest example of *impaled* arms in Scotland; the device shows two adjacent coats-of-arms as a shield divided vertically. A charter bearing a seal with these arms and Patrick Dunbar of Biel's own coat-of-arms is dated 2nd January 1352, engrossed at Wester Spott and witnessed by the 9th Earl of Dunbar. The charter confirms a grant of land in West Pitcorthie, Fife by Dunbar's vassal, Richard of Anstruther to his sister Cecilia and her husband John Strang. Also, the earliest example of a coat-of-arms is that of the 9th Earl of Dunbar which appears on a seal to a deed dated 13th May 1334 (Innes of Learney, *Scottish Heraldry; Book of the Old Edinburgh Club vol iii* p1 (Edinburgh 1911)
152 Man was an empty title; given to Randolph by Robert Bruce in 1324, it became English again after Neville's Cross in 1346 Riddell, *Inquiry into the Law and Practice in Scottish Peerages* erroneously states that George, 10th Earl of Dunbar inherited Man from his mother, Agnes; she was his great-aunt. Riddell also states that Robert II granted Dunbar 'a hundred pounds of land in Man, when it should be recovered from the English.' Writing in 1842, Riddell indicates that the arms of Man were 'yet to be seen on the remaining fragment of his [ie Dunbar's] castle'
153 *Miller, Dunbar* describes the Man and Annandale insignia on a cross-wall which was incorporated into the castle restored by James IV in 1497-1501
154 Miller, *Lamp of Lothian;* his title is misleading as it refers to the town of Haddington rather than the original Church of Minorites destroyed by Edward III
155 Sir Patrick of Biel was with the French army at Poitiers on 19th September 1356; afterwards, he went on pilgrimage to Jerusalem but died en route at the town of Candia, Crete (*CDS vol iv* p22)
156 Croft Dickinson, *A Source Book of Scottish History*
157 *CDS vol iii* No 1629
158 *Ibid* No 1657
159 *Ibid* No 1660
160 Historians have been unable to determine the reasons for and the extent of this so-called 'rebellion' but most consider these were of a personal nature. Also, the Steward and Dunbar had, in the king's eyes, deserted him at Neville's Cross and he probably treated them accordingly. *Buchanan,Hist.* states that David punished all three nobles, Dunbar losing part of his estates - probably the earldom of Moray
161 *Rot. Scot.*
162 Innes, *Sketches of Early Scottish History*
163 Nicholson, *Scotland and the Later Middle Ages*
164 *RRS vol I, The Acts of David II*
165 *CDS vol iv* No 92 which indicates that the king of Scotland would declare 'his own pleasure' regarding Annandale and Lochmaben Castle, then held by Henry de Bohun [pronounced Boon] Earl of Hertford but described as being in his [David II's] proper heritage.'
166 *RMS vol I* No 152 dated 2nd July 1363; *RRS vol I The Acts of David II* No 345 dated 18th April 1365
167 Tytler, *History of Scotland vol ii*
168 *CDS vol iv* No 83
169 *RMS vol I The Acts of David II* No 379; see also *Lawrie ESC* for the arrangement between Gospatric II and the monks of Coldingham-Durham
170 *SP;* Patrick Dunbar was born in c.1276 which means he was over 90 years old when he died. His son John, issue of his first wife Ermigarda, pre-deceased him; there may also have been a son Patrick who died in infancy
171 *RMS vol I* No 149
172 *Ibid* Nos 291 and 292
173 Lang, *A History of Scotland* erroneously describes her as Black Agnes' daughter. The *ERs* for 1369 show the Aberdeen ac counts including the cost of spices delivered to Agnes Dunbar; a payment of £25:2:5 (£2.12) occurs in the Chamberlain's Ac count for the same year. In 1370, there is an entry of £66:13:4 (£66.67) for Agnes' expenses.
174 *APS, vol vii* No 159 and *RMS vol I The Acts of David II* No 509
175 *Ibid*
176 *RMS vol i App 2* No 1652 gave Agnes Dunbar ' ane annual furthe [fourth]' of the customs of Aberdeen and Haddington; the *Handlist of Acts of David II* No 665 also gave her an annual pension of 1,000 merks from the *fermes* (rents from burgesses) and customs of Aberdeen and Haddington on 21st January 1371. This pension ceased after the king's death
177 James Douglas is of interest to historians as he left two wills engrossed in 1390 and 1392, the earliest surviving in Scottish archives. His wife Agnes Dunbar died some time between 1372 and 1390 as he left instructions in the first will that he wished to be buried beside her in the monastery at Newbattle, Midlothian. The wills itemise jewels and armour; his brother-in-law George, 10th Earl of Dunbar was to receive a ruby ring. Douglas died of influenza in 1420
178 *List of Charters of Robert II* No 19 (W Robertson, Edinburgh 1629)
179 Cockayne's *Peerage (GEC)* gives his age as 32; *Miller, Dunbar* says he was 29 or 30
180 *ERs vol ii* Nos 364, 366,433-35, 460 and 501
181 *CDS vol iv* No 231 dated 1st May 1376 which lists the paucity of receipts to Lochmaben Castle and.thus to the English be cause of the Scots' scorched earth policies in Annandale; the account also confirms that Lochmaben's governor, Henry de Bohun, Earl of Hertford died some time between 1375 and 1376

182 *Chron. Pluscarden*: 'No single Englishman escaped his slaughter.'

183 *CDS vol iv* No 260 dated 2nd April 1378; the new warden of Lochmaben Castle refused to reside there because of the hardship caused by the Earls of Dunbar and Douglas and Sir Archibald Douglas who were imprisoning and ransoming tenants in Annandale

184 *Ibid* No 859

185 *ERs vol iii* 1380

186 *ERs* indicate that Dunbar received loans from and lent money to Robert II between 1380 and 1382, amounts not repaid until 1391. From 1389 and until 1400, George Dunbar was exempt from the Great Customs of Dunbar for his services to Robert III and his son, the Earl of Carrick. Such payments rejoice in the name of money-fiefs which were replacing the old feudal system of knight-service. The former concept of token service was dying out in Europe; while a vassal might have served his king in the old way, his heirs were more likely to regard their inherited property as theirs by right of inheritance rather than on the whim of a king. Thus the feudal system was 'modernised', with cash payments made for service. This became known as *bastard feudalism*

187 Recounted with obvious relish by Bower and Andrew Wyntoun in their chronicles

188 *CDS vol iv* No 315 dated 1382. Just before this, Percy of Northumberland had allowed Dunbar to remove 400 quarters of malt from England for part payment of the ransom of two English esquires
'in aid of their deliverance from Dunbar.'

189 *CDS vol iv* No 336

190 *Ibid* No 372

191 Carr, *A History of Coldingham Priory, App 3*

192 The English force reputedly numbered 600 knights and 8000 foot; if this were so and the Scots under Douglas outnumbered them, the two Scottish 'battles' must have joined forces at some point before the fight

193 *CDS vol iv* No 392

194 Tytler, *History of Scotland vol iii*

195 *ERs vol iii* No 203

196 *Ibid* No 204

197 For example, Dunbar was allowed to visit Canterbury in 1390 with 30 followers (*CDS vol iv* No 417) and in 1393, when his safe conduct stipulated that he didn't harm the people of England (*CDS vol iv* No 446)

198 *ERs vol iii;* the burghs of Dunbar, Haddington and North Berwick met 10% of the cost

199 *SP;* Pope Benedict XIII granted a dispensation dated 28th August 1395; his letter to the Bishops of St Andrews and Brechin give clear indication of matrimonial intentions:

> 'David, earl of Carrick, first born of Robert, king of Scotland, to marry the noblewoman Elizabeth, daughter of the noble man George, earl of March, who although being related in the 3rd degree of consanguinity [they were second cousins] and in full knowledge of this fact had contracted marriage *per verba de futuro* [which in the marriage laws of medieval Scotland was a public admission of intent to marry, made before a priest] since if this marriage were not to come about, grave scandal and dissension would arise.'
> (*Calendar of Papal Letters to Scotland: Benedict XIII of Avignon)*

A second dispensation was issued on 10th March 1397:

> 'To the bishop of Aberdeen, the abbot of Kelso and the Dean of Dunbar in Mandate. David, earl of Carrick and eldest son of Robert, King of Scots, and Elizabeth, daughter of George, earl of March, wishing to marry and knowing they were related in the third degree of consanguinity [always a useful technicality for obtaining a divorce with Rome's blessing in the Middle Ages]on both sides, had nonetheless contracted marriage and then sought a dispensation which the pope gave mandate to certain judges to grant. Not, however, having received notice of this, David and Elizabeth had posted their banns for the 'three solemn days' as custom demanded and had then consummated the marriage; whereupon Walter, bishop of St Andrews, had instituted proceedings against them. David and Elizabeth had appealed to the pope for absolution which the pope now grants and which the mandatories are to the effect after a separation of the two parties for a period of time at the discretion of the said mandatories.'

Dunbar, *Scottish Kings* indicates that the couple had married under banns *copulata subsecuta*, or following physical consummation. If the parties hadn't been within the forbidden degree of consanguinity, the marriage would have been indissoluble under marital law.

200 *ERs vol iii* pp406, 428; *Scotichronicon vol viii* p5

201 *Liber Pluscarden*

202 'He would arrange something unheard of and unusual to be done in the kingdom' so that '......some people regarded the man's grandiloquence as perhaps dangerous and noted his words, slowly turning them over in their heads.' (Bower, *Scotichronicon*)

203 *Ibid vol iii* p33; *Chron. Wyntoun vol vi* pp393-4

204 St Leonard's and St Mary Magdalene's hospitals were suppressed by James I in 1436; their lands and revenues were given to the Carthusian convent in Perth, the sole Scottish house of that Order

205 *Scotichronicon* states that Dunbar attended the ceremony at Bothwell Church and that he

> 'went up to the king saying and beseeching him that he should either have the marriage with his own daughter......fulfilled, or restore to him entirely the sum of ready money paid to him [ie the king].'

206 New Style calendar = 18th February 1400

207 *National MSS of Scotland vol ii* No 53

208 Henry had recently appointed Westmoreland keeper of Lochmaben Castle and Annandale, Dunbar lands which were no longer occupied by the English

209 A safe conduct was issued on 8th June 1400; lasting until Easter 1401, it allowed Dunbar to bring 100 horsemen - knights and esquires - to visit England and return to Scotland (*CDS vol iv* No 529)

210 Carr, *A History of Coldingham Priory*

211 *Report of the Royal Commission on Historical Manuscripts* (1870) 15th R *vol viii* 33

212 *CDS vol iv* No 546 and *CPRs, Henry IV vols i-iv* 1399-1413 (London, 1903-09):

'Safe conduct until Michaelmas [29th September] for the king's kinsman, George Dunbarre, earl of March of Scotland coming within the realm for a colloquoy with the king, and his men to the number of 50.'

213 *CDS vol iv* Nos 551 and 552

214 *Ibid* No 553

215 *Ibid* No 563

215 It is difficult to ascertain precisely the cash and land grants made to Dunbar and his family over the period 1400-1407. However, *CDS vol.* iv (3rd May 1400 to 12th June 1407) contains many references to these payments; these amount to £2,357 in cash, with 3,000 marks (£1,960, an English mark being valued at 13/4 or 67p at the time) in revenue paid to George Dunbar from lands granted to him in England; his Countess received £41 and his son Gawain was paid £40 a year or the equivalent in land value for life. In addition to the cash payments and land revenues, Dunbar was granted Clippeston Manor in Sherwood Forest, revenue from the castle and Lordship of Somerton, Lincolnshire, the revenues from the manors of Kyme and Croftes, Lincolnshire which he received until the heir reached his majority and Thomas Percy's house in Bishopsgate, London. Dunbar's son Columba was appointed Dean of the Collegiate Church of St Mary Magdalen, Bridgenorth; he systematically 'diverted' the grants allowed for the upkeep and repair of the church into his own pocket, stripping the lead from its roof and selling it! When the Dunbars returned to Scotland, St Mary's required £600 to make it wind and waterproof.

216 It is certain that the Dunbars were inadequately compensated for their services to Henry IV; George Dunbar lost considerably more in revenue when his Scottish earldom's lands were forfeited. It cannot be said that Dunbar defected to England for gain; it was more a matter of family honour.

217 *ERs vol iv*

218 *Chron. Pluscarden; Scotichronicon;* Jacob, *The Fifteenth Century*

219 Tytler, *History of Scotland* calls the site of the battle Slaughter Hill; the *New Statistical Account* refers to it as Manslaughter Hill

220 Bower, *Scotichronicon* calls it Humbleton, modern day Homilton; *Miller, Dunbar* erroneously refers to it as Halidon, confus ing it with the site of the battle of 1333

221 Tytler, *History of Scotland* tells us that Dunbar held Percy's horse-bridle to prevent him from charging the Scots

222 *Ibid*

223 *CDS vol iv* and *Introduction* pxix and No 632

224 Some accounts give Henry's army as 12,000 and the Percies' forces at 10,000

225 *CDS vol iv* No 676

226 *Ibid* Nos 733 and 734

227 *RMS vol I* No 920

228 *CDS vol iv* No 791

229 Built on a breathtakingly precipitous rock overhanging the North Sea near St Abbs, Fast Castlewas impregnable; it is likely that Dunbar captured it by bribing the gatekeeper as it is virtually unassailable from land or sea. It was retaken from Patrick Dunbar, son of the 11th Earl by the English; destroyed in 1515, it was rebuilt in 1521. Fast Castle later came into the possession of the Homes

230 Thomson, *Coldingham Parish and Priory*

231 *Scotichronicon; SP*

232 *CDS vol iv* No 804

233 *Ibid vol v* No 942

234 Bower, *Scotichronicon* identifies his fatal illness as 'le quhew' or influenza

235 *The Donibristle Manuscript, MS D*

236 Dobson, *Durham Priory*

237 *CSR; SP* states that Dunbar died in 1423

238 *CDS vol iv* No 949 dated 28th March 1424

239 *Ibid* No 983

240 *Ibid vol v* No 999 dated 26th July 1426

241 *ERs vol iv* indicates that James' feather bed was sent to Haddington for his comfort. Some historians such as Tytler and Pinkerton have cast doubts on this meeting having taken place but this is confirmed by *ERs vol iv* pp466 and 477 as well as by the account of the Dunbar custumars - customs officers - although no record of the discussion between James and Beaufort appears to have survived

242 Cockayne's *Peerage (GEC)*

243 Tytler, *History of Scotland.* Lang, *A History of Scotland* is not alone in his view that James described Dunbar as the son of the renegade 10th Earl but he is wildly inaccurate in his view that the Dunbars 'had never been frankly Scottish' simply because they were related to the House of Lancaster

244 *ERs vol iv* indicates that the revenues due from Cockburnspath - one of Dunbar's tower houses - were paid to the Crown shortly afterwards

245 Dunbar reputedly inherited Kilconquhar from his mother; it was given to Thomas Randolph, Earl of Moray by Robert Bruce and probably formed part of the lands inherited by the 9th Earl of Dunbar through his wife, Agnes Randolph. The Barony of Kilconquhar appears to have been held of the Bishop of St Andrews. It remained in the Dunbars' possession until 1568 - ironically, the year Dunbar Castle was dismantled - when Andrew Wood of Largo was given the fourth part of 'the barony of Kilconquhere belonging to Elizabeth Dunbar, lying under the regality of St Andrews but now in the hands of the Crown, by the forfeitship of the archbishop of St Andrews.'
(Riddell, *Inquiry into the Law and Practices of Scottish Peerages vol I* (1842))

246 A warrant for the safe conduct of George Dunbar and 24 horsemen was issued on 31st October 1435 (*CDS vol v* No 1086); the reason for the visit is unspecified . A further warrant was issued on 18th November (*Rot. Scot. vol ii* p293)

247 For example in 1448, Patrick Hepburn of Hailes granted some of the former Dunbar lands to John Thome of North Hailes 'for his services and tenandry of land in North Hailes and a cotland in the territory of Beynston [Beanston]'. For these, Thome had to pay rent of six merks a year to the chapel of St Mary at Markle. The transaction was witnessed by Adam Hepburn of

Hailes, Dean of Dunbar Collegiate Church on 13th June 1448. Adam Hepburn assumed control of Dunbar Castle shortly afterwards as *ERs vol iv* records a payment to him as its keeper. (*Calendar of Laing Charters*)

248 Piperdean was situated between Coldingham and Cockburnspath, near Aldcambus

249 Ridpath, *Border History* gives the Scottish casualties as 200, the English as 1,500, which is suspect; other sources give casualties of 40 and 50 respectively which are more credible. Bower, *Scotichronicon,* states that no more than 40 from both sides were killed. Tytler, *History of Scotland* gives 40 English dead and a number of Scottish prisoners.

250 *ERs vol v*

251 *Acts of Lords in Council vol iii*

252 Each Earl of Dunbar had his own crest or seal; the coat-of-arms was a lion *rampant* charged with a *bordure* of 8 roses. The 11th Earl's crest was a helmet with a *capeline*, coronet and a horse's head bridled, two lions *sejant* with a tree beside each

253 Cockayne, *Peerage (GEC)* states that he died some time betwen 1455 and 1457, aged over 80

254 The Black Douglas lordship passed to the Red Douglas, George, 4th Earl of Angus, in 1489

255 Beaton, Chancellor of Scotland persecuted those intent on reforming the Church; he personally supervised the burning of George Wishart for heresy. Beaton was noted for his pride, cruelty and licentiousness

256 *Acta Parl. Jacobi VI* No 20. He received the castle and its policies as well as the 'landis and boundis of the great loch of Dunbar' - now known as Lochend – and all else pertaining to the lordship and barony of Dunbar

257 Watts and Watts, *From Border to Middle Shire* 1586-1625

258 *Calendar of State Papers, Domestic Series, James I* 1603-10 (HMSO 1857)

259 *Ibid*

260 *Ibid*

261 *Ibid*

262 His other daughter Anne married Sir James Home of Coldingknowes and their son became 3rd Earl of Home

263 *Calendar of State Papers, Domestic Series James I* 1603-1610

264 It wasn't until 1634 that a stone bridge costing £1,500 was completed

265 *Calendar of State Papers, Domestic Series James I* 1611-18 (HMSO 1858)

266 During the summer of 1725, the Old Pretender summoned James Moray to Rome and appointed him the 'Protector governor' of the Prince of Wales, Charles Edward Stuart aka Bonnie Prince Charlie

267 Moray had fought in the '15 and was present on the field of Sheriffmuir, from where he escaped to France

Chapter 5: Ecclesiastical

1 *Melrose Liber*

2 *St Andrews Liber*

3 Agnes Randolph didn't become Countess of Dunbar until c.1320; she was a child in 1296

4 Fairknowe was the original name for Whitekirk

5 *CPL Benedict XIII*

6 *CSSR ii* A footnote states that the ruins of the chapel - surely a reference to the hermitage - still survive in the undergrowth overlooking Seacliff Bay (see also *RCAHMS : East Lothian* and *TELAS* 1926). The hermitage was reputedly visited by pil grims, including Aeneas Sylvanus who became Pope Pius II (see Chapter 2). Waddell, *An Old Kirk Chronicle* believes the ruins are those of St Baldred's Priory but this is incorrect. Nearby is a shallow cave with a large stone at the entrance, reputedly the sacrificial altar of local Druids

7 The first Collegiate Church, St Mary-of-the-Rocks, was founded at St Andrews (1250), followed by Abernethy (early fourteenth century and possibly a few years before Dunbar in 1342; next was Maybole (1383), Lincluden (1389), Bothwell (1397), Dalkeith (1406), Bothans (Yester, 1421), Dunglass (1443), Dirleton (1444-50), Seton (1493) and Haddington (c1540). Between 1342 and 1545, about 40 such establishments were founded

8 Usually a provost in Scotland; it is thought that Dunbar's relative proximity to Durham was the reason why the senior appointments were given the English titles of Dean and Archpriest or Archdeacon

9 *SHS Misc. vol vi*

10 Watt, *Fasti*

11 In 1306, the 8th Earl of Dunbar used the church to store grain for the garrison of his castle, presumably in the hope that Bruce's guerrillas wouldn't desecrate a church by stealing from it

12 *Yester Writs* No 142

13 *Ibid* No 373

14 These terms were abolished after the Reformation in Scotland but not in England. In a free parish, the rector served it and received all the legal revenues; the vicar [Latin for substitute] undertook the parish duties of a monastery or collegiate church

15 *Yester Writs* No 27A dated 5th August 1366

16 *Ibid* No 28

17 *Ibid* Nos 191 and 193, signed at Dunbar Castle and No 194 signed at Belton; several local people were witnesses, including Malcolm Drummond, rector of Dunbar and David Home of Spott on 3rd, 5th and 7th November 1478

18 SRO ref. CH2/333. This refers to the defeat - and subsequent execution - of the Protestant Archibald, 9th Earl of Argyll; his rebellion was timed to coincide with Monmouth's rebellion to depose Catholic James VII and II. Monmouth was defeated at Sedgemoor in Somerset and Argyll's rising was botched. He was captured in Glasgow and executed, becoming a Protestant Martyr. James VII was deposed by William of Orange in the Glorious Revolution of 1688

19 British Museum; *Harleian MSS* 4637 c. folio 189

20 *RMS vol iv* No 3037

21 *Witch Hunting in East Lothian*

22 Larner, *A Source-Book of Scottish Witchcraft*

23 *Synod Records of Lothian and Tweeddale*

24 Bell, *An Ingenious and Scientific Discourse of Witchcraft* (1705)

25 Burt, *Letters from the North of Scotland*

26 I have been unable to identify the published sources of the records of the Edinburgh (Old Associate) Presbytery whose member ship numbered less than 1,300 in 1744 (*History of the Congregations of the United Presbyterian Church,* 1723-1900 ed. R Small, Edinburgh, 1904)
27 Waddell, *An Old Kirk Chronicle*
28 Andrews, *Bygone Days of Church Life in Scotland*
29 *Synod Records of Lothian and Tweeddale*
30 *RSS vol v* No 2774
31 *Bygone Days of Church Life in Scotland*
32 Dunbar (Old) Kirk Session Minutes:

SRO ref.	CH2/647/1	1659-1662
	/2	1709-1713
	/3	1718-1728
	/4	1728-1748
	/5	1748-1770
	/6	1779-1783 (gap between 1786 and 1821)
		1821-1842
	/7	1842-1864
	/8	1900-1906
	/9	1906-1932
	/10	1934-1947

33 Rogers, *Social Life in Scotland*
34 Extract from booklet *Dunbar Parish Church, Tribute to the Past Hope for the Future (TELAS,* October 1987)
35 *RPC Third Series* 1686-1689 *vol ixii* p235
36 *PSAS vol 39* 1904-05 and *vol 85* 1950-51

Chapter 6: The Protector

1 Waddell, *An Old Kirk Chronicle*
2 Miller, *Lamp of Lothian*
3 Carlyle, *Cromwell's Letters and Speeches*
4 There is no evidence to support this in official documents. According to Douglas, *Cromwell's Scotch Campaigns* the local people had simply helped themselves to the supplies; however, according to Whitelock's *Memorialls* quoted in *Miller, Dunbar,* Cromwell's officers distributed £240 in pease and wheat to a near-starving population
5 *Diary of Johnston of Wariston* 1650-54 (*SHS 2nd Series vol ii* 18)
6 Leslie afterwards blamed himself for concentrating his left flank so close to the English and along the banks of the Brox Burn, thus reducing the impact of his big battalions
7 Roxburghe, a Border noble received a charter granting him Pinkerton, then Oswald Dean in 1632 and finally the Barony of Broxfield [Broxburn] in 1642 (Miller, *Lamp of Lothian*). However Roxburghe occupied Broxmouth in 1639 (see chapter 3)
8 *Cromwell's Letters and Speeches*
9 *Cromwell's Letters and Speeches*
10 *APS vol vi Part 2* p808
11 *Ibid*
12 When the bush was dug up in the nineteenth century, some bones, military buttons and a coin of Charles I's reign were found; one of the buttons was inscribed *CR (Charles Rex) (Berwickshire Naturalists' Club)*
13 *Letters and Papers of State Addressed to Oliver Cromwell*
14 Wills, *Scottish Firsts; PSAS vol 66* 1931-32
15 SRO ref. B 18/39; *TELAS vol ix* 1968
16 Forbes-Gray, *A Short History of Haddington*
17 *Cromwell's Letters and Speeches*
18 *Ibid*
19 Douglas, *Cromwell's Scotch Campaigns;* Miller, *Lamp of Lothian*
20 *Cromwell's Letters and Speeches*
21 National Library of Scotland ref. MF SP 49. The letter was addressed to the Council of State for Irish and Scottish Affairs and was presented to the Council on 8th November 1650, about eight or nine weeks after the Scottish prisoners began their march south
22 The facts are that prisoners taken in the Civil Wars invariably went hungry. For example, in 1643, about a farthing a day (about 3p per month) was the rate allowed to feed one Welsh Royalist taken at the siege of Gloucester; a Parliamentary soldier could expect to receive sixpence (just under 3p) a day for his rations. Some Royalist prisoners fared better than others, receiving about a penny farthing a day (about 15p a month) but invariably, Parliamentary jailers starved their prisoners
23 They were probably sold
24 Possibly the 40 men assigned to sweep out the Castle and Cathedral at Durham
25 Smith, *Colonists in Bondage; White Servitude and Convict Labour in America*
26 Not 900 as suggested by Donaldson, *The Scots Overseas*. Smith; *Colonists in Bondage etc* states that it is possible that a further 150 may have joined Major Clark's 150 although the author admits this is difficult to confirm
27 Happily, when released from their indentured service in 1656, these men were granted land and prospered; their descendants in Boston are proud of their origins
28 *CSP Dom vol I* pp69 and 233. Colonels Rokeby and Killigrew were ordered to transport 300 and 200 respectively 'beyond the seas'. Rokeby was unable to comply with his orders and his 300 remained at Tynemouth
29 Tepper, *Passengers to America; Scottish prisoners deported to New England*
30 *CSP Dom vol I*

31 Page, *The Victorian History of the Counties of England, Durham.* The pre-Reformation font and its covers were destroyed and some family tombs were desecrated. It is thought that the Scots burnt most of the wooden furniture to keep themselves warm during the winter of 1650-51, which contradicts Sir Arthur Hesilrige's claim that he provided the prisoners with 100 fires each day (see Appendix H)
32 As late as 1685, Covenanters were still being deported. Tom Kellie of Dunbar was shipped to an American plantation that year in a sloop bound for New Jersey; he was followed later by Katherine Kellie, possibly his wife (Dobson, *Directory of Scots Banished to the American Plantations*)
33 It is thought that virtually all the rank-and-file were sent to Bermuda and the Bahamas (*CSP Dom vol. I*)
34 Some of the Scots Charitable Society Papers are located in the Massachussetts Historical Society, Boston
35 Notified by Thomas Purves, burgess of Dunbar and burgh commissioner to the Convention of Royal Burghs that year

Chapter 7: Forgotten Men

1 *Later Struggles in the Journey of Life etc* (the title runs to 44 words!)
2 Every 160 years, the former Julian Calendar had been inaccurate by one day; by 1752, when England finally accepted the Gregorian Calendar adopted by Scotland in 1600, it was incorrect by 11 days. Not everyone accepted the change at first and even after eleven days were removed from the calendar in September 1752, subsequent generations celebrated Hansel Monday in Scotland on different days, often within the same community
3 Trading today as Downie's Stationers and Newsagent
4 There were of course a few private libraries in East Lothian before Miller's; one of the earliest was that bequeathed to Haddington by the Rev. J Gray, minister at Aberlady. The minister at Saltoun also possessed a library for his personal use and there were 60 books at the parochial school in Ormiston. George Miller's circulating library differed both in size and the fact that it was available to any who wanted to use it. The controversy whether Samuel Brown of Haddington opened the first of the East Lothian libraries may be disregarded (see *Samuel Brown and George Miller: A Mystery* (Library Review 1971). Miller's biographer, W Couper states that Brown's Itinerating Library was started in 1817, over 25 years after Miller's library
5 It is thought that the Crombies, merchants in Stenton, were for generations suppliers of goods and chapbooks to the hawkers; they reputedly traded at the foot of Preston Tower. When the guild was revived in the late nineteenth century, Sir Walter Scott was made a gentleman chapman
6 Neuberg, *Popular Education in 18th Century Britain*
7 Miller also printed for the Earl of Haddington the signals which would warn the local population of a French landing on the coast between Berwick and Musselburgh. These were probably devised by General Sir George Don who was appointed sec ond-in-command of the troops stationed in Scotland in 1801
8 Doubt has been expressed whether Miller was East Lothian's first printer of literature; McNeills of Haddington, a bookselling and publishing business in 1771 was printing in 1833
9 Miller, *War, A System of Irreligion and Madness* (Edinburgh, 1796)
10 The *Third Statistical Account for Scotland* erroneously credits son James with this achievement; other accounts are equally guilty of the same error
11 The original appeal and subscription list may be inspected in the Scottish Record Office (SRO ref. B 42/3). Perhaps these were the copies referred to in the burgh council minutes of 13th May 1942 as having been offered to the town by a Mr F W McManus of Glasgow (SRO ref. B 18/13/21)
12 Couper, *The Millers of Haddington, Dunbar and Dunfermline*
13 In 2002, a second-hand copy of the *History of Dunbar* retailed at £75; in 1830, it cost a few shillings
14 Provost and Magistrates Committee Minutes 1943-47 (SRO ref. B 18/14/4)
15 *Ibid*

Chapter 8: Royal Burgh

1 *RMS vol I* No 340; Chambers, *Caledonia* ventures that Dunbar became the 47th royal burgh in 1370 but this is incorrect; full royal burgh status did not occur until 1445
2 *TELAS vol ii Part 1* 1929-30
3 Pryde, *The Burghs of Scotland; A Critical List; TELAS vol ii Part 1* 1929-30
4 *RMS vol vi* No 1418; James VI's charter confirmed (i) David II's charter of 1370 (ii) James II's of 1445 which conferred royal burgh status ie *burgus in liberum burgum regium* (iii) the charters enacted in the reign of Mary, Queen of Scots of 18th June 1555 (*RMS vol iv* No 999 which describes Dunbar as a *liberum burgum regalem* - free royal burgh) and 31st March 1567 (referred to in *RMS vol vii* - see note 5)
5 *RMS vol vii* No 1921 dated 23rd October 1618
6 *APS vol v* No 254
7 *Ibid vol ii* No 93 which confirms Dunbar's first representative in parliament; the burgh was represented at the first recorded meeting of the Convention of Royal Burghs in 1552 (*RCRB vol I* p1)
8 Although the burgh council minutes record that Bailie William Fall rode to the last parliament in Scotland for the opening cer emony, Robert Kellie attended as the burgh's representative
9 The effects of the Window Tax can still be seen in the many blocked-up windows in towns throughout Scotland, a local example being George Miller's former shop at No 71 High Street
10 Gross, *The Gild Merchants;* Bain, *Merchants and Craft Guilds*
11 *RPC vol ii Third Series* 1664-69 p543
12 *Ibid vol iv* 1673-76
13 *Poor Law Inquiry Commission for Scotland; Minutes of Evidence Appendix III* (Edinburgh, 1844)
14 *APS vol vi Part I* p718
15 *RPC vol iii* 1578-85 pp313, 690, *vol xi* 1616-19 p410 and *vol vi* 1635-37 p283

16 In 1833, there was a dispute between Mrs Hamilton Nisbet Ferguson and the magistrates of Dunbar as to the ownership of Dunbar Common. The magistrates argued that the Common was exclusively burgh property because of the former earldom of March. Their rights were proved to derive simply from servitude or vassalage created by Crown charter of 1618. Dunbar was ruled to possess only 200 acres which had been used to graze 50 of the town's cattle. The dispute arose because a joint stock company of burgesses had attempted to increase the acreage for cattle grazing and also to introduce sheep. After an extensive enquiry in which several witnesses appeared to verify rights of ownership by others, legal division of the land left Dunbar with 204acres valued at £33:10:3 (£33.51). The other owners were Mrs Nisbet Ferguson with 697 acres and Mr Sydserff of Ruchlaw with 192 acres; others included the Duke of Roxburghe, the Marquis of Tweeddale, Sir James Grant Suttie, the Earl of Haddington, Captain Hay of Belton and James Balfour of Whittingehame. Dunbar's portion was bounded in part by the Old Herring Road and contained the Mickle Moss and Priest's Well, near Deuchrie Dod (Dunbar Commonty (see reports RO ref. B 18/18/10)

17 *RCAHMS Report: East Lothian* 1924; *Friarscroft and the Trinitarians* (*PSAS* 1983)

18 *The Scottish Burgh Survey* gives 1734; Pevsner, *Buildings of Scotland: Lothian* says 1740

19 *The Scottish Burgh Survey;* Thomson, *Lauder and Lauderdale*

20 *Miller, Dunbar*

21 Cowan, *SHS Report* (1983); *PSAS vol 84* 1949-50

22 Next to the Tolbooth or Town House, Silver Street was reputedly named for a hoard of silver coins discovered when the street was being causeyed in the eighteenth century

23 Groome, *Gazetteer of Scotland*

24 Dramatised in the film *55Days at Peking*

25 *Reform of the Internal Government of the Royall Boroughs*[sic]*] of Scotland* 1787 (Edinburgh Public Library ref. XJS 4133)

26 Porteous, *Town Seals of Scotland*; Stevenson and Wood, *Scottish Heraldic Seals.* Dunbar's seal was only matriculated - registered - by Lord Lyon King-at-Arms on 20th October 1942 to allow the burgh to present its official plaque to the officers and men of *HMS Dunbar* (*Haddingtonshire Courier*). (See also Chapter 11 for details)

27 Dunbar Town Council Minutes: extracts quoted in the text can be found in the following:

SRO ref. B 18/13/1	1671-1687	B 18/13//9	1831-1841
/2	1688-1715	/10	1841-1859
	(1715-1719 missing)	/11	1859-1876
/3	1716-1728	/12	1876-1895
/4	1729-1746	/13	1895-1919
/5	1746-1770	/20	1936-1941
/6	1770-1799	/21	1941-1947
/7	1799-1818	/26	1950-1959
/8	1818-1831	to35	
/41/2-5	1698-1776		

Minute Books of Magistrates and Committees:

SRO ref. B 18/14/1	1833-1871
/2	1871-1910

Miscellaneous Papers
SRO ref. B 18/42

Chapter 9: Economic and Social
Agriculture

1 The boll contained 12 gallons of ale or 123 pounds of water; a chalder = 16 bolls. These measurements increased during the Middle Ages and by 1618, it required 4-6 bushels to make a boll ie 32-48 gallons (*A Source Book of Scottish History*)

2 The Dunbar parish entry in the *Old Statistical Account* reveals that the custom of *thirlage* was in decline; the contributor to the *Account* was aware of the demands to end this ancient and iniquitous residue of the feudal system. Thirlage was finally abolished under the *Thirlage Act,*1799. The enforced use of the local lord's mills was introduced by Alexander III and subsequent legislation outlawed the use of querns and handmills to avoid paying the lord his *multure,* or share of the corn ground

3 Standard units of Scots land measure:
1 davoch = 4 ploughgates: 1 ploughgate = 104 Scots acres (130 English acres) or 8 oxgangs*
1 husbandland = 2 oxgangs: 1 oxgang = 3 Scots acres
*a unit so-called as it was the amount of land a single 8 oxen - drawn plough could till in a single year

4 *Accounts of the Lord High Treasurer of Scotland*

5 *Birlaw* or *birlay* is Old Norse; the system is thought to have come to Scotland betwen the ninth and twelfth centuries but it is not known whether this was instigated by landowners or peasants

6 *Old Statistical Account;* Spott Parish

7 Smout, *Scottish Trade on the Eve of the Union* 1660-1707

8 James Meikle, the father, built the first barley mill and the first winnowing machine in Scotland for Fletcher of Saltoun; the latter drew up an agreement in which Meikle agreed to become an industrial spy in Holland to learn the art of perfecting pot or pearl barley. The agreement contained a clause whereby Fletcher would bail Meikle out Dutch prison and pay his expenses! (R Somerville, *A General View of the Agriculture of East Lothian)* Andrew Meikle invented the threshing machine and grand son George built the large waterwheel which drained and reclaimed Drumossie Moss

9 *TELAS vol xiii* 1968

10 Geoffrey Bles, *Agricultural Sir John; The Life of Sir John Sinclair of Ulbster* 1780-1811 (1962)

11 At Crowhill Farm near the Portland Cement Company works, a farmer created a 250-foot long shaft built in a tunnel to pro vide water for his water-mill; the remains are visible today
12 *A General View of the Agriculture of East Lothian*
13 Edward Topham, *Captain Topham's Letters from Edinburgh*
14 *Border Country Life,* Grieve Papers
15 *Royal Commission on Labour 1893 Part II*

Fishing and Sea Trade

16 *RMS vol ii 1609-20* No 1921
17 *Miller, Dunbar*
18 *RMS vol iv 1546-56* No 999
19 Hume Brown, *Early Travellers in Scotland*
20 *RPC vol ii 1569-78* pp417-418 (November 1574) and *RSS vol v* No 2732. The burgh council was allowed to levy two shillings (10p) on all goods entering and leaving the harbour and 12 pence (5p) on goods entering and leaving carried by Norwegian ves sels. The money thus raised was to be used specifically for harbour improvements
21 Pevsner, *The Buildings of Scotland: East Lothian.* On 10th November 1574, the Regent Moray made
'a gift to the burgh of Dunbar for the benefit of its harbour........eist the castell.' (*RSS vol vi 1574*)
In 1591, the Convention of Royal Burghs excused the commissioner from Dunbar from attending meetings so that he could repair the 'dekayitt harberie' on which £60 was spent (*RCRB vol I* p363)
22 *Early Travellers in Scotland* (see also Chapter 3)
23 *RPC vol x 1613-1616* pp436-439, 640-641
24 *CSP Dom vol x 1655-57*
25 *Early Travllers in Scotland* (see also Chapter 3)
26 *SBRS* p18
27 *An Abridged Statistical Account of Scotland*
28 The term seems to have assumed a different or extended meaning by the mid-nineteenth century; by then, it constituted an agreement between two or three fishermen and five or six landsmen, the latter providing the boat and equipment in return for a share of the catch
29 *Old Statistical Account*
30 The burgh council minutes of 1936 record the discovery of a whale's skeleton at the Pier Head, Old Harbour; examined by a Scottish Royal Museum official, it was found to be the remains of a whalebone whale, one of the largest Greenland species (SRO ref. B 18/13/20). Christian Salvesen of Leith operated the last whaler in 1963
31 *New Statistical Account*
32 *Board of White Fisheries for Scotland*: minutes of 1840-44 (SRO refs. AF 1/12 and AF 1/13)
33 Chambers, *Scottish Biographical Dictionary*
34 *APS vol v 1636* p494
35 *Old Statistical Account*
36 Letters from the Board of Customs and Excise to the Dunbar collector (SRO ref. CE 56 2/1-9)
37 SRO ref. CS 230/F1/1

Chapter 10, Trade, Industry, Commerce and Social

1 *ERs* Fig 13
2 The historian may enquire in vain about the reasons for these fluctuations (see fig 13). Also the relatively high return for wool exports probably dried up in the mid-fifteenth century when Berwick was given back to Scotland in 1461 and the export trade moved there
3 *SBRS; State and Condition of the Burgh of Dunbar on 18 April 1692* p120
4 Somerville, *Autobiography of a Working Man etc*
5 *Accounts of the Principal Limestone Quarries of Scotland*
6 *Old Statistical Account*
7 *The Life and Work of a Great Engineer*
8 Provost and Magistrates' Committee Minutes 1943-47, 5th April 1946 (SRO ref. B 18/14/4)

Education

9 Regulations of the burgh school, 1679; only articles 25-30 have survived (SRO ref. B 18/46/1)
10 Grant, *Burgh Schools of Scotland*
11 *RPC vol ii 1569-78* p479
12 *Report of Parishes* 1627

Social

13 *Kelso Liber*
14 Thomson. *Coldingham: Parish and Priory*
15 By comparison, Edinburgh's population in the fourteenth century was little more than 2,000; the population of Scotland was about half a million
16 There was also a Thomas de Ryklynton employed as a customs officer at Dunbar (*ERs*)
17 *RPC vol ii 1569-78; vol iii 1578-85* pp313 and 690

18 Correspondence between Dunbar Town Council and the Local Government Board about a dispute concerning the suitability of the Battery Hospital for the treatment of infectious diseases (SRO ref. B 18/45/9)
19 Papers concerning the opening of a soup kitchen for the relief of the deserving poor in 1863 (SRO ref B 18/48/13)
20 Criminal Complaints and Defaulters Books 1849-54 and 1854-61 (SRO ref. B 18/10/3-4)
21 *Beauties of Scotland*
22 Minute Book of Dunbar and District Curling Club 1901-38 (SRO ref. B 18/18/26)
23 *Picturesque Dunbar*
24 The Town Council Minutes of 11th February 1942 refer to a photograph taken on 1st September 1894 of a function at Belton which celebrated the conferring of the freedom of the burgh on Captain Hay and Mrs Baird for her generous gift of the West Promenade to the people of Dunbar (SRO ref. B 18/14/3). The Town Council Minutes of 10th February 1954 reported the death of Major James Hay of Belton, the last of a family which had resided there for some five centuries. The Town Council received a bequest of a portrait of Mrs Baird and Captain Hay, two caskets with the burgh arms which contained the freedom address of 1894, the Freedom Address in frame, a photograph of the presentation, a burgess brooch and a book entitled *Dunbar and the Hays of Belton* (SRO ref. B 18/13/30)
25 Provost and Magistrates' Committee Minutes 1943-47, 7th July 1947 (SRO ref. B 18/14/4)
26 Sixth Centennial Celebrations 1970-71 (SRO ref. B 18/20/20 and 21)

Chapter 11: The Prophet

1 Town Council Minutes 13th April 1938 (SRO ref. B 18/13/20)
2 Provost and Magistrates' Committee Meetings 1938-43 (SRO ref. B 18/14/3A)
3 Unless he meant No 134 High Street, the Muir home when the family emigrated in 1849; even so, both Muir houses in the High Street survived. Daniel Muir sold No 134 to Dr Lorn, a local physician on 1st February 1849; the property subsequently became the Lorne Temperance Hotel
4 The site is now occupied by a housing estate although the school boundary wall has survived
5 The house was owned by Provost Robert Fall, the merchant, then a Doctor Charles Wightman who sold it to Dr William Wightman his son, from whom Daniel Muir bought it
6 There are other examples in Dunbar; the Window Tax was obnoxious as light like water is a natural resource, although the latter requires capital investment to maintain its purity
7 *Edinburgh Evening News* of 27th November 1996; the Secretary of State granted permission for the erection of the statue in the autumn of 1997

Chapter 12: Military Annals

1 *APS vol v Part I*
2 *RPC Third Series vol I* 1664-69
3 *Ibid vol iii* 1667-72
4 *Ibid vol v* 1676-78
5 So-called as he became a general in the army of the Czar of Russia after escaping from the Royalist defeat at Worcester in 1651. Dalyell formed the regiment which was known as the Royal North British Dragoon Guards or Scots Greys. When he returned to Scotland after the Restoration, he was appointed commander-in-chief of the army; he was noted for his ferocity in suppress ing the Covenanters
6 Considerably less than the number of women executed as witches by the Covenanter Church - eg in one year (1661-62), at least 300 women were put to death
7 *APS vol ix* 1689-95
8 Town Council Minutes (TCM) 1746-70, 31st March 1747 (SRO ref. B 18/13/5)
9 *Ibid* 1729-46, April 1746 (SRO ref, B 18/13/4)
10 *Ibid* 1746-70 (SRO ref. B 18/13/5)
11 *Ibid* 1770-99 (SRO ref. B 18/13/6)
12 *New Statistical Account* : Dunbar parish
13 Miscellaneous Papers, Dunbar: 8th June 1781 (SRO ref. B 18/42/10)
14 TCM 1770-99, 18th March 1793 (SRO ref. B 18/13/6)
15 National Library of Scotland MS 1649Z 3156 6
16 TCM 1770-99, 23rd May 1794 (SRO ref. B 18/13/6
17 *TELAS vol ii* 1926-33
18 *Laing MSS Division II* No 500 (Edinburgh University)
19 They were, in the words of Tom Paine 'summer soldiers and sunshine patriots'; Paine wrote thus of certain lukewarm colo nists during the American War of Independence
20 TCM 1799-18118, 29th November 1803 (SRO ref, B 18/13/7)
21 Miscellaneous Papers, Dunbar (SRO ref. B 18/42/10)
22 The volume of TCM for 1799-1818 contains a map which indicates that the whole of Gallows Green [Gala Green] was desig nated for barrack accommodation in June 1803 (SRO ref. B 18/13/7)
23 War Office ref. WO 30/116 (1805, rep. 1880)
24 *New Statistical Account* for Berwickshire states that the fire was caused by whin burning and that the alarm was raised in Babchester. Other accounts state the fires were caused by charcoal-burners in Northumberland
25 *The False Alarm* (SRO ref. B 18/51/3)
26 Criminal Complaints and Defaulters Book, Dunbar 1854-61 (SRO ref. B 18/10/4)
27 *Ibid*
28 TCM 19th February 1855 (SRO ref. B 18/13/10)

29 *Picturesque Dunbar* p23 (printed c1899)
30 As portrayed in the film *55 Days at Peking*
31 Japanese troops (12,000), British (3,000), Russian (3,000), American (2,800) and French (1,000)
32 *Haddingtonshire Courier*
33 *Ibid,* 13th November 1899
34 *Ibid.* 27th November 1899; The report states that Tom Goodall was in 'the local yeomanry' implying the *Lothian and Border Yeomanry.* He was in fact in the *Kimberley Light Horse* as his memorial in Dunbar cemetery shows
35 *Haddingtonshire Courier*, 29th December 1899
36 Provost and Magistrates' Committee Minutes, 6th March 1900
37 These men were probably volunteers in *D* Company, 1st Haddingtonshire Militia Rifle Volunteers, part of the 7th Battalion, Royal Scots; the Company was stationed first at Dunglass, then West Barns and finally at East Linton. The volunteers wore riflemen green uniforms with scarlet piping and a busby-type shako (*Records of the Scottish Volunteer Force* 1859-1908, J Moncrieff Grierson, London, 1909)
38 Provost and Magistrates' Committee Minutes, 8th May 1902 (SRO ref. B 18/14/3A
39 *Haddingtonshire Courier,* 28th August 1914
40 *Ibid,* 14th August 1914
41 *Ibid*, 11th September 1914
42 *Ibid*
43 *Ibid*
44 *Ibid,* 25th September 1914
45 *Ibid,* 12th March 1915
46 *Ibid*, 19th March 1915
47 *Ibid,*14th May 1915
48 *Ibid*, 28th May 1915
49 *Ibid*, 25th June 1915. The wreath of laurel, iris and roses bore a small card depicting the figure of an artillery officer in the uniform worn in 1815; the card was inscribed as follows:

> '*Ubique.* Hundredth anniversary of the Battle of Waterloo, 18th June 1815. These flowers are sent by brother officers of today for remembrance of Major General William Cochran Anderson, who took part in the battle.
> *Quo fus et gloria defunct.'* (whither pours down glory)

50 *Haddingtonshire Courier,* 9th July 1915
51 *Ibid*, 2nd July 1915
52 *Ibid*, 26th May 1917
53 *Ibid,* 16th February 1917
54 *Ibid*, 22nd March 1918
55 *Ibid*, 12th April 191
56 *Ibid*, 21st June 1918
57 First World War Graves Commission (SRO ref. B 18/20/34)
58 Provost and Magistrates' Committee Minutes, 7th October 1938 (SRO ref. B 18/14/3A)
59 *Edinburgh Evening News*, 22nd September 1995; *East Lothian at War* (East Lothian District Library, 1996)
60 *Edinburgh Evening News,* 22nd September 1995
61 Provost and Magistrates' Committee Minutes, 3rd November 1939 (SRO ref. B 18/14/3A)
62 TCM 17th January 1941 (SRO ref. B 18/13/21)
63 Provost and Magistrates' Committee Minutes, 6th September 1940 (SRO ref. B 18/14/3A)
64 *This Present Emergency*
65 *Ibid*
66 TCM, 12th November 1941 (SRO ref. B 18/13/21)
67 Provost and Magistrates' Committee Minutes, 3rd April 1942 (SRO ref. B 18/14/3A)
68 TCM, 6th June 1941 (SRO ref. B 18/13/21)
69 *Ibid*, 8th August 1941
70 *Ibid*, 6th February 1942
71 *Ibid*, 11th March 1942
72 *Ibid*, 6th November 1942
73 *Ibid*, 8th September 1943
74 *Edinburgh Evening News*, 3rd July 1996
75 Miscellaneous Papers: Dunbar: Castle Park Barracks, 12th October 1944 (SRO ref. B 18/20/30)
76 *Haddingtonshire Courier*, 13th April 1945
77 *Ibid*
78 Some of the blocks were removed from Belhaven foreshore in 1945; the defence system at Winterfield wasn't dismantled until 1950 (TCM 1947-49 and 1950; SRO refs. B 18/13/22 and 26)
79 Victory Celebrations 1946 (SRO ref. B 18/20/13)
80 *Haddingtonshire Courier*, 22nd May 1964
81 *Edinburgh Evening News*, 22nd September 1995
82 TCM 12th October 1955 (SRO ref. B 18/13/31)

Notes and Bibliography

BIBLIOGRAPHY

General

The Bibliography includes all primary and secondary sources which appear more than once in the text and Notes to Chapters. Place and year of publication are shown in most cases.

Summary of Sources Consulted

1 Records and Original Documents: Royal, State and Local Government
2 History: Early Sources prior to 1800: Chronicles, Histories, Manuscripts and Letters
3 History: Modern Accounts, Biographies and accounts by historical/antiquarian clubs and socities etc compiled after 1800
4 Ecclesiatical: Records, Biographies and Histories
5 Peerages: Genealogical Collections and Family Histories
6 Counties, Towns, Burghs, Parishes and Villages
7 Economic: Agriculture, Fishing and Sea Trade, Trade and Industry:
Education and Social: Various Accounts, Government (central and local) Publications and Reports

1

RECORDS AND ORIGINAL DOCUMENTS: ROYAL, STATE AND LOCAL GOVERNMENT

Accounts of the Lord High Treasurer of Scotland (Compota Thesaurorium Scotorum) 1473-1574 *vols. i-xi* ed. J Dickson *et al* (Edinburgh, 1877-1973)
Acts of the Lords of Council in Public Affairs 1501-54 ed. R K Hannay (Edinburgh, 1932)
Acts of the Parliaments of Scotland 1124-1707 *vols i-xii* ed. T Thomson , C Innes (Edinburgh, 1814-75)
Ancient Laws and Customs of the Burghs of Scotland: Scottish Burgh Records 1124-1424 (Edinburgh, 1868)
Anglo-Scottish Relations 1174-1328: Some Selected Documents: Oxford Medieval Texts ed. E L G Stones (Edinburgh and London, 1965)
Annals of the Reigns of Malcolm and William, Kings of Scotland 1153-1214 ed. Sir A Lawrie (Glasgow, 1910)

Border Papers, The: Calendar of Letters and Papers Relating to the Affairs of the Borders of England and Scotland 1560-1603 *vols i-ii* ed. J Bain (Edinburgh, 1894-96)

Calendar of the Close Rolls, Edward I 1296-1302 *vol iv* (PRO, London, 1906)
Calendar of the Close Rolls, Henry IV 1399-1413 *vols i-iv* (PRO, London, 1903-09)
Calendar of Documents relating to Scotland 1104-1516 *vols i-v* and *Addenda* viz:

i	1104-1272
ii	1272-1307
iii	1307-1357
iv	1357-1509
Addenda	1221-1435
v	1108-1516 (Supplementary)

Vols i-iv and Addenda ed. J Bain (Edinburgh, 1881-88); vol v ed. G C Simpson and J Galbraith (Edinburgh, 1986)
Calendar of Fine Rolls, Edward I 1272-1307 *vol I* (PRO, London, 1911)
Calendar of Inquisitions Post Mortem, Edward I 1298 *vol iii* (PRO, London, 1912)
Calendar of the Laing Charters 854-1837 ed. J Anderson (Edinburgh, 1899)
Calendar of Patent Rolls 1216 - several vols (PRO, London, 1901-)
Calendar of State Papers Domestic Series (England) (PRO, London, 1856-77)
Calendar of the State Papers relating to Scotland 1509-1603 *vols i-ii* ed. M J Thorpe (London, 1858)
Calendar of the State Papers relating to Scotland and Mary, Queen of Scots 1547-1603 *vols i-xiii* ed. J Bain *et al* (Edinburgh & Glasgow, 1898-1969)
Criminal Trials of Scotland vols i-iii ed. R Pitcairn (Bannatyne Club, 1833)
Cromwellian Papers:
Harleian MSS: 'A list of Ye Scottish Army at Dunbarr' which gives 'The Horse at Dunbarr Bataille and the Foot at Dunbarr Bataille' (British Museum ref. 6844 folio 23)
Letters and Speeches of Oliver Cromwell, The, vols i-iii ed. T Carlyle (London, 1904)
Original Letters and Speeches of Oliver Cromwell found among the Political Collections of John Milton ed. J Nickolls (London, 1743)
Prisoners of the Battle of Dunbar 1650, *The*: Letter dated 31st October from Sir Arthur Hesilrige to the Committee of the Council of State for Irish and Scottish Affairs (National Library of Scotland microfiche ref. MF SP 49)
Documents and Records Illustrating the History of Scotland ed. F Palgrave (Record Commission, 1837)

Earliest Scottish Charters, The: ed A A M Duncan (*SHR vol xxxvii* 1958)
Early Scottish Charters Prior to AD 1153 ed. Sir A Lawrie (Glasgow, 1905)
English Historical Documents 1042-1189 *vol ii* ed. D C Douglas and G W Greenaway (London, 1953)
Exchequer Rolls of Scotland 1264-1600 *vols i-xxiii* (see also under *Rotuli Scaccarii Regum Scotorum*) ed. J Stuart *et al* (Edin burgh, 1878-1908)

Glasgow University Manuscripts
Great Seal of Scotland (see under *Registrum Magni Sigilli Regum Scotorum - Register of the Great Seal of Scotland*)

Hamilton Papers vols i-ii ed. J Bain (Edinburgh, 1890-92)
Handlist of Acts of Alexander II compiled by J M Soutar (Department of History, University of Edinburgh, 1959)
Handlist of Acts of David II compiled by B Webster (Department of History, University of Edinburgh, 1962)
Historical Documents of Scotland 1286-1706 ed. J Stevenson (Edinburgh, 1876)

National Manuscripts of Scotland (Facsimilies) (London, 1867-71)

Pipe Rolls of Henry II (*Pipe Roll Society*, 1884-97)
PRO ref. E 372/Note 177 160 m 50 (Public Record Office): this contains Edward II's decree that the 9th Earl of Dunbar had forfeited his lands in Beanley, Northumberland from 25th June 1314 ie after the battle of Bannockburn
Records of the Convention of Royal Burghs of Scotland 1295-1799 *vols i-vii* ed. J Marwick and T Hamilton (Edinburgh, 1866-1914)
Regesta Regum Scottorum (Acts and Charters of various Scottish kings):

Malcom IV	1153-65	ed. G W S Barrow *et al* (Edinburgh, 1960)
William I	1165-1214	ed. G W S Barrow (Edinburgh, 1990)
Alexander II	1214-49	see under *Handlist of Acts of Alexander II*
Robert I	1306-29	ed. A A M Duncan (Edinburgh, 1988)
David II	1329-71	ed. B Webster (Edinburgh, 1988) and see under *Handlist of Acts of David II*

Registrum Magni Sigilli Regum Scotorum (*Register of the Great Seal of Scotland*) 1306-1668 *vols i-ix* ed. J Thomson *et al* (Edinburgh, 1882-1914)
Registrum Secreti Sigilli Regum Scotorum (*Register of the Privy Seal of Scotland*) 1488-1584 *vols i-viii* ed. M Livingston *et al* (HMSO Einburgh, 1908-82)
Register of the Privy Council of Scotland , First Series 1545-1625 *vols i-xiv; Second Series* 1625-60 *vols i*-viii; *Third Series* 1661-1691 *vols i-xvi* ed. J Hill Burton *et al* Edinburgh, 1877-1970)
Rotuli Scaccarii Regum Scotorum (see under *Exchequer Rolls*)
Rotuli Scotiae in Turri Londinensi et in Domo Capitulari Westmonasteriensi Asservati vols i-ii ed. D MacPherson *et al* (*Record Commission,* 1814-19(; being a collection of records illustrative of Scotland from 1290 to 1516 and dealing with such matters as the succession to the Scottish throne in 1291, preparations for wars, the treatment and ransom of prisoners of war and grants made to Scottish subjects who gave assistance to English kings

Scottish Burgh Records Society, Miscellany of the ed. J Marwick (Edinburgh, 1881). (Contains Thomas Tucker's report of the Scottish customs and excise revenues during the Cromwellian Protectorate)
Source Book of Scottish History, A vols i-ii ed. W Croft Dickinson, G Donaldson and I A Milne (Edinburgh, 1956-58)

2

HISTORY; EARLY SOURCES, CHRONICLES, HISTORIES, MANUSCRIPTS AND LETTERS PRIOR TO 1800

Anglo-Saxon Chronicle, The ed. B Thorpe (*Rolls Series*, London, 1861 and rev. trans. by Dorothy Whitelock, London, 1961)
Annals of Tigernach (Ireland) ed. Whitley Stokes (*Revue Celtique vols xvi-xviii* 1895-97)
Antiquities of Scotland, The, Francis Grose (London, 1789)
Auchinleck Chronicle, The; ane Schort Memoriale of Scotis Cornikillis for Addiciuon ed. T Thomson (Edinburgh, 1819-77)
Asloan MSS vol I ed. W A Craigie (*Scottish Text Society,*1923-25). This is the sole substantial contemporary account of the reign of James II which has survived

Bruce, The J Barbour (1375) ed. W Mackenzie (London, 1909), P McDiarmid and J A C Stevenson (*Scottish Text Society,* 1980-85)

Caledonia: An Account, Historical and Topographic of North Britain vol I G Chalmers (London, 1807- 24)
Calendar of Manuscripts at Hatfield House: History and Treasures of Hatfield House, Marquis of Salisbury (London, 1959)
Chronica Gentis Scotorum (Chronicle of the Scottish Nation, Fordun's Chronicle): Johannis de Fordun trans. F J H Skene ed. W F Skene (Edinburgh 1871-72)
Chronica Magistri Rogeri de Houedene (Chronicle of Roger Hoveden, 1201) *vols i-iv* ed. W Stubbs (*Rolls Series,* 1868-71)
Chronici Majora Historia Anglorum (Chronicle of Matthew Paris and the History of England) Matthew Paris, monk of St Albans *vols i-iv* 1248-59 ed F H Madden (*Rolls Series,* 1872-80) and H Luard (*Rolls Series,* 1872-84)
Chronica Monasterii S. Albani Willemi Rishanger, Chronica et Annales (Chronicle of William Rishanger, 1259-1307) ed. H T Riley (*Rolls Series,* 1865)
Chronicle of England (15th century) J Capgrave ed. F G Hingeston (*Rolls Series,* 1858)
Chronicle of England, France, Spain of Jean Froissart trans. T Johnes (London, 1848); also *Chroniques,* 1325-1400, Jean Froissart, by Sir John Bourchier, Lord Berners, 1523-25 ed. W P Ker (London, 1901-03)
Chronicles of Englande, Scotlande and Irelande, Raphael Holinshed (London, 1577)
Chronicle of Holyrood ed. M O Anderson (*Scottish History Society,* 1938)
Chronicles of the Picts: Chronicles of the Scots and Other Memorials of Scottish History ed. W F Skene (Edinburgh, 1867)
Chronicles of the Reigns of Stephen, Henry II and Richard I vols i-iv ed. R Howlett (*Rolls* Series, 1888-89)
Chronicon Angliae de Regnis de Henrici IV, Henrici V et Henrici VI (anonymous) ed. J A Giles (London, 1848)
Chronicon de Lanercost (Chronicle of Lanercost Priory, 1201-1346) ed. J Stevenson (*Maitland Club,* 1839)

Chronicon de Mailros (Chronicle of Melrose Abbey) (*Bannatyne Club,* 1835); facsimile edition by A O Anderson and W Croft Dickinson (London, 1936)
Chroniques/Histoire de Ducs de Normandie (Chronicles of the Dukes of Normandy, Benoit de Sainte-Marie ed. F Michel (*Societe de l'Histoire de France,* Paris, 1836-44); also *Histoire de Ducs de Normandie et les Rois d'Angleterre* ed. F Michel (*Societe de l'Histoire de France,* Paris, 1840)

Diurnal of Occurrents in Scotland 1513-75, being 'A Diurnal of Remarkable Occurrents That Have Passed Within the Country of Scotland Since the Death of King James the Fourth' ed. T Thomson (*Bannatyne Club,* 1833)

Early Sources of Scottish History AD 500 to 1286: extracts from various chronicles ed. A O Anderson (Edinburgh, 1922, rep. 1990)
Expedicioune into Scotland....of Edward, Duke of Somerset, 1547 An Eye Witness Account of the Battle of Pinkie: W Patten (London, 1548)

Florentii Wigorniensis Monachi, Chronicon ex Chronicis (Chronicle of Florence of Worcester, 1171-1265) *vols i-ii* ed. B Thorpe (London, 1848-49)

Histoire de la Guerre d'Ecosse pendant les campagnes 1548 et 1549: An Eye Witness Account of the siege of Haddington: Jean de Beaugue (*Maitland Club,* 1862)
Historia Anglicana, Bartholomaei Cotton Monachi Norwicenses (History of England 449-1298, Bartholomew Cotton, monk of Norwich) ed. H R Luard (*Rolls Series,* 1859)
Historia Anglorum (Chronicle of Henry of Huntingdon, 1154) ed. T Arnold (*Rolls Series,*1879)
Historia Anglicana Thomae Walsingham (Chronicle of Thomas of Walsingham, monk of St Albans, 1272-1422) ed. H T Riley (*Rolls Series,* 1863-64)
Historia Regum in Symeonis monachi opera omnia (Chronicle of Symeon of Durham) *vols i-ii* ed. T Arnold (*Rolls Series*, 1875)
Historie and Cronicles of Scotland, The: 1437-1575, Robert Lindsay of Pitscottie *vols i-iii* ed. A J G Mackay (*Scottish Text Society,* 1899-1911)
History of Greater Britain, A: J Mair or Major (1517) (*Scottish History Society,* 1892)
History of Scotland, G Buchanan (1583) *vols i-iv* trans. and ed. J Aikman (Glasgow & Edinburgh, 1827-29)
History of Scotland, Bishop A Lesley (*Bannatyne Club,* 1840)

Letters from the North of Scotland vol I, E Burt (London, 1754) ed. R Jamieson (3rd edition, Edinburgh, 1974)

Melville, Sir James of Hallhill: Memoirs of His Own Life 1535-1617 ed. A F Stewart (London, 1929)
Memoirs of the Affairs of Scotland, D Moysie (*Bannatyne Club,* 1830)
Orygynale Cronikyl of Scotland, Andrew of Wyntoun (1246) ed. D Laing (Edinburgh, 1872-79) and F J Amours (*Scottish Text Society,* 1903-14)

Scalacronica, Sir Thomas Gray of Heton, Knight (1356) ed. J Stevenson (*Maitland Club,* 1836) trans. H Maxwell (Glasgow, 1907)
Schir William Walleis, The Actis and Deidis of the Illustere and Valzeand Campioun Schir William Walleis Knicht of Ellderslie, Henry the Minstrel, known as Blind Harry: ed. J Moir (1889) and M P McDiarmid (*Scottish Text Society,* 1968-69)
Scotichronicon (The Chronicle of Inchcolm 1440-45): A Continuation of Fordun's Chronicle by Walter Bower, Abbot of Inchcolm; *vols i-viii* ed. S Taylor, D E R Watt with B Scott (Aberdeen, 1987-89)
Scotorum Historiae (History of Scotland), Hector Boece (2nd edition Paris, 1574)
Scottish Annals from English Chroniclers AD 500 to 1286 ed. A O Anderson (London, 1908)
Scottish Correspondence of Mary of Lorraine 1543-60 ed. A I Cameron (*Scottish History Society, 1927)*
Society of Antiquarians of Sotland (established 1792); see under various headings

Topham's Letters from Edinburgh, Captain Edward Topham (London, 1770)

Vita Edwardi Secundi (Life of Edward II) by the so-called Monk of Malmsbury ed. N Denholm-Young (London & Edinburgh, 1957)

Wallace, William- see under *Schir William Walleis etc*
*Warrender Letters, The:*Correspondence of Sir George Warrender of Lochend, Dunbar, Lord Provost of Edinburgh, 1715 ed. W K Dickson (*Scottish History Society,* 1935)
Warrender Papers, The: ed. R S Rait (*Scottish History Society* , 1932)
Warrender Papers, The: King James' Secret ed. R S Rait and A I Cameron (London, 1927)
Warrender Papers, The: 1301-1603 vols i-ii ed. A I Cameron (*Scottish History Society,* 1930-32)

3

HISTORY: MODERN GENERAL HISTORIES, BIOGRAPHIES AND ACCOUNTS BY HISTORICAL CLUBS AND SOCIETIES COMPILED AFTER 1800

Anglo-Saxon England, Sir Frank Stenton (Oxford, 1976)
Annals of Scotland vols i-ii, Sir David Dalrymple of Hailes (Edinburgh, 1819)

Battlefields of Scotland, The: T F C Brotchie (Edinburgh, 1913)
Border History of England and Scotland, J Ridpath ed. P Ridpath (Berwick, 1848)
Border Antiquities of England and Scotland, The, Sir Walter Scott (Edinburgh, 1814-17)
Bothwell: Life of James Hepburn, Earl of Bothwell, F Schiern (Edinburgh, 1880)
Bruce, Robert and the Community of the Realm of Scotland , G W S Barrow (3rd edition, Edinburgh, 1988)

Casket Letters, The : M H Armstrong Davison (London, 1965)
Celtic Scotland, volsi-iii, W F Skene (Edinburgh, 1886-90)
Conquest of England, A : R J Adam (London, 1965)
Concise History of Scotland, Sir Fitzroy MacLean (London, 1970)
Cromwell:
Colonists in Bondage: White Servitude and Convict Labour in America, 1607-1776, Abbot Emerson Smith (University of North Carolina Press, Chapel Hill, 1947);
Cromwell's Generals: General Monck, M Ashley (London, 1977);
Cromwell's Scotch Campaigns, 1650-51, W S Douglas (London, 1898);
Cromwellian Union, The, 1651-52 ed. C S Terry (*Scottish History Society,* 1902);
Directory of Scots Banished to the American Plantations, 1650-1775 ed. David Dobson (Genealogical Publicating Co., Baltimore, 1984-86);
Passengers to America, J Tepper (Baltimore, 1977);
Regimental History of the Covenanting Armies, A: 1639-51, E M Furgol (Edinburgh, 1990);
Scots Overseas, The: G Donaldson (London, 1966);
Scottish Prisoners Deported to New England (Massachussetts HistoricalPublications 61, 1927-28;
Search for Scottish Ancestry, Gerald Hamilton (Edinburgh, 1972);
(see also Cromwellian Papers, Letters under Records)

Dictionary of National Biography, ed. L Stephen *et al* (London, 1885-1930)

East Lothian at War, J Tully Jackson and Ian Brown (East Lothian District Library, 1996)
East Lothian at War, vol. 2, J Tully Jackson and Ian Brown (East Lothian Council Library Service, 2001)
Edward the Confessor, F Barlow (London, 1970)
Edward III and the Scots, 1327-35: *The Formative Years of a Military Career,* R Nicholson (London, 1965)
Elgin Past and Present, H B Mackintosh (Elgin, 1914)
English Historical Review (London, 1896-)

Feudal England, J H Round (London, 1895, rep. several to 1964)
Fifteenth Century, The: 1399-1485: E F Jacob (Oxford, 1961)
Fourteenth Century, The: 1307-1399: May McKisac (Oxford, 1959)

History and Antiquarian Clubs and Societies:

Bannatyne Club	estabished 1823
Berwickshire Naturalists' Club	" " 1831
East Lothian Antiquarian and Field Naturalists' Society	" " 1924
Maitland Club	" " 1828
Scottish Burgh Records Society	" " 1868
Scottish History Society (with associated Miscellanies)	" " 1887
Scottish Record Society	" " 1897
Scottish Text Society	" " 1884
Spalding Club	" " 1841
Spottiswoode Society	" " 1844

History of Dunbar, J Miller (Dunbar, 1830, rep. 1859)
History of Scotland, vols i-viii, J Hill Burton (Edinburgh, 1897)
History of Scotland, A: vols i-iv, A Lang, (Edinburgh, 1900-07)
History of Scotland, 1249-1603: *vols i-ix,* P F Tytler (Edinburgh, 1828-43)
History of Scotland, vols i-iii, P Hume Brown (Cambridge, 1909-11)
Honour the Light Brigade, W M Lummis and K G Wynn (London, 1973)

James I, King of Scots, E W M Balfour-Melville (London, 1936)
James III, A Political Study, N Macdougall (Edinburgh, 1982)
James IV, N Macdougall (Edinburgh, 1989)
James VI and I, King, D H Wilson (London, 1956)

Kingdom of the Scots, The: Government, Church and Society from the Eleventh to the Fourteenth Century, G W S Barrow (London, 1973)

Lamp of Lothian, J Miller (Haddington, 1844)

Mary, Queen of Scots, Antonia Fraser (London, 1969)
Muster Roll of the French Garrison at Dunbar, Miscellany of the Scottish History Society, vol 2 ed. R S Rait (Edinburgh, 1904)
My Own Life and Times, 1741-1814, T Somerville (Edinburgh, 1861)

National Trust Book of Castles, P Johnson (London, 1978)
Normans in Scotland, The: R L G Ritchie (Edinburgh, 1954)

Prisoners Progress, The, Leslie C Hunt (London 1941)
Proceedings of the Society of Antiquaries of Scotland (see under *Society of Antiquaries*)
Provincial Antiquities of Scotland, The: Sir Walter Scott (Edinburgh, 1826)

Royal Commission on the Ancient and Historical Monuments of Scotland: East Lothian:8th Report (HMSO, Edinburgh, 1924)

Scotland, Sir R S Rait and G S Pryde (London, 1954)
Scotland and the Crusades 1095-1560, A McQuarrie (Edinburgh, 1996)
Scotland, the Ancient Kingdom, D A Mackenzie (London, 1930)
Scotland in the Middle Ages, Cosmo Innes (Edinburgh, 1860)
Scotland, the Later Middle Ages (The Edinburgh History of Scotland, *vol ii*) R Nicholson (Edinburgh, 1974)
Scotland: The Making of the Kingdom (The Edinburgh History of Scotland *vol I*) A A M Duncan (Edinburgh, 1975)
Scotland under Her Early Kings, volsi-ii, E W Robertson (Edinburgh, 1862)
Scottish Hazard:The Flemish Heritage, vol ii, Beryl Platts (London, 1990)
Scottish Heraldry, Sir Thomas Innes of Learney (Edinburgh & London, 1956)
Scottish Historical Review (Glasgow and Edinburgh, 1904-
Scottish Kings: A Revised Chronology of Scottish History, 1005-1625, Sir A Dunbar (Edinburgh, 1906)
Scottish Nation, The: W Anderson (Edinburgh, 1867)
Sketches of Early Scotch History and Social Progress, Cosmo Innes (Edinburgh, 1861
Society of Antiquaries of Scotland: Proceedings (after 1800):
Articles: Notes on the Old Earldom of Dunbar, March and Moray, A Hamilton (*vol 22,* 1888)
List of Travels and Tours Relating to Scotland, A; 1200-1900 ed. A H Mitchell (*vol 35,* 1902)
Notes on Ancient Graves at Belhaven, East Lothian, R Paul (*vol 39,* 1904-05)
Battle of Culblean 1335, The; W Douglas Simpson (*vol 64,*1929-30)
Bamburgh's Castle and Town Wall, Dunbar, G P H Watson (*vol 84,*1949-50)
Cemetery, Dunbar, East Lothian, C S T Calder and R W Peachem (*vol 85,* 1950-51)
Graveyard Monuments: East Lothian, A Graham (*vol 94,* 1960-61)
Massive Cist and Multiple Burial of Iron Age Date, A: Part 1, I H Longworth (*vol 98,* 1964-66)
Iron Age Peoples of Dunbar, The: Part 2, D R Brothwell and R Powers. (*vol 98,* 1964-66)
Old Harbours at Dunbar, The: A Graham (*vol 99,* 1966-67)
Friarscroft and the Trinitarians at Dunbar,: J Wordsworth (*vol 113,* 1983)
Castle Park Dunbar: Two Thousand Years of a Fortified Headland, D Perry *et al* (Scottish Monograph Series No. 16, Edinburgh, 2000) (See also muster roll of French garrison at Dunbar Castle, SHS)
Steel Bonnets, The: G M Fraser (London, 1971)

Thirteenth Century, The: 1216-1307, Sir Maurice Powicke (Oxford, 1991)
This Present Emergency: An Account of the Second World War, A Jeffrey (Edinburgh, 1992)

Warlords and holy men: Scotland AD80-1000, A P Smyth (Edinburgh, 1984)
William Wallace: The King's Enemy, D J Gray (London, 1955)

4

ECCLESIASTICAL SOURCES: RECORDS, BIOGRAPHIES AND HISTORIES

Ancient Church Dedications in Scotland, J M McKinlay (Edinburgh, 1914)
Annals of the Church in Scotland, T Ralegh (Oxford,1921)

Bede-see under *Historia Ecclesiastica Gentis Anglorum*
Bek, Beck, Antony: History of Antony Bek, Bishop of Durham, C M Fraser (Oxford, 1957)
Bishops of Scotland, The: J Dowden (Glasgow, 1912)
Blackadder, J: The Life of the Reverend J Blackadder, A Crichton (Edinburgh, 1826)
Bygone Days of Church Life in Scotland, W Andrews (London, 1899)

Calendar of Entries in the Papal Registers relating to Great Britain and Ireland: Papal Letters, ed W H Bliss *et al* (London, 1893-)
Calendar of Papal Letters to Scotland of Pope Benedict XIII of Avignon, 1394-1418 ed. F McGurk (*Scottish History Society,* 1976)
Calendar of Papal Letters to Scotland of Pope Clement VII of Avignon, 1378-94 ed. C Burns (*Scottish History Society,* 1976)
Calendar of Scottish Supplications to Rome, 1423-28 *vol ii* ed. A I Dunlop (*Scottish History Society,1956)*
Calendar of Scottish Supplications to Rome, *1428-32: 4th Series vol vii* ed. A I Dunlop and I B Cowan (*Scottish History Society,* 1970)
Church of Scotland in the Thirteenth Century (The Life and Times of David de Bernham of St Andrews AD 1239 to 1253), W Lockhart (Edinburgh, 1889)

Coldingham:

Coldingham : Parish and Priory, A Thomson (Galashiels, 1908);
The Priory of Coldingham ed. J Raine (*Surtees Society,*London, 1841)
A History of Coldingham Priory, A A Carr (Edinburgh, 1836)

Collections, Hutton - being a collection of *MSS* by General George Hutton held in the national Library of Scotland. These consist of several volumes on early monastic and religious houses (ref. *Advocate MSS,* 1829). The *MSS* are referred to by Anthony Ross, *Three Antiquaries (Innes Review No 2,* 1964)

Dunbar:

Dunbar Collegiate Church: Foundation Charter, ed. D Easson (*Miscellany of the Scottish History Society,vol vi* 1938-39);
Dunbar Collegiate Church: Deans from 1342-1617, D E R Watt, *Fasti Ecclesiae Scoticanae Medii Aevi ad Annum 1638,* St Andrews, 1969; *Scottish Text Society,* Edinburgh, 1969;
Old Parish Kirk Session Minutes 1709-1744 (SRO ref. CH2/99.4 and CH2/647)
Trinitarians at Friarscroft (see under section 3 - Society of Antiquaries of Scotland: Proceedings)

Durham:

Durham Charters; Durham cathedral Library ed R K Richardson (*Campden Miscellany,* 1924);
Symeonis monachi opera omnia vol I; Historiae Ecclesiae ed. T Arnold (*Rolls Series,* 1875); also *Symeonis Dunelmensis Opera et Collectanea* ed. J H Hinde (Durham, 1868;
Liber Vitae Ecclesiae Dunelmensis (*Surtees Society,* London, 1841 and ed. A Hamilton Thomson (1923);
Libellus de Amirandis Beati Cuthberti (Miracles of St Cuthbert) Reginald of Durham (*Surtees Society,* 1835)

Ecclesiastical Chronicle for Scotland vols i-iii ed. J F S Gordon (London & Dumfries, 1875)
Ecclesiastical History, The: Ordericus Vitalis, *vols i-iv* ed. M Chibnall (Oxford, 1969-78); also *Historia Ecclesiastica* (A Church History) 1123-41, Ordericus Vitalis *vols i-iv* (London, 1783) ed. A Le Prevost et L Delisle (*Societe de l'Histoire de France,* Paris, 1838-55)

Fasti Ecclesiae Scoticanae Medii Aevi as Annum 1638: A succession of ministers up to and beyond the Reformation ed. D E R Watt (St Andrews, 1969)
Fasti Ecclesiae Scoticanae: The succession of ministers of the Church of Scotland from the Reformation: Synod of Lothian and Tweeddale ed. Hew Scott *et al* (Edinburgh, 1915-)

Historia Ecclesiastica Gentis Anglorum (A Church History of the English Nation c731), The Venerable Bede ed. B Colgrove and R A B Mynors (Oxford, 1969); also *Opera Historia* (A History of the the Church of England) ed. T E Page (London, 1930)
Historical catalogue of the Scottish Bishops, An: R Keith ed. M Russel (Edinburgh, 1824)
History of the Church of Scotland vols i-iii, Archbishop J Spottiswoode (*Spottiswoode Society,* 1847-51)
History of the Kirk of Scotland, D Calderwood ed. T Thomson (*Wodrow Society,* Edinburgh, 1842-49)
History of the Reformation in Scotland, John Knox (1556) ed. W Croft Dickinson (Edinburgh, 1949)

Knox, John: A Biography, Lord Eustace Percy (London, 1937)

Liber Cartarum Prioratus Sancti Andree in Scotia (St Andrews' Cartulary) (*Bannatyne Club,* 1841)
Liber S. Marie de Calchou (Kelso Cartulary) ed. Cosmo Innes (*Bannatyne Club,* 1846)
Liber S. Marie de Dryburgh (Dryburgh Cartulary) ed. J Spottiswoode (*Bannatyne Club,* 1847)
Liber S. Marie de Melros (Melrose Cartulary) *vols i-ii* (*Bannatyne Club,* 1837)

Medieval Church in Scotland, The: Its Condition, Organisation and Law, J Dowden (Glasgow, 1910)
Medieval Religious Houses Scotland, I B Cowan and D Easson (London, 1957 and 1976)
Monuments and Monumental Inscriptions in Scotland, C Rogers (London, 1871)

Old Kirk Chronicle, An: A History of Auldhame, Tyninghame and Whitekirk Churches from Session Records, 1615-1850 ed. P H Waddell (Edinburgh, 1893)

St Margaret of Scotland:

Life of Margaret of Scotland 1093-1104 [?], Bishop Turgot; Turgot's contemporary account is reproduced in the British Museum (ref. *MSS Cotton Liber D III*); the *MSS* dates from the late twelfth century and was transcribed by Fr. Forbes-Leith;
St Margaret of Scotland and Hungary, K Nagy (Glasgow, 1973)

St Wilfrid of York, Eddius Stephanus (c710) pub. in J Raine's *York* (*Rolls Series,* 1879-94); also *Vita S. Wilfridi* (Life of St Wilfrid of York) Eddius Stephanus trans. B Colgrove (Cambridge, 1927)
Scoti-Monastichon: The Ancient Church of Scotland, M E C Walcott (London, 1874) Spott Kirk Session Minutes (SRO ref. CH2/333)
Spottiswoode Miscellany (Civil and Ecclesiatical) vols i-ii (*Spottiswoode Society,* 1844-45)
Statures of the Scottish Church ed. D Patrick (*Scottish History Society,* 1907)
Symeon of Durham - see under Durham
Synod Records of Lothian and Tweeddale ed. J Kirk (*Stair Society,* Edinburgh, 1977)

Tyninghame - see under *An Old Kirk Chronicle*

Witchcraft:

Calendar of Cases of Witchcraft in Scotland, A: 1510-1727, G F Black (New York, 1938);
Collection of Celebrated Criminal Trials in Scotland, A: 1536-1784, Hugo Arnot (Edinburgh, 1785);
Criminal Trials in Scotland 1488-1624 (and beyond), R Pitcairn (Edinburgh, 1833);
Deil's Ain, The: Roy J M Pugh (Balerno, 2001);
Enemies of God: The Witch Hunt in Scotland, C J Larner (Oxford, 1981);
Ingenious and Scientific Discourse on Witchcraft, An: J Bell, minister of Gladsmuir Church, East Lothian (1705);
Letters from the North of Scotland - see under History, Early Sources; Letter xii contains a description of the last witch executed in Scotland;
Malleus Maleficarum (Hammer of Witches) Jacob Sprenger and Heinrich Kramer trans. M Summer (London, 1948);
Memoirs of Extraordinary Popular Delusions, Charles Mackay (London,1869);
Registers of the Privy Council of Scotland - see under Records and Original Documents: Royal, State and Local Government
Satan's Invisible World Discovered,, George Sinclair (Edinburgh, 1685);
Scotland Social and Domestic, C Rogers (*Grampian Club,* Aberdeen, 1869);
Social England, R Steele (London, 1903);
Source-Book of Scottish Witchcraft, A: ed. C J Larner, C H Lee and H V MacLachlan (Glasgow, 1977);
Witchcraft in British History, R Holmes (London, 1976);
Witchcraft in Scotland, article by F Legge in *The Scottish Review, vol xviii* (London & Paisley, 1891)

5

PEERAGES, GENEALOGICAL COLLECTIONS AND FAMILY HISTORIES

Peerages

Baronage of Scotland, The: Sir Robert Douglas (Edinburgh, 1798)

Complete Peerage, The: G E Cockayne ed. V Gibbs *et al vols i-xiii* (London, 1910-59)

Histories of Noble British Families vol. I and 2 ed. H Drummond and G Pickering (London, 1846)

Inquiry into the Law and Practice of Scottish Peerages, J Riddell (Edinburgh, 1842)

Peerage of Scotland, The: Sir Robert Douglas (Edinburgh, 1764)
Peerage of Scotland, The: vols i-ii, J P Wood: A Correction of Douglas' *Peerage* of 1764 (Edinburgh, 1813)

Scots' Peerage, The: vols i-vii, Sir J Balfour Paul (Edinburgh, 1904-14)

Genealogical Collections

Dunbar Line, The: Prepared for Dunbar of Durn in Banffshire (1910), *The Dunbar Line* purports to have been drawn from 'authentic manuscripts and sources in the possession of E H W Butterworth, Liverpool'. *The Dunbar Line* is generally accurate although it contains detail which does not reconcile with *Scots' Peerage* or Dunbar of Kilconzie's *Dunbar's 1000 Years.* Several of the printed sources quoted in support of *The Dunbar Line* also do not reconcile; for example, it differs from the *Complete Peerage,* which is given as a confirmatory source. *The Dunbar Line* was printed at Stratford-on-Avon

Genealogical Collections concerning Families in Scotland made by Walter MacFarlane ed. J T Clark (*Scottish History Society,* 1906-08)

Family Histories

Ayton Bard, The: Robert Mennon 1797-1855, A Michael Mennim (York, 1989)
Douglas Book, The: vols i-iv, W Fraser (Edinburgh, 1855)
Douglas and Angus, A History of the House and Race of: D Hume of Godscroft (Edinburgh, 1748)

Lockharts of Lee and Carnwath, A History of: Seven Centuries, S M Lockhart (Carnwath, 1976)

Millers of Haddington, Dunbar and Dunfermline, The; W Couper (London, 1914)

Seton, A History of the Family of: G Seton (Edinburgh, 1896)

Wemyss, Memoirs of the Family of: W Fraser (Edinburgh, 1888)

6

COUNTIES, TOWNS, BURGHS, PARISHES AND VILLAGES

General

Beauties of Scotland, R Forsyth (rep. London, 1841)
Burghs of Scotland, The: A Critical List, G S Pryde (London, 1965)
Convention of the Royal Burghs of Scotland, T Pagan (Glasgow, 1926)
Early Burgh Organization in Scotland vols i-ii, D Murray (Glasgow, 1932)

Mercat Cross and Tolbooth, C Mair (Edinburgh, 1988)

Ordnance Gazetteer of Scotland, ed. F H Groome (Edinburgh, 1882)

Records of the Convention of Royal Burghs of Scotland, 1295-1779 *vols i-vii* ed. J Marwick and T Hunter (Edinburgh, 1866-1917) see under Records etc

Scottish Burghs, The: W Malcolm Mackenzie (Edinburgh, 1949)
Scottish Burgh and County Heraldry, J M Urquhart (Aberdeen, 1972)
Scottish Burgh Record Society, Miscellany of: ed. J Marwick (Edinburgh, 1881) - see under section 3 Records etc
Scottish Heraldic Seals, J H Stevenson and M Wood (Glasgow, 1940)

Town Council Seals of Scotland, A Porteous (Edinburgh, 1906)

Various

Bass Rock, The: T McRie (Edinburgh, 1848)
Berwickshire: The Royal Commission on the Ancient Monuments and Constructions in Scotland: On the County of Berwick (6th report HMSO, Edinburgh, 1915)
Berwickshire Naturalists' Club (1831-) - see under section 3

Cockburnspath: A Documentary History of a Border Parish, ed. E Rankin (Edinburgh, 1981)
Cockburnspath, Sally Smith (Dunglass Mill Press, 1999)
Coldingham - see under Ecclesiastical etc
Cullen, Annals of 961-1904, W Crammond (Buckie, 1904)
Cumberland, History of the County of: W Hutchison (Carlisle, 1794)
Cumberland and Westmoreland Antiquarian and Archaeological Society,Transactions of vols i-lxvii (Kendal, 1905-67)

Dunbar and Belhaven:
(see also Belhaven and Dunbar entries in section 3 (*Society of Antiquaries of Scotland: Proceedings*) and Dunbar entry in section 4 (Ecclesiastical)
Dunbar's 1000 Years, W Dunbar of Kilconzie (W Dunbar, Herne Bay, Kent, 1982 - copy available for reference at East Lothian Local History Centre, Haddington);
Burgh Register and Guide to Dunbar: Descriptive History of the Burgh,Castle and Battle [of 1650], JMcDonald (Haddington, 1895 rep. 1897)
Historic Dunbar: Scottish Burgh Survey: The Archaeological Implications of Development: University of Glasgow Department of Archaeology (1981);
History of Dunbar, The: James Miller (Dunbar, 1830 rep. 1859 with additional information, mainly about shipwrecks);
Picturesque Dunbar: An Illustrative Guide, J Horne (Edinburgh, 1899?);
Town Council and provost and magistrates' Committees Minute Books (1671-1959);
Criminal Complaints and Defaulters Books (1854-61);
Miscellaneous papers (SRO)

East Lothian, C E Greene (Edinburgh & London, 1907)
East Lothian, T S Muir (Cambridge, 1915)
East Lothian Monuments: The Royal Commission on the Ancient and Historical Monuments of Scotland (see under section 3)
East Lothian Buildings: *The Buildings of Scotland: Lothian* ed. N Pevsner (London, 1978)
East Lothian: Sketches from the Haddingtonshire Courier, D Croal (Edinburgh, 1904)
East Neuk of Fife, W Wood (Edinburgh, 1887)
Edinburgh, Cassells Old and New vols i-ii ed. J Grant (London & Edinburgh, 1880-87)
Edinburgh and the Lothians: The Queen's Scotland, Theo Lang (Edinburgh, 1952)
*Edwardian East Lothian,*W F Jackson (collection of photographs) (East Lothian District Library and Gullane Local History Society, 1989)
Elgin Past and Present, H B Mackintosh (Elgin, 1914)

Greenlaw: An Old Berwickshire Town, R Gibson (Edinburgh, 1905)

Haddingtonshire Courier 1859-1971 thereafter the *East Lothian Courier*: extracts by courtesy of the proprietors
Haddington: A Short History of; W Forbes Gray, (Edinburgh, 1944)

Haddington, Reminiscences and Notices of the County of, J Martine (Edinburgh & Glasgow, 1894)
Haddington, Reminiscences of the Royal Burgh of, J Martine (Edinburgh & Glasgow, 1883)

Jersey, the Balliewick of : G R Balleine (Jersey, 1951)
Jersey, Biographical Dictionary of : G R Balleine (Jersey, 1948)

Lauder and Lauderdale, A Thomson (Galashiels, 1902)

May, Isle of: A Scottish Nature Reserve, W J Eggeling (Edinburgh, 1960)
Moray, The History of the Province of : L Shaw (Glasgow & London, 1882)

Northumberland and Durham:

Historical Records of Remarkable Events in Northumberland and Durham, Newcastle-upon-Tyne, ed. J Sykes and T Fordyce (Newcastle, 1865-76);
Durham: *The History and Antiquities of North Durham, Appendix,* J Raine's *North Durham* (London, 1852);
The Victorian History of the Counties of England: Durham ed. W Page (London, 1928);
Northumberland and the Scottish Borders (Proceedings of the Archaeological Institute in 1852, Newcastle, *vol ii*) C Hartshone (London, 1858);
From Border to Middle Shire, 1586-1625 ed. Susan J Watts and Sheldon J Watts (Leicester, 1979). When James VI became James I of Britain, the Borders became known as the Middle Shire since the Border ceased to have any political or military significance;
Northumberland, The History of: The Northumberland County History Committee (Newcastle, 1893-1939) *vols i-xv viz*

vols i-ii	1893-95	ed. E Bateson
vol iii	1896	ed. A B Hinds
vols iv-vii	1897-1904	ed.. J C Hodgson
vols vii-x	1907-14	ed.. H H E Craster
vol ix	1922	ed. K H Vickers
vols xii-xv	1926-39	ed. M H Dodds

Spott -see under Ecclesiastical etc

Tyninghame - see under Ecclesiastical ie *An Old Kirk Chronicle*

Whittingehame: The Seven Ages of an East Lothian Parish, M D Lang (Edinburgh, 1929)

7

ECONOMIC; AGRICULTURE, FISHING AND SEA TRADE, TRADE, INDUSTRY; EDUCATION AND SOCIAL: VARIOUS ACCOUNTS, GOVERNMENT (CENTRAL AND LOCAL) PUBLICATIONS AND REPORTS

General and Miscellaneous

British Encyclopaedia vols i-xii ed J M Parrish (London, 1953)

Chambers Scottish Biographical Dictionary ed. R Goring (Edinburgh, 1992)

Directory of Land Ownership in Scotland c1770 ed. R Timperley (*Scottish Record Society,* 1976)

Encyclopaedia Britannica vols i-xxiv ed. H S Ashmore (London, & Chicago, 1961)

Memoirs of Extraordinary Popular Delusions, C Mackay (London, 1841)

Scottish Firsts: Innovation and Achievement, Elspeth Wills (Edinburgh, 1987)
Scottish Staple at Veere, The: J Davidson and A Gray (London, 1909)
Scottish Trade on the Eve of Union, T C Smout (Edinburgh, 1963)
Statistical Accounts:
Abridged Statistical Account of Scotland, An: East Lothian ed. J H Dawson (Edinburgh, 1853);
Old Statistical Account of Scotland, The: ed. Sir John Sinclair (Edinburgh, 1793);
New Statistical Account of Scotland, The: Linlithgow, Haddington and Berwick ed. J T Gordon (London, 1845);
Third Statistical Account of Scotland, The: East Lothian ed. C Snodgrass (Edinburgh, 1953)

Agriculture

Agricultural laboureres in Scotland Then and Now, R Hunter Pringle (*Transactions of the Highland and Agricultural Society of Scotland,* 5th Series VI, 1894)
Autobiography of a Working Man (Who Has Whistled Behind the Plough), A Somerville (London, 1848 rep. 1967)

Countrey Man's Rudiments by ABC, J Hamilton, 2nd Lord Belhaven (Edinburgh, 1699)

First report of the Select Committee to Inquire into the State of Agriculture, Parliamentary Papers *vol iii* (1836)

General View of the Agriculture of East Lothian (for the Board of Agriculture and Internal Improvement) R Somerville, surgeon of Haddington (London, 1805)

Report of the Board of Supervision by Sir John MacNeill on the Western Highlands and Islands vol 26
Royal Commission on the Employment of Children, Young Persons and Women in Agriculture, Fourth Report, Parliamentary Papers (1870)
Royal Commission on Labour, Part II (1893)

Transactions of the Highland and Agricultural Society of Scotland, New Series No XXI (1853-55)

Fisheries

Board of White Fisheries for Scotland (SRO refs. AF 1/12, AF 1/13)
British Fishery Society Records (SRO ref. GD9)

Committee Appointed to Inquire into the State of the British Fisheries, 1785: Reports to the House of Commons, 1803, *vol x*
Committee Appointed to Inquire into the State of the British Herring Fisheries, 1798: Reports to the House of Commons, 1803, *vol x*

Fishing Boats and Fishing Folk on the East Coast of Scotland, P F Anson (London, 1930)

Observations on the Report of the Committee of the House of Commons Appointed to Inquire into the State of the British Fishery, Robert Fall, (Dunbar, 1786)

Reports on and since the year 1848 on the Subject of the Fishery Board in Scotland, 1856, *vol lix*
Reports addressed to the Lords Commissioners of Her Majesty's Treasurer in Scotland in 1856 on the Subject of the Fishery Board in Scotland, 1857, *vol xv*
Report of the Commission Appointed to Inquire into Sea Fisheries of the United Kingdom, 1866, *vols xvii-xviii*
Report of the Select Committee on Harbour Accommodation, 1853, *vol xiv* and 1884, *vol xii*
Report for the Select Committee on Sea Fishing, 1893-94, *vol xv*
Reports of the Scottish Departmental Committee on the Scottish Sea Fishing Industry, 1914, *vol xxxi*

Select Committee on Harbour Accommodation: Reports from the House of Commons, 1803

Brewing

History of the Brewing Industry in the Lothians, A: I Donnachie (Edinburgh, 1979)

Lime Production

Accounts of the Principal Limestone Quarries of Scotland, 1837 ed. J Carmichael (*Transactions of the Highland and Agricultural Society of Scotland,* Series 2)
Autobiography of a Working Man etc, A Somerville

Lime Industry in the Lothians, The: B Skinner (Edinburgh, 1909)

Crafts

'The Gild Merchant' by Charles Gross (*Scottish Review, vol xxxii*)

Merchant and Craft Guilds, E Bain (Aberdeen, 1887)

Printing, Publishing and Libraries

Latter Struggles in the Journey of Life: or, the afternoon of my days....the period between my forty-fifth and the end of my sixtieth year: An autobiography by George Miller, printer, publisher and journalist, Dunbar, 1795-1833 (Edinburgh, 1833)

Millers of Haddington, Dunbar and Dunfermline, The: W J Couper (London, 1914)

Samuel Brown and George Miller: A Mystery by L Durbridge; this is an article about which of these men began the first public lending library in East Lothian (*Library Review,vol xxiii,*1971)

Education

Burgh Schools in Scotland, The: J Grant (London, 1876)
From Slate to Disk ed. Lena Glass (Haddington, 1997)

Popular Education in 18th Century Britain, Victor Neuberg (London, 1971)

Environmental

John Muir, From Scotland to the Sierra, Frederick Turner (Edinburgh, 1997)

John Muir, The Wilderness Journeys, intro. by G White (Edinburgh, 1996)

Works by John Muir quoted in Chapter 10:

The Mountains of California (1894)
Our National Parks (1901)
Stickeen (1909)
My First Summer in the Sierra (1911)
The Yosemite (1912)
The Story of My Boyhood and Youth (1913 - unfinished autobiography
Travels in Alaska (1915)*
A Thousand Mile Walk to the Gulf (1916)*
The Cruise of the Corwin (1917)*
Steep Trails (1918)*

* Published posthumously

Literature

Poems Moral and Religious, R Mennon (Edinburgh, 1869)
Poems and Songs by the Late Richard Gall, with a Memorial of the Author, A Murray (Edinburgh, 1819)
St Baldred of the Bass, the Seige of Berwick and Other Poems, J Miller (Edinburgh, 1834)
Verses to Lord Ramsay on His Marriage with Lady Susan Hay, J Miller (Edinburgh, 1836)
Verses to Sir T Buchan Hepburn, J Miller (Edinburgh, 1837)
Battles of Dunbar and Prestonpans and Other Verses (Old and New) James Lumsden (Haddington, 1896)

Social

Book of Days, The: A Miscellany of Popular Activities ed. R Chambers (London & Edinburgh, 1864)

Domestic Annals of Scotland, R Chambers (Edinburgh & London, 1874)

Scotland Social and Domestic, C Rogers (*Grampian Club,* 1869)
Social and Economic Life of Scotland before 1603, The: I F Grant (London, 1830)
Social Life in Scotland, C Rogers (*Grampian Club*, 1884)

Travels in Scotland:
Early Travellers in Scotland, P Hume Brown (Edinburgh, 1891);
In Scotland Again, H V Morton (London, 1965);
Journey Through Scotland, A: J Mackay (Edinburgh, 1723);
Journey to the Northern Parts of Great Britain (anon.) (*The East Lothian and Field Naturalists' Society vol ii* 1926-33);
Tour Through the Whole Island of Great Britain, vols i-ii, Daniel Defoe (rep. London, 1927);
Tours of Scotland, 1747, 1750, 1760, Bishop R Pococke (*Scottish History Society,* 1887);
Tours of Scotland, T Pennant (Chester, 1771);
Travels and Tours Relating to Scotland, 1200-1900 - see under section 3 Modern Histories

GENERAL INDEX

Index

INDEX OF NAMES

J. MASON,
Bootmaker,
DUNBAR.

Agent for . . .
"K" Boots,
"Adapted" Boots,
Scafe's Boots, &c.

A. LAING,
Tobacconist,
59 HIGH STREET,
DUNBAR.

5 and 7 Good Cigars for a Shilling.

M'KENZIE'S
LIBRARY
2 HIGH STREET,
DUNBAR.

Tobacconist & Stationer.

WILSON'S
Temperance Hotel & Dining Rooms,
HIGH STREET,
DUNBAR.

Home Comforts to Cyclists and Visitors.
Charges Moderate.

TAIT BROTHERS.
BUTCHERS.
Poulterers and
GAME DEALERS.
96 HIGH STREET
DUNBAR.
ARMY CONTRACTORS

J. DOWNIE,

Bookseller, Stationer,
rinter, and Newsagent,
56 HIGH STREET,
(Opposite George Hotel)
DUNBAR.
ESTABLISHED 1842.

Agency for . . .
rnished Houses and Apartments
In Dunbar and Neighbourhood.

The Roxburghe Marine Hotel.

This High-class
FAMILY HOTEL
occupies one of the
Finest Positions
in Dunbar
being situated
midway between the
Railway Station and
Golf Links
and commands a magnificent
and uninterrupted
SEA-VIEW of over 30 miles of
Rugged Coast-line.

TABLE D'HOTE at Separate
Tables at 7.30 daily.

REDUCED TARIFF FROM OCTOBER TO JUNE. For Terms, Address Manageress.

ALEX. SIMPSON,

Ladies' Tailor,
—:— AND —:—
Gentlemen's Outfitter,
5 FRIARSBANK TERRACE.

ESTABLISHED 1756.

St George Hotel,
DUNBAR.
First-class Commercial Hotel.

Ordinary Daily, One o'clock.
Headquarters for C. T. C.

EDMUND LEACH, Proprietor.

KEENEST PRICES IN TOWN CHARGED

Only the Finest Quality of Goods
stocked for a First-Class Family Trade.

ALEXANDER WOOD,

Family Grocer and Wine Merchant,

Sole Agent in District for—
RAGGETT & SONS,
CELEBRATED NOURISHING STOUT.
AUGIER FRERES,
COGNAC OLD LIQUEUR BRANDIES.
AUSTRALIAN WINE IMPORTERS, Limited,
CLARETS, BURGUNDIES, &c.

71 HIGH STREET,
(adjoining George Hotel)
DUNBAR.

Telegrams "WILSON" DUNBAR.

FRESH DRUGS
PURE CHEMICALS

LATEST REMEDIES
PHARMACEUTICAL PREPARATIONS

REGISTERED TRADE MARK
DUNBAR CASTLE

Physicians' Prescriptions accurately dispensed under personal supervision.

PROPRIETARY ARTICLES

DRUGGISTS' SUNDRIES.

PATENT MEDICINES

W. P. WILSON
CHEMIST,
67, HIGH STREET,
DUNBAR.

HOMŒOPATHIC MEDICINES.

VETERINARY PREPARATIONS.

PHOTOGRAPHIC REQUISITES.

AERATED WATERS
Manufactured by Gold Medal Machinery with the Latest Appliances.
Only the Finest Materials are used for the production of High-class Waters guaranteed of absolute Purity.

ROYAL HOTEL,

NEAREST HOTEL TO RAILWAY STATION

First-class Family and Commercial,
OCCUPYING BEST POSITION IN TOWN.
Has been considerably enlarged.

CONTAINS:—
COFFEE, DRAWING, SMOKING, BILLIARD ROOMS.
Private Sitting Rooms en Suite,
with
Comfortable Bedrooms, Bathroom, &c.
Decorated & Furnished on up-to-date lines.

EXCELLENT CUISINE.

Most Moderate Charges, combined with every comfort and attention.

Boarding Terms by arrangement. Special Week-end Terms for Golfers.
UNDER PERSONAL SUPERVISION OF THE PROPRIETOR.
Stabling in connection with Hotel. JAMES PETTIGREW, Proprietor.

ESTABLISHED 1849.

JAMES KNOX,

BOOKSELLER, STATIONER, AND NEWSAGENT,
64—HIGH STREET—64
DUNBAR.

VALENTINE'S VIEWS OF DUNBAR AND DISTRICT.
ALBUM OF VIEWS OF DUNBAR, PRICE 1s.
AGENT FOR PATERSON & SONS' PIANO TUNER.

Morning, Evening, and Weekly Newspapers. Magazines and Monthly Periodicals delivered or sent by post. Any Newspaper, Book, or Magazine not in stock, can be had on the shortest notice. All Orders by Post attended to.

ORDERS RECEIVED FOR BOOKBINDING IN ALL STYLES.